MODERN PORTFOLIO THEORY AND INVESTMENT ANALYSIS

SIXTH EDITION

EDWIN J. ELTON
Leonard N. Stern School of Business
New York University

MARTIN J. GRUBER
Leonard N. Stern School of Business
New York University

STEPHEN J. BROWN
Leonard N. Stern School of Business
New York University

WILLIAM N. GOETZMANN
Yale University

John Wiley & Sons, Inc.

To some of the future generation of our readers: Ned's grandchildren, Erik Bietel and Sophia Bietel, and Marty's grandchildren, Samuel Gruber, Jack Gruber and Ava Gruber.

ACQUISITIONS EDITOR Leslie Kraham

ASSOCIATE EDITOR Cindy Rhoads

SENIOR MARKETING MANAGER Charity Robey

SENIOR PRODUCTION EDITOR Norine M. Pigliucci

SENIOR DESIGNER Harry Nolan

PRODUCTION MANAGEMENT SERVICES Argosy Publishing

This book was set in Times Roman by Argosy Publishing and printed and bound by Hamilton Printing. The cover was printed by Lehigh Printing.

This book is printed on acid-free paper.

Library of Congress Cataloging-in-Publicaation Data

Elton, Edwin J.
   Modern portfolio theory and investment analysis / Edwin J. Elton, Martin J. Gruber.--
6th ed.
      p. cm.
   Includes bibliographical references and index.
   ISBN 0-471-23854-6 (cloth : alk. paper)
      1. Portfolio management. 2. Investment analysis. I. Gruber, Martin Jay, 1937- II. Title.

HG4529.5 .E47 2003
332.6--dc21   2002024598

Printed in the United States of America

10 9 8 7 6 5 4 3 2 1

About the Authors

EDWIN J. ELTON is Nomura Professor of Finance at the Stern School of Business of New York University. He has authored or coauthored eight books and more than 90 articles. These articles have appeared in journals such as *The Journal of Finance, The Review of Financial Studies, Review of Economics and Statistics, Management Science, Journal of Financial Economics, Journal of Business, Oxford Economic Papers,* and *Journal of Financial and Quantitative Analysis.* He has been coeditor of the *Journal of Finance.* Professor Elton has been a member of the Board of Directors of the American Finance Association and an Associate Editor of *Management Science.* He is Associate Editor of *Journal of Banking and Finance* and *Journal of Accounting Auditing and Finance.* Professor Elton has served as a consultant for many major financial institutions. A compendium of articles by Professor Elton and Professor Gruber has recently been published in two volumes by MIT press. Professor Elton is a past president of the American Finance Association, a fellow of that association, and a recipient of distinguished research award by the Eastern Finance Association.

MARTIN J. GRUBER is Nomura Professor of Finance and past Chairman of the Finance Department at the Stern School of Business of New York University. He is a fellow of the American Finance Association. He has published nine books and more than 90 journal articles in journals such as *The Journal of Finance, The Review of Financial Studies, Review of Economics and Statistics, Journal of Financial Economics, Journal of Business, Management Science, Journal of Financial and Quantitative Analysis, Operations Research, Oxford Economic Papers,* and *The Journal of Portfolio Management.* He has been coeditor of the *Journal of Finance.* He has been President of the American Finance Association, a Director of the European Finance Association, a Director of the American Finance Association, and a Director of both the Computer Applications Committee and the Investment Technology Symposium of the New York Society of Security Analysts. He was formerly Finance Department Editor for *Management Science.* Professor Gruber has consulted in the areas of Investment Analysis and Portfolio Management with many major financial institutions. He is currently a Trustee of TIAA-CREF, a director of Deutsche B. T. Asset Management Mutual Funds, and a Director of the Diawa closed-end funds.

STEPHEN J. BROWN is David S. Loeb Professor of Finance and Coordinator of Undergraduate Finance at the Leonard N. Stern School of Business, New York University. He has served on the Board of Directors of the American Finance Association, was a founding editor of *The Review of Financial Studies* and is currently a member of the Board of the Society of Quantitative Analysis. He is a Managing Editor of the *Journal of Financial and Quantitative Analysis* and has served on the editorial boards of *The Journal of Finance, Pacific-Basin Finance Journal*, and other journals. He has published numerous articles and four books on finance and economics related areas. In 1996 he served on the nominating committee for the Bank of Sweden Prize in Economic Sciences in Memory of Alfred Nobel. He has served as an expert witness for the U.S. Department of Justice.

WILLIAM N. GOETZMANN is Edwin J. Beinecke Professor of Finance and Management Studies at the Yale School of Management and Director, International Center for Finance at the Yale School of Management and has served on the Board of Directors of the American Finance Association. His published research topics include global investing, forecasting stock markets, selecting mutual fund managers, housing as investment, and the risk and return of art. Professor Goetzmann has a background in arts and media management. As a documentary filmmaker, he has written and coproduced programs for *Nova* and the *American Masters* series, including a profile of the artist Thomas Eakins. A former director of Denver's Museum of Western Art, Professor Goetzmann coauthored the award winning book, *The West of the Imagination*.

Preface

This book, as the title suggests, is concerned with the characteristics and analysis of individual securities, as well as with the theory and practice of optimally combining securities into portfolios. Part 1 of the book provides a description of securities and markets. Two new chapters have been added to provide the reader with the institutional background to place the analytics that follow in perspective.

The second, and longest, part of the book discusses modern portfolio theory. We begin Part 2 with a detailed presentation of the theory of modern portfolio analysis and show that the characteristics of portfolios are significantly different from those of the individual securities from which they are formed. In fact, portfolio analysis is the recipe for one of the few "free lunches" in economics. By the end of Chapter 6, the reader will have learned the basis of portfolio theory from the relationship of portfolio characteristics to security characteristics to the method of computing sets of portfolios that investors will find desirable.

Although the theory presented at the beginning of the book is relatively new (any economic theory less than 40 years old is new!), it has been around long enough that major breakthroughs have occurred in its implementation. These breakthroughs involve simplification of the amount and type of inputs to the portfolio problem (Chapters 7 and 8), as well as simplification of the computational procedure to find sets of desirable portfolios (Chapter 9). The major advantage in the latter simplification is that the portfolio selection process and the final portfolios selected have a structure with a clear-cut economic rationale, one to which both the practicing security analyst and the economist can relate.

The reader might note that up to now we have discussed sets of portfolios. These sets contain portfolios that would be desirable to any investor. In Chapters 10 and 11, we examine how an individual investor might choose the one optimal portfolio (for him or her) from among the sets of portfolios designed to appeal to any investor. We conclude Part 2 with a discussion of the potential benefits derived from diversifying portfolios internationally.

Part 3 provides a discussion of equilibrium in the capital markets. This material usually is included under the rubric of the capital asset pricing model or arbitrage pricing theory and shows how portfolio theory can be used to infer what equilibrium returns and prices will be for individual securities. This area is changing rapidly. But, as the reader will see, empirical tests suggest that the theory as it now stands provides great insight into the functioning of security markets and the pricing of individual issues. It also suggests ways that equilibrium theory can be used to manage portfolios more meaningfully.

Part 4 of this book deals with the characteristics and evaluation of individual securities. In this part we discuss whether security markets are efficient, the valuation of common stocks, the characteristics of earnings and their role in the valuation process, the valuation of bonds, the nature of and valuation of options, and finally the valuation and uses of futures.

Part 5 is a discussion of the evaluation of the investment analysis and portfolio management process. In writing this part we have stressed techniques for evaluating every stage of the process, from the forecasting of earnings by security analysts to the performance of portfolios that are finally selected. It seems fitting that a book that deals primarily with investment analysis and portfolio management should end with a discussion of how to tell if these functions are performed well.

The book was designed to serve as a text for courses both in portfolio theory and in investment analysis that have an emphasis on portfolio theory. We have used it for these purposes at New York University for several years. For the course in portfolio analysis, we use Chapters 4–16 plus Chapters 24 and 26. This thoroughly introduces the students to modern portfolio theory and general equilibrium models (capital asset pricing models and arbitrage pricing models).

The book can also be used in a course in investments where both portfolio analysis and security analysis are discussed. For these purposes, the institutional material in Chapters 1 and 2, the security analysis chapters of Part 4, as well as Chapter 25 on the Evaluation of Security Analysis, are appropriate, and some of the advanced portfolio theory and general equilibrium chapters of Parts 2 and 3 can be deleted. Each professor's preference and the dictates of the course will ultimately determine the final choice. One possible choice that has been successfully used was the replacement of much of Chapter 6 and Chapters 8, 11, 14, 15, and 16 with the chapters on security analysis contained in Part 4. Courses covering portfolio theory and investments vary greatly in their content. We have included in this book those areas that we view as most relevant.

We believe that this book will be an aid to the practicing security analyst and portfolio manager. It is remarkable how quickly the ideas of modern portfolio theory have found their way into investment practice. The manager who wishes an overview of modern portfolio theory and investment analysis will find that Chapters 4, 5, 7, 9, 12, and 17–25 will provide a thorough and readable understanding of the issues. Specialists who are concerned with issues on implementation will find that the other chapters will equip them with the most modern tools available.

As the reader may know, New York University has not only the normal MBA and undergraduate student, but also courses intended for full-time portfolio managers and securities analysts. The professional reader can be assured that the book has been used in these courses and that some of our most enthusiastic responses came from practicing managers who learned not only the ideas of modern portfolio theory and investment analysis, but also its strengths and weaknesses.

In writing this book, our purpose has been to make all the material accessible to students of portfolio analysis and investment management, both at the undergraduate and graduate levels. To the extent possible, the text stresses the economic intuition behind the subject matter. Mathematical proofs involving more than simple algebra are placed in footnotes, appendices, or specially noted sections of the text. They can be deleted without losing the general thrust of the subject matter. In addition, we have included problems both in the text and at the end of each chapter. We have tried to capture in this book the frontier of the state of the art of modern portfolio analysis, general equilibrium theory, and investment analysis while presenting it in a form that is accessible and has intuitive appeal.

A book must, of necessity, present material in a certain order. We have tried to present the material so that much of it can be used in alternative sequences. For example, we tend to teach formal utility analysis after many of the concepts of portfolio analysis. However, we realize that many professors prefer to begin with a discussion of utility analysis. Thus, this chapter in particular could be read immediately after the introductory chapter.

We wish to extend our thanks to the instructors who provided us with valuable feedback as we revised this edition. These reviewers include: Susan M. Mangiero; Sacred Heart University; Stephen J. Brown, Stern School of Business, New York University; Stuart L. Gillan, The University of Hong Kong; James Bradfield, Hamilton College; Gregory Kadlec, Virginia Polytechnic University; David Ikenberry, Rice University; and Brent Sorenson, Brown University.

Earlier editions of this work had the benefit of reviews by many of our colleagues. Those reviews have helped to shape the text you now hold. Those colleagues include Chris Blake at Fordham who was been especially helpful in all of the revisions; Ed Blomeyer, Louisiana State University; Gregg Brauer, University of Iowa; Tom Conine, Fairfield University; Cheol S. Eun, Georgia Institute of Technology; Jim Farrell, MPT Associates; Bob Ferguson, Fordham; Steve Figlewski, New York University; Ed Friedman, City College of New York; Gabriel Hawawini, INSEAD; Nancy Jacob, University of Washington; Charles Jones, North Carolina State University; Maurice Joy, University of Kansas; Bob Klemokosky, Indiana University; Dorothy Koehl, University of Maryland; Richard Kolodny, University of Maryland; Jerry Levine, Temple University; Joseph Liberman, University of Illinois, Chicago Circle; James Gale, Michigan Technological University; Richard McEnally, University of North Carolina; Don Tuttle, Indiana University; Stuart Wood, Tulane University; Ronald E. Copley, University of North Carolina, Wilmington; Edward A. Downe, University of New Haven; C. Thomas Howard, University of Denver; Robert A. Korajczyk, Northwestern University; Tom Schneeweis, University of Massachusetts; Maurry Tamarkin, Clark University; Thomas J. Zweirlein, Colorado State University; Robert F. Stambaugh, University of Pennsylvania; Roger Murray, Professor Emeritus at Columbia University; and William Fouse, Chairman of Mellon Capital Management Corporation. Earlier editions also benefited from the help of our colleagues at New York University, including Ramasastry Ambarish, Yahov Amihud, Steve Figlewski, Mustafa Gultekin (University of North Carolina), Tom Ho, Avner Kalay (University of Utah), Jerry Kallberg, Mike Keenan, Richard Levich, Prafulla Nabar, Bob Schwartz, and Marti Subrahmanyan. Matt Hlavka and Bruce Tuckman provided much help with the revision. We also thank Ingrid Persaud and Selma Rabinowitz for their help in typing the revisions. This new edition benefited from additional comments from Joseph Finnerty, University of Illinois, Champaign; Diana Harrington, Babson College; Frederick Puritz, SUNY Oneonta; Linda Richardson, Siena College; Anthony Sanders, Ohio State University; Ethel Silverstein, New York Institute of Technology; and Joan Lamm-Tennant, Villanova University.

The text of the present edition is quite similar to the successful versions of earlier editions. Those versions owed much to the help we received from Kirk Vandezande, Simon Frazer, Finbarr Bradley at Trinity College, and Seth Grossman. Finally, we wish to acknowledge Dr. Watson. We have noted her contribution to utility analysis and security valuation in previous books. Her contribution to earlier versions of this book were substantial. Her untimely death meant that we did not have the benefit of her excellent advice on this latest edition, though her help is still reflected in the book you have before you.

E.J. Elton
M.J. Gruber

Software Applications

We are especially pleased to announce the continued publication of the software program, The Investment Portfolio. This program is a self-contained, Windows-based tool that will allow the user to perform most of the analyses in this book.

We wish to thank Chris Blake of Fordham University for his help in designing, developing, and beta-testing this package. Philippe Marchal and Rick Clinton of Intellipro, Inc., developed the software, and their efficient and thorough development work was critical. To order this software package please call Wiley's Customer Service Department at 1-800-225-5945 or visit our web sites at www.wiley.com or www.wiley.co.uk (for customers in Europe, South Africa, and the Middle East). In addition to The Investment Portfolio, a complete *Instructor's Manual with Tests,* prepared by Chris Blake in conjunction with the authors, is available on the Book Companion Web Site at www.wiley.com/college/elton.

A NOTE TO THE SIXTH EDITION

This edition marks a change in authorship. Our long time friends Stephen Brown and Will Goetzmann have joined us as coauthors. We have taken major responsibility for changes in this edition. For subsequent editions Stephen and Will are going to play a major role. In this edition we updated all tables and changed the discussion to reflect these changes. We have added significant material on some of the issues involved in asset allocation, introduced value at risk, added some more discussion on multiperiod decision making, and significantly changed the bond chapter, option chapter, and the chapter on portfolio performance. In addition we have updated the biographical references. We wish to thank Chris Blake of Fordham, who we have often worked with on research for many helpful suggestions for this edition. This book is a labor of love. We are delighted to have Stephen and Will join us.

Final Thoughts

More than 20 years have passed since we began to write the first edition of this book. Progress has been made in several areas, and yet new changes have occurred that reopen old questions. The acceptance of quantitative techniques by the investment community both here and overseas has grown at a rate we would not have dreamed of then. The use of modern portfolio techniques for stocks and bonds, dividend discount models, concepts of passive portfolios, the incorporation of international assets in portfolios, and the use of futures and options as risk control techniques are very widespread. Yet the world of investments continues to change. No sooner do we begin to believe that the capital asset pricing model (CAPM) describes reality than the arbitrage pricing theory (APT) comes along. No sooner do we convince ourselves that markets are efficient than market anomalies become hot topics. No sooner do we say that security analysis does not pay than we justify the cost of analysis in a world of partially revealing prices. No sooner is market timing discredited than it arises again under the name of tactical asset allocation.

Will the field continue to evolve and will today's truths become less true tomorrow? Probably. We will continue to learn. We know more about the capital markets now than we did 20 years ago. There is still a lot more to learn. That is why there will no doubt be a Seventh Edition of this book, and why there are securities and strategies that have expected returns above the riskless rate.

E.J.E.
M.J.G.

Contents

Part 1

INTRODUCTION

1

Introduction

Almost everyone owns a portfolio (group) of assets. This portfolio is likely to contain real assets such as a car, a house, or a refrigerator, as well as financial assets such as stocks and bonds. The composition of the portfolio may be the result of a series of haphazard and unrelated decisions or it may be the result of deliberate planning. In this book we discuss the basic principles underlying rational portfolio choice and what this means for prices determined in the marketplace. We confine our attention to financial assets, although much of the analysis we develop is equally applicable to real assets.

An investor is faced with a choice from among an enormous number of assets. When one considers the number of possible assets and the various possible proportions in which each can be held, the decision process seems overwhelming. In the first part of this book we analyze how decision makers can structure their problems so that they are left with a manageable number of alternatives. Later sections of the book deal with rational choice among these alternatives, methods for implementing and controlling the decision process, and equilibrium conditions in the capital markets to which the previous analysis leads.

Let us examine the composition of this book in more detail.

OUTLINE OF THE BOOK

This book is divided into six parts. The first part provides background material on securities and financial markets. The reader already familiar with these topics can go directly to Part 2.

The second and longest part deals with the subject of portfolio analysis. Portfolio analysis is concerned with finding the most desirable group of securities to hold, given the properties of each of the securities. This part of the book is itself divided into four sections. The first of these sections is entitled "Mean Variance Portfolio Theory." This section deals with determining the properties of combinations (portfolios) of risky assets given the properties of the individual assets, delineating the characteristics of portfolios that make them preferable to others, and, finally, showing how the composition of the preferred portfolios can be determined.

At the end of this section readers will know almost all that they need to know about the theory of portfolio selection. This theory is more than 45 years old. In the ensuing years, a tremendous amount of work has been devoted to implementing this theory. The second section of Part 2 is concerned with the implementation and simplification of portfolio theory. The topics covered include simplifying the quantity and type of input needed to do portfolio analysis, and simplifying the computational procedure used to find the composition of the efficient portfolios.

The third section of Part 2 deals with the selection of that one portfolio that best meets the needs of an investor. This section has two chapters. The first one discusses selection from the viewpoint of maximizing expected utility. This concept should be familiar to any student who has had a basic course in economics. The second chapter discusses alternative ways to select the best alternative. The assumption here is that the investor will not go through the arithmetic of expected utility maximization, but will employ one of the alternative and simpler decision-making criteria suggested in the economic literature.

The final section of Part 2 deals with the impact of the opportunity to diversify a stock portfolio across international boundaries. As the reader might suspect, any increase in the set of possible investment opportunities should increase portfolio performance.

Part 3 deals with models of equilibrium prices and returns in the capital markets. If investors behave as portfolio theory suggests they should, then their actions can be aggregated to determine prices at which securities will sell.

The first two chapters of Part 3 deal with some alternative forms of equilibrium relationships. Different assumptions about the characteristics of capital markets and the way investors behave lead to different models of equilibrium. The third chapter in this part of the book deals with empirical tests of how well these theoretical models describe reality. The final chapter in Part 3 presents both the theoretical basis of and empirical evidence on the newest theory of relative prices: the Arbitrage Pricing Theory.

The fourth part of the book deals with some issues in investment analysis. The first question examined is the speed with which new information is incorporated into the share price. If new information is immediately and accurately incorporated into the share price, then there can be no payoff from security analysis, while if information is more slowly incorporated into the share price, it may pay to engage in certain types of analysis. The key to security analysis is the method used to turn forecasts of fundamental firm characteristics into forecasts of price performance. This is the subject of the second chapter in Part 4, entitled "Valuation Process." Virtually every valuation process employs forecasts of earnings as one important input. A detailed analysis of earnings is presented as an example of methods of forecasting inputs to valuation models. The next two chapters in Part 4 deal with the theory of interest rates, the pricing of bonds, and the management of bond portfolios. The final two chapters in Part 4 deal with the valuation of options and financial futures. The markets for security options and for futures are among the fastest growing markets in the country. In addition, the theory of option pricing has important implications for generating the inputs to portfolio analysis. Futures, because of their low transaction costs, are an important tool for modifying portfolio composition.

The fifth part of the book is concerned with evaluating the investment process. The first chapter in this section deals with the evaluation of portfolio performance. In this chapter we discuss the best methods of evaluating portfolio performance and how well-managed portfolios have performed. In contrast to the voluminous literature on portfolio performance, almost nothing has been written about how to evaluate the other steps in the investment process. For example, very little has been written about how to evaluate forecasts of security analysts or how to evaluate the valuation process. The second chapter in this part of the book deals with these problems. The final part of the book integrates the material contained in the earlier parts.

THE ECONOMIC THEORY OF CHOICE: AN ILLUSTRATION UNDER CERTAINTY

All decision problems have certain elements in common. Any problem involves the delineation of alternatives, the selection of criteria for choosing among those alternatives, and, finally, the solution of the problem. Furthermore, individual solutions can often be aggregated to describe equilibrium conditions that prevail in the marketplace. A large part of this book will be concerned with following these steps for the selection of risky assets. But before we start this problem, let us examine a simpler one, under certainty, to illustrate the elements of the solution to any economic problem.

Consider an investor who will receive with certainty an income of $10,000 in each of two years. Assume that the only investment available is a savings account yielding 5% per year. In addition, the investor can borrow money at a 5% rate.

How much should the investor save and how much should he or she consume each year? The economic theory of choice proposes to solve this problem by splitting the analysis into two parts. First, specify those options that are available to the investor. Second, specify how to choose among these options. This framework for analysis carries over to more complex problems.

The Opportunity Set

The first part of the analysis is to determine the options open to the investor. One option available is to save nothing and consume $10,000 in each period. This option is indicated by the point B in Figure 1.1.

Scrooge would choose another option. He would save all income in the first period and consume everything in the second. In the second period his savings account would be worth the $10,000 he saves in period 1 plus interest of 5% on the $10,000 or $10,500. Adding this to his second-period income of $10,000 gives him a consumption in period 2 of $10,500 + $10,000 = $20,500. This is indicated by point A in Figure 1.1.

Another possibility is to consume everything now and not worry about tomorrow. This would result in consumption of $10,000 from this period's income plus the maximum the investor could borrow against next period's income. If X is the amount borrowed, then X plus the interest paid for borrowing X equals the amount paid back. Since the investor's income in the second period is $10,000, the maximum amount is borrowed if X plus the interest on X at 5% equals $10,000.

$$X + 0.05X = 10,000$$

or

$$X = \frac{10,000}{1.05} = \$9,524$$

Thus, the maximum the investor can consume in the first period is $19,524. This is indicated by point C in Figure 1.1. Note that points A, B, and C lie along a straight line. This did not happen by accident. In fact, all of the enormous possible patterns of consumption in periods 1 and 2 will lie along this straight line. Let us see why.

The amount the investor consumes in the two periods is constrained by the amount of income the investor has available in the two periods. Let C_1 be the consumption in period 1 and C_2 be the consumption in period 2. The amount consumed in period 2 is the income in period 2 of $10,000 plus the period 2 value of the savings in period 1. Remember that the value of period 1 savings can be negative, for the investor could have dissaved. That is,

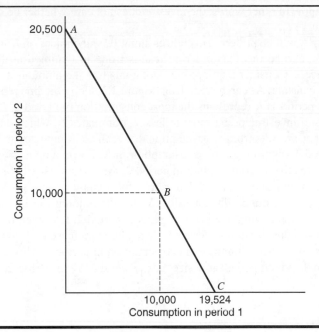

Figure 1.1   The investor's opportunity set.

he could have borrowed in period 1 and consumed more than his period 1 income. As of period 2, the value of the savings in period 1 is the amount saved in period 1 ($10,000 minus what is consumed) plus accumulated interest. Putting this in equation form we have

$$\begin{bmatrix} \text{Period 2} \\ \text{consumption} \end{bmatrix} = \begin{bmatrix} \text{Period 2} \\ \text{income} \end{bmatrix} + \begin{bmatrix} \text{Amount} \\ \text{saved in 1} \end{bmatrix}[1+0.05]$$

$$C_2 = \$10,000 + (10,000 - C_1)(1.05)$$

$$C_2 = \$20,500 - (1.05)C_1$$

This is, of course, the equation for a straight line and is the line shown in Figure 1.1. It has an intercept of $20,500, which results from zero consumption in period 1 ($C_1 = 0$) and is the point A we determined earlier. It has a slope equal to -1.05 or minus the quantity one plus the interest rate. The value of the slope reflects the fact that each dollar the investor consumes in period 1 is a dollar he cannot invest and, hence, reduces period 2 consumption by one dollar plus the interest he could earn on the dollar or a total of $1.05. Thus an increase in period 1's consumption of a dollar reduces period 2's consumption by $1.05.

The investor is left with a large number of choices. We usually refer to the set of choices facing the investor as the opportunity set. Let us now examine how an investor selects the optimum consumption pattern from the opportunity set.

The Indifference Curves

The economic theory of choice states that an investor chooses among the opportunities shown in Figure 1.1 by specifying a series of curves called utility functions or indifference curves. A representative set is shown in Figure 1.2. These curves represent the investor's preference for income in the two periods. The name "indifference curves" is used because the curves are constructed so that everywhere along the same curve the investor is assumed to be equally happy. In other words, the investor does not care whether he obtains point A, B, or C along curve I_1.

Choices along I_1 will be preferred to choices along I_2, and choices on I_2 will be preferred to choices on I_3, and so on. This ordering results from an assumption that the investor prefers more to less. Consider the line OM. Along this line the amount of consumption in period 1 is held constant. As can be seen from Figure 1.2, along the line representing equal consumption in period 1, I_1 represents the most consumption in period 2, I_2 the next most, and so on. Thus, if investors prefer more to less, I_1 dominates I_2, which dominates I_3.

The curved shape results from an assumption that each additional dollar of consumption forgone in period 1 requires greater consumption in 2. For example, if consumption in period 1 is large relative to consumption in period 2, the investor should be willing to give up a dollar of consumption in period 1 in return for a small increase in consumption in period 2. In Figure 1.2 this is illustrated by Δ_1 for the amount the investor gives up in period 1 and Δ_2 for the amount the investor gains in period 2. However, if the investor has very few dollars of consumption in period 1, then a large increase in 2 is required in order to be indifferent about giving up the extra consumption in period 1. This is represented by the Δ_1' in period 1 (which is the same size as Δ_1) and the Δ_2' in period 2, which is much larger than Δ_2.

The Solution

The indifference curves and the opportunity set represent the tools necessary for the investor to reach a solution. The optimum consumption pattern for the investor is determined by the

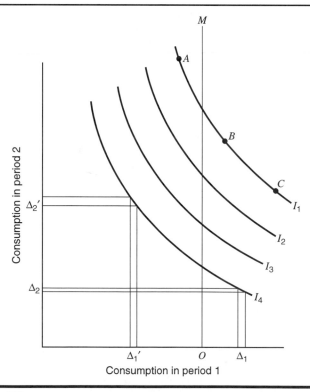

Figure 1.2   Indifference curves.

point at which a number of the set of indifference curves is tangent to the opportunity set (point D in Figure 1.3). Let us see why. The investor can select either of the two consumption patterns indicated by the points where I_3 intersects the line ABC in Figure 1.3. But we have argued that the investor is better off selecting a consumption pattern lying on an indifference curve located above and to the right of I_3 if possible. The investor will move to higher indifference curves until the highest one that contains a feasible consumption pattern is reached. That is the one just tangent to the opportunity set. This is I_2 in Figure 1.3, and the consumption pattern the investor will choose is given by the point of tangency point D. The question might be asked why doesn't the investor move up to a point along I_0 since this would be preferable to a point along I_2? The answer is that there is no investment opportunity available on line I_0.

An Example: Determining Equilibrium Interest Rates

We take another look at the investor's possible decision to see how it can help in determining equilibrium conditions in the market. The optimum decision could occur in three sections of Figure 1.3: A to B, point B, or B to C. If the optimum occurs in the segment AB, then the investor lends money at the 5% rate. If the optimum occurs at point B, then the investor is neither a borrower nor a lender. Finally, if the optimum occurs in segment BC, the investor borrows against future income at the 5% rate.

In this simple framework, equilibrium in the marketplace is easy to determine. At a 5% interest rate this investor wishes to lend $2,000, the difference between $10,000 in income and $8,000 in consumption. Summing across all investors who wish to lend when the interest rate is 5% gives one point on the supply curve. Similarly summing across investors who wish to borrow at a 5% interest rate gives one point on the demand curve. As the interest rate changes, the amount our hypothetical investor wishes to lend also changes. In fact, if the interest rate is low enough, the investor may change from a lender to a borrower. By

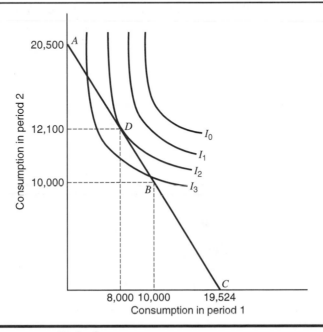

Figure 1.3   Investor equilibrium.

varying the interest rate, the supply and demand curve can be traced out and the equilibrium interest rate determined. The equilibrium interest rate is that rate at which the amount investors wish to borrow is equal to the amount investors wish to lend. This is often called a "market clearing condition." The equilibrium interest rate depends on what each investor's decision problem looks like or the characteristics of a figure like Figure 1.3 for each investor. Figure 1.3 depends on the investor's income in the two periods and the investor's tastes or preferences. Thus, in this simple world, equilibrium interest rates are also determined by the same influences: investors' tastes and investors' income.

CONCLUSION

What we have learned from this simple example is the elements that are necessary to analyze a portfolio problem. We need two components to reach a solution: a representation of the choices available to the investor—called the opportunity set—and a representation of the investor's tastes or preferences—called indifference or utility curves. With these two components we solved this simple problem and can solve the more realistic problems that follow. In addition, this simple example taught us that by aggregating across investors we can construct models of equilibrium conditions in the capital markets. Now we turn to an examination of why and how this framework must be modified to deal realistically with multiple investment alternatives.

MULTIPLE ASSETS AND RISK

If everyone knew with certainty the returns on all assets, then the framework just presented could easily be extended to multiple assets. If a second asset existed that yielded 10%, then the opportunity set involving investment in this asset would be the line $A'BC'$ shown in Figure 1.4. Its intercept on the vertical axis would be $10,000 + (1.10)(10,000) = \$21,000$ and the slope would be $-(1.10)$. If such an asset existed, the investor would surely prefer it if lending and prefer the 5% asset if borrowing. The preferred opportunity set would be A', B, C. Additional assets could be added in a straightforward manner. But this situation is inherently unstable. Two assets yielding different certain returns cannot both be available since everyone will want to invest in the higher yielding one and no one will purchase the lower yielding one. We are left with two possibilities: either there is only one interest rate available in the marketplace or returns are not certain.[1] Since we observe many different interest rates, uncertainty must play an important role in the determination of market rates of return. To deal with uncertainty, we need to develop a more complex opportunity set.

The remainder of this book is concerned with the development of the framework necessary to solve the more complex asset choice problems in the presence of risk. In the next two chapters we deal with the basic notions of the investor's opportunity set under risk.

QUESTIONS AND PROBLEMS

1. Walking down an unfamiliar street one day, you come across an old-fashioned candy store. They have red hots five for one penny, and rock candy—one small piece for

---

[1]Transaction costs, or alternative tax treatment of income from different securities, can explain the existence of some differential rates but nothing like the variety and magnitude of differentials found in the marketplace.

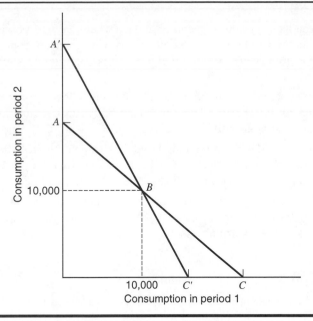

Figure 1.4 Investor's opportunity set with several alternatives.

one penny. You decide to purchase some for yourself and your friends, but you find that you only have $1.00 in your pocket. Construct your opportunity set both geometrically and algebraically. Draw in your indifference map (set of indifference curves). Explain why you have drawn your indifference curves as you have drawn them.

2. Let us solve a two-period consumption investment decision similar to the one presented in the text. Assume that you have income equal to $20 in each of two periods. Furthermore, you have the ability to both lend and borrow money at a 10% rate. Draw the opportunity set and your indifference map. Show the optimum amount of consumption in each period.

3. Assume you can lend and borrow at 10% and have $5,000 in income in each of two periods. What is your opportunity set?

4. Assume you can lend and borrow at 5% and have $20,000 in income in each of two periods. Further assume you have current wealth of $50,000. What is your opportunity set?

5. An individual has two employment opportunities involving the same work conditions, but different incomes. Job 1 yields $Y_1 = 50$, $Y_2 = 30$. Job 2 yields $Y_1 = 40$, $Y_2 = 40$. Given that markets are perfect and bonds yield 5%, which should be selected?

6. Assume you have income of $5,000 in each of two periods and can lend at 10% but pay 20% on borrowing. What is your opportunity set?

7. Assume your preference function P is $P = C_1 + C_2 + C_1 C_2$. Plot the location of all points with $P = 50$, $P = 100$.

8. In Problem 3 what is the preferred choice if the preference function discussed in

Problem 7 holds?

9. Suppose you have $10.00 to spend on dinner. There are two possibilities: pizza at $2.00 a slice or hamburgers at $2.50 apiece. Construct an opportunity set algebraically and graphically. Add indifference curves according to your own individual taste.

10. Using the two-period consumption model, solve the following problem. Assume you can lend and borrow at 5% and your income is $50 in each period. Derive the opportunity set and add your indifference curves.

11. Assume you earn $10,000 in periods 1 and 2. Also you inherit $10,000 in period 2. If the borrowing/lending rate is 20%, what is the opportunity set? What is the maximum that can be consumed in the first period? In the second period?

12. Assume the borrowing rate is 10% and the lending rate is 5%. Also assume your income is $100 in each period. What is the maximum you can consume in each period? What is the opportunity set?

BIBLIOGRAPHY

1. Hirshleifer, Jack. *Investment, Interest, and Capital.* (Englewood Cliffs, N.J.: Prentice-Hall, 1969).
2. Markowitz, Harry. *Portfolio Selection: Efficient Diversification of Investments.* (New York: John Wiley & Sons, Inc. 1959).
3. Sharpe, William. *Portfolio Theory and Capital Markets.* (New York: McGraw-Hill, 1970).

2

Financial Securities

This chapter is meant to introduce the reader to the principal financial instruments, their return characteristics, and the indexes that are used to represent their return. The nature of the material means that this chapter is much more descriptive than subsequent chapters. Those readers already familiar with financial instruments and the indexes that can be used to represent their return can skip to Chapter 3. Those readers who have had a prior finance course and are familiar with financial instruments but are not familiar with the principal indexes used to represent their returns can skip to the section in this chapter titled, "The Return Characteristics of Alternative Security Types." We can think of a *security* as a legal contract representing the right to receive future benefits under a stated set of conditions. There are a large number of financial securities. When you take out a mortgage on a house or lease a car, the contract you sign is a financial security. We are going to limit the set of financial securities we deal with by selecting primarily from among those that are traded in organized markets. In fact, Chapter 3 will focus on the nature of alternative market structures for the securities described in this chapter.

In the first section of this chapter, we will describe the characteristics of a broad sample of financial securities. In the second section, we will examine the performance of a representative sample of financial assets to begin to understand the relevant characteristics of different types of securities. Finally, we will discuss indexes that are used to represent the performance of classes of securities. This later material is included because in later chapters we will often discuss market performance. We will need an indication of performance and will use one or more of the indexes described in this chapter.

TYPES OF MARKETABLE FINANCIAL SECURITIES

There are many ways to categorize financial securities. We have found it useful to use the scheme diagrammatically shown at top of next page.

An investor can choose to purchase directly any one of a number of different securities, many of which represent a different type of claim on a private or government entity. Alternatively, an investor can invest in an intermediary (mutual fund), which bundles together a set of direct investments and then sells shares in the portfolio of financial instruments it holds. Because indirect investing involves purchasing shares of bundled direct

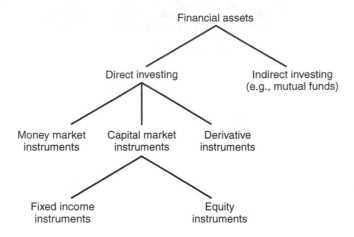

investments, we will discuss indirect investing at the end of this section. Direct investment can be divided by the time horizon of the investment. Investments in debt that have a life of less than one year are usually called *money market instruments*. These can be further divided according to whether the money market instrument is issued by a government entity or a private entity. Investments with maturities of more than one year are generally called *capital market instruments*. The latter can be divided according to whether they are debt or equity instruments, and debt instruments can be further divided according to whether they are issued by a government entity or a private entity. The final category of financial assets we discuss is derivative instruments. They are called *derivative instruments* because their payoff depends on (is derived from) the price of one of the primary assets already discussed. We will now discuss each of these categories of financial assets in turn.

Money Market Securities

Money market securities are short-term debt instruments sold by governments, financial institutions, and corporations. The important characteristic of these securities is that they have maturities when issued of one year or less. The minimum size of a transaction in a money market instrument is typically large, usually exceeding $100,000. In addition, some market securities that we will describe are not actively traded on exchanges. Given the minimum transaction size and the inactive trading of some securities, many individuals who wish to own these instruments will do so by holding a mutual fund (money market fund). These funds are discussed later in this chapter. The major money market instruments are listed in Table 2.1.

Table 2.1   Money Market Instruments

Treasury Bills
Repurchase Agreement (Repos or RPs)
LIBOR
Negotiable Certificate of Deposit (CDs)
Bankers Acceptances
Commercial Paper
Eurodollars

Table 2.1 contains a long list of securities, and we do not intend to discuss each in detail. We will discuss three securities that play a large role in later analysis in this book and briefly summarize some general characteristics of the remaining securities.

Treasury Bills U.S. Treasury bills are the least risky and the most marketable of all money market instruments. They represent a short-term IOU of the U.S. federal government. While most money market instruments are sold in minimum denominations of $100,000, Treasury bills (T-bills) are sold in minimum denominations of $10,000. New T-bills are issued by the federal government at frequent intervals. New 91- and 182-day T-bills are issued weekly, whereas 52-week T-bills are issued monthly. An active secondary market with very low transaction costs exists for trading T-bills. T-bills are sold at a discount from face value (*face value* is the cash payment the investor will receive at maturity) and pay no explicit interest payments. The difference between the purchase price and the face value constitutes the return the investor receives.[1]

Treasury bills play a special role in financial theory. Because they are considered to have no risk of default, have very short-term maturities, have a known return, and are traded in active markets, they are the closest approximations that exist to a riskless investment. The rate on 30-day Treasury bills will be used throughout the book to approximate the monthly riskless rate of interest.

Repurchase Agreements (Repos) A repurchase agreement is an agreement between a borrower and a lender to sell and repurchase a U.S. government security. A borrower, usually a government securities dealer, will institute the Repo by contracting to sell securities to a lender at a particular price and simultaneously contracting to buy back the government security at a future date at a specified price. The difference between the two prices represents the return to the lender. The maturity of a Repo is usually very short (less than 14 days) with overnight Repos being fairly common. Longer Repos exist and have been labeled "term Repos"; they frequently have maturities of 30 days or more. The institution on the opposite side of the Repo is said to have a reverse Repo. The party doing the reverse Repo contracts to buy a security at a particular price and to sell it back at a predetermined price and time.

Repos and reverse Repos play an important role in the pricing of derivative securities because they allow short positions to be taken in bonds. The ability to use Repos will be important in the type of arbitrage arguments made in future chapters.

Other Short-Term Instruments Although all short-term instruments are considered to have very low risk, they do tend to offer slight differences in returns according to the type and even specific institution that offers them. CDs (negotiable certificates of deposit) are time deposits with a bank. Bankers' acceptances are contracts by a bank to pay a specific sum of money on a particular date. Both instruments sell at rates which depend on the credit rating of the bank that backs them, although CDs are insured by the Federal Deposit Insurance Corporation up to a limit of $10,000. Eurodollar and Eurodollar CDs are dollar denominated deposits backed by a foreign bank or a European branch of an American bank. Because foreign banks are often subject to less regulation than U.S. banks, instruments issued by foreign banks usually carry larger interest payments than similar instruments issued by U.S. banks. Commercial paper is a short-term debt instrument issued by large well-known corporations, and rates are determined in part by the creditworthiness of the corporations.

In a later section of this chapter, we will use data on one-month Treasury bills to represent the behavior of money market instruments. Although this will serve as an example,

---

[1]The pricing conventions on T-bills are described in Chapter 20 on bond pricing.

keep in mind that other money market instruments will offer different returns because of both differences in maturity and differences in the risk of the issuing institutions. For example, when oil prices dropped dramatically and Texas real estate prices quickly followed, the creditworthiness of Texas banks declined, and CDs in Texas banks sold at much higher yields than did average CDs.

Before leaving this section, we will discuss an important element of money markets that is not an instrument but rather a rate.

The London Interbank Offered Rate (LIBOR)   LIBOR is the rate at which large international banks in London lend money among themselves. We single it out for special mention because it is used as a base rate for setting many types of longer-term loans even in the U.S. markets. Despite the fact that it is a rate between London banks, it is usually quoted for loans expressed in dollars. It is quite common to see longer-term debt instruments having rates that change periodically (and thus have some of the characteristics of shorter-term instruments). These changing rates are usually set at either the Treasury bill rate plus a fixed amount or the LIBOR rate plus a fixed amount.

Capital Market Securities

Capital market securities include instruments with maturities greater than one year and those with no designated maturity at all. The market is generally divided according to whether the instruments contain a promised set of cash flows over time, or offer participation in the future profitability of a company. The first sector is usually referred to as the Fixed Income Market, whereas the second is the Equity Market. Preferred stock, discussed last, is an instrument that has some of the characteristics of each of the other two types.

Fixed Income Securities   Fixed income securities have a specified payment schedule. Most are traditional bonds and promise to pay specific amounts at specific times.[2] Usually this is in the form of prespecified dates for the payment of interest and a specific date for the repayment of principal. In almost all cases, failure to meet any specific payment puts the bond into default with all remaining payments (missed interest plus principal) due immediately. Fixed income securities differ from each other in promised return because of differences which include the maturity of the bonds, the creditworthiness of the issuer, and the taxable status of the bond. We will start by examining the safest type of fixed income securities, those offered by the U.S. federal government.[3]

Treasury Notes and Bonds   The federal government issues fixed income securities over a broad range of the maturity spectrum. Debt instruments from 1 to 10 years in maturity are called *Treasury notes.* Debt instruments with a maturity beyond 10 years are known as *Treasury bonds.* Both notes and bonds pay interest twice a year and repay principal on the maturity date. One difference between Treasury bonds and notes is that some bonds are callable before maturity (most often during the last five years of the bond's life), while notes are not callable.[4] Callability means that the government can force the holder of the bond to sell the bond back to the government at a fixed schedule of prices before maturity. For

---

[2]The pricing and management of fixed income securities is discussed in more detail in Chapters 20 and 21.

[3]One should be aware that the quoted price of a fixed income security is not what the investor pays to purchase the security, rather the investor pays the quoted price plus interest accrued since the last coupon payment.

[4]Treasury bonds issued after 1985 do not contain call provisions.

example, if a bond is callable at $101, the government has the option of buying the bond back at $101. The government would likely exercise the option when it benefits itself, and thus this is disadvantageous to the investor. Thus callable bonds have to offer the investor a higher return to compensate for the possibility of a disadvantageous call.

Treasury instruments are generally considered to be safe from default, and thus differences in expected returns are due to differences in maturity, differences in liquidity, and the presence or absence of a call provision.[5]

Federal Agency Securities and Municipal Securities   Federal agency securities are issued by various federal agencies which have been granted the power to issue debt in order to help certain sectors of the economy. For example, the Farm Credit Banks make funds available for such things as research and short-term loans to farm cooperatives. Federal agency securities are often thought of as a close substitute for Treasury securities. Although they are not backed by the full faith and credit of the federal government, investors assume that the federal government would not allow an agency to default in its payments. However, the lack of an explicit guarantee from the federal government plus the fact that markets for agencies are frequently less liquid than markets for Treasury instruments has resulted in the agency instruments selling at slightly higher yields than Treasury notes and bonds.

Municipal Securities   Municipal bonds are debt instruments sold by political entities such as states, counties, cities, airport authorities, school districts, and such, other than the federal government or its agencies. They differ from agency bonds in that they can (and in rare instances do) default and that their interest is exempt from federal and usually (within the state that issues them) state taxes. The principal types of municipal bonds are general obligation bonds, which are backed by the full faith and credit (taxing power) of the issuer, and revenue bonds, which are backed either by the revenues of a particular project (e.g., a toll road) or the particular municipal agency operating the project.

Because of the tax-exempt feature of municipal bonds, they sell at lower promised yields than nonmunicipal bonds of the same risk. To find an equivalent yield one must explicitly compare the discounted value of after-tax cash flows with before-tax cash flows. It is common practice to use the following approximation to the tax equivalent yield:

$$\text{Taxable equivalent yield} = \frac{\text{Tax - exempt municipal yield}}{1 - \text{Marginal tax rate}}$$

This approximation holds exactly only if municipal bonds sell at par, the treasuries they are being compared to sell at par, and the yield curve is flat. One must be particularly careful using this approximation for municipal bonds selling below par. While the interest payment on municipal bonds is tax exempt, capital gains are subject to taxation.

Corporate Bonds   Corporate bonds are generally similar to government bonds in payment pattern. They promise to pay interest at periodic intervals and to return principal at a fixed date. The major difference is that these bonds are issued by business entities and thus have a risk of default. Corporate bonds are rated as to quality by several agencies, the best known of which are Standard and Poor's and Moody's.[6]

---

[5]The tax implications of different coupon rates can also explain differences in yield; this will be discussed in later chapters.

[6]See Chapter 20 on bond pricing for a more detailed description of bond ratings and their impact on bond prices.

Corporate bonds differ in risk not only because of differences in the probability of default of the issuing corporations, but also because of differences in the nature of their claims on the assets and earnings of the issuing corporations. For example, secured bonds have specific collateral backing them in the event of bankruptcy, whereas unsecured corporate bonds (called debentures) do not. An additional class of bonds called subordinated debentures not only have no specific collateral, but they have a still lower priority claim on assets in the event of default than unsubordinated debentures. In an attempt to gain some protection against bankruptcy, corporate bonds typically place certain restrictions on management behavior as part of the loan agreement (called the bond indenture). Such restrictions might include limiting the payment of dividends or the addition of new debt.

Another notable feature of corporate bonds is that they are most often callable, which means that corporations can force the holder of the bond to surrender them at a fixed price (usually above the price at which the bonds were initially sold) during a set period of time. Corporations usually call bonds at a time when interest rates are below those that existed when the bond was first sold. Thus, the bondholder risks reinvesting his or her proceeds from a call at lower rates than the interest rate of the bond at the time of issuance.

Not So Fixed Income Securities   It is evident from the preceding discussion that fixed income securities do not always pay the security holder the promised payment (because of calls or default). This leads to variability in cash flows received by the investor. Two classes of fixed income securities have even greater variability in cash flows: preferred stocks and mortgage-backed securities. In both cases, variability in cash flows is expected, and variability does not result in the holder's right to force bankruptcy.

Preferred Stock   Preferred stock at first blush resembles an infinite life bond. It promises to pay to the holder periodic payments like coupons, but called dividends rather than interest. There is no return of principal in this case because preferred stock is almost always infinite in life. Preferred stock is not really a fixed payment instrument, however, in that failure to pay the promised dividend does not result in bankruptcy. Usually when a firm fails to pay dividends these dividends are cumulated and all unpaid preferred stock dividends must be paid off before any common stock dividends can be paid.

Preferred stock occupies a middle position between bonds and common stock in terms of priority of payment of income and in terms of return on capital if the corporation is liquidated. In addition, most preferred stock does not actually have an infinite life, because the issues are frequently callable and many of the issues may be converted into common stock at the discretion of the holder. Of course, a combination of callability and convertibility allows the issuer to force conversion. These features affect the risk and reward from holding preferred stocks.

Mortgage-Backed Securities   The last "not so fixed income" security type that is most often classified as a fixed income security is mortgage-backed securities, which represent a share in a pool of mortgages. The best known mortgage-backed security is the Ginnie Mae (GNMA), which are issues of the Government National Mortgage Association. These instruments are backed by the full faith and credit of the U.S. government, so the investor bears no default risks. However, the investor is subject to considerable interest rate risk. These instruments are "pass through" securities, which means that all interest and principal payments on the individual mortgages making up the pool backing a particular GNMA certificate are paid (passed through) to the holder of a GNMA. The stated maturity in GNMAs may be as high as 40 years, but the average life is considerably shorter. The pass-through feature means that the holder will receive a very uncertain stream of future payments, because it's dependent on how fast mortgage holders pay off their mortgages. Furthermore, to the extent that mortgages are paid off when interest rates are low, the investor receives funds at the time when investment opportunities have expected returns below the promised return on the original GNMA. The added element of risk is compensated for by GNMAs selling at a higher promised return than government securities of similar expected life.

Mortgage-backed securities are also issued by several other government agencies and by financial institutions. These securities carry additional risk, since they may be backed by the credit of the issuing body or simply by the pool of mortgages themselves.

Common Stock (Equity)   Common stock represents an ownership claim on the earnings and assets of a corporation. After holders of debt claims are paid, the management of the company can either pay out the remaining earnings to stockholders in the form of dividends or reinvest part or all of the earnings in the business.

The unique feature of common stock (unlike simply owning the business) is that the holder of common stock has limited liability. If a company goes bankrupt, all that the holder of common stocks can lose is his or her original investment in the stock. The creditor cannot look to the general assets of stockholders to finance his claims.

Despite limited liability, because of the residual nature of its claim to earnings and assets, common stock as a class is the riskiest of the securities discussed to this point.[7]

Derivative Instruments

Derivative instruments are securities whose value derives from the value of an underlying security or basket of securities. The instruments are also known as contingent claims, since their values are contingent on the performance of underlying assets. The most common contingent claims are options and futures. An option on a security gives the holder the *right* to either buy (a call option) or sell (a put option) a particular asset or bundle of assets at a future date or during a particular period of time for a specified price. The buyer pays a price for this option, but is free not to exercise this option if prices move in the wrong direction. A future is the *obligation* to buy a particular security or bundle of securities at a particular time for a stated price. A future is simply a delayed purchase of a security. Futures and options are securities that represent side bets on the performance of individual or bundles of securities. There is always a buyer and a seller of an option or future, and the profit (or loss) to the seller is exactly equal to the loss (or profit) of the buyer. The action of the buyer or seller of options or futures does not affect the cash flows to the corporation, nor does it result in a change in the number or type of securities the corporation has outstanding.

The corporation can issue contingent claims, however, and in this case the value of the corporation is often impacted by the action of holders of its contingent claims. Corporate-issued contingent claims include rights and warrants, which allow the holder to purchase common stocks from the corporation at a set price for a particular period of time, and convertible securities (bonds and preferred stocks), which allow the holder to convert an instrument into common stock under specified conditions. Although these corporate contingent claims have many features in common with other derivative instruments, they differ in that if the holders execute them, it results in a change in the attributes of the corporation (e.g., the receipt of cash and or change in the nature and size of capital). This means that these contingent claims are more difficult to analyze than those not issued by the corporation.

---

[7]Common stock issued by some companies can be less risky than some high-risk debt issues.

Indirect Investing

While an investor can purchase any of the instruments described here (and several we haven't touched on), the investor can instead choose to invest indirectly by purchasing the shares of investment companies (mutual funds). A mutual fund holds a portfolio of securities, usually in line with a stated policy and objective. Mutual funds exist which hold only a small set of securities (e.g., short-term tax-free securities or stocks in a particular industry or sector), or broad classes of securities (such as stocks from major stock exchanges around the world, or a broad representation of American stocks and bonds).

Mutual funds come in two flavors: open-end funds and closed-end funds. Open-end fund shares are purchased (and sold) directly from (and to) the mutual fund. They are purchased (and sold) at the value of the net assets standing behind each share, where the net asset value is determined once a day, at a stated time. As a first approximation, if you own 1/100 of the shares outstanding in a mutual fund, your shares are worth 1/100 of the market value of the total portfolio of securities that the fund owns. The reason we say first approximation is that some mutual funds charge a fee when the investor buys a fund (front-end load) and some charge additional fees (back-end load) when an investor sells shares in a fund. For example, in the case of an 8% front-end load you only purchase assets with 92% of the money you put up. Similarly, in the case of a 6% back-end load, you will receive only 94% of the value of the assets your shares represent when you sell the fund. Very often back-end loads decrease as a function of the amount of time the investor holds the fund.

Closed-end funds differ from open-end funds in that they initially sell a predetermined number of shares in the fund. They then take the proceeds (minus costs) from the sale of fund shares and invest in stocks or stock and bonds. Shares in the fund are then traded on an exchange and take on a life of their own. Owning a share in a closed-end fund is like owning a share in any corporation, but the assets of the corporation are stocks and bonds.[8] Unlike open-end funds, the shares of a closed-end mutual fund can sell at a discount or a premium to their net asset value. Premiums and discounts are related to the perceived quality of management and certain tax liabilities. In fact, most closed-end funds sell at a discount from net asset value. The clear exceptions are funds such as the Korean funds, where the only way an American investor can own stocks in Korea is through buying a closed-end fund. These funds sell at a monopoly premium.

Mutual funds may offer the investor special services such as check-writing privileges or the ability to switch between mutual funds (types of investment) in the same family of funds at no costs. Although most offer liquidity, diversification, and "professional management," they do not offer these qualities without a cost. Investors pay a pro rata share of the expenses and management fees charged by the mutual fund company. In addition (for "open-end" funds), investors may pay a sales charge and/or a special charge known as a 12b-1 fee, which is a fee charged to the customer of a fund to compensate the fund for the cost of promoting (e.g., advertising) the fund. We will examine additional attributes of mutual funds in Chapter 24.

THE RETURN CHARACTERISTICS OF ALTERNATIVE SECURITY TYPES

When describing securities in the previous section, we alluded to risk and return. One of the basic tenets of this book is that investors like high return, but don't like high risk. Although we will be much more specific about measuring risk and return in future chapters, it is

---

[8]There is a difference in that income, if paid out to fund shareholders, is not subject to corporate taxes provided certain conditions are met by the fund.

useful to become familiar with the risk and return characteristics of some of the securities we have discussed.

First, we should discuss what we mean by return. We will in most instances use return to indicate the return on an investment over a particular span of time called *holding period return*. Return will be measured by the sum of the change in the market price of a security plus any income received over a holding period divided by the price of a security at the beginning of the holding period. Thus, if a stock started the year at $100, paid $5 in dividends at the end of the year, and had a price of $105 at the end of the year, the return would be 10%.[9]

In describing securities, we mentioned several factors that should affect risk. These included

1. The maturity of an instrument (in general the longer the maturity the more risky it is).
2. The risk characteristic and creditworthiness of the issuer or guarantor of the investment.
3. The nature and priority of the claims the investment has on income and assets.
4. The liquidity of the instrument and the type of market in which it is traded.[10]

If risk is related to these elements, then measures of risk such as the variability of returns should be related to these same factors.

In Figure 2.1, for example, we have plotted the history of annual returns over the 1946–2000 period for short-term Treasury bills, long-term Treasury bonds, and common

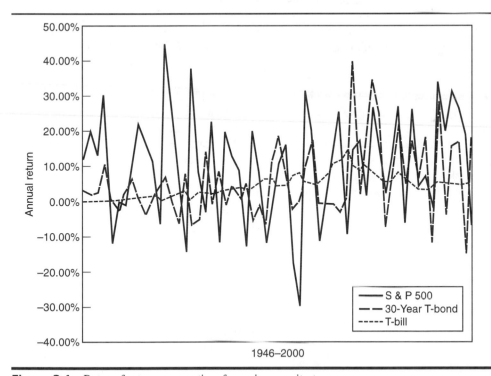

Figure 2.1   Rates of returns versus time for major security types.

---

[9]If dividends or other income is received during the period of time over which return is computed, an assumption must be made about the rate at which the cash flow is reinvested until the end of the period.

[10]This will be discussed in Chapter 3.

stock. Examination of the graph makes it clear that Treasury bonds have a more variable return pattern than Treasury bills due to the longer maturity of the claim. Common stocks show even more variability because the issuer has a higher risk and because the claims on income and earnings are more junior in nature.

Although we won't introduce formal measures of risk until Chapter 4, let us just state at this time that a widely accepted measure of risk (metric for capturing the type of variability shown in Figure 2.1) is called the standard deviation. The standard deviations of the return series on several instruments, including the securities shown in Figure 2.1, together with the average return for each series, are shown in Table 2.2.

As you can see, the ranking of standard deviation is consistent with the ranking you perceived by simply looking at the graph. We've added three more categories to the three assets graphed in Figure 2.1.

One of the major tenets of this book is that returns (over long periods of time) should be consistent with risk. In fact, the average historical returns presented earlier are broadly consistent with this.

An examination of historical returns on security types such as those presented earlier is frequently used as a starting point for preparing forecasts of the return expected from broad classes of assets.

For example, a forecaster might start with a forecast of the inflation rate over the next year. Economists argue that Treasury bills over long periods of time should compensate investors for any loss in purchasing power (inflation) plus the time value of money (giving up the use of funds for a short period of time). From Table 2.2 we see that the return on Treasury bills has averaged 0.5% per year over inflation. One forecast of the return for Treasury bills would simply be to add 0.5% to the forecast of inflation. Alternatively, one could simply use current rates.

In a similar manner we can note that the historic difference in returns between Treasury bills and long-term Treasury bonds is 1.7%. However, as with all historical premiums, the historical premium might be modified to reflect current beliefs about the future, relative to the past. However, historical data provide a useful starting place. This is often called a term premium. Although it depends on supply and demand conditions to the capital markets and the pattern of longer-term expectations about the movement in short-term rates, the term premium also depends on the risk preferences of investors. Longer-term bonds have more variable returns than short-term bonds.

The difference between long-term corporate bonds rates and the rate on long-term government bonds (0.5%) is compensation for the greater risk of default of corporate bonds.

The rate of return on large common stocks is 6.4% higher than the rate of return on long-term corporate bonds because of the greater risk associated with the future cash flows on large stocks. The rate on small stocks is 5.3% higher than the rate on larger stocks, due in part to the added risk associated with small stocks.

Table 2.2 Return and Risk for Selected Types of Securities in Percent Per Year

	Average Return	Standard Deviation
Treasury Bills	3.8	3.2
Treasury Bonds	5.5	9.3
Common Stock (Large Stocks)	13.3	20.1
Inflation	3.2	4.5
Corporate Bonds	5.9	8.7
Small Stocks	17.6	33.6

The type of building blocks approach to rates of return on security types presented earlier is frequently used to forecast rates of return in the future. That is, starting with either forecasts of inflation or the Treasury bill rate, management will modify historic differentials in order to estimate the expected returns on categories of securities. Modifications of the past differentials for forecasting are based on forecasts of supply and demand conditions in different capital markets as well as on forecasts of general economic activity.

We have indicated the return performance of some broad classes of securities. In doing so we have used a set of performance indexes without actually describing the indexes. Since we will often talk about indexes of general performance and "the market" in this book, it is worthwhile spending a short amount of time reviewing some widely used indexes.

STOCK MARKET INDEXES

The oldest continuously quoted index of stock price performance in the United States is the Dow Jones Industrial Average Index (DJIA); this index has been computed since 1896. Since 1928, it has consisted of a price-weighted average of 30 large "blue chip" stocks. When the index was originally constructed it contained 20 stocks and the value of the index was found by adding together the prices of the 20 stocks (assuming the investor bought one share of each stock). Today the average is computed by adding together the price of 30 stocks and dividing by an adjustment factor.[11] Despite the fact that this index is the most widely quoted stock market index it has some flaws. First of all, 30 stocks, particularly 30 stocks that are among the largest, represent at best a very narrow definition of the market.

Second and perhaps most important, the implicit price weighting in the index assumes that an investor is equally likely to buy one share of any stock. Another way to view this is that the investor is more likely to place a dollar in a share of stock if it sells at a higher price. The "market" represents the aggregate of the action of all investors. All investors in aggregate must hold all stocks in proportion to the fraction that the aggregate market value of any stock represents of the total market value of all stocks. This is clearly different than the Dow Jones index, which weighs each stock by the price of that stock relative to the sum of the market value of one share of each stock in the index. The absurdity to which this weighting can lead is evident by what happens if a stock splits. In a two for one stock split the weighting of the split stock after the split would be one half of the weighting before the split.

Despite these defects in the methodology used in computing this index, the Dow Jones Industrial Average continues to be widely employed and mimicked. For example, one of the most widely used indexes of the Japanese stock market, the Nikkei 225, is computed in the same manner as the Dow Jones index. The index does allow the rate of price increase to be computed for a well-defined strategy: buy one share of each stock in the index, selling off any additional shares received due to stock splits or stock dividends while reallocating the proceeds among all shares in the index. To compute the rate of price appreciation from this strategy one simply takes the change in the index over a certain period of time and divides by the value of the index at the beginning of the period. Note that this only provides a rate of price appreciation, not a total rate of return, for dividends are ignored in computing the index.

---

[11]The adjustment factor is computed so as to correct for discontinuities in the index caused when a stock is substituted for one previously in the index or when a stock in the index has a stock split or dividend.

Most stock price indexes are weighted by market capitalization. The next most popular index of the U.S. stock market is the Standard and Poor's Composite 500 stock index (S&P 500). In calculating this index, the price of each of the 500 stocks is multiplied by the market value of the company's shares outstanding, divided by the aggregate market value of all 500 companies. We can think of this index as reporting the price performance of a portfolio where the investor buys the same percentage of the total outstanding stock (in market value) of each company. Note that stock splits and dividends do not affect the index, since they have no effect on the total market value of the outstanding stock.[12]

The reader should note that the Standard and Poor's index does not include dividends; thus, using it directly allows the computation of a rate of price appreciation and not a rate of return. A crude adjustment for dividends (to get total return) can be achieved by splicing the Standard and Poor's Price index with the dividend yield index published by Standard and Poor. In recent years, however, a number of sources, most notably the Center for Research in Security Prices (CRSP), have computed a version of the S&P index corrected for dividends. This is the index we used in the previous section to represent common stocks (large stocks).[13]

In recent years the number of indexes measuring common stock performance here and abroad has proliferated. Large populations of stocks are represented in the United States by, among others, the New York Stock Exchange index (including all stocks listed on NYSE), the Amex index, the Wilshire 5000 stock index (NYSE, American Stock Exchange, actively traded over-the-counter stocks), and such. They are all market-weighted indexes, though they do not include dividends. CRSP has available a number of return indexes for different groups of stocks on the New York, American, and over-the-counter markets. These are calculated on a market-weighted basis and include return from reinvestment of dividends.

Finally, a number of international stock market indexes are market weighted and are computed with dividends. For example, Morgan Stanley International computes indexes for more than 20 countries as well as for different geographical sectors of the world and an Aggregate World index.

BOND MARKET INDEXES

Although almost all of the major stock market indexes exclude dividends and thus are not total return indexes, the major bond indexes are total return indexes, for they include interest payments as well as capital gains.[14] The best known bond indexes are constructed by Lehman Brothers, Merrill Lynch, and Salomon Brothers. They are all market-weighted total return indexes including all issues above a certain size. Furthermore, subindexes exist covering different parts of the bond market by maturity as well as by type of issuer.

Perhaps the use of market weighting and the inclusion of cash flows (interest) in the indexes reflects the fact that bond indexes were constructed more recently than stock indexes, when the concepts of market weighting and total return were better understood.

---

[12]The stock split could affect expectations about the future cash flows of the firm and its market value.

[13]The monthly version of the CRSP index treats all dividends paid on a stock as reinvested at the end of the month. The assumption is implicitly made that cash payments earn no return during the remainder of the month in which they are paid.

[14]Lehman Brothers and Salomon Brothers compute their indexes on a monthly basis and assume any interest paid during a month is reinvested at the end of the month. Merrill Lynch computes their indexes on a daily basis and reinvests paid interest at the end of the day. All prices used in computing these indexes are quoted price plus accrued interest. This is the price an investor would have to pay for the bond.

One caution on using these indexes is that a number of issues in the indexes are not actively traded. The prices of these issues represent price estimates based on issues that are traded; this estimation process can be a source of inaccuracy.

The set of bond indexes with the longest history are those compiled by Ibbotson and Associates. Ibbotson reports monthly returns from the beginning of 1926 to the present for Treasury bills, long-term government bonds, intermediate-term government bonds, and long-term corporate bonds. These series are excellent for gaining perspective on the major bond markets because of their long history. However, the user of these series should be aware that the number of bonds included in each of the series are not the same. For example (a) the long-term corporate bond series currently includes nearly all Aaa and Aa rated corporate bonds, whereas (b) the long-term government bond series is based on a single government bond of approximately 20 years maturity selected at the start of each year.[15]

The indexes mentioned earlier compiled by Merrill Lynch, Salomon, and Lehman both cover more bonds and include indexes for more sectors than the Ibbotson indexes; however, they are only available for a much shorter period of time.

CONCLUSION

We have described the attributes of a broad representation of financial assets in this chapter. We've looked at some indexes that are used to measure the performance of broad classes of assets, and we've examined in risk and return terms the characteristics of a representative set of assets. We have not discussed the markets these assets trade on nor the impact of market structure on the characteristics of assets; these will be discussed in Chapter 3.

---

[15]See Ibbotson annual yearbooks for a detailed description of the construction of each of the bond series.

3

Financial Markets

Almost every chapter in this book is concerned with selecting securities, constructing portfolios, and the evaluation of these decisions. In this chapter we will discuss how securities are traded and the nature of the markets in which they are traded. This chapter, like Chapter 2, is more descriptive and less analytical than the rest of the book. The reader who is familiar with the mechanics of the markets in which securities are traded or who is not concerned with this subject can go directly to Chapter 4 with no loss of continuity.

The characteristics of markets can influence trading costs, the speed with which information is reflected in prices, and the accuracy with which prices reflect available information. Thus, characteristics of markets can determine how often one should trade as well as the degree of mispricing of a security (or suboptimality of a portfolio) before a trade could be profitable.

The chapter is divided into four sections: (1) the mechanics of trading of a security, (2) margin, (3) the nature and structure of markets, and (4) special characteristics of trades, including their type and costs.

TRADING MECHANICS

An individual wishing to buy or sell a security would contact a salesperson at a brokerage firm (called an *account executive* or *registered representative*) and place an order. The order must specify

1. The name of the issuer of the security and the type of security the investor wishes to trade (e.g., a 20-year U.S. government bond or General Motors common stock).
2. Whether the order is a purchase or sale.
3. Order size.
4. What type of order is being placed and for some types of orders the order price.
5. The length of time the order is to be outstanding.

Each of the latter three characteristics will now be discussed in more detail.

Order Size

Trading on the stock markets in the United States is usually carried out in round lots. A round lot for most common stocks is considered 100 shares. An odd lot is a quantity different from 100 shares, such as 27 shares. Orders can be both round and odd lots. Thus an order for 227 shares is two round lots and an odd lot of 27 shares. Generally odd lots have higher transaction costs. For securities other than common stock there is no differential categorization by order size, but there may be a minimum order size. For example, orders of 10, 15, or 100 bonds are not designated as different types of orders.

Types of Orders

Investors may choose the type of order they place with their brokers.

Market Orders   These are the most common type of order placed by an individual investor on the New York Stock Exchange. A market order is an order to buy or sell at the best price currently available. For example, assume IBM is quoted at $80 bid and 80\frac{1}{4}$ ask. This price range means that there are investors in the marketplace willing to pay $80 a share to buy the stock and other investors willing to sell at $80.25. Thus, an investor placing a market order to purchase a security and having that market order filled at the ask price would pay $80.25 per share or $8025 per 100 shares plus commissions. Similarly, a market order for a sale that was executed at the bid price would result in a price of $80 per share less commissions. The purchase or sale price can differ from the bid or ask. First consider a market buy order. Other investors could simultaneously be placing market orders to sell and the shares could be traded inside the bid-ask spread. Since share prices are quoted in minimum differences of 12.5 cents, the price between the bid and ask would be $80.125. Second, the bid-ask spread could change between the time the order is placed and the time it is executed because of other preceding trades or because new information caused a change in the bid-ask spread. Thus an investor using a market order is ensuring execution with some uncertainty as to price.

Limit Orders   This is an order to buy or sell at a maximum or minimum price. An example of a limit order would be an order to sell 100 shares of Bethlehem Steel at $25. The investor placing this limit order would guarantee that the sale would be at a minimum of $25. The investor could receive more than $25 if, for example, the bid price was greater than $25 when the order reached the place of execution. If the limit order is between the bid and ask, it will likely be executed quickly. If it is outside the bid-ask spread, it will be recorded and executed if the trade price equals or passes through it. For example, if Bethlehem was quoted at 24 bid 24$\frac{1}{8}$ ask, a limit order to sell 100 shares at $25 will not be immediately executed. Rather the limit order will be recorded. Trades at $25 will not guarantee the investor's shares will be sold, since there may be other orders at that price. But trades at a price above $25 will mean all sales at $25 have been executed.[1] Limit orders control the price paid or received, but the investor has no way of knowing when and if the order will be filled. A limit order can be utilized by an investor who observes the price to be varying within a range and tries to sell or buy the stock at a favorable price within the range, and is willing to bear the risk of not filling the order.

---

[1]There are various rules to determine who trades first when there are multiple limit orders at the same price. On the New York and American Stock Exchanges it is first come–first served. On National Association of Security Dealers (Nasdaq) the limit orders are not at a central location so that there is no particular sequence in which orders are filled.

Short Sale Investors can sell securities they don't own. This type of trade is referred to as a short sale. When an investor short sells a security, a security is physically sold. Since the investor doesn't own the security, the brokerage firm borrows it from another investor or lends the security to the investor itself. The securities borrowed normally come from the securities held at the brokerage firm for other investors. Securities kept at a brokerage firm by investors are referred to as securities registered in street name. For example, an investor might wish to short sell 100 shares of General Motors. If the brokerage firm had 100 shares of General Motors in street name, and the owner of these shares had given the brokerage firm permission to use these shares for short sales, they would sell those shares. If the firm did not possess the shares it desired to sell, it would borrow the shares from someone else, often another broker. The investor whose shares were borrowed and sold normally would not know that the transaction had occurred and would definitely not know who had borrowed the shares. Since the shares are physically sold, the company would not pay dividends to the investor whose shares were borrowed but instead would pay the purchaser of the shares. For the investor whose shares were borrowed not to be hurt by the short sale, he or she must receive the dividends. The person who sold the shares short is responsible for supplying the funds so that the person whose shares were borrowed can receive any dividends paid on the stock that was sold short.

At a future time the short seller repurchases the shares and replaces the shares that were borrowed. Thus capital gains and losses are equal in magnitude but opposite in sign to a short seller compared to a purchaser of the shares. Since the short seller pays dividends to the person whose shares were borrowed, and the capital gains or losses to a short seller are exactly opposite those of a purchaser, the return to the short seller is minus the return of the purchaser.[2]

The textbook reason for short sales is that the short seller expects the shares to decline in value and wishes to profit from the decline. For example, assume General Motors shares are at $60 and the investor believes they will decline to $50. If the investor short sells the securities and is correct in the expectation of decline then the investor repurchases the securities when they decline to $50 and thus makes $10 a share. There are other reasons for short sales, however. The principal one is to decrease the sensitivity of a portfolio to market movements. Securities rise and fall because of general market conditions as well as events specific to the security or a subset of securities. Since the return on short sales is the opposite of the return on a long purchase, a portfolio that includes short sales as well as long purchases reduces the exposure to market movements.[3]

Stop Orders A fourth type of order is one that is activated only when the price of the stock reaches or passes through a predetermined limit. The price that activates the trade is called a stop price. Once a trade takes place at the stop price the order becomes a market order. For example, a stop loss order at $40 is activated only if trades of others take place at $40 or less. If trades take place at $40 or less, the order is activated and the order becomes a market sell order. Thus the stop loss order can be viewed as a conditional market order. A stop buy order becomes a market buy when the trades of others equal or exceed the stop price. For example, a stop buy order at $50 becomes a market order when trades take place at $50 or above.

---

[2]Normally the short seller neither receives interest on the proceeds of the sale nor pays interest to the person whose securities were borrowed, although either possibility can occur.

[3]There are alternative ways to reduce market exposure. See Chapter 23.

Stop loss orders are used to attempt to lock in a gain. For example, consider an investor who purchased shares at $20 and subsequently saw the price rise to $50. The investor might place a stop loss order at $45. If the share price declines, the investor still expects to gain ($45 − $20 = $25). If the price continues to rise, then the investor continues to hold the shares and benefits from the rise. A stop loss order might be appropriate if the investor believes that the stock is overpriced and might decline but believes it is likely to rise even more before other investors reach the same conclusion. In this case the investor might place a stop loss order increasing the stop price if the shares continue to rise. As with all market orders the actual price the shares will trade at is uncertain because the trade prices might move below the stop price before the stop loss order can be executed.

A stop buy order is often used in conjunction with a short sale. Recall that a short sale is a sale of a security one doesn't own. Since the share must be replaced at a later date, a price increase harms the short seller. A stop buy order serves to limit the amount of the loss the short seller can incur.

Length of Time an Order Is Outstanding

For orders other than market orders, an investor must specify the length of time the order is to be outstanding. A day order instructs the broker to fill the order by the end of the day. If the order is not filled by the end of the day, the order is automatically canceled. If the investor doesn't specify the length of time the order is to be outstanding, it is assumed to be a day order. A week or month order instructs the broker to fill the order by the end of the week or month or cancel the order. Good until canceled orders remain outstanding until the investor specifically cancels the order. Finally, fill or kill orders instruct the broker to fill the order immediately or to kill the order.[4]

MARGIN

Investors can buy securities either with cash or part cash and part borrowing. If the investor utilizes borrowing as well as cash, the investor is said to purchase the securities on margin. An investor utilizing margin borrows money from the brokerage firm, which in turn borrows the money from a bank. The securities purchased serve as collateral both for the brokerage firm and the bank. Thus an investor utilizing margin must leave the securities with the brokerage firm rather than take delivery (called leaving securities in "street name"). In addition, the investor signs a "hypothecation" agreement that allows the brokerage firm to use the customer's securities as collateral for their own loans and allows the brokerage firm to lend the securities to others.

The customer is charged an interest rate on the loan. This rate is determined by adding a premium (usually 1%) to the rate the brokerage firm is charged on its loan (designated as the call rate). The amount the customer can borrow to finance a purchase or short sale is carefully regulated; these regulations are referred to as initial margin requirements. There are separate regulations that monitor the amount of the loan relative to the value of the assets at each point in time; these are called maintenance margin requirements. Finally, the way margin is defined for an account with long purchases is different from the way margin is defined for an account with short sales. Thus, an account with both long purchases and short sales must meet both sets of margin requirements.

---

[4]There are other types of specialized instructions that can be given, such as specifying that a market order be executed at the close.

Margin Long Purchase

Margin for long purchases is defined as[5]

$$\text{Margin} = \frac{\text{market value of assets} - \text{amount borrowed}}{\text{market value of assets}}$$

For example, if 100 shares of AT&T were purchased at $50 a share and the purchase was partially financed with a loan of $2000, then the investor's account would look like this:

ASSETS		LIABILITIES	
100 shares of AT&T	$5000	Loan	$2000
		Net Worth	$3000
			$5000

and the margin is

$$\text{Margin} = \frac{3000}{5000} = 60\%$$

As time passes the margin in the account will vary as security prices change. For example, if AT&T increased to $70 a share, the account would be

ASSETS		LIABILITIES	
100 shares of AT&T	$7000	Loan	$2000
		Net Worth	$5000
			$7000

and the margin is

$$\text{Margin} = \frac{5000}{7000} = 71.43\%$$

Initial Margin Long Purchase

The minimum amount of margin that must be in the account immediately after a security is purchased is called initial margin. The initial margin requirement is set by the board of governors of the Federal Reserve System (although an individual brokerage firm can set it higher). This requirement has varied considerably over time and has been as high as 100%, which precludes any borrowing for new purchases.

Margin is one of the tools utilized by the Federal Reserve to influence the economy. Consider an initial margin requirement of 60%. Assume the investor opens an account and purchases 100 shares of AT&T at $50 a share, or a $5000 purchase. The investor would need 0.60 × $5000 or $3000 in cash and could borrow the remainder of $2000. If the initial margin requirement was 80%, then the investor would need 0.80 × $5000, or $4000 in cash with the remainder being borrowed. For accounts that already include borrowing, the amount of cash an investor needs for an additional purchase depends on the price movements of the securities owned and the amount of prior borrowing.

Consider the investor who bought 100 shares of AT&T at $50 a share, paying for the purchase with $3000 in cash and $2000 in borrowing. If subsequently AT&T increased in price to $70 a share and initial margin requirements were 60%, the investor could purchase

---

[5]Not all securities are counted in calculating margin. For example, securities that are not readily traded such as securitized partnerships in private deals are not counted in determining assets.

100 shares of Bethlehem Steel at $10 only utilizing borrowing since after the purchase the account would look like this:

ASSETS		LIABILITIES	
100 shares of AT&T	$7000	Loan	$3000
100 shares Bethlehem Steel	$1000	Net Worth	$5000
	$8000		$8000

and the margin would be above the initial margin requirement since

$$\text{Margin} = \frac{5000}{8000} = 62.50\%$$

Thus, initial margin regulates the amount that can be borrowed at the time when securities are purchased. The amount that can be borrowed can vary from zero to more than 100%. It could be more than 100% if the securities in the account had declined significantly in value, since at the time of any new purchase initial margin requirements must hold for the whole account.

The securities serve as collateral for the investor's loan and for the broker's loan. To guarantee that the loans can be paid there is a lower limit to which the margin can fall without the investor having to put up additional security. This is the subject of the next section.

Maintenance Margin Long Purchase

The minimum amount the margin can decline to without an investor having to take action is called the maintenance margin. The maintenance margin is set by the exchanges, although an individual brokerage firm can set it higher. If the stockholder's margin drops below the maintenance margin, then the brokerage firm issues a margin call. The shareholder must bring the margin above the maintenance margin by either adding additional cash or securities to the account, or by selling securities. If the investor fails to respond to the margin call or the investor is unable to be reached by the brokerage firm, the brokerage firm sells off sufficient securities to bring the margin above the maintenance margin. Usually initial margin requirements are substantially higher than maintenance margin requirements. Thus there could be a substantial decline in price without a margin call. The amount of decline in price before a margin call is easy to calculate. Let P be the price that will result in a margin call. We will calculate this price for our original example where 100 shares of AT&T were purchased at $50 a share using $3000 in cash and $2000 in borrowing.

If the maintenance margin requirement is 25%, then

$$0.25 = \frac{100P - 2000}{100P}$$

and

$$P = 26\frac{2}{3}$$

Effect of Margin on Return

Margin is the purchase of securities utilizing leverage. As such all gains and losses are accentuated. The amount of the accentuation depends on the percentage of the purchase the investor paid for in cash. Assume the share was purchased at $50. A $5 increase in price over six months would result in a six-month return for the security of

$$r_s = \frac{5}{50} = 10\%$$

Now assume the share was purchased with 50% margin and that the annual interest rate on the borrowing was 6% or 3% semiannually. With 50% margin the investor would put up $25 in cash and the interest paid over the six months would be 0.03 (25) = $0.75. A $5 increase in share price results in a return on the cash investment (r_c) of

$$r_c = \frac{5 - 0.75}{25} = 17\%$$

Of course this leverage works both ways. A $5 decrease in share value (share price declined 10%) would result in percentage loss to the investor utilizing margin of

$$r_c = \frac{-5 - 0.75}{25} = -23\%$$

The minimum amount the investor puts up in cash is the margin times the price. In this case the return on the cash invested is

$$r_c = \frac{\text{change in price} - \text{interest}}{\text{price} \times \text{margin}} = \frac{1}{\text{margin}} \frac{\text{change in price} - \text{interest}}{\text{price}}$$

$$= \frac{1}{\text{margin}} \left(r_s - \frac{\text{interest}}{\text{price}} \right)$$

There are also margin rules for short sales. The short seller receives the proceeds of the sale less the commission in the form of cash in the account. However, the short seller has to put up cash to protect against an increase in the stock price. Like long purchases there are margin requirements both at the time of the trade (initial margin) and margin requirements to be met at all times (maintenance margin). The margin for short sales is calculated somewhat differently than the margin for purchases. This is the subject of the next section.

Margin Requirements for Short Sales

Margin for short sales is calculated as a percentage of the market value of the short. For short sales, margin is defined as

$$\text{Margin} = \frac{\text{Value of the assets} - \text{market value of securities sold short}}{\text{Market value of securities sold short}}$$

For example, assume an investor just opened an account and short sold $10,000 worth of shares and the initial margin requirement was 50%. The investor would have to put up $5000 in cash. The account would then look like this:

ASSETS		LIABILITIES	
Cash from the short sale	$10,000	Market value of securities sold short	$10,000
Cash from investor	$ 5,000	Net Worth	$ 5,000
	$15,000		$15,000

and the account would meet the initial margin requirement since

$$\text{Margin} = \frac{15,000 - 10,000}{10,000} = 50\%$$

The amount of money that must be added to the account for additional short sales depends on what happened to share price subsequent to the short sales. If the stock price falls, then an account will be above the initial margin requirement and additional shares can be sold short without putting up as much additional money, or perhaps no money at all. If the margin is below the initial margin, then the investor must bring the account up to the initial margin for additional short selling; therefore additional short sales involve more than a normal cash contribution. With short sales like long purchases there is a minimum margin to be exceeded at all times; this is called a maintenance margin. Many accounts have both short sales and long purchases. These accounts would need to meet margin requirements for both types of trades.

MARKETS

In this section we discuss the markets in which trades take place. The section is divided into two parts. In the first part we discuss the general characteristics of markets. In the second part we discuss some of the principal U.S. markets.

Characteristics of Markets

There are a number of ways to classify markets. First, markets can be classified as primary or secondary. Primary markets are security markets where new issues of securities are initially sold. The Federal Reserve auctions off on a weekly basis new government bills and on a less frequent basis government bonds. This auction market is considered a primary market. A secondary market is a market where securities are resold. The New York Stock Exchange is a secondary market.

A second way to classify markets is as a call market or a continuous market. In a call market trading takes place at specified time intervals. One structure for a call market has prices announced verbally. In a verbal market prices are announced and the participants indicate the amount they are willing to sell or purchase at that price. This price is changed until a price is determined that most closely matches intended sales with intended purchases, at which time transactions are executed at that price.

A second structure for a call market uses a computer. Prices at which investors wish to buy or sell are entered into the computer and a preliminary price is displayed. Investors can change their orders or enter new orders until a specified execution time when the price that best matches buys and sells is determined. If there is no price that completely matches buys and sells, an allocation method is needed. One method is first come–first serve, which fills the oldest orders on the side with the surplus first.

Some call markets have a provision that limits the movement from the prior price. This is to prevent a temporary order imbalance from dramatically moving the price. Market orders are allowed in most call markets, and all market orders are filled at the clearing price. There is a greater price uncertainty for market orders in a call market than there is in a continuous market. In particular, the price movement between calls is likely to be greater than the price change in a continuous market from the time an order is placed until it is executed. Also, the trade need not be executed if the market has price limits and the clearing price exceeds the price limits. The New York Stock Exchange opens the market with a trade very much like those found in a call market, though it then becomes a continuous market. Stock markets in Austria and Belgium are call markets and Germany and Israel have call markets at some point in the day.

Continuous markets are markets where trading takes place on a continuous basis. For example, a market order placed in a continuous market will be executed quickly at the best available price.

A third way to classify markets is to determine whether they are dealer or broker markets. In a broker market a broker acts as agent for an investor and buys or sells shares on the investor's behalf. In a broker market shareholders are trading with other shareholders albeit utilizing an agent. In a dealer market the dealer purchases or sells shares for the investor utilizing the dealer's own inventory. In a dealer market investors' trades are not made directly with other investors but with the dealer, who serves as an intermediary between buyers and sellers.

A fourth way to classify markets is to determine whether the trading is executed by humans or done electronically. Execution on the NYSE involves people. Executions on the Toronto stock exchange, Paris, Australia, and for some stocks on the Tokyo stock exchange are done electronically. One advantage of an electronic market is that the power of the computer allows complex conditional trades to be handled. For example, electronic trading would allow an order to be executed conditional on the value of a market index. However we classify a market, there are a number of characteristics that are desirable for it to have. First, investors buy and sell assets based on information. Useful market information includes past prices, volume, current bids and offers, and the amount of short sales outstanding. Thus, it is desirable that this market information be promptly and accurately available to investors. Second, markets differ according to trading costs. The lower the costs of trading shares in the market, ceteris paribus, the better the market. Third, the markets should be liquid. Liquidity refers to the ability to transact a large number of shares at prices that don't vary substantially from past prices unless new information enters the market. Liquidity is often subdivided into continuity and depth. Price continuity means that an investor can expect to transact some shares at prices close to those at which the security recently traded absent any new information in the marketplace. A deep market is one that has a large number of buyers and sellers willing to trade at close to the current transaction price, so that a large number of shares can be transacted without a substantial change in price. Fourth, markets differ in the speed with which new information is incorporated in share prices. Investors would hope that the share price reflected all available information about the share. This is referred to as informational efficiency and is discussed in some detail in Chapter 17, "Efficient Markets."

Major Markets

In this section we will discuss some of the important markets in the United States, including both primary and secondary markets. First we will discuss markets that are principally secondary markets.

Stock Markets   There are a number of organized exchanges in the United States where stocks are traded, as well as an over-the-counter market and the so-called third and fourth markets. For a stock to be traded on an organized exchange it must be listed on the exchange.[6] Listing is primarily determined by the wishes of the company, the size of the company, and the trading activity of the stock. Unlisted stocks are traded in the over-the-counter market (OTC).[7] The third market involves trading of listed securities in the OTC market, whereas the fourth market refers to direct trades between institutions without using an exchange.

---

[6]Regional exchanges allow a stock to be traded without listing.

[7]Stocks on Nasdaq and Nasdaq National Market System must meet listing requirements.

In the United States the principal stock exchange is the New York Stock Exchange followed in importance by the American Stock Exchange and then the regional exchanges with the Chicago, Pacific, and PBW (Philadelphia-Baltimore-Washington) the most important. Because of its importance we will focus on the New York Stock Exchange.

New York Stock Exchange   The New York Stock Exchange is a corporation consisting of members who own seats on the exchange. A membership or seat allows the member to trade on the exchange. Brokerage firms are major owners of seats generally held by their employees. Members can serve any of four functions:

1. *Commission Brokers.* These members take the orders placed by the public at the brokerage firm they are affiliated with and execute them on the exchange.

2. *Floor Brokers.* Floor brokers aid commission brokers when the order flow becomes too large for a commission broker to handle.

3. *Floor Traders.* These people trade only for their own account and are prohibited from trading for the public. They attempt to make a profit by taking advantage of temporary mispricing due to order imbalances.

4. *Specialists.* These members keep the book that lists all limit orders that cannot be executed immediately because shares are not offered or demanded at prices that allow execution at the limit prices. In addition the specialists trade for their own account. In doing so the specialists are charged with maintaining a fair and orderly market. Thus, the specialists are supposed to trade to absorb temporary order imbalances in the marketplace. The specialist has an obligation to trade at all times, which ensures a continuous market. Finally, at the beginning of each day the specialist decides when the market for a particular stock will open so that order imbalances do not cause large stock price changes at the opening. Each stock has only one specialist, but a specialist can have several stocks.

How trading takes place is best described by an example. Assume a customer places an order for the purchase of 1000 shares of IBM stock with a broker. The broker can send the order either to the firm's booth on the floor of the exchange or enter the order on the superDOT system. If the order is entered on the superDOT system, it will be electronically transmitted to the firm's booth or entered on the specialist's book depending on predetermined rules set by the brokerage firm. In 1992, 75% of all trades were entered by the superDOT system, which represented 28% of total volume.[8]

If the order is sent to the firm's booth, then the firm's broker for IBM is paged, the broker goes to a nearby phone, receives the order, and then joins the crowd at the IBM trading post to work the order. The order can be executed in whole or in part through trades with other floor brokers, the specialist, or trades against limit orders on the book. Given the amount of labor involved, only large orders are generally sent to the firm's booth. Smaller orders are generally entered directly on the specialist display book via the superDOT system and are executed by the specialist.[9]

If the order is a market order, the specialist can execute the order against another market order, against the specialist inventory of public limit orders, with a floor trader, or the specialist can trade for his or her own account. Because public orders have priority, the specialist can trade only if it leads to price improvement. Alternatively the specialist can

---

[8]See Hasbrouck, Sofianos, and Sosebee [2].

[9]In rare cases, they are traded electronically without specialist intervention.

"stop" the order. In 1992, 26% of superDOT orders received after the opening were stopped.[10] If an order is stopped, the customer is guaranteed that the order will not be executed at a price worse than the existing bid or ask. The reason for stopping an order is a belief that price improvement is possible. An order is usually stopped when the bid-ask spread is greater than an $\frac{1}{8}$ and the specialist feels that, by exposing the order to floor brokers, a price within the spread can be obtained. If the spread is $\frac{1}{8}$, then the order is stopped only if there is a large order imbalance on the books and the specialist feels the price will move substantially. In 1992, 62% of the stopped orders led to price improvement and the average time from entry on the specialist books to execution was 28 seconds.[11]

Limit orders can also be entered using the superDOT system; however, there is a size limit to using the superDOT system. Currently market orders must be under 30,099 shares and limit orders under 99,999 shares.

The first trade of the day is an exception to the procedures just discussed. The specialist has discretion on when a stock will be opened for trading. He or she will indicate where the price will open and elicit expressions of interest. The specialist will continue to adjust these preliminary price indications until supply and demand are balanced, and he or she feels that interested buyers or sellers are aware of the probable price. Thus, the first trade of the day is executed in what is essentially a call market.

Large and medium trades, usually from institutional investors, may be handled differently than any of the methods described above. If they are of medium size (under 10,000 shares), they are likely to be executed over time by the traders on the floor of the exchange. This procedure, called working the crowd, may involve trading a few 1000-share units at a time to conceal the size of the order. For very large trades the use of the specialist and the crowd is not feasible. The limit orders on the specialist books are unlikely to accommodate a large trade without a substantial movement in the price. Furthermore, because the specialist is forbidden to solicit trades, he or she is unable to search out the other side of a large trade. Thus, large trades are likely to be negotiated in the upstairs market, which consists of block traders. These traders try to find other institutions that are interested in taking the other side of a block trade. In addition, part of the trade will likely be traded on the exchange.[12] Finally, if this is insufficient to trade all the shares, they may temporarily take part of the shares themselves.

Assume, for example, a large mutual fund wishes to sell 150,000 shares of Ford Motor Company. The mutual fund calls one of the block traders and begins the negotiation. The block trader may know of some investors who have already indicated an interest in purchasing Ford. In addition, the block trader will survey other investors' interest in the other side, explore how much could be sold on the exchange at various prices, and decide how much of the block he or she is willing to hold temporarily. The prices obtainable from the other large traders, the price on the floor plus the size of the position the block trader has to hold, will dictate the price offered to the seller. The original 150,000 shares might be split up into two lots of 60,000 and 40,000 shares to be purchased by other institutional investors, 20,000 to be traded on the exchange and the remaining 30,000 held by the block trader to be disposed of over time, each at different prices. The institution selling the 150,000 shares will be offered one price from the block trader. If the institution agrees to the trade, the institution will receive this price less an agreed commission. The initial

---

[10]See Hasbrouck, Sofianos, and Sosebee [2].

[11]See Hasbrouck, Sofianos, and Sosebee [2].

[12]Block traders must at least trade with all limit orders that are at a price better than that offered on the block.

choice of a block trader is important since the price that will be offered will depend on the block trader's knowledge of other investors interested in purchasing the shares and the relative negotiation skills.

One very useful facility for handling institutional trades is Reuter's Instinet. Instinet is an electronic system that records institutional limit orders and facilitates execution against them. Thus, Instinct is an information source for potential trading partners. The limit orders are expressions of interest and are not binding. However, Instinet has the desirable feature of allowing electronic on-line negotiation without revealing the name until the trade is agreed on. Instinet is widely used by institutional traders, block traders, and Nasdaq dealers.

Over-the-counter trading takes place for stocks not listed on the exchanges.

Over-the-Counter Market Most securities that are traded over the counter are listed on the National Association of Security Dealers (Nasdaq) automatic quote system. Nasdaq has a quote system that allows the potential trader to ascertain who is interested in trading and at what price. It is important to note that the Nasdaq quote system is an information source and not an electronic trading system. Brokers trading for a customer will note which brokers are interested and at what prices and then will directly contact the broker to negotiate a trade. Three levels of service are available from Nasdaq. Level III subscribers are given terminals with which to enter bids and asks. These dealers must be prepared to execute at least a minimum amount (usually 1000 shares) at these prices. Level II subscribers are usually traders who have access to all bids and asks as well as the name of the firm making the quote. This allows the traders to determine where to obtain the best price. Level 1 subscribers simply obtain the best bid and ask for any stock; these subscribers are normally salespersons (registered representatives) dealing with customers. Nasdaq classifies some of the stocks as part of the National market system (primarily on the basis of trading volume). Stocks designated as part of the National market system are eligible for short sales and margin purchases. OTC stocks not listed on the Nasdaq quote system have bids and offers recorded on paper available once a day; these are called "pink sheets." These quotes are not binding and simply give the trader an idea of who is potentially interested in the stock.[13]

Intermarket Trading System The Intermarket Trading System is a communications network that lists the most favorable quote across exchanges and the OTC market for eligible securities. When a market maker at an exchange receives an order at his or her exchange with an inferior quote, the market maker can either match the best quote from Intermarket Trading System (ITS) or the market maker can use ITS to send "a firm commitment" to the exchange with the superior quote to trade at the quote. Firm commitments are not subject to stops or exposed to the crowd but rather trade at the quote. Although the system was intended to guarantee the best price for the shares, this may not occur because of quote changes during the time the order is transmitted, the lack of exposure to the crowd, and the possibility of price improvement through "stop orders." The transmittal of the order to another exchange is not automatic but depends on an action by the market maker. If the market maker fails to make the transfer, the exchange with the best quote can complain; the market maker must then either adjust the price or make up for it by executing a trade with the exchange with the best quote for the full amount being offered.

---

[13]The National Association of Security Dealers now has an electronic bulletin board for many of these stocks. This facilitates more frequent trading.

Computerized Markets   A number of markets have been set up to exploit the power of the computer and to try to reduce transaction costs. Three systems are electronic crossing networks—Posit, Instinet, and the New York Stock Exchange afterhours systems. All three systems match buys and sells. The price at which trades are made is determined in the primary markets. Instinet has two crosses a day. First customers can enter unpriced orders before the market opens at 8:30 A.M. Eastern Standard Time; at the time the market opens, Instinet matches the orders. The trade price is the average price between the opening and the close on the day the order is placed. The weight attached to each trade price is the proportion of volume that trade represents of the daily volume. Instinet and the New York Stock Exchange also will match orders after the market closes at the closing price. Posit, like Instinet, has two crosses a day. For Posit the crosses are at randomly selected times. The trade price is the middle of the bid-ask spread at the time of the cross. Crossing networks feed off the primary markets. They play no role in price determination; rather, the price is determined in a primary market and these networks simply match buyers and sellers at this price. A customer using Instinet's premarket opening cross or Posit is uncertain as to the trade price. For all systems the customer is uncertain about whether or not the trade will take place; for example, not all buys will be executed if the amount of buy orders exceeds the amount of sell orders. These systems owe their existence to a perception of lower cost.

The Arizona stock exchange is an electronic call market where customers enter limit orders. The computer calculates where the price would be that best matched buys and sells. Customers can change orders or place new orders until 5 P.M. EST, at which point the trade is made.[14] Computers clearly have revolutionized much of industry, and these computerized trading systems are likely to play an even more important role in future security trading.

Bond Markets   Almost all bond trading in the secondary market occurs in the OTC market. While there is limited listing of bonds on the NYSE and AMEX, almost all the volume is OTC. The trading volume in government bonds is very large, and they are highly liquid. There are a number of government bond security dealers who are willing to trade on a continuous basis, and most trading occurs with or between these dealers. An institution interested in trading in government bonds would call a number of government bond dealers and get quotes. The institution would then take one of the quotes or attempt to negotiate a more attractive price. An individual purchasing through a broker would be offered whatever the current bid and ask are from that broker for retail accounts. Treasury dealers trade with each other in a different manner using intermediaries called government brokers. Five government brokers handle the majority of the trading volume. Treasury dealers give firm bids and offers to the government broker who displays the most attractive bid and offer on a monitor at each dealer. Dealers can execute the trade electronically, and the size and price of the trade are immediately available to all dealers. The government bond brokers deal with all the paperwork and maintain the confidentiality of the traders in return for a small fee. Thus, although there is a quote system for dealers, none exists for individuals or nondealer institutions. In addition, there is no record of transaction prices available to the general public.

---

[14]Economides and Schwartz [1] argue that at current volume the Arizona stock exchange acts as a crossing network.

The secondary markets for corporate bonds or Ginnie Maes are fairly illiquid. Only recent issues or some large issues have an active secondary market. An individual wishing to purchase a bond with certain characteristics will likely be offered a choice of bonds with these characteristics that are contained in the brokerage firm's inventory. Given the illiquidity, the characteristics will have to be stated in fairly general terms (e.g., AAA corporates with about 10 years' maturity). If the inquiry involves a sufficiently large order, the firm might survey other firms to determine other potential options. Given the illiquidity of the market the bid-ask spread will be much higher than in the government bond market.

Dealers have three sources of potential profit: (1) they can make money on the bid-ask spread; (2) they can make or lose money on the change in the value of the inventory;[15] (3) they can make or lose money on the difference between the interest earned on the inventory and the interest paid to finance it.

Primary Markets   Primary markets are markets that involve new issues of securities and hence, unlike secondary markets, provide a direct flow of cash to the issuing entity. In this section we will discuss some of the principal primary markets.

Government Bonds   Treasury securities are issued by auction on a regular basis where the frequency of issuance depends on the maturity of the security. For example, 91-day and 182-day Treasury bills are offered every Monday; 7-, 10-, and 30-year Treasury bonds are issued quarterly. There are two types of orders that can be placed: noncompetitive (market orders) or competitive (limit orders). Noncompetitive bids can be placed up to $1 million face value. Noncompetitive bids are filled at a price equal to the average price paid by all competitive bidders.

Competitive bids can be placed by banks or brokerage firms that are designated by the Federal Reserve. These institutions place bids for a particular quantity and at a particular price (limit orders) for themselves or their customers. The auction works as follows. First, the Federal Reserve deducts the aggregate value of all noncompetitive issues from the aggregate amount to be sold. It then ranks the competitive bids from highest to lowest, filling the bids until the amount it wishes to issue is sold. For the marginal bids (the lowest accepted) the volume is allocated among bidders proportional to the amount requested by each. Thus, competitive bidders can receive the amount they bid, a fractional amount, or none. Noncompetitive bidders have price uncertainty; competitive bidders face volume uncertainty.[16]

Corporate Issues   Corporate bonds and common stocks are usually sold using the services of an investment banker. The corporation normally has an ongoing relationship with an investment banker and when it has a need for funds negotiates the instruments and price with the investment banker. New issues are divided into two types: (1) seasoned new issues, which are issues of companies that already have publicly traded securities, such as new issues of Ford or IBM; (2) issues of companies without publicly traded securities,

---

[15]Many dealers will try to limit the susceptibility to price changes on inventory by taking an appropriate position in the futures market (for a discussion of how this is done see Chapter 23).

[16]The Treasury is experimenting with an alternative bidding system where everyone pays the same price and the price is the price of the last bidder needed to sell all the bonds (marginal bidder). The hope is that total revenues will be higher. This could occur if all bidders bid higher since the price they pay is the marginal bid rather than the amount they bid themselves.

referred to as initial public offerings. These issues are usually issues of small companies just starting out. However, they can be issues of companies that are recapitalizing, such as companies that had publicly traded securities, were bought out by the management and held privately, and then became public again. These companies can be quite large (e.g., Nabisco).

The investment banking firm can either purchase the shares directly from the firm at an agreed-upon price and then resell them to the general public (called firm commitment) or can simply help the firm in selling to the general public (called best efforts). Underwriters have a conflict of interest. As an adviser to the issuing firm, they have an obligation to obtain the best price possible. However, the lower the price the easier it is to market the securities to the public. The empirical evidence indicates that Initial Public Offerings (IPOs) earn abnormally large returns on the day of issuance but underperform similar risk securities in subsequent months.

Clearing Procedures   Most transactions require that settlement be made in five business days. A brokerage firm will engage in trades involving customers from a number of other brokerage firms in the same security. Some will be sales and some will be purchases. It would be very costly to have to settle each and every trade rather than the net of the purchases and sales. To facilitate settlement, clearing corporations have been established. At the end of the day all records of trades are sent to the clearing corporation, which then notifies the firm of the net amount of securities to be delivered and the net amount of money to be received or to pay.

Clearing corporations play an especially important role in the options and futures markets. Not only are all trades cleared through the clearing corporation, the clearing corporation guarantees all trades. With options and futures (unlike common stock) the profit or loss comes from the individual on the other side of the trade. With stocks and bonds the profit depends on the creditworthiness of a corporation and its earnings, and one can analyze the creditworthiness of a publicly held corporation. It would be much more difficult to determine the creditworthiness of the individual taking the opposite position in an option or future. In these markets the clearing corporation stands behind each trade, and thus the trade can be thought of as a trade with the corporation. The clearing corporation keeps a list of all buyers and sellers of each security, but there is no matching of trades. If a trader fails to meet their obligation, their margin is taken and the firm that executed the trade makes up any difference. If the firm that made the trade fails, there is a further system of backup involving the failing firm's margin, the margin of other firms, and the clearing corporation's own assets. In short, the risk of an investor in the options and futures markets not having their contract honored is the risk of the clearing corporation collapsing, and such a collapse would have to involve massive failure of much of the financial system.

The clearing corporation serves another role in the options and futures market. Since trades can be thought of as taking place with the clearing corporation, when the investor exercises an option or delivers on a futures contract, the clearing corporation has to decide who is on the other side. This is decided by using well-specified rules, which in some cases are random selection.

TRADE TYPES AND COSTS

In this section we will discuss motivations for trading and what factors influence the costs of a trade.

Types of Trades

There are generally considered to be two reasons for investors to trade. The first reason investors trade securities is because traders believe that the price is incorrect and they buy or sell based on a perceived mispricing. These traders are referred to as "information traders." The second reason for buying or selling securities is because of a surplus or need for money. An investor needing the down payment for a house or the money to purchase a car or boat might liquidate part of his or her portfolio to obtain the necessary funds. Similarly, an investor receiving an inflow of funds might purchase shares because stocks in general are a good investment rather than because of information indicating that the particular stock being purchased is mispriced. These investors are referred to as "liquidity traders."

Specialists and dealers have different profit possibilities trading with information-based or liquidity-based traders. For liquidity-based traders it is reasonable to assume that the side of the trade they are on (buy or sell) is unrelated to the future course of price movements. Thus, the bid-ask spread should provide profit to the dealer, because subsequent price movements will not systematically affect the value of any inventory held as a result of the trade. This is true whether we are discussing a specialist buying or selling for his or her own account or a dealer in the government bond market. An information-based trade is different. If the person initiating the trade has superior information, then one can anticipate that the short-run price movements on average will be unfavorable to the specialist or dealer. And although the specialist will gain on the bid-ask spread, he or she will lose on any inventory obtained or lost from the trade since subsequent price movements will likely on average be unfavorable. The specialist or dealer will expect to gain money from liquidity traders and information traders who do not have superior information but lose to information traders with superior information. The greater the proportion and the higher the quality of the superior information for information-based traders the more the specialist or dealer will have to make on the bid-ask spread and the higher the bid-ask spread must be. Thus, liquidity investors will do better if specialists and dealers are informed. Furthermore, a liquidity-based trader who can credibly convey this fact to the dealers should be able to obtain a better price. For example, an index fund that stays fully invested can often obtain better prices in purchases and sales because their trades are not information motivated, which is a credible message to convey to dealers.

Trading Costs

One of the important elements in markets is the cost of trading. The size of the trading costs affects how large the perceived mispricing must be before an investor can profitably swap one share for another. Substantial trading costs mean that investors will hold nonoptional portfolios because the transaction costs of adjusting them are too high.

There are three major sources of trading costs. First are the direct costs, commission to the brokers plus a tax on the trade. The second cost is the bid-ask spread. An investor buying and then subsequently selling the stock will purchase at the ask and sell at the bid.[17] The difference in the bid and ask is a cost to the investor buying and then selling the stock (called roundtrip). Third is the potential price impact of a large sale or purchase. Small

---

[17]If the bid-ask spread is more than $\frac{1}{8}$, the investor may trade within the spread; however, the same principal holds.

purchases and sales can be executed at the bid and ask, but large purchases or sales may cause an adverse change in the bid and ask.

There is another factor that affects the cost for liquidity traders. Since liquidity traders do not engage in a determination of equilibrium price, it is important that they feel confident that market prices are close to equilibrium prices. Quoted prices can differ from equilibrium prices because information takes a long time to be incorporated in share price, or because trading costs are sufficiently high that trade prices can differ substantially from equilibrium prices without information-based traders entering the market. Differences of trade prices from equilibrium prices can help or hurt the investor's return. However, these differences increase the variability of return the investor will receive and thus are a cost in the sense they increase the investor's risk.

These costs vary with the type of security purchased or sold, the exchange used (if any), and the size of the purchase or sale. Commissions as a percentage of the total value of the sale generally increase as the price of the share declines. The commission also varies widely from broker to broker. Full-service brokerage firms offering advice as well as transaction services generally charge substantially more than the discount brokers, who primarily offer order execution. The bid-ask spread also varies across securities. The less liquid the security the greater the bid-ask spread is likely to be. This is especially true in the bond market where very illiquid bonds are likely to have very large bid-ask spreads.

The size of the trade works both ways. The larger the trade the more likely the trade is to have an impact on price. Large traders, however, usually institutions, are in a better position to negotiate a more attractive price. This is especially true in dealer markets such as bond markets, where large investors have the ability to negotiate with a number of dealers and where small investors usually do not have access to negotiation with multiple dealers.

CONCLUSION

In this chapter we have described the markets in which securities are traded. This chapter and Chapter 2 have supplied the reader with the background necessary for the discussion of investment analysis. We start with a more detailed analysis of risk and portfolio management. This will allow us to return to an examination of many of the securities discussed to this point to see how they are priced and how they fit into a portfolio.

BIBLIOGRAPHY

1. Economides, Nicholas, and Schwartz, Robert. "Electronic Call Market Trading," *Journal of Portfolio Management*, Spring 1995, p. 10–18.
2. Hasbrouck, Jael, Sofianos, George, and Sosebee, Deborah. "New York Stock Exchange Systems and Trading Procedures," unpublished paper, New York Stock Exchange, 1994.
3. Schwartz, Robert. *Reshaping the Equity Markets: A Guide for the 1990s*, Harper Business, New York, NY, 1991.

Part 2

PORTFOLIO ANALYSIS

Section 1

Mean Variance
Portfolio Theory

4

The Characteristics of the
Opportunity Set Under Risk

In Chapter 1 we introduced the elements of a decision problem under certainty. The same elements are present when we recognize the existence of risk; however, their formulation becomes more complex. In the next two chapters we explore the nature of the opportunity set under risk. Before we begin the analysis we present a brief summary or roadmap of where we are going. The existence of risk means that the investor can no longer associate a single number or payoff with investment in any asset. The payoff must be described by a set of outcomes and each of their associated probability of occurrence, called a frequency function or return distribution. In this chapter we start by examining the two most frequently employed attributes of such a distribution: a measure of central tendency, called the expected return, and a measure of risk or dispersion around the mean, called the standard deviation. Investors shouldn't and in fact don't hold single assets; they hold groups or portfolios of assets. Thus a large part of this chapter is concerned with how one can compute the expected return and risk of a portfolio of assets given the attributes of the individual assets. One important aspect of this analysis is that the risk on a portfolio is more complex than a simple average of the risk on individual assets. It depends on whether the returns on individual assets tend to move together or whether some assets give good returns when others give bad returns. As we show in great detail there is a risk reduction from holding a portfolio of assets if assets do not move in perfect unison.

We continue this discussion in Chapter 5. Initially. we examine portfolios of only two assets. We present a detailed geometric and algebraic analysis of the characteristics of portfolios of two assets under different estimates of how they covary together (how related their returns are to each other). We then extend this analysis to the case of multiple assets. Finally, we arrive at the opportunity set facing the investor in a world with risk. Let us begin by characterizing the nature of the opportunity set open to the investor.

In the certainty case the investor's decision problem can be characterized by a certain outcome. In the problem analyzed in Chapter 1, the 5% return on lending (or the 5% cost of borrowing) was known with certainty. Under risk, the outcome of any action is not known with certainty and outcomes are usually represented by a frequency function. A frequency function is a listing of all possible outcomes along with the probability of the occurrence of each. Table 4.1 shows such a function. This investment has three possible returns. If event 1 occurs, the investor receives a return of 12%; if event 2 occurs, 9% is received; and if event 3 occurs, 6% is received. In our examples each of these events is assumed to be equally likely. Table 4.1 shows us everything there is to know about the return possibilities.

Table 4.1

Return	Probability	Event
12	$\frac{1}{3}$	1
9	$\frac{1}{3}$	2
6	$\frac{1}{3}$	3

Usually we do not delineate all of the possibilities as we have in Table 4.1. The possibilities for real assets are sufficiently numerous that developing a table like Table 4.1 for each asset is too complex a task. Furthermore, even if the investor decided to develop such tables, the inaccuracies introduced would be so large that he or she would probably be better off just trying to represent the possible outcomes in terms of some summary measures. In general, it takes at least two measures to capture the relevant information about a frequency function: one to measure the average value and one to measure dispersion around the average value.

DETERMINING THE AVERAGE OUTCOME

The concept of an average is standard in our culture. Pick up the newspaper and you will often see figures on average income, batting averages, or average crime rates. The concept of an average is intuitive. If someone earns $11,000 one year and $9,000 in a second, we say his average income in the two years is $10,000. If three children in a family are age 15, 10, and 5, then we say the average age is 10. In Table 4.1 the average return was 9%. Statisticians usually use the term "expected value" to refer to what is commonly called an average. In this book we use both terms.

An expected value or average is easy to compute. If all outcomes are equally likely, then to determine the average, one adds up the outcomes and divides by the number of outcomes. Thus, for Table 4.1 the average is $(12 + 9 + 6)/3 = 9$. A second way to determine an average is to multiply each outcome by the probability that it will occur. When the outcomes are not equally likely, this facilitates the calculation. Applying this procedure to Table 4.1 yields $\frac{1}{3}(12) + \frac{1}{3}(9) + \frac{1}{3}(6) = 9$.

It is useful to express this intuitive calculation in terms of formula. The symbol Σ should be read sum. Underneath the symbol we put the first value in the sum and what is varying. On the top of the symbol we put the final value in the sum. We use the symbol R_{ij} to denote the jth possible outcome for the return on security i. Thus,

$$\frac{\sum_{j=1}^{3} R_{ij}}{3} = \frac{R_{i1} + R_{i2} + R_{i3}}{3} = \frac{12 + 9 + 6}{3}$$

Using the summation notation just introduced and a bar over a variable to indicate expected return, we have for the expected value of the M equally likely returns for asset i

$$\bar{R}_i = \sum_{j=1}^{M} \frac{R_{ij}}{M}$$

If the outcomes are not equally likely and if P_{ij} is the probability of the jth return on the ith asset, then expected return is[1]

$$\bar{R}_i = \sum_{j=1}^{M} P_{ij} R_{ij}$$

We have up to this point used a bar over a symbol to indicate expected value. This is the procedure we adopt throughout most of this book. However, occasionally, this notation proves awkward. An alternative method of indicating expected value is to put the symbol E in front of the expression for which we wish to determine the expected value. Thus $E(R_i)$ should be read as the expected value of R_{ij} just as $\bar{R}_i$ is the expected value of R_{ij}.

Certain properties of expected value are extremely useful. These properties are:

1. The expected value of the sum of two returns is equal to the sum of the expected value of each return, that is,

$$E\left(R_{1j} + R_{2j}\right) = \bar{R}_1 + \bar{R}_2$$

2. The expected value of a constant "C" times a return is the constant times the expected return, that is,

$$E\left[C\left(R_{1j}\right)\right] = C\bar{R}_1$$

These principles are illustrated in Table 4.2. For any event the return on asset 3 is the sum of the return on assets 1 and 2. Thus, the expected value of the return on asset 3 is the sum of the expected value of the return on assets 1 and 2. Likewise, for any event the return on asset 3 is three times the return on asset 1. Consequently, its expected value is three times as large as the expected value of asset 1.

These two properties of expected values will be used repeatedly and are worth remembering.

Table 4.2   Return on Various Assets

Event	Probability		Asset 1	Asset 2	Asset 3
A	$\frac{1}{3}$		14	28	42
B	$\frac{1}{3}$		10	20	30
C	$\frac{1}{3}$		6	12	18
		Expected Return	10	20	30

A MEASURE OF DISPERSION

Not only is it necessary to have a measure of the average return, it is also useful to have some measure of how much the outcomes differ from the average. The need for this second

---

[1]This latter formula includes the formula for equally likely observations as a special case. If we have M observations each equally likely, then the odds of any one occurring are $1/M$. Replacing the P_{ij} in the second formula by $1/M$ yields the first formula.

characteristic can be illustrated by the old story of the mathematician who believed an average by itself was an adequate description of a process and drowned in a stream with an average depth of 2 inches.

Intuitively a sensible way to measure how much the outcomes differ from the average is simply to examine this difference directly; that is, examine $R_{ij} - \bar{R}_i$. Having determined this for each outcome, one could obtain an overall measure by taking the average of this difference. Although this is intuitively sensible, there is a problem. Some of the differences will be positive and some negative and these will tend to cancel out. The result of the canceling could be such that the average difference for a highly variable return need be no larger than the average difference for an asset with a highly stable return. In fact, it can be shown that the average value of this difference must always be precisely zero. The reader is encouraged to verify this with the example in Table 4.2. Thus, the sum of the differences from the mean tells us nothing about dispersion.

Two solutions to this problem suggest themselves. First, we could take absolute values of the difference between an outcome and its mean by ignoring minus signs when determining the average difference. Second, since the square of any number is positive, we could square all differences before determining the average. For ease of computation, when portfolios are considered, the latter procedure is generally followed. In addition, as we will see when we discuss utility functions, the average squared deviations have some convenient properties.[2] The average squared deviation is called the variance, the the square root of the variance is called the standard deviation. In Table 4.3 we present the possible returns from several hypothetical assets as well as the variance of the return on each asset. The alternative returns on any asset are assumed equally likely. Examining asset 1, we find the deviations of its returns from its average return are $(15 - 9)$, $(9 - 9)$, and $(3 - 9)$. The squared deviations are 36, 0, and 36, and the average squared deviation or variance is $(36 + 0 + 36)/3 = 24$.

To be precise, the formula for the variance of the return on the ith asset (which we symbolize as σ_i^2) when each return is equally likely is

$$\sigma_i^2 = \sum_{j=1}^{M} \frac{\left(R_{ij} - R_i\right)^2}{M}$$

Table 4.3   Returns on Various Investments[a]

Market Condition	Return[a]				Rainfall	Return[a] Asset 4
	Asset 1	Asset 2	Asset 3	Asset 5		
Good	15	16	1	16	Plentiful	16
Average	9	10	10	10	Average	10
Poor	3	4	19	4	Poor	4
Mean return	9	10	10	10		10
Variance	24	24	54	24		24
Standard deviation	4.9	4.9	7.35	4.90		4.9

[a]The alternative returns on each asset are assumed equally likely and, thus, each has a probability of $\frac{1}{3}$.

[2]Many utility functions can be expressed either exactly or approximately in terms of the mean and variance. Furthermore, regardless of the investor's utility function, if returns are normally distributed, the mean and variance contain all relevant informaton about the distribution. An elaboration of these points is contained in later chapters.

If the observations are not equally likely, then, as before, we multiply by the probability with which they occur. The formula for the variance of the return on the ith asset becomes

$$\sigma_i^2 = \sum_{j=1}^{M}\left[P_{ij}\left(R_{ij} - \bar{R}_i\right)^2\right]$$

Occasionally, we will find it convenient to employ an alternative measure of dispersion called standard deviation. The standard deviation is just the square root of the variance and is designated by σ_i.

In the examples discussed in this chapter we are assuming that the investor is estimating the possible outcomes and the associated probabilities. Often initial estimates of the variance are obtained from historical observations of the assets return. In this case, many authors and programs used in calculators multiply the variance formula given above by $M/(M-1)$. This produces an estimate of the variance that is unbiased but has the disadvantage of being inefficient (i.e., it produces a poorer estimate of the true variance). We leave it to readers to choose which they prefer. In our examples in this book, we will not make this correction.[3]

The variance tells us that asset 3 varies considerably more from its average than asset 2. This is what we intuitively see by examining the returns shown in Table 4.3. The expected value and variance or standard deviation are the usual summary statistics utilized in describing a frequency distribution.

There are other measures of dispersion that could be used. We have already mentioned one, the average absolute deviation. Other measures have been suggested. One such measure considers only deviations below the mean. The argument is that returns above the average return are desirable. The only returns that disturb an investor are those below average. A measure of this is the average (overall observations) of the squared deviations below the mean. For example, in Table 4.3 for asset 1 the only return below the mean is 3. Since 3 is 6 below the mean, the square of the difference is 36. The other two returns are not below the mean so they have 0 deviation below the mean. The average of $(0) + (0) + (36)$ is 12. This measure is called the semivariance.

Semivariance measures downside risk relative to a benchmark given by expected return. It is just one of a number of possible measures of downside risk. More generally, we can consider returns relative to other benchmarks, including a risk-free return or zero return. These generalized measures are, in aggregate, referred to as *lower partial moments*. Yet another measure of downside risk is the so-called *Value at Risk measure*, which is widely used by banks to measure their exposure to adverse events and to measure the least expected loss (relative to zero, or relative to wealth) that will be expected with a certain probability. For example, if 5% of the outcomes are below -30% and if the decision maker is concerned about how poor the outcomes are 5% of the time, then -30% is the value at risk.

---

[3]As stated, sometimes the formula is divided by M and sometimes it is divided by $M-1$. The choice is a matter of taste. However, the reader may be curious why some choose one or the other. The technical reason authors choose one or the other is as follows.

Employing M as the denominator gave the best estimate of the true value or the so-called maximum likelihood estimate. Although it is the best estimate as M gets large, it does not converge to the true value (it is too small). Dividing by $M-1$ produces a S_i^2 that converges to the true value as M gets large (technically unbiased) but is not the best estimate for a finite M. Some people consider one of these properties more important than the other, whereas some use one without consciously realizing why this might be preferred.

Intuitively, these alternative measures of downside risk are reasonable and some portfolio theory has been developed using them. However, they are difficult to use when we move from single assets to portfolios. In cases where the distribution of returns is symmetrical, the ordering of portfolios in mean variance space will be the same as the ordering of portfolios in mean semivariance space or mean and any of the other measures of downside risk discussed above. For well-diversified equity portfolios, symmetrical distribution is a reasonable assumption so variance is an appropriate measure of downside risk. Furthermore, since empirical evidence shows most assets existing in the market have returns that are reasonably symmetrical, semivariance is not needed. If returns on an asset are symmetrical, the semivariance is proportional to the variance. Thus, in most of the portfolio literature the variance, or equivalently the standard deviation, is used as a measure of dispersion.

In most cases, instead of using the full frequency function such as that presented in Table 4.1, we use the summary statistics mean and variance or equivalent mean and standard deviation to characterize the distribution. Consider two assets. How might we decide which we prefer? First, intuitively one would think that most investors would prefer the one with the higher expected return if standard deviation was held constant. Thus, in Table 4.3 most investors would prefer asset 2 to asset 1. Similarly, if expected return were held constant, investors would prefer the one with the lower variance. This is reasonable because the smaller the variance the more certain an investor is that she will obtain the expected return and the fewer poor outcomes she has to contend with.[4] Thus in Table 4.3 the investor would prefer asset 2 to asset 3.

VARIANCE OF COMBINATIONS OF ASSETS

This simple analysis has taken us partway toward an understanding of the choice between risky assets. However, the options open to an investor are not to simply pick between assets 1, 2, 3, 4, or 5 in Table 4.3 but also to consider combinations of these five assets. For example, an investor could invest part of his money in each asset. While this opportunity vastly increases the number of options open to the investor and hence the complexity of the problem, it also provides the raison d'être of portfolio theory. The risk of a combination of assets is very different from a simple average of the risk of individual assets. Most dramatically, the variance of a combination of two assets may be less than the variance of either of the assets themselves. In Table 4.4 there is a combination of asset 2 and asset 3 that is less risky than asset 2.

Table 4.4   Dollars at Period 2 Given Alternative Investments

Condition of Market	Asset 2	Asset 3	Combination of Asset 2 (60%) and Asset 3 (40%)
Good	$1.16	$1.01	$1.10
Average	1.10	1.10	1.10
Poor	1.04	1.19	1.10

[4]We will not formally develop the criteria for making a choice from among risky opportunities until the next chapter. However, we feel we are not violating common sense by assuming at this time that investors prefer more to less and act as risk avoiders. More formal statements of the properties of investor choice will be taken up in the next chapter.

Let us examine this property. Assume an investor has $1 to invest. If he selects asset 2 and the market is good, he will have at the end of the period $1 + 0.16 = $1.16. If the market's performance is average, he will have $1.10, and if it is poor $1.04. These outcomes are summarized in Table 4.4 along with the corresponding values for the third asset. Consider an alternative. Suppose the investor invests $0.60 in asset 2 and $0.40 in asset 3. If the condition of the market is good, the investor will have $0.696 at the end of the period from asset 2 and $0.404 from asset 3, or $1.10. If the market conditions are average, he will receive $0.66 from asset 2, $0.44 from asset 3, or a total of $1.10. By now the reader might suspect that if the market condition is poor the investor still receives $1.10, and this is, of course, the case. If the market condition is poor the investor receives $0.624 from his investment in 2 and $0.476 from his investment is asset 3, or $1.10. These possibilities are summarized in Table 4.4.

This example dramatically illustrates how the risk on a portfolio of assets can differ from the risk of the individual assets. The deviations on the combination of the assets was zero because the assets had their highest and lowest returns under opposite market conditions. This result is perfectly general and not confined to this example. When two assets have their good and poor returns at opposite times, an investor can always find *some* combination of these assets that yields the same return under all market conditions. This example illustrates the importance of considering combinations of assets rather than just the assets themselves and shows how the distribution of outcomes on combinations of assets can be different than the distributions on the individual assets.

The returns on asset 2 and asset 4 have been developed to illustrate another possible situation. Asset 4 has three possible returns. Which return occurs depends on rainfall. Assuming that the amount of rainfall that occurs is independent of the condition of the market, then the returns on the assets 2 and 4 are independent of one another. Therefore, if the rainfall is plentiful we can have good, average, or poor security markets. Plentiful rainfall does not change the likelihood of any particular market condition occurring. Consider an investor with $1.00 who invests $0.50 in each asset. If rain is plentiful he receives $0.58 from his investment in asset 4, and any one of three equally likely outcomes from his investment in asset 2: $0.58 if the market is good, $0.55 if it is average, and $0.52 if the market is poor. This gives him a total of $1.16, $1.13, or $1.10. Similarly, if the rainfall is average, the value of his investment in asset 2 and 4 is $1.13, $1.10, or $1.07, and if rainfall is poor, $1.10, $1.07, or $1.04. Since we have assumed that each possible level of rainfall is equally likely as is each possible condition of the market, there are nine equally likely outcomes. Ordering then from highest to lowest we have $1.16, $1.13, $1.13, $1.10, $1.10, $1.10, $1.07, $1.07, and $1.04. Compare this to an investment in asset 2 by itself, the results of which are shown in Table 4.3. The mean is the same. However, the dispersion around the mean is less. This can be seen by direct examination and by noting that the probability of one of the extreme outcomes occurring ($1.16 or $1.04) has dropped from $\frac{1}{3}$ to $\frac{1}{9}$.

This example once again shows how the characteristics of the portfolio can be very different than the characteristics of the assets that comprise the portfolio. The example illustrates a general principle. When the returns on assets are independent such as the returns on assets 2 and 4, a portfolio of such assets can have less dispersion than either asset.

Consider still a third situation, one with a different outcome than the previous two. Consider an investment in assets 2 and 5. Assume the investor invests $0.50 in asset 2 and $0.50 in asset 5. The value of his investment at the end of the period is $1.16, $1.10, or $1.04. These are the same values he would have obtained if he invested the entire $1.00 in either asset 2 or 5 (see Table 4.3). Thus, in this situation the characteristics of the portfolios were exactly the same as the characteristics of the individual assets, and holding a portfolio rather than the individual assets did not change the investor's risk.

We have analyzed three extreme situations. As extremes they dramatically illustrated some general principles that carry over to less extreme situations. Our first example showed that when assets have their good and bad outcomes at different times (assets 2 and 3), then investment in these assets can radically reduce the dispersion obtained by investing in one of the assets by itself. If the good outcomes of an asset are not always associated with the bad outcomes of a second asset, but the general tendency is in this direction, then the reduction in dispersion still occurs but the dispersion will not drop all the way to zero as it did in our example. However, it is still often true that appropriately selected combinations of the two assets will have less risk than the least risky of the two assets.

Our second example illustrated the situation where the conditions leading to various returns were different for the two assets. More formally, this is the area where returns are independent. Once again, dispersion was reduced but not in as drastic a fashion. Note that investment in asset 2 alone can result in a return of $1.04 and that this result occurs $\frac{1}{3}$ of the time. The same result can occur when we invested an equal amount in asset 2 and asset 4. However, a combination of asset 2 and 4 has nine possible outcomes, each equally likely, and $1.04 occurs only $\frac{1}{9}$ of the time. With independent returns, extreme observations can still occur. They just occur less frequently. Just as the extreme values occur less frequently, outcomes closer to the mean become more likely so that the frequency function has less dispersion.

Finally, our third example illustrated the situation where the assets being combined had their outcomes affected in the same way by the same events. In this case, the characteristics of the portfolio were identical to the characteristics of the individual assets. In less extreme cases this is no longer true. Insofar as the good and bad returns on assets tend to occur at the same time, but not always exactly at the same time, the dispersion on the portfolio of assets is somewhat reduced relative to the dispersion on the individual assets.

We have shown with some simple examples how the characteristics of the return on portfolios of assets can differ from the characteristics of the returns on individual assets. These were artificial examples designed to dramatically illustrate the point. To reemphasize this point it is worthwhile examining portfolios of some real securities over a historical period.

Three securities were selected: IBM, General Motors, and Alcoa Aluminum. The monthly returns, average return, and standard deviation from investing in each security is shown in Table 4.5. In addition, the return and risk of placing one half of the available funds in each pair of securities is shown in the table. Finally, we have plotted the returns from each possible pair of securities in Figure 4.1. In this figure we have the return from each of two securities as well as the return from placing one half of the available funds in each security. Both Figure 4.1 and Table 4.5 make it clear how diversification across real securities can have a tremendous payoff for the investor. For example, a portfolio composed of 50% IBM and 50% Alcoa had the same return as each stock but less risk than either stock over the period studied. Earlier we argued that an investor is better off working with summary characteristics rather than full frequency functions. We used two summary measures: average return and variance or standard deviation of return. We will now examine analytically how the summary characteristics of a portfolio are related to those of individual assets.

CHARACTERISTICS OF PORTFOLIOS IN GENERAL

The return on a portfolio of assets is simply a weighted average of the return on the individual assets. The weight applied to each return is the fraction of the portfolio invested in

Table 4.5　Monthly Returns on IBM, Alcoa, and GM (in percent)

Month	IBM	Alcoa	GM	$\frac{1}{2}$ IBM + $\frac{1}{2}$ Alcoa	$\frac{1}{2}$ GM + $\frac{1}{2}$ Alcoa	$\frac{1}{2}$ GM + $\frac{1}{2}$ IBM
1	12.05	14.09	25.20	13.07	19.65	18.63
2	15.27	2.96	2.86	9.12	2.91	9.07
3	−4.12	7.19	5.45	1.54	6.32	0.67
4	1.57	24.39	4.56	12.98	14.48	3.07
5	3.16	0.06	3.72	1.61	1.89	3.44
6	−2.79	6.52	0.29	1.87	3.41	−1.25
7	−8.97	−8.75	5.38	−8.86	−1.69	−1.80
8	−1.18	2.82	−2.97	0.82	−0.08	−2.08
9	1.07	−13.97	1.52	−6.45	−6.23	1.30
10	12.75	−8.06	10.75	2.35	1.35	11.75
11	7.48	−0.70	3.79	3.39	1.55	5.64
12	−.94	8.80	1.32	3.93	5.06	0.19
$\bar{R}$	2.95	2.95	5.16	2.95	4.05	4.05
σ	7.15	10.06	6.83	6.32	6.69	6.02

Correlation Coefficient: IBM and Alcoa = 0.05;
GM and Alcoa = 0.22; IBM and GM = 0.48

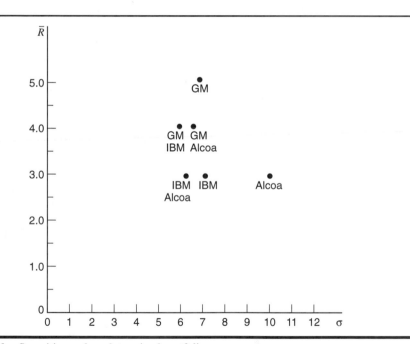

Figure 4.1　Securities and predetermined portfolios.

that asset. If R_{Pj} is the jth return on the portfolio and X_i is the fraction of the investor's funds invested in the ith asset, and N is the number of assets, then

$$R_{Pj} = \sum_{i=1}^{N} \left(X_i R_{ij} \right)$$

The expected return is also a weighted average of the expected returns on the individual assets. Taking the expected value of the expression just given for the return on a portfolio yields

$$\overline{R}_P = E(R_P) = E\left(\sum_{i=1}^{N} X_i R_{ij}\right)$$

But we already know that the expected value of the sum of various returns is the sum of the expected values. Therefore, we have

$$\overline{R}_P = \sum_{i=1}^{N} E(X_i R_{ij})$$

Finally, the expected value of a constant times a return is a constant times the expected return, or

$$\overline{R}_P = \sum_{i=1}^{N} (X_i \overline{R}_i)$$

This is a perfectly general formula, and we use it throughout the book. To illustrate its use, consider the investment in assets 2 and 3 discussed earlier in Table 4.3. We determined that no matter what occurred, the investor would receive \$1.10 on an investment of \$1.00. This is a return of 0.10/1.00 = 10%.

Let us apply the formula for expected return. In the example discussed earlier, \$0.60 was invested in asset 2 and \$0.40 in asset 4; therefore, the fraction invested in asset 4 is 0.40/1.00. Furthermore, the expected return on asset 2 and asset 4 is 10%. Applying the formula for expected return on a portfolio yields

$$\overline{R}_P = \left(\frac{0.60}{1.00}\right)(0.10) + \left(\frac{0.40}{1.00}\right)(0.10) = 0.10$$

The second summary characteristic was the variance. The variance on a portfolio is a little more difficult to determine than the expected return. We start out with a two-asset example. The variance of a portfolio P, designated by σ_P^2, is simply the expected value of the squared deviations of the return on the portfolio from the mean return on the portfolio, or $\sigma_P^2 = E(R_P - \overline{R}_P)^2$. Substituting in this expression the formulas for return on the portfolio and mean return yields in the two-security case

$$\sigma_P^2 = E(R_P - \overline{R}_P)^2 = E\left[X_1 R_{1j} + X_2 R_{2j} - \left(X_1 \overline{R}_1 + X_2 \overline{R}_2\right)\right]^2$$

$$= E\left[X_1\left(R_{1j} - \overline{R}_1\right) + X_2\left(R_{2j} - \overline{R}_2\right)\right]^2$$

where $\overline{R}_i$ stands for the expected value of security i with respect to all possible outcomes. Recall that

$$(X + Y)^2 = X^2 + XY + XY + Y^2 = X^2 + 2XY + Y^2$$

Applying this to the previous expression we have

$$\sigma_P^2 = E\left[X_1^2\left(R_{1j} - \overline{R}_1\right)^2 + 2X_1 X_2\left(R_{1j} - \overline{R}_1\right)\left(R_{2j} - \overline{R}_2\right) + X_2^2\left(R_{2j} - \overline{R}_2\right)^2\right]$$

Applying our two rules that the expected value of the sum of a series of returns is equal to the sum of the expected value of each return, and that the expected value of a constant times a return is equal to the constant times the expected return, we have

$$\sigma_P^2 = X_1^2 E\left[\left(R_{1j} - \overline{R}_1\right)^2\right] + 2X_1 X_2 E\left[\left(R_{1j} - \overline{R}_1\right)\left(R_{2j} - \overline{R}_2\right)\right] + X_2^2 E\left[\left(R_{2j} - \overline{R}_2\right)^2\right]$$

$$= X_1^2 \sigma_1^2 + 2X_1 X_2 E\left[\left(R_{1j} - \overline{R}_1\right)\left(R_{2j} - \overline{R}_2\right)\right] + X_2^2 \sigma_2^2$$

$E[(R_{1j} - \overline{R}_1)(R_{2j} - \overline{R}_2)]$ has a special name. It is called the covariance and will be designated as σ_{12}.[5] Substituting the symbol σ_{12} for $E[(R_{1j} - \overline{R}_1)(R_{2j} - \overline{R}_2)]$ yields

$$\sigma_P^2 = X_1^2 \sigma_1^2 + X_2^2 \sigma_2^2 + 2X_1 X_2 \sigma_{12}$$

Notice what the covariance does. It is the expected value of the product of two deviations: the deviations of the returns on security 1 from its mean $(R_{1j} - \overline{R}_1)$ and the deviations of security 2 from its mean $(R_{2j} - \overline{R}_2)$. In this sense it is very much like the variance. However, it is the product of two different deviations. As such it can be positive or negative. It will be large when the good outcomes for each stock occur together and when the bad outcomes for each stock occur together. In this case, for good outcomes the covariance will be the product of two large positive numbers, which is positive. When the bad outcomes occur, the covariance will be the product of two large negative numbers, which is positive. This will result in a large value for the covariance and a large variance for the portfolio. In contrast, if good outcomes for one asset are associated with bad outcomes of the other, the covariance is negative. It is negative because a plus deviation for one asset is associated with a minus deviation for the second and the product of a plus and a minus is negative. This was what occurred when we examined a combination of assets 2 and 3.

The covariance is a measure of how returns on assets move together. Insofar as they have positive and negative deviations at similar times, the covariance is a large positive number. If they have the positive and negative deviations at dissimilar times, then the covariance is negative. If the positive and negative deviations are unrelated, it tends to be zero.

For many purposes it is useful to standardize the covariance. Dividing the covariance between two assets by the product of the standard deviation of each asset produces a variable with the same properties as the covariance but with a range of -1 to $+1$. The measure is called the correlation coefficient. Letting ρ_{ik} stand for the correlation between securities i and k the correlation coefficient is defined as

$$\rho_{ik} = \frac{\sigma_{ik}}{\sigma_i \sigma_k}$$

[5]Note that when all joint outcomes are equally likely, the covariance can be expressed as

$$\sum_{j=1}^{M} \frac{\left(R_{1j} - \overline{R}_1\right)\left(R_{2j} - \overline{R}_2\right)}{M}$$

where M is the number of equally likely joint outcomes. Once again when estimates are based on a sample of data such as actual historical returns it is traditional to divide by $T - 1$ rather than T where T is the number of periods in the sample.

Table 4.6   Calculating Covariances

Condition of Market	Deviations Security 1	Deviations Security 2	Product of Deviations	Deviations Security 1	Deviations Security 3	Product of Deviations
Good	(15 − 9)	(16 − 10)	36	(15 − 9)	(1 − 10)	−54
Average	(9 − 9)	(10 − 10)	0	(9 − 9)	(10 − 10)	0
Poor	(3 − 9)	(4 − 10)	36	(3 − 9)	(19 − 10)	−54
			72			−108

Dividing by the product of the standard deviations does not change the properties of the covariance. It simply scales it to have values between −1 and +1. Let us apply these formulas. First, however, it is necessary to calculate covariances. Table 4.6 shows the intermediate calculations necessary to determine the covariance between securities 1 and 2 and securities 1 and 3. The sum of the deviations between securities 1 and 2 is 72. Therefore, the covariance is 72/3 = 24 and the correlation coefficient is $24/\sqrt{24}\ \sqrt{24}$. For assets 1 and 3 the sum of the deviations is −108. The covariance is −108/3 = −36 and the correlation coefficient is $-36/\sqrt{24}\ \sqrt{54}$. Similar calculations can be made for all other pairs of assets, and the results are contained in Table 4.7.

Earlier we examined the results obtained by an investor with $1.00 to spend who put $0.60 in asset 2 and $0.40 in asset 3. Applying the expression for variance of the portfolio we have

$$\sigma_P^2 = \left(\frac{0.60}{1.00}\right)^2 24 + \left(\frac{0.40}{1.00}\right)^2 54 + 2\left(\frac{0.60}{1.00}\right)\left(\frac{0.40}{1.00}\right)(-36) = 0$$

This was exactly the result we obtained when we looked at the combination of the full distribution. The correlation coefficient between securities 2 and 3 is −1. This meant that good and bad returns of assets 2 and 3 tended to occur at opposite times. When this situation occurs, a portfolio can always be constructed with zero risk.

Our second example was an investment in securities 1 and 4. The variance of this portfolio is

$$\sigma^2 = \left(\tfrac{1}{2}\right)^2 24 + \left(\tfrac{1}{2}\right)^2 24 = 12$$

In this case where the correlation coefficient was zero, the risk of the portfolio was less than the risk of either of the individual securities. Once again, this is a general result. When the return patterns of two assets are independent so that the correlation coefficient and

Table 4.7   Covariance and Correlation Coefficients (in Brackets) Between Assets

	1	2	3	4	5
1		24 (+1)	−36 (−1)	0 (0)	24 (+1)
2			−36 (−1)	0 (0)	24 (+1)
3				0 (0)	−36 (−1)
4					0 (0)
5					

covariance are zero, a portfolio can be found that has a lower variance than either of the assets by themselves.

As an additional check on the accuracy of the formula just derived, we calculate the variance directly. Earlier we saw there were nine possible returns when we combined assets 2 and 4. They were $1.16, $1.13, $1.13, $1.10, $1.10, $1.10, $1.07, $1.07, and $1.04. Since we started with an investment of $1.00, the returns are easy to determine. The return is 16%, 13%, 13%, 10%, 10%, 10%, 7%, 7%, and 4%. By examination it is easy to see that the mean return is 10%. The deviations are 6, 3, 3, 0, 0, 0, –3, –3, –6. The squared deviations are 36, 9, 9, 0, 0, 0, 9, 9, 36, and the average squared deviation or variance is $108/9 = 12$. This agrees with the formula developed earlier.

The final example analyzed previously was a portfolio of assets 1 and 5. In this case the variance of the portfolio is

$$\sigma_P^2 = \left(\tfrac{1}{2}\right)^2 24 + \left(\tfrac{1}{2}\right)^2 24 + 2\left(\tfrac{1}{2}\right)\left(\tfrac{1}{2}\right)24$$

$$= \tfrac{1}{4}(24) + \tfrac{1}{4}(24) + \tfrac{1}{2}(24)$$

$$= 24$$

As we demonstrated earlier, when two securities have their good and bad outcomes at the same time, the risk is not reduced by purchasing a portfolio of the two assets.

The formula for variance of a portfolio can be generalized to more than two assets. Consider first a three-asset case. Substituting the expression for return on a portfolio and expected return of a portfolio in the general formula for variance yields

$$\sigma_P^2 = E\left(R_P - \overline{R}_P\right)^2$$

$$= E\left[X_1 R_{1j} + X_2 R_{2j} + X_3 R_{3j} - \left(X_1 \overline{R}_1 + X_2 \overline{R}_2 + X_3 \overline{R}_3\right)\right]^2$$

Rearranging,

$$\sigma_P^2 = E\left[X_1\left(R_{1j} - \overline{R}_1\right) + X_2\left(R_{2j} - \overline{R}_2\right) + X_3\left(R_{3j} - \overline{R}_3\right)\right]^2$$

Squaring the right-hand side yields

$$\sigma_P^2 = E\Big[X_1^2\left(R_{1j} - \overline{R}_1\right)^2 + X_2^2\left(R_{2j} - \overline{R}_2\right)^2 + X_3^2\left(R_{3j} - \overline{R}_3\right)^2$$

$$+ 2X_1 X_2\left(R_{1j} - \overline{R}_1\right)\left(R_{2j} - \overline{R}_2\right) + 2X_1 X_3\left(R_{1j} - \overline{R}_1\right)\left(R_{3j} - \overline{R}_3\right)$$

$$+ 2X_2 X_3\left(R_{2j} - \overline{R}_2\right)\left(R_{3j} - \overline{R}_3\right)\Big]$$

Applying the properties of expected return discussed earlier yields

$$\sigma_P^2 = X_1^2 E\left(R_{1j} - \overline{R}_1\right)^2 + X_2^2 E\left(R_{2j} - \overline{R}_2\right)^2 + X_3^2 E\left(R_{3j} - \overline{R}_3\right)^2$$

$$+ 2X_1 X_2 E\left[\left(R_{1j} - \overline{R}_1\right)\left(R_{2j} - \overline{R}_2\right)\right] + 2X_1 X_3 E\left[\left(R_{1j} - \overline{R}_1\right)\left(R_{3j} - \overline{R}_3\right)\right]$$

$$+ 2X_2 X_3 E\left[\left(R_{2j} - \overline{R}_2\right)\left(R_{3j} - \overline{R}_3\right)\right]$$

Utilizing σ_i^2 for variance of asset i and σ_{ij} for the covariance between assets i and j, we have

$$\sigma_P^2 = X_1^2 \sigma_1^2 + X_2^2 \sigma_2^2 + X_3^2 \sigma_3^2 + 2X_1 X_2 \sigma_{12} + 2X_1 X_3 \sigma_{13} + 2X_2 X_3 \sigma_{23}$$

This formula can be extended to any number of assets. Examining the expression for the variance of a portfolio of three assets should indicate how. First note that the variance of each asset is multiplied by the square of the proportion invested in it. Thus, the first part of the expression for the variance of a portfolio is the sum of the variances on the individual assets times the square of the proportion invested in each, or

$$\sum_{i=1}^{N}\left(X_i^2\sigma_i^2\right)$$

The second set of terms in the expression for the variance of a portfolio is covariance terms. Note that the covariance between each pair of assets in the portfolio enters the expression for the variance of a portfolio. With three assets the covariance between 1 and 2, 1 and 3, and 2 and 3 entered. With four assets, covariance terms between 1 and 2, 1 and 3, 1 and 4, 2 and 3, 2 and 4, and 3 and 4 would enter. Further note that each covariance term is multiplied by two times the product of the proportions invested in each asset. The following double summation captures the covariance terms:

$$\sum_{j=1}^{N}\sum_{\substack{k=1\\k\neq j}}^{N}\left(X_j X_k \sigma_{jk}\right)$$

The reader concerned that a 2 does not appear in this expression can relax. The covariance between securities 2 and 3 comes about both from $j = 2$ and $k = 3$ and from $j = 3$ and $k = 2$. This is how the term "2 times the covariance between 2 and 3" comes about. Furthermore, examining the expression for covariance shows that order does not matter; thus $\sigma_{jk} = \sigma_{kj}$. The symbol $\neq$ means k should not have the same value as j. To reemphasize the meaning of the double summation, we examine the three-security case. We have

$$\sum_{j=1}^{3}\sum_{\substack{k=1\\k\neq j}}^{3}\left(X_j X_k \sigma_{jk}\right) = X_1 X_2 \sigma_{12} + X_1 X_3 \sigma_{13} + X_2 X_1 \sigma_{21}$$
$$+ X_2 X_3 \sigma_{23} + X_3 X_1 \sigma_{31} + X_3 X_2 \sigma_{32}$$

Since the order does not matter in calculating covariance and thus $\sigma_{12} = \sigma_{21}$, we have

$$\sum_{j=1}^{3}\sum_{\substack{k=1\\k\neq j}}^{3}\left(X_j X_k \sigma_{jk}\right) = 2X_1 X_2 \sigma_{12} + 2X_1 X_3 \sigma_{13} + 2X_2 X_3 \sigma_{23}$$

Putting together the variance and covariance parts of the general expression for the variance of a portfolio yields

$$\sigma_P^2 = \sum_{j=1}^{N}\left(X_j^2\sigma_j^2\right) + \sum_{j=1}^{N}\sum_{\substack{k=1\\k\neq j}}^{N}\left(X_j X_k \sigma_{jk}\right)$$

This formula is worth examining further. First, consider the case where all assets are independent and, therefore, the covariance between them is zero. This was the situation we observed for assets 2 and 4 in our little example. In this case $\sigma_{jk} = 0$ and the formula for variance becomes

$$\sum_{j=1}^{N}\left(X_j^2\sigma_j^2\right)$$

Furthermore, assume equal amounts are invested in each asset. With N assets the proportion invested in each asset is $1/N$. Applying our formula yields

$$\sigma_P^2 = \sum_{j=1}^{N} (1/N)^2 \sigma_j^2 = 1/N \left[\sum_{j=1}^{N} \frac{\sigma_j^2}{N} \right]$$

The term in the brackets is our expression for an average. Thus our formula reduces to $\sigma_P^2 = 1/N\bar{\sigma}_j^2$, where $\bar{\sigma}_j^2$ represents the average variance of the stocks in the portfolio. As N gets larger and larger, the variance of the portfolio gets smaller and smaller. As N becomes extremely large, the variance of the portfolio approaches zero. This is a general result. If we have enough *independent* assets, the variance of a portfolio of these assets approaches zero.

In general, we are not so fortunate. In most markets the correlation coefficient and the covariance between assets is positive. In these markets the risk on the portfolio cannot be made to go to zero but can be much less than the variance of an individual asset. The variance of a portfolio of assets is

$$\sigma_P^2 = \sum_{j=1}^{N} \left(X_j^2 \sigma_j^2 \right) + \sum_{j=1}^{N} \sum_{\substack{k=1 \\ k \neq j}}^{N} \left(X_j X_k \sigma_{jk} \right)$$

Once again, consider equal investment in N assets. With equal investment, the proportion invested in any one asset X_j is $1/N$ and the formula for the variance of a portfolio becomes

$$\sigma_P^2 = \sum_{j=1}^{N} (1/N)^2 \sigma_j^2 + \sum_{j=1}^{N} \sum_{\substack{k=1 \\ k \neq j}}^{N} (1/N)(1/N)\sigma_{jk}$$

Factoring out $1/N$ from the first summation and $(N-1)/N$ from the second yields

$$\sigma_P^2 = (1/N) \sum_{j=1}^{N} \left[\frac{\sigma_j^2}{N} \right] + \frac{(N-1)}{N} \sum_{j=1}^{N} \sum_{\substack{k=1 \\ k \neq j}}^{N} \left[\frac{\sigma_{jk}}{N(N-1)} \right]$$

Both of the terms in the brackets are averages. That the first is an average should be clear from the previous discussion. Likewise the second term in brackets is also an average. There are N values of j and $(N-1)$ values of k. There are $N-1$ values of k since k cannot equal j so that there is one less value of k than j. In total there are $N(N-1)$ covariance terms. Thus the second term is the summation of covariances divided by the number of covariances and it is, therefore, an average. Replacing the summations by averages, we have

$$\sigma_P^2 = \frac{1}{N} \bar{\sigma}_j^2 + \frac{N-1}{N} \bar{\sigma}_{jk}$$

This expression is a much more realistic representation of what occurs when we invest in a portfolio of assets. The contribution to the portfolio variance of the variance of the individual securities goes to zero as N gets very large. However, the contribution of the covariance terms approaches the average covariance as N gets large. The individual risk of securities can be diversified away, but the contribution to the total risk caused by the covariance terms cannot be diversified away.

Table 4.8 illustrates how this relationship looks when dealing with U.S. equities. The average variance and average covariance of returns were calculated using monthly data for all stocks listed on the New York Stock Exchange. The average variance was 46.619. The average covariance was 7.058. As more and more securities are added, the average variance on the portfolio declines until it approaches the average covariance. Rearranging the previous equation clarifies this relationship even further. Thus,

Table 4.8   Effect of Diversification

Number of Securities	Expected Portfolio Variance
1	46.619
2	26.839
4	16.948
6	13.651
8	12.003
10	11.014
12	10.354
14	9.883
16	9.530
18	9.256
20	9.036
25	8.640
30	8.376
35	8.188
40	8.047
45	7.937
50	7.849
75	7.585
100	7.453
125	7.374
150	7.321
175	7.284
200	7.255
250	7.216
300	7.190
350	7.171
400	7.157
450	7.146
500	7.137
600	7.124
700	7.114
800	7.107
900	7.102
1000	7.097
Infinity	7.058

$$\sigma_P^2 = (1/N)\left(\bar{\sigma}_j^2 - \bar{\sigma}_{kj}\right) + \bar{\sigma}_{kj}$$

The first term is $1/N$ times the difference between the variance of return on individual securities and the average covariance. The second term is the average covariance. This relationship clarifies the effect of diversification on portfolio risk. The minimum variance is obtained for very large portfolios and is equal to the average covariance between all stocks in the population. As securities are added to the portfolio, the effect of the difference between the average risk on a security and the average covariance is reduced.

Figures 4.2 and 4.3 and Table 4.9 illustrate this same relationship for common equities in a number of countries. In Figure 4.3 the vertical axis is the risk of the portfolio as a percentage of the risk of an individual security for the U.K. The horizontal axis is the number of securities in the portfolio. Figure 4.2 presents the same relationship for the United

Table 4.9 Percentage of the Risk on an Individual Security that Can Be Eliminated by Holding a Random Portfolio of Stocks within Selected National Markets and among National Markets [13]

United States	73
U.K.	65.5
France	67.3
Germany	56.2
Italy	60.0
Belgium	80.0
Switzerland	56.0
Netherlands	76.1
International stocks	89.3

States. Table 4.9 shows the percentage of risk that can be eliminated by holding a widely diversified portfolio in each of several countries as well as an internationally diversified portfolio. As can be seen, the effectiveness of diversification in reducing the risk of a portfolio varies from country to country. From the previous equation we know why. The average covariance relative to the variance varies from country to country. Thus, in Switzerland and Italy securities have relatively high covariance, indicating that stocks tend to move together. On the other hand, the security markets in Belgium and the Netherlands tend to have stocks with relatively low covariances. For these latter security markets, much more of the risk of holding individual securities can be diversified away. Diversification is especially useful in reducing the risk on a portfolio in these markets.

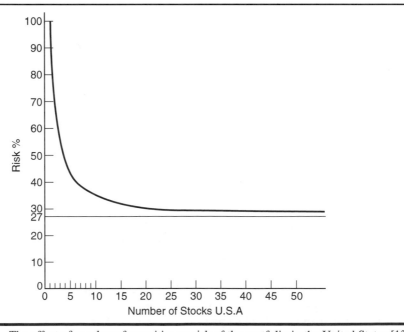

Figure 4.2 The effect of number of securities on risk of the portfolio in the United States [13].

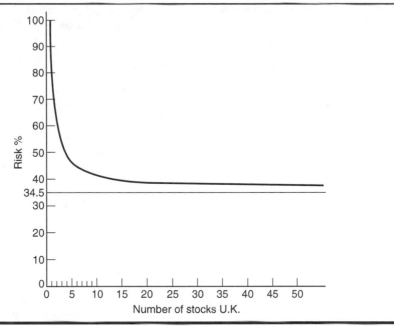

Figure 4.3   The effect of securities on risk in the U.K. [13].

TWO CONCLUDING EXAMPLES

We will close this chapter and several chapters that follow with realistic applications of the principles discussed in the chapter. These applications serve both to review the concepts presented and to demonstrate their usefulness. The two examples that follow are applications to the asset allocation decision. The first application analyzes the allocation between stocks and bonds; the second analyzes the allocation between domestic and foreign stocks.

Bond Stock Allocation

One of the major decisions facing an investor is the allocation of funds between stocks and bonds. In order to make this allocation one needs to have estimates of mean returns, standard deviations of return, and either correlation coefficients or covariances. In order to estimate these variables it is useful to begin by looking at historical data. Even in allocating among managed portfolios it is useful to start by assuming that the stock and bond portfolio managers you are allocating between have performance similar to that of broad representative indexes.

The principal index used to represent common stock portfolios is the Standard and Poor's index. As described in Chapter 2, the Standard and Poor's index is a value weighted index of 500 large stocks. Value weighting means that the weight each stock represents of the portfolio is the market value of that stock (price times number of shares) divided by the aggregate market value of all shares in the index. Thus large stocks are weighted more heavily.

The version of the Standard and Poor's index reported in the newspapers is a capital appreciation index and as such doesn't include the return from dividends. In order to get total return one has to add dividend income. We will use the S&P index plus dividends for examining the characteristics of stock returns.

The standard index used to represent bond performance is the Lehman Brothers aggregate bond index. It is a value weighted index of almost all bonds in the market, and includes both capital appreciation and interest income. Thus it is a total return index.

In Table 4.10 we report the standard deviation and correlation coefficients calculated using monthly data but expressed in annual terms. The data is for a 15-year period and three 5-year periods. The month of the major market crash, October 1987, was omitted in the belief that it was atypical. Examining Table 4.10 shows that the standard deviation over each of the five-year periods is fairly constant for the S&P index; thus, using the overall average is a reasonable estimate and we will use 14.9%. Because the standard deviation for bonds has declined as markets have become less volatile, an estimate closer to the latest five-year results is probably appropriate and we will use 4.8%. The correlation coefficient has risen over time. Placing more emphasis on recent data, .45 is a reasonable estimate. At the time of the revision of this book the average forecast by security analysts surveyed was a return of 12.5% for the S&P index and 6% for the Lehman Brothers aggregate index. Thus our inputs are

$$\overline{R}_{S\&P} = 12.5\% \quad \sigma_{S\&P} = 14.9\% \quad \rho_{S\&PB} = 0.45$$
$$\overline{R}_B = 6\% \quad\quad \sigma_B = 4.8\%$$

The means and standard deviation of return for combinations of stocks and bonds varying from 100% in the S&P, which is $X_{S\&P} = 1$ and $X_{SL} = 0$ to 0% in the S&P are presented in Table 4.11. Note that the expected return varies linearly from 12.5% to 6% as we decrease the amount in the S&P and increase it in bonds. Also the risk decreases as we put more in the bonds, but not linearly. Figure 4.4 shows the various choices diagrammatically.

Table 4.10   Historical Data on Bonds and Stocks

Date	Standard Deviations		Correlation Coefficients
	Bonds	Stocks	
77–81	9.70%	14.54%	0.34
82–86	6.63%	14.66%	0.41
87–91	4.72%	15.40%	0.49
77–91	7.46%	14.87%	0.41

Table 4.11   Mean Return and Standard Deviation for Combinations of Stocks and Bonds

Proportion Stocks	Proportion Bonds	Mean Return	Standard Deviation
1	0	12.5	14.90
0.9	0.1	11.85	13.63
0.8	0.2	11.2	12.38
0.7	0.3	10.55	11.15
0.6	0.4	9.9	9.95
0.5	0.5	9.25	8.80
0.4	0.6	8.6	7.70
0.3	0.7	7.95	6.69
0.2	0.8	7.3	5.82
0.1	0.9	6.65	5.16
0	1	6	4.80

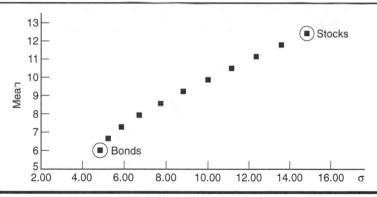

Figure 4.4   Combinations of bonds and stocks.

Domestic Foreign Allocation

As a second example consider the allocation decision between domestic and foreign stocks. In Chapter 12 we will review the characteristics of foreign portfolios in some detail. In that chapter we will show that on average foreign stock portfolios are somewhat less risky than domestic. Thus, if we are assuming domestic portfolios have a standard deviation of 14.9%, foreign portfolios can reasonably be assumed to have a standard deviation of 14%. Furthermore, a reasonable correlation coefficient is 0.33. This was the average correlation between a U.S. mutual fund and a foreign mutual fund for the most recent five years (as shown in Table 12.11). At the time of this revision analysts were more pessimistic about foreign markets than U.S. markets and were estimating returns 2% lower. Thus our inputs are

$$\overline{R}_{S\&P} = 12.5\% \quad \sigma_{S\&P} = 14.9\% \quad \rho_{S\&P\ Int} = 0.33$$
$$\overline{R}_{int} = 10.5\% \quad \sigma_{int} = 14.0\%$$

The expected return and standard deviation of return for all combinations of the two portfolios is shown in Table 4.12 and is plotted in Figure 4.5. Note that investment in the two portfolios combined substantially reduced risk. This is a powerful demonstration of the effect of diversification.

CONCLUSION

In this chapter we have shown how the risk of a portfolio of assets can be very different from the risk of the individual assets comprising the portfolio. This was true when we selected assets with particular characteristics such as those shown in Table 4.3. It was also true when we simply selected assets at random such as those shown in Tables 4.8 and 4.9.

In the following chapter we examine the relationship between the risk and return on individual assets in more detail. We then show how the characteristics on combinations of securities can be used to define the opportunity set of investments from which the investor must make a choice. Finally, we show how the properties of these opportunities taken together with the knowledge that the investor prefers return and seeks to avoid risk can be used to define a subset of the opportunity set that will be of interest to investors.

Table 4.12   Mean Return and Standard Deviation for Combinations of Domestic and
                 International Stocks

Proportion S&P	Proportion International	Mean Return	Standard Deviation
1	0	12.5	14.90
0.9	0.1	12.3	13.93
0.8	0.2	12.1	13.11
0.7	0.3	11.9	12.46
0.6	0.4	11.7	12.01
0.5	0.5	11.5	11.79
0.45	0.55	11.4	11.76
0.4	0.6	11.3	11.80
0.3	0.7	11.1	12.04
0.2	0.8	10.9	12.50
0.1	0.9	10.7	13.17
0	1	10.5	14.00

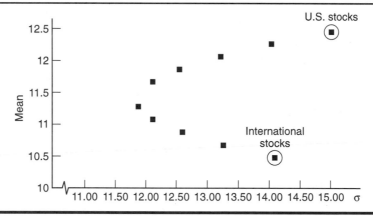

Figure 4.5   Combinations of U.S. stocks and international stocks.

QUESTIONS AND PROBLEMS

1. Assume that you are considering selecting assets from among the following four candidates:

Asset 1		
Market Condition	Return	Probability
Good	16	$\frac{1}{4}$
Average	12	$\frac{1}{2}$
Poor	8	$\frac{1}{4}$

Asset 2		
Market Condition	Return	Probability
Good	4	$\frac{1}{4}$
Average	6	$\frac{1}{2}$
Poor	8	$\frac{1}{4}$

Asset 3		
Market Condition	Return	Probability
Good	20	$\frac{1}{4}$
Average	14	$\frac{1}{2}$
Poor	8	$\frac{1}{4}$

Asset 4		
Rainfall	Return	Probability
Plentiful	16	$\frac{1}{3}$
Average	12	$\frac{1}{3}$
Light	8	$\frac{1}{3}$

Assume that there is no relationship between the amount of rainfall and the condition of the stock market.

A. Solve for the expected return and the standard deviation of return for each separate investment.

B. Solve for the correlation coefficient and the covariance between each pair of investments.

C. Solve for the expected return and variance of each of the portfolios shown below.

	Portions Invested in Each Asset			
Portfolio	Asset 1	Asset 2	Asset 3	Asset 4
a	$\frac{1}{2}$	$\frac{1}{2}$		
b	$\frac{1}{2}$		$\frac{1}{2}$	
c	$\frac{1}{2}$			$\frac{1}{2}$
d		$\frac{1}{2}$	$\frac{1}{2}$	
e			$\frac{1}{2}$	$\frac{1}{2}$
f	$\frac{1}{3}$	$\frac{1}{3}$	$\frac{1}{3}$	
g		$\frac{1}{3}$	$\frac{1}{3}$	$\frac{1}{3}$
h	$\frac{1}{3}$		$\frac{1}{3}$	$\frac{1}{3}$
i	$\frac{1}{4}$	$\frac{1}{4}$	$\frac{1}{4}$	$\frac{1}{4}$

D. Plot the original assets and each of the portfolios from Part C in expected return standard deviation space.

2. Below is actual price and dividend data for three companies for each of seven months.

	Security A		Security B		Security C	
Time	Price	Dividend	Price	Dividend	Price	Dividend
1	$57\frac{6}{8}$		333		$106\frac{6}{8}$	
2	$59\frac{7}{8}$		368		$108\frac{2}{8}$	
3	$59\frac{3}{8}$	0.725^a	$368\frac{4}{8}$	1.35	124	0.40
4	$55\frac{4}{8}$		$382\frac{2}{8}$		$122\frac{2}{8}$	
5	$56\frac{2}{8}$		386		$135\frac{4}{8}$	
6	59	0.725	$397\frac{6}{8}$	1.35	$141\frac{6}{8}$	0.42
7	$60\frac{2}{8}$		392		$165\frac{6}{8}$	

[a]A dividend entry on the same line as a price indicates that the return between that time period and the previous period consisted of a capital gain (or loss) and the receipt of the dividend.

    A. Compute the rate of return for each company for each month.

    B. Compute the average rate of return for each company.

    C. Compute the standard deviation of the rate of return for each company.

    D. Compute the correlation coefficient between all possible pairs of securities.

    E. Compute the average return and standard deviation for the following portfolios:

$$\tfrac{1}{2}A + \tfrac{1}{2}B$$
$$\tfrac{1}{2}A + \tfrac{1}{2}C$$
$$\tfrac{1}{2}B + \tfrac{1}{2}C$$
$$\tfrac{1}{3}A + \tfrac{1}{3}B + \tfrac{1}{3}C$$

3. Assume that the average variance of return for an individual security is 50 and that the average covariance is 10. What is the expected variance of an equally weighted portfolio of 5, 10, 20, 50, and 100 securities?

4. In Problem 3 how many securities need to be held before the risk of a portfolio is only 10% more than minimum?

5. For the Italy data and Belgium data of Table 4.9, what is the ratio of the difference between the average variance minus average covariance and the average covariance? If the average variance of a single security is 50, what is the expected variance of a portfolio of 5, 20, and 100 securities?

6. For the data in Table 4.8, suppose an investor desires an expected variance less than 8. What is the minimum number of securities for such a portfolio?

BIBLIOGRAPHY

1. Brennan, Michael J. "The Optimal Number of Securities in a Risky Asset Portfolio When There Are Fixed Costs of Transacting: Theory and Some Empirical Results." *Journal of Financial and Quantitative Analysis,* **X,** No. 3 (Sept. 1975), pp. 483–496.
2. Elton, Edwin J., and Gruber, Martin J. "Risk Reduction and Portfolio Size: An Analytical Solution," *Journal of Business,* **50,** No. 4 (Oct. 1977), pp. 415–437.
3. ——. "Modern Portfolio Theory: 1950 to Date," *Journal of Banking and Finance,* **21,** Nos. 11–12 (December 1997), pp. 1743–1759.
4. ——. "The Rationality of Asset Allocation Recommendations," *Journal of Financial and Quantitative Analysis,* **35,** No. 1, (March 2000), pp. 27–42.
5. Epps, Thomas W. "Necessary and Sufficient Conditions for the Mean-Variance Portfolio Model with Constant Risk Aversion," *Journal of Financial and Quantitative Analysis,* **XVI,** No. 2 (June 1981), pp. 169–176.
6. Evans, L. John, and Archer, N. Stephen. "Diversification and the Reduction of Dispersion: An Empirical Analysis," *Journal of Finance,* **XXIII,** No. 5 (Dec. 1968), pp. 761–767.
7. Fisher, Lawrence, and Lorie, James. "Some Studies of Variability of Returns on Investments in Common Stocks," *Journal of Business,* **43,** No. 2 (April 1970), pp. 99–134.
8. Jennings, Edward. "An Empirical Analysis of Some Aspects of Common Stock Diversification," *Journal of Financial and Quantitative Analysis,* **VI,** No. 2 (March 1971), pp. 797–813.
9. Johnson, K., and Shannon, D. "A Note of Diversification and the Reduction of Dispersion," *Journal of Financial Economics,* **1,** No. 4 (Dec. 1974), pp. 365–372.
10. Markowitz, Harry. "Markowitz Revisited," *Financial Analysts Journal,* **32,** No. 4 (Sept.–Oct. 1976), pp. 47–52.
11. Ross, Stephen A. "Adding Risks: Samuelson's Fallacy of Large Numbers Revisited," *Journal of Financial and Quantitative Analysis,* **34,** No. 3 (Sept. 1999), pp. 323–340.

12. Rubinstein, Mark. "The Fundamental Theorem of Parameter-Preference Security Valuation," *Journal of Financial and Quantitative Analysis,* **VIII,** No. 1 (Jan. 1973), pp. 61–69.
13. Solnick, Bruno. "The Advantages of Domestic and International Diversification," in Edwin J. Elton and Martin J. Gruber (eds.), *International Capital Markets* (Amsterdam: North Holland, 1975).
14. Statman, Meir. "How Many Stocks Make a Diversified Portfolio?" *Journal of Financial and Quantitative Analysis,* **22,** No. 3 (Sept. 1987), pp. 353–363.
15. Wagner, W., and Lau, S. "The Effect of Diversification on Risk," *Financial Analysts Journal,* **27,** No. 5 (Nov.–Dec. 1971), pp. 48–53.
16. Whitmore, G.A. "Diversification and the Reduction of Dispersion: A Note," *Journal of Financial and Quantitative Analysis,* **V,** No. 2 (May 1970), pp. 263–264.

5

Delineating Efficient Portfolios

In Chapter 4 we examined the return and risk characteristics of individual securities and began to study the attributes of combinations or portfolios of securities. In this chapter we look at the risk and return characteristics of combinations of securities in more detail. We start off with a reexamination of the attributes of combinations of two risky assets. In doing so we emphasize a geometric interpretation of asset combinations. It is a short step from the analysis of the combination of two or more risky assets to the analysis of combinations of all possible risky assets. After making this step we can delineate that subset of portfolios that will be preferred by all investors who exhibit risk avoidance and who prefer more return to less.[1] This set is usually called the efficient set or efficient frontier. Its shape will differ according to the assumptions that are made with respect to the ability of the investor to sell securities short as well as his ability to lend and borrow funds.[2] Alternative assumptions about short sales and lending and borrowing are examined.

COMBINATIONS OF TWO RISKY ASSETS REVISITED: SHORT SALES NOT ALLOWED

In Chapter 4 we began the analysis of combinations of risky assets. In this chapter we continue it. Previously, we treated the two assets as if they were individual assets, but nothing in the analysis so constrains them. In fact, when we talk about assets, we could equally well be talking about portfolios of risky assets.

Recall from Chapter 4 that the expected return on a portfolio of two assets is given by

$$\overline{R}_P = X_A \overline{R}_A + X_B \overline{R}_B \tag{5.1}$$

where

X_A is the fraction of the portfolio held in asset A

X_B is the fraction of the portfolio held in asset B

---

[1] In this chapter and most of those that follow, we assume that mean variance is the relevant space for portfolio analysts. See Chapter 11 for an examination of other portfolio models.

[2] Short selling is defined at a later point in this chapter.

$\bar{R}_P$ is the expected return on the portfolio

$\bar{R}_A$ is the expected return on the asset A

$\bar{R}_B$ is the expected return on the asset B

In addition, since we require the investor to be fully invested, the fraction she invests in A plus the fraction she invests in B must equal one, or

$$X_A + X_B = 1$$

We can rewrite this expression as

$$X_B = 1 - X_A \tag{5.2}$$

Substituting Equation (5.2) into Equation (5.1), we can express the expected return on a portfolio of two assets as

$$\bar{R}_P = X_A \bar{R}_A + (1 - X_A) \bar{R}_B$$

Notice that the expected return on the portfolio is a simple-weighted average of the expected returns on the individual securities, and that the weights add to one. The same is not necessarily true of the risk (standard deviation of the return) of the portfolio. In Chapter 4 the standard deviation of the return on the portfolio was shown to be equal to

$$\sigma_P = \left(X_A^2 \sigma_A^2 + X_B^2 \sigma_B^2 + 2 X_A X_B \sigma_{AB} \right)^{1/2}$$

where

σ_P is the standard deviation of the return on the portfolio

σ_A^2 is the variance of the return on security A

σ_B^2 is the variance of the return on security B

σ_{AB} is the covariance between the returns on security A and security B

If we substitute Equation (5.2) into this expression, we obtain

$$\sigma_P = \left[X_A^2 \sigma_A^2 + (1 - X_A)^2 \sigma_B^2 + 2 X_A (1 - X_A) \sigma_{AB} \right]^{1/2} \tag{5.3}$$

Recalling that $\sigma_{AB} = \rho_{AB} \sigma_A \sigma_B$ where ρ_{AB} is the correlation coefficient between securities A and B, then Equation (5.3) becomes

$$\sigma_P = \left[X_A^2 \sigma_A^2 + (1 - X_A)^2 \sigma_B^2 + 2 X_A (1 - X_A) \rho_{AB} \sigma_A \sigma_B \right]^{1/2} \tag{5.4}$$

The standard deviation of the portfolio is not, in general, a simple-weighted average of the standard deviation of each security. Cross-product terms are involved and the weights do not, in general, add to one. In order to learn more about this relationship, we now study some specific cases involving different degrees of co-movement between securities.

We know that a correlation coefficient has maximum value of $+1$ and minimum value of -1. A value of $+1$ means that two securities will always move in perfect unison, while a value of -1 means that their movements are exactly opposite to each other. We start with an examination of these extreme cases; then we turn to an examination of some intermediate values for the correlation coefficients. As an aid in interpreting results, we examine a specific example as well as general expressions for risk and return. For the example we consider two stocks: a large manufacturer of automobiles ("Colonel Motors") and an electric utility company operating in a large eastern city ("Separated Edison"). Assume the stocks have the following characteristics:

	Expected Return	Standard Deviation
Colonel Motors (*C*)	14%	6%
Separated Edison (*S*)	8%	3%

As you might suspect, the car manufacturer has a bigger expected return and a bigger risk than the electric utility.

Case 1—Perfect Positive Correlation ($\rho = +1$)

Let the subscript C stand for Colonel Motors and the subscript S stand for Separated Edison. If the correlation coefficient is $+1$, then the equation for the risk on the portfolio, Equation (5.4), simplifies to

$$\sigma_P = \left[X_C^2 \sigma_C^2 + \left(1 - X_C\right)^2 \sigma_S^2 + 2X_C\left(1 - X_C\right)\sigma_C\sigma_S \right]^{1/2} \tag{5.5}$$

Note that the term in square brackets has the form $X^2 + 2XY + Y^2$ and, thus, can be written as

$$\left[X_C\sigma_C + \left(1 - X_C\right)\sigma_S \right]^2$$

Since the standard deviation of the portfolio is equal to the positive square root of this expression, we know that

$$\sigma_P = X_C\sigma_C + \left(1 - X_C\right)\sigma_S$$

While the expected return on the portfolio is

$$\overline{R}_P = X_C\overline{R}_C + \left(1 - X_C\right)\overline{R}_S$$

Thus with the correlation coefficient equal to $+1$, both risk and return of the portfolio are simply linear combinations of the risk and return of each security. In footnote 3 we show that the form of these two equations means that all combinations of two securities that are perfectly correlated will lie on a straight line in risk and return space.[3] We now illustrate that this is true for the stocks in our example. For the two stocks under study

$$\overline{R}_P = \frac{\sigma_P - \sigma_S}{\sigma_C - \sigma_S}\,\overline{R}_C + \left(1 - \frac{\sigma_P - \sigma_S}{\sigma_C - \sigma_S}\right)\overline{R}_S$$

---

[3]Solving for X_C in the expression for standard deviation yields

$$X_C = \frac{\sigma_P - \sigma_S}{\sigma_C - \sigma_S}$$

Substituting this into the expression for expected return yields

$$\overline{R}_P = \frac{\sigma_P - \sigma_S}{\sigma_C - \sigma_S}\,\overline{R}_C + \left(1 - \frac{\sigma_P - \sigma_S}{\sigma_C - \sigma_S}\right)\overline{R}_S$$

$$\overline{R}_P = \left(\overline{R}_S - \frac{\overline{R}_C - \overline{R}_S}{\sigma_C - \sigma_S}\,\sigma_S\right) + \left(\frac{\overline{R}_C - \overline{R}_S}{\sigma_C - \sigma_S}\right)\sigma_P$$

which is the equation of a straight line connecting security C and security S in expected return standard deviation space.

Table 5.1   The Expected Return and Standard Deviation of a Portfolio of Colonel Motors and Separated Edison When $\rho = +1$

X_C	0	0.2	0.4	0.5	0.6	0.8	1.0
$\bar{R}_P$	8.0	9.2	10.4	11	11.6	12.8	14.0
σ_P	3.0	3.6	4.2	4.5	4.8	5.4	6.0

Table 5.1 presents the return on a portfolio for selected values of X_C and Figure 5.1 presents a graph of this relationship. Note that the relationship is a straight line. The equation of the straight line could easily be derived as follows. Utilizing the equation presented above for σ_P to solve for X_C yields

$$X_C = \frac{\sigma_P}{3} - 1$$

Substituting this expression for X_C into the equation for $\bar{R}_P$ and rearranging yields[4]

$$\bar{R}_P = 2 + 2\sigma_P$$

In the case of perfectly correlated assets, the return and risk on the portfolio of the two assets is a weighted average of the return and risk on the individual assets. There is no reduction in risk from purchasing both assets. This can be seen by examining Figure 5.1 and noting that combinations of the two assets lie along a straight line connecting the two assets. Nothing has been gained by diversifying rather than purchasing the individual assets.

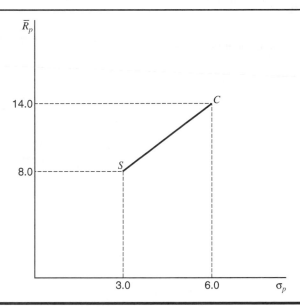

Figure 5.1   Relationship between expected return and standard deviation when $\rho = +1$.

[4]An alternative way to derive this equation is to substitute the appropriate values for the two firms into the equation derived in footnote 3. This yields

$$\bar{R}_P = 8 + 6\frac{(\sigma_P - 3)}{3} = 2 + 2\sigma_P$$

Case 2—Perfect Negative Correlation ($\rho = -1.0$)

We now examine the other extreme: two assets that move perfectly together but in exactly opposite directions. In this case the standard deviation of the portfolio is [from Equation (5.4) with $\rho = -1.0$]

$$\sigma_P = \left[X_C^2\sigma_C^2 + \left(1-X_C\right)^2\sigma_S^2 - 2X_C\left(1-X_C\right)\sigma_C\sigma_S\right]^{1/2} \tag{5.6}$$

Once again the equation for standard deviation can be simplified. The term in the brackets is equivalent to either of the following two expressions:

$$\left[X_C\sigma_C - \left(1-X_C\right)\sigma_S\right]^2$$

or

$$\left[-X_C\sigma_C + \left(1-X_C\right)\sigma_S\right]^2 \tag{5.7}$$

Thus σ_P is either

$$\sigma_P = X_C\sigma_C - \left(1-X_C\right)\sigma_S$$

or

$$\sigma_P = -X_C\sigma_C + \left(1-X_C\right)\sigma_S \tag{5.8}$$

Since we took the square root to obtain an expression for σ_P and since the square root of a negative number is imaginary, either of the above equations holds only when its right-hand side is positive. A further examination shows the right-hand side of one equation is simply -1 times the other. Thus, each equation is valid only when the right-hand side is positive. Since one is always positive when the other is negative (except when both equations equal zero), there is a unique solution for the return and risk of any combination of securities C and S. These equations are very similar to the ones we obtained when we had a correlation of $+1$. Each also plots as a straight line when σ_P is plotted against X_C. Thus, one would suspect that an examination of the return on the portfolio of two assets as a function of the standard deviation would yield two straight lines, one for each expression for σ_P. As we observe in a moment, this is, in fact, the case.[5]

The value of σ_P for Equation (5.7) or (5.8) is always smaller than the value of σ_P for the case where $\rho = +1$ [Equation (5.5)] for all values of X_C between 0 and 1. Thus the risk on a portfolio of assets is always smaller when the correlation coefficient is -1 than when it is $+1$. We can go one step further. If two securities are perfectly negatively correlated (i.e., they move in exactly opposite directions), it should always be possible to find some combination of these two securities that has zero risk. By setting either Equation (5.7) or (5.8) equal to 0, we find that a portfolio with $X_C = \sigma_S/(\sigma_S + \sigma_C)$ will have zero risk. Since $\sigma_S > 0$ and $\sigma_S + \sigma_C > \sigma_S$, this implies that $0 < X_C < 1$ or that the zero risk portfolio will always involve positive investment in both securities.

Now let us return to our example. Minimum risk occurs when $X_C = 3/(3 + 6) = \frac{1}{3}$. Furthermore, for the case of perfect negative correlation,

$$\overline{R}_P = 8 + 6X_C$$

$$\sigma_P = 6X_C - 3\left(1-X_C\right)$$

---

[5]This occurs for the same reason that the analysis for $\rho = +1$ led to one straight line and the mathematical proof is analogous to that presented for the case of $\rho = +1$.

or

$$\sigma_P = -6X_C + 3(1 - X_C)$$

there are two equations relating σ_P to X_C. Only one is appropriate for any value of X_C. The appropriate equation to define σ_P for any value of X_C is that equation for which $\sigma_P \geq 0$. Note that if $\sigma_P > 0$ from one equation, then $\sigma_P < 0$ for the other. Table 5.2 presents the return on the portfolio for selected values of X_C and Figure 5.2 presents a graph of this relationship.[6]

Notice that a combination of the two securities exists that provides a portfolio with zero risk. Employing the formula developed before for the composition of the zero-risk portfolio, X_C should equal $3/(3 + 6)$ or $\frac{1}{3}$. We can see this is correct from Figure 5.2 or by substituting $\frac{1}{3}$ for X_C in the equation for portfolio risk given previously. We have once again demonstrated the most powerful result of diversification: the ability of combinations of securities to reduce risk. In fact, it is not uncommon for combinations of two securities to have less risk than either of the assets in the combination.

We have now examined combinations of risky assets for perfect positive and perfect negative correlation. In Figure 5.3 we have plotted both of these relationships on the same graph. From this graph we should be able to see intuitively where portfolios of these two stocks should lie if correlation coefficients took on intermediate values. From the expression for the standard deviation [Equation (5.4)] we see that for any value for X_C between 0 and 1 the lower the correlation the lower is the standard deviation of the portfolio. The standard deviation reaches its lowest value for $\rho = -1$ (curve SBC) and its highest value for $\rho = +1$ (curve SAC). Therefore, these two curves should represent the limits within which all portfolios of these two securities must lie for intermediate values of the correlation coefficient. We would speculate that an intermediate correlation might produce a curve such as SOC in Figure 5.3. We demonstrate this by returning to our example and constructing the relationship between risk and return for portfolios of our two securities when the correlation coefficient is assumed to be 0 and +0.5.

Table 5.2 The Expected Return and Standard Deviation of a Portfolio of Colonel Motors and Separated Edison When $\rho = -1$

X_C	0	0.2	0.4	0.6	0.8	1.0
$\bar{R}_P$	8.0	9.2	10.4	11.6	12.8	14.0
σ_P	3.0	1.2	0.6	2.4	4.2	6.0

[6]The equation for $\bar{R}_P$ as a function of σ_P can be obtained by solving the expression relating σ_P and X_C for X_C and using this to eliminate X_C in the expression for $\bar{R}_P$. This yields

$$\bar{R}_P = 8 + 6\left(\frac{\sigma_P + 3}{6 + 3}\right) = 10 + \tfrac{2}{3}\sigma_P$$

or

$$\bar{R}_P = 8 + 6\left(\frac{\sigma_P - 3}{-6 - 3}\right) = 10 - \tfrac{2}{3}\sigma_P$$

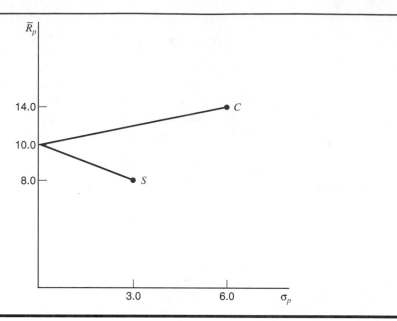

Figure 5.2   Relationship between expected return and standard deviation when $\rho = -1$.

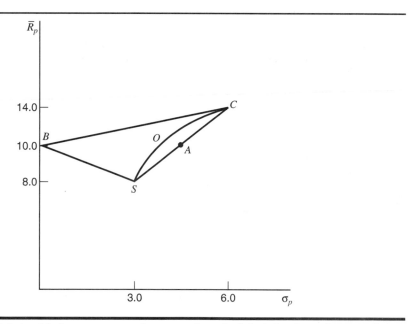

Figure 5.3   Relationship between expected return and standard deviation for various correlation coefficients.

Case 3—No Relationship between Returns on the Assets ($\rho = 0$)

The expression for return on the portfolio remains unchanged; but noting that the covariance term drops out, the expression for standard deviation becomes

$$\sigma_P = \left[X_C^2 \sigma_C^2 + \left(1 - X_C \right)^2 \sigma_S^2 \right]^{1/2}$$

For our example this yields

$$\sigma_P = \left[(6)^2 X_C^2 + (3)^2 (1 - X_C)^2\right]^{1/2}$$

$$\sigma_P = \left[45 X_C^2 - 18 X_C + 9\right]^{1/2}$$

Table 5.3 presents the returns and standard deviation on the portfolio of Colonel Motors and Separated Edison for selected values of X_C.

A graphical presentation of the risk and return on these portfolios is shown in Figure 5.4. There is one point on this figure that is worth special attention: the portfolio that has minimum risk. This portfolio can be found in general by looking at the equation for risk:

$$\sigma_P = \left[X_C^2 \sigma_C^2 + (1 - X_C)^2 \sigma_S^2 + 2 X_C (1 - X_C) \sigma_C \sigma_S \rho_{CS}\right]^{1/2}$$

To find the value of X_C that minimizes this equation, we take the derivative of it with respect to X_C, set the derivative equal to zero, and solve for X_C. The derivative is

$$\frac{\partial \sigma_P}{\partial X_C} = \left(\frac{1}{2}\right) \frac{\left[2 X_C \sigma_C^2 - 2 \sigma_S^2 + 2 X_C \sigma_S^2 + 2 \sigma_C \sigma_S \rho_{CS} - 4 X_C \sigma_C \sigma_S \rho_{CS}\right]}{\left[X_C^2 \sigma_C^2 + (1 - X_C)^2 \sigma_S^2 + 2 X_C (1 - X_C) \sigma_C \sigma_S \rho_{CS}\right]^{1/2}}$$

Setting this equal to zero and solving for X_C yields

$$X_C = \frac{\sigma_S^2 - \sigma_C \sigma_S \rho_{CS}}{\sigma_C^2 + \sigma_S^2 - 2 \sigma_C \sigma_S \rho_{CS}} \tag{5.9}$$

Table 5.3   The Expected Return and Standard Deviation for a Portfolio of Colonel Motors and Separated Edison with $\rho = 0$

X_C	0	0.2	0.4	0.6	0.8	1.0
$\bar{R}_P$	8.0	9.2	10.4	11.6	12.8	14.0
σ_P	3.00	2.68	3.00	3.79	4.84	6.0

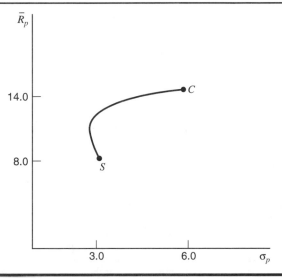

Figure 5.4   Relationship between expected return and standard deviation when $\rho = 0$.

In the present case ($\rho_{CS} = 0$) this reduces to

$$X_C = \frac{\sigma_S^2}{\sigma_C^2 + \sigma_S^2}$$

Continuing with the previous example, the value of X_C that minimizes risk is

$$X_C = \frac{9}{9+36} = \frac{1}{5} = 0.20$$

This is the minimum risk portfolio that was shown in Figure 5.4.

Case 4—Intermediate Risk ($\rho = 0.5$)

The correlation between any two actual stocks is almost always greater than 0 and considerably less than 1. To show a more typical relationship between risk and return for two stocks, we have chosen to examine the relationship when $\rho = +0.5$.

The equation for the risk of portfolios composed of Colonel Motors and Separated Edison when the correlation is 0.5 is

$$\sigma_P = \left[(6)^2 X_C^2 + (3)^2 (1 - X_C)^2 + 2X_C(1 - X_C)(3)(6)(\tfrac{1}{2})\right]^{1/2}$$

$$\sigma_P = \left(27X_C^2 + 9\right)^{1/2}$$

Table 5.4 presents the returns and risks on alternative portfolios of our two stocks when the correlation between them is 0.5.

This risk-return relationship is plotted in Figure 5.5 along with the risk-return relationships for other intermediate values of the correlation coefficient. Notice that in this example if $\rho = 0.5$, then the minimum risk is obtained at a value of $X_C = 0$ or where the investor has placed 100% of his funds in Separated Edison. This point could have been derived analytically from Equation (5.9). Employing this equation yields

$$X_C = \frac{9 - 18(0.5)}{9 + 36 - 2(18)(0.5)} = 0$$

In this example (i.e., $\rho_{CS} = 0.5$) there is no combination of the two securities that is less risky than the least risky asset by itself, though combinations are still less risky than they were in the case of perfect positive correlation. The particular value of the correlation coefficient for which no combination of two securities is less risky than the least risky security depends on the characteristics of the assets in question. Specifically, for all assets there is some value of ρ such that the risk on the portfolio can no longer be made less than the risk of the least risky asset in the portfolio.[7]

We have developed some insights into combinations of two securities or portfolios from the analysis performed to this point. First, we have noted that the lower (closer to -1.0) the correlation coefficient between assets, all other attributes held constant, the higher the

---

[7]The value of the correlation coefficient where this occurs is easy to determine. Equation (5.9) is the expression for the fraction of the portfolio to be held in X_C to minimize risk. Assume X_S is the least risky asset. When X_C equals zero in Equation (5.9), that means that 100% of the funds are invested in the least risky asset (i.e., X_S equals 1) to obtain the least risky portfolio. Setting X_C equal to zero in Equation (5.9) and solving for ρ_{CS} gives $\rho_{CS} = \sigma_S/\sigma_C$. So when ρ_{CS} is equal to σ_S/σ_C, X_C will equal zero, and the least risky "combination" assets will be 100% invested in the least risky asset alone. If ρ_{CS} is greater than σ_S/σ_C, then the least risky combination involves short selling C.

Table 5.4   The Expected Return and Standard Deviation of a Portfolio of Colonel Motors and Separated Edison When $\rho = 0.5$

X_C	0	0.2	0.4	0.6	0.8	1.0
$\bar{R}_P$	8.0	9.2	10.4	11.6	12.8	14.0
σ_P	3.00	3.17	3.65	4.33	5.13	6.00

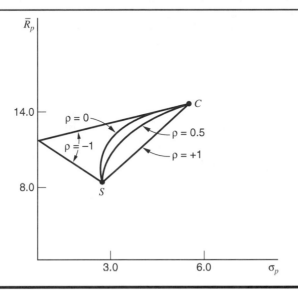

Figure 5.5   Relationship between expected return and standard deviation of return for various correlation coefficients.

payoff from diversification. Second, we have seen that combinations of two assets can never have more risk than that found on a straight line connecting the two assets in expected return standard deviation space. Finally, we have produced a simple expression for finding the minimum variance portfolio when two assets are combined in a portfolio. We can use this to gain more insight into the shape of the curve along which all possible combinations of assets must lie in expected return standard deviation space. This curve, which is called the portfolio possibilities curve, is the subject of the next section.

THE SHAPE OF THE PORTFOLIO POSSIBILITIES CURVE

Reexamine the earlier figures in this chapter and note that the portion of the portfolio possibility curve that lies above the minimum variance portfolio is concave while that which lies below the minimum variance portfolio is convex.[8] This is not due to the peculiarities of the examples we have chosen but rather is a general characteristic of all portfolio problems.

This can easily be demonstrated. Remember that the equations and diagrams we have developed are appropriate for all combinations of securities and portfolios. We now examine combinations of the minimum variance portfolio and an asset that has a higher return and risk.

---

[8]A concave curve is one where a straight line connecting any two points on the curve lies entirely under the curve. If a curve is convex, a straight line connecting any two points lies totally above the curve. The only exception to this is that a straight line is both convex and concave and so can be referred to as either.

Figures 5.6*a*, 5.6*b*, and 5.6*c* represent three hypothesized shapes for combinations of Colonel Motors and the minimum variance portfolio. The shape depicted in 5.6*b* cannot be possible since we have demonstrated that combinations of assets cannot have more risk than that found on a straight line connecting two assets (and that only in the case of perfect positive correlation). But what about the shape presented in Figure 5.6*c*? Here all portfolios have less risk than the straight line connecting Colonel Motors and the minimum variance portfolio. However, this is impossible. Examine the portfolios labeled *U* and *V*. These are simply combinations of the minimum variance portfolio and Colonel Motors. Since *U* and *V* are portfolios, all combinations of *U* and *V* must lie either on a straight line connecting *U* and *V* or above such a straight line.[9] Hence 5.6*c* is impossible and the only legitimate shape is that shown in 5.6*a*, which is a concave curve. Analogous reasoning can be used to show that if we consider combinations of the minimum variance portfolio and a security or portfolio with higher variance and lower return, the curve must be convex, that is, it must look like Figure 5.7*a* rather than 5.7*b* or 5.7*c*.

Now that we understand the risk-return properties of combinations of two assets, we are in a position to study the attributes of combinations of all risky assets.

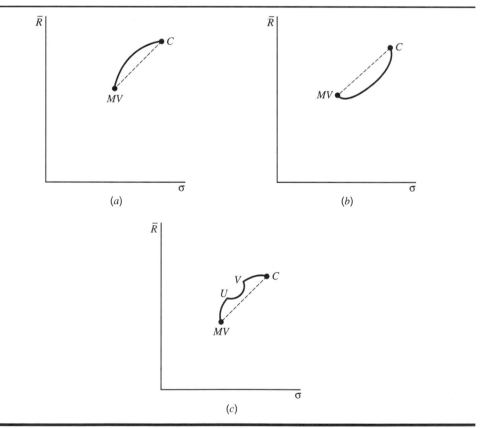

Figure 5.6   Various possible relationships for expected return and standard deviation when the minimum variance portfolio and Colonel Motors are combined.

---

[9]If the correlation between *U* and *V* equals +1, they will be on the straight line. If it is less than +1, the risk must be less, so combinations must be above the straight line.

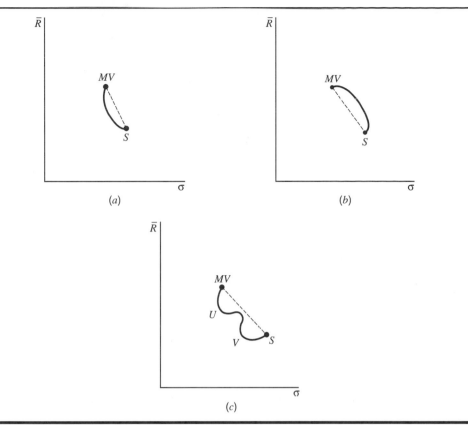

Figure 5.7   Various possible relationships between expected return and standard deviation of return when the minimum variance portfolio is combined with portfolio S.

The Efficient Frontier with No Short Sales

In theory we could plot all conceivable risky assets and combinations of risky assets in a diagram in return standard deviation space. We used the words "in theory," not because there is a problem in calculating the risk and return on a stock or portfolio, but because there are an infinite number of possibilities that must be considered. Not only must all possible groupings of risky assets be considered, but all groupings must be considered in all possible percentage compositions.

If we were to plot all possibilities in risk-return space, we would get a diagram like Figure 5.8. We have taken the liberty of representing combinations as a finite number of points in constructing the diagram. Let us examine the diagram and see if we can eliminate any part of it from consideration by the investor. In Chapter 4 we reasoned that an investor would prefer more return to less and would prefer less risk to more. Thus, if we could find a set of portfolios that

1. offered a bigger return for the same risk, or
2. offered a lower risk for the same return,

we would have identified all portfolios an investor could consider holding. All other portfolios could be ignored.

Let us take a look at Figure 5.8. Examine portfolios A and B. Note that portfolio B would be preferred by all investors to portfolio A because it offers a higher return with the same

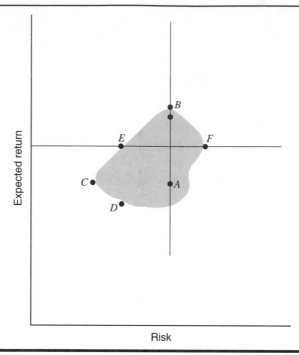

Figure 5.8 Risk and return possibilities for various assets and portfolios.

level of risk. We can also see that portfolio C would be preferable to portfolio A because it offers less risk at the same level of return. Notice that at this point in our analysis we can find no portfolio that dominates portfolio C or portfolio B. It should be obvious at this point that an efficient set of portfolios cannot include interior portfolios. We can reduce the possibility set even further. For any point in risk-return space we want to move as far as possible in the direction of increasing return and as far as possible in the direction of decreasing risk. Examine the point D, which is an exterior point. We can eliminate D from further consideration since portfolio E exists, which has more return for the same risk. This is true for every other portfolio as we move up the outer shell from D to point C. Point C cannot be eliminated since there is no portfolio that has less risk for the same return or more return for the same risk. But what is point C? It is the global minimum variance portfolio.[10] Now examine point F. Point F is on the outer shell, but point E has less risk for the same return. As we move up the outer shell curve from point F, all portfolios are dominated until we come to portfolio B. Portfolio B cannot be eliminated for there is no portfolio that has the same return and less risk or the same risk and more return than point B. Point B represents that portfolio (usually a single security) that offers the highest expected return of all portfolios. Thus the efficient set consists of the envelope curve of all portfolios that lie between the global minimum variance portfolio and the maximum return portfolio. This set of portfolios is called the efficient frontier.

Figure 5.9 represents a graph of the efficient frontier. Notice that we have drawn the efficient frontier as a concave function. The proof that it must be concave follows logically from the earlier analysis of the combination of two securities or portfolios. The efficient

---

[10]The global minimum variance portfolio is that portfolio that has the lowest risk of any feasible portfolio.

frontier cannot contain a convex region such as that shown in Figure 5.10 since as argued earlier U and V are portfolios and combinations of two portfolios must be concave.[11]

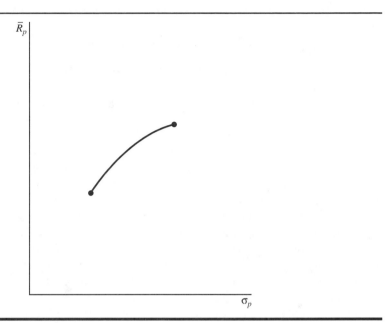

Figure 5.9 The efficient frontier.

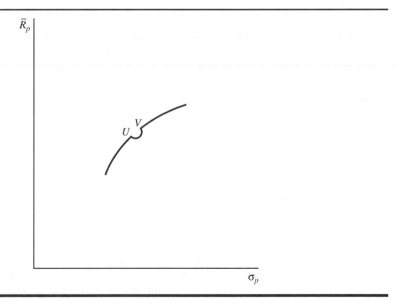

Figure 5.10 An impossible shape for the efficient frontier.

---

[11]Furthermore, there can be linear segments if the two efficient portfolios are perfectly correlated. Since a linear relationship is both concave and convex, we can still refer to the efficient frontier as concave.

Up to this point we have seen that the efficient frontier is a concave function in expected return standard deviation space that extends from the minimum variance portfolio to the maximum return portfolio. The portfolio problem, then, is to find all portfolios along this frontier. The computational procedures necessary to do so will be examined in Chapter 6.

The Efficient Frontier with Short Sales Allowed

In the stock market (and many other capital markets), an investor can often sell a security that he or she does not own. This process is called short selling and is described in Chapter 3; however, the mechanics of short sales are worth repeating here. It involves in essence taking a negative position in a security. Short sales exist in sizable amounts on the New York Stock Exchange (as well as other securities markets) and the amount of short sales in New York Stock Exchange stocks is reported in the *New York Times* every Monday. In a moment we will discuss the incorporation of short sales into our analysis. Before we do so, however, it is worthwhile pointing out that we have not been wasting our time by studying the case where short sales are disallowed. There are two reasons why this is true. The first is that most institutional investors do not short sell. Many institutions are forbidden by law from short selling, whereas still others operate under a self-imposed constraint forbidding short sales. The second is that the incorporation of short sales into our analysis involves only a minor extension of the analysis we have developed up to this point.

In this section we will employ a simplified description of the way short sales work. This has been the general description of short sales in the literature, but in footnotes and in Chapter 6 we present both the deficiencies of this description and an alternative, more realistic description of short sales. Our description of short sales, which treats short sales as the ability to sell a security without owning it, assumes that there are no special transaction costs involved in this process. Let us see how this process might work.

Let us assume an investor believed that the stock of ABC company, which currently sells for $100 per share, is likely to be selling for $95 per share (expected value) at the end of the year. In addition, the investor expects ABC company to pay a $3.00 dividend at the end of the year. If the investor bought one share of ABC stock, the cash flow would be $-$100.00 at time zero when the stock is purchased and $+$3.00 from the dividend, plus $+$95.00 from selling the stock at time 1. The cash flows are

	Time	
	0	1
Purchase Stock	-100	
Dividend		$+\ 3$
Sell Stock		$+95$
Total Cash Flow	-100	$+98$

Unless this stock had very unusual correlations with other securities, it is unlikely that an investor with these expectations would want to hold any of it in his own portfolio. In fact, an investor would really like to own negative amounts of it. How might the investor do so? Assume a friend, Joelle, owned a share of ABC company and that the friend had different expectations and wished to continue holding it. The investor might borrow Joelle's stock under the promise that she will be no worse off lending him the stock. The investor could then sell the stock, receiving $100. When the company pays the $3.00 dividend, the investor must reach into his own pocket and pay Joelle $3.00. He has a cash flow of $-$3.00. He has to do this because neither he nor Joelle now own the stock and he promised that Joelle would be no worse off by lending him the stock. Now at the end of the year, the investor could purchase the stock for $95 and give it back to Joelle. The cash flows for the investor are

	Time	
	0	1
Sell Stock	+100	
Pay Dividend		− 3
Buy Stock		−95
Total Cash Flow	+100	−98

Notice in the example that the lender of the stock is no worse off by the process and the borrower has been able to create a security that has the opposite characteristics of buying a share of the ABC company. In the real world Joelle might require some added compensation for lending her stock, but we will continue to use this simplified description of short selling in analyzing portfolio possibilities.[12]

It was clear that when an investor expected the return on a security to be negative, short sales made sense. Even in the case where returns are positive, short sales can make sense, for the cash flow received at time zero from short selling one security can be used to purchase a security with a higher expected return. Return to an example employing Colonel Motors and Separated Edison. Recall that the expected return for Separated Edison was 8% while it was 14% for Colonel Motors. If we disallow short sales, the highest return an investor can get is 14% by placing 100% of the funds in Colonel Motors. With short sales higher returns can be earned by short selling Separated Edison and placing the investor's original capital plus the initial cash flow from short sales in Colonel Motors. In doing so, however, there is a commensurate increase in risk. To see this more formally we return to the case where the correlation coefficient between the two securities is assumed to be 0.5 and see what happens when we allow short sales. The earlier calculations in Table 5.4 and the diagram in Figure 5.5 are still valid, but now they must be extended to consider values of X greater than 1 and less than 0. Some sample calculations are shown in Table 5.5.

Table 5.5   The Expected Return and Standard Deviation When Short Sales Are Allowed

X_C	−1	−0.8	−0.6	−0.4	−0.2	+1.2	+1.4	+1.6	+1.8	+2.0
$\bar{R}$	2.0	3.2	4.4	5.6	6.8	15.2	16.4	17.6	18.8	20.0
σ	6.0	5.13	4.33	3.65	3.17	6.92	7.87	8.84	9.82	10.82

The new diagram with short sales is shown in Figure 5.11. The reader should note that with short sales, portfolios exist that give infinite expected rates of return. This should not be too surprising since with short sales one can sell securities with low expected returns and use the proceeds to buy securities with high expected returns. For example, suppose an investor had $100 to invest in Colonel Motors and Separated Edison. The investor could

---

[12]In the case of actual short sales a broker plays the role of the friend and demands that funds be put up as security for the loan of the stock. These funds are in addition to the proceeds from the short sale. Since, in most cases, the amount of the funds that must be put up is quite large and the broker pays no return on these funds, the description of short sales commonly used in the literature overstates the return from short sales.

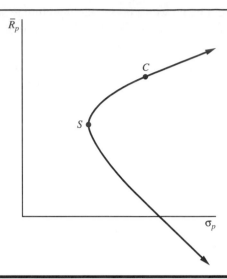

Figure 5.11   Expected return standard deviation combinations of Colonel Motors and Separated Edison when short sales are allowed.

place the entire $100 in Colonel Motors and get a return of $14, or 14%. On the other hand. the investor could sell $1,000 worth of Separated Edison stock short and buy $1,100 worth of Colonel Motors. The expected earnings on the investment in Colonel Motors is $154 while the expected cost of borrowing Separated Edison is $80. Therefore, the expected return would be $74, or 74%, on the original $100 investment. Is this a preferred position? The expected return would increase from 14% to 74% but the standard deviation would increase from 6% to 57.2%. Whether an investor should take the position offering the higher expected return would depend on the investor's preference for return relative to risk. We have more to say about this in Chapter 10.

In Figure 5.11 we have constructed the diagram for combinations of Colonel Motors and Separated Edison, assuming a correlation coefficient of 0.5. Notice that all portfolios offering returns above the global minimum variance portfolio lie along a concave curve. The reasoning for this is directly analogous to that presented when short sales were not allowed.

When we extend this analysis to the efficient frontiers of all securities and portfolios, we get a figure such as Figure 5.12, where *MVBC* is the efficient set. Since combinations of two portfolios are concave, the efficient set is concave. The efficient set still starts with the minimum variance portfolio, but when short sales are allowed it has no finite upper bound.[13]

THE EFFICIENT FRONTIER WITH RISKLESS LENDING AND BORROWING

Up to this point we have been dealing with portfolios of risky assets. The introduction of a riskless asset into our portfolio possibility set considerably simplifies the analysis. We can consider lending at a riskless rate as investing in an asset with a certain outcome (e.g.,

---

[13]Merton [19] has shown that the efficient set is the upper half of a hyperbola.

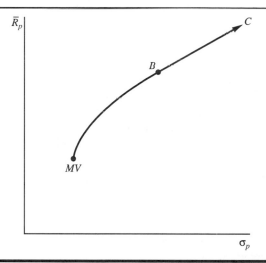

Figure 5.12   The efficient set when short sales are allowed.

a short-term government bill or savings account). Borrowing can be considered as selling such a security short, thus borrowing can take place at the riskless rate.

We call the certain rate of return on the riskless asset R_F. Since the return is certain, the standard deviation of the return on the riskless asset must be zero.

We first examine the case where investors can lend and borrow unlimited amounts of funds at the riskless rate. Initially assume that the investor is interested in placing part of the funds in some portfolio A and either lending or borrowing. Under this assumption we can easily determine the geometric pattern of all combinations of portfolio A and lending or borrowing. Call X the fraction of original funds that the investor places in portfolio A. Remember that X can be greater than 1 because we are assuming that the investor can borrow at the riskless rate and invest more than his initial funds in portfolio A. If X is the fraction of funds the investor places in portfolio A, $(1 - X)$ must be the fraction of funds that were placed in the riskless asset. The expected return on the combination of riskless asset and risky portfolio is given by

$$\overline{R}_C = (1 - X)R_F + X\overline{R}_A$$

The risk on the combination is

$$\sigma_C = \left[(1-X)^2\sigma_F^2 + X^2\sigma_A^2 + 2X(1-X)\sigma_A\sigma_F\rho_{FA}\right]^{1/2}$$

Since we have already argued that σ_F is zero,

$$\sigma_C = \left(X^2\sigma_A^2\right)^{1/2} = X\sigma_A$$

Solving this expression for X yields

$$X = \frac{\sigma_C}{\sigma_A}$$

Substituting this expression for X into the expression for expected return on the combination yields

$$\overline{R}_C = \left(1 - \frac{\sigma_C}{\sigma_A}\right)R_F + \frac{\sigma_C}{\sigma_A}\overline{R}_A$$

Rearranging terms,

$$\overline{R}_C = R_F + \left(\frac{\overline{R}_A - R_F}{\sigma_A} \right) \sigma_C$$

Note that this is the equation of a straight line. All combinations of riskless lending or borrowing with portfolio A lie on a straight line in expected return standard deviation space. The intercept of the line (on the return axis) is R_F, and the slope is $(\overline{R}_A - R_F)/\sigma_A$. Furthermore, the line passes through the point $(\sigma_A, \overline{R}_A)$. This line is shown in Figure 5.13. Note that to the left of point A we have combinations of lending and portfolio A, whereas to the right of point A we have combinations of borrowing and portfolio A.

The portfolio A we selected for this analysis had no special properties. Combinations of any security or portfolio and riskless lending and borrowing lie along a straight line in expected return standard deviation of return space. Examine Figure 5.14. We could have combined portfolio B with riskless lending and borrowing and held combinations along the line R_FB rather than R_FA. Combinations along R_FB are superior to combinations along R_FA since they offer greater return for the same risk. It should be obvious that what we would like to do is to rotate the straight line passing through R_F as far as we can in a counterclockwise direction. The furthest we can rotate it is through point G.[14] Point G is the tangency point between the efficient frontier and a ray passing through the point R_F on the vertical axis. The investor cannot rotate the ray further because by the definition of the efficient frontier there are no portfolios lying above the line passing through R_F and G.

All investors who believed they faced the efficient frontier and riskless lending and borrowing rates shown in Figure 5.14 would hold the same portfolio of risky assets—portfolio G. Some of these investors who were very risk-averse would select a portfolio along the

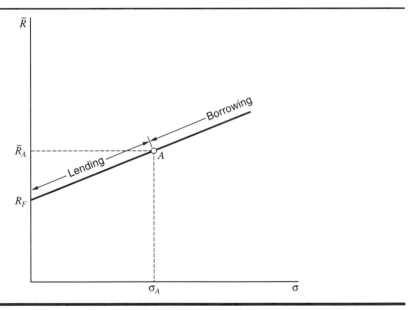

Figure 5.13   Expected return and risk when the risk-free rate is mixed with portfolio A.

---

[14]In this section we have drawn the efficient frontier as it would look if short sales were not allowed. However, the analysis is general and applies equally well to the case where short sales are allowed.

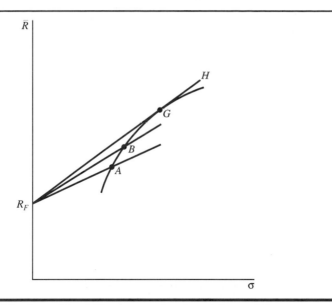

Figure 5.14   Combinations of the riskless asset and various risky portfolios.

segment R_F—G and place some of their money in a riskless asset and some in risky portfolio G. Others who were much more tolerant of risk would hold portfolios along the segment G—H, borrowing funds and placing their original capital plus the borrowed funds in portfolio G. Still other investors would just place the total of their original funds in risky portfolio G. All of these investors would hold risky portfolios with the exact composition of portfolio G. Thus, for the case of riskless lending and borrowing, identification of portfolio G constitutes a solution to the portfolio problem. The ability to determine the optimum portfolio of risky assets without having to know anything about the investor has a special name. It is called the separation theorem.[15]

Let us for a moment examine the shape of the efficient frontier under more restrictive assumptions about the ability of investors to lend and borrow at the risk-free rate. There is no question about the ability of investors to lend at the risk-free rate (buy government securities). If they can lend but not borrow at this rate, the efficient frontier becomes R_F—G—H in Figure 5.15. Certain investors will hold portfolios of risky assets located between G and H. However, any investor who held some riskless asset would place all remaining funds in the risky portfolio G.

Another possibility is that investors can lend at one rate but must pay a different and presumably higher rate to borrow. Calling the borrowing rate R'_F the efficient frontier would become R_F—G—H—I in Figure 5.16. Here there is a small range of risky portfolios that would be optional for investors to hold. If R_F and R'_F are not too far apart, the assumption of riskless lending and borrowing at the same rate might provide a good approximation to the optimal range G—H of risk portfolios that investors might consider holding.

---

[15]The words "separation theorem" have, at times, been used to describe other phenomena in finance. We continue to use it in the above sense throughout this book.

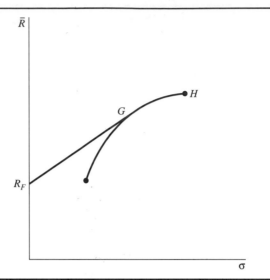

Figure 5.15   The efficient frontier with lending but not borrowing at the riskless rate.

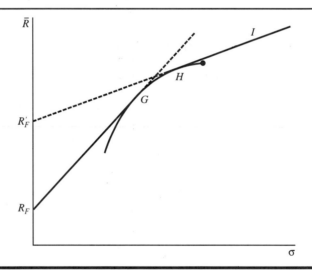

Figure 5.16   The efficient frontier with riskless lending and borrowing at different rates.

EXAMPLES AND APPLICATIONS

In this section, we will discuss some considerations that affect the choice of inputs to the portfolio selection problem and provide some examples of the use of the analysis just presented.

Considerations in Determining Inputs

Almost all asset allocation analysis starts out by estimating some of the inputs to the portfolio selection process using historical data. Analysts usually modify these historical estimates so that they better reflect beliefs about the future. In Chapters 7 and 8 on index models, we will discuss ways of using historical data to obtain estimates of variances and correlation coefficients that are more accurate than simply taking their historical value. However, before we do so, we will discuss some general considerations in using historical data.

Inflation-Adjusted Inputs to Optimization   The efficient frontier technology is widely used in practice to make asset allocation decisions for long-term investment, particularly for pension fund assets. When the investment horizon is measured in decades, it is important to consider how the change in the purchasing power of currency affects investment choice. In particular, investors may care more about the future purchasing-power value of the portfolio, that is the value after adjusting for the effects of inflation, than they care about the future nominal value of the portfolio. One approach to this problem is to apply the efficient frontier technology to *inflation-adjusted* returns. Table 5.6 compares historical statistics for U.S. stocks, government bonds, Treasury bills, and inflation. Notice that Treasury bill returns are correlated with inflation and have a larger return when inflation is higher and a lower return when inflation is less. This suggests that Treasury bills may serve as a partial inflation hedge.

Table 5.7 reports statistics for inflation-adjusted returns to stocks, bonds, and Treasury bills. The reader can use these inputs as a starting point when creating an efficient frontier for inflation-adjusted returns.

Although some securities like Treasury bills provide a partial hedge against inflation, there is no "riskless" asset in the above example—even Treasury bills have some exposure to inflation. One security recently developed in the United States and used for some time in other countries, such as the U.K., provides a near-perfect inflation hedge. Since 1997, the United States has issued inflation-linked securities whose value is determined, in part, by changes in the Consumer Price Index (an inflation measure). The return of these bonds varies with inflation, making the bonds a good hedge against inflation. At times, inflation has been over 10% per year in the United States, which means that the purchasing power of wealth invested in assets uncorrelated to changes in inflation effectively lose 10% of their purchasing power per year. Thus inflation-linked securities have the potential to protect against serious erosion of investor wealth in inflationary times.

Table 5.6   Returns with No Inflation Adjustment

	Arithmetic Mean	Standard Deviation	S&P	Correlations		
				Bonds	T-Bills	Inflation
Stocks	10.03	15.67	1.00			
Bonds	5.73	11.14	0.22	1.00		
T-Bills	4.56	3.19	−0.15	0.24	1.00	
Inflation	4.24	3.65	−0.36	−0.20	0.38	1.00

Table 5.7   Returns After Adjusting for Inflation

	Arithmetic Mean	Standard Deviation	S&P	Bonds	T-Bills
S&P	5.78	17.32	1.00		
Bonds	1.49	12.39	0.37	1.00	
T-Bills	0.31	3.83	0.33	0.54	1.00

In performing investment analysis, the analyst may well want to examine inflation-adjusted returns along with or instead of nominal returns. Furthermore, inflation-linked securities are increasingly likely to be an important asset class in portfolio optimization.

Input Estimation Uncertainty   Reliable inputs are crucial to the proper use of mean-variance optimization in the asset allocation decision. It is common to use historical risk, return, and correlation as a starting point in obtaining inputs for calculating the efficient frontier. If return characteristics do not change through time, then the longer the data are available the more accurate is the estimate of the mean. To see this, note that the formula for the standard error of the mean of a sequence of independent random variables is $\frac{\sigma^2}{N}$ where N is the sample size. For a sequence of independent returns observed through time, N is the number of time periods since the beginning of the historically observed data. Thus, under the assumption of stationary (or unchanging) expected returns and returns uncorrelated through time, more historical data will improve the estimate of expected return included in the mean-variance model, although the improvement is diminishing.

To illustrate the importance of this issue for portfolio choice, imagine that the investor is forced to choose between two investments, each with identical sample means and variances. Other things equal, the standard approach would view the two investments as equivalent. If you consider the additional information that the first sample mean was based on 1 year of data and the second on 10 years of data, common sense would suggest that the second alternative is less risky than the first. Furthermore, we can assume that the investor is mainly concerned about next month's return, which has a mean return of $\bar{R}$ and a variance of $\sigma^2_{\text{Pred}} = \sigma^2 + \frac{\sigma^2}{T}$ where

σ^2_{Pred} is the predicted variance series

σ^2 is the variance of monthly return

T is the number of time periods

The first part of the expression captures the inherent risk in the return. The second term captures the uncertainty that comes from lack of knowledge about the true mean return. In a Bayesian analysis, the sum of the two terms on the right-hand side of this equation is referred to as the variance of the *predictive distribution* of returns. Notice that predicted variance is always greater than historical variance because of uncertainty as to the future mean.

Characteristics of security returns usually change over time. Thus, there is a trade-off between using a long time frame to improve the estimates and having potentially inaccurate estimates from the longer time period because the security characteristics have changed. Because of this conflict, most analysts modify historical estimates to reflect their beliefs about how current conditions differ from past conditions.

The choice of the time period is more complicated when a relatively new asset class is added to the mix, and the available data for the new asset is much less than for other assets. For example, consider the addition of the International Financial Corporation's (IFC) index of emerging equity markets, which is available from 1985. An analyst who wishes to use historical data as a starting point for optimization could use all available data for calculating means, standard deviations, and correlations, or use data only from the common period of observation. Applying the first approach to U.S. capital market data would mean using the entire historical data from 1926 to the present from stocks and bonds. The second approach would only use data on U.S. markets from 1985 to the present. Table 5.8 shows the inputs for the two separate approaches.

Notice that the mean return for small stocks—that is, for companies with smaller capitalization—is greater than that for large stocks over the period from 1926, but less over

Table 5.8   Risk and Return over Different Horizons

	Beginning Date	Arithmetic Mean Return Starting in 1926	Arithmetic Mean Return Starting in 1985	Standard Deviation Starting in 1926	Standard Deviation Starting in 1985
S&P 500	1926	10.82	17.15	22.03	17.89
U.S. Small Stocks	1926	12.36	14.46	35.33	22.69
U.S. Government Bonds	1926	5.32	11.98	8.08	10.44
IFC Emerging Market Index	1985	11.91	11.91	26.17	26.17

Source: Courtesy of Ibbotson Associates.

the period since 1985. In both periods, however, the risk of smaller stocks is substantially higher than that of large stocks. Statistics over the longer term are consistent with an equilibrium in which a higher investor risk is compensated by higher investor expected return. Statistics over the period of common observation, beginning in 1985, are inconsistent with the argument of expected reward for additional risk. Which set of inputs makes more sense as the basis for optimization? Are the differences due to poor estimation, due to the small amount of data or changes in economic conditions? How will these different sets of inputs affect the efficient frontier? Correlations for the two different periods are provided in Table 5.9–5.11. The reader is urged to calculate the two different efficient frontiers and examine the differences. Even without performing the two optimizations, however, the reader will note that the highest mean portfolio on the frontier differs, depending upon which set of inputs is used.

Correlations over Different Time Periods   The entries to the right of 1.0 in Table 5.9 give the correlations calculated over the longest available period for both series. The entries to the left of 1.0 give the correlation over the period of common observation beginning in 1985.

Table 5.9   Correlation over Different Horizons

Top Triangle: All Periods	S&P 500	Small	Bonds	IFC
S&P 500	1.00	0.83	0.18	0.43
Small	0.67	1.00	0.09	0.46
Bonds	0.30	0.07	1.00	−0.15
IFC	0.43	0.46	−0.15	1.00
Bottom Triangle Common	S&P 500	Small	Bonds	IFC

Source: Courtesy of Ibbotson Associates.

Short Horizon Inputs and Long Horizon Portfolio Choice   Another important consideration in estimating inputs to the optimization process is the effect of the investment time horizon on variance. In the previous example, we saw that under the assumption that returns were uncorrelated from one period to the next, the standard error of the mean decreased with the square root of time. This is based on a more general result that the sum of the variance of a sequence of random variables is equal to the variance of the sum. When actual returns are examined, some securities have returns that are highly correlated over time (e.g., autocorrelated). Treasury bill returns, for example, tend to be highly autocorrelated, meaning that the return to investing in T-bills in one year does a good job at predicting the return to investing in T-bills the next year. High T-bill returns are more likely to be followed by high returns than low returns. Thus, although the standard deviation of T-bills is low over short intervals, on a percentage basis it significantly increases as the time period of observation increases from 1 to 5 to 10 years. Thus T-bills are effectively an increasingly risky asset as the investment time horizon grows. For example, research by Edwards and Goetzmann [11], shows that the estimated annualized standard deviation for Treasury bill returns over the 10-year horizon is about 6%, compared to the 3.2% annual standard deviation measured at the one-year horizon.

Table 5.10 shows the annualized means and standard deviations for 10-year returns, derived from a simulation procedure that takes into account their autocorrelation. It also reports the means and standard deviations based on the annual returns, not accounting for autocorrelation. Notice that the mean returns are not greatly affected by the correction for autocorrelation, however, the volatility for stocks is slightly reduced at longer horizons while the volatility for bonds and T-bills is increased.

Table 5.10   The Effect of Time Horizon on Risk

Time Period 1926–1991	Annualized Arithmetic Mean Return Based on Annualized 10-Year Returns	Arithmetic Mean Return Based on Annual Returns	Standard Deviation Based on Annualized 10-Year Returns	Standard Deviation Based on Annual Returns
S&P 500	9.8%	9.6%	20.7%	19.9%
U.S. Government Bonds	4.3%	4.8%	6.1%	7.7%
Treasury Bills	3.6%	3.6%	6.0%	3.2%

Source: F. Edwards and W. Goetzmann [11].

The reader can use the mean and standard deviations in Table 5.10, and the correlations provided in Table 5.11, to calculate the efficient frontier over the 1-year horizon and the 10-year horizon.

Table 5.11   Correlations over Different Time Horizons

Top Triangle: 10-Year	S&P	Bonds	T-Bills
S&P 500	1.00	0.06	0.19
Bonds	0.14	1.00	0.08
T-Bills	−0.03	0.22	1.00
Bottom Triangle: 1-Year			

THREE EXAMPLES

Let us return to the two examples discussed in Chapter 4. Consider first the allocation between equity and debt. The minimum variance portfolio is given by Equation (5.9). The estimated inputs for bonds and stocks are

$$\overline{R}_{S\&P} = 12.5\% \quad \sigma_{S\&P} = 14.9\% \quad \rho_{S\&P, B} = .45$$
$$\overline{R}_B = 6\% \qquad \sigma_B = 4.8\%$$

Plugging the values for standard deviation and correlation into Equation (5.9) gives

$$X_{S\&P} = \frac{(4.8)^2 - .45(4.8)(14.9)}{(4.8)^2 + (14.9)^2 - (2)(.45)(4.8)(14.9)}$$

$$X_{S\&P} = -.051$$

Thus the minimum variance portfolio involves short selling stock. The associated standard deviation is 4.75%, which is slightly less than the standard deviation associated with investing 100% in bonds. The dots in Figure 5.17 are plots of all combinations of the S&P index and Lehman Brothers aggregate bond index, ranging from the global minimum variance portfolio to the portfolio representing 150% in common stock and −50% in bonds. The dot next to the global minimum variance portfolio represents the expected return and standard deviation of the portfolio with 0% in common stocks. As we move to the right each dot represents the expected return and standard deviation of a portfolio with 10% more in common stock. This is the efficient frontier with short sales allowed (although it would continue to the right). The efficient frontier with no short sales is Figure 4.4. In this case the global minimum variance portfolio is 100% in bonds.

At the time of this revision the interest rate on Treasury bills was about 5%. Using this as a riskless lending and borrowing rate, the tangency portfolio is portfolio T shown in Figure 5.17. We will see how this is calculated in the next chapter. The expected return and risk for portfolio T as read from the graph are 13.54% and 16.95%, respectively. Thus the slope of the line connecting the tangency portfolio and the efficient frontier is

$$\frac{13.54 - 5}{16.95} = 0.50$$

and the equation of the efficient frontier with riskless lending and borrowing is

$$\overline{R}_P = 5 + 0.50\sigma_P$$

Once we know the expected return of portfolio T we can easily determine its composition. Simply recall that

$$\overline{R}_P = X_{S\&P}\overline{R}_{S\&P} + (1 - X_{S\&P})\overline{R}_B$$

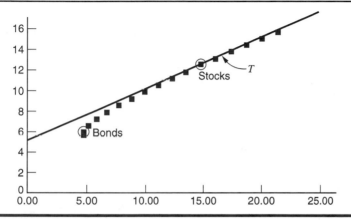

Figure 5.17   The efficient frontier.

Therefore

$$13.54 = X_{S\&P}(2.5) + (1 - X_{S\&P})6.0$$

and

$$X_{S\&P} = 116\% \quad X_B = -16\%$$

The second example we examined in Chapter 4 was a combination of a domestic portfolio represented by the S&P index and an international portfolio represented by an average international fund. All combinations of these two funds without short sales were represented by Figure 4.5. Note that part of these combinations is inefficient. The estimated inputs were

$$\overline{R}_{S\&P} = 12.5\% \quad \sigma_{S\&P} = 14.9\% \quad \rho_{S\&P,\,int} = 0.33$$
$$\overline{R}_{int} = 10.5\% \quad \sigma_{int} = 14.0\%$$

Solving for the global minimum variance portfolio we have

$$X_{S\&P} = \frac{(14)^2 - 0.33(14)(14.9)}{(14.9)^2 + (14)^2 + (2)(.33)(14)(14.9)}$$
$$X_{S\&P} = 0.45$$

Thus the global minimum variance portfolio is obtained by investing 0.45 in the S&P index and 0.55 in the foreign portfolio. The resulting standard deviation is 11.76, which is less than the standard deviation of both portfolios. This is an example of how diversification can reduce risk. Note that it is inefficient to hold the foreign portfolio by itself. An investor wishing to accept the risk of 14% on the foreign portfolio could obtain an expected return of 12.31% by putting 90.7% in the S&P index and 9.3% in the foreign portfolio. Thus at a 14% standard deviation the increase in expected return from using the optimum combination is 1.81% with no increase in risk. The efficient frontier with no short sales is the scatter of dots in Figure 5.18 from the global minimum variance portfolio to 100% in the S&P index. The dot to the right of the global minimum variance portfolio is the expected return and standard deviation of return when there is 50% in the S&P index. Each dot as we move to the right represents the expected return and standard deviation of return as we increase the amount in the S&P index by 10%. The efficient frontier with short sales allowed is the complete scatter of dots shown in Figure 5.18 (although it would continue to the right).

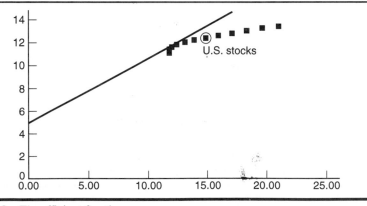

Figure 5.18   The efficient frontier.

If the riskless lending and borrowing rate is 5%, then the tangency portfolio is 61% in the S&P index and 39% in the international portfolio. The associated mean return is 11.72% and standard deviation of return is 12.04%. Thus the slope of the efficient frontier with riskless lending and borrowing is

$$\frac{11.72 - 5}{12.04} = .558$$

and the equation of the efficient frontier is

$$\overline{R}_P = 5 + .558\sigma_P$$

As a third example consider the asset allocation problem across bonds, domestic stocks, and international stocks. We continue to use all the inputs from the prior examples. We need one additional input, the correlation coefficient between bonds and the international portfolio. Past data indicate a value of 0.05 is reasonable. Various combinations of these three assets, some of which lie on the efficient frontier and some of which do not, are plotted as dots in Figure 5.19. Note that both the international portfolio and the bond portfolio are obviously dominated by other portfolios. The figure does not include portfolios involving short sales. Thus, since the S&P has the highest expected return it is not dominated. The efficient frontier would be the dots that have the highest mean return for a given standard deviation.

The tangency portfolio with a riskless lending and borrowing rate has the following proportions[16]:

$$X_{S\&P} = 0.581$$
$$X_B = 0.038$$
$$X_{int} = 0.381$$

The expected return of this portfolio is 11.49%, and the standard deviation is 11.64%. Thus the slope of the efficient frontier with riskless lending and borrowing is .558 and the equation of the efficient frontier is

$$R_P = 5 + 0.558\sigma_P$$

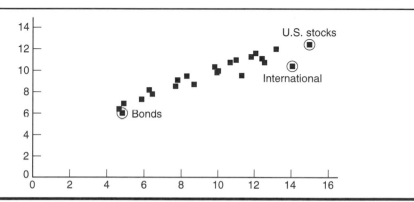

Figure 5.19. Combinations of bonds, domestic stocks, and international stocks.

---

[16]Techniques for obtaining this solution are presented in Chapter 6.

Comparing this to the efficient frontier derived with two risky assets and a riskless asset shows this efficient frontier dominates the efficient frontier using only the S&P and bonds as the risky assets but to three places to the right of the decimal point is identical to the efficient frontier using only the S&P and the international portfolio as the risky assets. Thus, adding bonds to the combination of the S&P and international portfolio doesn't lead to much improvement in the efficient frontier with riskless lending and borrowing.

CONCLUSION

In this chapter we have defined the geometric properties of that set of portfolios all risk-avoiding investors would hold regardless of their specific tolerance for risk. We have defined this set—the efficient frontier—under alternative assumptions about short sales and the ability of the investor to lend and borrow at the riskless rate. Now that we understand the geometric properties of the efficient frontier, we are in a position to discuss solution techniques to the portfolio problem. This is done in the following chapter.

QUESTIONS AND PROBLEMS

1. Return to the example presented in Problem 1, Chapter 4.

    A. Assuming short selling is not allowed:

    (1) For securities 1 and 2 find the composition, standard deviation, and expected return of that portfolio that has minimum risk.

    (2) On the same graph plot the expected return and standard deviation for all possible combinations of securities 1 and 2.

    (3) Assuming that investors prefer more to less and are risk avoiders, indicate in red those sections of the diagram in Part 2 that are efficient.

    (4) Repeat steps 1, 2, and 3 for all other possible pairwise combinations of the securities shown in Problem 1 of Chapter 4.

    B. Assuming short selling is allowed:

    (1) For securities 1 and 2 find the composition, standard deviation, and expected return of that portfolio that has minimum risk.

    (2) On the same graph plot the expected return and standard deviation for all possible combinations of securities 1 and 2.

    (3) Assuming that investors prefer more to less and are risk avoiders, indicate in red those sections of the diagram in Part 2 that are efficient.

    (4) Repeat steps 1, 2, and 3 for all other possible pairwise combinations of the securities shown in Problem 1 of Chapter 4.

    C. Assuming that the riskless lending and borrowing rate is 5%, and short sales are allowed, find the location of the optimal portfolio from among those considered. Repeat for a rate of 8%.

2. Answer the questions to Problem 1 with data from Chapter 4, Problem 2.

3. For Problem 2 find the composition of the portfolio that has minimum variance for each two security combinations you considered.

4. Derive the expression for the location of all portfolios of two securities in expected return standard deviation space when the correlation between the two securities is -1.

5.

	Expected Return	Standard Deviation
Security 1	10%	5%
Security 2	4%	2%

For the 2 securities shown plot all combinations of the 2 securities in $\bar{R}_p$ σ_p space. Assume $\rho = 1, -1, 0$. For each correlation coefficient what is the combination that yields the minimum σ_p and what is that σ_p? Assume no short selling.

6. In Problem 5, assume a riskless rate of 10%. What is the optimal investment?

BIBLIOGRAPHY

1. Bawa, Vijay. "Admissible Portfolios for All Individuals," *Journal of Finance*, **XXXI**, No. 3 (Sept. 1976), pp. 1169–1183.
2. Ben-Horim, Moshe, and Levy, Haim. "Total Risk, Diversifiable Risk and Non–Diversifiable Risk: A Pedagogic Note," *Journal of Financial and Quantitative Analysis*, **XV**, No. 2 (June 1980), pp. 289–298.
3. Brennan, Michael J., and Kraus, Allan. "The Geometry of Separation and Myopia," *Journal of Financial and Quantitative Analysis*, **XI**, No. 2 (June 1976), pp. 171–193.
4. Brown, Stephen, and Barry, Christopher. "Differential Information and the Small Firm Effect," *Journal of Financial Economics,* Vol. 13, pp. 283–294, 1984.
5. ———. "Differential Information and Security Market Equilibrium," *Journal of Financial and Quantitative Analysis,* **20,** (1985), pp.407–422.
6. Brumelle, Shelby. "When Does Diversification between Two Investments Pay?" *Journal of Financial and Quantitative Analysis*, **IX,** No. 3 (June 1974), pp. 473–483.
7. Buser, Stephen. "A Simplified Expression for the Efficient Frontier in Mean-Variance Portfolio Analysis," *Management Science*, **23,** (April 1977). pp. 901–903.
8. Canner, Niko. "An Asset Allocation Puzzle" *American Economic Review*, Nashville, **87,** No. 1 (Mar. 1997), pp. 181–193.
9. Cass, Davie, and Stiglitz, Joseph. "The Structure of Investor Preferences and Asset Returns, and Separability in Portfolio Allocation: A Contribution to the Pure Theory of Mutual Funds," *Journal of Economic Theory*, **2,** No. 2 (June 1970), pp. 122–160.
10. Dalal, Ardeshir J. "On the Use of a Covariance Function in a Portfolio Model," *Journal of Financial and Quantitative Analysis*, **XVIII,** No. 2 (June 1983), pp. 223–228.
11. Edwards, Franklin, and Goetzmann, William. "Short Horizon Inputs and Long Horizon Portfolio Choice," *Journal of Portfolio Management,* **20,** No. 4 (Summer 1994), pp. 76–81.
12. Elton, Edwin J., and Gruber, Martin J. "Dynamic Programming Applications in Finance," *Journal of Finance*, **XXVI,** No. 2 (May 1971), pp. 473–505.
13. ———."Portfolio Theory When Investment Relatives Are Lognormally Distributed," *Journal of Finance*, **XXIX,** No. 4 (Sept. 1974), pp. 1265–1273.
14. Friedman, Harris. "Real Estate Investment and Portfolio Theory," *Journal of Financial and Quantitative Analysis*, **VI,** No. 2 (March 1971), pp. 861–873.
15. Gibbons, Michael R., and Shanken, Jay. "Subperiod Aggregation and the Power of Multivariate Tests of Portfolio Efficiency," *Journal of Financial Economics*, Amsterdam, **19,** No. 2 (Dec. 1987), pp. 389–394.
16. Grauer, Robert R., and Hakansson, Nils H. "A Half Century of Returns on Levered and Unlevered Portfolios of Stocks, Bonds, and Bills, With and Without Small Stocks," *Journal of Business*, **59,** No. 2 (Apr. 1986), 287.
17. Hakansson, Nils. "Risk Disposition and the Separation Property in Portfolio Selection," *Journal of Financial and Quantitative Analysis*, **IV,** No. 4 (Dec. 1969), pp. 401–416.
18. ———. "An Induced Theory of the Firm under Risk: The Pure Mutual Fund," *Journal of Financial and Quantitative Analysis*, **V,** No. 2 (May 1970), pp. 155–178.

19. Merton, Robert. "An Analytic Derivation of the Efficient Portfolio Frontier," *Journal of Financial and Quantitative Analysis*, **VII,** No. 4 (Sept. 1972), pp. 1851–1872.
20. Mossin, Jan. "Optimal Multiperiod Portfolio Policies," *Journal of Business*, **41,** No. 2 (April 1968), pp. 215–229.
21. Ohlson, James. "Portfolio Selection in a Log-Stable Market," *Journal of Financial and Quantitative Analysis*, **X,** No. 2 (June 1975), pp. 285–298.
22. Ohlson, J.S., and Ziemba, W.T. "Portfolio Selection in a Lognormal Market When the Investor Has a Power Utility Function," *Journal of Financial and Quantitative Analysis*, **XI,** No. 1 (March 1976), pp. 57–71.
23. Pye, Gordon. "Lifetime Portfolio Selection in Continuous Time for a Multiplicative Class of Utility Functions," *American Economic Review*, **LXIII,** No. 5 (Dec. 1973), pp. 1013–1020.
24. Rosenberg, Barr, and Ohlson, James. "The Stationarity Distribution of Returns and Portfolio Separation in Capital Markets: A Fundamental Contradiction," *Journal of Financial and Quantitative Analysis*, **XI,** No. 3 (June 1973), pp. 393–401.
25. Shanken, Jay. "A Bayesian Approach to Testing Portfolio Efficiency," *Journal of Financial Economics*, **19,** No. 2 (Dec. 1987), pp. 195–216.
26. Smith, Keith. "Alternative Procedures for Revising Investment Portfolios," *Journal of Financial and Quantitative Analysis*, **III,** No. 4 (Dec. 1968), pp. 371–403.
27. Zhou, Guofu. "Small Sample Tests of Portfolio Efficiency," *Journal of Financial Economics*, **30,** No. 1 (Nov. 1991) pp. 165–192.

6

Techniques for Calculating the Efficient Frontier

In Chapters 4 and 5 we discussed the properties of the efficient frontier under alternative assumptions about lending and borrowing and alternative assumptions about short sales. In this chapter we describe and illustrate methods that can be used to calculate efficient portfolios. By necessity this chapter is more mathematically complex than those that preceded it and most of those that follow. The reader who is only concerned with a conceptual approach to portfolio management can skip this chapter and still understand later ones. However, we believe that knowledge of the solution techniques to portfolio problems outlined here yields a better understanding and appreciation of portfolio management.

We have not followed the same order in presenting solution techniques for portfolio problems as was followed in describing the properties of the efficient set (Chapter 5). Rather, we have rearranged the order so that solution techniques are presented from the simplest to the most complex. The first four sections of this chapter discuss the solution to the portfolio problem when it is assumed in turn that

1. Short sales are allowed and riskless lending and borrowing is possible.
2. Short sales are allowed but riskless lending or borrowing is not permitted.
3. Short sales are disallowed but riskless lending and borrowing exists.
4. Neither short sales nor riskless lending and borrowing are allowed.

A fifth section shows how additional constraints such as the need for a minimum dividend yield can be incorporated in the portfolio problem. The solution techniques discussed here are the ones used in actual applications. For most problems the calculations are lengthy enough that computers are used. Indeed computer programs exist for each of the techniques discussed. In addition, in Chapter 9 we present simplifications of the procedures discussed in the present chapter that are useful in solving most real problems. This chapter is necessary for an understanding of the computer programs and an appreciation of the simple rules discussed later. Thus although this chapter is more demanding than some others, it is well worth the effort needed to understand it.

SHORT SALES ALLOWED WITH RISKLESS LENDING AND BORROWING

The derivation of the efficient set when short sales are allowed and there is a riskless lending and borrowing rate is the simplest case we can consider. From Chapter 5 we know that the existence of a riskless lending and borrowing rate implies that there is a single portfolio of risky assets that is preferred to all other portfolios. Furthermore, in return standard deviation space, this portfolio plots on the ray connecting the riskless asset and a risky portfolio that lies furthest in the counterclockwise direction. For example, in Figure 6.1 the portfolio on the ray R_F—B is preferred to all other portfolios of risky assets. The efficient frontier is the entire length of the ray extending through R_F and B. Different points along the ray R_F—B represent different amounts of borrowing and/or lending in combination with the optimum portfolio of risky assets portfolio B.

An equivalent way of identifying the ray R_F—B is to recognize that it is the ray with the greatest slope. Recall that the slope of the line connecting a riskless asset and risky portfolio is the expected return on the portfolio minus the risk-free rate divided by the standard deviation of the return on the portfolio. Thus, the efficient set is determined by finding that portfolio with the greatest ratio of excess return (expected return minus risk-free rate) to standard deviation that satisfies the constraint that the sum of the proportions invested in the assets equals 1. In equation form we have: maximize the objective function

$$\theta = \frac{\overline{R}_P - R_F}{\sigma_P}$$

subject to the constraint[1]

$$\sum_{i=1}^{N} X_i = 1$$

This is a constrained maximization problem. There are standard solution techniques available for solving it. For example, it can be solved by the method of Lagrangian multipliers. There is an alternative. The constraint could be substituted into the objective function and the objective function maximized as in an unconstrained problem. This latter procedure will be followed below. We can write R_F as R_F times 1. Thus we have

$$R_F = 1R_F = \left(\sum_{i=1}^{N} X_i\right) R_F = \sum_{i=1}^{N} \left(X_i R_F\right)$$

Making this substitution in the objective function and stating the expected return and standard deviation of return in the general form, derived in Chapter 4, yields

---

[1]Lintner [25] has advocated an alternative definition of short sales, one that is more realistic. He assumes correctly that when an investor sells stock short, cash is not received but rather is held as collateral. Furthermore, the investor must put up an additional amount of cash equal to the amount of stock he or she sells short. The investor generally does not receive any compensation (interest) on these funds. However, if the investor is a broker-dealer, interest can be earned on both the money put up and the money received from the short sale of securities. As shown in Appendix A, this leads to the constraint, $\Sigma|X_i| = 1$, and leaves all other equations unchanged.

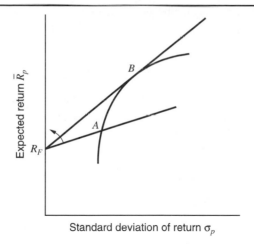

Figure 6.1   Combinations of the riskless asset in a risky portfolio.

$$\theta = \frac{\sum_{i=1}^{N} X_i \left(\overline{R}_i - R_F \right)}{\left[\sum_{i=1}^{N} X_i^2 \sigma_i^2 + \sum_{i=1}^{N} \sum_{\substack{j=1 \\ j \neq 1}}^{N} X_i X_j \sigma_{ij} \right]^{1/2}}$$

The problem stated above is a very simple maximization problem and as such can be solved using the standard methods of basic calculus. In calculus it is shown that to find the maximum of a function you take the derivative with respect to each variable and set it equal to zero.[2] Thus the solution to the maximization problem just presented involves finding the solution to the following system of simultaneous equations:

1. $\dfrac{d\theta}{dX_1} = 0$

2. $\dfrac{d\theta}{dX_2} = 0$

3. $\dfrac{d\theta}{dX_3} = 0$

$\vdots$

N. $\dfrac{d\theta}{dX_N} = 0$

---

[2]Solving the problem without constraining the solution by

$$\sum_{i=1}^{N} X_i = 1$$

does not work in every maximization problem. It works here because the equations are homogeneous of degree zero.

In Appendix B at the end of this chapter we show that

$$\frac{d\theta}{dX_i} = -\left(\lambda X_1 \sigma_{1i} + \lambda X_2 \sigma_{2i} + \lambda X_3 \sigma_{3i} + \cdots + \lambda X_i \sigma_i^2 + \cdots\right.$$

$$\left. + \lambda X_{N-1} \sigma_{N-1i} + \lambda X_N \sigma_{Ni}\right) + \overline{R}_i - R_F = 0$$

where λ is a constant.[3] A mathematical trick allows a useful modification of the derivative. Note that each X_k is multiplied by a constant λ. Define a new variable $Z_k = \lambda X_k$. The X_k are the fraction to invest in each security, and the Z_k are proportional to this fraction. Substituting Z_k for the λX_k simplifies the formulation. To solve for the X_k after obtaining the Z_k, one divides each Z_k by the sum of the Z_k. Substituting Z_k for $\lambda_k X_k$ and moving the variance covariance terms to the right-hand side of the equality yields

$$\overline{R}_i - R_F = Z_1 \sigma_{1i} + Z_2 \sigma_{2i} + \cdots + Z_i \sigma_i^2 + \cdots + Z_{N-1} \sigma_{N-1i} + Z_N \sigma_{Ni}$$

We have one equation like this for each value of i. Thus the solution involves solving the following system of simultaneous equations.

$$\overline{R}_1 - R_F = Z_1 \sigma_1^2 + Z_2 \sigma_{12} + Z_3 \sigma_{13} + \cdots + Z_N \sigma_{1N}$$

$$\overline{R}_2 - R_F = Z_1 \sigma_{12} + Z_2 \sigma_2^2 + Z_3 \sigma_{23} + \cdots + Z_N \sigma_{2N}$$

$$\overline{R}_3 - R_F = Z_1 \sigma_{13} + Z_2 \sigma_{23} + Z_3 \sigma_3^2 + \cdots + Z_N \sigma_{3N} \qquad (6.1)$$

$$\vdots$$

$$\overline{R}_N - R_F = Z_1 \sigma_{1N} + Z_2 \sigma_{2N} + Z_3 \sigma_{3N} + \cdots + Z_N \sigma_N^2$$

The Zs are proportional to the optimum amount to invest in each security. To determine the optimum amount to invest, we first solve the equations for the Zs. Note that this does not present a problem. There are N equations (one for each security) and N unknowns (the Z_k for each security). Then the optimum proportions to invest in stock k is X_k, where

$$X_k = Z_k \bigg/ \sum_{i=1}^{N} Z_i$$

Let us solve an example. Consider three securities: Colonel Motors with expected return of 14% and standard deviation of return of 6%, Separated Edison with average return of 8% and standard deviation of return of 3%, and Unique Oil with mean return of 20% and standard deviation of return of 15%. Furthermore, assume that the correlation coefficient between Colonel Motors and Separated Edison is 0.5, between Colonel Motors and Unique Oil is 0.2, and between Separated Edison and Unique Oil is 0.4. Finally assume that the riskless lending and borrowing rate is 5%. Equation (6.1) for three securities is

$$\overline{R}_1 - R_F = Z_1 \sigma_1^2 + Z_2 \sigma_{12} + Z_3 \sigma_{13}$$

$$\overline{R}_2 - R_F = Z_1 \sigma_{12} + Z_2 \sigma_2^2 + Z_3 \sigma_{23}$$

$$\overline{R}_3 - R_F = Z_1 \sigma_{13} + Z_2 \sigma_{23} + Z_3 \sigma_3^2$$

Substituting in the assumed values, we get the following system of simultaneous equations:

$$14 - 5 = 36 Z_1 + (0.5)(6)(3) Z_2 + (0.2)(6)(15) Z_3$$

$$8 - 5 = (0.5)(6)(3) Z_1 + 9 Z_2 + (0.4)(3)(15) Z_3$$

$$20 - 5 = (0.2)(6)(15) Z_1 + (0.4)(3)(15) Z_2 + 225 Z_3$$

---

[3]The constant is equal to $(\overline{R}_P - R_F)$ divided by σ_P^2.

Simplifying,

$$9 = 36Z_1 + 9Z_2 + 18Z_3$$
$$3 = 9Z_1 + 9Z_2 + 18Z_3$$
$$15 = 18Z_1 + 18Z_2 + 225Z_3$$

Further simplifying,

$$1 = 4Z_1 + Z_2 + 2Z_3$$
$$1 = 3Z_1 + 3Z_2 + 6Z_3$$
$$5 = 6Z_1 + 6Z_2 + 75Z_3$$

The solution to this system of simultaneous equations is

$$Z_1 = \frac{14}{63}, \quad Z_2 = \frac{1}{63}, \quad \text{and} \quad Z_3 = \frac{3}{63}$$

The reader can verify this solution by substituting these values of Z_k into the foregoing equations.[4] The proportion to invest in each security is easy to determine. We know that each Z_k is proportional to X_k. Consequently, all we have to do to determine X_k is to scale the Z_k so that they add to 1.[5] For the foregoing problem

$$\sum_{i=1}^{3} Z_i = \frac{18}{63}$$

Thus the proportion to invest in each security is

$$X_1 = \frac{14}{18}, \quad X_2 = \frac{1}{18}, \quad \text{and} \quad X_3 = \frac{3}{18}$$

The expected return on the portfolio is

$$\bar{R}_P = \frac{14}{18}(14) + \frac{1}{18}(8) + \frac{3}{18}(20) = 14\tfrac{2}{3}\%$$

The variance of the return on the portfolio is[6]

$$\sigma_P^2 = \left(\frac{14}{18}\right)^2(36) + \left(\frac{1}{18}\right)^2 9 + \left(\frac{3}{18}\right)^2(225) + 2\left(\frac{14}{18}\right)\left(\frac{1}{18}\right)(6)(3)(0.5)$$
$$+ 2\left(\frac{14}{18}\right)\left(\frac{3}{18}\right)(6)(15)(0.2) + 2\left(\frac{1}{18}\right)\left(\frac{3}{18}\right)(3)(15)(0.4) = \frac{203}{6} = 33\tfrac{5}{6}$$

---

[4]See Appendix C at the end of this chapter for a description of solution techniques for systems of simultaneous equations.

[5]In the case of Lintnerian short sales, simply scale so that

$$\sum_{i=1}^{3} |X_i| = 1$$

[6]The variance of the portfolio could have been determined in another way. Recall that λ is the ratio of the excess return on the optimum portfolio divided by the variance of the optimum portfolio. Thus

$$\lambda = \frac{\bar{R}_P - R_F}{\sigma_P^2} = \frac{14\tfrac{2}{3} - 5}{\sigma_P^2}$$

Also recall that $Z_i = \lambda X_i$ so that $\Sigma Z_i = \lambda \Sigma X_i = \lambda$. Earlier we determined that $\Sigma Z_i = \lambda = 18/63$. Equating these two equations and solving for σ_P^2 yields the value presented above.

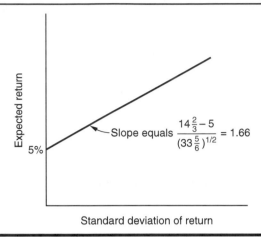

Slope equals $\dfrac{14\frac{2}{3}-5}{(33\frac{5}{6})^{1/2}} = 1.66$

Figure 6.2   The efficient set with riskless lending and borrowing.

The efficient set is a straight line with an intercept at the risk-free rate of 5% and a slope equal to the ratio of excess return to standard deviation. (See Figure 6.2.) There are standard computer packages for the solution of a system of simultaneous equations. Appendix C at the end of this chapter presents some methods of solving them when the number of securities involved is limited so that hand calculations are reasonable.

SHORT SALES ALLOWED: NO RISKLESS LENDING AND BORROWING

When the investor does not wish to make the assumption that he can borrow and lend at the riskless rate of interest, the solution developed in the last section must be modified. However, much of the analysis can still be utilized. Consider Figure 6.3. The riskless lending and borrowing rate of 5% led to the selection of portfolio B. If the riskless lending and borrowing rate had been 4%, the investor would invest in portfolio A. If the investor's lending and borrowing rate was 6%, the investor would select portfolio C. These observations suggest the following procedure. Assume that a riskless lending and borrowing rate exists and find the optimum portfolio. Then assume that a different riskless lending and borrowing rate exists and find the optimum portfolio that corresponds to this second rate. Continue changing the assumed riskless rate until the full efficient frontier is determined.[7]

In Appendix D we present a general solution to this problem. We show that the optimal proportion to invest in any security is simply a linear function of R_F. Furthermore, since the entire efficient frontier can be constructed as a combination of any two portfolios that lie along it, the identification of the characteristics of the optimal portfolio for any two arbitrary values of R_F is sufficient to trace out the total efficient frontier.

RISKLESS LENDING AND BORROWING WITH SHORT SALES NOT ALLOWED

This problem is analogous to the case of riskless lending and borrowing with short sales allowed. One portfolio is optimal. Once again, it is the one that maximizes the slope of the

---

[7]This only works for the standard definition of short sales. The Lintner definition of short sales assumes riskless lending and borrowing at a particular rate for each point on the original (curved) efficient frontier.

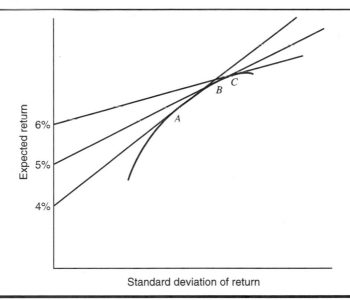

Figure 6.3   Tangency portfolios for different riskless rates.

line connecting the riskless asset and a risky portfolio. However, the set of portfolios that is available to combine with lending and borrowing is different because a new constraint has been added. Investors cannot hold securities in negative amounts. More formally, the problem can be stated as

$$\text{Maximize } \theta = \frac{\overline{R}_P - R_F}{\sigma_P}$$

Subject to

$$(1) \quad \sum_{i=1}^{N} X_i = 1$$

$$(2) \quad X_i \geq 0 \qquad \text{all } i$$

This is a mathematical programming problem because of the inequality restriction on X_i. At first glance this might look like a linear programming problem. In fact, the constraints (1) and (2) are linear constraints. The problem is that the objective function (the expression we are maximizing) is not linear. σ_P contains terms involving X_i^2 and $X_i X_j$. Equations involving squared terms and cross-product terms are called quadratic equations. Since this looks like a linear programming problem except that the objective function is quadratic rather than linear, it is called a quadratic programming problem. There are standard computer packages for solving quadratic programming problems just as there are for linear programming problems, and the reader interested in solving a large-scale problem would utilize one of them. Some discussion of solution techniques is contained in Appendix E at the end of this chapter.

NO SHORT SELLING AND NO RISKLESS LENDING AND BORROWING

Recall that an efficient set is determined by minimizing the risk for any level of expected return. If we specify the return at some level and minimize risk, we have one point on the efficient frontier. Thus, to get one point on the efficient frontier, we minimize risk subject to the return being some level plus the restriction that the sum of the proportions invested in each security adds to 1 and that all securities have positive or zero investment. This yields the following problem:

$$\text{Minimize} \sum_{i=1}^{N}\left(X_i^2 \sigma_i^2\right) + \sum_{i=1}^{N}\sum_{\substack{j=1 \\ j \neq i}}^{N}\left(X_i X_j \sigma_{ij}\right)$$

Subject to

$$(1) \quad \sum_{i=1}^{N} X_i = 1$$

$$(2) \quad \sum_{i=1}^{N}\left(X_i \overline{R}_i\right) = \overline{R}_P$$

$$(3) \quad X_i \geq 0, \qquad i = 1,\ldots,N$$

Varying $\overline{R}_P$ between the return on the minimum variance portfolio and the return on the maximum return portfolio traces out the efficient set. Once again, the problem is a quadratic programming problem because of the presence of terms such as X_i^2 and $X_i X_j$ (squared and cross-product terms). However, there are standard packages available that solve this problem.

THE INCORPORATION OF ADDITIONAL CONSTRAINTS

The imposition of short sales constraints has complicated the solution technique, forcing us to use quadratic programming. Once we resort to this technique, however, it is a simple matter to impose other requirements on the solution. Literally any set of requirements that can be formulated as linear functions of the investment weights can be imposed on the solution. For example, some managers wish to select optimum portfolios given that the dividend yield on the optimum portfolios is at least some number (e.g., 2%). If we let D stand for the target dividend yield and d_i stand for the dividend yield on stock i, then we can impose this requirement by adding a fourth constraint to the problem described in the previous section

$$(4) \quad \sum_{i=1}^{N}\left(X_i d_i\right) \geq D$$

If we desire the dividend constraint but want to allow short sales, we simply eliminate the third constraint

$$(3) \quad X_i \geq 0, \qquad i = 1,\ldots,N$$

from the problem.

Note that once we impose inequality constraints, like the one described for dividends, we must solve a quadratic programming problem instead of a system of simultaneous equations, even if short sales are allowed.

Other types of constraints are frequently employed in solving portfolio problems. Perhaps, the most frequent constraints are those that place an upper limit on the fraction of the portfolio that can be invested in any stock. Upper limits on the amount that can be invested in any one stock are often part of the charter of mutual funds. Also, upper limits (and occasionally lower limits) are often placed on the fraction of a portfolio that can be invested in any industry. Finally, it is possible to build in constraints on the amount of turnover in a portfolio and to allow the consideration of transaction costs in computing returns.

AN EXAMPLE

This chapter has presented techniques for obtaining the efficient frontier when there are a large number of assets to choose from. A computer package is available from John Wiley & Sons to use with this book which performs the necessary calculations. We will now present an actual solution to a realistic problem for a pension fund manager. Table 6.1 shows the data for the asset allocation problem we will examine. The manager is considering an allocation across three U.S. categories, and international stocks. The three U.S. categories are large stocks, small stocks, and bonds. Large stocks are represented by the Standard and Poor's index including dividends, bonds by the Lehman Brothers aggregate index and small stocks by the CRSP small stock index.[8] The international data were obtained by using returns on international stock mutual funds. The international portfolios are selected to divide the world into as many nonoverlapping segments as possible. Thus there is a Canadian fund, a European fund, a Japanese fund, a Pacific fund, and an emerging market fund. There is some overlap. The Pacific fund and the Japanese fund have stocks in Japan in common. Similarly, the emerging market and Pacific fund have some countries in common. The effect of overlap can be seen by examining the correlation coefficients. The correlation between the Japan fund and the Pacific fund is 0.73, which is the highest correlation between Japan and any other fund. The emerging market is interesting. Before examining the data one would expect that the correlations would be very low with the major countries. However, the correlations are high with major markets, implying that the performance of emerging markets is very much affected by what happens in major markets.

The correlation matrix was calculated by using return data over the prior five years, and was calculated for returns expressed in U.S. dollars. It was modified in several ways. First,

Table 6.1   Input Data for Asset Allocation

	S&P	Bonds	Canadian	Japan	Emerging Market	Pacific	Europe	Small Stock
Expected return	14.00	6.50	11.00	14.00	16.00	18.00	12.00	17.00
Standard deviation	18.50	5.00	16.00	23.00	30.00	26.00	20.00	24.00
			Correlation Coefficients					
S&P	1.00	0.45	0.70	0.20	0.64	0.30	0.61	0.79
Bonds		1.00	0.27	−0.01	0.41	0.01	0.13	0.28
Canadian			1.00	0.14	0.51	0.29	0.48	0.59
Japan				1.00	0.25	0.73	0.56	0.13
Emerging Market					1.00	0.28	0.61	0.75
Pacific						1.00	0.54	0.16
Europe							1.00	0.44
Small stock								1.00

---

[8]The CRSP small stock index is roughly the smallest quintile of stocks on the NYSE plus AMEX and Nasdaq stocks of similar size. See the footnote to Table 17.1 for a detailed description of the construction of the CRSP small stock index.

the crash of October 1987 was omitted in the belief that this was an atypical period. Second, security analysts at a major investment banking firm compared the correlations calculated using returns from the most recent five-year period with prior five-year periods. Using these data and their judgment, analysts modified some historic numbers in order to obtain their best estimate of what the future correlations would be. However, very little modification was done and the correlations shown in Table 6.1 are very close to those obtained using the prior five years' data.

The standard deviations are expressed in annual returns. They were also calculated over the prior five years. Once again, however, analysts modified them slightly utilizing both data from earlier periods and their experience in order to obtain their best subjective estimates for the future. The mean returns are the estimates of a major financial intermediary concerned with the allocation decisions analyzed here. At this time they were fairly pessimistic about U.S. bond markets, Canadian stocks, and European stocks, and this is reflected in their estimates. The final input needed is a riskless rate of interest which was 5% for U.S. investors in this period.

The efficient frontier without riskless lending and borrowing but with short sales is the curved figure shown in Figure 6.4. Each asset class as a separate investment is represented by a dot in Figure 6.4. The global minimum variance portfolio has a mean return of 6.41% and a standard deviation of 3.91%. Note that bonds are by far the least risky asset. However, a portfolio of assets is less risky than bonds even though the next least risky asset has a standard deviation more than three times larger than bonds. Alternatively, the optimum portfolio with the same risk as bonds has a mean return of 8.42% or 1.92% more than bonds. This is an illustration of the power of diversification. Note that all assets are held either long or short. Furthermore, note that for the higher returns (above portfolio 2) the short sales involved are substantial and would involve short selling more than margin requirements would allow. Thus the efficient frontier would terminate after portfolio 2. At

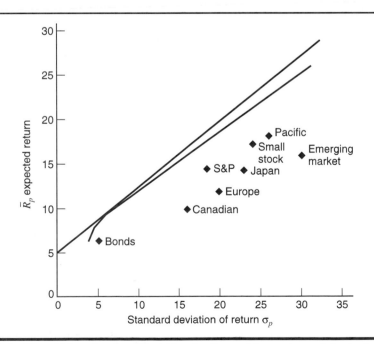

Figure 6.4   The efficient frontier with riskless lending and borrowing and short sales allowed.

low risks, the major long purchase is bonds. As expected return is increased, the S&P, small stocks, and Pacific fund all are held long in substantial amounts with Japan held long in a somewhat smaller proportion. These are all relatively high expected return portfolios. Notice, however, that the other high mean return portfolio emerging markets does not enter into the optimum. This is because it has a very high correlation with the other countries and thus does not contribute much to the diversification. Europe and bonds are sold short for portfolios with higher mean returns. These are both low expected return assets. In addition, Europe has the advantage of being relatively highly correlated with the assets held long. When an asset is sold short the covariance term with a long asset is negative, thus reducing risk. It is therefore desirable for a short sold asset to be highly correlated with an asset held long.

Now consider the solution when short sales are not allowed and there is no riskless lending and borrowing. The efficient frontier is the curved region in Figure 6.5. The composition for a number of portfolios is shown in Table 6.2. Short sales not allowed is probably the realistic case to consider for the pension fund manager whose problem we are analyzing. As shown in Table 6.2, the global minimum variance portfolio has an expected return of 6.89% and a standard deviation of 4.87%. This is of course a higher standard deviation than if short sales were allowed. Comparing the numbers Figures 6.1 and 6.2, shows that the efficient frontier with short sales allowed offers a higher mean return for a given risk (either with or without riskless lending and borrowing). This is because short sales offer additional investment opportunities that are used.

As shown in Table 6.2, the minimum risk portfolio is primarily investment in bonds. Without short sales the minimum risk is only slightly less than the risk of bonds alone—4.87% compared to 5%—and the expected return is only 0.39% higher. As we increase the risk on the portfolio, the percent invested in bonds goes down and we start to invest primarily in small stocks and Pacific. A minor amount is invested in Japan. The highest mean return portfolio is of course 100% in the highest return asset, Pacific bond.

When riskless lending and borrowing is allowed, the efficient frontier is the straight line shown in Figures 6.4 and 6.5. The equations of the straight lines are

Short sales allowed

$$\overline{R}_P = 5 + 0.714\sigma_P$$

Table 6.2   Proportions Invested When Short Sales Not Allowed

	Global Minimum	1	2	3	4	5
Mean return	6.89	9.36	11.83	14.30	16.77	18.00
Standard deviation	4.88	6.66	10.03	13.86	17.87	26.00
			Proportions			
S&P	0.00	0.00	0.00	0.00	0.63	0.00
Bond	95.16	72.91	50.51	28.12	5.51	0.00
Canadian	0.06	0.00	0.00	0.00	0.00	0.00
Japan	3.96	3.57	3.17	2.77	2.41	0.00
Emerging market	0.00	0.00	0.00	0.00	0.00	0.00
Pacific	0.81	12.42	22.86	33.29	43.62	100.00
Europe	0.00	0.00	0.00	0.00	0.00	0.00
Small stock	0.00	11.10	23.46	35.82	47.82	0.00

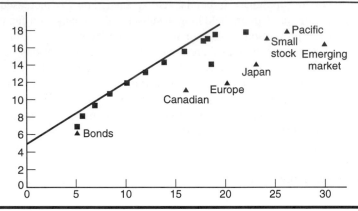

Figure 6.5   The efficient frontier with no riskless lending and borrowing and no short sales.

Short sales not allowed

$$\overline{R}_P = 5 + 0.685_P$$

Obviously the efficient frontier with short sales allowed is steeper. The tangency portfolio for short sales not allowed has a mean return of 11.51%. Higher returns involve borrowing at the riskless rate. For the pension manager whose problem is being analyzed this is likely infeasible. For this manager the efficient frontier is likely to be the straight line segment from R_F to the tangency point and the curved shape from there to the right. Given the low return of the tangency portfolio the choice would likely lie on the curve to the right of the tangency portfolio. This would involve bonds, small stocks, Pacific, and a little invested in Japan. It would be important to vary the inputs in a reasonable range to see how this composition would change given reasonable changes in the inputs.

CONCLUSION

In this chapter we discussed and illustrated the use of techniques that can be employed to solve for the set of all possible portfolios that are efficient. All of the solution techniques discussed are feasible and have been used to solve problems. However, the techniques require gigantic amounts of input data and large amounts of computation time. Furthermore, the input data are in a form to which the security analyst and portfolio manager cannot easily relate. For this reason it is difficult to get estimates of the input data or to get practitioners to relate to the final output.

The next logical step is to simplify the number and type of input requirements for portfolio selection and, in turn, to see if this reduction in data complexity can also be used to simplify the computational procedure. This is the subject of the next three chapters.

APPENDIX A

AN ALTERNATIVE DEFINITION OF SHORT SALES

Modeling short sales from the viewpoint of the broker-dealer, we first note that the broker-dealer has a fixed sum of money to invest. A short sale involves putting up an amount of money equal to the short sale. Thus, the short sale is a use rather than a source of funds to the short seller. The total funds the broker-dealer invests short, plus the funds invested long, must add to the original investment. Since for short sales $X_i < 0$, the proportion of the funds invested in the short sale is $|X|_i$. In addition, the short seller (if a broker-dealer) receives interest on both the money put up against short sales and the money received from the short sale. Thus, the expected return from short selling 0.10 of stock i is $-0.1\overline{R}_i + 0.2R_F$. Since X_i is negative for short sales, this can be written as $X_i(\overline{R}_i - 2R_F)$. Assume stocks 1 to k are held long and stocks $k + 1$ to N are sold short. Then

$$\overline{R}_P = \sum_{i=1}^{k} X_i(\overline{R}_i) + \sum_{i=k+1}^{N} X_i(\overline{R}_i - 2R_F)$$

$$\overline{R}_P = \sum_{i=1}^{N} X_i\overline{R}_i - 2\sum_{i=k+1}^{N} X_i(R_F)$$

The constraint with the Lintner definition of short sales is

$$\sum_{i=1}^{N} |X| = 1$$

Substituting this for 1 times R_F yields

$$R_F = \sum_{i=1}^{N} |X_i|R_F = \sum_{i=1}^{k} X_iR_F - \sum_{i=k+1}^{N} X_iR_F \tag{A.1}$$

This is the expression used for R_F. Subtracting R_F from both sides of the equation for $\overline{R}_P$ and using (A.1) for R_F on the right-hand side of the equation yields

$$\overline{R}_P - R_F = \left[\sum_{i=1}^{N} X_i\overline{R}_i - 2\sum_{i=k+1}^{N} X_iR_F\right] - \left[\sum_{i=1}^{k} X_iR_F - \sum_{i=k+1}^{N} X_iR_F\right]$$

$$\overline{R}_P - R_F = \sum_{i=1}^{N} X_i\overline{R}_i - \sum_{i=1}^{N} X_iR_F = \sum_{i=1}^{N} X_i(\overline{R}_i - R_F)$$

This is identical to the equation given in the text. The reader should note that in the Lintnerian definition of short sales, the final portfolio weights must be scaled so that the sum of the absolute value of the weights, rather than their sum, adds to 1.

APPENDIX B

DETERMINING THE DERIVATIVE

In the text we discussed that in order to solve the portfolio problem when short sales are allowed the derivative of θ with respect to X_k was needed.[9] In the text we presented the value of the derivative. In this appendix we will derive its value. To determine the derivative rewrite the θ shown in the text as

$$\theta = \left[\sum_{i=1}^{N} X_i(\overline{R}_i - R_F)\right]\left[\sum_{i=1}^{N} X_i^2\sigma_i^2 + \sum_{i=1}^{N}\sum_{\substack{j=1 \\ j\neq i}}^{N} X_iX_j\sigma_{ij}\right]^{-1/2}$$

---

[9]To ensure a maximum, the second derivative should be negative. The structure of this problem guarantees this.

Two rules from calculus are needed:

1. **The product rule:** θ is the product of two functions. The product rule states that the derivative of the product of two functions is the first function times the derivative of the second function plus the second times the derivative of the first. In symbols,

$$\frac{d}{dx}\left[\left[F_1(x)\right]\left[F_2(x)\right]\right]=\left[F_1(x)\right]\frac{dF_2(x)}{dx}+\left[F_2(X)\right]\frac{dF_1(x)}{dx} \tag{B.1}$$

Let

$$F_1(X)=\sum_{i=1}^{N}X_i\left(\overline{R}_i-R_F\right) \tag{B.2}$$

$$F_2(X)=\left(\sum_{i=1}^{N}X_i^2\sigma_i^2+\sum_{i=1}^{N}\sum_{\substack{j=1\\j\neq i}}^{N}X_iX_j\sigma_{ij}\right)^{-1/2} \tag{B.3}$$

Consider first the derivative of $F_1(X)$. At first glance the reader may believe it is difficult. However, it turns out to be trivial. An expression like

$$\sum_{i=1}^{N}X_i\left(\overline{R}_i-R_F\right)$$

involves a lot of terms that do not contain an X_k and one term involving X_k. The derivatives of the terms not involving X_k are zero (they are constants as far as X_k is concerned). The derivative of the term involving X_k is $\overline{R}_k-R_F$. Thus

$$\frac{dF_1(X)}{dX_k}=\overline{R}_k-R_F \tag{B.4}$$

Now consider the derivative of $F_2(X)$. To determine this a second rule from calculus is needed.

2. **The chain rule:** $F_2(X)$ involves a term in brackets to a power (the power $-\frac{1}{2}$). The chain rule states that its derivative is the power, times the expression in parentheses to the power minus one, times the derivative of what is inside the brackets. Thus,

$$\frac{dF_2(X)}{dX_k}=\left(-\frac{1}{2}\right)\left(\sum_{i=1}^{N}X_i^2\sigma_i^2+\sum_{i=1}^{N}\sum_{\substack{j=1\\j\neq i}}^{N}X_iX_j\sigma_{ij}\right)^{-3/2}$$

$$\times\left(2X_k\sigma_k^2+2\sum_{\substack{j=1\\j\neq k}}^{N}X_j\sigma_{jk}\right) \tag{B.5}$$

The only term that requires comment is the last one. The derivative of

$$\sum_{i=1}^{N}X_i^2\sigma_i^2$$

follows the same principles discussed earlier. All terms not involving k are constant as far as k is concerned and thus their derivative is zero. The term involving k is $X_k^2 \sigma_k^2$ and has a derivative of $2X_k \sigma_k^2$. The derivation of the double summation is more complex. Consider the double summation term

$$\left(\sum_{i=1}^{N} \sum_{\substack{j=1 \\ j \neq i}}^{N} X_i X_j \sigma_{ij} \right)$$

We get X_k twice, once when $i = k$ and once when $j = k$. When $i = k$, we have

$$\sum_{\substack{j=1 \\ j \neq k}}^{N} X_k X_j \sigma_{kj} = X_k \left[\sum_{\substack{j=1 \\ j \neq k}}^{N} X_j \sigma_{kj} \right]$$

The derivative of this is, of course

$$\sum_{\substack{j=1 \\ j \neq k}}^{N} X_j \sigma_{kj}$$

Similarly, when $j = k$, we have

$$\sum_{\substack{i=1 \\ i \neq k}}^{N} X_i X_k \sigma_{ik} = X_k \left(\sum_{\substack{i=1 \\ i \neq k}}^{N} X_i \sigma_{ik} \right)$$

The derivative of this is also

$$\left(\sum_{\substack{i=1 \\ i \neq k}}^{N} X_i \sigma_{ik} \right)$$

i and j are simply summonds. It does not matter which we use. Further, $\sigma_{ik} = \sigma_{ki}$. Thus,

$$\sum_{\substack{j=1 \\ j \neq k}}^{N} X_j \sigma_{kj} = \sum_{\substack{i=1 \\ i \neq k}}^{N} X_i \sigma_{ik}$$

and we have the expression shown in the derivative, namely,

$$2 \sum_{\substack{j=1 \\ j \neq k}}^{N} X_j \sigma_{kj}$$

Substituting (B.2), (B.3), (B.4), and (B.5) into the product rule, expression (B.1) yields

$$\frac{d\theta}{dX_k} = \left[\sum_{i=1}^{N} X_i\left(\overline{R}_i - R_F\right)\right]\left[\left(-\frac{1}{2}\right)\left(\sum_{i=1}^{N} X_i^2\sigma_i^2 + \sum_{i=1}^{N}\sum_{\substack{j=1\\j\neq i}}^{N} X_iX_j\sigma_{ij}\right)^{-3/2}\right.$$

$$\times\left.\left(2X_k\sigma_k^2 + 2\sum_{\substack{j=1\\j\neq k}}^{N} X_j\sigma_{kj}\right)\right] + \left[\sum_{i=1}^{N} X_i^2\sigma_i^2 + \sum_{i=1}^{N}\sum_{\substack{j=1\\j\neq i}}^{N} X_iX_j\sigma_{ij}\right]^{-1/2}$$

$$\times\left[\left(\overline{R}_k - R_F\right)\right] = 0$$

Multiplying the derivative by

$$\left(\sum_{i=1}^{N} X_i^2\sigma_i^2 + \sum_{i=1}^{N}\sum_{\substack{j=1\\j\neq i}}^{N} X_iX_j\sigma_{ij}\right)^{1/2}$$

and rearranging yields

$$-\left[\frac{\sum_{i=1}^{N} X_i\left(\overline{R}_i - R_F\right)}{\sum_{i=1}^{N} X_i^2\sigma_i^2 + \sum_{i=1}^{N}\sum_{\substack{j=1\\j\neq i}}^{N} X_iX_j\sigma_{ij}}\right]\left[X_k\sigma_k^2 + \sum_{\substack{j=1\\j\neq k}}^{N} X_j\sigma_{kj}\right] + \left[\overline{R}_k - R_F\right] = 0$$

Defining λ as

$$\frac{\sum_{i=1}^{N} X_i\left(\overline{R}_i - R_F\right)}{\sum_{i=1}^{N} X_i^2\sigma_i^2 + \sum_{i=1}^{N}\sum_{\substack{j=1\\j\neq i}}^{N} X_iX_j\sigma_{ij}}$$

yields

$$-\lambda\left[X_k\sigma_k^2 + \sum_{\substack{j=1\\j\neq k}}^{N} X_j\sigma_{kj}\right] + \left(\overline{R}_k - R_F\right) = 0$$

Multiplying the terms in the brackets by λ yields

$$-\left[\lambda X_k\sigma_k^2 + \sum_{\substack{j=1\\j\neq k}}^{N} \lambda X_j\sigma_{kj}\right] + \left(\overline{R}_k - R_F\right) = 0$$

This is the expression shown in the text.

APPENDIX C

SOLVING SYSTEMS OF SIMULTANEOUS EQUATIONS

To solve large systems of simultaneous equations, one would use any of the large number of standard computer packages that exist for this purpose. However, small systems can be solved by hand. The simplest way is by repetitive substitution. Consider the following system of simultaneous equations:

$$4X_1 + X_2 = 7 \qquad\qquad\qquad (C.1)$$

$$3X_1 + 2X_2 = 5 \qquad\qquad\qquad (C.2)$$

Equation (C.1) can be rearranged so that X_2 is expressed as a function of X_1. This rearrangement yields

$$X_2 = 7 - 4X_1$$

Substituting this into Equation (C.2) yields

$$3X_1 + 2(7 - 4X_1) = 5$$
$$3X_1 + 14 - 8X_1 = 5$$
$$-5X_1 = -9$$
$$X_1 = \tfrac{9}{5}$$

Substituting the value for X_1 into rearranged Equation (C.1) yields

$$X_2 = 7 - 4\left(\tfrac{9}{5}\right) = 7 - \tfrac{36}{5} = -\tfrac{1}{5}$$

This technique is extremely easy and can be applied to solving any number of simultaneous equations, although with lots of equations it becomes extremely time consuming. For a second example consider the problem analyzed in the section "Short Sales Allowed":

$$1 = 4Z_1 + Z_2 + 2Z_3 \qquad\qquad\qquad (C.3)$$

$$1 = 3Z_1 + 3Z_2 + 6Z_3 \qquad\qquad\qquad (C.4)$$

$$5 = 6Z_1 + 6Z_2 + 75Z_3 \qquad\qquad\qquad (C.5)$$

Solving Equation (C.3) for Z_2 and eliminating Z_2 from Equation (C.4) yields

$$Z_2 = 1 - 4Z_1 - 2Z_3 \qquad\qquad\qquad (C.3')$$

$$1 = 3Z_1 + 3(1 - 4Z_1 - 2Z_3) + 6Z_3 \qquad\qquad\qquad (C.4')$$

Simplifying (C.4') yields

$$-2 = -9Z_1$$

Following the same procedure for Equation (C.5) yields

$$5 = 6Z_1 + 6(1 - 4Z_1 - 2Z_3) + 75Z_3 \qquad\qquad\qquad (C.5')$$

Simplifying (C.5') yields

$$-1 = -18Z_1 + 63Z_3$$

Equation (C.4′) gives an immediate solution for Z_1; it is $Z_1 = \frac{2}{9}$. Substituting this into Equation (C.5′) allows us to solve for Z_3.

$$-1 = -18\left(\tfrac{2}{9}\right) + 63Z_3$$
$$-1 = -4 + 63Z_3$$
$$Z_3 = \tfrac{3}{63}$$

Substituting the value of Z_3 and Z_1 into (C.3′) yields for Z_2

$$Z_2 = 1 - \tfrac{8}{9} - \tfrac{6}{63} = \tfrac{1}{63}$$

This is the solution stated in the text. When the number of equations and variables becomes large, it is usually more convenient to solve the problem by working on a tableau. A tableau for the last problem is presented below.

Z_1	Z_2	Z_3	= Constant
4	1	2	= 1
3	3	6	= 1
6	6	75	= 5

Under each of the variables is the coefficient shown in the system of Equations (C.3), (C.4), and (C.5). If c_1, c_2, c_3 are arbitrary constants, the solution is reached when the tableau looks like

Z_1	Z_2	Z_3	= Constant
1	0	0	c_1
0	1	0	c_2
0	0	1	c_3

To move from the first tableau to the second, three operations are allowed:

1. You can multiply or divide any row by a constant.
2. You can add or subtract a constant times one row from another row.
3. You can exchange any two rows.

Let us apply this to the problem discussed earlier. Subtracting twice row 2 from row 3 yields

Z_1	Z_2	Z_3	= Constant
4	1	2	1
3	3	6	1
0	0	63	3

Dividing row 3 by 63 yields

Z_1	Z_2	Z_3	= Constant
4	1	2	1
3	3	6	1
0	0	1	$\frac{3}{63}$

Subtracting two times row 3 from row 1 and 6 times row 3 from row 2 yields

Z_1	Z_2	Z_3	= Constant
4	1	0	$\frac{57}{63}$
3	3	0	$\frac{45}{63}$
0	0	1	$\frac{3}{63}$

Subtracting $\frac{1}{3}$ of row 2 from row 1 yields

Z_1	Z_2	Z_3	= Constant
3	0	0	$\frac{42}{63}$
3	3	0	$\frac{45}{63}$
0	0	1	$\frac{3}{63}$

Taking $\frac{1}{3}$ of row 1 and $\frac{1}{3}$ of row 2 yields

Z_1	Z_2	Z_3	= Constant
1	0	0	$\frac{14}{63}$
1	1	0	$\frac{15}{63}$
0	0	1	$\frac{3}{63}$

Subtracting row 1 from row 2 yields the final tableau

Z_1	Z_2	Z_3	= Constant
1	0	0	$\frac{14}{63}$
0	1	0	$\frac{1}{63}$
0	0	1	$\frac{3}{63}$

The now familiar solution can be read directly from this tableau. It is

$$Z_1 = \frac{14}{63}, \qquad Z_2 = \frac{1}{63}, \qquad \text{and} \qquad Z_3 = \frac{3}{63}$$

Either of these methods can be used to solve a system of simultaneous equations.

APPENDIX D

A GENERAL SOLUTION

While we have just outlined a feasible procedure for identifying the efficient frontier, there is a simpler one. When we assumed a particular riskless lending and borrowing rate, we determined that the optimum portfolio is the one that solves the following system of simultaneous equations:

$$\overline{R}_1 - R_F = Z_1\sigma_1^2 + Z_2\sigma_{12} + Z_3\sigma_{13} + \cdots + Z_N\sigma_{1N}$$

$$\overline{R}_2 - R_F = Z_1\sigma_{12} + Z_2\sigma_2^2 + Z_3\sigma_{23} + \cdots + Z_N\sigma_{2N}$$

$$\overline{R}_3 - R_F = Z_1\sigma_{13} + Z_2\sigma_{23} + Z_3\sigma_3^2 + \cdots + Z_N\sigma_{3N}$$

$$\vdots$$

$$\overline{R}_N - R_F = Z_1\sigma_{1N} + Z_2\sigma_{2N} + Z_3\sigma_{3N} + \cdots + Z_N\sigma_N^2$$

When we solved this system of simultaneous equations we substituted, in particular, values of $\overline{R}$, R_F, σ_i^2, and σ_{ij}. However, we do not have to substitute in a particular value of R_F. We can simply leave R_F as a general parameter and solve for Z_k in terms of R_F. This results in a solution of the form

$$Z_k = C_{0k} + C_{1k}R_F$$

where C_{0k} and C_{1k} are constants. They have a different value for each security k but that value does not change with changes in R_F. Once the Z_k are determined as functions of R_F, we could vary R_F to determine the amount to invest in each security at various points along the efficient frontier. Let us apply this to the example following Equation (6.1). The system of simultaneous equations for a general R_F is

$$14 - R_F = 36Z_1 + 9Z_2 + 18Z_3 \tag{D.1}$$

$$8 - R_F = 9Z_1 + 9Z_2 + 18Z_3 \tag{D.2}$$

$$20 - R_F = 18Z_1 + 18Z_2 + 225Z_3 \tag{D.3}$$

The solution to this system of simultaneous equations is

$$Z_1 = \frac{42}{189} \tag{D.4}$$

$$Z_2 = \frac{118}{189} - \frac{23}{189}R_F \tag{D.5}$$

$$Z_3 = \frac{4}{189} + \frac{1}{189}R_F \tag{D.6}$$

This solution can be confirmed by substituting these values into Equations (D.1), (D.2), and (D.3). Also, as a further check, note that the substitution of $R_F = 5$ (which was the value we assumed in the last section) into Equations (D.4), (D.5), and (D.6) yields

$$Z_1 = \frac{42}{189} = \frac{14}{63}$$

$$Z_2 = \frac{118}{189} - \frac{23}{189}(5) = \frac{118 - 115}{189} = \frac{3}{189} = \frac{1}{63}$$

$$Z_3 = \frac{4}{189} + \frac{1}{189}(5) = \frac{9}{189} = \frac{3}{63}$$

the same solution we obtained earlier. The values of Z_k just determined can be scaled to sum to 1 exactly as was done before so that the optimum proportions can be determined.

Determining the General Coefficient from Two Portfolios

In the last section we determined that

$$Z_2 = \frac{118}{189} - \frac{23}{189} R_F$$

Assume that we had not determined this general expression. Rather we simply solved the system of simultaneous equations for two arbitrary values of R_F. The value of Z_2 corresponding to R_F of 5 is $\frac{1}{63}$ and the Z_2 corresponding to an R_F of 2 is $\frac{72}{189}$. Can we determine the general expression? The answer is clearly *yes*. As an example, assume we had solved the equations for an R_F of 2 and 5. We know the general expression has the form

$$Z_2 = C_{02} + C_{12} R_F$$

Further, we know that

$$Z_2 = \tfrac{1}{63} \quad \text{if } R_F = 5$$
$$Z_2 = \tfrac{72}{189} \quad \text{if } R_F = 2$$

Utilizing this in the previous equation we have

$$\tfrac{1}{63} = C_{02} + C_{12}(5)$$
$$\tfrac{72}{189} = C_{02} + C_{12}(2)$$

This is a system of two equations and two unknowns. We can use it to solve for $C_{02} = \frac{118}{189}$ and $C_{12} = -\frac{23}{189}$. Thus, if we have the optimum portfolio for any two values of R_F, we can obtain the value for C_{0k} and C_{1k} and then by varying R_F obtain the full efficient frontier.

This is an extremely powerful result. It means that the solution of the system of simultaneous equations for any two values of R_F allows us to trace out the full efficient frontier.

The tracing out of the efficient frontier can be done in two ways. First, we could solve for the general expression for Z_k in terms of R_F by determining Z_k for any two arbitrary values of R_F. Then, by varying R_F over the relevant range, we could trace out the efficient frontier.

A second procedure is suggested by the previous discussion. We showed that solving the system of simultaneous equations for any two values of R_F allowed us to obtain a general expression for Z_k in terms of R_F, thus enabling us to trace out the efficient frontier. This suggests that the efficient frontier can be determined directly by simply calculating any two optimum portfolios rather than indirectly by first determining Z_k as a function of R_F. It can be shown that this direct procedure is appropriate.[10] Thus, the entire efficient frontier can be traced out by determining the composition of any two portfolios and then determining all combinations of these two portfolios. This is an extremely powerful result and is the preferred way to determine the efficient set.

In the previous chapter we showed how to trace out all combinations (portfolios) of two assets. Nothing prevents the two assets from being efficient portfolios. Thus, given that the efficient frontier can be traced out by combining two efficient portfolios, if we find two efficient portfolios, we can utilize the procedures discussed in the last chapter to trace out the full efficient frontier. Let's see how this is done.

---

[10]See Black [7] for a rigorous proof that this holds.

Tracing Out the Efficient Frontier

The Z_k that correspond to an $R_F = 2$ are from Equations (D.4) and (D.5), and (D.6):

$$Z_1 = \frac{42}{189}, \qquad Z_2 = \frac{72}{189}, \qquad Z_3 = \frac{6}{189}$$

The proportions to invest in each security are

$$X_1 = \frac{42}{120} = \frac{7}{20}$$

$$X_2 = \frac{72}{120} = \frac{12}{20}$$

$$X_3 = \frac{6}{120} = \frac{1}{20}$$

The expected return associated with this portfolio is

$$\overline{R}_P = \left(\frac{7}{20}\right)(14) + \left(\frac{12}{20}\right)(8) + \left(\frac{1}{20}\right)(20) = 10\tfrac{7}{10}$$

The variance of return on this portfolio is

$$\sigma_P^2 = \left(\frac{7}{20}\right)^2 (36) + \left(\frac{12}{20}\right)^2 9 + \left(\frac{1}{20}\right)^2 (225)$$

$$+2\left(\frac{7}{20}\right)\left(\frac{12}{20}\right)9 + 2\left(\frac{7}{20}\right)\left(\frac{1}{20}\right)(18) + 2\left(\frac{12}{20}\right)\left(\frac{1}{20}\right)18 = \frac{5481}{400}$$

If we knew the covariance between the portfolios associated with an $R_F = 5$ and the one associated with an $R_F = 2$, we could trace out the full efficient frontier by treating each portfolio as an asset and utilizing the method discussed in Chapter 5. The covariance is determined as follows. Consider a portfolio consisting of $\frac{1}{2}$ of each of the two portfolios already determined. The investment proportions are

$$X_1'' = \frac{1}{2}\frac{7}{20} + \frac{1}{2}\frac{14}{18} = \frac{203}{360}$$

$$X_2'' = \frac{1}{2}\frac{12}{20} + \frac{1}{2}\frac{1}{18} = \frac{118}{360}$$

$$X_3'' = \frac{1}{2}\frac{1}{20} + \frac{1}{2}\frac{3}{18} = \frac{39}{360}$$

Its variance is

$$\sigma_P^2 = \left(\frac{203}{360}\right)^2 36 + \left(\frac{118}{360}\right)^2 9 + \left(\frac{39}{360}\right)^2 225$$

$$+2\left(\frac{203}{360}\right)\left(\frac{118}{360}\right)9 + 2\left(\frac{203}{360}\right)\left(\frac{118}{360}\right)18$$

$$+2\left(\frac{118}{360}\right)\left(\frac{39}{360}\right)18 = 21.859$$

But we know that this portfolio is a weighted average of the other two portfolios. In Chapter 5 we showed that the variance of a portfolio comprised of two assets or portfolios was

$$\sigma_P^2 + X_1^2\sigma_1^2 + X_2^2\sigma_2^2 + 2X_1X_2\sigma_{12}$$

Thus, the variance of a portfolio consisting of $\frac{1}{2}$ of portfolio 1 and $\frac{1}{2}$ of portfolio 2 is

$$\sigma^2 = \left(\frac{1}{2}\right)^2\left(\frac{203}{6}\right) + \left(\frac{1}{2}\right)^2\left(\frac{5481}{400}\right) + 2\left(\frac{1}{2}\right)\left(\frac{1}{2}\right)\sigma_{12}$$

We know the variance of this portfolio is 21.859. Thus, σ_{12} can be determined from

$$21.859 = \left(\frac{1}{2}\right)^2\left(\frac{203}{6}\right) + \left(\frac{1}{2}\right)^2\left(\frac{5481}{400}\right) + 2\left(\frac{1}{2}\right)\left(\frac{1}{2}\right)\sigma_{12}$$

and

$$\sigma_{12} = 19.95$$

Knowing the expected returns variance and covariance, we can trace out the efficient frontier exactly as we did for combinations of two assets in Chapter 5. We have done so in Figure 6.6.

The Number of Securities Included

Before leaving this section, some observations are in order. First, when short sales are allowed, the investor takes a position in almost all securities. Each security will have, in general, one value of R_F for which it is not held, namely, when $C_{0k} + C_{1k}R_F = 0$. But for all other values of R_F, it will be held either long or short. In fact, for all values of R_F above this value, the security will be held only long or short and vice versa for values of R_F below the value. Let us examine the expressions for Z_k as a function of R_F from our previous example.

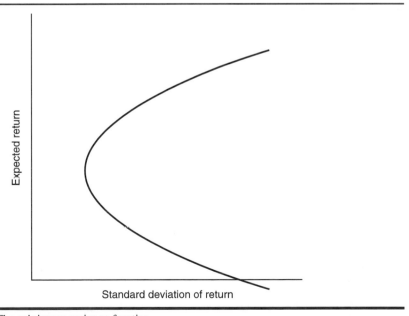

Figure 6.6   The minimum variance frontier.

$$Z_1 = \frac{42}{189}$$

$$Z_2 = \frac{118}{189} - \frac{23}{189} R_F$$

$$Z_3 = \frac{4}{189} + \frac{1}{189} R_F$$

Security 1 is always held long. Security 2 is held long if R_F is less than $\frac{118}{23}$ and is held short for all values of R_F greater than $\frac{118}{23}$. Finally, security 3 is held long if R_F is greater than -4 and held short for values of R_F below -4. The various values of Z as a function of R_F are shown in Figure 6.7.

The inclusion of almost all or all securities in the optimum portfolio makes intuitive sense. If a security's characteristics make it undesirable to hold, then the investor should issue it by selling it short. Thus, "good" securities are held and "bad" securities are issued to someone else. Of course, for someone else to be willing to take "bad" securities, there has to be a difference of opinion of what is good and bad.

APPENDIX E

QUADRATIC PROGRAMMING AND KUHN–TUCKER CONDITIONS

These quadratic programming algorithms are based on a technique from advanced calculus called Kuhn–Tucker conditions. For small-scale problems these conditions may be able to be used directly. Furthermore, an understanding of the nature of the solution to this type of portfolio problem can be gained by understanding the Kuhn–Tucker conditions.

Earlier we simply took the derivative of θ with respect to each X_i and set it equal to zero to find a maximum value of θ. This maximum is indicated by point M in Figure 6.8a or

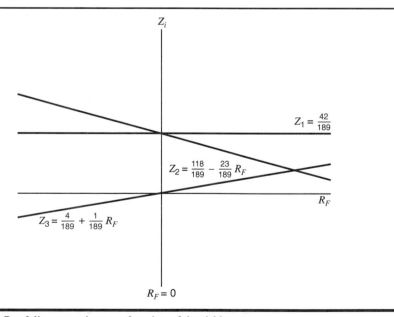

Figure 6.7 Portfolio proportion as a function of the riskless rate.

6.8b. When X_i must be non-negative, a problem can occur because the unconstrained maximum may be at a value of X_i, which is infeasible. θ as a function of X_i might look like Figure 6.8b rather than Figure 6.8a. In this case (Figure 6.8b) the maximum feasible value of θ occurs at point M' rather than M. Notice that if the maximum value for X_i occurs at M', then $d\theta/dX_i < 0$ at the maximum feasible value ($X_i = 0$), whereas if it occurs when X_i is positive, then $d\theta/dX_i = 0$. Thus, in general, with X_i constrained to be larger than or equal to zero, we can write

$$\frac{d\theta}{dX_i} \leq 0$$

We could make this an equality by writing

$$\frac{d\theta}{dX_i} + U_i = 0$$

This is the first Kuhn–Tucker condition for a maximum.

Note two things about U_i. If the optimum occurs when X_i is positive, then the $d\theta/dX_i = 0$ and U_i is zero. Furthermore, if the optimum occurs when the maximum occurs at $X_i = 0$, then $d\theta/dX_i < 0$ and U_i is positive. To summarize at the optimum we have

$$X_i > 0, \qquad U_i = 0$$
$$X_i = 0, \qquad U_i > 0$$

This is the second Kuhn–Tucker condition. It can be written compactly as

$$X_i U_i = 0$$
$$X_i \geq 0$$
$$U_i \geq 0$$

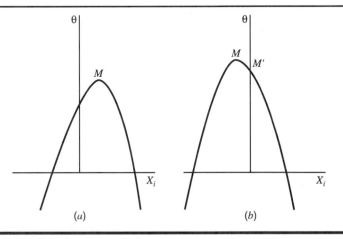

Figure 6.8   Value of the function as X changes.

The four Kuhn–Tucker conditions are

$$(1) \quad \frac{d\theta}{dX_i} + U_i = 0$$

$$(2) \quad X_i U_i = 0$$

$$(3) \quad X_i \geq 0$$

$$(4) \quad U_i \geq 0$$

If someone suggested a solution to us and it satisfied the Kuhn–Tucker conditions, then we could be sure that he had indeed given us the optimum portfolio.[11]

For example, assume the lending and borrowing rate was 6% and the securities being considered are the three securities considered throughout this chapter. Furthermore, assume the solution was

$$X_1 = \frac{43}{53}, \qquad U_1 = 0$$

$$X_2 = 0, \qquad U_2 = \frac{5}{8}$$

$$X_3 = \frac{10}{53}, \qquad U_3 = 0$$

Since this solution meets all the Kuhn–Tucker conditions, it is optimal.

To see that this solution meets the Kuhn–Tucker conditions, consider the following. First all X's and U's are positive, thus conditions 3 and 4 are met. U_1, X_2, and $U_3 = 0$, thus either X or U is zero for any pair of securities and condition 2 is met. Finally, recall that

$$\frac{d\theta}{dX_i} = \bar{R}_i - R_F - \lambda \left[X_i \sigma_i^2 + \sum_{\substack{j=1 \\ j \neq i}}^{N} X_j \sigma_{ij} \right]$$

Adding U_i to this equation and substituting in the returns, variances, and covariances for the various securities, we have

$$8 - \lambda \left[36X_1 + 9X_2 + 18X_3 \right] + U_1$$

$$2 - \lambda \left[9X_1 + 9X_2 + 18X_3 \right] + U_2$$

$$14 - \lambda \left[18X_1 + 18X_2 + 225X_3 \right] + U_3$$

$\lambda = (\bar{R}_P - R_F)/\sigma_P^2$. A little calculation shows that $\lambda = \frac{53}{216}$.

Substituting for X_1, X_2, and X_3 yields

$$8 - \frac{53}{216} \left[36 \left(\frac{43}{53} \right) + 9(0) + 18 \left(\frac{10}{53} \right) \right] + 0$$

$$2 - \frac{53}{216} \left[9 \left(\frac{43}{53} \right) + 9(0) + 18 \left(\frac{10}{53} \right) \right] + \frac{5}{8}$$

$$14 - \frac{53}{216} \left[18 \left(\frac{43}{53} \right) + 18(0) + 225 \left(\frac{10}{53} \right) \right] + 0$$

---

[11]There are conditions on the shape of θ for this to be optimum, but they are always met for the portfolio problem and so can be safely ignored here.

Since all three equal zero, the Kuhn–Tucker conditions are met.

QUESTIONS AND PROBLEMS

1. Assume analysts provide the following types of information. Assume (standard definition) short sales are allowed. What is the optimum portfolio if the lending and borrowing rate is 5%?

Security	Mean Return	Standard Deviation	Covariance with A	Covariance with B	Covariance with C
A	10	4		20	40
B	12	10			70
C	18	14			

2. Given the following information, what is the optimum portfolio if the lending and borrowing rate is 6%, 8%, or 10%? Assume the Lintner definition of short sales.

Security	Mean Return	Standard Deviation	Covariance with A	Covariance with B	Covariance with C
A	11	2		10	4
B	14	6			30
C	17	9			

3. Assume the information given in Problem 1, but that short sales are not allowed. Set up the formulation necessary to solve the portfolio problem.

4. Consider the following data. What is the optimum portfolio, assuming short sales are allowed (standard definition)? Trace out the efficient frontier.

Number	$\bar{R}_i$	σ_i
1	10	5
2	8	6
3	12	4
4	14	7
5	6	2
6	9	3
7	5	1
8	8	4
9	10	4
10	12	2

$$\rho_{ij} = 0.5 \text{ for all } ij$$
$$R_F = 4$$

5. Assume that the data below apply to two efficient portfolios. What is the efficient frontier? Assume the standard definition of short sales.

Portfolio	$\bar{R}_i$	σ_i
A	10	6
B	8	4

$$\sigma_{ij} = 20$$

BIBLIOGRAPHY

1. Alexander, Gordon. "The Derivation of Efficient Sets," *Journal of Financial and Quantitative Analysis*, **XI,** No. 5 (Dec. 1976), pp. 817–830.
2. ——. "Mixed Security Testing of Alternative Portfolio Selection Modes," *Journal of Financial and Quantitative Analysis*, **XII,** No. 4 (Dec. 1977), pp. 817–832.
3. ——. "A Reevaluation of Alternative Portfolio Selection Models Applied to Common Stocks," *Journal of Financial and Quantitative Analysis*, **XIII,** No. 1 (March 1978), pp. 71–78.
4. Bawa, Vijay. "Mathematical Programming of Admissible Portfolios," *Management Science*, **23,** No. 7 (March 1977), pp. 779–785.
5. Bawa, Vijay S., Brown, Stephen J., and Klein, Roger W. *Estimation Risk and Optimal Portfolio Choice* (Amsterdam: North Holland, 1979).
6. Bertsekas, Dimitris. "Necessary and Sufficient Conditions for Existence of an Optimal Portfolio," *Journal of Economic Theory*, **8,** No. 2 (June 1974), pp. 235–247.
7. Black, Fisher. "Capital Market Equilibrium with Restricted Borrowing," *Journal of Business*, **45,** No. 3 (July, 1972), pp. 444–445.
8. Bowden, Roger. "A Dual Concept and Associated Algorithm in Mean-Variance Portfolio Analysis," *Management Science*, **23,** No. 4 (Dec. 1976), pp. 423–432.
9. Breen, William, and Jackson, Richard. "An Efficient Algorithm for Solving Large-Scale Portfolio Problems," *Journal of Financial and Quantitative Analysis*, **VI,** No. 1 (Jan. 1971). pp. 627–637.
10. Buser, Stephen. "Mean-Variance Portfolio Selection with Either a Singular or Non-Singular Variance-Covariance Matrix," *Journal of Financial and Quantitative Analysis*, **XII,** No. 3 (Sept. 1977), pp. 436–461.
11. Chen, Andrew. "Portfolio Selection with Stochastic Cash Demand," *Journal of Financial and Quantitative Analysis*, **XII,** No. 2 (June 1977), pp. 197–213.
12. Chen, Andrew, Jen, Frank, and Zionts, Stanley. "The Optimal Portfolio Revision Policy," *Journal of Business*, **44,** No. 1 (Jan. 1971), pp. 51–61.
13. ——. "Portfolio Models with Stochastic Cash Demands," *Management Science*, **19,** No. 3 (Nov. 1972), pp. 319–332.
14. Chen, Andrew, Kim, Han, and Kon, Stanley. "Cash Demands, Liquidation Costs and Capital Market Equilibrium Under Uncertainty," *Journal of Financial Economics*, **2,** No. 3 (Sept. 1975), pp. 293–308.
15. ——. "Cash Demand...Reply," *Journal of Financial Economics*, **3,** No. 3 (June 1976), pp. 297–298.
16. Constantinides, George. "Comment on Chen, Kim and Kon," *Journal of Financial Economics*, **3,** No. 3 (June 1976), pp. 295–296.
17. Dybvig, Philip H. "Short Sales Restrictions and Kinks on the Mean Variance Frontier," *Journal of Finance*, **39,** No. 1 (March 1984), pp. 239–244.
18. Faaland, Bruce. "An Integer Programming Algorithm for Portfolio Selection," *Management Science*, **20,** No. 10 (June 1974), pp. 1376–1384.
19. Fishburn, Peter, and Porter, Burr. "Optimal Portfolios with One Safe and One Risky Asset: Effects of Change in Rate of Return and Risk," *Management Science*, **22,** No. 10 (June 1976), pp. 1064–1073.
20. Hill, Rowland. "An Algorithm for Counting the Number of Possible Portfolios Given Linear Restrictions on the Weights," *Journal of Financial Economics*, **XI,** No. 3 (Sept. 1976), pp 479–487.
21. Jacob, Nancy. "A Limited-Diversification Portfolio Selection Model for the Small Investor," *Journal of Finance*, **XXIX,** No. 3 (June 1974), pp. 847–856.
22. Jones-Lee, M.W. "Some Portfolio Adjustment Theorems for the Case of Non-Negativity Conditions on Security Holdings," *Journal of Finance*, **XXVI,** No. 3 (June 1971), pp. 763–775.
23. Jorion, Philippe. "Bayes-Stein Estimation for Portfolio Analysis," *Journal of Financial and Quantitative Analysis*, Seattle, **21,** No. 3 (Sept. 1986), pp. 279–292.

24. Lewis, Alan L. "A Simple Algorithm for the Portfolio Selection Problem," *Journal of Finance*, **43,** No. 1 (March 1988), pp. 71–82.

25. Lintner. John. "The Valuation of Risk Assets and the Selection of Risky Investments in Stock Portfolios and Capital Budgets," *Review of Economics and Statistics*, **XLVII,** (Feb. 1965). pp. 13–37.

26. Shanken, Jay. "Testing Portfolio Efficiency When the Zero-Beta Rate Is Unknown: A Note," *Journal of Finance*, Cambridge, **41,** No. 1 (Mar. 1986), pp. 269–276.

27. Tucker, James, and Defaro, Clovis. "A Simple Algorithm for Stone's Version of the Portfolio Selection Problem," *Journal of Financial and Quantitative Analysis*, **X,** No. 5 (Dec. 1975), pp. 859–870.

28. Ziemba. William. "Solving Nonlinear Programming Problems with Stochastic Objective Functions." *Journal of Financial and Quantitative Analysis*, **VII,** No. 3 (June 1972), pp. 1809–1827.

Section 2

Simplifying the Portfolio Selection Process

7

The Correlation Structure of Security Returns

THE SINGLE-INDEX MODEL

In the first four chapters of this book we outlined the basics of modern portfolio theory. The core of the theory, as described in these chapters, is not new; in fact, it was presented as early as 1956 in Markowitz's pioneering article and subsequent book. The reader, noting that the theory is over 30 years old, might well ask what has happened since the theory was developed. Furthermore, if you had knowledge about the actual practices of financial institutions, you might well ask why the theory took so long to be used by financial institutions. The answers to both these questions are closely related. Most of the research on portfolio management in the last 30 years has concentrated on methods for *implementing* the basic theory. Many of the breakthroughs in implementation have been quite recent, and it is only with these new contributions that portfolio theory becomes readily applicable to the management of actual portfolios.

In the next three chapters we are concerned with the implementation of portfolio theory. Breakthroughs in implementation fall into two categories: The first concerns a simplification of the amount and type of input data needed to perform portfolio analysis. The second involves a simplification of the computational procedure needed to calculate optimal portfolios. As will soon become clear, these issues are interdependent. Furthermore, their resolution vastly simplifies portfolio analysis. This results in the ability to describe the problem and its solution in relatively simple terms—terms that have intuitive as well as analytical meaning, and terms to which practicing security analysts and portfolio managers can relate.

In this chapter we begin the problem of simplifying the inputs to the portfolio problem. We start with a discussion of the amount and type of information needed to solve a portfolio problem. We then discuss the oldest and most widely used simplification of the portfolio structure: the single-index model. The nature of the model as well as some estimating techniques are examined.

In Chapter 8 we discuss alternative simplified representations of the portfolio problem. In particular, we will be concerned with other ways to represent and predict the correlation structure between returns. Finally, in the last chapter dealing with implementation we will show how each of the techniques that have been developed to simplify the input to portfolio analysis can be used to reduce and simplify the calculations needed to find optimal portfolios.

Most of Chapters 7 and 8 will be concerned with simplifying and predicting the correlation structure of returns. Many of the single- and multi-index models discussed in these chapters were developed to aid in portfolio management. Lately, however, these models have been used for other purposes that are often viewed as being as important as their use in portfolio analysis. Although many of these other uses will be detailed later in the book, we briefly describe some of them at the end of this chapter and in Chapter 8.

THE INPUTS TO PORTFOLIO ANALYSIS

Let us return to a consideration of the portfolio problem. From earlier chapters we know that to define the efficient frontier we must be able to determine the expected return and standard deviation of return on a portfolio. We can write the expected return on any portfolio as

$$\overline{R}_P = \sum_{i=1}^{N} X_i \overline{R}_i \tag{7.1}$$

while the standard deviation of return on any portfolio can be written as

$$\sigma_P = \left[\sum_{i=1}^{N} X_i^2 \sigma_i^2 + \sum_{i=1}^{N} \sum_{\substack{j=1 \\ j \neq i}}^{N} X_i X_j \sigma_i \sigma_j \rho_{ij} \right]^{1/2} \tag{7.2}$$

These equations define the input data necessary to perform portfolio analysis. From Equation (7.1) we see that we need estimates of the expected return on each security that is a candidate for inclusion in our portfolio. From Equation (7.2) we see that we need estimates of the variance of each security, plus estimates of the correlation between each possible pair of securities for the stocks under consideration. The need for estimates of correlation coefficients differs both in magnitude and substance from the two previous requirements. Let's see why.

The principal job of the security analyst traditionally has been to estimate the future performance of stocks he or she follows. At a minimum this means producing estimates of expected returns on each stock he follows.[1]

With the increased attention that "risk" has received in recent years, more and more analysts are providing estimates of risk as well as return. The analyst who estimates the expected return of a stock should also be in a position to estimate the uncertainty of that return.

Correlations are an entirely different matter. Portfolio analysis calls for estimates of the pairwise correlation between all stocks that are candidates for inclusion in a portfolio. Most firms organize their analysts along traditional industry lines. One analyst might follow steel stocks or, perhaps in a smaller firm, all metal stocks. A second analyst might follow chemical stocks. But portfolio analysis calls for these analysts not only to estimate how a particular steel stock will move in relationship to another steel stock, but also how a particular steel stock will move in relationship to a particular chemical stock or drug stock. There is no nonoverlapping organizational structure that allows such estimates to be directly produced.

---

[1]Whether the analyst's estimates contain information or whether one is better off estimating returns from an equilibrium model (such as those to be presented in Chapters 13 and 14) is an open question. We have more to say about this later. However, the reader should note that portfolio selection models can help to answer this question.

The problem is made more complex by the number of estimates required. Most financial institutions follow between 150 and 250 stocks. To employ portfolio analysis, the institution needs estimates of between 150 and 250 expected returns and 150 and 250 variances. Let us see how many correlation coefficients it needs. If we let N stand for the number of stocks a firm follows, then it has to estimate ρ_{ij} for all pairs of securities i and j. The first index i can take on N values (one for each stock); the second can take on $(N-1)$ values (remember $j \neq i$). This gives us $N(N-1)$ correlation coefficients. However, since the correlation coefficient between stocks i and j is the same as that between stocks j and i, we have to estimate only $N(N-1)/2$ correlations. The institution that follows between 150 and 250 stocks needs between 11,175 and 31,125 correlation coefficients. The sheer number of inputs is staggering.

It seems unlikely that analysts will be able to directly estimate correlation structures. Their ability to do so is severely limited by the nature of feasible organizational structures and the huge number of correlation coefficients that must be estimated. Recognition of this has motivated the search for the development of models to describe and predict the correlation structure between securities. In this chapter and in Chapter 8 we discuss some of these models and examine empirical tests of their performance.

The models developed for forecasting correlation structures fall into two categories: index models and averaging techniques. The most widely used technique assumes that the co-movement between stocks is due to a single common influence or index. This model is appropriately called the single-index model. The single-index model is used not only in estimating the correlation matrix, but also in efficient market tests (discussed later) and in equilibrium tests, where it is called a return-generating process. The rest of this chapter is devoted to a discussion of the properties of this model.

SINGLE-INDEX MODELS: AN OVERVIEW

Casual observation of stock prices reveals that when the market goes up (as measured by any of the widely available stock market indexes), most stocks tend to increase in price, and when the market goes down, most stocks tend to decrease in price. This suggests that one reason security returns might be correlated is because of a common response to market changes, and a useful measure of this correlation might be obtained by relating the return on a stock to the return on a stock market index. The return on a stock can be written as[2]

$$R_i = a_i + \beta_i R_m$$

where

> a_i is the component of security i's return that is independent of the market's performance—a random variable.
>
> R_m is the rate of return on the market index—a random variable.
>
> β_i is a constant that measures the expected change in R_i given a change in R_m.

This equation simply breaks the return on a stock into two components, that part due to the market and that part independent of the market. β_i in the expression measures how

---

[2]The return on the index is identical, in concept, to the return on a common stock. It is the return the investor would earn if he or she held a portfolio with a composition identical to the index. Thus, to compute this return, the dividends that would be received from holding the index should be calculated and combined with the price changes on the index.

sensitive a stock's return is to the return on the market. A β_i of 2 means that a stock's return is expected to increase (decrease) by 2% when the market increases (decreases) by 1%. Similarly, a β of 0.5 indicates that a stock's return is expected to increase (decrease) by $\frac{1}{2}$ of 1% when the market increases (decreases) by 1%.[3]

The term a_i represents that component of return insensitive to (independent of) the return on the market. It is useful to break the term a_i into two components. Let α_i denote the expected value of a_i and let e_i represent the random (uncertain) element of a_i. Then

$$a_i = \alpha_i + e_i$$

where e_i has an expected value of zero. The equation for the return on a stock can now be written as

$$R_i = \alpha_i + \beta_i R_m + e_i \qquad (7.3)$$

Once again, note that both e_i and R_m are random variables. They each have a probability distribution and a mean and standard deviation. Let us denote their standard deviations by σ_{ei} and σ_m, respectively. Up to this point we have made no simplifying assumptions. We have written return as the sum of several components but these components, when added together, must by definition be equal to total return.

It is convenient to have e_i uncorrelated with R_m. Formally, this means that

$$\mathrm{cov}(e_i\, R_m) = E\big[(e_i - 0)(R_m - \overline{R}_m)\big] = 0$$

If e_i is uncorrelated with R_m, it implies that how well Equation (7.3) describes the return on any security is independent of what the return on the market happens to be. Estimates of α_i, β_i, and σ_{ei}^2 are often obtained from time series-regression analysis.[4] Regression analysis is one technique that guarantees that e_i and R_m will be uncorrelated, at least over the period to which the equation has been fit. All of the characteristics of single-index models described to this point are definitions or can be made to hold by construction. There is one further characteristic of single-index models: it holds only by assumption. This assumption is the characteristic of single-index models that differentiates them from other models used to describe the covariance structure.

The key assumption of the single-index model is that e_i is independent of e_j for all values of i and j or, more formally, $E(e_i e_j) = 0$. This implies that the only reason stocks vary together, systematically, is because of a common co-movement with the market. There are no effects beyond the market (e.g., industry effects) that account for co-movement between securities. We will have more to say about this in our discussion of multi-index models in Chapter 8. However, at this time, note that, unlike the independence of e_i and R_m, there is nothing in the normal regression method used to estimate α_i, β_i, and σ_{ei}^2 that forces this to be true. It is a simplifying assumption that represents an approximation to reality. How well this model performs will depend, in part, on how good (or bad) this approximation is. Let us summarize the single-index model:

BASIC EQUATION

---

[3] We are illustrating the single-index model with a stock market index. It is not necessary that the index used be a stock market index. The selection of the appropriate index is an empirical rather than a theoretical question. However, anticipating the results of future chapters, the results should be better when a broad-based market-weighted index is used, such as the S&P 500 index or the New York Stock Exchange Index.

[4] This will be discussed in more detail later in the chapter.

$$R_i = \alpha_i + \beta_i R_m + e_i \qquad \text{for all stocks } i = 1, \ldots, N$$

BY CONSTRUCTION
1. Mean of $e_i = E(e_i) = 0$ for all stocks $i = 1, \ldots, N$

BY ASSUMPTION
1. Index unrelated to unique return: for all stocks $i = 1, \ldots, N$
   $E[e_i(R_m - \bar{R}_m)] = 0$
2. Securities only related through common   for all pairs of stocks $i = 1, \ldots, N$
   response to market: $E(e_i e_j) = 0$ and $j = 1, \ldots, N$ but $i \neq j$

BY DEFINITION
1. Variance of $e_i = E(e_i)^2 = \sigma_{ei}^2$ for all stocks $i = i, \ldots, N$
2. Variance of $R_m = E(R_m - \bar{R}_m)^2 = \sigma_m^2$

In the subsequent section we derive the expected return, standard deviation, and covariance when the single-index model is used to represent the joint movement of securities. The results are

1. The mean return, $\bar{R}_i = \alpha_i + \beta_i \bar{R}_m$.
2. The variance of a security's return, $\sigma_i^2 = \beta_i^2 \sigma_m^2 + \sigma_{ei}^2$.
3. The covariance of returns between securities i and j, $\sigma_{ij} = \beta_i \beta_j \sigma_m^2$.

Note that the expected return has two components: a unique part α_i and a market-related part $\beta_i \bar{R}_m$. Likewise, a security's variance has the same two parts, unique risk σ_{ei}^2 and market-related risk $\beta_i^2 \sigma_m^2$. In contrast, the covariance depends only on market risk. This is what we meant earlier when we said that the single-index model implied that the only reason securities move together is a common response to market movements. In this section of the text delineated by the solid line we derive these results. The reader uninterested in the derivation can note the results and then skip to the end of the section.

The expected return on a security is

$$E(R_i) = E[\alpha_i + \beta_i R_m + e_i]$$

Since the expected value of the sum of random variables is the sum of the expected values, we have

$$E(R_i) = E(\alpha_i) + E(\beta_i R_m) + E(e_i)$$

α_i and β_i are constants and by construction the expected value of e_i is zero. Thus,

$$E(R_i) = \alpha_i + \beta_i \bar{R}_m \qquad\qquad \textbf{Result 1}$$

The variance of the return on any security is

$$\sigma_i^2 = E(R_i - \bar{R}_i)^2$$

Substituting for R_i and $\bar{R}_i$ from the expression above yields

$$\sigma_i^2 = E\left[(\alpha_i + \beta_i R_m + e_i) - (\alpha_i + \beta_i \bar{R}_m)\right]^2$$

Rearranging and noting that the α's cancel yields

$$\sigma_i^2 = E\left[\beta_i(R_m - \bar{R}_m) + e_i\right]^2$$

Squaring the terms in the brackets yields

$$\sigma_i^2 = \beta_i^2 E\left(R_m - \bar{R}_m\right)^2 + 2\beta_i E\left[e_i\left(R_m - \bar{R}_m\right)\right] + E(e_i)^2$$

Recall that by assumption (or in some cases by construction) $E[e_i(R_m - \bar{R}_m)] = 0$. Thus,

$$\sigma_i^2 = \beta_i^2 E\left(R_m - \bar{R}_m\right)^2 + E(e_i)^2$$

$$\sigma_i^2 = \beta_i^2 \sigma_m^2 + \sigma_{ei}^2 \qquad \textbf{Result 2}$$

The covariance between any two securities can be written as

$$\sigma_{ij} = E\left[\left(R_i - \bar{R}_i\right)\left(R_j - \bar{R}_j\right)\right]$$

Substituting for R_i, $\bar{R}_i$, R_j, and $\bar{R}_j$ yields

$$\sigma_{ij} = E\Big\{\left[\left(\alpha_i + \beta_i R_m + e_i\right) - \left(\alpha_i + \beta_i \bar{R}_m\right)\right]$$
$$\cdot \left[\left(\alpha_j + \beta_j R_m + e_j\right) - \left(\alpha_j + \beta_j \bar{R}_m\right)\right]\Big\}$$

Simplifying by canceling the α's and combining the terms involving β's yields

$$\sigma_{ij} = E\left[\left(\beta_i\left(R_m - \bar{R}_m\right) + e_i\right)\left(\beta_j\left(R_m - \bar{R}_m\right) + e_j\right)\right]$$

Carrying out the multiplication

$$\sigma_{ij} = \beta_i \beta_j E\left(R_m - \bar{R}_m\right)^2 + \beta_j E\left[e_i\left(R_m - \bar{R}_m\right)\right]$$
$$+ \beta_i E\left[e_j\left(R_m - \bar{R}_m\right)\right] + E(e_i e_j)$$

Since the last three terms are zero, by assumption

$$\sigma_{ij} = \beta_i \beta_j \sigma_m^2 \qquad \textbf{Result 3}$$

These results can be illustrated with a simple example. Consider the returns on a stock and a market index shown in the first two columns of Table 7.1. These returns are what an investor might have observed over the prior five months. Now consider the values for the single-index model shown in the remaining columns of the table. Column three just reproduced column one and is the return on the security. Accept for the moment that $\beta_i = 1.5$. The fifth column is just the second column times 1.5 or the market return times a Beta of 1.5. Where does e_i come from? Recall that the average value of e_i is zero. If the average value of e_i is zero, then the sum of e_i is also zero. The single-index model is an equality. The return over the 5 periods for the stock is 40; 30 of the 40 is market-related return, hence 10 must be non-market-related or unique. If e_i sums to zero, then for the single-index model to be an equality, α_i must sum to 10. Since α_i is a constant and there are 5 periods, α_i is $\frac{10}{5}$ or 2 per period.

Given the values for α_i and for $\beta_i R_m$, and since the single-index model is an equality, e_i

Table 7.1 Decomposition of Returns for the Single-Index Model

Month	1 Return on Stock	2 Return on Market	3 R_i	=	4 α_i	+	5 $\beta_i R_m$	6 e_i
1	10	4	10	=	2	+	6	+ 2
2	3	2	3	=	2	+	3	− 2
3	15	8	15	=	2	+	12	+ 1
4	9	6	9	=	2	+	9	− 2
5	3	0	3	=	2	+	0	+ 1
	40	20	40		10		30	0

is whatever is necessary to make the left- and right-hand sides the same. For example, in the first period the sum of α_i and $\beta_i R_m$ is 8. Since the return on the security in the first period is 10, e_i is $+ 2$.

The reader should now understand where all the values of the single-index model come from except β_i. β_i divides return into market-related and unique return. When β_i is set equal to 1.5, the market return is independent of the residual return e_i. A lower value of e_i leaves some market return in e_i and the covariance of e_i with the market is positive. A β_i greater than 1.5 removes too much market return and results in a negative covariance between e_i and the market. Thus the value of β_i is unique and is the value that exactly separates market from unique return, making the covariance between R_m and e_i zero.

Before leaving the simple example, let's apply the formulas presented earlier. The mean return on the security is

$$\overline{R}_i = 40/5 = 8$$

using the formula from the single-index model.

$$\overline{R}_i = \alpha_i + \beta_i \overline{R}_m = 2 + 1.5(4) = 8$$

The variance of security i is calculating from the formula derived for the single-index model.

$$\sigma_i^2 = \beta_i^2 \sigma_m^2 + \sigma_{ei}^2$$
$$= (1.5)^2 (8) + 2.8$$
$$= 20.8$$

Having explained the simple example, we can turn to the calculation of the expected return and variance of any portfolio if the single-index model holds. The expected return on any portfolio is given by

$$\overline{R}_P = \sum_{i=1}^{N} X_i \overline{R}_i$$

Substituting for $\overline{R}_i$ we obtain

$$\overline{R}_P = \sum_{i=1}^{N} X_i \alpha_i + \sum_{i=1}^{N} X_i \beta_i \overline{R}_m \tag{7.4}$$

We know that the variance of a portfolio of stocks is given by

$$\sigma_P^2 = \sum_{i=1}^{N} X_i^2 \sigma_i^2 + \sum_{i=1}^{N} \sum_{\substack{j=1; \\ j \neq i}}^{N} X_i X_j \sigma_{ij}$$

Substituting in the results stated above for σ_i^2 and σ_{ij}, we obtain

$$\sigma_P^2 = \sum_{i=1}^{N} X_i^2 \beta_i^2 \sigma_m^2 + \sum_{i=1}^{N} \sum_{\substack{j=1 \\ j \neq i}}^{N} X_i X_j \beta_i \beta_j \sigma_m^2 + \sum_{i=1}^{N} X_i^2 \sigma_{ei}^2 \tag{7.5}$$

There are many alternative ways of estimating the parameters of the single-index model. From Equations (7.4) and (7.7) it is clear that expected return and risk can be estimated for any portfolio if we have an estimate of α_i for each stock, an estimate of β_i for each stock, an estimate of σ_{ei}^2 for each stock, and, finally, an estimate of both the expected return ($\overline{R}_m$) and variance (σ_m^2) for the market. This is a total of $3N + 2$ estimates. For an institution following between 150 and 250 stocks, the single-index model required between 452 and 752 estimates. Compare this with the 11,175–31,125 correlation estimates or 11,475–31,625 total estimates required when no simplifying structure was assumed. Furthermore, note that there is no requirement for direct estimates of the joint movement of securities, only estimates of the way each security moves with the market. A nonoverlapping organizational structure can produce all the required estimates.

The model can also be employed if analysts supply estimates of expected return for each stock, the variance of the return on each stock, the Beta (β_i) for each stock, and the variance of the market return.[5] This is $3N + 1$ estimates. This alternative set of estimates has the advantage that they are in more familiar terms.

We have discussed means and variances before. The only new variable is Beta. The Beta is simply a measure of the sensitivity of a stock to market movements.

Before we discuss alternative ways of estimating Betas, let us examine some of the characteristics of the single-index model.

CHARACTERISTICS OF THE SINGLE-INDEX MODEL

Define the Beta on a portfolio β_P as a weighted average of the individual β_is on each stock in the portfolio where the weights are the fraction of the portfolio invested in each stock. Then

$$\beta_P = \sum_{i=1}^{N} X_i \beta_i$$

Similarly define the Alpha on the portfolio α_P as

$$\alpha_P = \sum_{i=1}^{N} X_i \alpha_i$$

Then Equation (7.4) can be written as

$$\overline{R}_P = \alpha_P + \beta_P \overline{R}_m$$

If the portfolio P is taken to be the market portfolio (all stocks held in the same proportions as they were in constructing R_m), then the expected return on P must be $\overline{R}_m$. From the above equation the only values of β_P and α_P that guarantee $\overline{R}_P = \overline{R}_m$ for any choice of $\overline{R}_m$ is α_P equal to 0 and β_P equal to 1. Thus, the Beta on the market is 1 and stocks are thought of as being more or less risky than the market, according to whether their Beta is larger or smaller than 1.

Let us look further into the risk of an individual security. Equation (7.5) is

---

[5]The fact that these inputs are equivalent to those discussed earlier is easy to show. The expected returns can be used directly to estimate the expected return on a portfolio

$$\overline{R}_P = \sum_{i=1}^{N} X_i \overline{R}_i$$

The estimates of the variance of return on a stock, the variance of the market, and the Beta on each stock can be used to derive estimates of its residual risk by noting that

$$\sigma_i^2 = \beta_i^2 \sigma_m^2 + \sigma_{ei}^2$$

In addition, this structure is natural for those institutions that want analysts' estimates of means and variances and model estimates of correlations or covariances.

$$\sigma_P^2 = \sum_{i=1}^{N} X_i^2 \beta_i^2 \sigma_m^2 + \sum_{i=1}^{N} X_i^2 \sigma_{ei}^2 + \sum_{i=1}^{N} \sum_{\substack{j=1 \\ j\neq i}}^{N} X_i X_j \beta_i \beta_j \sigma_m^2$$

In the double summation $i \neq j$, if $i = j$, then the terms would be $X_i X_i \beta_i^2 \sigma_m^2$. But these are exactly the terms in the first summation. Thus, the variance on the portfolio can be written as

$$\sigma_P^2 = \sum_{i=1}^{N} \sum_{j=1}^{N} X_i X_j \beta_i \beta_j \sigma_m^2 + \sum_{i=1}^{N} X_i^2 \sigma_{ei}^2$$

Or by rearranging terms

$$\sigma_P^2 = \left(\sum_{i=1}^{N} X_i \beta_i \right) \left(\sum_{j=1}^{N} X_j \beta_j \right) \sigma_m^2 + \sum_{i=1}^{N} X_i^2 \sigma_{ei}^2$$

Thus, the risk of the investor's portfolio could be represented as

$$\sigma_P^2 = \beta_P^2 \sigma_m^2 + \sum_{i=1}^{N} X_i^2 \sigma_{ei}^2$$

Assume for a moment that an investor forms a portfolio by placing equal amounts of money into each of N stocks. The risk of this portfolio can be written as[6]

$$\sigma_P^2 = \beta_P^2 \sigma_m^2 + \frac{1}{N} \left(\sum_{i=1}^{N} \frac{1}{N} \sigma_{ei}^2 \right)$$

Look at the last term. This can be expressed as $1/N$ times the average residual risk in the portfolio. As the number of stocks in the portfolio increases, the importance of the average residual risk,

$$\sum_{i=1}^{N} \frac{\sigma_{ei}^2}{N}$$

diminishes drastically. In fact, as Table 7.2 shows, the residual risk falls so rapidly that most of it is effectively eliminated on even moderately sized portfolios.[7]

The risk that is not eliminated as we hold larger and larger portfolios is the risk associated with the term β_P. If we assume that residual risk approaches zero, the risk of the portfolio approaches

$$\sigma_P = \left[\beta_P^2 \sigma_m^2 \right]^{1/2} = \beta_P \sigma_m = \sigma_m \left[\sum_{i=1}^{N} X_i \beta_i \right]$$

Since σ_m is the same, regardless of which stock we examine, the measure of the contribution of a security to the risk of a large portfolio is β_i.

The risk of an individual security is $\beta_i^2 \sigma_m^2 + \sigma_{ei}^2$. Since the effect of σ_{ei}^2 on portfolio risk

---

[6]Examining the expression for the variance of portfolio P shows that the assumptions of the single-index model are inconsistent with $\sigma_P^2 = \sigma_m^2$. However, the approximation is very close. See Fama [34] for a detailed discussion of this issue.

[7]To the extent that the single-index model is not a perfect description of reality and residuals from the market model are correlated across securities, residual risk does not fall this rapidly. However, for most portfolios the amount of positive correlation present in the residuals is quite small and residual risk declines rapidly as the number of securities in the portfolio increases.

Table 7.2   Residual Risk and Portfolio Size

Number of Securities	Residual Risk (Variance) Expressed as a Percent of the Residual Risk Present in a One-Stock Portfolio with σ^2_{ei} a Constant
1	100
2	50
3	33
4	25
5	20
10	10
20	5
100	1
1000	0.1

can be made to approach zero as the portfolio gets larger, it is common to refer to σ^2_{ei} as diversifiable risk.[8] However, the effect of $\beta^2_i \sigma^2_m$ on portfolio risk does not diminish as N gets larger. Since σ^2_m is a constant with respect to all securities, β_i is the measure of a security's nondiversifiable risk.[9] Since diversifiable risk can be eliminated by holding a large enough portfolio, β_i is often used as the measure of a security's risk.

ESTIMATING BETA

The use of the single-index model calls for estimates of the Beta of each stock that is a potential candidate for inclusion in a portfolio. Analysts could be asked to provide subjective estimates of Beta for a security or a portfolio. On the other hand, estimates of future Beta could be arrived at by estimating Beta from past data and using this historical Beta as an estimate of the future Beta. There is evidence that historical Betas provide useful information about future Betas. Furthermore, some interesting forecasting techniques have been developed to increase the information that can be extracted from historical data. Because of this, even the firm that wishes to use analysts' subjective estimates of future Betas should start with (supply analysts with) the best estimates of Beta available from historical data. The analyst can then concentrate on the examination of influences that are expected to change Beta in the future. In the rest of this chapter we examine some of the techniques that have been proposed for estimating Beta. These techniques can be classified as measuring historical Betas, correcting historical Betas for the tendency of historical Betas to be closer to the mean when estimated in a future period, and correcting historical estimates by incorporating fundamental firm data.

Estimating Historical Betas

In Equation (7.3) we represented the return on a stock as

$$R_i = \alpha_i + \beta_i R_m + e_i$$

This equation is expected to hold at each moment in time, although the values of α_i, β_i, or σ^2_{ei} might differ over time. When looking at historical data, one cannot directly observe α_i, β_i, or σ^2_{ei}. Rather, one observes the past returns on the security and the market. If α_i, β_i,

---

[8]An alternative nomenclature calls this nonmarket or unsystematic risk.

[9]An alternative nomenclature calls this market risk or systematic risk.

and σ_{ei}^2 are assumed to be constant through time, then the same equation is expected to hold at each point in time. In this case, a straightforward procedure exists for estimating α_i, β_i, and σ_{ei}^2.

Notice that Equation (7.3) is an equation of a straight line. If σ_{ei}^2 were equal to zero, then we could estimate α_i and β_i with just two observations. However, the presence of the random variable e_i means that the actual return will form a scatter around the straight line. Figure 7.1 illustrates this pattern. The vertical axis is the return on security i and the horizontal axis is the return on the market. Each point on the diagram is the return on stock i over a particular time interval, for example, one month (t) plotted against the return on the market for the same time interval. The actual observed returns lie on and around the true relationship (shown as a solid line). The greater σ_{ei}^2, the greater the scatter around the line, and since we do not actually observe the line, the more uncertain we are about where it is. There are a number of ways of estimating where the line might be, given the observed scatter of points. Usually, we estimate the location of the line using regression analysis.

This procedure could be thought of as first plotting R_{it} versus R_{mt} to obtain a scatter of points such as that shown in Figure 7.1. Each point represents the return on a particular stock and the return on the market in one month. Additional points are obtained by plotting the two returns in successive months. The next step is to fit that straight line to the data that minimized the sum of the squared deviation from the line in the vertical (R_{it}) direction. The slope of this straight line would be our best estimate of Beta over the period to which the line was fit, and intercept would be our best estimate of Alpha (α_i).[10]

More formally, to estimate the Beta for a firm for the period from $t = 1$ to $t = 60$ via regression analysis use

$$\beta_i = \frac{\sigma_{im}}{\sigma_m^2} = \frac{\sum_{t=1}^{60}\left[\left(R_{it} - \overline{R}_{it}\right)\left(R_{mt} - \overline{R}_{mt}\right)\right]}{\sum_{t=1}^{60}\left(R_{mt} - \overline{R}_{mt}\right)^2}$$

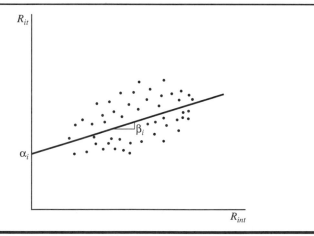

Figure 7.1

---

[10]If R_{it} and R_{mt} come from a bivariate normal distribution, the unbiased and most efficient estimates of α_i and β_i are those that come from regressing R_{it} against R_{mt}, the procedure described above.

and to estimate Alpha use[11]

$$\alpha_i = \overline{R}_{it} - \beta_i \overline{R}_{mt}$$

To learn how this works on a simple example let us return to Table 7.1. We used the data in 7.1 to show how Beta interacted with returns. But now assume that all you observed was columns 1 and 2 or the return on the stock and the return on the market. To estimate Beta we need to estimate the covariance between the stock and the market. The average return on the stock was 40/5 = 8, whereas on the market it was 20/5 = 4. The Beta value for the stock is the covariance of the stock with the market divided by the variance of the market or

$$\beta_i = \frac{\left[\sum_{t=1}^{5}\left(R_i - \overline{R}_i\right)\left(R_m - \overline{R}_m\right)\right]\Big/5}{\sum_{t=1}^{5}\left(R_m - \overline{R}_m\right)^2 \Big/ 5}$$

The covariance is found as follows:

Month	Stock Return Minus Mean		Market Return Minus Mean		Value
1	$(10 - 8)$	×	$(4 - 4)$	=	0
2	$(3 - 8)$	×	$(2 \;\; 4)$	=	10
3	$(15 - 8)$	×	$(8 - 4)$	=	28
4	$(9 - 8)$	×	$(6 - 4)$	=	2
5	$(3 - 8)$	×	$(0 - 4)$	=	20
				Total	60

The covariance is 60/5 = 12. The variance of the market return is the average of the sum of squared deviation from the mean

$$\sigma_m^2 = \left[(4-4)^2 + (2-4)^2 + (8-4)^2 + (6-4)^2 + (0-4)^2\right]\Big/5 = 8$$

Thus Beta = 12/8 = 1.5

This value of Beta is identical to the number used in constructing Table 7.1.

Alpha can be computed by taking the difference between the average security return and Beta times the average return on the market.

$$\alpha_i = 8 - (1.5)(4) = 2$$

---

[11]Two other statistics of interest can be produced by this analysis. First, the size of σ_{ei}^2 over the estimation period can be found by looking at the variance of the deviations of the actual return from that predicted by the model:

$$\sigma_{ei}^2 = \frac{1}{60}\sum_{t=1}^{60}\left[R_{it} - \left(\alpha_i + \beta_i R_{mt}\right)\right]^2$$

Remember that, in performing regression analysis, one often computes a coefficient of determination. The coefficient of determination is a measure of association between two variables. In this case, it would measure how much of the variation in the return on the individual stock is associated with variation in the return on the market. The coefficient of determination is simply the correlation coefficient squared, and the correlation coefficient is equal to

$$\rho_{im} = \frac{\sigma_{im}}{\sigma_i \sigma_m} = \frac{\beta_i \sigma_m^2}{\sigma_i \sigma_m} = \beta_i \frac{\sigma_m}{\sigma_i}$$

The values of α_i and β_i produced by regression analysis are estimates of the true α_i and β_i that exist for a stock. The estimates are subject to error. As such, the estimate of α_i and β_i may not be equal to the true α_i and β_i that existed in the period.[12] Furthermore, the process is complicated by the fact that α_i and β_i are not perfectly stationary over time. We would expect changes as the fundamental characteristics of the firm change. For example, β_i as a risk measure should be related to the capital structure of the firm and, thus, should change as the capital structure changes.

Despite error in measuring the true β_i and the possibility of real shifts in β_i over time, the most straightforward way to forecast β_i for a future period is to use an estimate of β_i obtained via regression analysis from a past period. Let us take a look at how well this works.

Accuracy of Historical Betas

The first logical step in looking at Betas is to see how much association there is between the Betas in one period and the Betas in an adjacent period. Both Blume [13] and Levy [61] have done extensive testing of the relationship between Betas over time. Let us look at some representative results from Blume's [13] study. Blume computed Betas using time series regressions on monthly data for nonoverlapping seven-year periods. He generated Betas on single stock portfolios, 2 stock portfolios, 4 stock portfolios, and so forth up to 50 stock portfolios and for each size portfolio examined how highly correlated the Betas from one period were with the Betas for a second period. Table 7.3 presents a typical result showing how highly correlated the Betas are for the period 7/54–6/61 and 7/61–6/68.

It is apparent from this table that, while Betas on very large portfolios contain a great deal of information about future Betas on these portfolios, Betas on individual securities contain much less information about the future Betas on securities. Why might observed Betas in one period differ from Betas in a second period? One reason is that the risk (Beta) of the security or portfolio might change. A second reason is that the Beta in each period is measured with a random error, and the larger the random error, the less predictive power Betas from one period will have for Betas in the next period.

Changes in security Betas will differ from security to security. Some will go up, some will go down. These changes will tend to cancel out in a portfolio, and we observe less change in the actual Beta on portfolios than on securities.

Table 7.3　Association of Betas Over Time

Number of Securities in the Portfolio	Correlation Coefficient	Coefficient of Determination
1	0.60	0.36
2	0.73	0.53
4	0.84	0.71
7	0.88	0.77
10	0.92	0.85
20	0.97	0.95
35	0.97	0.95
50	0.98	0.96

---

[12]In fact, the analysis will produce an estimate of the standard error in both α_i and β_i. This can be used to make interval estimates of future Alphas and Betas under the assumption of stationarity.

Likewise, one would expect that the errors in estimating Beta for individual securities would tend to cancel out when securities are combined, and therefore, there would be less error in measuring a portfolio's Beta.[13] Since portfolio Betas are measured with less error, and since Betas on portfolios change less than Betas on securities, historical Betas on portfolios are better predictors of future Betas than are historical Betas on securities.

Adjusting Historical Estimates

Can we further improve the predictive ability of Betas on securities and portfolios? To aid in answering this question, let us examine a simple hypothetical distribution of Betas. Assume the true Betas on all stocks are really one. If we estimate Betas for all stocks, some of our estimated Betas will be one, but some will be above or below one due to sampling error in the estimate. Estimated Betas above one would be above one simply due to positive sampling errors. Estimated Betas below one would be below one due to negative sampling errors. Furthermore, since there is no reason to suspect that a positive sampling error for a stock will be followed by a positive sampling error for the same stock, we would find that historical Beta did a worse job of predicting future Beta than did a Beta of one for all stocks. Now, assume we have different Betas for different stocks. The Beta we calculate for any stock will be, in part, a function of the true underlying Beta and, in part, a function of sampling error. If we compute a very high estimate of Beta for a stock, we have an increased probability that we have a positive sampling error, while if we compute a very low estimate of Beta, we have an increased chance that we have a negative sampling error. If this scenario is correct, we should find that Betas, on the average, tend to converge to one in successive time periods. Estimated Betas that are a lot larger than one should tend to be followed by estimated Betas that are closer to one (lower), and estimated Betas below one should tend to be followed by higher Betas. Evidence that this does, in fact, happen has been presented by Blume [15] and Levy [61]. Blume's results are reproduced in Table 7.4. The reader should examine the table and confirm the tendency of Betas in the forecast period to be closer to one than the estimates of these Betas obtained from historical data.[14]

---

[13]Assuming that the relationship between R_{jt} and R_{mt} is described by a stationary bivariate normal distribution, then the standard error in the measurement of Beta for a security is given by

$$\sigma_{\beta i} = \sigma_{ei}/\sigma_m$$

The standard error for the β on a portfolio is given by

$$\sigma_{\beta P} = \sigma_{ep}/\sigma_m$$

where

$$\sigma_{ep}^2 - \frac{1}{T}\sum_{t=1}^{T}\left(e_{pt}\right)^2 = \frac{1}{T}\sum_{t=1}^{T}\left(\sum_{i=1}^{N}X_ie_{it}\right)^2$$

where N is the number of securities in the portfolio and T is the number of time periods.

To the extent that the residuals for different stocks are not perfectly correlated, averaging them across stocks will lower the value of the residuals and, hence, the value of σ_{ep}^2 on the portfolio. In particular, if the assumptions of the single-index model are met and if stocks are held in equal proportions, the standard error of the Beta on the portfolio would equal the average standard error on all stocks times the reciprocal of the number of stocks in the portfolio.

[14]Through this section when we speak of Betas we are referring to estimates of Betas.

Table 7.4   Betas on Ranked Portfolios for Two Successive Periods

Portfolio	7/54–6/61	7/61–6/68
1	0.393	0.620
2	0.612	0.707
3	0.810	0.861
4	0.987	0.914
5	1.138	0.995
6	1.337	1.169

Source: Blume, Marchell. "On the Assessment of Risk," *Journal of Finance*, VI, No. 1 (March 1971).

Measuring the Tendency of Betas to Regress Toward One— Blume's Technique

Since Betas in the forecast period tend to be closer to one than the estimate obtained from historical data, the next obvious step is to try to modify past Betas to capture this tendency. Blume [15] was the first to propose a scheme for doing so. He corrected past Betas by directly measuring this adjustment toward one and assuming that the adjustment in one period is a good estimate of the adjustment in the next.

Let us see how this could work. We could calculate the Betas for all stocks for the period 1948–1954. We could then calculate the Betas for these same stocks for the period 1955–1961. We could then regress the Betas for the later period against the Betas for the earlier period as shown in Figure 7.2. Note that each observation is the Beta on the same stock for the period 1948–1954 and 1955–1961. Following this procedure we would obtain a line that measures the tendency of the forecasted Betas to be closer to one than the estimates from historical data. When Blume did this for the period mentioned, he obtained

$$\beta_{i2} = 0.343 + 0.677\beta_{i1}$$

where β_{i2} stands for the Beta on stock i in the later period (1955–1961) and β_{i1} stands for the β for stock i for the earlier period (1948–1954). The relationship implies that the Beta in the later period is 0.343 + 0.677 times the Beta in the earlier period. Assume we wish

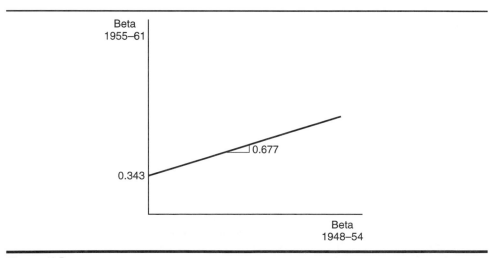

Figure 7.2

to forecast the Beta for any stock for the period 1962–1968. We then compute (via regression analysis) its Beta for the years 1955–1961. To determine how this Beta should be modified, we substitute it for β_{i1} in the equation. We then compute β_{i2} from the foregoing equation and use it as our forecast.

Notice the effect of this on the Beta for any stock. If β_{i1} were 2.0, then our forecast would be $0.343 + 0.677(2) = 1.697$, rather than 2.0. If β_{i1} were 0.5, our forecast would be $0.343 + 0.677(0.5) = 0.682$ rather than 0.5. The equation lowers high values of Beta and raises low values. One more characteristic of this equation should be noted. It modifies the average level of Betas for the population of stocks. Since it measures the relationship between Betas over two periods, if the average Beta increased over these two periods, it assumes that average Betas will increase over the next period. Unless there is reason to suspect a continuous drift in Beta, this will be an undesirable property. If there is no reason to expect this trend in the average Beta to continue, then the estimates can be improved by adjusting the forecasted Betas so that their mean is the same as the historical mean.

To make this point more concrete, let us examine an example. Assume that in estimating the equation Blume found the average Beta in 1948–1954 was one and the average Beta in 1955–1961 was 1.02. These numbers are consistent with his results, though there are other sets of numbers that would also be consistent with his results. Now, to determine what the average forecasted Beta should be for the period 1962–1968, we simply substitute 1.02 in the right-hand side of the estimating equation. The answer is 1.033. As discussed earlier, Blume's technique results in a continued extrapolation of the upward trend in Betas observed in the earlier periods.

If there is no reason to believe that the next period's average Beta will be more than this period's, then the forecasts should be improved by adjusting the forecast Beta to have the same mean as the historical mean. This involves subtracting a constant from all Betas after adjusting them toward their mean. In our example, this is achieved by subtracting 1.033 from each forecast of Beta and adding 1.02.

Measuring the Tendency of Betas to Regress Toward One— Vasicek's Technique

Recall that the actual Beta in the forecast period tends to be closer to the average Beta than is the estimate obtained from historical data. A straightforward way to adjust for this tendency is to simply adjust each Beta toward the average Beta. For example, taking one-half of the historical Beta and adding it to one-half of the average Beta moves each historical Beta halfway toward the average. This technique is widely used.[15]

It would be desirable not to adjust all stocks the same amount toward the average but rather to have the adjustment depend on the size of the uncertainty (sampling error) about Beta. The larger the sampling error, the greater the chance of large differences from the average, being due to sampling error, and the greater the adjustment. Vasicek [92] has suggested the following scheme that incorporates these properties: If we let $\overline{\beta}_1$ equal the average Beta, across the sample of stocks, in the historical period, then the Vasicek procedure involves taking a weighted average of $\overline{\beta}_1$ and the historical Beta for security i. Let $\sigma_{\overline{\beta}1}^2$ stand for the variance of the distribution of the historical estimates of Beta over the sample of stocks. This is a measure of the variation of Beta across the sample of stocks under consideration. Let $\sigma_{\beta1}^2$ stand for the square of the standard error of the estimate of Beta for

---

[15]For example, Merrill Lynch has used a simple weighting technique like this to adjust its Betas.

security i measured in time period 1. This is a measure of the uncertainty associated with the measurement of the individual securities Beta. Vasicek [92] suggested weights of

$$\frac{\sigma^2_{\bar{\beta}1}}{\sigma^2_{\bar{\beta}1}+\sigma^2_{\beta i1}} \text{ for } \beta_{i1} \quad \text{and} \quad \frac{\sigma^2_{\beta i1}}{\sigma^2_{\bar{\beta}1}+\sigma^2_{\beta i1}} \text{ for } \bar{\beta}_1$$

Note that these weights add up to 1 and that the more the uncertainty about either estimate of Beta, the lower the weight that is placed on it. The forecast of Beta for security i is

$$\beta_{i2} = \frac{\sigma^2_{\beta i1}}{\sigma^2_{\bar{\beta}1}+\sigma^2_{\beta i1}}\bar{\beta}_1 + \frac{\sigma^2_{\bar{\beta}1}}{\sigma^2_{\bar{\beta}1}+\sigma^2_{\beta i1}}\beta_{i1}$$

This weighting procedure adjusts observations with large standard errors further toward the mean than it adjusts observations with small standard errors. As Vasicek has shown, this is a Bayesian estimation technique.[16]

While the Bayesian technique does not forecast a trend in Betas as does the Blume technique, it suffers from its own potential source of bias. In the Bayesian technique, the weight placed on a stock's Beta, relative to the weight on the average Beta in the sample, is inversely related to the stock's standard error of Beta. High Beta stocks have larger standard errors associated with their Betas than do low Beta stocks. This means that high Beta stocks will have their Betas lowered by a bigger percentage of the distance from the average Beta for the sample than low Beta stocks will have their Betas raised. Hence, the estimate of the average future Beta will tend to be lower than the average Beta in the sample of stocks over which Betas are estimated.

Unless there is reason to believe that Betas will continually decrease, the estimate of Beta can be further improved by adjusting all Betas upward so that they have the same mean as they had in the historical period.

Accuracy of Adjusted Beta

Let us examine how well the Blume and the Bayesian adjustment techniques worked as forecasters, compared to unadjusted Betas. Klemkosky and Martin [57] tested the ability of these techniques to forecast over three 5-year periods for both one-stock and ten-stock portfolios. As would be suspected, in all cases both the Blume and Bayesian adjustment techniques led to more accurate forecasts of future Betas than did the unadjusted Betas. The average squared error in forecasting Beta was often cut in half when one of the adjustment techniques was used. Klemkosky and Martin used an interesting decomposition technique to search for the source of the forecast error. Specifically, the source of error was decomposed into that part of the error due to a misestimate of the average level of Beta, that part due to the tendency to overestimate high Betas and underestimate low Betas, and that part that is unexplained by either of the first two influences. As might be expected, when the Blume and Bayesian techniques were compared with the unadjusted Betas, almost all of the decrease in error came from the reductions in the tendency to overestimate high Betas and underestimate low Betas. This is not surprising because this is exactly what the two techniques were designed to achieve. Klemkosky and Martin found that the Bayesian technique had a slight tendency to outperform the Blume technique. However,

---

[16]The reader should note that this is just one of an infinite number of ways of forming prior distributions. For example, priors could have been set equal to 1 (the average for all stocks market weighted) or to an average Beta for the industry to which the stock belongs, and so on.

the differences were small and the ordering of the techniques varied across different periods of time.

Most of the literature dealing with Betas have evaluated Beta adjustment techniques by their ability to better forecast Betas. However, there is another, and perhaps more important criterion by which the performance of alternative Betas can be judged. At the beginning of this chapter we discussed the fact that the necessary inputs to portfolio analysis were expected returns, variances, and correlations. We believe that analysts can be asked to provide estimates of expected returns and variances, but that correlations will probably continue to be generated from some sort of historical model.[17] One way Betas can be used is to generate estimates of the correlation between securities. The correlations between stocks (given the assumptions of the single-index model) can be expressed as a function of Beta.

$$\rho_{ij} = \frac{\sigma_{ij}}{\sigma_i \sigma_j} = \frac{\beta_i \beta_j \sigma_m^2}{\sigma_i \sigma_j}$$

Another way to test the usefulness of Betas, as well as the performance of alternative forecasts of Betas, is to see how well Betas forecast the correlation structure between securities.

Betas as Forecasters of Correlation Coefficients

Elton, Gruber, and Urich [31] have compared the ability of the following models to forecast the correlation structure between securities:

1.   The historical correlation matrix itself
2.   Forecasts of the correlation matrix prepared by estimating Betas from the prior historical period
3.   Forecasts of the correlation matrix prepared by estimating Betas from the prior two periods and updating via the Blume technique
4.   Forecasts prepared as in the third model but where the updating is done via the Vasicek Bayesian technique

One of the most striking results of the study was that the historical correlation matrix itself was the poorest of all techniques. In most cases it was outperformed by all of the Beta forecasting techniques at a statistically significant level. This indicates that a large part of the observed correlation structure between securities, not captured by the single-index model, represents random noise with respect to forecasting. The point to note is that the single-index model, developed to simplify the inputs to portfolio analysis and thought to lose information due to the simplification involved, actually does a better job of forecasting than the full set of historical data.

The comparison of the three Beta techniques is more ambiguous. In each of two five-year samples tested, the Blume adjustment technique outperformed both the unadjusted Betas and the Betas adjusted via the Bayesian technique. The difference in the techniques was statistically significant. However, the Bayesian adjustment technique performed better than the unadjusted Beta in one period and worse in a second. In both cases, the results were statistically significant. This calls for some further analysis. The performance of any forecasting technique is, in part, a function of its forecast of the average correlation between all stocks and, in part, a function of its forecast of previous differences from the

---

[17]It is possible that analysts will be used to subjectively modify historical estimates of Beta to improve their accuracy. Several firms currently use analysts' modified estimates of Beta.

mean. We might stop for a moment and see why each of the Beta techniques might produce forecasts of the average correlation coefficient between all stocks that are different from the average correlation coefficient in the data to which the technique is fitted.

Let us start with the unadjusted Betas. This model assumes that the only correlation between stocks is one due to common correlation with the market. It ignores all other sources of correlation such as industry effects. To the extent that there are other sources of correlation that are, on the whole, positive, this technique will underestimate the average correlation coefficient in the data to which it is fitted. This is exactly what Elton, Gruber, and Urich [31] showed happened in both periods over which the model was fitted.

The Blume technique suffers from the same bias, but it has two additional sources of bias. One is that the Blume technique adjusts all Betas toward one. This tends to raise the average correlation coefficient estimated from the Blume technique. The correlation coefficient is the product of two Betas. To the extent that Betas are reduced to one symmetrically (with no change in mean), the cross products between them will tend to be larger. For example, the product of 1.1 and 0.9 is larger than the product of 1.2 and 0.8. There is another source of potential problems in the Blume technique. Remember that the Blume technique adjusts the Betas in period two for the changes in Betas between period one and two. If the average change in Beta between periods one and two is positive (negative), the Blume technique will adjust the average Beta for period two up (down).[18] In the Elton, Gruber, and Urich study there was an upward drift in Betas over the period studied and this, combined with the tendency of the Blume technique to shrink all Betas toward one, resulted in forecasts of an average correlation coefficient well above the average correlation coefficient for the sample to which the model was fitted.

The Bayesian adjustment to Betas, like the Blume adjustment, has some upward forecast bias because of its tendency to shrink Betas toward one, but it does not continue to project a trend in Betas and, hence, correlation coefficients as the Blume technique does. However, as pointed out earlier, it has a new source of bias: one that tends to pull Betas and correlation coefficients in a downward direction. This occurs because high Beta stocks are adjusted more toward the mean than low Beta stocks.

Short of empirical tests, it is difficult to say whether, given any set of data, the alternative sources of bias, which work in different directions, will increase or decrease the forecast accuracy of the result. We do know that unless there are predictable trends in average correlation coefficient, the effect of these biases on forecast accuracy will be random from period to period. This source of randomness can be eliminated. One way to do it is to force the average correlation coefficient, estimated by each technique, to be the same and to be equal to the average correlation coefficient that existed in the period over which the model was fitted. If correlation coefficients do not have stable trends, this will be an efficient forecast procedure. It uses only available data and is also easy to do.

When the adjustments were made, the Bayesian adjustment produced the most accurate forecasts of the future correlation matrix. Its difference from the Blume technique, the unadjusted Beta, and the historical matrix was statistically significant in all periods tested. The second-ranked technique varied through time with the Blume adjustment, outperforming the unadjusted Beta in one period and the unadjusted Beta outperforming Blume in one period.[19]

---

[18]This would be a desirable property if trends in average correlation coefficients were expected to persist over time, but we see no reason to expect them to do so.

[19]In addition, tests were made that forced the average correlation coefficient from each technique to be the same and equal to the average correlation coefficient that occurred in the forecast period. This is equivalent to perfect foresight with respect to the average correlation coefficient. The rankings were the same as those discussed above when this was done.

The forecasts from the three Beta techniques were compared with the forecasts from a fourth Beta estimate, Beta equals one for all stocks, as well as with the historical correlation matrix, as a forecast of the future. The mean forecast was adjusted to be the same for all techniques. The performance of the historical correlation matrix and the Beta-equals-one model was inferior to the performance of all other models at a statistically significant level.

Let us stop a minute and review the work on estimating Betas. There are two reasons for estimating Betas: The first is in order to forecast future Betas. The second is to generate correlation coefficients as input to the portfolio problem. Empirical evidence strongly suggests that to forecast future Betas one should use either the Bayesian adjustment or the Blume adjustment rather than unadjusted Betas. The evidence on the choice between the Blume and Bayesian adjustment is mixed, but the Bayesian adjustment seems to work slightly better.

If the goal is estimating the future correlation matrix as an input to the portfolio problems, things get more complex. Unadjusted Betas and adjusted Betas, both by the Bayesian and the Blume techniques, all contain potential bias as forecasters of future correlation matrices.[20] The forecasts from all of these techniques can be examined directly or the forecasts can be adjusted to remove bias in the forecast of the average correlation coefficient. The first fact to note is that each of these three estimates of Beta outperforms the historical correlation matrix as a forecast of the future correlation matrix. Second, note that when compared to a Beta of one, all produce better forecasts. The ranking among these three techniques is a function of whether we make the adjustment to the average forecast. Since we believe it is appropriate to do so, we find that the Bayesian adjustment technique performs best.

Recently, attempts have been made to incorporate more data than past return information into the forecasts of Betas. We will now take a brief look at some of the work that has been done in this area.

Fundamental Betas

Beta is a risk measure that arises from the relationship between the return on a stock and the return on the market. However, we know that the risk of a firm should be determined by some combination of the firm's fundamentals and the market characteristics of the firm's stock. If these relationships could be determined, they would help us both to better understand Betas and to better forecast Betas.

One of the earliest attempts to relate the Beta of a stock to fundamental firm variables was performed by Beaver, Kettler, and Scholes [7]. They examined the relationship between seven firm variables and the Beta on a company's stock. The seven variables they used were

1. Dividend payout (dividends divided by earnings).
2. Asset growth (annual change in total assets).
3. Leverage (senior securities divided by total assets).
4. Liquidity (current assets divided by current liabilities).
5. Asset size (total assets).
6. Earning variability (standard deviation of the earnings price ratio).
7. Accounting Beta (the Beta that arises from a time series regression of the earnings of the firm against average earnings for the economy, often called the earnings Beta).

---

[20]As discussed earlier, a smaller set of potential biases is present when Betas are estimated.

An examination of these variables would lead us to expect a negative relationship between dividend payout and Beta under one of two arguments:

1. Since management is more reluctant to cut dividends than raise them, high payout is indicative of confidence on the part of management concerning the level of future earnings.

2. Dividend payments are less risky than capital gains; hence, the company that pays out more of its earnings in dividends is less risky.

Growth is usually thought of as positively associated with Beta. High-growth firms are thought of as more risky than low-growth firms.

Leverage tends to increase the volatility of the earnings stream, hence to increase risk and Beta.

A firm with high liquidity is thought to be less risky than one with low liquidity and, hence, liquidity should be negatively related to market Beta.

Large firms are often thought to be less risky than small firms, if for no other reason than that they have better access to the capital markets. Hence, they should have lower Betas.

Finally, the more variable a company's earning stream and the more highly correlated it is with the market, the higher its Beta should be.

Table 7.5 reports some of the results from the Beaver et al. [7] study. Note all variables had the sign that we expected.

The next logical step in developing fundamental Betas is to incorporate the effects of relevant fundamental variables simultaneously into the analysis. This is usually done by relating Beta to several fundamental variables via multiple regression analysis.

An equation of the following form is estimated:

$$\beta_i = a_0 + a_1 X_1 + a_2 X_2 + \cdots + a_N X_N + e_i \tag{7.6}$$

where each X_i is one of the N variables hypothesized as affecting Beta. Several studies have been performed that link Beta to a set of fundamental variables, such as that studied by Beaver et al. [7].[21] The list of variables that has been studied and linked to Betas is too long to review here. For example, Thompson [91] reviews 43 variables while Rosenberg [79]

Table 7.5   Correlation between Accounting Measures of Risk and Market Beta

Variable	Period 1 1947–1956		Period 2 1957–1965	
	One-Stock Portfolio	Five-Stock Portfolio	One-Stock Portfolio	Five-Stock Portfolio
Payout	−0.50	−0.77	−0.24	−0.45
Growth	0.23	0.51	0.03	0.07
Leverage	0.23	0.45	0.25	0.56
Liquidity	−0.13	−0.44	−0.01	−0.01
Size	−0.07	−0.13	−0.16	−0.30
Earnings variability	0.58	0.77	0.36	0.62
Earnings Beta	0.39	0.67	0.23	0.46

[21]For examples of the use of fundamental data to estimate Betas, see [40], [63], [67], [78], [79], and [91]. The ability of fundamental data to aid in the prediction of future Betas has been mixed. Some studies find large improvements in forecasting ability while others do not.

reviews 101. Rather than discuss the long list of variables that has been used to generate fundamental Betas, let us review the relative strengths and weaknesses of fundamental and historical Betas as well as one system, that proposed by Barr Rosenberg [76–79], which has been put forth to combine both types of Betas.

The advantage of Betas based on historical return data is that they measure the response of each stock to market movements. The disadvantage of this type of Beta is that it reflects changes in the size or importance of company characteristics only after a long period of time has passed. For example, assume a company increased its debt-to-equity ratio. We would expect its Beta to increase. However, if we are using 60 months of return data to estimate Beta, one month after the company increased its debt-to-equity ratio, only one of the 60 data points will reflect the new information. Thus, the change in debt-to-equity ratio would have only a very minor impact on the Beta computed from historical return data. Similarly, one full year after the event only 12 of the 60 data points used to measure Beta will reflect the event.

On the other hand, fundamental Betas respond quickly to a change in the companies' characteristics since they are computed directly from these characteristics. However, the weakness of fundamental Betas is that they are computed under the assumption that the responsiveness of all Betas to an underlying fundamental variable is the same. For example, they assume that the Beta for IBM will change in exactly the same way with a given change in its debt-to-equity ratio as will the Beta of General Motors (GM).[22]

By combining the techniques of historical Betas and fundamental Betas into one system, Barr Rosenberg hopes to gain the advantages of each without being subject to the disadvantages of either. In addition, because Rosenberg and McKibben [78] found that there were persistent differences between the Betas of different industries, Rosenberg and Marathe [79] introduced a set of industry dummy variables into the analysis to capture these differences. Rosenberg's system can be described as follows:[23]

$$\beta_i = a_0 + a_1 x_1 + a_2 x_2 + a_3 x_3 + \cdots + a_7 x_7 + a_8 x_8 + \cdots + a_{46} x_{46} \tag{7.7}$$

where

x_1 represents 14 descriptions of market variability. These 14 descriptions include historical values of Beta as well as other market characteristics of the stock such as share trading, volume, and stock price range.

x_2 represents seven descriptors of earnings variability. These descriptors include measures of earnings variability, earnings Betas, and measures of the unpredictability of earnings such as the amount of extraordinary earnings reported.

x_3 represents eight descriptors of unsuccess and low valuation. These descriptors include growth in earnings, the ratio of book value to stock price, relative strength, and other indicators of perceived success.

x_4 represents nine descriptors of immaturity and smallness. These descriptors include total assets, market share, and other indicators of size and age.

x_5 represents nine descriptors of growth orientation. These descriptors include dividend yield, earnings price ratios, and other measures of historical and perceived growth.

---

[22]Each of the regression coefficients of Equation (7.6) (e.g., a_1) has only one value for all firms. This means that a change of 1 unit in X_1 will change the Beta of every firm by a_1 units.

[23]Rosenberg changes the variables in his system over time. This description is based on his system as it existed at a point in time as described in [79].

x_6 represents nine descriptors of financial risk. These include measures of leverage, interest coverage, and liquidity.

x_7 represents six descriptors of firm characteristics. These include indicators of stock listings and broad types of business.

x_8 through x_{46} are industry dummy variables. These variables allow the fact that different industries tend to have different Betas, all other variables held constant, to be taken into account.

While conceptually the Rosenberg technique is easy to grasp, the multitude of variables (101) makes it difficult to grasp the meaning of the parameterized model. The reason for moving to this complex model is to improve forecasting ability. While the model is too new for extensive testing to have been performed, Rosenberg and Marathe's [79] initial testing indicates that the model involving both fundamental data and historical Betas leads to better estimates of future Betas than the use of either type of estimate in isolation.

Before ending this chapter, we should mention one more type of model that is beginning to attract attention. The Rosenberg system quickly reflects changes in Beta that have occurred because it uses data that reflect present conditions (fundamental firm variables) to modify historical Betas as forecasts of the future. A more ideal system would employ forecasts of future fundamental firm variables to modify historical estimates of Beta—in other words, substitute estimates of future values on the right-hand side of Equation (7.7) rather than concurrent values. Now it seems unlikely that analysts can do this for the 101 variables used in Rosenberg's system. However, simpler systems employing a much smaller number of variables are being used in this way.

THE MARKET MODEL

Although the single-index model was developed to aid in portfolio management, a less restrictive form of it—known as the market model—has found increased usage in finance. The market model is identical to the single-index model except that the assumption that $\text{cov}(e_i e_j) = 0$ is not made.[24]

The model starts with the simpler linear relationship of returns and the market

$$R_i = \alpha_i + \beta_i R_m + e_i$$

and produces an expected value for any stock of

$$\bar{R}_i = \alpha_i + \beta_i \bar{R}_m$$

Since it does not make the assumption that all covariances between stocks are due to a common covariance with the market, however, it does not lead to the simple expressions of portfolio risk that arise under the single-index model.

We will meet the market model again as we progress through this book. It is used extensively in the efficient market chapter. The point to keep in mind is that the discussion of estimating Beta is equally as applicable whether we are talking about the market model or the single-index model.

---

[24]Actually, although the single-index model can be defined in terms of any influence (e.g., the rate of return on liverwurst), we usually think of the index as the rate of return on some market portfolio. The market model is always defined in terms of a market portfolio.

AN EXAMPLE

A manager of a large pension fund will often utilize several domestic stock managers. The pension fund sponsor (manager) can view the asset allocation problem as equivalent to selecting among various stock mutual funds. The data for the portfolios being considered by a large pension fund are as follows:

NAME		α_I	β_i	σ^2_{ei}
1.	Small stock	6	1.4	65
2.	Value	4	0.8	20
3.	Growth	4.5	1.3	45
4.	Large capitalization	0.8	0.90	24
5.	Special situation	0.2	1.1	45

The Alphas, Betas, and residual risks were initially computed by running a regression of each fund's return on the return of the S&P index using five years of monthly returns. These estimates were then modified by the plan sponsor to reflect their beliefs. Management projected that the S&P index at this point had an expected return of 12.5% and an estimated standard deviation of return of 14.9%. The expected returns, standard deviations of return, and covariance using the single-index model are

$$\overline{R}_1 = 6 + 1.4(12.5) = 23.5$$

$$\overline{R}_2 = 4 + 0.8(12.5) = 14$$

$$\overline{R}_3 = 4.5 + 1.3(12.5) = 20.75$$

$$\overline{R}_4 = 0.8 + 0.9(12.5) = 12.05$$

$$\overline{R}_5 = 0.2 + 1.1(12.5) = 13.95$$

$$\sigma_1 = \left[(1.4)^2(14.9)^2 + 65\right]^{1/2} = 22.36$$

$$\sigma_2 = \left[(0.8)^2(14.9)^2 + 20\right]^{1/2} = 12.73$$

$$\sigma_3 = \left[(1.3)^2(14.9)^2 + 45\right]^{1/2} = 20.5$$

$$\sigma_4 = \left[(.90)^2(14.9)^2 + 24\right]^{1/2} = 14.28$$

$$\sigma_5 = \left[(1.1)^2(14.9)^2 + 45\right]^{1/2} = 17.71$$

$$\sigma_{12} = (1.4)(0.8)(14.9)^2 = 249$$

$$\sigma_{13} = (1.4)(1.3)(14.9)^2 = 404$$

$$\sigma_{14} = (1.4)(0.9)(14.9)^2 = 280$$

$$\sigma_{15} = (1.4)(1.1)(14.9)^2 = 342$$

$$\sigma_{23} = 231$$

$$\sigma_{24} = 160$$

$$\sigma_{25} = 195$$

$$\sigma_{34} = 260$$

$$\sigma_{35} = 317$$

$$\sigma_{45} = 220$$

These estimates for portfolio inputs are not necessarily the same as would be obtained from historical data. However, the Betas for fund 1 and 2 were the historical betas using the prior five years of data. Thus if the covariance between the residuals for fund 1 and 2 were zero, the estimate of the covariance using the single-index model and the historical estimate would be the same. The covariance between assets 1 and 2 computed directly from the historical data was 271. The estimate from the single-index model was 249. The difference arose because there was a small positive correlation between residuals for fund 1 and fund 2. The justification for using the single-index model to estimate inputs is a belief that this positive residual resulted by chance and zero is a better estimate of its future value than the actual past value. The optimum proportions using these inputs, a riskless rate of 5%, and the procedures discussed in Chapter 6 are

FUND A	WITH SHORT SALES	NO SHORT SALES
1	6926%	78%
2	5797%	0
3	4218%	22%
4	−10,143%	0
5	−5797%	0

The solution with short sales is of course unreasonable both because pension managers cannot short sell and because of the magnitude of the numbers. The large numbers come about because mutual funds are very highly correlated with one another and small differences result in large positions being taken. In Chapter 9 we will analyze the problem when we have developed the tools for a simpler analysis.

QUESTIONS AND PROBLEMS

1. Monthly return data are presented below for each of three stocks and the S&P index (corrected for dividends) for a 12-month period. Calculate the following quantities:

    A. Alpha for each stock
    B. Beta for each stock
    C. The standard deviation of the residuals from each regression
    D. The correlation coefficient between each security and the market
    E. The average return on the market
    F. The variance of the market

	Security			
Month	A	B	C	S&P
1	12.05	25.20	31.67	12.28
2	15.27	2.86	15.82	5.99
3	−4.12	5.45	10.58	2.41
4	1.57	4.56	−14.43	4.48
5	3.16	3.72	31.98	4.41
6	−2.79	10.79	−0.72	4.43
7	−8.97	5.38	−19.64	−6.77
8	−1.18	−2.97	−10.00	−2.11
9	1.07	1.52	−11.51	3.46
10	12.75	10.75	5.63	6.16
11	7.48	3.79	−4.67	2.47
12	−0.94	1.32	7.94	−1.15

2. **A.** Compute the mean return and variance of return for each stock in Problem 1
    using

    (1) The single-index model.

    (2) The historical data.

    B. Compute the covariance between each possible pair of stocks using

    (1) The single-index model.

    (2) The historical data.

    C. Compute the return and standard deviation of a portfolio constructed by placing
    one-third of your funds in each stock, using

    (1) The single-index model.

    (2) The historical data.

    D. Explain why the answers to parts A.1 and A.2 were the same, while the answers
    to parts B.1, B.2 and C.1, C.2 were different.

3. Show that the Vasicek technique leads to a simple proportional weighting of the market Beta and the stock's Beta if the standard error of all Betas is the same.

4. **A.** If the Blume adjustment equation is fit and the appropriate equation is

    $$\beta_{it+1} = 0.41 + 0.60\beta_{i,t}$$

    what is your best forecast of Beta for each of the stocks in Question 1?

    B. If the parameters of the Vasicek technique are fit, and they are

    $$\sigma_{\bar{\beta}1}^2 = 0.25, \quad \sigma_{\beta1A}^2 = 0.22,$$

    $$\beta_1 = 1.00$$

    $$\sigma_{\beta1B}^2 = 0.36, \quad \sigma_{\beta1C}^2 = 0.41$$

    what is your best forecast of Beta for each of the stocks in Question 1?

5.

	Security			
	A	B	C	D
α	2	3	1	4
β	1.5	1.3	.8	.9
σ_{ei}	3	1	2	4

Given the data above and the fact that $\bar{R}_m = 8$ and $\sigma_m = 5$, calculate the following:

(a) The mean return for each security.

(b) The variance of each security's return.

(c) The covariance of returns between each security.

6. Using the data in Problem 5 and assuming an equally weighted portfolio, calculate the
    following:

    (a) β_p

    (b) α_p

    (c) σ_p^2

    (d) $\bar{R}_p$

7. Using Blume's technique where $\beta_{i2} = 0.343 + 0.677\beta_{i1}$ calculate β_{i2} for the securities in Problem 5.

8. Suppose $\bar{\beta}_1 = 1$ and $\sigma_{\bar{\beta}1} = 0.25$ $\sigma_{\beta A} = 0.21$ $\sigma_{\beta B} = 0.32$ $\sigma_{\beta C} = 0.18$ $\sigma_{\beta D} = 0.20$, forecast each security's Beta using the Vasicek technique.

BIBLIOGRAPHY

1. Alexander, Gordon J., and Benston, P. George. "More on Beta as a Random Coefficient," *Journal of Financial and Quantitative Analysis*, **XVII,** No. 1 (March 1982), pp. 27–36.
2. Alexander, Gordon J., and Chervany, Norman L. "On the Estimation and Stability of Beta," *Journal of Financial and Quantitative Analysis*, **XV,** No. 1 (March 1980), pp. 123–138.
3. Ali, Mukhtar M., and Giaccotto, Carmelo. "Optimum Distribution-Free Tests and Further Evidence of Heteroscedasticity in the Market Model," *Journal of Finance*, **37,** No. 5 (Dec. 1982), pp. 1247–1258.
4. Altman, Edward, Jacquillat, Bertram, and Levasseur, Michael. "Comparative Analysis of Risk Measures: France and the United States," *Journal of Finance*, **IX,** No. 5 (Dec. 1974), pp. 1495–1511.
5. Baesel, Jerome. "On the Assessment of Risk: Some Further Consideations," *Journal of Finance*, **IX,** No. 5 (Dec. 1976), pp. 1491–1494.
6. Barry, Christopher, and Winkler, Robert. "Nonstationarity and Portfolio Choice," *Journal of Financial and Quantitative Analysis*, **XI,** No. 2 (June 1976), pp. 217–235.
7. Beaver, W., Kettler, P., and Scholes, M. "The Association Between Market Determined and Accounting Determined Risk Measures," *The Accounting Review*, **45** (Oct. 1970), pp. 654–682.
8. Beja, Avraham. "On Systematic and Unsystematic Components of Financial Risk," *Journal of Finance*, **VII,** No. 1 (March 1972), pp. 37–45.
9. Bey, Roger P., and Pinches, George E. "Additional Evidence of Heteroscedasticity in the Market Model," *Journal of Financial and Quantitative Analysis*, **XV,** No. 2 (June 1980), pp. 299–322.
10. Bick, Avi. "On Viable Diffusion Price Processes of the Market Portfolio," *Journal of Finance*, **45,** No. 2 (June 1990), pp. 673–680.
11. Bickler, J. L. "Comment: on [51]," *Journal of Financial and Quantitative Analysis*, **IX,** No. 2 (March 1974), pp. 277–230.
12. Bildersee, John S., and Roberts, Gordon S. "Beta Instability When Interest Rate Levels Change," *Journal of Financial and Quantitative Analysis*, **XVI,** No. 3 (Sept. 1981), pp. 375–380.
13. Blume, Marchall. "Portfolio Theory: A Step Toward Its Practical Application," *Journal of Business*, **43,** No. 2 (April 1970), pp. 152–173.
14. ——. "On the Assessment of Risk," *Journal of Finance*, **VI,** No. 1 (March 1971), pp. 1–10.
15. ——. "Betas and Their Regression Tendencies," *Journal of Finance*, **X,** No. 3 (June 1975), pp. 785–795.
16. Breen, William. "Homogeneous Risk Measures and the Construction of Composite Assets," *Journal of Financial and Quantitative Analysis*, **III,** No. 4 (Dec. 1968), pp. 405–413.
17. Brenner, Menachem, and Smidt, Seymour. "A Simple Model of Non-Stationarity of Systematic Risk," *Journal of Finance*, **XII,** No. 4 (Sept. 1977), pp. 1081–1092.
18. Brenner, Menachem. "On the Stability of the Distribution of the Market Component in Stock Price Changes," *Journal of Financial and Quantitative Analysis*, **IX,** No. 6 (Dec. 1974), pp. 945–961.
19. Brown, Steve. "Heteroscedasticity in the Market Model: A Comment on [61]," *Journal of Business*, **50,** No. 1 (January 1977), pp. 80–83.
20. Carleton, Willard T., and Lakonishok, Josef. "Risk and Return on Equity: The Use and Misuse of Historical Estimates," *Financial Analysts Journal*, **41,** No. 1 (Jan./Feb. 1985), pp. 38–47.
21. Chan, Louis, K. C. "The Risk and Return from Factors," *Journal of Financial and Quantitative Analysis*, Seattle, **33,** No. 2 (June 1998), pp. 159–189.

22. Chen, Son-Nan. "Beta Nonstationarity, Portfolio Residual Risk and Diversification," *Journal of Financial and Quantitative Analysis*, **XVI,** No. 1 (March 1981), pp. 95–112.

23. ——. "An Examination of Risk-Return Relationship in Bull and Bear Markets Using Time-Varying Betas," *Journal of Financial and Quantitative Analysis*, **XVII,** No. 2 (June 1982), pp. 265–286.

24. Cohen, K., Maier, S., Schwartz, R., and Whitecomb, D. "The Returns Generation Process, Returns Variance, and the Effect of Thinness in Security Markets," *Journal of Finance*, **XIII,** No. 1 (March 1978), pp. 149–167.

25. ——. "Limit Orders, Market Structure, and the Returns Generation Process," *Journal of Finance*, **XIII,** No. 3 (June 1978), pp. 723–736.

26. Cohen, Kalman, Ness, Walter, Okuda, Hitashi, Schwartz, Robert, and Whitcomb, David. "The Determinants of Common Stock Returns Volatility: An International Comparison," *Journal of Finance*, **XI,** No. 2 (May 1976), pp. 733–740.

27. Cooley, P., Roenfeldt, R., and Modani, N. "Interdependence of Market Risk Measures," *Journal of Business*, **50,** No. 3 (July 1977), pp. 356–363.

28. Cornell, Bradford, and Dietrich, Kimball, "Mean-Absolute-Deviation versus Least-Squares Regression Estimation of Beta Coefficients," *Journal of Financial and Quantitative Analysis*, **XIII,** No. 1 (March 1978), pp. 123–131.

29. Dickinson, J. P. "The Reliability of Estimation Procedures in Portfolio Analysis," *Journal of Financial and Quantitative Analysis*, **IX,** No. 3 (June 1974), pp., 447–462.

30. Dimson, Elroy, and Marsh, P. "The Stability of UK Risk Measures and the Problem in Thin Trading," *Journal of Finance*, **38,** No. 3 (June 1983), pp. 753–784.

31. Elton, Edwin J., Gruber, Martin J., and Urich, Thomas. "Are Betas Best?" *Journal of Finance*, **XIII,** No. 5 (Dec. 1978), pp. 1375–1384.

32. Fabozzi, Frank, and Francis, Clark. "Stability Tests for Alphas and Betas over Bull and Bear Market Conditions," *Journal of Finance*, **XII,** No. 4 (Sept. 1977), pp. 1093–1099.

33. ——. "Beta as a Random Coefficient," *Journal of Financial and Quantitative Analysis*, **XIII,** No. 1 (March 1978), pp. 101–116.

34. Fama, Eugene. "Risk, Return, and Equilibrium: Some Clarifying Comments," *Journal of Finance*, **23** (March 1968), pp. 29–40.

35. Fielitz, Bruce. "Stationarity of Random Data: Some Implications for the Distribution of Stock Price Changes," *Journal of Financial and Quantitative Analysis*, **VI,** No. 3 (June 1971), pp. 1025–1034.

36. Fouse, W., Jahnke, W., and Rosenberg, B. "Is Beta Phlogiston?" *Financial Analysts Journal*, **30,** No. 1 (Jan.–Feb. 1974), pp. 70–80.

37. Frankfurter, George, and Phillips, H. "Alpha-Beta Theory: A Word of Caution," *Journal of Financial Management*, **3,** No. 4 (Summer 1977), pp. 35–40.

38. Frankfurter, George, Phillips, Hervert, and Seagle, John. "Performance of the Sharpe Portfolio Selection Model: A Comparison," *Journal of Financial and Quantitative Analysis*, **XI,** No. 2 (June 1976), pp. 195–204.

39. Francis, Jack Clark. "Intertemporal Differences in Systematic Stock Price Movements," *Journal of Financial and Quantitative Analysis*, **X,** No. 2 (June 1975), pp. 205–219.

40. Gonedes, Nicholas J. "Evidence on the Information Content of Accounting Numbers: Accounting-based and Market-based Estimates of Systematic Risk," *Journal of Financial and Quantitative Analysis*, **8** (June 1973), pp. 407–443.

41. Gooding, Arthur, and O'Malley, Terence. "Market Phase and the Stationarity of Beta," *Journal of Financial and Quantitative Analysis*, **XII,** No. 4 (Dec. 1977), pp. 833–857.

42. Gordon, Edward. "Comment: on [67]," *Journal of Financial and Quantitative Analysis*, **IX,** No. 2 (March 1974), pp. 234–245.

43. Hamada, S. Robert. "The Effect of the Firm's Capital Structure on the Systematic Risk of Common Stocks," *Journal of Finance*, **VII,** No. 2 (May 1971), pp. 435–452.

44. Handa, Puneet, Kothari, S. P., and Wasley, Charles. "The Relation Between the Return Interval and Betas: Implications for the Size Effect," *Journal of Financial Economics*, Amsterdam, **23,** No. 1 (June 1989), pp. 79–101.

45. Hasty, John, and Fielitz, Bruce. "Systematic Risk for Heterogeneous Time Horizons," *Journal of Finance*, **X**, No. 2 (May 1975), pp. 659–673.

46. Hawawini, Gabriel A. "Intertemporal Cross-Dependence in Securities Daily Returns and the Short-Run Intervaling Effect on Systematic Risk," *Journal of Financial and Quantitative Analysis*, **XV**, No. 1 (March 1980), pp. 139–150.

47. ———. "An Analytical Examination of the Intervaling Effect on Skewness and Other Moments," *Journal of Financial and Quantitative Analysis*, **XV**, No. 5 (Dec. 1980), pp. 1121–1128.

48. Hawawini, Gabriel A., and Vora, Ashok. "Evidence of Intertemporal Systematic Risks in the Daily Price Movements of NYSE and AMEX Common Stocks," *Journal of Financial and Quantitative Analysis*, **XV**, No. 2 (June 1980), pp. 331–340.

49. Hawawini, Gabriel A., Michel, Pierre A., and Corhay, Albert. "New Evidence on Beta Stationarity and Forecasting for Belgium Common Stocks," *Journal of Business Finance*, **9**, No. 4 (December 1985), pp. 553–560.

50. Hill, Ned C., and Stone, Bernell K. "Accounting Betas, Systematic Operating Risk, and Financial Leverage: A Risk-Composition Approach to the Determinants of Systematic Risk," *Journal of Financial and Quantitative Analysis*, **XV**, No. 3 (Sept. 1980), pp. 595–638.

51. Hsu, D. A. "The Behavior of Stock Returns: Is it Stationary or Evolutionary?" *Journal of Financial and Quantitative Analysis*, **19**, No. 1 (March 1984), pp. 11–28.

52. Jacob, Nancy. "The Measurement of Systematic Risk for Securities and Portfolios: Some Empirical Results," *Journal of Financial and Quantitative Analysis*, **VI**, No. 2 (March 1971), pp. 815–833.

53. ———. "Comment on [23]," *Journal of Financial and Quantitative Analysis*, **VIII**, No. 2 (March 1973), pp. 351–354.

54. Joehnk, Michael, and Nielsen, James. "The Effects of Conglomerate Merger Activity on Systematic Risk," *Journal of Financial and Quantitative Analysis*, **IX**, No. 2 (March 1974), pp. 215–225.

55. Johnson, James, and Baesel, Jerome. "The Nature and Significance of Trend Betas," *Journal of Financial Management*, **4**, No. 3 (Spring 1978), pp. 36–40.

56. Klemkosky, Robert, and Martin, John. "The Effect of Market Risk on Portfolio Diversification," *Journal of Finance*, **X**, No. 1 (March 1975), pp. 147–153.

57. ———. "The Adjustment of Beta Forecasts," *Journal of Finance*, **X**, No. 4 (Sept. 1975), pp. 1123–1128.

58. Latane, Henry, Tuttle, Don, and Young, Allan. "How to Choose a Market Index," *Financial Analysts Journal*, **27**, No. 4 (Sept.–Oct. 1971), pp. 75–85.

59. Lee, Cheng. "On the Relationship Between the Systematic Risk and the Investment Horizon," *Journal of Financial and Quantitative Analysis*, **XI**, No. 5 (Dec. 1976), pp. 803–815.

60. Levy, Haim. "Measuring Risk and Performance over Alternative Investment Horizons," *Financial Analysts Journal*, **40**, No. 2 (March/April 1984), pp. 61–67.

61. Levy, Robert. "On the Short-Term Stationarity of Beta Coefficients," *Financial Analysts Journal*, **27**, No. 5 (Dec. 1971), pp. 55–62.

62. ———. "Beta Coefficients as Predictors of Return," *Financial Analysts Journal*, **30**, No. 1 (Jan.–Feb. 1974), pp. 61–69.

63. Logue, Dennis, and Merville, Larry. "Financial Policy and Market Expectations," *Financial Management*, **1** (Summer 1972), pp. 37–44.

64. Martin, John, and Keown, Arthur. "A Misleading Feature of Beta for Risk Measurement," *Journal of Financial Management*, **3**, No. 4 (Summer 1977), pp. 31–34.

65. Martin J., and Klemkosky, R. "Evidence of Heteroscedasticity in the Market Model," *Journal of Business*, **48**, No. 1 (Jan. 1975), pp. 81–86.

66. McDonald, Bill. "Beta Nonstationarity and the Use of the Chen and Lee Estimator: A Note," *The Journal of Finance*, **38**, No. 3 (June 1983), pp. 1005–1010.

67. Melicher, Ronald. "Financial Factors which Influence Beta Variations within an Homogeneous Industry Environment," *Journal of Financial and Quantitative Analysis*, **IX**, No. 2 (March 1974), pp. 231–241.

68. Officer, R. R. "The Variability of the Market Factor of the New York Stock Exchange," *Journal of Business*, **46,** No. 3 (July 1973), p. 434.

69. Owen, Joel, and Rabinovitch, Ramon. "The Cost of Information and Equilibrium in the Capital Asset Market," *Journal of Financial and Quantitative Analysis*, **XV,** No. 3 (Sept. 1980), pp. 497–508.

70. Pinches, E. George, and Kinney, R. William, Jr. "The Measurement of the Volatility of Common Stock Prices," *Journal of Finance*, **VI,** No. 1 (March 1971), pp. 119–125.

71. Pogue, Gerald, and Solnik, Bruno. "The Market Model Applied to European Common Stocks: Some Empirical Results," *Journal of Financial and Quantitative Analysis*, **IX,** No. 6 (Dec. 1974), pp. 917–944.

72. Rentz, William, and Vandenberg, Pieteo. "The Impact of Changes in Trading Location on a Security's Systematic Risk," *Journal of Financial and Quantitative Analysis*, **X,** No. 5 (Dec. 1975), pp. 881–890.

73. Robichek, Alexander, and Cohn, Richard. "The Economic Determinants of Systematic Risk," *Journal of Finance*, **XXIX,** No. 2 (May 1974), pp. 439–447.

74. Roenfeldt, R., Griepentrog, G., and Pflaum, C. "Further Evidence on the Stationarity of Beta Coefficients," *Journal of Financial and Quantitative Analysis*, **XIII,** No. 1 (March 1978), pp. 117–121.

75. Roll, Richard. "Bias in Fitting the Sharpe Model to Time Series Data," *Journal of Financial and Quantitative Analysis*, **IV,** No. 3 (Sept. 1969), pp. 271–289.

76. Rosenberg, Barr, and Guy, James. "Prediction of Beta from Investment Fundamentals," *Financial Analysts Journal*, **32,** No. 3 (May–June 1976), pp. 60–72.

77. ——. "Prediction of ...: Part II," *Financial Analysts Journal*, **32,** No. 3 (July–Aug. 1976), pp. 62–70.

78. Rosenberg, Barr, and McKibben, Walt. "The Prediction of Systematic and Specific Risk in Common Stocks," *Journal of Financial and Quantitative Analysis*, **VIII,** No. 2 (March 1973), pp. 317–333.

79. Rosenberg, Barr, and Marathe, Vinary. "The Prediction of Investment Risk: Systematic and Residual Risk," Reprint 21, Berkeley Working Paper Series.

80. Rudd, Andrew, and Rosenberg, Barr. "The 'Market Model' in Investment Management," *The Journal of Finance*, **35,** No. 2 (May 1980), pp. 597–606.

81. Schaefer, Stephen, Brealey, Richard, and Hodges, Steward. "Alternative Models of Systematic Risk," in Edwin J. Elton and Martin J. Gruber (eds.), *International Capital Markets* (Amsterdam: North-Holland, 1976).

82. Scheller, Meir I. "Are Better Betas Worth the Trouble?" *Financial Analysts Journal*, **39**, No. 4 (July/Aug. 1983), pp. 74–77.

83. Schmalensee, Richard, and Trippi, Robert. "Common Stock Volatility Expectations Implied by Option Premi," *Journal of Finance*, **XIII,** No. 1 (March 1978), pp. 129–147.

84. Schneller, Meir. "Regression Analysis for Multiplicative Phenomenon and Its Implications for the Measurement of Investment Risk," *Management Science*, **2,** No. 4 (Dec. 1975), pp. 422–426.

85. Scholes, M., and Williams, J. "Estimating Betas from Non-Synchronous Data," *Journal of Financial Economics*, **5,** No. 3 (Dec. 1977), pp. 309–328.

86. Scott, Elton, and Brown, Stewart. "Biased Estimators and Unstable Betas," *The Journal of Finance*, **35,** No. 1 (March 1980), pp. 49–56.

87. Sharpe, William. "Mean-Absolute-Deviation Characteristic Lines for Securities and Portfolios," *Management Science*, **18,** No. 2 (Oct. 1971), pp. B1–B13.

88. Smith, Keith. "Stock Price and Economic Indexes for Generating Efficient Portfolios," *Journal of Business*, **42,** No. 3 (July 1969), pp. 226–326.

89. Sunder, Shyam. "Stationarity of Market Risk: Random Coefficients Tests for Individual Stocks," *Journal of Finance*, **35,** No. 4 (Sept. 1980), pp. 883–896.

90. Theobald, Michael. "Beta Stationarity and Estimation Period: Some Analytical Results," *Journal of Financial and Quantitative Analysis*, **XVI,** No. 5 (Dec. 1981), pp. 747–758.

91. Thompson II, Donald. "Sources of Systematic Risk in Common Stocks," *Journal of Business*, **40,** No. 2 (April 1978), pp. 173–188.
92. Vasicek, Oldrich. "A Note on Using Cross-Sectional Information in Bayesian Estimation of Security Betas," *Journal of Finance*, **VIII,** No. 5 (Dec. 1973), pp. 1233–1239.
93. Young, S. David, Berry, Michael A., Harvey, David W., and Page, John R. "Macroeconomic Forces, Systematic Risk, and Financial Variables: An Empirical Investigation," *Journal of Financial and Quantitative Analysis*, Seattle, **26,** No. 4 (Dec. 1991), pp. 559–565.

8

The Correlation Structure of Security Returns

MULTI-INDEX MODELS AND GROUPING TECHNIQUES

In Chapter 7 we argued that because of both the huge number of forecasts required and the necessary restrictions on the organizational structure of security analysts, it was not feasible for analysts to directly estimate correlation coefficients. Instead, some structural or behavioral model of how stocks move together should be developed. The parameters of this model can be estimated either from historical data or by attempting to get subjective estimates from security analysts. We have already examined one such model, the single-index model, which assumes that stocks move together only because of a common co-movement with the market. There are two other approaches that have been widely used to explain and estimate the correlation structure of security returns: multi-index models and averaging techniques.

Multi-index models are an attempt to capture some of the nonmarket influences that cause securities to move together. The search for nonmarket influences is a search for a set of economic factors or structural groups (industries) that account for common movement in stock prices beyond that accounted for by the market index itself. While it is easy to find a set of indexes that is associated with nonmarket effects over any period of time, as we will see, it is quite another matter to find a set that is successful in predicting covariances that are not market related.

Averaging techniques are at the opposite end of the spectrum from multi-index models. Multi-index models introduce extra indexes in the hope of capturing additional information. The cost of introducing additional indexes is the chance that they are picking up random noise rather than real influences. Averaging techniques smooth the entries in the historical correlation matrix in an attempt to "damp out" random noise and so produce better forecasts. The potential disadvantage of averaging models is that real information may be lost in the averaging process.

In this chapter we examine both multi-index models and averaging models. Several of the models put forth in the finance literature are discussed as well as some of the empirical evidence on their relative merits.

At this point, we should mention that there are other uses for multi-index models besides predicting correlation coefficients. Multi-index models can be used to form expectations about returns and study the impact of events, as a method for tailoring the return distribution of a portfolio to the specific needs of an investor, and as a method for attributing the cause of good or bad performance on a portfolio. These are subjects which we will return to later in the book. However, the reader should be alerted to these other possible uses. We will close this chapter with a discussion of some multi-index models using fundamental data that have recently been developed as a step toward building a general equilibrium model of security returns. We will return to this class of model in Chapter 16.

MULTI-INDEX MODELS

The assumption underlying the single-index model is that stock prices move together only because of common movement with the market. Many researchers have found that there are influences beyond the market that cause stocks to move together. For example, as early as 1966, King [43] presented evidence on the existence of industry influences. Two different types of schemes have been put forth for handling additional influences. We have called them the general multi-index model and the industry index model.

General Multi-Index Models

Any additional sources of covariance between securities can be introduced into the equations for risk and return, simply by adding these additional influences to the general return equation. Let us hypothesize that the return on any stock is a function of the return on the market, changes in the level of interest rates, and a set of industry indexes. If R_i is the return on stock i, then the return on stock i can be related to the influences that affect its return in the following way:

$$R_i = a_i^* + b_{i1}^* I_1^* + b_{i2}^* I_2^* + \cdots + b_{iL}^* I_L^* + c_i$$

In this equation I_j^* is the actual level of index j, b_{ij}^* is a measure of the responsiveness of the return on stock i to changes in the index j. Thus, b_{ij}^* has the same meaning as β_i in the case of the single-index model. A b_{ij}^* of 2 would mean that if the index increased (decreased) by 1%, the stock's return is expected to increase (decrease) by 2%. As in the case of the single-index model, the return of the security not related to indexes is split into two parts; a_i^* and c_i. a_i^* is the expected value of the unique return. This is the same meaning it had in the single-index model. c_i is the random component of the unique return. It has a mean of zero and a variance we will designate as σ_{ci}^2.

While a multi-index model of this type can be employed directly, the model would have some very convenient mathematical properties if the indexes were uncorrelated (orthogonal). This would allow us to simplify both the computation of risk and the selection of optimal portfolios. Fortunately, this presents no theoretical problems because it is always possible to take any set of correlated indexes and convert them into a set of uncorrelated indexes. The method for doing so is outlined in Appendix A. Using this methodology, the equation can be rewritten as[1]

$$R_i = a_i + b_{i1} I_1 + b_{i2} I_2 + b_{i3} I_3 + \cdots + b_{iL} I_L + c_i$$

where all I_j are uncorrelated with each other. The new indexes still have an economic interpretation. Assume I_1^* was a stock market index and I_2^* an index of interest rates. I_2 is now an index of the difference between actual interest rates and the level of interest rates that

---

[1]The asterisks have been removed to indicate that the indexes and coefficients are now different. Actually, if the procedure in Appendix A at the end of this chapter is followed, $I_1 = I_1^*$, but all others are different. In applications it may be easier for analysts to estimate the model with correlated indexes. This model can then be transformed into one with uncorrelated indexes for purposes of portfolio selection.

would be expected given the rate of return on the stock market (I_1). Similarly, b_{i2} becomes a measure of the sensitivity of the return on stock i to this difference. We can think of b_{i2} as the sensitivity of stock i's return to a change in interest rates when the rate of return on the market is fixed.

Not only is it convenient to make the indexes uncorrelated, but it is also convenient to have the residual uncorrelated with each index. Formally, this implies that $E[c_i(I_j - \bar{I}_j)] = 0$ for all j. The implication of this construction is that the ability of Equation (8.1) to describe the return on any security is independent of the value any index happens to assume. When the parameters of this model are estimated via regression analysis, as is usually done, this will hold over the period of time to which the model is fitted.

The standard form of the multi-index model can be written as follows:

BASIC EQUATION:

$$R_i = a_i + b_{i1}I_1 + b_{i2}I_2 + b_{i3}I_3 + \cdots + b_{iL}I_L + c_i$$

$$\text{for all stocks } i = 1, ..., N \quad (8.1)$$

BY DEFINITION

1. Residual variance of stock i equals σ_{ci}^2 where $i = 1, ..., N$.
2. Variance of index j equals σ_{Ij}^2 where $j = 1, ..., L$.

BY CONSTRUCTION

1. Mean of c_i equals $E(c_i) = 0$ for all stocks, where $i = 1, ..., N$.
2. Covariance between indexes j and k equals $E[(I_j - \bar{I}_j)(I_k - \bar{I}_k)] = 0$ for all indexes, where $j = 1, ..., L$ and $k = 1, ..., L$ ($j \neq k$).
3. Covariance between the residual for stock i and index j equals $E[c_i(I_j - \bar{I}_j)] = 0$ for all stocks and indexes, where $i = 1, ..., N$ and $j = 1, ..., L$.

BY ASSUMPTION

1. Covariance between c_i and c_j is zero ($E(c_i c_j) = 0$) for all stocks where $i = 1, ..., N$ and $j = 1, ..., N$ ($j \neq i$).

The assumption of the multi-index model is that $E(c_i c_j) = 0$. This assumption implies that the only reason stocks vary together is because of common co-movement with the set of indexes that have been specified in the model. There are no factors beyond these indexes that account for co-movement between any two securities. There is nothing in the estimation of the model that forces this to be true. This is a simplification that represents an approximation to reality. The performance of the model will be determined by how good this approximation is. This, in turn, will be determined by how well the indexes that we have chosen to represent co-movement really capture the pattern of co-movement between securities.

The expected return, variance, and covariance between securities when the multi-index model describes the return structure is derived in Appendix B and is equal to

1. Expected return is

$$\bar{R}_i = a_i + b_{i1}\bar{I}_1 + b_{i2}\bar{I}_2 + \cdots + b_{iL}\bar{I}_L \quad (8.2)$$

2. Variance of return is

$$\sigma_i^2 = b_{i1}^2\sigma_{I1}^2 + b_{i2}^2\sigma_{I2}^2 + \cdots + b_{iL}^2\sigma_{IL}^2 + \sigma_{ci}^2 \quad (8.3)$$

3. Covariance between security i and j is

$$\sigma_{ij} = b_{i1}b_{j1}\sigma_{I1}^2 + b_{i2}b_{j2}\sigma_{I2}^2 + \cdots + b_{iL}b_{jL}\sigma_{IL}^2 \qquad (8.4)$$

From Equations (8.2), (8.3), and (8.4) it is clear that the expected return and risk can be estimated for any portfolio if we have estimates of a_i for each stock, and estimates of b_{ik} for each stock with each index, an estimate of σ_{ci}^2 for each stock and, finally, an estimate of the mean $(\bar{I}_j)$ and variance σ_{Ij}^2 of each index. This is a total of $2N + 2L + LN$ estimates. For an institution following between 150 and 250 stocks and employing 10 indexes, this calls for between 1820 and 3020 inputs. This is larger than the number of inputs required for the single-index model but considerably less than the inputs needed when no simplifying structure was assumed. Notice that now analysts must be able to estimate the responsiveness of each stock they follow to several economic and industry influences.

This model can also be used if analysts supply estimates of the expected return for each stock, the variance of each stock's returns, each index loading (b_{ik} between each stock i and each index k), and the means and variances of each index. This is the same number of inputs ($2N + 2L + LN$). However, the inputs are in more familiar terms. As discussed at several points in this book, the inputs needed to perform portfolio analysis are expected returns, variances, and correlation coefficients. By having the analysts estimate means and variances directly, it is clear that the only input derived from the estimates of the multi-index models are correlation coefficients. We stress this point because later in this chapter we evaluate the ability of a multi-index model to aid in the selection of securities by examining its ability to forecast correlation coefficients.

There is a certain type of multi-index model that has received a large amount of attention. This class of models restricts attention to market and industry influences. Alternative industry index models result from different assumptions about the behavior of returns and, hence, differ in the type and amount of input data needed. We now examine these models.

Industry Index Models

Several authors have dealt with multi-index models that start with the basic single-index model and add indexes to capture industry effects. The early precedent for this work can be found in King [43], who measured effects of common movement between securities beyond market effects and found this extra market covariance was associated with industries. For example, two steel stocks had positive correlation between their returns, even after the effects of the market had been removed.[2]

If we hypothesize that the correlation between securities is caused by a market effect and industry effects, our general multi-index model could be written as

$$R_i = a_i + b_{im}I_m + b_{i1}I_1 + b_{i2}I_2 + \cdots + b_{iL}I_L + c_i$$

where

I_m is the market index

I_j are industry indexes that are constrained to be uncorrelated with the market and uncorrelated with each other

---

[2]King [43] found that over the entire period studied, 1927–1960, about half of the total variation in a stock's price was accounted for by a market index while an average of another 10% was accounted for by industry factors. In the latter part of the period he studied, the importance of the market factor dropped to 30%, while the industry factors continued to explain 10% of price movement.

The assumption behind this model is that a firm's return can be affected by the market plus several industries. For some companies this seems appropriate as their lines of business span several traditional industries. However, some companies gain the bulk of their return from activities in one industry and, perhaps of more importance, are viewed by investors as members of a particular industry. In this case the effects on the firm's return of indexes for industries to which they do not belong are likely to be small and their inclusion may introduce more random noise into the process than the information they supply. This has prompted some authors to advocate a simpler form of the multi-index model: one that assumes that returns of each firm are affected only by a market index and one industry index. Furthermore, the model assumes that each industry index has been constructed to be uncorrelated with the market and with all other industry indexes. For firm i in industry j, the return equation can be written as

$$R_i = a_i + b_{im}I_m + b_{ij}I_j + c_i$$

The covariance between securities i and k can be written as

$$b_{im}b_{km}\sigma_m^2 + b_{ij}b_{kj}\sigma_{Ij}^2$$

for firms in the same industry and

$$b_{im}b_{km}\sigma_m^2$$

for firms in different industries. Notice that the number of inputs needed for portfolio selection has been cut to $4N + 2L + 2$.

The data needed are the expected return and variance for each stock, the loading of each stock on the market and industry index, and, finally, the mean and variance of each industry index and the market index.[3]

How Well Do Multi-Index Models Work?

At this point it is worth examining how well these multi-index models have performed when the parameters are estimated from historical data.[4] Remember, multi-index models lie in an intermediate position between the full historical correlation matrix itself and the single-index model in ability to reproduce the historical correlation matrix. The more indexes added, the more complex things become and the more accurately the historical correlation matrix is reproduced. However, this does not imply that future correlation matrices will be forecast more accurately. Since there are an infinite number of multi-index models that can be tried, one cannot unequivocally say that multi-index models are better or worse than single-index models. However, we can examine some typical results on several multi-index models to see how well they work.

---

[3]As the reader can imagine, there is more than one way to write any model. This particular type of multi-index model has been popularized in another form by Cohen and Pogue [16].

It can be shown that the model Cohen and Pogue call the diagonal form of the multi-index model is identical to the form we have been discussing. The advantage of expressing the input data as suggested by Cohen and Pogue is that the analyst can deal directly with responsiveness of industries to the market. This may be easier than dealing with the responsiveness of stocks to industry indexes with market influences removed.

[4]All of the tests of the various models we've discussed have estimated the models using historical data. There is no reason that the estimates could not come from analysts. The ability of analysts to make these estimates and their value is still an open question.

Let us start with the most general form of the multi-index model:

$$R_i = a_i + b_{i1}I_1 + b_{i2}I_2 + b_{i3}I_3 + \cdots + b_{iL}I_L + c_i$$

This model explains firm returns in terms of a set of uncorrelated indexes.[5]

Before discussing the results, it is worth digressing for a moment to see how we might judge the performance of these models. Remember that all index models lead to the same estimates of expected returns and a stock's own variance (as opposed to covariances) when estimated from historical returns and variances. Furthermore, if analysts are used to estimate expected return and variance, the only estimate from a model is an estimate of the covariance. However, the covariance is the product of standard deviations and correlation coefficients. If analysts are used to estimate standard deviations, any differences in performance that exist must arise from differences in estimating the correlation structure of security returns. The most direct test of alternative models is to examine how well they estimate the future correlation matrix of security returns. Differences between forecasts and actual results can be measured and the statistical significance of these differences can be judged. While tests of statistical significance are useful for judging the superiority of forecasting techniques, tests of economic significance are often of more interest. Tests of economic significance examine the difference in return or profit that results from basing forecasts on one technique rather than on another. In this case the future returns (at alternative specified risk levels) that would result from selecting portfolios based on each forecasting model can be examined.

Now let us discuss the results of both the statistical tests and tests of economic significance. In general, Elton and Gruber [19] found (that on both statistical grounds and economic grounds) adding additional indexes to the single-index model led to a decrease in performance. Although adding more indexes led to a better explanation of the historical correlation matrix, it led both to a poorer prediction of the future correlation matrix and to the selection of portfolios that, at each risk level, tended to have lower returns. In short, these added indexes introduced more random noise than real information into the forecasting process.

The evidence that a generalized multi-index model, where the indexes are extracted according to explanatory power from past data, does not perform as well as a single-index model is very strong. This does not imply that a different form of a multi-index model

---

[5]A mathematical technique exists that allows a set of indexes that meets the criteria for this model to be constructed from a set of returns. The technique is called principal components analysis. Principal components analysis will extract from a historical variance-covariance matrix of returns that index (weighting of the individual returns) that best explains (reproduces) the variance of the original data. This index is called the first principal component. Principal components analysis then proceeds to extract the index that explains as much as possible of the variance of the original data unexplained by the first principal component, given that this second index is constrained to be uncorrelated with the first index. It proceeds to sequentially form additional indexes, ensuring that each index formed explains as much as possible of the variation in the data that has not been explained by previous indexes, given that each index extracted is uncorrelated with each index previously extracted. This technique can be used until the number of indexes extracted equals the number of stocks whose variance-covariance matrix is being examined. At this point the principal components can exactly reproduce the historical variance-covariance matrix. However, since the first principal component explains as much as possible of the historical variance-covariance matrix, the second explains as much as possible of the remaining variance, and so on, we would expect the last few principal components to have almost no explanatory power. In fact, to the extent that there is any real underlying structure to the data, most of the correlation matrix should be explained by the first few principal components.

Elton and Gruber [20] used principal component analysis on 76 firms and found that the percentage of the variance in the original data explained with 1, 3, 8, and 17 principal components was 36%, 45%, 61%, and 75%, respectively.

might not work better than a single-index model. Indexes based on interest rates or oil prices or other fundamental factors affecting different companies in different ways may lead to better performance. One would expect that other influences exist that should have a major and lasting influence on the correlation structure of stock prices. Whether they do or not is a matter for empirical research.

Another test of the multi-index model was performed by Cohen and Pogue [16]. They examined the use of a specialized multi-index model to select portfolios (test of economic significance).[6] Standard industrial classifications were used to divide the stocks in their sample into industries. Standard industrial classifications group firms by end product such as steel or chemical. Single-index models and a multi-index model, with a market and industry index, were then run. While Cohen and Pogue tested results, both over the period to which the models were fit and over the forecast period, only the latter set of tests is of interest to a person considering the adoption of these models. Cohen and Pogue conclude that with respect to these tests, the single-index model has more desirable properties. The single-index model led to lower expected risks and is much simpler to use.[7]

While Cohen and Pogue accepted standard industrial classifications in their analysis, other authors have sought to employ industry index models where industries were defined, not in terms of a standard classification but in terms of the tendency of firms to act alike. Procedures for forming homogeneous groups of firms or pseudo-industries were first examined in Elton and Gruber [18] and later again in Elton and Gruber [20] and Elton, Martin, and Blake [22]. Farrell [28] was the first to use the concepts and procedures of pseudo-industries to form indexes as input to a multi-index model.

The following question may occur to the reader. Why bother with a statistical alternative to traditional industry classification? After all, the traditional grouping partitions firms into sets according to end product or service produced or sold. There are at least two problems with the use of these codes. One is that the increase in the number of multiproduct firms and the prevalence of company diversification have made classification by product difficult and, sometimes, arbitrary. Second, and even more important, classification by product or service may be useful for some purposes but it is far from a universal classification for all purposes. For example, General Motors and American Motors are in the same industry but there are major differences in their performance and the risk to which they are subject.

Given the problems with traditional industry classifications, it is useful to develop an alternative or group of alternative classifications. In fact, it is logical to have techniques for grouping that allow groups to be formed according to the objective in mind and the nature of the process under investigation. In the case of the multi-index model, the purpose is clear: develop groups such that the indexes for them predict as much as possible of the correlation between securities that is not predicted (explained) by the market index. One logical way to do this is to remove the market index from stock returns and then to examine the correlation structure of residuals. Stocks that have highly correlated residuals are combined into a pseudo-industry. Indexes for each pseudo-industry can be developed, and these indexes used in a multi-index model. This is similar to the procedure that was followed by Farrell [28, 29]. He found that the large sample of stocks he analyzed could be

---

[6]The specialized form of the model they tested was their diagonal form of the multi-index model.

[7]Cohen and Pogue [16] also tested a more elaborate form of the multi-index industry model. In this form the entire covariance structure between industry indexes was employed. However, the performance of this model was inferior to the simpler diagonal form of the industry multi-index model and, hence, inferior to the single-index model.

classified into four pseudo-industries. Furthermore, because of the nature of the stocks in each group, he could associate characteristics with each group. He labeled the four groups growth stocks, cyclical stocks, stable stocks, and oil stocks. Note that, in his sample, only one traditional industry was sufficiently homogeneous to show up in his groupings. The significance of these pseudo-industry indexes over the period studied can be seen by the fact that, while the market index accounted for 30% of the variance in stock prices, the use of an appropriate pseudo-industry index with each stock accounted for an additional 15%. As would be expected, when multi-index models were used, the models were able to account for a larger percentage of historical correlation than the single-index model. This is not surprising. Extracting more indexes from this historical correlation matrix, according to their ability to explain it, has to mean that a model that includes these additional indexes reproduces the correlation matrix from which they were extracted better than a model that excludes them. Remember that both Elton and Gruber [20] and Cohen and Pogue [16] found that their multi-index model did a better job of reproducing the historical correlation matrix, but it did not do a better job of forecasting than the single-index model.

The relevant question is how well a model employing pseudo-industries performs when it is used to predict future correlation matrices or to select portfolios. Perhaps the first question to ask is whether pseudo-industries are stable over time. To have any predictive ability, the composition of pseudo-industries must show a high degree of stability. Farrell tests for stability and concludes it is quite high. He next uses both the single-index model and a four-index model (based on his four groups) to select portfolios based on data from the period 1961–1969 and observes how well these portfolios perform for the period 1970–1974. Farrell concludes that his multi-index model based on homogeneous groups outperformed the single-index model.[8] Some caution is warranted in generalizing Farrell's results. An examination of them shows that, while on average the multi-index model does perform slightly better, it leads to inferior performance at some risk levels and superior performance at others. The dominance is not complete. Furthermore, the conclusions are based on one sample over one time period. Before his conclusion can be accepted, more testing is needed. Nevertheless, Farrell's work holds out hope for the development of multi-index models based on security groupings that can outperform single-index models.[9]

Up to this point we have discussed the use of multi-index models as a way of forecasting the future correlation structure between security returns. While this use holds great promise for the future, the results, to date, have been mixed. A natural question arises: If the addition of more indexes to a single-index model can, at times, introduce more random noise than real information into the forecasting process, might not a technique that smooths more of the historical data lead to better results?

Recently there has been a renewed interest in multi-index models. The testing has been to see how many indexes best explain the historical variance-covariance or correlation matrix. Roll and Ross [57] report that at least three indexes are needed to explain the historical variance-covariance matrix. Dhrymes, Friend, and Gultekin [17] show that the

---

[8]Leonard Fertuck [30] followed a procedure similar to Farrell's to form pseudo-industries. He then compared the ability of multi-index models based on pseudo-industries with multi-index models based on traditional industries to explain the variance of returns over a subsequent period. He found that the traditional industry grouping outperformed the pseudo-industry indexes in most cases.

[9]In selecting all portfolios, Farrell forces his intercept for both the single-index and multi-index models to be zero. In Chapter 13 we show that the theoretical values of these intercepts is not zero and so this could bias his results.

number of indexes that are needed is very dependent on the number of firms that are being analyzed. Depending on the sample size, they find that many more than three are needed. Finally Gibbons [32], analyzing bond and stock data, finds that six or seven indexes are needed. Chen, Roll, and Ross [13], and Burmeister writing with others [7–10] have recently produced a set of multi-index models based on an a priori-hypothesized set of macroeconomic variables. Those models are extremely interesting and have several potential applications in finance. Because of their growing importance we will devote a special section to their description at the end of this chapter. Unfortunately, none of these studies or other similar recent studies make an attempt to examine whether multi-index models are better as forecasters than single-index models of the future variance-covariance matrix. It would not be at all surprising if multi-index models better explained the historical variance-covariance matrix or correlation matrix but led to poorer forecasting due to a change in the structure over time. Thus although the recent research should encourage future work in this area, it does not provide evidence in favor of the use of multi-index models to forecast the correlation structure in portfolio analysis.

AVERAGE CORRELATION MODELS

The idea of averaging (smoothing) some of the data in the historical correlation matrix as a forecast of the future has been tested by Elton and Gruber [20] and Elton, Gruber, and Urich [22].

The most aggregate type of averaging that can be done is to use the average of all pairwise correlation coefficients over some past period as a forecast of each pairwise correlation coefficient for the future. This is equivalent to the assumption that the past correlation matrix contains information about what the average correlation will be in the future but no information about individual differences from this average. This model can be thought of as a naive model against which more elaborate models should be judged. We refer to this model as the overall mean model.

A more disaggregate averaging model would be to assume that there was a common mean correlation within and between groups of stocks. For example, if we employ the idea of traditional industries as a method of grouping, we would assume that the correlation between any two steel stocks was the same as the correlation between any other two steel stocks and was equal to the average historical correlation between steel stocks. The averaging is done across all pairwise correlations between steel stocks in a historical period. Similarly, the correlation between any steel stocks and any chemical stocks is assumed to be equal to the correlation between any other steel stock and any other chemical stock and is set equal to the average of the correlations between each chemical and each steel stock. When this is done, with respect to traditional industry classifications, it will be referred to as the traditional mean model. The same technique has been used [20] with respect to pseudo-industries.

The overall mean has been extensively tested against single-index models, general multi-index models, and the historical correlation matrix itself. Tests have been performed using three different samples of stocks over a total of four different time periods. In every case, the use of the overall mean model outperformed the single-index model, the multi-index model, and the historical correlation matrix. The differences in forecasting future correlation coefficients were almost always statistically significant at the 0.05 level. Furthermore, for most risk levels, the differences in portfolio performance were large enough to have real economic significance. Using the overall mean technique, as opposed to the best of the single-index model, the multi-index model, or the historical correlation model, often led to a 25% increase in return (holding risk constant).

The next logical question is what happens when we introduce some disaggregation into the results by using the traditional mean or pseudo-mean model. Here the results are much more ambiguous. Averaging models based on either traditional industries or pseudo-industries outperformed single-index models, multiple-index models, and the historical correlation matrix both on statistical and economic criteria. However, their differences from each other and from the overall mean were much less clear. The ordering of these three techniques was different over different time periods and at different risk levels in the same time period. At this point all we can say is that, although it is worth continuing to investigate the performance of traditional mean and pseudo-mean averaging models, their superiority over the overall mean model has not yet been demonstrated.

MIXED MODELS

Another model that has received attention is a combination of the models discussed in Chapter 7 and those introduced in this chapter. We call them mixed models. In a mixed model, the single-index model is used as the basic starting point. However, rather than assume that the extramarket covariance is zero, a second model is constructed to explain extramarket covariance. This concept should not be new to the reader. If we consider a general multi-index model, where the first index is the market, then we can consider all other indexes as indexes of extramarket covariance. What is new is the way that extramarket covariance is predicted. The most widely known model of this type is that described by Rosenberg [58]. In Chapter 7 we discussed Rosenberg's methods of relating Beta to a set of fundamental and technical data. Rosenberg has used the same method for predicting extramarket covariance. He relates extramarket covariance to the same type of fundamental variables and industry membership coefficients that were discussed in Chapter 7. After removing the market index, he regresses the extramarket covariance on 114 variables. These variables include traditional industry classification as well as firm variables such as debt-equity ratios and dividend payout measures. Initial results with this type of analysis appear quite promising, although extensive tests of the forecast ability have not been performed.

Another approach worth exploring is to apply the same type of averaging techniques discussed earlier directly to the extramarket covariance. That is, instead of performing the averaging on the correlation coefficients themselves, perform the averaging on the correlations of the residuals from the single-index model. For example, a traditional industry averaging scheme might be used. In this case, after removing the market influence, the residuals for each stock could be averaged within and between industries. Then the correlation between any two stocks would be predicted by combining their predicted correlation from the single-index model with the extramarket correlation predicted from the averaging model.

FUNDAMENTAL MULTI-INDEX MODELS

As mentioned earlier, a number of multi-index models have recently been developed relating security return to macroeconomic variables.

The first of the recent group of multi-index models of stock returns was published by Chen, Roll, and Ross [13]. Although the purpose of their article was to explain equilibrium returns (a subject we will discuss at great length in Chapter 16), their analysis laid the groundwork for many of the models that were to follow. Chen, Roll, and Ross hypothesized a broad set of influences that could affect security returns. Their work is based on two concepts. The first is that the value of a share of stock is equal to the present value of future cash flows to the equity holder. Thus an influence that affects either the size of future cash flows or the function (discount rates) used to value cash flows impacts price. Once a set of variables that affects prices is identified, their second concept comes into play. They argue that because current beliefs about these variables are incorporated in price, it is only innovations or unexpected changes in these variables that can affect return.

In a series of articles, Burmeister, McElroy, and others [7–10] have continued the development of a multi-index model building on the work of Chen, Roll, and Ross. They find that five variables are sufficient to describe security returns. They employ two variables that are related to the discount rate used to find the present value of cash flows, one related to both the size of the cash flows and discount rates, one related only to cash flows, and a remaining variable that captures the impact of the market not incorporated in the first four variables. Let's briefly discuss each of the variables.

Prices are affected by the rate at which future cash flows are discounted by an investor. They argue that the average rate used depends on two influences. The first depends on how much more an investor requires to buy a more risky instrument rather than a safe one. The second is the shape of the discount function (the rate at which the investor discounts cash flows far in the future versus the rate used to discount near cash flows). Remember, it is unexpected changes or innovations in these variables rather than their level that affect returns.

The first variable employed by Burmeister et al. is the unexpected difference in return between 20-year government bonds and 20-year corporate bonds. The interest payments on government bonds are considered to be riskless, whereas corporations may default on their payments. Thus return differences in these series measure default risk. They argue that differences in this series from its average value are unexpected. Because the average monthly difference between corporate bonds and government bonds over a long time period is one-half of 1 percent per month, their first variable is[10]

I_1 = one-half of 1 percent plus the return on long-term government bonds minus the return on long-term corporate bonds.

The second variable measures the shape of the interest rate relationship with maturity. Called *term structure*, it is measured as

I_2 = return on long-term government bonds minus return on the one-month Treasury bill one month in the future.

The authors find that this variable has a zero mean and zero autocorrelation and thus argue any nonzero value is unexpected.[11]

The third variable is a measure of unexpected deflation. To the extent that investors are concerned with real cash flows (cash flows after adjusting for inflation) or adjust discount rates to real values, the rate of deflation should affect stock prices. Thus unexpected changes in deflation should affect returns.

I_3 = rate of inflation expected at the beginning of month minus the actual rate of inflation realized at the end of the month

The fourth variable uses the unexpected change in the growth rate in real final sales as a proxy for the unexpected changes in long-run profits for the economy.

---

[10]The authors use the data of Ibbotson and Sinquefield [40] for their return series.

[11]Data for the first two variables are taken from Ibbotson and Sinquefield [40].

I_4 = expected long-run growth rate in real final sales expected at the beginning of the month minus the expected long-run growth rate in real final rates expected at the end of the month[12]

To the extent that these four influences do not capture all of the macroeconomic (and psychological) factors affecting stock returns, there may be an impact of the market itself. More specifically, Burmeister et al. wish to examine the impact of the market on stock returns after the influence of their first four variables is removed. To do this, they form a fifth variable. As a proxy for the market they use the return on the S&P index. The fifth variable is the return on the S&P 500 index, which is uncorrelated with any of the four indexes already discussed. To obtain this variable, they first run a time series regression of the S&P index on the four variables discussed previously and obtain the following results:

$$R_M - R_F = .0022 - 1.33I_1 + 0.56I_2 + 2.29I_3 - 0.93I_4$$

$$R_2 = .24$$

t values in parentheses

The author's last variable I_5 is simply the differences between the excess return on the market for any month and the excess return predicted from the estimated equation or the time series of

$$I_5 = (R_m - R_F) - (.0022 - 1.33I_1, +0.56I_2 + 2.29I_3 - 0.93I_4)$$

How can we judge whether this model makes sense? If the model is a reasonable return generating process, we would expect the first four variables to be related to the market in a sensible manner, and we would expect returns on individual stocks to be related to the five variables in a sensible manner. Let's first look at the relationship between the S&P index and the first four variables.

As shown previously, the first four influences account for about 25% of the movement in the S&P index. In addition, the coefficient on each variable is statistically significant at the 5% level and has the sign that theory would lead us to expect.

Consider the second variable I_2. If the premium for holding longer maturity instruments is high, the rate of return required by the market should also be high and stock returns should be high. Hence the sign of the coefficient of I_2 should be positive. Similarly, if I_1 is large, it indicates a small risk premium is demanded by the market and stock returns should be low. Thus the coefficient I_1 should have a negative sign. I_3 measures deflation. Deflation, I_3, should be and is associated with an increase in stock returns. Thus its sign should be and is positive. The fourth variable measures the decrease in expectations of sales growth. If expectations decrease during a period, prices should drop and returns should be high. Hence the negative relationship found by the authors.[13]

---

[12]The third and fourth variables are constructed from the National Income Accounts. Expected inflation is found by time series treatment (Kalyman Filter) of past inflation series. Expectations are forecast by using a lagged autoregressive model involving lagged values of growth in final sales and growth in disposable income.

[13]Recall that the five variables are supposed to be surprises or innovations and as such they should not be able to be predicted from their own past values. Burmeister, McElroy, and others test this by examining the time series of the indexes themselves and conclude that they cannot predict the value of the index from their past values (all autocorrelations are close to zero).

How well does this five-index model explain returns? Fitting the model to 70 firms, the authors find that 215 out of the 350 regression parameters (b_{ij}s) are significantly different from zero at the 5% level (have t values of 1.98 or greater) and the model typically accounts for between 30% and 50% in the variation of the return of individual stocks. Furthermore, they form portfolios of securities in industries or sectors and regress returns on these port-folios against the indexes. The results have intuitive appeal. For example, Berry, Burmeister, and McElroy [4] examine the sensitivities (b_{ij}s) of seven economic sectors to their five risk indexes. The seven sectors they examined are Cyclical, Growth, Stable, Oil, Utility, Transportation, and Financial. These results are shown in Table 8.1. Note that the financial sector has the highest sensitivity (of any of the seven sectors) on I_1 (default risk) and I_2 (term structure). Firms in this industry are highly leveraged and we would expect their perform-ance to be very sensitive to changes in the term structure or risk structure of interest rates. As another example, utilities have the lowest sensitivity to deflation I_3 and growth in prof-its I_4. Utilities are governed by rate-of-return regulation and so can pass on much of the impact of deflation and profit changes to their customers in the form of higher (or lower) prices. As a final example, note that the highest sensitivity to the market influence is asso-ciated with growth stocks and the lowest sensitivity is utilities. The impact of other influ-ences not captured by the first four indexes is captured in I_5, including market psychology. It seems reasonable that growth stocks are most sensitive to this influence, and utility stocks that are often described as pseudo bonds are least sensitive to it.

The model we have just described represents an example of the type of fundamental risk models that is beginning to have an impact on industry as well as the academic profession. A recent return-generating process developed by Salomon Brothers [65, 66] is in the spirit of the type of model we have been discussing. This model uses seven variables to explain the return on securities. They are as follows:

1. **Economic growth.** As a proxy for long-run growth trends in the economy, it uses year-to-year changes in total industrial production. This series provides a gauge of general economic well-being.[14]

2. **Business cycle.** They argue that the shorter-term cyclical behavior of the economy is captured by the difference in return on investment-grade corporate bonds and U.S.

Table 8.1   Sector Sensitivities

Sector Name	I_1 Default	I_2 Term Structure	I_3 Deflation	I_4 Growth	I_5 Residual Market	R^2
Cyclical	−1.63	0.55	2.84	−1.04	1.14	0.77
Growth	−2.08	0.58	3.16	−0.92	1.28	0.84
Stable	−1.40	0.68	2.31	−0.22[a]	0.74	0.73
Oil	−0.63[a]	0.31	2.19[a]	−0.83[a]	1.14	0.50
Utility	−1.06	0.72	1.54	0.23[a]	0.62	0.67
Transportation	−2.07	0.58	4.45	−1.13	1.37	0.66
Financial	−2.48	1.00	3.20	−0.56[a]	0.99	0.72

[a]Indicates *not* statistically different from zero at the 5% level.

---

[14]Salomon Brothers argue that year-to-year changes are better than shorter time interval fluctuations, because shorter sampling intervals result in greater volatility and, therefore, do not provide a reliable indicator of eco-nomic growth.

Treasuries. They use bonds with about a 20-year maturity. They argue that changes in the spread between the two instruments capture the risk of default.

3. ***Long-term interest rates.*** They argue that changes in the long rate reflect an alteration in the relative attractiveness of financial assets and should induce a change in the portfolio mix. This model uses the yield change in 10-year Treasuries as an indicator of the attractiveness of default-free bonds.

4. ***Short-term interest rates.*** Similarly, a change in short-term interest rates would alter the supply of assets for investment in longer-term instruments, such as stocks and bonds. The model uses the yield change in one-month U.S. Treasury bills as an indicator of changes at the short end of the yield curve.

5. ***Inflation stock.*** The Consumer Price Index (CPI) is used to measure inflation. The stock element is measured as the difference between realized inflation and expected inflation.[15]

6. ***U.S. dollar.*** The impact of currency fluctuations on the stock market is measured by changes in a 15-country, trade-weighted basket of currencies. Salomon finds a statistically stable relationship between returns on stocks and currency fluctuations.

7. That part of the market index that is uncorrelated with the six indexes previously described.

Salomon Brothers has been employing their multi-index model for some time. They report that using monthly data, this model explains on average 41% of the fluctuations in return for individual stocks contained in a sample of 1000 institutional quality stocks. Models of this type are most promising. We will return to examine this again when we discuss equilibrium prices in Chapter 16.

CONCLUSION

In this chapter we have discussed alternatives to the single-index model for predicting future correlation coefficients. There are an infinite number of such models. Thus, we cannot give definitive answers concerning their performance relative to single-index models. Many of the results are promising. This probably does not surprise the reader. What surprises most students is the ability of simple models such as the single-index model and overall mean to outperform more complex models in many tests. Although complex models better describe the historical correlation, they often contain more noise than information with respect to prediction. There is still a great deal of work to be done before complicated models consistently outperform simpler ones.

APPENDIX A

PROCEDURE FOR REDUCING ANY MULTI-INDEX MODEL TO A MULTI-INDEX MODEL WITH ORTHOGONAL INDEXES

We illustrate the procedure with a two-index model. Let

$$R_i = a_i^* + b_{i1}^* I_1^* + b_{i2}^* I_2^* + c_i$$

---

[15]Based on the generally accepted premise that the current default-free rate of interest (on Treasury bills) is composed of the cost of credit when inflation is zero, plus the expected rate of inflation, Salomon extracts an expected inflation series from returns on Treasury bills using econometric methods.

For example, I_1^* might be a market index and I_2^* a sector index (e.g., aggregate index for companies producing capital goods). If two indexes are correlated, the correlation may be removed from either index.

Define I_1 as equal to I_1^*. Now to remove the impact of the market from the sector index, we can establish the parameters of the following equation via regression analysis:

$$I_2^* = \gamma_0 + \gamma_1 I_1 + d_t$$

where γ_0 and γ_1 are regression coefficients and d_t is the random error term. By the techniques of estimation used in regression analysis, d_t is uncorrelated with I_1. Thus

$$d_t = I_2^* - (\gamma_0 + \gamma_1 I_1)$$

is an index of the performance of the sector index with the effect of I_1 (the market) removed.[16]

If we define

$$I_2 = d_t = I_2^* - \gamma_0 - \gamma_1 I_1$$

we have defined an index of sector performance that is uncorrelated with the market. Solving for I_2^* and substituting into the return equation yields

$$R_i = a_i^* + b_{i1}^* I_1 + b_{i2}^* I_2 + b_{i2}^* \gamma_0 + b_{i2}^* \gamma_1 I_1 + c_i$$

Rearranging terms gives

$$R_i = \left(a_i^* + b_{i2}^* \gamma_0\right) + \left(b_{i1}^* + b_{i2}^* \gamma_1\right) I_1 + b_{i2}^* I_2 + c_i$$

The first term is a constant we define as a_i. The coefficient on the second term is a constant we define as b_{i1}. Now let $b_{i2} = b_{i2}^*$. Then this equation becomes

$$R_i = a_i + b_{i1} I_1 + b_{i2} I_2 + c_i$$

where I_1 and I_2 have been defined so that they are uncorrelated, and we have accomplished our task.

If the model contained a third index, for example, an industry index, then this index could be made orthogonal to the other two indexes by running the following regression:

$$I_3^* = \theta_1 + \theta_2 I_2 + \theta_3 I_2 + e_i$$

The index I_3 could be defined as

$$I_3 = I_3^* - \left(\theta_1 + \theta_2 I_1 + \theta_3 I_2\right)$$

The proof that this leads to a three-index model with uncorrelated indexes of the form

$$R_i = a_i + b_{i1} I_1 + b_{i2} I_2 + b_{i3} I_3 + c_i$$

is left as an exercise to the reader.

APPENDIX B

MEAN RETURN, VARIANCE, AND COVARIANCE OF A MULTI-INDEX MODEL

In this appendix we derive the mean return variance and covariance of return when the multi-index model is assumed to describe the return structure in the market.

---

[16]The index could also be written as $d_t + \gamma_0$. Each is appropriate. The way we have defined it the mean is zero.

Expected Return

The expected return on a security with the multi-index model is

$$E(R_i) = E(a_i + b_{i1}I_1 + b_{i2}I_2 + \cdots + b_{iL}I_L + c_i)$$

Since the expected value of the sum of random variables is the sum of the expected values, we have

$$E(R_i) = E(a_i) + E(b_{i1}I_1) + E(b_{i2}I_2) + \cdots + E(b_{iL}I_L) + E(c_i)$$

Recognizing that a and b are constants and that by construction $E(c_i) = 0$, we have

$$E(R_i) = a_i + b_{i1}\bar{I}_1 + b_{i2}\bar{I}_2 + \cdots + b_{iL}\bar{I}_L$$

This is the result stated in the text.

Variance of Return

The variance of the return on a security is

$$\sigma_i^2 = E(R_i - \bar{R}_i)^2$$

Substituting for R_i and $\bar{R}_i$, we have

$$\sigma_i^2 = E\big[(a_i + b_{i1}I_1 + b_{i2}I_2 + \cdots + b_{iL}I_L + c_i)$$
$$- (a_i + b_{i1}\bar{I}_1 + b_{i2}\bar{I}_2 + \cdots + b_{iL}\bar{I}_L)\big]^2$$

Canceling the a_i's and rearranging yields

$$\sigma_i^2 = E\big[b_{i1}(I_1 - \bar{I}_1) + b_{i2}(I_2 - \bar{I}_2) + \cdots + b_{iL}(I_L - \bar{I}_L) + c_i\big]^2$$

The next step is to square the terms in the brackets. The results of this can be seen if we examine all terms involving the first index. The first index times itself and each of the other terms is

$$E\big[b_{i1}^2(I_1 - \bar{I}_1)^2 + b_{i1}b_{i2}(I_1 - \bar{I}_1)(I_2 - \bar{I}_2) + \cdots$$
$$+ b_{i1}b_{iL}(I_1 - \bar{I}_1)(I_L - \bar{I}_L) + b_{i1}(I_1 - \bar{I}_1)(c_i)\big]$$

The expected value of the sum of random variables is the sum of the expected values and, since the b_i's are constants, we have

$$b_{i1}^2 E(I_1 - \bar{I}_1)^2 + b_{i1}b_{i2}E\big[(I_1 - \bar{I}_1)(I_2 - \bar{I}_2)\big] + \cdots$$
$$+ b_{i1}b_{iL}E\big[(I_1 - \bar{I}_1)(I_L - \bar{I}_L)\big] + b_{i1}E\big[(I_1 - \bar{I}_1)(c_i)\big]$$

By construction

$$E\big[(I_i - \bar{I}_i)(I_j - \bar{I}_j)\big] = 0$$

and

$$E\big[(I_1 - \bar{I}_1)(c_i)\big] = 0$$

thus, the only nonzero term involving index one is

$$b_{i1}^2 E(I_1 - \bar{I}_1)^2 = b_{i1}^2 \sigma_{I1}^2$$

When we examine terms involving the c_i, we get the c_i with each index that has an expected value of zero. We also get $E(c_i)^2 = \sigma_{ci}^2$; thus,

$$\sigma_i^2 = b_{i1}^2\sigma_{I1}^2 + b_{i2}^2\sigma_{I2}^2 + \cdots + b_{iL}^2\sigma_{IL}^2 + \sigma_{ci}^2$$

The Covariance

The covariance between securities i and j is

$$\sigma_{ij} = E\left[\left(R_i - \overline{R}_i\right)\left(R_j - \overline{R}_j\right)\right]$$

Substituting in the expressions for R_i and R_j yields

$$\sigma_{ij} = E\Big\{\left[b_{i1}\left(I_1 - \overline{I}_1\right) + b_{i2}\left(I_2 - \overline{I}_2\right) + \cdots + b_{iL}\big(. \\ \cdot\left[b_{j1}\left(I_1 - \overline{I}_1\right) + b_{j2}\left(I_2 - \overline{I}_2\right) + \cdots + b_{jL}\big(I$$

Noting that the a's cancel, and combining the terms involving the same b's yields

$$E\Big[b_{i1}b_{j1}\left(I_1 - \overline{I}_1\right)^2 + b_{i1}b_{j2}\left(I_1 - \overline{I}_1\right)\left(I_2 - \overline{I}_2\right) + b_{i1}b_{j3}\left(I_1 - \overline{I}_1\right)\big(\\ + \cdots + b_{i1}b_{jL}\left(I_1 - \overline{I}_1\right)\left(I_L - \overline{I}_L\right) + b_{i1}\left(I_1 - \overline{I}_1\right)c_j\Big]$$

The next step is to multiply out the terms. The results of this multiplication can be seen by considering the terms involving b_{i1}. They are

$$E\Big[b_{i1}b_{j1}\left(I_1 - \overline{I}_1\right)^2 + b_{i1}b_{j2}\left(I_1 - \overline{I}_1\right)\left(I_2 - \overline{I}_2\right) + b_{i1}b_{j3}\left(I_1 - \overline{I}_1\right)\left(I_3 - \overline{I}_3\right) \\ + \cdots + b_{i1}b_{jL}\left(I_1 - \overline{I}_1\right)\left(I_L - \overline{I}_L\right) + b_{i1}\left(I_1 - \overline{I}_1\right)c_j\Big]$$

The expected value of all terms involving different indexes, for example, $(I_1 - \overline{I}_1)(I_k - \overline{I}_k)$ is zero by construction. Furthermore, the expected value of $b_{i1}(I_1 - \overline{I}_1)c_j$ is zero by construction. Thus, the only nonzero term is

$$b_{i1}b_{j1}E\left(I_1 - \overline{I}_1\right)^2 = b_{i1}b_{j1}\sigma_{I1}^2$$

There are two types of terms involving the cs. First, there are terms like $b_{ik}(I_k - \overline{I}_k)c_j$, which is zero by construction. Second, there is the term c_ic_j. This is zero by assumption. Thus

$$\sigma_{ij} = b_{i1}b_{j1}\sigma_{I1}^2 + b_{i2}b_{j2}\sigma_{I2}^2 + b_{i3}b_{j3}\sigma_{I3}^2 + \cdots + b_{iL}b_{jL}\sigma_{IL}^2$$

QUESTIONS AND PROBLEMS

1. Given that the correlation coefficient between all securities is the same, call it ρ^*, and the assumption of the single-index model is accepted, derive an expression for the Beta on any stock in terms of ρ^*.

2. Complete the procedure in Appendix A for reducing a general three-index model to a three-index model with orthogonal indexes.

3. Assume that all assumptions of the single-index model hold, except that the covariance between residuals is a constant K instead of zero. Derive the covariance between the two securities and the variance on a portfolio.

4. Given a three-index model such that all indexes are orthogonal, derive the formulas for the expected return, variance, and covariance of any stock.

5.

	Security		
	A	B	C
a_i	2	3	1
b_{i1}	0.8	1.1	0.9
b_{i2}	0.9	1.3	1.1
σ_{ci}	2.0	1.0	1.5

Assuming Is are uncorrelated and $\bar{I}_1 = 8$, $\bar{I}_2 = 4$, $\sigma_{I1} = 2.0$, $\sigma_{I2} = 2.5$ calculate the following using the general multi-index model

(1) Expected returns.

(2) Variance of return.

(3) Covariance of return.

6. Using the data from Problem 5, assume the model is now an Industry Index Model where $I_1 = I_m$ and I_2 is now an industry index. Assuming that firms A and B are in the same industry, calculate the covariance of returns.

7. Repeat Problem 6, assuming now that firms B & C are in the same industry.

8. Given the following multi-index model

$$R_i = 2 + 1.1I_1^* + 1.2I_2^* + C_i$$

where I_1^* and I_2^* are correlated and given the regression equation $I_2^* = 1 + 1.3I_1 + d_t$, transform the equation for R_i into one with orthogonal indexes.

BIBLIOGRAPHY

1. Aber, John. "Industry Effects and Multivariate Stock Price Behavior," *Journal of Financial and Quantitative Analysis*, **XI,** No. 4 (Nov. 1976), pp. 617–624.
2. Altman, Edward, and Schwartz, Robert. "Common Stock Price Volatility Measures and Patterns," *Journal of Financial and Quantitative Analysis*, **IV,** No. 5 (Jan. 1970), pp. 603–625.
3. Bell, Frederick. "The Relation of the Structure of Common Stock Prices to Historical, Exceptional and Industrial Variables," *Journal of Finance*, **IX,** No. 1 (March 1976), pp. 187–197.
4. Berry, Michael, Brumeister, Edwin, and McElroy, Marjorie. "Sorting Out Risks Using Known APT Factors," *Financial Analysts Journal* (March 1988), pp. 29–42.
5. Best, Michael J., and Grauer, Robert R. "Positively Weighted Minimum-Variance Portfolios and the Structure of Asset Expected Returns," *Journal of Financial and Quantitative Analysis*, Seattle, **27,** No. 4 (Dec. 1992), pp. 513–538.
6. Brown, Stephen J. "The Number of Factors in Security Returns," *Journal of Finance*, **44,** No. 5 (1989), pp. 1247–1262.
7. Burmeister, Edwin, and McElroy, Marjorie. "APT and Multifactor Asset Pricing Models with Measured and Unobserved Factors: Theoretical and Econometric Issues," *Discussion Paper, Department of Economics, University of Virginia and Duke University* (1987).

8. ———. "Joint Estimation of Factor Sensitivities and Risk Premia for the Arbitrage Pricing Theory," *Journal of Finance*, **43,** No. 3 (July 1988), pp. 721–733.

9. Burmeister, Edwin, and Wall, Kent. "The Arbitrage Pricing Theory and Macroeconomic Factor Measures." *The Financial Review* (Feb. 1986).

10. Burmeister, Edwin, Wall, Kent, and Hamilton, James. "Estimation of Unobserved Expected Monthly Inflation Using Kalman Filtering," *Journal of Business and Economic Statistics*, **4** (April 1986), pp. 147–160.

11. Chan, K. C., Chen, Nai-fu, and Hsieh, David. "An Explanatory Investigation of the Firm Size Effect," *Journal of Financial Economics*, **14** (Sept. 1985), pp. 451–471.

12. Chen, Nai-fu. "Some Empirical Tests of the Theory of Arbitrage Pricing," *Journal of Finance*, **38** (Dec. 1983), pp. 1392–1414.

13. Chen, Nai-fu, Roll, Richard, and Ross, Stephen. "Economic Forces and the Stock Market," *Journal of Business*, **59** (July 1986), pp. 386–403.

14. Cho, D. Chinhyung, and Taylor, William. "The Seasonal Stability of the Factor Structure of Stock Returns," *Journal of Finance*, **42** (Dec. 1987), pp. 1195–1211.

15. Chung, Peter. "An Investigation of the Firm Effects Influence in the Analysis of Earnings to Price Ratios of Industrial Common Stocks," *Journal of Financial and Quantitative Analysis*, **IX,** No. 6 (Dec. 1974), pp. 1009–1031.

16. Cohen, Kalman, and Pogue, Jerry. "An Empirical Evaluation of Alternative Portfolio Selection Models," *Journal of Business*, **46** (April 1967), pp. 166–193.

17. Dhrymes, Phoebus, Friend, Irwin, and Gultekin, Bulent. "A Critical Reexamination of the Empirical Evidence on the Arbitrage Pricing Theory," *The Journal of Finance*, **39** (June 1984), pp. 323–346.

18. Elton, Edwin J., and Gruber, Martin J. "Homogeneous Groups and the Testing of Economic Hypotheses," *Journal of Financial and Quantitative Analysis*, **IV,** No. 5 (Jan. 1970), pp. 581–602.

19. ———. "Improved Forecasting Through the Design of Homogenous Groups," *Journal of Business*, **44,** No. 4 (Oct. 1971).

20. ———. "Estimating the Dependence Structure of Share Prices—Implications for Portfolio Selection," *Journal of Finance*, **VIII,** No. 5 (Dec. 1973), pp. 1203–1232.

21. ———. "Multi-Index Models and Performance Measurement," in Edward I. Altman and Irwin T. Vanderhoof (eds.), *The Financial Dynamics of the Insurance Industry*, (Homewood, IL: Irwin Professional Publishing, 1997).

22. Elton, Edwin J., Gruber, Martin J., and Blake, Christopher R. "Common Factors in Fund Returns," *European Finance Review*, **3,** No. 4, pp. 320–332.

23. Elton, Edwin J., Gruber, Martin J., and Urich, Thomas. "Are Betas Best?" *Journal of Finance*, **23,** No. 5 (Dec. 1978), pp. 1375–1384.

24. Eun, Cheol S., and Resnick, Bruce G. "Estimating the Correlation Structure of International Share Prices," *The Journal of Finance*, **39,** No. 5 (Dec. 1984), pp. 1311–1324.

25. Fama, Eugene. "Stock Returns, Real Activity, Inflation and Money," *American Economic Review*, **71** (1981), pp. 545–565.

26. Fama, Eugene, and Gibbons, Michael. "A Comparison of Inflation Forecasts," *Journal of Monetary Economics*, **13** (1984), pp. 327–348.

27. Fama, Eugene, and MacBeth, James. "Risk, Return, and Equilibrium: Empirical Tests," *Journal of Political Economy*, **38** (1973), pp. 607–636.

28. Farrell, James. "Analyzing Covariation of Returns to Determine Homogeneous Stock Groupings," *Journal of Business*, **47,** No. 2 (April 1974), pp. 186–207.

29. ———. *The Multi-Index Model and Practical Portfolio Analysis*, The Financial Analysts Research Foundation Occasional Paper No. 4 (1976).

30. Fertuck, Leonard. "A Test of Industry Indexes Based on SIC Codes," *Journal of Financial and Quantitative Analysis*, **X,** No. 5 (Dec. 1975), pp. 837–848.

31. Frankfurter, George, Phillips, Herbert, and Seagle, John. "Portfolio Selection: The Effects of Uncertain Means, Variances and Covariances," *Journal of Financial and Quantitative Analysis*, **VI,** No. 5 (Dec. 1971), pp. 1251–1262.

32. Gibbons, Michael R. "Multivariate Tests of Financial Models, A New Approach," *Journal of Financial Economics*, **10** (March 1982), pp. 3–27.

33. Grinblatt, Mark, and Titman, Sheridan. "Factor Pricing in a Finite Economy," *Journal of Financial Economics*, **12** (1983), pp. 497–507.

34. ——. "Approximate Factor Structures: Interpretations and Implications for Empirical Tests," *Journal of Finance*, **40** (1985), pp. 1367–1373.

35. Gultekin, Mustafa, and Gultekin, N. Bulent. "Stock Return Anomalies and Tests of the APT," *Journal of Finance*, **42** (Dec. 1987), pp. 1213–1224.

36. Hansen, Lars, and Singleton, Kenneth. "Stochastic Consumption, Risk Aversion, and the Temporal Behavior of Assets Returns," *Journal of Political Economy*, **91** (1983), pp. 249–265.

37. Huberman, Gur. "A Simple Approach to Arbitrage Pricing Theory," *Journal of Economic Theory*, **78** (1982), pp. 183–191.

38. Huberman, Gur, and Kandel, Shmuel. "Mean-Variance Spanning," *Journal of Finance*, **42** (Sept. 1987), pp. 873–888.

39. Huberman, Gur, and Stambaugh, Robert. "Mimicking Portfolios and Exact Arbitrage Pricing," *Journal of Finance*, **42** (March 1987), pp. 1–9.

40. Ibbotson, Roger, and Sinquefield, Rex. *Stocks, Bonds, Bills and Inflation: The Past and the Future.* Charlottesville, Va.: Financial Analysts Research Foundation (1982).

41. Ingersoll, Jonathan E., Jr. "Some Results in the Theory of Arbitrage Pricing," *Journal of Finance*, **39** (1984), pp. 1021–1039.

42. Ingersoll, Jonathan E., Jr. *Theory of Financial Decision Making* (Totowa, N.J.: Rowman and Littlefield, 1987).

43. King, Benjamine. "Market and Industry Factors in Stock Price Behavior," *Journal of Business*, **39** (Jan. 1966), pp. 139–140.

44. Kryzanowski, Lawrence, and To, Minh Chan. "General Factor Models and the Structure of Security Returns," *Journal of Financial and Quantitative Analysis*, **18** (1983), pp. 31–52.

45. Lee, Cheng. "A Note on the Interdependent Structure of Security Returns," *Journal of Financial and Quantitative Analysis*, **XI**, No. 1 (March 1976), pp. 73–86.

46. Lloyd, William, and Shick, Richard. "A Test of Stone's Two-Index Model of Returns," *Journal of Financial and Quantitative Analysis*, **XII,** No. 3 (Sept. 1977) pp. 363–376.

47. Lucas, Robert E., Jr. "Asset Prices in an Exchange Economy," *Econometrica*, **46** (1978), pp. 1429–1445.

48. Martin, John, and Klemkosky, Robert. "The Effect of Homogeneous Stock Groupings on Portfolio Risk," *Journal of Business*, **49,** No. 3 (July 1976) pp. 339–349.

49. McElroy, Marjorie, and Burmeister, Edwin. "Arbitrage Pricing Theory as a Restricted Nonlinear Multivariate Regression Model: ITNLSUR Estimates," *Journal of Business and Economic Statistics*, **VI,** No. 1 (Jan. 1988), pp. 29–42.

50. McElroy, Marjorie, and Wall, Kent. "Two Estimators for the APT Model When Factors Are Measured," *Economics Letters*, **19** (1985), pp. 271–275.

51. Merton, Robert C. "An Intertemporal Capital Asset Pricing Model," *Econometrica*, **41** (1973), pp. 867–887.

52. Meyers, Stephen. "A Re-examination of Market and Industry Factors in Stock Price Behavior," *Journal of Finance*, **VIII**, No. 3 (June 1973), pp. 695–705.

53. Morgan, I. G. "Grouping Procedures for Portfolio Formation," *Journal of Finance*, **XI,** No. 5 (Dec. 1977), pp. 1759–1765.

54. Ohlson, James, and Garman, Mark. "A Dynamic Equilibrium for the Ross Arbitrage Model," *Journal of Finance*, **35** (1980), pp. 675–684.

55. Pallmann, Nils. "Recent Empirical Tests of the APT and the Consumption-Based CAPM," *Discussion Paper, Department of Finance, New York University* (1989).

56. Reilly, Frank, and Drzycimski, Eugene. "Alternative Industry Performance and Risk," *Journal of Financial and Quantitative Analysis*, **IX**, No. 3 (June 1974), pp. 423–446.

57. Roll, Richard, and Ross, Stephen. "An Empirical Investigation of the Arbitrage Pricing Theory," *The Journal of Finance*, **35** (Dec. 1980), pp. 1073–1103.

58. Rosenberg, Barr. "Extra-Market Components of Covariance in Security Returns," *Journal of Financial and Quantitative Analysis*, **IX,** No. 2 (March 1974), pp. 263–274.

59. Rush, David. "Comment: The Interdependent Structure of Security Returns," *Journal of Financial and Quantitative Analysis*, **VIII,** No. 2 (March 1973), pp. 289–291.

60. Schwartz, Robert, and Altman, Edward. "Volatility Behavior of Industrial Stock Price Indexes," *Journal of Finance*, **VIII,** No. 4 (Sept. 1973), pp. 957–970.

61. Shanken, Jay. "The Arbitrage Pricing Theory: Is It Testable?" *Journal of Finance*, **37** (1982), pp. 1129–1140.

62. ———. "Multi-Beta CAPM or Equilibrium-APT? A Reply," *Journal of Finance*, **40** (1985a), pp. 1186–1189.

63. ———. "Multivariate Tests of the Zero-Beta CAPM," Journal of Financial Economics, **14** (Sept. 1985), pp. 327–348.

64. Simkowitz, Michael, and Logue, Dennis. "The Interdependent Structure of Security Returns." *Journal of Financial and Quantitative Analysis*, **VIII,** No. 2 (March 1973), pp. 259–272.

65. Sorensen, Eric, Mezrich, Joseph, and Thum, Chee. The Salomon Brothers U.S. Stock Risk Attribute Model, Salomon Brothers (Oct. 1989).

66. Sorensen, Eric, Salomon, R. S. Davenport, Caroline, and Fiore, Maria. *Risk Analysis: The Effect of Key Macroeconomic and Market Factors on Portfolio Returns*, Salomon Brothers (Nov. 1989).

67. Stevens, Guy V. G. "On the inverse of the Covariance Matrix in Portfolio Analysis," *The Journal of Finance*, **53,** No. 5 (Oct. 1998), pp. 1821–1828.

9

Simple Techniques for Determining the Efficient Frontier

In Chapters 7 and 8 we examined several models that were developed to simplify the inputs to the portfolio selection problem. Each of these models makes an assumption about why stocks covary together. Each leads to a simplified structure for the correlation matrix or covariance matrix between securities. These models were developed to cut down on the number of inputs and simplify the nature of the inputs needed to forecast correlations between securities. The use of these models was expected to lead to some loss of accuracy in forecasting correlations, but the ease of using the models was expected to compensate for this loss of accuracy. However, we have seen in Chapters 7 and 8 that when fitted to historical data, these simplifying models result in an increase, not a decrease, in forecasting accuracy. The models are of major interest because they both reduce and simplify the inputs needed to perform portfolio analysis *and* increase the accuracy with which correlations and covariances can be forecast.

In this chapter we see that there is yet another advantage to these models. Each allows the development of a system for computing the composition of optimum portfolios that is so simple it can often be performed without the use of a computer. Perhaps even more important than the ease of computation is the fact that the methods of portfolio selection described in this chapter make it very clear why a stock does or does not enter into an optimal portfolio. Each model of the correlation structure discussed in Chapters 7 and 8 leads to a unique ranking of stocks, such that if a stock enters an optimal portfolio, any higher ranked stock must also enter the optimal portfolio. Similarly, if a stock does not enter an optimal portfolio, any lower ranked stock does not enter the optimal portfolio. This allows the analyst to judge the relative desirability of stocks even before the portfolio selection process is begun. Furthermore, as we will see, the optimum ranking of stocks depends on variables that are already familiar to security analysts and portfolio managers, as well as to readers of this book. This should minimize the institutional barriers to their adoption.

In this chapter we describe, in detail, the methods for selecting optimal portfolios that are appropriate when the single-index model and the constant-correlation model are accepted as descriptions of the covariance structure between securities. In the text of this chapter we present the rules for optimal portfolio selection and show how to use them. This may appear as magic to the reader because, while we declare that the rules lead to the selection of optimal portfolios, the text does not contain a proof that this is so. For the reader who prefers science to magic, the appendices at the end of this chapter present the derivations of all of the rules described in the text. These derivations also act as proof of the optimality of the rules. We have separated the material in this way because the mathematical sophistication needed to understand the derivation of the rules is so much greater than the mathematical sophistication needed to use the rules.

We close this chapter with a brief discussion of the types of rules that some of the other models of correlation structure (presented in Chapter 8) lead to. The discussion here is quite concise, but, for the reader interested in learning more about these rules, the appropriate references are noted.

THE SINGLE-INDEX MODEL

In this section we present and demonstrate the optimum procedure for selecting portfolios when the single-index model is accepted as the best way to forecast the covariance structure of returns.

First we present the ranking criteria that can be used to order stocks for selection for the optimal portfolio. We next present the technique for employing this ranking device to form an optimum portfolio, along with a logical explanation for why it works. While the technique for forming optimum portfolios is easy to understand, the formal proof that it leads to the same portfolio that would be produced by the optimum procedure, presented in Chapter 6, is complex and is presented in Appendix A and Appendix C at the end of this chapter.

After presenting the criteria for the composition of an optimal portfolio, we demonstrate its use with some simple examples. In the first part of the section we assume that short sales are forbidden. In the latter part we allow short sales. In addition, we start by assuming unlimited borrowing and lending at the riskless rate. This assumption is dropped later in the chapter.

The Formation of Optimal Portfolios

The calculation of optimal portfolios would be greatly facilitated, and the ability of practicing security analysts and portfolio managers to relate to the construction of optimal portfolios greatly enhanced, if there were a single number that measured the desirability of including a stock in the optimal portfolio. If one is willing to accept the standard form of the single-index model as describing the co-movement between securities, such a number exists. In this case, the desirability of any stock is directly related to its excess return to Beta ratio. Excess return is the difference between the expected return on the stock and the riskless rate of interest such as the rate on a Treasury bill. The excess return to Beta ratio measures the additional return on a security (beyond that offered by a riskless asset) per unit of nondiversifiable risk. The form of this ratio should lead to its easy interpretation and acceptance by security analysts and portfolio managers, because they are used to thinking in terms of the relationship between potential rewards and risk.[1] The numerator of this ranking device is the extra return over the riskless asset that we earn from holding

---

[1] In Chapter 18 we see that one commonly used measure to rank portfolio performance is the portfolio's excess return to Beta ratio with the best portfolio being the one with the highest ratio. It is intuitively appealing to rank stocks by the same criteria as one uses to rank portfolios and, in fact, it is shown in the appendix that it is optimal to do so.

a security other than the riskless asset. The denominator is the nondiversifiable risk (the risk we cannot get rid of) that we are subject to by holding a risky security rather than the riskless asset.

More formally, the index we use to rank stocks is "excess return to Beta," or

$$\frac{\overline{R}_i - R_F}{\beta_i}$$

where

$\overline{R}_i$ = the expected return on stock i

R_F = the return on a riskless asset

β_i = the expected change in the rate of return on stock i associated with a 1% change in the market return

If stocks are ranked by excess return to Beta (from highest to lowest), the ranking represents the desirability of any stock's inclusion in a portfolio. In other words, if a stock with a particular ratio of $(\overline{R}_i - R_F)/\beta_i$ is included in an optimal portfolio, all stocks with a higher ratio will also be included. On the other hand, if a stock with a particular $(\overline{R}_i - R_F)/\beta_i$ is excluded from an optimal portfolio, all stocks with lower ratios will be excluded (or if short selling is allowed, sold short). When the single-index model is assumed to represent the covariance structure of security returns, then a stock is included or excluded, depending only on the size of its excess return to Beta ratio. How many stocks are selected depends on a unique cut-off rate such that all stocks with higher ratios of $(\overline{R}_i - R_F)/\beta_i$ will be included and all stocks with lower ratios excluded. We call this cut-off ratio C^*.

The rules for determining which stocks are included in the optimum portfolio are as follows:

1. Find the "excess return to Beta" ratio for each stock under consideration, and rank from highest to lowest.

2. The optimum portfolio consists of investing in all stocks for which $(\overline{R}_i - R_F)/\beta_i$ is greater than a particular cut-off point C^*. Shortly, we will define C^* and interpret its economic significance.

The preceding procedure is extremely simple. Once C^* has been determined, the securities to be included can be selected by inspection. Furthermore, the amount to invest in each security is equally simple to determine, as will be discussed shortly.

Ranking Securities

In Tables 9.1 and 9.2 we present an example that illustrates this procedure. Table 9.1 contains the data necessary to apply our simple ranking device to determine an optimal portfolio. It is the normal output generated from a single-index or Beta model, plus the ratio of excess return to Beta. These same data could alternatively be generated by analysts' subjective estimates. There are 10 securities in the tables. For the readers' convenience, we have already ranked the securities according to $(\overline{R}_i - R_F)/\beta_i$ and have used numbers that make the calculations easy to follow. The application of rule 2 involves the comparison of $(\overline{R}_i - R_F)/\beta_i$ with C^*. Accept that $C^* = 5.45$ for the moment; we will shortly present a procedure for its calculation. Examining Table 9.1 shows that for securities 1 to 5 $(\overline{R}_i - R_F)/\beta_i$ is greater than C^* while for security 6 it is less than C^*. Hence, an optimal portfolio consists of securities 1 to 5.

Table 9.1 Data Required to Determine Optimal Portfolio $R_F = 5\%$

1	2	3	4	5	6
Security No. i	Mean Return $\bar{R}_i$	Excess Return $\bar{R}_i - R_F$	Beta β_i	Unsystematic Risk σ^2_{ei}	Excess Return over Beta $\dfrac{(\bar{R}_i - R_F)}{\beta_i}$
1	15	10	1	50	10
2	17	12	1.5	40	8
3	12	7	1	20	7
4	17	12	2	10	6
5	11	6	1	40	6
6	11	6	1.5	30	4
7	11	6	2	40	3
8	7	2	0.8	16	2.5
9	7	2	1	20	2
10	5.6	0.6	0.6	6	1.0

Table 9.2 Calculations for Determining Cut-off Rate with $\sigma^2_m = 10$

1	2	3	4	5	6	7
Security No. i	$\dfrac{(\bar{R}_i - R_F)}{\beta_i}$	$\dfrac{(\bar{R}_i - R_F)\beta_i}{\sigma^2_{ei}}$	$\dfrac{\beta_i^2}{\sigma^2_{ei}}$	$\displaystyle\sum_{j-1}^{i} \dfrac{(\bar{R}_j - R_F)\beta_j}{\sigma^2_{ej}}$	$\displaystyle\sum_{j=1}^{i} \dfrac{\beta_j^2}{\sigma^2_{ej}}$	C_i
1	10	2/10	2/100	2/10	2/100	1.67
2	8	4.5/10	5.625/100	6.5/10	7.625/100	3.69
3	7	3.5/10	5/100	10/10	12.625/100	4.42
4	6	24/10	40/100	34/10	52.625/100	5.43
5	6	1.5/10	2.5/100	35.5/10	55.125/100	5.45
6	4	3/10	7.5/100	38.5/10	62.625/100	5.30
7	3	3/10	10/100	41.5/10	72.625/100	5.02
8	2.5	1/10	4/100	42.5/10	76.625/100	4.91
9	2.0	1/10	5/100	43.5/10	81.625/100	4.75
10	1.0	0.6/10	6/100	44.1/10	87.625/100	4.52

Setting the Cut-off Rate (C*)

As discussed earlier, C^* is the cut-off rate. All securities whose excess-return-to-risk ratio is above the cut-off rate are selected and all whose ratios are below are rejected. The value of C^* is computed from the characteristics of all of the securities that belong in the optimum portfolio. To determine C^* it is necessary to calculate its value as if there were different numbers of securities in the optimum portfolio. Designate C_i as a candidate for C^*. The value of C_i is calculated when i securities are assumed to belong to the optimal portfolio.

Since securities are ranked from highest excess return to Beta to lowest, we know that if a particular security belongs in the optimal portfolio, all higher ranked securities also belong in the optimal portfolio. We proceed to calculate values of a variable C_i (the procedure is outlined below) as if the first ranked security was in the optimal portfolio ($i = 1$), then the first and second ranked securities were in the optimal portfolio ($i = 2$), then the first, second, and third ranked securities were in the optimal portfolio ($i = 3$), and so forth. These C_i are candidates for C^*. We know we have found the optimum C_i—that is

C^*—when all securities used in the calculation of C_i have excess returns to Beta above C_i and all securities not used to calculate C_i have excess returns to Beta below C_i. For example, column 7 of Table 9.2 shows the C_i for alternative values of i. Examining the table shows that C_5 is the only value of C_i for which all securities used in the calculation of i (1 through 5 in the table) have a ratio of excess return to Beta above C_i and all securities not used in the calculation of C_i (6 through 10 in the table) have an excess return to Beta ratio below C_i. C_5 serves the role of a cut-off rate in the way a cut-off rate was defined earlier. In particular, C_5 is the only C_i that when used as a cut-off rate selects only the stocks used to construct it. There will always be one and only one C_i with this property and it is C^*.

Calculating the Cut-off Rate C*

Recall that stocks are ranked by excess return to risk from highest to lowest. For a portfolio of i stocks C_i is given by

$$C_i = \frac{\sigma_m^2 \sum_{j=1}^{i} \frac{\left(\overline{R}_j - R_F\right)\beta_j}{\sigma_{ej}^2}}{1 + \sigma_m^2 \sum_{j=1}^{i} \left(\frac{\beta_j^2}{\sigma_{ej}^2}\right)} \tag{9.1}$$

where

σ_m^2 = the variance in the market index

σ_{ej}^2 = the variance of a stock's movement that is not associated with the movement of the market index. This is usually referred to as a stock's unsystematic risk.

This looks horrible. But a moment's reflection combined with a peek at the example below will show that it is not as hard to compute as it appears. While Equation (9.1) is the form that should actually be used to compute C_i, this expression can be stated in a mathematically equivalent way that clarifies the meaning of C_i.[2]

$$C_i = \frac{\beta_{iP}\left(\overline{R}_P - R_F\right)}{\beta_i} \tag{9.2}$$

where

β_{iP} = the expected change in the rate of return on stock i associated with a 1% change in the return on the optimal portfolio

$\overline{R}_P$ = the expected return on the optimal portfolio
All other terms as before.

β_{iP} and $\overline{R}_P$ are, of course, not known until the optimal portfolio is determined. Hence, Equation (9.2) could not be used to actually determine the optimum portfolio; rather, Equation (9.1) must be used. However, this expression for C_i is useful in interpreting the economic significance of our procedure. Recall that securities are added to the portfolio as long as

$$\frac{\overline{R}_i - R_F}{\beta_i} > C_i$$

---

[2]See Appendix A at the end of this chapter for a derivation of this expression.

Rearranging and substituting in Equation (9.2) yields

$$\left(\overline{R}_i - R_F\right) > \beta_{iP}\left(\overline{R}_P - R_F\right)$$

The right-hand side is nothing more than the expected excess return on a particular stock based solely on the expected performance of the optimum portfolio. The term on the left-hand side is the security analyst's estimate of the expected excess return on the individual stock. Thus, if the analysis of a particular stock leads the portfolio manager to believe that it will perform better than would be expected, based on its relationship to the optimal portfolio, it should be added to the portfolio.

Now let us look at how Equation (9.1) can be used to determine the value of C_i for our example. While Equation (9.1) might look complex, the ease with which it can be calculated is demonstrated by Table 9.2. This table presents the intermediate calculations necessary to determine Equation (9.1).

Let's work through the intermediate calculations shown in Table 9.2 and find the value for C_i for the first security in our list of securities. The numerator of Equation (9.1) is

$$\sigma_m^2 \sum_{j=1}^{i} \frac{\left(\overline{R}_j - R_F\right)\beta_j}{\sigma_{ej}^2}$$

Column 3 of Table 9.2 presents the value of

$$\frac{\left(\overline{R}_j - R_F\right)\beta_j}{\sigma_{ej}^2}$$

for each security. This is necessary in order to determine the summation. For example, for the first security using the values shown in Table 9.1, it is

$$\frac{(15-5)1}{50} = \frac{2}{10}$$

Column 5 gives the value of the summation, or the running cumulative total of column 3. For the first security $i = 1$ and

$$\sum_{j=1}^{1} \frac{\left(\overline{R}_j - R_F\right)\beta_j}{\sigma_{ej}^2} = \frac{\left(\overline{R}_1 - R_F\right)\beta_1}{\sigma_{e1}^2}$$

Thus column 5 of Table 9.2 is the same as column 3 for security 1. The last term in the denominator of expression 9.1 is

$$\sum_{j=1}^{i} \frac{\beta_j^2}{\sigma_{ej}^2}$$

Since $i = 1$ for the first security, it is simply

$$\frac{\beta_1^2}{\sigma_{e1}^2} = \frac{(1)^2}{50} = \frac{2}{100}$$

This result is shown in column 4 and cumulated in column 6. We can now put these terms together to find C_i. Remembering that $\sigma_m^2 = 10$,

$$C_i = \frac{\sigma_m^2 \sum_{j=1}^{i} \frac{\left(\overline{R}_j - R_F\right)\beta_j}{\sigma_{ej}^2}}{1 + \sigma_m^2 \sum_{j=1}^{i} \frac{\beta_j^2}{\sigma_{ej}^2}}$$

$$= \frac{\sigma_m^2 (\text{column 5})}{1 + \sigma_m^2 (\text{column 6})} = \frac{10\left(\dfrac{2}{10}\right)}{1 + 10\left(\dfrac{2}{100}\right)} = 1.67$$

We now follow through the calculations for security 2 ($i = 2$). Column 3 is found to be

$$\frac{(17 - 5)1.5}{40} = \frac{4.5}{10}$$

Now column 5 is the sum of column 3 for security 1 and security 2 or

$$\frac{2}{10} + \frac{4.5}{10} = \frac{6.5}{10}$$

Column 4 is

$$\frac{(1.5)^2}{40} = \frac{5.625}{100}$$

Column 6 is the sum of column 4 for security 1 and 2, or

$$\frac{2}{100} + \frac{5.625}{100} = \frac{7.625}{100}$$

We can now find C_2 as

$$C_2 = \frac{\sigma_m^2 (\text{column 5})}{1 + \sigma_m^2 (\text{column 6})} = \frac{10 \dfrac{6.5}{10}}{1 + 10 \dfrac{7.625}{100}} = 3.68$$

Proceeding in the same fashion we can find all the C_i's.

Constructing the Optimal Portfolio

Once the securities that are contained in the optimum portfolio are determined, it remains to show how to calculate the percent invested in each security. The percentage invested in each security is

$$X_i = \frac{Z_i}{\sum_{\text{included}} Z_j}$$

where

$$Z_i = \frac{\beta_i}{\sigma_{ei}^2}\left(\frac{\bar{R}_i - R_F}{\beta_i} - C*\right)$$ (9.3)

The second expression determines the relative investment in each security while the first expression simply scales the weights on each security so they sum to one and, thus, ensure full investment. Note that the residual variance on each security σ_{ei}^2 plays an important role in determining how much to invest in each security. Applying this formula to our example we have

$$Z_1 = \frac{2}{100}(10 - 5.45) = 0.091$$

$$Z_2 = \frac{3.75}{100}(8 - 5.45) = 0.095625$$

$$Z_3 = \frac{5}{100}(7 - 5.45) = 0.0775$$

$$Z_4 = \frac{20}{100}(6 - 5.45) = 0.110$$

$$Z_5 = \frac{2.5}{100}(6 - 5.45) = 0.01375$$

$$\sum_{i=1}^{5} Z_i = 0.387875$$

Dividing each Z_i by the sum of the Z_i, we find that we should invest 23.5% of our funds in security 1, 24.6% in security 2, 20% in security 3, 28.4% in security 4, and 3.5% in security 5.

Let us stress that this is identical to the result that would be achieved had the problem been solved using the established quadratic programming codes. However, the solution has been reached in a fraction of the time with a set of relatively simple calculations.

Notice that the characteristics of a stock that make it desirable and the relative attractiveness of stocks can be determined before the calculations of an optimal portfolio are begun. The desirability of any stock is solely a function of its excess return to Beta ratio. Thus, a security analyst following a set of stocks can determine the relative desirability of each stock before the information from all analysts is combined and the portfolio selection process begun.

Up to this point we have assumed that all stocks have positive Betas. We believe that there are sound economic reasons to expect all stocks to have positive Betas and that the few negative Beta stocks that are found in large samples are due to measurement errors. However, as pointed out in [6], negative Beta stocks (and zero Beta stocks) are easily incorporated in the analysis.

Another Example

We have included a second example to illustrate the use of these formulas. This example is presented in Tables 9.3 and 9.4. Once again, securities are ranked by excess return to Beta. Examining Table 9.4 shows that the C_i associated with security 4 is the only C_i

Table 9.3   Data Required to Determine Optimal Portfolio; $R_F = 5$

1	2	3	4	5	6
Security Number i	Mean Return $\bar{R}_i$	Excess Return $\bar{R}_i - R_F$	Beta β_i	Unsystematic Risk σ_{ei}^2	Excess Return over Beta $\dfrac{(\bar{R}_i - R_F)}{\beta_i}$
1	19	14	1.0	20	14
2	23	18	1.5	30	12
3	11	6	0.5	10	12
4	25	20	2.0	40	10
5	13	8	1.0	20	8
6	9	4	0.5	50	8
7	14	9	1.5	30	6
8	10	5	1.0	50	5
9	9.5	4.5	1.0	50	4.5
10	13	8	2.0	20	4
11	11	6	1.5	30	4
12	8	3	1.0	20	3
13	10	5	2.0	40	2.5
14	7	2	1.0	20	2

Table 9.4   Calculations for Determining Cut-off Rate with $\sigma_m^2 = 10$

Security Number i	$\dfrac{(\bar{R}_i - R_F)}{\beta_i}$	$\dfrac{(\bar{R}_i - R_F)\beta_i}{\sigma_{ei}^2}$	$\dfrac{\beta_i^2}{\sigma_{ei}^2}$	$\displaystyle\sum_{j=1}^{i} \dfrac{(\bar{R}_j - R_F)\beta_j}{\sigma_{ej}^2}$	$\displaystyle\sum_{j=1}^{i} \dfrac{\beta_j^2}{\sigma_{ej}^2}$	C_i
1	14	$\dfrac{70}{100}$	$\dfrac{5}{100}$	$\dfrac{70}{100}$	$\dfrac{5}{100}$	4.67
2	12	$\dfrac{90}{100}$	$\dfrac{7.5}{100}$	$\dfrac{160}{100}$	$\dfrac{12.5}{100}$	7.11
3	12	$\dfrac{30}{100}$	$\dfrac{2.5}{100}$	$\dfrac{190}{100}$	$\dfrac{15}{100}$	7.6
4	10	$\dfrac{100}{100}$	$\dfrac{10}{100}$	$\dfrac{290}{100}$	$\dfrac{25}{100}$	8.29
5	8	$\dfrac{40}{100}$	$\dfrac{5}{100}$	$\dfrac{330}{100}$	$\dfrac{30}{100}$	8.25
6	8	$\dfrac{4}{100}$	$\dfrac{0.5}{100}$	$\dfrac{334}{100}$	$\dfrac{30.5}{100}$	8.25
7	6	$\dfrac{45}{100}$	$\dfrac{7.5}{100}$	$\dfrac{379}{100}$	$\dfrac{38}{100}$	7.9
8	5	$\dfrac{10}{100}$	$\dfrac{2}{100}$	$\dfrac{389}{100}$	$\dfrac{40}{100}$	7.78
9	4.5	$\dfrac{9}{100}$	$\dfrac{2}{100}$	$\dfrac{398}{100}$	$\dfrac{42}{100}$	7.65
10	4	$\dfrac{80}{100}$	$\dfrac{20}{100}$	$\dfrac{478}{100}$	$\dfrac{62}{100}$	6.64
11	4	$\dfrac{30}{100}$	$\dfrac{7.5}{100}$	$\dfrac{508}{100}$	$\dfrac{69.5}{100}$	6.39
12	3	$\dfrac{15}{100}$	$\dfrac{5}{100}$	$\dfrac{523}{100}$	$\dfrac{74.5}{100}$	6.19
13	2.5	$\dfrac{25}{100}$	$\dfrac{10}{100}$	$\dfrac{548}{100}$	$\dfrac{84.5}{100}$	5.8
14	2	$\dfrac{10}{100}$	$\dfrac{5}{100}$	$\dfrac{558}{100}$	$\dfrac{89.5}{100}$	5.61

consistent with our definition of C^*. That is, it is the only value of C_i such that stocks ranked i or higher all have excess returns to Beta above C_i and all stocks ranked below i have excess returns to Beta below C_i. Thus the cut-off rate

$$C^* = C_4 = \frac{58}{7} = 8.29$$

The optimum amount to invest is determined using Equation (9.3). For this example, it is

$$Z_1 = \frac{1}{20}\left(14 - \frac{58}{7}\right) = \frac{40}{140} = \frac{240}{840}$$

$$Z_2 = \frac{1.5}{30}\left(12 - \frac{58}{7}\right) = \frac{39}{210} = \frac{156}{840}$$

$$Z_3 = \frac{0.5}{10}\left(12 - \frac{58}{7}\right) = \frac{13}{70} = \frac{156}{840}$$

$$Z_4 = \frac{2}{40}\left(10 - \frac{58}{7}\right) = \frac{24}{280} = \frac{72}{840}$$

Scaling the Z's so that they add to one we have

$$X_1 = \frac{240}{240 + 156 + 156 + 72} = \frac{240}{624} = 0.38$$

$$X_2 = \frac{156}{240 + 156 + 156 + 72} = \frac{156}{624} = 0.25$$

$$X_3 = \frac{156}{240 + 156 + 156 + 72} = \frac{156}{624} = 0.25$$

$$X_4 = \frac{72}{240 + 156 + 156 + 72} = \frac{72}{624} = 0.12$$

Thus, in this example the optimum portfolio consists of four securities with the largest investment in security 1 and the smallest in security 4.

In solving this problem there is no need to fill in all the entries in Table 9.4. Clearly, all the intermediate calculations associated with the lower ranked securities are not needed. One could start by ranking all securities by excess return to Beta. Then proceed to calculate C_i for larger values of i (higher ranked stocks) until a value of i is found so that the ith + 1 stock is excluded. At that point we can ignore stocks ranked below the ith stock. Notice that, though excess return to Beta had to be computed for all stocks, the calculation of C_i and Z_i need only be done for i stocks or, in the case of this example, four stocks.

Short Sales Allowed

The procedures used to calculate the optimal portfolio when short sales are allowed are closely related to the procedures in the no short sales case. As a first step all stocks are ranked by excess return to Beta just as they were in the previous case. However, the cut-off point for stocks, C^*, now has a different meaning, as well as a different procedure for calculation. When short sales are allowed, all stocks will either be held long or sold short.[3]

---

[3]Actually, it is possible for one or more stocks to have return and risk characteristics so that they are held in exactly zero proportions. This does not affect the procedure described in this section.

Thus, all stocks enter into the optimum portfolio and all stocks affect the cut-off point. Equation (9.1) still represents the cut-off point, but now the numerator and denominator of this equation are summed over all stocks. In addition, although Equations (9.1) and (9.3) still hold (with respect to the new C^*), the meaning of Z_i is now changed. We now have to calculate a value for Z_i for each stock. A positive value of Z_i indicates the stock will be held long, and a negative value indicates it will be sold short. Thus, the impact of C^* has changed. Stocks that have an excess return to Beta above C^* are held long (as before), but stocks with an excess return to Beta below C^* are now sold short.

Let us illustrate this by returning to the first example presented earlier in Table 9.2. Remember in order to calculate C^* we must employ Equation (9.1) with i set equal to the number of stocks under consideration. In this case we have a population of 10 stocks so that

$$C^* = C_{10} = 4.52$$

Employing Equation (9.3) for each security we find

$$Z_1 = \frac{1}{50}\left[10 - 4.52\right] = 0.110 \qquad Z_7 = \frac{2}{40}\left[3 - 4.52\right] = -0.076$$

$$Z_2 = \frac{1.5}{40}\left[8 - 4.52\right] = 0.131 \qquad Z_8 = \frac{0.8}{16}\left[2.5 - 4.52\right] = -0.101$$

$$Z_3 = \frac{1}{20}\left[7 - 4.52\right] = 0.124 \qquad Z_9 = \frac{1}{20}\left[2 - 4.52\right] = -0.126$$

$$Z_4 = \frac{2}{10}\left[6 - 4.52\right] = 0.296 \qquad Z_{10} = \frac{0.6}{6}\left[1.0 - 4.52\right] = -0.352$$

$$Z_5 = \frac{1}{40}\left[6 - 4.52\right] = 0.037$$

$$Z_6 = \frac{1.5}{30}\left[4 - 4.52\right] = -0.026 \qquad \sum_{i=1}^{10} Z_i = 0.017$$

The last step in the procedure involves the scaling of the Z_i's so they represent the optimum proportions to invest in each stock (X_i's). There are actually two ways to do this scaling. These methods exactly parallel the two definitions of short sales we examined in earlier chapters. Under the standard definition of short sales, which presumes that a short sale of a stock is a source of funds to the investor, the appropriate scaling factor is given by

$$X_i = \frac{Z_i}{\sum_{j=1}^{N} Z_j}$$

where Z_i can be positive or negative. This scaling factor is arrived at by realizing that under this definition of short sales the constraint on the X_i's is that

$$\sum_{i=1}^{N} X_i = 1$$

The second definition of short sales we referred to earlier is Lintner's definition. Under this definition short sales are a use of the investor's funds; however, the investor receives the riskless rate of the funds involved in the short sale.[4] We have seen that this translates into the constraint

$$\sum_{i=1}^{N}|X_i|=1$$

The analogous scaling factor is

$$X_i = \frac{Z_i}{\sum_{j=1}^{N}|Z_j|} \tag{9.4}$$

In Table 9.5 we have presented the fraction of funds that the investor should place in each security when short sales are not allowed, when the standard definition of short sales is employed, and when Lintner's definition of short sales is used.

Note that under the two alternative definitions of short sales, not only are the same stocks always held long and sold short, but any two stocks are always held in the same ratio to each other. This is true because the two solutions differ by only a scale factor. From the foregoing analysis it is obvious that this scale factor is simply

$$\frac{\sum_{i=1}^{N}|Z_i|}{\sum_{i=1}^{N}Z_i}$$

One point of interest this example makes clear is that employing the normal definition of short sales can really change the scale of the optimal solution. While the proportions invested under the Lintner definition seem reasonable, for example, place 8% of your money in security 1 and use 25.5% of your funds to short sell security 10, the solution that can be reached under the standard definition of short sales can seem extreme. In this example the standard

Table 9.5   Optimum Percentages

Security	Short Sales Disallowed	Lintner Definition of Short Sales	Standard Definition of Short Sales
1	23.5	8.0	647.1
2	24.6	9.5	770.6
3	20.0	9.0	729.4
4	28.4	21.5	1741.2
5	3.5	2.7	217.6
6	0	−1.9	−152.9
7	0	−5.5	−447.1
8	0	−7.3	−594.1
9	0	−9.1	−741.2
10	0	−25.5	−2070.6

[4]To be precise, the Lintner definition assumes that the proceeds of the short sale are not available for investment. Furthermore, the investor must put up an amount of funds equal to the proceeds of the short sale as collateral to protect against adverse price movements. The return on the short sale is the opposite of a long purchase. A negative value for X is required in determining the return on a portfolio. However, in analyzing the constraint on the amount invested, the additional funds invested must be considered—hence the absolute value sign in the constraint of the sum of X's. See footnote 1 in Chapter 6 for a further explanation.

definition of short sales would involve investing in stock 1 a sum of money equal to 6.47 times the amount originally available for investment and selling short an amount of security 10 equal to 20.7 times the amount originally available for investment.

If we now compare either of the short sales examples with the short sales disallowed examples, we can see some interesting differences. First note that the proportion placed in any stock relative to a second stock need bear no relationship between the two cases. As an example examine security 1 and security 4 in the short sales allowed and short sales not allowed examples. Both call for security 1 and security 4 to be held long. When short sales are not allowed, we hold 1.21 as much of security 4 as we hold of security 1. When short sales are allowed, we hold 2.69 as much of security 4 as we hold of security 1. This demonstrates that the proportions held of securities under short sales allowed need bear no particular relationship to the proportions held of the securities when short sales are not allowed.

In fact, although this particular example does not demonstrate it, the set of securities that is held long can be different according to whether short sales are allowed or not. This can be seen by reexamining example 2. When short sales were not allowed, we have seen that the first four securities are held long. If short sales are allowed, the appropriate value for C (all securities included) is 5.61 from Table 9.4. Examining Table 9.4 we now see that the first seven rather than the first four securities should be held long in the optimal portfolio.

The fact that allowing short sales changes the nature of the optimal solution should not come as a surprise to the reader. Allowing short sales is equivalent to adding new securities to the set from which the optimal portfolio will be selected. It is equivalent to adding a set of securities with the opposite characteristics from those included in the set when short sales are not allowed.

SECURITY SELECTION WITH A PURCHASABLE INDEX

Oftentimes the index used in the single-index model is a portfolio of securities. For example, the index could be the S&P index. If the portfolio used as an index is an asset the investor is considering investing in (buy an index fund), then the simple rules described earlier are even simpler. As shown in Appendix E, in this case, Equation (9.3) collapses to

$$Z_i = \frac{\alpha_i'}{\sigma_{ei}^2}$$

where

$$\alpha_i' = \overline{R}_i - \left[R_F + \beta_i\left(\overline{R}_m - R_F\right)\right]$$

and the subscript m designates the index.

Once again the amount to invest in any asset involves dividing each Z_i by the sum of the Z_i's. The preceding expression, which works only if short sales are allowed, was first derived by Treynor and Black. The intuition is that a mixture of a riskless asset and the index having the same Beta as asset i would have an expected return of $R_F + \beta_i(\overline{R}_m - R_F)$. Thus if asset i has a higher mean return than a passive mixture with the same Beta $\alpha_i' > 0$, it should be held long. If it has a lower expected return than a passive mixture with the same Beta $\alpha_i' < 0$, it should be sold short.[5]

---

[5]Since the riskless asset has a Beta of zero and the index a Beta of 1, the combination of a riskless asset and the portfolio with the same Beta as asset i would involve investing β_i in the index portfolio and 1 minus β_i in the riskless portfolio. This has an expected return of $(1 - \beta_i)R_F + \beta_i\overline{R}_m$ or rearranging $R_F + \beta_i(\overline{R}_m - R_F)$. This is the term in the brackets in the definition of α_i'.

Constructing an Efficient Frontier

The procedure just described assumes the existence of a riskless lending and borrowing rate. It produces the composition of the optimal portfolio that lies at the point where a ray passing through the riskless asset is tangent to the efficient frontier in expected return standard deviation space. If the investor does not wish to assume the existence of a riskless asset, then it is necessary to derive the full efficient frontier.

Two cases need to be analyzed: when short sales are allowed and when they are forbidden. If short sales are allowed, then, as was shown in Chapter 6, the full efficient frontier can be constructed from combinations of any two portfolios that lie on the efficient frontier. The composition of two portfolios on the efficient frontier can be found easily by assuming two different values for R_F and repeating the procedure just described for each. From these two efficient portfolios, the full frontier can be traced. The efficient frontier is a little more difficult to determine when short sales are not allowed.

The brute force solution is to solve the portfolio composition problem for a large number of values of R_F and, thus, approximate the full efficient frontier. An alternative procedure that solves directly for the R_F associated with each corner portfolio is described in [6].[6] Since the frontier between corner portfolios can be found as combinations of corner portfolios, this procedure allows the full efficient frontier to be easily traced out.

THE CONSTANT CORRELATION MODEL

We now present and demonstrate the use of simple procedures for selecting optimum portfolios when the constant correlation model is accepted as the best way to forecast correlation coefficients. The reader will recall from earlier chapters that the constant correlation model assumes that the correlation between all pairs of securities is the same. The procedures assuming a constant correlation coefficient exactly parallel those presented for the case of the single-index model. Once again, the derivation of these procedures and the proof that they are, indeed, optimum is left for Appendix B at the end of this chapter.

If the constant correlation model is accepted as describing the co-movement between securities, then all securities can be ranked by their excess return to standard deviation. To be precise, if σ_i is the standard deviation of the return on security i, then a security's desirability is determined by

$$\frac{\left(\overline{R}_i - R_F\right)}{\sigma_i}$$

Notice that we are still ranking on the basis of excess return to risk; but standard deviation has taken the place of Beta as the relevant risk measure.[7] This ratio provides an ordering of securities for which the top ranked securities are purchased and the lower ranked securities are not held in the case of short sales prohibited or are sold short if such sales are allowed. Once again, there is a unique cut-off rate.

---

[6]Recall that a corner portfolio is one in which a security either enters the efficient set or is deleted from the efficient set as we move along the efficient frontier.

[7]In Chapter 18 we see that excess return to standard deviation like excess return to Beta has been used as a technique for ranking portfolios.

Ranking and Selecting from Among Securities—Short Sales Not Allowed

We illustrate the manner in which an optimal portfolio can be designed with a simple example presented in Table 9.6. First, as has been done in Table 9.6, all stocks are ranked by excess return to standard deviation. Then, the optimal value of C_i, called C^*, is calculated and all stocks with higher excess returns to standard deviation are included in the optimal portfolio. All stocks with lower excess returns to standard deviation are excluded. For the moment accept that C^* equals 5.25. Shortly we will discuss how to calculate it. Since securities 1 through 3 have higher excess returns to standard deviations, they are included in the optimum portfolio. Securities 4 through 12 have excess returns to standard deviation below 5.25 and, hence, are not included in the optimal portfolio.

Setting the Cut-off Rate

The procedure for setting the cut-off rate is directly analogous to that presented for the case of the single-index model. First, we need a general expression for C_i, where i represents the fact that the first i securities are included in the computation of C_i. As shown in Appendix D at the end of this chapter, C_i can be found from

$$C_i = \frac{\rho}{1-\rho+i\rho} \sum_{j=1}^{i} \frac{\bar{R}_j - R_F}{\sigma_j}$$

where ρ is the correlation coefficient—assumed constant for all securities. The subscript i indicates that C_i is calculated, using data on the first i securities.

Just as in the single-index model case, we have determined the appropriate level of the cut-off rate C^* when we have found a C_i such that

1. All stocks ranked 1 through i have a value of excess return to standard deviation lower than C_i.

2. All stocks ranked $i + 1$ through N have a value of excess return to standard deviation lower than C_i.

Table 9.6   Data to Determine Ranking $R_F = 5\%$

Security No. i	Expected Return $\bar{R}_i$	Excess Return $\bar{R}_i - R_F$	Standard Deviation σ_i	Excess Return to Standard Deviation $\dfrac{(\bar{R}_i - R_F)}{\sigma_i}$
1	29	24	3	8.0
2	19	14	2	7.0
3	29	24	4	6.0
4	35	30	6	5.0
5	14	9	2	4.5
6	21	16	4	4.0
7	26	21	6	3.5
8	14	9	3	3.0
9	15	10	5	2.0
10	9	4	2	2.0
11	11	6	4	1.5
12	8	3	3	1.0

Tables 9.6 and 9.7 present an example and some of the intermediate calculations needed to design an optimal portfolio. Examine the two columns at the extreme right of Table 9.7. Note that only for a value of $C_i = C_3$ do all stocks 1 to i have higher excess returns to standard deviation and all stocks $i + 1$ to 12 have lower excess return to standard deviation. Thus, $C^* = C_3 = 5.25$.

As we show in Appendix B at the end of this chapter, the optimum amount to invest in any security is

$$X_i = \frac{Z}{\sum_{j=1}^{N} Z_j}$$

where

$$Z_i = \frac{1}{(1-\rho)\sigma_i}\left[\frac{\overline{R}_i - R_F}{\sigma_i} - C^*\right]$$

For our example we have

$$Z_1 = \frac{1}{1.5}\left[8 - \frac{21}{4}\right] = \frac{11}{6} = \frac{44}{24}$$

$$Z_2 = \frac{1}{1}\left[7 - \frac{21}{4}\right] = \frac{7}{4} = \frac{42}{24}$$

$$Z_3 = \frac{1}{2}\left[6 - \frac{21}{4}\right] = \frac{3}{8} = \frac{9}{24}$$

Table 9.7   Determining the Cut-off Rate $\rho = 0.5$

Security No. i	$\dfrac{\rho}{1-\rho+i\rho}$	$\sum_{j=1}^{i} \dfrac{\overline{R}_j - R_F}{\sigma_j}$	C_i	$\dfrac{\overline{R}_i - R_F}{\sigma_i}$
1	$\frac{1}{2}$	8	$\frac{8}{2} = 4$	8
2	$\frac{1}{3}$	15	$\frac{15}{3} = 5$	7
3	$\frac{1}{4}$	21	$\frac{21}{4} = 5.25$	6
4	$\frac{1}{5}$	26	$\frac{26}{5} = 5.2$	5
5	$\frac{1}{6}$	30.5	$\frac{30.5}{6} = 5.08$	4.5
6	$\frac{1}{7}$	34.5	$\frac{34.5}{7} = 4.93$	4
7	$\frac{1}{8}$	38	$\frac{38}{8} = 4.75$	3.5
8	$\frac{1}{9}$	41	$\frac{41}{9} = 4.56$	3
9	$\frac{1}{10}$	43	$\frac{43}{10} = 4.3$	2
10	$\frac{1}{11}$	45	$\frac{45}{11} = 4.09$	2
11	$\frac{1}{12}$	46.5	$\frac{46.5}{12} = 3.88$	1.5
12	$\frac{1}{13}$	47.5	$\frac{47.5}{13} = 3.65$	1

Dividing each Z_i by the sum of the Z_i's gives the optimum amount to invest in each security. This calculation results in

$$X_1 = \frac{44}{44 + 42 + 9} = \frac{44}{95} \text{ or } 46.3\%$$

$$X_2 = \frac{42}{95} \text{ or } 44.2\%$$

$$X_3 = \frac{9}{95} \text{ or } 9.5\%$$

Short Sales Allowed

If short sales are allowed, then, as in the single-index case, all stocks will either be held long or sold short. This suggests, once again, that C^* should include all stocks, and this is correct. The C^* when all stocks are included is $C^* = C_{12} = 3.65$. Once again, C^* is the cut-off rate that separates securities that are purchased long from those that are sold short. In this example $C^* = 3.65$ implies that the first six securities are purchased long and securities 7 to 12 are sold short. The optimum amount to invest in any security is given by the same formula Equation (9.4) with C^* defined to incorporate all securities.

OTHER RETURN STRUCTURES

We have presented two simple ranking devices based on different correlation structures. As discussed in the last two chapters, there are a number of other models for estimating the covariance structure. For each of these other structures a simple ranking device exists; the references listed at the end of the chapter show where. However, a few comments are in order. There are two types of models for estimating correlation structure: index models and group models. The single- and multi-index models are examples of the former, while constant correlation and multi-group models are examples of the latter.

For index models the ranking is done by excess return to Beta. This is true for both single- and multi-index models. However, the cut-off rate for multi-index models is different than the cut-off rate for single-index models. For example, assume a multi-index model where securities are related to a general market index and an industry index. In this model the cut-off rate is different for each industry but depends on the members of all industries.

If a multi-group model is employed, then the ranking is always in terms of excess return to standard deviation. The cut-off rate varies from group to group and depends on which securities are included and in which groups.

Beta is important in index models because it is a measure of the securities' contribution to the risk of the portfolio. In multi-group or constant correlation models, the contribution to portfolio risk depends on the standard deviation and, hence, standard deviation is the risk measure in the portfolios.

AN EXAMPLE

Let us return to the problem analyzed in Chapter 7. The problem involved an allocation among five common stock funds. The input data were

FUND	$\bar{R}_i$	β_i	$\sigma^2_{\epsilon i}$	$R_F = 5\%$
1. Small stock	23.5	1.4	65	

2. Value	14	0.8	20
3. Growth	20.75	1.3	45
4. Large capitalization	12.05	0.9	24
5. Special situation	13.95	1.1	45

Utilizing the simple rules discussed earlier we can complete their rank in order of desirability.

FUND	$\dfrac{\overline{R}_i - R_F}{\beta_i}$
1.	13.21
2.	11.25
3.	12.12
4.	7.83
5.	8.14

Thus the ranking is 1, 3, 2, 5, 4. Calculating a cut-off rate assuming two securities in the optimum portfolio (1 + 3) yields

$$C^* = 11.82$$

This is optimum since security 1 + 3 are above the cut-off and 2, 4, and 5 below. Security 2 would be the next to enter. It is 0.57 below the cut-off. Thus if the management is confident that the value fund has an expected return of 14 and the Beta is estimated correctly, security 3 shouldn't enter. Securities 4 and 5 are much farther below the cut-off. Security 4 is 3.99 and 5 is 3.68 below. These are sufficiently far from the cut-off that reasonable adjustments in inputs are unlikely to lead to their inclusion. However, management might well wish to refine their estimates for securities 1, 2, and 3.

Computing the optimum proportions with no short sales we have

$$Z_1 = \frac{1.4}{65}[13.21 - 11.82] = 0.02994$$

$$Z_3 = \frac{1.3}{45}[12.12 - 11.82] = 0.00867$$

and

$$X_1 = \frac{0.02994}{0.03861} = 0.775$$
$$X_2 = 0.225$$

It is left as an exercise for the reader to show that this solution is identical to the solution obtained using the technique discussed in Chapter 6.

CONCLUSION

In this chapter we have discussed several simple rules for optimal portfolio selection. These simple ranking devices allow the portfolio manager to quickly and easily determine the optimum portfolio. Furthermore, the manager uncertain about some of the estimates can easily manipulate them in order to determine if reasonable changes in the estimates lead to a different selection decision. The existence of a cut-off rate allows the manager to quickly determine if a new security should or should not be included in the portfolio.

Finally, the existence of simple ranking devices makes clear the characteristics of a security that are important and why a security is included, or excluded, from a portfolio.

APPENDIX A

SINGLE-INDEX MODEL—SHORT SALES ALLOWED

In this appendix we derive the simple ranking device when the investor is allowed to short sell securities and where he wishes to act as if the single-index model adequately reflects the correlation structure between securities. As we showed in Chapter 6, if the investor wishes to assume a riskless lending and borrowing rate, then he can obtain an optimum portfolio by solving a system of simultaneous equations. If, on the other hand, he desires to trace out the full efficient frontier, then he must solve this same system of simultaneous equations for two risk-free rates. This allows him to determine the characteristics of any two efficient portfolios and allows him to trace out the efficient frontier. The system of simultaneous equations the investor solves is

$$\bar{R}_i - R_F = Z_i \sigma_i^2 + \sum_{\substack{j=1 \\ j \neq i}}^{N} Z_j \sigma_{ij} \qquad i = 1, \ldots, N \qquad \text{(A.1)}$$

where

$\bar{R}_i$　is the expected return of security i

R_F　is the return on the riskless asset

σ_i^2　is the variance of security i

σ_{ij}　is the covariance between securities i and j

Z_i　is proportional to the amount invested in security i

From Chapter 7 we know that if the single-index model is used to describe the structure of security returns, then the covariance between securities i and j is $\beta_i \beta_j \sigma_m^2$ and the variance of security i is $\beta_i^2 \sigma_m^2 + \sigma_{ei}^2$. Substituting these relationships that hold for the single-index model into the general system of simultaneous equations, (A.1) yields

$$\bar{R}_i - R_F = Z_i \left(\beta_i^2 \sigma_m^2 + \sigma_{ei}^2 \right) + \sum_{\substack{j=1 \\ j \neq i}}^{N} Z_j \beta_i \beta_j \sigma_m^2 \qquad i = 1, \ldots, N$$

Look at the summation term. If $j = i$, it would be $Z_i \beta_i \beta_j \sigma_m^2$. But, this is exactly the first term on the right-hand side of the equality sign. Eliminating the $j \neq i$ underneath the summation sign by incorporating the term $Z_i \beta_i \beta_i \sigma_m^2$ within it yields

$$\bar{R}_i - R_F = Z_i \sigma_{ei}^2 + \sum_{j=1}^{N} Z_j \beta_i \beta_j \sigma_m^2 \qquad i = 1, \ldots, N$$

Solving for Z_i and taking the constants outside the summation yields

$$Z_i = \frac{\bar{R}_i - R_F}{\sigma_{ei}^2} - \frac{\beta_i \sigma_m^2}{\sigma_{ei}^2} \sum_{j=1}^{N} Z_j \beta_j \qquad i = 1, \ldots, N \qquad \text{(A.2)}$$

This can be written as

$$Z_i = \frac{\beta_i}{\sigma_{ei}^2}\left[\frac{\overline{R}_i - R_F}{\beta_i} - C*\right] \qquad i = 1,\ldots,N$$

where

$$C* = \sigma_m^2 \sum_{j=1}^{N} Z_j \beta_j \qquad\qquad (A.3)$$

This is the equation presented in the text. To get the $C*$ in terms of known variables, we must express (A.2) and (A.3) in terms that do not invoke

$$\sum_{j=1}^{N} Z_j \beta_j$$

To do so, first multiply Equation (A.2) by β_i and sum over all values of $i = 1, \ldots, N$. This yields

$$\sum_{j=1}^{N} Z_j \beta_j = \sum_{j=1}^{N} \frac{(\overline{R}_j - R_F)\beta_j}{\sigma_{ej}^2} - \sigma_m^2 \sum_{j=1}^{N} \frac{\beta_j^2}{\sigma_{ej}^2} \sum_{j=1}^{N} Z_j \beta_j$$

Notice that the term

$$\sum_{j=1}^{N} Z_j \beta_j$$

is found on both the left-hand and right-hand sides of the equation. Solving for this yields

$$\sum_{j=1}^{N} Z_j \beta_j = \frac{\displaystyle\sum_{j=1}^{N} \frac{(\overline{R}_j - R_F)\beta_j}{\sigma_{ej}^2}}{1 + \sigma_m^2 \displaystyle\sum_{j=1}^{N} \frac{\beta_j^2}{\sigma_{ej}^2}}$$

From Equation (A.3) we see that

$$C* = \frac{\sigma_m^2 \displaystyle\sum_{j=1}^{N} \frac{(\overline{R}_j - R_F)\beta_j}{\sigma_{ej}^2}}{1 + \sigma_m^2 \displaystyle\sum_{j=1}^{N} \frac{\beta_j^2}{\sigma_{ej}^2}}$$

The alternative form for C_i (Equation 9.2) employed in the text can be derived from Equation (A.3). From Equation (A.3) we see that

$$C* = \sigma_m^2 \sum_{j=1}^{N} Z_j \beta_j$$

We also note from Chapter 6 that Z_j is proportional to the optimal fraction of the portfolio the investor should hold in each stock X_j. The constant is equal to the ratio of the excess return of the optimal portfolio to the variance of its return. Thus,

$$C^* = \sigma_m^2 \sum_{j=1}^{N} \frac{\overline{R}_P - R_F}{\sigma_P^2} X_j \beta_j$$

Recognizing

$$\sum_{j=1}^{N} X_j \beta_j$$

as the Beta on the investor's portfolio

$$C^* = \left(\overline{R}_P - R_F \right) \beta_P \frac{\sigma_m^2}{\sigma_P^2}$$

Dividing and multiplying the equation by β_i and recognizing that $\beta_i \beta_p \sigma_m^2$ is $cov(ip)$ under the assumption of the single-index model, we have

$$C^* = \left(\overline{R}_P - R_F \right) \frac{cov(ip)}{\sigma_P^2} \frac{1}{\beta_i} = \frac{\beta_{ip}}{\beta_i} \left(\overline{R}_P - R_F \right)$$

where β_{ip} is the regression coefficient of the return on security i to the return on portfolio p.

APPENDIX B

CONSTANT CORRELATION COEFFICIENT—SHORT SALES ALLOWED

In this appendix we derive the simple ranking devices discussed in the text when the investor believes that the constant correlation coefficient adequately describes the structure of security returns. Once again, we utilize the result shown in Chapter 6 that the efficient frontier can be determined by solving a system of simultaneous equations. The system of simultaneous equations is

$$\overline{R}_i - R_F = Z_i \sigma_i^2 + \sum_{\substack{j=1 \\ j \neq i}}^{N} Z_i \sigma_{ij} \qquad i = 1, \ldots, N \tag{B.1}$$

If the constant correlation model holds, then $\sigma_{ij} = \rho \sigma_i \sigma_j$. Note that the correlation coefficient between stocks i and j is by assumption the same for all i and j. Making the substitution into (B.1) yields

$$\overline{R}_i - R_F = Z_i \sigma_i^2 + \sum_{\substack{j=1 \\ j \neq i}}^{N} Z_j \rho \sigma_i \sigma_j \qquad i = 1, \ldots, N$$

If $j = i$, then the term in the summation is $Z_i \rho \sigma_i \sigma_i$. Adding this to the summation and subtracting the same term yields

$$\overline{R}_i - R_F = Z_i \sigma_i^2 - Z_i \rho \sigma_i \sigma_i + \sum_{j=1}^{N} Z_j \rho \sigma_i \sigma_j \qquad i = 1, \ldots, N$$

Solving for Z_i yields

$$Z_i (1 - \rho) \sigma_i^2 = \overline{R}_i - R_F - \rho \sigma_i \sum_{j=1}^{N} Z_j \sigma_j \qquad i = 1, \ldots, N$$

or

$$Z_i = \frac{1}{(1-\rho)\sigma_i}\left[\frac{\overline{R}_i - R_F}{\sigma_i} - C^*\right] \qquad i = 1,\ldots,N \qquad (B.2)$$

where

$$C^* = \rho \sum_{j=1}^{N} Z_j \sigma_j$$

This is the equation used in the text. To express C^* in known terms, multiply (B.2) by σ_i and ρ and add up the N equations. This yields

$$C^* = \rho \sum_{j=1}^{N} Z_j \sigma_j = \frac{\rho}{1-\rho}\sum_{j=1}^{N}\frac{\overline{R}_j - R_F}{\sigma_j} - \frac{N\rho C^*}{1-\rho}$$

Solving for C^*

$$C^*\left(1 + \frac{N\rho}{1-\rho}\right) = \frac{\rho}{1-\rho}\sum_{j=1}^{N}\frac{\overline{R}_j - R_F}{\sigma_j}$$

or

$$C^* = \left(\frac{\rho}{1-\rho}\right)\left(\frac{1-\rho}{1-\rho+N\rho}\right)\sum_{j=1}^{N}\frac{\overline{R}_j - R_F}{\sigma_j} = \frac{\rho}{1-\rho+N\rho}\sum_{j=1}^{N}\frac{\overline{R}_j - R_F}{\sigma_j}$$

Appendix C

SINGLE-INDEX MODEL WITH SHORT SALES NOT ALLOWED

In this appendix we derive simple ranking rules when the investor wishes to act as if the single-index model is a reasonable method of describing the structure of security returns. In Chapter 6 we showed that if we could find a solution that met the Kuhn–Tucker conditions, then we could be certain we had the optimum portfolio. In this appendix we show that our simple ranking procedure does, in fact, lead to a solution that meets the Kuhn–Tucker conditions.

The Kuhn–Tucker conditions were

1. $\overline{R}_i - R_F = Z_i \sigma_i^2 + \sum_{\substack{j=1 \\ j\neq i}}^{N} Z_j \sigma_{ij} - M_i \qquad i = 1,\ldots,N.$

2. $Z_i M_i = 0 \qquad i = 1,\ldots,N.$

3. $Z_i \geq 0$ and $M_i \geq 0 \qquad i = 1,\ldots,N.$ $\qquad\qquad$ (C.1)

where M_i is a variable added to make Equation (C.1) an equality.

If the single-index model is assumed to adequately describe the return structure, then

$$\sigma_{ij} = \beta_i \beta_j \sigma_m^2 \quad \text{and} \quad \sigma_i^2 = \beta_i^2 \sigma_m^2 + \sigma_{ei}^2$$

Substituting this into the first Kuhn–Tucker condition yields

$$\overline{R}_i - R_F = Z_i\left(\beta_i^2 \sigma_m^2 + \sigma_{ei}^2\right) + \sum_{\substack{j=1 \\ j\neq i}}^{N} Z_j \beta_i \beta_j \sigma_m^2 - M_i \qquad i = 1,\ldots,N$$

Once again, noting that when $j = i$, the term in the summation would be $Z_i\beta_i\beta_i\sigma_m^2$, and this is the first term on the right-hand side of the equality. Incorporating this term into the summation, we have

$$\overline{R}_i - R_F = Z_i\sigma_{ei}^2 + \beta_i\sigma_m^2 \sum_{j=1}^{N} Z_j\beta_j - M_i \qquad i = 1,\ldots,N$$

If the security is not in the optimum portfolio, then $Z_j = 0$. Thus, the summation only has to include the Z_i and β_i for those securities in the optimum portfolio. We will call the set of securities in the optimum set k. Further, we will use the symbol

$$\sum_{j\epsilon k}$$

to indicate that the summation is to include all securities in the optimum. Rewriting the equation yields

$$\overline{R}_i - R_F = Z_i\sigma_e^2 + \beta_i\sigma_m^2 \sum_{j\epsilon k} Z_j\beta_j - M_i \qquad i = 1,\ldots,N \qquad \text{(C.2)}$$

Examine conditions 2 and 3. Condition 3 says that Z_i and M_i must each be either zero or positive. Condition 2 states that their product must be zero. Thus, if Z_i is positive, M_i must be zero. For any security included in the optimum, Z_i is positive. Hence, we can drop the M_i for included securities (those in set k). Setting $M_i = 0$ in Equation (C.2) yields

$$\overline{R}_i - R_F = Z_i\sigma_{ei}^2 + \beta_i\sigma_m^2 \sum_{j\epsilon k} Z_j\beta_j \qquad \text{for } i\epsilon k$$

or

$$Z_i = \frac{\beta_i}{\sigma_{ei}^2}\left[\frac{\overline{R}_i - R_F}{\beta_i} - \sigma_m^2 \sum_{j\epsilon k} Z_j\beta_j\right] \qquad \text{for } i\epsilon k \qquad \text{(C.3)}$$

We can eliminate

$$\sum_{j\epsilon k} Z_j\beta_j$$

by multiplying (C.3) by β_j and summing over set k

$$\sum_{j\epsilon k} Z_j\beta_j = \sum_{j\epsilon k}\frac{(\overline{R}_j - R_F)\beta_j}{\sigma_{ej}^2} - \sigma_m^2 \sum_{j\epsilon k}\frac{\beta_j^2}{\sigma_{ej}^2}\sum_{j\epsilon k} Z_j\beta_j$$

Rearranging

$$\sum_{j\epsilon k} Z_j\beta_j = \frac{\displaystyle\sum_{j\epsilon k}\frac{(\overline{R}_j - R_F)\beta_j}{\sigma_{ej}^2}}{1 + \sigma_m^2 \displaystyle\sum_{j\epsilon k}\frac{\beta_j^2}{\sigma_{ei}^2}}$$

(C.3) can be written as

$$Z_i = \frac{\beta_i}{\sigma_{ei}^2}\left[\frac{\overline{R}_i - R_F}{\beta_i} - C^*\right] \qquad i\epsilon k \qquad \text{(C.4)}$$

where

$$C^* = \sigma_m^2 \sum_{j \in k} Z_j \beta_j = \frac{\sigma_m^2 \sum_{j \in k} \dfrac{\left(\overline{R}_j - R_F\right)\beta_j}{\sigma_{ej}^2}}{1 + \sigma_m^2 \sum_{j \in k} \dfrac{\beta_j^2}{\sigma_{ej}^2}}$$

This is the expression utilized in the text.

Let us see how to determine a portfolio that meets the Kuhn–Tucker conditions. First condition 2 ($Z_i M_i = 0$) is met by construction. M_i was set to zero for all securities included in the optimum portfolio, those with $Z_i > 0$. For those not included in the optimum, $Z_i = 0$ guaranteeing $Z_i M_i = 0$.

Now consider the first and third conditions. Assume we have found a set of securities for which Z_i as determined by (C.4) is greater than zero for securities in the set and less than zero for securities not in the set.

For securities in the set Equation (C.4) is equivalent to condition 1 if $M_i = 0$. $Z_i > 0$ and $M_i = 0$ meets condition 3. Thus, conditions 1 and 3 are met.

For securities not in this set, (C.4) is not equivalent to condition 1. However, comparing these two shows that $M_i > 0$ will make condition 1 hold, and also Z_i is equal to zero so that condition 3 holds.

Thus, the Kuhn–Tucker conditions will be met if a set k can be determined for which (C.4) is positive for members of the set and negative for securities not in the set.

Examine (C.4). C^* is a constant. Assume for the moment that $\beta_i > 0$. Then the term outside the brackets is positive. The term in the brackets is positive if $(\overline{R}_i - R_F)/\beta_i > C^*$ and is negative if $(\overline{R}_i - R_F)/\beta_i > C^*$. The procedure discussed in the text assures that this will occur.

APPENDIX D

CONSTANT CORRELATION COEFFICIENT—SHORT SALES NOT ALLOWED

The analysis in this section closely parallels the analysis of the last section. Once again, if the Kuhn–Tucker conditions are met, then the solution is an optimum. The Kuhn–Tucker conditions are as shown in (C.1). If an investor wishes to act as if the return structure is adequately described by the assumption of a constant correlation coefficient, then the covariance terms are $\sigma_{ij} = \rho \sigma_i \sigma_j$. Making this substitution into the first Kuhn–Tucker condition and adding and subtracting $\rho \sigma_i \sigma_i Z_i$ to eliminate $j \neq i$ under the summation sign yields

1. $\overline{R}_i - R_F = Z_i \sigma_i^2 (1 - \rho) + \sum_{j=1}^{N} Z_j \rho \sigma_i \sigma_j - M_i \qquad i = 1, \dots, N.$

2. $Z_i M_i = 0, \qquad i = 1, \dots, N.$

3. $Z_i \geq 0$ and $M_i \geq 0 \qquad i = 1, \dots, N.$ \hfill (D.1)

The same considerations hold here as did in Appendix C. If set k is the set of included securities, then $Z_i = 0$ for securities not in set k and, thus,

$$\sum_{j \in k} Z_j \sigma_j = \sum_{j=1}^{N} Z_j \sigma_j$$

Furthermore, if $Z_i > 0$, then $M_i = 0$ so that $M_i = 0$ for set k. Using these two observations, Equation (D.1) becomes

$$\bar{R}_i - R_F = Z_i\sigma_i^2(1-\rho) + \rho\sigma_i\sum_{j\in k} Z_j\sigma_j \qquad i\in k \tag{D.2}$$

Rearranging and solving for Z_i

$$Z_i = \frac{1}{(1-\rho)\sigma_i}\left[\frac{\bar{R}_i - R_F}{\sigma_i} - \rho\sum_{j\in k} Z_j\sigma_j\right] \tag{D.3}$$

We can eliminate

$$\sum_{j\in k} Z_j\sigma_j$$

by multiplying each equation by σ_i and then adding together all the equations in set k. This yields

$$\sum_{j\in k} Z_j\sigma_j = \frac{1}{1-\rho}\left[\sum_{j\in k}\frac{\bar{R}_j - R_F}{\sigma_j} - \rho N_k\sum_{j\in k} Z_j\sigma_j\right]$$

where N_k is the number of securities in k. Rearranging

$$\sum_{j\in k} Z_j\sigma_j = \frac{1}{1-\rho}\left(\frac{1-\rho}{1-\rho+\rho N_k}\right)\sum_{j\in k}\frac{\bar{R}_j - R_F}{\sigma_j}$$

Thus, (D.3) becomes

$$Z_i = \frac{1}{(1-\rho)\sigma_i}\left[\frac{\bar{R}_i - R_F}{\sigma_i} - \phi_k\right] \qquad i\in k$$

$$\phi_k = \rho\sum_{j\in k} Z_j\sigma_j = \frac{\rho}{1-\rho+\rho N_k}\sum_{j\in k}\frac{\bar{R}_j - R_F}{\sigma_j} \tag{D.4}$$

The same considerations hold here as did in Appendix C. Namely, if (D.4) is positive for members of set k and negative for all other securities, the Kuhn–Tucker conditions are met. The procedures discussed in the text lead to this solution.

APPENDIX E

SINGLE-INDEX MODEL, SHORT SALES ALLOWED, AND A MARKET ASSET

If one can buy a portfolio that exactly replicates the index used in the single-index model, the solution is simpler. In fact investors can often replicate the index. For example, the Standard & Poor's (S&P) index is often used as the index in the single-index model, and an investor can buy an index fund matching the S&P index.

We will now examine this case. Let the subscript m represent this asset. Furthermore, note that portfolio m regressed on itself has zero residual risk and a slope of 1. Thus, $\sigma_{em}^2 = 0$ and $\beta_m = 1$. With these substitutions the equation above (A.2) becomes $\bar{R}_m - R_F = \sigma_m^2\sum_{j=1}^{N}\beta_j Z_j$ and thus the cut-off rate in (A.3) is $C^* = \bar{R}_m - R_F$. Substituting this into (9.3) results in

$$Z_i = \frac{\beta_i}{\sigma_{ei}^2}\left(\frac{\overline{R}_i - R_F}{\beta_i} - \left(\overline{R}_m - R_F\right)\right)$$

or

$$Z_i = \frac{1}{\sigma_{ei}^2}\left[\overline{R}_i - R_F - \beta_i\left(\overline{R}_m - R_F\right)\right]$$

defining α_i' as the term in the brackets we have $Z_i = \frac{\alpha_i'}{\sigma_{ei}^2}$ which is the expression shown in the text. This expression does not hold when short sales are not allowed. In particular the solution when short sales are not allowed does not involve holding long all securities with a positive Z_i.

QUESTIONS AND PROBLEMS

1. Given the following data: $\sigma_m^2 = 10$

Security Number	Expected Return	Beta	σ_{ei}^2
1	15	1.0	30
2	12	1.5	20
3	11	2.0	40
4	8	0.8	10
5	9	1.0	20
6	14	1.5	10

What is the optimum portfolio assuming no short sales if $R_F = 5\%$?

2. What is the optimum portfolio assuming short sales if $R_F = 5\%$ and the data from Problem 1 are used?

3. Using the data from Problem 1, what is the optimum portfolio assuming short sales are allowed but riskless lending and borrowing are forbidden?

4. Given the following data

Security Number	Expected Return	Standard Deviation
1	15	10
2	20	15
3	18	20
4	12	10
5	10	5
6	14	10
7	16	20

What is the optimum portfolio assuming no short sales if $R_F = 5\%$ and $\rho = 0.5$?

5. What is the optimum portfolio assuming short sales if $R_F = 5\%$ and $\rho = 0.5$? Use the data in Problem 4.

6. What is the optimum portfolio assuming short sales but no riskless lending and borrowing with $\rho = 0.5$ for all pairs of securities? Use the data in Problem 4.

BIBLIOGRAPHY

1. Alexander, Gordon J., and Resnick, Bruce G. "More on Estimation Risk and Simple Rules for Optimal Portfolio Selection," *The Journal of Finance*, **40,** No. 1 (March 1985), pp. 125–134.
2. Bawa, Vijay, Elton, Edwin J., and Gruber, Martin J. "Simple Rules for Optimal Portfolio Selection in a Stable Paretian Market," *Journal of Finance*, **34,** No. 2 (June 1979).
3. Chen, Son-Nan, and Brown, Stephen J. "Estimation Risk and Simple Rules for Optimal Portfolio Selection," *The Journal of Finance*, **38,** No. 4 (Sept. 1983), pp. 1087–1094.
4. Elton, Edwin J., Gruber, Martin J., and Padberg, Manfred W. "Simple Criteria for Optimal Portfolio Selection," *Journal of Finance,* **XI,** No. 5 (Dec. 1976), pp. 1341–1357.
5. ——. "Simple Rules for Optimal Portfolio Selection: The Multi Group Case," *Journal of Financial and Quantitative Analysis*, **XII,** No. 3 (Sept. 1977), pp. 329–345.
6. ——. "Simple Criteria for Optimal Portfolio Selection: Tracing Out the Efficient Frontier," *Journal of Finance*, **XIII,** No. 1 (March 1978), pp. 296–302.
7. ——. "Optimal Portfolios from Simple Ranking Devices," *Journal of Portfolio Management,* **4,** No. 3 (Spring 1978), pp. 15–19.
8. ——. "Simple Criteria for Optimal Portfolio Selection with Upper Bonds," *Operation Research,* **8,** (Nov.–Dec. 1978).
9. ——. "Simple Criteria for Optimal Portfolio Selection: The Multi-Index Case," in Edwin J. Elton and Martin J. Gruber, (eds.), *Portfolio Theory: 25 Years Later* (Amsterdam: North-Holland, 1979).
10. Frankfurter, George M., and Lamourex, Christopher G. "The Relevance of the Distributional Form of Common Stock Returns to the Construction of Optimal Portfolios," *Journal of Financial and Quantitative Analysis*, **22,** No. 4 (Dec. 1987), pp. 505–511.
11. Green, Richard C., and Hollifield, Burton. "When Will Mean-Variance Efficient Portfolios Be Well Diversified," *The Journal of Finance*, **47,** No. 5 (Dec. 1992), p. 1784.
12. Kwan, Clarence C. Y. "Portfolio Analysis Using Single Index, Multi-Index, and Constant Correlation Models: A Unified Treatment," *The Journal of Finance*, **39,** No. 5 (Dec. 1984), pp. 1469–1484.
13. Lee, Sang, and Lerro, A. J. "Optimizing the Portfolio Selection for Mutual Funds," *Journal of Finance*, **VIII,** No. 5 (Dec. 1973), pp. 1087–1101.
14. Mao, C. T. James. "Essentials of Portfolio Diversification Strategy," *Journal of Finance*, **V,** No. 5 (Dec. 1970), pp. 1109–1121.
15. Porter, Burr, and Bey, Roger. "An Evaluation of the Empirical Significance of Optimal Seeking Algorithms in Portfolio Selection." *Journal of Finance*, **IX,** No. 5 (Dec. 1974), pp. 1479–1490.
16. Sharpe, W. F. "Simple Strategies for Portfolio Diversification: Comment," *Journal of Finance*, **VII,** No. 1 (March 1972), pp. 127–129.
17. ——. "Simple Strategies for Portfolio Diversification: Comment, A Correction," *Journal of Finance*, **VII,** No. 3 (June 1972), p. 733.
18. Sharpe, William, and Stone, Bernell. "A Linear Programming Formulation of the General Portfolio Selection Model," *Journal of Financial and Quantitative Analysis*, **VIII,** No. 4 (Sept. 1973), pp. 621–636.

Section 3

Selecting the Optimum Portfolio

10

Utility Analysis

In Chapter 1 we pointed out that to solve any decision problem one had to define an opportunity set and define a preference function. In the preceding chapters we have discussed how an investor could construct this opportunity set and how, with some very general assumptions about preferences, he or she could limit this set to the efficient frontier.[1] The subject of this chapter is how to choose among the investor's opportunity set or, alternatively, how to specify a preference function.

Although the previous chapters dealt with the definition of the investor's opportunity set, we quite often made use of assumptions about the attributes of the investors' preference functions in order to limit the opportunity set. For example, we have shown that, if the investor prefers more to less and is a risk avoider, the opportunity set can be reduced to the efficient frontier. We have also shown that if riskless lending and borrowing can take place at the same rate in unlimited quantities, then there is only one preferred portfolio of risky assets for each investor. That is, there is one portfolio of risky assets that will be preferred by a risk-avoiding investor, regardless of the investor's preference function. This means that the manager of a portfolio of risky assets can select the optimal portfolio of risky assets for an investor without regard to the investor's preference function. Does this mean that the investor's preference function plays no role in the decision process when riskless lending and borrowing is allowed? The answer is no. In this case, the investor's preference function determines what combination of the optimum risky portfolio and riskless asset the investor will hold, and how much this investor will consume and invest.

Thus, whatever the opportunity set facing the investor, his or her preference function will play a key role in his optimal decision. We devote the remainder of this chapter to a discussion of preference functions. We start off with a general description of the characteristics of choice functions. Appendix A at the end of this chapter contains a more rigorous axiomatic treatment of the material contained in the text. Then we explore the desirable economic features of preference functions and the types of preference functions

---

[1]This analysis assumed that means and variances constituted the relevant information for any decision problem. The analysis in this chapter is applicable whether the relevant decision space is formulated in terms of means and variances or higher movements of the probability distribution of returns are used.

that possess these characteristics. Finally, we explore the limited evidence on the types and characteristics of utility functions that are consistent with investor behavior.

AN INTRODUCTION TO PREFERENCE FUNCTIONS

We start our discussion of the choice between risky assets with a simple example. Consider the two alternatives shown in Table 10.1. Investment A and investment B each have three possible outcomes, each equally likely. Investment A has less variability in its outcomes but has a lower average outcome.

Table 10.1   Two Alternative Investments

Investment A		Investment B	
Outcome	Probability of Outcome	Outcome	Probability of Outcome
15	1/3	20	1/3
10	1/3	12	1/3
5	1/3	4	1/3

There are several ways to decide between A and B. First, we could simply ask the decision maker which he prefers or whether he is indifferent between them. With the simple problem presented in Table 10.1, this probably is sufficient. Even for the more complicated problems, the direct analysis of the options may be the most sensible alternative.

Another approach is to specify how much more valuable the large outcomes are relative to the small outcomes and then to weight the outcomes by their value and find the expected value of these weighted outcomes. The idea of adding up or averaging weighted outcomes is very common. Consider, for example, how the winning team is selected in hockey. Table 10.2 shows the hypothetical records for two hockey teams. Current practice weights wins by two, ties by one, and losses by zero. With this weighting scheme, the Islanders would be leading the Flyers 100 to 95. But there is nothing special about this weighting scheme. A league interested in deemphasizing the incentive for ties might weight wins by four, ties by one, and losses by zero. In this case, the Flyers would be considered the dominant team 185 to 180. If we denote W as the result (win, tie, lose), $U(W)$ as the value of this result, and $N(W)$ as the number of times (games) that W occurs, then to determine the better team we calculate[2]

$$\sum_{W} U(W)N(W)$$

Table 10.2   Data for Ranking Hockey Teams

	Islanders	Flyers
Wins	40	45
Ties	20	5
Losses	10	20

---

[2] $\sum_{W}$ should read as the sum over all results.

The team with the higher U is considered the better team. For example, utilizing current practice U (win) = 2, U (tie) = 1, and U (loss) = 0. Applying the formula to the Islanders yields[3]

$$U = 2(40) + 1(20) + 0(10) = 100$$

This is the 100 we referred to earlier. While the particular function $U(W)$ differs between situations, the principle is the same. Traditionally, instead of using the number of outcomes of a particular type, the proportion is used. There were 70 hockey games in our example. If $P(W)$ is the proportion of the total games that resulted in outcome W, then $P(W) = N(W)/70$. Dividing through by 70 will not affect our choice. Weighting a function by the proportion of each outcome is equivalent to calculating an average or expected value. Letting $E(U)$ designate the expected value of U yields

$$E(U) = \sum_{W} U(W)P(W)$$

When we apply this principle to the decision problem shown in Table 10.1, we have special names for the principle. The weighting function is called a utility function and the principle is called the expected utility theorem. Consider the example shown in Table 10.1. The weighting function could look like this

Outcome	Weight	Value of Outcome
20	0.9	18
15	1.0	15
12	1.1	13.2
10	1.2	12
5	1.4	7
4	1.5	6

We have called the last column in the table the value of the outcome. Alternatively, it could be called the utility of an outcome. If this was the weighting function the investor felt was appropriate, then he or she would compare the expected utility of investments A and B, using this function. For example, the expected utility of A is

$$U(15)(1/3) + U(10)(1/3) + U(5)(1/3)$$

Referring to the weighting function, we have

$$15(1/3) + 12(1/3) + 7(1/3) = 34/3$$

and the expected utility of investment B is

$$U(20)\left(\frac{1}{3}\right) + U(12)\left(\frac{1}{3}\right) + U(4)\left(\frac{1}{3}\right) = 18\left(\frac{1}{3}\right) + 13.2\left(\frac{1}{3}\right) + 6\left(\frac{1}{3}\right) = \frac{37.2}{3}$$

In this situation the investor would select investment B because it offers the higher average or expected utility. In general we can say that the investor will choose among alternatives by maximizing expected utility or maximizing

$$E(U) = \sum_{W} U(W)P(W)$$

---

[3]These numbers are hypothetical.

Table 10.3   Outcomes and Associated Probabilities for Three Investments

Investment A		Investment B		Investment C	
Outcome	Probability	Outcome	Probability	Outcome	Probability
20	3/15	19	1/5	18	1/4
18	5/15	10	2/5	16	1/4
14	4/15	5	2/5	12	1/4
10	2/15			8	1/4
6	1/15				

Consider a second example. Table 10.3 lists three separate investments. Assume the investor has the following utility function:

$$U(W) = 4W - (1/10)W^2$$

Then the utility of 20 is $80 - (1/10)(400) = 40$; the utility of 18 is $72 - (1/10)(324) = 39.6$; and the utility of 14 is $56 - (1/10)(196) = 36.4$.

The rest of the values are shown in Table 10.4. The expected utility of the three investments is found by multiplying the probability of each outcome times the value of the outcome.

Expected utility $A = (40)(3/15) + (39.6)(5/15) + (36.4)(4/15)$
$$+ (30)(2/15) + (20.4)(1/15)$$

$$= \frac{544}{15} = 36.3$$

Expected utility $B = (39.9)(1/5) + (30)(2/5) + (17.5)(2/5)$

$$= \frac{134.9}{5} = 26.98$$

Expected utility $C = (39.6)(1/4) + (38.4)(1/4) + (33.6)(1/4) + (25.6)(1/4)$

$$= \frac{137.2}{4} = 34.4$$

Thus, an investor with the utility function discussed earlier would select investment A.

An important attribute of utility analysis is that utility functions are unique up to a positive linear transformation. This means that $A + bv(W)$ will lead to the same investments being selected as $v(W)$. To see this, assume in the last example that the utility function was

Table 10.4   Including Utility

Investment A			Investment B			Investment C		
Outcome	Utility of Outcome	Probability	Outcome	Utility of Outcome	Probability	Outcome	Utility of Outcome	Probability
20	40	3/15	19	39.9	1/5	18	39.6	1/4
18	39.6	5/15	10	30	2/5	16	38.4	1/4
14	36.4	4/15	5	17.5	2/5	12	33.6	1/4
10	30	2/15				8	25.6	1/4
6	20.4	1/15						

$2 + 4W - (1/10)W^2$ rather than $4W - (1/10)W^2$. The only difference between the two functions is the addition of the number 2. Thus, the value of each outcome would be increased by two times the probability of the outcome. Furthermore, expected utility would be increased by two times the sum of the probabilities of each outcome. But the probabilities must sum to 1. Thus, the expected utility of each investment increases by 2. If the expected utility of each investment increases by 2, the ranking is unchanged. A similar argument can be made for the effect of multiplication by a positive constant. In this case the expected utility is also multiplied by a positive constant. But such a multiplication does not change the order, and the same investment would be selected.

If the investor acts in certain ways (obeys certain postulates of behavior), then the choice of preferred investment, using the expected utility theorem, is identical to the choice made by examining the investment directly. For the reader interested in a formal statement and demonstration of these postulates, see Appendix A at the end of this chapter. It follows that, having an investor make choices between a series of simple investments, we can attempt to determine the weighting (utility) function that the investor is implicitly using. Applying this weighting function to more complicated investments, we should be able to determine which one the investor would choose.

A number of brokerage firms and banks have developed programs to extract the utility function of investors by confronting them with a choice between a series of simple investments. These have not been particularly successful. Many investors do not obey all the rationality postulates when faced with a series of choice situations, even though they may find the underlying principles perfectly reasonable. Also, many investors, when faced with more complicated choice situations, encounter aspects of the problem that were not of concern to them in the simple choice situations.

Even if the investor, or manager, does not believe in formally deriving utility functions, there is still a lot to be learned from utility analysis. An understanding of the properties of alternative utility functions can lead to insight into the process of rational choice. This will allow the investor to eliminate some portfolios from further consideration and will reduce the chances of making a really bad decision.

In the next section we examine more formally the characteristics of utility functions.

THE ECONOMIC PROPERTIES OF UTILITY FUNCTIONS

The first restriction placed on a utility function is that it be consistent with more being preferred to less. This attribute, known in the economic literature as nonsatiation, simply says that the utility of more $(X + 1)$ dollars is always higher than the utility of less (X) dollars. Thus, if we want to choose between two certain investments, we always take the one with the largest outcome. In this section we will formulate utility functions in terms of end of period wealth. This property then states that more wealth is always preferred to less wealth. If utility increases as wealth increases, then the first derivative of utility, with respect to wealth, is positive.[4] Thus, the first restriction placed on the utility function is a positive first derivative.

---

[4]The reader might note that in this chapter we discuss utility functions of end of period wealth. Earlier chapters discussed opportunity sets in terms of returns rather than wealth. This should present no conceptual problems as end of period wealth is simply beginning wealth times 1 plus the appropriate rate of return. Therefore, all the properties discussed with respect to wealth also hold with respect to returns.

Table 10.5   An Example of a Fair Gamble

Invest		Do Not Invest	
Outcome	Probability	Outcome	Probability
2	1/2	1	1
0	1/2		

The second property of a utility function is an assumption about an investor's taste for risk. Three assumptions are possible: the investor is averse to risk, the investor is neutral toward risk, and the investor seeks risk. Risk aversion, risk neutrality, and risk seeking can all be defined in terms of a fair gamble. Consider the gambles (options) shown in Table 10.5.

The option "invest" has an expected value of $(1/2)(2) + (1/2)(0) = \$1$. Assume that an investor would have to pay $1 to undertake this investment and obtain these outcomes. Thus, if the investor chooses not to invest, the $1 is kept. This is the alternative: do not invest. The expected value of the gamble is exactly equal to the cost. The position of the investor may be improved or hurt by undertaking the investment, but the expectation is that there will be no change in position. Because the expected value of the gamble shown in Table 10.5 is equal to its cost, it is called a fair gamble.

Risk aversion means that an investor will reject a fair gamble. In terms of Table 10.5, it means $1 for certain will be preferred to an equal chance of $2 or $0. Risk aversion implies that the second derivative of utility, with respect to wealth, is negative. If $U(W)$ is the utility function and $U''(W)$ is the second derivative, then risk aversion is usually equated with an assumption that $U''(W) < 0$. Let us examine why this is true.

If an investor prefers not to invest, then the expected utility of not investing must be higher than the expected utility of investing or

$$U(1) > (1/2)U(2) + (1/2)U(0)$$

Multiplying both sides by 2 and rearranging, we have

$$U(1) - U(0) > U(2) - U(1)$$

Examine the preceding expression. The expression means that a one-unit change from 0 to 1 is more valuable than a one-unit change from 1 to 2. This latter change involves larger values of outcomes. A function where an additional unit increase is less valuable than the last unit increase is a function with a negative second derivative.

The assumption of risk aversion means an investor will reject a fair gamble because the disutility of the loss is greater than the utility of an equivalent gain. Functions that exhibit this property must have a negative second derivative. Therefore, the rejection of a fair gamble implies a negative second derivative.

Risk neutrality means that an investor is indifferent to whether or not a fair gamble is undertaken. In the context of Table 10.5, a risk-neutral investor would be indifferent to whether or not an investment was made. Risk neutrality implies a zero second derivative. Let us examine why. For the investor to be indifferent between investing and not investing, the expected utility of investing, or not investing, must be the same, or

$$U(1) = (1/2)U(2) + (1/2)U(0)$$

Multiplying by 2 and rearranging yields

$$U(1) - U(0) = U(2) - U(1)$$

This expression implies that the change in utility from a one-unit change in wealth is independent of whether we are moving from 0 to 1 or 1 to 2. This characteristic is associated with functions that exhibit a zero second derivative. Thus, indifference to a fair gamble implies a zero second derivative, and utility functions of risk-neutral investors should have zero second derivatives.

Risk seeking means that an investor would select a fair gamble. In the context of Table 10.5, the risk-seeking investor would choose to invest. Risk-seeking investors have utility functions with positive second derivatives. The reason why exactly parallels previous discussion. Since the risk-seeking investor chooses the investment, the expected utility of investment must be higher than the expected utility of not investing, or

$$(1/2)U(2) + (1/2)U(0) > U(1)$$

Once again, multiplying by 2 and rearranging yields

$$U(2) - U(1) > U(1) - U(0)$$

This expression indicates that the utility of a one-unit change from 1 to 2 is greater than the utility of a one-unit change from 0 to 1. Functions that exhibit the property of greater change in value for larger unit changes in the argument are functions with positive second derivatives. Thus, the acceptance of a fair gamble implies a positive second derivative. These conditions are summarized in Table 10.6.

Table 10.6   Implications of Attitude Toward Risk

Condition	Definition	Implication
1. Risk aversion	Reject fair gamble	$U''(0) < 0$
2. Risk neutrality	Indifferent to fair gamble	$U''(0) = 0$
3. Risk preference	Select a fair gamble	$U''(0) > 0$

Figures 10.1*a* and 10.1*b* show preference functions exhibiting alternative properties with respect to risk aversion. Figure 10.1*a* presents the shape of utility functions in utility of wealth space that exhibit risk aversion, risk neutrality, and risk preference. Figure 10.1*b* presents the shape of the indifference curves in expected return standard deviation space that would be associated with each of these three types of utility functions.

As discussed in earlier chapters, investors who can state their feelings toward a fair gamble can significantly reduce the set of risky investments they must consider. For example, risk-averse investors must consider only the efficient frontier when choosing among alternative portfolios. Thus, an understanding of utility theory can simplify the selection problem of investors even if they are unwilling to more formally specify their utility function.

The third property of utility functions is an assumption about how the investor's preferences change with a change in wealth. If the investor's wealth increases, will more or less of that wealth be invested in risky assets? For example, assume that an investor with $10,000 to invest puts $5000 into risky assets. Now assume the same investor's wealth increases to $20,000. Will the investor invest more than $5000, less than $5000, or $5000 in risky assets? If the investor increases the amount invested in risky assets as wealth increases, then the investor is said to exhibit decreasing absolute risk aversion. If the investor's investment in risky assets is unchanged as wealth changes, then the investor is said to exhibit constant absolute risk aversion. Finally, if the investor invests fewer dollars in risky assets as wealth increases, then the investor is said to exhibit increasing absolute

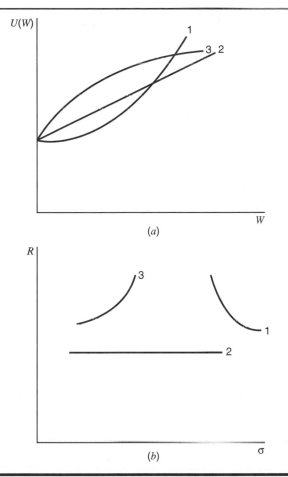

Figure 10.1   Characteristics of functions with different risk-aversion coefficients. (1) Utility
function of a risk-seeking investor. (2) Utility function of a risk-neutral investor.
(3) Utility function of a risk-averse investor.

risk aversion. When we discussed risk aversion, we showed that different degrees of risk
aversion were associated with different derivatives of the utility function. A similar result
is true for absolute risk aversion. If $U'(W)$ and $U''(W)$ are the first and second derivatives
of the utility function at wealth level W, then we show in Appendix B, at the end of this
chapter that

$$A(W) = \frac{-U''(W)}{U'(W)}$$

can be used to measure an investor's absolute risk aversion. Then $A'(W)$, the derivative of
$A(W)$ with respect to wealth, is an appropriate measure of how absolute risk aversion
behaves with respect to changes in wealth. Table 10.7 summarizes the important relationship between $A'(W)$ and changes in risk aversion and presents an example of a utility function exhibiting each type of behavior described in the table.

Most evidence would indicate that, as wealth increases, the dollar amount invested in

Table 10.7   Changes in Absolute Risk Aversion with Wealth

Condition	Definition	Property of $A(W)^a$	Example[b]
Increasing absolute risk aversion	As wealth increases hold fewer dollars in risky assets	$A'(W) > 0$	W^{-cW^2}
Constant absolute risk aversion	As wealth increases hold same dollar amount in risky assets	$A'(W) = 0$	$-e^{-cW}$
Decreasing absolute risk aversion	As wealth increases hold more dollars in risky assets	$A'(W) < 0$	$\ln W$

[a]$A'(W)$ is the first derivative of $A(W)$ with respect to wealth.
[b]The proof is left to the reader.

risky assets should increase, or that investors exhibit decreasing absolute risk aversion. Regardless of which condition of absolute risk aversion best describes investors' behavior, if they can specify their feelings regarding absolute risk aversion, then the number of possible options they need consider can be reduced. Furthermore, this assumption restricts the possible utility functions that could describe their preferences.

The final characteristic that is used to restrict the investor's utility function is how the percentage of wealth invested in risky assets changes as wealth changes. For example, if the investor puts 50% of her wealth in risky investments when her wealth is $10,000, does she still put 50% of her wealth in risky assets when her wealth increases to $20,000? If she does, then the investor's behavior is said to be characterized by constant *relative* risk aversion. If she invests a greater percentage of her wealth in risky investments, she is said to exhibit decreasing relative risk aversion, and if she invests a smaller percentage, she is said to exhibit increasing relative risk aversion. Relative risk aversion is closely related to absolute risk aversion. Relative risk aversion refers to the change in the percentage investment in risky assets as wealth changes. In contrast, absolute risk aversion refers to the change in dollar amount invested in risky assets as wealth changes. The measure of relative risk aversion is

$$R(W) = \frac{-WU''(W)}{U'(W)} = WA(W)$$

If $R'(W)$ is the first derivative of W, then $R'(W) < 0$ indicates that the utility function exhibits decreasing relative risk aversion. If $R'(W) = 0$, then the utility function is said to exhibit constant relative risk aversion. Finally, if $R'(W) > 0$, then the function is said to exhibit increasing relative risk aversion. This is summarized in Table 10.8.

While there is general agreement that most investors exhibit decreasing absolute risk aversion, there is much less agreement concerning relative risk aversion. Often people assume constant relative risk aversion. The justification for this, however, is often one of convenience rather than belief about descriptive accuracy. In any case, if investors can articulate their feelings about the percentage they would invest in risky assets as wealth changes, then they can reduce the number of portfolios they must consider or further restrict the utility functions that might describe their behavior.

Table 10.8 Changes in Relative Risk Aversion with Wealth

Condition	Definition	Property of $R'(W)$	Examples of Utility Functions
Increasing relative risk aversion	Percentage invested in risky assets declines as wealth increases	$R'(W) > 0$	$W - bW^2$
Constant relative risk aversion	Percentage invested in risky assets is unchanged as wealth increases	$R'(W) = 0$	$\ln W$
Decreasing relative risk aversion	Percentage invested in risky assets increases as wealth increases	$R'(W) < 0$	$-e^{2W-1\backslash 2}$

Let us examine some utility functions that have been used in the economics and finance literature to describe investor behavior and explore the characteristics of each. The most frequently used function is probably the quadratic. It is

$$U(W) = W - bW^2$$

Its derivatives are

$$U'(W) = 1 - 2bW$$

$$U''(W) = -2b$$

If the investor displays a utility function that exhibits risk aversion, then the second derivative must be negative or b must be positive. If the investor is assumed to prefer more to less, then the first derivative must be positive. No matter how small b is, as long as it is positive there is always some value of W that will make the first derivative negative. Thus, for investors who prefer more to less, the quadratic utility could represent their desires over only a restricted range of wealth. To be consistent with non-satiation, the following restriction must be placed on W: $1 - 2bW > 0$ or $W < 1/2b$. The absolute and relative risk-aversion measures are

$$A(W) = \frac{-U''(W)}{U'(W)} = \frac{+2b}{(1 - 2bW)}$$

$$A'(W) = \frac{4b^2}{(1 - 2bW)^2} > 0$$

$$R(W) = \frac{-Wu''(W)}{u'(W)} = \frac{2bW}{1 - 2bW}$$

$$R'(W) = \frac{4b^2 W}{(1 - 2bW)^2} + \frac{2b(1 - 2bW)}{(1 - 2bW)^2} = \frac{2b}{(1 - 2bW)^2} > 0$$

Examining the absolute risk-aversion function shows that the quadratic utility function exhibits increasing absolute risk aversion. Thus, the quadratic function is consistent with investors who reduce the dollar amount invested in risky assets as wealth increases. Since they decrease the dollar amount invested, it is clear the percentage amount also decreases. Thus, the quadratic utility function must exhibit increasing relative risk aversion, also. A glance at the relative risk-aversion function confirms that this is so.

The quadratic utility function has always had a special place in mean variance analysis because the assumption of a quadratic utility function leads to mean variance analysis being optimum.[5] As we have just discussed, the quadratic utility function has some characteristics that are undesirable. However, a number of authors (e.g., [14]) have shown that a quadratic function can be found that approximates very closely a function with more desirable properties. This approximation may well depend on the wealth of the investor. However, by changing the parameters of the quadratic function as wealth changes, one can obtain a function that closely resembles a function with more desirable characteristics and that still satisfies mean variance analysis. As a second example of a utility function, consider the following log function

$$U(W) = \ln W$$

The first and second derivatives of this function are

$$U'(W) = W^{-1}$$
$$U''(W) = -W^{-2}$$

An examination of the first derivative shows that the derivative is positive over all values of W. An examination of the second derivative shows that it is negative over all values. Thus, the log function is a candidate for an investor who prefers more to less and is risk averse. The absolute and relative risk-aversion coefficients are

$$A(W) = \frac{-\left(-W^{-2}\right)}{W^{-1}} = W^{-1}$$

$$A'(W) = -W^{-2} < 0$$

$$R(W) = \frac{-W\left(-W^{-2}\right)}{W^{-1}} = 1$$

$$R'(W) = 0$$

Thus, the log function exhibits decreasing absolute risk aversion and constant relative risk aversion. The log function is consistent with the behavior of a risk-averse investor who prefers more to less and whose percentage invested in risky assets remains constant as wealth increases.

---

[5]The variance of a random variable is defined as $\sigma_w^2 = E[W - E(W)]^2$. Performing the squaring yields $\sigma_w^2 = E\{W^2 - 2W \cdot E(W) + [E(W)]^2\}$. Since the expected value of the sum of random variables is the sum of the expected values, we have

$$\sigma_w^2 = E\left(W^2\right) - E\left[2W \cdot E(W)\right] + \left[E(W)\right]^2$$

Since the expected value of a constant times a random variable is the constant times the expected value of the random variable, σ_w^2 can be written as

$$\sigma_w^2 = E\left(W^2\right) - 2E(W) \cdot E(W) + E(W)^2 \qquad \text{or} \qquad \sigma_w^2 = E\left(W^2\right) - \left[E(W)\right]^2$$

Taking the expected value of a quadratic utility function yields

$$E[U(W)] = E(W) - bE\left(W^2\right)$$

Rearranging the previously derived relationship to solve for $E(W^2)$ yields $E(W^2) = \sigma_w^2 + [E(W)]^2$. Substituting this for $E(W^2)$ in the utility equation shows

$$E[U(W)] = E(W) - b\left\{\sigma_w^2 + \left[E(W)\right]^2\right\}$$

Thus, expected utility can be defined in terms of means and variances when utility is quadratic.

UTILITY AND THE INVESTOR HORIZON

The utility functions introduced in this chapter are, in general, based upon investor choice over a single-time horizon. In reality, investors confront a multiperiod choice problem. Any asset allocation chosen today can be undone tomorrow. The infinite possibilities of revising the allocation decision through time under static or changing market conditions make the multiperiod investment problem a very difficult one. Later in this book, we will introduce some multiperiod equilibrium and hedging models. In this section, however, we consider the multiperiod investment policies implied by basic utility functions. As an example, let us return to the log-utility function which we just examined. Suppose a log-utility investor with $1000 faces a multiperiod investment opportunity. That is, he or she has the choice to invest in a risky asset for two periods, one period, or not to invest at all. The risky asset is forecast to either double or halve in value each period, with equal probability. The expected utility calculation for the risky investment in the first period would be

$$U(\text{one period investment}) = \frac{1}{2}\log(\$2000) = \frac{1}{2}\log(\$500) = 6.9077$$

If the investor simply held the cash, the utility would be

$$\text{Log}(\$1000) = 6.9077$$

Thus, this investor is indifferent between investing for one period or not investing at all.

The number $1000 is called the *certainty equivalent* for the risky investment because it is the certain value that will make you indifferent between taking and not taking a gamble. Under the same conditions for a second investment period, the log-utility investor will also be indifferent. Calculating the expected utility for the four potential outcomes in period 2 (i.e., two doublings in a row, two halvings in a row, a doubling and then a halving, and a halving then a doubling), the expected utility is

$$U(\text{two period investment}) = \frac{1}{4}\log(\$4000) + \frac{1}{2}\log(\$1000) + \frac{1}{4}\log(\$250) = 6.9077$$

Thus, for the log-utility investor, for all classes of utility functions that display constant relative risk aversion for multiplicative investments, the horizon of the investment will not affect investor choice.[6] One important exception to this rule is when the returns of the risky asset are correlated. If, for example, asset prices tend to go down after a rise, or up after a fall. In this case risky investments are more attractive (less risky) in the long run than they are in the short run. Also, the proportion invested in risky assets will increase as the horizon gets longer.

Although log-utility has many attractive features as a description of investor preferences, scholars have recently pointed out that the special "time-indifference" characteristic of log-utility with uncorrelated returns depends upon somewhat extreme aversion to large losses. For example, consider changing the two-period investment described above to a 50-50 of doubling or, decreasing wealth by 95% in each period. The log-utility function implies that the investor is willing to pay $900—nearly all of his or her wealth—to avoid this gamble—even though the certain loss of $900 is nearly the same percentage decrease as the loss that may occur with 50% probability.[7] If investors don't exhibit time indifference, how do they act?

---

[6]For further details and related examples, see Kritzmann, Mark, and Dan Rich [12].

[7]For more on the investor time horizon and utility functions, see Ross, Stephen A. [22].

Recent analysis by Stephen A. Ross [22], from which this example is adapted, suggests that investors who have some tolerance for very large losses may be willing to invest in risky assets over long horizons, but not necessarily over short horizons. This increased willingness to invest in the risky asset as the investment horizon grows suggests that the asset allocation choice of many investors can depend on how long they expect keep their money invested before using it for retirement, education, or to meet other future liabilities.

EMPIRICAL EVIDENCE ON THE SUITABILITY OF ALTERNATIVE PREFERENCE FUNCTIONS

In the earlier sections we continuously discussed the consistency of assumptions about investor behavior with observations of actual behavior. In this section, we elaborate on these statements.

Empirical evidence as to the form of a utility function that might reasonably represent behavior is of two types:

1.   Experimental evidence from simple choice situations.

2.   Survey data on investor's asset choices.

The assumption that investors prefer more to less is consistent with most evidence. Few investors, faced with a choice of securities with identical properties, except for expected return, select the one with the lowest expected return unless there are differences in transaction costs or control.

The assumption of risk aversion is also generally consistent with empirical evidence. Most investors purchase insurance on homes and cars. Since the insurance premiums are always larger than the expected loss (to cover insurance company profit and costs), the purchase of insurance is risk-averse behavior. In experimental situations, if return is held constant, most individuals choose the gamble with the least risky alternatives. A number of people have been disturbed by the observation that people buy lottery tickets or gamble. These activities are the opposite of insurance. The expected return on the gamble is negative, and a gamble is risk-seeking behavior. In order to accommodate both gambling and insurance in an individual's utility function, Friedman and Savage suggested a function that exhibited risk aversion for some levels of wealth and risk-seeking behavior for others. This is one alternative. The other alternative is to argue that gambling provides entertainment value as well as risky outcomes. Accounting for the entertainment value means that a risk-averse individual might still gamble.

There are two major studies that attempt to determine investors' relative and absolute risk-aversion behavior. Both studies used survey data of individuals' asset holdings and wealth to draw inferences concerning investors' relative and absolute risk aversion. Ideally, to draw this type of inference, one would prefer to have observations concerning each investor's portfolio behavior over time as his or her wealth changes. Unfortunately, these data do not exist. Thus, one must resort to drawing inferences from different investors at different wealth levels.

One set of studies by Blume and Friend [4] examined the Federal Reserve Board survey of the financial characteristics of consumers. They found that the percentage invested in risky assets remained virtually unchanged when they examined asset holdings of investors with very different wealth. They concluded that their evidence was supportive of an assumption of constant relative risk aversion and this, of course, implies decreasing absolute risk aversion. The second major study was by Cohn, Lewellen, Lease, and Schlarbaum [7]. This study examined survey data obtained from questionnaires mailed by a brokerage firm to its customers. They examined the amount held in risky assets for investors with different wealth. They conclude that investors exhibit decreasing relative risk aversion, which also implies decreasing absolute risk aversion.

As mentioned earlier, some caution must be exercised with regard to these studies since they examined different investors with different levels of wealth, rather than the same investor at different wealth levels. However, these imaginative studies are very suggestive of the types of absolute or relative risk-aversion behavior that are consistent with actual behavior.

APPENDIX A

AN AXIOMATIC DERIVATION OF THE EXPECTED UTILITY THEOREM

The expected utility theorem can be developed from a set of axioms or postulates concerning investor behavior. If an investor acts in accordance with these postulates, then the investor's behavior is indistinguishable from one who makes decisions on the basis of the expected utility theorem. The first two axioms concern the preference ordering of certain outcomes. The remaining two axioms concern rationality when ordering random prospects. The axioms are

1. **Comparability.** An investor can state a preference among all alternative certain outcomes. Thus, if the investor has a choice of outcome A or B, a preference for A to B or B to A can be stated or indifference between them can be expressed. An assumption that investors can make comparisons between outcomes (that are certain) is a standard assumption of economic theory.

2. **Transitivity.** If an investor prefers A to B and B to C, then A is preferred to C. This is an assumption that investors are consistent in their ranking of outcomes. Although it would seem reasonable that most investors would behave in this manner in experimental situations, this is not always so. The difficulty occurs because some situations are sufficiently complex that the investor is unable to understand all of the implications of the choice. In experimental situations when the intransitivities are pointed out and the implication of the choice explored, most individuals want to revise their decisions in a way that is consistent with this axiom.

3. **Independence.** Consider two certain prospects X and Y and assume the investor is indifferent between them. Designate a third prospect by Z. Independence implies that the investor is indifferent between the following two gambles:

    > X with probability P and Z with probability $1 - P$, and
    > Y with probability P and Z with probability $1 - P$.

    The investor may like both or neither, but the point is she will feel equally good or bad about each.

    For example, if a person were indifferent between having a Chevrolet or a Ford, then that person would be indifferent to buying a raffle ticket for $10 that gave a 1 in 500 chance of winning a Ford or a raffle ticket for $10 that gave a 1 in 500 chance of winning a Chevrolet. This person might prefer to buy neither ticket, but if the decision to buy a ticket was made, then the person would not care which one was bought.

4. **Certainty Equivalent.** For every gamble there is a value (called certainty equivalent) such that the investor is indifferent between the gamble and the certainty equivalent. This assumption simply states that everything has a price.

Using these axioms, we can derive the expected utility theorem. What follows is an intuitive explanation. For a more rigorous derivative, see Fama and Miller [10]. Consider a security G with two possible outcomes

$$G = \begin{bmatrix} b \text{ with probability } h \\ 0 \text{ with probability } 1-h \end{bmatrix}$$

Let C be the amount of money that would make the investor indifferent between taking gamble G and receiving the money C, which is the certainty equivalent. Clearly C depends on the probability of receiving b (i.e., the value of h). However, from axiom 4, C must exist. If we vary h, then a different value of C would be appropriate. If we varied h over a large number of values and then plotted all values of h versus C, we might have a diagram such as Figure 10.2. The curve in this figure is the investor's preference curve. It separates combinations of C and h for which the investor prefers the security from points where the investor prefers the certain amount. Consider the point X', which represents the same gamble as X but a higher certainty equivalent. The investor has stated he is indifferent between X' and C', where C is a lower certainty equivalent than C'. Most investors prefer more to less, thus they would prefer the security X to the certainty equivalent C. This would imply that points above the curve are points where the gamble is preferred and points below the curve are points where the certainty equivalent is preferred.[8] Now consider a portfolio of securities S_1 with N possible outcomes defined as

$$S_1 = \begin{bmatrix} W_1 \text{ with probability } P_1 \\ W_2 \text{ with probability } P_2 \\ \vdots \\ W_N \text{ with probability } P_N \end{bmatrix}$$

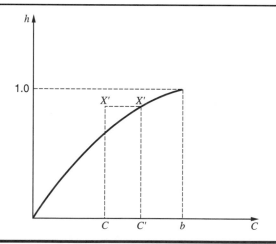

Figure 10.2   An investor's preference curve.

---

[8]Strictly speaking, all we know is that the preference curve separates the area where the investor prefers the security from the area where he prefers the certain amount. It would be possible that above the curve he selects the certain amount. In this case he prefers less to more.

Since each W_i is a known payoff and since C_i's of all sizes exist, we can replace each W_i with a C_i of the same size. Thus, portfolio S_1 can be represented as

$$S_1 = \begin{bmatrix} C_1 \text{ with probability } P_1 \\ C_2 \text{ with probability } P_2 \\ \vdots \\ C_N \text{ with probability } P_N \end{bmatrix}$$

Since for every C_i there exists an equivalent lottery, we can represent an equivalent portfolio as

$$S_2 = \begin{matrix} \begin{bmatrix} b \text{ with probability } h_1 \\ 0 \text{ with probability } 1-h_1 \end{bmatrix} & \text{with probability } P_1 \\[2ex] \begin{bmatrix} b \text{ with probability } h_2 \\ 0 \text{ with probability } 1-h_2 \end{bmatrix} & \text{with probability } P_2 \\[2ex] \vdots & \\[1ex] \begin{bmatrix} b \text{ with probability } h_N \\ 0 \text{ with probability } 1-h_N \end{bmatrix} & \text{with probability } P_N \end{matrix}$$

The investor declared indifference between each C_i and the lottery. Thus, it is reasonable that S_1 and S_2 should be equivalent.

Let us explore this in more detail. Assume that outcome i occurs. Then, if the investor selects S_1, C_i is received. If the investor selects S_2, then b with probability h_i and 0 with probability $1 - h_i$ is received. However, the investor has indicated in the construction of the preference curve an indifference between C_i and this lottery. Further, W_i is equal to C_i. Thus the investor is indifferent between W_i and this lottery. Thus, security 2 is equivalent to security 1. Note that from axiom 3 the investor does not change preference simply because the alternatives are part of a lottery.

A tree diagram might clarify this choice further. Figure 10.3 represents the portfolio S_1 and Figure 10.4 the portfolio S_2. Note that while S_2 is equivalent to S_1, S_2 has only two possible outcomes: b and 0. We could equivalently write S_2 as b with probability $\Sigma_i P_i h_i$ and 0 with probability $1 - \Sigma_i P_i h_i$. Utilizing the technique just discussed, we can do the same with any portfolio. Thus, any portfolio can be reduced to two outcomes, b and 0, with known probabilities.

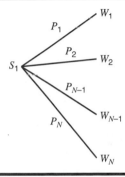

Figure 10.3   Outcomes for S_1.

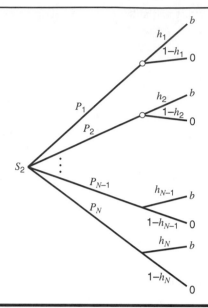

Figure 10.4 Outcomes for S_2.

How do we choose between these portfolios? To decide, the individual need consider only the probability of receiving b, and the one with the higher probability is to be preferred. Define $H_i = \Sigma P_i h_i$, where the P and h are the values appropriate for the security under question. Then if $H_K > H_L$, security K is to be preferred to security L. This leads directly to the expected utility theorem. Earlier, we replaced every W_i with a C_i; associated with the C_i was an h_i. Thus, for each W_i there corresponds an h_i. Let us call the function that relates W_i to h_i a utility function and denote it by $U(\ )$. Then, noting that h_i is a function of W_i is equivalent to writing $h_i = U(W_i)$. Furthermore, our feelings about a gamble can be expressed as

$$H_i = \Sigma_i P_i h_i = \Sigma_i P_i U(W_i)$$

But $\Sigma_i P_i U(W_i)$ is simply expected utility. Thus, expressing the feelings about an investment in terms of H_i is equivalent to expressing them in terms of expected utility. Further ranking by H_i is equivalent to ranking by expected utility.

APPENDIX B

ABSOLUTE AND RELATIVE RISK AVERSION

Assume an investor has wealth W and a security with outcomes represented by the random variable Z. Let Z be a fair gamble so that $E(Z) = 0$. Let σ_z^2 equal the variance of Z and $U(\ )$ the investor's utility function. Let W_c be the level of wealth such that the investor is indifferent between having W_c and having wealth W plus the gamble Z. Thus, the two choices are

Choice A	Choice B
$W + Z$	W_c

By assumption, the investor is indifferent between these positions, thus

$$E\big[(U(W+Z))\big] = EU(W_c) = U(W_c) \tag{B.1}$$

The last equality holds because W_c is received with certainty. The difference between W and W_c is the dollars the investor is willing to give up not to have to face the gamble. If the investor could take out an insurance policy, $W - W_c$ would be the maximum the investor would be willing to pay to avoid the risk of the investment. The greater this difference, the greater the amount of dollars the investor is willing to give up to avoid the gamble. Thus, it is natural to think of $\pi = W - W_c$ as a measure of the investor's absolute risk aversion.

Expanding $U(W + Z)$ in a Taylor series around W, we have[9]

$$U(W+Z) = U(W) + U'(W)\big[(W+Z) - W\big] + (1/2)U''(W)$$
$$\big[(W+Z) - W\big]^2 + \cdots$$

Taking the expected value of both sides and ignoring terms involving the third and higher order derivatives, we have

$$E\big[U(W+Z)\big] \simeq E\big[U(W)\big] + U'(W)E(Z) + (1/2)U''(W)E(Z-0)^2$$

Recalling that $U(W)$ is a constant and that

$$E(Z-0)^2 = E\big[Z - E(Z)\big]^2$$

is the variance of Z yields

$$E\big[U(W+Z)\big] \simeq U(W) + (1/2)U''(W)\sigma_Z^2 \tag{B.2}$$

Recall that W_c is equal to $W - \pi$. Expanding $U(W - \pi)$ in a Taylor series around W, we have

$$U(W_c) = U(W - \pi) \simeq U(W) + U'(W)\big[(W - \pi) - W\big] + \cdots$$

Ignoring terms above the first derivative, we have

$$U(W_c) \simeq U(W) + U'(W)(-\pi) \tag{B.3}$$

From Equation (B.1) $E[U(W + Z)] = U(W_c)$ and Equation (B.2) equals Equation (B.3), or

$$U(W) + (1/2)U''(W)\sigma_Z^2 = U(W) + U'(W)(-\pi)$$

Rearranging

$$\pi = -(1/2)\sigma_Z^2 \frac{U''(W)}{U'(W)}$$

Since $(1/2)\sigma_Z^2$ is a constant, $A(W) = -U''(W)/U'(W)$ measures the amount of risk aversion.

Note that $A(W)$ has some special properties. First, if $U'(W) > 0$, then the sign of $A(W)$ depends on the sign of $U''(W)$. If $A(W)$ has the same sign for all values of W, then the investor has the same risk preference for all values of W and we refer to the investor as

---

[9]A Taylor series is a method of approximating a function using its derivatives. Let primes indicate derivatives. For example, $U'(\ )$ is the first derivative and $U''(\ )$ is the second derivative. Let $\simeq$ mean "approximately equal to." Then, the Taylor approximation in the vicinity of a is

$$U(X) \simeq U(a) + \frac{U'(a)}{1}[X-a] + \frac{U''(a)}{2 \cdot 1}[X-a]^2 + \frac{U'''(a)}{3 \cdot 2 \cdot 1}[X-a]^3 + \cdots$$

"globally" risk averse or globally risk neutral, or as a global risk seeker. Second, note that $A(W)$ is equivalent for investors with similar utility functions. Earlier we noted utility functions are unique only up to a linear transform. Thus, $U(W)$ and $V(W) = a + bU(W)$ lead to identical choices. Note that $V'(W) = bU'(W)$ and that $V''(W) = bU''(W)$. Computing $A(W)$ for function $V(W)$ yields

$$A(W) = \frac{-bU''(W)}{bU'(W)} = \frac{-U''(W)}{U'(W)}$$

Thus, both functions $U(W)$ and $V(W)$ not only rank investment identically but have the same absolute risk-aversion coefficient.

The relative risk-aversion coefficient is derived as follows. The percentage insurance premium one would pay is $\pi = (W - W_c)/W$, where π is the fraction of wealth an investor is giving up in order to avoid the gamble. With π defined in this manner, $W_c = W(1 - \pi)$. Change the definition of Z so that it represents outcome per dollar invested. Let $E(Z) = 1$ and variance of $Z = \sigma_Z^2$. Thus, if we invest Z dollars, we obtain WZ as a dollar return. Expanding WZ in a Taylor series around W yields

$$U(WZ) = U(W) + U'(W)E(WZ - W) + \frac{U''(W)}{2}E(ZW - W)^2 + \cdots$$

Taking the expected value of both sides and simplifying yields

$$EU(WZ) = U(W) + 0 + \frac{U''(W)}{2}W^2\sigma_Z^2$$

Expanding W_c in a Taylor expansion around W yields

$$U(W_c) = U[W(1 - \pi)]$$
$$= U(W) + U'(W)[W(1 - \pi) - W] + \cdots$$

Ignoring higher-order terms,

$$U(W_c) = U(W) + U'(W)(-\pi W)$$

Equating $E[U(WZ)]$ with $U(W_c)$ yields

$$U(W) + (1/2)U''(W)\sigma_Z^2 W^2 = U(W) - \pi WU'(W)$$

Simplifying,

$$\pi = -\frac{\sigma_Z^2}{2}\frac{WU''(W)}{U'(W)}$$

π is a measure of the percentage change in the risk premium. Define

$$R(W) = \frac{-WU''(W)}{U'(W)}$$

Then $R(W)$ is a measure of proportional or relative risk aversion.

In the derivation shown above, we dropped some higher-order terms. In this sense, it is an approximation. It is possible to derive the absolute and relative risk coefficients directly without using the Taylor expansion. (See, for example, Mossin [17].) However, this derivation, while mathematically correct, conveys less economic intuition behind the meaning of relative and absolute risk aversion. Because of this, we have chosen to present the derivation using the approximation. It might also bother the reader that we dropped terms involving different derivatives in our expansion. However, note that the coefficients of the terms involved are π in one case and moments of Z in the other. Thus, the magnitude of the terms dropped are roughly the same.

QUESTIONS AND PROBLEMS

1. Consider the following three investments. Which are preferred if $U(W) = W - (1/2)W^2$?

Investment A		Investment B		Investment C	
$ Outcome	Probability	$ Outcome	Probability	$ Outcome	Probability
5	1/3	4	1/4	1	1/5
6	1/3	7	1/2	9	3/5
9	1/3	10	1/4	18	1/5

2. Assume the utility function is $U(W) = -W^{-1/2}$. What is the preferred investment in Problem 1?

3. Consider the following two investments:

Investment A		Investment B	
$ Outcome	Probability	$ Outcome	Probability
7	2/5	5	1/2
10	1/5	12	1/4
14	2/5	20	1/4

Which is preferred if the utility function is $U(W) = 2W - 0.04W^2$?

4. Consider the choice shown in Problem 3. The probability of a $5 return is $\frac{1}{2}$ and $12 return is $\frac{1}{4}$. How much would these probabilities have to change so that the investor is indifferent between investments A and B?

5. Consider the utility function $U(W) = W^{-1/2}$. What are the characteristics of this function with respect to absolute and relative risk aversion?

6. Consider the function $U(W) = ae^{-bW}$, where a and b are constants. What are the signs of a and b if the investor is assumed to prefer more to less and to exhibit risk aversion?

7. Assume that an investor's utility function is $U(W) = a + be^{cW}$ where (a) a, b, c, are constants, and (b) W is wealth. Assuming that the investor prefers more to less and is risk averse, what can be said about the sign of a, b, c? What are the properties of this utility function in terms of absolute and relative risk aversion?

8. What are the properties of the utility function $U(W) = -W^{-1/2}$?

9. What are the properties of the function $U(W) = -e^{-w}$?

10. Consider the following investments.

Investment A		Investment B	
Outcome	Probability	Outcome	Probability
5	0.20	6	0.30
7	0.50	8	0.60
10	0.30	9	0.10

Which is preferred if $U(W) = W - 0.05W^2$?

11. In Problem 10 what is the minimum amount that the $5 outcome would have to be changed so that the investor is indifferent between the two investments?

BIBLIOGRAPHY

1. Baker, Kent, Hargrove, Michael, and Haslem, John. "An Empirical Analysis of the Risk-Return Preferences of Individual Investors," *Journal of Financial and Quantitative Analysis*, **XII,** No. 3 (Sept. 1977), pp. 377–389.

2. Baron, David. "On the Utility Theoretic Foundations of Mean-Variance Analysis," *Journal of Finance*, **XII,** No. 5 (Dec. 1977), pp. 1683–1697.

3. Bernoulli, Daniel. "Exposition of a New Theory on the Measurement of Risk," *Econometrica*, **32** (Jan. 1954), pp. 23–26.

4. Blume, Marshall, and Friend, Irwin. "The Asset Structure of Individual Portfolios and Some Implications for Utility Functions," *Journal of Finance*, **X,** No. 2 (May 1975), pp. 585–603.

5. Campbell, John Y. "Consumption and Portfolio Decisions When Expected Returns are Time Varying," *The Quarterly Journal of Economics*, **114,** No. 2 (May 1999), pp. 433–492.

6. Caplin, Andrew. "Psychological Expected Utility Theory and Anticipatory Feelings," *The Quarterly Journal of Economics*, **116,** No. 1 (Feb. 2001), pp. 55–79.

7. Cohn, Richard, Lewellen, Wilbur, Lease, Ronald, and Schlarbaum, Gary. "Individual Investor Risk Aversion and Investment Portfolio Composition," *Journal of Finance,* **X,** No. 2 (May 1975), pp. 605–620.

8. Diamond, Peter, and Stiglitz, Joseph. "Increases in Risk and in Risk Aversion," *Journal of Economic Theory*, **8,** No. 3 (July 1974), pp. 337–360.

9. Engelbrecht, Richard. "A Note on Multivariate Risk and Separable Utility Functions," *Management Science*, **23,** No. 10 (June 1977), pp. 1143–1144.

10. Fama, Eugene, and Miller, Merton. *Theory of Finance* (New York: Holt, Rinehart and Winston, 1972).

11. Friedman, Milton, and Savage, Leonard J. "The Utility Analysis of Choices Involving Risk," *Journal of Political Economy* (Aug. 1948), pp. 279–304

12. Kritzmann, Mark, and Rich, Dan. "Beware of Dogma," *Journal of Portfolio Management,* **24,** No. 4 (Summer 1998), pp. 66–67.

13. Kroll, Yoram, Levi, Haim, and Markovits, Henry M. "Mean-Variance Versus Direct Utility Maximization," *Journal of Finance*, **39,** No. 1 (March 1984), pp. 47–60.

14. Lease, Ronald, Lewellen, Wilbur, and Schlarbaum, Gary. "The Individual Investor: Attributes and Attitudes," *Journal of Finance*, **IX,** No. 2 (May 1974), pp. 413–433.

15. Levy, Haim, and Sarnat, Marshall. "A Note on Portfolio Selection and Investor's Wealth," *Journal of Financial and Quantitative Analysis*, **VI,** No. 1 (Jan. 1971), pp. 639–642.

16. Markowitz, Harry. *Portfolio Selection: Efficient Diversification of Investments* (New York: John Wiley & Sons, 1959).

17. Mossin, Jan. *Theory of Financial Markets* (Englewood Cliffs, N.J.:Prentice Hall, 1973).

18. Pratt, J. "Risk Aversion in the Small and in the Large," *Econometrica* (Jan.–April 1964), pp. 122–136.

19. Reid, Donald W., and Tew, Bernard V. "Mean-Variance Versus Direct Utility Maximization: A Comment," *The Journal of Finance*, **41,** No. 5 (Dec. 1986), pp. 1177–1179.

20. Remaley, William. "Suboptimization in Mean-Variance Efficient Set Analysis," *Journal of Finance*, **VIII,** No. 2 (May 1973), pp. 397–403.

21. Richard, Scott. "Multivariate Risk Aversion, Utility Independence, and Separable Utility Functions," *Management Science*, **22,** No. 1 (Sept. 1975), pp. 12–21.

22. Ross, Stephen. "Adding Risks; Samuelsons Fallacy of Large Numbers Revisited, *The Journal of Financial And Quantitative Analysis*, **34,** No. 3 (Sept. 1999), pp. 323–389.

23. Sarnat, Marshall. "A Note on the Implications of Quadratic Utility for Portfolio Theory," *Journal of Financial and Quantitative Analysis*, **IX,** No. 4 (Sept. 1974), pp. 687–689.

24. Sennetti, John. "On Bernoulli, Sharpe Financial Risk and the Petersburg Paradox," *Journal of Finance*, **XI,** No.3 (June 1976), pp. 960–962.

25. Singleton, J. Clay, and Wingender, John. "Skewness Persistence in Common Stock Returns," *Journal of Financial and Quantitative Analysis*, **21,** No. 3 (Sept. 1986), pp. 335–341.

26. "A Simple Algorithm for the Portfolio Selection Problem" *The Journal of Finance*, **43,** No. 1 (Mar. 1988), pp. 71–82.

27. Von Neumann, J. and Morgenstern, O. *Theory of Games and Economic Behavior*, 2nd ed. (Princeton, N.J.: Princeton University Press, 1947).

28. Williams, Joseph. "A Note on Indifference Curves in the Mean-Variance Model," *Journal of Financial and Quantitative Analysis*, **XII,** No. 1 (March 1977), pp. 121–126.

29. Wippern, Ronald. "Utility Implications of Portfolio Selection and Performance Appraisal Models," *Journal of Financial and Quantitative Analysis*, **VI,** No. 3 (June 1977), pp. 913–924.

30. Zeckhauser, R., and Keeler, E. "Another Type of Risk Aversion," *Econometrica*, **38,** No. 4 (Sept. 1970), pp. 661–665.

11

Other Portfolio Selection Models

In all previous chapters and, in fact, in most of those that follow, we have assumed that investors are attempting to maximize the expected utility of the returns from an investment portfolio. Usually we have assumed that the expected utility of any opportunity could be meaningfully measured in terms of means and variances. This is the traditional and widely accepted mean-variance approach to portfolio management. While this is the central approach of this book, we would be remiss if we did not mention some of the other approaches that have been advocated in the finance and economic literature.

First, let us note that the mean-variance approach as we have presented it holds exactly when investors are expected utility maximizers, prefer more to less, are risk averse, and either (1) security returns are normally distributed or (2) utility functions are quadratic. Furthermore, the analysis is robust in that, as Markowitz [72] has shown, it frequently holds approximately even when assumptions (1) or (2) are violated. For example, quadratic approximations are almost always good local approximations to nonquadratic utility functions.

Other approaches to the portfolio problem make less stringent assumptions about the investor's choice framework, the form of the utility function, and/or the form of the distribution of security returns. In this chapter we examine four other criteria for portfolio selection: the geometric mean return, safety first, stochastic dominance, and analysis in terms of characteristics of the return distribution.

The geometric mean criterion is a choice framework that purports to select optimum portfolios without the need to consider the form of investors' utility functions or the distribution of security returns. The geometric mean return criterion was developed to represent what its proponents felt was commonsense behavior on the part of investors (rather than because it was consistent with maximization of expected utility). This criterion can be viewed as maximizing the expected value of terminal wealth. It is not surprising that this criterion can lead to the selection of different portfolios than the expected utility framework. What is surprising is that, under several alternative assumptions, this criterion leads to the selection of a portfolio that is on the efficient set. Thus, under broad sets of assumptions, the advocate of maximum geometric mean criterion will find useful most of the analysis in the preceding chapters.

The alternative forms of safety first imply that investors cannot, or will not, go through the expected utility calculations, but rather will employ a simpler decision criterion concentrating on the avoidance of "bad" outcomes. As in the case of the geometric mean, we will find that the portfolio that optimizes a safety first criterion will often lie on the efficient set and so most of the analysis presented to this point is still useful.

While the first two criteria discussed in this chapter do not utilize the idea of expected utility, the last two criteria, like mean-variance analysis, utilize this idea.

Stochastic dominance defines efficient sets of investments under alternative (progressively more stringent) conditions on the behavior of utility functions. While stochastic dominance rules are more general than mean-variance analysis, they are, under certain assumptions, consistent with mean-variance analysis and lead to the same efficient set.

The final criterion we examine in this chapter is portfolio selection in terms of three moments. The introduction of skewness into the portfolio problem, in addition to mean and variance, complicates the analysis and requires an extension of the analysis needed to perform mean variance analysis.

MAXIMIZING THE GEOMETRIC MEAN RETURN

One alternative to mean-variance analysis is simply to select that portfolio that has the highest expected geometric mean return. Many researchers have put this forth as a universal criterion. That is, they advocate its use without qualifications as to the form of utility function or the characteristics of the probability distribution of security returns. The proponents of the geometric mean usually proceed with one of the following arguments. Consider an investor saving for some purpose in the future, for example, retirement in 20 years. One reasonable portfolio criterion for such an investor would be to select that portfolio that has the highest expected value of terminal wealth. Latane [60] has shown that this is the portfolio with the highest geometric mean return. The proponents have also argued that the maximum geometric mean[1]

1. Has the highest probability of reaching, or exceeding, any given wealth level in the shortest possible time.[2]

2. Has the highest probability of exceeding any given wealth level over any given period of time.[3]

These characteristics of the maximum geometric mean portfolio are extremely appealing and have attracted many advocates.

Opponents quickly point out that, in general, maximizing the expected value of terminal wealth (or either of the other benefits discussed above) is not identical to maximizing the utility of terminal wealth.[4] Since opponents accept the tenets of utility theory, and, in particular, the idea that investors should maximize the expected utility of terminal wealth, they reject the geometric mean return criteria.

---

[1]The accuracy of these statements is not universally accepted.

[2]See Brieman [18] for a discussion of this property. Roll [88] argues that this is true only in the limit.

[3]See Brieman [18] for a discussion of this property. Roll [88] and Hakansson [38] make a similar argument.

[4]It has been shown that the portfolio that maximizes the expected value of a logarithmic utility function is identical to the portfolio that maximizes the geometric mean return. This is not, in general, true for other utility functions.

In short, some researchers find the characteristics of the geometric mean return so appealing they accept it as a universal criterion. Others find any criterion that is inconsistent with expected utility maximization unacceptable. Readers must judge for themselves which of these approaches is more appealing.

Having discussed the arguments in favor of and against the use of the geometric mean as a portfolio selection criterion, let us examine the definition of the geometric mean and some properties of portfolios that maximize the geometric mean criterion.

The geometric mean is easy to define. Instead of adding together the observations to obtain the mean, you multiply them. If R_{ij} is the ith possible return on the jth portfolio and each outcome is equally likely, then the geometric mean return on the portfolio ($\bar{R}_{Gj}$) is

$$\bar{R}_{Gj} = \left[\left(1 + R_{1j}\right)^{1/N} \left(1 + R_{2j}\right)^{1/N} \cdots \left(1 + R_{Nj}\right)^{(1/N)} - 1.0 \right]$$

If the likelihood of each observation is different and P_{ij} is the probability of the ith outcome for portfolio j, then the geometric mean return is

$$\bar{R}_{Gj} = \left(1 + R_{1j}\right)^{P_{1j}} \left(1 + R_{2j}\right)^{P_{2j}} \cdots \left(1 + R_{N-1j}\right)^{P_{N-1j}} \left(1 + R_{Nj}\right)^{P_{Nj}} - 1.0$$

This is sometimes written in compact form. The symbol Π means product. Thus, the above series can be written as

$$\bar{R}_{Gj} = \prod_{i=1}^{N} \left(1 + R_{ij}\right)^{P_{ij}} - 1.0$$

The portfolio that has the maximum geometric mean is usually a diversified portfolio. This can be illustrated with an example. Table 11.1 shows three possible investments listed as securities A, B, and C. Each of these investments has two possible outcomes, each equally likely. The portfolio shown consists of equal proportions of each of the three securities. As can be seen from the table, the portfolio has a higher geometric mean return than any of the individual securities. This result is easily explained. The geometric mean return penalizes extreme observations. In fact, a strategy with any probability of bankruptcy would never be selected as it would have a zero geometric mean.[5] As we have seen in other chapters, portfolios have less extreme observations than individual securities. Thus, the geometric mean strategy usually leads to a diversified strategy.

While that portfolio that maximizes the geometric mean is likely to be highly diversified, it will not (except in special circumstances) be mean-variance efficient. Furthermore, portfolios that are mean-variance efficient may have very low geometric mean returns. However, there are two cases where mean-variance analysis is meaningful for locating the portfolio with the highest geometric mean return.

Table 11.1   Geometric Mean Returns

Outcome	Securities			Portfolio
	A	B	C	
1	0.80	−0.10	−0.20	0.16 2/3
2	−0.30	0.30	0.60	0.20
Geometric mean	0.12	0.08	0.13	0.18

[5]If one possible outcome is a return of −1, then for that outcome $(1 + R_{ij}) = (1 − 1) = 0$. The geometric mean is the product of the $(1 + R_{ij})$. The whole product becomes zero if one element is zero. Thus, the geometric mean criteria would never select an investment with any probability of bankruptcy.

First, maximizing the geometric mean return is equivalent to maximizing the expected value of a log utility function.[6] We know from earlier chapters that if returns are normally distributed, then mean-variance portfolio analysis is appropriate for investors interested in maximizing expected utility. Investors with log utility functions are such investors. Thus, investors interested in maximizing the geometric mean return could use mean-variance analysis if returns were normally distributed.

It has also been shown that the portfolio that maximizes the geometric mean return is mean-variance efficient if returns are log-normally distributed. In this case, a very simple formula exists that indicates which portfolio in the mean-variance efficient set is to be preferred.[7] With the exception of these two cases, the portfolio with the maximum geometric mean return need not be mean-variance efficient.

When returns are not normally, or log-normally, distributed, more general procedures are needed in order to determine the optimum portfolio. Ziemba [101] discusses one possible approach. Maier, Peterson, and Vanderweide [71] discuss a second approach.

The geometric mean return is more often advocated than any other alternative to mean-variance analysis. While we leave the choice of these two criteria up to the reader, our preference for the tenets of expected utility theory and mean-variance analysis is unavoidably revealed by the amount of material we devote to each in this book. Note, also, that if returns are either normally or log-normally distributed, then mean-variance analysis can aid in finding that portfolio that has the highest geometric mean return.

SAFETY FIRST

A second alternative to the expected utility theorem that is advocated by many is a group of criteria called safety first models. The origin of these models stems from a belief that decision makers are unable, or unwilling, to go through the mathematics of the expected utility theorem, but rather will use a simpler decision model that concentrates on bad outcomes. The name "safety first" comes about because of the emphasis each of the criteria places on limiting the risk of bad outcomes. Three different safety first criteria have been

---

[6]The log utility function can be written as

$$\max E \ln W_1$$

where W_1 is end of period wealth, a random variable. Since utility functions are unchanged up to a linear transformation, if we let W_0 stand for the funds the investor can invest, then we can write the problem as

$$\max E(\ln W_1 - \ln W_0) = \max E \ln \left(\frac{W_1}{W_0} \right)$$

$$= \max E \ln(1 + R_i)$$

$$= \max \sum_i P_i \ln(1 + R_i)$$

$$= \max \sum_i \ln(1 + R_i)^{P_i}$$

Since the sum of the logs of a set of variables is the same as the log of the products, this problem can be written as

$$\max \ln \prod_i (1 + R_i)^{P_i}$$

But this is just the log of 1 plus the geometric mean return. Since taking the log of a set of numbers maintains the rank order, then that portfolio with the highest geometric mean return will also be the preferred portfolio if the investor has a log utility function.

[7]See Elton and Gruber [26, 27]. The mathematics is sufficiently complex that we have not included the proofs, but rather refer the interested reader to the original source.

put forth. The first, developed by Roy, states that the best portfolio is the one that has the smallest probability of producing a return below some specified level. If R_P is the return on the portfolio and R_L is the level below which the investor does not wish returns to fall, Roy's criterion is

$$(1) \quad \text{minimize Prob}\left(R_p < R_L\right)$$

If returns are *normally* distributed, then the optimum portfolio would be the one where R_L was the maximum number of standard deviations away from the mean.[8] For example, consider the three portfolios shown in Table 11.2. Assume 5% is the minimum return the investor desires. The investor wishes to minimize the chance of getting a return below 5%. If the investor selects portfolio A, then 5% is 1 standard deviation below the mean. The chance of getting a return below 5% is the probability of obtaining a return more than 1 standard deviation below the mean. If the investor selects investment B, then 5% is $2\frac{1}{4}$ standard deviations below the mean. The probability of obtaining a return below 5% is the probability of obtaining a return more than $2\frac{1}{4}$ standard deviations below the mean. If he selects investment C, the probability of obtaining a return below 5% is the probability of obtaining a return more than 1.5 standard deviations below the mean. Since the odds of obtaining a return more than $2\frac{1}{4}$ standard deviations below the mean are less than the odds of obtaining a return more than 1.5 or 1 standard deviation less than the mean, investment B is to be preferred. In order to determine how many standard deviations R_L lies below the mean, we calculated R_L minus the mean return divided by the standard deviation. To satisfy Roy's criterion if returns are normally distributed, we

$$\text{minimize } \frac{R_L - \overline{R}_P}{\sigma_P}$$

This is equivalent to maximizing minus this ratio or

$$\text{maximize } \frac{\overline{R}_P - R_L}{\sigma_P}$$

This criterion should look familiar. If R_L were replaced by R_F—the riskless rate of interest—this would be the criterion we used throughout much of the book. All portfolios that are equally desirable under Roy's criterion would have the same value for this ratio. That is, they could be described by the following expression:

$$\frac{\overline{R}_P - R_L}{\sigma_P} = K$$

Furthermore, if K was larger, the portfolio would be more desirable under Roy's criterion. Rearranging this expression yields

$$\overline{R}_P = R_L + K\sigma_P$$

Table 11.2   Mean Returns, Standard Deviations, and Lower Limits

	Portfolio		
	A	*B*	*C*
Mean return	10	14	17
Standard deviation (σ)	5	4	8
Difference from 5%	-1σ	-2.25σ	-1.5σ

[8]Assuming the mean return is above R_L.

This is the equation of a straight line with an intercept of R_L and a slope of K. Thus, all points of equal desirability (i.e., constant K) plot on a straight line and the preferred line is one with the highest slope. This is shown in Figure 11.1 where the K's are ordered such that $K_4 > K_3 > K_2 > K_1$. The Roy criterion with normally distributed returns produces a decision problem of exactly the same form as the portfolio problem with riskless lending and borrowing. In this case, R_L serves the role of the riskless rate, R_F. The desired portfolio is the feasible portfolio lying on the line in the most counterclockwise direction and is easy to find, utilizing the standard techniques discussed earlier. Notice that the portfolio that maximizes Roy's criterion must lie along the efficient frontier in mean standard deviation space.[9]

Although the analysis was performed assuming normally distributed returns, a similar result holds for any distribution that has first and second moments. The very same maximization problem follows from the use of Tchebyshev's inequality.[10]

---

[9]The location of portfolios that satisfy Roy's criterion when lending and borrowing are allowed is discussed in Appendix A at the end of this chapter. This conclusion assumes $R_P > R_L$.

[10]One of the ways to determine the probability of some outcome is the use of Tchebyshev's inequality. Tchebyshev's inequality allows one to determine the maximum probability of obtaining an outcome less than some value. It does not assume any distribution for returns. If a distribution was assumed, a more precise statement about probability could be made. Rather, it is a general statement applicable for all distributions.

The Tchebyshev inequality is

$$\text{Prob}\left(\left|\frac{R - \overline{R}_P}{\sigma_P}\right| > K\right) \le \frac{1}{K^2}$$

where

R is the outcome
$\overline{R}_P$ is the mean return
σ_P is the standard deviation
K is a constant

Since we are interested in the case where the lower limit is less than $\overline{R}_P$, the returns we are interested in are those less than $\overline{R}_P$. Therefore, the term in the absolute value sign is negative. Noting this, we can write the term in the parentheses as

$$\left(\frac{R - \overline{R}_P}{\sigma_P} < -K\right)$$

and the expression as

$$\text{Prob}\left(\frac{R - \overline{R}_P}{\sigma_P} < -K\right) \le \frac{1}{K^2} \tag{11.1}$$

We can express the lower limit in Roy's criterion as the number of standard deviations K lies below the mean, or

$$K = \frac{\overline{R}_P - R_L}{\sigma_P} \tag{11.2}$$

Since Tchebyshev's inequality holds for any value of K, we can substitute the expression for K shown in Equation (11.2) into the left-hand side of Equation (11.1). Doing so, and simplifying, yields

$$\text{Prob}\left(R < R_L\right) \le \frac{1}{K^2}$$

Since this is precisely Roy's criterion, we want to maximize K or maximize Equation (11.2). But this is exactly what we did in the case of the normal distribution.

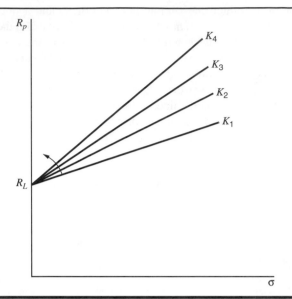

Figure 11.1 Lines of constant preference—Roy's criterion.

The Tchebyshev inequality makes very weak assumptions about the underlying distribution. It gives an expression that allows the determination of the maximum odds of obtaining a return less than some number. The use of this inequality leads to the same maximization problem and the same analysis as previously discussed. Thus, mean-variance analysis follows from the Roy safety first criterion.

The second safety first criterion was developed by Kataoka. Kataoka suggests the following criterion: maximize the lower limit subject to the constraint that the probability of a return less than, or equal to, the lower limit is not greater than some predetermined value. For example, maximize R_L subject to the constraint that the chance of a return below R_L is less than or equal to 5%. If α is the probability (in the example 5%), then in symbols this is

$$\text{maximize} \quad R_L$$
$$\text{subject to} \quad (1)\ \text{Prob}\left(R_P < R_L\right) \le \alpha$$

If returns are normally distributed, we can analyze this criterion in mean standard deviation space. Earlier, we noted that if returns are normally distributed, then the probability of obtaining returns below some number depends on the number of standard deviations below the mean that the number lies. Thus the odds of obtaining a return more than 3 standard deviations below the mean is 0.13% while the odds of obtaining a return more than 2 standard deviations below the mean is 2.28%. As an example set $\alpha = 0.05$. From the table of the normal distribution, we see that this is met as long as the lower limit is at least 1.65 standard deviations below the mean. With $\alpha = 0.05$, the constraint becomes

$$R_L \le \overline{R}_P - 1.65\sigma_P$$

Since we want to make R_L as large as possible, this inequality can be written as an equality. Writing it as an equality and rearranging, we obtain for a constant R_L

$$\overline{R}_P = R_L + 1.65\sigma_P$$

This is the equation of a straight line. Since the intercept is R_L as R_L changes, the line shifts in a parallel fashion. Figure 11.2 illustrates this for various values of R_L. The objective is

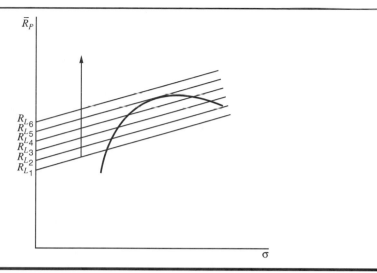

Figure 11.2   The portfolio choice problem with Kataoka's safety first rule.

to maximize R_L or to move as far up as possible (in the direction of the arrow). If there is no lending or borrowing, then a unique maximum exists and it is the tangency point on the highest R_L line (R_{L5} in the example). Note that, as in the case of Roy's criterion, the optimum portfolio must be on the efficient frontier in mean standard deviation space. Once again, the same analysis follows if one chooses to use the Tchebyshev inequality, rather than assuming normally distributed returns.

The final safety first criterion was put forth by Telser. He suggested that a reasonable criterion would be for an investor to maximize expected return, subject to the constraint that the probability of a return less than, or equal to, some predetermined limit was not greater than some predetermined number. In symbols, we have

$$\text{maximize } \overline{R}_P$$

$$\text{subject to (1) Prob}\big(R_P \le R_L\big) \le \alpha$$

Once again, it is convenient to rearrange the constraint. In the discussion of the Kataoka criterion, it was shown that if returns are normally distributed, this constraint becomes

$$R_L \le \overline{R}_P - (\text{constant})\sigma$$

Rearranging yields

$$\overline{R}_P \ge R_L + (\text{constant})\sigma$$

In the last section, the constant was set equal to 1.65 for the example. In general, it depends on the value of α. As discussed earlier, when the equality holds, this expression is the equation of a straight line. Consider Figure 11.3. The efficient frontier and the constraint are plotted in that figure. All points above the line meet the constraint. In Figure 11.3 the feasible set is bounded by the straight line and the efficient frontier (the shaded area). In this case the optimum is point A. If the portfolio with the overall highest return lies above the line, it will be selected. If it does not, the constraint line excludes part of the efficient set. In this case, the feasible portfolio with the highest mean return will lie at the highest intersection of the efficient frontier and the constraint. In either case, the point selected will be on the efficient set. It is possible that there are no feasible points that meet the constraint.

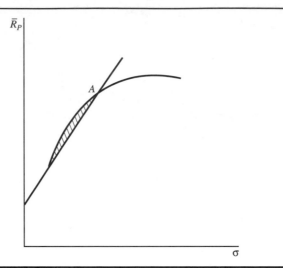

Figure 11.3   The investor's choice problem—Telser's criterion.

For example, in Figure 11.4 the constraint lies above the efficient set. In this case, there is no feasible portfolio lying above the constraint and the criterion fails to select any portfolios.

Note that with the Telser criterion, the optimum portfolio either lies on the efficient frontier in mean standard deviation space or it does not exist.

As with the other two criteria, the same analysis follows if we use the Tchebyshev inequality rather than assuming normal returns.

The safety first criteria were originally suggested as appealing decision making and an alternative to the expected utility framework of traditional analysis. We see in this section that, under reasonable sets of assumptions, they lead to mean-variance analysis and to the selection of a particular portfolio in the efficient set. As shown in Appendix A, at the end of this chapter, with unlimited lending and borrowing at a riskless rate, the analysis may lead to infinite borrowing, an unreasonable prescription for managers. However, the difficulties lie, not with the criteria, but with the original assumption that investors can borrow

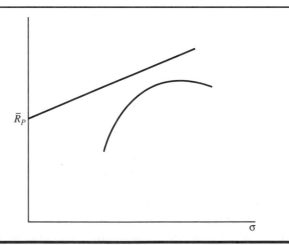

Figure 11.4   No feasible portfolio—Telser's criterion.

unlimited amounts at a riskless rate of interest. Whether the safety first criteria are reasonable criteria can be answered only by the readers themselves. To some, they seem sensible as a description of reality. To others, the fact that they may be inconsistent with expected utility maximization leads to their rejection. If one accepts one of the safety first criteria and believes that the probability distribution of returns is normal or sufficiently well behaved that the Tchebyshev inequality holds, then the discussion in all previous chapters concerning the generation of the efficient frontier is useful in finding the optimal portfolio.

STOCHASTIC DOMINANCE

A third set of alternatives to mean-variance analysis that has been advocated in the literature is stochastic dominance. The most general form of stochastic dominance makes no assumptions about the form of the probability distribution of returns. Furthermore, when we employ stochastic dominance we do not have to assume the specific form of investors' utility functions. Rather, we can define efficient sets under alternative assumptions about the general characteristics of investors' utility functions. These characteristics are consistent with whole families of utility functions. There are three progressively stronger assumptions about investor behavior that are employed in the stochastic dominance literature. They lead directly to first-, second-, and third-order stochastic dominance. First-order stochastic dominance assumes an investor prefers more to less. Second-order stochastic dominance assumes that, in addition to investors preferring more to less, they are risk averse. Finally, third-order stochastic dominance adds to the two assumptions of second-order dominance the assumption that investors have decreasing absolute risk aversion.[11]

Associated with each level of stochastic dominance is a theorem that allows the investor to eliminate many portfolios from consideration. Appendix B at the end of this chapter contains a proof of each of the theorems. In the chapter proper we intend to state the theorem and illustrate its use with a simple example.

Consider the example shown in Table 11.3. If an investor preferred more to less, then investment in asset A is preferable to investment in asset B because no matter which outcome occurs, A will always yield a higher return than B. For example, if market conditions are good, then A will return 10% and B will return 9%. The theorem of first-order stochastic dominance would, in fact, show that A dominated B. Now, consider the choices shown in Table 11.4. Investment A has the better outcomes. However, it is no longer certain that an investor will do worse by investing in B. For example, it is possible the return

Table 11.3   Outcomes Associated with Alternative Market Conditions

Market Condition	Outcome	
	A	B
Very good	11	10
Good	10	9
Average	9	8
Poor	8	7
Very poor	7	6

---

[11]Third-order stochastic dominance assumes the third derivative of utility is positive. A positive third derivative is a necessary condition for decreasing absolute risk aversion.

Table 11.4 Two Investment Alternatives: Outcomes and Associated Probabilities

Investment A		Investment B	
Outcome	Probability	Outcome	Probability
12	1/3	11	1/3
10	1/3	9	1/3
8	1/3	7	1/3

will be 11% if B is invested in and 10% or 8% if A is invested in. However, the chances are the investor will do worse with B. Let us rearrange this example (see Table 11.5). Note that no matter what the return is, the probability of obtaining less than that return (worse outcomes) are always as high with B as with A, or higher. Since we are assuming that the investor prefers more to less, A is preferred to B. Once again, A is preferred to B, not because the investor will always obtain a higher return, but rather because for all returns the odds of obtaining that return or less (doing worse) are as high with B as with A, or higher.

Table 11.5 shows the cumulative probability of any particular return. The cumulative probability is the likelihood of obtaining a given return or less. The example shown in Table 11.5 is plotted in Figure 11.5. Note that B coincides with A or lies above A at all levels of return. This implies that the odds of obtaining any return or less are as high with B as A, or higher.

The examples we have been discussing illustrate the ideas behind first-order stochastic dominance. The formal theorem is: if investors prefer more to less, and if the cumulative probability of A is never greater than the cumulative probability of B and sometimes less, then A is preferred to B.

The cumulative probability of A is never greater than the cumulative probability of B if, in diagrams such as Figure 11.5, the two curves do not cross and A does not lie above B. If the two curves cross, it is not possible to make a choice between A and B based on first-order stochastic dominance. To make a choice, we must make a stronger assumption about the characteristics of utility functions. To illustrate this, consider Table 11.6, which shows two possible investments, each with four equally likely outcomes. The cumulative probability for these two investments is shown in Table 11.7. At a return of 5%, B has a higher probability of a poor return than A, while at 8% A has a higher probability of a poorer return. Thus, we cannot select between A and B using first-order stochastic dominance. In order to be able to choose between these two investments, we have to be able to decide

Table 11.5 A Cumulative Probability Distribution

Return	Odds of Obtaining a Return Equal to or Less Than That Shown in Column 1	
	A	B
7	0	1/3
8	1/3	1/3
9	1/3	2/3
10	2/3	2/3
11	2/3	1
12	1	1

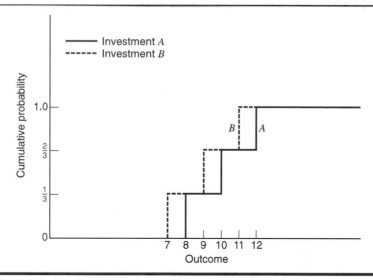

Figure 11.5   Cumulative frequency function for gambles A and B.

whether the higher probability of low returns in the range between 5% and 6% for B is more important than the higher probability of a low return from A in the range of 8% to 9%. If we assume risk aversion, in addition to preferring more to less, we can answer this question. Risk aversion means that the investor must be compensated for bearing risk. It arises when each increment in return is less valuable to the investor than the last. We still

Table 11.6   Two Investment Alternatives: Outcomes and Associated Probabilities

A		B	
Outcome	Probability	Outcome	Probability
6	1/4	5	1/4
8	1/4	9	1/4
10	1/4	10	1/4
12	1/4	12	1/4

Table 11.7   The Sum of the Cumulative Probability Distribution

Return	Cumulative Probability		Sum of Cumulative Probability		Sum of Cumulative Probabilities	
	A	B	A	B	A	B
4	0	0	0	0	0	0
5	0	1/4	0	1/4	0	1/4
6	1/4	1/4	1/4	1/2	1/4	3/4
7	1/4	1/4	1/2	3/4	3/4	1 1/2
8	1/2	1/4	1	1	1 3/4	2 1/2
9	1/2	1/2	1 1/2	1 1/2	3 1/4	4
10	3/4	3/4	2 1/4	2 1/4	5 1/2	6 1/4
11	3/4	3/4	3	3	8 1/2	9 1/4
12	1	1	4	4	12 1/2	13 1/4

prefer obtaining 9% to 8%. However, the 1% increment in return from 8% to 9% is less valuable than the 1% increment from 5% to 6%. Examine Table 11.6. A differs from B in the lowest two returns. If both investments turn out as badly as possible, the investor obtains 6% from A and only 5% from B. The investor gets an extra 1% from A if the worst occurs. The cost of selecting A rather than B is that, if the second worst return occurs, the investor obtains 8% from A rather than 9% from B. He loses the extra 1%. If he is risk averse, then he should be willing to lose 1% in return at a higher level of return in order to obtain an extra 1% at a lower return level. This is exactly the idea behind second-order stochastic dominance, and second-order stochastic dominance implies A dominates B.

The same result can be seen by examining the cumulative probability distributions. Figure 11.6 is a plot of Table 11.6. The area between 5% and 6% is identical to the area between 8% and 9%. Since risk aversion is being assumed, it is preferable to have a lower probability of a low return in the 5% to 6% range than the 8% to 9% range. Thus, A is preferred to B. The areas have been designated by + and −. If, for all returns, the + area below that return is no smaller than the − area and for some returns it is larger, then A dominates B by second-order stochastic dominance.

These ideas can be formalized in the following theorem: If

1. Investors prefer more to less, and

2. Investors are risk averse, and

3. The sum of the cumulative probabilities for all returns is never more with A than B and sometimes less,

then A dominates B with second-order stochastic dominance.

The application of this theorem is shown in Table 11.7. We have already seen that A dominates B by examining the cumulative probability distribution. We can see it more easily simply by applying point 3 above to the sum of the cumulative probability distribution

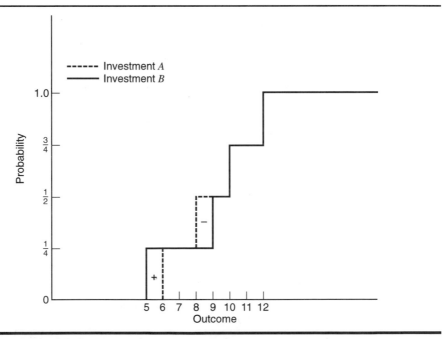

Figure 11.6   The choice between investments A and B.

shown in columns 4 and 5 of Table 11.7 entitled "Sum of Cumulative Probability." Applying point 3 shows clearly that A dominates B.

The reader might be curious how this analysis relates to mean-variance analysis. If returns are normally distributed, then the answer is clear. First-order stochastic dominance assumes investors prefer more to less. The first part of the efficient set theorem utilizes this same assumption and leads to the result that, at any level of standard deviation, the investor preferred a higher mean return. Thus, first-order stochastic dominance implies the first part of the efficient set theorem if returns are normally distributed. When short sales are allowed, preferring a higher mean for any standard deviation leads to the efficient frontier. When short sales are disallowed, first-order stochastic dominance produces a set of portfolios that lies on the upper half of the outer boundary of the feasible set. These portfolios include the efficient set produced by mean-variance analysis, plus all portfolios that have the highest return possible for each level of risk. In Figure 11.7, the portfolios along the boundary segment BC are not in the efficient set AB but satisfy the first-order stochastic dominance condition.

Second-order stochastic dominance assumes investors are risk averse, as well as prefer more to less. These are the same assumptions that lead to the efficient set theorem. Thus, it should not surprise the reader that with normally distributed returns the only set of portfolios that is not dominated, using second-order stochastic dominance, is the mean-variance efficient set.

We have just seen that, when returns are normally distributed, second-order stochastic dominance (and, with short sales, first-order stochastic dominance) leads to a definition of an optimal set of portfolios that is consistent with the efficient set produced by mean-variance analysis. The advantage of stochastic dominance is that it can be used to derive sets of desirable portfolios when returns follow other distributions, or when one is unwilling to assume specific utility functions.

One should be careful not to overemphasize the importance of this advantage. In general, stochastic dominance involves pairwise comparisons of all alternatives. Since there is an infinite set of alternatives to consider in portfolio selection, the direct use of stochastic

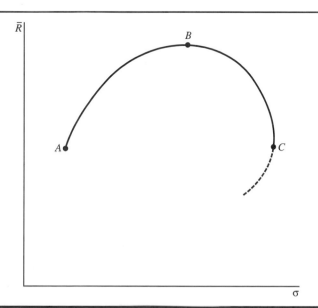

Figure 11.7 Portfolios having first-order stochastic dominance.

dominance becomes infeasible.[12] However, if returns follow any of a variety of well-behaved distributions, then the use of stochastic dominance shows that portfolios can be selected in simpler ways. We have already seen that, when returns are normally distributed, stochastic dominance leads to the familiar mean-variance analysis. Bawa [13] has shown that when returns follow any two-parameter distribution, stochastic dominance can be used to derive simple two-parameter rules for portfolio selection.

Before leaving this section, it is useful to examine third-order stochastic dominance.

Figure 11.8 plots the sum of the cumulative distribution function for the example presented in Table 11.7. The sum of the cumulative frequency function can be thought of as the cumulative of the cumulative frequency function. Note that A never lies to the left of B or above B. This allows us to choose among the alternatives using second-order stochastic dominance. If the curves cross, then neither A nor B can be eliminated by second-order stochastic dominance and third-order is necessary.

Third-order stochastic dominance assumes investors exhibit decreasing absolute risk aversion. One of the properties of a function exhibiting decreasing absolute risk aversion is a positive third derivative.[13] The theorem for third-order stochastic dominance utilizes this fact. Since there are other characteristics of decreasing absolute risk aversion, a more powerful theorem awaits development.[14]

A dominates B using third-order stochastic dominance if:

1. Investors prefer more to less,
2. Investors are risk averse,
3. The third derivative of the investors utility function is positive,
4. The mean of A is greater than the mean of B, and
5. The sum of the sum of the cumulative probability distribution for all returns is never more with A than B and sometimes less.

Columns 4 and 5 of Table 11.7 are the sums of the cumulative distributions. Columns 6 and 7 are the sums of the sum of the cumulative distribution.

As can be seen from this table, A dominates B using third-order stochastic dominance. This is to be expected since A dominates B under second-order stochastic dominance and third-order is more restrictive.

The stochastic dominance analysis may seem to the reader to be a lot of analysis with few results. Many of the results in portfolio analysis that can be obtained from using stochastic

---

[12]This drawback is not as important in other areas. For example, in looking at the selection of investment alternatives by the firm we are dealing with, a limited set of alternatives and stochastic dominance would seem to be a very useful tool.

[13]A utility function exhibits decreasing absolute risk aversion. If $A'(W) < 0$ where $U'(W)$ and $U''(W)$ are the first and second derivatives of the utility function, respectively, then

$$A(W) = -\frac{U''(W)}{U'(W)}$$

$$A'(W) = +\left(\frac{U''(W)}{U'(W)}\right)^2 - \frac{U'''(W)}{U'(W)}$$

The first term is positive since it is a ratio of squared terms. $U'(W) > 0$ by assumption. Therefore, for the second term to be negative, it is necessary for $U'''(W) > 0$. Note that $U'''(W)$ is a necessary, but not sufficient, condition for $A'(W) < 0$.

[14]For some distributions, such a theorem exists.

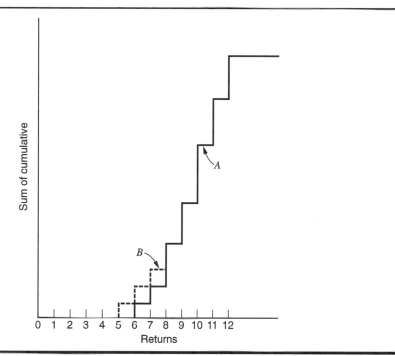

Figure 11.8   Sum of cumulative probabilities for two investments.

dominance are well known and more easily obtainable in other ways. However, stochastic dominance is a set of tools that is likely to lead to substantial additional breakthroughs. Knowledge of these tools should help the reader understand future research in this area.

SKEWNESS AND PORTFOLIO ANALYSIS

A number of authors have proposed selecting portfolios on the basis of the first three moments of return distributions, rather than the first two (mean and variance). The third moment is called skewness. Skewness is a measure of the asymmetry of a distribution. The normal distribution has zero skewness since the shape of the distribution above the mode is a mirror image of the shape below the mode. The log-normal distribution shown in Figure 11.9 has positive skewness. Point A indicates the mode or most likely value. The log-normal has more observations above this value than below. It is said to be skewed toward high values or exhibit positive skewness. Researchers interested in skewness believe investors should prefer positive skewness. All else constant, they should prefer portfolios with a larger probability of very large payoffs. This is not only logical, but is also consistent with some empirical evidence that investors exhibit this preference.[15]

If three moments are important to the investor, then the portfolio problem is best represented in three-dimensional space with mean on one axis, variance on the second, and skewness on the third. The efficient set would be the outer shell of the feasible set with maximum mean return, minimum variance, and maximum skewness.

---

[15]See Arditti [4] for evidence concerning investors' preferences for positive skewness. Kraus and Litzenburger [57] have criticized Arditti for not differentiating between diversifiable and nondiversifiable skewness.

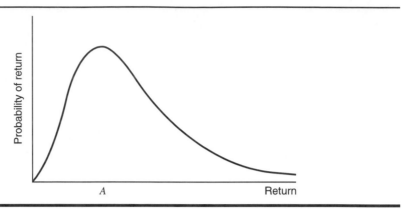

Figure 11.9　The log-normal distribution.

The skewness of a portfolio of securities is not simply a weighted average of the skewness of the component securities. Like variance, it depends on the joint movement of securities. This means that to measure the skewness on a portfolio, a great number of estimates of joint movement must be made. For these estimates to be feasible, it requires the type of model development discussed in Chapters 7 and 8 and the development of simple rules such as those discussed in Chapter 9. This developmental work has not been done. Thus, practical portfolio analysis in three moments must await development of a set of analytical techniques for estimating and solving problems involving skewness measures.[16]

VALUE AT RISK (VaR)

The principal argument in favor of introducing skewness preferences into the portfolio problem is that variance is not a complete measure of risk in the case where the distribution of returns is asymmetric. An alternative to introducing skewness is to consider alternative measures of downside risk. One such measure of downside risk is the semivariance which is discussed in Chapter 3 (the average squared difference from the mean for all returns below the mean). As we mentioned, the semivariance measures downside risk relative to a benchmark given by expected return. More generally, we can consider return variability relative to any other benchmark, such as a risk-free return or zero return. These measures in aggregate are called *lower partial moments*. Bawa [13] shows how using a range of lower partial moments as measures of downside risk is consistent with stochastic dominance criteria. If the differences from the benchmark are squared, it is called a second lower partial moment. If they are not squared, it is a first lower partial moment. If alternative A has a smaller second lower partial moment across the range of all possible benchmarks than alternative B, then alternative A will be preferred on second-order stochastic dominance criteria. Similarly, if alternative B has a smaller lower partial moment across the range of all possible benchmarks, then alternative B will be preferred on first-order stochastic dominance criteria.

---

[16]There are two justifications for three-moment portfolio theory. First, it is appropriate if investors have cubic utility functions. However, the cubic utility function does not always exhibit risk aversion and exhibits increasing absolute risk aversion over part of its domain. The other argument for three-moment portfolio theory is that distributions are nonnormal and the introduction of skewness better approximates the distribution. See Samuelson [91].

This first-order stochastic dominance result gives us an interesting way of thinking about a measure of downside risk and has become almost a standard measure of downside risk for banks: Value at Risk, or VaR. VaR measures the least expected loss (relative to zero, or relative to expected wealth) that will be obtained with a probability, P. In other words, for initial wealth W_0 the VaR is given as $VaR = -W_0(1 + R_{min})$, where R_{min} is the value of returns defined by Prob $(R \geq R_{min}) \geq P$. For example, if P is 0.05, then R_{min} is the highest return in the poorest 5% of returns. The motivation is that R_{min} defines the investor's worst-case scenario. In a typical application, the investor would maximize expected return $\bar{R}$ subject to a VaR no greater than a certain prespecified amount. This corresponds to the Telser criterion mentioned earlier. This VaR measure is dependent on an accurate measure of the tail area probability of the distribution of returns. An alternative metric referred to as the Tail Conditional Expectation (TCE) measures downside risk not in terms of a certain value of the returns distribution, but rather by a measure of the expected return less than the benchmark.[17] This alternative measure corresponds precisely to the first lower partial moment of returns, and gives rise to a first-order stochastic dominance criterion for choosing among portfolios.

Just like the case of the stochastic dominance criteria, the results of Bawa [13] can be used to show that when returns follow any two-parameter distribution, ordering by VaR will be the same as an ordering by the second parameter. For example, suppose that portfolio returns are approximately normal. With a 5% probability the minimum return relative to expectation will be given by (on a per-dollar basis) $R_{min} = \bar{R} - 1.65\sigma$ which implies that the least expected loss with 95% probability is given as VaR $= -R_{min}$. Under these circumstances, a ranking of portfolios by VaR given the mean return $\bar{R}$ is equivalent to a ranking by variance given the mean return $\bar{R}$. This statistic is used both for portfolio management and risk diagnostic purposes.

The use of VaR and other downside risk metrics is motivated by the fact that in many cases variance is inadequate as a measure of risk. A simple example is where returns follow an asymmetrical distribution, and portfolios begin to be characterized by more than two moments of the distribution of returns, giving rise to concerns about the relevance of skewness in determining appropriate preference orderings. Since downside risk measures give the same orderings as would the use of variance and can be applied where variance is not appropriate as a measure of risk, it appears that they would dominate the use of variance under all circumstances. Unfortunately they are difficult to compute and work with in cases where the distribution of returns is asymmetrical.

One important special case is when the asymmetry arises through the inclusion of derivative securities in the total portfolio of assets. It is possible under these circumstances to characterize the worst-case scenarios, and by a careful analysis of the way in which payoffs are related to the underlying security returns, we can infer the VaR of an entire portfolio under the assumption that the underlying security returns are normally distributed. This is referred to as the *delta-normal* method. A criticism of this approach is its sensitivity to the assumption that returns are in fact normally distributed. If the return distribution is in fact fat-tailed, or there are unusual or extreme events possible but not encountered in

---

[17]Artzner, et al. [8] argue that VaR is not a coherent risk measure, as it does not satisfy the subadditivity property—in other words, the VaR associated with a combination of two portfolios can be higher than the sum of the VaRs of the two individual portfolios, and give this as a reason for using the first lower partial moment measure LCE. Cuoco, et al. [24] show that it is always possible to transform a TCE limit into an equivalent VaR limit, and conversely.

a given historical data set, the portfolio VaR will be an underestimate of the VaR that would be computed appropriately accounting for these factors.[18]

CONCLUSION

In this chapter we have analyzed several alternatives to the traditional mean-variance portfolio model. Perhaps the most noteworthy point is that, if returns follow a normal distribution, many of these criteria produce optimal portfolios that lie on the mean-variance efficient frontier. This is true though some techniques like maximizing the geometric mean would, without analysis, seem to lead to very different results. Thus, if returns follow a normal distribution, the analysis performed in earlier chapters is still relevant to portfolio decision making even when the alternative decision criteria discussed in this chapter are utilized.

APPENDIX A

SAFETY FIRST WITH RISKLESS LENDING AND BORROWING

In the text we discuss the choice of portfolios that satisfies each of the three standard formulations of the safety first criteria, assuming choices are to be made from among risky assets. In this appendix we extend the analysis to include riskless lending and borrowing.

Roy Criteria

If a riskless lending and borrowing rate exists and returns are normally distributed, then the Roy criteria lead to infinite borrowing or only investment in the riskless asset depending on the relationship between R_L and R_F.[19] Figures 11.10 and 11.11 illustrate two possible patterns.

In both cases the investor wishes to rotate the line passing through R_L as much as possible in the counterclockwise direction. In Figure 11.10 this leads to investing in the riskless portfolio. This makes intuitive sense. If the riskless asset yields more than R_L (as it does in Figure 11.10), then by investing in the riskless asset the investor has zero chance of obtaining a return below R_L. Since returns are assumed normally distributed, any policy involving a risky asset has some probability of a return below R_L; thus 100% investment in the riskless asset is optimal.

If R_F is below R_L, then investment in R_F guarantees a return below R_L. Examining the figure shows that borrowing an infinite amount at R_F and investing in a risky asset is optimal.

Kataoka Criteria

If lending and borrowing at the riskless rate of interest exists, then using Kataoka's criteria, the optimum policy is to invest 100% in the riskless asset or borrow an infinite amount, depending on the slope of the R_L lines in relation to the slope of the R_F line.[20] Figure 11.12

---

[18]Another limitation of this so-called *delta-normal* approach is that it fails to account appropriately for sources of risk that arise from changes in volatility or the other characteristics of returns. Phillipe Jorion [55] describes this and other more advanced procedures referred to as *delta-gamma* approximations which attempt to account for these additional sources of risk.

[19]There are an infinite number of solutions if $R_L = R_F$.

[20]There are an infinite number of solutions if the slope of the R_L lines is the same as the slope of the lending-borrowing line.

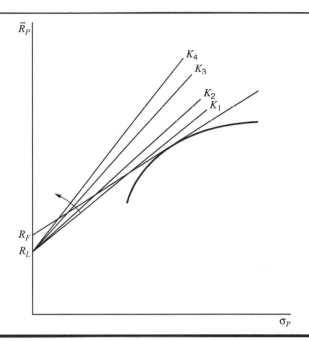

Figure 11.10 Investment alternatives leading to 100% investment in the riskless asset.

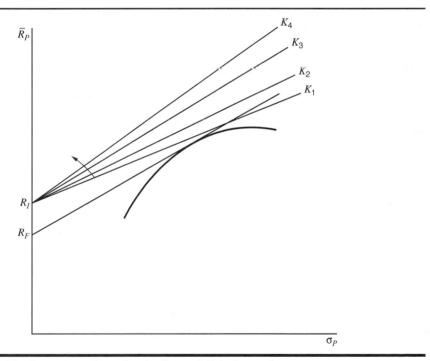

Figure 11.11 Investment alternatives leading to infinite borrowing.

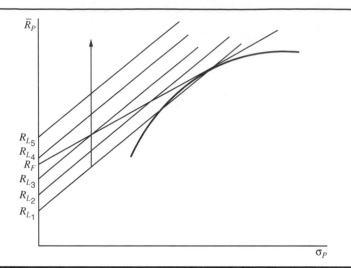

Figure 11.12   Investment alternatives leading to 100% investment in riskless asset.

shows a situation where the optimum policy is to invest 100% in the riskless asset. (Slope of R_L lines greater than slope of lending-borrowing line.) Figure 11.13 shows a case where the optimum policy is infinite borrowing (slope of lending-borrowing line greater than slope of R_L line).

Telser Criteria

With riskless lending and borrowing, employing Telser's criteria leads to three possible solutions:

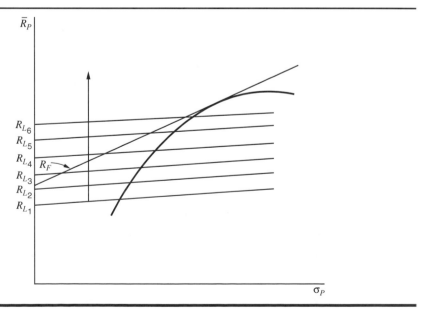

Figure 11.13   Investment alternatives leading to infinite borrowing.

1. The optimum occurs at the intersection of the constraint with the lending and borrowing line.
2. The optimum occurs at infinite borrowing.
3. There is no portfolio that meets the constraint and thus no feasible solution.

Figure 11.14 shows the situation where the optimum is the intersection of the constraint with the lending and borrowing line. Figure 11.15 shows the situation where the optimum is infinite borrowing. The case where there was no feasible solution was demonstrated in

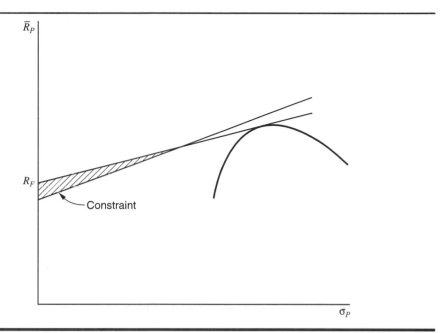

Figure 11.14 Investment alternatives where a mixed policy is optimum.

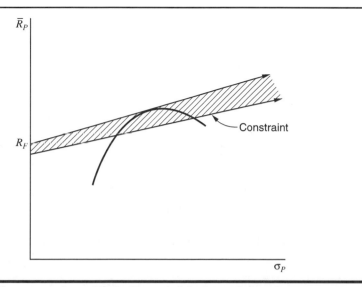

Figure 11.15 Investment alternatives leading to infinite borrowing.

Figure 11.4. The same analysis would follow with lending and borrowing at a riskless rate of interest. Once again, the optimum depends on the slope of the lending-borrowing line and the constraint.

APPENDIX B

PROOF OF THE SUFFICIENCY OF THE STOCHASTIC DOMINANCE THEOREMS[21]

Theorem   First-order stochastic dominance. F dominates G if:

1.   The investor prefers more to less $U'(X) > 0$, and
2. $F(X) \leq G(X)$ for all X and $F(X) < G(X)$ for at least one value, where $F(X)$ and $G(X)$ are cumulative distribution functions of F and G, respectively.

Proof F is preferred to G if the expected utility of distribution F is greater than the expected utility of G. The expected utility of

$$F = \int_a^b U(X)\, dF(X)$$

and the expected utility of

$$G = \int_a^b U(X)\, dG(X)$$

a and b are simply the smallest and largest values F and G can take on. Thus, for F to be preferred to G,

$$\int_a^b U(X)\, dF(X) > \int_a^b U(X)\, dG(X)$$

or

$$\int_a^b U(X)\, dF(X) - \int_a^b U(X)\, dG(X) > 0$$

Recall that $d(uw) = u\, dw + w\, du$. Integrating both sides and rearranging shows that $\int_a^b u\, dw = uw\big|_a^b - \int_a^b w\, du$. This expression is integration by parts. Defining u as $U(x)$ and dw as $d[F(X) - G(X)]$ and integration by parts yields

$$\int_a^b U(X)\, d\big[F(x) - G(x)\big] = U(x)\big[F(x) - G(x)\big]\Big|_a^b - \int_a^b U'(x)\big[F(x) - G(x)\big]\, dx$$

$F(b) = G(b) = 1$ and $F(a) = G(a) = 0$ by definition. Thus, F dominates G if the last term is positive (i.e., the integral negative). By assumption, $U'(x)$ is positive. The integral adds up values of $U'(x)$ and $F(x) - G(x)$. For this integral to be negative no matter what pattern $U'(x)$ takes on (and, thus, for the last term to be positive), $F(x)$ must be less than or equal to $G(x)$ for all x. For it to have a value different from zero, the strict inequality must hold for some value. This completes the proof.

Theorem   Second-order stochastic dominance. F is preferred to G if:

---

[21]These proofs follow Bawa [13]. For a proof of sufficiency and necessity, see Bawa [13].

1. Investors prefer more to less $U'(x) > 0$,
2. Investors are risk averse $U''(x) < 0$, and
3. $\int_a^x F(y)\, dy \le \int_a^x G(y)\, dy$ for all x with the strict inequality holding for some value.

Proof F is preferred to G if the expected utility of F is greater than the expected utility of G. In the last section we showed this is equivalent to

$$-\int_a^b U'(x)\left[F(x)-G(x)\right] dx < 0$$

Integrating once more by parts yields

$$-U'(x)\int_a^x\left[F(y)-G(y)\right]dy\,\Big]_a^b + \int_a^b U''(x)\int_a^x\left[F(y)-G(y)\right]dy\,dx$$

or

$$-U'(b)\int_a^b\left[F(y)-G(y)\right]dy + \int_a^b U''(x)\int_a^x\left[F(y)-G(y)\right]dy\,dx$$

$U'(b) > 0$ by definition. Therefore, the first term is positive if the integral is negative. $U''(x) < 0$ by definition. Thus the second term is positive if the integral is negative or zero for all values of X. For the terms to be nonzero, the integral must be strictly negative for at least one value of X. The theorem is proven.

Theorem The theorem for third-order stochastic dominance is F dominates G if:

1. Investors prefer more to less $U'(x) > 0$,
2. Investors are risk averse $U''(x) < 0$,
3. The third derivative of the utility function is positive $U''(x) > 0$,
4. The mean of F is greater than the mean of G, and
5. $\int_a^x \int_a^t [F(y) - G(y)]\, dy\, dt \le 0$ for all x and the strict inequality holds for some value, where t lies between a and b.

Proof F dominates G if the expected utility of F is greater than the expected utility of G. In the last section this required that

$$-U'(b)\int_a^b\left[F(y)-G(y)\right]dy + \int_a^b U''(x)\int_a^x\left[F(y)-G(y)\right]dy\,dx > 0$$

Integrating the second term by parts yields

$$-U'(b)\int_a^b\left[F(y)-G(y)\right]dy + U''(b)\int_a^t\int_a^b\left[F(y)-G(y)\right]dy\,dt$$

$$-\int_a^b U'''(x)\int_a^x\int_a^t\left[F(y)-G(y)\right]dy\,dx\,dt$$

Note that

$$\int_a^b\left[F(y)-G(y)\right]dy$$

is the difference in means between G and F. Since, by assumption, the mean of G is less than the mean of F, this is negative. $U'(x) > 0$ by assumption; thus the first term is positive. Similarly, $U''(x) < 0$ and $U''' > 0$; thus the last two terms are positive if the double integral is negative. This completes the proof.

QUESTIONS AND PROBLEMS

1. Consider the following investments. What can be said about their desirability using first- or second-order stochastic dominance?

A		B		C	
Probability	Outcome	Probability	Outcome	Probability	Outcome
0.2	4%	0.1	5%	0.4	6%
0.3	6%	0.3	6%	0.3	7%
0.4	8%	0.2	7%	0.2	8%
0.1	10%	0.3	8%	0.1	10%
		0.1	9%		

2. If R_L equals 5%, what is the preferred investment shown in Problem 1 using Roy's safety first criterion?
3. If α equals 10%, what is the preferred investment shown in Problem 1 using Kataoka's safety first criterion?
4. If $R_L = 5\%$ and $\alpha = 10\%$, what is the preferred investment shown in Problem 1 using Telser's safety first criterion?
5. Using geometric mean return as a criterion, which investment is to be preferred in Problem 1?
6. Given the following investments:

A		B		C	
Probability	Outcome %	Probability	Outcome %	Probability	Outcome %
0.4	3	0.1	5	0.1	5
0.3	4	0.2	6	0.1	7
0.1	6	0.1	8	0.2	8
0.1	7	0.2	9	0.2	9
0.1	9	0.4	10	0.4	11

What can be said about the desirability of the investments using first- and second-order dominance?

7. If R_L is 3%, what investment in Problem 6 is preferred using Roy's safety first criterion?
8. Using geometric mean, which investment is preferred in Problem 6?

BIBLIOGRAPHY

1. Alderfer, Clayton, and Bierman, Harold. "Choices with Risk: Beyond the Mean and Variance," *Journal of Business*, **43,** No. 3 (July 1970), pp. 341–353.
2. Ali, Mukhtar. "Stochastic Dominance and Portfolio Analysis," *Journal of Financial Economics*, **2,** No. 2 (June 1975), pp. 205–230.
3. Ang, James. "A Note on the E, SL Portfolio Selection Model," *Journal of Finance and Quantitative Analysis*, **X,** No. 5 (Dec. 1975), pp. 849–857.

4. Arditti, Fred. "Risk and the Required Return on Equity," *Journal of Finance*, **XXII,** No. 1 (March 1967), pp. 19–36.

5. ——. "Skewness and Investors' Decisions: A Reply," *Journal of Financial and Quantitative Analysis*, **X,** No. 1 (March 1975), pp. 173–176.

6. Arditti, Fred, and Levy, Haim. "Distribution Moments and Equilibrium: A Comment," *Journal of Financial and Quantitative Analysis*, **VII,** No. 1 (Jan. 1972), pp. 1429–1433.

7. ——. "Portfolio Efficiency Analysis in Three Moments: The Multiperiod Case," *Journal of Finance*, **XXX,** No. 3 (June 1975), pp. 797–809.

8. Artzner, P., Delbaen, F., Eber, J.-M., and Heath, D. "Coherent Measures of Risk," *Mathematical Finance*, **9,** No. 2 (1999), pp. 203–228.

9. Arzac, Enrique. "Utility Analysis of Change-Constrained Portfolio Selection," *Journal of Financial and Quantitative Analysis*, **IX,** No. 6 (Dec. 1974), pp. 993–1007.

10. ——. "Utility Analysis of Chance-Constrained Portfolio Selection: A Correction," *Journal of Financial and Quantitative Analysis*, **XII,** No. 2 (June 1977), p. 321–323.

11. Aucamp, Donald. "A Comment on Geometric Mean Portfolios," *Management Science*, **24,** No. 8 (April 1978), pp. 859–868.

12. Banz, Rolf, and Miller, Merton. "Prices for State-Contingent Claims: Some Estimates and Applications," *Journal of Business*, **51,** No. 4 (Oct. 1978), pp. 653–672.

13. Bawa, Vijay. "Optimal Rules for Ordering Uncertain Prospects," *Journal of Financial Economics*, **2,** (1975), pp. 95–121.

14. ——. "Safety-First, Stochastic Dominance, and Optimal Portfolio Choice," *Journal of Financial and Quantitative Analysis*, **XIII,** No. 2 (June 1978), pp. 225–271.

15. Bawa, Vijay B., Bodurtha, James N., Jr., Rao, M. R., and Suri, Hira L. "On Determination of Stochastic Dominance Optimal Sets," *Journal of Finance*, **40,** No. 2 (June 1985), pp. 417–432.

16. Bey, Roger P., and Howe, Keith M. "Gini's Mean Difference and Portfolio Selection: An Empirical Evaluation," *Journal of Financial and Quantitative Analysis*, **XIX,** No. 3 (Sept. 1984), pp. 329–338.

17. Brennan, Michael J., and Schwartz, Eduardo S. "On the Geometric Mean Index: A Note," *Journal of Financial and Quantitative Analysis*, **XX,** No. 1 (March 1985), pp. 119–122.

18. Brieman, Leon. "Investment Policies for Expanding Businesses Optimal in A Long Run Sense," *Naval Research Logistics Quarterly*, **7** (Dec. 1960), pp. 647–651.

19. Campbell, Rachel. "Optimal Portfolio Selection in a Value-at-Risk Framework," *Journal of Banking & Finance*, **25,** No. 9 (Sept. 2001), 789.

20. Cheng, Lee. "Functional Form, Skewness Effect, and the Risk-Return Relationship," *Journal of Financial and Quantitative Analysis*, **XII,** No. 1 (March 1977), pp. 55–72.

21. Cheng, Pao, and Deets, King. "Test of Portfolio Building Rules: Comment," *Journal of Finance*, **XXVI,** No. 4 (Sept. 1971), pp. 965–972.

22. Cheung, C. Sherman, and Kwan, Clarence C.Y. "A Note on Simple Criteria for Optimal Portfolio Selection," *The Journal of Finance*, **43,** No. 1 (Mar. 1988), pp. 41–46.

23. Coles, Jeffrey L., Loewenstein, Uri, and Suay, Jose. "On Equilibrium Pricing Under Parameter Uncertainty," *Journal of Financial and Quantitative Analysis*, **30,** No. 3 (Sept. 1995), pp. 347–364.

24. Cuoco, Domenico, He, Hua, and Issaenko, Sergei. "Optimal Dynamic Trading Strategies with Risk Limits," Unpublished working paper, New Haven, Conn., Yale University, 2001.

25. Ekern, Steinar. "Time Dominance Efficiency Analysis," *The Journal of Finance*, **36,** No. 5 (Dec. 1981), pp. 1023–1034.

26. Elton, Edwin J., and Gruber, Martin J. "On the Optimality of Some Multiperiod Portfolio Selection Criteria," *Journal of Business*, **47,** No. 2 (April 1974), pp. 231–243.

27. ——. "An Algorithm for Maximizing the Geometric Mean." *Management Science* (Dec. 1974), pp. 483–488.

28. Fama, Eugene, and Macbeth, James. "Long-Term Growth in a Short Term Market," *Journal of Finance*, **XXIX,** No. 3 (June 1974), pp. 857–885.

29. Fishburn, Peter. "Mean-Risk Analysis with Risk Associated with Below-Target Returns," *American Economic Review*, **67,** No. 2 (March 1977), pp. 116–126.

30. Francis, Jack Clark. "Skewness and Investors' Decisions," *Journal of Financial and Quantitative Analysis*, **X,** No. 1 (March 1975), pp. 163–172.

31. Frankfurther, George, and Phillips, Herbert. "Efficient...: Comment," *Journal of Financial and Quantitative Analysis*, **X,** No. 1 (March 1975), pp. 177–179.

32. Gennotte, Gerard, and Feldman, David. "Optimal Portfolio Choice Under Incomplete Information/Comment," *The Journal of Finance*, **41,** No. 3 (July 1986), pp. 733–749.

33. Granito, Michael, and Walsh, Patrick. "Portfolio Efficiency Analysis in Three Moments—The Multiperiod Case: Comment," *Journal of Finance*, **XXXIII,** No. 1 (March 1978), pp. 345–361.

34. Grauer, Robert R. "A Comparison of Growth Optimal and Mean Variance Investment Policies," *Journal of Financial and Quantitative Analysis*, **XVI,** No. 1 (March 1981), pp. 1–22.

35. ———. "Normality, Solvency, and Portfolio Choice," *Journal of Financial and Quantitative Analysis*, **21,** No. 3 (Sept. 1986), pp. 265–278.

36. Green, Richard C. "Positively Weighted Portfolios on the Minimum-Variance Frontier," *The Journal of Finance*, **41,** No. 5 (Dec. 1986), pp. 1051–1068.

37. Hadar, Josef, and Russel, William. "Stochastic Dominance and Diversification," *Journal of Economic Theory*, **3,** No. 3 (Sept. 1971), pp. 288–305.

38. Hakansson, Nils. "Capital Growth and the Mean-Variance Approach to Portfolio Selection," *Journal of Financial and Quantitative Analysis*, **VI,** No. 1 (Jan. 1971), pp. 517–557.

39. ———. "Comment on Merton and Samuelson," *Journal of Financial Economics*, **1,** No. 1 (May 1974), pp. 950–970.

40. Hakansson, Nils, and Ching Liu Tien. "Optimal Growth Portfolios When Yields Are Serially Correlated," *Review of Economics and Statistics*, **LII,** No. 4 (Nov. 1970), pp. 385–394.

41. Hakansson, Nils, and Miller, Bruce. "Compound-Return Mean-Variance Portfolios Never Risk Ruin," *Management Science*, **22,** No. 4 (Dec. 1975), pp. 391–400.

42. Hanoch, Giora, and Levy, Haim. "Efficient Portfolio Selection with Quadratic and Cubic Utility," *Journal of Business*, **43,** No. 2 (April 1970), pp. 191–198.

43. Hanssmann, Fred. "Probability of Survival as an Investment Criterion," *Management Science*, **15,** No. 1 (Sept. 1968), pp. 33–48.

44. Hogan, William, and Warren, James. "Computation of the Efficient Boundary in the E-S Portfolio Selection Model," *Journal of Financial and Quantitative Analysis*, **VII,** No. 4 (Sept. 1972), pp. 1881–1896.

45. Jahankhani, Ali. "E-V and E-S Capital Asset Pricing Models: Some Empirical Tests," *Journal of Financial and Quantitative Analysis*, **XI,** No. 4 (Nov. 1976), pp. 513–528.

46. Jarrow, Robert. "The Relationship between Arbitrage and First Order Stochastic Dominance," *Journal of Finance*, **41,** No. 4 (Sept. 1986), pp. 915–921.

47. Jean, William. "The Extension of Portfolio Analysis to Three or More Parameters," *Journal of Financial and Quantitative Analysis*, **VI,** No. 1 (Jan. 1971), pp. 505–515.

48. ———. "Distribution Moments and Equilibrium: Reply," *Journal of Financial and Quantitative Analysis*, **VII,** No. 1 (Jan. 1972), pp. 1435–1437.

49. ———. "More on Multidimensional Portfolio Analysis," *Journal of Financial and Quantitative Analysis*, **VIII,** No. 3 (June 1973), pp. 475–490.

50. ———. "A General Class of Three-Parameter Risk Measures: Comment," *Journal of Finance*, **XXX,** No. 1 (March 1975), pp. 224–225.

51. Jean, William H. "The Geometric Mean and Stochastic Dominance," *The Journal of Finance*, **35,** No. 1 (March 1980), pp. 151–158.

52. Jean, William H., and Helms, Billy P. "Geometric Mean Approximations," *Journal of Financial and Quantitative Analysis*, **XVIII,** No. 3 (Sept. 1983), pp. 287–294.

53. Johnson, Keith, and Burgess, Richard. "The Effects of Sample Sizes on the Accuracy of EV and SSD Efficiency Criteria," *Journal of Financial and Quantitative Analysis*, **X,** No. 5 (Dec. 1975), pp. 813–830.

54. Jones, E. Irwin. "Test of Portfolio Building Rules: Comment," *Journal of Finance*, **XXVI,** No. 4 (Sept. 1971), pp. 973–975.

55. Jorion, Phillipe. *Value at Risk: The New Benchmark for Controlling Derivatives Risk* (New York: McGraw Hill, 1997).

56. Kane, Alex. "Skewness Preference and Portfolio Choice," *Journal of Financial and Quantitative Analysis*, **XVII,** No. 1 (March 1982), pp. 15–26.

57. Kraus, Alan, and Litzenberger, Robert. "Skewness Preference and the Valuation of Risky Assets," *Journal of Finance*, **21,** No. 4 (Sept. 1976), pp. 1085–1094.

58. Kritzmann, Mark, and Rich, Don. "Beware of Dogma," *Journal of Portfolio Management*, **24,** No. 4 (Summer 1998), pp. 66–77.

59. Kumar, P., Philippatos, G., and Ezzell, J. "Goal Programming and the Selection of Portfolios by Dual-Purpose Funds," *Journal of Finance*, **XXXIII,** No. 1, (March 1978), pp. 303–310.

60. Latane, Henry. "Criteria for Choice Among Risky Ventures," *Journal of Political Economy* (April 1959), pp. 144–155.

61. Latane, Henry, and Young, E. Williams, "Test of Portfolio Building Rules," *Journal of Finance*, **XXIV,** No. 4 (Sept. 1969), pp. 595–612.

62. ———. "A Reply," *Journal of Finance*, **XXVI,** No. 4 (Sept. 1971), pp. 976–981.

63. Lean, William H., and Helms, Billy P. "The Identification of Stochastic Dominance Efficient Sets by Moment Combination Orderings," *Journal of Business Finance*, **12,** No. 2 (June 1988), pp. 243–253.

64. Levy, Haim. "Stochastic Dominance, Efficiency Criteria, and Efficient Portfolios: The Multi-Period Case," *American Economic Review*, **LXIII,** No. 5 (Dec. 1973), pp. 986–994.

65. ———. "Stochastic Dominance Rules for Truncated Normal Distributions: A Note," *The Journal of Finance*, **37,** No. 4 (Sept. 1982), pp. 1299–1304.

66. Levy, Haim, and Hanoch, Giora. "Relative Effectiveness of Efficiency Criteria for Portfolio Selection," *Journal of Financial and Quantitative Analysis*, **V,** No. 1 (March 1970), pp. 63–76.

67. Levy, Haim, and Kroll, Yoram. "Stochastic Dominance with Riskless Assets," *Journal of Financial and Quantitative Analysis*, **XI,** No. 5 (Dec. 1976), pp. 743–777.

68. Levy, Haim, and Sarnat, Marshall. "Alternative Efficiency Criteria: An Empirical Analysis," *Journal of Finance*, **XXV,** No. 5 (Dec. 1970), pp. 1153–1158.

69. ———. "Two-Period Portfolio Selection and Investors' Discount Rates," *Journal of Finance*, **XXVI,** No. 3 (June 1971), pp. 757–761.

70. Litzenberger, Robert, and Budd, A. P. "A Note on Geometric Mean Portfolio Selection and the Market Prices of Equities," *Journal of Financial and Quantitative Analysis*, **VI,** No. 5 (Dec. 1971), pp. 1277–1282.

71. Maier, Steven, Peterson, David, and Vanderweide, James. "A Monte Carlo Investigation of Characteristics of Optimal Geometric Mean Portfolios," *Journal of Financial and Quantitative Analysis*, **XII,** No. 2 (June 1977), pp. 215–233.

72. Markowitz, Harry. *Portfolio Selection Efficient Diversification of Investments.* (New York: John Wiley & Sons, 1959).

73. ———. "Investment for the Long-Run: New Evidence for an Old Rule," *Journal of Finance*, **XXXI,** No. 5 (Dec. 1976), pp. 1273–1286.

74. Merton, Robert. "Lifetime Portfolio Selection Under Uncertainty: The Continuous Time Case," *Review of Economics and Statistics*, **LI,** No. 3 (Aug. 1969), pp. 247–257.

75. ———. "Optimum Consumption and Portfolio Rules in a Continuous-Time Model," *Journal of Economic Theory*, **3,** No. 4 (Dec. 1971), pp. 373–413.

76. Nielscn, Lars Tyge. "Portfolio Selection in the Mean Variance Model: A Note," *The Journal of Finance*, **42,** No. 5 (Dec. 1987), pp. 1371–1376.

77. Ohlson, James. "Quadratic Approximations of the Portfolio Selection Problem When the Means and Variances Are Infinite." *Management Science*, **23,** No. 6 (Feb. 1977), pp. 576–584.

78. Owen, Joel, and Ravinovitch, Ramon. "On the Class of Elliptical Distributions and Their Applications to the Theory of Portfolio Choice," *The Journal of Finance*, **38,** No. 3 (June 1983), pp. 745–752.

79. Perrakis, Stylianos, and Zerbinis, John. "Identifying the SSD Portion of the EV Frontier: A Note," *Journal of Financial and Quantitative Analysis*, **XIII,** No. 1 (March 1978), pp. 167–171.

80. Philippatos, Goerge, and Gressis, Nicolas. "Conditions of Equivalence Among E-V, SSD, and E-H Portfolio Selection Criteria; The Case for Uniform, Normal, and Lognormal Distributions," *Management Science*, **21,** No. 6 (Feb. 1975), pp. 617–625.

81. Porter, Burr. "An Empirical Comparison of Stochastic Dominance and Mean-Variance Portfolio Choice Criteria," *Journal of Financial and Quantitative Analysis*, **VIII,** No. 4 (Sept. 1973), pp. 587–608.

82. ——. "Semivariance and Stochastic Dominance: A Comparison," *American Economic Reivew*, **LXIV,** No. 1 (March 1974), pp. 200–204.

83. Price, Kelly, Price, Barbara, and Nantell, Timothy J. "Variance and Lower Partial Moment Measures of Systematic Risk: Some Analytical and Empirical Results," *The Journal of Finance*, **37,** No. 3 (June 1982), pp. 843–906.

84. Pye, Gordon. "Minimax Portfolio Policies," *Financial Analysts Journal*, **28,** No. 2 (March-April 1972), pp. 56–60.

85. Pyle, David, and Turnovsky, Stephen. "Safety-First and Expected Utility Maximization in Mean-Standard Deviation Portfolio Analysis," *Review of Economics and Statistics*, **LII,** No. 1 (Feb. 1970), pp. 75–81.

86. ——. "Risk Aversion in Chance Constrained Portfolio Selection," *Management Science*, **18,** No. 3 (Nov. 1971), pp. 218–225.

87. Rentz, William, and Westin, Richard. "A Note on First-Degree Stochastic Dominance and Portfolio Composition," *Management Science*, **22,** No. 4 (Dec. 1975), pp. 501–504.

88. Roll, Richard. "Evidence on the 'Growth-Optimum' Model," *Journal of Finance*, **XXVIII,** No. 3 (June 1973), pp. 551–556.

89. Ross, Stephen A. "Adding Risks: Samuelson's Fallacy of Large Numbers Revisited," *Journal of Financial and Quantitative Analysis*, **34,** No. 3 (Sept. 1999), pp. 323–339.

90. Roy, A.D. "Safety-First and the Holding of Assets," *Econometrics*, **20** (July 1952), pp. 431–449.

91. Samuelson, Paul. "The Fundamental Approximation Theorem of Portfolio Analysis in Terms of Means Variances and Higher Moments," *Review of Economic Studies*, **25** (Feb. 1958), pp. 65–86.

92. Saunders, Anthony, Ward, Charles, and Woodward, Richard. "Stochastic Dominance and the Performance of U.K. Unit Trusts," *Journal of Financial and Quantitative Analysis*, **XV,** No. 2 (June 1980), pp. 323–330.

93. Shalit, Haim, and Yitzhaki, Shlomo. "Mean-Gine, Portfolio Theory and the Pricing of Risky Assets," *The Journal of Finance*, **39,** No. 5 (Dec. 1984), pp. 1449–1468.

94. Singleton, J. Clay, and Wingender, John. "Skewness Persistence in Common Stock Returns," *Journal of Financial and Quantitative Analysis*, **21,** No. 3 (Sept. 1986), pp. 335–341.

95. Stein, William, Pfaffenberg, Roger, and Kumar, P. C. "On the Estimation Risk in First-Order Stochastic Dominance: A Note," *Journal of Financial and Quantitative Analysis*, **XVIII,** No. 4 (Dec. 1983), pp. 471–476.

96. Tehranian, Hassan, and Helms, Billy P. "An Empirical Comparison of Stochastic Dominance among Lognormal Prospects," *Journal of Financial and Quantitative Analysis*, **XVII,** No. 2 (June 1982), pp. 217–226.

97. Vanderweide, James, Peterson, David, and Maier, Steven. "A Strategy Which Maximizes the Geometric Mean Return on Portfolio Investments," *Management Science*, **23,** No. 10 (June 1977), pp. 1117–1123.

98. ——. "Reply to Aucamp," *Management Science*, **24,** No. 8 (April 1978), p. 860.

99. Vickson, R. G. "Stochastic Dominance for Decreasing Absolute Risk Aversion," *Journal of Financial and Quantitative Analysis*, **X,** No. 5 (Dec. 1975), pp. 799–811.

100. Young, Williams, and Trent, Roberts. "Geometric Mean Approximations of Individual Securities and Portfolio Performance," *Journal of Financial and Quantitative Analysis*, **IV,** No. 2 (June 1969), pp. 179–199.

101. Ziemba, William. "Note on 'Optimal Growth Portfolios When Yields Are Serially Correlated'," *Journal of Financial and Quantitative Analysis*, **VII,** No. 4 (Sept. 1972), pp. 1995–2000.

Section 4

Widening the
Selection Universe

12

International Diversification

Portfolio managers in France, Germany, and England have for decades routinely invested a large fraction of their portfolio in securities that were issued in other countries. In contrast only in the last decade has there been a significant amount of foreign securities held by U.S. investors. Was the historical emphasis on U.S. securities by U.S. investors provincialism that is now disappearing, or are there sound economic reasons for the historical differences in the behavior of managers in different countries and for the current changes on the part of U.S. managers? In this chapter we attempt to present sufficient evidence for the readers to decide for themselves.

In the first section of this chapter we examine the market value of equities and debt worldwide. It turns out that no country comprises most of the world's wealth. Given the great number of opportunities worldwide, we discuss whether international diversification is a sensible strategy for investors. To analyze this question, we first show how returns on foreign assets are computed. The reasonableness of international diversification depends on the correlation coefficient across markets, the risk of each market, and the returns in each market. This is the subject of the next section of the chapter. One of the major sources of risk in international investment are changes in exchange rates. The impact of exchange risk on international diversification and the possibility of eliminating part of the risk through hedging is examined next. The next two sections of this chapter examine the key role of return expectations in determining the benefits of international diversification. Break-even returns are derived and evidence is presented from actively managed international portfolios. After discussing the reasonableness of international diversification, we focus on active and passive strategies for international investment.

THE WORLD PORTFOLIO

In discussing the size of capital markets it is interesting to employ the concept of a world portfolio. The world portfolio represents the total market value of all stocks (or bonds) that an investor would own if he or she bought the total of all marketable stocks on all the major stock exchanges in the world. Table 12.1 shows the percentage that each nation's equity securities represented of the world portfolio in 2000. Table 12.2 shows similar percentages for the various publicly traded bond markets in 1999.

Table 12.1 Comparative Sizes of World Equity Markets 2000

Area or Country	Percent of Total[a]
Austria	0.1%
Belgium	0.4%
Denmark	0.4%
Finland	1.6%
France	5.5%
Germany	4.3%
Ireland	0.2%
Italy	2.1%
Netherlands	2.5%
Norway	0.2%
Portugal	0.2%
Spain	1.3%
Sweden	1.6%
Switzerland	2.8%
U.K.	9.7%
Europe	**32.8%**
Australia	1.1%
Hong Kong	1.0%
Japan	12.6%
Malaysia	0.5%
New Zealand	0.1%
Singapore	0.4%
Pacific	**15.5%**
Canada	2.1%
United States	49.5%
North America	**51.6%**
Total	**100.0%**

Source: From *Morgan Stanley Capital International Perspectives,* June 2000.
[a]Since the Morgan Stanley index does not include all shares traded in a market the proportions are approximate. Column sums may not equal totals because of rounding.

Table 12.2 Comparative Sizes of Major Bond Markets 1999

Area or Country	Percent of Total
United States	47.0%
Euroland	22.9%
Japan	18.3%
United Kingdom	3.0%
Canada	1.7%
Switzerland	0.9%
Denmark	0.8%
Australia	0.6%
Sweden	0.6%
Norway	0.2%
New Zealand	0.1%
Asia	2.3%
Latin America	0.8%
Eastern Europe/Middle East/Africa	0.7%
Total	**100.0%**

Source: From Salomon Brothers.

In 2000 the largest equity market was the United States, which represented 50% of the total. The second largest was Japan with 13% of the world market. All of the European markets combined accounted for about 33% of the world market.[1] Table 12.2 shows that the U.S. bond market represented 47% of the world value and the European Monetary Union bond market was 23% of world value. Next was Japan with 18.3% of the world market.

Even for U.S. investors a large part of the investment opportunities lie outside the domestic market. For investors from any other country the opportunities (in terms of the market value of securities) outside the home country are much greater than those within the country of domicile. Thus for all investors a large part of the world's wealth lies outside the investor's home country. International assets could be duplicates of those found in the home country, in which case they do not offer new opportunities, or they could represent opportunities not duplicated in the home country. Which of these possibilities holds needs to be analyzed in order to determine whether international diversification should be an important part of each investor's portfolio. To examine this question we need to analyze the correlation between markets and the risk and return of each market. But before we do this we must first examine how to calculate returns on foreign investments.

CALCULATING THE RETURN ON FOREIGN INVESTMENTS

The return on a foreign investment is affected by the return on the assets within its own market and the change in the exchange rate between the security's own currency and the currency of the purchaser's home country. Thus the return on a foreign investment can be quite different than simply the return in the asset's own market and can differ according to the domicile of the purchaser. From the viewpoint of an American investor, it is convenient to express foreign currency as costing so many dollars.[2] Thus it is convenient to express an exchange rate of 2 marks to the dollar, or the cost of 1 mark is $0.50. Assume the following information:

	1	2	
Time	Cost of 1 Mark	Value of German Shares	Value in Dollars (1 × 2)
0	$0.50	40 DM	0.50 × 40 = $20
1	$0.40	45 DM	0.40 × 45 = $18

Furthermore assume that there are no dividends paid on the German shares. In this case the return to the German investor expressed in the home currency (marks) is

$$\left(1 + R_H\right) = \frac{45}{40} \quad \text{or} \quad R_H = 0.125 \text{ or } 12.5\%$$

---

[1]The percentage shown for Japan is an overstatement since Japanese companies have a greater tendency to own other companies than do companies in other countries and thus have more double counting.

[2]Foreign currency exchange rates can be quoted in two ways. If an exchange rate is stated as the amount of dollars per unit of foreign currency, the exchange rate is quoted in direct (or American) terms. If the exchange rate is given as the amount of foreign currency per dollar, the quote is in indirect (or foreign) terms. The form of quotes differs across markets. In the interbank market indirect quotes are used, whereas direct quotes are the norm in futures and options markets.

However, the return to the U.S. investor is

$$(1+R_{US}) = \frac{0.40 \times 45}{0.50 \times 40} = \frac{18}{20} \qquad \text{or} \qquad R_{US} = -0.10 \text{ or } -10\%$$

The German investor received a positive return, whereas the U.S. investor lost money because marks were worth less at time one than at time zero. It is convenient to divide the return to the American investor into a component due to return in the home or German market and the return due to exchange gains or losses. Letting R_x be the exchange return we have

$$(1+R_{US}) = (1+R_x)(1+R_H)$$

$$1+R_x = \frac{0.40}{0.50} = 1-0.20 \qquad \text{or} \qquad R_x = -0.20$$

$$1+R_H = \frac{45}{40} = 1-0.125 \qquad \text{or} \qquad R_H = 0.125$$

$$(1+R_{US}) = (1-0.20)(1+0.125) = 1-0.10 \qquad \text{or} \qquad R_{US} = -0.10$$

Thus the 12 1/2% gain on the German investment was more than offset by the 20% loss on the change in the value of the mark. Restating the preceding equation

$$(1+R_{US}) = (1+R_x)(1+R_H)$$

Simplifying

$$R_{US} = R_x + R_H + R_x R_H$$

In the example

$$-0.10 = -0.20 + 0.125 + (-0.20) \times (0.125)$$
$$= -0.20 + 0.125 - 0.025$$

The last term (the cross-product term) will be much smaller than the other two terms, so that return to the U.S. investor is approximately the return of the security in its home market plus the exchange gain or loss. Using this approximation, we have the following expressions for expected return and standard deviation of return on a foreign security.

Expected return

$$\overline{R}_{US} = \overline{R}_x + \overline{R}_H$$

Standard deviation of return

$$\sigma_{US} = \left[\sigma_x^2 + \sigma_H^2 + 2\sigma_{Hx} \right]^{1/2}$$

As will be very clear when we examine real data, the standard deviation of the return on foreign securities (σ_{US}) is much less than the sum of the standard deviation of the return on the security in its home country (σ_H) plus the standard deviation of the exchange gains and losses (σ_x). This relationship results from two factors. First, there is very low correlation between exchange gains (or losses) and returns in a country (and therefore the last term σ_{Hx} is close to zero). Second, squaring the standard deviations, adding them, and then taking the square root of the sum is less than adding them directly. To see this let

$$\sigma_x = 0.10$$
$$\sigma_H = 0.15$$
$$\rho_{Hx} = 0 \qquad \text{(to make the covariance zero)}$$

then

$$\sigma_{US}^2 = 0.10^2 + 0.15^2$$

and

$$\sigma_{US} = 0.18$$

Thus the standard deviation of the return expressed in dollars is considerably less than the sum of the standard deviation of the exchange gains and losses and the standard deviation of the return on the security in its home currency. The reader should be conscious of this difference in the tables that follow.

Having developed some preliminary relationships it is useful to examine some actual data on risk and return.

THE RISK OF FOREIGN SECURITIES

Table 12.3 presents the correlation between the equity markets of several countries for the period 1991–2000. These correlation coefficients have been computed using monthly returns on market indexes. The indexes are computed by Morgan Stanley Capital International. They are market-weighted indexes with each stock's proportion in the index determined by its market value divided by the aggregate market value of all stocks in that market. The indexes include securities representing approximately 60% of the aggregate market value of each country. All returns were converted to U.S. dollars at prevailing exchange rates before correlations were calculated. Thus, Table 12.3 presents the correlation from the viewpoint of a U.S. investor. These are very low correlation coefficients relative to those found within a domestic market. The average correlation coefficient between a pair of U.S. common stocks is about 0.40, and the correlation between U.S. indexes is much higher. For example, the correlation between the S&P index of 425 large stocks and the rest of the stocks on the New York Stock Exchange is about 0.97. The correlation between a market-weighted portfolio of the 1000 largest stocks in the U.S. market and a market-weighted portfolio of the next 2000 largest stocks is approximately 0.92. Finally, the correlation coefficient between two 100-security portfolios drawn at random from the New York Stock Exchange is on the order of 0.95. The numbers in the table are much smaller than this, with the average correlation being 0.48.

The correlations between international indexes are only slightly larger than the correlation between two securities in the United States and less than the correlation between two securities in most other markets. The correlations shown in Table 12.3 are very similar to those found in other studies. Thus Table 12.3 is representative of typical correlation coefficients.[3] In each edition of this book we do the same calculation using the prior 10 years' returns. The numbers in Table 12.3 are somewhat higher than prior editions, 0.48 rather than 0.40. This is primarily due to the increased correlation among countries within the European Monetary Union because of the elimination of exchange rates charges and greater integration of the economies.

---

[3]Similar results have been found by other researchers. For example, Solnik [59] studied the 15-year period 1971–1986 and found an average correlation of 0.35 between countries. Similarly, Kaplanis and Schaefer [41], studying the period February 1978–June 1987, found an average correlation of 0.32. Furthermore, Eun and Resnick [22], studying the period 1973–1982, found an average correlation of 0.41. Finally, in the prior edition of this book, using data from 1980 to 1988, the average correlation was 0.40.

Table 12.3   Correlations among Stock Indexes Measured in U.S. Dollars

	Australia	Austria	Belgium	Canada	France	Germany	Hong Kong	Italy	Japan	Netherlands	Spain	Sweden	Switzerland	United Kingdom	United States
Australia															
Austria	0.279														
Belgium	0.304	0.459													
Canada	0.608	0.316	0.299												
France	0.400	0.505	0.677	0.465											
Germany	0.393	0.671	0.612	0.454	0.749										
Hong Kong	0.501	0.350	0.225	0.572	0.387	0.395									
Italy	0.248	0.358	0.396	0.361	0.487	0.495	0.231								
Japan	0.430	0.245	0.317	0.355	0.415	0.307	0.289	0.330							
Netherlands	0.480	0.578	0.738	0.514	0.758	0.740	0.424	0.429	0.432						
Spain	0.460	0.422	0.523	0.455	0.681	0.606	0.415	0.575	0.482	0.599					
Sweden	0.490	0.364	0.348	0.486	0.600	0.639	0.393	0.480	0.461	0.577	0.693				
Switzerland	0.363	0.530	0.610	0.410	0.598	0.537	0.327	0.304	0.465	0.697	0.567	0.494			
United Kingdom	0.543	0.519	0.577	0.460	0.642	0.594	0.437	0.313	0.474	0.722	0.602	0.523	0.494		
United States	0.505	0.281	0.504	0.709	0.534	0.489	0.491	0.301	0.348	0.592	0.530	0.466	0.523	0.646	

Average Correlation Coefficient   0.475

Table 12.4   Correlations among Bond Indexes Measured in U.S. Dollars

	Canada	France	Germany	Japan	Netherlands	Switzerland	U.K.
Canada							
France	0.191						
Germany	0.157	0.910					
Japan	0.112	0.391	0.495				
Netherlands	0.217	0.917	0.960	0.408			
Switzerland	0.076	0.697	0.803	0.540	0.751		
U.K.	0.433	0.599	0.580	0.314	0.614	0.467	
United States	0.567	0.456	0.357	0.177	0.430	0.257	0.478

Table 12.4 shows the correlation between the Salomon Brothers long-term bond indexes of eight countries for the years 1990–2000. These indexes are value-weighted indexes of the major issues in each country. Once again the correlations are very low relative to the correlations of two intracountry indexes or bond portfolios. The average correlation between countries shown in Table 12.4 is 0.54. In contrast, Kaplanis and Schaefer [41] show an average correlation between countries of 0.43 for long-term bond indexes in their sample period, and Chollerton, Pieraerts, and Solnik [17] find 0.43. This can be contrasted with the correlation between two typical American bond mutual funds of 0.94 and the correlation between the U.S. government and corporate bond index of 0.98.

Finally, Table 12.5 shows correlation coefficients for short-term bonds, in particular, monthly returns of three-month debt. The average correlation for the same eight countries shown in Table 12.4 is 0.34. The low correlation across markets for stocks, bonds, and Treasury bills (T-bills) is the strongest evidence in favor of international diversification. The low correlation suggests that international diversification could reduce the risk on an investor's portfolio.

Risk depends not only on correlation coefficients but also on the standard deviation of return. Tables 12.6a, 12.6b, and 12.6c show the standard deviation of return for an investment in the common equity indexes, the long-term bond indexes, and the short-term bond indexes discussed earlier. It should be emphasized once again that the standard deviation is calculated on market indexes and is therefore a measure of risk for a well-diversified portfolio, consisting only of securities traded within the country under examination.

As shown in the last section, there are two sources of risks. The return on an investment in foreign securities varies because of variation of security prices within the securities home market and because of exchange gains and losses. Note that in some cases the total risk is less than the domestic risk. The reduction in correlation when exchange rates are

Table 12.5   Correlations for Three-Month Bond Indexes Measured in U.S. Dollars

	Canada	France	Germany	Japan	Netherlands	Switzerland	U.K.
Canada							
France	−0.178						
Germany	−0.163	0.978					
Japan	−0.015	0.393	0.426				
Netherlands	−0.167	0.983	0.998	0.422			
Switzerland	−0.146	0.915	0.933	0.477	0.931		
U.K.	−0.006	0.696	0.697	0.282	0.695	0.660	
United States	0.097	−0.073	−0.073	0.113	−0.068	−0.060	−0.106

Table 12.6a Risk for U.S. Investor in Stocks 1990–2000

Stocks	Domestic Risk	Exchange Risk	Total Risk
Australia	13.94	8.66	17.92
Austria	24.80	10.59	24.50
Belgium	16.15	10.21	15.86
Canada	15.02	4.40	17.13
France	18.87	10.61	17.76
Germany	20.41	10.55	20.13
Hong Kong	29.75	0.43	29.79
Italy	24.55	11.13	25.29
Japan	22.04	12.46	25.70
Netherlands	16.04	10.59	15.50
Spain	22.99	11.18	23.27
Sweden	24.87	11.18	24.21
Switzerland	17.99	11.61	17.65
U.K.	14.45	10.10	15.59
United States	13.59	0.00	13.59
Equally Weighted Index (Non-U.S.)	21.57	10.03	23.43
Value-Weighted Index (Non-U.S.)			16.70

Table 12.6b Risk for U.S. Investor in Bonds 1990–2000

Stocks	Domestic Risk	Exchange Risk	Total Risk
Canada	8.67	4.40	10.75
France	8.71	10.61	12.61
Germany	5.38	10.55	11.20
Japan	9.18	12.46	15.10
Netherlands	7.03	10.59	11.68
Switzerland	6.64	11.61	12.06
U.K.	9.23	10.10	12.78
United States	7.89	0.00	7.90
Equally Weighted (Non-U.S.)	7.95	10.33	12.38
Value-Weighted Index (Non-U.S.)			9.45

Table 12.6c Risk for U.S. Investor in Three-Month Securities 1990–2000

Stocks	Domestic Risk	Exchange Risk	Total Risk
Canada	0.77	4.40	4.42
France	0.86	10.61	10.53
Germany	0.72	10.55	10.49
Japan	0.79	12.46	12.42
Netherlands	0.72	10.59	10.52
Switzerland	0.82	11.61	11.52
U.K.	0.82	10.10	10.04
United States	0.35	0.00	0.35
Equally Weighted Index (Non-U.S.)	0.79	10.33	10.27
Value-Weighted Index (Non-U.S.)			6.77

taken into account comes about because for these countries in this period exchange fluctuations were negatively correlated with movements in the local market.

The column headed "Domestic Risk" in Tables 12.6a–c shows the standard deviation of return when returns are calculated in the indexes' own currency. Thus the standard deviation of 20.41 for Germany is the standard deviation when returns on German stocks are calculated in marks. The second source of risk is exchange risk. Exchange risk arises because the exchange rate between the mark and dollar changes over time, affecting the return to a U.S. investor on an investment in German securities. The variability of the exchange rate for each currency converted to dollars is shown in the column titled "Exchange Risk." As discussed in the last section, the exchange risk and the within country risk are usually relatively independent (in this period they were negatively correlated for many countries) and standard deviations are not additive. Thus total risk to the U.S. investor is much less than the sum of exchange risk and within country risk. For example, the standard deviation of German stocks in marks is 20.41%. The standard deviation of changes in the mark dollar exchange rate is 10.55%. However, the risk of German stocks in dollars when both fluctuations are taken into account is 20.13%. It should be emphasized that the variability of exchange rates is calculated by examining the variability of each currency in dollars. Thus the total risk is measured from a U.S. investor's point of view.

As shown in Table 12.6a over the 1990–2000 time period, the standard deviation of an index of the U.S. equity market was less than the standard deviation of other market indexes when the standard deviation of returns was calculated in its own currency (domestic risk). When the effect of exchange risk is taken into account, the higher risk of foreign markets was even more pronounced. These results are not atypical. Solnik [65], Kaplanis and Schaefer [41], and Eun and Resnick [23] find the same results for different periods. We found the same results in all earlier editions of this book. For long-term bonds, the standard deviation of the U.S. bond index is about average when the standard deviation of each index is calculated in its own currency. When returns are adjusted for changes in exchange rates and all returns are expressed in dollars, the risk for the U.S. bond index is much lower than for any foreign index. This illustrates the importance of exchange rate fluctuations on returns and risk. Finally, for short-term bonds (Table 12.6c) the effect of exchange rates is even more dramatic. The exchange rate risk is by far the largest component of total risk. When the standard deviation is calculated for a U.S. investor, the standard deviation of U.S. T-bills is much less than the standard deviation for non-U.S. investments. For the case of T-bills and perhaps bonds, although the relatively low correlation strongly suggests that international diversification pays, the higher standard deviation suggests it may not.

Table 12.7 shows the combination of a value-weighted index of non-U.S. markets and the corresponding U.S. index. The numbers in the table are standard deviations of this combination when various percentages are invested in the international portfolio. When considering equities the minimum risk is achieved with 74% in the U.S. portfolio and 26% in the market-weighted world portfolio (excluding U.S. securities), and total risk is reduced by 3.7% compared with exclusive investment in the U.S. market. The risk reduction for long-term bonds is much less dramatic because the relative risk of a non-U.S. market-weighted international bond portfolio is much higher and the correlation slightly higher. Nevertheless a slight risk reduction is achieved. Finally, for T-bills some international diversification lowers risk (slightly less than 1%). Because of exchange risk the standard deviation of a value-weighted non-U.S. international short-term bond portfolio is dramatically higher than the standard deviation of U.S. T-bills. In this time period, however, the correlation of U.S. T-bills and a value-weighted index of foreign T-bills was about

Table 12.7   Risk from Placing X Percent in a World Index Excluding U.S. Securities and the Rest in U.S. Index 1990–2000

X	Value-Weighted Index		
Proportion in World Index (%)	Stocks	Long-Term Bonds	T-Bills
0%	13.59	7.90	0.35
10%	13.28	7.63	0.75
20%	13.12	7.45	1.38
30%	13.10	7.37	2.05
40%	13.23	7.39	2.72
50%	13.51	7.52	3.39
60%	13.93	7.75	4.06
70%	14.47	8.06	4.74
80%	15.12	8.46	5.42
90%	15.87	8.93	6.09
100%	16.70	9.45	6.77

zero. Thus, even with the high standard deviation, a modest amount of international diversification lowered risk.

These results were derived using data from 1990 to 2000. An interesting question to analyze is whether the results are unique to the period examined or if we can safely generalize them. The conclusions depend on the correlation between the world portfolio and the U.S. index and the standard deviation of each index. As discussed earlier, the correlations used in this analysis are very similar to the correlations other researchers have found in other periods and somewhat higher than the correlations discussed in prior editions of this book. The variability of return for foreign markets during this period is higher than the variability of return that most other researchers have found.

Thus the risk reduction shown in Table 12.7 would hold if data from other periods were used and the results are likely to be robust across periods. Furthermore, for stocks, rather substantial errors in selecting the optimal mix could be made and risk would still be reduced. Therefore, using data from a prior period to decide on a mixture of an international and domestic portfolio would likely result in a less risky portfolio than pure domestic investment. For example, if one took any minimum shown in a prior edition of this text, the overall risk of the stock portfolio would be less than investing 100% in domestic stocks. For long-term bonds and T-bills, the risk reduction via international diversification is so small that errors in determining the risk-minimizing mix of international and domestic portfolios could easily result in a portfolio more risky than the domestic one held alone.

RETURNS FROM INTERNATIONAL DIVERSIFICATION

The decade of the 1990s was an especially favorable time for U.S. markets relative to foreign markets. Tables 12.8a and 12.8b show the average annual returns from January 1990 to December 2000 on several international markets. The "Exchange Gain" column is the difference between the return in the assets home country and the assets return in the United States.[4] The average non-U.S. equity index had a return of 12.54% in its home country

---

[4]Earlier we showed that the expected return to a U.S. investor is not the sum of exchange gains and losses and the return in the investor's home country. Thus column two includes not only the exchange return but also includes all joint effects of the country and exchange return.

Table 12.8a   Return to U.S. Investor in Stocks 1990–2000 (percent per annum)

Stocks	Own Country	Exchange Gain	To U.S. Investor
Australia	10.51	−2.82	7.69
Austria	2.37	−1.55	0.82
Belgium	11.85	−1.39	10.46
Canada	13.53	−2.29	11.24
France	14.78	−1.40	13.37
Germany	13.89	−1.56	12.32
Hong Kong	16.90	0.02	16.92
Italy	12.55	−4.34	8.22
Japan	−4.80	2.47	−2.32
Netherlands	17.38	−1.55	15.83
Spain	16.13	−4.17	11.96
Sweden	21.22	−3.40	17.81
Switzerland	15.81	−0.43	15.38
U.K.	12.71	−0.42	12.28
United States	16.17	0.00	16.17
Equally Weighted Index (Non-U.S.)	12.54	−2.22	10.31
Value-Weighted Index (Non-U.S.)			8.77

Table 12.8b   Return to U.S. Investor in Bonds 1990–2000 (percent per annum)

Bonds	Own Country	Exchange Gain	To U.S. Investor
Canada	11.50	−2.08	9.42
France	11.08	−1.77	9.31
Germany	7.89	−1.89	6.00
Japan	8.13	3.62	11.75
Netherlands	8.84	−1.93	6.91
Switzerland	6.63	−0.55	6.08
U.K.	12.21	−0.54	11.67
United States	8.93		
Equally Weighted Index (Non-U.S.)	9.47	−0.73	8.73
Value-Weighted Index (Non-U.S.)			9.59
Three-Month Securities			
Canada	6.34	−2.16	4.18
France	6.44	−1.63	4.81
Germany	5.73	−1.82	3.91
Japan	2.72	3.67	6.39
Netherlands	5.58	−1.80	3.78
Switzerland	4.35	−0.38	3.97
U.K.	7.65	−0.44	7.21
United States	4.92		
Equally Weighted Index (Non-U.S.)	5.54	−0.65	4.89
Value-Weighted Index (Non-U.S.)			6.77

compared with 16.17% for the U.S. market with an exchange loss averaging -2.22%, when converted to dollars the average non-U.S. equity index returned 10.31%.

The column in Table 12.8a that presents returns in U.S. dollars shows only three countries, Hong Kong, Netherlands, and Sweden, that had returns above the United States. Thus, most internationally diversified equity portfolios would have had a lower return than the U.S. market index over this period. During this period international diversification had the advantage of lowering risk but resulted in lower average returns.

The results for long-term bonds are similar. The equally weighted portfolio of country return indexes (excluding the United States) did slightly worse than the U.S. market index. The value-weighted portfolio performed better. This was due primarily to the performance of Japanese bonds. In yen, Japanese bonds returned about 8.13% but over this period, the dollar value of the yen increased by 3.62% resulting in an 11.75% return to U.S. investors. A fair number of countries underperformed the U.S. bond market. Thus many international portfolios would have also underperformed a portfolio of U.S. bonds.

For three-month T-bills the return on the equally weighted index was slightly worse and value-weighted index was slightly better than the return on U.S. T-bills. Given the higher risk discussed earlier, many international portfolios would have been inferior to an exclusive U.S. portfolio.

Although these results are appropriate for the period discussed, it is useful to examine other periods. Solnik [65] studied equity indexes for 17 countries for the years 1971–1985. For all but two countries the return on the foreign index expressed in dollars was greater than the return on the U.S. equity index. The exchange gain from holding foreign equities added 0.2% on average to this return. For long and short bonds only, Canada and the United Kingdom had a lower return when return was expressed in U.S. dollars. For bonds, however, a major factor contributing to the return being above the U.S. return was exchange gains. The period covered in the last edition, primarily the 1980s, was a better period for non-U.S. markets and many international portfolios would have outperformed their U.S. counterparts.

For portfolio decisions, estimates of future values of mean return, standard deviation, and correlation coefficients are needed. The correlation coefficients between international markets have been very low historically relative to intracountry correlations. As Europe integrates its markets and as all countries move toward greater integration, these coefficients are likely to rise.[5] However, they are still likely to be low relative to intracountry correlation. For example, the correlation coefficient between countries whose economies are relatively highly integrated, such as Canada and the United States, the Benelux countries, or the Scandinavian countries is still much lower than the intracountry correlation coefficients. Thus international diversification is likely to continue to lead to risk reduction in the foreseeable future. However, we know of no economic reason to argue that returns in foreign markets will be higher or lower than for domestic markets.

THE EFFECT OF EXCHANGE RISK

Earlier we showed how the return on a foreign investment could be split into the return in the security's home market and the return from changes in exchange rates. In each of the prior tables we separated out the effect of changes in the exchange rate on return and risk. In Table 12.8b, the column entitled "Exchange Return or Exchange Risk" calculated the

---

[5]In particular, exchange rates between European currencies are fixed. Although European currencies will continue to fluctuate with the U.S. currency, any advantage in diversifying across currencies will be eliminated.

effect of converting all currencies into dollars. Obviously if we were presenting the same tables from a French or Norwegian point of view, the "Exchange Rate Expected Return" and "Risk" columns would be different, because they would contain results as if all currencies were converted to francs (for the French investor) or kroner (for the Norwegian investor). Because francs and kroner have not fluctuated perfectly with the dollar, these columns would be different. Thus the country of domicile affects the expected returns and risk (including correlation coefficients) from international diversification.

Table 12.9 illustrates this by computing expected return and risk from the U.S. investor's point of view (which is a repeat of prior tables) and from the French point of view. The numbers are clearly quite different. It is possible to protect partially against exchange rate fluctuations. An investor can enter into a contract for future delivery of a currency at a price that is fixed now. For example, an American investor purchasing German securities could simultaneously agree to convert marks into dollars at a future date and at a known rate. If the investor knew exactly what the security would be worth at the end of the period, he or she would be completely protected against rate fluctuations by agreeing to switch an amount of marks exactly equal to the value of the investment. However, given that, in general, the end of period value of the investment is random, the best the investor can do is protect against a particular outcome (e.g., its expected value).[6]

As shown earlier, the standard deviation of foreign investments generally increases as a result of exchange risk. If exchange risk was completely hedged, then the "Domestic Risk" column in Tables 12.6a, 12.6b, and 12.6c would be the relevant column used to measure risk.

When examining risk for common stocks in most periods, total risk is higher for most countries. However, in the period of the '90s, this was not true. Therefore, in the '90s, hedging increased risk for many countries. The increase in risk due to exchange fluctuations is clearest for long- and short-term bonds. Although we will not present the tables,

Table 12.9   The Effect of Country of Domicile on Mean Return and Risk

Country	Mean Return		Variance	
	In Francs	In Dollars	In Francs	In Dollars
Australia	9.15	7.69	21.58	17.92
Austria	2.29	0.82	25.62	24.50
Belgium	11.92	10.46	16.77	15.86
Canada	12.70	11.24	21.73	17.13
France	14.78	13.37	18.87	17.76
Germany	13.79	12.32	21.02	20.13
Hong Kong	18.38	16.92	32.72	29.79
Italy	9.68	8.22	27.91	25.29
Japan	−0.86	−2.32	26.67	25.70
Netherlands	17.29	15.83	16.44	15.50
Spain	13.42	11.96	25.08	23.27
Sweden	19.28	17.81	26.37	24.21
Switzerland	16.84	15.38	18.67	17.65
U.K.	13.74	12.28	17.03	15.59
United States	17.63	16.17	18.45	13.59

---

[6]Procedures exist for changing the hedge through time in order to eliminate most of the exchange risk. See Kaplanis and Schaefer [41].

the correlation coefficients are somewhat lower when we calculate the correlation between returns assuming exchange risk is fully hedged away. Exchange movement increases the correlation among countries' returns. The average correlation coefficient between two countries is 0.46 assuming exchange risk is hedged away for the countries shown in Table 12.3. This contrasts with 0.48 when exchange risk is fully borne. Similarly, Kaplanis and Schaefer [41] found an average correlation of 0.37 when including the effect of exchange risk and 0.32 when exchange risk was fully hedged. Risk in international stock portfolios is normally reduced if exchange risk is hedged away and always reduced in bond markets.

The effect on expected return is less clear. Table 12.8 shows that during the 1990–2000 period, exchange movements caused losses to U.S. investors for most countries. The same table in the 1970s would have shown mostly gains. Also, the loss to the U.S. investor is the gain to the foreign investor, so that a different table would hold if we expressed returns in, for example, Swiss francs. Thus the effect of eliminating exchange gains or losses on expected return varies from country to country and period to period.

One way to determine whether international diversification will be a useful strategy in the future is to analyze how low expected returns in foreign countries would have to be for an investor not to gain via international diversification.

RETURN EXPECTATIONS AND PORTFOLIO PERFORMANCE

Most of the literature on domestic and international diversification tells us that history is a much better guide in forecasting risk than it is in forecasting returns. If we accept the historical data on risk as indicative of the future, for any assumed return on the U.S. market we can solve for the minimum return that must be offered by any foreign market to make it an attractive investment from the U.S. standpoint.

We did this under two assumptions: that the U.S. market would return 12% and that it would return 16%. These numbers were selected because 16% is approximately the return for the U.S. equity market in the 1990s and 12% is roughly the historical long-term return on U.S. equities. The calculations used the correlation coefficients shown in Table 12.3 and the standard deviations shown in Table 12.6, and a risk-free rate of 6%. These numbers are shown in Table 12.10. The basic formula to determine these numbers is as follows:

Hold non-U.S. securities as long as[7]

$$\frac{\bar{R}_N - R_F}{\sigma_N} > \frac{\bar{R}_{US} - R_F}{\sigma_{US}} \rho_{N.US} \qquad (12.1)$$

where

$\bar{R}_N$ is the expected return on the non-U.S. securities in dollars

$\bar{R}_{US}$ is the expected return on U.S. securities

---

[7]From Chapter 4 the first-order conditions are

$$\bar{R}_N - R_F = Z_N \sigma_N^2 + Z_{US} \rho_{N.US} \sigma_{US} \sigma_N$$
$$\bar{R}_{US} - R_F = Z_N \rho_{N.US} \sigma_{US} \sigma_N + Z_{US} \sigma_{US}^2$$

Setting Z_N equal to zero and eliminating Z_{US} results in the preceding equation as an equality. Increasing $\bar{R}_N$ would cause Z_N to be greater than zero. For a more detailed derivation see Elton, Gruber, and Rentzler [20].

This analysis assumes foreign securities cannot be shorted. If they can be shorted, then markets for which Equation (12.1) doesn't hold are candidates for short sales.

Table 12.10 Minimum Returns on Foreign Markets Necessary for International Diversification to Be Justified

	U.S. Return	
Country	12%	16%
Australia	9.99	12.66
Austria	9.04	11.07
Belgium	9.53	11.88
Canada	11.36	14.94
France	10.19	12.98
Germany	10.35	13.24
Hong Kong	12.46	16.76
Italy	9.36	11.60
Japan	9.95	12.58
Netherlands	10.05	12.75
Spain	11.44	15.07
Sweden	10.98	14.30
Switzerland	10.08	12.79
U.K.	10.45	13.41
Equally Weighted Index (Non-U.S.)		
Value-Weighted Index (Non-U.S.)	10.17	12.95

σ_N is the standard deviation of the non-U.S. securities in dollars

σ_{US} is the standard deviation of U.S. securities

$\rho_{N.US}$ is the correlation between U.S. securities and non-U.S. securities

R_F is the risk-free rate of interest

Although this equation is written from a U.S. investor's point of view, a similar equation holds true for investors in any country considering foreign investment. The reader would simply redefine the symbols presently subscripted U.S. to the country of interest.

Note that in Table 12.10 the return required on a foreign investment is, for most markets, considerably less than the return on the U.S. investment. For an assumed U.S. expected return of 12%, Austrian securities would have to have an expected return of less than 9.04% for it not to pay to invest in Austrian securities at all. Diversification into Canada and Spain requires higher expected returns than diversification into other countries and Hong Kong would have to have an expected return above U.S. securities. For Canadian securities this result is caused by high correlation of the U.S. and Canadian markets. For Spain and Hong Kong it is primarily very high standard deviation that makes diversification less attractive. Thus, the expected return in these markets must be higher or almost as high as the U.S. market for diversification to pay.

If we rearrange the expression (12.1), we have hold non-U.S. securities as long as[8]

$$\bar{R}_N - R_F > \left[\bar{R}_{US} - R_F\right]\left[\frac{\sigma_N \rho_{N.US}}{\sigma_{US}}\right] \qquad (12.2)$$

---

[8]Multiplying the numerator and denominator of the expression in the brackets by σ_{US} shows that the expression in the brackets is the Beta of the non-U.S. markets on the U.S. index.

As long as the expression in the last bracket is less than one, foreign securities should be held even with expected returns lower than those found in the domestic market. For all the countries except Hong Kong, the expression in the last bracket was less than one so the expected return on non-U.S. securities could be less than U.S. securities and international diversification would still pay. Thus, for the period studied, expected returns in non-U.S. countries could have been considerably less than in U.S. countries and international diversification would still have paid.

All the entries in Table 12.10 with the exception of those in the last row showed the minimum expected return when one country was added to the U.S. portfolio. Thus the portfolio was composed of two countries' securities. The last row shows the expected return on a value-weighted index necessary to justify adding it to U.S. securities. Although not the lowest return, it is less than most countries' return considered separately. If the expected return on U.S. securities is 16%, a value-weighted portfolio should be added if its expected return is greater than 12.95%. This is a general result. Portfolios of securities from many countries will be less risky than portfolios of a single country's securities. Examining Equation (12.2) shows that for a given correlation, the lower the standard deviation the lower the expected return on a foreign portfolio can be and still have international diversification pay.

We argued in the first section that international diversification lowers risk. In this section we have shown that returns in foreign markets would have to be much lower than returns in the domestic market or international diversification pays. What is foreign to one investor is domestic to another, however. Are there any circumstances where international diversification does not pay for investors of all countries?

To understand this issue, consider the U.S. and U.K. markets and refer to Table 12.10. This table shows that if the return in the U.K. market is not less than 13.41% when returns in the U.S. market are 16%, a U.S. investor should purchase some U.K. securities. Furthermore, it is easy to show that if a U.K. investor believed expected returns in the U.K. would be less than in the U.S., then the U.K. investor should purchase U.S. stocks. If investors in the two markets agree on expected returns, we have one of three situations: both gain from diversification, the U.S. investor gains, or the U.K. investor gains. In all three cases, however, at least one investor should diversify internationally. If the investors do not agree on returns in the two markets, then it is possible that neither the U.S. investor nor the U.K. investor will benefit from international diversification. For example, assume U.S. investors believe that U.K. markets have an expected return of 5%, whereas U.S. markets would have an expected return of 10%. Further assume that U.K. investors believe U.K. markets have an expected return of 10%, whereas U.S. markets have an expected return of 5%. Under this set of expected returns neither U.S. nor U.K. investors would wish to diversify internationally. Are there any circumstances where investors in all countries could rationally believe that returns are higher in their country relative to the rest of the world? The answer is *yes*!

If governments tax foreign investments at rates very different from domestic investments, then the pattern just discussed would be possible for aftertax returns. Differential taxation has occurred in the past, continues to occur today, and will likely persist into the future.[9] Second, many countries impose a withholding tax on dividends. Taxable investors may receive a domestic credit for the foreign tax withheld and thus not have lowered returns. However, for nontaxable investors (or for a nontaxable part of an investor's

---

[9]A government's ability to enforce payment of taxes may be lower on foreign than domestic securities. Tax cheating could mitigate tax rate differentials.

portfolio such as pension assets), the withholding is a cost that lowers the return of foreign investment. A third situation that could cause foreign investments to have a lower return than domestic investments for all investors is if there were differential transaction costs for domestic and foreign purchases. This could occur if there was difficulty in purchasing foreign securities or currency controls existed. For example, there may be restrictions in converting domestic to foreign currency that could affect returns. The exchange of currency A for B might take place at an official rate higher than the free market rate, and there might be an expectation of a later reversal. A fourth situation that can result in investors in all countries having an expectation of higher returns from domestic investments relative to foreign, is a danger of a government restricting the ability of foreigners to withdraw funds. Governments can and do place such restrictions on foreigners, and this can reduce returns to foreigners. The considerations just discussed are real and can affect the returns from international diversification.

Before leaving this section, one other issue needs to be discussed. It has been suggested that investors could confine themselves to a national market and receive most of the benefits of international diversification by purchasing stocks in multinational corporations. Jacquillat and Solnik [37] have tested this for the American investor. They found that stock prices of multinational firms do not seem to be affected by foreign factors and behave much like the stocks of domestic firms. The American investor cannot gain much of the advantage of international diversification by investing in the securities of the multinational firm.

OTHER EVIDENCE ON INTERNATIONALLY DIVERSIFIED PORTFOLIOS

In prior sections we have presented the considerations that are important in deciding on the reasonableness of international diversification. Obviously, we feel that the type of analysis we have presented is the relevant way to analyze the problem. However, several studies analyze the reasonableness of international diversification by examining the characteristics of international portfolios selected using historical data. The most common approach attempts to show the advantages of international diversification by forming an optimal portfolio of international and domestic securities using historical data and comparing the return to an exclusively domestically held portfolio over the same time period. It should not surprise the reader that knowing the exact values of mean returns, variance, and covariances for international markets allows construction of portfolios that dominate investment exclusively in the domestic portfolio. A variant of this analysis presents the efficient frontier using historical data with and without international securities and "shows" that adding international securities improves the efficient frontier.

While examining historical data is interesting, the real of test of international diversification is the performance of funds that hold internationally diversified portfolios. Table 12.11 shows data for 20 of the largest international mutual funds (funds that invest only in international securities) that existed in the '90s together with data on the Standard & Poor's (S&P) index.

Table 12.11 shows data for a random sample of 20 international funds (funds that invest only in international securities) that existed in the 90s together with data on the S&P index.

The major promise of international diversification is the low correlation between domestic securities and foreign securities. As shown in Table 12.11, the average correlation between the fund return and the S&P index was 0.61. These correlations are somewhat higher than the correlations between the international stock indexes and the U.S. indexes presented in Table 12.3.

Table 12.11   Performance Data on Stock Funds

	1990–1999			
	Mean Return Monthly	Standard Deviation	Beta	Correlation with Market
Canada General Fund	1.05	4.27	0.92	0.93
Keystone International Fund	0.76	3.96	0.58	0.63
Japan Fund	0.76	7.08	0.41	0.25
Scudder International Fund	1.12	4.30	0.62	0.62
G.T. Pacific Fund	0.23	6.52	0.81	0.53
Alliance International Fund/A	0.65	4.55	0.66	0.62
Templeton Foreign Fund	0.98	3.88	0.60	0.66
T. Rowe Price International Stock Fund	1.00	4.30	0.63	0.64
Fidelity Overseas Fund	0.97	4.36	0.64	0.63
Vanguard World—International Growth	0.89	4.40	0.61	0.60
Managers Funds: International	1.06	3.68	0.56	0.66
Morgan Stanley Instl. Fund—International Eq.	1.12	3.93	0.53	0.58
Warburg Pincus International Equity	1.09	4.72	0.64	0.59
G.T. Global Growth—Europe Growth	0.78	4.90	0.71	0.62
T. Rowe Price International Discovery	1.17	5.41	0.54	0.43
Schroder Captial Funds: International	0.84	4.24	0.56	0.57
Smith Barney World Funds International	1.19	4.86	0.72	0.64
Thompson McKinnon Invest Trust Global	0.84	4.67	0.76	0.71
Fidelity International Growth and Income	1.01	4.05	0.58	0.62
Ivy Fund International	1.03	4.40	0.67	0.66
Average	0.93	4.62	0.64	0.61
S&P	1.48	3.58	1.00	1.00

Correlations this low would never be found for a U.S. mutual fund investing primarily in common stock. Rather, the average correlation with the S&P index would be above 0.90. This is strong evidence that the extensive analysis discussed earlier concerning low correlation among countries can be reflected in actual performance of international mutual funds. Similarly, the column entitled "Beta" shows the responsiveness of international funds to a change in the S&P index. The Beta is the Beta introduced in Chapter 5, where we discussed the single-index model. The Beta for the common stock portion of a fund invested in U.S. securities would be close to one. For the 20 funds the average Beta is 0.64. In the fifth edition we examined a similar sample for the 1980s. The average Beta was 0.71. Thus, there is a fair amount of stability in historical risk numbers.

As shown in Table 12.6, the U.S. market is less risky than other national markets from a U.S. perspective. Given the low correlation between non-U.S. markets, however, the relative riskiness of U.S. portfolios and an internationally diversified portfolio is less clear.

Table 12.11 shows that the average standard deviation of an international portfolio was somewhat higher than the S&P index. This evidence would suggest that the higher risk of individual countries relative to U.S. markets was balanced by low correlation between countries, and the interaction of these two effects produced a portfolio with risk somewhat higher than that of a U.S. portfolio.

The realized return on international portfolios relative to U.S. portfolios is very dependent on the time period studied.

This 10-year period had very high returns in the U.S. market. There were other 10-year periods where international portfolios outperformed U.S. portfolios.

There are many fewer international bonds funds than there are stock funds, and their history is much more limited. Table 12.12 shows summary statistics for the six funds for which data were available. The last column is the correlation coefficient of each fund with the Shearson–Lehman bond index, which is the standard index used to calculate the performance of U.S. bond funds. It is the bond market equivalent of the S&P index. For U.S. domestic bond funds the correlation with the Shearson-Lehman index would be 0.85 to 0.90. Examining the last column shows that once again the promise of low correlation is met. The average correlation of 0.51 is considerably less than for U.S. bond funds. The standard deviation of a bond fund is very dependent on the maturity of the portfolio. Portfolios of bonds with long maturities have a higher standard of deviation than portfolios of short-maturity bonds. We have no information on the maturity of the foreign bond funds relative to the Shearson–Lehman index. Thus, it is not meaningful to compare standard deviations.

The risk structure between various countries has been studied for 20 years, and the result of low correlation among international markets relative to intracountry portfolios has been consistently found. Thus the risk characteristics of international funds that have been found in the past are likely to be found in the future. It is hard, however, to develop a convincing economic case that the U.S. market will outperform or underperform other markets consistently in the future. Thus, once again, we believe the relevant way to utilize mutual fund data to examine the reasonableness of international diversification is to examine the proportions to invest in the United States and an international portfolio at various levels of assumed differences between returns in the United States and returns in other countries. Table 12.13 shows the optimal investment proportions for a portfolio of the S&P index and the typical international fund.

In calculating the proportions, the standard deviations shown in Table 12.11 for the S&P index and the average international fund were used as well as the average correlation coefficient. An expected return of 12% was assumed for the S&P index and a 6% riskless lending and borrowing rate.

Using data for the typical fund in the 10-year sample shows that international diversification pays as long as the return on the international portfolio is no less than 1 1/4% below the return on the S&P index.[10] With equal expected return, the optimum is 80% U.S and 20% international.

MODELS FOR MANAGING INTERNATIONAL PORTFOLIOS

Prior sections present analysis that suggests that a portfolio of international equities should be a part of an optimum portfolio. Furthermore, examining the performance of international funds shows that the analysis is confirmed by actual performance. The conclusions were less clear for international bond funds.

The obvious strategy for an investor deciding to diversify internationally but not wishing to determine how to construct an international portfolio is to hold an international

---

[10]One consideration an investor in an international portfolio needs to be aware of is that there is some evidence that international managers underperform domestic managers. At a number of conferences the authors have listened to industry speakers who specialize in evaluating international portfolios. They estimate a U.S. manager of a portfolio of foreign securities (such as Japanese) underperforms the foreign (Japanese) manager. The estimates we have heard range from 2% to 4%. The underperformance may well hold. Estimates of the exact amount should be treated with some skepticism.

Table 12.12   Performance Data on Bond Funds

Fund Name	Sample Period (years)	Fund Mean Return Monthly	Standard Deviation	Beta	Correlation with Shearson-Lehman Index
Fidelity Global Bond Fund	10	0.42%	1.85%	0.76	0.48
T. Rowe Price International Bond Fund	10	0.60%	2.41%	0.80	0.38
PaineWebber Master Global Income Fund	10	0.50%	1.32%	0.66	0.58
Putnam Global Governmental Income Trust	10	0.52%	1.85%	0.87	0.54
Scudder International Bond Fund	10	0.58%	2.05%	0.87	0.49
Morgan Stanley Dean Witter World Wide Inc.	10	0.46%	1.50%	0.78	0.60
Average	10.00	0.51%	1.83%	0.69	0.51

index fund. The parallel to holding a domestic index fund is to hold a value-weighted portfolio of international securities. The Morgan Stanley Capital International index excluding the United States is a value-weighted index, and an investment matching this index would be a value-weighted index fund.[11]

The justification for holding a U.S. index fund rests with the equilibrium models discussed in Chapters 13–16. If expected return is related to a market index and if securities are in equilibrium, then bearing nonmarket or unique risk does not result in additional compensation. The way to eliminate nonmarket risk is to hold an index fund. Even an investor who believes that securities are out of equilibrium but does not profess to know which securities give a positive or negative nonequilibrium return (has no forecasting ability) should hold the index fund. In this case, bearing nonmarket risk on average does not improve expected return because the investor on average selects securities with zero nonmarket return. Thus the investor should eliminate nonmarket risk by holding an index fund.

Table 12.13   Optimal Investment Proportions

Return on International Portfolio Relative to U.S. Portfolio	15-Year Data Optimal Proportions U.S.	International	10-Year Data Optimal Proportions U.S.	International
+3	27%	73%	40%	60%
+2	40%	60%	53%	47%
+1	53%	47%	66%	34%
0	68%	32%	80%	20%
−1	85%	15%	96%	4%
−2	99%	1%	100%	0%
−3	100%	0%	100%	0%

R_F = the return on the riskless and = 6%,
$R_{S\&P}$ = the total return on the Standard and Poor index = 12%.

[11]Although the Morgan Stanley index is the most widely used index, differences by country in the cross holdings of securities (one company owning shares in another) means that its weighting is very different than an index using the value of a country's equity assets. Japan in particular is very much overweighted. In addition, the Morgan Stanley index is a sample of each country's securities and the proportion sampled varies from country to country. Thus it is not an appropriately weighted market index.

If there was good evidence that individual securities' expected returns were determined by an international equilibrium model, and if a value-weighted index was the factor affecting expected returns, a parallel argument could be presented for holding an international value-weighted index fund. However, the evidence in favor of any international model determining expected return is still controversial.

A disturbing aspect of an international index fund is the proportion that Japan represents of the world excluding the United States (about 25%). If one believes in an international equilibrium asset pricing model and Japan represents about 25% of the market portfolio, then this is appropriate. Otherwise it makes sense only if Japan is expected to have an abnormally high return; for diversification or risk arguments it is clearly inappropriate. The authors have heard a number of presentations suggesting other weighting schemes, such as trade or GNP that lower the percentage in Japan. The correct justification for any weighting should come from equilibrium arguments; otherwise any weighting is as arbitrary as another.

If one is not willing to accept an international equilibrium model that partitions risk into that part that results in higher expected return and that part that is unique, it is appropriate for an investor without an ability to forecast expected returns to minimize total risk. The risk structure is reasonably predictable through time. The low correlation on average among country portfolios, and the pattern of relatively high correlation among countries with close economic links (such as the United States and Canada) is likely to continue in the future. Both Jorion [38] and Eun and Resnick [23] have examined the stability of the correlation structure and have found predictability. Thus the past correlation matrices can be used to predict the future. Similarly, Jorion [38] has shown that standard deviations are predictable, and thus a low-risk international portfolio can be developed.

If one wishes to develop an active international portfolio, then many of the same considerations are involved as are present in developing an active domestic portfolio. However, international investment adds two elements to the investment process not present in pure domestic investment—country selection and exchange exposure.[12]

The decision concerning how much to invest in each country depends on the factors discussed earlier, namely, intercountry correlation, the variance of return for each country's securities, and the expected return in each country. There is good evidence that the past standard deviations and correlations are useful in predicting the future.

Recently a number of researchers have also found predictable in returns. Harvey [35], Solnick [67], and Campbell and Hammo [15] find predictability in many country's returns. The predictability is low with 1%–2% of the variation in returns explained by past variables. However, Kandel and Stambaugh [40] provide evidence that even with this low explanatory power, improvement in portfolio allocation can be achieved. What variables seem to predict returns? Lagged returns, price levels (dividend price, earnings price, and book price ratios), interest rate levels, yield spreads, and default premiums have all been used. How is this done?

In Chapter 8 we discussed how to estimate the coefficients in a multi-index model. For example, we could estimate the relationship between return in a country (e.g., France) and some of the variables that have been found to predict return. Performing this analysis we could find the relationship

---

[12]Technically the amount to invest in any security should depend on securities selected in other countries. Thus our treatment of first selecting each portfolio within a country and then doing country selection is nonoptimal. However, it captures much of practice. Furthermore, intercountry factors are relatively unimportant in determining each securities' return, so this assumption may be a simplification that improves performance.

Return $= -1 + 1$ (return in the prior period) $+ \frac{1}{2}$ (interest rate in the prior period)

The coefficients, -1, 1, and $\frac{1}{2}$, are estimated by running a time series regression. To forecast return in the next period, one simply substitutes the current value of this period's return and interest rates in the right side of the equation.

These predictions of return plus past values of correlations and standard deviations can be used as input to the portfolio optimization process.

A second possibility for predicting expected returns is to utilize any of the valuation models discussed in Chapter 18. For example, the infinite constant growth model states that

$$\text{Expected return} = \frac{\text{Dividend}}{\text{Price}} + \text{growth}$$

Estimates of next period's dividend could be obtained by estimating earnings and estimating the proportion of earnings paid out as dividends (the payout rate). The payout ratio for a country portfolio is very stable over time, and forecasts of earnings are widely available and at an economy level quite accurate. Estimates of growth rates in earnings are also widely available internationally. Thus valuation models are a feasible way to estimate expected returns.[13]

One of the few studies that examines some alternative ways of estimating expected return is Arnott and Henriksson [9]. They forecast the relative performance of each country's stocks compared to the country's bonds on the basis of current risk premiums and economic variables. They define the risk premium as the difference in expected return between common equity and bonds. They measure expected return on bonds by using the yield to maturity. They measure expected return on equity by calculating the earnings divided by price. Comparing this measure with the valuation model just presented shows that growth should be added and differences in payout taken into account. These differences, as well as differences in accounting conventions across countries and the impact of this on earnings, could affect risk premium comparisons across countries. They recognize these influences and instead of using risk premiums directly, they use current risk premiums relative to past risk premiums. Their forecast equation states that future performance is related to current risk premiums divided by average risk premiums in the past. In equation form this is

Future returns on equities relative to debt $=$ constant

$+$ constant (current risk premium/average risk premium prior two years)

They find for many countries that this equation is a useful predictor and that for some countries it can be improved by adding other macroeconomic variables, such as prediction of trade and production statistics. This model could be used to estimate which countries have higher expected future returns on equities by using current bond yields as expected returns for bonds, and the preceding equation to estimate the difference between bond and equity returns. Clearly, further testing of all of these models is necessary. However, they are suggestive of the type of analysis that can be done in active international asset allocation.

The second new consideration that international investment introduces is exchange risk. As discussed earlier, entering into futures contracts can reduce the variability because of the exchange risk. Considering only risk, this is generally useful. Entering into futures

---

[13]Testing of the accuracy of forecasts produced by these models is unavailable, so all we can do is to suggest types of analysis; we cannot report results.

contracts can also affect expected return, however. As discussed in Chapter 23, entering into a futures contract could lower expected returns. Furthermore, the investor may have some beliefs about changes in exchange rates different from those contained in market prices.[14] In this case the sacrifice in expected return may lead the investor to choose not to eliminate exchange risk.

Finally, Black [13] has shown that taking some exchange risk can increase expected return. Thus exchange rate exposure involves a risk return tradeoff.

Active Short-Term Bond Management

Risk-free interest rates differ from country to country. For example, the interest rate on six-month government issues could be 7% in England and 4% in the United States. The expected return for a U.S. investor buying an English bond would be the expected return to a British investor plus the exchange gains and losses.

Theory says the exchange gain or loss should be related to the interest rate differential. Thus the U.S. investor should expect to lose about 3% in exchange rate changes by buying the British bond. However, empirical evidence does not support the claim that exchange rate changes have a close relationship to interest rate differentials.

The empirical evidence strongly supports that investment in the high interest rate country gives the higher return.[15] Three explanations have been suggested: a peso explanation, extra risk, and an investment opportunity. The peso explanation is named after the investors who invested their money in Mexican government bonds. For a number of years they earned a return greater than they would have earned in the United States. When the devaluation occurred, however, it more than eliminated all past gains. The peso argument is that although the empirical evidence suggests gains by investing in the higher interest rate countries, some future devaluation will eliminate all gains. The return gains have been so persistent that the size of a devaluation necessary to eliminate past gains seems too large to be plausible. Thus, most analysts reject this explanation.

The second explanation is that the extra return is simply compensation for risk. Although some of the extra return may be compensation for risk, studies to date do not support this as a complete explanation. Thus, there seems to be an investment opportunity and there are a number of funds that follow the strategy of investing in the higher-yielding country [21].[16]

---

[14]Levich ([45] and [46]) has shown that some forecasters are able to predict exchange rate movements.

[15]For example, Cumby [19] finds on average that exchange rate changes increase the return of buying the higher interest rate counting (e.g., British bonds would be expected to return more than 7%).

[16]There is a variation in this strategy that some funds follow. Assume we observe the following interest rates on six-month government debt:

U.S. rate   = 4%

English rate = 7%

German rate   = 5%

In this scenario, one investment strategy is to buy English bonds and hedge exchange risk by buying a futures contract of Deutsche marks for dollars. The investor will lose 1% on the futures contract since there is a 1% difference in T-bill rates and empirical evidence supports that the interest rate differential is reflected in the futures contract. If the English-deutsche mark exchange rate stays constant, the investor will earn 7% on the bond less 1% on the futures contract or 6%, which is superior to the return on U.S. bills.

CONCLUSION

In this chapter we have discussed the evidence in support of international diversification. The evidence that international diversification reduces risk is uniform and extensive. Given the low risk, international diversification is justified even if expected returns are less internationally than domestically. Unless there are mechanisms such as taxes or currency restrictions that substantially reduce the return on foreign investment relative to domestic investment, international diversification has to be profitable for investors of some countries, and possibly all.

QUESTIONS AND PROBLEMS

1. Assume that you expect that the average return on a security in various markets is as shown in the following table. Assume further that the historical correlation coefficients shown in Table 12.3 are a reasonable estimate of future correlation coefficients. Finally, assume the standard deviations shown in Table 12.6. Which markets are attractive investments for an American investor if the riskless lending and borrowing rate is 6%?

	Market	Expected Return (%)
1.	Austria	14
2.	France	16
3.	Japan	14
4.	U.K.	15
5.	United States	20

2. Assume the information shown in Table 12.6. What is the minimum risk portfolio of the U.S. and value-weighted index for:

   (1) Common equities when $\rho_{N,US} = 0.423$
   (2) Bonds when $\rho_{N,US} = 0.527$
   (3) T-bills when $\rho_{N,US} = -0.220$

3. Consider the following returns:

Period	United States	U.K.	Exchange Rate[a]
1	10%	5%	$3
2	15%	−5%	2.5
3	−5%	15%	2.5
4	12%	8%	2.0
5	6%	10%	1.5
6			2.5

[a]Beginning of period dollars for pounds.

   What is the average return in each market from the point of view of a U.S. investor and of a U.K. investor?

4. Given the data in the prior question, what is the standard deviation of return from the point of view of a U.S. investor and of a U.K. investor?

5. For the following returns:

Period	United States	Japan	Exchange Rate[a]
1	12%	18%	200
2	15%	12%	180
3	5%	10%	190
4	10%	12%	150
5	6%	7%	170
6			180

[a]Beginning of period value of yen for dollars.

What is the average return in each market from the point of view of a U.S. and Japanese investor?

6. What is the standard deviation of return from the point of view of a U.S. and Japanese investor?

7. What is the correlation of return between markets from the point of view of each investor?

BIBLIOGRAPHY

1. Adler, Michael. "The Cost of Capital and Valuation of a Two-Country Firm," *Journal of Finance*, **XXIX,** No. 1 (March 1974), pp. 119–132.
2. Adler, Michael, and Horesh, Reuven. "The Relationship Among Equity Markets: Comment on [3]," *Journal of Finance*, **XXIX,** No. 4 (Sept. 1974), pp. 1131–1317.
3. Adler, Michael, and Dumas, Bernard. "International Portfolio Choice and Corporate Finance: A Synthesis," *Journal of Finance*, **38,** No. 3 (June 1983), pp. 925–984.
4. Adler, Michael, and Prasad, Bhaskar. "On Universal Currency Hedges," *Journal of Financial and Quantitative Analysis*, **27,** No. 1 (Mar. 1992), pp. 19–38.
5. Agmon, Tamir. "The Relations Among Equity Markets: A Study of Share Price Co-Movements in the United States, United Kingdom, Germany and Japan," *Journal of Finance*, **XXVII,** No. 3 (June 1972), pp. 839–855.
6. ———. "Country Risk: The Significance of the Country Factor for Share-Price Movements in the United Kingdom, Germany, and Japan," *Journal of Business*, **46,** No. 1 (Jan. 1973), pp. 24–32.
7. ———. "Reply to [2]," *Journal of Finance*, **XXIX,** No. 4 (Sept. 1974), pp. 1318–1319.
8. Agmon, Tamir, and Lessard, Donald. "Investor Recognition of Corporate International Diversification," *Journal of Finance*, **XXXII,** No. 4 (Sept. 1977), pp. 1049–1055.
9. Arnott, A., and Henriksson, N. "A Disciplined Approach to Global Asset Allocation," *Financial Analyst Journal* (March–April 1989), pp. 17–28.
10. Baxter, Marianne. "The International Diversification Puzzle Is Worse Than You Think," *The American Economic Review*, **87,** No. 1 (Mar. 1997), pp. 170–180.
11. Bennett, James A. "International Stock Market Equilibrium with Heterogenous Tastes," *The American Economic Review*, **89,** No. 3 (June 1999), pp. 639–648.
12. Black, F. "International Capital Market Equilibrium with Investment Barriers," *Journal of Financial Economics*, **1,** No. 4 (Dec. 1974), pp. 337–352.
13. Black, F. "Equilibrium Exchange Rate Hedging," National Bureau of Economic Research (NBER) Working Paper, No. 2947 (April 1989).
14. Branch, Ben. "Common Stock Performance and Inflation: An International Comparison," *Journal of Business*, **47,** No. 1 (Jan. 1973), pp. 48–52.
15. Campbell, J., and Hammo, Y. "Predictable Stock Returns in the United States and Japan: A Study of Long-Term Capital Market Integration," *Journal of Finance*, **47,** (1992), pp. 43–70.

16. Cho, Chinhyung D., Eun, Cheol S., and Senbet, Lemma. "International Arbitrage Pricing Theory: An Empirical Investigation," *Journal of Finance*, **41,** No. 2 (June 1986), pp. 313–329.

17. Chollerton, Kenneth, Pieraerts, Pierre, and Solnik, Bruno. "Why Invest in Foreign Currency Bonds?" *Journal of Portfolio Management,* **22** (Summer 1986), pp. 4–8.

18. Cumby, Robert. "Is It Risk? Explaining Deviations from Uncovered Interest Rate Parity," *Journal of Monetary Economics,* **22,** No. 2 (1988), pp. 297–300.

19. Cumby, Robert, and Glen, Jack. "Evaluating the Performance of International Mutual Funds," *Journal of Finance,* **24** (1990), pp. 408–435.

20. Elton, Edwin J., Gruber, Martin J., and Rentzler, Joel. "Professionally Managed, Publicly Traded Community Funds," *The Journal of Business,* **60,** No. 2 (April 1987), pp. 175–199.

21. Eun, Cheol, Kolodny, Richard, and Resnick, Bruce. "U.S. Based International Mutual Funds: A Performance Evaluation," *Journal of Portfolio Management,* forthcoming.

22. Eun, Cheol S., and Resnick, Bruce G. "Exchange Rate Uncertainty, Forward Contracts, and International Portfolio Selection," *The Journal of Finance*, **43,** No. 1 (Mar. 1988), pp. 197–215.

23. Eun, Cheol, and Resnick, Bruce. "Exchange Rate Uncertainty, Forward Contracts and International Portfolio Selection," *Journal of Finance,* **43,** No. 8 (1988), pp. 197–215.

24. Fama, Eugene, and French, Kenneth. "Business Conditions and Expected Return on Stocks and Bonds," *Journal of Financial Economics*, **25,** (1993), pp. 23–50.

25. Farber, Andre L. "Performance of Internationally Diversified Mutual Funds," in Edwin J. Elton and Martin J. Gruber (eds.), *International Capital Markets* (Amsterdam: North-Holland, 1975).

26. Fatemi, Ali M. "Shareholder Benefits from Corporate International Diversification," *The Journal of Finance*, **39,** No. 5 (Dec. 1984), pp. 1325–1344.

27. French, Kenneth R., and Poterba, James M. "Investor Diversification and International Equity Markets," *The American Economic Review*, **81,** No. 2 (May 1991), pp. 222–226.

28. Grauer, R., and Hakansson, Nils. "Gains from Internation Diversification: 1968–85 Returns on Portfolios of Stocks and Bonds," *Journal of Finance* (July 1987), pp. 721–738.

29. Grauer, Robert R., Hakansson, Nils H., and Crouhy, Michel. "Gains from International Diversification: 1968–85 Returns on Portfolios of Stocks and Bonds/Discussion," *The Journal of Finance*, **42,** No. 3 (July 1987), pp. 721–741.

30. Grauer, F., Litzenberger, R., and Stehle, R. "Sharing Rules and Equilibrium in an International Capital Market Under Uncertainty," *Journal of Financial Economics*, **3,** No. 3 (June 1976), pp. 233–256.

31. Grubel, Herbert. "Internally Diversified Portfolios: Welfare Gains and Capital Flows," *American Economic Review*, **LVIII,** No. 5, Part 1 (Dec. 1968), pp. 1299–1314.

32. Grubel, G. Herbert, and Fadner, Kenneth. "The Interdependence of International Equity Markets," *Journal of Finance*, **XXVI,** No. 1 (March 1971), pp. 89–94.

33. Gultekin, N. Bulent. "Stock Market Returns and Inflation: Evidence from Other Countries," *The Journal of Finance*, **38,** No. 1 (March 1983), pp. 49–68.

34. Guy, J. "The Performance of the British Investment Trust Industry," *Journal of Finance* (May 1978), pp. 443–455.

35. Harvey, Campbell R. "Predictable Risk and Returns in Emerging Markets." *Review of Financial Studies,* **8,** No. 3 (1995), pp. 773–816.

36. Ibbotson, Roger, Siegal, Lawrence, and Love, Kathryn. "World Wealth: Market Values and Returns," *Journal of Portfolio Management*, **4,** No.2 (Fall 1985), pp. 4–23.

37. Jacquillat, Bertrand, and Solnik, Bruno. "Multi-Nationals Are Poor Tools for Diversification," *Journal of Portfolio Management*, **11,** No. 1 (Winter 1978), pp. 8–12.

38. Jorion, Philippe. "International Diversification with Estimation Risk," *Journal of Business,* **12,** No. 1 (July 1985), pp. 259–278.

39. Joy, Maurice, Panton, Don, Reilly, Frank, and Martin, Stanley. "Co-Movements of International Equity Markets," *The Financial Review*, **58,** No. 3 (1976), pp. 1–20.

40. Kandel, Shmuel, and Stambaugh, Robert. "On the Predictability of Stock Returns: An Asset-Allocation Perspective," *Journal of Finance,* **51** (1996) pp. 385–424.

41. Kaplanis, C.E., and Schaefer, Steve. "Exchange Risk and International Diversification in Bond and Equity Portfolios," unpublished manuscript, London Business School.

42. Lessard, Donald. "International Portfolio Diversification: A Multivariate Analysis for a Group of Latin American Countries," *Journal of Finance*, **XXVIII**, No. 3 (June 1973), pp. 619–633.

43. ———. "World, National and Industry Factors in Equity Returns," *Journal of Finance*, **XXIV**, No. 2 (May 1974), pp. 379–391.

44. ———. "The Structure of Returns and Gains from International Diversification: A Multivariate Approach," in Edwin J. Elton and Martin J. Gruber (eds.), *International Capital Markets* (Amsterdam: North-Holland, 1975).

45. Levich, Richard. "On the Efficiency of Markets for Foreign Exchange," in Frenkel, J. and Dornbusch, R. (eds.), *International Economic Policy: Theory and Evidence,* **42** (Baltimore, Md.: Johns Hopkins Press, 1970).

46. ———. "The Efficiency of Markets for Foreign Exchange: A Review and Extension," in Donald Lessard (ed.), *International Financial Management: Theory and Application* (New York: Warren, Gorham and Lamont, 1979).

47. Levich, Richard, and Frenkel, Jacob. "Covered Interest Arbitrage: Unexplored Profits?" *Journal of Political Economy* (April, 1975), pp. 325–338.

48. ———. "Transaction Costs and Interest Arbitrage: Tranquil versus Turbulent Periods," *Journal of Political Economy* (Dec. 1977), pp. 1209–1286.

49. Levy, Haim, and Sarnat, Marshall. "International Diversification of Investment Portfolios," *American Economic Review*, **LX**, No. 4 (Sept. 1970), pp. 668–675.

50. ———. "Devaluation Risk and the Portfolio Analysis of International Investment," in Edwin J. Elton and Martin J. Gruber (eds.), *International Capital Markets* (Amsterdam: North-Holland, 1975).

51. Makin, John. "Portfolio Theory and the Problem of Foreign Exchange Risk," *Journal of Finance*, **XXXIII**, No. 2 (May 1978), pp. 517–534.

52. McDonald, John. "French Mutual Fund Performance: Evaluation of Internationally-Diversified Portfolios," *Journal of Finance*, **XXVIII**, No. 5 (Dec. 1973), pp. 1161–1180.

53. Obstfeld, Maurice. "Risk-Taking, Global Diversification, and Growth," *The American Economic Review*, **84**, No. 5 (Dec. 1994), pp. 1310–1329.

54. Panton, Don, Lessig, Parket, and Joy, Maurice. "Co-Movement of International Equity Markets: A Taxonomic Approach," *Journal of Financial and Quantitative Analysis*, **XI**, No. 3 (Sept. 1976), pp. 415–432.

55. Ripley, Duncan. "Systematic Elements in the Linkage of National Stock Market Indices," *Review of Economics and Statistics*, **LV**, No. 3 (Aug. 1973), pp. 356–361.

56. Robicher, Alexander, and Eaker, Mark. "Foreign Exchange Hedging and the Capital Asset Pricing Model," *Journal of Finance*, **XXXIII**, No. 3 (June 1978), pp. 1011–1018.

57. Severn, Alan. "Investor Evaluation of Foreign and Domestic Risk," *Journal of Finance*, **XXIX**, No. 2 (May 1974), pp. 545–550.

58. Sharma, J. L., and Kennedy, Robert. "A Comparative Analysis of Stock Price Behavior on the Bombay, London, and New York Stock Exchanges," *Journal of Financial and Quantitative Analysis*, **XII**, No. 3 (Sept. 1977), pp. 391–413.

59. Solnik, Bruno. "The International Pricing of Risk: An Empirical Investigation of the World Capital Market Structure," *Journal of Finance*, **XXIX**, No. 2 (May 1974), pp. 365–378.

60. ———. "Why Not Diversify Internationally?" *Financial Analysts Journal*, **20**, No. 4 (July/Aug. 1974), pp. 48–54.

61. ———. "An Equilibrium Model of the International Capital Market," *Journal of Economic Theory*, **8**, No. 4 (Aug. 1974), pp. 500–524.

62. ———. "An International Market Model of Security Price Behavior," *Journal of Financial and Quantitative Analysis*, **IX**, No. 4 (Sept. 1974), pp. 537–554.

63. ———. "The Advantages of Domestic and International Diversification," in Edwin J. Elton and Martin J. Gruber (eds.), *International Capital Markets* (Amsterdam: North-Holland, 1975).

64. ———. "Testing International Asset Pricing: Some Pessimistic Views," *Journal of Finance*, **XXXII**, No. 2 (May 1977), pp. 503–512.

65. Solnik, Bruno. *International Investments* (Reading, Mass.: Addison-Wesley, 1988).
66. Solnick, Bruno. "The Performance of International Asset Allocations Strategies Using Conditioning Information," *Journal of Empirical Finance*, **1,** No. 1 (June 1993), pp. 33–55.
67. ——. "Global Asset Management," *The Journal of Portfolio Management*, (Summer 1998), pp. 43–51.
68. Solnik, Bruno, and Noetzlin, B. "Optimal International Asset Allocation," *Journal of Portfolio Management,* **2** (Fall 1982), pp. 11–21.
69. Stehle, Richard. "An Empirical Test of the Alternative Hypotheses of National and International Pricing of Risky Assets," *Journal of Finance*, **XII,** No. 2 (May 1977), pp. 493–502.
70. Subrahmanyam, Marti. "International Capital Markets, Equilibrium, and Investor Welfare with Unequal Interest Rates," in Edwin J. Elton and Martin J. Gruber (eds.), *International Capital Markets* (Amsterdam: North-Holland, 1975).
71. ——. "On the Optimality of International Capital Market Integration," *Journal of Financial Economics*, **2,** No. 1 (March 1975), pp. 3–28.
72. Uppal, Raman. "A General Equilibrium Model of International Portfolio Choice," *The Journal of Finance*, **48,** No. 2 (June 1993), pp. 529–553.

Part 3

MODELS OF
EQUILIBRIUM IN THE
CAPITAL MARKETS

13

The Standard Capital Asset Pricing Model

All of the preceding chapters have been concerned with how an individual or institution, acting upon a set of estimates, could select an optimum portfolio, or set of portfolios. If investors act as we have prescribed, then we should be able to draw on the analysis to determine how the aggregate of investors will behave, and how prices and returns at which markets will clear are set. The construction of general equilibrium models will allow us to determine the relevant measure of risk for any asset and the relationship between expected return and risk for any asset when markets are in equilibrium. Furthermore, though the equilibrium models are derived from models of how portfolios should be constructed, the models, themselves, have major implications for the characteristics of optimum portfolios.

The subject of equilibrium models is so important that we have devoted four chapters to it. In this chapter we develop the simplest form of an equilibrium model, called the standard capital asset pricing model, or the one-factor capital asset pricing model. This was the first general equilibrium model developed, and it is based on the most stringent set of assumptions. The second chapter on general equilibrium models deals with models that have been developed under more realistic sets of assumptions. The third chapter in this sequence deals with tests of general equilibrium models. The final chapter deals with a new theory of asset pricing: arbitrage pricing theory.

It is worthwhile pointing out, at this time, that the final test of a model is not how reasonable the assumptions behind it appear but how well the model describes reality. As readers proceed with this chapter they will, no doubt, find many of its assumptions objectionable. Furthermore, the final model is so simple readers may well wonder about its validity. As we will see, despite the stringent assumptions and the simplicity of the model, it does an amazingly good job of describing prices in the capital markets.

THE ASSUMPTIONS UNDERLYING THE STANDARD CAPITAL ASSET PRICING MODEL (CAPM)

The real world is sufficiently complex that to understand it and construct models of how it works, one must assume away those complexities that are thought to have only a small (or no) effect on its behavior. As the physicist builds models of the movement of matter in a frictionless environment, the economist builds models where there are no institutional frictions to the movement of stock prices.

The first assumption we make is that there are no transaction costs. There is no cost (friction) of buying or selling any asset. If transaction costs were present, the return from any asset would be a function of whether or not the investor owned it before the decision period. Thus, to include transaction costs in the model adds a great deal of complexity. Whether it is worthwhile introducing this complexity depends on the importance of transaction costs to investors' decisions. Given the size of transaction costs, they are probably of minor importance.

The second assumption behind the CAPM is that assets are infinitely divisible. This means that investors could take any position in an investment, regardless of the size of their wealth. For example, they can buy one dollar's worth of IBM stock.

The third assumption is the absence of personal income tax.[1] This means, for example, that the individual is indifferent to the form (dividends or capital gains) in which the return on the investment is received.

The fourth assumption is that an individual cannot affect the price of a stock by his buying or selling action. This is analogous to the assumption of perfect competition. While no single investor can affect prices by an individual action, investors in total determine prices by their actions.

The fifth assumption is that investors are expected to make decisions solely in terms of expected values and standard deviations of the returns on their portfolios. In other words, they make their portfolio decision, utilizing the framework discussed in other chapters.

The sixth assumption is that unlimited short sales are allowed. The individual investor can sell short any amount of any shares.[2]

The seventh assumption is unlimited lending and borrowing at the riskless rate. The investor can lend or borrow any amount of funds desired at a rate of interest equal to the rate for riskless securities.

The eighth and ninth assumptions deal with the homogeneity of expectations. First, investors are assumed to be concerned with the mean and variance of returns (or prices over a single period), and all investors are assumed to define the relevant period in exactly the same manner. Second, all investors are assumed to have identical expectations with respect to the necessary inputs to the portfolio decision. As we have said many times, these inputs are expected returns, the variance of returns, and the correlation matrix representing the correlation structure between all pairs of stocks.

The tenth assumption is that all assets are marketable. All assets, including human capital, can be sold and bought on the market.

Readers can now see the reason for the earlier warning that they might find many of the assumptions behind the CAPM untenable. It is clear that these assumptions do not hold in the real world just as it is clear that the physicist's frictionless environment does not really exist. The relevant questions are: How much is reality distorted by making these assumptions? What conclusions about capital markets do they lead to? Do these conclusions seem to describe the actual performance of the capital market?

THE CAPITAL ASSET PRICING MODEL

The standard form of the general equilibrium relationship for asset returns was developed independently by Sharpe, Lintner, and Mossin. Hence, it is often referred to as the Sharpe–Lintner–Mossin form of the capital asset pricing model. This model has been

---

[1]The major results of the model would hold if income tax and capital gains taxes were of equal size.

[2]This model can be derived under either of the descriptions of short sales discussed in Chapter 5.

derived in several forms involving different degrees of rigor and mathematical complexity. There is a trade-off between these derivations. The more complex forms are more rigorous and provide a framework within which alternative sets of assumptions can be examined. However, because of their complexity, they do not convey as readily as some of the simpler forms the economic intuition behind the capital asset pricing model. Because of this, we approach the derivation of the model at two distinct levels. The first derivation consists of a simple intuitively appealing derivation of the CAPM. This is followed by a more rigorous derivation.

Deriving the CAPM—A Simple Approach

Recall that in the presence of short sales, but without riskless lending and borrowing, each investor faced an efficient frontier such as that shown in Figure 13.1. In this figure BC represents the efficient frontier while ABC represents the set of minimum variance portfolios. In general the efficient frontier will differ among investors because of differences in expectations.

When we introduced riskless lending and borrowing, we showed that the portfolio of risky assets that any investor would hold could be identified without regard to the investor's risk preferences. This portfolio lies at the tangency point between the original efficient frontier of risky assets and a ray passing through the riskless return (on the vertical axis). This is depicted in Figure 13.2 where P_i denotes investor i's portfolio of risky assets.[3] The investors satisfy their risk preferences by combining portfolio P_i with lending or borrowing.

If all investors have homogeneous expectations and they all face the same lending and borrowing rate, then they will each face a diagram such as in Figure 13.2 and, furthermore, all of the diagrams will be identical. The portfolio of risky assets P_i held by any investor will be identical to the portfolio of risky assets held by any other investor. If all investors

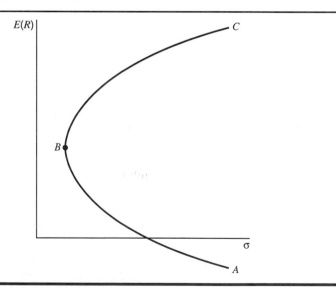

Figure 13.1   The efficient frontier—no lending and borrowing.

---

[3]We have subscripted P because each individual can face a different efficient frontier and, thus select a different P_i. This is true, though the composition of P_i does not depend on investor i's risk preference.

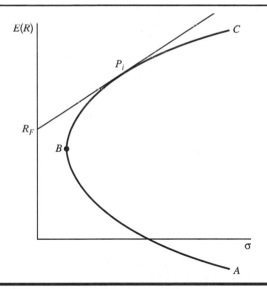

Figure 13.2   The efficient frontier with lending and borrowing.

hold the same risky portfolio, then, in equilibrium, it must be the market portfolio. The market portfolio is a portfolio comprised of all risky assets. Each asset is held in the proportion that the market value of that asset represents of the total market value of all risky assets. For example, if IBM stock represents 3% of all risky assets, then the market portfolio contains 3% IBM stock and each investor will take 3% of the money that will be invested in all risky assets and place it in IBM stock.

Notice that we have already learned something important. All investors will hold combinations of only two portfolios: the market portfolio (M) and a riskless security. This is sometimes referred to as the two mutual fund theorem because all investors would be satisfied with a market fund, plus the ability to lend or borrow a riskless security.

The straight line depicted in Figure 13.2 is usually referred to as the capital market line. All investors will end up with portfolios somewhere along the capital market line and all *efficient portfolios* would lie along the capital market line. However, not all securities or portfolios lie along the capital market line. In fact, from the derivation of the efficient frontier, we know that all portfolios of risky and riskless assets, except those that are efficient, lie below the capital market line. By looking at the capital market line we can learn something about the market price of risk. In Chapter 5 we showed that the equation of a line connecting a riskless asset and a risky portfolio (the line we now call the capital market line) is

$$\bar{R}_e = R_F + \frac{\bar{R}_M - R_F}{\sigma_M} \sigma_e$$

where the subscript e denotes an efficient portfolio.

The term $[(\bar{R}_M - R_F)/\sigma_M]$ can be thought of as the market price of risk for all efficient portfolios.[4] It is the extra return that can be gained by increasing the level of risk (standard deviation) on an efficient portfolio by one unit. The second term on the right-hand side of

---

[4]The reader should be alerted to the fact that many authors have defined $(\bar{R}_M - R_F)/\sigma_M^2$ as the market price of risk. The reason we have selected $(\bar{R}_M - R_F)/\sigma_M$ will become clear as you proceed with this chapter.

this equation is simply the market price of risk times the amount of risk in a portfolio. The second term represents that element of required return that is due to risk. The first term is simply the price of time or the return that is required for delaying potential consumption, one period given perfect certainty about the future cash flow. Thus, the expected return on an efficient portfolio is

(Expected return) = (Price of time) + (Price of risk) × (Amount of risk)

Although this equation establishes the return on an efficient portfolio, it does not describe equilibrium returns on noneffient portfolios or on individual securities. We now turn to the development of a relationship that does so.

Earlier (in Chapter 7) we argued that, for very well-diversified portfolios, Beta was the correct measure of a security's risk. For *very* well-diversified portfolios, nonsystematic risk tends to go to zero and the only relevant risk is systematic risk measured by Beta. As we have just explained, given the assumptions of homogeneous expectations and unlimited riskless lending and borrowing, all investors will hold the market portfolio. Thus the investor will hold a *very* well-diversified portfolio. Since we assume that the investor is concerned only with expected return and risk, the only dimensions of a security that need be of concern are expected return and Beta.

Let us hypothesize two portfolios with the characteristics shown here:

Investment	Expected Return	Beta
A	10	1.0
B	12	1.4

We have already seen (Chapter 5) that the expected return from portfolio A is simply the sum of the products of the proportion invested in each stock and the expected return on each stock. We have also seen that the Beta on a portfolio is simply the sum of the product of the proportion invested in each stock times the Beta on each stock. Now consider a portfolio C made up of one half of portfolio A and one half of portfolio B. From the facts stated earlier, the expected return on this portfolio is 11 and its Beta is 1.2. These three potential investments are plotted in Figure 13.3. Notice they lie on a straight line. This is no accident. All portfolios composed of different fractions of investments A and B will lie along a straight line in expected return Beta space.[5]

Now hypothesize a new investment D that has a return of 13% and a Beta of 1.2. Such an investment cannot exist for very long. All decisions are made in terms of risk and return. This portfolio offers a higher return and the same risk as portfolio C. Hence, it would pay

---

[5]If we let X stand for the fraction of funds invested in portfolio A, then the equation for return is

$$\overline{R}_P = X\overline{R}_A + (1-X)\overline{R}_B$$

The equation for Beta is

$$\beta_P = X\beta_A + (1-X)\beta_B$$

Solving the second equation for X and substituting in the first equation, we see that we are left with an equation of the form

$$\overline{R}_P = a + b\beta_P$$

or the equation of a straight line.

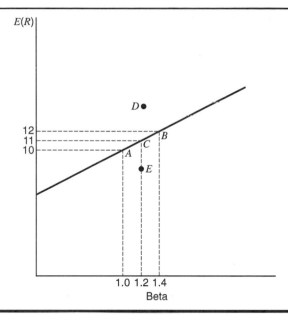

Figure 13.3   Combinations of portfolios.

all investors to sell C short and buy D. Similarly, if a security were to exist with a return of 8% and a Beta of 1.2 (designated by E), it would pay arbitragers to step in and buy portfolio C while selling security E short. Such arbitrage would take place until C, D, and E all yielded the same return. This is just another illustration of the adage that two things that are equivalent cannot sell at different prices. We can demonstrate the arbitrage discussed earlier in a slightly more formal manner. Let us return to the arbitrage between portfolios C and D. An investor could sell $100 worth of portfolio C short and with the $100 buy portfolio D. If the investor were to do so, the characteristics of this arbitraged portfolio would be as follows:

	Cash Invested	Expected Return	Beta
Portfolio C	−$100	−$11	−1.2
Security D	+$100	$13	1.2
Arbitrage portfolio	0	$ 2	0

From this example it is clear that as long as a security lies above the straight line, there is a portfolio involving zero risk and zero net investment that has a positive expected profit. An investor will engage in this arbitrage as long as any security or portfolio lies above the straight line depicted in Figure 13.3. A similar arbitrage will exist if any amount lies below the straight line in Figure 13.3.

We have now established that all investments and all portfolios of investments must lie along a straight line in return-Beta space. If any investment were to lie above or below that straight line, then an opportunity would exist for riskless arbitrage. This arbitrage would continue until all investments converged to the line. There are many different ways that this straight line can be identified, for it takes only two points to identify a straight line. Since we have shown that, under the assumptions of the CAPM, everybody will hold the market portfolio and since all portfolios must lie on the straight line, we will use this as one point. Recall in Chapter 7 we showed that the market portfolio must have a Beta of one. Thus, in Figure 13.4 the market portfolio is point M with a Beta of one and an expected return of $\bar{R}_M$. It is often convenient to choose the second point to identify a straight line as the intercept. The intercept occurs when Beta equals zero, or when the asset has zero systematic risk. One asset with zero systematic risk is the riskless asset. Thus, we can treat the intercept as the rate of return on a riskless asset. These two points identify the straight line shown in Figure 13.4. The equation of a straight line has the form

$$\bar{R}_i = a + b\beta_i \tag{13.1}$$

One point on the line is the riskless asset with a Beta of zero. Thus,

$$R_F = a + b(0)$$

or

$$R_F = a$$

A second point on the line is the market portfolio with a Beta of one. Thus,

$$\bar{R}_M = a + b(1)$$

or

$$\left(\bar{R}_M - a\right) = b$$

Putting these together and substituting into Equation (13.1) yields

$$\bar{R}_i = R_F + \beta_i\left(\bar{R}_M - R_F\right) \tag{13.2}$$

Think about this relationship for a moment. It represents one of the most important discoveries in the field of finance. Here is a simple equation, called the security market line, that describes the expected return for all assets and portfolios of assets in the economy. The expected return on any asset, or portfolio, whether it is efficient or not, can be determined from this relationship. Notice that $\bar{R}_M$ and R_F are not functions of the assets we examine.

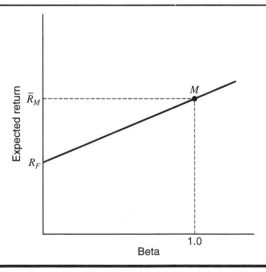

Figure 13.4   The security market line.

Thus, the relationship between the expected return on any two assets can be related simply to their difference in Beta. The higher Beta is for any security, the higher must be its equilibrium return. Furthermore, the relationship between Beta and expected return is linear. One of the greatest insights that comes from this equation arises from what it states is unimportant in determining return. Recall that in Chapter 7 we saw that the risk of any stock could be divided into systematic and unsystematic risk. Beta was the index of systematic risk. This equation validates the conclusion that systematic risk is the only important ingredient in determining expected returns and that nonsystematic risk plays no role.[6] Put another way, the investor gets rewarded for bearing systematic risk. It is not total variance of returns that affects expected returns, but only that part of the variance in returns that cannot be diversified away. This result has great economic intuition for, if investors can eliminate all nonsystematic risk through diversification, there is no reason they should be rewarded, in terms of higher return, for bearing it. All of these implications of the CAPM are empirically testable. Indeed, in Chapter 15 we examine the results of these tests. Provided the tests hold, we have, with a simple model, gained great insight in the behavior of the capital markets.

We digress for a moment and point out one seeming fallacy in the potential use of the CAPM. Invariably, when a group of investors is first exposed to the CAPM, one or more investors will find a high Beta stock that last year produced a smaller return than low Beta stocks. The CAPM is an equilibrium relationship. High Beta stocks are expected to give a higher return than low Beta stocks because they are more risky. This does not mean that they will give a higher return over all intervals of time. In fact, if they always gave a higher return, they would be less risky, not more risky, than low Beta stocks. Rather, because they are more risky, they will sometimes produce lower returns. However, over long periods of time, they should on the average produce higher returns.

We have written the CAPM model in the form

$$\overline{R}_i = R_F + \beta_i \left(\overline{R}_M - R_F \right)$$

This is the form in which it is most often written and the form most amenable to empirical testing. However, there are alternative forms that give added insight into its meaning. Recall that

$$\beta_i = \frac{\sigma_{iM}}{\sigma_M^2}$$

We could then write the security market line as

$$\overline{R}_i = R_F + \left(\frac{\overline{R}_M - R_F}{\sigma_M} \right) \frac{\sigma_{iM}}{\sigma_M} \tag{13.3}$$

This, in fact, is the equation of a straight line located in expected return σ_{iM}/σ_M space. Recall that earlier in our discussion of the capital market, line $(\overline{R}_m - R_F)/\sigma_M$ was described as the market price of risk. Since σ_{iM}/σ_M is a definition of the risk of any security, or portfolio, we would see that the security market line, like the capital market line, states that the

---

[6]This result is somewhat circular for, in this proof, we assumed that Beta was the relevant risk measure. In the more rigorous proof that follows, we make no such assumption, yet we end up with the same equation for the security market line.

expected return on any security is the riskless rate of interest plus the market price of risk times the amount of risk in the security or portfolio.[7]

Many authors write the CAPM equation as

$$\overline{R}_i = R_F + \left(\frac{\overline{R}_M - R_F}{\sigma_M^2}\right)\sigma_{iM}$$

They define $(\overline{R}_M - R_F)/\sigma_M^2$ as the market price of risk and σ_{iM} as the measure of the risk of security i. We have chosen the form we used because σ_{iM}/σ_M is the measure of how the risk on a security affects the risk of the market portfolio. It seems to us that this is the appropriate way to discuss the risk of a security.

We have now completed our intuitive proof of the CAPM. We are about to present a more complex mathematical proof. There are two reasons for presenting this mathematical proof. The first is that it is more rigorous. The second, and more important, reason is that one needs a richer framework to incorporate modifications of the assumptions of the standard CAPM. The method of proof used before is too restrictive to allow forms of general equilibrium equations that make more realistic assumptions about the world to be derived. The framework presented subsequently can be used to derive equilibrium models under alternative assumptions and, indeed, will be used to do so in the next chapter. The reader who finds both these reasons unappealing can skip the next section and the derivations in the next chapter with no loss of continuity.

Deriving the CAPM—A More Rigorous Approach

To derive the CAPM more rigorously, we return to the analysis presented in Chapter 6. Recall that in the first section of Chapter 6 we solved for the optimal portfolio when short sales were allowed and the investor could lend and borrow unlimited amounts of money at

---

[7]Below we offer theoretical justification that σ_{iM}/σ_M is the relevant measure of the risk of any security in equilibrium. Recall that the standard deviation of the market portfolio is given by

$$\sigma_M = \left[\sum_{i=1}^{N} X_i^2\sigma_i^2 + \sum_{i=1}^{N}\sum_{\substack{j=1\\j\neq i}}^{N} X_iX_j\sigma_{ij}\right]^{1/2}$$

where all X_i's are market proportions. Since all investors hold the market portfolio, the relevant definition of the risk of a security is the change in the risk of the market portfolio, as the holdings of that security are varied. This can be found as follows:

$$\frac{d\sigma_M}{dX_i} = \frac{d\left[\sum_{i=1}^{N} X_i^2\sigma_i^2 + \sum_{i=1}^{N}\sum_{\substack{j=1\\j\neq i}}^{N} X_iX_j\sigma_{ij}\right]^{1/2}}{dX_i}$$

$$= \frac{\left(\frac{1}{2}\right)\left[2X_i\sigma_i^2 + (2)\sum_{\substack{j=1\\j\neq 1}}^{N} X_j\sigma_{ij}\right]}{\left[\sum_{i=1}^{N} X_i^2\sigma_i^2 + \sum_{i=1}^{N}\sum_{\substack{j=1\\j\neq 1}}^{N} X_iX_j\sigma_{ij}\right]^{1/2}} = \frac{X_i^2\sigma_i^2 + \sum_{\substack{j=1\\j\neq 1}}^{N} X_j\sigma_{ij}}{\sigma_M} = \frac{\sigma_{iM}}{\sigma_M}$$

Therefore, the relevant risk of security is equal to σ_{iM}/σ_M.

the riskless rate of interest. The solution involved finding the composition of the portfolio that maximized the slope of a straight line passing through the riskless rate of interest on the vertical axes and the portfolio itself. As shown in Chapter 6, this involved maximizing the function

$$\theta = \frac{\bar{R}_P - R_F}{\sigma_P}$$

When the derivative of θ was taken with respect to all securities in the portfolio and each equation was set equal to zero, a set of simultaneous equations of the following form was derived:

$$\lambda \left(X_1 \sigma_{1k} + X_2 \sigma_{2k} + \cdots + X_k \sigma_k^2 + \cdots + X_N \sigma_{Nk} \right) = \bar{R}_k - R_F \tag{13.4}$$

This equation held for each security and there is one such equation for each security in the market. If there are homogeneous expectations, then all investors must select the same optimum portfolio. If all investors select the same portfolio, then, in equilibrium, that portfolio must be a portfolio in which all securities are held in the same percentage that they represent of the market. In other words, in equilibrium, the proportion invested in security 1 must be that fraction of the total market value of all securities that security 1 represents. To get from Equation (13.4) to the CAPM involves simply recognizing that the left-hand side of Equation (13.4) is $\lambda \, \text{cov}(R_k R_M)$. To see this, first note that

$$R_M = \sum_{i=1}^{N} R_i X_i'$$

where the prime indicates market proportions. Thus

$$\text{cov}(R_k R_M) = E\left[\left(R_k - \bar{R}_k \right) \left(\sum_{i=1}^{N} R_i X_i' - \sum_{i=1}^{N} \bar{R}_i X_i' \right) \right] \tag{13.5}$$

Rearranging the second term

$$\text{cov}(R_k R_M) = E\left[\left(R_k - \bar{R}_k \right) \left(\sum_{i=1}^{N} X_i' (R_i - \bar{R}_i) \right) \right]$$

Multiplying out the terms

$$\begin{aligned}
\text{cov}(R_k R_M) = E\Big[&X_1' \left(R_k - \bar{R}_k \right) \left(R_1 - \bar{R}_1 \right) \\
&+ X_2' \left(R_k - \bar{R}_k \right) \left(R_2 - \bar{R}_2 \right) + \cdots \\
&+ X_k' \left(R_k - \bar{R}_k \right) \left(R_k - \bar{R}_k \right) + \cdots + X_N' \left(R_k - \bar{R}_k \right) \left(R_N - \bar{R}_N \right) \Big]
\end{aligned}$$

Since the expected value of the sum of random variables is the sum of the expected values, factoring out the X's yields

$$\begin{aligned}
\text{cov}(R_k R_M) = &X_1' E\left(R_k - \bar{R}_k \right) \left(R_1 - \bar{R}_1 \right) + X_2' E\left(R_k - \bar{R}_k \right) \left(R_2 - \bar{R}_2 \right) + \cdots \\
&+ X_k' E\left(R_k - \bar{R}_k \right)^2 + \cdots + X_N' E\left(R_k - \bar{R}_k \right) \left(R_N - \bar{R}_N \right)
\end{aligned}$$

Earlier we argued that the X's in Equation (13.4) were market proportions. Comparing Equation (13.5) with the left-hand side of Equation (13.4) shows that they are, indeed, equal. Thus, Equation (13.4) can be written as

$$\lambda \, \text{cov}(R_k R_M) = \bar{R}_k - R_F \tag{13.6}$$

Since this must hold for all securities (all possible values of k), it must hold for all portfolios of securities. One possible portfolio is the market portfolio. Writing Equation (13.6) for the market portfolio involves recognizing that $\text{cov}(R_M R_M) = \sigma_M^2$.

$$\lambda \, \sigma_M^2 = \overline{R}_M - R_F$$

or

$$\lambda = \frac{\overline{R}_M - R_F}{\sigma_M^2}$$

Substituting this value for λ in Equation (13.6) and rearranging yields

$$\overline{R}_k = R_F + \frac{\overline{R}_M - R_F}{\sigma_M^2} \text{cov}(R_k R_M) = R_F + \beta_k (\overline{R}_M - R_F)$$

This completes the more rigorous derivation of the security market line.

The advantages of this proof over that presented earlier are that we have not had to assume that Beta is the relevant measure of risk and we have established a framework that, as we see in the next chapter, can be used to derive general equilibrium solutions when some of the present assumptions are relaxed.

PRICES AND THE CAPM

Up to now we have discussed equilibrium in terms of rate of return. In the introduction to this chapter we mentioned that the CAPM could be used to describe equilibrium in terms of either return or prices. The latter is of importance in certain situations, for example, the pricing of new assets. It is very easy to move from the equilibrium relationship in terms of rates of return to one expressed in terms of prices. All that is involved is a little algebra.

Let us define

P_i as the present price of asset i.

P_M as the present price of the market portfolio (all assets).

Y_i as the dollar value of the asset one period hence. It is market value plus any dividends.

Y_M as the dollar value of the market portfolio one period hence including dividends.

$\text{cov}(Y_i Y_M)$ as the covariance between Y_i and Y_M.

$\text{var}(Y_M)$ as the variance in Y_M.

r_F as $(1 + R_F)$.

The return on asset i is

$$R_i = \frac{\text{Ending value} - \text{Beginning value}}{\text{Beginning value}}$$

In symbols,

$$R_i = \frac{Y_i - P_i}{P_i} = \frac{Y_i}{P_i} - 1$$

Similarly,

$$R_M = \frac{Y_M - P_M}{P_M} = \frac{Y_M}{P_M} - 1$$

Substituting these expressions into Equation (13.3) yields

$$\frac{\overline{Y}_i}{P_i} - 1 = R_F + \left(\frac{\overline{Y}_M}{P_M} - 1 - R_F\right)\frac{\text{cov}(R_iR_M)}{\sigma_M^2} \tag{13.7}$$

Now we can rewrite $\text{cov}(R_iR_M)$ as

$$\text{cov}(R_iR_M) = E\left[\left(\frac{Y_i - P_i}{P_i} - \frac{\overline{Y}_i - P_i}{P_i}\right)\left(\frac{Y_M - P_M}{P_M} - \frac{\overline{Y}_M - P_M}{P_M}\right)\right]$$

$$= E\left[\left(\frac{Y_i}{P_i} - \frac{\overline{Y}_i}{P_i}\right)\left(\frac{Y_M}{P_M} - \frac{\overline{Y}_M}{P_M}\right)\right] = \frac{1}{P_iP_M}\text{cov}(Y_iY_M)$$

Similarly,

$$\sigma_M^2 = \frac{1}{P_M^2}\text{var}(Y_M)$$

Substituting these into Equation (13.7) adding 1 to both sides of the equation and recalling that $r_F = 1 + R_F$,

$$\frac{\overline{Y}_i}{P_i} = r_F + \left(\frac{\overline{Y}_M}{P_M} - r_F\right)\frac{\dfrac{1}{P_i}\dfrac{1}{P_M}\text{cov}(Y_iY_M)}{\dfrac{1}{P_M^2}\text{var}(Y_M)}$$

Multiplying both sides of the equation by P_i and simplifying the last term on the right-hand side,

$$\overline{Y}_i = r_FP_i + \left(\overline{Y}_M - r_FP_M\right)\frac{\text{cov}(Y_iY_M)}{\text{var}(Y_M)}$$

Solving this expression for P_i,

$$P_i = \frac{1}{r_F}\left[\overline{Y}_i - \left(\overline{Y}_M - r_FP_M\right)\frac{\text{cov}(Y_iY_M)}{\text{var}(Y_M)}\right]$$

Valuation formulas of this type have often been suggested in the security analysis literature. The equation involves taking the expected dollar return next year, $(\overline{Y}_i)$, subtracting off some payment as compensation for risk taking, and then taking the present value of the net result. The term in square brackets can be thought of as the certainty equivalent of the horizon cash payment, and to find the present value of the certainty equivalent, we simply discount it at the riskless rate of interest. While this general idea is not new, the explicit definition of how to find the certainty equivalent is one of the fundamental contributions of the CAPM. It can be shown that

$$\frac{\overline{Y}_M - r_FP_M}{\left[\text{var}(Y_M)\right]^{1/2}}$$

is equal to a measure of the market price of risk and that

$$\frac{\text{cov}(Y_iY_M)}{\left[\text{var}(Y_M)\right]^{1/2}}$$

is the relevant measure of risk for any asset.

CONCLUSION

In this chapter we have discussed the Sharpe–Lintner–Mossin form of a general equilibrium relationship in the capital markets. This model, usually referred to as the capital asset pricing model or standard CAPM, is a fundamental contribution to understanding the manner in which capital markets function. It is worthwhile highlighting some of the implications of this model.

First, we have shown that, under the assumptions of the CAPM, the only portfolio of risky assets that any investor will own is the market portfolio. Recall that the market portfolio is a portfolio in which the fraction invested in any asset is equal to the market value of that asset divided by the market value of all risky assets. Each investor will adjust the risk of the market portfolio to his or her preferred risk-return combination by combining the market portfolio with lending or borrowing at the riskless rate. This leads directly to the two mutual fund theorem. The two mutual fund theorem states that all investors can construct an optimum portfolio by combining a market fund with the riskless asset. Thus, all investors will hold a portfolio along the line connecting R_F with $\overline{R}_M$ in expected return, standard deviation of return space. See Figure 13.5.

This line, usually called the capital market line, which describes all efficient portfolios, is a pictorial representation of the equation

$$\overline{R}_e = R_F + \frac{\overline{R}_M - R_F}{\sigma_M} \sigma_e$$

Thus, we can say that the return on an efficient portfolio is given by the market price of time plus the market price of risk times the amount of risk on an efficient portfolio. Note that risk is defined as the standard deviation of return on any efficient portfolio.

From the equilibrium relationship for efficient portfolios we were able to derive the equilibrium relationship for any security or portfolio (efficient or inefficient). This relationship, presented in Figure 13.6, is given by

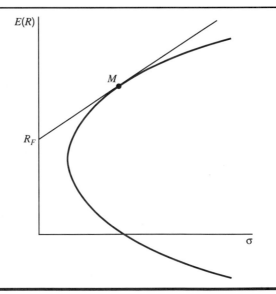

Figure 13.5   The efficient frontier.

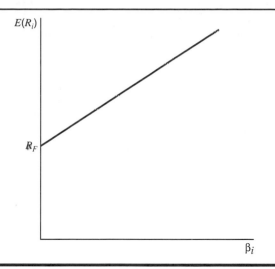

Figure 13.6   The security market line.

$$\overline{R}_i = R_F + \left(\frac{\overline{R}_M - R_F}{\sigma_M} \right) \frac{\sigma_{iM}}{\sigma_M}$$

or

$$\overline{R}_i = R_F + \beta_i \left(\overline{R}_M - R_F \right)$$

This relationship is usually called the security market line. Notice that it might have been called the security-portfolio market line for it describes the equilibrium return on all portfolios, as well as all securities.

Examination of the first form of the security market line shows that it is analogous in many ways to the capital market line. As we have shown, the impact of a security on the risk of the market portfolio is given by σ_{iM}/σ_M. Thus, we can state that the equilibrium return on any security is equal to the price of time plus the market price of risk times the relevant definition of risk for the security.

The security market line clearly shows that return is an increasing function, in fact, a linearly increasing function, of risk. Furthermore, it is only market risk that affects return. The investor receives no added return for bearing diversifiable risk.

The capital asset pricing model has been derived under a set of very restrictive assumptions. The test of a model is how well it describes reality. The key test is: Does it describe the behavior of returns in the capital markets? These tests will be taken up in Chapter 15. Before we turn to these tests, however, it is logical to examine forms of the general equilibrium relationship that exist under less restrictive assumptions. Even if the standard CAPM model explains the behavior of security returns, it obviously does not explain the behavior of individual investors. Individual investors hold nonmarket and, in fact, quite often, very small portfolios. Furthermore, by developing alternative forms of the general equilibrium relationship, we can test whether observed returns are more consistent with one of these than they are with the standard CAPM.

QUESTIONS AND PROBLEMS

1. Assume that the following assets are correctly priced according to the security market line. Derive the security market line. What is the expected return on an asset with a Beta of two?

$$\overline{R}_1 = 6\% \qquad \beta_1 = 0.5$$
$$\overline{R}_2 = 12\% \qquad \beta_2 = 1.5$$

2. Assume the security market line given below. Assume that analysts have estimated the Beta on two stocks as follows: $\beta_x = 0.5$ and $\beta_y = 2$. What must the expected return on the two securities be in order for them to be a good purchase?

$$\overline{R}_i = 0.04 + 0.08\beta_i$$

3. Assume that over some period a CAPM was estimated. The results are shown below. Assume that over the same period two mutual funds had the following results:
   Fund A   Actual return = 10%   Beta = 0.8
   Fund B   Actual return = 15%   Beta = 1.2
   What can be said about the fund performance?

$$\overline{R}_i = 0.06 + 0.19\beta_i$$

4. Consider the CAPM line shown below. What is the excess return of the market over the risk-free rate? What is the risk-free rate?

$$\overline{R}_i = 0.04 + 0.10\beta_i$$

5. Write the CAPM shown in Problem 4 in price form.

6. Show that the standard CAPM should hold even if short sales are not allowed.

7. Assume that an asset exists with $\overline{R}_3 = 15\%$ and $\beta_3 = 1.2$. Further assume the security market line discussed in Problem 1. Design the arbitrage opportunity.

8. If the following assets are correctly priced on the security market line, what is the return of the market portfolio? What is the risk-free rate?

$$\overline{R}_1 = 9.40\% \qquad \beta_1 = 0.80$$
$$\overline{R}_2 = 13.40\% \qquad \beta_2 = 1.30$$

9. Given the following security market line

$$\overline{R}_i = 0.07 + 0.09\beta_i$$

What must be the returns for two stocks assuming their β's are 1.2 and 0.9?

BIBLIOGRAPHY

1. Aivazian, Varouj. "The Demand for Assets under Conditions of Risk: Comment," *Journal of Finance*, **XXXII**, No. 3 (June 1976), pp. 927–929.
2. Benninga, Simon, and Protopapadakis, Aris. "The Stock Market Premium, Production, and Relative Risk Aversion," *The American Economic Review*, **81**, No. 3 (June 1991), pp. 591–599.
3. Bernstein, Peter L. "What Rate of Return Can You 'Reasonably' Expect?" *Journal of Finance*, **XXVIII**, No. 2 (May 1973), pp. 273–282.
4. Chen, Nai-Fu, Grundy, Bruce, and Stambaugh, Robert F. "Changing Risk, Changing Risk Premiums, and Dividend Yield Effects," *The Journal of Business*, **63**, No. 1 (Jan. 1990), pp. 551–570.

5. Fama, Eugene. "Risk, Return and Equilibrium: Some Clarifying Comments," *Journal of Finance*, **XXIII,** No. 1 (March 1968), pp. 29–40.
6. ——. "Risk, Return and Equilibrium," *Journal of Political Economy*, **79,** No. 1 (Jan./Feb. 1971), pp. 30–55.
7. ——. "Risk, Return and Portfolio Analysis: Reply to [20]," *Journal of Political Economy*, **81,** No. 3 (May/June 1973), pp. 753–755.
8. Fama, Eugene F. "Determining the number of priced state variables in the ICAPM" *Journal of Financial and Quantitative Analysis*, **33,** No. 2 (June 1998), pp. 217–231.
9. Ferson, Wayne E., Harvey, C., and Campbell, R. "The Variation of Economic Risk Premiums," *The Journal of Political Economy*, **99,** No. 2 (Apr. 1991), pp. 385–416.
10. Ferson, Wayne E., Kandel, Shmuel, and Stambaugh, Robert F. "Tests of Asset Pricing with Time-Varying Expected Risk Premiums and Market Betas," *The Journal of Finance*, **42,** No. 2 (June 1987), pp. 201–220.
11. Green, Richard C. "Benchmark Portfolio Inefficiency and Deviations from the Security Market Line," *The Journal of Finance*, **41,** No. 2 (June 1986), pp. 295–312.
12. Hietala, Pekka T. "Asset Pricing in Partially Segmented Markets: Evidence from the Finnish Market," *The Journal of Finance*, **44,** No. 3 (July 1989), pp. 697–718.
13. Kroll, Yoram, and Levy, Haim. "Further Tests of the Separation Theorem and the Capital Asset Pricing Model," *The American Economic Review*, **82,** No. 3 (June 1992) pp. 664–670.
14. Kroll, Yoram, Levy, Haim, and Rapoport, Amnon. "Experimental Tests of the Separation Theorem and the Capita" *The American Economic Review*, **78,** No. 3 (June 1988), pp. 500–519.
15. Levy, Haim. "The Demand for Assets under Conditions of Risk," *Journal of Finance*, **XXVIII,** No. 1 (March 1973), pp. 79–96.
16. ——. "The Demand for Assets under Conditions of Risk: Reply to [1]," *Journal of Finance*, **XXXII,** No. 3 (June 1976), pp. 930–932.
17. Lintner, John. "Security Prices, Risk, and Maximal Gains from Diversification," *Journal of Finance* (Dec. 1965), pp. 587–615.
18. ——. "The Aggregation of Investor's Diverse Judgments and Preferences in Purely Competitive Security Markets," *Journal of Financial and Quantitative Analysis*, **IV,** No. 4 (Dec. 1969), pp. 347–400.
19. ——. "The Market Price of Risk, Size of Market and Investor's Risk Aversion," *Review of Economics and Statistics*, **LII,** No. 1 (Feb. 1970), pp. 87–99.
20. Markowitz, Harry M. "Nonnegative or not Nonnegative: A Question about CAPM's," *The Journal of Finance,* **38,** No. 2 (May 1983), pp. 283–296.
21. Modigliani, Franco, and Pogue, Jerry. "An Introduction to Risk and Return," *Financial Analysts Journal*, **30,** No. 2 (Mar./Apr. 1974), pp. 68–80.
22. ——. "An Introduction to Risk and Return: Part II," *Financial Analysts Journal*, **30,** No. 3 (May/June 1974), pp. 69–86.
23. Ng, Lilian. "Tests of the CAPM with Time-Varying Covariances: A Multivariate GARCH Approach," *The Journal of Finance*, **46,** No. 4 (Sept. 1991), pp. 1507–1521.
24. Ross, Stephen. "A Simple Approach to the Valuation of Risky Streams," *Journal of Business*, **51,** No. 3 (July 1978), pp. 453–475.
25. Rubinstein, Mark. "An Aggregation Theorem for Securities Markets," *Journal of Financial Economy*, **1,** No. 3 (Sept. 1974), pp. 225–244.
26. Rubinstein, Mark E. "A Mean-Variance Synthesis of Corporate Financial Theory," *Journal of Finance*, **XXXVIII,** No. 1 (March 1973), pp. 167–181.
27. Sharpe, W.F. "Capital Asset Prices: A Theory of Market Equilibrium Under Conditions of Risk," *Journal of Finance* (Sept. 1964), pp. 425–442.
28. ——. "Bonds Versus Stocks: Some Lessons from Capital Market Theory," *Financial Analysts Journal*, **29,** No. 6 (Nov./Dec. 1973), pp. 74–80.
29. ——. "Capital Asset Prices with and Without Negative Holdings," *The Journal of Finance*, **46,** No. 2 (June 1991), pp. 489–509.
30. Stapleton, C. Richard. "Portfolio Analysis, Stock Valuation and Capital Budgeting Decision Rules for Risky Projects," *Journal of Finance*, **XXVI,** No. 1 (Mar. 1971), pp. 95–117.

31. Tinic, Seha M., and West, Richard R. "Risk, Return, and Equilibrium: A Revisit" *The Journal of Political Economy*, **94,** No. 1 (Feb. 1986), pp. 126–147.

32. Tsiang, S.C. "Risk, Return and Portfolio Analysis: Comment on [4]," *Journal of Political Economy*, **81,** No. 3 (May/June 1973), pp. 748–752.

33. Turnbull, Stuart. "Market Value and Systematic Risk," *Journal of Finance*, **XXXII,** No. 4 (Sept. 1977), pp. 1125–1142.

14

Nonstandard Forms of Capital Asset Pricing Models

The CAPM model developed in the previous chapter would provide a complete description of the behavior of capital markets if each of the assumptions set forth held. The test of the CAPM model is how well it describes reality. But even before we examine these tests, it is useful to develop equilibrium models based on more realistic assumptions. Most of the assumptions underlying the CAPM violate conditions in the real world. This does not mean that we should disregard the CAPM model, for the differences from reality may be sufficiently unimportant that they do not materially affect the explanatory power of the model. On the other hand, the incorporation of alternative, more realistic assumptions into the model has several important benefits. While the CAPM may describe equilibrium returns on the macro level, it certainly is not descriptive of micro (individual investor) behavior. For example, most individuals and many institutions hold portfolios of risky assets that do not resemble the market portfolio. We might get better insight into investor behavior by examining models developed under alternative and more realistic assumptions. Another reason for examining other equilibrium models is that it allows us to formulate and test alternative explanations of equilibrium returns. The CAPM may work well; but do other models work better and explain discrepancies from the CAPM? Finally, and perhaps most important, because the CAPM assumes several real-world influences away, it does not provide us with a mechanism for studying the impact of those influences on capital market equilibrium or on individual decision making. Only by recognizing the presence of these influences can their impact be investigated. For example, if we assume personal taxes do not exist, there is no way the equilibrium model can be used to study the effects of taxes. By constructing a model that includes taxes, we can study the impact of taxes on individual investor behavior and on equilibrium returns in the capital market.

The effects of modifying most of the assumptions of the CAPM model have been examined in the economics and finance literature. We review much of this work in this chapter. We place special emphasis on two assumptions: the ability to lend and borrow infinite sums of money at the riskless rate and the absence of personal taxes. The reason we do so is not only because there are important influences, but also because they lead to the development of full-fledged general equilibrium models of a form that are amenable to testing.

In the remainder of this chapter we discuss general equilibrium models derived under more realistic assumptions about each of the following influences:

Short sales

Riskless lending and borrowing

Personal taxes

Nonmarketable assets

Heterogeneous expectations

Non-price-taking behavior

Multiperiod analysis

SHORT SALES DISALLOWED

One of the assumptions made in deriving the capital asset pricing model is that the investor can engage in unlimited short sales. Furthermore, short sales were defined in the broadest sense of the term in that the investor was allowed to sell any security (whether owned or not) and to use the proceeds to buy any other security.[1] This was a convenient assumption and it simplified the mathematics of the derivation, but it was *not* a necessary assumption. Exactly the same result would have been obtained had short sales been disallowed. The economic intuition behind this is quite simple.[2] In the CAPM framework all investors hold the market portfolio in equilibrium. Since in equilibrium no investor sells any security short, prohibiting short selling cannot change the equilibrium.[3] Thus, the same CAPM relationship would be derived irrespective of whether short sales are allowed or prohibited.

MODIFICATIONS OF RISKLESS LENDING AND BORROWING

A second assumption of the CAPM is that investors can lend and borrow unlimited sums of money at the riskless rate of interest. Such an assumption is clearly not descriptive of the real world. It seems much more realistic to assume that investors can lend unlimited sums of money at the riskless rate but cannot borrow at a riskless rate. The lending assumption is equivalent to investors being able to buy government securities equal in maturity to their single-period horizon. Such securities exist and they are, for all intents and purposes, riskless. Furthermore, the rate on such securities is virtually the same for all investors. On the other hand, it is not possible for investors to borrow unlimited amounts at a riskless rate. It is convenient to examine the case where investors can neither borrow nor lend at the riskless rate first, and then to extend the analysis to the case where they can lend but not borrow at the riskless rate.

No Riskless Lending or Borrowing

This model is the second most widely used general equilibrium model. The simple capital asset pricing model developed in the last chapter is the most widely used. Because of the importance of this model, we derive it twice. The first derivation stresses economic rationale, the second is more rigorous.

---

[1]The allowance of short sales was reflected in the constraint on our basic problem in Chapter 6 that $\Sigma X_i = 1$ while simultaneously not constraining X_i to be positive.

[2]For a formal proof, see Lintner [80].

[3]The more mathematically inclined reader can reach this same conclusion by using the Kuhn–Tucker conditions on the basic problem outlined in the previous chapter. The derivative of the Lagrangian with respect to each security will have a Kuhn–Tucker multiplier added to it; but since each security is contained in the market portfolio, the value of each Kuhn–Tucker multiplier will be zero. Hence, the solution will be unchanged.

Simple Proof   In the last chapter we argued that systematic risk was the appropriate measure of risk and that two assets with the same systematic risk could not offer different rates of return. The essence of the argument was that the unsystematic risk of large diversified portfolios was essentially zero. Thus, even if an individual asset had a great deal of unsystematic risk, it would have little impact on portfolio risk and, therefore, unsystematic risk would not require a higher return. This was formalized in Figure 13.3, and an analogous diagram, Figure 14.1, will be used here.

Let us recall why all assets are plotted on a straight line. First, we showed that combinations of two risky portfolios lie on a straight line connecting them in expected return Beta space. For example, positive combinations of portfolios A and D lie on the line segment A–D. Thus, if securities or portfolios happened to lie on a straight line in expected return Beta space, all combinations of securities (e.g., portfolios) would lie on the same line.

Now consider securities C and D in Figure 14.1. They both have the same systematic risk, but C has a higher return. Clearly, an investor would purchase C rather than D until the prices adjusted so that they offered the same return. In fact, an investor could purchase C and sell D short and have an asset with positive expected return and no systematic risk. Such an opportunity cannot exist in equilibrium. In short, all portfolios and securities must plot along a straight line.

One portfolio that lies along the straight line is the market portfolio. This can be seen in either of two ways. If it did not lie along the straight line, two assets would exist with the same systematic risk and different return, and in equilibrium, equivalent assets must offer the same return. In addition, note that all combinations of securities lie on the line and the market portfolio is a weighted average of the securities.

A straight line can be described by any two points. One convenient point is the market portfolio. A second convenient portfolio is where the straight line cuts the vertical axis (where Beta equals zero).[4]

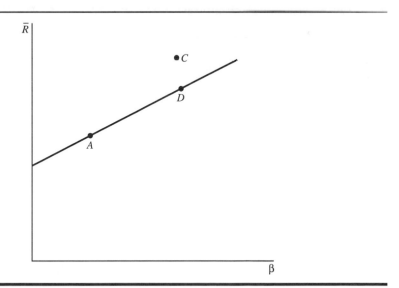

Figure 14.1   Portfolios in expected return Beta space.

---

[4]To see that such a point exists, note that the straight line must go indefinitely in both directions. All positive combinations of A and D lie on the line segment between A and D. However, if we purchase D and sell A short, we move above D, and vice versa. Thus, the line continues indefinitely and, in particular, cuts the vertical axis.

The equation of a straight line is

$$\text{Expected return} = a + b(\text{Beta})$$

This must hold for a portfolio with zero Beta. Letting $\bar{R}_Z$ be the expected return on this portfolio, we have

$$\bar{R}_Z = a + b(0) \qquad \text{or} \qquad a = \bar{R}_Z$$

The equation must also hold for the market portfolio. If $\bar{R}_M$ is the expected return on the market and, recalling that the Beta for the market portfolio is one, we have

$$\bar{R}_M = \bar{R}_Z + b(1) \qquad \text{or} \qquad b = \bar{R}_M - \bar{R}_Z$$

Putting this together and letting $\bar{R}_i$ and β_i be the expected return and Beta on an asset or portfolio, the equation for the expected return on any security or portfolio becomes

$$\bar{R}_i = \bar{R}_Z + \left(\bar{R}_M - \bar{R}_Z\right)\beta_i \qquad\qquad (14.1)$$

This is the so-called zero Beta version of the capital asset pricing model and is plotted in Figure 14.2. This form of the general equilibrium relationship is often referred to alternatively as a two-factor model.

Rigorous Derivation   Assume for the moment that the market portfolio lies on the efficient frontier in expected return standard deviation space. Later in this chapter we show that it must, indeed, do so. In Chapter 6 we showed that the entire efficient frontier can be traced out by allowing the riskless rate of interest to vary and finding the tangency point between the efficient frontier and a ray passing through the riskless rate (on the vertical axis). Corresponding to every "risk-free rate" there was one point on the efficient frontier, and vice versa. There is, of course, one unique riskless rate in the market (if any). Thus, the procedure of varying the riskless rate was simply a method of obtaining the full efficient frontier. In all cases but one what we called the riskless rate was an artificial construct we used to obtain one point on the efficient frontier. Define R'_F as the riskless rate such that

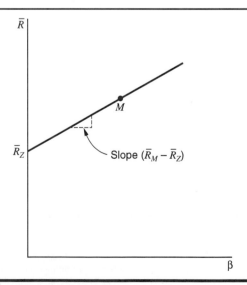

Figure 14.2   The zero Beta capital asset pricing line.

if investors could lend and borrow unlimited amounts of funds at the rate R'_F, they would hold the market portfolio.

The investor who could lend and borrow at the riskless rate R'_F would face an investment opportunity set as depicted in Figure 14.3. To solve for optimal proportions, he or she would face a set of simultaneous equations directly analogous to Equation (13.4). One such equation is[5]

$$\lambda\left(X_1\sigma_{1j} + X_2\sigma_{2j} + \cdots + X_j\sigma_j^2 + \cdots + X_N\sigma_{Nj}\right) = \overline{R}_j - R'_F \tag{14.2}$$

Note that in the equation the X_i's are market proportions because R'_F is defined as that value of the riskless rate that causes investors to hold the market portfolio.

In the previous chapter we showed that the term in parentheses in the left-hand side of Equation (14.2) was simply the covariance between the return on security j and the return on the market portfolio. Thus, Equation (14.2) can be written as

$$\lambda \operatorname{cov}\left(R_j R_M\right) = \overline{R}_j - R'_F$$

or

$$\overline{R}_j = R'_F + \lambda \operatorname{cov}\left(R_j R_M\right) \tag{14.3}$$

The expected return on the market portfolio is a weighted average of the expected return on individual securities. Since Equation (14.3) holds for each security, it must also hold for the market. Thus,

$$\overline{R}_M = R'_F + \lambda \operatorname{cov}\left(R_M R_M\right)$$

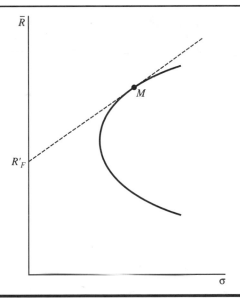

Figure 14.3   The opportunity set with rate R_F.

---

[5]These equations are first-order conditions and must hold for the tangency point of any line drawn from the vertical axis and the efficient frontier.

But $\text{cov}(R_M R_M)$ is the variance of M so that

$$\overline{R}_M = R'_F + \lambda \sigma_M^2 \qquad \text{or} \qquad \lambda = \frac{\overline{R}_M - R'_F}{\sigma_M^2}$$

Substituting the expression for λ into Equation (14.3) and rearranging yields

$$\overline{R}_j = R'_F + \frac{\overline{R}_M - R'_F}{\sigma_M^2} \text{cov}\left(R_j R_M\right)$$

or

$$\overline{R}_j = R'_F + \beta_j\left(\overline{R}_M - R'_F\right) \tag{14.4}$$

Note that a riskless asset with a return of R'_F does not really exist. However, there are an infinite number of assets and portfolios giving a return of R'_F. They are located along the solid portion of the line segment $R'_F - C$ shown in Figure 14.4. Examine Equation (14.4). For R_j to be equal to R'_F the last term must be zero. Thus, any security or portfolio that has an expected return of R'_F must have a Beta (covariance with the market portfolio) equal to zero.

While equilibrium can be expressed in terms of any of the zero Beta portfolios on the solid portion of the line segment $R'_F - C$, it makes sense to utilize the least risky zero Beta portfolio. This is equivalent to the zero Beta portfolio that has the least total risk. We designate the minimum variance zero Beta portfolio as Z and its expected return as $\overline{R}_Z$.

Then, since $\overline{R}_Z = R'_F$, the security market line can be written as

$$\overline{R}_j = \overline{R}_Z + \left(\overline{R}_M - \overline{R}_Z\right)\beta_j$$

This is exactly the expression [Equation (14.1)] we found for the security market line earlier in this chapter.

Let us see if we can learn anything about the location of this minimum variance zero Beta portfolio. First, we know that the expected return on the zero Beta portfolio must be lower than the expected return on the market portfolio. The market portfolio is on the

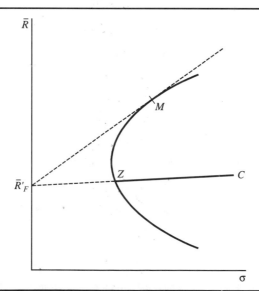

Figure 14.4   The location of portfolios with return R'_F.

efficient segment of the minimum variance frontier, and the slope at this point must be positive. Thus, as we move along the line tangent to $\bar{R}_M$ toward the vertical axis, we lower return. Since $\bar{R}_Z$ is the intercept of the tangency line and the vertical axis, it has a return less than $\bar{R}_M$. Second, as we prove below, the minimum variance zero Beta portfolio cannot be efficient.

Proof Denote by s the portfolio that has the smallest possible variance. This portfolio can be formed as a combination of the market portfolio and the zero Beta portfolio.

$$\sigma_s^2 = X_Z^2 \sigma_Z^2 + \left(1 - X_Z\right)^2 \sigma_M^2$$

There is no covariance term since the covariance between these two assets is zero. To find the weights in each portfolio that minimize variance, take the derivative with respect to X_Z and set it equal to zero, or

$$\frac{d\sigma_s^2}{dX_Z} = 2X_Z\sigma_Z^2 - 2\sigma_M^2 + 2X_Z\sigma_M^2 = 0$$

Solving for X_Z

$$X_Z = \frac{\sigma_M^2}{\sigma_M^2 + \sigma_Z^2}$$

Since both σ_M^2 and σ_Z^2 must be positive numbers, that portfolio with the smallest possible variance must involve positive weights on both the zero Beta and market portfolio. Since $\bar{R}_Z < \bar{R}_M$, portfolios of Z and M with positive weights must have higher expected returns than Z. Since *the* minimum variance portfolio has higher return and smaller variance than Z, Z cannot be on the efficient portion of the minimum variance frontier.

We can locate portfolios Z, M, and s on the minimum variance frontier of all portfolios in expected return standard deviation space.[6] This is done in Figure 14.5. This figure presents the location of all efficient portfolios in expected return standard deviation space. All investors will hold some portfolio that lies along the efficient frontier (*SMC*). Investors who hold portfolios offering returns between s and $\bar{R}_M$ will hold combinations of the zero Beta portfolio and the market portfolio.[7] Investors who choose to hold portfolios to the right of M (choose returns above $\bar{R}_M$) will hold a portfolio constructed by selling portfolio Z short and buying the market portfolio. No investor will choose to hold only portfolio Z for this is an inefficient portfolio. Furthermore, since investors in the aggregate hold the market portfolio, the aggregate holding of portfolio Z (long positions minus short positions) must be exactly zero. Note also that we still have a two mutual fund theorem. All investors can be satisfied by transactions in two mutual funds: the market portfolio and the minimum variance zero Beta portfolio.

We started out this section by assuming that the market portfolio is efficient. While we do not intend to provide a rigorous proof of its efficiency, a few comments should convince the reader of its truth. Those interested in a rigorous proof are referred to Fama [29].

With homogeneous expectations, all investors face the same efficient frontier. Recall that with short sales allowed all combinations of any two minimum variance portfolios are

---

[6]The minimum variance curve or minimum variance frontier contains the set of portfolios that offers the lowest risk at any obtainable level of return. The efficient set (frontier) is a subset of these minimum variance portfolios.

[7]Recall from Chapter 6 that the entire efficient frontier can be generated as portfolios of any two portfolios on the efficient frontier.

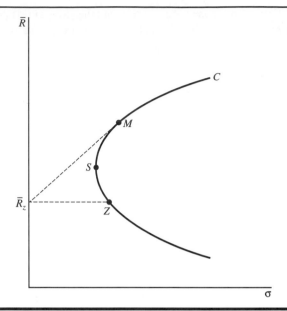

Figure 14.5   The minimum variance frontier.

minimum variance. Thus, if we combine any two investors' portfolios, we have a minimum variance portfolio. The market portfolio is a weighted average or portfolio of each investor's portfolio where the weights are the proportion each investor owns of the total of all risky assets. Thus, it is minimum variance. Since each investor's portfolio is efficient and since the return on the market is an average of the return on the portfolios of individual investors, the return on the market portfolio is the return of a portfolio on the efficient segment of the minimum variance frontier. Thus, the market portfolio is not only minimum variance but efficient.

Riskless Lending But No Riskless Borrowing

We have gone too far in changing our assumptions. As we agreed earlier, while it is unrealistic to assume that individuals can borrow at the riskless rate, it is realistic to assume that they can lend at a rate that is riskless. Individuals can place funds in government securities that have a maturity equal to their time horizon and, thus, be guaranteed of a riskless payoff at the horizon.

If we allow riskless lending, then the investor's choice can be pictured as in Figure 14.6.[8] As we argued in earlier chapters, all combinations of a riskless asset and a risky portfolio lie on the straight line connecting the asset and the portfolio. The preferred combination lies on the straight line passing through the risk-free asset and tangent to the efficient frontier. This is the line $R_F T$ in Figure 14.6.

Notice that we have drawn T below and to the left of the market portfolio M and, hence, $\bar{R}_Z > R_F$. This was not an accident. Let us examine why this must hold. Before we introduced the ability to lend at the riskless rate, all investors held portfolios along the efficient frontier SMC (portfolios along the line $\bar{R}_Z M$ do not exist). With riskless lending the investor can hold portfolios of riskless and risky assets along the line $R_F T$. If the investor chooses to hold an investment on the line $R_F T$, he would be placing some of his funds in

---

[8]Once again we are assuming short sales are allowed. This is a necessary assumption.

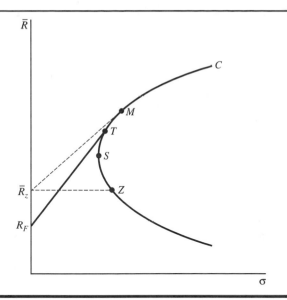

Figure 14.6   The opportunity set with riskless lending.

the portfolio of risky assets denoted by T and some in the riskless asset. The choice to hold any portfolio of risky assets other than T would never be made. Now, why can't T and M be the same portfolio? As long as any investor has a risk-return trade-off such that he or she chooses to hold a portfolio of investments to the right of T, the market must lie to the right of T. For example, assume that all investors but one choose to lend money and hold portfolio T. Now this one investor who does not choose T must hold a portfolio to the right of T on the efficient frontier STC. If the investor did not, then he or she would be better off holding a portfolio on the line $R_F T$ and, hence, holding portfolio T. Since the market portfolio is an average of the portfolios held by all investors, the market portfolio must be a combination of the investor's portfolio and T. Thus, it lies to the right of T. M, being to the right of T, leads directly to $\bar{R}_Z$ being larger than R_F. R_F is the intersection of the vertical axis and a line tangent to the efficient frontier at T. Similarly, $\bar{R}_Z$ is the intersection of the vertical axis and a line tangent at M. Since the slope of the efficient frontier at M is less than at T and since M lies above T, the line tangent at M must intersect the vertical axis above the line tangent at T.[9] Thus, $\bar{R}_Z$ must be greater than R_F.

The efficient frontier is given by the straight line segment $R_F T$ and curve TMC.[10] Notice that, in the case of no lending and borrowing, combinations of all efficient portfolios were efficient. In the case where riskless lending is allowed, not all combinations of efficient portfolios are efficient. It should be obvious to the reader that combinations of a portfolio from the line segment $R_F T$ and a portfolio from the curve TMC are dominated by a portfolio lying along the curve TMC.

Portfolio T can be obtained by combining portfolios Z and M. Examining the efficient frontier we see that investors who select a portfolio along the line segment $R_F T$ are placing some of their money in portfolio T (which is constructed from the market portfolio plus

---

[9]The property of the two slopes follows directly from the concavity of the efficient frontier proved in Chapter 5.

[10]The reader might note that portfolio T is a corner portfolio, a portfolio whose composition is different from those immediately adjacent to it. All portfolios to the right of T on the efficient frontier are made up of combinations of portfolios M and Z while those to the left of T are made up of portfolios M and Z plus the riskless security.

portfolio Z) and some in the riskless asset. (Those that select a portfolio on the segment TM are placing some of their money in portfolio M and some in Z.) Those that select a portfolio on MC are selling portfolio Z short and investing all of the proceeds in M. (Notice that our two mutual fund theorem has been replaced with a three mutual fund theorem.) All investors can be satisfied by holding (long or short) some combination of the market portfolio, the minimum variance zero Beta portfolio, and the riskless asset.[11]

Having examined all efficient portfolios in expected return standard deviation space, let us turn our attention to the location of securities and portfolios in expected return Beta space. Let us develop the security market line.

The market portfolio M is still an efficient portfolio. Thus, the analysis of the last section holds. All securities contained in M have an expected return given by

$$\bar{R}_j = \bar{R}_Z + \beta_j\left(\bar{R}_M - \bar{R}_Z\right) \tag{14.5}$$

Similarly, all portfolios composed solely of risky assets have their return given by Equation (14.5). This splits as a straight line in expected return Beta space and is the line $\bar{R}_Z TMC$ in Figure 14.7. This equation holds only for risky assets and for portfolios of risky assets. It does not describe the return on the riskless asset or the return on portfolios that contain the riskless asset.

In the previous chapter we examined combinations of the riskless asset and a risky portfolio and found that they lie on the straight line connecting the two points in expected return Beta space. Since investors who lend all hold risky portfolio T, the relevant line segment is $R_F T$ in Figure 14.7.

Thus, while the straight line $\bar{R}_Z M$ can be thought of as the security market line for all risky assets and for all portfolios composed entirely of risk assets, it does not describe the return on portfolios (and, of particular note, on those efficient portfolios) that contain the

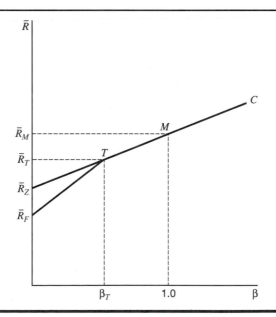

Figure 14.7   The location of investments in expected return Beta space.

---

[11]Note that while we continually speak of using the market portfolio and the minimum variance zero Beta portfolio to obtain the efficient frontier, any other two minimum variance portfolios would serve equally well.

riskless asset. Efficient portfolios have their return given by the two line segments R_FT and
TC in Figure 14.7. The fact that efficient portfolios have lower return for a given level of
Beta than individual assets may seem startling. But remember that securities or portfolios
on $\bar{R}_ZT$ have a higher standard deviation than portfolios with the same return on segment
R_FT. (In order to understand this, remember that the return on portfolio Z is uncertain, even
though it has a zero Beta, while the return on the riskless asset is certain.)

Before moving on to other models, it is well worth reviewing certain characteristics of
those we have been discussing, particularly insofar as they resemble or are different from
the characteristics of the simple capital asset pricing model.

First, note that, under either of these models, all investors no longer hold the same portfolio in equilibrium. This is comforting for it is more consistent with observed behavior.
Of less comfort is that investors still hold most securities (either long or short) and hold
many securities short. In the case where neither lending nor borrowing is allowed, we have
a two mutual fund theorem. In the case where riskless lending is allowed, we have a three
mutual fund theorem.

As in the case of the simple CAPM, we still get a security market line. In addition, many
of the implications of this relationship are the same. For risky assets or portfolios expected
return is still a linearly increasing function of risk as measured by Beta. It is only market
risk that affects the return on individual risky securities and portfolios of risky securities.
On these securities the investor gains no extra return from bearing diversifiable risk. In
fact, the only difference lies in the intercept and slope of the security market line.[12]

Other Lending and Borrowing Assumptions

Brennan [10] has analyzed the situation where riskless lending and borrowing is available,
but at different rates. The efficient frontier for the individual when riskless borrowing and
lending at different rates is possible was analyzed in Chapter 5. If all investors face the
same efficient frontier, this efficient frontier must appear as in Figure 14.8.

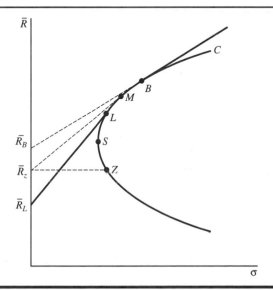

Figure 14.8   The opportunity set with a differential lending and borrowing rate.

[12]In all models the efficient frontier itself is affected by diversifiable risk. Since the shape of the frontier affects
the location of the tangency portfolio, diversifiable risk has some effect on security returns.

In this diagram L stands for the portfolio of risky securities that will be held by all investors who lend money and B stands for the portfolio of all securities that will be held by investors who borrow money. The market portfolio must lie on the efficient frontier and it must lie between L and B.

Let us examine why. The only portfolios of risky securities held by investors are L and B and intermediate portfolios on the curve LB. Earlier we showed that combinations of efficient portfolios were efficient. In the earlier section lending and borrowing was not allowed so that the proof was that combinations of portfolios on the efficient portion of the minimum variance frontier were also on the efficient portion. The market portfolio is a weighted average of all portfolios held by individuals. Since these are efficient, we know from the earlier discussion that the market portfolio lies on the efficient portion of the minimum variance curve. But we can be even more precise. The return on the market portfolio is a weighted average of the return of portfolio L, portfolio B, and all intermediate portfolios. Thus, its return must be between L and B. Therefore, the market portfolio must lie somewhere on the efficient frontier between L and B. Having established that the market portfolio lies on the efficient frontier between L and B, we derive, in the same manner, the same security market line as we derived in the last section of this chapter. Equation (14.1) still holds. However, remember that this equation only describes the return on securities and portfolios that do not have any investment in the riskless asset (long or short). Thus, the equation will not describe the return on portfolios along the straight line between $\bar{R}_L$ and L or with return more than R_B.

Brennan [10] has also examined the case where the borrowing rate differed from the lending rate and where these rates were different for each investor. Once again, because the market portfolio lies on the efficient frontier, an equation identical in form to Equation (14.1) describes the return on all risky assets and on all portfolios composed entirely of risky assets.

PERSONAL TAXES

The simple form of the capital asset pricing model ignores the presence of taxes in arriving at an equilibrium solution. The implication of this assumption is that investors are indifferent between receiving income in the form of capital gains or dividends and that all investors hold the same portfolio of risky assets. If we recognize the existence of taxes and, in particular, the fact that capital gains are taxed, in general, at a lower rate than dividends, the equilibrium prices should change. Investors should judge the return and risk on their portfolio after taxes. This implies that, even with homogeneous expectations about the before-tax return on a portfolio, the relevant (after-tax) efficient frontier faced by each investor will be different. However, a general equilibrium relationship should still exist since, in the aggregate, markets must clear. In the appendix at the end of this chapter we derive the general equilibrium pricing equation for all assets and portfolios, given differential taxes on income and capital gains. The return on any asset or portfolio is given by

$$E(R_i) = R_F + \beta_i\left[\left(E(R_M) - R_F\right) - \tau\left(\delta_M - R_F\right)\right] + \tau\left(\delta_i - R_F\right) \tag{14.6}$$

where

δ_M = the dividend yield (dividends divided by price) of the market portfolio

δ_i = the dividend yield for stock i

τ = a tax factor that measures the relevant market tax rates on capital gains and income. τ is a complex function of investors' tax rates and wealth. However, it should be a positive number. See the appendix for further discussion.

The equilibrium relationship for expected returns has now become very complex. When dividends are on average taxed at a higher rate than capital gains (as they are in the U.S. economy), τ is positive and expected return is an increasing function of dividend yield. This is intuitively appealing since the larger the fraction of return paid in the form of dividends the more taxes the investor will have to pay and the larger the pretax return required. The reader may wonder why the last term contains R_F as well as the dividend yield. The reason for this is the tax treatment of interest on lending and borrowing. Since interest payments are for all intents and purposes taxed at the same rate as dividends, they enter the relationship in a parallel manner although with an opposite sign.[13] The fact that the term in square brackets has the correct form can be seen by letting security i be the market portfolio and noting that (since Beta equals one for the market portfolio) the equation reduces to $E(R_M) = E(R_M)$.

Examination of Equation (14.6) reveals that a security market line is no longer sufficient to describe the equilibrium relationship. In previous versions of general equilibrium relationships the only variable associated with the individual security that affected expected return was its Beta. Now we see from Equation (14.6) that both the securities Beta and its dividend yield affect expected return. This means that equilibrium must be described in three-dimensional spaces (R_i, β_i, δ_i) rather than two-dimensional space. The resultant equilibrium relationship [Equation (14.6)] will be a plane rather than a straight line. The plane will be located such that for any value of Beta expected return goes up as dividend yield goes up, and for any value of dividend yield expected return goes up as Beta goes up. We will have more to say about the location of the plane (the parametrization of this equation) in the next chapter.

If returns are determined by an equilibrium model like that presented in Equation (14.6), it should be possible to derive optimal portfolios for any investor as a function of the tax rates paid on capital gains and dividends. While the mathematics of the solution are rather complex, the economic intuition behind the results is strong.[14] All investors will hold widely diversified portfolios that resemble the market portfolio, except they will be tilted in favor of those stocks in which the investor has a competitive advantage. For example, investors whose tax bracket is below the average effective rate in the market should hold more of high-dividend stocks in their portfolio than the percentage these stocks constitute of the market portfolio, while they should hold less (and in extreme cases even short sell) stocks with very low dividends. Low-tax-bracket investors have a comparative advantage in holding high-dividend stocks for the tax disadvantage of these stocks is less disadvantageous to them than it is to the average stockholder. Individual investors in the market seem to behave as the analysis suggests they should.[15] The optimization rules described in Elton and Gruber [27] ensure that markets will clear at the returns established in Equation (14.6).

NONMARKETABLE ASSETS

Up to now we have assumed that all assets are readily marketable so that each investor was free to adjust his or her portfolio to an optimum. In truth, every investor has nonmarketable

---

[13]The implications of this for investor behavior are interesting. For example, an investor could convert a dividend-paying stock into one with only a capital gains return by borrowing a sum of money such that when the sum borrowed plus the initial planned investment in a stock is invested in the stock, interest payments exactly equal the dividend payments on the stock.

[14]See Elton and Gruber [27] for the derivation of the composition of optimal portfolios under taxation.

[15]Pettit and Stanley [93] have found that investors tend to behave as this model suggests they should behave.

assets or assets that he or she will not consider marketing. Human capital is an example of a nonmarketable asset. People are forbidden by law from selling themselves into slavery in the United States. There is no direct way that an investor can market his or her claims to future labor income. Similarly, the investor has other future monetary claims such as social security payments or the future payments from a private retirement program that cannot be marketed. There are categories of marketable assets that, although the investor might be able to market them, he or she considers them a fixed part of the portfolio. For example, investors who own their own home can market it, but they will often not consider switching houses as part of changes in their "optimum investment portfolio." This is due, in part, to large transaction costs but also because of nonmonetary factors.

If we divide the world up into marketable and nonmarketable assets, then a simple equation exists for the equilibrium return on all assets. Let

R_H equal the one period rate of return on nonmarketable assets

P_H equal the total value of all nonmarketable assets

P_M equal the total value of all marketable assets

All other terms are defined as before. Then, it can be shown that[16]

$$E(R_j) = R_F + \frac{E(R_M) - R_F}{\sigma_M^2 + P_H/P_M \, \text{cov}(R_M R_H)} \left[\text{cov}(R_j R_M) + \frac{P_H}{P_M} \text{cov}(R_j R_H) \right]$$

To contrast this with the simple capital asset pricing model we can write the simple model as

$$E(R_j) = R_F + \frac{E(R_M) - R_F}{\sigma_M^2} \left[\text{cov}(R_j R_M) \right]$$

Notice that the inclusion of nonmarketable assets leads to a general equilibrium relationship of the same form as the simple model that excluded nonmarketable assets. However, the market trade-off between return and risk is different, as is the measure of risk for any asset. Including nonmarketable assets, the market risk-return trade-off becomes

$$\frac{E(R_M) - R_F}{\sigma_M^2 + \frac{P_H}{P_M} \text{cov}(R_M R_H)}$$

rather than

$$\frac{E(R_M) - R_F}{\sigma_M^2}$$

It seems reasonable to assume that the return on the total of nonmarketable assets is positively correlated with the return on the market, which would suggest that the market return-risk trade-off is lower than that suggested by the simple form of the model. How much lower is a function of both the covariance between the return on the nonmarketable assets and the marketable assets and the total value of nonmarketable assets relative to

---

[16]For a derivation see Mayers. Although this equation does not appear in Mayers [85], it can be derived from his Equation (19) with a little algebra. The reader may be bothered by the fact that P_H appears in our equation while the Mayers' equations make use of the income (actually income plus value) of the asset one period hence. However, there is no inconsistency as Mayers' Equation (15) allows for the determination of P_H.

marketable assets. If nonmarketable assets had a very small value relative to marketable assets or if there was an extremely low correlation between the return on marketable and nonmarketable assets, there would be little harm done in using the standard CAPM. However, it seems likely that, since nonmarketable assets include at a minimum human capital and since wage rates as well as market performance are correlated with the performance of the economy, there will be important differences between these models.

In addition, the definition of the risk of any asset has been changed. With nonmarketable assets it is a function of the covariance of an asset with the total stock of nonmarketable assets, as well as with the total stock of marketable assets. The weight this additional term receives in determining risk depends on the total size of nonmarketable assets relative to marketable assets. The risk on any asset that is positively correlated with the total of nonmarketable assets will be higher than the risk implied by the simple form of the CAPM.

Considering the difference in both the reward-risk ratio and the size of risk itself, we can see that the equilibrium return for an asset can be either higher or lower than it is under the standard form of the CAPM. If the asset is negatively correlated with the total of nonmarketable assets, its equilibrium return will be lower for its risk and the price of risk will be lower. However, if its return is positively correlated with the return on marketable assets, its equilibrium return could be higher or lower, depending on whether the increased risk is high enough to offset the decreased market price of risk.

Mayers [85] explores the implications of his model for the optimal portfolio holdings of individuals. As you would suspect, investors tilt their portfolio, holding a smaller percentage of those stocks (than found in the market) with which their nonmarketable securities are most highly correlated.

Brito [12, 13] has examined, in more detail, the optimum portfolio holdings of individuals in equilibrium when nonmarketable assets are present. He finds that each individual can select an optimal portfolio from among three mutual funds. The first mutual fund is a portfolio that has a covariance with each marketable asset equal in magnitude but opposite in sign to the covariance between the investor's nonmarketable portfolio and each marketable asset. Note two things about this fund: First, it will have a different composition for different investors, according to the nonmarketable assets they hold. Second, the reason for its optimality has an intuitive explanation. It is that portfolio that diversifies away as much of the nonmarketable risk as it is possible to diversify away. In short, it allows the investor to "market" as much of his or her nonmarketable assets as is possible. Brito then shows that each individual will allocate the remainder of his or her wealth between the riskless security (the second fund) and a third fund that is the market portfolio minus the *aggregate* of all investments made in the first type of fund by all investors. Note that, while the second and third funds are the same for all investors, the first fund has a different composition for each investor, according to the composition of his or her nonmarketable assets.

While Mayers' analysis is important for the insight it provides into the pricing of nonmarketable assets, it is at least as important for the insight it gives us into the missing asset problem. Empirical tests of general equilibrium models will always have to be conducted with the market defined as including something less than the full set of assets in the economy. The equilibrium equations described previously are perfectly valid for examining the missing asset problem, where R_M is now defined as the return on the collection of assets selected to represent the market and R_H is the return on the assets that were left out. In a manner exactly parallel to that presented, they allow us to think through the influence of missing assets on both the markets risk-return trade-off and the equilibrium return from missing assets.

HETEROGENEOUS EXPECTATIONS

Several researchers have examined the existence and characteristics of a general equilibrium solution when investors have heterogeneous expectations.[17] Although all of these models lead to forms of an equilibrium pricing equation that have some similarity to those presented earlier in this chapter and in the last chapter, there are important differences. Equilibrium can still be expressed in terms of expected returns, covariances, and variance, but now these returns, covariances, and variances are complex weighted averages of the estimates held by different individuals. The weightings are very complex because they involve information about investor utility functions. In particular, they involve information about investors' trade-offs (marginal rate of substitution) between expected return and variance. But this trade-off for most utility functions is a function of wealth and, hence, prices. This means that prices are required to determine the risk-return trade-offs that we need to determine prices. Thus, in general, an explicit solution to the heterogeneous expectation problem cannot be reached. The problem can be made simpler by placing additional restrictions either on investor utility functions or on the characteristics of opportunities facing the investor.

The first approach was taken by Lintner [79]. He could not derive a simple capital asset pricing model under heterogeneous expectations because the marginal rate of substitution between expected return and variances was, itself, a function of equilibrium prices. If we assume a utility function such that the marginal rate of substitution is not a function of wealth, then we will not face this problem. We have already studied such a class of utility functions in Chapter 10. They were the functions exhibiting constant absolute risk aversion. Lintner assumed this type of function (to be precise, he assumed a negative exponential utility function).[18] Utilizing this function, he showed that the Sharpe–Lintner–Mossin form of the CAPM model holds and that the term $(\bar{R}_M - R_F)/\sigma_M^2$ in Equation (13.2) is proportional to the harmonic mean of the risk-avoidance coefficient, and all expected values, variances, and covariances are complicated averages of the probability beliefs and risk preferences of all individuals.

A second way to arrive at more testable models of equilibrium under heterogeneous assumptions is to place restrictions on the form that the heterogeneity can assume. Gonedes [41] assumes that a set of basic economic activities exist such that any firm can be viewed as some combination of these basic economic activities and the heterogeneous expectations arise because of disagreement about the exact combination (weighting) of those basic economic activities that represent a firm. Gonedes analyzes the case where this is the one source of heterogeneous expectations. He shows that, under this assumption, the minimum variance frontier is the same for all investors, even though they have heterogeneous expectations about the returns from different securities. Furthermore, the market portfolio is a minimum variance portfolio for each and every investor. Gonedes then proceeds to show that Beta is a sufficient measure of risk and that the equilibrium models lead to a linear relationship between expected return and Beta parallel to that found under simpler forms of the CAPM.

NON-PRICE-TAKING BEHAVIOR

Up to now we have assumed that individuals act as price takers in that they ignore the impact of their buying or selling behavior on the equilibrium price of securities and, hence, on their

---

[17]See Lintner [79], Sharpe [118], Fama [32], and Gonedes [41].

[18]Lintner assumes the negative exponential utility function given by $u(w) = e^{-a_i W_i}$. The measure of risk aversion is given by a_i.

optimal portfolio holdings. The obvious question to ask is what happens if there are one or more investors, such as mutual funds or large pension funds, who believe that their behavior impacts price. The method of analysis used by Lindenberg [77, 78] derives equilibrium conditions under all possible demands by the price affector. The price affector selects her portfolio to maximize utility given the equilibrium prices that will result from her action. Assuming that the price affector operates so as to maximize utility, we can then arrive at equilibrium conditions. Lindenberg finds that all investors, including the price taker, hold some combination of the market portfolio and the riskless asset. However, the price affector will hold less of the riskless asset (will be less of a risk avoider) than would be the case if the price affector did not recognize the fact that her actions affected price. By doing so the price affector increases utility. Because the price affector still holds a combination of the riskless asset and the market portfolio, we still get the simple form of the CAPM, but the market price of risk is lower than it would be if all investors were price takers.

Lindenberg [77] goes on to analyze collective portfolio selection and efficient allocation among groups of investors. He finds that by colluding or merging, individuals or institutions can increase their utility. This analysis provides us with one reason for the existence of large financial institutions.

MULTIPERIOD CAPM

Up to now we have assumed that all investors make investment decisions based on a single-period horizon. In fact, the portfolio an investor selects, at any point in time, is really one step in a series of portfolios that he intends to hold over time to maximize his utility of lifetime consumption. Two questions immediately become apparent:

1. What are the conditions under which the simple CAPM adequately describes market equilibrium?

2. Is there a fully general multiperiod equilibrium model?

Fama [29] and Elton and Gruber [25, 26] have explored the conditions under which the multiperiod investment consumption decision can be reduced to the problem of maximizing a one-period utility function. These conditions are

1. The consumer's tastes for particular consumption goods and services are independent of future events (any future sets of conditions).

2. The consumer acts as if consumption opportunities in terms of goods and their prices are known at the beginning of the decision period (are not state dependent.)[19]

3. The consumer acts as if the distribution of one-period returns on all assets are known at the beginning of the decision period (are not state dependent).

Furthermore, Fama [29] has shown that if the investor's multiperiod utility function, expressed in terms of multiperiod consumption, exhibits both a preference of more to less and risk aversion with respect to each period's consumption, then the derived one-period utility has the same properties with respect to that period's consumption.

Recall earlier that risk aversion and preferring more to less were two assumptions necessary to obtain an efficient frontier. If we make the additional assumptions of the standard CAPM, we obtain the standard CAPM even for investors with a multiperiod horizon. If we make the additional assumptions underlying the zero Beta version of the CAPM, the zero

---

[19]A process is not state dependent if its outcomes do not depend on which one of a set of events occurs.

Beta model is appropriate for investors with a multiperiod horizon. In short, the Fama multiperiod assumptions make single-period capital asset pricing models appropriate for investors with multiperiod horizons. The particular single-period model that results depends on the additional assumptions that are being made.

It is comforting to know that there are conditions under which the standard CAPM is appropriate when investors treat the portfolio selection problem in a multiperiod framework. However, we would expect that future utilities, returns, and prices are state dependent. For an excellent treatment of multiperiod equilibrium, under some general assumptions, the reader is referred to Stapleton and Subrahmanyam [120]. The reader should be warned that the mathematics involved are beyond any attempted in this book.

There are three cases of a multiperiod general equilibrium model that deserve special attention: the consumption CAPM, a CAPM explicitly including inflation, and the multi-Beta CAPM. The consumption CAPM is based on the assumption that in a multiperiod world an investor is concerned with the utility of lifetime consumption. It proceeds logically with a derivation under which growth in consumption rather than the return on the market drives security returns. A second approach, an inflation CAPM, recognizes that in a multiperiod world the investor must be concerned with inflation risk and that inflation must be recognized as a factor in an investor's preference function. The third approach is the multi-Beta model of Merton [88]. In this model the assumptions that allow us to reduce the portfolio and equilibrium model to a single-period framework are dropped and a larger set of economic factors is found to affect security returns. We will now briefly discuss each of these models in turn.

THE CONSUMPTION-ORIENTED CAPM

A number of authors, starting with Breeden [5] and Rubinstein [104], have taken a different approach to defining equilibrium in the capital markets. They start with a set of assumptions: investors maximize a multiperiod utility function for lifetime consumption; have homogeneous beliefs concerning return characteristics of assets; there is an infinitely lived fixed population; there is a single consumption good; and there exists a capital market that allows investors to reach a consumption pattern such that they cannot jointly fare better by additional trades. They are able to show, under these assumptions, that return on assets should be linearly related to the growth rate in aggregate consumption if the parameters of the linear relationship can be assumed constant over time. Furthermore, the residuals from the linear relationship are uncorrelated with the growth rate in aggregate consumption, have zero mean, and are uncorrelated with one another.

To be more explicit, define:

C_t = the growth rate in aggregate consumption per capita at time t

R_{it} = the rate of return on asset i in period t

$$R_{it} = \alpha_i + \beta_i C_t + e_{it} \tag{14.7}$$

where

1. $E(e_{it}) = 0$
2. the covariance between residuals and the index is zero. $E(e_{it}, C_t) = 0$
3. $\beta_i = \dfrac{\text{Cov}(R_{it}, C_t)}{\text{Var}(C_t)}$

Having established Equation (14.7) there are a number of ways (including using the same type of arguments introduced at the start of this chapter) to show that the equilibrium condition is[20]

$$\overline{R}_i = \overline{R}_Z + \gamma_1 \beta_1 \tag{14.8}$$

where

1. γ_1 is the market price of the consumption Beta.
2. $\overline{R}_Z$ is the expected return on a portfolio with zero consumption Beta.

This model is directly analogous to the simple form of the CAPM. The growth rate of per capita consumption has replaced the rate of return on the market portfolio as the influence affecting the time series of returns and hence equilibrium returns.

INFLATION RISK AND EQUILIBRIUM

One specific case of a multiperiod general equilibrium model that has received special attention is the case where all of Fama's assumptions are met except that there is uncertain inflation. Friend, Landskroner, and Losq [39] derive a general equilibrium relationship for the expected return on any asset under uncertain inflation, assuming that all utility functions exhibit constant proportional risk aversion. Their equilibrium appears similar to the simple form of the CAPM, but both the definition of the market price of risk and the risk on an asset are modified. In particular, they show that as long as the correlation between the rate of return on the market and the rate of inflation is positive, the market price of risk is higher than that depicted in the standard CAPM. Furthermore, they show that the risk of any asset is not just a function of its covariance with the market; it is also a function of its covariance with the rate of inflation. If an asset's rate of return is positively correlated with the rate of inflation, the standard CAPM formulation overstates the risk of the asset. Finally, they show that the traditional CAPM will understate (overstate) the equilibrium rate of return on any asset if the correlation of the return on that asset with the rate of inflation is less than (greater than) the product of the correlation of the rate of return on the asset with the market return, and the correlation between the market return and the inflation rate.

THE MULTI-BETA CAPM

Although Friend, Landskroner, and Losq [39] identified two (one new) forms of priced uncertainty in their equilibrium model, Merton [88] has constructed a generalized intertemporal capital asset pricing model in which a number of sources of uncertainty would be priced. Merton models investors as solving lifetime consumption decisions when faced with multiple sources of uncertainty. In this multiperiod setting uncertainty exists about not only the future value of securities, but also about such other influences as future labor income, future prices of consumption goods, future investment opportunities, and so on. Investors will form portfolios to hedge away each of these risks (to the extent possible). If sources of risk are a general concern to investors, then these sources of risk will affect the expected returns on securities. The inflation model is the simplest form of a

---

[20]These arguments are the no arbitrage conditions discussed more formally in Chapter 16 on Arbitrage Pricing Theory (APT).

multi-Beta CAPM where the expected return on any security can be expressed as a function of two sensitivities

$$\overline{R}_i - R_F = \beta_{iM}\left(\overline{R}_M - R_F\right) + \beta_{iI}\left(\overline{R}_I - R_F\right)$$

This expression represents the standard CAPM plus a new term. The new term is the product of a new Beta (which is the sensitivity of any security to the portfolio of securities that is held to hedge away inflation risk) and the price of inflation risk.

The multi-Beta CAPM tells us that the expected return on any security should be related to the security's sensitivity to a set of influences. The form of the expected return is

$$\overline{R}_i - R_F = \beta_{iM}\left(\overline{R}_M - R_F\right) + \beta_{iI1}\left(\overline{R}_{I1} - R_F\right) + \beta_{iI2}\left(\overline{R}_{I2} - R_F\right) + \cdots$$

In this relationship, all of the $\overline{R}_{Ij}$'s are expected returns on a set of portfolios that allows the investor to hedge a set of risks with which he or she is concerned. Although the theory tells us that these should be additional influences present in pricing securities and that these influences should be related to the investor's multiperiod utility functions, it does not tell us explicitly what these influences are or exactly how to form portfolios to hedge whatever risks they represent. One set of risks we might consider as potentially important is the four risks (in addition to the market) that we examined in Chapter 8: default risk, term structure risk, deflation risk, and profit risk.

We will leave this subject at this point, but will return to it in a later chapter when we discuss arbitrage pricing theory.

CONCLUSION

In this chapter we have shown that the simple form of the CAPM is remarkably robust. Modifying some of its assumptions leaves the general model unchanged, whereas modifying other assumptions leads to the appearance of new terms in the equilibrium relationship or, in some cases, to the modification of old terms. That the CAPM changes with changes in the assumptions is not unusual. What is unusual is (1) the robustness of the methodology in that it allows us to incorporate these changes, and (2) the fact that many of the conclusions of the original model hold, even with changes in assumptions.

The reader should be warned, however, that these results may seem stronger than they are. We have modified the assumptions one at a time. When assumptions are modified, simultaneously, the departure from the standard CAPM may be much more serious. For example, when short sales were disallowed but lending and borrowing were allowed, the standard CAPM held. When riskless lending and borrowing were disallowed but short sales were allowed, we got a model that very much resembled the standard CAPM, except that the slope and intercept were changed. Ross [100] has shown that when both riskless lending and borrowing and short sales are disallowed, one cannot derive a simple general equilibrium relationship.

There is no doubt that the general equilibrium models we now have are imperfect. The question is how well they describe conditions in the capital markets. We shall turn to this subject in the next chapter.

APPENDIX

DERIVATION OF THE GENERAL EQUILIBRIUM WITH TAXES

Earlier in this chapter we saw that any security or portfolio has an equilibrium return given by

$$\overline{R}_j = \overline{R}_Z + \left(\overline{R}_M - \overline{R}_Z\right)\frac{\sigma_{jM}}{\sigma_M^2}$$

We derived this expression by maximizing

$$0 = \frac{\overline{R}_P - R_F'}{\sigma_P}$$

for the investor's portfolio (P) equal to the market portfolio M and the riskless rate defined as the intercept of a line tangent to point M. $\overline{R}_Z$ in the foregoing solution is the return on the minimum variance portfolio that is uncorrelated with the portfolio M.

We could have repeated this analysis for any portfolio P different from M, and for assets included in portfolio P we would get the following equilibrium relationship:

$$\overline{R}_j = \overline{R}_{0P} + \left(\overline{R}_P - \overline{R}_{0P}\right)\frac{\sigma_{jP}}{\sigma_P^2}$$

Where $\overline{R}_{0P}$ is the expected return on the minimum variance portfolio that is uncorrelated with portfolio P.

We will now make several changes in this expression. In a world of taxes, investors will reach equilibrium in terms of after-tax returns. The superscript A will be added to each variable to show that it holds in after-tax terms. In addition, the portfolio selected by each investor may be different because homogeneous before-tax expectations will produce heterogeneous after-tax expectations. Thus, we will use the subscript i to stand for investor i. Finally, since we are assuming unlimited lending and borrowing, an asset exists (the riskless asset) that is uncorrelated with all portfolios. Thus we can replace $\overline{R}_{0P}$ with R_F. With these changes, the equation above can be written as

$$\overline{R}_{ji}^A = R_{Fi}^A + \left(R_{Pi}^A - R_{Fi}^A\right)\frac{\mathrm{cov}\left(R_{ji}^A R_{Pi}^A\right)}{\left(\sigma_{Pi}^A\right)^2} \tag{A.1}$$

While expectations of after-tax returns are heterogeneous, expectations of before-tax returns are homogeneous. We can write this expression in terms of before-tax returns.

Let

δ_j = the dividend yield on stock j
t_{di} = stockholder i's marginal tax rate on interest and dividends
t_{gi} = stockholder i's marginal tax rate on capital gains
w_i = the amount of stockholder i's wealth invested in risky assets
W = the sum of all wealth invested in risky assets

$$W = \sum_i w_i$$

Then,

$$\overline{R}_{ji}^A = \left(\overline{R}_j - \delta_j\right)\left(1 - t_{gi}\right) + \delta_j\left(1 - t_{di}\right)$$
$$= \overline{R}_j\left(1 - t_{gi}\right) - \delta_j\left(t_{di} - t_{gi}\right)$$
$$R_{Fi}^A = R_F\left(1 - t_{di}\right)$$

If we assume that next period's dividend is sufficiently predictable, then we can treat it as a certain stream and

$$\text{cov}\left(R_{ji}^A R_{Pi}^A\right) = \text{cov}\left(R_j R_{Pi}\right)\left(1 - t_{gi}\right)^2$$

$$\left(\sigma_{Pi}^A\right)^2 = \sigma_{Pi}^2\left(1 - t_{gi}\right)^2$$

Substituting in Equation (A.1),

$$\left(\overline{R}_j - R_F\right)\left(1 - t_{gi}\right) - \left(\delta_j - R_F\right)\left(t_{di} - t_{gi}\right) = \frac{\overline{R}_{Pi}^A - R_{Fi}^A}{\sigma_{Pi}^2}\text{cov}\left(R_j R_{Pi}\right)$$

Dividing through by $1 - t_{gi}$ and multiplying through by w_i and dividing through by λ_i where λ_i is defined as

$$\frac{\overline{R}_{Pi}^A - R_{Fi}^A}{\sigma_{Pi}^2}\frac{1}{\left(1 - t_{gi}\right)}$$

we get

$$\frac{w_i}{\lambda_i}\left(\overline{R}_j - R_F\right) - \left(\delta_j - R_F\right)\frac{\left(t_{di} - t_{gi}\right)}{\left(1 - t_{gi}\right)}\frac{w_i}{\lambda_i} = w_i\,\text{cov}\left(R_j R_{Pi}\right) \tag{A.2}$$

Summing this equation across all investors and dividing by Σw_i,

$$\left(\overline{R}_j - R_F\right)\frac{\sum\limits_i\left(w_i/\lambda_i\right)}{\sum\limits_i w_i} - \left(\delta_j - R_F\right)$$

$$\times\left[\sum_i\frac{\left(t_{di} - t_{gi}\right)w_i}{\left(1 - t_{gi}\right)\lambda_i}\bigg/\sum_i w_i\right] = \frac{\sum\limits_i w_i\,\text{cov}\left(R_j R_{Pi}\right)}{\sum\limits_i w_i}$$

But note that since

$$\frac{\sum\limits_i w_i R_{Pi}}{\sum\limits_i w_i} = R_M$$

the right-hand side of this equation is equal to $\text{cov}(R_j R_M)$. Define the following symbols:

$$H = \left(\sum_i w_i\right)\bigg/\left(\sum_i w_i/\lambda_i\right)$$

$$\tau = H\left(\sum_i\frac{\left(t_{di} - t_{gi}\right)w_i}{\left(1 - t_{gi}\right)\lambda_i}\right)\bigg/\sum_i w_i$$

We can see that the tax factor τ is a complex weighted average of the investor's tax rates where the weights on each investor's tax rate is a function of the wealth he places in risky securities and his degree of risk avoidance as expressed by the ratio of excess return to variance on the portfolio he chooses to hold. Equation (A.2) can now be written as

$$\left(\overline{R}_j - R_F\right) - \left(\delta_j - R_F\right)\tau = H\,\text{cov}\left(R_j R_M\right) \tag{A.3}$$

Since expression (A.3) must hold for any asset or portfolio, it must hold for the market portfolio. Thus,

$$\left(\overline{R}_M - R_F\right) - \left(\delta_M - R_F\right)\tau = H\sigma_M^2$$

or

$$H = \frac{\left(\overline{R}_M - R_F\right) - \left(\delta_M - R_F\right)\tau}{\sigma_M^2}$$

Substituting the expression for H into the equation and rearranging yields

$$\overline{R}_j = R_F + \frac{\left(\overline{R}_M - R_F\right) - \left(\delta_M - R_F\right)\tau}{\sigma_M^2}\ \text{cov}\left(R_j R_M\right) + \left(\delta_j - R_F\right)\tau$$

or

$$\overline{R}_j = R_F + \beta_j\left[\left(\overline{R}_M - R_F\right) - \left(\delta_M - R_F\right)\tau\right] + \left(\delta_j - R_F\right)\tau$$

QUESTIONS AND PROBLEMS

1. Assume the equilibrium equation shown below. What is the return on the zero Beta portfolio and the return on the market assuming the zero Beta model holds?

$$\overline{R}_i = 0.04 + 0.10\beta_i$$

2. In the previous chapter we showed that the standard CAPM model could be written in price form. What is the zero Beta model in price form?

3. Given the model shown below, what is the risk-free rate if the post-tax equilibrium model describes returns?

$$\overline{R}_i = 0.05 + 0.10\beta_i + 0.24\delta_i$$

4. Given the following situation:

$$\overline{R}_M = 15 \quad \sigma_M = 22$$
$$\overline{R}_Z = 5 \quad \ \ \sigma_Z = 8$$
$$R_F = 3$$

    draw the minimum variance curve and efficient frontier in expected return standard deviation space. Be sure to give the coordinates of all key points. Draw the security market line.

5. You have just lectured two tax-free institutions on the necessity of including taxes in the general equilibrium relationship. One believed you and one did not. Demonstrate that if the model holds, the one that did could engage in risk-free arbitrage with the one that did not in a manner such that:

    A.   Both parties believed they were making an arbitrage profit in the transaction.

    B.   The one who believed in the post-tax model actually made a profit; the other institution incurred a loss.

6. Assume that returns are generated as follows

$$R_i = \overline{R}_i + a_i\left(R_M - \overline{R}_M\right) + b_i\left(C - \overline{C}\right)$$

where C is the rate of change in interest rates. Derive a general equilibrium relationship for security returns.

7. If $\bar{R}_M = 15\%$ and $R_F = 5\%$ and risk-free lending is allowed but riskless borrowing is not, sketch what the efficient frontier might look like in expected return standard deviation space. Sketch the security market line and the location of all portfolios in expected return Beta space. Label all points and explain why you have drawn them as you have.

8. Assume you paid a higher tax on income than on capital gains. Furthermore, assume that you believed that prices were determined by the post-tax CAPM. Now another investor comes along who believes that prices are determined by the pre-tax CAPM. Demonstrate that you can make an excess return by engaging in a two-security swap with him.

9. As we will see in the next chapter, most tests of the CAPM involve tests on common stock data and perform the tests using the S&P index. You have just had a revelation that bonds are also marketable assets and thus should belong in the market return. Show what effect leaving them out might have on stocks with different characteristics.

BIBLIOGRAPHY

1. Alexander, Gordon. "An Algorithmic Approach to Deriving the Minimum-Variance Zero-Beta Portfolio," *Journal of Financial Economics*, **4,** No. 2 (March 1977), pp. 231–236.
2. Arzac, Enrique, and Bawa, Vijay. "Portfolio Choice and Equilibrium in Capital Markets with Safety-First Investors," *Journal of Financial Economics*, **4,** No. 3 (May 1977), pp. 277–288.
3. Black, Fischer. "Capital Market Equilibrium with Restricted Borrowing," *Journal of Business*, **45,** No. 3 (July 1972), pp. 444–455.
4. Borch, Karl. "Equilibrium, Optimum and Prejustices in Capital Markets," *Journal of Financial and Quantitative Analysis*, **IV,** No. 1 (March 1969), pp. 4–14.
5. Breeden, D. "An Intertemporal Asset Pricing Model with Stochastic Consumption and Investment Opportunities," *Journal of Financial Economics*, **7** (1979), pp. 265–296.
6. ——. "Consumption Risk in Futures Markets," *Journal of Finance*, **35** (1980), pp. 503–520.
7. Breeden, D., and Litzenberger, R. "Prices of State-Contingent Claims Implicit in Option Prices," *Journal of Business*, **51** (1978), pp. 621–651.
8. Breeden, D., Gibbons, M., and Litzenberger, R. "Empirical Tests of the Consumption-Oriented CAPM," *Journal of Finance*, **44** (1989), pp. 231–262.
9. Brennan, Michael J. "Taxes, Market Valuation, and Corporate Financial Policy," *National Tax Journal*, **25** (1970), pp. 417–427.
10. ——. "Capital Market Equilibrium with Divergent Borrowing and Lending Rates," *Journal of Financial and Quantitative Analysis*, **VI,** No. 5 (Dec. 1971), pp. 1197–1205.
11. Brenner, Menachem, and Subrahmanyam, Marti. "Intra-Equilibrium and Inter-Equilibrium Analysis in Capital Market Theory: A Clarification," *Journal of Finance*, **XXII,** No. 4 (Sept. 1977), pp. 1313–1319.
12. Brito, O. Ney. "Marketability Restrictions and the Valuation of Capital Assets under Uncertainty," *Journal of Finance*, **XXXII,** No. 4 (Sept. 1977), pp. 1109–1123.
13. ——. "Portfolio Selection in an Economy with Marketability and Short Sales Restrictions," *Journal of Finance*, **XXXIII,** No. 2 (May 1978), pp. 589–601.
14. Chamberlain, G., and Rothschild, M. "Arbitrage, Factor Structure, and Mean-Variance Analysis on Large Asset Markets," *Econometrica*, **51** (1983), pp. 1281–1304.
15. Chen, N., Roll, R., and Ross, S. "Economic Forces and the Stock Market," *Journal of Business*, **59** (1986), pp. 386–403.
16. Connor, G. "A Unified Beta Pricing Theory," *Journal of Economic Theory*, **34** (1984), pp. 13–31.

17. Connor, G., and Korajczyk, R. "Performance Measurement with the Arbitrage Pricing Theory: A New Framework for Analysis," *Journal of Financial Economics*, **15** (1986), pp. 373–394.
18. Constantinides, George M. "Admissible Uncertainty in the Intertemporal Asset Pricing Model," *Journal of Financial Economics*, **8,** No. 1 (March 1980), pp. 71–87.
19. Cornell, B. "The Consumption Based Asset Pricing Model: A Note on Potential Tests and Applications," *Journal of Financial Economics*, **9** (1981), pp. 103–108.
20. Dhrymes, Phoebus, Friend, Irwin, and Gultekin, Bulent, "A Critical Reexamination of the Empirical Evidence on the Arbitrage Pricing Theory," *The Journal of Finance*, **39** (June 1984), pp. 323–346.
21. Dybvig, Philip H. "An Explicit Bound on Deviations from APT Pricing in a Finite Economy," *Journal of Financial Economics*, **12** (1983), pp. 483–496.
22. ———. "Distributional Analysis of Portfolio Choice," *The Journal of Business*, **61,** No. 2 (July 1988), pp. 369–393.
23. Dybvig, P., and Ross, S. "Yes, the APT Is Testable," *Journal of Finance*, **40** (1985), pp. 1173–1188.
24. Easley, David, and Jarrow, Robert A. "Consensus Beliefs Equilibrium and Market Efficiency," *The Journal of Finance*, **38,** No. 3 (June 1983), pp. 903–912.
25. Elton, Edwin J., and Gruber, Martin J. "The Multi-Period Consumption Investment Decision and Single Period Analysis," *Oxford Economic Papers,* **26** (Sept. 1974) pp. 180–195.
26. ———. *Finance as a Dynamic Process* (Englewood Cliffs, N.J.: Prentice Hall, 1975).
27. ———. "Taxes and Portfolio Composition, *Journal of Financial Economics*, **6** (1978), pp. 399–410.
28. Errunza, Vihang, and Losq, Etienne. "International Asset Pricing Under Mild Segmentation: Theory and Test," *The Journal of Finance*, **40,** No. 1 (March 1985), pp. 105–124.
29. Fama, Eugene. "Multi-Period Consumption-Investment Decision," *American Economic Review*, **60** (Mar. 1970), pp. 163–174.
30. ———. "Risk, Return and Equilibrium," *Journal of Political Economy*, **79,** No. 1 (Jan.-Feb. 1971), pp. 30–55.
31. ———. "A Note on the Market Model and the Two-Parameter Model," *Journal of Finance*, **XXVIII,** No. 5 (Dec. 1973), pp. 1181–1185.
32. ———. *Foundations of Finance* (New York: Basic Books, 1976).
33. Fama, E., MacBeth, J., and Schwert, G. "Asset Returns and Inflation," *Journal of Financial Economics*, **5** (1977), pp. 115–146.
34. ———. "Inflation, Interest and Relative Prices," *Journal of Business*, **52** (1979), pp. 183–209.
35. Ferson, W. "Expected Real Interest Rates and Consumption in Efficient Financial Markets: Empirical Tests," *Journal of Financial and Quantitative Analysis*, **18** (1983), pp. 477–498.
36. Figlewski, Stephen. "Information Diversity and Market Behavior," *The Journal of Finance*, **37,** No. 1 (March 1982), pp. 87–102.
37. Foster, F. Douglas. "Assessing Goodness-of-Fit of Asset Pricing Models: The Distribution the Maximal R2," *The Journal of Finance*, **52,** No. 2 (June 1997), pp. 591–607.
38. Friend, Irwin, and Westerfield, Randolph. "Co-Skewness and Capital Assets Pricing," *The Journal of Finance*, **35,** No. 4 (Sept. 1980), pp. 897–914.
39. Friend, Irwin, Landskroner, Yoram, and Losq, Etienne. "The Demand for Risky Assets and Uncertain Inflation," *Journal of Finance*, **XXXI,** No. 5 (Dec. 1976), pp. 1287–1297.
40. Gibbons, M., and Ferson, W. "Testing Asset Pricing Models with Changing Expectations and an Unobservable Market Portfolio," *Journal of Financial Economics*, **14** (1985), pp. 217–236.
41. Gonedes, Nicholas. "Capital Market Equilibrium for a Class of Heterogeneous Expectations in a Two-Parameter World," *Journal of Finance*, **XXXI,** No. 1 (March 1976), pp. 1–15.
42. Grinblatt, Mark, and Titman, Sheridan. "Factor Pricing in a Finite Economy," *Journal of Financial Economics*, **12** (1983), pp. 497–507.
43. Grossman, S., and Shiller, R. "Consumption Correlatedness and Risk Measurement in Economies with Non-Traded Assets and Heterogeneous Information," *Journal of Financial Economics*, **10** (1982), pp. 195–210.

44. Grossman, S., Melino, A., and Shiller, R. "Estimating the Continuous-Time Consumption-Based Asset-Pricing Model," *Journal of Business and Economic Statistics*, **5** (1987), pp. 315–328.

45. Guiso, Luigi, Jappelli, Tullio, and Terlizzese, Daniele. "Income Risk, Borrowing Constraints, and Portfolio Choice," *The American Economic Review*, **86,** No. 1 (Mar. 1996), pp. 158–172.

46. Hagerman, Robert, and Kim, Han. "Capital Asset Pricing with Price Level Changes," *Journal of Financial and Quantitative Analysis*, **XI,** No. 3 (Sept. 1976), pp. 381–391.

47. Hall, R. "Stochastic Implications of the Life Cycle-Permanent Income Hypothesis: Theory and Evidence," *Journal of Political Economy*, **86** (1978), pp. 971–987.

48. Hansen, L., and Singleton, K. "Generalized Instrumental Variables Estimation of Nonlinear Rational Expectations Models," *Econometrica*, **50** (1982), pp. 1269–1286.

49. ——. "Stochastic Consumption, Risk Aversion, and the Temporary Behavior of Asset Returns," *Journal of Political Economy*, **91** (1983), pp. 249–265.

50. Hart, Oliver. "On the Existence of Equilibrium in a Securities Model," *Journal of Economic Theory*, **9,** No. 3 (Nov. 1974), pp. 293–311.

51. Heckerman, Donald. "Portfolio Selection and the Structure of Capital Asset Prices When Relative Prices of Consumption Goods May Change," *Journal of Finance*, **XXVII,** No. 1 (March 1972), pp. 47–60.

52. ——. "Reply to [52]," *Journal of Finance*, **XXVIII,** No. 5 (Dec. 1973), p. 1361.

53. Hilliard, Jimmy E. "Asset Pricing under a Subset of Linear Risk Tolerance Functions and Log-Normal Market Returns," *Journal of Financial and Quantitative Analysis*, **XV,** No. 5 (Dec. 1980), pp. 1041–1062.

54. Hogan, William, and Warren, James. "Toward the Development of an Equilibrium Capital-Market Model Based on Semi-Variance," *Journal of Financial and Quantitative Analysis*, **IX,** No. 1 (Jan. 1974), pp. 1–11.

55. Hopewell, Michael. "Comment on [88]: A Model of Capital Asset Risk," *Journal of Financial and Quantitative Analysis*, **VII,** No. 2 (March 1972), pp. 1673–1677.

56. Ibbotson, Roger, and Sinquefield, Rex. *Stocks, Bonds, Bills and Inflation: The Past and the Future* (Charlottesville, Va.: Financial Analysts Research Foundation, 1982).

57. Ingersoll, Jonathan E., Jr. "Some Results in the Theory of Arbitrage Pricing," *Journal of Finance*, **39** (1984), pp. 1021–1039.

58. Jarrow, Robert. "Heterogeneous Expectations, Restrictions on Short Sales, and Equilibrium Asset Prices," *The Journal of Finance*, **35,** No. 5 (Dec. 1980), pp. 1105–1114.

59. Jobson, J., and Korkie, B. "Estimation for Markowitz Efficient Portfolios," *Journal of the American Statistical Association*, **75** (1980), pp. 544–554.

60. Jobson, J., and Korkie, R. "Potential Performance Tests of Portfolio Efficiency," *Journal of Financial Economics*, **10** (1982), pp. 433–466.

61. Kamoike, Osamu. "Portfolio Selection When Future Prices of Consumption Goods May Change: Comment on [36]," *Journal of Finance*, **XXVIII,** No. 5 (Dec. 1973), pp. 1357–1360.

62. Kandel, S. "On the Exclusion of Assets from Tests of the Mean Variance Efficiency of the Market Portfolio," *Journal of Finance*, **39** (1984), pp. 63–75.

63. Kandel, S. "The Likelihood Ratio Test Statistic of Mean-Variance Efficiency without a Riskless Asset," *Journal of Financial Economics*, **13** (1984), pp. 575–592.

64. Kandel S., and Stambaugh, R. "On Correlations and the Sensitivity of Inferences about Mean-Variance Efficiency," *Journal of Financial Economics*, **18** (1987), pp. 61–90.

65. Keim, D. "Size Related Anomalies and Stock Return Seasonability: Further Empirical Evidence," *Journal of Financial Economics*, **12** (1983), pp. 13–32.

66. Korkie, Bob. "Comment: on [73]," *Journal of Financial and Quantitative Analysis*, **IX,** No. 5 (Nov. 1974), pp. 723–725.

67. Kraus, Alan, and Litzenberger, Robert. "Market Equilibrium in a Multi-Period State Preference Model with Logarithmic Utility," *Journal of Finance*, **XXX,** No. 5 (Dec. 1975), pp. 1213–1227.

68. ——. "Skewness Preference and the Valuation of Risk Assets," *Journal of Finance*, **XXXI,** No. 4 (Sept. 1976), pp. 1085–1100.

69. Kryzanowski, Lawrence, and Chau, To Hinh. "Asset Pricing Models When the Number of Securities Held Is Constrained: A Comparison and Reconciliation of the Mao and Levy Models," *Journal of Financial and Quantitative Analysis*, **XVII**, No. 1 (March 1982), pp. 63–74.

70. Kumar, Prem. "Market Equilibrium and Corporation Finance: Some Issues," *Journal of Finance*, **XXIX**, No. 4 (Sept. 1974), pp. 1175–1188.

71. Landskroner, Yoram. "Nonmarketable Assets and the Determinants of the Market Price of Risk," *Review of Economics and Statistics*, **LIX**, No. 4 (Nov. 1977), pp. 482–514.

72. ———. "Intertemporal Determination of the Market Price of Risk," *Journal of Finance*, **XXXII**, No. 5 (Dec. 1977), pp. 1671–1681.

73. Lee, Chang. "Investment Horizon and the Functional Form of the Capital Asset Pricing Model," *Review of Economics and Statistics*, **LVIII**, No. 3 (Aug. 1976), pp. 356–363.

74. Lehari, David, and Levy, Haim. "The Capital Asset Pricing Model and the Investment Horizon," *Review of Economics and Statistics*, **LIX**, No. 1 (Feb. 1977), pp. 92–104.

75. Levy, Haim. "The Capital Asset Pricing Model, Inflation, and the Investment Horizon: The Israeli Experience," *Journal of Financial and Quantitative Analysis*, **XV**, No. 3 (Sept. 1980), pp. 561–594.

76. Levy, Haim, and Levy, Azriel. "Equilibrium Under Uncertain Inflation: A Discrete Time Approach," *Journal of Financial and Quantitative Analysis*, **22**, No. 3 (Sept. 1987), pp. 285–297.

77. Lindenberg, Eric. "Imperfect Competition Among Investors in Security Markets," Ph.D. Dissertation, New York University, 1976.

78. ———. "Capital Market Equilibrium with Price Affecting Institutional Investors, in Edwin J. Elton and Martin J. Gruber (eds.), *Portfolio Theory 25 Years Later* (Amsterdam: North-Holland, 1979).

79. Lintner, John. "The Aggregation of Investors Diverse Judgments and Preferences in Purely Competitive Security Markets," *Journal of Financial and Quantitative Analysis*, **4**, No. 4 (Dec. 1969), pp. 347–400.

80. ———. "The Effect of Short Selling and Margin Requirements in Perfect Capital Markets," *Journal of Financial and Quantitative Analysis*, **VI**, No. 5 (Dec. 1971), pp. 1173–1195.

81. Litzenberger, R., and Ronn. E. "A Utility Based Model of Common Stock Returns," *Journal of Finance*, **41** (1986), pp. 67–92.

82. Long, John. "Stock Prices, Inflation, and the Term Structure of Interest Rates," *Journal of Financial Economics*, **1**, No. 2 (July 1974), pp. 131–170.

83. Losq, Etienne, and Chateau, John Peter D. "A Generalization of the CAPM Based on a Property of the Covariance Operator," *Journal of Financial and Quantitative Analysis*, **XVII**, No. 5 (Dec. 1982), pp. 783–798.

84. Lucas, R. "Asset Prices in an Exchange Economy," *Econometrica*, **46** (1978), pp. 1429–1445.

85. Mayers, D. "Nonmarketable Assets and Capital Market Equilibrium under Uncertainty," in M.C. Jensen (ed.), *Studies in Theory of Capital Markets* (New York: Praeger, 1972).

86. Mayers, David. "Nonmarketable Assets and the Determination of Capital Asset Prices in the Absence of a Riskless Asset." *Journal of Business*, **46**, No. 2 (April 1973), pp. 258–267.

87. ———. "Nonmarketable Assets. Market Segmentation and the Level of Asset Prices," *Journal of Financial and Quantitative Analysis*, **XI**, No. 1 (March 1976), pp. 1–37.

88. Merton, Robert. "An Intertemporal Capital Asset Pricing Model," *Econometrica*, **41**, No. 5 (Sept. 1973), pp. 867–888.

89. Milne, Frank, and Smith, Clifford, Jr. "Capital Asset Pricing with Proportional Transaction Cost," *Journal of Financial and Quantitative Analysis*, **XV**, No. 2 (June 1980), pp. 253–266.

90. Ohlson, James. "Equilibrium in Stable Markets," *Journal of Political Economy*, **85**, No. 4 (Aug. 1977), pp. 859–864.

91. Paxson, Christina. "Borrowing Constraints and Portfolio Choice," *The Quarterly Journal of Economics*, **105**, No. 2 (May 1990), pp. 535–543.

92. Peles, Yoram. "A Note on Risk and the Theory of Asset Value," *Journal of Financial and Quantitative Analysis*, **VI**, No. 1 (Jan. 1971), pp. 643–647.

93. Pettit, R. Richardson, and Stanley, L. "Consumption-Investment Decisions with Transaction Costs and Taxes: A Study of the Clientele Effect of Dividends," *Journal of Financial Economics*, **5,** No. 3 (1979).

94. Pettit, R. Richardson, and Westerfield, Randolph. "A Model of Capital Asset Risk," *Journal of Financial and Quantitative Analysis*, **VII,** No. 2 (March 1972), pp. 1649–1668.

95. Rabinovitch, Ramon, and Owen, Joel. "Non-Homogeneous Expectations and Information in the Capital Asset Market," *Journal of Finance*, **XXXIII,** No. 2 (May 1978), pp. 575–587.

96. Reinganum, Marc R. "A New Empirical Perspective on the CAPM," *Journal of Financial and Quantitative Analysis*, **XVI,** No. 4 (Nov. 1981), pp. 439–462.

97. Roberts, Gordon. "Endogenous Endowments and Capital Asset Prices," *Journal of Finance*, **XXX,** No. 1 (March 1975), pp. 155–162.

98. Roll, Richard, and Ross, Stephen. "An Empirical Investigation of Arbitrage Pricing Theory," *Journal of Finance* (Dec. 1980), pp. 1073–1105.

99. Rosenberg, B., and Guy, J. "Prediction of Beta from Investment Fundamentals," *Financial Analysts Journal*, **32** (1976), pp. 60–72.

100. Ross, Stephen. "Return, Risk, and Arbitrage," in I. Friend and J. Bickster (eds.), *Risks and Return in Finance* (Cambridge, Mass.: Ballinger, 1977).

101. ——. "The Capital Asset Pricing Model (CAPM), Short-Sale Restrictions and Related Issues," *Journal of Finance*, **XXXII,** No. 1 (March 1977), pp. 177–183.

102. ——. "Mutual Fund Separation in Financial Theory—The Separating Distributions," *Journal of Economic Theory*, **17,** No. 2 (April 1978), pp. 254–286.

103. ——. "The Current Status of the Capital Asset Pricing Model (CAPM)," *Journal of Finance*, **XXXIII,** No. 3 (June 1978), pp. 885–901.

104. Rubinstein, M. "The Valuation of Uncertain Income Streams and the Pricing of Options," *Bell Journal of Economics and Management Science*, **7** (1976), pp. 407–425.

105. Rubinstein, Mark. "The Strong Case for the Generalized Logarithmic Utility Model as the Premier Model of Financial Markets," *Journal of Finance*, **XXXI,** No. 2 (May 1976), pp. 551–571.

106. Samuelson, Paul. "Lifetime Portfolio Selection by Dynamic Stochastic Programming," *Review of Economics and Statistics*, **LI,** No. 3 (Aug. 1969), pp. 239–246.

107. Samuelson, Paul, and Merton, Robert. "Generalized Mean-Variance Tradeoffs for Best Perturbation Corrections to Approximate Portfolio Decisions," *Journal of Finance*, **XXIX,** No. 1 (March 1974), pp. 27–40.

108. Sandmo, Agnar. "Capital Risk, Consumption and Portfolio Choice," *Econometrica*, **37,** No. 4 (Oct. 1969), pp. 586–599.

109. Scholes, M., and Williams, J. "Estimating Betas from Nonsynchronous Data," *Journal of Financial Economics*, **5** (1977), pp. 309–327.

110. Shanken, J. "An Asymptotic Analysis of the Traditional Risk-Return Model," Unpublished Manuscript, School of Business Administration, University of California, Berkeley, 1982.

111. ——. "Multi-Beta CAPM or Equilibrium-APT? A Reply," *Journal of Finance*, **40** (1985), pp. 1186–1189.

112. ——. "Multivariate Tests of the Zero-Beta CAPM," *Journal of Financial Economics*, **14** (Sept. 1985), pp. 327–348.

113. ——. "On Exclusion of Assets from Tests of the Mean Variance Efficiency of the Market Portfolio: An Extension," *Journal of Finance*, **41** (1986), pp. 331–337.

114. ——. "A Posterior-Odds Ratio Approach to Testing Portfolio Efficiency," Working Paper, Graduate School of Management, University of Rochester, Rochester, N.Y., 1986.

115. ——. "Testing Portfolio Efficiency when the Zero-Beta Rate Is Unknown: A Note," *Journal of Finance*, **41** (1986), pp. 269–276.

116. ——. "Multivariate Proxies and Asset Pricing Relations," *Journal of Financial Economics*, **18** (1987), pp. 91–110.

117. Shanken, Jay. "The Arbitrage Pricing Theory: Is it Testable?" *Journal of Finance*, **37** (1982), pp. 1129–1140.

118. Sharpe, William. *Portfolio Theory and Capital Markets* (New York: McGraw-Hill, 1970).

119. Siegel, Jeremy, and Warner, Jarold. "Indexation, The Risk-Free Asset, and Capital Market Equilibrium," *Journal of Finance*, **XXXII,** No. 4 (Sept. 1977), pp. 1101–1107.
120. Stapleton, Richard, and Subrahmanyam, Marti. "Multi-Period Equilibrium Asset Pricing Model," *Econometrica*, **46** (1977).
121. Stone, Bernell. "Systematic Interest-Rate Risk in a Two-Index Model of Returns," *Journal of Financial and Quantitative Analysis*, **IX,** No. 5 (Nov. 1974), pp. 709–721.
122. Viard, Alan D. "The Asset Pricing Effects of Fixed Holding Costs: An Upper Bound," *Journal of Financial and Quantitative Analysis*, **30,** No. 1 (Mar. 1995), pp. 43.
123. Williams, Joseph. "Risk, Human Capital, and the Investor's Portfolio," *Journal of Business*, **51,** No. 1 (Jan. 1978), pp. 65–89.

15

Empirical Tests of Equilibrium Models

In the two previous chapters we stressed the fact that the construction of a theory necessitates a simplification of the phenomena under study. To understand and model any process, elements in the real world are simplified or assumed away. While a model based on simple assumptions can always be called into question because of these assumptions, the relevant test of how much damage has been done by the simplification is to examine the relationship between the predictions of the model and observed real-world phenomena. In our case the relevant test is how well the simple CAPM, or perhaps some other general equilibrium model, describes the behavior of actual capital markets.

The principle is easily stated and intuitively appealing. However, it opens up a new series of problems. Namely, how does one design meaningful empirical tests of a theory? In particular, how can one test the CAPM or any of its numerous variants? In this chapter we review several of the tests of the general equilibrium models that have been presented in the literature. In doing so, we discuss many of the problems encountered in designing these tests. Finally, we discuss fundamental work by Roll [65] that suggests certain problems with all of the tests of general equilibrium models and opens up the area to further questions.

THE MODELS—EX-ANTE EXPECTATIONS AND EX-POST TESTS

Most tests of general equilibrium models deal with either the standard CAPM or the zero Beta (two-factor) form of a general equilibrium model. The basic CAPM can be written as

$$E(R_i) = R_F + \beta_i \left[E(R_M) - R_F \right]$$

The no lending or borrowing version, often called the two-factor model, can be written as

$$E(R_i) = E(R_Z) + \beta_i \left[E(R_M) - E(R_Z) \right]$$

Recall that $E(R_Z)$ is the expected return on the minimum variance portfolio that is uncorrelated with the market portfolio.

Notice that these models are formulated in terms of expectations. All variables are expressed in terms of future values. The relevant Beta is the future Beta on the security. Furthermore, both the return on the market and the return on the minimum variance zero Beta portfolio are expected future returns.

Since large-scale systematic data on expectations do not exist, almost all tests of the CAPM have been performed using ex-post or observed values for the variables. This raises the logical question of how one justifies testing an expectational model in terms of realizations.

There are two lines of defense that have commonly been used by researchers. The simpler defense is to argue that expectations are on average and, on the whole, correct. Therefore, over long periods of time, actual events can be taken as proxies for expectations.

The more complex defense starts by assuming that security returns are linearly related to the return on a market portfolio (a version of the single-index model of Chapter 7). This model, called the market model, can be written as

$$\tilde{R}_{it} = \alpha_i + \beta_i \tilde{R}_{Mt} + \tilde{e}_{it} \tag{15.1}$$

The squiggle over a variable indicates that the variable is random.

The expected value of the return on security i is

$$E(R_i) = \alpha_i + \beta_i E(R_M)$$

Thus,

$$E(R_i) - \alpha_i - \beta_i E(R_M) = 0$$

Adding this equation to the right-hand side of Equation (15.1) and rearranging yields

$$\tilde{R}_{it} = E(R_i) + \beta_i \left[\tilde{R}_{Mt} - E(R_M)\right] + \tilde{e}_{it}$$

The simple form of the CAPM model is

$$E(R_i) = R_F + \beta_i \left[E(R_M) - R_F\right]$$

Substituting the expression for $E(R_i)$ into the previous equation and simplifying,

$$\tilde{R}_{it} = R_F + \beta_i \left(\tilde{R}_{Mt} - R_F\right) + \tilde{e}_{it} \tag{15.2}$$

Testing a model of this form with ex-post data seems appropriate. However, notice that there are three assumptions behind this model:

1. The market model holds in every period.
2. The CAPM model holds in every period.
3. The Beta is stable over time.

A test of this model on ex-post data is really a simultaneous test of all three of these hypotheses.

The reader should note that, if one had used the two-factor model instead of the Sharpe–Lintner–Mossin form, we would have found

$$\tilde{R}_{it} = \tilde{R}_{Zt} + \beta_i \left(\tilde{R}_{Mt} - \tilde{R}_{Zt}\right) + \tilde{e}_{it} \tag{15.3}$$

rather than Equation (15.2). As in the previous case, a test of this model is really a simultaneous test of three hypotheses: the zero Beta version of the CAPM model holds in every period, the market model holds in every period, and Beta is stable over time. However, making these assumptions does express the model in terms of realized returns.

EMPIRICAL TESTS OF THE CAPM

There has been a huge amount of empirical testing of the standard form and the two-factor form of the CAPM model. A discussion of all empirical work would require a volume by itself. The approach we have adopted is to review the hypotheses that should be tested, to review some of the early work on testing the CAPM, then to discuss briefly a few of the problems inherent in any test of the CAPM. Finally, we review, in more detail, some of the more rigorous tests.

Some Hypotheses of the CAPM

Certain hypotheses can be formulated that should hold whether one believes in the simple CAPM or the two-factor general equilibrium model.

The first is that higher risk (Beta) should be associated with a higher level of return.

The second is that return is linearly related to Beta; that is, for every unit increase in Beta, there is the same increase in return.

The third is that there should be no added return for bearing nonmarket risk.

In addition, if some form of general equilibrium model holds, then investing should constitute a fair game with respect to it. That is, deviations of a security or portfolio from equilibrium should be purely random and there should be no way to use these deviations to earn an excess profit.

In addition to the hypotheses common to both the standard and the two-factor form of the CAPM, we can formulate hypotheses that attempt to differentiate between these general equilibrium models. In particular, the standard version implies that the security market line, drawn in return Beta space, should have an intercept of R_F and a slope of $(\bar{R}_M - R_F)$, while the two-factor version requires that it should have an intercept of $\bar{R}_Z$ and a slope of $(\bar{R}_M - \bar{R}_Z)$.

A Simple Test of the CAPM

Before we become involved in a discussion of the history and methodology of tests of the CAPM model, it seems worthwhile examining the results of a simple test of the CAPM to see if, over long periods of time, higher return has been associated with higher risk (as measured by Beta). Sharpe and Cooper [80] examined whether following alternative strategies, with respect to risk over long periods of time, would produce returns consistent with modern capital theory. In order to get portfolios with different Betas they divided stocks into deciles once a year on the basis of the Beta of each security.[1] To be more precise, Beta at a point in time was measured using 60 months of previous data. Once a year, for each year 1931–1967, all New York Stock Exchange stocks were divided into deciles based on their rank by Beta. An equally weighted portfolio was formed of the stocks that comprised each decile. A strategy consisted of holding the stocks of a particular decile over the entire period. The stocks one holds change both because of the reinvestment of dividends and because the stocks that make up a particular decile change as the decile's composition is revised once a year. Notice that the strategy outlined by Sharpe and Cooper could actually be followed by an investor. Each year the investor divides stocks into deciles by Beta based on the previous five years' (60 months) returns. If investors want to pursue the high Beta strategy, they simply divide their funds equally among the stocks in the highest Beta decile. They do this every year and observe the outcomes. Table 15.1 shows what would have happened, on average, if an investor had done this each year from 1931 to 1967.

---

[1]The measure of Beta they used was analogous to the standard Beta computed by regressing the returns from any security against the market. The difference was that dividends were excluded both from the market and the stocks' return. The authors found the coefficient of determination between standard Beta and their measure was 0.996.

Table 15.1   Average Returns and Betas on Portfolios Ranked by Betas

Strategy	Average Return	Portfolio Beta
10	22.67	1.42
9	20.45	1.18
8	19.116	1.14
7	21.77	1.24
6	18.49	1.06
5	19.13	0.98
4	18.88	1.00
3	14.99	0.76
2	14.63	0.65
1	11.58	0.58

While the relationship between strategy and return is not perfect, it is very close. In general, stocks with higher Betas have produced higher future returns. In fact, the rank correlation coefficient between strategy and return is over 0.93, which is statistically significant at the 0.01 level. Similarly, buying stocks with higher forecast Beta would lead to holding portfolios with higher realized Betas. The rank correlation between strategy and Beta is 95%, which is significant at the 0.01 level.

The next logical step is to examine the relationship between the return that would have been earned and the risk (Beta) from following alternative strategies. Figure 15.1 from Sharpe and Cooper [80] shows this relationship. The equation of this graph is

$$\overline{R}_i = 5.54 + 12.75\beta_i$$

More than 95% of the variation in expected return is explained by differences in Beta. Thus, Beta has explained a very significant portion of the difference in return between these portfolios (strategies).

Sharpe and Cooper's work presents rather clear and easily interpreted evidence that, as general equilibrium theory suggests, there is a positive relationship between return and Beta. Furthermore, an examination of Figure 15.1 provides confidence that the relationship

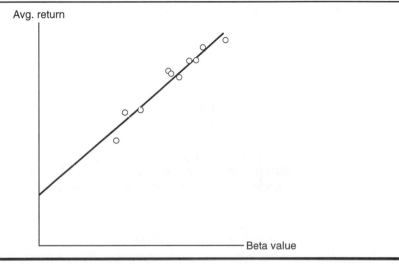

Figure 15.1   Estimated security market line.

is both strong and linear. The intercept of 5.54 is considerably higher than the riskless rate (rate on Treasury bills) that was below 2% during this period. This lends support to the two-factor form of the CAPM. Let us now turn to some more sophisticated tests of the CAPM.

Some Early Empirical Tests

Most of the early empirical tests of the CAPM involved the use of a time series (first pass) regression to estimate Betas and the use of a cross-sectional (second pass) regression to test the hypotheses we derived from the CAPM model. To make this more concrete, let us turn to an early empirical study of the CAPM performed by Lintner and reproduced in Douglas [23]. Lintner first estimated Beta for each of the 301 common stocks in his sample. He estimated Beta by regressing each stock's yearly return against the average return for all stocks in the sample using data from 1954 to 1963. The first-pass regression had the form

$$R_{it} = \alpha_i + b_i R_{Mt} + e_{it}$$

where b_i (the regression coefficient) was the estimate of the true Beta for stock i. Lintner then performed the second-pass cross-sectional regression

$$\bar{R}_i = a_1 + a_2 b_i + a_3 S_{ei}^2 + \eta_i$$

where S_{ei}^2 is the residual variance from the first-pass regression (the variance of e_i). Each parameter of this model has a theoretical value. a_3 should be equal to zero, a_1 should be equal to either R_F or $\bar{R}_Z$, and a_2 should be equal to either $\bar{R}_M - R_F$ or $\bar{R}_M - \bar{R}_Z$, according to the form of the CAPM that is being tested.[2] The values he obtained were

$$a_1 = 0.108$$
$$a_2 = 0.063$$
$$a_3 = 0.237$$

These results seem to violate the CAPM.[3] The term representing residual risk was statistically significant and positive. The intercept term a_1 would seem to be larger than any reasonable estimate of either R_F or $\bar{R}_Z$ and a_2, although statistically significant, has a value slightly lower than we could reasonably expect. Douglas [23] employed a similar methodology and found results that were similar to Lintner's.

Some Problems in Methodology

Miller and Scholes [63] in a classic article provide an analysis of the statistical problems inherent in all empirical tests of the CAPM. In addition to discussing the various theoretical problems associated with these tests, they also conducted a series of carefully constructed simulations designed to measure the extent to which certain previous studies have produced results that were biased by these statistical problems.

Miller and Scholes start with a discussion of possible biases due to misspecification of the basic estimation equations. One of the first considerations here is that, if returns are

---

[2]These theoretical values arise from Equations (15.2) and (15.3).

[3]Both a_2 and a_3 are statistically different from zero at the 0.01 level. The t values for these coefficients are 6.9 and 6.8, respectively.

really generated by the simple form of the CAPM, then the time series equation used to estimate Beta should be consistent with the CAPM. The CAPM in time series form is

$$\tilde{R}_{it} = R_{Ft} + \beta_i \left(\tilde{R}_{Mt} - R_{Ft} \right)$$

or

$$\tilde{R}_{it} = \left(1 - \beta_i \right) R_{Ft} + \beta_i \tilde{R}_{Mt}$$

But the equation used by both Lintner and Douglas was the market model

$$\tilde{R}_{it} = \alpha_i + \beta_i \overline{R}_{Mt}$$

Now, if R_F is a constant over the estimation period, no damage is done. The estimate of α_i should be equal to $(1 - \beta_i)R_{Ft}$. However, if R_{Ft} fluctuates over time and, if it is correlated with R_{Mt}, we have a classic case of missing variable bias and β_i will be a biased estimate of the true β_i. Furthermore, Miller and Scholes prove that if R_{Ft} and R_{Mt} are negatively correlated, then this will have the effect of biasing the intercept of the second-pass regression upward and its slope downward and this could, in part, explain the inconsistencies found by Lintner and Douglas. Miller and Scholes examine historical data and find a negative correlation. This is not surprising, for the stock market usually declines when interest rates go up. They test for the importance of this in explaining the Lintner findings. Although they find the influence is in the direction discussed herein, the order of magnitude of the bias is so small that it had almost no effect on Lintner's results.

Another possible source of equation misspecification that could account for finding an intercept too high and a slope too low is if the relationship between expected return and Beta was, in reality, nonlinear. Miller and Scholes test for nonlinearity and conclude that any nonlinearity that was present did not lead to the increased intercept and decreased slope.

A third possible source of distortion is the presence of heteroscedasticity. Heteroscedasticity is an often encountered problem in econometric tests. It occurs when the variance of the error is larger for higher values of the independent variable than it is for smaller values. In this case, it would imply that higher Beta stocks have a higher variance of return, unexplained by the market (nonmarket risk), than lower Beta stocks. Although Miller and Scholes found evidence of heteroscedasticity, they did not find that heteroscedasticity accounted for the high intercept and low slope. In fact, if anything, it biased the results in the other direction.[4]

Having demonstrated that errors in estimating the basic equations did not account for the differences between the Lintner results and those predicted by some form of the CAPM, Miller and Scholes next consider the effect of possible errors in the definition of the variables.

One form of the bias that we know is present is due to the error in measuring Beta for the second-pass regression. The β_i we arrive at in the first-pass regression is an estimate of the "true" Beta for stock i. Even if a true and stable Beta exists for stock i, all we have is an estimate of it, an estimate that may be unbiased but subject to sampling error. Any error in the estimate of Beta will cause the coefficient of β_i in the second-pass regression to be downward biased and the intercept to be upward biased.[5] Miller and Scholes show that this has an important effect on the results they estimate, that this resulted in the second-pass

---

[4]The reader should note that heteroscedasticity does reduce the estimate of the errors in the regression coefficients and so may lead you to conclude that a relationship is statistically significant when it, in fact, is not.

[5]A proof of this is contained in the appendix at the end of this chapter.

regression coefficient on Beta being only 64% of its true value, and that it caused a commensurate increase in the intercept.

There is a second effect of the Betas being measured with error that is also extremely important. To the extent that the true value of Beta is positively correlated with a company's residual variance, residual variance will serve as a proxy for the true Beta and return will be positively correlated with residual risk. Miller and Scholes conclude that this is, in fact, the case in the Lintner tests. Thus, although return is not dependent on residual variance, residual variance may show up as being statistically related to return in cross-sectional regression analysis because residual risk acts as a proxy variable for the true, but unobserved, Beta.

Miller and Scholes finally demonstrate that return distributions appear to be positively skewed and, if there is skewness, that the cross-sectional regression will show an association between residual risk and return, even though there is no such association.[6]

Having been able, thanks to Miller and Scholes, to catalog the potential problems present in any test of the CAPM, let us turn to an examination of two of the classic tests of the CAPM.

Tests of Black, Jensen, and Scholes

Black, Jensen, and Scholes [6] were the first to conduct an in-depth time series test of the CAPM. They took as their basic time series model

$$R_{it} - R_{Ft} = \alpha_i + \beta_i \left(R_{Mt} - R_{Ft} \right) + e_{it}$$

When this equation is estimated on time series data, the regression coefficient α_i should be equal to zero if the simple CAPM describes returns.

In order to test the CAPM, it is desirable to use a large number of securities. The obvious method is to estimate the equation for each of a series of securities and then examine the distribution of α_i. However, this is inappropriate because tests of the distribution of α's assume that the residuals (e_{it}, e_{jt}) are independent, and they are not.

One way to alleviate the problem is to run the time series regression on portfolios. Now $\tilde{R}_{it}$ is the return on portfolio i and β_i is the Beta on portfolio i. Since portfolios utilized data on more than one security and, since the residual variance from the regression using portfolios will incorporate the effect of any cross-sectional interdependencies, the standard error of the intercept can be used to test the difference of α_i from zero.

When they form portfolios, Black, Jensen, and Scholes want to maximize the spread in Betas across portfolios so they can examine the effect of Beta on return. The most obvious way to do this is to rank stocks into portfolios by true Beta. But all we have is observed Beta. To rank into portfolios by observed Beta would introduce selection bias. Stocks with high observed Beta (in the highest group) would be more likely to have a positive measurement error in estimating Beta. This would introduce a positive bias into the Beta for high Beta portfolios and would introduce a negative bias into an estimate of the intercept α_i. In an attempt to avoid this problem, an instrumental variable was used to rank stocks into portfolios. An instrumental variable is one that ideally is highly correlated with the true Beta but can be observed independently. The instrumental variable used in this study and, indeed in most studies of the CAPM, is the Beta for each security in the previous time period.

The exact procedure Black, Jensen, and Scholes used was to employ five years of monthly data to estimate Betas and rank stocks into deciles (from highest to lowest). Each

---

[6]In addition to these considerations, Miller and Scholes also examine the sensitivity of the results to the index Lintner chooses for the market. They find that the results are reasonably insensitive to the choice of the stock market index. Roll [65], as discussed later, questions this result.

decile was then considered the portfolio in the next (e.g., sixth) year. Then data for the second through sixth year were used to rank stocks and form deciles that were considered portfolios for the seventh year. This was done until deciles and the return for each decile was computed for 35 years. Then the return for decile one in each year was considered a series of returns from a portfolio, the return for decile two in each year considered a series of returns on a portfolio, and so forth. Each of the 10 portfolios could then be regressed against the market and an intercept, a Beta, and a correlation coefficient for the equation computed.

Table 15.2 shows the Beta, excess return, intercept, and correlation coefficient for each decile reported by Black, Jensen, and Scholes. Note, first, how well the model explains excess return (the high value of correlation coefficients). This would tend to support the structure of the linear equation as a good explanation of security returns. Note, however, that the intercepts vary quite a bit from zero. In fact, when $\beta > 1$ the intercepts tend to be negative and when $\beta < 1$ the intercepts tend to be positive. This, as explained below, is consistent with the two-factor capital asset pricing model rather than the standard CAPM. The implications of the zero Beta form of the CAPM are that

$$R_{it} = \overline{R}_Z(1 - \beta_i) + \beta_i R_{Mt} + e_{it}$$

The model tested is

$$R_{it} = \alpha_i + R_F(1 - \beta_i) + \beta_i R_{Mt} + e_{it}$$

If the zero Beta model really explains security prices, then rearranging these equations to eliminate $B_i R_{Mt}$ and solving for α_i yields

$$\alpha_i = (\overline{R}_Z - R_F)(1 - \beta_i)$$

As shown in Chapter 14, $\overline{R}_Z$ should be larger than R_F. Thus, $(\overline{R}_Z - R_F)$ should be positive. Therefore, if β_i is less than 1, α_i should be positive; and if β_i is greater than 1, α_i should be negative. This is exactly what the empirical results show. Black, Jensen, and Scholes repeat these tests for four subperiods and find, by and large, the same type of behavior we have described for the overall period.

Table 15.2   Tests of the CAPM as reported by Black, Jensen, and Scholes [6]

	β	Excess Return[a]	α_i Intercept	ρ[b]
1	1.561	0.0213	−0.0829	0.963
2	1.384	0.0177	−0.1938	0.988
3	1.248	0.0171	−0.0649	0.988
4	1.163	0.0163	−0.0167	0.991
5	1.057	0.0145	−0.0543	0.992
6	0.923	0.0137	0.0593	0.983
7	0.853	0.0126	0.0462	0.985
8	0.753	0.0115	0.0812	0.979
9	0.629	0.0109	0.1968	0.956
10	0.490	0.0091	0.2012	0.898
Market	1.000	0.0142		

[a]On monthly terms 0.0213 should be read as 2.13% return per month. Excess return is average return on the portfolio minus the risk-free rate.
[b]Correlation coefficient.

To this point we have described the time series tests of the CAPM performed by Black, Jensen, and Scholes. We now very briefly describe their cross-sectional tests. Recall that one of the major problems in cross-sectional tests (second-pass regressions) was an inability to identify the true Beta. This biased the intercept of the second-pass regression upward, biased its slope downward, and caused residual risk to serve as a proxy variable for Beta risk. One way to decrease substantially the error in estimating Beta is to measure Betas for portfolios rather than for securities. To the extent that errors in measuring each stock's Betas are random, they will cancel out and the aggregate error will be very small when Betas are estimated for portfolios.[7] The grouping procedures we have already described are an excellent way of forming portfolios to estimate Betas for second-pass regressions. When the excess returns for the 10 portfolios described in Table 15.2 are regressed against the Betas for each portfolio, the results are

$$\bar{R}_i - R_F = 0.00359 + 0.01080\beta_i, \qquad \rho^2 = 0.98$$

The results are shown diagrammatically in Figure 15.2.

The positive value of the intercept that emerges from this analysis is powerful evidence in support of the two-factor model.[8] The high percentage of the variation in returns explained (98%) shows that a straight line describes returns very well as predicted by the theory. Let us now turn to an examination of the Fama and MacBeth tests of the CAPM.

Tests of Fama and MacBeth

Fama and MacBeth [30] used an interesting methodology to test the CAPM. They formed 20 portfolios of securities to estimate Betas from a first-pass regression, using the same procedure as Black et al. However, they then performed one second-pass regression for each month over the time period 1935–1968. The equation they tested was

$$\tilde{R}_{it} = \hat{\gamma}_{0t} + \hat{\gamma}_{1t}\beta_i - \hat{\gamma}_{2t}\beta_i^2 + \hat{\gamma}_{3t}S_{ei} + \eta_{it} \qquad (15.4)$$

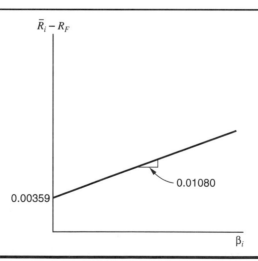

Figure 15.2   Excess return versus Beta.

---

[7]See the appendix in Black, Jensen, and Scholes [6] for a formal proof of this statement.

[8]Black et al. analyze the intercept of the second-pass regression over several subperiods. This analysis provides further evidence that the two-factor model is a better description of security returns than the one-factor model.

By estimating this equation (in cross section) for each month, it is possible to study how the parameters change over time.

This form of the equation allows the test of a series of hypotheses regarding the CAPM. The tests are:

1. $E(\hat{\gamma}_{3t}) = 0$ or residual risk does not affect return.
2. $E(\hat{\gamma}_{2t}) = 0$ or there are no nonlinearities in the security market line.
3. $E(\hat{\gamma}_{1t}) > 0$ that is, there is a positive price of risk in the capital markets.

If both $E(\hat{\gamma}_{2t})$ and $E(\hat{\gamma}_{3t})$ are not different from zero, we can also examine both $E(\hat{\gamma}_{0t})$ and $E(\hat{\gamma}_{1t})$ to see whether the standard CAPM or zero Beta model is a better description of market returns.

Finally, we can examine all of the coefficients and the residual term to see if the market operates as a fair game. If the market is a fair game, then there is no way that one should be able to use knowledge about the value of the parameters in previous periods to make an excess return. For example, if the standard CAPM or the zero Beta model holds, then, regardless of the prior values of γ_{2t} and γ_{3t}, each of their expected values at time $t + 1$ should be zero. Furthermore, if the zero Beta model is the best description of general equilibrium, then deviations of $\hat{\gamma}_{0t}$ from its mean $E(R_Z)$ and $\hat{\gamma}_{1t}$ from its mean $E(R_M) - E(R_Z)$ are random, regardless of what happened at time period $t - 1$ or any earlier time period. If the simple form of the CAPM holds the same, statements should be true with R_F substituted for $\bar{R}_Z$.

Fama and MacBeth have estimates of $\hat{\gamma}_{0t}$, $\hat{\gamma}_{1t}$, $\hat{\gamma}_{2t}$, and $\hat{\gamma}_{3t}$ and η_{it} for each month over the period January 1935–June 1968. The average value of any $\hat{\gamma}_{it}$ (denoted by $\bar{\hat{\gamma}}_i$) can be found simply by averaging the individual values, and this mean can be tested to see if it is different from zero.[9]

Table 15.3 from [30] presents the results of estimating Equation (15.4) and several variations of it over the full time period of 1935–1968, as well as for several subperiods. Notice that Fama and MacBeth have estimated the full Equation (15.4), as well as forms of the equation with all values of $\hat{\gamma}_{2t}$ and $\hat{\gamma}_{3t}$ both separately and simultaneously forced to zero. If both theory and empirical evidence indicate that one or more variables have no influence on an equation, better estimates of the remaining coefficients can be made when these influences do not enter the estimating equation. For example, theory and the initial empirical results (as we will see) indicate that neither β^2 nor residual risk affect return. Therefore, better estimates of the effect of Beta on return can be made when these variables are excluded because the coefficient on Beta will not be affected by the multicollinearity between Beta and Beta square and between Beta and residual risk.

Examining panels C and D of Table 15.3 reveals that, when measured over the entire period, $\bar{\hat{\gamma}}_3$ is small and is not statistically different from zero. Furthermore, when we examine it over several subperiods, we find that it remains small in each subperiod, is not significantly different from zero, and, in fact, exhibits different signs in different subperiods. We can safely conclude that residual risk has no effect on the expected return of a security. However, it is still possible that the market does not constitute a fair game with respect to any information contained in $\hat{\gamma}_{3t}$. That is, it is possible that the fact that $\hat{\gamma}_{3t}$ differs from zero in any period gives us insight into what its value (and, therefore, returns) will be next period. The easiest way to test this is to examine the correlation of $\hat{\gamma}_{3t}$ in one period with

---

[9]The statistical significance of each parameter can be found by calculating the standard deviation of the mean and testing to see if the mean is a significant number of standard deviations from zero. From the central limit theorem the mean is normally distributed with standard deviation equal to the standard deviation of the $\hat{\gamma}_{it}$'s divided by the square root of the number of observations on $\hat{\gamma}_{it}$.

Table 15.3 Tests of the Two-Parameter Model

Panel A — $R_{it} = \hat{\gamma}_{0t} + \hat{\gamma}_{1t}\beta_i + \eta_{it}$

Period	$\bar{\hat{\gamma}}_0$	$\bar{\hat{\gamma}}_1$	$\bar{\hat{\gamma}}_2$	$\bar{\hat{\gamma}}_3$	$\overline{\hat{\gamma}_0 - R_F}$	$s(\hat{\gamma}_0)$	$s(\hat{\gamma}_1)$	$s(\hat{\gamma}_2)$	$s(\hat{\gamma}_3)$	$\hat{\rho}_0(\hat{\gamma}_0 - R_F)$	$\hat{\rho}(\hat{\gamma}_1)$	$\hat{\rho}_0(\hat{\gamma}_2)$	$\hat{\rho}_0(\hat{\gamma}_3)$	$t(\bar{\hat{\gamma}}_0)$	$t(\bar{\hat{\gamma}}_1)$	$t(\bar{\hat{\gamma}}_2)$	$t(\bar{\hat{\gamma}}_3)$	$t(\hat{\gamma}_0 - R_F)$	$\bar{\rho}^2$	$s(\rho^2)$
1935–6/1968	0.0061	0.0085			0.0048	0.038	0.066			0.15	0.02			3.24	2.57			2.55	0.29	0.30
1935–1945	0.0039	0.0163			0.0037	0.052	0.098			0.10	−0.03			0.86	1.92			0.82	0.29	0.29
1946–1955	0.0087	0.0027			0.0078	0.026	0.041			0.18	0.07			3.71	0.70			3.31	0.31	0.32
1956–6/1968	0.0060	0.0062			0.0034	0.030	0.044			0.27	0.15			2.45	1.73			1.39	0.28	0.29
1935–1940	0.0024	0.0109			0.0023	0.064	0.116			0.07	−0.09			0.32	0.79			0.31	0.23	0.30
1941–1945	0.0056	0.0229			0.0054	0.034	0.069			0.23	0.15			1.27	2.55			1.22	0.37	0.28
1946–1950	0.0050	0.0029			0.0044	0.031	0.047			0.20	0.04			1.27	0.48			1.10	0.39	0.33
1951–1955	0.0123	0.0024			0.0111	0.019	0.035			0.20	0.08			5.06	0.53			4.56	0.24	0.29
1956–1960	0.0148	−0.0059			0.0128	0.020	0.034			0.37	0.18			5.68	−1.37			4.89	0.22	0.31
1961–6/1968	0.0001	0.0143			−0.0029	0.034	0.048			0.22	0.09			0.03	2.81			−.80	0.32	0.27

Panel B — $R_{it} = \hat{\gamma}_{0t} + \hat{\gamma}_{1t}\beta_i + \hat{\gamma}_{2t}\beta_i^2 + \eta_{it}$

Period	$\bar{\hat{\gamma}}_0$	$\bar{\hat{\gamma}}_1$	$\bar{\hat{\gamma}}_2$	$\bar{\hat{\gamma}}_3$	$\overline{\hat{\gamma}_0 - R_F}$	$s(\hat{\gamma}_0)$	$s(\hat{\gamma}_1)$	$s(\hat{\gamma}_2)$	$s(\hat{\gamma}_3)$	$\hat{\rho}_0(\hat{\gamma}_0 - R_F)$	$\hat{\rho}(\hat{\gamma}_1)$	$\hat{\rho}_0(\hat{\gamma}_2)$	$\hat{\rho}_0(\hat{\gamma}_3)$	$t(\bar{\hat{\gamma}}_0)$	$t(\bar{\hat{\gamma}}_1)$	$t(\bar{\hat{\gamma}}_2)$	$t(\bar{\hat{\gamma}}_3)$	$t(\hat{\gamma}_0 - R_F)$	$\bar{\rho}^2$	$s(\rho^2)$
1935–6/1968	0.0049	0.0105	−0.0008		0.0036	0.052	0.118	0.056		0.03	−0.11	−0.11		1.92	1.79	−0.29		1.42	0.32	0.31
1935–1945	0.0074	0.0079	0.0040		0.0073	0.061	0.139	0.074		−0.10	−0.31	−0.21		1.39	0.65	0.61		1.36	0.32	0.30
1946–1955	−0.0002	0.0217	−0.0087		−0.0012	0.036	0.095	0.034		0.04	0.00	0.00		−0.07	2.51	−2.83		−0.38	0.36	0.32
1956–6/1968	0.0069	0.0040	0.0013		0.0043	0.054	0.116	0.053		0.17	0.07	0.03		1.56	0.42	0.29		0.97	0.30	0.30
1935–1940	0.0013	0.0141	−0.0017		0.0012	0.069	0.160	0.075		−0.13	−0.36	−0.35		0.16	0.75	−0.19		0.14	0.24	0.30
1941–1945	0.0148	0.0004	0.0108		0.0146	0.050	0.111	0.073		−0.04	−0.19	−0.04		2.28	0.03	1.15		2.24	0.39	0.29
1946–1950	−0.0008	0.0152	−0.0051		−0.0015	0.037	0.104	0.032		0.14	0.04	0.00		−0.18	1.14	−1.24		−0.32	0.44	0.32
1951–1955	0.0004	0.0281	−0.0122		−0.0008	0.030	0.085	0.035		−0.17	−0.14	−0.01		0.10	2.55	−2.72		−0.20	0.28	0.29
1956–1960	0.0128	−0.0015	−0.0020		0.0108	0.030	0.072	0.029		0.35	0.11	0.26		3.38	−0.16	−0.54		2.84	0.25	0.31
1961–6/1968	0.0029	0.0077	0.0034		−0.0000	0.066	0.138	0.064		0.14	0.06	−0.01		0.42	0.53	0.51		−0.01	0.34	0.29

Panel C

$$R_{it} = \hat{\gamma}_{0t} + \hat{\gamma}_{1t}\beta_i + \hat{\gamma}_{3t}s_{e_i} + \eta_{it}$$

Period	(1)	(2)	(3)	(4)	(5)	(6)	(7)	(8)	(9)	(10)	(11)	(12)	(13)	(14)	(15)	(16)
1935–6/1968	0.0054	0.0072	0.0198	0.0041	0.065	0.052	0.868	0.04	−0.12	−0.04	2.10	2.20	0.46	1.59	0.32	0.31
1935–1945	0.0017	0.0104	0.0841	0.0015	0.083	0.073	0.921	−0.00	−0.26	−0.08	0.26	1.41	1.05	0.24	0.32	0.31
1946–1955	0.0110	0.0075	−0.1052	0.0100	0.056	0.032	0.609	0.08	0.02	−0.20	3.78	1.47	−1.89	3.46	0.34	0.32
1956–6/1968	0.0042	0.0041	0.0633	0.0016	0.052	0.040	0.984	0.12	0.08	0.03	1.28	0.96	0.79	0.50	0.30	0.29
1935–1940	0.0036	0.0119	−0.0170	0.0035	0.105	0.082	0.744	−0.03	−0.26	−0.18	0.37	0.97	−0.19	0.36	0.25	0.30
1941–1945	−0.0006	0.0085	0.2053	−0.0009	0.052	0.061	1.091	0.07	−0.29	−0.02	−0.08	1.25	1.46	−0.11	0.41	0.30
1946–1950	0.0069	0.0081	−0.0920	0.0062	0.066	0.034	0.504	0.14	0.06	−0.02	1.56	0.95	−1.41	1.40	0.42	0.33
1951–1955	0.0150	0.0069	−0.1185	0.0138	0.043	0.029	0.702	0.06	−0.18	−0.32	4.05	1.24	−1.31	3.72	0.27	0.29
1956–1960	0.0127	−0.0081	−0.0728	0.0107	0.045	0.037	1.164	0.15	0.15	0.21	2.68	−1.40	0.48	2.26	0.26	0.30
1961–6/1968	−0.0014	0.0122	0.0570	−0.0044	0.055	0.042	0.850	0.10	0.00	−0.19	−0.32	2.12	0.64	−0.98	0.33	0.27

Panel D

$$R_{it} = \hat{\gamma}_{0t} + \hat{\gamma}_{1t}\beta_i + \hat{\gamma}_{2t}\beta_i^2 + \hat{\gamma}_{3t}s_{ei} + \eta_{it}$$

Period	(1)	(2)	(3)	(4)	(5)	(6)	(7)	(8)	(9)	(10)	(11)	(12)	(13)	(14)	(15)	(16)	(17)	(18)	(19)	(20)
1935–6/1968	0.0020	0.0114	−0.0026	0.0516	0.0008	0.123	0.075	0.060	0.929	−0.09	−0.09	−0.12	−0.10	0.55	1.85	−0.86	1.11	0.20	0.34	0.31
1935–1945	0.0011	0.0118	−0.0009	0.0817	0.0010	0.146	0.103	0.079	1.003	−0.20	−0.23	−0.24	−0.15	0.13	0.94	−0.14	0.94	0.11	0.34	0.31
1946–1955	0.0017	0.0209	−0.0076	−0.0378	0.0008	0.096	0.042	0.038	0.619	−0.10	−0.00	−0.01	−0.20	0.44	2.39	−2.16	−0.67	0.20	0.36	0.32
1956–6/1968	0.0031	0.0034	−0.0000	0.0966	0.0005	0.122	0.065	0.055	1.061	0.12	0.03	0.01	−0.05	0.59	0.34	−0.00	1.11	0.10	0.32	0.29
1934–1940	0.0009	0.0156	−0.0029	0.0025	0.0008	0.171	0.112	0.085	0.826	−0.16	−0.23	−0.26	−0.12	0.07	0.78	−0.29	0.03	0.06	0.26	0.30
1941–1945	0.0015	0.0073	0.0014	0.1767	0.0012	0.109	0.092	0.072	1.181	−0.28	−0.21	−0.22	−0.18	0.12	0.52	0.15	1.16	0.10	0.43	0.31
1946–1950	0.0011	0.0141	−0.0040	−0.0313	0.0004	0.106	0.047	0.042	0.590	−0.10	0.03	−0.01	−0.12	0.18	1.03	−0.73	−0.41	0.07	0.44	0.33
1951–1955	0.0023	0.0277	−0.0112	−0.0443	0.0011	0.085	0.037	0.034	0.651	−0.11	−0.13	−0.01	−0.28	0.48	2.53	−2.54	−0.53	0.23	0.29	0.30
1956–1960	0.0103	−0.0047	−0.0020	0.0979	0.0083	0.078	0.049	0.032	1.286	−0.16	0.19	−0.01	0.02	1.63	−0.47	−0.49	0.59	1.31	0.28	0.30
1961–6/1968	−0.0017	0.0088	0.0013	0.0957	−0.0046	0.144	0.073	0.066	0.887	0.20	0.00	0.01	−0.15	−0.21	0.58	0.19	1.02	−0.60	0.35	0.29

Source: Eugene F. Fama and James D. MacBeth [31].

its value in the prior period where the mean of all periods is assumed to be zero.[10] Panels C and D show that the value of this correlation coefficient $[\rho_0(\gamma_3)]$ is close to zero and not statistically significant.[11] Fama and MacBeth also compute the correlation between $\hat{\gamma}_{3t}$ and its prior value for lags of more than one period. They find, once again, that there is no usable information contained in $\hat{\gamma}_{3t}$.

The results of Fama and MacBeth are opposite to those of Lintner and Douglas regarding the importance of residual risk. The earlier discussion provides a clue. Recall that Miller and Scholes showed that if Beta had large sampling error, then residual risk served as a proxy for true Beta. Fama and MacBeth have much less sampling error than Lintner and Douglas because of their use of portfolios. When Beta is estimated more accurately, residual risk no longer shows up as important.

The results, with respect to $\bar{\hat{\gamma}}_{2t}$, are very similar. Examining panels B and D we see that $\bar{\hat{\gamma}}_2$ is small, is not statistically significant, and changes sign over alternative subperiods. Furthermore, an examination of the correlation of $\hat{\gamma}_{2t}$ with its previous value (with means assumed to be zero) shows that there is no information contained in individual values of $\hat{\gamma}_{2t}$. Thus, the Beta squared term neither affects the expected return on securities, nor does its coefficient contain information with respect to an investment strategy.

Having concluded that neither Beta squared nor residual risk has an influence on returns, the correct form of the equation to examine for further tests is that displayed in panel A.

Fama and MacBeth examine the performance of $\bar{\hat{\gamma}}_1$ for the entire period and conclude that there is evidence that the relationship between expected return and Beta is positive as well as linear. Furthermore, by testing the correlation of the difference between $\hat{\gamma}_{1t}$ and its mean with prior values of the same variable, they show that difference in $\hat{\gamma}_{1t}$ from its mean cannot be employed to produce a better forecast of a future value of $\hat{\gamma}_{1t}$ than simply using the mean.

Fama and MacBeth find that $\bar{\hat{\gamma}}_0$ is generally greater than R_F and over the entire period $\bar{\hat{\gamma}}_1$ is statistically significantly greater than zero. In addition, they find that $\bar{\hat{\gamma}}_1$ is generally less than $\bar{R}_M - R_F$. The fact that $\bar{\hat{\gamma}}_0$ is substantially greater than R_F and $\bar{\hat{\gamma}}_1$ is substantially less than $\bar{R}_M - R_F$ would seem to indicate that the zero Beta model is more consistent with equilibrium conditions than is the simple CAPM.[12]

Before finishing our discussion of these tests one more point is worth mentioning. If the equilibrium model describes market conditions, then an individual security's deviation from the model should contain no information. That is, a positive residual value for any one stock at any moment in time should convey no information about the differential performance of that stock (from the expected value produced by the model) in future periods. For this to be true, there should be no correlation (with any lag) between the residuals in Equation (15.4). This is, in fact, what Fama and MacBeth found.

Two Additional Tests of the CAPM

Two more recent articles have developed new methodologies for testing whether the simple CAPM adequately describes returns. Gibbons [38] employs the fact that the CAPM

---

[10]This is often called the autocorrelation around zero.

[11]Fama and MacBeth point out that the standard deviation of the correlation coefficient can be approximated by one divided by the square root of the number of observations or 0.05 for the overall period, 0.09 for the 10-year subperiod, and 0.13 for the 5-year subperiod.

[12]A warning is in order. Roll [65] demonstrates that this difference could be due to the choice of a market index and Fama [30] also indicates that this might be true.

places a nonlinear restriction on a set of N regression equations, one for each security. More specifically, we know that the market model requires

$$R_{it} = \alpha_i + \beta_i (R_{mt}) + e_{it} \qquad (15.5)$$

If the market model and the CAPM hold simultaneously, then

$$R_{it} = \gamma_1 (1 - \beta_i) + \beta_i (R_{mt}) + e_{it}$$

or

$$\alpha_i = \gamma_1 (1 - \beta_i) \qquad (15.6)$$

where γ_1 is a constant for all securities. For the standard form of the CAPM, γ_1 should equal R_F, for the zero-Beta form, γ_1 should equal $\bar{R}_Z$, which should be larger than R_F. Now a set of N equations (one for each security) like (15.5) can be estimated simultaneously.

The same set of equations can be estimated under the constraint that all α_i's equal a constant times the sum of one minus β_i. Obviously the constrained equation cannot have more explanatory power than the unconstrained equation. However, if it has less at a statistically significant level, it would be strong evidence for rejecting both the standard and zero-Beta form of the CAPM. Gibbons performs this test using the methodology of seemingly unrelated regression and does a likelihood ratio test on the difference in explanatory power between the constrained and unconstrained regression. Defining the market as an equally weighted portfolio of New York Stock Exchange stocks, Gibbons rejects both the standard form and the zero-Beta form of the CAPM.

Stambaugh [84] takes a similar approach to Gibbons in examining the CAPM. However, he uses a different statistical test (a Lagrangian Multiplier test rather than a likelihood ratio test). Stambaugh claims that his test is more powerful for samples of the size studied by both authors, and based on his tests he reaches very different conclusions than does Gibbons. Stambaugh finds strong support for the zero-Beta form of the CAPM and evidence against the standard form. Furthermore, Stambaugh performs these tests using several alternative definitions of the market portfolio, including corporate bonds, government bonds, Treasury bills, home furnishings, residential real estate, and automobiles as well as common stocks. His major conclusions appear robust over alternative definitions of the market portfolio.

TESTING SOME ALTERNATIVE FORMS OF THE CAPM MODEL

It is difficult to state that any form of the CAPM is right or wrong. In fact, in the next section of this chapter we will see that there are additional problems we have not as yet faced. Although it may be impossible to accept or reject a model as correct for all purposes, it may be possible to say that one form of a model works better for a specific purpose or explains historical returns better than another form of a model. The nonstandard forms of the CAPM described in Chapter 14 have not been subject to the intense investigation that has been performed on the more standard CAPMs. However, there are two models that have been investigated in some detail: the post-tax form of the CAPM and the consumption-based CAPM. We will discuss each briefly.

TESTING THE POST-TAX FORM OF THE CAPM MODEL

While a great deal of attention has been paid to tests of the zero Beta (two-factor) CAPM model, almost no testing has been done on the other forms of general equilibrium models described in the previous chapter. The one exception to this is tax-adjusted versions of the general equilibrium model. Black and Scholes [5] have tested a form of the CAPM that includes a dividend term and concluded that dividends do not affect the equilibrium relationship. Since a dividend term is present in the post-tax CAPM, this would seem to indicate that a pre-tax CAPM is more descriptive of equilibrium returns. However, subsequently Litzenberger and Ramaswamy [60] have found strong, positive support for dividends affecting equilibrium prices. Their results differ from Black and Scholes at least in part because while Black and Scholes assumed that dividends were received in equal amounts each month, Litzenberger and Ramaswamy formulated their tests so that dividends were assumed to be received in the month in which they could reasonably be expected to occur.[13] They tested a model of the form

$$R_{it} - R_{Ft} = \gamma_0 + \gamma_1 \beta_{it} + \gamma_2 (\delta_{it} - R_{Ft}) + e_{it}$$

where δ_{it} is the dividend divided by price for stock i in month t. This model appears like a test of the two-factor model with the addition of a new term involving dividend yields. The form of this new term is consistent with the post-tax model presented in Chapter 14 with γ_2 interpreted as τ.[14]

When Litzenberger and Ramaswamy tested this model using maximum likelihood estimates on monthly data, they found the following results for the period 1936–1977.[15]

$$R_{it} - R_{Ft} = 0.0063 + 0.0421 \beta_{it} + 0.236 (\delta_{it} - R_{Ft})$$

$$(2.63) \qquad (1.86) \qquad (8.62)$$

t - statistics in parentheses

The key point to note from this analysis is that the dividend term is positive and statistically significant. Furthermore, it is obvious that the dividend term is of economic significance. This term indicates that for every $1 of dividends paid, stock investors require 23.6¢ in extra return. The model also allows us to infer the effective tax rates for determining equilibrium in the market. Recall that γ_2 is equal to τ.

In Chapter 14 we demonstrated that τ was equal to an average of τ_i

$$\tau_i = \frac{t_{di} - t_{gi}}{1 - t_{gi}}$$

where

t_{di} = tax rate paid on dividend income

t_{gi} = tax rate paid on capital gain income

The assumption behind this derivation was that capital gains taxes as well as ordinary income taxes were paid at the end of each period (e.g., year). Litzenberger and Ramaswamy developed an analogous model under the assumption that capital gains taxes are postponed indefinitely and are essentially equal to zero. Under this assumption t_{gi}

---

[13]Other differences are that Litzenberger and Ramaswamy based the form of their dividend term on the general equilibrium equation. Black and Scholes simply added a dividend term to the standard CAPM. In addition, Litzenberger and Ramaswamy used maximum likelihood methods for estimating their equation, rather than relying on the portfolio grouping techniques of Black and Scholes.

[14]τ is related to tax rates as explained below.

[15]Litzenberger and Ramaswamy estimate this equation for six subperiods during the 1936–1977 time span. In each subperiod the dividend yield term has positive signs. It is statistically significant in five of the six periods. This is the best behaved of the three coefficients as each of the other coefficients have the wrong sign in two subperiods and are statistically significant in only one or two of the subperiods.

equals zero and τ equals an average of t_{di}. The truth probably lies somewhere between these two extremes. Using their estimate of τ, the effective income tax rate lies in the following range[16]:

$$0.236 \leq t_{di} \leq 0.382$$

They also tested for and found evidence supporting the presence of a clientele effect. That is, stockholders in high tax brackets tended to hold stocks with low dividend yields, while investors in low tax brackets tended to hold stocks with high dividend yields. These results are consistent with the findings of Elton and Gruber [27].

Testing the Consumption Based CAPM (CCAPM)

A series of papers have formulated tests of the consumption based CAPM.[17] One of the most comprehensive sets of tests are found in a paper by Breeden, Gibbons, and Litzenberger [13]. The form of the model they test has been examined in Chapter 14 and is briefly summarized below. Returns are assumed to be generated by the following process

$$R_{it} = \alpha_i + \beta_i C_t + e_{it}$$

Where by assumption

$E(e_{it}) = 0$ and the covariance between e_{it} and C_t is zero or

$E(e_{it}C_t) = 0$

Under this model

$$\beta_i = \frac{\mathrm{Cov}(R_{it}, C_t)}{\mathrm{Var}(C_t)}$$

and the equilibrium return for any security is given by

$$\overline{R}_i = \overline{R}_z + \gamma_1 \beta_i$$

where

C_t = the rate of growth in per capita consumption at time t

γ_1 = the market price of consumption risk (Beta)

As pointed out earlier, this set of equations is analogous to the equations for the zero Beta form of the CAPM, with the return on the market portfolio replaced by the rate of growth in consumption between two points in time.

Testing the consumption capital asset pricing models has many econometric problems in common with testing the zero Beta form of the standard capital asset pricing model. The major problem both have in common is identifying the variable that drives return (in this case the growth rate in per capita consumption).

Breeden, Gibbons, and Litzenberger [13] have recognized and attempted to solve four types of problems that arise in measuring the rate of growth in per capita consumption. These measurement problems stem from the fact that:

---

[16]The lower estimate is of course their coefficient on the dividend term. The higher estimate is obtained by setting

$$\frac{t_{di} - t_{gi}}{1 - t_{gi}} = 0.236 \qquad \text{and} \qquad t_{gi} = (1/2)t_{di}$$

[17]See [10], [11], [12], [13].

1. Any estimate of consumption contains sampling error.

2. Statistics are reported on expenditures not on consumption.

3. Total expenditures over some period of time (a month or a quarter) are reported rather than expenditures at a point in time.

4. After 1958 monthly numbers are reported, but only quarterly expenditures are reported for the period prior to 1958.[18]

Breeden, Gibbons, and Litzenberger show that if errors in measuring consumption are random and uncorrelated with economic variables, the estimate of the price of risk (γ_1) will be upward biased but their tests of the significance of the model will not be biased. Breeden, Gibbons, and Litzenberger deal with the second problem by assuming that expenditures on nondurable goods plus services act as a good proxy for consumption. They ignore any consumption flow from durable goods and any pattern in the storage of nondurables.

The third problem is more difficult to solve. Because consumption expenditures are reported for a period of time rather than at a point in time, expenditures are averaged. Estimated Betas on averaged consumption are less than they would be if consumption was reported at a point in time. They estimate the size of this difference and rescale the growth in a consumption so that the Betas are as if consumption was reported at a point in time.[19]

Having shown this, the authors are left with the last remaining problem, the unavailability of monthly data. Breeden [10] has shown that the CAPM holds when the growth in aggregate per capita consumption is replaced with the rate of return on a portfolio of assets that has maximum correlation with the appropriate consumption series. By designing such a portfolio using quarterly data, the authors can then proceed to test the consumption CAPM using monthly observations on this portfolio (called the consumption portfolio). Breeden, Gibbons, and Litzenberger employ data from 1929–1982 to find the consumption portfolio (MCP), which has maximum correlation with consumption. The portfolio is formed from among return series on each of 13 industries plus return series for U.S. Treasury bills, long-term government bonds, long-term corporate bonds, and a junk bond premium. The composition of the MCP portfolio is assumed to be the same over the entire time period, 1929–1982. The MCP is a portfolio of stocks and debt instruments that is clearly related to but different from many of the proxies that have been used for the market portfolio. For the period of study, 1929–1982, the correlation between the MCP and the CRSP value-weighted index is 0.67.

Tests of the consumption-based CAPM model using the MCP portfolio produced mixed results. The consumption CAPM has certain test characteristics that are appealing. Average return seems to be linearly related to Beta. Furthermore, the intercept seems to support a riskless asset version rather than a zero Beta version of the consumption CAPM. In all periods examined the market price of risk γ_1 is positive, and in most periods it is statistically significantly different from zero.

---

[18]The authors use expenditures on nondurable goods and services based on national income accounting. The Commerce Department statistics on average U.S. population are used to obtain per capita statistics.

[19]In the next paragraph we discuss construction of a matching portfolio. Betas are needed to construct this matching portfolio. The adjustment is determined as follows. Breeden, Gibbons, and Litzenberger show analytically that the variance in this smoothed series should be equal to two-thirds of the variance of the unsmoothed series, that the covariance of the smoothed series with spot quarterly returns on securities should be equal to one-half of the spot covariance with the unsmoothed series, and that thus the smoothed Beta of return with consumption should be equal to three-quarters of the unsmoothed Beta. This analysis is used to adjust the growth in consumption so that Betas will be the appropriate size.

However, when tests of efficiency similar to those performed by Gibbons [38] and Stambaugh [83] using Equation (15.6) are performed, the efficiency of the MCP is rejected. So is the CRSP value-weighted index. The methodology employed does not allow us to draw a conclusion as to the superiority of either model.

SOME RESERVATIONS ABOUT TRADITIONAL TESTS OF GENERAL EQUILIBRIUM RELATIONSHIPS AND SOME NEW RESEARCH

In this chapter we have reviewed some of the classic tests of general equilibrium relationships. These tests were intended to validate the theories we have described in the previous two chapters. Roll has argued [65] that general equilibrium models of the form of the CAPM are not amenable to testing or, at least, that the tests performed so far provide little evidence in support of, or against, CAPM. Roll raised some legitimate questions, and his arguments are well worth reviewing.

Perhaps the easiest way to understand Roll's case is to start with his proof that if *any* ex-post mean variance efficient portfolio is selected as the market portfolio and Betas are computed using this as the market proxy, then the equation

$$\overline{R}_i = \overline{R}_{ZP} + \beta_{iP}\left(\overline{R}_P - \overline{R}_{ZP}\right)$$

must hold.[20] In fact, it is a tautology that has nothing to do with the way equilibrium is set in the capital markets or with investor's attitude toward risk.

Proof   Return to Equation (13.4). Assume a riskless asset exists with a return R_F. Then

$$\lambda\left(X_1\sigma_{1k} + X_2\sigma_{2k} + \cdots + X_k\sigma_k^2 + \cdots + X_N\sigma_{kN}\right) = \overline{R}_k - R_F$$

If all X_i's stand for the proportion of stock i in portfolio P, we can write this expression as

$$\lambda\sigma_{kP} = \overline{R}_k - R_F \tag{15.7}$$

Since this expression must hold for each security in portfolio P, it must also hold for portfolio P itself or

$$\lambda\sigma_P^2 = \overline{R}_P - R_F$$

Solving for λ, substituting in Equation (15.5) and rearranging,

$$\overline{R}_k = R_F + \frac{\sigma_{kP}}{\sigma_P^2}\left(\overline{R}_P - R_F\right)$$

Recognizing that $(\sigma_{kP}/\sigma_P^2) = \beta_{kP}$, we can write this as

$$\overline{R}_k = R_F + \beta_{kP}\left(\overline{R}_P - R_F\right) \tag{15.8}$$

Now, as we did in Chapter 14, assume that lending and borrowing cannot take place at the riskless rate R_F. However, as we have seen, an infinite number of portfolios will exist that have the return R_F. From Equation (15.8) they all must be uncorrelated with portfolio

---

[20]In this expression P is the proxy for the market portfolio, $\overline{R}_P$ is the expected return on the proxy for the market portfolio, β_{iP} is the Beta for security i with the proxy market portfolio, and R_{ZP} is the minimum variance portfolio that has a zero Beta with the market proxy portfolio.

P. Let $\overline{R}_{ZP}$ stand for the minimum variance portfolio that is uncorrelated with portfolio *P*. Then, since $\overline{R}_{ZP} = R_F$, Equation (15.8) can be written as

$$\overline{R}_k = \overline{R}_{ZP} + \beta_{kP}\left(\overline{R}_P - \overline{R}_{ZP}\right)$$

From the proof it follows that the return on an asset or portfolio is an *exact* linear function of Beta if Betas are computed using any efficient portfolio. Conversely, if the portfolio used to compute Betas is not efficient, then return is not an exact linear function of Beta.

From this proof it follows that the two-factor form of the CAPM must always hold with respect to ex-post data if the proxy chosen for the market portfolio is ex-post efficient. Furthermore, Roll argues that tests performed with any portfolio other than the true market portfolio are not tests of the CAPM. They are simply tests of whether the portfolio chosen as a proxy for the market is efficient or not. Since over an interval of time efficient portfolios exist, a market proxy may be chosen that satisfies all the implications of the CAPM model, even when the market portfolio is inefficient. On the other hand, an inefficient portfolio may be chosen as a proxy for the market and the CAPM rejected when the market itself is efficient. Roll demonstrates that the high correlation that exists among most reasonable proxies for the market does not mean that the choice of a proxy is unimportant. Though they are highly correlated, some may be efficient while others are inefficient.

Roll proceeds to show that the choice between alternative forms of the CAPM model is extremely sensitive to the choice of a market proxy. For example, while the Black, Jensen, and Scholes results did not support the Sharpe–Lintner–Mossin form of the CAPM, Roll shows there was a mean variance efficient market proxy that had a correlation of 0.895 with the market proxy used by Black et al., which supported the Sharpe–Lintner–Mossin form of the model perfectly.

The logical conclusion of Roll's work is that equilibrium theory is not testable unless the exact composition of the true market portfolio is known and used in the tests. The true test of the generalized two-parameter CAPM is whether the market portfolio is mean-variance efficient. Alternative forms of the CAPM can be judged against one another only if the true market portfolio is used in these tests.

Perhaps Roll's feelings about the state of testing of the capital asset pricing theory can best be summarized by a quote from his work: "Unfortunately, it [capital asset pricing theory] has never been subjected to an unambiguous empirical test. There is considerable doubt, moreover, at least by me, that it ever will."

The logic behind Roll's statement is that we don't know the composition, much less the return, on the true market portfolio. Most tests of CAPM use some portfolio of common stocks as the market, but the true market contains all risky assets. These include not only traded assets like stocks, bonds, and preferred stocks, but assets on which data are not as readily available, such as diamonds, gold, old coins, and items we are only beginning to measure (like human capital).

Several attempts have been made to deal with Roll's criticism of tests of the CAPM. Many involve trying alternative definitions of the market portfolio to test for linearity or the reasonableness of the intercept. One problem with most empirical work on the efficiency of a market proxy is that most reasonable proxies are highly correlated with each other (and perhaps with the true market), and despite this high correlation small differences in the choice from among a set of highly correlated proxies can lead to very different inferences.

The most imaginative attempt to deal with this problem is an approach advocated by Jay Shanken [77]. He recognized that the acceptance or rejection of the CAPM depends on how well the proxy for the market replicates the true but unobserved market portfolio.

Shanken develops a joint test that allows acceptance or rejection of the joint hypothesis that the correlation of the proxy with the market portfolio exceeds some limit and the CAPM is valid. For example, Shanken tests the joint hypothesis that the correlation between the CRSP equally weighted portfolio of common stocks and the market portfolio exceeds 0.7 (50% association), and the CAPM holds with respect to the unobserved market portfolio. The joint hypothesis is rejected at the 10% level. Thus on the basis of this test one can conclude that either the unobserved market portfolio is inefficient or its correlation with the CRSP equally weighted index is below 0.7.

Shanken's technique is sufficiently flexible that it allows sets of variables (or portfolios) to be tested as proxies for the market portfolio. For example, Shanken repeats his tests using a combination of the CRSP equally weighted stock portfolio and the return on long-term government bonds as a proxy for the market portfolio. He concludes that the results are substantially the same (rejection of the CAPM) with the more complex proxy rather than just the stock portfolio.

The Roll criticism, that we cannot test the CAPM unless we can identify the market portfolio, although still correct, has been at least made less severe. Thanks to Shanken we can test whether the CAPM holds conditional on an a priori belief about the correlation between a portfolio or a set of portfolios and the unobserved market portfolio. However, to use it we still need an elusive number: the correlation between the proxy chosen and the unobservable true market portfolio.

CONCLUSION

This is, perhaps, the most difficult chapter in this book to conclude. On the one hand, we have a host of evidence that purports to support the CAPM. On the other hand, we have Roll's very cogent arguments questioning this evidence. Can we conclude anything positive from all this?

First, we should be careful to note that Roll has not cast aspersions on any specific form of the CAPM; he has not said that they do not hold. What he has simply said is that we have not tested whether they do or do not hold, nor, in his opinion, are we likely to be able to do so.

If we reexamine the tests in this chapter, not as tests of the CAPM but as inputs to the portfolio process, do we gain useful information? We would argue that we do. The fact that return and risk appear to be linearly related for securities and portfolios over long periods of time, when risk is defined as systematic risk, is important. The same can be said for the fact that return is not related to residual risk. Even if these statements do not constitute tests of the CAPM, they have important implications for behavior. Investors are not rewarded for taking nonmarket risk, but they are rewarded for bearing added market risk. These statements seem to hold under alternative methods of calculating systematic risk. Furthermore, they seem to hold even more firmly when systematic risk is calculated using a value-weighted, rather than equally weighted, market proxy.[21] The fair game nature of the model is also important. Not only does the model seem to hold over long periods of time, but intertemporal deviations from the model cannot be used to make an extra return.

In summary, while the empirical work is not fully a satisfactory test of the CAPM, it produces results that are consistent with what one would expect from a test of the CAPM.

---

[21]See, for a comparison, Foster [35]. CAPM tests have usually been performed utilizing an equally weighted index for all New York Stock Exchange (NYSE) stocks. Foster compares tests employing an equally weighted index with those employing a market-weighted index.

Furthermore, these results are produced with respect to observables variables (market proxies). While we should continue to search for true tests of the CAPM, we can, with some care, proceed on the basis of the results produced by tests of observable, but not optimum, phenomena.

There is another direction that testing can take. In this chapter we have attempted to see whether we could prove the CAPM was "true" or not. We have concluded that although we couldn't tell whether it was true or not, it does give us insight into behavior in capital markets. A very practical question to ask is if there is another model of asset prices that gives us added insight into capital markets. The existence of competing models might not allow us to determine that one is right, but it might allow us to determine that one is better or at least better for some purposes.

In the next chapter we will describe a competing paradigm for describing asset prices. We will then examine tests of that model to see if in fact it allows us to gain new insights into portfolio management and to help explain what happens in capital markets.

APPENDIX

RANDOM ERRORS IN BETA AND BIAS IN THE PARAMETERS OF THE CAPM

This appendix contains a proof that a random (unbiased) error in identifying Beta leads to a downward bias slope and upward biased intercept in the second-pass (cross-sectional) regression used to test the CAPM.

Define the correct model for the second-pass regression as

$$R_i - R_F = \gamma_1 \beta_i + e_i \tag{A.1}$$

where β_i is the true, but unobserved, value of Beta for security i. Furthermore, note that β_i has a cross-sectional mean of 1 and a variance of $\sigma^2(\beta_i)$.

Now assume that the estimate of β_i from the first-pass regression has an error that is independent of β_i and e_i (unbiased), and is drawn from the same distribution for all stocks. Let b_i equal the observed value of β_i; then we can write

$$b_i = \beta_i + v_i \tag{A.2}$$

where $E(v_i) = 0$ and variance $(v_i) = \sigma^2(v_i)$,

$$\text{cov}(v_i, e_i) = 0 \qquad \text{cov}(v_i, \beta_i) = 0$$

The second-pass regression that is actually run is

$$R_i - R_F = \gamma_0 + \gamma_1 b_i + e_i$$

For very large sample sizes, the limit of

$$\plim_{n \to \infty} \hat{\gamma}_1 = \frac{\text{cov}(R_i - R_F, b_i)}{\sigma^2(b_i)}$$

Substituting (A.1) for $R_i - R_F$ and (A.2) for b_i,

$$\plim_{n \to \infty} \hat{\gamma}_1 = \frac{\text{cov}(\gamma_1 \beta_i + e_i, \beta_i + v_i)}{\sigma^2(\beta_i + v_i)}$$

Recalling that $\mathrm{cov}(e_i, v_i) = 0$, $\mathrm{cov}(e_i, \beta_i) = 0$, and $\mathrm{cov}(v_i, \beta_i) = 0$,

$$\operatorname*{plim}_{n \to \infty} \hat{\gamma}_1 = \gamma_1 \frac{\sigma^2(\beta_i)}{\sigma^2(\beta_i) + \sigma^2(v_i)} \qquad (\text{A.3})$$

As long as there is a measurement error, $\sigma^2(v_i)$ is positive and $\hat{\gamma}_1$ is a downward biased estimate of the true γ_1.

To examine the bias in the intercept, recall that the regression must pass through the mean of both the dependent and independent variable, or

$$\frac{1}{N} \sum_{i=1}^{N} (R_i - R_F) = \hat{\gamma}_0 + \hat{\gamma}_1 \frac{1}{N} \sum_{i=1}^{N} \beta_i$$

By summing (A.1) across securities and dividing by N,

$$\frac{1}{N} \sum_{i=1}^{N} (R_i - R_F) = \gamma_1 \frac{1}{N} \sum_{i=1}^{N} \beta_i$$

But,[22]

$$\frac{1}{N} \sum_{i=1}^{N} \beta_i = 1$$

therefore,

$$\frac{1}{N} \sum_{i=1}^{N} (R_i - R_F) = \gamma_1 = \hat{\gamma}_0 + \hat{\gamma}_1 \qquad \text{or} \qquad \hat{\gamma}_0 = \gamma_1 - \hat{\gamma}_1$$

If $\hat{\gamma}_1$ was equal to γ_1, then $\hat{\gamma}_0$ would, indeed, be zero. Substituting in Equation (A.3),

$$\operatorname*{plim}_{n \to \infty} \hat{\gamma}_0 = \gamma_1 \left[1 - \frac{\sigma^2(\beta_i)}{\sigma^2(\beta_i) + \sigma^2(v_i)} \right]$$

Thus, $\hat{\gamma}_0$ is an upward biased estimate of the true intercept.

Based on the cross-sectional variance of b_i [as a proxy for $\sigma(\beta_i)$] and the square of the standard error of b_i [as a proxy for $\sigma(v_i)$], Miller and Scholes conclude plim $\hat{\gamma}_1 = 0.64\gamma_1$.

QUESTIONS AND PROBLEMS

1. We have sometimes heard investment managers say: "I followed that (expletive deleted) theory and bought high Beta stocks last year and they did worse than low Beta stocks. That theory is 'expletive deleted.'" Is this a valid test and is this empirical evidence inconsistent with the theory?

2. A new theory has been proposed. The expected percentage increase in alcoholism in each city is equal to the rate of change in the price of gold plus the product of two terms. The first is the covariance of the percentage change in alcoholism in the city with the percentage change in professors' salaries divided by the variance of the percentage change in professors' salaries. The second term is the percentage change in professors' salaries minus the percentage increase in gold. How would you test this proposition?

---

[22]The average Beta equals one only for equally weighted market portfolios. Otherwise the following equation is an approximation.

3. Show that if the market portfolio is not an efficient portfolio, then

$$\bar{R}_i = \bar{R}_Z + \beta_i \left(\bar{R}_M - \bar{R}_Z \right)$$

cannot in general hold.

4. Explain how you might use general equilibrium theory to evaluate the performance of one or more common stocks managers.

5. Assume the post-tax CAPM holds but the Sharpe–Lintner model is tested. What would you expect the empirical results to look like?

BIBLIOGRAPHY

1. Alder, Michael. "On the Risk-Return Trade-Off in the Valuation of Assets," *Journal of Financial and Quantitative Analysis*, **IV,** No. 4 (Dec. 1969), pp. 492–512.
2. Bar-Yosef, Sasson, and Kolodny, Richard. "Dividend Policy and Capital Market Theory," *Review of Economics and Statistics*, **LVIII,** No. 2 (May 1976), pp. 181–190.
3. Belkaoui, Ahmed. "Canadian Evidence of Heteroscedasticity in the Market Model," *Journal of Finance*, **XII,** No. 4 (Sept. 1977), pp. 1320–1324.
4. Best, Michael J., and Grauer, Robert R. "Capital Asset Pricing Compatible with Observed Market Value Weights," *The Journal of Finance*, **40,** No. 1 (March 1985), pp. 85–104.
5. Black, F., and Scholes, M. "The Effects of Dividend Yield and Dividend Policy on Common Stock Prices and Returns," *Journal of Financial Economics*, **1,** 1974, pp. 1–22.
6. Black, F., Jensen, M.C., and Scholes, M. "The Capital Asset Pricing Model: Some Empirical Tests," in Jensen (ed.), *Studies in the Theory of Capital Markets* (New York: Praeger, 1972).
7. Blume, Marshall, and Friend, Irwin. "A New Look at the Capital Asset Pricing Model," *Journal of Finance,* **VIII,** No. 1 (March 1973), pp. 19–33.
8. ——. "Risk, Investment Strategy, and the Long-Run Rates of Return," *Review of Economics and Statistics*, **LVI,** No. 3 (Aug. 1974), pp. 259–269.
9. Blume, Marshall, and Husic, Frank. "Price, Beta, and Exchange Listings," *Journal of Finance*, **VIII,** No. 2 (May 1973), pp. 283–299.
10. Breeden, D. "An Intertemporal Asset Pricing Model with Stochastic Consumption and Investment Opportunities," *Journal of Financial Economics*, **7** (1979), pp. 265–296.
11. ——. "Consumption Risk in Futures Markets," *Journal of Finance*, **35** (1980), pp. 503–520.
12. Breeden, D., and Litzenberger, R. "Prices of State-Contingent Claims Implicit in Option Prices," *Journal of Business*, **51** (1978), pp. 621–651.
13. Breeden, D., Gibbons, M., and Litzenberger, R. "Empirical Tests of the Consumption-Oriented CAPM," *Journal of Finance*, **44** (1989), pp. 231–262.
14. Brown, David P., and Gibbons, Michael R. "A Simple Econometric Approach for Utility-Based Asset Pricing Models," *The Journal of Finance*, **40,** No. 2 (June 1985), pp. 359–382.
15. Brown, Stephen J., and Weinstein, Mark I. "A New Approach to Testing Asset Pricing Models: The Bilinear Paradigm," *The Journal of Finance,* **38,** No. 3 (June 1983), pp. 711–744.
16. Chamberlain, G., and Rothschild, M. "Arbitrage, Factor Structure, and Mean-Variance Analysis on Large Asset Markets," *Econometrica*, **51** (1983), pp. 1281–1304.
17. Chen, N., Rolls, R., and Ross, S. "Economic Forces and the Stock Market," *Journal of Business*, **59** (1986), pp. 386–403.
18. Clarkson, Pete, Guedes, Jose, and Thompson, Rex. "On the Diversification, Observability, and Measurement of Estimation Risk," *Journal of Financial and Quantitative Analysis*, **31,** No. 1 (Mar. 1996), pp. 69–84.
19. Connor, G. "A Unified Beta Pricing Theory," *Journal of Economic Theory*, **34** (1984), pp. 13–31.
20. Connor, G., and Korajczyk, R. "Performance Measurement with the Arbitrage Pricing Theory: A New Framework for Analysis," *Journal of Financial Economics,* **15** (1986), pp. 373–394.

21. Cornell, B. "The Consumption Based Asset Pricing Model: A Note on Potential Tests and Applications," *Journal of Financial Economics*, **9** (1981), pp. 103–108.

22. Dhrymes, Phoebus, Friend, Irwin, and Gultekin, Bulent. "A Critical Reexamination of the Empirical Evidence on the Arbitrage Pricing Theory," *The Journal of Finance*, **39** (June 1984), pp. 323–346.

23. Douglas, George. *Risk in the Equity Markets: An Empirical Appraisal of Market Efficiency* (Ann Arbor, Mich.: University Microfilms, Inc., 1968).

24. Dybvig Phillip H. "An Explicit Bound on Deviations from APT Pricing in a Finite Economy," *Journal of Financial Economics*, **12** (1983), pp. 483–496.

25. Dybvig, P., and Ross, S. "Yes, the APT Is Testable," *Journal of Finance*, **40** (1985), pp. 1173–1188.

26. Elton, Edwin J. "Presidential Address: Expected Return, Realized Return and Asset Pricing Tests," *Journal of Finance*, **54** (Aug. 1999) pp. 1199–1220.

27. Elton, Edwin J., and Gruber, Martin J. "Marginal Stockholder Tax Rates and the Clientele Effect," *Review of Economics and Statistics*, **52** (1970), pp. 68–74.

28. Eubank, Arthur. "Risk-Return Contrasts: NYSE, AMEX, and OTL," *Journal of Portfolio Management*, **3,** No. 4 (Summer 1977), pp. 25–30.

29. Fama, Eugene. *Foundations of Finance* (New York: Basic Books, 1976).

30. Fama, Eugene, and MacBeth, J. "Risk, Return, and Equilibrium: Empirical Tests," *Journal of Political Economy*, **71** (May/June 1973), pp. 607–636.

31. ———. "Tests of the Multiperiod Two-Parameter Model," *Journal of Financial Economics*, **1,** No. 1 (May 1974), pp. 43–66.

32. Fama, E., MacBeth, J., and Schwert, G. "Asset Returns and Inflation," *Journal of Financial Economics*, **5** (1977), pp. 115–146.

33. ———. "Inflation, Interest and Relative Prices," *Journal of Business*, **52** (1979), pp. 183–209.

34. Ferson, W. "Expected Real Interest Rates and Consumption in Efficient Financial Markets: Empirical Tests," *Journal of Financial and Quantitative Analysis*, **18** (1983), pp. 477–498.

35. Foster, George. "Asset Pricing Models: Further Tests," *Journal of Financial and Quantitative Analysis*, **XIII,** No. 1 (Mar. 1978), pp. 39–53.

36. Friend, Irwin, Westerfield, Randolf, and Granito, Michael. "New Evidence on the Capital Asset Pricing Model," *Journal of Finance*, **XII,** No. 3 (June 1978), pp. 903–917.

37. Gentry, James, and Pike, John. "An Empirical Study of the Risk-Return Hypothesis Using Common Stock Portfolios of Life Insurance Companies," *Journal of Financial and Quantitative Analysis*, **V,** No. 2 (May 1970), pp. 179–185.

38. Gibbons, Michael R. "Multivariate Tests of Financial Models: A New Approach," *Journal of Financial Economics*, **X,** No. 1 (March 1982), pp. 3–28.

39. Gibbons, Michael R., and Ferson, Wayne. "Testing Asset Pricing Models with Changing Expectations and an Unobservable Market Portfolio," *Journal of Financial Economics*, **XIV,** No. 2 (June 1985), pp. 217–236.

40. Grinblatt, Mark, and Titman, Sheridan. "Factor Pricing in a Finite Economy," *Journal of Financial Economics*, **12** (1983), pp. 497–507.

41. Grinblatt, Mark, and Titman, Sheridan. "The Relation Between Mean-Variance Efficiency and Arbitrage," *The Journal of Business*, **60,** No. 1 (Jan. 1987), pp. 97–112.

42. Grossman, S., and Shiller, R. "Consumption Correlatedness and Risk Measurement in Economies with Non-Traded Assets and Heterogeneous Information," *Journal of Financial Economics*, **10** (1982), pp. 195–210.

43. Grossman, S., Melino, A., and Shiller, R. "Estimating the Continuous-Time Consumption-Based Asset-Pricing Model," *Journal of Business and Economic Statistics*, **5** (1987), pp. 315–328.

44. Hall, R. "Stochastic Implications of the Life Cycle-Permanent Income Hypothesis: Theory and Evidence," *Journal of Political Economy*, **86** (1978), pp. 971–987.

45. Hansen, L., and Singleton, K. "Generalized Instrumental Variables Estimation of Nonlinear Rational Expectations Models," *Econometrica*, **50** (1982), pp. 1269–1286.

46. ——. "Stochastic Consumption, Risk Aversion, and the Temporary Behavior of Asset Returns," *Journal of Polticial Economy*, **91** (1983), pp. 249–265.

47. Ibbotson, Roger, and Sinquefield, Rex. *Stocks, Bonds, Bills and Inflation: The Past and the Future* (Charlottesville, Va.: Financial Analysts Research Foundation, 1982).

48. Ingersoll, Jonathan E., Jr. "Some Results in the Theory of Arbitrage Pricing," *Journal of Finance*, **39** (1984), pp. 1021–1039.

49. Jobson, J., and Korkie, B. "Estimation for Markowitz Efficient Portfolios," *Journal of the American Statistical Association*, **75** (1980), pp. 544–554.

50. Jobson, J., and Korkie, R. "Potential Performance Tests of Portfolio Efficiency," *Journal of Financial Economics*, **10** (1982), pp. 433–466.

51. Kandel, S. "On the Exclusion of Assets from Tests of the Mean Variance Efficiency of the Market Portfolio," *Journal of Finance*, **39** (1984), pp. 63–75.

52. ——. "The Likelihood Ratio Test Statistic of Mean-Variance Efficiency without a Riskless Asset," *Journal of Financial Economics*, **13** (1984), pp. 575–592.

53. Kandel, Shmuel. "The Geometry of the Maximum Likelihood Estimator of the Zero-Beta Return," *The Journal of Finance*, **41,** No. 2 (June 1986), pp. 339–346.

54. Kandel, S., and Stambaugh, R. "On Correlations and the Sensitivity of Inferences about Mean-Variance Efficiency," *Journal of Financial Economics*, **18** (1987), pp. 61–80.

55. Keim, D. "Size Related Anomalies and Stock Return Seasonality: Further Empirical Evidence," *Journal of Financial Economics*, **12** (1983), pp. 13–32.

56. Lau, Sheila, Quay, Stuart, and Ramsey, Carl. "The Tokyo Stock Exchange and the Capital Asset Pricing Model," *Journal of Finance*, **IX,** No. 2 (May 1974), pp. 507–514.

57. Lehmann, Bruce N., and Modest, David M. "The Empirical Foundations of the Arbitrage Pricing Theory," *Journal of Financial Economics*, **21,** No. 2 (Sept. 1988), pp. 213–254.

58. Litzenberger, R., and Ronn, E. "A Utility Based Model of Common Stock Returns," *Journal of Finance*, **41** (1986), pp. 67–92.

59. Litzenberger, R.H., and Budd, A. P. "Secular Trends in Risk Premiums," *Journal of Finance*, **VII,** No. 3 (June 1972), pp. 857–864.

60. Litzenberger, R.H., and Ramaswamy, K. "The Effect of Personal Taxes and Dividends on Capital Asset Prices: Theory and Empirical Evidence," *Journal of Financial Economics*, **7,** No. 2 (June 1979), pp. 163–195.

61. Lucas, R. "Asset Prices in an Exchange Economy," *Econometrica*, **46** (1978), pp. 1429–1445.

62. Merton, Robert C. "An Intertemporal Capital Asset Pricing Model," *Econometrica*, **41** (1973), pp. 867–887.

63. Miller, M.H., and Scholes, M. "Rates of Return in Relation to Risk: A Re-Examination of Some Recent Findings," in Jensen, M. (ed.). *Studies in the Theory of Capital Markets* (New York: Praeger, 1972).

64. Morgan. I.G. "Prediction of Return with the Minimum Variance Zero-Beta Portfolio," *Journal of Financial Economics*, **2,** No. 4 (Dec. 1975), pp. 361–376.

65. Roll, Richard, "A Critique of the Asset Pricing Theory's Tests; Part I: On Past and Potential Testability of the Theory," *Journal of Financial Economics*, **4,** No. 2 (March 1977), pp. 129–176.

66. ——. "Orthogonal Portfolios," *Journal of Financial and Quantitative Analysis*, **XV,** No. 5 (Dec. 1980), pp. 1005–1024.

67. Roll, Richard, and Ross, Stephen. "An Empirical Investigation of the Arbitrage Pricing Theory," *Journal of Finance,* **35,** No. 5 (Dec. 1980), pp. 1073–1105.

68. Rosenberg, B., and Guy, J. "Prediction of Beta from Investment Fundamentals," *Financial Analysts Journal*, **32** (1976), pp. 60–72.

69. Rubinstein, M. "The Valuation of Uncertain Income Streams and the Pricing of Options," *Bell Journal of Economics and Management Science*, **7** (1976), pp. 407–425.

70. Scholes, M., and Williams, J. "Estimating Betas from Nonsynchronous Data," *Journal of Financial Economics*, **5** (1977), pp. 309–327.

71. Shanken, J. "An Asymptotic Analysis of the Traditional Risk-Return Model," Unpublished Manuscript, School of Business Administration, University of California, Berkeley, 1982.

72. ——. "Multivariate Tests of the Zero-Beta CAPM," *Journal of Financial Economics*, **14,** No. 3 (Sept. 1985), pp. 327–348.

73. ——. "Multi-Beta CAPM or Equilibrium-APT? A Reply," *Journal of Finance*, **40,** No. 4 (1985a), pp. 1186–1189.

74. ——. "On Exclusion of Assets from Tests of the Mean Variance Efficiency of the Market Portfolio: An Extension," *Journal of Finance*, **41,** No. 2 (1986), pp. 331–337.

75. ——. "A Posterior-Odds Ratio Approach to Testing Portfolio Efficiency," Working Paper, Graduate School of Management, University of Rochester, Rochester, NY, 1986.

76. ——. "Testing Portfolio Efficiency when the Zero-Beta Rate is Unknown: A Note," *Journal of Finance*, **41,** No. 1 (1986), pp. 269–276.

77. ——. "Multivariate Proxies and Asset Pricing Relations," *Journal of Financial Economics*, **18,** No. 1 (1987), pp. 91–110.

78. Shanken, Jay. "The Arbitrage Pricing Theory: Is it Testable?" *Journal of Finance*, **37** (1982), pp. 1129–1140.

79. Sharpe, W.F., "Risk, Market Sensitivity, and Diversification," *Financial Analysts Journal*, **28,** No. 1 (Jan.–Feb. 1972), pp. 74–79.

80. Sharpe, W.F., and Cooper, G. M. "Risk-Return Class of New York Stock Exchange Common Stocks, 1931–1967," *Financial Analysts Journal*, **28,** No. 2 (March–April 1972), pp. 46–52.

81. Sharpe, W.F., and Sosin, H. "Risk, Return, and Yield: New York Stock Exchange Common Stocks, 1928–1969," *Financial Analysts Journal*, **32,** No. 2 (March–April 1976), pp. 33–42.

82. Smith, Keith. "The Effect of Intervaling on Estimating Parameters of the Capital Asset Pricing Model," *Journal of Financial and Quantitative Analysis*, **XIII,** No. 2 (June 1978), pp. 313–332.

83. Stambaugh, Robert F. "On the Exclusion of Assets from Tests of the Two-Parameter Model: A Sensitivity Analysis," *Journal of Financial Economics*, **X,** No. 3 (Nov. 1982), pp. 237–268.

84. Upson, Roger, and Jessup, Paul. "Risk-Return Relationships in Regional Securities Markets," *Journal of Financial and Quantitative Analysis*, **IV,** No. 5 (Jan. 1970), pp. 677–695.

16

The Arbitrage Pricing Model APT—A New Approach to Explaining Asset Prices

All of the equilibrium models discussed in Chapters 13, 14, and 15 have their basis in mean-variance analysis. All require that it is optimal for the investor to choose investments on the basis of expected return and variance. However, definitions of returns for which means and variances are calculated differ between models. For example, in the version of the capital asset pricing model (CAPM) involving taxes, investors examine means and variances of after-tax returns. As a second example, Elton and Gruber [34] have shown that the alternative version of CAPM under conditions of uncertain inflation can be derived by assuming that investors maximize a utility function defined in terms of the mean and variance of real as compared to nominal returns. As noted in the previous chapter, there are major obstacles to testing any of these equilibrium theories.

Ross [99, 100] has proposed a new and different approach to explaining the pricing of assets. Ross had developed a mechanism that, given the process that generates security returns, derives asset prices from arbitrage arguments analogous to (but more complex than) those used in the beginning of Chapters 11 and 13 to derive CAPMs. In this chapter we first present the mechanism of arbitrage pricing theory (APT). This is the derivation of equilibrium conditions given any prespecified return-generating process.

Following this we discuss implementation of the APT. APT theory provides interesting insight into the nature of equilibrium. However, the theory is far from easy to implement. Empirical research is still in the early stages in this area. Furthermore, alternative approaches have been advocated for implementing the theory. After discussing some of those alternatives, we present an examination of whether evidence supporting APT is necessarily inconsistent with the standard form or any alternative form of the CAPM as a model of equilibrium. We close with a discussion of both applications and advantages of APT.

APT—WHAT IS IT?

Arbitrage pricing theory is a new and different approach to determining asset prices. It is based on the law of one price: two items that are the same can't sell at different prices. The strong assumptions made about utility theory in deriving the CAPM are not necessary. In fact, the APT description of equilibrium is more general than that provided by a CAPM-type model in that pricing can be affected by influences beyond simply means and variances. An assumption of homogeneous expectations is necessary. The assumption of investors utilizing a mean variance framework is replaced by an assumption of the process generating security returns. APT requires that the returns on any stock be linearly related to a set of indexes as shown in Equation (16.1).[1]

$$R_i = a_i + b_{i1}I_1 + b_{i2}I_2 + \cdots + b_{ij}I_j + e_i \tag{16.1}$$

where

a_i = the expected level of return for stock i if all indices have a value of zero

I_j = the value of the jth index that impacts the return on stock i

b_{ij} = the sensitivity of stock i's return to the jth index

e_i = a random error term with mean equal to zero and variance equal to σ_{ei}^2

For the model to fully describe the process generating security returns[2]:

$$E(e_i e_j) = 0 \qquad \text{for all } i \text{ and } j \text{ where } i \neq j$$

$$E\left[e_i\left(I_j - \bar{I}_j\right)\right] = 0 \qquad \text{for all stocks and indexes}$$

If you are beginning to get the feeling that you have seen all this before, you are right. This representation is nothing more or less than the description of the multi-index model presented in Chapter 8. APT is the description of the expected returns that can be derived when returns are generated by a single- or multi-index model meeting the conditions defined before. The contribution of APT is in demonstrating how (and under what conditions) one can go from a multi-index model to a description of equilibrium.

In the following pages we will demonstrate the derivation of an APT equilibrium in two different ways. The first proof stresses the economic rationale behind APT whereas the second proof is mathematically more rigorous.

A Simple Proof of APT

We will demonstrate the expected returns that must arise from the APT with a two-index model. Suppose that the following two-index model describes returns:

$$R_i = a_i + b_{i1}I_1 + b_{i2}I_2 + e_i \tag{16.2}$$

Furthermore assume that $E(e_i e_j) \approx 0$

If an investor holds a well-diversified portfolio, residual risk will tend to go to zero and only systematic risk will matter. The only terms in the preceding equation that affect the systematic risk in a portfolio are b_{i1} and b_{i2}. Since the investor is assumed to be concerned with expected return and risk he or she need be concerned only with three attributes of any portfolio (p): $\bar{R}_p$, b_{p1}, and b_{p2}.

Let us hypothesize the existence of the three widely diversified portfolios shown in the following table.

---

[1]The linearity assumption is not as restrictive as it might at first appear. Any of the indexes can be a nonlinear function of a variable. It could be a variable squared, the log of a variable, or any other nonlinear transformation that seems appropriate.

[2]It is convenient, though unnecessary, to assume the indexes are uncorrelated with each other. We show in Chapter 8 that a set of correlated indexes can always be converted to a set of uncorrelated indexes. The results remain the same with uncorrelated indexes but the mathematics is more complex.

Portfolio	Expected Return	b_{i1}	b_{i2}
A	15	1.0	.6
B	14	.5	1.0
C	10	.3	.2

We know from the concepts of geometry that three points determine a plane just as two points determine a line. The equation of the plane in $\overline{R}_p$, b_{p1}, and b_{p2} space defined by these three portfolios is[3]

$$\overline{R}_i = 7.75 + 5b_{i1} + 3.75b_{i2}$$

The expected return and risk measures of any portfolio of these three portfolios are given by

$$\overline{R}_P = \sum_{i=1}^{N} X_i \overline{R}_i$$

$$b_{p1} = \sum_{i=1}^{N} X_i b_{i1}$$

$$b_{p2} = \sum_{i=1}^{N} X_i b_{i2}$$

$$\sum_{i=1}^{N} X_i = 1$$

Since a weighted combination of points on a plane (where the weights sum to one) also lies on the plane, all portfolios constructed from portfolios A, B, and C lie on the plane described by portfolios A, B, and C.[4]

What happens if we consider a new portfolio not on this plane? For example, assume a portfolio E exists with an expected return of 15%, a b_{i1} of 0.6, and a b_{i2} of 0.6.

Compare this with a portfolio (call it D) constructed by placing $\frac{1}{3}$ of the funds in portfolio A, $\frac{1}{3}$ in portfolio B, and $\frac{1}{3}$ in portfolio C. The b_{pj}'s on this portfolio are

$$b_{p1} = \frac{1}{3}(1.0) + \frac{1}{3}(0.5) + \frac{1}{3}(0.3) = .6$$

$$b_{p2} = \frac{1}{3}(0.6) + \frac{1}{3}(1.0) + \frac{1}{3}(0.2) = .6$$

The risk for portfolio D is identical to the risk on portfolio E. The expected return on portfolio D is

$$\frac{1}{3}(15) + \frac{1}{3}(14) + \frac{1}{3}(10) = 13$$

---

[3]The reader interested in verifying this can recall that the equation of a plane can be written as $R_i = \lambda_0 + \lambda_1 b_{i1} + \lambda_2 b_{i2}$. By substituting in the values of R_i, b_{i1}, and b_{i2} for portfolios A, B, and C, we obtain three equations with three unknowns: λ_0, λ_1, and λ_2. Solving the three equations gives the values of λ_0, λ_1, and λ_2 shown in the equation in the text.

[4]The reader is encouraged to form a portfolio of portfolios A, B, and C with any set of X_i summing to one. One can then see that this portfolio lies on the plane given by $\overline{R}_i = 7.75 + 5\,b_{i1} + 3.75\,b_{i2}$. One example of this is portfolio D analyzed shortly in the text.

Alternatively, since portfolio D must lie on the plane described above, we could have obtained its expected return from the equation of the plane:

$$\overline{R}_i = 7.75 + 5(0.6) + 3.75(0.6) = 13$$

By the law of one price, two portfolios that have the same risk cannot sell at a different expected return. In this situation it would pay arbitrageurs to step in and buy portfolio E while selling an equal amount of portfolio D short. Buying portfolio E and financing it by selling D short would guarantee a riskless profit with no investment and no risk. We can see this quite easily. Assume the investor sells $100 worth of portfolio D short and buys $100 worth of portfolio E. The results are shown in the following table.

	Initial Cash Flow	End of Period Cash Flow	b_{i1}	b_{i2}
Portfolio D	+$100	−$113.0	−0.6	−0.6
Portfolio E	−$100	$115.0	0.6	0.6
Arbitrage portfolio	0	2.0	0	0

The arbitrage portfolio involves zero investment, has no systematic risk (b_{i1} and b_{i2}), and earns $2. Arbitrage would continue until portfolio E lies on the same plane as portfolio A, B, and C.

We have established that all investments and portfolios must be on a plane in expected return, b_{i1}, b_{i2} space. If an investment were to lie above or below the plane, an opportunity would exist for riskless arbitrage. The arbitrage would continue until all investments converged to a plane.

The general equation of a plane in expected return, b_{i1}, b_{i2} space is

$$\overline{R}_i = \lambda_0 + \lambda_1 b_{i1} + \lambda_2 b_{i2} \qquad (16.3)$$

This is the equilibrium model produced by the APT when returns are generated by a two-index model. Notice that λ_1 is the increase in expected return for a one-unit increase in b_{i1}. Thus λ_1 and λ_2 are returns for bearing the risks associated with I_1 and I_2, respectively.

More insight can be gained into the meaning of the λ_i's by using Equation (16.3) to examine a particular set of portfolios. Examine a portfolio with b_{i1} and b_{i2} both equal to zero. The expected return on this portfolio equals λ_0. This is a zero b_{ij} portfolio, and we denote its return by R_F. If the riskless asset is not available, R_F is replaced with $\overline{R}_Z$ the return on a zero Beta portfolio. Most researchers in this area assume that the intercept is in fact R_F.

Substituting $\overline{R}_F$ for λ_0 and examining a portfolio with a b_{i2} of zero and a b_{i1} of one, we see that

$$\lambda_1 = \overline{R}_1 - R_F$$

where $\overline{R}_1$ is the return on a portfolio having a b_{i1} of one and a b_{i2} of zero. In general, $\lambda_i = \overline{R}_j - R_F$ or λ_j is the expected excess return on a portfolio only subject to risk of index j and having a unit measure of this risk.

The analysis in this section can be generalized to the J index case

$$R_i = a_i + b_{i1}I_1 + b_{i2}I_2 + \cdots + b_{iJ}I_J + e_i$$

By analogous arguments it can be shown that all securities and portfolios have expected returns described by the J-dimensional hyperplane

$$\overline{R}_i = \lambda_0 + \lambda_1 b_{i1} + \lambda_2 b_{i2} + \cdots + \lambda_J b_{iJ} \qquad (16.4)$$

with $\lambda_0 = R_F$ and $\lambda_j = \overline{R}_j - R_F$.

A More Rigorous Proof of APT

Once again we will derive APT assuming a two-index return-generating process. This derivation is sufficiently rich to allow generalization to any arbitrary number of indices. The two-index model we use is that presented in Equation (16.2).

Taking the expected value of Equation (16.2) and subtracting it from Equation (16.2), we have

$$R_i = \bar{R}_i + b_{i1}\left(I_1 - \bar{I}_1\right) + b_{i2}\left(I_2 - \bar{I}_2\right) + e_i \tag{16.5}$$

Now a sufficient condition for an APT proof to hold is that there are enough securities in the market so that a portfolio with the following characteristics can be formed:

$$\sum_{i=1}^{N} X_i = 0$$

$$\sum_{i=1}^{N} X_i b_{i1} = 0$$

$$\sum_{i=1}^{N} X_i b_{i2} = 0$$

$$\sum_{i=1}^{N} X_i e_i \approx 0$$

The last condition is a requirement that residual risk be approximately zero.[5] The first of these four equations states that this portfolio involves zero investment. The remaining equations imply that this portfolio has no risk. This portfolio involves no investment and no risk; therefore, it must produce an expected return of zero. In other words, the three equations plus the condition on residual risk just discussed imply that

$$\sum_{i=1}^{N} X_i \bar{R}_i = 0$$

Now there is another more mathematical interpretation of these equations. The equation

$$\sum_{i=1}^{N} X_i b_{i1} = 0$$

means that the vector of security proportions is orthogonal to the vector of b_{i1}'s. Similarly, the first equation

$$\sum_{i=1}^{N} X_i = 0$$

means that the vector of security proportions is orthogonal to a vector of ones. We have just shown, in the previous paragraph, that if the vector of portfolio proportions is orthogonal to

---

[5]The assumption of zero residual risk might seem bothersome. Original proofs of APT assumed an infinite number of securities and well-diversified arbitrage portfolios. Because with uncorrelated residuals each residual variance enters with a weight equal to the square of the fraction of money placed in that security, for well-diversified portfolios selected from an infinite or in fact a very large population of securities, residual risk will be very close to zero. A series of papers by Dybvig [33], Grinblatt and Titman [52, 53], and Ingersoll [68] investigate how closely the APT holds for finite economies and economies where residual risks are not uncorrelated. APT continues to hold although it does not necessarily hold exactly the same for all securities (there can be very small errors for many securities and there can be large pricing errors for a few securities).

a vector of ones, a vector of b_{i1}'s, and a vector of b_{i2}'s, this implies that the vector of security proportions is orthogonal to the vector of expected returns. But there is a well-known theorem in linear algebra that states that if the fact that a vector is orthogonal to $N - 1$ vectors implies it is orthogonal to the Nth vector, then the Nth vector can be expressed as a linear combination of the $N - 1$ vectors. In this case, the vector of expected returns can be expressed as a linear combination of a vector of ones, a vector of b_{i1}'s, and a vector of b_{i2}'s. Thus we can write the expected value for any security as a constant times 1, plus a second constant times b_{i1}, plus a third constant times b_{i2} or

$$\overline{R}_i = \lambda_0 + \lambda_1 b_{i1} + \lambda_2 b_{i2}$$

This equation must hold for all securities and all portfolios. The λ's can be evaluated by following the procedure used in the previous section of this chapter, namely, forming three portfolios with the following characteristics

1. $b_{p1} = 0$ and $b_{p2} = 0$

2. $b_{p1} = 1$ and $b_{p2} = 0$

3. $b_{p1} = 0$ and $b_{p2} = 1$

we find that

$$\overline{R}_i = R_F + b_{i1}\left(\overline{R}_1 - R_F\right) + b_{i2}\left(\overline{R}_2 - R_F\right)$$

or for the general case

$$\overline{R}_i = R_F + b_{i1}\left(\overline{R}_1 - R_F\right) + \cdots + b_{iJ}\left(\overline{R}_J - R_F\right)$$

Defining λ_0 as R_F and λ_j as $\overline{R}_j - R_F$, we can write this equation as

$$\overline{R}_i = \lambda_0 + \lambda_1 b_{i1} + \lambda_2 b_{i2} + \cdots + \lambda_J b_{iJ}$$

The principal strength of the APT approach is that it is based on the no arbitrage condition. Because the no arbitrage conditions should hold for any subset of securities, it is not necessary to identify all risky assets or a "market portfolio" to test the APT. It is reasonable to test it over a class of assets such as common stocks or even a smaller set such as the stocks making up the Standard & Poor's (S&P) index or all stocks on the New York Stock Exchange. One has to be somewhat careful in that the correct APT model for a larger class of securities can be different from (contain more influences than) an APT model appropriate for a smaller set of securities. Failure to find a model for a small set (type) of securities does not mean that a model does not exist across different types of securities. However, it is appropriate to use the APT to describe relative prices for a set of securities of interest to the investigator rather than deal with the whole population of risky assets. In fact, it has been argued that many tests of the CAPM were really tests of a single- or multiple-factor APT model.

An important characteristic of the APT theory is that it is extremely general. This generality is both a strength and a weakness. Although it allows us to describe equilibrium in terms of any multi index model, it gives us no evidence as to what might be an appropriate multi-index model. Furthermore, APT tells us nothing about the size or the signs of the λ_j's. This makes interpretation of tests difficult. We'll have more to say about this shortly.

ESTIMATING AND TESTING APT

The proof of any economic theory is how well it describes reality. Tests of APT are particularly difficult to formulate because all the theory specifies is a structure for asset pricing: the economic or firm characteristics that should affect expected return are not specified. Let us review the structure of APT that will enter any test procedure.

We can write the multifactor return-generating process as

$$R_i = a_i + \sum_{j=1}^{J} b_{ij} I_j + e_i \tag{16.6}$$

The APT model that arises from this return-generating process can be written as

$$\overline{R}_i = R_F + \sum_{j=1}^{J} b_{ij} \lambda_j \tag{16.7}$$

It's worth spending a little time discussing the meaning of the variables b_{ij}, I_j, and λ_j.

Notice from Equation (16.6) that each security i has a unique sensitivity to each I_j but that any I_j has a value that is the same for all securities. Any I_j affects more than one security (if it did not, it would have been compounded in the residual term e_i). These I_j's have generally been given the name factors in the APT literature. They are identical to the influences we called indexes in earlier chapters. The factors affect the returns on more than one security and are the sources of covariance between securities. The b_{ij}'s are unique to each security and represent an attribute of the security. This attribute may be simply the sensitivity of the security to a particular factor, or it can be a characteristic of the security such as dividend yield.

Finally, from Equation (16.7) we see that λ_j is the extra expected return required because of a security's sensitivity to the jth attribute of the security. At this point the reader might note that Equation (16.6) looks suspiciously like the type of relationship we used in first-pass regression tests of the CAPM in Chapter 15, whereas Equation (16.7) bears a close resemblance to the type of equation used in second-pass tests. This intuition is correct. The problem is that, whereas for the CAPM the correct I_j is defined (e.g., the excess return on the market portfolio for the simple CAPM), for the multifactor model and the APT the set of I_j's is not defined by the theory. In order to test the APT, one must test Equation (16.7), which means that one must have estimates of the b_{ij}'s. Most tests of APT use Equation (16.6) to estimate the b_{ij}'s. However, to estimate the b_{ij}'s we must have definitions of the relevant I_j's. The most general approach to this problem is to estimate simultaneously factors (I_j's) and firm attributes (b_{ij}'s) for Equation (16.7). Most of the early tests of the APT employed this methodology. It still continues to be widely used in the finance literature and in practice. We examine this type of simultaneous estimation technique shortly. Before we do so, however, let us point out two alternative methods.

One alternative method is to specify a set of attributes (firm characteristics) that might affect expected return. When using this method the b_{ij}'s are directly specified. The b_{ij}'s might include such characteristics as divided yield and the firm's Beta with the market. Once the b_{ij}'s are specified, Equation (16.7) is used to estimate the λ's and thus the APT model.

The second alternative method is to specify the factors I_j's in Equation (16.6) and then to estimate the security attributes b_{ij}'s and market prices of risk λ_j's. Two approaches have been used to specify the factors. One approach is to first hypothesize (we hope on the basis of economic theory) a set of macroeconomic influences that might affect return and then to use Equation (16.6) to estimate the b_{ij}'s. These influences might include variables such as the rate of inflation and the rate of interest.[6]

---

[6]Recently BIRR has offered a commercial version of this research. A detailed description of their model can be found in Burmeister, Roll, and Ross [13].

A second approach is to specify a set of portfolios as factors which the researcher believes captures the relevant influences affecting security returns. As in the previous case Equation (16.6) is used to estimate the b_{ij}'s with the return on the hypothesized portfolios used as the I_j's and b_{ij}'s estimated via regression analysis. For either approach Equation (16.7) is then estimated to obtain the λ_j's and the associated APT model.

If any method other than factor analysis is used to obtain the b_{ij}'s for testing APT, one is really conducting a joint test of the APT and the relevancy of the factors or characteristics that have been hypothesized as determining equilibrium. Each of these general approaches will now be discussed in more detail.

Simultaneous Determination of Factors and Characteristics

A complete specification of Equation (16.6) would call for all factors (I_j) and attributes (b_{ij}) to be defined, so that the covariance between any residual return (the e_i's not explained by the equation) was zero. While it is not possible to produce this exact result, there is a body of statistical methodology that is very well suited to approximating this result. These techniques are called *factor analysis*. We present a simple example of a factor analytic solution in Appendix A to provide the reader who has not worked with this technique some feel for what it accomplishes.

Factor analysis determines a specific set of I_j's and b_{ij}'s such that the covariance of residual returns (returns after the influence of these indexes has been removed) is as small as possible.[7] In the terminology of factor analysis the I_j's are called factors and the b_{ij}'s are called factor loadings. A specific factor analysis is performed for a specific number of hypothesized factors. By repeating this process for alternative hypotheses about the number of factors, a solution for two factors, three factors, . . . , and j factors is obtained. One can stop when the probability that the next factor explains a statistically significant portion of the covariance matrix drops below some level—for example, 50%.[8] Using this technique, it is not possible to be sure that one has captured all relevant factors. At best, statements such as the following can be made: "There is less than a 50% probability that another factor is needed." Whether one chooses to stop extracting factors when there is a 50% chance that no more are needed, or a 10% chance, or some other level is a matter of taste rather than mathematical rigor. Without a theory of how many factors should be present, the decision as to how many to extract from the data has to be made subjectively.

Factor analysis produces estimates of the factor loadings (b_{ij}) and the factors (I_j). Recall that the factor loadings b_{ij} are sensitivity measures and are like the β_i's of the simple CAPM. At this point a set of tests analogous to the first-pass regression tests discussed in Chapter 15 has been performed. The major difference is that one has not only identified the b_{ij}'s but one has estimated how many factors (indices) there should be and has determined the definition of each I_j. Each I_j is an index consisting of a (different) weighted average of the securities on which the factor analysis is performed.

---

[7]Principal component analysis is somewhat analogous to factor analysis. Recall from Chapter 8 that principal component analysis extracts from the data a set of indexes that best explains the variance of the data. Indexes are extracted in order of importance and as many indexes are extracted as the smaller of the number of stocks or the number of observations. Factor analysis is covariance rather than variance driven. For a specified number of indexes it finds the set of that many indexes that best explains the covariance in the original data. There are alternative ways of performing factor analysis. Most empirical work in this area uses maximum likelihood factor analysis, and the techniques developed by Joreskog [71–73] are often used.

[8]See Lawley and Maxwell [78] for a discussion of the test procedure described. The reader should be aware that these tests are based on the assumption of multivariate normality. This is the procedure applied by Roll and Ross [97].

The next step in testing the APT is to form a set of tests directly analogous to the second-pass tests performed by Fama and MacBeth [46] on the simple CAPM.[9] By running a cross-sectional test, estimates of λ's can be computed for each time period and the average value of each λ_j and its variance over time computed. Roll and Ross [97] were the first to perform this type of test. The mathematics of factor analysis allows this to be done more easily than with regression techniques, but the results are analogous to those that would be obtained by using the generalized least squares regression procedure. However, there are some problems with the use of factor analysis of which the reader should be aware. First, we have the same error in variables problem that we had when testing the standard CAPM. The factor loading b_{ij}'s, like the Betas from the first-pass regression, are estimated with error. This means that significance tests of λ_j's are only asymptotically correct. There are three additional problems that are unique to factor analysis. First, there is no meaning to the signs of the factors produced by factor analysis, so the signs on the b_{ij}'s and on the λ_j's could be reversed. Second, the scaling of the b_{ij}'s and the λ_j's is arbitrary. For example, all b_{ij}'s could be doubled and the resultant λ_j's halved. Third, there is no guarantee that factors are produced in a particular order, so when analysis is performed on separate samples the first factor from one sample may be the third from another sample.

The procedure discussed above is that used by Roll and Ross [97] in their classic study of APT. They applied factor analysis to 42 groups of 30 stocks using daily data for the time period July 3, 1962, to December 1972. The results of their first-pass test are rather striking. These tests show that, in over 38% of the groups, there was less than a 10% chance that a sixth factor had explanatory power and in over three-fourths of the groups there was a 50% chance that five factors were sufficient. While Roll and Ross try several different second-pass tests, their major results are that at least three factors are significant in explaining equilibrium prices but that it is unlikely that four are significant. On the surface it would appear that they find more factors significant than one would expect to find under the standard CAPM model or the zero Beta version of the CAPM.

It is logical to question whether there is any way these results could be consistent with the CAPM or whether there seem to be additional factors at work in the market. Although we cannot answer definitely, the analysis of Cho, Elton, and Gruber [25] would seem to indicate that there are additional influences at work. They repeat the Roll and Ross methodology for a later period and find more factors to be significant than do Roll and Ross. They then simulate a set of data using the zero Beta form of CAPM while enforcing the same means and variances on the returns for each stock that were present in the original data. In doing so, they allow the rate on the zero Beta portfolio and the Beta on each asset to change over time. When the Roll and Ross methodology is applied to these data, the number of factors that are found to be significant is consistent with the zero Beta form of the CAPM. The fact that many more factors were found to be significant when actual returns were analyzed lends support to Roll and Ross's argument that additional factors beyond those embodied by the zero Beta form of the CAPM determine equilibrium prices. While this analysis would seem to suggest that more than one or two factors are important in determining both returns and equilibrium returns, there still remain some questions about the implementation of APT through the use of factor analysis.[10]

The usefulness of an APT model cannot be differentiated from the methodology used to estimate it. The theory may well be correct, but if it cannot be implemented or estimated

---

[9]Alternate tests such as those advocated by Gibbons [51] described in the previous chapter or those advocated by Burmeister et al. [11] described later in this chapter can be used instead of the second-pass test.

[10]In the last section of this chapter we discuss an alternative way in which the zero Beta form of the CAPM could be consistent with the Roll and Ross results.

in a meaningful sense, then, while it remains useful as a way of thinking about the world, it cannot be used as part of the investment process. A test of the APT is a joint test of the theory and the methodology used to implement the theory.

Factor analysis is the principal methodology used to estimate simultaneously the factors that affect equilibrium return and the sensitivity of firms to these factors. One problem with employing this methodology to estimate factors is that the mathematics of factor analysis is so complex that only a limited number of securities can be analyzed at one time.[11] A set of factors and factor loadings are extracted that can best describe the behavior of a small sample of risky assets rather than all risky assets. Roll and Ross used groups of 30 assets. The reader may well ask, "So what? If the arbitrage pricing theory is correct, why don't we obtain the true factors whether we use 30 securities or 2000 securities?" Dhrymes, Friend, and Gultekin [32] present evidence that the number of factors that appear significant is an increasing function of the size of the group analyzed. In their samples the number of significant factors increased from 3 for groups of 15 securities to 7 for groups of 60 securities, the largest groups studied. The authors suggest that dividing the sample into subgroups may ignore important sources of covariance between the securities in different groups and, further, that the factors identified within any subgroup may not be the same as the factor identified in a second subgroup.

While the necessity of estimating the APT for small groups provides some major problems with respect to the applicability of the result, it does provide a unique opportunity for testing the theory and methodology jointly. According to the theory,

$$\overline{R}_i = \overline{R}_Z + \sum_{j=1}^{J} b_{ij}\lambda_j$$

Now if the theory is correct and if through factor analysis we have identified the correct factors in the return-generating process, and thus the b_{ij}'s, then the value of the market price of all factor λ_j's and the intercept should be the same for each group. Testing this is not as easy as it may seem at first. Remember that the sign of the b_{ij}'s and λ_j's are not uniquely determined, nor is the order in which factors appear in different groups uniquely determined.

Methodology does exist for evaluating whether the intercept is constant across groups and whether the factor prices estimated are the same across groups. The methodology and test results have been described very well in an article by Brown and Weinstein [9]. They are able to test (1) whether the intercept term is the same for all groups, (2) whether the factor prices are the same for all groups given that the intercept is constrained to be the same, and (3) whether both the intercept and factor prices are the same for all groups, a joint hypothesis. Unfortunately their results are ambiguous. Although they cast some doubt on the use of the maximum likelihood factor analysis to explain equilibrium return successfully, as Brown and Weinstein recognize, their "results cannot be viewed as compelling evidence against the APT." Dhrymes, Friend, and Gultekin [32] in another set of tests find that, depending on the method of grouping stocks employed, the intercept term may be significantly different or not significantly different across groups.

Other tests of the APT have failed to demonstrate its clear superiority over other models although results are mixed. Dhrymes, Friend, and Gultekin find that a multifactor

---

[11]Chen [18] has described a procedure that allows APT to be estimated and tested across large numbers of securities. However, his procedure, which involves forming a small number of portfolios of securities based on an initial factor solution for use in further tests, has been questioned by Dhrymes, Friend, and Gultekin [32]. The resolution of the adequacy of this procedure, and in particular the value of estimates for some securities versus the loss of information involved in his portfolio aggregation technique, will have to await further study.

model of the APT has better explanatory power than a one-factor model. This tends to support the existence of more than one factor. However, they find that the explanatory power of either model is modest and that there is some doubt about whether the risk premia (prices) of the five risk factors employed by Roll and Ross are significantly different from zero.

Other tests of the Roll and Ross type APT have produced equally ambiguous results. For example, one test of the APT that would give us great confidence is if a stock's residual risk was not priced when added as another factor in the equilibrium pricing equation. Recall that the b_{ij}'s are supposed to capture the impact of all systematic components of risk. Any other attribute of a security, and in particular its residual risk, should be unique to each security and therefore diversifiable. Roll and Ross test for the impact of residual risk and find almost no evidence that it is priced. Dhrymes, Friend, and Gultekin also test and find that both a stock's own standard deviation and skewness generally yield insignificant coefficients. However, they find that these two influences are significant at least as frequently as the factors suggested by Roll and Ross.[12]

The literature has contained a number of tests of empirically estimated factor models and APT models. Although a detailed description of the empirical methodology goes beyond the level of analysis, we wish to present here two articles that are well worth mentioning.

Lehmann and Modest [79] implemented the idea of forming portfolios of assets that mimic factor realizations (returns). By forming a portfolio that has minimum residual risk for each factor they can then use this set of portfolios as independent variables to estimate the sensitivities of each of a large number of securities to each influence (factor). Each portfolio is identified by finding a set of weights summing to one across stocks, so that the portfolio has minimum residual risk and a sensitivity of zero to all factors except the one under study. Lehmann and Modest are able to explain certain phenomena not explained by the standard CAPM. In Chapter 17 on efficient markets we show that the standard CAPM does not satisfactorily account for extra returns associated with high dividends, the stock's own variance, small size (low capitalization), and the January effect. Lehmann and Modest show that a multi-index APT can explain away discrepancies due to dividend yield and own variance, but that the extra return on small firms and in January are only partially accounted for by the model. Nevertheless, the ability of the model to account for some influences not explained by the CAPM is in fact support for the model as an alternative to the simple CAPM. Lest we get too excited, recall that an after-tax CAPM tested by Litzenberger and Ramaswamy [82] was also successful in accounting for returns varying with dividend yield.

Connor and Korajczyk [30] provide a test of APT using the asymmetric principle components technique proposed by Chamberlain and Rothschild [15]. They find that with five factors, they can explain the extra return on small firms and in January better than the CAPM based on a value-weighted index.

The ability of an APT model employing a small number of factors to account for return patterns unexplained by the CAPM strongly suggests that the APT is a useful model for explaining relative prices.

---

[12]One other type of test has been performed on Roll and Ross type of multifactor models. In applying the standard CAPM and zero Beta CAPM, certain anomalies have been noted. For example, small (low capitalization) firms tend consistently to produce returns in excess of those we would expect based on CAPM. This anomaly is either due to a market inefficiency or a deficiency in the CAPM as a model of equilibrium returns. If a Roll and Ross type of multifactor of equilibrium better explained anomalies, such as the small-firm effect, one would have added faith in such models. Reinganum [94] has investigated this issue and finds that a Roll and Ross multifactor model could not explain the size anomaly any better than the standard CAPM.

All of the tests just described are joint tests of the APT and a particular statistical methodology used to identify both the b_{ij}'s and I_j's of the factor model. The results of this research are inconclusive. There is fairly strong indication that more than two factors affect returns and that more than two factors are priced. Statistical methodology has been developed and continues to be developed that allows us to better define the factors and to better form portfolios that mimic them. However, research is just beginning to explore the stability of the factor structure over time.

In Japan, APT has been tested and shows a clear superiority over the CAPM in selecting securities as well as in explaining past returns. For example, Elton and Gruber [34, 35] find that a five-factor APT model does a better job of explaining and predicting expected returns than does a single-factor or CAPM model. In particular, in the Japanese stock market the CAPM model appears to break down. In Japan, unlike other markets, small stocks have smaller Betas than large stocks. This should imply a lower expected return given the CAPM and yet small stocks have significantly higher excess returns. This happens when small is defined as anything but the largest 100 stocks on the Tokyo Stock Exchange. These problems are not nearly as great when a multifactor model is used. Furthermore, a multifactor model does a much better job of allowing mimicking portfolios to be constructed (both as index funds and hedge portfolios for futures and option trading) than does a single-index model. The APT model is almost universally used by industry as a replacement for the CAPM model in Japan.

An Alternative Approach to Testing the APT

If we could specify a priori either the factors that affected stock returns or the characteristics of stocks that affected returns, we would then have a much easier estimation problem to solve. A debate exists among academics and practitioners about whether part of the model should be prespecified on the basis of theory or whether all of the parameters should be determined empirically. This type of debate has gone on since the dawn of modern science. The issue is discussed by Roll and Ross [97]. They state that "we do consider the basic underlying causes of the generating process of returns to be a potentially important area of research but we think it is an area that can be investigated separately from testing asset pricing theories." The problem is that, without a theory, the empirical tools one uses are a lot weaker and the results of tests harder to interpret. For example, in the APT we have no idea of what the size or even the sign of factor prices should be. All we can say is that we expect some of them to be statistically different from zero. On the other hand, in the Sharpe–Lintner CAPM the price of Beta was supposed to be $\bar{R}_m - R_F$, a quantity that we expected to be positive and about which we have some rough idea of magnitude.

The controversy we are discussing would be easy to resolve if we had a theory of the appropriate factors or characteristics that determine security returns. Someday we hope to have one. In the absence of such a theory all we can do is examine three attempts to prespecify one set of variables in the multifactor model. One attempt hypothesized a set of firm characteristics, another hypothesized a set of macroeconomic indexes, and the third specifies a set of portfolios as the indexes.

Specifying Attributes of Securities

In the preceding section of this chapter we examined the use of maximum likelihood factor analysis to determine simultaneously the characteristics that affect return and the extra return required because of a security's sensitivity to these characteristics. If a set of characteristics that affects return could be specified a priori, then the market price of these characteristics over any period of time could be measured fairly easily.

The estimating equation would be the form

$$\overline{R}_i = \lambda_0 + \lambda_1 b_{i1} + \lambda_2 b_{i2} + \cdots + \lambda_J b_{iJ}$$

for the case of J characteristics. In this equation the b_{ij}'s would be the value each characteristic took on, and the λ_j's the average extra return required because of these characteristics. The values of the λ_j's would be estimated via regression analysis. This procedure is directly analogous to a second-pass test of the CAPM. In fact, we have already examined two models that could be viewed as this type of test. The first was the model tested by Fama and MacBeth [46] and reviewed in Chapter 15; although they viewed the model as a test of the CAPM, it could be viewed as a test of APT. The model they tested was

$$\overline{R}_i = \lambda_0 + \lambda_1 \beta_i + \lambda_2 \beta_i^2 + \lambda_3 S_{ei}$$

The firm characteristics examined were the Beta for each firm, the Beta for each stock squared, and the residual risk of each stock. These tests clearly show that, at least with respect to the hypothesized set of characteristics, a multifactor model did not outperform the zero Beta form of the CAPM. None of the added characteristics were priced. Remember that tests of this type are a joint test of the APT in general and the specific characteristics that were hypothesized as explaining equilibrium returns. Fama and MacBeth tested characteristics that on the basis of economic theory should not explain equilibrium returns and concluded that they did not.

We examined a second model in Chapter 15 that hypothesized an additional firm characteristic as affecting equilibrium return. Recall that Litzenberger and Ramaswamy [82] included dividend yield as an added variable and found its impact was statistically significant. This should encourage the pursuit of models containing more characteristics.

One such model has been constructed and tested by Sharpe [106]. He starts with the hypothesis that equilibrium returns should be affected by the following characteristics: a stock's Beta with the S&P index, its dividend yield, the size of the firm (market value of equity), its Beta with long-term bonds, its past value of Alpha (the intercept of the regression of past excess return against excess returns on the S&P index), and eight-sector membership variables. Sharpe does not attempt an elaborate economic rationale for these variables but rather states that he has selected them more or less "ex cathedra." We would expect both Beta and dividend yield to be related positively to expected returns based on the theory discussed in Chapters 13, 14, and 15. Size may well be, at least in part, a proxy for liquidity. If so, size should enter the model with a negative sign. If sensitivity to interest rates is an important variable, we would expect bond Beta to play a role in determining equilibrium returns. If the past value of Alpha proves significant, it would be evidence of autocorrelation of the residuals from the CAPM. This might indicate that there are some added variables explaining cross-sectional returns that were not captured in the model. The use of sector membership as an additional set of variables implies that membership in a particular sector of the economy has an important effect on equilibrium return.

The results of applying this model to 2197 stocks on a monthly basis for all months between 1931 and 1979 are summarized in Table 16.1, which reports the average coefficients (on an annualized basis) over the entire period and the percent of months in which the coefficients were significantly different from zero at the 5% level. Note that for those variables where we had clear expectations about the sign of the relationship and return, our expectations are borne out. Furthermore, note that while on the basis of chance we would expect any firm characteristic to be significant about 5% of the time, each characteristic was significant a much higher percentage of the time.

Table 16.1   Cross-sectional Data on Sharpe's Multifactor Model

Attribute	Annualized Value of Associated λ	Percent of Months in Which Associated λ Was Significantly Different from Zero
Beta	5.36	58.3
Yield	0.24	39.5
Size	−5.56	56.5
Bond Beta	−0.12	28.2
Alpha	−2.00	43.5
Sector Membership		
Basic industries	1.65	32.5
Capital goods	0.16	18.7
Construction	−1.59	15.3
Consumer goods	−0.18	39.3
Energy	6.28	36.9
Finance	−1.48	16.3
Transportation	−0.57	43.9
Utilities	−2.62	35.0

Another way to judge the importance of including more than one characteristic in the description of equilibrium is by examining the explanatory power (coefficient of determination) of the model as more characteristics are employed. The average coefficient of determination for monthly data when Beta is used as the only characteristic to explain cross-sectional returns is 0.037. This might seem low relative to the results reported in Chapter 15, but recall that monthly data are being used and portfolio grouping is not being done. This is in fact consistent with other studies employing similar research designs. When the security characteristics of yield, size, bond Beta, and Alpha are added, the coefficient of determination adjusting for added variables more than doubles to 0.079. When all the characteristics in Table 16.1 are used, it goes up to 0.104. The use of firm characteristics in addition to Beta has increased the explanatory power of the model. In addition, these factors seem to be significant a considerably higher percentage of the time than chance alone would explain.

Sharpe seems to have identified some additional characteristics, beyond a stock's Beta with a proxy for the market portfolio, that are useful for explaining cross-sectional returns over time. He recognizes that his model is rather ad hoc in nature, but it is an indication that increased research into significant economic characteristics of a stock should allow us to build better models of equilibrium.

A second model which is widely used in industry and which specifies a set of firm characteristics is that employed by Barra.[13] This model uses nine firm characteristics in place of the five characteristics used by Sharpe. These are volatility, momentum, size, liquidity, growth, value, earnings volatility, financial leverage, and industry membership.

Specifying the Influences Affecting the Return-Generating Process

Another alternative to the joint determination of factor loadings and factors discussed in the earlier section of this chapter is the specification (one hopes on the basis of economic

---

[13]See Grinold and Kahn [55] for a description of this model. As explained in this article, the model actually makes use of a combination of firm specific characteristics and macroeconomic variables.

theory) of the set of influences or indexes (I_j's) that should enter the return-generating process.

Chen, Roll, and Ross [21] have hypothesized and tested a set of economic variables. They reason that return on stocks should be affected by any influence that affects either future cash flows from holding a security or the value of these cash flows to the investor (e.g., changes in the appropriate discount rate on future cash flows). Chen, Roll, and Ross construct sets of alternative measures of unanticipated changes in the following influences:

1. *Inflation.* Inflation impacts both the level of the discount rate and the size of the future cash flows.

2. *The term structure of interest rates.* Differences between the rate on bonds with a long maturity and a short maturity affect the value of payments far in the future relative to near-term payments.

3. *Risk premia.* Differences between the return on safe bonds (Aaa) and more risky bonds (Baa) are used to measure the market's reaction to risk.

4. *Industrial production.* Changes in industrial production affect the opportunities facing investors and the real value of cash flows.

Chen, Roll, and Ross then examined these measures or indexes

1. To see if they were correlated with the set of indexes extracted by the factor analysis used by Roll and Ross as described in a previous section of this chapter.

2. To see if they explained equilibrium returns.

When they examine the relationship between the macroeconomic variables and the factors (indexes) over the period to which the factors were formed (fit), they find a strong relationship. Furthermore, when the relationship is tested over a hold-out period (a period following the fit period) the relationship continues to be strong. There appears to be a significant relationship between the hypothesized macroeconomic variables and the statistically identified systematic factors in stock market returns.

The second set of tests involves investigating whether returns are related to the sensitivity of a stock to their macroeconomic variables. The procedure is analogous to the two-step procedure used by Fama and MacBeth (and discussed in the previous chapter) to investigate the CAPM. In the first stage, time-series regressions are run for each of a series of portfolios to estimate each portfolio's sensitivity to each macroeconomic variable [the b_{ij}'s of Equation (16.6)]. Then the market price of risk [the λ_j's of Equation (16.7)] is estimated by running a cross-sectional regression each month and looking at the average of the market price in each month. Chen, Roll, and Ross find that the macrovariables are significant explanatory influences on pricing. Furthermore, when the Beta of each portfolio with the market was introduced as an additional variable along with the sensitivity of each portfolio to the macroeconomic variables, it did not show up as significant in the second stage (cross-sectional) regression.

Chen, Roll, and Ross recognize that they cannot claim to have found the (correct) state variables for asset pricing. However, they certainly have made an important start in that direction.

Their work is continued in a series of papers by Burmeister and McElroy. Burmeister and McElroy have integrated tests of the factor models, CAPM, and APT. It is worthwhile reviewing two of their tests. The first test is constructed using the multi-index model described in Chapter 8. More specifically, returns are assumed to be generated by the following five indexes (see Chapter 8).

I_1 = Default risk as measured by the return on long-term government bonds minus the return on long-term corporate bonds plus one-half of 1 percent.

I_2 = Time premium as measured by the return on long-term government bonds minus the one-month Treasury bill rate one month ahead.

I_3 = Deflation as measured by expected inflation at the beginning of the month minus actual inflation during the month.

I_4 = Change in expected sales.

I_5 = The market return not captured by the first four variables.

The fifth variable is a proxy for any unobserved general influences. As explained in the appendix, it is estimated by taking the residuals from a regression of a diversified portfolio (the authors use the S&P composite index) against the first four observable variables described earlier. The regression the authors found was

$$R_M - \lambda_0 = 0.00224 - 1.330I_1 + 0.558I_2 + 2.286I_3 - 0.935I_4$$
$$(0.619) \quad (-3.94) \quad (4.96) \quad (1.997) \quad (-2.27)$$

The first four factors account for about 25% (R^2 = .24) of the variation in the return on the S&P composite index and each of the four coefficients is significant.

When the sensitivities (b_{ij}) are estimated for each firm, more than two-thirds of the sensitivities are statistically different from zero at the 5% level, and the five variables typically account for 30% to 50% of the variation of returns of individual firms. In general, b_{i1} appears with a significant negative coefficient, whereas b_{i2} and b_{i5} appear with significant positive coefficients. The remaining two variables have a more ambiguous impact on stock returns.

The prices (λ_i) of each of the five sensitivities implied by the model are all positive and all statistically significantly different from zero. The average value of the λ's using monthly returns is contained in the following table:

	Mean λ Value	t Statistic
λ_1	0.44	4.27
λ_2	1.00	4.76
λ_3	0.04	1.83
λ_4	0.15	2.21
λ_5	0.51	3.21

Additional interesting questions can be addressed with the author's methodology. The first is whether the APT form of the return equation [Equation (A-6) in the appendix] explains returns significantly better than the return-generating process (five-index model). The difference between these two models is that in estimating the APT form, the expected return on each stock is constrained to take on a value that does not allow arbitrage opportunities between securities. This difference is analogous to earlier tests of the CAPM where the intercept was constrained to be $R_F(1 - \beta_i)$, the no-arbitrage condition from the market model. Imposing this constraint cannot increase the explanatory power of the model; it can only decrease it. If the APT is correct, however, the decrease should be small. The fact that the decrease is not statistically significant shows that we can't reject the APT version of the return-generating process and is at least weak evidence in support of it.

Another test the authors perform is to restrict the coefficients to see if the market index alone explains a statistically different amount than the five-index model. The additional explanation of the four variables is statistically significant even when the APT form of the return-generating process is used.

In a later paper, Burmeister and McElroy [11] continue their attempt to differentiate between three models: the return-generating model (the factor model), APT, and CAPM. This study differs from their previous work in two ways. They modify their definition of the observable factors, but more important, they assume there are three unobservable factors rather than one. They use three portfolios to represent these unobservable factors: the return on the S&P 500 stock index, the return on 20-year corporate bonds, and the return on 20-year government bonds.

Burmeister and McElroy conclude that at the 1% significance level the CAPM model can be rejected in favor of their APT model. Furthermore, the APT restrictions cannot be rejected at any reasonable significance level in favor of the more general factor model. This work represents the strongest evidence so far in favor of the APT model as a useful explanation of expected return.

Specifying a Set of Portfolios Affecting the Return-Generating Process

Another alternative is to specify a set of portfolios (I_j's) (which may or may not include the market portfolio) which a priori are thought to capture the influences affecting security returns. These portfolios are selected on the basis of a belief about the types of securities and/or economic influences that affect security returns.[14]

An example of this type of approach is that used by Fama and French [44] to construct a model to explain returns and expected returns on both stocks and bonds. In addition to using the returns on a market portfolio of stocks, they use the returns on other portfolios to represent the I_j's in the return-generating process. These portfolios are

1. The difference in return on a portfolio of small stocks and a portfolio of large stocks (small minus large).

2. The difference in return between a portfolio of high book to market stocks and a portfolio of low book to market stocks (high minus low).

3. The difference between the monthly long-term government bond return and the one-month Treasury bill return.

4. The difference in the monthly return on a portfolio of long-term corporate bonds and a portfolio of long-term government bonds.

Note that all variables are either the return on portfolios of assets or the difference in the return of two portfolios of assets.[15] The latter can be considered a portfolio with a set of stocks sold short. Clearly this model has elements in common with the models that have been presented earlier in this chapter. We saw that Chen, Roll, and Ross and Burmeister

---

[14]We should point out that this is fundamentally different from the approach of factor replicating portfolios that has been discussed by Lehmann and Modest [79] and Huberman, Kandel, and Stambaugh [64] among others. In these approaches either factor analysis is used to extract factors or macroeconomic variables are hypothesized as important and then a mathematical programming problem is solved to find portfolios that mimic the underlying factors.

[15]Elton, Gruber, Das, and Hlavka [41], Blake, Elton, and Gruber [5], and Elton, Gruber, and Blake [38] investigate alternative return-generating processes. In the latter paper, they develop an APT model where some or all of the indexes represent portfolios of assets. This work is discussed more fully in Chapter 24, "Evaluation of Portfolio Performance."

and McElroy use bond return variables similar to those used in this model. Whether one describes these as measures of macroeconomic variables or portfolios is largely a matter of taste. The unique aspect of this model is in the formulation of the variables representing size and book to market ratios. In Sharpe's model (described earlier), size enters as a firm characteristic or a b_{ij}. Size is measured in dollars (actually the natural logarithm of dollars) and a λ is associated with it via cross-sectional regression. What Fama and French have done is to convert the size component from a direct measure to a return concept by constructing a portfolio to capture this influence. The b_{ij} associated with size is not the log of size for any company i, but rather is the sensitivity of that company to the return on the size portfolio. Because size is measured by the return on a portfolio, it now enters the return-generating process as well as the pricing equation. This allows Fama and French to investigate both the time-series and cross-sectional properties of size.[16]

Fama and French test the model described above in a number of time-series tests. The cross-sectional implications are tested by examining whether the intercepts of the time series of excess returns indeed equals zero as APT would suggest.[17] They find that in fact the intercepts are zero and that this portfolio model is successful in explaining expected stock returns. More specifically, they conclude that "at a minimum, our results show that five factors do a good job explaining a) common variations in bond and stock returns and b) the cross-section of average returns."

APT AND CAPM

Before continuing our examination of APT models, we should discuss the fact that the APT model and, in fact, the existence of a multifactor model, including one where more than one factor is priced, is not necessarily inconsistent with the Sharpe–Lintner–Mossin form or one of the other forms of the CAPM.

The simplest case in which an APT model is consistent with the simple form of the CAPM is the case where the return-generating function is of the form

$$R_i = a_i + \beta_i R_m + e_i$$

If returns are generated by a single-index model, the single index is the return on the market portfolio, and a riskless rate exists, then the methodology at the beginning of the chapter can be used to show that

$$\overline{R}_i = R_F + \beta_i \left(\overline{R}_m - R_F \right)$$

If the return-generating function is more complex than this, does it imply that the simple CAPM cannot hold? The answer is no. Recall that the simple CAPM does not assume that the market is the only source of covariance between returns. Let us assume that the return-generating function is of the multi-index type

$$R_i = a_i + b_{i1} I_1 + b_{i2} I_2 + e_i \qquad (16.8)$$

The indexes can be industry indexes, sector indexes, or indexes of broad economic influences such as the rate of inflation. All we assume is that the set of indexes used captures all the sources of covariance between securities: [e.g., $E(e_i e_j) = 0$].

---

[16]Which of these approaches (measuring the b_{ij} directly from firm size or estimating it from a regression on a portfolio) is better awaits further empirical investigation.

[17]This is basically a multi-variable form of the Black, Jensen, and Scholes [4] procedure discussed in Chapter 15.

The APT equilibrium model for this multifactor return-generating process with a riskless asset is

$$\overline{R}_i = R_F + b_{i1}\lambda_1 + b_{i2}\lambda_2 \tag{16.9}$$

Recall that if the CAPM is the equilibrium model, it holds for all securities, as well as all portfolios of securities. Assume the indexes can be represented by portfolios of securities. Actually, we have seen that λ_j is the excess return on a portfolio with a b_{ij} of one on one index and a b_{ij} of zero on all other indices. If the CAPM holds, the equilibrium return on each λ_j is given by the CAPM or

$$\lambda_1 = \beta_{\lambda 1}\left(\overline{R}_m - R_F\right)$$

$$\lambda_2 = \beta_{\lambda 2}\left(\overline{R}_m - R_F\right)$$

Substituting into Equation (16.9) yields

$$\overline{R}_i = R_F + b_{i1}\beta_{\lambda 1}\left(\overline{R}_m - R_F\right) + b_{i2}\beta_{\lambda 2}\left(\overline{R}_m - R_F\right)$$

$$\overline{R}_i = R_F + \left(b_{i1}\beta_{\lambda 1} + b_{i2}\beta_{\lambda 2}\right)\left(\overline{R}_m - R_F\right)$$

Defining β_i as $(b_{i1}\beta_{\lambda 1} + b_{i2}\beta_{\lambda 2})$ results in the expected return of $\overline{R}_i$ being priced by the CAPM.

$$\overline{R}_i = R_F + \beta_i\left(\overline{R}_m - R_F\right)$$

The APT solution with multiple factors appropriately priced is fully consistent with the Sharpe–Lintner–Mossin form of the CAPM.

We wish to stress this point. Employing the Roll and Ross procedure and finding that more than one λ_j is significantly different from zero is not sufficient proof to reject any CAPM. If the λ_j's are not significantly different from $\beta_{\lambda j}(\overline{R}_m - R_F)$, the empirical results could be fully consistent with the Sharpe–Lintner–Mossin form of the CAPM. It is perfectly possible that more than one index explains the covariance between security returns but that the CAPM holds.

While we have demonstrated this with the simple CAPM, it should be apparent to the reader that other values of λ_j's can exist that are fully consistent with the more complex nonstandard forms of the CAPM reviewed in Chapter 14.

RECAPITULATION

The APT theory remains the newest and most promising explanation of relative returns. The theory promises to supply us with a more complete description of returns than the CAPM. Recent work, some of which employs a set of macro variables and some of which employs a set of portfolios is quite encouraging. The fact that a number of studies have found a set of macro variables and portfolios that impact average returns and are not only priced but are priced differently than the CAPM would imply is of both practical and theoretical significance. One word of caution is in order. It is possible that these additional influences are priced not because the APT is the correct model for expected returns, but because we have not correctly identified the market in constructing our model. The residual market plus the other variable employed in the model may together simply serve as a proxy for the (true but unobserved) market in the manner suggested in Chapter 15. Even if this is correct, the use of these multi-index models is, on a practical level, a better explanation for returns than any of the market proxies that have been proposed to date.

We could conclude the chapter at this point and in fact in previous editions have done so. We have instead decided to include a section on the uses of multi-index models and APT. Although there are many reasons for adding this section, most of which are discussed later, perhaps the key reason is that after teaching APT so many of our students have remarked that it seems more complex than the CAPM and asked why bother with it.

Multi-Index Models, APT, and Portfolio Management

The use of multi-index models and multi-index equilibrium models (APT models) in the selection of securities and the management and evaluation of portfolios is growing rapidly. Many brokerage firms, financial institutions, and financial consulting firms have developed their own multi-index models to aid in the investment process. These models have become increasingly popular because they allow risk to be more tightly controlled and they allow the investor to protect against specific types of risk to which he or she is particularly sensitive or to make specific bets on certain types of risk.

In this section we will discuss the use of APT and multi-index models to aid in passive management, active management, and portfolio evaluation. Before we do so we will review multi-index models and APT briefly and present a simple example of an APT model that we will use to illustrate some of the phenomena we discuss in this section.

Review of Multi-Index Models and APT

Earlier in this chapter we presented a return-generating process that expressed the return on any security as a linear function of a series of indexes:

$$R_i = a_i + b_{i1}I_1 + b_{i2}I_2 + b_{i3}I_3 + \cdots + e_i \tag{16.1a}$$

It is convenient for purposes of this section to assume that each index has been either formulated or adjusted to have a mean equal to zero. Since the indexes and residuals have a mean of zero, taking the expected value of both sides of Equation (16.1) results in

$$\overline{R}_i = a_i$$

Thus setting the mean of each index equal to zero has the effect of assuring that a_i is equal to the expected return on security i.

We saw that Equation (16.1a) leads to a description of expected returns given by

$$\overline{R}_i - R_F = \lambda_1 b_{i1} + \lambda_2 b_{i2} + \lambda_3 b_{i3} + \cdots \tag{16.10}$$

where

b_{ij}'s represent the sensitivity of a security's return to index j and is a measure of the risks inherent in the security under study λ's represent the reward for bearing these risks (price of risk).

Combining Equations (16.1) and (16.10) by recognizing that $a_i = \overline{R}_i$

$$R_i = R_F + \lambda_1 b_{i1} + \lambda_2 b_{i2} + \lambda_3 b_{i3} + \cdots \\ + b_{i1}I_1 + b_{i2}I_2 + b_{i3}I_3 + \cdots + e_i \tag{16.11}$$

There are several ways of identifying the I's in Equation (16-1) and the b_{ij}'s and λ_j's in Equation (16.11). However, for illustrating the use of these types of models it helps to deal with a specific model.

Let's assume that we have identified four influences in the return-generating model (Equation 16.1) and that

I_1 = unexpected change in inflation, denoted by I_I

I_2 = unexpected change in aggregate sales, denoted by I_S

I_3 = unexpected change in oil prices, denoted by I_O

I_4 = the return in the S&P index constructed to be orthogonal to the other influences, denoted by I_M

Furthermore, assume that oil risk is not priced ($\lambda_O = 0$). Equation (16.10) becomes

$$\overline{R}_i - R_F = \lambda_I b_{iI} + \lambda_S b_{iS} + \lambda_M b_{iM}$$

while Equation (16.11) becomes

$$R_i - R_F = \lambda_I b_{iI} + \lambda_S b_{iS} + \lambda_M b_{iM} + b_{iI}I_I + b_{iS}I_S + b_{iO}I_O + b_{iM}I_M + e_i$$

Recall that all I's have an expected value of zero.[18]

The set of λ's on these factors consistent with the results reported by Burmeister, Roll, and Ross are

$\lambda_I = -4.32$

$\lambda_S = 1.49$

$\lambda_M = 3.96$

While the sensitivities (b) values for the S&P index were

$b_{S\&P\ I} = -0.37$

$b_{S\&P\ S} = 1.71$

$b_{S\&P\ O} = 0.00$

$b_{S\&P\ M} = 1.00$

The parameterization of the model allows us to recognize the importance of any factor in determining the expected excess return on the S&P index. To do so, simply multiply the b associated with a factor times the associated price of risk (λ).

Factor	b	λ	Contribution to S&P Expected Excess Return (%)
Inflation	−0.37	−4.32	1.59
Sales growth	1.71	1.49	2.54
Oil prices	0.00	0.00	0.00
Market	1.00	3.96	3.96
Expected excess return for S&P index			8.09

This table shows that the expected excess return (return above the riskless rate) for the S&P index is 8.09%. Sales growth contributes 2.54% to the expected return for the S&P. In other words, sensitivity to sales growth accounts for 2.54 ÷ 8.09 or 31.4% of the total expected excess return.

[18]The model we describe here and the values we present represent a simplified version of the model and parameters described in Burmeister, Roll, and Ross [13]. Their model contains additional influences to those cited and does not contain an oil index. We wanted to include an unpriced index to show the role of unpriced indexes in portfolio management. The Salomon Brothers risk index model discussed in Chapter 8, on Multi-Index Models also does not include an oil index for U.S. stocks though they find this index is an important influence in Japan, the U.K., Germany, and France.

The same type of analysis can be used to examine the importance of the sources of risk for the expected excess return on any security or portfolio. For example, for a portfolio of growth stocks the b's, λ's, and contribution to expected excess return are shown later:[19]

Factor	b	λ	Contribution to Growth Stock Portfolio Expected Excess Return (%)
Inflation	$-.50$	-4.32	2.16
Sales growth	2.75	1.49	4.10
Oil prices	-1.00	0.00	0.00
Market	1.30	3.96	5.15
Expected excess return for growth stock portfolio			11.41

Notice that the expected excess return for the growth stock portfolio (11.41) is higher than it was for the S&P index (8.09). This is not surprising because the growth stock portfolio has more risk, with respect to each index, than the S&P portfolio.[20]

Individual influences (indexes) have a different absolute and relative contribution to the expected excess return on a growth stock portfolio than they have on the S&P index. For example, the contribution of sales growth to expected excess return is now 4.10%. Sales growth accounts for 35.9% of the excess return on the growth stock portfolio. It is not surprising that growth stocks are more sensitive to sales growth than the typical stock. What might be surprising, though it is generally true, is that growth stocks are more sensitive to all important indexes. So although the increase in sensitivity to sales growth causes the largest increase in expected excess returns, changes in all influences lead to greater excess return.

Let's now turn to the use of this model for investment and portfolio management. Portfolio managers can be divided into passive and active managers. Passive managers believe that mispriced securities can't be identified and thus try to hold a portfolio that mimics some set of stocks. The most common way passive management is practiced is to hold a portfolio of stocks that closely tracks a selected index. Active management involves making bets about some securities or set of securities in the sense of designing a portfolio based on a belief that one or more securities are mispriced.

Passive Management

The multi-index model can play a major role in improving passive management. It can be used to do a better job of tracking an index or to design a passive portfolio that is appropriate for a particular client.

The simplest use of a multi-index model is to create a portfolio of stocks that closely tracks an index. An obvious way to construct an index fund is to hold stocks in the same

---

[19]Although estimating the cost of equity capital falls beyond the scope of this book, the preceding analysis leads naturally to estimates of cost of capital. For example, the cost of capital of any stock or portfolio can be found by adding the riskless rate to the estimate of excess return from the APT model. For growth stocks this would be $R_F + 11.41$. For a detailed explanation of using APT to determine cost of equity capital, see Elton, Gruber, and Mei [39].

[20]Note that all b values, except for sensitivity to inflation, are larger for the growth stock portfolio than for the S&P portfolio. Though the b value for inflation is smaller for the growth stock portfolio, this portfolio is still less desirable with respect to inflation sensitivity because (unlike other λ's) the price of inflation sensitivity (λ_1) is negative.

proportion they represent of the index. However, many index funds do not simply hold each stock in an index in the proportion the stock represents of the index, but rather attempt to replicate the index with a smaller number of stocks. The more issues in an index, the smaller the companies represented in an index, and the less liquid the stocks in an index, the more costly it is to match the index by purchasing stocks in the same proportion they represent in the index. Clearly, once one becomes concerned with tracking an index that represents a very large segment of a market, exact matching of proportions becomes less and less appropriate. An index fund can be created using the single-index model by finding the portfolio that has a Beta of one with the desired index and that has minimum residual risks for a given portfolio size (minimum variance of the e_i's in a single index form of Equation [16.1]).

Employing a multi-index model rather than a one-index model allows the creation of an index fund that more closely matches the desired index.[21] The reason for this is clear. A properly constructed multi-index model ensures that the index has been matched in terms of all important sources of return movements (risk). On the other hand, just matching on market risk can leave the portfolio and the index with different sensitivities to the common factors affecting both, such as sensitivity to inflation. Let's consider a simple example of this. Reviewing the sensitivity coefficients associated with the market from Table 8.1, in Chapter 8, we see that both oil stocks and cyclical stocks have a sensitivity with the S&P index of 1.14, Thus, in a single-index model except for residual risk one would be indifferent to holding oil stocks or cyclical stocks in matching the S&P index. However, oil stocks and cyclical stocks have very different sensitivities (b's) to sales growth. Thus, a portfolio that was matched to an index on sensitivity with the S&P but was not matched on the b value with sales growth might not track the index very well in periods when unexpected changes in sales growth were large.

In general, the fewer stocks in an index-matching portfolio the less likely that the portfolio will be matched on the common factors affecting the portfolio and the index and the greater the superiority of multi-index models over single-index models.[22] This is true because unexpected changes in the missing indices will differentially impact the residual risk in future periods if sensitivity to these missing indices is not held constant. Portfolios are often formed to serve as arbitrage portfolios in the trading of options or futures on an index. Firms typically attempt to form a small basket of stocks (25 or 50) that they can actively trade as they change their futures or options position. The number must be kept small, because the basket of stocks will be bought and sold frequently. The use of multi-index models becomes critical in these instances.

Another problem frequently encountered in passive management is the desire to match an index with a portfolio that excludes certain types of stocks. Social goals or management preferences frequently restrict the set of stocks that can be used to match an index. In the last 10 years, for example, it was not uncommon for a pension fund to declare that it would not own tobacco stocks or that it would not invest in companies that were heavily engaged in business in South Africa. It is likely that a sector of the market such as tobacco stocks has sensitivity to inflation or interest rates that is different from the average stock. If an index fund is formed from a set of stocks that precludes tobacco stocks using the single-index model, then the sensitivity to the single-index will be matched but the sensitivity to

---

[21]See Elton and Gruber [35] for a demonstration of the improvement in index tracking that results from using a four-index as opposed to a one-index model.

[22]See Elton and Gruber [35] for empirical evidence on this issue.

other important influences will probably be different. Use of a multi-index model improves tracking an index.[23]

Multi-index models also help improve performance under a set of conditions that are directly opposite to those just described. An investor may decide to match an index with a portfolio that must contain certain stocks. This is very common in Japan where stocks are often held for reasons that have their foundations in the business relationship between firms. In the United States, an investor may want to maintain (or add) certain holdings in a portfolio for business reasons or because the investor does not want to recognize certain accumulated but unrealized capital losses or gains for either tax purposes or reporting purposes.[24] The problem then is to find an overall portfolio matching as closely as possible an index but including a defined set of stocks. Because these stocks may have sensitivities to important influences that are different from the index being matched, it is important to explicitly match on each of the key risk factors.

There is one type of passive management which can be performed with a multi-index model, which is fundamentally different from what can be done with a single-index model. The multi-index model allows one to closely match an index while purposely taking positions with respect to certain types of risk different from the positions contained in the index. For example, consider a pension fund that has cash outflows affected by inflation (COLA or cost-of-living adjustments). The payments for such a pension fund increase with inflation. Thus the overseers want a portfolio that will perform especially well when the rate of inflation increases. This can be illustrated more fully by returning to the data presented for the S&P index earlier in this chapter. The b value (sensitivity) for the S&P index with inflation was -0.37, which implies (other things held constant) that an investment in the S&P index will tend to go down by 0.37% if the rate of inflation goes up by 1%. If a pension fund is particularly sensitive to inflation risk (because its liability payments go up with inflation), it might wish to hold a portfolio that has a zero sensitivity to inflation (or even a positive sensitivity). It could form a portfolio that had the same response to all factors affecting the S&P (except for the inflation factor) by solving a quadratic programming problem to form a portfolio that matched all S&P b's except for the b on inflation, had a zero or positive b with inflation, and had minimum residual risk.

The applications we have just discussed can be done using a multi-index model; however, assuming an APT adds additional insight into the process. It tells the investor the expected cost of changing the exposure to inflation. Observing the λ with inflation we see that the market will accept a lower return of 4.32 for every one unit increase in sensitivity to inflation. This is because the aggregate of investors prefer stocks that offer higher return when inflation goes up. The investor who wanted zero sensitivity to inflation would expect to have a $(-4.32) \times 0.37 = -1.60$ change (decrease) in expected return to obtain the preferred position. Like most of economics this is not a free lunch. Instead, it is a method of allowing the investor to make specified trade-offs between types of risk and expected returns.[25]

There is one variable in our model that allows the investor to take an action that is very close to a free lunch. Let's reexamine our model. One of the factors, oil price changes, had

---

[23]See Elton and Gruber [35] for empirical evidence.

[24]An example of the latter occurs in insurance companies where the realization of gains or losses impacts the surplus account and thus the ability of the firm to write new business.

[25]Deviating from market b's to better match liabilities is different from deviating in order to take active bets on the change in one or more underlying influences. This active use of factor bets will be discussed shortly.

a zero λ (was given a zero price by the market). While oil prices affect returns on some stocks, changes in oil prices are not a pervasive enough influence to be priced by the market. At first glance one might think that the sensitivity on a portfolio to oil should be set to zero. After all, why take on a risk (increased variability in returns) with no commensurate increase in expected returns? For the average investor this is correct. However, think of an investor whose cash *outflow* increases with increases in oil prices. Such an investor would want to hold a portfolio of securities that has a positive sensitivity with oil prices. Furthermore, because oil sensitivity is not priced by the market, increasing the sensitivity to oil prices does not change expected return. Of course, if everybody wanted to hold portfolios that exhibited increased return with increases in oil prices, then the λ associated with oil prices would be positive. The fact that an investor desires, with respect to oil sensitivity, a position different from the aggregate allows the investor to improve his or her portfolio with no decrease in expected return, although there will be some increase in total risk.

Keep in mind that matching an index while making quantitative judgments on the amount of a particular type of risk to take can only be done if indexes representing these risks are contained in the multi-index model. Furthermore, the expected return (or expected cost) of these nonaverage risk positions can only be determined from an APT model.

Active Management

Most uses of multi-index models for active management parallel their use in passive management. It's easier to discuss them in reverse order to that presented previously. What a multi-index model does that cannot be done with a single-index model is allow the user to make factor bets. If you believe that unexpected inflation will accelerate at a rate above that anticipated by the market ($I_I > 0$), then you may want to place a bet by increasing your exposure (b value) with inflation. This can be done holding a portfolio with a sensitivity to inflation larger than the S&P index.[26] Obviously the more indexes included in the model the more active bets you can make. For example, in the Salomon model described earlier in this chapter, you can take active bets on economic growth, the stage of the business cycle, long-term interest rates, short-term interest rates, inflation rates, the value of the U.S. dollar, or the state of the stock market.

Return to the simple model we have been discussing, assume that the S&P index is the appropriate benchmark and that an analyst believed that sales were going to increase by 1% more than the market expected. The analyst might increase the b value with respect to sales on the portfolio from the 1.71 value found for the S&P index to 2.21. Under the APT model and recognizing the λ for sales is 1.49 the increase in sales sensitivity of 0.5% would lead to a $0.5(1.49) = 0.745\%$ increase in *expected return*, which is just sufficient to reward the investor for the additional risk. However, the additional 1% increase in sales would lead to an additional 2.21% increase in the return on the portfolio should it materialize. Of this 2.21% increase, 0.5% arose from increasing the sensitivity to sales while 1.71 would have arisen had the b been left at the level of the S&P index. The 0.5% increase is often called the excess risk adjusted return that arises from an ability to forecast factors better than the market.

Multi-index models and APT models can be used just as the single-index model and CAPM models are used to form optimal portfolios building upon estimates of the per-

---

[26]We assume the S&P index is the relevant benchmark in this section. Actually the analysis holds with the sensitivities of any benchmark (growth stocks or the New York Stock Exchange index) substituted for sensitivities to the S&P index.

formance of individual securities. The simplest approach is that discussed back in Chapter 8, where a multi-index model is used to generate the convariance between securities while expected returns and variances are supplied by some combination of analysts' forecasts and historical data.

Another application of APT is to use APT to determine stocks that are under- or over-valued. In this procedure an analyst produces a forecast of the return on a stock. The APT is then used together with estimates of the sensitivity of the stock to the factors to calculate a required return for the stock (using an equation such as 16.10). If the estimated return is above what's required given the stock's sensitivity and the λ's, the stock is purchased.

This is a generalization of the analysis that is used when the CAPM rather than the APT is used as an equilibrium model. Recall as shown in Chapter 14, that the CAPM is a straight line in expected return Beta space (see Figure 14.2). If a firm's expected return and Beta are such that it plots above the CAPM line, it offers a higher return (given its Beta) than is required in equilibrium and is a buy. Similarly, if it plots below the line, its expected return is less than required in equilibrium and it should be sold. The analysis with APT has the same logic. Consider a two-factor APT model. In this case, the APT plots as a plane in a three-dimensional space where the axes are sensitivities to the two factors and expected return. Firms that plot above the plane offer a higher expected return than is required given the sensitivities and λ's and should be purchased.[27]

Why the APT rather than the CAPM? If the APT is the appropriate equilibrium model and the CAPM is used, then stocks with different sensitivities to the factors but the same market Beta will be incorrectly classified as equally risky. The CAPM model incorrectly implies that they have the same expected return.

To better understand this, let's return to the example we have been discussing in this chapter. Note that the lambda on growth is positive. This implies that investors require a higher expected return for stocks that have higher sensitivity to unexpected changes in growth. A stock with a high sensitivity to growth will tend (because growth has a positive price or lambda) to have a higher expected return than a stock with a lower sensitivity to growth. But this is ignored (except for the part captured in the market Beta) by the standard CAPM models. Thus the extra return investors require (as reflected in the market price of risk or lambda associated with high sensitivity to growth) will be interpreted as underpricing by the standard CAPM model. Stocks that are very sensitive to unexpected changes in growth will tend to lie above the security market line. Stocks that are sensitive to other priced influences not included in the single-index model are likely to show up as systematically underpriced or overpriced by the CAPM and to lie above or below the security market line.

One of the most common uses of the APT model is to form a portfolio of stocks that while closely tracking a target will also produce a return in excess of that index. One way to implement this type of procedure is simply to employ the index-matching procedure described earlier in this chapter, but only allow selection from among a set of stocks that analysts have earmarked as superior performers. Other techniques use either numeric discrete ranking of stocks or expected return on stocks in an attempt to produce an excess return above an index while using the multi-index model to track an index as closely as possible.[28] Portfolios designed this way have become known as research titled index funds.

---

[27]The market prices of risk (λ's) for the CAPM or APT models can be specified by theory or estimated using analysts' forecasts of expected return and sensitivities for a set of stocks. See Chapter 19 for a discussion of how firm forecasts are used.

[28]Many firms have their analysts place stocks into groups (often five) with group 1 being the best purchases and 5 the stocks that should be sold.

Although some additional risk is involved (the index can't be matched as closely when selecting from a restricted set of stocks), investors who use this technique feel that an excess return can be earned with only a slight loss in the ability to track the index. The advantage of the multi-index model over the simple-index model is that the target index can be tracked more closely because the different sources of risk are explicitly taken into consideration.

The more the target being tracked differs from a diversified market portfolio the more important it is to use a multi-index model. The extreme case and one that has received a lot of attention is the long-short investment strategy or risk neutral strategy. If one has superior ability to identify stocks that will perform above average on an APT risk-adjusted basis and stocks that will perform below average on an APT risk-adjusted basis, then using the APT index one can form portfolios that offer an excess return and have no risk (zero b risk) with respect to any factor (e.g., no risk due to change in the market level, inflation, or interest rate movements). Obviously there is also no expected return due to any factor, because the Beta on each factor is set to zero. What one gets is a pure payoff from security selection with all factors including the market neutralized. We can examine this by returning to Equation (16.11). If we believe that an analyst can predict the extra return from any security over a period of time (return from security selection) Equation (16.11) can be written as

$$R_i = R_F + \alpha_i + \lambda_1 b_{i1} + \lambda_2 b_{i2} + \lambda_3 b_{i3} +$$
$$\cdots + b_{i1}I_1 + b_{i2}I_2 + b_{i3}I_3 + \cdots + e_i$$

where α_i is the extra return the security analyst predicts on security i.

Think of this equation for each of two portfolios: portfolio L is a portfolio of long positions and portfolio S is a portfolio of short positions. Furthermore, assume that the portfolios are formed so that $b_{Lj} + b_{Sj} = 0$ for all j's. Then, combining the preceding equation for each of the two portfolios, we get a risk neutral (or more specifically systematic risk neutral) portfolio denoted by N with a return given by

$$R_N = R_F + \alpha_L + \alpha_S$$

and with a risk given by

$$e_N = e_L + e_S$$

Burmeister, Roll, and Ross [13] examined the payoff from such a model from the period April 1991 to March 1992, assuming α's could be correctly identified. They found that over this period the S&P index has a return of 11.57% per year and a standard deviation of 18.08%. Their factor-neutral portfolio had a return of 30.04% per year and a standard deviation of 6.26% per year. While these are obviously optimistic figures, for they assume perfect foresight, they do indicate the ability of factor-neutral portfolios to lower risk and, if forecasting ability exists, increase return.

Although one can perform the same type of analysis with a single-index model rather than a multi-index model, the overall risks of the portfolio will be greater and the user likely to find he or she is undertaking factor bets (inflation, interest rate, etc.) rather than pure security selection bets.

Performance Measurement and Attribution

The last use of multi-index and APT models we should examine is in the area of portfolio performance evaluation. It is difficult to discuss the use of APT in performance measurement and evaluation without reviewing the whole literature in this area. Because of this we will leave a detailed discussion and the continuation of the example we started in this chapter until Chapter 24. However, consideration of the model we have discussed shows that the expected performance of any portfolio is not just a function of the portfolio's sensitivity to the market but also a function of the portfolio's sensitivity to sales growth and inflation. If influences that enter the return-generating process and APT are ignored in doing performance evaluation, not only can't the analyst's performance be attributed to the type of management decisions he or she is making, but perhaps more important, incorrect conclusions may be reached about how well managers are performing.

CONCLUSION

In this chapter, we have reviewed

1. Modern concepts of arbitrage pricing.

2. Alternative approaches to estimating arbitrage pricing models.

3. Some uses of arbitrage pricing models.

Considerable evidence continues to be produced on the usefulness of arbitrage pricing models.

APPENDIX A

A SIMPLE EXAMPLE OF FACTOR ANALYSIS

In order to provide the reader who has never used any form of factor analysis with a demonstration of how it works we include a simple example in this appendix. We choose to use principal component analysis for the example, because this leads to a solution that is easiest to interpret.[29]

We choose 10 years of monthly data on the Morgan Stanley Capital International stock indexes for each of four countries: the United States, Canada, France, and Belgium. Remember that principal components analysis extracts from this data the index that explains as much as possible of the correlation in returns between the four countries and then finds a second index that explains as much as possible of the correlation in returns not explained by the first index.[30] The indexes produced by principal components are formed by combining (weighting) the time series of return for each country with the mean return for each country extracted.

Before we perform principal component analysis, let's think about what we would expect the results to look like. We might hypothesize that the first index would be some sort of measure of how stocks in general did, that is, some general aggregation of the returns under study. In thinking about the problem one would expect Canada and the United States to act somewhat alike and France and Belgium to act somewhat alike, whereas we would expect the differences between these paired countries to be greater. In fact, the correlations between the four countries as shown in Table 16.2 bear out this speculation.

---

[29]See Elton and Gruber [37] for a detailed discussion on the use of factor analysis in multi-index models.

[30]Principal components then extract a third and fourth index. In this case, we only report the first two, since the third and fourth are not statistically significant.

Table 16.2 Correlation Coefficient Between Returns in Four Countries

	Belgium	France	Canada	U.S.
Belgium	1.0			
France	0.65	1.0		
Canada	0.38	0.41	1.0	
United States	0.41	0.43	0.72	1.0

The indexes that are the first two principal components estimated from this data are presented below. Remember that in performing principal components analysis we do not specify the indexes we expect to find, we simply let the data determine the indexes.

The indexes are

$$I_{1t} = 0.67\left(R_{Bt} - \overline{R}_B\right) + 0.76\left(R_{Ft} - \overline{R}_F\right) + .076\left(R_{ct} - \overline{R}_c\right) + 0.77\left(R_{ut} - \overline{R}_u\right)$$

$$I_{2t} = -0.40\left(R_{Bt} - \overline{R}_B\right) - 0.37\left(R_{Ft} - \overline{R}_F\right) + 0.73\left(R_{ct} - \overline{R}_c\right) + 0.41\left(R_{ut} - \overline{R}_u\right)$$

where

I_{1t} and I_{2t} are the two indexes extracted from the data.

The R's are monthly returns, and the subscripts B, C, F, U, and t represent Belgium, Canada, France, United States, and time.

Note that the first index is very close to an equally weighted index of all four markets, and thus meets our expectation that the index that would explain as much as possible of returns is the general return index. The second index is long in North America and short in Europe. It meets our expectation that the second index should capture the fact that North American and European markets are less associated with each other than with markets within their own region.

To see how well these two indexes work we can regress the returns from each country against the two indexes. When we did so, the R^2 were: 0.81 for Belgium, 0.95 for Canada, 0.84 for France, and 0.74 for the United States.

APPENDIX B

SPECIFICATION OF THE APT WITH AN UNOBSERVED MARKET FACTOR

This appendix is a brief recapping of the procedures put forth in a series of articles by Burmeister, McElroy, and others. For further details see [10–12] and [84].

We can represent a return-generating process (multi-index model) with observable indices plus an unobservable index designated by index k as

$$R_{it} = \overline{R}_{it} + \sum_{j=1}^{J} b_{ij} F_{jt} + b_{ik} F_{kt} + \epsilon_{it} \tag{B.1}$$

Making the no arbitrage assumption of APT, expected return is approximately given by

$$\overline{R}_{it} = \lambda_{Ot} + \sum_{j=1}^{J} b_{ij} \lambda_{jt} + b_{ik} \lambda_{kt} \tag{B.2}$$

We will make the assumption of [84] that all λ_{ot}, equal the risk-free rate and all other λ's are constant over time, substituting (B.2) into (B.1).

$$R_{it} = R_{Ft} + \sum_{j=1}^{J} b_{ij}\lambda_j + \sum_{j=1}^{J} b_{ij}F_{jt} + b_{ik}\lambda_k + b_{ik}F_{kt} + \epsilon_{it} \tag{B.3}$$

Now assume a very well-diversified portfolio called m. For this portfolio residual risk approaches zero and[31]

$$R_{mt} = \lambda_m + R_{Ft} + \sum_{j=1}^{J} b_{mj}F_{jt} + F_{kt} \tag{B.4}$$

where $\lambda_m = \sum_{j=1}^{J} b_{mj}\lambda_j + \lambda_k$

Burmeister and McElroy assume the market portfolio has no residual risk $\epsilon_{mt} = 0$, this F_{kt} is the unobserved error term.

However, F_{kt} can be estimated by the residual of an Ordinary Least Squares (OLS) time-series regression of R_{mt} on the observed variables as in Equation (B.4) or rearranging (B.4) yields

$$\hat{F}_{kt} = (R_{mt} - R_{Ft}) - \left[\lambda_m + \sum_{j-1}^{J} b_{mj}F_{jt} \right] \tag{B.5}$$

McElroy and Burmeister [84] show that $\hat{F}_{kt}$ is an unbiased estimate of the common stocks F_{kt}. Thus substituting $\hat{F}_{kt}$ for F_{kt} in (B.3) and adjusting the residual yields

$$R_{it} = R_{Ft} + \sum_{j=1}^{J} b_{ij}\lambda_j + b_{ik}\lambda_k + \sum_{j=1}^{J} b_{ij}F_{jt} + b_{ik}\hat{F}_{kt} + e_{it} \tag{B.6}$$

To estimate this equation McElroy and Burmeiser [84] first use time-series analysis to estimate Equations (B.4 and B.5) and then nonlinear seemingly unrelated regressions to estimate (B.6).[32]

In doing so, they make one more interesting change in this model. They allow for the possibility that although APT correctly prices every security in their sample, it may not correctly price every security in the highly diversified portfolio.

QUESTIONS AND PROBLEMS

1. Assume that the following two-index model describes returns

$$R_i = a_i + b_{i1}I_1 + b_{i2}I_2 + e_i$$

Assume that the following three portfolios are observed.

Portfolio	Expected Return	b_{i1}	b_{i2}
A	12.0	1	0.5
B	13.4	3	0.2
C	12.0	3	−0.5

---

[31]The assumption is made that the unobserved variable F_{kt} is recalled to have a Beta of one with the portfolio m.

[32]Conditions on the relationship between e_{it} and ϵ_{it} are delineated in [84].

Find the equation of the plane that must describe equilibrium returns.

2. Referring to the results of Problem 1, illustrate the arbitrage opportunities that would exist if a portfolio called D with the following properties were observed.

$$\bar{R}_D = 10 \quad b_{D1} = 2 \quad b_{D2} = 0$$

3. Repeat Problem 1 if the three portfolios observed have the following characteristics.

Portfolio	Expected Return	b_{i1}	b_{i2}
A	12	1.0	1
B	13	1.5	2
C	17	0.5	−3

4. Referring to the results of Problem 3, illustrate the arbitrage opportunities that would exist if a portfolio called D with the following characteristics were observed.

$$\bar{R}_i = 15 \quad b_{i1} = 1 \quad b_{i2} = 0$$

5. If we accept the Sharpe model as a description of expected returns, using the data in Table 16.1 find the expected return on a stock in the construction industry with the following characteristics. Assume a riskless rate of 8%.

$$\begin{aligned}
\text{Beta} &= 1.2 \\
\text{Yield} &= 6 \\
\text{Size} &= 0.4 \\
\text{Bond Beta} &= 0.2 \\
\text{Alpha} &= 1
\end{aligned}$$

6. Return to Problem 1. If $(\bar{R}_m - R_F) = 4$, find the values for the following variables that would make the expected returns from Problem 1 consistent with equilibrium determined by the simple (Sharpe–Lintner–Mossin) CAPM.

A. $\beta_{\lambda 1}$ and $\beta_{\lambda 2}$

B. β_p for each of the three portfolios

C. R_F

BIBLIOGRAPHY

1. Admati, Anat, and Pfleiderer, Paul. "Interpreting the Factor Risk Premia in Arbitrage Pricing Theory," *Journal of Economic Theory*, **35** (Feb. 1985), pp. 191–195.
2. Berry, Michael, Burmeister, Edwin, and McElroy, Marjorie. "Sorting Out Risks Using Known APT Factors," *Financial Analysts Journal* (March 1988), pp. 29–42.
3. Black, F. "Capital Market Equilibrium with Restricted Borrowing," *Journal of Business*, **45** (July 1972), pp. 444–454.
4. Black, Fisher, Jensen, Nick, and Scholes, Myron. "The Capital Asset Pricing Model: Some Empirical Tests." In Jensen, M. (ed.) *Studies in the Theory of Capital Markets* (New York: Praeger, 1972).
5. Blake, Christopher, Elton, Edwin J., and Gruber, Martin J. "The Performance of Bond Mutual Funds," *Journal of Business*, **66**, No. 3 (July 1993), pp. 371–403.
6. Bower, Dorothy H., Bower, Richard S., and Logue, Dennis E. "Arbitrage Pricing Theory and Utility Stock Returns," *The Journal of Finance*, **39,** No. 4 (Sept. 1984), pp. 1041–1054.

7. Brennan, M. "Capital Asset Pricing and the Structure of Security Returns," Working Paper, University of British Columbia, 1971.

8. ———. "Discussion," *Journal of Finance*, **36** (May 1981), pp. 352–357.

9. Brown, S. J., and Weinstein, M. I. "A New Approach to Testing Asset Pricing Models: The Bilinear Paradigm," *Journal of Finance*, **38**, No. 3 (June 1983).

10. Burmeister, Edwin, and McElroy, Marjorie. "APT and Multifactor Asset Pricing Models with Measured and Unobserved Factors: Theoretical and Econometric Issues," Discussion Paper, Department of Economics, University of Virginia and Duke University, 1987.

11. Burmeister, Edwin, and McElroy, Marjorie. "Joint Estimation of Factor Sensitivities and Risk Premia for the Arbitrage Pricing Theory," *Journal of Finance*, **43**, No. 3 (July 1988), pp. 721–733.

12. Burmeister, Edwin, and Wall, Kent. "The Arbitrage Pricing Theory and Macroeconomic Factor Measures," *The Financial Review* (Feb. 1986).

13. Burmeister, Edwin, Roll, Richard, and Ross, Stephen, "A Practitioner's Guide to Arbitrage Pricing Theory," in *A Practitioner's Guide to Factor Models*, (Charlottesville, Va., The Research Foundation of the Institute of Chartered Financial Analysts, 1994).

14. Burmeister, Edwin, Wall, Kent, and Hamilton, James. "Estimation of Unobserved Expected Monthly Inflation Using Kalman Filtering," *Journal of Business and Economic Statistics*, **4** (April 1986), pp. 147–160.

15. Chamberlain, G., and Rothschild, M. "Arbitrage, Factor Structure, and Mean-Variance Analysis on Large Asset Markets," Working Paper, University of Wisconsin at Madison, 1981.

16. Chamberlain, Gary. "Funds, Factors and Diversification in Arbitrage Pricing Models," *Econometrica*, **51** (Sept. 1983), pp. 1305–1323.

17. Chan, K. C., Chen, Nai-fu, and Hsiech, David. "An Explanatory Investigation of the Firm Size Effect," *Journal of Financial Economics*, **14** (Sept. 1985), pp. 451–471.

18. Chen, N. "The Arbitrage Pricing Theory: Estimation and Applications," Working Paper, Graduate School of Management, UCLA, 1981.

19. Chen, Nai-fu. "Some Empirical Tests of the Theory of Arbitrage Pricing," *The Journal of Finance*, **38**, No. 5 (Dec. 1983), pp. 1393–1414.

20. Chen, Nai-fu, and Ingersoll, Jonathan E., Jr. "Exact Pricing in Linear Factor Models with Finitely Many Assets: A Note," *The Journal of Finance*, **38**, No. 3 (June 1983), pp. 985–988.

21. Chen, Nai-fu, Roll, Richard, and Ross, Stephen. "Economic Forces and the Stock Market," *Journal of Business*, **59** (July 1986), pp. 386–403.

22. Cho, D. Chinhyung. "On Testing the Arbitrage Pricing Theory: Inter-Battery Factor Analysis," *The Journal of Finance*, **39**, No. 5 (Dec. 1984), pp. 1485–1502.

23. ———. "Some fundamental factors effecting asset prices," Working Paper, University of Wisconsin, 1984.

24. Cho, D. Chinhyung, and Taylor, William. "The Seasonal Stability of the Factor Structure of Stock Returns," *Journal of Finance*, **42** (Dec. 1987), pp. 1195–1211.

25. Cho, D. Chinhyung, Elton, Edwin J., and Gruber, Martin J. "On the Robustness of the Roll and Ross Arbitrage Pricing Theory," *Journal of Financial and Quantitative Analysis*, **XIX,** No. 1 (March 1984), pp. 1–10.

26. Cho, D. Chinhyung, Eun, Cheol S., and Senbet, Lemma W. "International Arbitrage Pricing Theory: An Empirical Investigation," *The Journal of Finance*, **41,** No. 2 (June 1986), pp. 313–329.

27. Cochrane, John H. "Production-Based Asset Pricing and the Link Between Stock Returns and Economic Fluctuations," *The Journal of Finance*, **46**, No. 1 (Mar. 1991), pp. 209–237.

28. Connor, G. "A Factor Pricing Theory for Capital Assets," Working Paper, Kellog Graduate School of Management, Northwestern University, 1981.

29. Connor, Gregory. "A Unified Beta Pricing Theory," *Journal of Economic Theory*, **34,** No. 3 (Oct. 1984), pp. 13–31.

30. Connor, G., and Korajczyk, R. "Performance Measurement with the Arbitrage Pricing Theory: A New Framework for Analysis," *Journal of Financial Economics*, **15**, No. 3 (1986), pp. 373–394.

31. Conway, Delores, and Reinganum, Marc. "Capital Market Factor Structure: Identification through Cross Validation," *Journal of Business and Financial Statistics*, **6**, No. 1 (Jan. 1988).

32. Dhrymes, Pheobus J., Friend, Irwin, and Gultekin, N. Bulent. "A Critical Reexamination of the Empirical Evidence on the Arbitrage Pricing Theory," *The Journal of Finance*, **39,** No. 2 (June 1984), pp. 323–346.

33. Dybvig, Phillip H. "An Explicit Bound on Deviations from APT Pricing in a Finite Economy," *Journal of Financial Economics*, **12** (1983), pp. 483–496.

34. Elton, E., and Gruber, M. "Non-Standard CAPMs and the Market Portfolio," Working Paper, New York University, Graduate School of Business, 1982.

35. Elton, Edwin J., and Gruber, Martin J. "A Multi-Index Risk Model of the Japanese Stock Market," *Japan and the World Economy* **1,** No. 1 (1988).

36. Elton, Edwin J., and Gruber, Martin J. "Expectational Data and Japanese Stock Prices," *Japan and the World Economy*, **1** (1989), pp. 391–401.

37. Elton, Edwin J., and Gruber, Martin J. "Multi-Index Models Using Simultaneous Estimation of all Parameters." In *A Practitioner's Guide to Factor Models*, (The Research Foundation of the Institute of Chartered Financial Analysts, Charlottesville, Va., 1994), pp. 31–58.

38. Elton, Edwin J., Gruber, Martin J., and Blake, Christopher. "Fundamental Variables, APT, and Bond Fund Performance," Working Paper, New York University, 1994.

39. Elton, Edwin J., Gruber, Martin J., and Mei, Jianping. "Cost of Capital Using Arbitrage Pricing Theory: A Case Study of Nine New York Utilities." In *Estimating the Cost of Capital: Methods and Practice, Journal of Financial Markets, Institutions & Instruments*, **3,** No. 3, Blackwell Publishers (1994).

40. Elton, Edwin J., Gruber, Martin J., and Rentzler, Joel. "The Arbitrage Pricing Model and Returns on Assets Under Uncertain Inflation," *The Journal of Finance*, **38,** No. 2 (May 1983), pp. 525–538.

41. Elton, Edwin J., Gruber, Martin J., Das, Sanjiv, and Hlavka, Matthew. "Efficiency with Costly Information: A Reinterpretation of Evidence from Managed Portfolios," *Review of Financial Studies*, **6,** No. 1 (1993), pp. 1–22.

42. Fama, Eugene. "Stock Returns, Real Activity, Inflation and Money," *American Economic Review*, **71** (1981), pp. 545–565.

43. Fama, Eugene, and French, Kenneth. "The Cross Section of Expected Stock Returns," *The Journal of Finance*, **47,** No. 2 (June 1992), pp. 427–466.

44. Fama, Eugene, and French, Kenneth. "Common Factors in the Returns on Bonds and Stocks," Working Paper, Center for Research in Security Prices, University of Chicago, 1993.

45. Fama, Eugene, and Gibbons, Michael. "A Comparison of Inflation Forecasts," *Journal of Monetary Economics*, **13** (1984), pp. 327–348.

46. Fama, Eugene, and MacBeth, James. "Risk, Return, and Equilibrium: Empirical Tests," *Journal of Political Economy*, **38** (1973), pp. 607–636.

47. Fogler, H. Russell, John, Kose, and Tipton, James. "Three Factors Interest Rate Differentials and Stock Groups," *The Journal of Finance*, **36,** No. 2 (May 1981), pp. 323–336.

48. Garman, Mark B., and Ohlson, James A. "A Dynamic Equilibrium for the Ross Arbitrage Model," *The Journal of Finance*, **35,** No. 3 (June 1980), pp. 675–684.

49. Gehr, A., Jr. "Some Tests of the Arbitrage Pricing Theory," *Journal of the Midwest Finance Association* (1975), pp. 91–105.

50. Gibbons, M. "Multivariate Tests of Financial Models: A New Approach," *Journal of Financial Economics*, **10,** No. 1 (March 1982), pp. 3–27.

51. Gibbons, M.R. "Empirical Examination of the Return Generating Process of the Arbitrage Pricing Theory," Working Paper, Stanford University, 1981.

52. Grinblatt, Mark, and Titman, Sheridan. "Factor Pricing in a Finite Economy," *Journal of Financial Economics*, **12** (1983), pp. 497–507.

53. ——. "Approximate Factor Structures: Interpretations and Implications for Empirical Tests," *Journal of Finance*, **40** (1985), pp. 1367–1373.

54. ——. "The Relation Between Mean-Variance Efficiency and Arbitrage Pricing," *Journal of Business*, **60** (1987), pp. 97–113.

55. Grinold, Richard and Kahn, Ronald. "Multi Factor Models for Portfolio Risk," in *A Practitioner's Guide to Factor Models*, (Charlottesville, Va.: The Research Foundation of the Institute of Chartered Financial Analysts, 1994).

56. Gultekin, Mustafa, and Gultekin, N. Bulent. "Stock Return Anomalies and Tests of the APT," *Journal of Finance*, **42** (Dec. 1987), pp. 1213–1224.

57. Hansen, Lars, and Singleton, Kenneth. "Stochastic Consumption, Risk Aversion, and the Temporal Behavior of Assets Returns," *Journal of Political Economy*, **91** (1983), pp. 249–265.

58. Harman, H. *Modern Factor Analysis*, third edition (Chicago: University of Chicago Press, 1976).

59. Huberman, Gur. "A Simple Approach to Arbitrage Pricing Theory," *Journal of Economic Theory*, **78** (1982), pp. 183–191.

60. ——. "A Review of the Arbitrage Pricing Theory," in Eatwell; John, Milgate, Murray, and Newman, Peter (eds.), *The New Palgrave: A Dictionary of Economic Theory and Doctrine* (New York: Stockton Press, 1987).

61. Huberman, Gur, and Kandel, Shmuel. "Mean-Variance Spanning," *The Journal of Finance*, **42,** No. 4 (Sept. 1987), pp. 873–888.

62. ——. "Mean-Variance Spanning," *Journal of Finance*, **42** (Sept. 1987), pp. 873–888.

63. Huberman, Gur, and Stambaugh, Robert. "Mimicking Portfolios and Exact Arbitrage Pricing," *Journal of Finance*, **42** (March 1987), pp. 1–9.

64. Huberman, Gur, Kandel, Shmuel, and Stambaugh, Robert F. "Mimicking Portfolios and Exact Arbitrage Pricing," *The Journal of Finance*, **42,** No. 1 (Mar. 1987), pp. 1–9.

65. Hughes, P. "A Test of the Arbitrage Pricing Theory," Working Paper, University of British Columbia, 1981.

66. Ibbotson, Roger, and Sinquefield, Rex. *Stocks, Bonds, Bills and Inflation: The Past and the Future* (Charlottesville, Va.: Financial Analysts Research Foundation, 1982).

67. Ikeda, Shinsuke. "Arbitrage Asset Pricing Under Exchange Risk," *The Journal of Finance*, **46,** No. 1 (Mar. 1991), pp. 447–455.

68. Ingersoll, Jonathan E., Jr. "Some Results in the Theory of Arbitrage Pricing," *Journal of Finance*, **39** (1984), pp. 1021–1039.

69. ——. *Theory of Financial Decision Making*. Totowa, N.J.: Rowman and Littlefield (1987).

70. Jobson, J.D. "A Multivariate Linear Regression Test for the Arbitrage Pricing Theory," *The Journal of Finance*, **37,** No. 4 (Sept. 1982), pp. 1037–1042.

71. Joreskog, K.G. "Some Contributions to Maximum Likelihood Factor Analysis," *Psychometrika*, **32,** No. 4 (Dec. 1967), pp. 443–482.

72. Joreskog, K.G. "Factor Analysis by Least Squares and Maximum Likelihood Methods," in K. Enslein, A. Ralston, and H. S. Wilf (eds.), *Statistical Methods of Digital Computers* (New York: John Wiley & Sons, 1977).

73. Joreskog, K.J. *Statistical Estimation in Factor Analysis* (Stockholm: Almqvist & Wiksell, 1963).

74. King, B. "Market and Industry Factors in Stock Price Behavior," *Journal of Business*, **39** (Jan. 1966), pp. 139–190.

75. Kristof, W. "Orthogonal Inter-Battery Factor Analysis," *Psychometrika*, **32,** No. 2 (June 1967), pp. 199–227.

76. Kryzanowski, L., and To, M.C. "General Factor Models and the Structure of Security Returns," *Journal of Financial and Quantitative Analysis*, **18,** No. 1 (March 1983), pp. 31–37.

77. Lawley, D.N. "The Estimation of Factor Loadings by the Method of Maximum Likelihood," *Proceedings of the Royal Society of Edinburgh, Section A*, **60** (1940), pp. 64–82.

78. Lawley, D.N., and Maxwell, M.A. *Factor Analysis as a Statistical Method* (London, U.K.: Butterworths, 1963).

79. Lehmann, Bruce, and Modest, David. "The Empirical Foundations of the Arbitrage Pricing Theory I: The Empirical Tests," *Journal of Financial Economics*, **21** (1988), pp. 213–254.

80. Levine, M.S. *Canonical Analysis and Factor Comparison* (Beverly Hills, Calif.: Sage Publications, 1977).

81. Lintner, J. "The Valuation of Risk Assets and the Selection of Risky Investments in Stock Portfolios and Capital Budgets," *Review of Economics and Statistics*, **47** (Feb. 1965), pp. 13–37.
82. Litzenberger, R. H., and Ramaswamy, K. "The Effect of Personal Taxes and Dividends on Capital Asset Prices: Theory and Empirical Evidence," *Journal of Financial Economics*, **7** (1979), pp. 163–196.
83. Lucas, Robert E., Jr. "Asset Prices in an Exchange Economy," *Econometrica*, **46** (1978), pp. 1429–1445.
84. McElroy, Marjorie, and Burmeister, Edwin. "Arbitrage Pricing Theory as a Restricted Nonlinear Multivariate Regression Model: ITNLSUR Estimates," *Journal of Business and Economic Statistics*, **VI,** No. 1 (Jan. 1988), pp. 29–42.
85. McElroy, Marjorie, and Wall, Kent. "Two Estimators for the APT Model When Factors Are Measured," *Economics Letters*, **19** (1985), pp. 271–275.
86. Merton, Robert C. "An Intertemporal Capital Asset Pricing Model," *Econometrica*, **41** (1973), pp. 867–887.
87. Morrison, D. F. *Multivariate Statistical Methods* (New York: McGraw-Hill, 1976).
88. Mossin, J. "Equilibrium in a Capital Asset Market," *Econometrika*, **34** (Oct. 1966), pp. 768–783.
89. Neyman, J., and Pearson, E.S. "On the Use and Interpretation of Certain Test Criteria for Purposes of Statistical Inferences," *Biometrika*, **20A** (1928), pp. 175–240, 263–294.
90. Ohlson, James, and Garman, Mark. "A Dynamic Equilibrium for the Ross Arbitrage Model," *Journal of Finance*, **35** (1980), pp. 675–684.
91. Oldfield, George S., Jr., and Rogalski, Richard J. "Treasury Bill Factors and Common Stock Returns," *The Journal of Finance*, **36,** No. 2 (May 1981), pp. 337–349.
92. Pallmann, Nils. "Recent Empirical Tests of the APT and the Consumption-Based CAPM," Discussion Paper, Department of Finance, New York University, 1989.
93. Pastor, Luxos. "Comparing Asset Pricing Models: An Investment Perspective," *Journal of Financial Economics*, **56,** No. 3 (June 2000), p. 335.
94. Reinganum, M. "The Arbitrage Pricing Theory: Some Empirical Results," *Journal of Finance*, **36** (May 1981), pp. 313–321.
95. Roll, R. "A Critique of the Asset Pricing Theory's Tests," *Journal of Financial Economics*, **4** (May 1977), pp. 129–176.
96. Roll, R. "Ambiguity When Performance Is Measured by the Securities Market Line," *Journal of Finance*, **33** (Sept. 1978), pp. 1051–1069.
97. Roll, R., and Ross, S. A. "An Empirical Investigation of the Arbitrage Pricing Theory," *Journal of Finance*, **35,** No. 5 (Dec. 1980), pp. 1073–1103.
98. Roll, Richard, and Ross, Stephen A. "A Critical Reexamination of the Empirical Evidence on the Arbitrage Pricing Theory: A Reply," *The Journal of Finance*, **39,** No. 2 (June 1984), pp. 347–350.
99. Ross, S.A. "The Arbitrage Theory of Capital Asset Pricing," *Journal of Economic Theory*, **13** (Dec. 1976), pp. 341–360.
100. ——. "Return Risk, and Arbitrage." In Irwin Friend and James L. Bicksler (eds.), *Risk and Return in Finance*, Vol. 1 (Cambridge, Mass.: Ballinger, 1977).
101. Rubinstein, M. "The Valuation of Uncertain Income Streams and the Pricing of Options," *Bell Journal of Economics*, **7** (1976), pp. 407–425.
102. Shanken, J. "The Arbitrage Pricing Theory: Is It Testable?" *Journal of Finance*, **37,** No. 5 (Dec. 1982), pp. 1129–1140.
103. ——. "Multi-Beta CAPM or Equilibrium-APT? A Reply," *Journal of Finance*, **40** (1985a), pp. 1186–1189.
104. ——. "Multivariate Tests of the Zero-Beta CAPM," *Journal of Financial Economics*, **14** (Sept. 1985), pp. 327–348.
105. Sharpe, W. "Capital Asset Prices: A Theory of Market Equilibrium under Conditions of Risk," *Journal of Finance*, **19** (Sept: 1964), pp. 425–442.

106. ———. "Factors in NYSE Security Returns, 1931–1979," *Journal of Portfolio Management*, **8,** No. 2 (Summer 1982), pp. 5–19.

107. Shukla, Ravi, and Trzcinka, Charles. "Sequential Tests of the Arbitrage Pricing Theory: A Comparison of Principal Components and Maximum Likelihood Factors," *The Journal of Finance*, **45,** No. 5 (Dec. 1990), pp. 1541–1564.

108. Sinclair, N.A. "Security Return Data and 'Blind' Factor Analysis," Working Paper, Australian Graduate School of Management, 1981.

109. Solnik, Bruno. "International Arbitrage Pricing Theory," *The Journal of Finance*, **38,** No. 2 (May 1983), pp. 449–458.

110. Sorensen, Eric, Mezrich, Joseph, and Thum Chee. "The Salomon Brothers U.S. Stock Risk Attribute Model." Published by The Salomon Brothers (Oct. 1989).

111. Sorensen, Eric, Salomon, R. S., Davenport, Caroline, and Fiore, Maria. Risk Analysis: The Effect of Key Macroeconomic and Market Factors on Portfolio Returns. Published by The Salomon Brothers (Nov. 1989).

112. Stambaugh, Robert. "On the Exclusion of Assets from Tests of the Two-Parameter Model," *Journal of Financial Economics*, **10** (Nov. 1982), pp. 237–268.

113. ———. "Testing the CAPM with Broader Market Indexes: A Problem of Mean Deficiency," *Journal of Banking and Finance*, **7** (March 1985), pp. 5–16.

114. Tiemann, Jonathan. "Exact Arbitrage Pricing And The Minimum-Variance Frontier," *The Journal of Finance*, **43,** No. 2 (June 1988), pp. 327–338.

115. Trzcinka, Charles. "On the Number of Factors in the Arbitrage Pricing Model," *The Journal of Finance*, **41,** No. 2 (June 1986), pp. 347–368.

Part 4

SECURITY ANALYSIS AND PORTFOLIO THEORY

17

Efficient Markets

One of the dominant themes in the academic literature since the 1960s has been the concept of an efficient capital market.[1] Although the reader may well be able to visualize several meanings of the term *efficient market* and although it has, in fact, been used to denote different phenomena at different times, it has come to have a very specific meaning in finance. When someone refers to efficient capital markets, they mean that *security prices fully reflect all available information.*

This is a very strong hypothesis. A necessary condition for investors to have an incentive to trade until the prices fully reflect all the information is that the cost of information acquisition and trading be zero. Since these costs are clearly positive, a more realistic definition is that prices reflect information until the marginal costs of obtaining information and trading no longer exceed the marginal benefit. Throughout this chapter when we are reviewing the evidence on market efficiency, some deviations from efficient markets will be observed. We will often comment on the likely size of transaction costs. However, the ultimate judgment in deciding if these deviations exceed reasonable transaction costs will be left to the reader.

Some authors require that prices accurately reflect fundamental information for a market to be efficient. However, most tests of the efficient market hypothesis simply deal with how fast information is incorporated, but don't deal with whether it is correctly incorporated in prices. We will refer to the hypothesis that prices reflect fundamental values as market rationality and discuss these tests at the end of the chapter.

The efficient market hypothesis has historically been subdivided into three categories, each dealing with a different type of information. *Weak* form tests are tests of whether all information contained in historical prices is fully reflected in current prices. *Semistrong form* tests of the efficient market hypothesis are tests of whether publicly available information is fully reflected in current stock prices. Finally, *strong form* tests of the efficient market hypothesis are tests of whether all information, whether public or private, is fully reflected in security prices and whether any type of investor can make an excess profit.[2]

---

[1]This chapter benefited greatly from the review article by Fama [77].

[2]Our definition of strong form tests is different from that contained in the literature. Fama defines strong form tests as tests of whether markets fully reflect nonpublic information. This is examined by analyzing whether any group of investors can earn excess returns. We believe that if excess returns were found, the tests could not differentiate as to whether the excess returns arose from monopoly access to information or superior use of publicly available information. Thus, a more general definition of strong form efficiency than Fama's is necessary.

These classifications were originally suggested by Fama [80]. In a recent review article Fama expanded the definition of the first type of efficiency. He changed the classification weak form tests to the more general category tests of return predictability. We will adopt this generalization. Under this classification we will examine patterns in security returns such as high returns in January and on Mondays as well as whether or not returns can be predicted from past data. Consistent with this new classification, Fama has changed semi-strong form efficiencies to event studies or studies of announcements, and we will also adopt this classification.

Careful consideration will show that much of the efficient market literature is actually concerned with the speed with which information is impounded into security prices. For example, assume a firm announces that earnings will be three times larger than expected next year with no additional investment on the part of the firm. Furthermore, suppose that there have been fundamental changes in the company that imply that this increase in the level of earnings is permanent. Finally, assume that investors believe this announcement. Clearly the company is worth considerably more than before. The share price should go up to reflect this increase in value. The efficient market hypothesis does not deny the useful-ness of this information, nor does it deny that prices should increase. What the efficient market hypothesis is concerned with is under what conditions an investor can earn excess returns on this security. Consider several scenarios.

First, assume that after the announcement, the price gradually increases over the week in response to the announcement. Investors examining the price sequence would observe that the price was moving away from that level at which it had previously traded. If they purchased securities when the securities started to trade away from historical prices, they would purchase the security a day or two after the announcement (after they had observed this new price behavior). If it took a week for the price to fully reflect the announcement, however, investors purchasing securities on the basis of movements away from historical prices would benefit from part of the price increase and make excess returns. Tests of the predictability of returns (formerly tests of the weak form of the efficient market hypothe-sis) are in part tests of whether this type of trading behavior can lead to excess profits. If returns are not predictable from past returns, then new information is incorporated in the security price sufficiently fast that, by the time an investor could tell from the price move-ments themselves that there had been a fundamental change in company prospects, the fundamental change is already fully reflected in price.

Consider a second scenario. Assume the investor hears the announcement of the improved prospects and believes it. The investor immediately buys shares of the company in anticipation of a price rise. The semistrong form tests of the efficient markets hypothe-sis are tests of whether this strategy leads to excess profits. The semistrong form of the effi-cient markets hypothesis assumes that investors who wish to sell the security, as well as those who wish to buy, hear the announcement and reassess the value of the security. This reassessment leads an immediate increase in price. The new price need not be the new equilibrium price, but it is not systematically lower or higher than the equilibrium price.[3] Thus, an investor who buys the security after the announcement may be paying too little or too much for the security. If the semistrong form of the efficient markets hypothesis holds, then over a large number of similar situations the investor would be paying on

---

[3]It may take several days or weeks before investors can fully assess the impact of the change in firm conditions. Thus, the price may be very volatile for a number of days. In efficient markets, the price immediately after the announcement is an unbiased estimate of the equilibrium after investors have fully assessed the impact of the earnings increase.

average about what the securities are worth. The investor would be unable to earn an excess profit by purchasing securities on the basis of such announcements.

The strong form of the efficient market hypothesis is concerned with two different ideas. Both can be demonstrated in terms of our previous example. One idea involves whether anyone can earn money by acting on the basis of information such as the announcement discussed earlier. Tests of the semistrong form of the efficient market hypothesis would examine all announcements such as the one under discussion, assume an investor purchased immediately after the announcement, and see if this leads to excess returns. There is nothing in this type of test that considers the value of the information contained in the announcement. Assume the investor hears the announcement and can fairly accurately reassess its effect on the value of the company. When the price after the announcement is below the reassessed value, the investor purchases; when it is above, the investor sells if the shares are owned or shorts the stock (or does nothing) if the shares are not owned. The strong form of the efficient market hypothesis states that there is no investor with this superior ability. Since it is impossible to determine exactly how investors might utilize the announcement to reassess the value of the firm, tests of the strong form of the efficient markets hypothesis are examinations of whether an investor or groups of investors have earned excess returns. Because of the lack of data on most types of investors, the group most frequently tested is managers of mutual funds.

The strong form of the efficient market hypothesis has a second facet that can also be illustrated with this example. Suppose the managers of the firm knew about the improved prospects in advance of the announcement; they had access to the information before it was publicly available. Could they purchase the security on the basis of the private information and make money? The most extreme form of the strong form of the efficient market hypothesis says no.[4] It should not surprise the reader that the evidence does not support this extreme form of the efficient market hypothesis. What might surprise the reader, initially, is the strength of the evidence in favor of the less extreme forms. Once the reader considers the ideas behind these hypotheses, however, it should not be as surprising. Information about securities is rapidly disseminated. There are thousands of people who follow securities professionally. Information should be rapidly incorporated in price.

The efficient market hypothesis has strong implications for security analysis. If, for example, empirical tests find that future return can't be predicted from past return, then trading rules based on an examination of the sequence of past prices are worthless. If the semistrong form of the hypothesis is supported by empirical evidence, then trading rules based on publicly available information are suspect. Finally, if the strong form tests show efficiency, then the value of security analysis itself would be suspect. Thus, an understanding of efficient market tests should provide guidance for the reader in determining what types of analysis are useful.

This chapter is divided into five sections. The first section provides some additional background on the efficient market hypothesis. The next three sections discuss efficient market tests, and the last section discusses market rationality.

SOME BACKGROUND

In order to test any of the three forms of the efficient market hypothesis it is necessary to be a little more precise regarding terms such as excess return. The purpose of this section is to introduce some of the terminology of the efficient market literature.

---

[4]The law in most countries also says no, because this type of insider trading in many countries is illegal.

The discussion in the previous section is consistent with the process determining prices being a "fair game." "Fair game" is a very descriptive term. It says that there is no way to use "information" available at a point of time (t) to earn a return above normal. To clarify this further, let ϕ_t represent a set of information that is available to investors at a time t. Now, based on this information, the investor can make an estimate of what a stock's return will be between time t and time $t + 1$. The investor can then compare the estimated return with the equilibrium return. Perhaps the estimate of equilibrium return comes out of one of the models discussed in Chapters 13 and 16. Deviations of the investor's estimated return from the equilibrium return should contain no information about future returns. Whether the investor's estimate of return is above or below equilibrium should be unrelated to whether actual return is above or below equilibrium. There is no way the investor can use the information in the set ϕ_t to make a profit beyond that which is consistent with the risk inherent in the security.

This discussion may seem either intuitively obvious or completely unappealing. To further clarify, let us specify some conditions under which it would not be correct. Let us assume the information set ϕ_t contains real information that is not incorporated in stock price at time t but that will be incorporated at time $t + 1$. For example, assume that a government employee in charge of military contracts is about to approve a large contract for a small and previously unused supplier of butter to the Army. This contract will result in a huge increase in profit for the company, but the market has assessed the probability of the company getting it as very small. Thus, only a fraction of the potential profits is incorporated in price. The procurement officer could make a much larger return than the equilibrium return for this company by purchasing its stock. The fair game model would not hold with respect to him or her. Thus, if the information set available to an investor is not incorporated in price, the fair game model does not hold with respect to that information set.

For the fair game model to hold, there must be no way in which the information set ϕ_t can be used to earn above equilibrium returns. For tests of return predictability ϕ_t is defined as the past history of stock prices, company characteristics, market characteristics, and the time of the year. For semistrong tests, it is defined as the announcement of one or more pieces of information. For strong form tests it is defined as all information, whether publicly available or not, that is at the disposal of some group of investors.

The reader should note that there is no implication in any of our discussion that the expected return on any security is zero. One would expect that, in general, it would not only be different from zero but, in fact, be positive. Further, one would expect that the return is related to risk with the more risky securities offering the higher return.

The reader might well wonder why we bother mentioning such an obvious point. This point has been a source of great confusion to many writers. One frequently reads that, if the efficient market hypothesis holds, then the best estimate of tomorrow's price is today's price, or an expected return of zero. This is not a correct implication of the efficient market model. Rather, the implication is that the past information contains nothing about the magnitude of the deviation of today's return from expected return.

Before leaving this section one additional term should be introduced—the random walk model. The random walk model assumes that successive returns are independent and that the returns are identically distributed over time. To understand the random walk model, visualize a roulette wheel with various returns written on it. Each period the wheel is spun, and the return for the next period is read from the wheel. The outcomes from spins of the wheel are unrelated through time so that past returns are unrelated to future returns. Furthermore, the same wheel is spun each period, which causes the returns to be identically distributed.

The random walk model is a restricted version of the fair game model discussed earlier. The fair game model does not require identical return distributions in the various periods. Furthermore, the fair game model does not imply that returns are independent through time. For example, a firm could be increasing its debt and risk over successive periods of time and show increasing expected and increasing actual returns. In this case we would observe a correlation in the sequence of returns and past returns that could be used to predict future returns. However, since risk is increasing and therefore expected return, this information could not be used to earn an excess return. If the random walk hypothesis holds, the efficient market hypothesis must hold with respect to past returns (though not vice versa). Thus, evidence supporting the random walk model is evidence supporting efficiency with respect to past returns.

TESTS OF RETURN PREDICTABILITY

In this section we review the studies examining the predictability of return from past data. In the first section we examine seasonal patterns in returns. A number of studies find that returns are different depending on the day of the week or time of the year. In the second section we discuss the predictability of return using past return. We analyze both short-term predictability and long-term predictability. In the third section we examine return and firm characteristics. In particular, we discuss evidence that abnormal returns are associated with small firms, firms with low market to book ratios and low earnings to price ratios. Finally, we discuss research showing a relationship between average firm or market characteristics and long-run return.

Time Patterns in Security Returns

A number of studies have reported time patterns in security returns. Returns are systematically higher or lower depending on the time of the day, the day of the week, and the month of the year. It is hard to know what conclusions should be drawn from this literature. One explanation is that with hundreds of researchers examining the same data set, patterns will be found, and that these patterns are simply random. If this is true then evidence from other markets and other time periods should not find similar patterns. A second possible explanation is that these patterns are induced by the market structure and order flow. The third possible answer is that markets are inefficient because one would expect that the patterns would disappear as investors exploited them. Until they are fully understood the best advice we can give the reader is that in most cases, because of transaction costs, the return differences are not large enough to develop a trading strategy to take advantage of them; if one is trading anyway, however, one might time the trade to try to exploit the pattern.

Intraday and Day-of-the-Week Patterns   One pattern that has been extensively examined is the difference in return for various days of the week. Returns on Mondays are much lower than on other days of the week on the New York Stock Exchange. Gibbons and Hess [100] examined the 17-year period 1962–1978. They found that Monday's return was a negative -33.5% on an annualized basis. Furthermore, when they split the data into two subperiods 1962–1970 and 1970–1978, the same large negative Monday return occurred. Gibbons and Hess also report a large positive return on Wednesdays and Fridays. In a more recent study Harris [113] examined intraday and day-of-the-week patterns for the 14-month period from December 1981 to January 1983. He confirmed the large negative Monday return but found returns on the other four days to be positive and of roughly the same order of magnitude. The larger negative Monday return was not evenly spread over the day. Rather, half of it occurred between Friday's market close and Monday's open, the weekend return. Of the remaining decline most occurred within the first 45 minutes of trading on Monday. After the first 45 minutes, returns on Monday closely resembled returns on any other day. On all days he found prices rose in the last 30 minutes of the day.[5] To date, no one has demonstrated profitable trading strategies based on these patterns. However, the result suggests an investor should sell late Friday and purchase on Monday after the first 45 minutes. As usual the reader should be cautioned that the study covers a short period of time and the market may have adjusted to these patterns.

Monthly Patterns Extensive research finds that returns in January are substantially higher than returns in other months. This is especially true for small stocks. Table 17.1 taken from Fama [77] reports the results for the period 1941–1981 and 1982 through January 1991. Consider first the results for 1941 to 1981. In this period small stocks averaged a return of 8.06% in January. Large stocks had a January return of 1.342%. In both cases the January return was higher than the average return in other months. However, the differences for small stocks are much larger than for large stocks, and thus most of the high January return effect is associated with small stocks. For the 10 years ending in January

Table 17.1 Comparison of Returns on the S&P 500, and the Smallest Quintile of CRSP Stocks: 1941–81 and 1982–91

| | Average Monthly Returns for January, February to December, and All Months | | | | | |
| | 1941–1981 | | | 1982–1990 (91 for January) | | |
Portfolio	Jan.	Feb.–Dec.	All	Jan.	Feb.–Dec.	All
S&P 500	1.34	0.92	0.96	3.20	1.23	1.39
CRSP Small	8.06	0.88	1.48	5.32	0.17	0.60

| | Year-by-Year Comparison of January Returns for 1982–1991 | | |
Year	S&P	CRSP Small	CRSP–S&P
1982	−1.63	−1.53	0.10
1983	3.48	10.01	6.53
1984	−0.65	0.26	0.91
1985	7.68	13.41	5.73
1986	0.44	3.82	3.38
1987	13.43	10.91	−2.52
1988	4.27	7.58	3.31
1989	7.23	4.79	−2.44
1990	−6.71	−6.38	0.33
1991	4.42	10.28	5.86

The value-weighted Center Research in Security Prices (CRSP) small-stock portfolio (CRSP Small) contains the bottom quintile of NYSE stocks, and the American Stock Exchange (AMEX) and National Association of Stock Dealers (NASDAQ) stocks that fall below the size (price times shares) breakpoint for the bottom quintile of NYSE stocks. The portfolio is formed at the end of each quarter and held for one quarter. Prior to June 1962, CRSP Small contained only the bottom quintile of NYSE stocks. AMEX stocks were added in July 1962 and NASDAQ stocks in January 1973.

[5]Keim [140] finds that there is some tendency for Friday's closing prices to be at the ask rather than the bid. This would make Monday prices somewhat lower even if there was no change in the bid and ask. However, Keim and Stambaugh [141] still find the weekend effect after accounting for this.

1991, the difference in returns in January between large and small stocks was not as pronounced. Small stocks had a January return of 5.32%, whereas large stocks had a January return of 3.2%. The extra return in January for small stocks is especially high in the first few days of January.

The January effect has been studied abroad as well as in the United States. Gultekin and Gultekin [112] studied January return patterns in 17 countries including the United States. They find much higher returns in January than in non-January months for all the countries they studied. In fact, for the period they studied the effect was bigger in the 16 non-U.S. markets. Kato and Shallheim [137] examined excess returns in January and the relationship between size and the January effect for the Tokyo stock exchange. They find no relationship between size and return in non-January months. However, they find excess returns in January and a strong relationship between return and size, with the smallest firms returning 8% and the largest less than 3%.

The January effect has also been documented in bonds. Keim and Stambaugh studied returns in bond markets from 1926–1978. They find that, on average, only in January do lower quality bonds give an extra return.

Keim [140] offers a microstructure explanation for part of the January effect. The CRSP tape calculates returns by using the closing price each month or the average of the bid and ask if the stock didn't trade. Keim finds that the last trade in December was primarily at the bid, which causes the return to appear high in the first few days of January. For example, assume a stock was 20 bid $20\frac{1}{4}$ ask. The last trade in December was likely to be at 20, whereas the first trade in January was somewhere between 20 and $20\frac{1}{4}$ on average $20\frac{1}{8}$. Thus, even without a change in the bid and ask, computing return using trading prices would imply a return of $\frac{1}{8}/20$ per day or a very large annual return.

Keim found that the tendency for stocks to be at the bid price for the last trade in December was much more pronounced for small stocks. In addition, small stocks have a higher bid-ask spread and a lower price. Therefore, the effect would be bigger for small stocks and would partly explain the differences in the January effect between large and small stocks. Thus, part of the January effect can be explained by the prices having a tendency to be at the bid in December.

A second explanation that has been offered for the high returns in January (especially in the first few days of January) is a tax-selling hypothesis. A popular suggestion of investment advisers, at year end, is to sell securities for which an investor has incurred substantial losses before the end of the year and purchase an equivalent security. This creates a tax loss for the investor. If the tax loss is substantial, it should more than cover transaction costs. Since the selling is in late December and the purchasing in early January, the argument is that prices are depressed at the end of December and rebound in January, creating high returns in January.

Both Reinganum [191] and Branch [23] find that the purchase of a security that has declined substantially by December has excess return in January. For example, Branch [22] analyzed a trading rule that involved the purchase of a security that reached its annual low in the last week of trading in December. He found that these securities rose faster in the first four weeks of the new year than the market as a whole, with very little difference in risk. He obtained average returns 8% above the market for a four-week holding period. Reinganum [191] finds similar results.

For this to be a partial explanation of the January seasonal it needs to be true that small stocks are an unusually high percentage of the stocks that are candidates for tax swapping. This is exactly what Reinganum [191] finds. However, Reinganum argues it is not the full explanation since he still finds a January effect (although much smaller) for firms that show gains in the prior year. Securities that are being sold for tax-loss purposes are more likely to be at the bid in December. Thus, the tax-selling hypothesis and microstructure explanation are likely to be partially measuring the same effect.

Several studies have provided evidence that is difficult to reconcile with the tax-selling hypothesis. Jones, Pearce, and Wilson [135] study a period from 1821 to 1917 before the introduction of the income tax. They find a January effect that isn't significantly different from the January effect found after the introduction of the income tax. Similarly, Japan and Belgium, which were found to have a January effect, do not have a capital gain tax. Furthermore, Australia has a non-December tax year so that if the extra returns were tax related the effect should be present in a different month. However, there are excess returns in January for Australia.

In an efficient market we should not observe a seasonal pattern. Investors observing high returns in January should start to purchase at the end of December to take advantage of the extra return. This adjustment of the pattern of investor purchases should cause the pattern to disappear. Furthermore, the explanations we have can only explain part of the extra return. Thus the January seasonal is difficult to reconcile with efficient markets.

Predicting Return from Past Return

In this section, we discuss the predictability of return from past return. In the first section we discuss short-term predictability. In the second section long-run predictability will be examined.

Short-term Predictability   Tests of short-term predictability examine whether return in the prior period (usually a day or days) can predict today's return. The tests range from simple ways of using past return data to complex trading rules. We will discuss a few representative tests from this voluminous literature on short-term price movements.

Correlation Tests   Correlation tests are tests of a linear relationship between today's returns and past returns. A regression of the following form is estimated.

$$r_t = a + b\, r_{t-1-T} + e_t \tag{17.1}$$

The term a measures the expected return, unrelated to previous return. Since most securities give a positive return, a should be positive. The term b measures the relationship between the previous return and today's return. If $T = 0$, then it is the relationship between today's return and yesterday's return. If $T = 1$, it is the relationship between today's return and the return two periods previously; e_t is a random number and incorporates the variability of the return not related to previous return.[6]

In the process of estimating Equation (17.1), the researcher obtains the correlation coefficient between r_t and r_{t-1-T}. The square of the correlation coefficient is the fraction of the variation of today's return explained by the return shown on the right-hand side of the

---

[6]Return has been defined both as change in price plus dividends divided by the prior period's price and as the log of the ratio of the price plus dividends divided by the prior period's price. The latter is the continuously compounded rate of return. In addition, some researchers have used change in price on both sides of the equation. It has been shown that for correlation tests it makes little difference which is used (see Granger [104]). For example, if a test utilizing price changes shows no relationship, then a test utilizing log price relatives would also show no relationship. Equation (17.1) is clearly a linear equation. In any test, b could be no different from zero, suggesting no relationship between the previous price change and next price change, and yet there may be a nonlinear relationship between successive price changes. For example, $P_t - P_{t-1}$ might be related to complex combinations of $(P_{t-1} - P_{t-2})$ raised to various powers.

equation. For example, a correlation coefficient of 0.5 means that $(0.5)^2 = 0.25$ or 25% of the variation of the term on the left-hand side of the equation is explained by the term on the right-hand side.

Table 17.2 reports the results of one study examining the correlation between today's return and return in prior periods (both continually compounded). The first column is a test of the relationship between today's return and yesterday's return. The second column is a test of the relationship between today's return and the return two days prior. As discussed earlier, the square of the number in the table is a measure of how much of the variation in return the equation explains. For example, the largest number (in absolute magnitude) in the first column is -0.123 associated with Goodyear. This implies that relating yesterday's return to today's return explains $(-0.123)^2$ or 1.51% of the variation in today's return. This is extremely small. The negative number implies that today's return is affected negatively by yesterday's return.

Table 17.2   Daily Correlation Coefficients (from Fama [78])

	Lag				
Stock	1	2	3	4	5
Allied Chemical	0.017	-0.042	0.007	-0.001	0.027
Alcoa	0.118^a	0.038	-0.014	0.022	-0.022
American Can	-0.087^a	-0.024	0.034	-0.065^a	-0.017
A.T.&T.	-0.039	-0.097^a	0.000	0.026	0.005
American Tobacco	0.111^a	-0.109^a	-0.060^a	-0.065^a	0.007
Anaconda	0.067^a	-0.061^a	-0.047	-0.002	0.000
Bethlehem Steel	0.013	-0.065^a	0.009	0.021	-0.053
Chrysler	0.012	-0.066^a	-0.016	-0.007	-0.015
Du Pont	0.013	-0.033	0.060^a	0.027	-0.002
Eastman Kodak	0.025	0.014	-0.031	0.005	-0.022
General Electric	0.011	-0.038	-0.021	0.031	-0.001
General Foods	0.061^a	-0.003	0.045	0.002	-0.015
General Motors	-0.004	-0.056^a	-0.037	-0.008	-0.038
Goodyear	-0.123^a	0.017	-0.044	0.043	-0.002
International Harvester	-0.017	-0.029	-0.031	0.037	-0.052
International Nickel	0.096^a	-0.033	-0.019	0.020	0.027
International Paper	0.046	-0.011	-0.058^a	0.053^a	0.049
Johns Manville	0.006	-0.038	-0.027	-0.023	-0.029
Owens Illinois	-0.021	-0.084^a	-0.047	0.068^a	0.086^a
Procter & Gamble	0.099^a	-0.009	-0.008	0.009	-0.015
Sears	0.097^a	0.026	0.028	0.025	0.005
Standard Oil (Calif.)	0.025	-0.030	-0.051^a	-0.025	-0.047
Standard Oil (N.J.)	0.008	-0.116^a	0.016	0.014	-0.047
Swift & Co.	-0.004	-0.015	-0.010	0.012	0.057^a
Texaco	0.094^a	-0.049	-0.024	-0.018	-0.017
Union Carbide	0.107^a	-0.012	0.040	0.046	-0.036
United Aircraft	0.014	-0.033	-0.022	-0.047	-0.067^a
U.S. Steel	0.040	-0.074^a	0.014	0.011	-0.012
Westinghouse	-0.027	-0.022	-0.036	-0.003	0.000
Woolworth	0.028	-0.016	0.015	0.014	0.007

[a]Coefficient is twice its computed standard error.

Despite the small size of the numbers, looking at the table might provide some evidence in favor of a weak relationship between returns over time. Twenty-two of the 30 numbers are positive, which is fairly high if there is no relationship. Furthermore, 11 of the numbers are significantly larger than would be expected by chance (although 2 of these are negative). Once again, this is more than one would expect. However, lest one get too excited by the relationship, the average absolute value of column 1 is 0.026. This implies that 0.067% of the variation in today's return is explained by yesterday's return.

As a second example consider Table 17.3.[7] This table shows the average correlation coefficient from a number of studies performed on both American and foreign stock exchanges. As the reader can see, none of the correlations is very strong.

Earlier we noted that a was the expected return in Equation (17.1). Investigators using correlation tests are, in essence, fitting Equation (17.1) to a body of data. The estimate of expected return arrived at for a security is the average unexplained by past return. This is very close to the average historical return. Different results might be obtained if the term a was set equal to different estimates of expected return. In the next section we see that, in

Table 17.3   Correlation of Return with Returns in Prior Periods for Various Countries

Author	Data	Variables	Time Interval	Average Correlation Coefficient
1. Kendall & Alexander [51]	19 indexes U.K.	Price	1 week 2 weeks 4 weeks 8 weeks 16 weeks	0.131 0.134 0.006 −0.054 0.156
2. Moore [51]	30 companies United States	Log prices	1 week	−0.056
3. Cootner [49]	45 companies United States	Log prices	1 week 14 weeks	−0.047 0.131
4. Fama [79]	30 companies United States	Log prices	1 day 4 days 9 days 16 days	0.026 −0.039 −0.053 −0.057
5. King [51]	63 companies United States	Log prices	1 month	0.018
6. Niarchos [171]	15 companies Greece	Log prices	1 month	0.036
7. Praetz [186]	16 indexes 20 companies Australia	Log prices	1 week 1 week	0.000 −0.118
8. Griffiths [107]	5 companies U.K.	Prices	9 days 1 month	−0.026 0.011
9. Jennergren [129]	15 companies Norway	Log prices	1 day 2 days 5 days	0.068 −0.070 −0.004
10. Jennergren and Korsvold [130]	30 companies Sweden	Log prices	1 day 3 days 5 days	0.102 −0.021 −0.016

[7]This table is based on Granger [104], but some additional data have been added.

semistrong tests of the efficient market hypothesis, expected return is usually obtained by the single-index model discussed in Chapter 7. It is possible that there may be a different correlation in the returns series when average return is defined using some other model, such as the single-index model. This issue has been examined by a number of authors.

An interesting set of tests using a different way of estimating expected return was performed by Fama and MacBeth [82]. Although the details of the Fama and MacBeth study are discussed in Chapter 15, it is worthwhile to briefly review them here. Fama and MacBeth used the capital asset pricing model of Chapter 13 to estimate expected return for a security. They then examined the correlation of excess returns (actual return minus expected return) and found virtually no correlation.[8] Thus deviations from expected return were random.

Other researchers have used more complicated models of expected return and then examined the correlation of excess returns. Galai [99] used a model developed by Black and Scholes to estimate expected returns in the option market and then examined the correlation of excess returns. Similarly, Roll used the term "structure" of interest rates to estimate expected return in the Treasury bill market and then looked at the correlation of excess return. In both cases they found no significant correlation.

Runs Tests   Most of the tests of the usefulness of past return in predicting future return utilize correlation coefficients to examine efficiency. The correlation coefficient tends to be heavily influenced by extreme observations. Thus, results can be due to one or two unusual observations. An alternative analysis, which eliminates the effect of extremely large observations, is to examine the sign of the price change. Designate a price increase by $+$ and a price decrease by $-$. Then, if price changes were positively related, it would be more likely that $a +$ was followed by $a +$ and $a -$ by $a -$, than to have a reversal in sign. This would mean that an investigator analyzing a sequence of correlated price changes would expect to find longer sequences of $+$'s and $-$'s than could be attributed to chance. A sequence of the same sign is called a run. Thus, $+ - - - + + + 0$ has four runs, a run of one $+$, a run of three $-$'s, followed by a run of three $+$'s, followed by a run of one no change. If there were a positive relationship between price changes, there should be more long sequences of $+$ and $-$ than could be attributed to chance and fewer runs.[9]

Many of the authors who examined correlation also examined runs. Table 17.4 is a typical example taken from Fama [75]. For one-day intervals 760 runs were expected and 735 were obtained. Thus, there were fewer runs than were expected, which is evidence of a small positive relationship between successive returns. The results for longer intervals are very striking. The actual number of runs in each case was almost exactly equal to the expected number.

In summary, correlation and runs tests seem to show some small positive relationship between today's return and yesterday's return, but on average it is very small, and frequently negative for individual securities.

Some correlations could be observed and the market still be efficient. An investor must incur transaction costs to trade securities. Thus, if the correlation is very low, transaction costs should more than eliminate any potential profits from attempting to take advantage of correlated series. In fact, in an efficient market, transaction costs would set an upper

---

[8]If we let (1) $\bar{r}_t$ be expected return in t and (2) r_t be actual return in t, then Fama and MacBeth correlated $(r_t - \bar{r}_t)$ with previous values of this difference; for example $(r_{t-1} - \bar{r}_{t-1})$.

[9]Because runs tests depend only on the sign, they are insensitive to whether price changes are being used or log price changes or rates of return.

limit to the amount of correlation. One indication that markets are efficient would be if we observed higher correlation in markets with higher transaction costs. This is exactly what Jennergren and Korsvold [130] found when they examined the higher transactions costs of Norwegian stocks.[10]

Although this is an indication that the correlation is insufficient to cover transaction costs, more direct tests are necessary. It is to these tests and tests of more complicated ways of using past return that we now turn.

Filter Rules   We have discussed tests of whether returns are linearly related to past returns. Even in the absence of such regular and simple patterns, it is possible that complex patterns exist that allow excess profits to be made. The simplest way to test for the existence of more complex patterns is to formulate a trading rule appropriate for a particular pattern of returns and see what would have happened if one had actually traded on these rules.

Table 17.4   Total Actual and Expected Numbers of Runs for One-, Four-, Nine-, and Sixteen-Day Differencing Intervals (from Fama [75]).

Stock	Daily		Four-day		Nine-day		Sixteen-day	
	Actual	Expected	Actual	Expected	Actual	Expected	Actual	Expected
Allied Chemical	683	713.4	160	162.1	71	71.3	39	38.6
Alcoa	601	670.7	151	153.7	61	66.9	41	39.0
American Can	730	755.5	169	172.4	71	73.2	48	43.9
A.T.&T.	657	688.4	165	155.9	66	70.3	34	37.1
American Tobacco	700	747.4	178	172.5	69	72.9	41	40.6
Anaconda	635	680.1	166	160.4	68	66.0	36	37.8
Bethlehem Steel	709	719.7	163	159.3	80	71.8	41	42.2
Chrysler	927	932.1	223	221.6	100	96.9	54	53.5
Du Pont	672	694.7	160	161.9	78	71.8	43	39.4
Eastman Kodak	678	679.0	154	160.1	70	70.1	43	40.3
General Electric	918	956.3	225	224.7	101	96.9	51	51.8
General Foods	799	825.1	185	191.4	81	75.8	43	40.5
General Motors	832	868.3	202	205.2	83	85.8	44	46.8
Goodyear	681	672.0	151	157.6	60	65.2	36	36.3
International Harvester	720	713.2	159	164.2	84	72.6	40	37.8
International Nickel	704	712.6	163	164.0	68	70.5	34	37.6
International Paper	762	826.0	190	193.9	80	82.8	51	46.9
Johns Manville	685	699.1	173	160.0	64	69.4	39	40.4
Owens Illinois	713	743.3	171	168.6	69	73.3	36	39.2
Procter & Gamble	826	858.9	180	190.6	66	81.2	40	42.9
Sears	700	748.1	167	172.8	66	70.6	40	34.8
Standard Oil (Calif.)	972	979.0	237	228.4	97	98.6	59	54.3
Standard Oil (N.J.)	688	704.0	159	159.2	69	68.7	29	37.0
Swift & Co.	878	877.6	209	197.2	85	83.8	50	47.8
Texaco	600	654.2	143	155.2	57	63.4	29	35.6
Union Carbide	595	620.9	142	150.5	67	66.7	36	35.1
United Aircraft	661	699.3	172	161.4	77	68.2	45	39.5
U.S. Steel	651	662.0	162	158.3	65	70.3	37	41.2
Westinghouse	829	825.5	198	193.3	87	84.4	41	45.8
Woolworth	847	868.4	193	198.9	78	80.9	48	47.7
Averages	735.1	759.8	175.7	175.8	74.6	75.3	41.6	41.7

[10]Jennergren and Korsvold [130] found 338.2 runs per stock over a period when uncorrelated returns would have led to 394.6.

One price pattern that has frequently been hypothesized for price movements is depicted in Figure 17.1. The argument behind this figure proceeds as follows. As long as no new information enters the market, the price fluctuates randomly within the two barriers around the "fair" price. If the actual price differs too much from the "fair" price, then "professionals" will step in and purchase or sell the security. This will keep the security price within the security price barriers. However, if new information comes into the market, then a new equilibrium price will be determined. If the news is very favorable, then the price should move up to a new equilibrium, well above the old price. Investors will know that this is occurring when the price breaks through the old barriers. If investors purchase at this point, they will benefit from the price increase to the new equilibrium level. Similarly, if bad news concerning the company is forthcoming, the stock will drop to a new equilibrium level. If investors sell the stock as it breaks the lower barrier, they will avoid much of the decline. If they sell the stock short as it breaks through the barrier, they will benefit from the decline. This argument is intuitively appealing; it is closely analogous to the idea of control charts and is put forth as an appropriate investment strategy by many who believe price series can be used to make superior profits. The strategy is called a filter rule. The filter rule is usually stated in the following way: Purchase the stock when it rises by $X\%$ from the previous low and hold it until it declines by $Y\%$ from the subsequent high. At this point, sell the stock short or hold cash.

Filter rules are a timing strategy. They show investors when they should be long in a security and when they should sell it short. The alternative to timing is to buy and hold the security. Thus, filter rules are analyzed by comparing them to a buy and hold strategy.[11]

The most extensive tests of filter rules were performed by Fama and Blume [78]. Table 17.5 reproduces their major results. The numbers under the letter F are the returns using the filter rule; the numbers under the letter B are returns from the buy and hold strategy. The only filter that showed a profit was a filter of 0.5%. However, Fama and Blume show

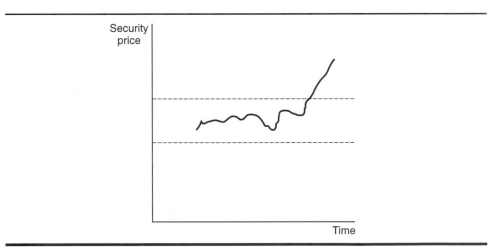

Figure 17.1   Security price and time.

[11]A number of tests of filter rules have analyzed returns during periods of market decline. During these periods, any rule that randomly caused the investor to sell a security and hold cash or go short should, on average, outperform a buy and hold strategy, at least before transaction costs are considered. The filter rule is purported to be a rule that utilizes past price behavior to lead to superior timing. It is important (if the rule is tested during periods of price decline) to determine that the rule outperforms a rule that randomly causes an investor to sell the security.

elsewhere in their article that the long purchases were profitable for filters of 1% and 1.5%. The average profits on each trade were very small, but, over long periods of time, they substantially outperformed buy and hold strategies. However, even with small transaction costs, these strategies are unprofitable. The profitability of these very small filter rules is consistent with a slight positive correlation of security price changes and is consistent with the evidence discussed earlier.

Jennergren and Korsvold [130] found some of the highest correlation coefficients of any investigators when they examined the lightly traded Norwegian and Swedish stocks. The relatively high correlations suggest that these securities are prime candidates for profitable filter rules. Jennergren examined filter rules for these securities. Norwegian and Swedish stocks cannot be sold short so that the alternative to holding securities long was to invest in a savings account. Some of the filter rules outperformed a buy and hold strategy. When taxes and transaction costs were considered, however, only the Queen (the only tax-exempt investor) had any prospects of making a profit.

We have examined one type of filter rule that purports to aid in timing decisions. We could test other types that suggest trades on the basis of alternative price patterns. Indeed, technical analysts are fond of talking about such things as head-and-shoulder patterns and other esoteric perceived price phenomena. But there is no evidence that trading on the basis of any of these patterns can lead to an excess profit. Rather than review other timing models that are based on historic price movements, let us review a system put forth to select stocks based on past price performance.

Relative Strength   One of the most popular ways of combining past price information about securities in order to select stocks is relative strength. An example of a relative strength rule is the one suggested by Levy [154]. Define $\overline{P}_{jt}$ as the average price over the last 27 weeks for stock j at time t. Further define P_{jt} as the price of the stock at time t. Then, the relative strength of the stock is its current price relative to its average price, or $P_{jt}/\overline{P}_{jt}$. According to Levy the securities to select are the $X\%$ with the highest ratio and they should be purchased in equal dollar amounts. In subsequent periods if the relative strength of a security drops below the relative strength of $K\%$ of securities, sell and invest the proceeds in the top $X\%$ of the securities. Levy tested a number of values for X and K, with the most profitable being $X = 5\%$ and $K = 70\%$.

Note that the relative strength rule causes funds to be invested in securities that have appreciated the most in the recent past. The most risky securities are usually those with the greatest variability of return. This suggests that the group of securities with greatest relative strength is likely to include a predominance of risky securities and the return earned from this investment must be adjusted for risk.

Also note that this rule does not involve the selection of a single security. Rather, it involves the selection of a set of securities. In testing the rule the relevant comparison is the rate of return on the securities that are selected by the relative strength rule adjusted for risk compared to the rate of return on the full population of securities from which the selection was made.

When Jensen and Bennington [134] tested several relative strength rules (including the one used by Levy and discussed previously), they found that the return after transaction costs for the relative strength rule was no more than the return on the full population. Furthermore, after adjustment for risk, it was inferior to purchasing the full set of securities.

We are continually shown various forms of relative strength rules along with the tests that purport to demonstrate their superiority. Even with the simple rule discussed earlier,

Table 17.5 Comparison of Rates of Return, before Commissions, under the Filter Technique and under a Buy and Hold Policy

Security	Filter size															
	0.005		0.010		0.015		0.020		0.025		0.030		0.035		0.040	
	F	B	F	B	F	B	F	B	F	B	F	B	F	B	F	B
Allied Chemical	0.155	0.068	0.037	0.069	0.042	0.063	−0.030	0.066	−0.105	0.069	0.008	0.066	−0.002	0.064	−0.010	0.051
Alcoa	0.401	0.025	0.308	0.023	0.318	0.016	0.330	0.021	0.241	0.022	0.303	0.025	0.270	0.008	0.182	0.006
American Can	0.121	0.085	−0.065	0.075	−0.123	0.075	−0.088	0.078	−0.057	0.074	−0.129	0.072	−0.201	0.071	−0.226	0.070
A.T.&T.	0.150	0.189	0.146	0.189	0.158	0.189	0.133	0.185	0.135	0.182	0.131	0.180	0.143	0.176	0.076	0.182
Amer. Tobacco	0.165	0.170	0.019	0.168	0.018	0.172	0.012	0.168	−0.057	0.170	−0.080	0.168	0.002	0.163	0.048	0.162
Anaconda	0.288	0.047	0.101	0.049	−0.012	0.046	−0.048	0.042	−0.038	0.059	−0.005	0.057	−0.030	0.055	−0.019	0.055
Beth. Steel	0.082	0.032	0.051	0.033	0.030	0.036	−0.004	0.038	−0.038	0.054	−0.128	0.052	−0.250	0.049	−0.169	0.044
Chrysler	0.031	0.004	−0.090	−0.002	−0.090	0.002	−0.183	0.016	−0.234	0.015	−0.152	0.015	−0.082	0.012	0.029	0.012
Du Pont	0.152	0.107	0.125	0.106	0.087	0.108	0.100	0.105	0.032	0.097	0.054	0.097	0.084	0.098	0.058	0.103
Eastman Kodak	0.078	0.194	0.025	0.195	0.005	0.189	0.057	0.185	0.085	0.183	0.009	0.183	0.032	0.178	0.133	0.175
G.E.	0.080	0.078	0.046	0.075	−0.015	0.075	−0.016	0.069	0.013	0.069	−0.052	0.069	0.011	0.072	−0.010	0.070
General Foods	0.122	0.257	0.122	0.256	0.146	0.257	0.028	0.251	0.084	0.250	0.062	0.246	0.112	0.250	0.080	0.250
General Motors	0.107	0.088	0.108	0.091	0.065	0.091	0.048	0.094	−0.063	0.093	−0.101	0.098	−0.151	0.099	−0.171	0.095
Goodyear	−0.229	0.086	−0.195	0.083	−0.151	0.085	−0.109	0.076	−0.092	0.070	0.048	0.077	−0.013	0.077	0.076	0.112
Int. Harvester	−0.088	0.180	−0.082	0.177	−0.206	0.176	−0.112	0.174	−0.142	0.170	−0.113	0.178	−0.036	0.175	−0.018	0.178
Int. Nickel	0.218	0.148	0.170	0.136	0.118	0.136	0.077	0.137	0.005	0.155	0.088	0.148	0.105	0.147	0.041	0.160
Int. Paper	0.205	0.010	0.156	0.007	0.095	0.005	0.063	0.003	0.034	0.010	0.026	0.011	0.014	0.011	−0.013	0.015
Johns Manville	0.021	0.094	−0.016	0.093	−0.162	0.087	−0.159	0.085	−0.070	0.077	−0.194	0.072	−0.204	0.074	−0.157	0.074

Owens Illinois	0.008	0.113	-0.036	0.116	-0.043	0.115	-0.130	0.119	-0.120	0.120	-0.112	0.120	-0.091	0.124	-0.037	0.106
Procter & Gamble	0.315	0.210	0.290	0.212	0.221	0.206	0.176	0.208	0.130	0.212	0.066	0.212	0.015	0.219	0.100	0.222
Sears	0.337	0.258	0.249	0.256	0.225	0.252	0.167	0.252	0.196	0.251	0.181	0.255	0.238	0.247	0.203	0.241
Std. Oil (Calif.)	0.076	0.093	0.052	0.090	-0.079	0.094	-0.106	0.099	-0.124	0.099	-0.123	0.094	-0.117	0.097	-0.158	0.098
Std. Oil (N.J.)	0.036	0.077	-0.072	0.067	-0.094	0.067	-0.093	0.070	-0.084	0.068	-0.083	0.064	-0.084	0.057	-0.086	0.056
Swift & Co.	0.010	0.047	0.002	0.042	-0.026	0.037	0.016	0.035	-0.044	0.037	-0.115	0.037	-0.052	0.034	-0.060	0.031
Texaco	0.172	0.188	0.165	0.192	0.105	0.189	0.095	0.188	0.109	0.186	0.166	0.184	0.144	0.183	0.115	0.178
Union Carbide	0.290	0.052	0.124	0.052	0.145	0.049	0.097	0.050	0.067	0.049	0.028	0.047	0.038	0.038	0.089	0.037
United Aircraft	-0.025	0.054	-0.020	0.052	-0.023	0.054	-0.110	0.059	-0.134	0.053	-0.189	0.048	-0.025	0.049	-0.026	0.046
U.S. Steel	0.101	0.014	-0.039	0.010	0.036	0.014	0.049	0.027	0.077	0.028	0.072	0.035	0.027	0.030	0.032	0.025
Westinghouse	0.008	0.038	-0.103	0.040	-0.047	0.038	-0.215	0.054	-0.216	0.048	-0.097	0.049	-0.083	0.051	-0.015	0.047
Woolworth	0.068	0.128	0.012	0.132	0.088	0.131	0.029	0.129	-0.058	0.131	-0.076	0.132	-0.052	0.141	-0.061	0.140
Average	0.115	0.104	0.055	0.103	0.028	0.102	0.002	0.103	-0.016	0.103	-0.017	0.103	-0.008	0.102	0.001	0.101

Source: From Fama and Blume [78].

there are many parameters that may be varied in the search for a rule that works. For example, should average price be calculated over 27 weeks, 20 weeks, or 30 weeks? Should one purchase the upper 5% or 7.2% of the securities? More complicated versions of relative strength rules make these decisions as a function of market conditions. Levy in his work tested some 68 variations of his basic rule. Given enough parameters to vary, one can find a mechanical trading rule that works on a given set of random numbers. It is extremely important that the rules be tested on a fresh sample of data and over several market conditions. For example, a rule designed to work under certain market conditions (e.g., selects high growth stocks) will work in periods when growth stocks did well. Using such a period to test this rule will "show the value of the rule," but is, of course, useless unless accompanied by a method of selecting such a period in the future. Each time we have been involved in or seen tests of these rules, their performance has been worse than buying the full population when tested in a different period. While the preponderance of evidence causes us to doubt the existence of a good relative strength or general technical trading rule, one can never prove that one doesn't exist.

The discussion up to this point has been concerned with price movements of days or weeks. Very short-term price changes have also been investigated, and these results are different.

Very Short-term Correlation   Neiderhoffer and Osborne [170] have examined the correlation between the price changes from transaction to transaction. They found a number of departures from randomness. More interesting, they found that reversals in price changes (a decline followed by an increase) was two to three times as likely as a continuation of the same price change.

The explanation of this is found in the structure of the New York Stock Exchange. Assume a stock is $49\frac{7}{8}$ bid and 50 ask. Suppose a market purchase order is placed. The order is executed at 50. If it is followed by a market sell order, the price will decline to $49\frac{7}{8}$. Thus, an increase will be followed by a decrease, a negative correlation. If the purchase order is followed by another purchase order, the price may not change if there were a number of limit orders at 50. It will change only if the purchase is for sufficient shares, so that the number of shares at 50 is insufficient to fill the order. Thus, an increase is likely to be followed by a decrease or no change and negative correlation is obtained.

The reader can likely see a number of ways an investor who did not pay transaction costs might benefit from this correlation. However, most of us, who are not so fortunate, cannot gain.

Correlation for Portfolios of Securities   There is evidence of somewhat higher correlation between past return and future return for portfolios of stocks compared to individual stocks. Lo and MacKinlay [156] and Conrad and Kaul [47] put together portfolios that are grouped by size (number of shares times price per share). They find that this week's return is related to the prior week's return and that this relationship is stronger for portfolios of small stocks. The weekly correlation coefficients from Conrad and Kaul for the largest portfolios is 0.09, so that 0.81% of this week's return is explained by the prior week's. However, the correlation coefficient for the smallest portfolio is 0.3, implying that 9% of this week's return can be explained by return in the prior week. The results suggest that because of the variance reduction of diversification, correlation of weekly returns is higher for portfolios than individual stocks. However, one must be somewhat cautious in interpreting these results. Portfolios will show correlation between past return and future return because some securities don't trade continually, and important information might be reflected in the securities at different times. Thus a major release of market information might affect securities in different weeks, causing returns to be correlated not because past returns predict future returns but because of infrequent trading. This latter hypothesis is consistent with the correlation of portfolios being greater for small portfolios than large portfolios.

Correlation over Long-run Horizons

Fama and French [79] and Poterba and Summers [185] have examined the correlation in returns computed over longer periods. Fama and French [79] find, using data from 1926–1985, that the correlation between this period's returns and return in the prior period is −0.25 for three-year periods to −0.40 for five-year periods. Poterba and Summers find similar results using a somewhat different methodology.

Fama and French argue that these results should not be given a lot of weight because both their procedures and those of Poterba and Summers have very little statistical power (could easily result from chance), and because the correlation is much smaller and insignificant after 1940. Furthermore, Fama [77] argues the results could be due to a combination of a changing expected return and expected return reverting to its mean over time.

Returns and Firm Characteristics

In this section we examine firm characteristics and returns. In particular we will examine what characteristics of firms are associated with excess returns. It has been found that a number of firm characteristics such as size, market value divided by book value, and earnings divided by price are related to excess return.

The relationship between firm characteristics and excess returns is a difficult set of empirical findings to reconcile with the concept of efficient markets. Indeed these are often referred to as market anomalies, since in an efficient market it shouldn't be possible to earn an excess return on the basis of observable firm characteristics.

There are five possible explanations for the existence of a relationship between firm characteristics and excess returns.

The first explanation is that the relationship observed is not real. With hundreds of researchers examining the same data for patterns, some relationship between firm variables and returns will be found. Furthermore, the conventional statistical test utilized to examine the statistical significance of the relationship they found is inappropriate, since they test the likelihood of one study finding a relationship, not one study out of hundreds of studies. Thus the tests that find a significant statistical relationship overstate the significance.

The second explanation is that these firm characteristics serve as a proxy for an omitted risk variable and that once this variable is taken into account the relationship between firm characteristics and excess return disappears. For example, small firms have excess returns when measuring expected return using the CAPM. However, some researchers argue that small firms have lower probability of survival and that "survival probability" isn't adequately measured by Beta. Furthermore, once this risk variable is taken into account the excess returns associated with size disappear.

The third explanation is that the CAPM is a reasonable model of expected returns but has been misestimated, causing apparent large returns when none exist. For example, assume Betas are systematically underestimated for small firms, then the estimate of expected returns for small firms would be too low and they would appear to have excess return when none would exist if Betas were estimated properly.

A fourth explanation of why the phenomena can continue to exist in an efficient market but not why it occurs in the first place is that trading costs eliminate the profitability of any trading rules designed to exploit the strategy.

Finally, markets may simply be inefficient.

The "Size Effect"   Banz [8] published one of the earliest and most often quoted empirical articles on the size effect. Employing a methodology similar to that used by Fama and MacBeth [83] (see Chapter 15), Banz documented that excess returns (Alphas) would have been earned over the period 1936–1977 by holding small firms. The striking aspects of Banz's analysis is that the size effect appeared to be important in terms of both statistical significance and empirical relevancy. The size term had roughly the same statistical significance in explaining returns as did Beta. Furthermore, the differential returns from buying very small firms versus very large firms were 19.8% per year. Other points should be mentioned. The real payoff from holding small stocks came from holding the smallest 20% of the firms in Banz's sample of New York Stock Exchange firms. The differential between other quintiles was quite small. Second, while on average the return from holding the smallest firms was large and statistically significant, there were periods of time where large firms outperformed small firms.

Subsequent to Banz's study it has been documented that a substantial part of the size effect occurs in January. For example, Keim reports that the difference in the returns in January due to size are about half of the annual difference. Thus, the size effect and January effect are strongly related.

The size effect was the first of the firm variables that was shown to be related to excess return; there has been extensive research into possible explanations. One research avenue has been to hypothesize that the CAPM was inappropriately measured causing apparent excess returns. The argument is that the Betas estimated for small firms were too low. If Beta is too low, then the estimate of expected return using the CAPM is too low and the difference between actual return and expected return would be positive even if it was zero when expected return was correctly estimated. Two reasons have been offered for why estimated Betas are too low for small firms. Roll [194] and Reinganum [187] have shown that the Beta for small firms will be biased downward because they trade less often than large firms and nonsynchronous trading leads to an underestimate of Beta. Christie and Hertzel [44] present a second reason why Beta might be downward biased. Beta is measured using historical returns. Firms that become small have changed their economic characteristics; these changes mean they are riskier and Beta measured over a prior period doesn't capture this increased risk. These factors could partially explain the relationship of excess return to size.

A second approach to explaining the small firm effect is to argue that expected return was miscalculated because the CAPM or zero beta CAPM are inappropriate models for measuring expected return. Perhaps a multifactor model better explains expected returns and when these models are used to measure expected return, the size effect disappears. An example of this research is Chan, Chen, and Hsieh [38]. They use the APT model of Chen, Roll, and Ross to measure expected return on 20 portfolios formed on the basis of size. They find that the difference in return between the smallest portfolios and the largest portfolio was 1.5% per year. In contrast, using the standard CAPM resulted in a difference in return of 11.5% per year. Thus they conclude that the size effect disappears when a more appropriate model of expected returns is used. The additional variable in their APT model that explains most of the variation in return between portfolios of different size is the difference in return between high risk corporate bonds and government bonds. In a later paper Chan and Chen [37] argue that the reason small firms are riskier is that they have low production efficiency and high leverage, and are in their terms "marginal firms" with lower probability of surviving economic hard times. They point out that size is serving as a proxy for this more fundamental risk.

Another reason why the CAPM may misestimate expected return was studied by Amihud and Mendleson [231]. They reason that investors should demand a higher expected return for less-liquid stocks since trading them involves higher transaction costs. Empirically small stocks have higher bid-ask spreads and the price impact of larger purchases would be considerable for small stocks. Thus they show the small stock effect is in part compensation for illiquidity.

Finally, a number of researchers have argued that transaction costs are very high in small stocks, so that markets are still efficient with substantial excess returns on small stocks. First, Roll [197] and Blume and Stambaugh [21] have estimated that the magnitude of the small firm effect is cut in half if small stock portfolios are reformed annually rather than rebalanced daily as assumed by a number of authors. If the reader wonders why not simply buy small firms and rebalance daily, the answer is that large transaction costs would be incurred. Second, a number of authors have estimated transaction costs for small stocks and then argued that the excess return is eliminated or at least reduced if realistic transaction costs are taken into account.[12]

Market to Book   Fama and French [89], Lakonishok, Shleifer, and Vishny [151], and Chan, Hamao, and Lakonishok [39] have all examined the relationship between market to book and excess return or return.

For example, Lakonishok, Shleifer, and Vishny [151] examine returns on portfolios of stocks bought on the basis of a stock's book to market value. To control for size effects they first classify stocks into five size categories. Within each of the five size categories they classify stocks into 10 equal-size groups on the basis of market to book value. The average difference in return between the high book to market firms and the low book to market firms is 7.8% per year. They attempt to examine whether this difference could be explained by risk. The normal procedure would be to use one of the equilibrium models of Chapters 13–16. However, they take a different and a very interesting approach. They separate out good market periods and bad market periods. They argue that if a stock is less risky, it is because it gives its good outcomes when it is needed most, namely, in bad markets. They find that low market to book stocks do not give a higher return when markets are poor, and thus argue that the higher return on high market to book firms is not compensation for risk.

Earnings Price   Basu [13] has shown that when expected returns are measured by the CAPM model, excess returns (return minus expected return) are positively related to the firm's earnings/price (E/P) ratio.

There has been much less work on the E/P effect than the size effect. Reinganum [188] presents empirical evidence that the E/P effect is highly correlated with the size effect. Fama and French [81] argue that once size and market to book are accounted for, the E/P effect disappears.

Chan, Hamao, and Lakonishok [39] get similar results. Thus, most researchers have seen the E/P relationship as a proxy for other effects.[13]

---

[12]There is a counterargument. Small stock index funds are able to match the small stock index. They do this in part by utilizing trading strategies that reduce transaction costs. Thus the estimates of transaction costs that have been presented may not be a realistic estimate for portfolio managers.

[13]Basu [14] was able to find an earnings price effect even after adjusting for size. However, he did not simultaneously control for market/book. This is probably because the market/book effect has only been documented recently.

Predicting Long-Run Returns from Firm and Market Characteristics

Long-run returns of bonds and common stocks seem to be predictable using past variables related to the general level of the stock market and the term and risk structure of interest rates. For example, five-year returns on the Standard & Poor's (S&P) index might be regressed on the dividend price ratio and the difference in yield on corporate bonds compared to government bonds. Since the dividend price ratio and the yield difference is known at the beginning of the period, this relationship could be used to predict returns in subsequent periods. Some authors interpret evidence of predictability as showing that expected return changes over time and that these changes can be predicted. Other authors view this evidence as an indication of inefficiency in the stock and bond markets.

The variables that have been used to predict return include

LEVEL OF MARKET VARIABLES

1. Dividends on S&P index/price of S&P index

2. Earnings of S&P index/price of S&P index

3. Current S&P index/long-run average of S&P index

INTEREST RATE VARIABLES

1. Term premium (yield on long-term bonds minus yield on short-term bonds)

2. Risk premium (yield on low-rated debt minus yield on high-rated debt)

The proportion of long-term return that can be explained by these variables is quite high. Fama and French [80] report that 25% of the returns on a value and equally weighted market index over two to four years can be explained by past dividends/price. Furthermore, the sign is positive: a high dividend over price (low level of price) implies high returns. Similarly, Campbell and Shiller [32] find that earnings/price where earnings are averaged over 30 years can explain more than 57% of the yearly returns on a market index.

In a later article Fama and French [82] find that dividend/price plus the term and risk premiums explain a significant proportion of the returns not only for the aggregate stock market index but also for an index of small stock returns, and indexes of high-and low-grade bonds. Furthermore, they find that the effect of dividend over price and risk spread bear a logical relationship to the return on the different instruments. For example, an increase in dividend/price predicts a greater increase in return for small stocks compared to large stocks, stocks compared to bonds, and low-grade debt compared to high-grade debt.

Finally, Harvey [114] finds that the S&P dividend/price and the U.S. term structure variables predict long-term returns on portfolios of foreign stocks.

ANNOUNCEMENT AND PRICE RETURN

The greatest amount of research in finance has been devoted to the effect of an announcement on share price. These studies are known as "event studies." Initially event studies were undertaken to examine whether markets were efficient, in particular, how fast the information was incorporated in share price.

For example, when a firm announces earnings will be much larger than expected, will this news be reflected in share price the same day or over the next week? Dozens of studies confirmed that share prices reacted rapidly to announcements, and in expected ways where the direction of the price change and the likely impact were clear. Consequently, many authors accept that information is rapidly incorporated in share price and use event studies to determine what information is reflected in price and, if its impact is unclear, to determine whether the announcement is good or bad news.

METHODOLOGY OF EVENT STUDIES

The methodology of event studies is fairly standard and proceeds as follows:

1. **Collect a sample of firms that had a surprise announcement (the event).** What causes prices to change is an announcement that is a surprise to investors. For many studies, such as an announcement of a merger, any announcement can be treated as a surprise. For other studies such as the impact of earnings announcements, it is more complicated. For these studies it is necessary to define a surprise. This is normally done by comparing announcements to what was expected as reflected in the average estimate of professional analysts. A number of services provide these data. To form a sample of surprises one first separates out a group of firms where the announcement is significantly different from what is being forecast. Since positive and negative surprises would affect price differently, this group is further separated into two groups, one for positive and one for negative earnings surprises.

2. **Determine the precise day of the announcement and designate this day as zero.** Most current studies use daily data, whereas the original studies used monthly data. The use of monthly data made measurement much more difficult because there are many surprises in a month besides the announcement effect being studied. Thus for measuring market efficiency it is important to measure the impact of the announcement using the smallest feasible intervals. A number of recent studies have used intraday data.

3. **Define the period to be studied.** If we studied 60 days around the event, then we would designate $-30, -29, -28, \ldots, -1$ as the 30 days prior to the event, 0 as the event day, and $+1, +2, +3, \ldots, +30$ as the 30 days after the event.

4. **For each of the firms in the sample, compute the return on each of the days being studied.** In the example this is 61 days (30 before the event plus the event day plus the 30 days after the event).

5. **Compute the "abnormal" return for each of the days being studied for each firm in the sample.** Abnormal return is actual return less the expected return. Different authors use different models for expected return. Any of the equilibrium models discussed in Chapters 13, 14, and 16 could be used to define expected return. Other authors use the market model of Chapter 7. Finally, a number of studies simply use the return on a market index as the expected return.[14]

6. **Compute for each day in the event period the average abnormal return for all the firms in the sample.** When this is done we can examine the data in a figure such as Figure 17.2. We normally look at the average effect of the announcement rather than examine each firm separately, because other events are occurring and averaging across all firms should minimize the effect of these other events, thereby allowing a better examination of the event under study. However, for studies where the magnitude of the announcement should vary across firms (such as earnings surprises), it may be useful to examine individual firm behavior as well.

---

[14]See Brown and Warner [29] for a comparison of these techniques. One must be sure that the sample does not have special characteristics such as small size that have been shown to produce abnormal returns.

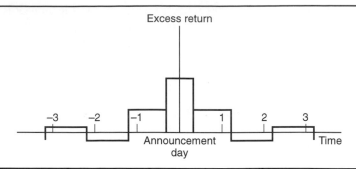

Figure 17.2   Excess return around announcement day.

7. **Often the individual day's abnormal return is added together to compute the cumulative abnormal return from the beginning of the period.** In this case for a 61-day period (30 before the event day, and 30 days after) the entry for -20 would be the sum of the daily average abnormal returns for days -30 to -20 and the entry for -10 would be the sum of the average daily abnormal returns for -30 to -10. Using the data for average daily abnormal returns shown in Figure 17.2, this produces a chart such as that shown in Figure 17.3. Notice that Figure 17.2 has a large positive abnormal return shown on day zero and nothing but randomness on other days. However, in Figure 17.3, which is the cumulative abnormal return, the positive abnormal return on day zero persists because it is part of the cumulative returns on days $+1$ through $+30$.

Figures 17.2 and 17.3 are the pattern of abnormal returns you would expect to find if markets are semi-strong form efficient. Thus, on the day of the announcement you

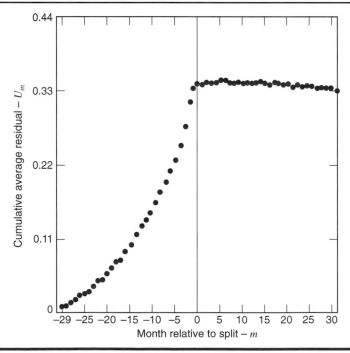

Figure 17.3   Cumulative excess return around split rate.

would expect an abnormal return but not on other days. However, normally some abnormal return is found on the days surrounding the announcement. Abnormal return after the announcement day is either due to information taking time to be reflected in share price or the announcement taking place so late in day zero, possibly even after the markets close, that its effect can only be reflected in trades and prices on the day following the announcement. Abnormal returns prior to the announcement day can come from three sources. First, the fact that an important announcement will take place is often released to the public prior to the announcement, and the news release that an announcement will take place and the way the release is handled may convey information. Thus a message conveyed to analysts and the financial press that there will be an important announcement at a luxury hotel with drinks and hors d'oeuvres afterward may convey information that there will be a welcome surprise. In an efficient market this should be reflected in price before the announcement takes place.

Second, if the announcement is at the discretion of the firm, it may be partially caused by prior abnormal returns, and an event study of this announcement will show prior abnormal returns. For example, firms split their stock generally after a substantial price rise. Event studies of stock splits will find abnormal returns prior to the announcement because firms with abnormal returns are more likely to split their shares. Third, abnormal returns prior to the announcement day could reflect leakage of the information by those with access to it.

8. **Examine and discuss the results.** Having performed the analysis the results are examined and conclusions drawn.

Results of Some Event Studies

We will not review all types of event studies in this chapter. Rather, we will concentrate on issues that are especially important for investment strategy. In particular, in this section we will examine the pattern of abnormal returns around the announcement day and whether there is a long-term abnormal return after the announcement (post-announcement drift). These questions are concerned with whether an investor can make short-term profits by buying on the announcements or make long-term abnormal profits by buying on the announcements and holding (or short selling if the drift is downward) over the longer period of time. Both strategies provide evidence on market efficiency.

The interpretation of abnormal returns earned around the announcement day is fairly noncontroversial. If annual market returns are 10%, then daily market returns are about 0.04%. Since most studies find abnormal returns of several percent at the time of the announcement, any way of measuring expected returns will show about the same results unless announcements are clustered on days of extreme market movements. Thus, how expected returns are calculated is not important in interpreting results on event days. In the following pages we will discuss three typical studies.

A number of studies have examined whether markets are efficient with respect to the announcement of the purchase or sale of securities (see Kraus and Stoll [144], Grier and Albin [106], and Dodd and Ruback [61]). In general, these studies find that markets are efficient. One of the more interesting studies of this type was by Firth [91]. He examined the efficiency with respect to an announcement that an individual or firm had acquired 10% of a firm. In the U.K. (which Firth analyzed) as well as in the United States, ownership of more than some percentage must be made public. Firth examined the market efficiency with respect to these announcements. One would expect that the purchase of a substantial percentage of a company might be an indication of a takeover or merger attempt, and Firth showed that this is an appropriate expectation. Empirical evidence indicates that mergers and takeovers normally involve premiums being paid to the stockholders of the company being taken over. Thus, the announcement of someone taking a large position in a security should be an indication of favorable prospects. Firth uses the single-index model to calculate expected return.

Figure 17.4 shows the cumulative excess returns from 30 days prior to the announcement. The cumulative excess return through the first day after the announcement is, in general, increasing. An investor with inside information that someone was accumulating a large block could make excess profits possibly larger than transaction costs. There is a substantial increase in cumulative excess returns on the day of the announcement. However, Firth shows the bulk of this increase occurs between the last trade before the announcement and the next trade. Thus, an investor without prior information about the announcement could not benefit from the price increase. From the first trade after the announcement until 30 days after the announcement, there is a slight decline in the cumulative excess return. In general, this evidence is consistent with market efficiency.

Another example of semistrong form tests of efficiency was performed by Davies and Canes [54]. They analyzed whether analysts' information could be used to earn excess returns or if it was already incorporated in share price. An enormous amount of information is sold to investors, including stock recommendations as well as detailed information

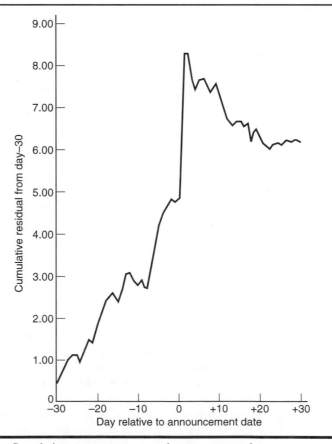

Figure 17.4   Cumulative excess return around announcement date.

on individual securities. One would expect that recommendations that are purchased contain sufficient information to justify their cost. Davies and Canes [54] analyze this by examining the usefulness of the "Heard on the Street" column in *The Wall Street Journal.* This column usually consists of a number of opinions on different stocks. The publication of the analysts' opinions in *The Wall Street Journal* usually occurs one or two weeks after the opinion was circulated to the firms' clients. However, *The Wall Street Journal* is usually the first large-scale dissemination of the opinions of several analysts.

The method of analysis was very similar to that discussed previously. The market model was used to estimate the relationship between each security's return and the market.[15] This equation was then used to estimate the expected return on each day given the actual level of the market. The difference between actual return and expected return was then tabulated. Figure 17.5 shows the results. As can be seen by examining the figure, the publication of the information seems to have an impact on returns. Davies and Canes tested to see if the large differences were statistically significant, and found they were.

The excess returns on the printing in *The Wall Street Journal* indicate that the column contains information that investors had not received directly from the analysts, or that the material in *The Wall Street Journal* conveys information possibly by certifying the analysts' recommendations.

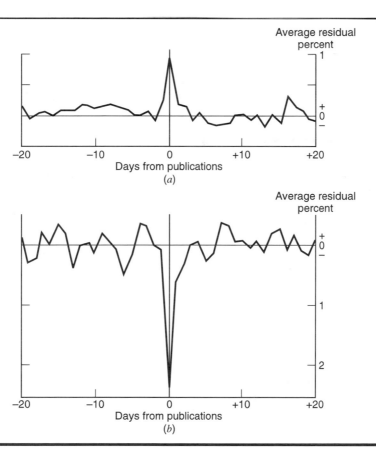

Figure 17.5 Excess return around publication date.

---

[15]The market model is the single-index of Chapter 7 without the assumption of uncorrelated residuals.

As a final example of announcements and market efficiency tests, consider the examination of dividend announcements by Pettit [179], Watts [224], Charest [40], Aharony and Swary [1], and Agrawal and Mullins [3]. Two aspects of these studies are different from those discussed previously. First, they must carefully define the event relative to expectations. What should affect security prices is surprises, not events that are anticipated. It is reasonable to assume that an announcement of a stock split, or the acquisition by one investor of a large position in a security, is a surprise. However, changes in dividends may well be anticipated. It has been shown that firms tend to follow a stable dividend policy. Thus, when earnings increase, the firm may have a policy of increasing dividends. This implies that a dividend increase may have been anticipated.

To determine whether the dividend is good news (above anticipations), bad news (below anticipations), or no news (anticipated), each of the authors employs a model of dividend policy. For example, Watts relates changes in dividends to the level of previous dividends and earnings. Firms are then dichotomized into two groups: those firms whose dividends are above those predicted using the model, and those that are below. Examining the excess return for these two groups allows one to examine the effect of unanticipated dividend changes.

The second difference in these studies is the need to disentangle the dividend changes from other effects. For example, stock splits and dividend increases often occur simultaneously, but in some cases they do not. Furthermore, dividend announcements almost always occur simultaneously with earnings announcements and it is important to deal with contemporaneous earnings surprises. Pettit handles this by splitting his firms, not only by size of dividend surprise, but also by the earnings change.

Other than these two aspects, the studies use methodology similar to that discussed earlier. Furthermore, their conclusions are similar. The market seems to adjust rapidly to new information.

The other finding of interest to investment professionals is that for a number of types of announcements, investigators have found a long-term drift in abnormal return (called post-announcement drift). For example, Agrawal, Jaffe, and Mandelker [5], and Jaffe and Mandelker [123] find that firms that acquire other firms have significant abnormal returns on average over the next five years. Similarly, Ritter [193] studied initial public offerings and found that on average new issues after the first day substantially underperform other securities on a risk-adjusted basis.

When we examine long-run abnormal returns the choice of how expected return is measured is important, and there is significant controversy of whether the results of a long-term drift are real or the result of using the wrong model for measuring expected returns.

STRONG FORM EFFICIENCY

In this section we discuss two issues. The first issue is whether insiders in their trading earn an excess return. Working at Atlantic Richfield and learning that your geologist had discovered massive oil fields off Alaska then trading on that information clearly leads to excess returns. It also likely leads to jail, since trading on inside information in the United States is illegal. Thus, examining the profitability of insider trading is both an examination of the usefulness of insider information and the regulation of the SEC. The second issue is whether professional investors, security analysts, and mutual fund managers have profitable information.

Insider Trading

All investors who own more than a certain percentage of the outstanding shares or are at a sufficiently high management level are considered insiders. In the United States insiders must list their purchases and sales with the SEC. If insiders trade on privileged information, then one would expect to see insiders purchase in months before the security price increases and sell in months before the security price declines. This pattern is, in fact, the pattern found by Jaffe [122] and Lorie and Niederhoffer [159]. Furthermore, they found, using methodology similar to that discussed earlier, that insiders earned returns in excess of expected return. Unless these insiders just happened to possess superior analytical ability, their excess return must be due to the illegal exploitation of insider information.

Another indication of the usefulness of insider trading is a legal action involving the person who set the type for the Value Line forecasts. Value Line is an investment advisory service; it divides firms into five groups, depending on its estimate of next period's performance. The typesetter knew what the recommendations of Value Line would be before the paper was printed and sold these to two brokers at a large brokerage firm. The brokers, in turn, used it to manage money for their clients. As reported in *The Wall Street Journal* [223], the brokers made a fair amount of money trading in the securities before they were apprehended.

Information in Analysts' Forecasts

Many authors have analyzed whether or not security analysts have information not incorporated in security prices. The majority of these studies suffer from selection bias and survivorship bias. Selection bias occurs because most studies analyze a set of historical analysts' forecasts, and access to these forecasts is controlled. Security analysts generally work for an investment organization that controls whether outsiders have access to prior analysts' forecasts. Furthermore, the investment organization is likely to systematically evaluate the forecasts of their analysts. The organizations that provide prior analysts' forecasts to academics are likely to be those where the organization knows normal evaluation techniques will show superior information. Thus, even if analysts had no information, academic studies would likely find information because the organizations supplying data for outside studies are the ones whose analysts by chance did well. We know of two studies that do not suffer from selection bias, since the forecasts they analyzed were prepared after the organizations to be studied were selected.[16]

These studies are by Dimson and Marsh [58] and Elton, Gruber, and Grossman [67].[17] Dimson and Marsh analyzed 4,000 return forecasts made for 200 of the largest U.K. common stocks provided by 35 different firms of analysts. The data were gathered by a large fund that requested their brokers to forecast excess return on shares assuming a zero excess return on the market (difference from the riskless rate). Dimson and Marsh correlated actual return with forecasted returns and found an average correlation coefficient of 0.08. This result is consistent with other research in the area. Recall that the square of the correlation coefficient is the percentage explained. Thus $(0.08)^2 = 0.0064$ of realized return is explained by analysts' forecasts of return. Forecasting ability differed across the 35 firms. The range of correlation coefficients for brokers recording more than 50 forecasts was -0.19 to $+0.26$. Furthermore, past forecasting ability was not predictive of future forecasting ability. The best estimate of which firm forecasted best in the next period was that all firms were equal. However, combining the forecasts did lead to improvement. The correlation between realized return and the average analyst's forecast was 0.12.

---

[16]The only possible bias was if the organizations with poor analysts refused to participate. In each case, however, the request was made by a major financial institution, so that no one refused to supply the information.

[17]Dimson and Marsh [58] present an extensive bibliography and review of previous research on analysts' forecasts. The reader interested in further research in this area should consult their article.

The forecasts of return were utilized by a fund for actual trades. Despite the small amount of information contained in the forecasts, as indicated by the size of the correlation presented earlier, the performance of the fund exceeded the market by 2.2%. Tests showed that more than one-half of the information contained in the forecasts was incorporated in share price in the first month following the forecast. Thus a rapid reaction to analyst forecasts was necessary.

Elton, Gruber, and Grossman [67] employed a database that was constructed by a large bank and disseminated under the name of I/B/O/S/S. This database contained the rankings of stocks into five groups: best buys, buys, holds, and two classes of sells. The data contained more than 10,000 classifications per month prepared by more than 720 analysts at 34 brokerage houses. An analysis of forecasts prepared in the form of discrete classifications is interesting because this is the form in which most decision makers in the financial community receive information. Elton, Gruber, and Grossman found that both a change in classification (e.g., from a hold to a buy or from a best buy to a buy) and the classification itself contained information. Excess risk-adjusted returns could be earned by buying upgraded stocks or stocks that were in a better classification, and selling downgraded stocks or stocks that were in a lower classification. Excess returns were found in the forecast (classification) month and for two months following the classification or change in classification.

Acting on changes in classification produced larger excess returns than acting on the recommendations themselves. In addition, no superior forecasters could be identified. One was better off following the advice of the average or consensus forecaster than the advice of any set of forecasters who performed best over a previous period.

Both Dimson and Marsh and Elton, Gruber, and Grossman find information in analysts' forecasts. There seems to be very little information about acting on the advice of single brokerage firms. By aggregating across brokerage firms, however, there appears to be real information that persists for short periods of time.

Publicly available analysts' information can suffer from selection bias and potentially suffers from survivorship bias. Survivorship bias occurs if the selection of the organization to be studied is based on knowledge concerning past forecasting skill. Survivorship bias can occur because one would expect that the firms that continue to be able to sell information to the public are those for which past information appears to be valuable. If analysts had no information, but by chance some were right in their forecasts and some were wrong, then a researcher who selected firms to study on the basis of currently existing firms and analyzes past data would likely find information in analysts' forecasts even if none existed.

Despite these problems the most studied data on security analysts' information is the Value Line investment survey. As discussed earlier, Value Line publishes weekly rankings where securities are divided into five groups, with one being the firms with the best prospects and five the worst. Stickel [213] analyzes the effect of a change in ranking using the event study methodology discussed earlier. He finds that prices change for those stocks that are moved from group 3 to group 2. For all stocks, the three-day price change averaged 2.44%, with the price change averaging 5.18% for small stocks. Furthermore, the price change was not reversed in subsequent periods. This is either additional evidence that analysts have information not fully incorporated in share price, or confirmation that value Line's reputation for having had good forecasts was confirmed.

Mutual Fund Performance

Dozens of researchers have examined the performance of mutual funds. A detailed discussion of mutual fund performance will be postponed to Chapter 24; however, a few comments will be made here.

Most of the studies evaluating mutual funds contain a serious survivorship bias in the sample analyzed. Putting together a sample of funds that exists today and then gathering historical data excludes funds that went out of business over the period studied. The funds that go out of business have below average performance. An investor purchasing a fund at the beginning of the period could potentially purchase a fund that disappears or survives. Since most studies look only at the performance of funds that survive, this makes performance look better than it actually is. Furthermore, because survivorship varies inversely with risk, analyzing a sample with survivorship bias will lead to high-risk groups appearing to have superior relative performance.

The performance of funds is clearly sensitive to the measure used to evaluate them. We know from prior sections that small stocks have excess returns when measured relative to the standard CAPM. Therefore, small stocks' managers would also show excess return relative to the standard CAPM even when small stocks' managers have no selection ability.

Studies that are survivorship free and measure performance relative to multiple indexes, such as those done by Elton, Gruber, Das, and Hklarka [68], find that managers underperform a combination of passive indexes combined to have the same risk as the fund being evaluated after management fees and expenses are taken into account. Furthermore, this underperformance is related to the management fees and expenses they charge. Thus, mutual fund managers on average are unable to earn enough to compensate for the fees they charge and expenses they incur.

MARKET RATIONALITY

In the prior sections we discussed the speed with which information is incorporated in share price. We referred to this as "informational efficiency." A number of authors are also concerned with whether prices accurately reflect investors' expectations about the present value of future cash flows. We will refer to this hypothesis as market rationality to distinguish it from informational efficiency, while recognizing that some authors use the word "efficiency" to apply to both ideas.

If markets exhibit rationality, there should be no systematic differences between share prices and the value of the security based on the present value of the cash flow to security holders. Much of the evidence on informational efficiency bears on market rationality. For example, if prices can be shown to respond to noneconomic variables such as stock splits, this would be powerful evidence against market rationality.

The existence of excess return as a function of firm characteristics and time patterns in security returns provides evidence against market rationality. Examples of these relationships include the size effect, the market/book effect, the January effect, and the day of the week effect. For informational inefficiency it is necessary to show that a profitable trading strategy (including trading costs) can be constructed to exploit the anomaly. However, the mere presence of a persistent anomaly calls into question market rationality.

The major direct evidence on stock market rationality involves volatility tests, stock market crashes, and tests of market overreaction. Each will be discussed in turn.

Volatility Tests

Volatility tests examine the volatility of share prices relative to the volatility of the fundamental variables that affect share prices. Markets would be seen as irrational if share prices deviated a great deal more than variance in the fundamental variables affecting share prices would imply.

The volatility tests of LeRoy and Porter [153] and Shiller [208, 209] are based on three assumptions:

1. Stock prices reflect the expectations of future dividends.
2. The real expected return on stock is constant over time.
3. Dividends can be described by a stationary process with a constant growth rate.

With these assumptions they devise tests based on the volatility of real prices relative to the volatility of theoretical prices (determined by the present value of future dividends). They find that actual prices vary considerably more than theoretical prices and reject market rationality. The results found by LeRoy and Porter and Shiller have been reexamined by a number of authors. Marsh and Merton [165] change the assumption of how dividends are determined assuming that it's a positive function of past prices and get results in direct opposition to those of Shiller.

Winners—Losers

DeBondt and Thaler [55, 56] have written several papers in which they argue that investors overreact. In particular, they find that stocks that are the most extreme losers have abnormally good subsequent performance and that stocks that have been the biggest winners have subsequent poor performance. They attribute this to overreaction on the part of investors. In particular, they construct portfolios each December of the 50 stocks that did the best and worst in the prior three or five years. They then measure performance in the subsequent three or five years. The portfolio of the 50 most extreme losers has high abnormal returns (especially in January), whereas the portfolio of 50 winners has negative abnormal returns.

Several aspects of the study are worth noting. First, this study is closely related to the tax-selling studies discussed elsewhere in this chapter. Second, the selection rule is exactly opposite the selection rule used in relative strength where past winners are selected. Third, one would expect that losers would have more small firms (partly because they are losers) than the winners category; we have discussed elsewhere the extra return of small firms in January.

The DeBondt and Thaler articles are an important challenge to market rationality and as such have received a fair amount of attention. Other authors have supported or refuted the finding. One area of controversy involves how expected return and thus abnormal return is calculated. Depending on the method of calculating expected return, evidence in support of DeBondt and Thaler (see Chopra, Lakonishok, and Ritter [43]) or refute (see Ball and Khothari [7]) is found. The second issue is how much of this effect is really another effect, such as the small firm effect or the tax-selling effect.[18]

Market Crash of October 1987

The stock market declined 23% in one day in October 1987. This decline followed a substantial decline on the prior Friday. For markets to be rational, people's expectations had to undergo substantial changes on Friday and Monday. Numerous researchers have tried to find news items that could have led to a major revision in expectations. Although there

---

[18]There is also a survivorship issue, since the losers must still exist for five subsequent years; thus losers who went bankrupt are excluded.

were clearly news items around the crash, it is hard to argue that they caused such a large change in expectations. Rather, panic, failure of the trading mechanism, and formula trading are usually given as reasons for the crash. The crash is not a challenge for informational efficiency unless one can show that it was predictable. It is however a greater challenge to market rationality. Nevertheless, it is possible that formula trading and market structure combined to allow a crash to occur and once it occurred people reevaluated their fundamental values because of the crash.

CONCLUSION

Although it is difficult to conclude a chapter that discusses such a diverse set of literature, we will try.

The size of the abnormal return around announcement days is sufficiently large that any measure of expected return will show similar results. Thus, the results of these studies are relatively insensitive to the measure chosen. These studies show that information is rapidly incorporated in share price and support efficient markets.

The results of studies of longer-term reaction such as post-announcement drift and the relationship of firm characteristics and abnormal returns depend on the model of expected return chosen. It is no coincidence that the implication of these studies for market efficiency is controversial.

Finally, the results of studies that find calendar patterns in security returns are inconsistent with market efficiency. However, the consistent finding of an inability of market professionals to outperform indexes raises questions as to the usefulness of these patterns.

QUESTIONS AND PROBLEMS

1. Discuss a trading strategy to utilize information such as that analyzed by Davies and Canes. How low would transaction costs have to be for the rule to be profitable? How would risk affect the usefulness of the rule?

2. Filter rules are one way to use past price movements to predict future movements. Discuss an alternative way to use past data. How would you test this alternative?

3. One rule for selecting stocks that has been suggested is to buy high growth, low P/E stocks. How could this rule be tested?

4. It has been suggested that the efficient market hypothesis could be used to determine whether you have monopoly access to a type of information. Explain how this might be done.

5. If the market is semistrong form efficient, must it be weak form efficient?

6. You have been hired as a consultant to a large brokerage firm. The firm thinks it has discovered an inefficiency in the market. At certain times large blocks of stocks that are held by individuals and institutions under restrictive agreements become available for trading. The date on which this happens is a matter of public record. How would you test whether the market is efficient with respect to the potential increased supply in stock?

7. A number of different models can be used to estimate return. Derive the circumstances under which the use of the zero Beta model might lead to the market being considered inefficient when the standard CAPM indicated efficiency.

8. Is the betting market at roulette an efficient market?

9.   You have just become convinced that whenever the president of a company retires, an excess return can be made by buying the stock. Design a study to test this hypothesis.

BIBLIOGRAPHY

1. Aharony, Joseph, and Swary, Itzhak. "Quarterly Dividend and Earnings Announcements and Stockholders' Returns: An Empirical Analysis," *The Journal of Finance*, **35,** No. 1 (March 1980), pp. 1–12.
2. Albin, Peter. "Information Exchange in Security Markets and the Assumption of 'Homogeneous Beliefs,'" *Journal of Finance*, **XXIX,** No. 4 (Sept. 1974), pp. 1217–1227.
3. Agrawal, A., and Mullins, David W. "The Impact of Initiating Dividend Payments on Shareholders' Wealth," *Journal of Business*, **56,** No. 1 (Jan. 1983).
4. ———. "Equity Issues and Offering Dilution," *Journal of Financial Economics*, **15** (1986), pp. 61–89.
5. Agrawal, A., Jaffe, J., and Mandelker, G. "The Post-Merger Performance of Acquiring Firms: A Reexamination of an Anomaly." *The Journal of Finance*, **47** (Dec. 1990), pp. 1605–1621.
6. Ball, Ray, and Kothari, S. "Anomalies in Relationships Between Securities' Yields and Yield-Surrogates," *Journal of Financial Economics*, **6** (1978), p. 103.
7. ———. "Nonstationary Returns: Implications for Tests of Market Efficiency and Serial Correlation in Returns," *Journal of Financial Economics*, **25,** No. 1 (Nov. 1989), pp. 51–74.
8. Banz, Rolf W. "The Relationship Between Return and Market Value of Common Stock," *Journal of Financial Economics*, **9** (1981), pp. 3–18.
9. Banz, Rolf W., and Breen, William J. "Sample-Dependent Results Using Accounting and Market Data: Some Evidence," *Journal of Finance*, **41,** No. 4 (Sept. 1986), pp. 779–793.
10. Barry, Christopher B., and Brown, Stephen J. "Anomalies in Security Returns and the Specification of the Market Model," *The Journal of Finance*, **39,** No. 3 (July 1984), pp. 807–818.
11. ———. "Differential Information and the Small Firm Effect," *Journal of Financial Economics*, **13** (1984), pp. 283–294.
12. Bar-Yosef, Sasson, and Brown, Lawrence. "A Reexamination of Stock Splits Using Moving Betas," *Journal of Finance*, **XXXII,** No. 4 (Sept. 1977), pp. 1069–1080.
13. Basu, S. "Investment Performance of Common Stocks in Relation to Their Price-Earnings Ratios: A Test of the Efficient Market Hypothesis," *Journal of Finance*, **XXXII,** No. 2 (June 1977), p. 663.
14. ———. "The Relationship Between Earnings' Yield, Market Value and the Return for NYSE Common Stocks: Further Evidence," *Journal of Financial Economics*, **12,** No. 1 (1983).
15. Berges, Angel, McConnell, John, J., and Schlarbaum, Gary C. "The Turn-of-the-Year in Canada," *Journal of Finance*, **39,** No. 1 (March 1984), pp. 185–192.
16. Bernard, Victor L., and Thomas, Jacob K. "Post-Earnings-Announcement Drift: Delayed Response or Risk Premium?" *Journal of Accounting Research*, **27** (Supplement, 1989), pp. 1–36.
17. Bernard, Victor L."Evidence that Stock Prices Do Not Fully Reflect the Implications of Current Earnings for Future Earnings," *Journal of Accounting and Economics*, **13,** No. 4 (Dec. 1990), pp. 305–340.
18. Bhandari, Laxmi Chand. "Debt/Equity Ratio and Expected Common Stock Returns: Empirical Evidence," *Journal of Finance*, **43,** No. 2 (June 1988), pp. 507–528.
19. Black, Fisher. "Yes, Virginia, There Is Hope: Tests of the Value Line Ranking System," *Financial Analysis Journal*, **29** (Sept./Oct. 1973), pp. 10–14.
20. Blanchard, Olivier, Rhee, Changyong, and Summers, Lawrence. "The Stock Market, Profit, and Investment," *The Quarterly Journal of Economics*, **108,** No. 1 (Feb. 1993), pp. 115–136.
21. Blume, Marshall E., and Stambaugh, Robert F. "Biases in Computed Returns," *Journal of Financial Economics*, **12** (1983), pp. 387–404.

22. Bradley, Michael. "Interfirm Tender Offers and the Market for Corporate Control," *Journal of Business*, **53,** No. 4 (Oct. 1980), pp. 345–376.

23. Branch, Ben. "A Tax Loss Trading Rule," *Journal of Business*, **50,** No. 2 (April 1977), pp. 198–207.

24. Brauer, Greggory A. "Using Jump-Diffusion Return Models to Measure Differential Information by Firm Size," *Journal of Financial and Quantitative Analysis*, **21,** No. 4 (Dec. 1986), pp. 447–458.

25. Brenner, Menachem. "A Note on [57]: Risk, Return and Equilibrium: Empirical Tests," *Journal of Political Economy*, **84,** No. 2 (April 1976), pp. 407–409.

26. ——. "The Effect of Model Misspecification on Tests of the Efficient Market Hypothesis," *Journal of Finance*, **XXXII,** No. 1 (March 1977), pp. 57–66.

27. Brown, Philip, Kleidon, Allan W., and Marsh, Terry A. "New Evidence on the Nature of Size Related Anomalies in Stock Prices," *Journal of Financial Economics*, **12,** No. 1 (1983), pp. 33–56.

28. Brown, Philip, Keim, Donald B., Kleidon, Allan W., and Marsh, Terry A. "Stock Return Seasonalities and the 'Tax-Loss Selling' Hypothesis: Analysis of the Arguments and Australian Evidence," *Journal of Financial Economics*, **12,** No. 1 (1983).

29. Brown, Stephen J., and Warner, Jerold B. "Using Daily Stock Returns: The Case of Event Studies," *Journal of Financial Economics*, **14,** No. 1 (March 1985), pp. 3–32.

30. Brown, Stewart L., and Nichols, William D. "Assimilating Earnings and Split Information: Is the Capital Market Becoming More Efficient?" *Journal of Financial Economics*, **9,** No. 3 (Sept. 1981), pp. 309–314.

31. Campbell, John Y. "Stock Returns and the Term Structure," *Journal of Financial Economics*, **18** (June, 1987), pp. 373–399.

32. Campbell, John Y., and Shiller, Robert. "Stock Prices, Earnings and Expected Dividends," *Journal of Finance*, **43,** No. 3 (July 1988), pp. 661–676.

33. ——. "The Dividend-Price Ratio and Expectations of Future Dividends and Discount Factors," *Review of Financial Studies*, **1,** No. 3 (1988–1989), pp. 195–228.

34. Casatis, Patrick, Miles, James, and Woolridge, Randall. "Restructuring Through Spinoffs: The Stock Market Evidence," *Journal of Financial Economics*, **33,** No. 3 (June 1993), pp. 293–313.

35. Chan, K. C. "On the Contrarian Investment Strategy," *Journal of Business*, **61,** No. 2 (April 1988), p. 147.

36. Chan, K. C., and Chen, Nai-Fu. "An Unconditional Asset-Pricing Test and the Role of Firm Size as an Instrument Variable for Risk," *Journal of Finance*, **43,** No. 2 (June 1988), pp. 309–325.

37. Chan, K. C., and Chen, Nai-Fu. "Structural and Return Characteristics of Small and Large Firms," *Journal of Finance*, **46,** No. 4 (Sept. 1991), pp. 1467–1484.

38. Chan, K. C., Chen, Nai-Fu, and Hsieh, David A. "An Exploratory Investigation of the Firm Size Effect," *Journal of Financial Economics*, **14** (1985), pp. 451–471.

39. Chan, Louis K. C., Hamao, Yasushi, and Lakonishok, Josef. "Fundamentals and Stock Returns in Japan," *Journal of Finance*, **46,** No. 5 (Dec. 1991), pp. 1739–1764.

40. Charest, Guy. "Dividend Information, Stock Returns, and Market Efficiency II," *Journal of Financial Economics*, **6,** No. 2/3 (June/Sept. 1978), pp. 297–330.

41. Chari, V. V., Jagannathan, Ravi, and Ofer, Aharon R. "Seasonalities in Security Returns: The Case of Earnings Announcements," *Journal of Finance Economics*, **21** (1988), pp. 101–121.

42. Cheng, L. Pao. "Reply to [189]," *Journal of Finance*, **XXVIII,** No. 3 (June 1973), pp. 742–745.

43. Chopra, N., Lakonishok, J., and Ritter, J. "Measuring Abnormal Performance: Do Stocks Overreact?" *Journal of Financial Economics*, **31,** No. 2 (April 1992), pp. 235–268.

44. Christie, Andrew A., and Hertzel, Michael. "Capital Asset Pricing 'Anomalies': Size and Other Correlations," Unpublished manuscript (1981), Rochester, N.Y.: University of Rochester.

45. Cochrane, John H. "Volatility Tests and Efficient Markets: A Review Essay," *Journal of Monetary Economics*, **27,** No. 3 (June 1991), pp. 463–485.

46. Connolly, Robert A. "An Examination of the Robustness of the Weekend Effect," *Journal of Financial and Quantitative Analysis*, **24,** No. 2 (June 1989), pp. 133–169.

47. Conrad, Jennifer, and Kaul, Gautam. "Time-variation in expected returns," *Journal of Business*, **61,** No. 4 (Oct. 1988), pp. 409–425.

48. Conway, Delores A., and Reinganum, Marc R. "Stable Factors in Security Returns: Identification Using Cross-Validation," *Journal of Business and Economic Statistics*, **6** (1988), pp. 1–15.

49. Cootner, Paul. *The Random Character of Stock Market Prices* (Cambridge, Mass.: MIT Press, 1974).

50. Copeland, Thomas E., and Mayers, David. "The Value Line Enigma (1965–1978): A Case Study of Performance of Evaluation Issues," *Journal of Financial Economics*, **X,** No. 3 (Nov. 1982), pp. 289–322.

51. Corhag, Albert, Hawawini, Gabriel, and Michel, Pierre. "Seasonality in the Risk-Return Relationship: Some International Evidence," *Journal of Finance*, **42,** No. 1 (March 1987), pp. 49–68.

52. Damodaran, Aswath. "Economic Events, Information Structure, and the Return-Generating Process," *Journal of Financial Quantitative Analysis*, **20,** No. 4 (Dec. 1985), pp. 423–433.

53. Dann, Larry, Mayers, David, and Raab, Robert. "Trading Rules, Large Blocks, and the Speed of Price Adjustment," *Journal of Financial Economics*, **4,** No. 1 (Jan. 1977), pp. 3–22.

54. Davies, Peter Lloyd, and Canes, Michael. "Stock Prices and the Publication of Second-Hand Information," *Journal of Business*, **51,** No. 1 (Jan. 1978), pp. 43–56.

55. DeBondt, Werner F. M., and Thaler, Richard H. "Does the Stock Market Overreact?" *Journal of Finance*, **40** (July 1985), pp. 793–805.

56. DeBondt, Werner F. M., and Thaler, Richard H. "Further Evidence on Investor Overreaction and Stock Market Seasonality," *Journal of Finance*, **42,** No. 3 (July 1987), pp. 557–581.

57. Desai, Hemang, and Jain, Prem C. "An Analysis of the Recommendations of the "Superstar" Money Managers at Barron's Annual Roundtable," *The Journal of Finance*, **50,** No. 4 (Sept. 1995), pp. 1257–1273.

58. Dimson, Elroy, and Marsh, Paul. "An Analysis of Brokers' and Analysts' Unpublished Forecasts of UK Stock Returns," *The Journal of Finance*, **39,** No. 5 (Dec. 1984), pp. 1257–1292.

59. Divecha, Arjun, and Morse, Dale. "Market Responses to Dividend Increases and Changes in Payout Ratios," *Journal of Financial and Quantitative Analysis*, **18,** No. 2 (June 1983), pp. 163–173.

60. Dodd, Peter. "Merger Proposals, Management Discretion and Stockholder Wealth," *Journal of Financial Economics*, **8,** No. 2 (June 1980), pp. 105–137.

61. Dodd, Peter, and Ruback, Richard. "Tender Offers and Stockholders' Returns," *Journal of Financial Economics*, **5,** No. 3 (Dec. 1977), pp. 351–375.

62. Dryden, Myles. "A Source of Bias in Filter Tests on Share Prices," *Journal of Business*, **42,** No. 3 (July 1969), pp. 321–325.

63. Dyl, Edward. "Capital Gains Taxation and Year-End Stock Market Behavior," *Journal of Finance*, **XXXII,** No. 1 (March 1977), pp. 165–175.

64. Dyl, Edward A., and Maberly, Edwin D. "Odd-Lot Transactions Around the Turn of the Year and the January Effect," *Journal of Financial and Quantitative Analysis*, **27,** No. 4 (Dec. 1992), p. 591.

65. Eades, Kenneth M., Hess, Patrick J., and Kim, E. Han. "On Interpreting Security Returns During the Ex-Dividend Period," *Journal of Financial Economics*, **13** (1984), pp. 3–34.

66. Elton, Edwin J., Gruber, Martin J., and Busse, Jeff. "Do Investors Care about Sentiment," *The Journal of Business*, **71,** No. 4 (Oct. 1998), pp. 477–500.

67. Elton, Edwin J., Gruber, Martin J., and Grossman, Seth. "Discreet Expectational Data and Portfolio Performance," *Journal of Finance*, **XXXXI,** No. 3 (July 1986), pp. 699–712.

68. Elton, Edwin J., Gruber, Martin J., Das, Sanjiv, and Hklarka, Matt. "Efficiency with Costly Information: A Reinterpretation of Evidence from Managed Portfolios," *Unpublished Manuscript*, New York University, 1990.

69. Emery, John. "The Information Content of Daily Market Indicators," *Journal of Financial and Quantitative Analysis*, **VIII,** No. 2 (March 1973), pp. 183–190.

70. ———. "Efficient Capital Markets and the Information Content of Accounting Numbers," *Journal of Financial and Quantitative Analysis*, **IX,** No. 2 (March 1974), pp. 139–149.

71. Epps, Thomas. "Security Price Changes and Transaction Volumes: Theory and Evidence," *American Economic Review*, **LXV,** No. 4 (Sept. 1975), pp. 586–597.

72. ———. "Security Price Changes and Transaction Volumes: Some Additional Evidence," *Journal of Financial and Quantitative Analysis*, **XII,** No. 1 (March 1977), pp. 141–146.

73. ———. "Security Price Changes and Transaction Volumes: Additional Evidence: Reply to [179]," *American Economic Review*, **68,** No. 4 (Sept. 1978), pp. 698–700.

74. Eskew, Robert, and Wright, William. "An Empirical Analysis of Differential Capital Market Reactions to Extraordinary Accounting Items," *Journal of Finance*, **XXXI,** No. 2 (May 1976), pp. 631–674.

75. Fama, Eugene. "The Behavior of Stock Market Prices," *Journal of Business*, **38** (Jan. 1965), pp. 34–105.

76. ———. "Efficient Capital Markets: A Review of Theory and Empirical Work," *Journal of Finance*, **XXV,** No. 2 (March 1970), pp. 383–417.

77. ———. Efficient Capital Markets II, *Journal of Finance*, **26,** No. 5 (Dec. 1991), pp. 1575–1617.

78. Fama, Eugene, and Blume, Marshall. "Filter Rules and Stock Market Trading," *Journal of Business*, **39** (Jan. 1966), pp. 226–241.

79. Fama, Eugene, and French, Kenneth R. "Permanent and Temporary Components of Stock Prices," *Journal of Political Economy*, **96** (April 1988), pp. 246–273.

80. ———. "Dividend Yields and Expected Stock Returns," *Journal of Financial Economics*, **22,** No. 1 (Oct. 1988), pp. 3–25.

81. ———. "Business Conditions and Expected Returns on Stocks and Bonds," *Journal of Financial Economics*, **25,** No. 1 (Nov. 1989), pp. 23–49.

82. ———. "The cross section of expected stock returns," Unpublished manuscript, Graduate School of Business, University of Chicago, 1991.

83. Fama, Eugene, and MacBeth, James. "Risk, Return and Equilibrium: Empirical Tests," *Journal of Political Economy*, **81,** No. 3 (May/June 1973), pp. 607–636.

84. Fama, E., Fisher, L., Jensen, M., and Roll, R. "The Adjustment of Stock Prices to New Information," *International Economic Review*, **10,** No. 1 (Feb. 1969), pp. 1–21.

85. Ferson, Wayne E., "Stock market regularities: A synthesis of the evidence and explanations," in Elroy Dimson (ed.), *Stock Market Anomalies*, Cambridge, U.K.: Cambridge University Press, 1988.

86. ———. "Trading Patterns, Bid-Ask Spreads, and Estimated Security Returns: The Case of Common Stocks at Calendar Turning Points," *Journal of Financial Economics*, **25,** No. 1 (Jan. 1989), pp. 75–97.

87. Ferson, Wayne E., and Harvey, Campbell R. "The Variation of Economic Risk Premiums," *Journal of Political Economy*, **99,** No. 2 (April 1991), pp. 385–415.

88. Finnerty, Joseph. "Insiders' Activity and Inside Information: A Multivariate Analysis," *Journal of Financial and Quantitative Analysis*, **XI,** No. 2 (June 1976), pp. 205–215.

89. ———. "Insiders and Market Efficiency," *Journal of Finance*, **XXXI,** No. 4 (Sept. 1976), pp. 1141–1148.

90. ———. "The Chicago Board Options Exchange and Market Efficiency," *Journal of Financial and Quantitative Analysis*, **XIII,** No. 1 (March 1978), pp. 29–38.

91. Firth, Michael. "The Information Content of Large Investment Holdings," *Journal of Finance*, **XXX,** No. 5 (Dec. 1975), pp. 1265–1281.

92. Flannery, Mark J., and Protopapdakis, Aris A. "From T-Bills to Common Stocks Investigating the Generality of Intra-Week Return Seasonality," *Journal of Finance*, **43,** No. 2 (June 1988), pp. 431–450.

93. Flavin, Marjorie A. "Excess Volatility in the Empirical Evidence," *Journal of Political Economics*, **91,** No. 6 (Dec. 1983), pp. 929–956.

94. Flood, Robert P., and Hodrick, Robert J. "Asset Price Volatility, Bubbles, and Process Switching," *Journal of Finance*, **41** (Sept. 1986), pp. 831–842.

95. French, Kenneth R. "Stock Returns and the Weekend Effect," *Journal of Financial Economics*, **8** (1980), pp. 55–70.

96. French, Kenneth R., Schwert, G. William, and Stambaugh, Robert F. "Expected Stock Returns and Volatility," *Journal of Financial Economics*, **19** (1987), pp. 3–29.

97. Friend, Irwin, and Lang, Larry H. D. "The Size Effect on Stock Returns: Is it Simply a Risk Effect not Adequately Reflected by the Usual Measures?" *Journal of Business Finance*, **12,** No. 1 (March 1988), pp. 13–30.

98. Furst, Richard. "Does Listing Increase the Market Price of Common Stocks?" *Journal of Business*, **43,** No. 2 (April 1970), pp. 174–180.

99. Galai, Dan. "Tests of Market Efficiency of the Chicago Board Options Exchange," *Journal of Business*, **50,** No. 2 (April 1977b), pp. 421–442.

100. Gibbons, Michael R., and Hess, Patrick J. "Day of the Week Effects and Asset Returns," *Journal of Business*, **54** (1981), pp. 579–596.

101. Givoly, Dan, and Ovadia, Arie. "Year-End Tax Induced Sales and Stock Market Seasonality," *Journal of Finance*, **38,** No. 1 (March 1983), pp. 171–185.

102. Givoly, Dan, and Pulman, Dan. "Insider Trading and the Exploitation of Inside Information: Some Empirical Evidence," *Journal of Business*, **58,** No. 1 (Jan. 1985), pp. 69–87.

103. Granger, C. W. "Some Aspects of the Random Walk Model of Stock Market Prices," *International Economic Review*, **9,** No. 2 (June 1968), pp. 253–257.

104. ——. "A Survey of Empirical Studies on Capital Markets," in Edwin J. Elton and Martin J. Gruber (eds.), *International Capital Markets* (Amsterdam: North-Holland, 1975).

105. Granger, C. W., and Morgenstern, O. *Predictability of Stock Market Prices* (Boston, Mass.: Heath, 1970).

106. Grier, Paul, and Albin, Peter. "Non-Random Price Changes in Association with Trading in Large Blocks," *Journal of Business*, **46,** No. 3 (July 1973), pp. 425–433.

107. Griffiths, R. J. "Relative Strength—An Indicator for Investment in the Equity Market," thesis (Department of Statistics, Cranfield College, Cambridge, U.K., 1970).

108. Grinblatt, Mark, and Titman, Sheridan. "The Persistence of Mutual Fund Performance, *The Journal of Finance*, **47,** No. 5 (Dec. 1992), pp. 1977–1984.

109. Grossman, S. J., and Hart, O. D. "Disclosure Law and Takeover Bids," *The Journal of Finance*, **35,** No. 2 (May 1980), pp. 323–334.

110. Grossman, Sanford. "On the Efficiency of Competitive Stock Markets Where Trades Have Diverse Information," *Journal of Finance*, **XXXI,** No. 2 (May 1976), pp. 573–585.

111. Grossman, Sanford J., and Shiller, Robert J. "The Determinants of the Variability of Stock Market Prices," *American Economic Review*, **71,** No. 2 (May 1981), pp. 222–227.

112. Gultekin, Mustafa N., and Gultekin, N. Bulent. "Stock Market Seasonality: International Evidence," *Journal of Financial Economics*, **12** (1983), pp. 469–481.

113. Harris, Lawrence. "A Transaction Data Study of Weekly and Intradaily Patterns in Stock Returns," *Journal of Financial Economics*, **14** (May 1986), pp. 99–117.

114. Harvey, Campbell. "The World Price of Covariance Risk," *Journal of Finance*, **46,** No. 1 (March 1991), pp. 111–157.

115. Hodrick, Robert J. "Dividend Yields and Expected Stock Returns: Alternative Procedures for Inference and Measurement," Unpublished Manuscript (1990), Northwestern University, and National Bureau of Economic Research.

116. Holthausen, Robert W., and Leftwich, Richard W. "The Effect of Bond Rating Changes on Common Stock Prices," *Journal of Financial Economy*, **17** (1986), pp. 57–89.

117. Huberman, Gur, and Kandel, Shmuel. "Value Line Rank and Firm Size," *Journal of Business*, **60,** No. 4 (Oct. 1987), pp. 577–589.

118. ——. "Market Efficiency and Value Line's Record," *Journal of Business*, **63,** No. 2 (April 1990). pp. 187–216.

119. Hausman, W. H., West, R. R., and Largay. J. A. "Stock Splits, Price Changes, and Trading Profits: A Synthesis," *Journal of Business*, **44,** No. 1 (Jan. 1971), pp. 69–77.

120. Hawkins, Eugene H., Chamberlin. Stanley C., and Daniel Wayne E. "Earnings Expectations and Security Prices." *Financial Analyst Journal*, **40,** No. 5 (Sept./Oct. 1984), pp. 24–39.

121. Ibbotson, Roger, and Jaffe, Jeffrey. "Hot Issue Markets," *Journal of Finance*, **XXX,** No. 2 (Sept. 1975), pp. 1027–1042.

122. Jaffe, Jeffrey. "Special Information and Insider Trading," *Journal of Business*, **47,** No. 3 (July 1974), pp. 410–428.

123. Jaffe, Jeffrey, and Mandelker, Gershon. "The Fisher Effect for Risky Assets: An Empirical Investigation," *Journal of Finance*, **XXXI,** No. 2 (May 1976), pp. 447–458.

124. Jaffe, Jeffrey, and Westerfield, Randolph. "The Week-end Effect in Common Stock Returns: The International Evidence," *Journal of Finance*, **40,** No. 2 (June 1985), pp. 433–454.

125. Jaim, Prem C. "The Effect of Voluntary Sell-off Announcements on Shareholder Wealth," *Journal of Finance*, **40,** No. 1 (March 1985), pp. 209–224.

126. ——. "Responses of Hourly Stock Prices and Trading Volume to Economic News," *Journal of Business*, **61,** No. 2 (April 1988), pp. 219–231.

127. James, Christopher, and Edmister, Robert O. "The Relation Between Common Stock Return, Trading Activity and Market Value," *Journal of Finance*, **38,** No. 4 (Sept. 1983), pp. 1075–1086.

128 Jegadeesh, Narasimhan, and Titman, Sheridan. "Returns to Buying Winners and Selling Losers: Implications for Stock Market Efficiency," *The Journal of Finance*, **48,** No. 1 (Mar. 1993), pp. 65–91.

129. Jennergren, Peter. "Filter Tests of Swedish Share Prices," in Edwin J. Elton and Martin J. Gruber (eds.), *International Capital Markets* (Amsterdam: North-Holland, 1975).

130. Jennergren, Peter, and Korsvold, Paul. "The Non-Random Character of Norwegian and Swedish Stock Market Prices," in Elton and Gruber, *International Capital Markets* (Amsterdam: North-Holland, 1975).

131. Jennings, Robert, and Starks, Laura. "Earnings Announcements, Stock Price Adjustment, and the Existence of Option Markets," *Journal of Finance*, **41,** No. 1 (March 1986), pp. 107–125.

132. Jensen, Michael. "Accounting Changes and Stock Prices," *Financial Analysts, Journal*, **29,** No. 1 (Jan./Feb. 1973), pp. 48–53.

133. ——. "Some Anomalous Evidence Regarding Market Efficiency," *Journal of Financial Economics*, **6,** No. 2/3 (June/Sept. 1978), pp. 95–101.

134. Jensen, Michael, and Bennington, George. "Random Walks and Technical Theories: Some Additional Evidence," *Journal of Finance*, **XXV,** No. 2 (May 1970), pp. 469–482.

135. Jones, C.D., Pearce, O.K., and Wilson, J.W. "Can Tax-Loss Selling Explain the January Effect? A Note," *Journal of Finance*, **42,** No. 2 (June 1987), pp. 453–461.

136. Kaplan, Steven. "The Effect of Management Buyouts on Operating Performance and Value," *Journal of Financial Economics*, **24,** No. 2 (Oct. 1989), pp. 217–254.

137. Kato, K., and Shallheim, J. "Seasonal and Size Anomalies in the Japanese Stock Market," *Journal of Financial and Quantitative Analysis*, **20,** No. 2 (June 1985), pp. 243–260.

138. Katz, Steven. "The Price Adjustment Process of Bonds to Rating Reclassifications: A Test of Bond Market Efficiency," *Journal of Finance*, **XXIX,** No. 2 (May 1974), pp. 551–559.

139. Keim, Donald B. "Size Related Anomalies and Stock Return Seasonality Further Empirical Evidence," *Journal of Financial Economics*, **12** (1983).

140. ——. "Trading Patterns, Bid-Ask Spreads, and Estimated Security Returns: The Case of Common Stocks at Calendar Turning Points," *Journal of Financial Economics*, **25,** No. 1 (Nov. 1989), pp. 75–97.

141. Keim, Donald B., and Stambaugh, Robert F. "A Further Investigation of the Weekend Effect in Stock Returns," *The Journal of Finance*, **39,** No. 3 (July 1984), pp. 819–840.

142. ——. "Predicting Returns in the Stock and Bond Markets," *Journal of Financial Economics*, **17,** No. 2 (Dec. 1986), pp. 357–390.

143. Kleidon, Allan W. "Bubbles, Fads and Stock Price Volatility Tests: A Partial Evaluation: Discussion," *Journal of Finance*, **43,** No. 3 (July 1988), pp. 656–659.

144. Kraus, Alan, and Stoll, Hans. "Price Impacts of Block Trading on the New York Stock Exchange," *Journal of Finance*, **XXVII,** No. 3 (June 1972), pp. 569–588.

145. Lakonishok, Josef, and Shapiro, Alan C. "Systematic Risk, Total Risk and Size as Determinants of Stock Market Returns," *Journal of Business Finance*, **10,** No. 1 (March 1986), pp. 115–132.

146. Lakonishok, Josef, and Smidt, Seymour. "Volume and Turn-of-the-Year Behavior," *Journal of Financial Economics*, **13** (1984), pp. 435–455.

147. ———. "Are Seasonal Anomalies Real?: A Ninety-Year Perspective," *Review of Financial Studies*, **1** (Winter 1988), pp. 435–455.

148. Lakonishok, Josef, Shleifer, Andrei, and Vishny, W. Robert, "Contrarian Investment, Extrapolation, and Risk," Unpublished Paper (1993), University of Illinois.

149. Larcker, David F., and Lys, Thomas. "An Empirical Analysis of the Incentives to Engage in Costly Information Acquisition: The Case of Risk Arbitrage," *Journal of Financial Economics*, **18** (1987), pp. 11–26.

150. Larcker, David F., Gordon, Lawrence A., and Pinches, George E. "Testing for Market Efficiency: A Comparison of the Cumulative Average Residual Methodology and Intervention Analysis," *Journal of Financial and Quantitative Analysis*, **XV,** No. 2 (June 1980), pp. 267–288.

151. Laurence, Martin M. "Weak Form Efficiency in the Kuala Lumpur and Singapore Stock Markets," *Journal of Business Finance*, **10** (Oct. 1986), pp. 431–445.

152. Lehmann, Bruce N. "Fads, Martingales, And Market Efficiency," *The Quarterly Journal of Economics*, **105,** No. 1 (Feb. 1990), pp. 1–27.

153. LeRoy, Stephen F., and Richard D. Porter. "The Present-Value Relation: Tests Based on Implied Variance Bounds," *Econometrica* (1981), pp. 555–574.

154. Levy, Robert. "Relative Strength as a Criterion for Investment Selection," *Journal of Finance*, **22** (Dec. 1967), pp. 595–610.

155. Liu, Pu, Smith, Stanley D., and Syed, Azmat A. "Security Price Reaction to the *Wall Street Journal*'s Securities' Recommendations," *Journal of Financial and Quantitative Analysis*, **25,** No. 3 (Sept. 1990), pp. 399–410.

156. Lo, Andrew W., and MacKinlay, A. Craig. "Stock Market Prices Do Not Follow Random Walks: Evidence from a Simple Specification Test," *Review of Financial Studies*, **1,** No. 1 (Spring 1988), pp. 41–66.

157. ———. "When Are Contrarian Profits Due to Stock Market Overreaction?" *Review of Financial Studies*, **3,** No. 2 (1990), pp. 175–205.

158. Logue, Dennis. "On the Pricing of Unseasoned Equity Issues: 1965–1969," *Journal of Financial and Quantitative Analysis*, **VIII,** No. 1 (Jan. 1973), pp. 91–103.

159. Lorie, James, and Neiderhoffer, Victor. "Predictive and Statistical Properties of Insider Trading," *Journal of Law and Economics*, **11** (April 1968), pp. 35–53.

160. Malkiel, Burton G. "Returns from Investing in Equity Mutual Funds 1971 to 1991," *The Journal of Finance*, **50,** No. 2 (June 1995), pp. 549–572.

161. Mandelbrot, Benoit. "Some Aspects of the Random Walk Model of Stock Market Prices," *International Economic Review*, **9,** No. 2 (June 1968), pp. 258–259.

162. ———. "When Can Price Be Arbitraged Efficiently? A Limit to the Validity of the Random Walk and Martingale Models," *Review of Economics and Statistics*, **LIII,** No. 3 (Aug. 1971), pp. 225–236.

163. Mandelker, Gershon. "Risk and Return: The Case of Merging Firms," *Journal of Financial Economics*, **1,** No. 4 (Dec. 1974), pp. 303–336.

164. Mankin, N. Gregory, Romer, David, and Shapiro, Matthew D. "An Unbiased Reexamination of Stock Market Volatility," *Journal of Finance*, **40,** No. 3 (July 1985), pp. 677–687.

165. Marsh, Terry A., and Robert C. Merton. "Dividend Variability and Variance Bounds Tests for the Rationality of Stock Market Prices," *American Economic Review* (1986), pp. 483–498.

166. Mech, Timothy S. "Portfolio return autocorrelation." *Journal of Financial Economics*, **34,** No. 3 (Dec. 1993), pp. 307–344.

167. Merton, Robert C. "On the Current State of the Stock Market Rationality Hypothesis," in Rudiger Dornbusch, Stanley Fisher, and John Bossons (eds.), *Macro-economics and Finance: Essays in Honor of Franco Modigliani* (Cambridge, Mass.: MIT Press, 1987).

168. Mitchell, Mark L., and Kenneth Lehn. "Do Bad Bidders Become Good Targets?" *Journal of Political Economy*, **98,** No. 2 (April 1990), pp. 372–398.

169. Niederhoffer, Victor. "The Analysis of World Events and Stock Prices," *Journal of Business*, **44,** No. 2 (April 1971), pp. 193–219.

170. Neiderhoffer, Victor, and Osborne, M. F. M. "Market Making and Reversal on the Stock Exchange," *Journal of the American Statistical Association*, **61** (1966), pp. 897–916.

171. Niarchos, N. A. "Statistical Analysis of Transactions on the Athens Stock Exchange," Thesis (Nottingham U.K.: Nottingham College), 1971.

172. Officer, Robert R. "Seasonality in the Australian Capital Markets: Market Efficiency and Empirical Issues," *Journal of Financial Economics*, **2** (1975), pp. 29–52.

173. Ohlson, James A., and Penman, Stephen H. "Volatility Increases Subsequent to Stock Splits: An Empirical Aberration," *Journal of Financial Economics*, **14,** No. 2 (June 1985), pp. 251–266.

174. Oppenheimer, Henry R., and Schlarbaum, Gary G. "Investing with Ben Graham: An Ex Ante Test of the Efficient Market Hypothesis," *Journal of Financial and Quantitative Analysis*, **XVI,** No. 3 (Sept. 1981), pp. 341–360.

175. Patel, Jayendu, Zeckhauser, Richard, and Hendricks, Darryll. "The Rationality Struggle: Illustrations from Financial Markets," *The American Economic Review*, **81,** No. 2 (May 1991), p. 232.

176. Patell, James M., and Wolfson, Mark A. "The Intraday Speed of Adjustment of Stock Prices to Earnings and Dividend Announcements," *Journal of Financial Economics*, **13,** No. 2 (June 1983), pp. 223–252.

177. Penman, Stephen H. "Insider Trading and the Dissemination of Firm's Forecast Information," *Journal of Business*, **55,** No. 4 (Oct. 1982), pp. 479–503.

178. ———. "The Distribution of Earnings News Over Time and Seasonalities in Aggregate Stock Returns," *Journal of Financial Economics*, **18** (1987), pp. 199–228.

179. Pettit, R. Richardson. "Dividend Announcements, Security Performance, and Capital Market Efficiency," *Journal of Finance*, **XXVII,** No. 5 (Dec. 1972), pp. 993–1007.

180. ———. "The Impact of Dividend and Earnings Announcements: A Reconciliation," *Journal of Business*, **49,** No. 1 (Jan. 1976)), pp. 86–89.

181. Pettit, R. Richardson, and Westerfield, Randolph. "Using the Capital Asset Pricing Model and the Market Model to Predict Security Returns," *Journal of Financial and Quantitative Analysis*, **IX,** No. 4 (Sept. 1974), pp. 579–605.

182. Pinches, George. "The Random Walk Hypothesis and Technical Analysis," *Financial Analysts Journal*, **26,** No. 2 (March/April 1970), pp. 104–110.

183. Pinches, George, and Simon, Gary. "An Analysis of Portfolio Accumulation Strategies Employing Low-Priced Common Stocks," *Journal of Financial and Quantitative Analysis*, **VII,** No. 3 (June 1972), pp. 1773–1796.

184. Poterba, James M., and Summers, Lawrence H. "The Persistence of Volatility and Stock Market Fluctuation," *American Economic Review* (Dec. 1986), **76,** No. 5, pp. 1142–1151.

185. Poterba, James, and Summers, Lawrence. "Mean Reversion in Stock Prices: Evidence and Implications," *Journal of Financial Economics*, **22,** No. 1 (Oct. 1988), pp. 27–59.

186. Praetz, Peter. "The Distribution of Share Price Changes," *Journal of Business*, **45,** No. 1 (Jan. 1972), pp. 49–55.

187. Reinganum, Marc. R. "The Arbitrage Pricing Theory: Some Empirical Results," *Journal of Finance*, **37** (1981), pp. 27–35.

188. ———. "Misspecification of Capital Asset Pricing: Empirical Anomalies Based on Earnings Yields and Market Values," *Journal of Financial Economics*, **9** (March 1981), pp. 19–46.

189. ———. "The Anomalous Stock Market Behavior of Small Firms in January: Empirical Tests for Tax-Loss Selling Effect," *Journal of Financial Economics*, **12,** No. 1 (1983).

190. ——. "A Direct Test of Roll's Conjecture on the Firm Size Effect," *The Journal of Finance*, **37,** No. 1 (March 1982), pp. 27–36.

191. ——. "The Anomalous Stock Market Behavior of Small Firms in January," *Journal of Financial Economics*, **12** (June 1983), pp. 89–104.

192. Reinganum, Marc R., and Shapiro, Alan C. "Taxes and Stock Return Seasonality: Evidence from the London Stock Exchange," *Journal of Business*, **60,** No. 2 (April 1987), pp. 281–295.

193. Ritter, Jay R. "The Buying and Selling Behavior of Individual Investors at the Turn of the Year," *Journal of Finance* (July 1983), pp. 701–717.

194. Roll, Richard. *The Behavior of Interest Rates: An Application of the Efficient Market Model to U.S. Treasury Bills* (New York: Basic Books, 1970).

195. ——. "A Possible Explanation of the Small Firm Effect," *Journal of Finance*, **36** (1981), pp. 879–888.

196. ——. "The Turn of the Year Effect and the Return Premium of Small Firms," *Journal of Portfolio Management* (1982).

197. ——. "On Computing Mean Returns and the Small Firm Premium," *Journal of Financial Economics*, **12** (1983), pp. 371–386.

198. Ross, Stephen A. "The Arbitrage Theory of Capital Asset Pricing," *Journal of Economic Theory*, **13** (1976), pp. 341–360.

199. Rozeff, Michael S., and Kinney, Jr., William R. "Capital Market Seasonality: The Case of Stock Returns," *Journal of Financial Economics*, **3** (1976), pp. 379–402.

200. Rozeff, Michael S., and Zaman, Mir A. "Market Efficiency and Insider Trading: New Evidence," *Journal of Business*, **61,** No. 1 (Jan. 1988), pp. 25–44.

201. Scholes, Myron, and Williams, Joseph. "Estimating Betas from Nonsynchronous Data, *Journal of Financial Economics*, **5,** No. 3 (Dec. 1977), pp. 309–329.

202. Schultz, Paul. "Transaction Costs and the Small Firm Effect: A Comment," *Journal of Financial Economics*, **12** (1983).

203. Schwartz, Robert, and Whitcomb, David. "Evidence on the Presence and Causes of Serial Correlation in Market Model Residuals," *Journal of Financial and Quantitative Analysis*, **XII,** No. 2 (June 1977), pp. 291–313.

204. Schwert G. William. "The Adjustment of Stock Prices to Information about Inflation," *The Journal of Finance*, **36,** No. 1 (March 1981), pp. 15–30.

205. ——. "Size and Stock Returns, and Other Empirical Regularities," *Journal of Financial Economics*, **12,** No. 1 (1983).

206. Seyhum, N. Nejat. "The January Effect and Aggregate Insider Trading," *Journal of Finance*, **43,** No. 1 (March 1988), pp. 129–141.

207. Shiller, Robert J. "The Volatility of Long-term Interest Rates and Expectations' Models of the Term Structure," *Journal of Political Economy*, **87,** No. 6 (Dec. 1979), pp. 1190–1219.

208. ——. "Do Stock Prices Move Too Much to Be Justified by Subsequent Changes in Dividends?" *American Economic Review* (June 1981), pp. 421–436.

209. ——. "Theories of Aggregate Stock Price Movements," *The Journal of Portfolio Management* (Winter 1984), pp. 28–37.

210. ——. "The Marsh-Merton Model of Managers' Smoothing of Dividends," American Economic Review (*AER*), **76,** No. 3 (June 1986), pp. 499–503.

211. ——. "Comovements In Stock Prices And Comovements In Dividends," *The Journal of Finance*, Jul 1989; Vol. 44, Iss. 3; pg. 719–729.

212. Shleifer, Andrei. "Do Demand Curves for Stocks Slope Down?" *Journal of Finance*, **41,** No. 3 (July 1980), pp. 579–590.

213. Stickel, Scott E. "The Effect of Value Line Investment Survey Rank Changes on Common Prices," *Journal of Financial Economics*, **14,** No. 1 (March 1985), pp. 121–144.

214. Smidt, Seymour. "A New Look at the Random Walk Hypothesis," *Journal of Financial and Quantitative Analysis*, **III,** No. 3 (Sept. 1968), pp. 235–261.

215. Smirlock, Michael, and Starks, Laoura. "Day-of-the-Week and Intraday Effects in Stock Returns," *Journal of Financial Economics*, **17** (1986), pp. 197–210.

216. Solnik, Bruno. "Note on the Validity of the Random Walk for European Stock Prices," *Journal of Finance*, **XXVIII**, No. 5 (Dec. 1973), pp. 1151–1159.

217. Stoll, Hans R., and Whaley, Robert E. "Transaction Costs and the Small Firm Effect," *Journal of Financial Economics*, **12**, No. 1 (1983).

218. Summers, Lawrence H. "Does the Stock Market Rationally Reflect Fundamental Volumes?" *Journal of Finance*, **41**, No. 3 (July 1986). pp. 591–601.

219. Taylor, Stephen J. "Tests of the Random Walk Hypothesis Against a Price-Trend Hypothesis," *Journal of Financial and Quantitative Analysis*, **XVII**, No. 1 (March 1982), pp. 37–62.

220. Tinic, Seha M., and West, Richard R. "Risk and Return: January vs. the Rest of the Year," *Journal of Financial Economics*, **13** (1984), pp. 561–574.

221. Tinic, Seha M., Barone-Adesi, Giovanni, and West, Richard R. "Seasonality in Canadian Stock Prices: A Test for the Tax-Loss-Selling Hypothesis," *Journal of Financial and Quantitative Analysis*, **22**, No. 1 (March 1987). pp. 51–63.

222. Vermaelen, Theo. "Common Stock Repurchases and Market Signalling: An Empirical Study," *Journal of Financial Economics*, **9**, No. 2 (June 1981), pp. 139–183.

223. *The Wall Street Journal*, June 1982.

224. Watts, Ross. "The Information Content of Dividends," *Journal of Business*, **45**, No. 2 (April 1973), pp. 191–211.

225. ——. "Comment on [125]...On the Informational Content of Dividends," *Journal of Business*, **49**, No. 1 (Jan. 1976). pp. 81–85.

226. ——. "Comments on [153]...The Impact of Dividend and Earnings Announcements: A Reconciliation," *Journal of Business*, **49**, No. 1 (Jan. 1976), pp. 97–106.

227. West, Kenneth D. "Bubbles, Fads, and Stock Price Volatility Tests: A Partial Evaluation," *Journal of Finance*, **43**, No. 3 (July 1988), pp. 639–655.

228. West, Richard, and Tinic, Seha. "Portfolio Returns and the Random Walk Theory: Comment on [25]," *Journal of Finance*, **XXVIII**, No. 3 (June 1973), pp. 733–741.

229. Westerfield, Randolph. "The Distribution of Common Stock Price Changes: An Application of Transaction, Time and Subordinated Stochastic Models," *Journal of Financial and Quantitative Analysis*, **10**, No. 4 (Dec. 1977), pp. 743–765.

230. Yakov, Amihud, and Mendleson, Haim. "Asset Pricing and the Bid-Ask Spread," *Journal of Financial Economics*, **17**, No. 2 (Dec. 1986), pp. 223–250.

231. ——. "Liquidity, Asset Prices, and Financial Policy," *Financial Analysts Journal*, **47** (Nov./Dec. 1991), pp. 56–66.

232. Zarowin, Paul. "Does the Stock Market Overreact to Corporate Earnings Information?" *Journal of Finance*, **44**, No. 5 (Dec. 1989), pp. 1385–1399.

18

The Valuation Process

The search for the "correct" way to value common stocks, or even one that works, has occupied a huge amount of effort over a long period of time. Attempts have ranged from simple mechanical techniques for picking winners to hypotheses about the broad influences affecting stock prices. At one extreme, the attempt to find a simple rule for selecting stocks that will have above-average performance can be likened to the search for a perpetual motion machine. Just as the laws of thermodynamics tell us we cannot build a perpetual motion machine, the theory of efficient markets tells us there is no simple mechanical way to pick winners in the stock market, or at least none that will recover its cost of operation. Yet people continue to spend a disproportionate amount of time on both of these endeavors.

At the other extreme the determinants of common stock prices are quite easy to specify in general terms. The price of common stock is a function of the level of a company's earnings, dividends, risk, the cost of money, and future growth rate. While it is easy to specify these broad influences, the implementation of a system that uses these concepts to successfully value or select common stocks is a difficult task. This is the task that a valuation model purports to accomplish.

A valuation model is a mechanism that converts a set of forecasts of (or observations on) a series of company and economic variables into a forecast of market value for the company's stock. The input to a valuation model is in terms of economic variables, for example, future earnings, dividends, variability of earnings, and so forth. The output is in terms of expected market value or expected return from holding the stock or, at the very least, a buy, sell, hold recommendation. The valuation model can be considered a formalization of the relationship that is expected to exist between a set of corporate and economic factors and the market's valuation of these factors.

Every financial organization employs a valuation model. Often the valuation model is implicit in the way the organization makes decisions rather than an explicit model. For example, the organization that holds an index fund is implicitly accepting the simple form of the capital asset pricing model, though it may not explicitly invoke the model every time it makes a decision.[1] The company that buys low price earnings ratio stocks is implicitly

---

[1] An index fund is a portfolio designed to replicate the market portfolio.

stating that only the present price earnings ratios, and not predictions of future growth or risk, affect the return that can be earned on stocks. The advantages of employing an explicit valuation model are tremendous. An explicit model requires the definition of relevant inputs. Furthermore, it assures that these inputs will be systematically collected and used in a consistent manner over time. Finally, the use of a valuation model allows for feedback and control in the functioning of a financial institution. By breaking the process of portfolio analysis into forecasting inputs, valuing securities, and forming portfolios, the ability of the organization to perform in each of these areas can be measured and those areas where the organization has ability can be capitalized upon.

For example, it is possible that an organization has a superior ability to forecast corporate variables but that the informational content of the forecasts is lost either in the valuation process or when securities are formed into portfolios. Only by breaking the process into logical steps can an institution see what it does well and what it does poorly. Only then can it capitalize on any special abilities it does have and improve its performance.[2]

In this chapter we review some of the more widely used approaches to security valuation. We have made no attempt to be exhaustive in the models we have selected. Rather we have attempted to present some typical models with perhaps some bias toward those that we find more appealing. We start this chapter with a review of the general discounted cash flow approach to security valuation.

DISCOUNTED CASH FLOW MODELS

Discounted cash flow models are based on the concept that the value of a share of stock is equal to the present value of the cash flow that the stockholder expects to receive from it.[3] We will argue that this is equivalent to the present value of all future dividends. To facilitate this argument, let us assume that a stockholder intends to hold a share of stock for one period. In this one period the stockholder will receive a dividend and the value of the stock when he or she sells it. If the dividend occurs at the end of the period, then the value of this share of stock should be given by

$$P_t = \frac{D_{t+1}}{(1+k)} + \frac{P_{t+1}}{(1+k)} \tag{18.1}$$

where

$$P_t = \text{the price of a share at time } t$$
$$D_{t+1} = \text{the dividend received at time } t+1$$
$$P_{t+1} = \text{the price at time period } t+1$$
$$k = \text{the appropriate discount rate}$$

To value this share the stockholder must estimate the price at which the stock will sell one period hence. Using the method employed previously,

$$P_{t+1} = \frac{D_{t+2}}{(1+k)} + \frac{P_{t+2}}{(1+k)} \tag{18.2}$$

---

[2]We will have more to say about evaluation and control in Chapters 24 and 25.

[3]There is a long history of discussion in the academic literature about what should be discounted. Some authors argued earnings, some dividends, and others earnings plus non-cash expenses such as depreciation. It turns out that, properly defined, these approaches are equivalent. See Miller and Modigliani [71].

Substituting Equation (18.2) into Equation (18.1),

$$P_t = \frac{D_{t+1}}{(1+k)} + \frac{D_{t+2}}{(1+k)^2} + \frac{P_{t+2}}{(1+k)^2} \tag{18.3}$$

If we, in turn, solved for P_{t+2} and substituted in Equation (18.3), then solved for P_{t+3} and so on, we would find that

$$P_t = \frac{D_{t+1}}{(1+k)} + \frac{D_{t+2}}{(1+k)^2} + \frac{D_{t+3}}{(1+k)^3} + \cdots + \frac{D_{t+n+1}}{(1+k)^{n+1}} + \cdots \tag{18.4}$$

or that the value of share of stock is equal to the present value of all future dividends. Stating the problem in terms of a stream of dividends plus a terminal price as in Equation (18.3) does not avoid the problem of forecasting how the future price will be set. It is not incorrect to state the problem in this way, but it may confuse the real issue that dividends have (at least in theory) to be forecast into the indefinite future.[4]

At this point a question invariably arises: What happened to earnings? The reader instinctively feels that earnings should be worth something, whether they are paid out as dividends or not, and wants to know why they do not appear in the valuation equation. In fact, they do appear in the equation but in the correct form. Earnings can be used for one of two purposes: they can be paid out to stockholders in the form of dividends or they can be reinvested in the firm. If they are reinvested in the firm, they should result in increased future earnings and increased future dividends. To the extent earnings at any time, say, time t, are paid out to stockholders, they are measured by the term D_t, and to the extent they are retained in the firm and used productively they are reflected in future dividends and should result in future dividends being larger than D_t. To discount the future earnings stream of a share of stock would be double counting since we would count retained earnings both when they were earned and when they, or the earnings from their reinvestment, were later paid to stockholders.

It might be worth noting that Equation (18.4), like any of the discounted cash flow (DCF) models discussed in this chapter, can be employed in any of three ways. First, P_t can be treated as the unknown and a value of P_t computed based on estimates of future dividends and the appropriate discount rate. This should be an estimate of the value of the stock, and a market price very different from value should be an indication that price will move in the direction of value.

Second, the present market price can be used for P_t, estimates of future dividends substituted in the equation, and the equation solved for k. The value arrived at for k should be the rate of return the stockholder will earn on the stock.[5] If the value of k arrived at is higher than is warranted by the risk of the stock, then price should adjust upward and rates of return greater than k be earned.[6]

---

[4]In practice, because of the discounting process, dividends that are expected to be received in the very distant future have very little impact on price.

[5]It should be obvious that the appropriate level of k is related to the risk of a stock. One way to determine the appropriate level of k is to employ capital market theory and to determine k from the security market line and an estimate of the firm's risk.

[6]If a stock is incorrectly priced, the rate of return earned may be different from the computed value of k. For example, if the value of k arrived at is higher than that warranted by the risk of the stock, the price of the stock should adjust upward. If this adjustment takes place rapidly, the return earned by buying the stock may be much greater than that implied by the computed value of k.

Finally, this equation can be converted to a price earnings ratio by simply dividing each side by earnings. The left-hand side of the equation would then represent the normal price earnings ratio at which the stock should sell.

To use an infinite dividend stream model in its purest form, it would be necessary to forecast the growth rate in dividends each year from now to infinity, use this infinite series of growth rates to derive a dividend stream, and then discount it back to the present. It is impractical to use the model in its purest form. No individual or institution can differentiate between short-term growth forecasts in the distant future. All users of infinite horizon Discounted Cash Flow (DCF) models make some simplifying assumptions about the pattern that growth will follow over time. A number of different assumptions about growth-rate patterns have been made and embodied in valuation models. We review a few of the more widely used ones here. In particular, we examine three sets of growth assumptions. They are

1. Constant growth over an infinite amount of time.[7]

2. Growth for a finite number of years at a constant rate, then growth at the same rate as a typical firm in the economy from that point on.[8]

3. Growth for a finite number of years at a constant rate, followed by a period during which growth declines to a steady-state level over a second period of years.[9] Growth is then assumed to continue at the steady-state level into the indefinite future.

We can, for obvious reasons, refer to these three models respectively as one-period, two-period, and three-period growth models. It should be equally as obvious that we could have a four-period, five-period, or *N*-period growth model.

As we move down this list of models, we are assuming more complex growth patterns for a company. We may be gaining the potential to more accurately forecast what a company will do, but we are asking the analyst to supply not only more data, but data increasingly difficult to forecast. As the type of data we ask to have forecasted becomes more difficult and the amount of information grows, forecasts are likely to contain less information and more random noise. As models become more complex, a point of diminishing returns is reached. Where this point is cannot be answered in the abstract; it is a function of the forecasting skills of the organization employing the model. Thus, the question can be answered only by examining the forecast ability of the organization that is using, or proposes using, one or more valuation models. Let us now turn to an examination of some of the DCF models mentioned earlier.

Constant Growth Model

One of the best known and certainly the simplest DCF model assumes that dividends will grow at the same rate (g) into the indefinite future. Defining P_0 as today's price, and D_1 as next period's dividend the value of a share of stock is

$$P_0 = \frac{D_1}{(1+k)} + \frac{D_1(1+g)}{(1+k)^2} + \frac{D_1(1+g)^2}{(1+k)^3} + \cdots + \frac{D_1(1+g)^{N-1}}{(1+k)^N} + \cdots$$

---

[7]See Williams [80] or Gordon [45] for discussion of models of this type.

[8]See Malkiel [67] for the presentation of a model of this type.

[9]See Molodovsky, May, and Chottinger [72] for the presentation of a model of this type.

Using the formula for the sum of a geometric progression,[10]

$$P_0 = \frac{D_1}{k - g} \tag{18.5}$$

This model states that the price of a share of stock should be equal to next year's expected dividend divided by the difference between the appropriate discount rate for the stock and its expected long-term growth rate. Alternatively, this model can be stated in terms of the rate of return on a stock as

$$k = D_1/P_0 + g \tag{18.6}$$

The constant growth model is often defended as the model that arises from the following assumptions: The firm will maintain a stable dividend policy (keep its retention rate constant) and earn a stable return on new equity investment over time. If we let b stand for the fraction of earnings retained within the firm, r stand for the rate of return the firm will earn on all new investments, and I_t stand for investment at t, we get a very simple expression for growth. The formula requires an estimate of the growth in dividends over time. We can derive an expression for the growth in dividends by first examining the growth in earnings. Growth in earnings arises from the return on new investments. We can write earnings at any moment as

$$E_t = E_{t-1} + rI_{t-1}$$

If the firm's retention rate is constant, then

$$E_t = E_{t-1} + rbE_{t-1} = E_{t-1}(1 + rb)$$

Growth in earnings is the percentage change in earnings, or

$$g = \frac{E_t - E_{t-1}}{E_{t-1}} = \frac{E_{t-1}(1 + rb) - E_{t-1}}{E_{t-1}} = rb$$

Since a constant proportion of earnings is assumed to be paid out each year, the growth in earnings equals the growth in dividends, or

$$g_E = g_D = rb$$

---

[10]The sum of a geometric progression is given by Sum = First term $[1 - (\text{common ratio})^N]/(1 - \text{common ratio})$, where N is the number of terms over which we are summing. For this model we have

$$P_0 = \frac{\dfrac{D_1}{1+k}\left[1 - \left(\dfrac{1+g}{1+k}\right)^N\right]}{1 - \dfrac{1+g}{1+k}}$$

As N goes to infinity and

$$\left(\frac{1+g}{1+k}\right)^N$$

goes to zero, we obtain the formula in the text.

Using this expression for growth, we can rewrite Equations (18.5) and (18.6) as[11]

$$P_0 = \frac{D_1}{k - rb} \qquad k = \frac{D_1}{P_0} + rb \qquad (18.5a)$$

It is worthwhile examining the implications of this model for the growth in stock prices over time. The growth in stock price is

$$g_P = \frac{P_{t+1} - P_t}{P_t}$$

Recognizing that P_t can be defined by Equation (18.5b) and that $P_t + 1$ is also given by Equation (18.5a) except that D_1 must be replaced by $D_1(1 + br)$, we find

$$g_P = br$$

Thus, under the one-period model dividends, earnings and prices are all expected to grow at the same rate. It might be worthwhile to point out the key role expectations about the future profitability of investment opportunities play in this model. The rate of return on new investments can be expressed as a fraction (perhaps larger than one) of the rate of return security holders require,

$$r = ck$$

Substituting this in Equation (18.5b) noting that $D_1 = (1 - b)E_1$ and rearranging yields

$$k = \frac{(1 - b)E_1}{(1 - cb)P_0}$$

Notice that if the firm has no extraordinary investment opportunities ($r = k$), then $c = 1$ and the rate of return that security holders require is simply the inverse of the stock's price earnings ratio. On the other hand, if the firm has investment opportunities that are expected to offer a return above that required by the firm's stockholders ($c > 1$), the earnings price ratio at which the firm sells will be below the rate of return required by investors.[12]

Let us spend a moment examining how the single-period model might be used to select stocks. One way is to predict next year's dividends, the firm's long-term growth rate, and the rate of return stockholders require for holding the stock. Equation (18.5) could then be solved for the theoretical price of the stock that could be compared with its present price. Stocks that have theoretical prices above their actual prices are candidates for purchase; those with theoretical prices below their actual price are candidates for sale. The same procedure could be followed using the equation in footnote 11 with respect to price earnings ratios.

Another way to use the DCF approach is to find the rate of return implicit in the price at which the stock is now selling. This can be done by substituting the current price,

---

[11]Analysts frequently like to work in terms of price earnings multiples. Since $D_1 = (1 - b)E_1$, if we divide both sides of Equation (18.5b) by earnings, we have

$$\frac{P_0}{E_1} = \frac{1 - b}{k - br}$$

[12]For a detailed analysis of the role that investment opportunities play in the valuation of securities, see Elton and Gruber [32].

estimated dividend, and estimated growth rate into Equation (18.6) and solving for the discount rate that equates the present price with the expected flow of future dividends. If this rate is higher than the rate of return considered appropriate for the stock, given its risk, it is a candidate for purchase.

We illustrate the use of the single-period model with a simple example. In the past, xyz's stock was selling for $65 a share. At that time xyz's earnings were $3.99 per share and it paid a $2.00 dividend. At that time a major brokerage firm was estimating xyz's long-term growth rate at 12% and its dividend payout rate at 50%. If we assume 13% is an appropriate discount rate of xyz, we would compute a theoretical price of

$$P_0 = \frac{2.00}{0.13 - 0.12} = \$200$$

While xyz's stock would seem to be undervalued selling at $65 a share, notice the sensitivity of this valuation equation to both the estimate of the appropriate discount rate and the estimate of the long-term growth rate. For example, if xyz's growth rate was estimated to be 9% rather than 12%, its theoretical price would be one-fourth as large or $50.

The single-period model has the advantage of being the simplest of all the models we will examine. Furthermore, multiperiod growth models assume that after a number of years the firm grows at a constant rate forever. The one-period model derived in this section is used to determine firm value at the beginning of this constant growth period. Thus this simple model is used as a part of all subsequent models.

It seems logical to assume that firms that have grown at a very high rate will not continue to do so into the infinite future. Similarly, firms with very poor growth might improve in the future. While a single growth rate can be found that will produce the same value as a more complex pattern, it is so hard to estimate this single number, and the resultant valuation is so sensitive to this number, that many investment firms have been reluctant to use the single-period growth model. As a result, they have turned to two- and three-period growth models.

The Two-Period Growth Model

The simplest extension of the one-period model is to assume that a period of extraordinary growth (good or bad) will continue for a certain number of years, after which growth will change to a level at which it is expected to continue indefinitely.

The assumption that growth is constant after some point in time follows from the following line of reasoning. After some point in time (5 years, 10 years, 15 years) the analyst has no ability to differentiate between firms on the basis of growth. Many current high-growth firms will no longer have high growth and many firms that are currently viewed as stodgy will be the dynamic high-growth firms of the future. Thus after some years it is sensible to not differentiate between firms but simply to assume they all grow at the same rate. At this point the constant growth model is used.

Let us assume that the length of the first period is N years, that the growth rate in the first period is g_1, and that P_N is the price at the end of period N. We can write the value of the firm as[13]

$$P_0 = \left[\frac{D_1}{1+k} + \frac{D_1(1+g_1)}{(1+k)^2} + \frac{D_1(1+g_1)^2}{(1+k)^3} + \cdots + \frac{D_1(1+g_1)^{N-1}}{(1+k)^N} \right] + \frac{P_N}{(1+k)^N}$$

---

[13]Many authors write the first term's dividend as $D_0(1 + g_1)$. In this case. the dividend is the current dividend rather than next period's dividend.

This can, of course, be simplified using the formula for the sum of a geometric progression. The result is

$$P_0 = D_1 \left[\frac{1 - \left(\dfrac{1+g_1}{1+k} \right)^N}{k - g_1} \right] + \frac{P_N}{(1+k)^N}$$

In the two-period model we are assuming that after N periods the firm exhibits a constant infinite growth. Thus, the model developed in the earlier section describes P_N. If g_2 is the growth in the second period and D_{N+1} is the dividend in the $N+1$ period, we have

$$P_N = \frac{D_{N+1}}{k - g_2}$$

The dividend in the $N+1$ period can be expressed in terms of the dividend in the first period

$$D_{N+1} = D_1 (1 + g_1)^{N-1} (1 + g_2)$$

With these substitutions we have

$$P_0 = D_1 \left[\frac{1 - \left(\dfrac{1+g_1}{1+k} \right)^N}{k - g_1} \right] + \left[\frac{D_1 (1 + g_1)^{N-1} (1 + g_2)}{(k - g_2)} \right] \left[\frac{1}{(1+k)^N} \right]$$

This formula can easily be solved for the theoretical price of any stock. However, the two-period model is often used in a slightly different form.

In one form of this model in year N the stock is assumed to change its characteristics so that it resembles the average stock in the economy. After year N the stock is expected to grow at the same rate, have the same dividend policy, and be subject to the same risk as the average stock in the economy. In this case the *P/E* ratio at which it sells in year N must be the same as the average *P/E* ratio for the economy. Let us define this as M_g.[14] The price in year N can be then defined as the expected earnings in year N times the appropriate *P/E* ratio or

$$P_N = \frac{P_N}{E_N} (E_N) = M_g E_N$$

If earnings grow at the same rate as dividends, then earnings in year N are next period's earnings E times $(1 + g_1)^{N-1}$ and price can be expressed as

$$P_0 = D_1 \left[\frac{1 - \left(\dfrac{1+g_1}{1+k} \right)^N}{k - g_1} \right] + \left[M_g E (1 + g_1)^{N-1} \right] \left[\frac{1}{(1+k)^N} \right]$$

Some rearrangement of the first term yields an expression that is more convenient to calculate.

---

[14]See Malkiel [67] for a formal derivation of this model.

$$P_0 = \frac{D_1}{k-g_1}\left[\frac{(1+k)^N - (1+g_1)^N}{(1+k)^N}\right] + M_g E(1+g_1)^{N-1}\left[\frac{1}{(1+k)^N}\right]$$

Notice that while we started with the value of a share of stock being equal to the present value of all future dividends, we could state the valuation in terms of the present value of a stream of dividends and terminal N year earnings plus a terminal P/E ratio. While this has no mathematical advantages over the sum of an infinite stream of dividends, it does have the advantage of being expressed in terms with which the security analyst feels more at home.

Like the constant growth model, this type of model can be used to arrive at a theoretical price that can then be compared with actual price, or alternatively the rate of return implicit in the present price can be solved for. To illustrate the first of these calculations, let us return to our xyz example. Let us assume that the analyst expects xyz's 12% growth rate to continue for 15 years, after which the analyst expects xyz to become an average company. Furthermore, assume that after 16 years the P/E ratio for the market is expected to be 9.5. Then the theoretical value of xyz's stock would be[15]

$$P = \frac{2.00}{0.13-0.12}\left[\frac{(1.13)^{15} - (1.12)^{15}}{(1.13)^{15}}\right] + \frac{(9.5)(3.99)(1.12)^{14}}{(1.13)^{15}} = \$54.59$$

With a constant growth model, earnings, prices, and dividends all grow at the same rate. With two-period and three-period models this is no longer true. With the model just described dividends and earnings had two distinct growth rates. In the first period dividends and earnings grow at g_1 and in the second period they grow at g_2. Price grows at neither. If g_1 is greater than g_2, then price grows initially at a rate above g_2 but below g_1 and declines to g_2. The longer the time of growth the closer the original growth in price is to g_1.

As with all valuation models the discount rate is the expected return on the stock if the price of the stock over time conforms to the valuation model. Table 18.1 illustrates these ideas for the XYZ example discussed earlier.

This table was constructed as follows. First the price each year was computed by recalculating the price formula presented previously but by successively shortening the number of years for which extraordinary growth was expected to continue. For example, the entry for price opposite year 10 was found as follows[16]:

$$P_{10} = \left[\frac{2.00(1.12)^{10}}{(1.13)^1} + \frac{2.00(1.12)^{11}}{(1.13)^2} + \frac{2.00(1.12)^{12}}{(1.13)^3}\right.$$

$$\left. + \frac{2.00(1.12)^{13}}{(1.13)^4} + \frac{2.00(1.12)^{14}}{(1.13)^5}\right] + \frac{9.5(3.99)(1.12)^{14}}{(1.13)^5}$$

$$P_{10} = [26.99] + 185.25(0.5427) = 127.55$$

---

[15]In the example we assume that both the $2.00 dividend and the $3.99 earnings will arise one period after the time of the valuation.

[16]This equation can also be written using the form shown immediately above in the text as

$$P_0 = \frac{2.00(1.12)^{10}}{(0.13-0.12)}\left[\frac{(1.13)^5 - (1.12)^5}{(1.13)^5}\right] + \frac{9.5(3.99)(1.12)^{14}}{(1.13)^5}$$

Table 18.1   Price and Dividend Behavior under a Two-Period Growth Model

	Price		Dollar Return		Percent Return		
	At Beginning of Period 1	At End after Dividend Is Paid 2	Dividend at End of Period 3	Capital Gain 4	Dividend Yield 5	Price Appreciation 6	Total Return 7
0	54.58	59.68	2.00	5.10	3.66	9.34	13.00
1	59.68	65.20	2.24	5.52	3.75	9.25	13.00
2	65.20	71.17	2.51	5.97	3.85	9.16	13.01
3	71.17	77.61	2.81	6.44	3.95	9.05	13.00
4	77.61	84.55	3.15	6.94	4.06	8.94	13.00
5	84.55	92.02	3.52	7.47	4.16	8.84	13.00
6	92.02	100.03	3.95	8.01	4.29	8.70	12.99
7	100.03	108.61	4.42	8.58	4.42	8.58	13.00
8	108.61	117.78	4.95	9.17	4.56	8.44	13.00
9	117.78	127.55	5.55	9.77	4.71	8.30	13.01
10	127.55	137.92	6.21	10.37	4.87	8.13	13.00
11	137.92	148.89	6.97	10.97	5.05	7.95	13.00
12	148.89	160.45	7.79	11.56	5.23	7.76	12.99
13	160.45	172.58	8.77	12.13	5.47	7.50	12.97
14	172.58	185.25	9.77	12.67	5.66	7.34	13.00
15	185.25						

The expected dividend in year 11 was found by assuming the present dividend (2.00) would continue to grow at the 12% rate, giving it a value of $2.00 \times (1.12)^{10}$. Dividends from year 11 through year 15 are expected to grow each year at the 12% rate and each dividend must be discounted back to year 10. The term in the large brackets is the value as of year 10 of the dividend received from year 11 to year 15. The last term is simply the price as of year 15 discounted back to year 10.

By successively employing this formula we can arrive at the prices shown in columns 1 and 2 of Table 18.1. Dividends (column 3) are computed by applying the growth rate of 12% to the initial dividend. Once prices and dividends are computed it is a simple matter to compute the percentage return from dividends and capital gains shown in columns 5 and 6. Adding the dividend return to the return from price appreciation we get the total return shown in column 7.

There are a few concepts that are made explicit by this example. First, note that the investor will get the 13% discount rate implied by our assumption even though the contribution of capital gains and dividends to this return changes drastically over time. As the period of high growth draws to an end, more of the contribution comes from dividends and less from capital gains. In fact, if we examine growth in price for a moment, we can see an interesting pattern. We know that once steady state occurs, the single-period growth model is appropriate, and earnings, dividends, and price will grow at the same rate. For our example this rate can be found from

$$P_0 = \frac{D_1}{k - g_2}$$

where the price at the beginning of year 15 is $185.25, $k = 0.13$, and the dividend is $2.00 $\times (1.12)^{14} (1 + g_2)$. Solving for g_2 produces a value of 7.34%. Reexamining column 6 with this number in mind shows that prices start growing at a rate in between the short- and long-run growth rates. The growth in price declines each period until the period of extraordinary growth is over and the growth in price equals the long-term growth rate in earnings and dividends.

Although we have chosen to present this model to solve for a theoretical price the model could just as easily be used in a second way. The analysts would estimate all of the variables that enter the model except the discount rate. The price used in the formula would be the current price. The formula can then be used to estimate the expected return.

An abrupt change from one growth rate to another for most stocks is probably not descriptive of reality. The three-period growth models discussed in the next section deal directly with this issue. Before discussing this model, however, a variation of the two-period growth model will be presented. It is perfectly feasible to allow the analyst to make specific forecasts of dividends for each year prior to the time that a steady-state growth rate is reached. This is a more detailed version of the model under discussion, for we don't impose a uniform growth rate for the first period. For illustration, assume that the analyst is willing to make forecasts for five years, but after that does not wish to differentiate among firms.

Define D_t as the dividend at period t. If the constant growth model is used to value the firm from period 5 onward, then the price of a firm at zero is

$$P_0 = \frac{D_1}{(1+k)} + \frac{D_2}{(1+k)^2} + \frac{D_3}{(1+k)^3} + \frac{D_4}{(1+k)^4} + \frac{\frac{D_5}{k-g_2}}{(1+k)^4}$$

where g_2 is the growth rate after five years.

The analyst would explicitly forecast the first five dividends and then utilize long-term averages for the market to estimate g_2. Because most analysts view earnings as the fundamental valuable being forecast, dividends would likely be forecast by forecast earnings and payout ratios. Explicitly forecasting dividends until a period of steady growth allows a gradual change in growth rate. An alternative way to allow a gradual change in growth is to use a three-period model.

The Three-Period Model

The usual two-period model assumes that during the initial period, earnings would continue to grow at some constant rate. At year N the second period started and growth was assumed to drop instantly to some steady-state value. Normally, the change to a new long-term growth rate would not occur instantly; rather, it would occur over a period of time. Thus, a logical extension is to assume a third period. The resultant model would assume that in period one growth is expected to be constant at some level. The analyst must forecast both the level of growth and the duration of period one. During period two the growth changes from its value in period one to a long-run-steady-state level. The analyst must forecast both the duration of period two and the pattern of change in growth. Although some firms (e.g., Wells Fargo) allow the analyst to select from among a predetermined set of patterns, most firms employ one pattern (usually linear) for all firms. The third and final period is the period of steady-state growth. Many organizations assume that once a firm reaches steady-state growth, it will have the same characteristics as the average firm in the economy. When this happens, the contribution of the third period to value can be found in a manner directly analogous to the formulation of the second period in the two-period model. Other users of the three-period model have assumed zero growth in the third period, whereas still others allow the analyst to forecast whatever growth is deemed appropriate.

Figure 18.1 shows the growth rate in dividends for a typical three-period model. For the first four years the firm is assumed to grow at a rate of 10%. After year 4 the growth rate of dividends is assumed to decline linearly to 6%. After year 7, the firm is assumed to grow at a rate of 6% forever. If we continue to assume a discount rate of 13%, the next dividend is $2 and that the next dividend payment is one year; hence, the value of the firm would be

$$
\text{Value} = \left[\frac{2}{(1.13)^1} + \frac{2(1.1)^1}{(1.13)^2} + \frac{2(1.1)^2}{(1.13)^3} + \frac{2(1.1)^3}{(1.13)^4} \right]
$$

$$
+ \left[\frac{2(1.1)^3(1.09)}{(1.13)^5} + \frac{2(1.1)^3(1.09)(1.08)}{(1.13)^6} + \frac{2(1.1)^3(1.09)(1.08)(1.07)}{(1.13)^7} \right]
$$

$$
+ \left[\frac{2(1.1)^3(1.09)(1.08)(1.07)(1.06)}{(0.13-0.06)} \right] \frac{1}{(1.13)^7}
$$

The first two terms in brackets are the present value of the dividends received in the first and second growth period, respectively.

The last term in brackets is the value as of year 7 of this firm. This is simply an application of the constant growth model developed earlier. The numerator is the dividend as of year 8, one year from the valuation date. The denominator is the difference between the discount rate and the long-term constant growth rate of $(k - g)$. To calculate the impact of the value of the firm in year 7 on the firm today, simply discount the value back to the present by multiplying it by

$$
\left[\frac{1}{1.13} \right]^7
$$

In the preceding expression we chose to solve for the value of the stock. This value could then be compared with actual price to see if the stock should be purchased. An alternative way to employ this model is to set the right-hand side of the preceding equation equal to actual price, but to leave the discount rate unspecified. The equation could then be solved for the discount rate implied by the analyst's expectation and the present price. This rate can be viewed as the analyst's estimate of expected return. The stock would be

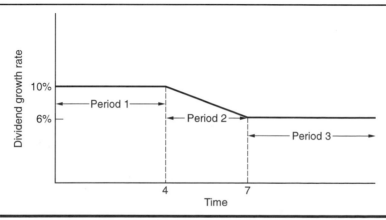

Figure 18.1   Growth-rate pattern for a three-period model.

purchased or sold depending on the relationship between the analyst's estimate of expected return and what the firm considers a fair return for the stock given its risk.

As we move from a constant growth model to a two-period growth model to a three-period growth model, and perhaps even beyond this, we have increased the number and the complexity of the inputs the analyst must provide. If growth patterns are overly simplified, insufficient information will be provided by the forecasts. If they are made too complex, the forecasts are likely to be inaccurate. This trade-off is most apparent in the two extreme models discussed earlier. Analysts cannot develop year-by-year growth estimates into the indefinite future. At the other extreme, asking the analysts to provide only a single average growth forecast means losing the chance for the analyst to provide information about the future pattern of the company's growth. The trade-off between complexity and manageability will have to be made on the basis of the forecasting skills of an organization. No matter how this is decided, one of the principal benefits of using a valuation model can be the preparation of a comparable and explicit set of forecasts over time. Only if forecasts are made explicit can an organization evaluate and improve its performance over time.

Before leaving DCF models, it is worth noting another type of DCF model that is sometimes used by security analysts.

Finite Horizon Models

We have just seen that a model based on discounting a finite stream of dividends and a terminal price can be consistent with discounting an infinite stream of dividends. In this case, the finite nature of the model arose from consideration of future growth. Let us now look at a finite horizon model that arises from the way many organizations work, rather than from discounting an infinite stream of dividends.

Many organizations make short-run earnings forecasts for stocks (one- and two-year forecasts) and intermediate (five-year) growth forecasts. Analysts frequently predict future prices on *P/E* ratios rather than patterns of growth into the indefinite future. These forecasts can be incorporated into a valuation model by discounting expected dividends for the five years and the terminal price (the product of the expected *P/E* ratio and expected earnings based on the forecasted growth rate). Keep in mind that the five-year horizon used in this approach is not a function of the economics of the firm, the period over which a steady growth is expected to continue; rather, it arises from the forecasting pattern of the organization analyzing the stock. While the model is mathematically equivalent to that discussed in the previous section, the rationale for the model is entirely different. Five years may not be an appropriate time horizon for the firm under study.

The major factor that separates this model from those we have previously discussed is the selection of a terminal *P/E* ratio without a specification of the economic rationale or assumptions behind either that *P/E* ratio or the five-year horizon. If the terminal *P/E* ratio is determined by assumptions about the future growth of the company, then the model reduces to one of those already discussed. If the terminal *P/E* ratio is simply asserted by the analyst, based on experience or sense of the market, the analyst has implicitly made an assumption about the future growth pattern for the company. Assumptions about future growth cannot be avoided. If they are not made explicitly, they will be made implicitly by the selection of a terminal *P/E* ratio.

It would seem preferable to make growth assumptions explicitly, rather than implicitly. If the analyst is going to use this type of model, he or she should at least explore the future growth rate implicit in the use of a terminal *P/E* ratio.

In fact, perhaps the most interesting aspect of this type of model is that it makes explicit the market expectations of future *P/E* ratios necessary to justify the price of a stock. That is, it can be used to answer the following question: Given my estimate of both growth rates and the appropriate discount rate, what *P/E* ratio five years in the future justifies the present price? Returning to our IBM example, we find that a *P/E* ratio of 16.50 would be necessary five years from now to justify the price of the stock today.[17]

The analyst could proceed to use one of the other growth models to discover the growth rate implicit in the expected future *P/E* ratio of 16.5. For example, using the constant growth rate assumption, we find that the implicit growth rate is close to 13% from year 5 into the indefinite future.

CROSS-SECTIONAL REGRESSION ANALYSIS

While DCF models are enjoying a rapidly increased popularity in the investment community, they have been adopted by only a small fraction of the practicing security analysts.[18] The majority of security analysts still values common stocks by applying some sort of earnings multiple (price earnings ratio) to either present earnings, normalized earnings, or forecasted earnings. Approaches to the establishment of the *P/E* ratio cover a vast range. Some firms use the historical *P/E* ratios for companies or the historical *P/E* ratio for a company relative to the market *P/E* ratio. Another approach, and one popular in many of the standard texts of security analysis, is to list and discuss large numbers of factors that should affect *P/E* ratios but leave the weighting and often the explicit definition of these factors up to the security analyst.[19] Still another approach is to take the broad determinants of common stock prices, earnings, growth, risk, time value of money, and dividend policy and to measure these and weight them together in some manner to form an estimate of the *P/E* ratio. This section reviews one way to do this. We discuss the use of cross-sectional regression analysis to define the weights the market places on a set of hypothesized determinants of common stock prices. Attempts to use this technique to measure the influence of potential determinants of common stock prices were very popular in the 1960s, and there is an indication that interest in them has recently revived.

The relationship that exists in the market at any point in time between price or price earnings ratios and a set of specified variables can be estimated using regression analysis. This is the same tool that was used to determine Betas in Chapter 5. Figure 18.2 presents the relationship between *P/E* ratios and forecasted growth for a sample of stocks as of the end of 1971. Each point in the diagram represents the *P/E* ratio and forecasted growth rate for a company as of the end of 1971. The straight line is fitted via regression analysis and its equation is given by[20]

$$\text{Price/Earnings} = 4 + 2.3 \text{ (growth rate in earnings)}$$

The usual technique of relating price or price earnings ratios to more than one variable is directly analogous to this. Called multiple regression analysis, it finds that linear combination of a set of variables that best explains price earnings ratios.

---

[17]This comes from an assumption of a constant payout ratio. The solution is

$$\$65 = P_0 = \frac{2.00}{1.13} + \frac{2(1.12)}{(1.13)^2} + \frac{2(1.12)^2}{(1.13)^3} + \frac{2(1.12)^3}{(1.13)^4} + \frac{2(1.12)^4}{(1.13)^5} + \left(\frac{P}{E}\right)(3.99)\frac{(1.12)^4}{(1.13)^5}$$

[18]For one survey in this area, see Bing [12].

[19]Graham, Dodd, and Cottle [46], perhaps the best-known book on security analysis, takes this approach.

[20]This example comes from Cohen, Zinbarg, and Zeikel [25], p. 244.

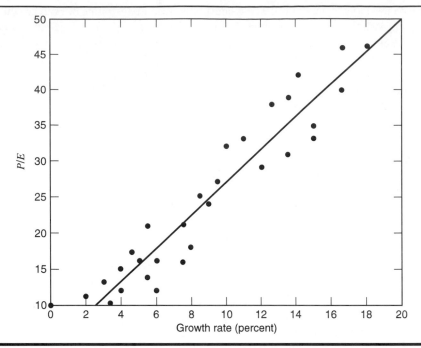

Figure 18.2   *P/E* ratios versus growth rates.

One of the earliest attempts to use multiple regression to explain price earnings ratios, which received wide attention, was the Whitbeck–Kisor model [79]. We indicated earlier that the price of a share of stock was related to earnings, dividend policy, growth, and risk. We could have said, equally well, that the price earnings ratio of a stock was related to dividend policy, growth, and risk. It was exactly this relationship that Whitbeck and Kisor set out to measure. In particular, they obtained estimates of earnings growth rates, dividend payouts, and the variation (standard deviation) of growth rates from a group of security analysts. Then, using multiple regression analysis to define the average relationship between each of these variables and price earnings ratios, they found (as of June 8, 1962) that

Price earnings ratio = 8.2

+ 1.50 (earnings growth rate)

+ 0.067 (dividend payout rate)

− 0.200 (standard deviation in growth rate)

This equation represents the estimate at a *point in time* of the simultaneous impact of the three variables on the price earnings ratio. The numbers represent the weight that the market placed on each variable at that point in time. The signs represent the direction of the impact of each variable on the price earnings ratio. We might take some comfort from the fact that the signs are consistent with what theory and common sense would lead us to expect: the higher growth, the higher the dividends (growth held constant), and the lower risk, the higher the price earnings ratio. The equations tell us that on average a 1% increase in earnings growth is associated with a 1.5-unit increase in the price earnings ratio, a 1%

increase in the dividend payout ratio is associated with a 0.067-unit increase in the price earnings ratio, and a 1% increase in the standard deviation of growth is associated with a 0.2-unit decrease in the *P/E* ratio.

An equation such as this can be used to arrive at the theoretical *P/E* ratio for any stock. Simply by substituting the forecasted earnings growth rate, dividend payout ratio, and risk for the stock on the right-hand side of the equation, one arrives at a theoretical *P/E* ratio. We can illustrate this with the IBM example used previously.[21] When IBM's price was $65, IBM's growth was forecast at 12%, its dividend payout ratio was 50%, and its standard deviation in growth rate was about 5. Substituting these numbers in the expression for price earnings ratios presented earlier, we get a theoretical *P/E* ratio of 28.55. Many researchers have taken what seems like a small step from here and advocated buying stocks with theoretical price earnings ratios above their actual price earnings ratios, and selling short stocks with theoretical prices below their market price earnings ratio.

Literally hundreds of models like the Whitbeck–Kisor model have appeared in print since the 1960s.

Every conceivable variable and combination of variables has been tried.[22] The common element of almost all of these models is that they are highly successful in explaining stock prices at a point in time. but they are much less successful in selecting the appropriate stocks to buy or sell short. It is not uncommon for these models to explain more than 80% of the difference in stock prices at a point in time. This gives us confidence that the models can be helpful in finding the variables and set of weights that determine price at a point in time. Why, then, haven't they been more successful in picking winners? The theory behind their use in finding under- and overvalued securities is that the market price will converge to the theoretical price before the theoretical price itself changes. There are at least three reasons why this might, in fact, not happen[23]:

1. Market tastes change. With changes in market tastes, the weight on each variable changes over time.

2. The values of the inputs, such as dividends and growth in earnings, change over time.

3. There are firm effects not captured by the model.

We discuss each of these in turn.

Market Tastes

One reason that price might not converge to theoretical price before theoretical price itself changes is that the parameters that determine theoretical price might change. Tastes, or the importance of certain variables in the market, change over time, and these changes are often rapid and drastic.

---

[21]The reader should be warned that this example is intended solely to illustrate the use of the model. The parameters of the model were estimated in 1962, and we are using 1976 data. The parameters of the model should not be expected to be stable over this period of time. We have more to say later about the stability of the parameters of regression models.

[22]Some of the more interesting models are Bower and Bower [17], Gordon [45], Gruber [48], and Malkiel and Cragg [69].

[23]A fourth reason should be briefly mentioned. The values in the equations are only estimates. Many researchers have tried large numbers of alternative definitions of variables or alternative variables in search of a "good" fit. Often what they are finding is spurious correlation (the variables happened to move together over the period). In this case there is no reason to believe the model will help select securities.

Let us return to the relationship between *P/E* ratios and growth examined earlier. The relationship found at the end of 1971 in a period of a bull market was

$$\text{Price earnings ratio} = 4 + 2.3 \text{ growth}$$

When the relationship was measured as of 1970 in a bear market using the same firms, it was

$$\text{Price earnings ratio} = 3 + 1.8 \text{ growth}$$

Notice that the importance of growth was higher in the bull market than it was in the bear market. For a stock with an expected growth rate of 20% per year, the estimated multiple rose from 39 in 1970 to 50 in 1971 or by more than 25%. The result is not surprising; it indicates the large magnitude of shift in market tastes that occurs over time. A similar shift with respect to a fuller set of determinants of common stock prices was reported by Gruber [48]. He examined the weight the market placed on dividends, growth, and three risk variables (earnings instability, financial leverage, and size) in each of 13 consecutive years. He found that the weights shifted drastically from year to year and were different at a statistically significant level.[24] Furthermore, the weights moved in a reasonable pattern, with growth becoming more important as the market moved up, and dividends less important. The opposite phenomenon occurred during downturns in the market. The shifts in the importance of the variables were more dramatic in those years when the market changed direction.

Input Data

Even if the market preference for variables remained stable over time, the theoretical value for a stock would change because the estimates of the variables like growth and dividends change. Input data are arrived at either by historical extrapolation or by the use of analysts' expectations. In any case, both the value of the inputs (earnings, growth, etc.) and expectations about these variables can and do change drastically over time. Every change in one of these variables—for example, expected growth—changes the theoretical value for a stock.

Firm Effects

Even when a model is constructed that explains a high fraction of the difference in stock prices, there are firms that have actual prices that lie above (or below) their theoretical prices and continue to do so period after period. Economists usually refer to this as firm effects. They are probably due to persistent influences that are not captured by the variables in the mode.[25] For example, in the early 1960s, tobacco stocks always had theoretical prices above their actual prices. This may well have been because theoretical prices did not take into consideration the threat of government intervention, while actual prices did.

Although cross-sectional regression models have been successfully used to examine the major determinants of common stock prices and the weight the market places on these determinants, the results from their use as a stock-selection tool have been mixed. Some authors, for example, Whitbeck and Kisor [79], have reported an ability to outperform random selection; others, for example, Bower and Bower [16] and Malkiel and Cragg [69],

---

[24]This means that it is inappropriate to pool cross-sectional samples in an attempt to define average weights.

[25]See Bower and Bower [16] for a discussion of firm effects.

have reported the failure of their models to lead to superior selection. The differences may be caused by the test periods used, the sample selected, or the authors' access to a better, or inferior, set of forecasts.

There is no doubt that cross-sectional regression models are helpful in understanding what has happened in the market over time. In addition, they may prove of some use in selecting stocks. However, the evidence at this time is not conclusive. It is clear that their usefulness is very dependent on the forecasting ability of the institution utilizing the model.

AN ONGOING SYSTEM

In this chapter we have considered several techniques for valuing common stock. The one with the strongest theoretical base involves the discounting of future dividends where the discount rate is appropriately formulated in terms of risk. In recent years several firms have attempted to implement stock valuation and selection systems that incorporate the DCF approach to stock selection and modern capital market theory. Perhaps the best known is the Wells Fargo stock evaluation system.

The first step in the Wells Fargo analysis is to estimate the rate of return implicit in the price at which a stock is selling. They do this by finding the discount rate that equates the present value of all future dividends with price. The growth model they use to predict dividends is similar to the three-period model discussed earlier in the chapter.

In the Wells Fargo system the analyst is required to estimate

1. Dividends (and earnings per share) for each of the next five years.
2. The fifth-year normalized earnings per share, growth rate, and payout.
3. An eventual steady-state payout and growth rate [the assumption here is that after a large number of years (larger than the five mentioned earlier), there will be a growth rate and payout rate that adequately describes the future behavior of the firm].
4. The number of years that are expected to elapse before the steady-state condition is reached.
5. The pattern of growth expected between the fifth year and the time that steady-state growth is expected to begin. The analyst is free to select one from among several typical patterns that are presented to him.

This gives an expected flow of dividends from the time of the analysis to infinity. This is used to find the expected rate of return, that is, the rate that equates expected dividends with present price.

In addition to dividend flows, the analyst provides estimates of the risk (Beta) of each security. The analyst is given a measure of Beta developed using historical data and is allowed to modify these estimates according to his analysis of the fundamental characteristics of the firm.

This results in an expected return and an expected Beta for each stock. Now the expected return and expected Beta for each of the companies in Wells Fargo's sample are plotted and the straight line that fits these points is used as an estimated security market line.[26] Note that the Wells Fargo security market line is an expectational construct. Most security market lines (see Chapter 15) have been estimated on historical data (realizations)

---

[26]Actually, Wells Fargo divides stocks into risk groups by Beta range and examines the return on a stock against the average Beta for its group.

rather than expectations. The Wells Fargo security market line is a representation of a set of expectations. It represents the relationship between expected return and expected Betas.

If stock has a return (given its Beta) above the security market line, it should offer a superior risk-adjusted return; if below, an inferior risk-adjusted return.

Perhaps an alternative explanation of this methodology might help. Analysts, by forecasting dividends, provide an estimate of the return expected from each stock. To understand whether this return is sufficient to compensate for risk, we need to know what the risk of the security is and average expected rate of return the market requires for bearing that risk. The analyst estimates the risk (Beta) on the stock. The average relationship between expected return and expected risk (the security market line) is found by looking at all stocks that analysts follow. If the stock offers a return above the return that should be warranted, given its risk (from the security market line), the stock should be a good buy. If it has a lower return, it should not be a good buy.

Let's consider a specific example. Table 18.2 shows a set of hypothetical data for a firm. It is divided into three periods. In the first period the analyst provides explicit forecasts of earnings and payout ratios for each year. The entries under the column dividends are then calculated by multiplying the first two columns. For the second period (the transitional period) the analyst forecasts the payout ratio (60%) the length of the period (three years), the long-term growth rate (6%), and the pattern of change in growth from the first period to the third period (linear). The growth rate in the first period averaged 10%. Given the analyst's forecasts, a growth rate of 9%, 8%, and 7% would be calculated for the three transitional years. The earnings in the last period are the earnings in period 8 compounded by the long-term growth rate of 6%. Finally the stock price was assumed to be $77.40. Thus the expected return is found by

$$\$77.40 = \frac{1.60}{(1+k)^1} + \frac{2.03}{(1+k)^2} + \frac{2.50}{(1+k)^3} + \frac{3.16}{(1+k)^4} + \frac{3.90}{(1+k)^5}$$

$$+ \frac{4.25}{(1+k)^6} + \frac{4.59}{(1+k)^7} + \frac{4.91}{(1+k)^8} + \left[\frac{5.21}{k-0.06}\right]^6 \frac{1}{(1+k)^8}$$

$$k = 0.10$$

Note that the first eight terms are the dividends shown in Table 18.2 discounted back to time zero. The last term has two parts, one in square brackets and the discount factor. The term in square brackets is the value of the firm as of period 8 using the constant growth

Table 18.2   Forecasts for Company 1

Period	Year	Earnings	Payout Ratio	Dividends
First	1	4.00	40%	1.60
	2	4.50	45%	2.03
	3	5.00	50%	2.50
	4	5.75	55%	3.16
	5	6.50	60%	3.90
Transitional	6	6.50(1.09)	60%	4.25
	7	6.50(1.09)(1.08)	60%	4.59
	8	6.50(1.09)(1.08)(1.07)	60%	4.91
Final	9^a	8.68	60%	5.21

[a]Earnings are 6.50(1.09) (1.08) (1.07) (1.06) = 8.68.

model. Recall that the constant growth model is $D/k - g$. The D in the expression is the dividend one period later than the time of valuation. For determining the value at period 8, the relevant dividend is the one paid at 9, whereas g is, of course, the 6% long-term growth rate. The value determined using the constant growth model is the value of the firm as of period 8. This value is discounted back eight periods to find the current value.

To decide if this company is a purchase or sale the capital asset pricing model is used. The forecasted return of 10% determined by the dividend discount model is shown for company 1 in Table 18.3, together with the firm's Beta. This Beta is determined using the techniques discussed in Chapter 7 with the analyst allowed to modify it if he or she believes that the future Beta is different from the best estimate using historical data.

Similar forecasts were made for the companies 2 through 10 shown in Table 18.3. At this point a CAPM is estimated by fitting a relationship to the data shown in Table 18.3. Running a least squares regression using the data shown in Table 18.3 results in

$$\overline{R}_i = 4.1 + 7.2\beta_i$$

Utilizing this equation to estimate equilibrium return allows the calculation of excess return for each stock that is shown in the last column. For example, for company 1 the expected return using the capital asset pricing model is

$$\overline{R}_i = 4.1 + 7.2(1.2) = 12.47$$

$$\text{Excess return} = 10 - 12.74 = -2.74$$

Thus the return of 10% that analysts forecast for company 1 is 2.74 below what is required given the risk of company 1, and company 1 would be a candidate for sale.

This approach has much to commend it. It uses the concept of the value of a share of stock being equal to the present value of future dividends, as well as the concepts of modern capital market theory. That is, it provides a consistent and theoretically defensible framework for the collection and use of output from security analysts. These are qualities that we have described earlier as being highly desirable.

Does this guarantee that the system will work? No. To be effective, the estimates from security analysts must contain real information. That is, their estimates of future dividends, future Betas, and the security market line must, in combination, provide information about future returns.

Does the system work? An independent study done on the forecasting ability of the Wells Fargo Stock Advisory Service on the 250 stocks followed by TIAA CREF found that

Table 18.3   Determining Mispriced Assets

Company	Expected Return	Beta	Excess Return
1	10%	1.2	−2.74
2	8	.8	−1.86
3	15	1.4	+.82
4	22	1.2	9.26
5	6	.9	−4.58
6	18	1.6	2.38
7	16	1.8	−1.06
8	12	1.0	+.70
9	4	1.2	−8.74
10	16	.8	+6.14

the service provided useful information on the relative value of stocks over a four-year period. Although this is not conclusive, it does suggest that systematic use of the data supplied by security analysts can lead to superior performance.

An Evolving System of Security Selection

Just as the capital asset pricing model (CAPM) can be used as a tool in the stock selection process, the new models evolving from the arbitrage pricing theory (APT) and multifactor model literature can be used to enrich the stock selection process. Because the models employ more information about the process driving security returns, they allow for a more detailed structure for selecting stocks or designing stock selection systems. To illustrate some of the ways in which a multi-index model can be used, let's assume a particular return-generating process. We can think of this process as a simplified representation of the more detailed models described in Chapters 8, 14, and 16.

Assume

$$R_i = \overline{R}_i + b_{iD}I_D + b_{iy}I_y + b_{ip}I_p + b_{iO}I_O + e_i \qquad (18.6a)$$

where

$R_i =$ the return on security i

$R_{\overline{i}} =$ the expected return on security i

$I_D =$ innovations (unexpected changes) in default premiums

$I_y =$ innovations in the difference between long- and short-term government securities

$I_p =$ innovations (unexpected changes) in inflation

$I_O =$ innovations in oil prices

$b_{ij} =$ sensitivities to each of the influences generating returns

$e_i =$ random error term

Under the assumptions of APT the equilibrium return for any asset should be the riskless rate of return (the T-bill rate) plus compensation for the sensitivity to different types of risks (b_{ij}'s) inherent in the asset. Thus Equation (18.6a) leads to

$$R_i = R_F + \lambda_D b_{iD} + \lambda_y b_{iy} + \lambda_p b_{ip} + \lambda_O b_{iO} \qquad (18.7)$$

where the λ's are the expected return for bearing sensitivity to each index (the market price of each type of risk). It is quite possible that a particular economic variable impacts returns over time but that the investor expects zero extra return for bearing sensitivity to it (the influence is not priced). For example, Roll and Ross [75] found many more influences present in the return-generating process than were present in the equilibrium model (priced by the market).

There are a number of ways in which a model such as those depicted in Equations (18.6a) and (18.7) can be used to manage a stock portfolio. The way in which the model can be used depends in part both on what an institution believes it can or cannot forecast and on the special characteristics of the institution's customer. We will discuss each of these in turn.

Forecasting Ability

The simplest use of this model is analogous to the use of the CAPM to select securities, as discussed in the previous section of this chapter. In this section we assume that analysts can forecast the return on individual stocks but have no ability to forecast the risks (b_{ij}'s) of any security, future innovations in the macro variable driving the return-generating process (I's), or the market price of the factor influences (λ's).[27]

The b_{ij}'s for any stock can be estimated just like the β_i's of the CAPM by using Equation (18.6) as a time-series multiple regression equation for each stock. Equation (18.7) can be run as a cross-sectional regression to estimate the λ's by utilizing the analyst's forecast of the expected return for each stock and the estimate of the b_{ij}'s for each stock arrived at from Equation (18.8). The results of this regression will be an equation such as

$$\bar{R}_i = 6 + 2b_{iD} + 0.8b_{iy} + 3b_{ip} \tag{18.8}$$

Note that in this example $\lambda_O = 0$, and thus the term $b_{iO}\lambda_O$ drops out of the equation. This implies that in equilibrium the investor does not believe the market gives an extra return to securities with sensitivity to oil prices. We made this assumption to reemphasize that some factors in the return-generating process need not be priced. This represents (just like the security market line) the *forecasted* equilibrium return on all stocks. For each security an equilibrium return is determined by substituting the sensitivities (b_{ij}'s) for that stock into Equation (18.8). The analyst then compares his or her forecasted return for each stock with the equilibrium return. If security analysts believe a stock will have a return above the equilibrium return determined by Equation (18.8), it is a good candidate to be purchased.

Although this use of the APT is directly analogous to what has become a popular use of the CAPM, there are other ways to employ this model in a forecast mode. The next most obvious use involves Equation (18.6). We have assumed that the expected value of all innovations in the relevant macro variables is zero. Although this is true for the market as a whole, an institution may feel it can successfully forecast nonzero innovations in one or more of the macro variables. If so, it might choose to weight any portfolio it holds toward stocks with higher (or lower) sensitivities to these variables. For example, financial stocks have particularly high sensitivities with respect to the default variable. Therefore if a manager expected a large positive innovation in the default variable, he or she might want to overweight (or underweight, depending on the direction of the innovation), the fraction of financial stocks in the portfolio.

Similar forecasting arguments can be made with respect to differences between the manager's estimate of sensitivities (b_{ij}'s) and consensus beliefs or differences in the manager's estimate of market price of any risks and the consensus beliefs.

All of these uses are based on an organization believing that it can forecast sensitivities (b_{ij}), market prices of risk λ_j, or innovations (I_j) more accurately than the average or consensus belief that is incorporated in market prices. Even in the absence of differential forecasting belief, however, there is a potential use for the models under discussion.

Portfolios Customized for User Characteristics

Even if the institution employing the type of multi-index model under discussion does not believe that it possess superior forecasting ability, it can take advantage of certain attributes of these models. The simplest use of this type of model is in the construction of index funds from a small number of stocks. Empirical evidence suggests that portfolios can be constructed that more closely mimic a target portfolio of securities (e.g., an index) when the target portfolio is matched with respect to several indices rather than one.[28]

---

[27]Actually the system we describe involves implicit forecasts of the λ's, but the forecasts result from a regression of the expected return forecast on each stock on the sensitivities rather than from a direct estimate.

[28]See Elton and Gruber [34].

Replicating portfolios involving a small number of securities are especially useful in exploiting relative mispricing between markets. [See, for example, the discussion of the use of futures on the Standard & Poor's (S&P) index in Chapter 23.]

An even more appealing use of the APT is to construct portfolios that are suited to an individual customer's needs. For example, a pension fund that has future pension liabilities which are heavily sensitive to inflation might want to construct a portfolio that tends to give high payoffs when inflation is high. By examining the b_{ip} for individual stocks and industries, a portfolio can be constructed that resembles a market portfolio, but that has returns that are more highly sensitive to inflation.

In deciding what position to take with respect to each source of risk portrayed in Equations (18.6) and (18.7), the investor is balancing extra risks against extra return. Although the market makes one particular trade-off, the investor may choose a different one because of his or her personal situation. As was just pointed out, an investor may choose to bear a high level of inflation risk because he or she has liabilities that are affected by inflation. Perhaps this can be seen most clearly by examining oil price risk. We assumed that the multiple regression resulted in an estimate of λ_o of zero (the investor believes that the oil price risk was not priced by the market). At first glance we would conclude that no investor should hold a portfolio that has a value of b_{io} other than zero. After all, there is no expected return from this risk, so why take it? But think of an investor where total consumption expenditures are affected by oil prices. Such an investor will want to hold stocks with positive b_{io} and bear this risk to cancel out some of the costs of consumption.

The use of an APT and multi-index model for stock selection is relatively new. We are only beginning to explore forecasting within the confines of the APT model. We are only starting to think about how the structure of the multi-index model can be used to design portfolios that have particular sets of multidimensional risk return characteristics that should appeal to specified groups of customers. This research, while still in its infancy, is promising.[29]

CONCLUSION

A valuation model can be considered as the black box that converts forecasts of fundamental data about companies and/or the economy into forecasts or evaluations of market price. In this chapter we have reviewed several approaches to valuation models. No valuation model can perform well if the forecasts on which it is based are of poor quality. On the other hand, good forecasts can be capitalized upon only if their effect on prices is evaluated in a sensible manner.

QUESTIONS AND PROBLEMS

1. A firm has just paid (the moment before valuation) a dividend of 55¢ and is expected to exhibit a growth rate of 10% into the indefinite future. If the appropriate discount rate is 14%, what is the value of the stock?

2. Consider the one-period growth model shown in Equation (18.5b). Assume the next period's dividend is $1, that stockholders require a 12% return, that new investment is expected to yield 14%, and that the retention rate is 50%. What is the implied fair price?

---

[29]See Elton and Gruber [35, 36] for an example.

3. Assume that price of the security discussed in Problem 2 was $30. Assume that all other information is the same except for the stockholders' required return. What does a $30 price imply for return?

4. Assume the information in Problem 2 and a price of $60. Furthermore, assume that the stockholder was most unsure concerning the return on new investment. How much would return have to change before the security was fairly priced?

5. The analyst who supplied you with the information in Problem 1 has just revised her forecast. She now realizes that the growth rate of 10% can continue for only five years, after which the company will have a long-term growth rate of 6%. Furthermore, at the end of the five years she expects the company's payout rate to increase from its present 30% up to 50%. What value would you assign to the company?

6. Assume that the forecast for the company in Problem 5 was such that at the end of the fifth year its growth was to decline linearly for four years to reach the steady-state 6% growth rate. Assume that the payout ratio was constant at 30% until it is changed to 50% at the end of the ninth year. What is the value of the company?

7. In Problem 2, assume that the price of the stock was $9 and solve for the expected rate of return from buying the stock.

8. In Problem 1, assume that the price of the stock was $9 and solve for the expected rate of return from buying the stock.

9. Consider the two-period model. Assume the same information as Problem 2, except that after 10 years growth would change to 5%. What is the implied price?

10. Assume the security sold for $25, the two-period growth model is appropriate, and all other information is identical to Problem 9. What is the implied return?

11. Assume the same information as Problem 9. However, assume the length of time of the higher growth is uncertain. How long would it have to last to justify an $18 price?

12. Derive a three-period valuation model where the transitional period was N_2 years and involved a linear change from the first growth rate to a steady-state growth rate.

BIBLIOGRAPHY

1. Altman, Ed. "Bankrupt Firm's Equity Securities as an Investment Alternative," *Financial Analysts Journal*, **25,** No. 4 (July/Aug. 1969), pp. 129–133.
2. Ambachtsheer, Keith. "Portfolio Theory and the Security Analyst," *Financial Analysts Journal*, **28,** No. 5 (Nov./Dec. 1972), pp. 53–57.
3. Arditti, Fred, and Pinkerton, John. "The Valuation and Cost of Capital of the Levered Firm with Growth Opportunities," *Journal of Finance*, **XXXIII,** No. 1 (March 1978), pp. 54–73.
4. Baker, Kent, and Haslem, John. "Toward the Development of Client-Specified Valuation Models," *Journal of Finance*, **XXIX,** No. 4 (Sept. 1974), pp. 1255–1263.
5. Baron, David. "Firm Valuation, Corporate Taxes, and Default Risk," *Journal of Finance*, **XXX,** No. 5 (Dec. 1975), pp. 1251–1264.
6. Baylis, Robert, and Bhirud, Suresh. "Growth Stock Analysis: A New Approach," *Financial Analysts Journal*, **29,** No. 4 (July/Aug. 1973), pp. 63–70.
7. Beaver, W., and Morse, D. "What Determines Price-Earnings Ratios?" *Financial Analysts Journal*, **34,** No. 4 (July/Aug. 1978), pp. 65–76.
8. Beidelman, Carl. "Pitfalls of the Price-Earnings Ratio," *Financial Analysts Journal*, **27,** No. 4 (Sept./Oct. 1971), pp. 86–91.
9. Bierman, Harold, and Hass, Jerome. "Normative Stock Price Models," *Journal of Financial and Quantitative Analysis*, **VI,** No. 4 (Sept. 1971), pp. 1135–1144.

10. Bierman, Harold, Downes, David, and Hass, Jerome. "Closed-Form Price Models," *Journal of Financial and Quantitative Analysis*, **VII,** No. 3 (June 1972), pp. 1797–1808.

11. Bildersee, John. "Some Aspects of the Performance of Non-Convertible Preferred Stocks," *Journal of Finance*, **XXVIII,** No. 5 (Dec. 1973), pp. 1187–1201.

12. Bing, Ralph. "Survey of Practitioners' Stock Evaluation Methods," *Financial Analysts Journal*, **27,** No. 3 (May/June 1971), pp. 55–69.

13. Black, Fischer. "The Dividend Puzzle," *Journal of Portfolio Management*, **2,** No. 2 (Winter 1976), pp. 5–8.

14. Black, Fischer, and Scholes, M. "The Effects of Dividend Yield and Dividend Policy on Common Stock Prices and Returns," *Journal of Financial Economics*, **1,** No. 1 (May 1974), pp. 4–22.

15. Boness, James, Chen, Andrew, and Jatusipitak, Som. "On Relations among Stock Price Behavior and Changes in the Capital Structure of the Firm," *Journal of Financial and Quantitative Analysis*, **VII,** No. 4 (Sept. 1972), pp. 1967–1982.

16. Bower, Dorothy, and Bower, S. Richard. "Test of a Stock Valuation Model," *Journal of Finance*, **XXV,** No. 2 (May 1970), pp. 483–492.

17. Bower, Richard, and Bower, Dorothy. "Risk and the Valuation of Common Stock," *Journal of Political Economy*, **77,** No. 3 (May/June 1969), pp. 349–362.

18. Bower, Richard, and Wippern, Ronald. "Risk-Return Measurement in Portfolio Selection and Performance Appraisal Models: Progress Report," *Journal of Financial and Quantitative Analysis*, **IV,** No. 4 (Dec. 1969), pp. 417–447.

19. Breen, William, and Lerner, Eugene M. "Corporate Financial Strategies and Market Measures of Risk and Return," *Journal of Finance*, **XXVIII,** No. 2 (May 1973), pp. 339–351.

20. Breen, William, and Savage, James. "Portfolio Distributions and Tests of Security Selection Models," *Journal of Finance*, **XXIII,** No. 5 (Dec. 1968), pp. 805–819.

21. Brennan, M. J. "An Approach to the Valuation of Uncertain Income Streams," *Journal of Finance*, **XXVIII,** No. 3 (June 1973), pp. 661–674.

22. Brennan, Michael. "Valuation and the Cost of Capital for Regulated Industries: Comment on [30]," *Journal of Finance*, **XVII,** No. 5 (Dec. 1972), pp. 1147–1149.

23. Brigham, Eugene, and Pappas, James. "Rates of Return on Common Stock," *Journal of Business*, **42,** No. 3 (July 1969), pp. 302–316.

24. Chen, Nai-Fu. "Risk and Return of Value Stocks," *The Journal of Business*, **71,** No. 4 (Oct. 1998), pp. 501–535.

25. Cohen, J., Zinbarg, E., and Zeikel, A. *Investment Analysis and Portfolio Management* (Homewood, Ill.: Richard D. Irwin, 1973).

26. Dennis, Charles N. "An Investigation into the Effects of Independent Investor Relations Firms on Common Stock Prices," *Journal of Finance*, **XXVIII,** No. 2 (May 1973), pp. 373–380.

27. Elton Edwin J., and Gruber, Martin J. "The Effect of Share Repurchases on the Value of the Firm," *Journal of Finance*, **XXIII,** No. 1 (Mar. 1968), pp. 135–149.

28. ——. "Marginal Stockholder Tax Rates and the Clientele Effect," *Review of Economics and Statistics*, **LII,** No. 1 (Feb. 1970), pp. 68–74.

29. ——. "Valuation and the Cost of Capital for Regulated Industries," *Journal of Finance*, **XXVI,** No. 3 (June 1971), pp. 661–670.

30. ——. "Valuation and the Cost of Capital for Regulated Industries: Reply to [21]," *Journal of Finance*, **XXVII,** No. 5 (Dec. 1972), pp. 1150–1155.

31. ——. "Asset Selection with Changing Capital Structure," *Journal of Financial and Quantitative Analysis*, **VIII,** No. 3 (June 1973), pp. 459–474.

32. ——. "Valuation and the Asset Selection Under Alternative Investment Opportunities," *Journal of Finance*, **XXXI,** No. 2 (May 1976), pp. 525–539.

33. ——. "Optimal Investment and Financing Patterns for a Firm Subject to Regulation with a Lag," *Journal of Finance*, **XXXII,** No. 5 (Dec. 1977), pp. 1485–1500.

34. ——. "A Multi-Index Risk Model of the Japanese Stock Market," *Japan and the World Economy*, **1,** No. 1 (1989).

35. ———. "Expectational Data and Japanese Stock Prices," *Japan and the World Economy*, **1**, No. 4 (1990).

36. ———. "Portfolio Analysis with a Non-Normal Multi-Index Return Generating Process," Working Paper, New York University, 1990.

37. Elton, Edwin, Gruber, Martin, and Lieber, Zvi. "Valuation, Optimum Investment, and Financing for the Firm Subject to Regulation," *Journal of Finance*, **XXX**, No. 2 (Mar. 1975), pp. 401–425.

38. Estep, Preston W. "A New Method for Valuing Common Stock," *Financial Analysts Journal*, **41**, No. 6 (Nov.–Dec. 1989), pp. 26–33.

39. Fewings, David. "The Impact of Corporate Growth on the Risk of Common Stocks," *Journal of Finance*, **XXX**, No. 2 (May 1975), pp. 525–531.

40. Foster, Earl. "Price-Earnings Ratio and Corporate Growth," *Financial Analysts Journal*, **26**, No. 1 (Jan.–Feb. 1970), pp. 96–99.

41. ———. "Price-Earnings and Corporate Growth: A Revision," *Financial Analysts Journal*, **26**, No. 3 (May–June 1970), pp. 115–118.

42. Fouse, W. "Risk and Liquidity: The Keys to Stock Price Behavior," *Financial Analysts Journal*, **32**, No. 3 (May–June 1976), pp. 35–45.

43. Fuller, Russel L., and Hsiu, Chi-Cheng. "A Simplified Common Stock Valuation Model," *Financial Analysts Journal*, **40**, No. 5 (Sept.–Oct. 1984), pp. 49–56.

44. Good, Walter. "Valuation of Quality-Growth Stocks," *Financial Analysts Journal*, **28**, No. 4 (Sept.–Oct. 1972), pp. 47–59.

45. Gordon, Myron. *The Investment, Financing, and Valuation of the Corporation* (Homewood, Ill.: Richard D. Irwin, 1962).

46. Graham, B., Dodd, D., and Cottle, S. *Security Analysis Principles and Techniques*, 4th ed. (New York: McGraw-Hill, 1962).

47. Granger, Clive W. J. "Some Consequences of the Valuation Model When Expectations Are Taken to Be Optimum Forecasts," *Journal of Finance*, **XXX**, No. 1 (Mar. 1975), pp. 135–145.

48. Gruber, Martin J. *The Determinants of Common Stock Prices* (University Park, Pa.: Pennsylvania State University Press, 1971).

49. Gupta, Manak. "Money Supply and Stock Prices: A Probabilistic Approach," *Journal of Financial and Quantitative Analysis*, **IX**, No. 1 (Jan. 1976), pp. 57–68.

50. Hakansson, Nils. "On the Dividend Capitalization Model Under Uncertainty," *Journal of Financial and Quantitative Analysis*, **IV**, No. 1 (March 1969), pp. 65–87.

51. Hamburger, Michael, and Kochin, Levis. "Money and Stock Prices: The Channels of Influence," *Journal of Finance*, **XXVII**, No. 2 (May 1972), pp. 231–249.

52. Haugen, Robert. "Expected Growth, Required Return, and the Variability of Stock Prices," *Journal of Financial and Quantitative Analysis*, **V**, No. 3 (Sept. 1970), pp. 297–307.

53. Haugen, Robert, and Kumar, Prem. "The Traditional Approach to Valuing Levered-Growth Stocks: A Clarification," *Journal of Financial and Quantitative Analysis*, **IX**, No. 6 (Dec. 1974), pp. 1031–1044.

54. Haugen, Robert, and Pappas, J. L. "Equilibrium in the Pricing of Capital Assets, Risk-Bearing Debt Instruments, and the Question of Optimal Capital Structure," *Journal of Financial and Quantitative Analysis*, **VI**, No. 3 (June 1971), pp. 943–953.

55. ———. "Equilibrium in the Pricing of Capital Assets, Risk-Bearing Debt Instruments, and the Question of Optimal Capital Structure: A Reply," *Journal of Financial and Quantitative Analysis*, **VII**, No. 4 (Sept. 1972), pp. 2005–2008.

56. Haugen, Robert, and Udell, John. "Rates of Return to Stockholders of Acquired Companies," *Journal of Financial and Quantitative Analysis*, **VII**, No. 1 (Jan. 1972), pp. 1387–1398.

57. Hawkins, D. "Toward an Old Theory of Equity Valuation," *Financial Analysts Journal*, **33**, No. 6 (Nov.–Dec. 1977), pp. 48–53.

58. Hunt, Lacy. "Determinants of the Dividend Yield," *Journal of Portfolio Management*, **3**, No. 3 (Spring 1977), pp. 43–48.

59. Imai, Yutaka, and Rubinstein, Mark. "Equilibrium in the Pricing of Capital Assets, Risk-Bearing Debt Instruments, and the Question of Optimal Capital Structure: Comment," *Journal of Financial and Quantitative Analysis*, **VII,** No. 4 (Sept. 1972), pp. 2001–2003.

60. Jaffee, Jeffrey, and Mandelker, Gershon. "The Value of the Firm Under Regulation," *Journal of Finance*, **XXXI,** No. 2 (May 1976), pp. 701–713.

61. Joy, Maurice, and Jones, Charles. "Another Look at the Value of *P/E* Ratios," *Financial Analysts Journal*, **26,** No. 4 (Sept.–Oct. 1970), pp. 61–64.

62. Keenan, Michael. "Models of Equity Valuation: The Great Bubble," *Journal of Finance*, **XXV,** No. 2 (May 1970), pp. 243–273.

63. Kraft, John, and Kraft, Arthur. "Determinants of Common Stock Prices: A Time Series Analysis," *Journal of Finance*, **XXXII,** No. 2 (May 1977), pp. 417–325.

64. Kummer, Donald, and Hoffmeister, Ronald. "Valuation Consequences of Cash Tender Offers," *Journal of Finance*, **XXXIII,** No. 2 (May 1978), pp. 505–515.

65. Latane, Henry, Joy, Maurice, and Jones, Charles. "Quarterly Data, Sort-Rank Routines, and Security Evaluation," *Journal of Business*, **43,** No. 3 (July 1970), pp. 427–438.

66. Litzenberger, Robert, and Budd, Alan. "Corporate Investment Criteria and the Valuation of Risk Assets," *Journal of Financial and Quantitative Analysis*, **V,** No. 4 (Dec. 1970), pp. 385–419.

67. Malkiel, Burton. "Equity Yields, Growth, and the Structure of Share Prices," *American Economic Review*, **53** (Dec. 1963), pp. 1004–1031.

68. ———. "The Valuation of Closed-End Investment-Company Shares," *Journal of Finance*, **XXXII,** No. 3 (June 1977), pp. 847–859.

69. Malkiel, Burton, and Cragg, John. "Expectations and the Structure of Share Prices," *American Economic Review*, **LX,** No. 4 (Sept. 1970), pp. 601–617.

70. Mehta, Dileep. "The Impact of Outstanding Convertible Bonds on Corporate Dividend Policy," *Journal of Finance*, **XXXI,** No. 2 (May 1976), pp. 489–506.

71. Miller, M., and Modigliani, F. "Dividend Policy, Growth, and the Valuation of Shares," *Journal of Business*, **34** (Oct. 1961), pp. 411–433.

72. Molodovsky, N., May, C., and Chottinger, S. "Common Stock Valuation," *Financial Analysts Journal*, **21** (Mar.–Apr. 1965), pp. 104–123.

73. Myers, Stewart. "A Time-State Preference Model of Security Valuation." *Journal of Financial and Quantitative Analysis*, **III,** No. 1 (Mar. 1968), pp. 1–33.

74. Nerlove, Marc. "Factors Affecting Differences among Rates of Return on Investments in Individual Common Stocks," *Review of Economics and Statistics*, **L,** No. 3 (Aug. 1968), pp. 312–331.

75. Roll, R., and Ross, S. A. "An Empirical Investigation of the Arbitrage Pricing Theory," *Journal of Finance*, **35,** No. 5 (Dec. 1980), pp. 1073–1103.

76. Sloane, William, and Reisman, Arnold. "Stock Evaluation Theory: Classification, Reconciliation, and General Model," *Journal of Financial and Quantitative Analysis*, **III,** No. 2 (June 1968), pp. 171–204.

77. Sorenson, Eric H., and Williamson, David A. "Some Evidence on the Value of Dividend Discount Models," *Financial Analysts Journal*, **41,** No. 6 (Nov.–Dec. 1985), pp. 60–69.

78. Warren, James. "A Note on the Algebraic Equivalence of the Holt and Malkiel Models of Share Valuation," *Journal of Finance*, **XXIX,** No. 3 (June 1974), pp. 1007–1010.

79. Whitbeck, V., and Kisor, M. "A New Tool in Investment Decision Making," *Financial Analysts Journal* (May–June 1963), pp. 55–62.

80. Williams, J.B. *The Theory of Investment Value* (Cambridge, Mass.: Harvard University Press, 1938).

19

Earnings Estimation

In the previous chapter we saw that both earnings and growth in earnings play a key role in valuation models. In this chapter we examine both the nature of earnings and some models for forecasting future earnings.

We start this chapter by briefly reviewing some of the ambiguities associated with the term "earnings." Different firms and even the same firm, at different times, can define earnings in alternative ways. A logical question is: If earnings can be defined differently, does the figure earnings per share, which shows up on the firm's income statement, have any impact on valuation? This question is examined in the second section of this chapter. As we will see, despite the ambiguous meaning of reported earnings, there is a real payoff from being able to forecast it.

The final two sections of this chapter examine models for forecasting future earnings. The first of the two sections examines the time-series behavior of earnings while the second discusses the relationship between earnings and other fundamental firm characteristics.

THE ELUSIVE NUMBER CALLED EARNINGS

The value of any asset is determined by its future earning power and not by what it cost at some time in the past. An economist would define earnings as cash flow plus the change in market value of an asset. Consider a bond originally purchased for $100 that carries a 10% interest rate. Assume the bond is worth $95 after one period. What has the earnings been on this investment over the period? The economist would say the earnings were $10 in interest plus the $5 decrease in value or a net of $5. An economist would apply the same principles to a physical investment. For example, if a manager purchases a machine, what are the earnings of the machine over the period? Clearly, one component of earnings is the profits earned from producing a product using the machine. An economist would argue that the change in the market value of the machine is also a part of earnings. The economist's concept of earnings is, of course, closely related to the idea of return we discussed in earlier chapters.

If an accountant reported the economist's definition of earnings and it was accurate, the analyst's job of valuing the asset or firm would be over. He or she could simply use the estimate of the change in the value of the asset or firm together with the old selling price to determine the new price. However, there is circularity. The best estimate of the change in the value of the asset is, of course, the actual change in the value of the asset. If the actual change is determined by the accountant's estimate, then how can the actual change be used as the estimate? The accountant can still look at the fundamental characteristics of the firm and try to estimate the change in value. Similarly, the accountant could just try to report the income earned in the single period and leave the estimating of the change in value to others. The accounting profession pursues a policy somewhere in between. The number the accountant calls earnings is a mixture of the income earned and an attempt to measure some part of the change in the value of the asset. The accountant's treatment of depreciation, research and development expenditures, and pension liabilities have elements associated with them that are related to change in value. However, these attempts to measure changes in value tend to be related more to the allocation or using up of historic costs than they are related to changes in market value. For example, depreciation reflects a somewhat arbitrary assumption about allocating the historical cost of an asset, as a change in value, over the life of an asset. The number the accountant uses for change in value (depreciation) is, at least in theory, related to the change in market value of an asset because the asset is used up. However, it makes no attempt to capture changes in the value of the asset due to either general or specific price changes. Thus, accounting earnings are a mixture of the within-period earnings and an easily replicated but somewhat arbitrary allocation of some of the change in value of the asset. This is not the end of the story. There are still more difficulties with accounting earnings.

The most often cited problem is the lack of consistency in defining the components of earnings for different firms.

Ashwinpaul Sondhi has prepared Table 19.1 to illustrate how, under current generally accepted accounting principles, a firm could show earnings of $1.98 or $4.41, depending on the choices made. Companies A and B are essentially the same company but have chosen different accounting methods in reporting income and cost.

The footnotes discuss in detail the differences between the assumptions made by the two companies. These include differences in assumptions concerning lives of investments, depreciation methods, pension costs, and forms of compensation.

Let us consider a few of these changes in detail. When the economy experiences very high inflation rates, the differences in the treatment of the costs of material used from inventory becomes important for many firms. There are two generally accepted methods of determining the cost of material used from inventory LIFO and FIFO. LIFO (last in first out) uses as the cost of an item taken from inventory, the cost of the last identical item purchased for inventory. FIFO (first in first out) uses as the cost of an item taken from inventory, the cost of the oldest identical item in inventory. In periods of inflation the cost of the oldest item in inventory is often much lower than the cost of the most recent purchase of the same item. Using LIFO during periods of increasing inflation leads to lower reported earnings than the use of FIFO.

As a second case, consider pension liabilities. Pension liabilities are a source of increasing cost to firms. A firm makes a payment to the pension trustees to cover future liabilities. This payment is an expense to the firm and lowers earnings. The size of the payment a firm has to make depends, in part, on the assumed rate of return of the pension fund assets. Different rates of return can result in very different contributions and very different impacts on a firm's reported earnings.

There are no simple rules that allow an analyst to adjust the firm's earnings so that they are on a comparable basis. The impact of alternative accounting methods depends on the characteristics of the various firms. For example, the effect of differences in depreciation policies depends on the importance of fixed assets in the firm's costs, the age of the assets,

Table 19.1   Accounting Magic Using Generally Accepted Accounting Principles

	Company A	Adjustments ($ in 000s)	Company B
Sales Revenue[a]	25,000	1,000	26,000
Other Income:			
Equity/Cost Method Affiliates[b]	1,500	(250)	1,250
Total Revenues	26,500	750	27,250
Costs and Expenses:			
Cost of Goods Sold	15,000		15,000
Selling, General and Administrative	3,550		3,550
LIFO Effect[c]	900	(900)	
Depreciation[d]	1,000	(400)	600
Amortization Expense[e]	400	(250)	150
Exploration Costs[f]	1,200	(550)	650
Pension Costs[g]	750	(200)	550
Other Post-employment Costs[h]	300	(200)	100
Asset Impairments[i]	300	(300)	
Compensation:			
Base Salaries	400		400
Bonuses[j]	200	(200)	
Total Costs/Expenses	24,000	(3,000)	21,000
Pretax Income	2,500		6,250
Tax Expense[k]	525		1,837.5
Net Income	1,975		4,412.5
Per Share on 1000 Shares	1.975		4.4125

[a]*Revenue Recognition Methods*
Firms have considerable latitude concerning when they recognize revenue. For example, variations can occur because of differences in estimates of the degree and cost of completion in long-term construction contracts where the percentage-of-completion method is used, in revenue recognition of installment sales, and in the use of sales-type or direct-financing leases where operating leases should be used by the lessor. The impact of different revenue recognition is $1,000 more in income recognized by Company B. We assume this amount has not yet been received in cash; however, deferred taxes must be reported.

[b]*Equity/Cost Method Affiliates*
Company A owns 20% or more of the voting common stock in another company. Its proportionate share of the earnings of this investment, $1500, is reported as a component of other income. It is assumed that Company A has received dividends of $1250 from the investment. Company B owns less than the 20% threshold and cannot use the equity method. Under the cost method, it reports as other income, the $1250 received as dividends, but it does not report the additional $250 that would have been recorded under the equity method. This is the one instance where Company A or B are slightly different. It is included because it's an important difference between companies.

   The investment in other companies also affects taxes. Eighty percent of dividends received from other corporations are tax-exempt. Thus, Company A recognizes a tax expense and liability for 20% of the $1250 received in dividends. Assuming a 35% corporate tax rate the tax liability is $87.50 or [0.20 × $1250 × 0.35]. Company B recognizes the same tax expense and liability on the $1,250 received as dividends. However, deferred taxes must be recorded on the additional $250 recorded by Company A. Company A may assume that it will receive this amount as dividends or capital gains in the future. We use the latter because it is more conservative. Company A records an additional tax expense and deferred taxes payable. Since for corporations that tax is payable on the full amount of the capital gain, the tax is $87.50 or [0.35 × 250].

   Note: Companies may assume either indefinite reinvestment of undistributed earnings [$250 in this case] or that these earnings will be received in a tax-free liquidation. Both assumptions would allow the company to record the $250 as income without any tax impact. This election is available only for companies with more than a 50% ownership share.

(continues on next page)

cLIFO Effect

Company A uses the LIFO inventory valuation method and Company B uses FIFO. In periods of increasing prices and stable or increasing inventories, LIFO firms will report higher cost of goods sold. The difference between FIFO and LIFO Cost of Goods Sold is the LIFO effect, $900 in this case.

dDepreciation

Company A uses accelerated depreciation methods with shorter lives, whereas Company B uses straight-line depreciation with longer lives.

eAmortization Expense

Company B amortizes goodwill, patents, and copyrights over the maximum periods allowed, whereas Company A uses shorter lives.

fExploration Costs

Company B capitalizes all exploration costs, whereas Company A expenses dry-hole costs.

gPension Costs

The difference in pension costs, $200 lower for Company B, is due to difference in assumptions of discount rates, assumed rates of return on assets, and different allocation to expense of the difference between actual results and actuarial assumptions.

hOther Post-employment Contracts

Costs of health-care and life-insurance benefits promised to employees are recognized as incurred by Company B. Current accounting does not require accrual of these costs (as in pensions). However, Company A has recorded current costs and accrued future costs. The values we used may understate the true differences, because studies have reported accrued amounts of as much as 20–30 times the periodic cost.

iAsset Impairments

Accounting guidelines for the timing and measurement of impairments (loss in value) to long-lived assets are at best vague and inconsistently applied. Firms also have considerable discretion with respect to reporting impairments to the carrying values of receivables, marketable securities, and investments in affiliates. Here, Company A has recognized loss due to impairment, whereas Company B has not yet done so.

jCompensation

Company B uses stock options for bonuses, whereas Company A pays them in cash.

kTax

For both companies that tax is the tax on the difference between sales revenue and total costs plus the tax on other income. Assuming a 35% corporate tax rate for Company A is $0.35 (25,000 - 24,000) + 87.50 + 87.50 = \$525$ the tax for Company B is $0.35 (26,000 - 21,000) + 87.50$.

and the life of the assets. The effect of differences in assumptions concerning the return on the pension assets depends on the size of the pension assets relative to the size of the firm's earnings. Thus, in comparing the earnings across firms, individual adjustments are necessary if they are to be put on a comparable basis.

The fact that different accounting methods can lead to different reported earnings, together with the belief held by many accountants and managers that earnings are important to the valuation process, has led to another problem. Accountants and management may attempt to manage the level and growth of earnings. There are a number of studies that have examined whether or not investors can see through attempts to manage earnings. While these studies support the hypothesis that they can, many firms believe the opposite strongly enough that they continue to incur costs in an attempt to manage reported earnings.

In the next part of this chapter we show that, despite the problems with accounting earnings, they still represent one of the important inputs in judging a firm's value.

THE IMPORTANCE OF EARNINGS

Several studies have shown that the ability to predict reported earnings, despite all the ambiguity in the meaning of "earnings," will lead to the investor earning superior returns.

An often-quoted example is the study by Niederhoffer and Regan [23]. They determined the 50 best and worst performing stocks in 1970 and examined their characteristics.

Table 19.2 Change in Earnings by Performance Category

	Worst 50 Performers[a]	Best 50 Performers[a]	Random 100 Firms
Median actual change in earnings	−83%	+21.4%	−10.5%
Median predicted change in earnings	+15.3%	+7.7%	+5.8%
Median actual change in stock price	−56.7%	+48.4%	−3.2%

[a]Some stocks were deleted in order to ensure common fiscal year.
Source: Niederhoffer and Regan [23].

Compared to a random sample of 100 stocks, the 50 best performing stocks increased in value by between 37% and 125%. The 50 worst performing stocks declined in value by −49% to −78%. Table 19.2 shows the changes in earnings associated with each of these three groups of stocks.

The most striking difference between the best and worst performing securities is the actual change in earnings. The earnings for the worst performing securities declined dramatically while the earnings for the best performing firms increased substantially. This suggests strongly that stocks that perform well are stocks that have huge increases in earnings. Reported earnings would seem to be an important determinant of stock prices. The relationship between predicted earnings and price changes is much less clear. The worst performing firms had the higher predicted change in earnings.[1] However, in all cases where data were available, the actual change was less than predicted. In contrast, the best performing firms had a predicting earnings change only slightly higher than the random sample. However, in all but five cases examined, the actual change was higher than the predicted. This study suggests that stock price movements are associated with earnings changes and that differences between actual and predicted change lead to substantial price adjustments.

Elton, Gruber, and Gultekin [12] examined the effect of earnings estimates and price changes in greater detail. While Niederhoffer and Regan [23] examined the attributes of stocks that had high and low rates of return, Elton, Gruber, and Gultekin directly looked at the risk-adjusted excess return that could be earned by purchasing stocks on the basis of earnings and earnings forecast data. The first question they examined was, Do earnings affect prices? If reported earnings are important, then buying those stocks that will experience the largest growth in earnings should lead to an excess risk-adjusted return. To study this question, Elton, Gruber, and Gultekin divided stocks into deciles by the size of the next year's growth in earnings. Then the examined the excess risk-adjusted return that would be earned if each decile were purchased and held until after actual earnings were announced.[2] Stocks that had the highest future growth in earnings provided the highest excess return. The results were statistically significant at the 1% level. Furthermore, the results seem to be economically significant. For example, the 30% of firms that had the highest growth provided an excess risk-adjusted return of 7.48%, while the 30% of firms with the lowest growth (candidates for short sale) provided an excess risk-adjusted return of −4.93%. This provides strong evidence that reported earnings, despite their deficiencies, do impact stock prices.

---

[1]Predictions were collected from a large number of security analysts as reported in Standard and Poor's (S&P) earnings forecaster.

[2]To define excess risk-adjusted return, Elton, Gruber, and Gultekin used the methodology outlined in "Efficient Markets," Chapter 17. Each portfolio has its return adjusted by subtracting from actual returns expected returns based on the market model $R_i = \alpha_i + \beta_i R_m$.

The next logical subject to look at is the impact of expectational data on stock prices. Economists believe that expectations determine stock prices. If this is true, and the market is efficient, then expectations about future earnings should be incorporated into stock prices. It follows logically that the investor should not be able to make an excess return by either buying or selling stock on the basis of the average (consensus) expectations about future earnings.[3] On the other hand, if prices reflect the consensus estimate, then the investor should be able to earn large excess returns by acting on either the difference between consensus estimates and realizations or changes in the consensus estimates.

Elton, Gruber, and Gultekin examined whether an investor could make an excess return by buying and selling stocks on the basis of the consensus estimate of earnings growth. They divided stocks into deciles based on the consensus forecast of earnings growth. They found that there was no difference in excess return between the deciles. The investor who bought the stocks that were expected to have low growth would have done just as well as the one who bought the stocks with high expected growth. This is what one would expect if markets are reasonably efficient and expectations are reflected in security prices. Their second test involved dividing firms into deciles by the error in the forecast of earnings growth. Here the results were dramatically different. The firms for which the actual earnings growth was higher than the forecasted earnings growth had returns well above normal. The firms with actual earnings growth below estimated earnings growth had returns well below normal. An investor who could forecast earnings better than average could earn excess returns. Finally, Elton, Gruber, and Gultekin divided firms into deciles by the change in the forecast of earnings. This led to even higher returns. While it was profitable to forecast earnings, it was even more profitable to forecast the change in expectations about future earnings. A number of mutual funds have a strategy of buying high-growth firms. By itself this should not be a useful strategy. What is important is to find high-growth firms that the market believes will be low-growth firms. Even more valuable would be to forecast changes in the market's belief about the future growth of a firm.

The studies just discussed provide strong evidence that earnings affect returns and that superior forecasts of earnings can lead to excess returns. The question is, How much better does the analyst have to be in order to earn excess returns? Table 19.3, taken from the Elton, Gruber, and Gultekin study, provides a partial answer to this question. The table shows the excess return that can be earned if analysts are able to identify the firms whose earnings will be less than the consensus forecast. For example, the second entry in the second column is 1.56%. If the analysts were able to eliminate the 10% of the stocks with the largest overestimate of growth, they would earn 1.56% more than normal, given the risk of the stocks. Similarly, if they were able to eliminate the 20% of stocks with the greatest overestimate of actual growth, an extra 2.88% return above normal would be earned. Columns 3 and 4 show the excess return if there is error in the analysts' ability to select firms with inaccuracies in the average estimate of earnings. The second column assumes that 50% of the time the analyst picks stocks, she picks one in the category shown (e.g., the 70% of the stocks with the least overestimate of average growth) and 50% of the time she picks stocks that have the average characteristics of the population of stocks. Column 4 is similar, except that it is assumed that the analyst can select from the best category only 10% of the time. As can be seen by examining these columns, even information with little accuracy can lead to excess returns.

---

[3]The consensus estimate was defined as the average estimate of security analysts at major brokerage houses following a stock. Only stocks followed by three or more analysts were included in the study.

Table 19.3   Excess Returns by Eliminating from Portfolio Those Firms that Had Earnings Estimates the Most Above (or Least Below) Realizations

Percentage of Firms Eliminated	Excess Return If Completely Accurate	Excess Return If 50% Error	Excess Return If 90% Error
0%	0	0	0
10%	1.56	0.78	0.16
20%	2.88	1.44	0.29
30%	3.07	1.53	0.31
40%	4.32	2.16	0.43
50%	5.77	2.88	0.58
60%	7.35	3.67	0.74
70%	9.08	4.54	0.91
7.110%	9.90	4.95	0.99
90%	10.42	5.21	1.04

Source: Elton, Gruber, and Gultekin [12].

This section illustrates the importance of earnings to the valuation process and the importance of being able to forecast earnings. In the next section we examine some time series characteristics of earnings and some methods for forecasting it.

CHARACTERISTICS OF EARNINGS AND EARNINGS FORECASTS

In this section we are going to analyze the characteristics of earnings. Are earnings changes highly related to the performance of the economy? Are future changes in earnings highly related to past earnings? Can analysts forecast earnings? In the last section we saw that good forecasts of earnings can lead to profitable returns. Hence, it is important to understand the characteristics of earnings and earnings changes.

The Influence of the Economy and Industry

In earlier chapters we showed that a stock's returns are strongly affected by market movements and by industry or sector returns. A similar phenomenon exists with respect to earnings. Earnings of a firm are strongly influenced by changes in aggregate earnings for the economy and there is some evidence that they are influenced by changes in the earnings of the industry to which the firm belongs. Table 19.4 illustrates the strength of these influences. The sample used in calculating this table was the earnings from 217 firms for the years 1948–1966. The earnings on the companies that comprise the S&P 425 index were used to represent the market index. The companies in the sample were divided into industries and the earnings averaged across each of the companies in the industry to obtain an industry index. The percentage of changes in each firm's earnings that could be attributed to the market and the industry was then determined. The results for individual firms were then averaged across an industry.

As can be seen by examining the table, on average 21% of the changes in firm's earnings can be accounted for by changes in the market's earnings, and an additional 21% of the changes in a firm's earnings can be accounted for by the changes in the industry earnings. The strength of these influences varied considerably. Earnings for companies in industries such as autos, chemicals, and steel seemed to be heavily influenced by market-wide changes. The earnings of firms in the oil industry and the rubber industry seemed to

Table 19.4   Proportion of Earnings Movement Attributable to Economy or Industry Influences

Industry	Economy Influence (%)	Industry Influence (%)
Aircraft	11	5
Autos	48	11
Beer	11	7
Cement	6	32
Chemical	41	8
Cosmetics	5	6
Department Stores	30	37
Drugs	14	7
Electricals	24	8
Food	10	10
Machinery	19	16
Nonferrous Metals	26	25
Office Machinery	14	6
Oil	13	49
Paper	27	28
Rubber	26	48
Steel	32	21
Supermarkets	6	33
Textiles and Clothing	25	29
Tobacco	8	19
All Companies	21	21

Source: Brealey [3].

be strongly influenced by industry changes. Many of the differences shown in the table may well be unique to the period examined. However, the large effects of market and industry factors are probably indicative of real influences.[4] A forecast of economy-wide changes and industry-wide changes may be useful first steps in estimating the companies' earnings.

The important effect of the economy on a company's earnings can be illustrated in another way. A number of authors have divided earnings by the book value of the assets to obtain a return on assets. This is then correlated with a similar measure for the market. Gonedes [15] performed this correlation for 316 firms using data from 1946–1969. He found on average that 23% of the variation of return on book assets can be explained by variation in the market return on book assets.

Gonedes [16] also analyzed the correlation of total income (rather than earnings per share) and a similar measure for the economy and industry. His sample consisted of 99 firms in the years 1946–1968. Gonedes used the average of the total income for the firms in his sample as a measure of the economy's earnings. Similarly, he used the firms in his sample to obtain an average for each industry. Since the earnings of each industry are affected by the economy's earnings, he removed this influence before calculating the correlations. Gonedes found that the industry influence was insignificant once the effect of the economy was taken into account. However, he did find a strong influence of the economy. Over his full period he found that variations in aggregate income for the economy explained about 50% of the variation in the firm's total income.

---

[4]There is some overstatement of the correlation since the firms themselves are part of the industry and economy.

All of these studies strongly suggest that changes in the economy's earnings influence the earnings of many firms. Furthermore, there is some evidence that industry earnings are also important.

In order to be able to utilize relationships such as those described previously, it is necessary that the relationships be reasonably stable over time and that economy and industry earnings be more easily forecasted than the earnings for individual companies. There is no evidence concerning this. Thus, at this time, while we can say that economy-wide and industry-wide earnings are useful in explaining the earnings of individual companies, demonstration that this is useful in improving prediction must await further research.

Past Earnings and Future Earnings

Two separate issues have been examined with respect to the time-series behavior of earnings. One is whether past growth is an indication of future growth. The second is whether the concept of normal earnings is meaningful. We discuss each of these in turn.

One of the popular terms used in the financial literature is the term "growth stock." This term often refers to a stock that has had substantial growth in the past and is expected to in the future. Names like IBM and Xerox come to mind. From this, one would expect that stocks that have had high growth in the past would have high growth in the future. A number of studies have seriously questioned this assumption. Lintner and Glauber [18] examined the correlation of aggregate earnings and earnings per share for 323 companies during 1946–1965. The 20 years of data were divided in four 5-year periods and two 10-year periods. Growth was estimated for each of these periods and correlations between the growth rates in adjacent periods was calculated.[5] The results give little comfort to anyone expecting past growth to predict the future. The highest association between successive growth rates implied that less than 2% of the variation in growth in the latter period was explained by growth in the earlier period. Lintner and Glauber introduced two modifications to try to improve the correlation in growth rates. First they deflated earnings by a measure of aggregate economic conditions. Second, they divided firms into groups by stability of growth rate and ran correlations within each group. This did lead to improvement. In one time period they were able to explain almost 50% of the variation in future growth rates by past growth rates. However, for most periods and most cases studied, less than 10% of the variation in future growth rates was explained by past growth.

Brealey [3] analyzed the same question in a slightly different way. He analyzed the growth of 610 industrial companies from 1950 to 1964. Each year he determined the 305 firms with the highest growth and the 305 firms with the lowest. If past growth is helpful in predicting future growth, then one would expect that firms would tend to have long periods when they were in the high-growth group and long periods when they were in the low-growth groups. The alternative is that the odds of being in either group is 50–50, independent of the firm's position in the previous period. Table 19.5 shows the results. The first column indicates the number of years the firms were in the same group. For example, the first entry in the second column is 1,152. This means 1,152 times firms were in the high-growth group one year and not in that group the next. The second entry, 562, means that 562 times firms were in the high-growth group two years in a row and in the low-growth group the next year. The first two columns look very similar to the last. In fact, the odds of long runs are, in general, higher for the last column than in the first two. The most striking place where the first two columns have higher odds than the last is for lengths of

---

[5]Growth was estimated using a logarithmic regression on time.

Table 19.5 Persistence of Growth

Length of Time in Same Group	No. of Consecutive Years of High Growth	No. of Consecutive Years of Low Growth	Expected No. of Consecutive Years of Low or High Growth if Odds Are 50–50 Regardless of Past Performance
1	1,152	1,102	1,068
2	562	590	534
3	266	300	267
4	114	120	133
5	55	63	67
6	24	20	33
7	23	12	17
8	5	6	8
9	3	3	4
10	6	0	2
11	2	0	1
12	1	0	1
13	0	0	0
14	0	0	0

Source: Brealey [3].

time one. But this implies that a good year follows a bad year more than expected by chance and vice versa.[6] This is the opposite of what one expects if past growth was a good predictor of the future.

These two studies are typical of the results found by a number of authors. These results have led them to speculate that earnings changes might be independent from period to period. The economic argument of why this might be so goes as follows: The economy is highly competitive. The earnings of a company are subject to a large number of uncertainties not under management control. These include strikes, mineral discoveries, regulatory changes, foreign competition, changing tastes, and so on. These kinds of uncertainties are the dominant influences on a company's fortunes on a year-to-year basis.

The counterargument is that there are a number of companies with monopoly control of the markets, with patent protection on unique products, or superior management, and these companies are able to sustain a high level of growth over a long period of time.

The argument for independence in earnings is much less persuasive than the argument for the independence of security prices presented in Chapter 17. Earnings are determined

---

[6]There is a potential bias here. One plus growth from t to $t + 1$ is

$$\frac{\text{Earnings } t + 1}{\text{Earnings } t}$$

Likewise, one plus growth from $t - 1$ to t is

$$\frac{\text{Earnings } t}{\text{Earnings } t - 1}$$

Thus, earnings in t appear on both sides of the equation. Under certain circumstances (such as the reversion to the mean process of generating earnings discussed in the next section), this can cause a negative basis and could account for the results just discussed.

by a physical process while stock prices are determined by expectations. It is reasonable to assume that changes in expectations cannot be predicted from past data or they would already be incorporated in the expectations. It is a more stringent requirement to assume that past levels of a physical process do not convey information about the future. However, the empirical evidence reviewed earlier is a useful cautionary note to those who would place too heavy a reliance on past earnings to predict the future.

The second major issue concerning the time series of earnings is the concept of normal earnings. To understand this issue, it is easiest to ignore growth for the moment and to assume independence of earnings between time periods. One view of a firm's earnings is as follows: The firm's earnings are on average $1.00, but there is some variation. Table 19.6 shows a possible scenario. If this is the process that describes earnings, then one would expect, if earnings were at an extreme, they would be closer to the mean the next period. For example, if you observed earnings of $1.20 in one period, you would expect, on average, that they would be less the next period. Extremes followed by observations closer to the mean would tend to introduce a negative correlation in the time series.

The second alternative scenario is illustrated in Table 19.7. The distinctive element of this process is that there is no tendency to revert to some mean level of earnings. The change occurs from the last level of earnings. If earnings are $1.20, then 10% of the time they will increase by 10% to $1.32, 20% of the time they will increase by 5% to $1.26, and so forth. This period's earnings serve as a starting point for the change to next period's earnings. If we observe earnings of $1.20, we are just as likely to have an increase in the earnings as a decrease. With this view of earnings there is no such thing as extreme earnings and one would not expect the negative correlation discussed earlier.

The issue of which process describes earnings is important. If the first process is a better description, then the starting point for any forecast of future earnings is an estimate of the mean or "normal" earnings. If the second process is more descriptive, then the starting point of any forecast is the latest observed level of earnings.

Throughout the discussion we assumed zero growth. This just simplified the discussion. The same discussion holds with growth. If a process like that in Table 19.6 is descriptive of earnings patterns except for the presence of a growth rate, then the starting point for the estimate of earnings using historical earnings is normal earnings plus an estimate of growth. If the second model is more descriptive, then the starting point is this period's earnings plus an estimate of growth. We also assumed independence. If there is positive dependence, then this should mitigate the negative correlation in the first case and impart positive correlation in the second. There are two types of evidence on this issue. The first is correlation in successive earnings changes. Brealey examined this question and found slight negative correlation in the series. While this is supportive of the concept of normal earnings, it was so small that it is not very strong support. The second type of evidence is forecast evidence. Does this concept of normalized earnings lead to a better forecast of earnings or does using last period's earnings produce a better forecast?

Table 19.6   Possible Levels of Earnings

Earnings	Odds
1.20	10%
1.10	20%
1.00	40%
0.90	20%
0.80	10%

Table 19.7   Possible Changes in Earnings

Earnings Change	Odds
+10%	10%
+5%	20%
0%	40%
−5%	20%
−10%	10%

Elton and Gruber [11] examined this question and found that allowing smoothing over a longer period of time led to better forecasts than did the simple use of last period's earnings. Ball and Watts, in contrast, found that last periods's earnings worked best. There were two major differences in the studies. First, Elton and Gruber utilized much more complicated forecasting models than Ball and Watts.[7] Second, Ball and Watts required that the same forecasting model be used to forecast the earnings of all firms. Elton and Gruber allowed a different model for each firm and selected the one to use in making comparisons that had provided the most accurate forecasting of earnings in prior periods. For many firms this was, in fact, last period's earnings, but in other cases it was a smoothed value of past earnings. When Elton and Gruber allowed this variation, they achieved improved forecasts. Lieber and Ronen [17] repeated this for the Ball and Watts sample and found that allowing individual variation led to improved forecasting. Thus, reality probably includes both of the models of firm's earnings discussed in Tables 19.6 and 19.7. For many firms the concept of normal earnings is superior, while for other firms last period's earnings provide a better forecast of next period's earnings.

The research that has been done on using the time series of past earnings to predict future earnings is not very encouraging. The evidence seems to suggest that in many cases the naive model of next year's earnings equals this year's earnings seems to do as well as more sophisticated extrapolations. This should serve as a cautionary note to anyone predicting future earnings using the past levels.

Forecasting Earnings with Additional Types of Historical Data

Firms make available a great deal more information than past levels of earnings per share. Perhaps this information can be used to forecast future levels of earnings per share or future growth in earnings per share. For example, changes in sales or research and development expense or new investment might be related to future earnings. If such a relationship exists, then past values could be used to estimate the relationship and this relationship could be used to forecast the future.

---

[7]Elton and Gruber [11] used an exponential smoothing model with an arithmetic change in growth. Their model is presented here:

Let E be earnings, g be growth, and subscripts indicate time periods. Let a and b be constants with a value between 0 and 1, and carets (^) indicate smoothed values. Then

1. Forecast of earnings $= \hat{E}_t + \hat{g}_t$
2. $\hat{E}_t = (\hat{E}_{t-1} + \hat{g}_{t-1}) + a[E_t - (\hat{E}_{t-1} + \hat{g}_{t-1})]$
3. $\hat{g}_t = (\hat{g}_{t-1}) + b[(\hat{E}_t - \hat{E}_{t-1}) - \hat{g}_{t-1}]$

In contrast, the Ball and Watts model [1] was:

1. Forecast of earnings $= \hat{E}_t$
2. $\hat{E}_t = a\hat{E}_{t-1} + (1 - a)E_t$

How can this be done? Assume that a set of variables is important in estimating earnings per share for firms in the same industry. Then a forecasting equation could be determined by estimating across the firms in the industry the best relationship between this set of variables and future earnings. Elton and Gruber [11] tried this with 180 firm samples. They estimated for each industry in their sample a relationship between earnings and past values of other firm variables. They compared the forecasting equations derived for each industry with a method using past earnings alone. The method using past earnings alone was superior.

This does not necessarily mean that the basic idea is unsound. It is possible that the variables they selected were poor or the industry groupings they utilized were not homogeneous with respect to the variables affecting future earnings or the relationship between these variables and future earnings.

Elton and Gruber [11] explored this latter explanation. They divided firms into groups by similarity in the pattern of their previous growth. They argued that if firms had similar growth patterns, they probably had responded to similar influences. Their procedure yielded a set of 10 groups or pseudo-industries. They then repeated the same analysis done previously, treating each of these 10 groups the same way they had treated traditional industries. This yielded a set of 10 forecast equations, one for each group. When they examined the accuracy of the forecasts generated in this way with the accuracy of a model utilizing only past earnings, they found that the forecasting equations utilizing other firm variables were superior. They repeated the analysis over several periods and several samples and the results were similar.

These results suggest that firm information, other than past earnings, may be useful in predicting future earnings.

Analysts' Forecasts

We have seen in earlier sections that accurate forecasts can lead to superior returns. Given this, it should not be surprising that security analysts spend a great deal of time forecasting earnings. In this section we intend to analyze the properties of these forecasts.

There seems to be a great deal of agreement among security analysts concerning the future earnings of a company. Cragg and Malkiel [7] examined the correlation between estimates of the growth in earnings forecasted by five different organizations in 1963 (labeled A to E) and four in 1962 (labeled A to D). Table 19.8 reproduces their results. An examination of the table shows that there is a high degree of agreement among analysts concerning the future prospects of a company. They tested to see if this agreement came about because of a common agreement concerning the prospects of particular industries

Table 19.8   Agreement among Growth-Rate Predictions

					Correlation Coefficients				
	1962					1963			
	A	B	C	D		A	B	C	D	E
A	1.000				A	1.000				
B	0.840	1.000			B	0.832	1.000			
C	0.889	0.819	1.000		C	0.854	0.764	1.000		
D	0.563	0.621	0.848	1.000	D	0.537	0.567	0.898	1.000	
					E	0.827	0.835	0.889	0.704	1.000

Source: Cragg and Malkiel [7].

and found that it was not a major factor. Rather, the agreement comes about because of similar forecasts of individual companies.

The second characteristic of analysts' estimates is that they are heavily influenced by past growth. Table 19.9 shows the correlations of the analysts' forecasts with a number of historical growth measures. Comparing this table with the previous one indicates that the correlation with past growth is just about as high as the correlation among the analysts. Analysts seem to place a heavy reliance on past growth rates in making their estimates of the future. Cragg and Malkiel went on to examine whether or not the correlation among analysts' estimates can be explained completely in terms of the correlation with past growth. Although the common reliance of analysts on past growth is an important reason for the similarity of forecasts, it is not the sole reason. After adjusting for the influence of past growth on analysts' forecasts, there is still a substantial amount of commonality in their forecasts.

In Chapter 25 we return to the question of the accuracy of analysts' forecasts. We place special emphasis on techniques for determining the accuracy of these forecasts.

CONCLUSION

In Chapter 25, we will analyze the accuracy of analysts' estimates in some detail. It is sufficient to state here that most studies have not found a great deal of predictive content in their estimates.

The studies discussed in this section do not provide a magic formula for predicting earnings. This should not be surprising, nor especially disturbing. Even if such a formula existed, its value would already be mitigated as investors utilized it to obtain superior predictions, and this was reflected in security price. We view the studies discussed in this section as suggestive of the kinds of analysis that might be worthwhile as well as the types of

Table 19.9   Predictions and Past Growth Rates[a] (Correlations of Predicted with Past Growth Rates)

	1962				1963				
	A	*B*	*C*	*D*	*A*	*B*	*C*	*D*	*E*
g_{p1}	0.78	0.68	0.75	0.41	0.85	0.73	0.84	0.56	0.67
g_{p2}	0.75	0.67	0.72	0.51	0.79	0.69	0.80	0.58	0.76
g_{p3}	0.77	0.71	0.82	0.61	0.75	0.72	0.79	0.70	0.74
g_{p4}	0.34	0.37	0.59	0.44	0.33	0.45	0.70	0.75	0.58
g_{c1}	0.55	0.46	0.65	0.32	0.63	0.52	0.61	0.30	0.58
g_{c2}	0.67	0.60	0.68	0.18	0.72	0.58	0.73	0.20	0.56
g_{c3}	0.75	0.63	0.73	0.17	0.79	0.66	0.76	0.17	0.57
g_{c4}	0.82	0.68	0.79	0.24	0.83	0.69	0.79	0.29	0.60

[a]g_{p1} is 8–10 year historic growth rate supplied by *A*.
g_{p2} is 4–5 year historic growth rate supplied by *A*.
g_{p3} is 6 year historic growth rate supplied by *D*.
g_{p4} is preceding 1 year growth rate supplied by *D*.
g_{c1} is log-regression trend fitted to last 4 years.
g_{c2} is log-regression trend fitted to last 6 years.
g_{c3} is log-regression trend fitted to last 8 years.
g_{c4} is log-regression trend fitted to last 10 years.
Source: Cragg and Malkiel [7].

behavior and research that are unlikely to be productive. Research is under way and should continue in this area.

QUESTIONS AND PROBLEMS

1. Write down the forecast of next period's earnings if

   A. Earnings are a mean reverting process with no trend or cycle.

   B. Earnings are a mean reverting process with a trend but not a cycle.

   C. Earnings are a mean reverting process with a trend and a cycle.

2. How would earnings be forecast if there was a strong relationship between the firm's earnings and the industry's and economy's earnings?

3. Is a strong relationship between a firm's earnings and an economy's earnings consistent with a mean reversion process for earnings generation?

4. Is a strong relationship between a firm's earnings and an economy's earnings consistent with last period's earnings being a better estimate of next period's earnings than normal earnings?

5. If expectations determine share price, what is a valuable analyst?

BIBLIOGRAPHY

1. Ball, Ray, and Watts, Ross. "Some Time Series Properties of Accounting Numbers," *Journal of Finance*, **27** (June 1972), pp. 663–681.
2. Bar-Yosef, Sasson, Callan, Jeffrey R. and Livnot, Joshua: Causality and Autoregressive Modeling of Earnings-Investment," *Journal of Finance*, **42,** No. 1 (March 1987), pp. 11–28.
3. Brealey, Richard. *An Introduction to Risk and Return from Common Stocks* (Cambridge, Mass.: MIT Press, 1969).
4. Brown, Lawrence, and Rozeff, Michael. "The Superiority of Analyst Forecasts as Measures of Expectations: Evidence from Earnings," *Journal of Finance*, **XXXIII,** No. 1 (Mar. 1978), pp. 1–16.
5. Chant, Peter D. "On the Predictability of Corporate Earnings per Share Behavior," *The Journal of Finance*, **35,** No. 1 (Mar. 1980), pp. 13–22.
6. Copelåd, Ronald, and Marioni, Robert. "Executives' Forecasts of Earnings per Share Versus Forecasts of Naive Models," *Journal of Business*, **45,** No. 4 (Oct. 1972), pp. 497–512.
7. Cragg, J. G., and Malkiel, Burton. "The Consensus and Accuracy of Some Predictions of the Growth of Corporate Earnings," *Journal of Finance*, **XXIII,** No. 1 (Mar. 1968), pp. 67–84.
8. Deschamps, Benôit, and Mehta, Dileep R. "Predictive Ability and Descriptive Validity of Earnings Forecasting Models," *The Journal of Finance*, **35,** No. 4 (Sept. 1980), pp. 933–950.
9. Edwards, Charles, and Hilton, James. "Some Comments on Short-Run Earnings Fluctuation Bias," *Journal of Financial and Quantitative Analysis*, **V,** No. 2 (May 1970), pp. 187–201.
10. Elton, Edwin J., and Gruber, Martin. "Improved Forecasting Through the Design of Homogeneous Groups," *Journal of Business*, **44,** No. 4 (Oct. 1971), pp. 432–450.
11. ——. "Earnings Estimation and the Accuracy of Expectational Data," *Management Science*, **18,** No. 2 (April 1972), pp. 409–424.
12. Elton, Edwin, Gruber, Martin, and Gultekin, M. "The Usefulness of Analyst Estimates of Earnings," Unpublished Manuscript, 1978.
13. ——. "Professional Expectations: Accuracy and Diagnosis of Errors," *Journal of Financial and Quantitative Analysis*, **19,** No. 4 (Dec. 1984), pp. 351–364.
14. Givoly, Dan, and Lakonishok, Josef. "The Quality of Analysts' Forecasts of Earnings," *Financial Analyst Journal*, **40,** No. 5 (Sept./Oct. 1984), pp. 40–48.

15. Gonedes, Nicholas. "Evidence on the Information Content of Accounting Numbers: Accounting-Based and Market-Based Estimates of Systematic Risk," *Journal of Financial and Quantitative Analysis*, **VIII,** No. 3 (June 1973), pp. 407–443.

16. ——. "A Note on Accounting-Based and Market-Based Estimates of Systematic Risk," *Journal of Financial and Quantitative Analysis*, **X,** No. 2 (June 1975), pp. 355–367.

17. Lieber, Zvi, and Ronen, Joshua. "Earnings Estimates and Historical Data," Unpublished Manuscript, Ross Center, New York University, 1975.

18. Lintner, John, and Glauber, Robert. "Higgeldy-Piggeldy Growth in America," Unpublished Manuscript, 1969.

19. Lorie, J., and Hamilton, M. *The Stock Market: Theories and Evidence* (Homewood, Ill.: Richard D. Irwin, 1973).

20. Mastrapasqua, Frank, and Bolten, Steven. "A Note on Financial Analyst Evaluation," *Journal of Finance*, **XXVIII,** No. 3 (June 1973), pp. 707–712.

21. McEnally, Richard. "An Investigation of the Extrapolative Determinants of Short-run Earnings Expectations," *Journal of Financial and Quantitative Analysis*, **VI,** No. 2 (March 1971), pp. 687–706.

22. Newell, Gale. "Revisions of Reported Quarterly Earnings," *Journal of Business*, **44,** No. 3 (July 1971), pp. 282–285.

23. Niederhoffer, V., and Regan, P. "Earnings Changes, Analysts' Forecasts, and Stock Prices," *Financial Analysts Journal*, **28,** No. 3 (May–June 1972), pp. 65–71.

24. Penman, Stephen H. "The Predictive Content of Earnings Forecasts and Dividends," *The Journal of Finance*, **38,** No. 4 (Sept. 1983), pp. 1181–1200.

25. ——. "A Comparison of the Information Content of Insider Trading and Management Earnings Forecasts," *Journal of Financial and Quantitative Analysis*, **20,** No. 1 (Mar. 1985), pp. 1–18.

26. Richards, Malcolm. "Analysts' Performance and the Accuracy of Corporate Earnings Forecasts," *Journal of Business*, **49,** No. 3 (July 1976), pp. 350–357.

20

Interest Rate Theory and the Pricing of Bonds

Until the last few decades, bond valuation was considered a rather dull subject. After all, a bond is easier to value than a stock because the issuer has agreed to a certain stream of payments (coupon and principal) and the bond has a maximum life (maturity).

Two factors led to a change in the difficulty of valuation. First, the timing of cash flows became more variable and their payment less certain because new types of instruments were issued. For example, bonds were issued with more complex options, which could affect both the timing and magnitude of the cash flows. In addition, more risky debt was issued with less certain cash flows. Second, valuation became more difficult because interest rates become more volatile. When interest rates go up, bond prices fall so that outstanding bonds offer returns similar to those earned by new issues. Interest rates were volatile during the 1970s and the 1980s. Accompanying this increased volatility were huge swings in the market value of bond portfolios. This increased volatility in market values was viewed as an opportunity and as a risk. Active bond portfolio management began to receive a lot of attention.

Table 20.1 presents the yearly holding period return that would have been earned by holding four different portfolios of bonds from 1990 to 2000, as well as the average interest rate on 10-year government bonds. Returns from holding long-term corporate bonds were extremely volatile during this period. For example, the return from this portfolio was −5.45 in 1994 and 25.03 in 1995. These returns bear little resemblance to the interest rate on long-term bonds during those years. Given the variability of bond returns, you might suspect that we are heading toward a consideration of a portfolio theory for bonds. In fact, that is the subject of the next chapter. But before we attempt to construct portfolio strategies, we must understand the pricing of bonds—discussed in this chapter. The first part of this chapter, after briefly introducing the major types of bonds, discusses the many meanings of interest rates and places special emphasis on the role of one of these rates, the spot rate, in determining bond prices. The second part of the chapter discusses the determination of bond prices. The third and longer part of the chapter deals with the factors that explain bond prices.

Table 20.1   Yields and Rates of Return on Selected Diversified Bond Portfolios

	1990	1991	1992	1993	1994	1995	1996	1997	1998	1999	2000
Average Yield											
Government 10 Year	8.07	6.70	6.69	5.80	7.83	5.58	6.42	5.75	4.65	6.44	5.12
Yearly Returns											
1. Intermediate Government	9.21	13.28	6.78	7.91	−1.72	13.57	4.03	7.49	8.21	0.51	10.02
2. Long Government	6.55	17.46	8.05	16.38	−7.69	27.47	−0.45	14.49	12.83	−8.97	18.74
3. Intermediate Corporate	7.42	15.49	7.98	10.65	−2.60	17.57	3.98	8.11	8.04	0.20	8.94
4. Long Corporate	6.51	19.28	9.11	12.98	−5.65	25.03	2.47	12.95	8.84	−5.84	8.41

AN INTRODUCTION TO DEBT SECURITIES

Bonds are primarily traded over the counter rather than on organized exchanges. For some bond issues the bond markets are highly liquid. Other bonds rarely trade. There are four major categories of long-term fixed income securities:

1. Federal government bonds
2. Corporate bonds
3. Mortgages
4. Municipal bonds

Although these were discussed in Chapter 2, we will review their major characteristics here.

Government Bonds

Government bonds represent the borrowing of the federal government. They represent the largest percentage of the total debt market and are by far the most liquid. Since they are backed by the government, they are considered default free. They are the simplest to value; they pay interest at a fixed rate and have a stated principal. The only complicating factor in valuing government bonds is that some issues are callable; that is, the government can force the investor to give up the bond at a stated price at the government's discretion.[1]

Corporate Bonds

Corporate bonds are debt obligations of corporations. Corporate issues can be publicly traded or privately placed, usually with a bank or insurance company. The publicly traded corporate market is much less active than the government market, with many of the issues rarely if ever trading after the initial offering. Corporate bonds are backed by the credit of the issuing corporation. It is the corporation's ability to earn money and meet the obligations of the debt issue that determines the bond's default risk. Generally, corporate bonds are divided into investment grade, where the risk of default is low and high yield or junk where the risk of default is substantial. Although many different types of option features can be present on corporate bonds, callability, sinking funds, and convertibility are the most common. A call

[1] All government bonds issued since 1985 are noncallable.

provision on a bond gives the issuing corporation the right to force the bondholder to sell the bond back to the corporation at a particular price. The price is known and may vary over time. The right to call rests with the corporation, and hence callable bonds must offer a higher return to compensate the holder for a disadvantageous call. Sinking funds options are like the call option. A large corporate bond issue may have a sinking fund provision. Consider a 100 million 10-year bond issue. The sinking fund provision may require the corporation to retire 10 million in face value of bonds a year for each of the 10 years. The sinking fund is intended to prevent the corporation from having to make one large repayment. The corporation generally has the option of purchasing the bonds in the open market or calling them back from the investors. Thus the investor risks having the bond called back to meet the sinking fund. Once again, because the corporation has the option, the investor will require a higher return, everything else held constant, to compensate for the disadvantageous call; everything else isn't constant, however. The presence of a sinking fund lowers the risk that the firm will default on the entire issue of bonds or perhaps on any of it. The presence of a sinking fund with the ability to call bonds to meet it results in a lower default risk but a higher interest rate risk for the bondholder. Finally, convertible bonds are bonds that can be exchanged for another security, usually common equity. Since the option rests with the bondholder, the bondholder has a potentially valuable option and these bonds are issued with lower interest payments than noncallable bonds.

Mortgage Bonds

Mortgages are debt obligations backed by real estate. Most mortgages are owned by a bank, insurance company, or other financial institution. However, many mortgage loans are publicly traded by pooling a group of mortgages and issuing bonds against the pool. The most liquid of the publicly traded mortgage instruments are Ginnie Maes, which are bonds backed by a pool of mortgages. The government insures the payment of principal and interest on the mortgages and extracts a fee for the insurance. In addition, a fee for collection of the mortgage payments is extracted. The remainder of the principal and interest payments on the mortgage is passed along to the Ginnie Mae owner. Since mortgages are paid monthly, interest on Ginnie Maes is also paid monthly. Ginnie Maes have interesting risk characteristics in that the default risk has been removed by the issuer, but there is major risk from the uncertainty associated with the timing of the payment stream. Homeowners have the option to prepay their mortgages and they will generally do so if they sell the home or if interest rates fall sufficiently. Since these options rest with the payer of the mortgage, the purchaser of a Ginnie Mae is uncertain about the size of the payment that will be received. To compensate for this uncertainty, investors in Ginnie Maes will require a higher return than on comparable governments.

Municipal Bonds

The final major category of bonds is municipals. These are debt obligations of states, cities, and state or city authorities. Municipal bonds are generally divided into two broad categories—bonds that are backed by the full faith and credit of the city or state, and those that are backed by a government agency or authority. The latter, called revenue bonds, would be issued by a government agency such as a port authority or turnpike authority and are backed by the revenues generated by the agency. Municipal bonds have default risk. Their major distinguishing characteristic is that the interest on municipal bonds is exempt from federal tax and sometimes from state tax, depending on the issuing state and the residence of the purchaser.

THE MANY DEFINITIONS OF RATES

An investor who examines the literature on bond valuation will find a confusing array of terms all seemingly related to interest rates—terms like spot rates, future rates, yield to maturity, and current yield. In the following we define and explain these alternative rates.

The rate most investment professionals use to compare bonds is yield to maturity. The method used to calculate the yield to maturity varies across bond categories. Thus, yield to maturities on different types of instruments may not be comparable. In what follows we will discuss general principles underlying the calculation of yield to maturity, the variations in calculations across bond categories, and how to make the calculations comparable. The yield to maturity is the internal rate of return earned from holding a bond to maturity. The yield to maturity on a three-year bond with annual interest payments of $100, a principal payment of $1000, and a cost $900 is that rate ($y$) that equates the present value of the three cash flows on the bond with its present price or[2]

$$900 = \frac{100}{(1+y)} + \frac{100}{(1+y)^2} + \frac{100+1000}{(1+y)^3}$$

Therefore,

$$y = 14.3\%$$

This expression for yield to maturity can also be written in summation notation. Let $C(t)$ be the cash flow in t. The cash flow in the example is either the coupon of $100 or the principal plus interest of $1100. Then in summation notation yield to maturity is the value of y that solves the following expression.

$$\text{Price} = \sum_t \frac{C(t)}{(1+y)^t}$$

The frequency of compounding assumed in computing the yield to maturity varies across types of bonds. We will review several compounding conventions here.

Government bonds and notes and most corporate bonds pay interest semiannually. The yield to maturity on these bonds is calculated differently from the earlier example. Assume a three-year bond with semiannual interest payments of $50, a principal payment of $1000, and a cost of $900. The yield to maturity is calculated as follows.

$$900 = \frac{50}{\left(1+\dfrac{y}{2}\right)} + \frac{50}{\left(1+\dfrac{y}{2}\right)^2} + \frac{50}{\left(1+\dfrac{y}{2}\right)^3} +$$

$$\frac{50}{\left(1+\dfrac{y}{2}\right)^4} + \frac{50}{\left(1+\dfrac{y}{2}\right)^5} + \frac{1050}{\left(1+\dfrac{y}{2}\right)^6}$$

Thus,

$$y = 14.2\%$$

The yield to maturity calculated in this way is also called the bond equivalent yield. This method of determining the yield to maturity is based on a rather arbitrary assumption about

---

[2]Eurobonds, which are bonds not registered with the Securities and Exchange Commission (SEC), pay annual interest, and their yield to maturity is calculated in the manner just shown.

reinvestment. Although it assumes discounting and compounding on a semiannual basis, it assumes no compounding in converting semiannual yield to an annual yield. That is, the semiannual rate of return is converted to an annual return by multiplying it by 2. This ignores the fact that the investor can earn interest on the first coupon received any year for the second half of the year. If one assumes that interest can be earned on the first payment received in a year, then the actual annual return is the value at the half year $(1 + y/2)$ times the return in the second half year $(1 + y/2)$ or on the example $[(1.071)^2] - 1 = 14.7\%$. This is often called the effective annual yield (y_E) and it is always higher than the yield to maturity stated on the bond.

The effective annual yield represents the annual return the investor will receive if he or she holds the bond to maturity and if coupons are reinvested every six months at one-half the bond equivalent yield for each six-month period.[3] Similar methodology and terminology apply for debt instruments that pay interest at more frequent intervals than semiannually. For example, Ginnie Maes have monthly cash flows of interest and principal. A 30-year Ginnie Mae would have 360 payments (12×30). If $C(t)$ is the payment, then the yield to maturity is y where

$$\text{price} = \sum_{t}^{360} \frac{C(t)}{\left(1 + \dfrac{y}{12}\right)^t}$$

In computing the yield to maturity the monthly interest rate $y/12$ is annualized by multiplying by 12. Once again no compounding is assumed in annualizing. The effective annual yield is one plus the monthly interest rate to the 12th power.

$$y_E = \left(1 + \frac{y}{12}\right)^{12} - 1$$

For example, if $C(t)$ is \$8482 and the price is \$1000, then

$$1,000,000 = \sum_{t}^{360} \frac{8482}{\left(1 + \dfrac{y}{12}\right)^t}$$

the yield to maturity is

$$y = 9.6\%$$

The effective annual yield is

$$y_E = \left(1 + \frac{0.096}{12}\right)^{12} - 1$$

$$y_E = 10.03\%$$

The quoted yield on Treasury bills is computed very differently than quoted yields on other instruments. Since Treasury bills are an important instrument, it is worthwhile discussing how rates are calculated.

Treasury bills are government debt issued with maturities of one year or less, There are only two cash flows associated with Treasury bills, one with the original purchase and one when the Treasury bill matures (they don't pay interest). A Treasury bill with a maturity of

---

[3]The reader should be alerted to the fact that the quoted price on bonds is not the trade price. The trade price includes accrued interest. (See Appendix A.)

60 days may be issued at 99 and mature at 100. The return is earned by the appreciation from 99 to 100. The interest rate on Treasury bills is calculated by the following formula called the bankers discount yield,

$$b = \frac{P_1 - P_0}{P_1} \cdot \frac{360}{N}$$

where

P_1 is ending price

P_0 is beginning price

N is number of days to maturity

In the example presented above, the bankers' discounted yield would be

$$b = \frac{100 - 99}{100} \times \frac{360}{60} = 6.00\%$$

as we have shown, the method used to calculate yield to maturity varies across instruments. Those investors using yield to maturity to compare bonds should adjust the calculations so that a common set of assumptions is being used. This is true when comparing Treasury bills to other government bonds. This is also true when comparing Ginnie Maes or Eurobonds to governments. Most institutions either calculate the effective annual yield on all instruments or adjust all instruments to have the same assumptions as government bonds by calculating a semiannual interest rate and doubling it (the bond equivalent yield).[4] Methods for doing this are presented in Appendix C.

Although the yield to maturity is the most common rate used in the investment community, there are problems with it. The yield to maturity is the return if all cash flows received before the horizon are invested at the yield to maturity to the horizon. Since different bonds have different yield to maturities, an investment organization choosing among bonds with different yields to maturity is making different assumptions concerning the reinvestment rate.

---

[4]For example, for Ginnie Maes, one would take the monthly interest rate y/12 and compute the semiannual interest rate

$$\left[\left(1 + \frac{y}{12}\right)^6 - 1\right]$$

The semiannual interest rate is then doubled to get an annual rate. Similarly for Treasury bills, the return earned over the life of the Treasury bill can be calculated by

$$r = b \cdot N/360 \cdot \frac{P_1}{P_0}$$

and the bond equivalent yield is

$$2 \times \left[(1 + r)^{365/2N} - 1\right]$$

See Appendix C for the calculations for all instruments.

As an illustration of the difficulty this causes, consider the following example:

	Bond A	Bond B
Coupon	10%	3%
Principal	100	100
Price	$138.90	$70.22
Maturity	15 years	15 years
Frequency of Payment	Annual	Annual
Yield to Maturity	6%	6.1%

In calculating the yield to maturity the implicit assumption is that cash flows are reinvested at 6% for bond A and 6.1% for bond B (the respective yield to maturities).

For an organization there will be some rate at which funds are invested, and this will be the same rate no matter which bond the coupon payments come from. For any reinvestment rate above 6.43% the value in 15 years will be higher for bond A than B.[5]

In addition, because of the differing reinvestment assumptions, yields are not additive. The yield to maturity on a portfolio is not a weighted average of the yields on the bonds that comprise it, where the weights are the proportion invested in each bond.

This is illustrated in Table 20.2. The yield to maturity is calculated for each of the three bonds as well for portfolios of the bonds. In addition, a weighted yield to maturity is calculated where the weights are the proportion invested in each bond. For example, the weights for $A + C$ are

$$\frac{100}{192} \text{ for } A \text{ and } \frac{92}{192} \text{ for } C$$

Note that the weighted average yield to maturity is not the yield to maturity when it is calculated using the cash flows on the portfolio as a whole. Yields are not additive. Investment professionals and some academics often talk about a yield pickup swap as a trading strategy. A yield pickup swap is trading one bond for another bond with a higher yield. Since the yield on a portfolio is not additive, a yield pickup swap can actually lower the yield on a portfolio. Finally, the yield to maturity is not generally the expected return on the bond if the bond is sold before the maturity.

Table 20.2   Illustrating the Nonadditivity of Yields

Outlay Bond	(Price)	Periods 1	2	3	Yield to Maturity	Weighted Average Yield
A	−100	15	15	115	15.00%	
B	−100	6	106		6.00%	
C	−92	9	9	109	12.35%	
A + B	−200	21	121	115	11.29%	10.50%
B + C	−192	15	115	109	9.65%	9.04%
A + C	−192	24	24	224	13.71%	13.73%

[5]In the next section we will show that the price of a bond is determined by discounting the cash flows at spot rates. In calculating the prices, a sharply rising yield curve was assumed with subsequent one-period rates above 5.9% throughout and in fact above 7.7% by period 2. Thus the anticipated reinvestment rate is well above 6.43% and the organization should prefer bond A.

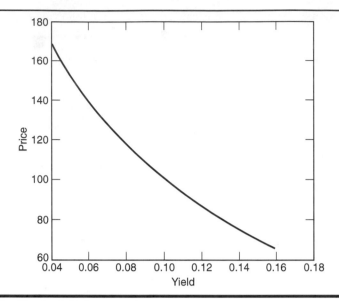

Figure 20.1   Graph of yield versus price.

Before leaving this section we should point out that price bears an inverse relationship with yield to maturity. Figure 20.1 plots the price of a bond for yields ranging from 4% to 16%. The bond is a 10-year bond with an interest rate of 10% and paying interest semiannually. Note as yield increases the price declines. Furthermore, the plot has curvature and is not a straight line. This curvature is known as convexity and will be discussed in the next chapter.

A second type of rate frequently quoted in the financial community is current yield. Current yield is simply the annual coupon payment divided by the price. If a bond pays $50 semiannually and costs $800, its current yield is 12.5%. This is determined by 100/800 = 12.5%. Current yield is the "interest rate" normally quoted in the financial press. It has very limited usefulness. Current yield is not the expected return over the year, nor is it the return if the bond is held to maturity. For example, the current yield on a bond that does not pay interest (a zero coupon bond) is zero. An investor who selects investment on the basis of current yield will reject bonds with low coupons but large return in the form of capital gains.

A third type of rate of interest is the spot rate. Spot interest rates are yields to maturity on loans or bonds that pay only one cash flow to the investor. A bond with only one cash flow paid the investor is called a pure discount bond or a zero coupon bond. Spot rates have special importance in bond valuation. As we will show in the next section unless bonds are priced at a price equal to the present value of their cash flows discounted at the spot rate, profitable swaps will exist.

A bond that involves an investment of $970.87 and returns a principal of $1000 in six months is a six-month pure discount bond. The return on such a bond is the six-month spot rate.

Spot rates are usually calculated for six-month intervals and then annualized by doubling the six-month rate. In what follows, subscripts will designate time and time will be in six-month intervals. More specifically in what follows, 0 will designate today, 1 six months from now, 2 12 months from now, and so on.

Defining S_{01} as the annualized spot rate between zero and one.

$$970.87 = \frac{1000}{\left(1 + \dfrac{S_{01}}{2}\right)} \qquad S_{01} = 6\%$$

Table 20.3 presents a number of other examples of spot rates. Each bond is assumed to cost the amount shown. The cash flows associated with each bond are as indicated. Note that these cash flows involve only a principal payment. Until the early 1980s the only pure discount bonds were those issued by the U.S. government with maturities of one year or less (Treasury bills). As a result, more complex techniques involving the inference of spot rates from coupon-paying bonds were necessary in order to estimate longer-term spot rates. The techniques used in this calculation are discussed in Appendix B.

In the early 1980s, corporations started to issue pure discount instruments with longer maturities, and brokerage firms put together packages of coupon bonds and sold off each year's payment separately, thereby creating pure discount bonds. These bonds were called "stripped coupon" bonds.

A fourth type of interest rate is the forward rate. Forward rates are interest rates on bonds where the date the commitment is made and the date the money is loaned are different. If a commitment is made now on a one-year loan to commence in six months, then the interest rate on this loan is a forward rate. For example, assume $924.56 is to be lent in 6 months and $1000 is to be repaid in 18 months; the rate of interest on this loan is a forward rate. As with spot rates, forward rates are estimated for six-month intervals and then the six-month rate is doubled to annualize.

Thus the forward rate from 6 months to 18 months (f_{13}) is calculated by

$$\left(1 + \frac{f_{13}}{2}\right)^2 = \frac{1000}{924.56}$$

Table 20.3   Cash Flow with Pure Discount Bonds

Maturity in Half Years	Cost	Cash Flows of Pure Discount Bond Cash Inflows						Determination of Spot Rate	
		1	2	3	4	5	6	Calculation	6-month Spot Rate (annualized)
1	970.87	1000						$\left(1 + \dfrac{S_{01}}{2}\right)^1 = \dfrac{1000}{920.87}$	$S_{01} = 6\%$
2	933.51	0	1000					$\left(1 + \dfrac{S_{02}}{2}\right)^2 = \dfrac{1000}{933.51}$	$S_{02} = 7\%$
3	889.00	0	0	1000				$\left(1 + \dfrac{S_{03}}{2}\right)^3 = \dfrac{1000}{889.00}$	$S_{03} = 8\%$
4	838.56	0	0	0	1000			$\left(1 + \dfrac{S_{04}}{2}\right)^4 = \dfrac{1000}{838.56}$	$S_{04} = 9\%$
5	783.53	0	0	0	0	1000		$\left(1 + \dfrac{S_{05}}{2}\right)^5 = \dfrac{1000}{783.53}$	$S_{05} = 10\%$
6	725.25	0	0	0	0	0	1000	$\left(1 + \dfrac{S_{06}}{2}\right)^6 = \dfrac{1000}{725.25}$	$S_{06} = 11\%$

As a second example, consider the interest rate on a two-year loan to be made in one year. Since periods are six-month periods, the loan started at period 2 goes to period 6. If $845.80 is lent at 2 and $1000 is repaid at 6, the annualized forward rate is

$$\left(1 + \frac{f_{26}}{2}\right)^4 = \frac{1000}{(845.80)}$$

or

$$f_{26} = 8\%$$

Forward rates and spots have a very specific relationship. Consider an investor wishing to hold money for two periods. The investor could buy a two-period pure discount instrument. The ending value per $1 invested would be

$$\$1\left(1 + \frac{S_{02}}{2}\right)^2$$

Alternatively the investor could buy a one-period pure discount instrument and simultaneously agree to invest the proceeds at one at the forward rate from one to two. The ending value per $1 invested would be

$$\$1\left(1 + \frac{S_{01}}{2}\right)\left(1 + \frac{f_{12}}{2}\right)$$

Since the forward rate is known at time zero and the commitment is made at zero, the investor can analyze which is better at zero. For there not to be arbitrage opportunities (buying the more attractive and financing this by issuing the less attractive) the return must be the same or

$$\left(1 + \frac{S_{02}}{2}\right)^2 = \left(1 + \frac{S_{01}}{2}\right)\left(1 + \frac{f_{12}}{2}\right)$$

therefore,

$$\left(1 + \frac{f_{12}}{2}\right) = \frac{\left(1 + \frac{S_{02}}{2}\right)^2}{\left(1 + \frac{S_{01}}{2}\right)}$$

The return equivalency is an application of the law of one price. Similarly, an investor with a three-period horizon could hold a three-period spot or buy a two-period spot and simultaneously enter into a forward commitment from two to three. For there to be no arbitrage the return must be the same or

$$\left(1 + \frac{S_{03}}{2}\right)^3 = \left(1 + \frac{S_{02}}{2}\right)^2\left(1 + \frac{f_{23}}{2}\right)$$

thus,

$$\left(1 + \frac{f_{23}}{2}\right) = \frac{\left(1 + \frac{S_{03}}{2}\right)^3}{\left(1 + \frac{S_{02}}{2}\right)^2}$$

As a further example, consider the spot rates shown in Table 20.3 for period 1 and period 2.

$$S_{01} = 6\%$$
$$S_{02} = 7\%$$

These can be used to determine the forward rate from period 1 to 2. Thus,

$$\left(1 + \frac{f_{12}}{2}\right) = \frac{\left(1 + \frac{0.07}{2}\right)^2}{\left(1 + \frac{0.06}{2}\right)}$$

$$f_{12} = 8\%$$

A number of additional examples are shown in Table 20.4. Having examined alternative definitions of rates on bonds, it is time to explain the key role that spot rates play in the pricing of bonds.

BOND PRICES AND SPOT RATES

Table 20.5 shows the cash flows associated with three different bonds. The bonds have cash flows in two periods. The cash flows from bond A can be reproduced by taking $\frac{22}{21}$ of bond B and $\frac{1}{21}$ of bond C. Thus an investor who desires the cash flow pattern of bond A can either purchase bond A directly or $\frac{22}{21}$ of bond B and $\frac{1}{21}$ of bond C. Don't be disturbed that the weights don't add up to one. These are not portfolio weights representing the proportion of the money placed in each asset; rather, they represent how much of B and C must be purchased to duplicate the cash flows of bond A. If the fractions are bothersome, the equivalent transaction is the purchase of 22 bond B's and 1 bond C to duplicate the cash flow of 21 bond A's.

Assume that bond A is more expensive than the corresponding portfolio of bonds B and C. Then an investor wishing to hold bond A could purchase the equivalent more cheaply by buying a combination of bonds B and C. Similarly, an investor holding bond A could sell bond A and replace it with $\frac{22}{21}$ of bond B and $\frac{1}{21}$ of bond C. The portfolio would still

Table 20.4 Determination of Forward Rates

Maturity	6-month Spot Rate	Forward Calculation	Forward Rate (annualized)
1	3%		
2	3.5%	$\left(1 + \frac{f_{12}}{2}\right) = \frac{(1.035)^2}{(1.03)}$	$f_{12} = 8\%$
3	4.0%	$\left(1 + \frac{f_{23}}{2}\right) = \frac{(1.04)^3}{(1.035)^2}$	$f_{23} = 10.01\%$
4	4.5%	$\left(1 + \frac{f_{34}}{2}\right) = \frac{(1.045)^4}{(1.04)^3}$	$f_{34} = 12.03\%$
5	5.0%	$\left(1 + \frac{f_{45}}{2}\right) = \frac{(1.05)^5}{(1.045)^4}$	$f_{45} = 14.05\%$
6	5.5%	$\left(1 + \frac{f_{56}}{2}\right) = \frac{(1.055)^6}{(1.05)^5}$	$f_{56} = 16.07\%$

Table 20.5   Cash Flows Associated with Three Different Bonds

Bond	Price	Cash Inflows 1	Cash Inflows 2
A	P_A	10	110
B	P_B	5	105
C	P_C	100	0

have the same cash flow but the investor would obtain an immediate riskless profit equal to the difference in price of bond A and the price of the portfolio of bonds B and C less transaction costs.

A similar argument can be made if bond A is cheaper. In this case, any investor holding bonds B and C could replace an appropriate mixture of them with bond A, maintain the same cash flows, and obtain an immediate riskless profit. The belief that the price of A should be equal to the price of an appropriate mixture of B and C is an application of the law of one price.

The law of one price states that two identical items should sell at the same price. In this case, the identical items are the cash flows of bond A and the cash flows from the portfolio of $\frac{22}{21}$ of bond B and $\frac{1}{21}$ of bond C. If these items do not sell at the same price, then everyone interested in the bonds will buy the cheaper, or anyone holding the more expensive bond will swap the more expensive for the cheaper, until they are the same price.

The law of one price has an important implication for bond pricing. It implies that if bonds A, B, and C are of identical risk, such as all government bonds, then alternative cash flows arising in the same period must be discounted at an identical rate. This does not imply that the same rate is used each period, just that all cash flows that occur in the same period must be discounted at an identical rate. We can demonstrate why this is true with an example: If

1. $S_{01} = 6\%$
2. $S_{02} = 7\%$

then,

$$P_A = \frac{10}{(1+0.06/2)} + \frac{110}{(1+0.07/2)^2} = \$112.39$$

$$P_B = \frac{5}{(1+0.06/2)} + \frac{105}{(1+0.07/2)^2} = \$102.87$$

$$P_C = \frac{100}{(1+0.06/2)} = \$97.09$$

With these prices the price of bond A is equal to the sum of $\frac{22}{21}$ of the price of bond B and $\frac{1}{21}$ of the price of bond C: $\frac{22}{21}$ ($102.87) + $\frac{1}{21}$ ($97.09) = $112.42. If the discount rate for the cash flows of any of the three bonds is different, then the price of bond A is not the same as the price of the portfolio and the law of one price is violated. For example, if the first-period cash flow for bond B is discounted at 8% annually or 4% semiannually, its price is $102, and the price of the portfolio is less expensive than bond A. This general principle has to hold for all bonds, including pure discount bonds. Thus, the rate used to discount the cash flows is the spot rate. In summary, either bonds are priced so that their price is equal to the present value of their cash flows discounted at the spot rates, or the law of one price is violated and swap opportunities are available. As discussed previously, forward rates can be derived from spot rates; therefore, forward rates can be used equally well to determine bond prices.

DETERMINING SPOT RATES

More details on the techniques for determining spot rates or equivalent discount functions are discussed in Appendix B and the associated references. However, because spot rates and discount functions play such an important role in bond pricing, some understanding of how they are obtained is useful. To illustrate how spot rates are estimated, assume we observe the following two bond prices and cash flows

		Cash Flows	
Bond	Price	1	2
A	$100	106	
B	$ 96.54	6	106

Bond A is a one-period pure discount instrument. Thus, the one-period spot rate can be determined directly

$$100 = \frac{106}{1 + \frac{S_{01}}{2}}$$

By inspection, S_{01} is 12%. Having calculated the one-period spot rate, the two-period spot rate can be determined. In the prior section we learned that the price of a bond was the cash flows brought back to present at the spot rate. In symbols this is

$$96.54 = \frac{6}{\left(1 + \frac{S_{01}}{2}\right)} + \frac{106}{\left(1 + \frac{S_{02}}{2}\right)^2}$$

Since the one-period spot rate was calculated using the one-period bond (bond A), the value of the one-period spot rate can be substituted into the equation.

Substituting 12% for S_{01} leaves S_{02} as the only unknown and the equation becomes

$$96.54 = \frac{6}{(1.06)} + \frac{106}{\left(1 + \frac{S_{02}}{2}\right)^2}$$

Solving for S_{02} we obtain $S_{02} - 16\%$. Clearly, a three-period bond could be used to determine S_{03} and so forth until all spots were determined. There are generally a number of bonds with the same pattern of cash flows, and each of these could be used to derive the spot rates. Because in equilibrium the price of each of these is determined by the same spot rates, it shouldn't matter which was used. In practice, it does matter, and very different spot rates would be estimated, depending on which set of bonds was used to estimate the spots. Some of the reasons for these differences are that bonds differ in tax treatment and callability features. These differences could and should be specifically taken into account. Even without differences in bond characteristics, however, it would matter which bonds were utilized to calculate discount functions and spot rates because of bid-ask spreads and because the prices used in the calculation are often from trades that occurred at different points in time (nonsynchronous trades). For example, a bond dealer might be willing to pay $85\frac{1}{4}$ for a bond but would require $85\frac{1}{2}$ to sell it. Depending on whether the trade was a purchase or sale, the trade price could be $85\frac{1}{4}$ or $85\frac{1}{2}$. Small differences such as this and nonsynchronous trades can result in large differences in estimated discount functions.[6]

What is desired then is an average estimate of the spot rates. Multiple regression is an averaging technique. For ease of discussion, we will work with discount functions where

$$d_t = \frac{1}{\left(1 + \dfrac{S_{0t}}{2}\right)^t}$$

obviously knowing d_t allows calculation of spot rates. The price of bond i can be expressed as the present value of the cash inflows or

$$P_i = d_1 C_i(1) + d_2 C_i(2) + d_3 C_i(3)$$

where

P_i is the price of bond i

$C_i(t)$ is the cash flow on bond i in period t

d_t are the discount functions

We expect to have many bonds with the same cash flow patterns. As discussed previously, they will have prices different from this equation because of nonsynchronous trading, bid-ask spreads, and possibly nonequilibrium prices as well as differences in bond characteristics. To account for these differences, a random error term (e_i) is added

$$P_i = d_1 C_i(1) + d_2 C_i(2) + d_3 C_i(3) + e_i \tag{20.1}$$

For any bond the price (P_i) and cash flows ($C_i(t)$) would be known. The discount functions are analogous to coefficients in a normal regression. The data used are the prices and cash flows on a sample group of bonds. The discount factors are outputs of the normal regression. Thus, Equation (20.1) could be used to estimate discount functions and hence spot rates. In practice, terms to account for tax considerations and callability are usually added to the equation. Because most bonds do not pay interest on the same dates, the procedures used by many firms for estimating discount functions are somewhat more complicated. These are discussed in Appendix B and the associated references.

Spot rate estimation is important and is the starting point for most organizations involved in bond management. Many organizations simply use spot rates to understand the

---

[6]In the last few years a large number of pure discount or zero coupon bonds have been introduced in the market. Many of these are stripped governments. Each could be used to easily estimate spot rates. Several factors affect the accuracy and usefulness of direct observation. First, a number of the zero coupon bonds are inactive so that current prices may not exist. Of more importance, the sum of the prices of strips generally is more than the price of the original bond. A higher price implies that spot rates calculated from strips are less than rates used to value coupon bonds. Differences of 1/2% for strips with a long maturity are not uncommon.

Obviously the differences just discussed violate the law of one price because the aggregate value of the strips is higher than the value of the bond or bonds that were stripped. The relevant question is how can this exist in equilibrium. The action that would force identical prices is to buy the least expensive (the bond or bonds being stripped) and sell the more expensive zero coupon strips. However, individual investors cannot issue strips. A creator of strips must be able to obtain the trust of investors, and this requires a large brokerage firm like Salomon, or Merrill Lynch. The difference in the aggregate value of the strips and the cost of the bonds being stripped is their profit. Competition will narrow the difference but not eliminate the difference entirely, because the brokerage firms will only issue strips if there is a profit to be made. Thus, in equilibrium the aggregate value of the strips can be different from the value of the underlying securities.

returns in the market for different holding periods. Others use estimated spots to price strips or zero coupon debt. The organization estimates the spot rates and then prices zeros to yield a rate so many hundredths of a percent different from the spot. A third use for spots is finding mispriced bonds. Those bonds with model prices (as determined by Equation [20.1]) very different from actual price are examined to see if there is an explanation for the mispricing. If there isn't, these bonds become candidates for purchase or sale.

A final use of estimated spots is in pricing private placements. A large portion of the debt market involves loans from financial intermediaries such as banks or insurance companies to corporations. One of the advantages of private placements relative to the public market is that unusual cash flow patterns can be set (involving uneven interest and principal payments) to better match the corporation's cash generation pattern. These unusual patterns cannot be priced relative to the public market, since public counterparts don't exist. Estimated spot rates are used to price private placements with unusual cash flow patterns.

THE DETERMINANTS OF BOND PRICES

Bonds can differ in a number of respects. These differences affect bond prices, spot rate, yields to maturity, the expected return in the next period, and the risk associated with next period's return. Standard bond theory deals with the determination of the yield to maturity or price. The yields to maturity on bonds differ for a number of reasons. Among the more important are the following:

1. The length of time before the bond matures.
2. The risk of not receiving coupon and principal payments.
3. The tax status of the cash flows.
4. The existence of provisions that allow the corporation or government to redeem the debt before maturity.
5. The amount of the coupon.

Term to Maturity and Term Structure Theory

In order to gain insight into the effect of maturity on the yield or price of a bond, it is necessary to understand the relationship between yield and time. This relationship is usually called the term structure. More precisely, the theory of the term structure of interest rates deals with why pure discount bonds of different maturities have different yields to maturity.[7] In the last section, it was pointed out that spot rates are equivalent to the yield to maturity on pure discount instruments. Thus, term structure theory could be described equally well as dealing with the determination of spot rates.

In analyzing the effect of maturity on yield, all other influences are held constant. Pure discount instruments are chosen to eliminate the effect of coupon payments. In addition, most analysis is done using government bonds without early redemption features. Therefore, bonds of different maturities are similar with respect to risk, tax liabilities, and redemption possibilities.

Figures 20.2 and 20.3 depict two different yield curves. Figure 20.2 shows a yield curve where the yield to maturity declines as maturity increases. In Figure 20.3 the yield curve

---

[7]Term structure theory is often incorrectly defined as explaining why coupon paying bonds of different maturities have different yields to maturity.

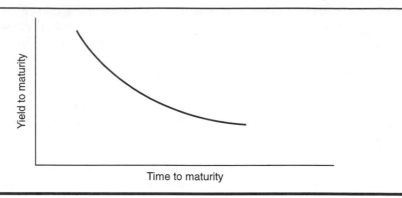

Figure 20.2   Possible term structure.

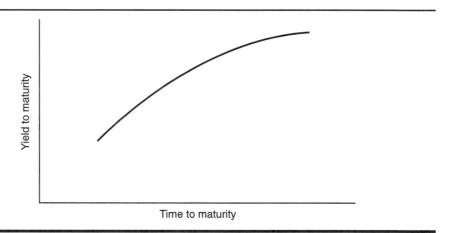

Figure 20.3   Possible term structure.

has a more normal upward slope. Term structure theory deals with why we observe these different shapes. In the next sections we will discuss four different explanations.

Segmented Market Theory   Segmented market theory has its origin in the observation that many investors and issuers of debt seem to have a strong preference for debt of a certain maturity. Furthermore, they seem to be insensitive to differentials in yields between debt of this maturity and debt of a different maturity.

Consider first debt with a long maturity. Let us examine the problem of maturity selection from the viewpoint of an insurance company. Life insurance companies offer insurance policies that are unlikely to require any payment for a long time. An insurance policy issued to a 25-year-old individual may involve 25 or more years before the company anticipates having to make a payment. The size of the premium payments is determined in part by the anticipated interest rate. If the insurance company invests in a long-term bond, the interest earned on the bond is known, and if it exceeds what was promised on the insurance contract, it substantially reduces the insurance company's risk. There is still some risk because the coupon payments will have to be reinvested at some future unknown rate. However, the principal remains invested at a known rate, which substantially reduces the risk. Alternatively, the insurance company could meet its long-term obligation by buying a sequence of one-year bonds. However, in this case, all earnings beyond the first year are unknown. If interest rates decline below what was anticipated in the insurance contract, the company may have difficulty meeting its obligations. Not only is there uncertainty associated with the rate that will be earned on the investment of the coupon payments, there is also uncertainty about the rate earned on the principal. Consequently, many insurance companies invest in long-term bonds even when short-term rates are considerably higher than long-term rates.

Let us examine the maturity selection problem from the viewpoint of the issuers of long-term debt. The construction of a manufacturing plant or warehouse or other physical facility can involve a large expenditure of funds for a corporation. These structures are long-lived assets. Corporations normally wish to pay for them over a long period of time. They can achieve this payment pattern by issuing long-term debt. Alternatively, they can issue short-term debt and keep reissuing it for a long period of time. If they issue the long-term debt, their costs are known ahead of time and there is no interest rate risk associated with the investment. This suggests that corporations will generally issue long-term debt to meet these types of obligations.

Similar considerations apply to short-term debt. Corporations have a number of known short-term obligations that occur at fixed intervals: tax payments and wages are two examples. Money is normally put aside to meet these obligations. If the corporation buys pure discount securities maturing exactly on the date the payment is due, they have zero risk concerning the amount of money they will have available. If they buy a longer-term security, the treasurer faces the risk that interest rates will increase, the price of the security will fall, and the amount that will be available to meet the obligations will be less than anticipated. Commercial banks hold a large number of short-term securities. For example, checking accounts make up a large percentage of the liabilities of commercial banks. Commercial banks engage in short-term lending in order to match the maturity of their assets with the maturity of their debt.

Market segmentation theory argues that investors are sufficiently risk averse that they operate only in their desired maturity spectrum. No yield differential will induce them to change maturities. Thus, what determines long-term rates is solely the supply and demand of long-term funds. Similarly, short-term rates are determined only by supply and demand of short-term funds. People who believe in market segmentation theory examine flows of funds into these market segments in order to predict changes in the yield curve.

Market segmentation theory is very popular with practitioners. Statements in the popular press often display an implicit belief in the market segmentation theory. The theory is much less popular with academics, who maintain that while there are investors who have strong maturity preferences, there are others who are attracted by relative yields. The effects of segmentation on interest rates will be offset if there are enough such investors.

Pure Expectations Theory   The pure expectations theory explains the term structure in terms of expected one-period spot rates. Advocates of the expectations theory believe that the yield on a one-year bond is set so that the return on the one-year bond is the same as the return on a six-month bond plus the expected return on a six-month bond purchased six months hence.

If the expectations theory is correct, then an upward sloping yield curve is an indication that short-term rates are expected to increase. Similarly, a flat yield curve is an indication that short-term rates are expected to remain the same. Finally, a downward sloping yield curve indicates that short-term rates are expected to decline.

The easiest way to understand the expectations theory is to assume that the investors setting prices don't care about risk (are risk neutral). In this case, no matter what their time horizon, they will select the security or securities that give them the highest expected return. This is exactly the opposite of the market segmentation theory.

Consider an investor with a one-year time horizon. Assume that the yield to maturity on a pure discount six-month bond is 10% and on a one-year pure discount bond is 12%. Furthermore assume that the investor expects the six-month spot rate to be 16% in six months. The one-year investment can be accomplished by holding a one-year bond with earnings per dollar invested assuming semiannual compounding of

$$\left(1+\frac{0.12}{2}\right)^2 - 1 = 1.1236 - 1 = 12.4 \quad \text{or } 12.4\%$$

Alternatively, the investor can hold two six-month bonds with expected earnings per dollar invested of

$$\left(1+\frac{0.10}{2}\right)\left(1+\frac{0.16}{2}\right) - 1 = 1.134 - 1 = 13.4 \quad \text{or } 13.4\%$$

The 16% is, of course, the expected one-period spot rate six months in the future. Given this combination of observed and expected rates, holding two six-month bonds gives the higher return, and all two-period investors will wish to hold the two one-period bonds.[8]

We have analyzed the return for investors with two period horizons. The same results apply to investors with any other horizon. Given this universal preference, prices should adjust until the expected return from holding a one-year bond is exactly the same as the expected return from holding two six-month bonds.

Under the expectations theory the yield curve can be derived directly from a series of expected one-period spot rates. Table 20.6 shows two hypothesized sequences of expected one-period rates. One of these sequences produces an upward sloping yield curve, whereas the other sequence produces a downward sloping yield curve.

Let us examine an example of the calculations. Under the expectations theory investing in a two-period bond and earning the spot rate from 0 to 2 must produce the same expected return as investing in two one-period bonds earning the spot rate from 0 to 1 and the expected spot rate from 1 to 2. Thus in Table 20.6, S_{02} is calculated from

$$\left(1+S_{02}/2\right)^2 = \left(1+0.10/2\right)\left(1+0.11/2\right)$$
$$S_{02} = 10.5\%$$

---

[8]The same choice would be made by investors with six-month horizons. These investors have the choice of buying the six-month bond or the one-year bond and selling it in six months. In six months the one-year bond will have six months remaining in its life. At that point it will have to offer the same yield as a newly issued bond. With semiannual compounding the one-year bond will pay $1.1236 at maturity for each dollar invested. For it to have a 16% annual return with six months left before it matures, its price per dollar invested must be

$$\frac{1.1236}{\left(1+\frac{0.16}{2}\right)} = 1.0404$$

If instead the investor buys a six-month bond, its value will be

$$\$1\left(1+\frac{0.10}{2}\right) = \$1.05$$

Table 20.6   Two Hypothesized Sequences of Expected One-period Rates

	Upward Yield Curve		Downward Yield Curve	
Period	Expected One-period Spot Rates	Yield to Maturity	Expected One-period Spot Rates	Yield to Maturity
1	10	10.0	10	10.0
2	11	10.5	9	9.5
3	12	11.0	8	9.0
4	13	11.5	7	8.5
5	14	12.0	6	8.0
6	15	12.5	5	7.5
7	16	13.0	5	7.1
8	16	13.4	5	6.9
9	16	13.7	5	6.7
10	16	13.9	5	6.5

Similarly,

$$\left(1 + S_{03}/2\right)^3 = \left(1 + 0.10/2\right)\left(1 + 0.11/2\right)\left(1 + 0.12/2\right)$$
$$S_{03} = 11\%$$

Not only can the yield curve be derived from the expected spot rates but under the expectations theory the market's belief about future one-period rates can easily be derived from an observed yield curve.

It is important to keep in mind the distinction between the six-month rate expected to prevail six months from now ($\overline{S}_{12}$) and the forward rate, f_{12}. The expectations theory simply states that the two must be equal.[9] In the next two sections we examine alternative theories under which they are no longer equal.

Liquidity Premium Theory   Liquidity premium theory is also based on investors analyzing the returns from holding bonds of varying maturities. However, unlike expectations theory, liquidity premium theory assumes investors must be offered a higher expected return to hold a bond with a horizon different from their preferred horizon. Furthermore, it is assumed that there is a shortage of longer-term investors so that extra return must be offered on long-term bonds to induce investors to hold them.

In the prior example, we considered investors with one- and two-period time horizons. We assumed the one-period rate was 10% and the one-period rate that was expected to prevail one period hence was 16%. Under the expectations theory, the two-period rate would be 13%. With the liquidity premium theory, this rate would have to be higher. The assumption is that there is an excess of investors with short-term horizons.

These investors have a choice of holding a six-month bond or of holding a one-year bond and selling it in six months. The investment in the one-year bond involves risk to the six-month investor. In order to induce some six-month investors to hold one-year bonds, a premium will have to be offered. Thus, the return from holding a one-year bond will be above the expected return from holding two six-month bonds.

For an investor with a six-month horizon, a bond with a maturity longer than one year is even riskier than a one-year bond. Thus, an even larger premium would be required on

[9]S_{12} is the spot rate that is expected to prevail at time 1. The expectation is as of time 0.

three-and four-period bonds. If the market is dominated by short-term investors, then the longer-term bonds will require larger premiums. This is the basic idea behind liquidity premium theory. Note that if the liquidity premium theory holds, an investor with a long-term horizon can hold a bond matching his or her horizon and earn the liquidity premium. Thus, such an investor earns an extra return without any extra risk.

In Table 20.7 we have taken the returns from Table 20.6 and added the liquidity premium. These are then used to construct a term structure. For example, for period 3 the yield to maturity was calculated by solving for S_{03} where

$$\left(1+\frac{S_{03}}{2}\right)^3 = \left(1+\frac{0.10}{2}\right)\left(1+\frac{0.11+0.002}{2}\right)\left(1+\frac{0.12+0.004}{2}\right)$$
$$S_{03} = 11.2\%$$

Liquidity premium theory modifies the conclusions drawn in the prior section concerning the shape of the yield curve and the implied one-period rates in future periods. If expectations are for an unchanged one-period rate, then the presence of a liquidity premium imparts an upward sloping shape to the yield curve. Even if expectations are for a declining series of one-period rates, it is still possible to observe an upward sloping yield curve. This would occur if the risk premiums were sufficiently large to overcome the expectations of a decline in one-period rates. Thus, an upward sloping yield curve would be consistent with any pattern of expectations concerning one-period rates. A flat or downward sloping yield curve is only consistent with a decrease in one-period rates.

Figure 20.4 depicts two yield curves and the associated liquidity premiums.

Preferred Habitat   Preferred habitat theory rests on the premise that investors who match the life of their assets with the life of their liabilities are in the lowest risk position. Matching the life of the assets and liabilities is their preferred position. If there is sufficient extra return to be earned on assets of other lives, they will adjust their position to include more of these higher yielding assets.

If this theory is correct, premiums will exist for maturities where there is insufficient demand. These premiums are necessary in order to induce investors to leave their preferred habitat. If there are a large number of firms issuing long-term debt relative to the number

Table 20.7   Yield Curve with a Liquidity Premium (expressed in percent)

	Upward Sloping Yield Curve			Downward Sloping Yield Curve		
Period	Expected One-period Spot Rate	Liquidity Premium	Yield to Maturity	Expected One-period Spot Rates	Liquidity Premium	Yield to Maturity
1	10	0	10.00	10	0	10.00
2	11	0.2	10.60	9	0.2	9.60
3	12	0.4	11.20	8	0.4	9.20
4	13	0.6	11.80	7	0.6	8.80
5	14	0.8	12.39	6	0.8	8.40
6	15	1.0	12.99	5	1.0	8.00
7	16	1.2	13.59	5	1.2	7.74
8	16	1.4	14.06	5	1.6	7.57
9	16	1.6	14.45	5	2.0	7.46
10	16	1.8	14.79	5	2.4	7.40

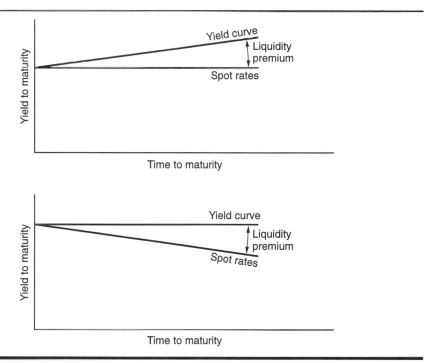

Figure 20.4   Yield curves with liquidity premiums.

of investors interested in long-term debt, a premium will have to be offered on long-term debt. If many firms and institutions wish to issue short-term debt and there are few investors who wish to invest short terms, a premium will have to be offered on short-term debt.

What is meant by a premium? For simplicity consider two periods. Let S_{01} be the spot interest rate in the first period and $\overline{S}_{12}$ be the expected one-period spot rate in the second. If the expectations theory holds, the two-period rate expressed as a rate per period is

$$\left(1+\frac{S_{02}}{2}\right)^2 = \left(1+\frac{S_{01}}{2}\right)\left(1+\frac{\overline{S}_{12}}{2}\right)$$

Assume that there is a surplus of short-term investors and therefore an extra return is necessary to induce investors to hold the two-period bond. If P is the size of the premium, then

$$\left(1+\frac{S_{02}}{2}\right)^2 = \left(1+\frac{S_{01}}{2}\right)\left(1+\frac{\overline{S}_{12}}{2}+\frac{P}{2}\right)$$

$$P > 0$$

In this case, preferred habitat theory would result in a set of spot rates that could have been derived equally well from the liquidity premium theory. If, on the other hand, there is a need to move investors to the short term, holding the two-period bond will be less profitable than holding two one-period bonds or

$$\left(1+\frac{S_{02}}{2}\right)^2 = \left(1+\frac{S_{01}}{2}\right)\left(1+\frac{\overline{S}_{12}}{2}+\frac{P}{2}\right)$$

with

$$P < 0$$

With the preferred habitat theory, the premiums can be positive or negative. Without an idea of the sign and size of the premiums, nothing can be concluded about future one-period rates from observing the yield curve.

Term Structure and Coupon Bonds   In the last section we examined the term structure for pure discount bonds. We will now examine the term structure for coupon paying bonds. A coupon paying bond can be considered a portfolio of pure discount bonds. Consider a three-period bond with a coupon of $75 and a principal repayment of $1000. Its price is calculated as follows.

$$\text{Price} = \frac{75}{\left(1+\frac{S_{01}}{2}\right)} + \frac{75}{\left(1+\frac{S_{02}}{2}\right)^2} + \frac{1075}{\left(1+\frac{S_{03}}{2}\right)^3} \tag{20.2}$$

This bond can be viewed as one bond or as a portfolio of three bonds—one-period, two-period, and three-period pure discount bonds paying $75, $75, and $1075, respectively. The price on this portfolio is given by Equation (20.2).

The price of the portfolio is, of course, the same as the price of the bond. The yield to maturity on the bond lies between the spot rates. Let us examine what this implies for yield curves of coupon bonds relative to yield curves of pure discount bonds. Consider a downward sloping yield curve. The spot rates associated with the earlier coupon payments are higher than the spot rate associated with the final maturity. Since the yield to maturity lies between these rates, the yield to maturity on the coupon bond lies above the spot rate associated with the final payment (see Figure 20.5). The higher the coupon payments, the greater the importance of earlier payments relative to the last payment and the more important the influence of earlier spot rates on the yield to maturity. Thus the higher the coupon payment, the greater the difference between the yield to maturity on the coupon paying bond and the spot rate on the final payment.

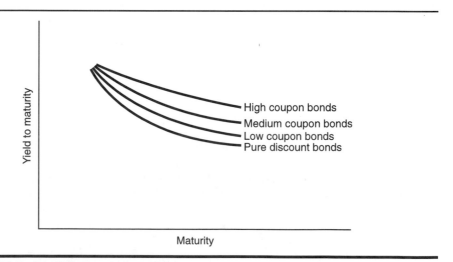

Figure 20.5   Possible term structure curves.

Figure 20.5 shows the plot of yield to maturity on coupon bonds compared to pure discount bonds. As just discussed, the greater the coupon, the greater the difference between yields to maturity and the spot rate of the final payment.

If the yield curve is upward sloping, then the yield to maturity on coupon bonds lies below the yield to maturity on discount bonds. The larger the coupon, the greater the difference between the yield on the coupon and noncoupon debt. Figure 20.6 plots the yield to maturity on bonds with various coupons with upward sloping yield curves.

A number of organizations examine yield curves on coupon paying debt. Pure discount debt for government bonds did not exist at all for bonds with maturities over one year until the 1980s. When pure discount debt for longer maturities was first offered, it was created by brokerage firms removing coupons from coupon bonds and selling them off separately. These instruments are not quite equivalent to pure discount government bonds, since they may be less marketable than when the government originally issued them, and there is some risk of the brokerage firm defaulting. Furthermore, even now there are not enough of them to allow accurate estimation of the yield curve. Most firms plot yield curves of coupon paying debt rather than go through the process of estimating the yield curve for pure discount debt using techniques discussed in the appendix at the end of the chapter. Examining Figures 20.5 and 20.6 shows that the general shape of the yield curve is preserved if the coupon rate on bonds of varying maturities is the same. The problem is that they are not the same. Most bonds with intermediate maturity are long-term bonds that were issued several years before. For example, a bond with a 7-year maturity might be a 30-year bond issued 23 years ago. Interest rates change dramatically over time. Thus the coupon rate on bonds of different maturities is likely to be very different. A yield curve drawn from coupon paying bonds is likely to be a mixture of the yield curves shown in Figures 20.5 and 20.6. In this case, even the shape need not be preserved.

Organizations examine yield curves for investment decisions and for determining interest rates to be offered their customers. Using coupon bonds can lead to very misleading yield curves and incorrect decisions.

Summary of the Term Structure of Interest Rates   We have shown how spot rates can be used to arrive at the correct price of any bond. To estimate spot rates one should use

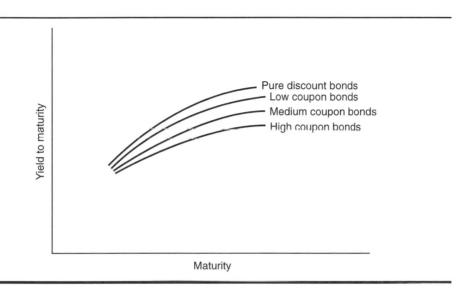

Figure 20.6 Possible term structure curves.

the methodology outlined in the appendix at the end of this chapter. Spot rates are determined by current one-period rates, expectations about future one-period rates, theories of institutional behavior, and risk preferences. Although we have not attempted to find a categorical answer to which of these term structure theories is correct, we have provided you with enough information about the contrasting theories to give insight into the term structure of interest rates.

Default Risk

Unlike government bonds, for corporate bonds and municipal bonds there is a risk that the coupon or principal payments will not be met. For these bonds it is necessary to make a distinction between promised return and expected return. A bond could promise a return of 12%, but if there were some probability that the principal or coupon might not be paid, its expected return could be 10%. In addition, since there is risk associated with these bonds, investors should require that the expected return be greater than the return on a similar bond that is default free. These concepts are illustrated in Table 20.8.

We have referred to the difference between the promised return and the expected return as the default premium. The difference between the expected return and the return on a default-free instrument is the risk premium. The investor requires this extra return because of the chance that a particular bond selected may default, resulting in a very poor and probably negative return.

Three large investment services estimate the likelihood of default for most corporate bonds: Moody's, Standard & Poor's, and Fitch. The estimates from Moody's and from Standard & Poor's are widely available. Their services are similar in that they classify bonds by likelihood of loss. Likelihood of loss includes both the probability of a missed, delayed, or partial payment and the size of the loss if a loss occurs. For example, consider two bonds with the same probability of a missed principal payment. If one of them has significant odds of paying a substantial portion of the principal payment if missed, while the odds are that the other will pay none, then the bond with the higher payment receives the higher rating. Bond rating services divide bonds into discrete classes. Table 20.9 shows Moody's classification of bonds and their discussion of what the various classifications mean.

Many organizations are restricted to buying bonds that have achieved at least a certain rating. These restrictions may be imposed by regulatory authority, by perception of legal requirements of prudent investment, or by organizational policy. In addition, many brokerage firms put together pools of bonds and then issue shares in these pools. These pools are normally restricted to A-rated bonds or better. These restrictions suggest the possibility of a segmented market between higher rated bonds and lower rated bonds; however, we know of no conclusive evidence on this issue.

Table 20.8   Components of Interest Rates on Corporate Bonds

2%	Default premium	
1%	Risk premium	
		12% Total return
9%	Return on default-free bonds	

Table 20.9   Key to Moody's Corporate Ratings

Aaa	Bonds which are rated Aaa are judged to be of the best quality. They carry the smallest degree of investment risk and are generally referred to as "gilt edge." Interest payments are protected by a large or by an exceptionally stable margin and principal is secure. While the various protective elements are likely to change, such changes as can be visualized are most unlikely to impair the fundamentally strong position of such issues.
Aa	Bonds which are rated Aa are judged to be of high quality by all standards. Together with the Aaa group they comprise what are generally known as high-grade bonds. They are rated lower than the best bonds because margins of protection may not be as large as in Aaa securities or fluctuation of protective elements may be of greater amplitude or there may be other elements present that make the long-term risks appear somewhat larger than in Aaa securities.
A	Bonds which are rated A possess many favorable investment attributes and are to be considered as upper medium-grade obligations. Factors giving security to principal and interest are considered adequate but elements may be present that suggest a susceptibility to impairment sometime in the future.
Baa	Bonds which are rated Baa are considered as medium-grade obligations (i.e., they are neither highly protected nor poorly secured). Interest payments and principal security appear adequate for the present, but certain protective elements may be lacking or may be characteristically unreliable over any great length of time. Such bonds lack outstanding investment characteristics and in fact have speculative characteristics as well.
Ba	Bonds which are rated Ba are judged to have speculative elements; their future cannot be considered as well assured. Often the protection of interest and principal payments may be very moderate and thereby not well safeguarded during both good and bad times over the future. Uncertainty of position characterizes bonds in this class.
B	Bonds which are rated B generally lack characteristics of the desirable investment. Assurance of interest and principal payments or of maintenance of other terms of the contract over any long period of time may be small.
Caa	Bonds which are rated Caa are of poor standing. Such issues may be in default or there may be present elements of danger with respect to principal or interest.
Ca	Bonds which are rated Ca represent obligations which are speculative in a high degree. Such issues are often in default or have other marked shortcomings.
C	Bonds which are rated C are the lowest rated class of bonds and issues so rated can be regarded as having extremely poor prospects of ever attaining any real investment standing.

Moody's and Standard & Poor's classifications can be duplicated fairly accurately by utilizing a weighted average of firm characteristics as follows. A number of firm characteristics are hypothesized as influencing Moody's or Standard & Poor's classifications. These characteristics usually include variables such as the amount of earnings compared to the interest payments, the variability of earnings, the amount of debt in the capital structure, the net worth, and the amount of short-term assets compared to short-term liabilities. Data on these variables are collected for a number of publicly traded bonds along with the classification of each bond by one of the bond rating services. Mathematical techniques exist for finding the combination of firm variables that best duplicates the classification of the rating agency. The combination is best in the sense that it most accurately reproduces the ratings. Once the best combination is determined, it is then tested using data on other publicly traded bonds to see how well it classifies them. Accurate classification of 70–80% of the bonds is not uncommon, with most bonds being only one rating away from the published ratings.

Reproducing public ratings is useful in order that bonds not classified by the public rating services can be inexpensively and accurately classified. The most obvious utilization of this system is in classifying private placements. Banks and insurance companies lend money to firms directly. These private placements are usually loans to small- or medium-sized companies that wish to avoid the expenses of issuing publicly traded debt (e.g., SEC registration, brokerage costs). Analysts make judgments concerning the likelihood and size of loss, the appropriate interest rate on the potential loan, and the decision on whether to lend. When individual lending officers are judged in part by the volume of loans they make, they tend to be optimistic about the likelihood of the firm repaying the loan in the future. A scheme that fairly accurately reproduces public ratings is a check on this optimism. These schemes are frequently used to rate all loans under consideration. The analyst is then required to justify any difference in interest rates he or she wishes to offer compared to what is normal given the rating the bond receives.

Table 20.10 shows the default experience in recent years on average for junk or high-yield bonds. Junk bonds are bonds rated below Baa if using Moody's ratings or below BBB if using Standard & Poor's. The default experience for this category of bonds is significantly higher than for other bonds, averaging about 3% between 1978 and 2000.

Another way of examining the default experience is to examine it over the life of the bond. Table 20.11 shows the cumulative default experience for newly issued bonds in each year subsequent to issue. Thus, the 31.51% for CCC bonds implies that 31.51% of the bonds rated CCC defaulted in the first 10 years. The default experience over the life of the bond is quite substantial for low-rated bonds outstanding for a number of years. Note also that as discussed earlier, the default experience in the first year tends to be less than in subsequent years.

Table 20.10   Historical Default Rate-Low Rated, Straight Debt Only 1978–2000

Year	Par Value Outstanding	Par Value Default	Default Rate
2000	$597,200	$30,248	5.06%
1999	567,400	23,532	4.15%
1998	465,500	7,464	1.60%
1997	335,400	4,200	1.25%
1996	271,000	3,336	1.23%
1995	240,000	4,551	1.90%
1994	235,000	3,418	1.45%
1993	206,907	2,287	1.11%
1992	163,000	5,545	3.40%
1991	183,600	18,862	10.27%
1990	181,000	18,354	10.14%
1989	189,258	8,110	4.29%
1988	148,187	3,944	2.66%
1987	129,557	7,486	5.78%
1986	90,243	3,156	3.50%
1985	58,088	992	1.71%
1984	40,939	344	0.84%
1983	27,492	301	1.09%
1982	18,109	577	3.19%
1981	17,115	27	0.16%
1980	14,935	224	1.50%
1979	10,356	20	0.19%
1978	8,946	119	1.33%
Average Default Rate 1978–2000			2.95%

Source: Altman and Nammacher [5].

Table 20.11   Cumulative Mortality Losses by Original S&P Bond Rating Covering Defaults and Issues from 1971 to 2000 (in %)

Original Rating	Year After Issuance									
	1	2	3	4	5	6	7	8	9	10
AAA	0.00	0.00	0.00	0.00	0.03	0.03	0.03	0.03	0.03	0.03
AA	0.00	0.00	0.35	0.54	0.54	0.54	0.54	0.54	0.57	0.59
A	0.00	0.00	0.02	0.09	0.12	0.20	0.25	0.34	0.40	0.40
BBB	0.12	0.60	1.14	1.73	2.28	2.85	3.55	3.70	3.75	3.98
BB	0.96	2.59	6.50	7.12	9.12	9.98	11.47	11.87	13.41	16.66
B	1.60	6.46	12.03	17.85	22.73	25.94	28.25	29.76	30.92	31.51
CCC	4.35	17.03	31.00	36.62	38.53	44.15	46.70	48.44	48.44	50.58

Source: Altman and Nammacher [5].

Tax Effects

The cash flows from certain bonds have a tax advantage. These bonds should sell at a different yield to maturity than bonds without this tax advantage. The most obvious example of such bonds is municipal bonds. The coupon payments from municipal bonds are not subject to federal taxation and usually are not subject to tax in the state where they are issued. Because of the benefits of such favorable tax treatment, the yield to maturity on these bonds is less than the yield to maturity on comparable taxable issues. Generally the yield to maturity is 30–40% lower on municipal bonds than on similar taxable issues.

The second example of the effect of tax on bonds are the so-called flower bonds. Flower bonds were designated as such at time of issue. These bonds were originally issued at times of relatively low interest rates. Normally they would sell at a value well below face value so that their yield to maturity would be comparable to other bonds. However, they have a unique provision that substantially affects their value. Flower bonds are accepted at face value in payment of estate taxes. Thus a wealthy individual might find it attractive to add flower bonds to his or her portfolio if an imminent demise were anticipated. Because of this special provision, flower bonds will sell at much higher prices than they otherwise would, leading to lower yields to the investor.

While flower bonds are the most colorful bond with special tax treatment, the most common type of bond subject to special tax treatment is one with a sufficiently low or high coupon to cause it to sell at a price very different than its face value. For these bonds, capital appreciation or loss is a significant part of the investor's return in addition to interest income. Consider a low coupon bond. The coupon payments are subject to taxation at ordinary income tax rates. Low coupon bonds would have two components to their return: the return from the coupon plus the return from the price appreciation. The total return must be competitive with other bonds of similar characteristics. The portion of return from the price appreciation is taxable as a capital gain. For most investors the capital gain rate is lower than the income tax rate. Thus low coupon bonds have a tax advantage because a portion of their return receives favorable tax treatment. Given this tax advantage low coupon bonds should and do have a lower (before tax) yield to maturity. McCulloch [55] has estimated that bonds are priced consistent with investors being in a 20–30% tax bracket. This means that the after-tax yield on a low coupon versus a normal coupon bond with similar characteristics is the same as if flows were adjusted by assuming a 20–30% tax bracket.[10]

---

[10]High coupon bonds have a tax disadvantage. Coupon payments are subject to the high ordinary tax rate. The price decline is a long-term loss. However, some of the loss in price may need to be amortized and can be used to reduce the ordinary income.

The tax bracket that is consistent with observed prices is important information to investors. If bonds are priced consistent with a 20–30% tax bracket, then investors in higher tax brackets will favor low coupon issues, all else held constant. Similarly, tax-exempt investors should primarily be holding the high coupon, high-yield bonds.

Option Features of Bonds

Bonds sometimes contain a feature that constitutes an option for either the issuer of the bond or the holder of the bond. Since the valuation of options is discussed in detail in Chapter 22, we limit our discussion in this chapter to a description of bond features that can be valued as options. Applying the option valuation formula to these features will not be specifically treated, although the option chapter together with the bibliography at the end of this chapter will allow the interested reader to pursue this subject.

The most common option included in bond contracts is the possibility of a call by the issuing firm. The call privilege is the right by the issuing firm to repurchase the bond at a fixed price. The price is generally the par value (face value) of the bond plus a premium (called the call premium). For example, the bond might be callable at par plus 5% of par. Generally the call premium declines over time, making the likelihood of a call higher in the later years than in earlier years. For example, the call premium might be 5% in the first year, 4% in the second year, 3% in the third year, and so forth. In addition, it is common to preclude a call for a number of years. The possibility of a call reduces the value of the bond to the investor. An investor can assume that the firm will call at times when the bond without the call feature is worth more than the price at which it is actually called. This difference is a loss to the investor. The value of a comparable noncallable bond will lie above the call price when interest rates decline compared to the original issue price. Thus an investor wishing to lock up high interest rates by buying a bond at a time of high rates might find that he or she earns these rates only for a short time because the bond is called away when rates decline and the proceeds are invested at these lower rates. Many firms calculate return to the first time at which a bond is callable in order to compare return on callable and noncallable bonds. This procedure makes the unrealistic assumption that firms will call as soon as a bond is callable. This underestimates its value, just as a return to maturity that ignores the possibility of call is an overestimate of the expected return over this horizon. The only accurate way to estimate the value of the call is to use the option models discussed in Chapter 22.

Another option associated with bonds is the sinking fund option. Many bond issues require that part of the issue be retired over the life of the bond. For example, bond covenants may require that 5% of the issue be retired at the end of each year over the bond's 10-year life. The corporation has the option of purchasing the bonds directly or of calling the bonds it needs to meet its sinking fund obligation. Obviously it will meet its obligation in the least expensive way. Since the bonds are chosen in a random way, all investors risk having their bonds called to meet the sinking fund obligation. The discussion of the call option is relevant in this case.

A third option found in certain bond contracts is the conversion option. This option benefits the bondholders. The bondholder has the option of converting the bond into common equity. The bond is used to pay for the equity. Assume a $1000 par bond is convertible into 50 shares of common equity. Then the investor is paying $20 per share. The convertible bond can be viewed as a bond plus an option to buy 50 shares at $20 per share.

Corporate Bonds

Having discussed some of the factors that affect bond prices, it is useful to examine corporate bonds in more detail.

Corporate Bond Spreads   Corporate bonds have a higher promised interest rate than government bonds. This difference in interest rates is called the spread. Table 20.12 shows the average spread between the spot rate on corporate bonds and the spot rate on government bonds for various maturities and ratings. For example, the four-year spot rate on AA corporate bonds was 7.38% and for four-year governments was 6.925%, resulting in a spread of

$$\text{Four-year AA Spread} = 7.38 - 6.925 = 0.455$$

Note that the empirical spread increases with maturity and with a decrease in rating.

Three factors affect the spread:

1. Expected default loss: some corporate bonds will default and investors require a higher promised payment to compensate for the expected loss from defaults.

2. Tax premium: interest payments on corporate bonds are taxed at the state level whereas interest payments on government bonds are not.

3. Risk premium: the return on corporate bonds is riskier than the return on government bonds, and investors should require a premium for the higher risk. As we will discuss, this occurs because a large part of the risk on corporate bonds is systematic rather than diversifiable.

The first two factors have already been discussed, while the third requires some elaboration. In Chapters 13–16 we presented evidence that an asset with systematic risk requires a higher expected return. Corporate bonds are systematically related to the same factors as common stock. If common stock requires a risk premium, then so should corporate bonds. Furthermore, as shown in Elton, et al. [31], the sensitivity to the common stock factors increases as rating decreases.

How much of the spread can be attributed to each of the three factors? Figure 20.7 shows the corporate bond spread for A-rated bonds. Most people focus on default as the major determinant of corporate bond spread. For A-rated bonds relatively little of the spread is explained by the fact that some bonds rated A ultimately default. The fact that corporate

Table 20.12   Corporate Bond Spreads for Industrial Bonds and Various Ratings, 1987–1996

Maturity	Treasuries	Spreads		
		AA	A	BBB
2	6.414	0.414	0.621	1.167
3	6.689	0.419	0.680	1.205
4	6.925	0.455	0.715	1.210
5	7.108	0.493	0.738	1.205
6	7.246	0.526	0.753	1.199
7	7.351	0.552	0.764	1.193
8	7.432	0.573	0.773	1.188
9	7.496	0.589	0.779	1.184
10	7.548	0.603	0.785	1.180

Source: Elton, et al. [31].

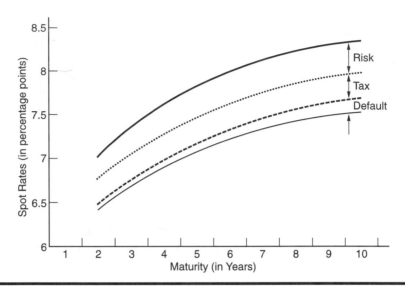

Figure 20.7   Spot rates for A-rated industrial bonds and for Treasuries.

bonds are subject to state taxes and government bonds are not, explains more of the pre-mium. Finally, the sensitivity of corporate bonds to systematic risk factors and the need to receive a higher return to be compensated for this systematic risk explains the largest part of the spread for A-rated bonds.

Floating Rate Bonds   A *floater* is a bond with coupon payments that varies as a func-tion of some interest rate. Consider a floating rate note with a maturity of two years that pays the 6-month Treasury bill rate. So that the next coupon is a known amount, and the rate is always fixed at the beginning of each period. Assume the coupon is paid every six months. Thus, the coupon that is paid in six months is the current 6-month Treasury bill rate. The rate that is paid in one year is the 6-month Treasury bill rate that exists six months from now. The rate that is paid in 18 months is the 6-month Treasury bill rate that exists in one year. Assume the bond is riskless and consider the value of the floating rate bond in 18 months. In 18 months there will be one remaining payment of the coupon and it will be paid at maturity in 24 months and since it is set in 18 months it will be known at that time with certainty. Since the bond is riskless by assumption, the value in 18 months is the payment to be made in 24 months brought back at the riskless rate. Since the coupon was fixed at the 6-month rate at that time and the discount rate is the 6-month rate, the dis-counted value will be the bond's par value. Let's consider an example. Assume that in 18 months the 6-month rate is 6% per year, or 3% per 6-month period. If the bond has a par value of $100, the final payment is $103. The value of this final payment in 18 months will be 103/1.03 or $100. The same logic applies at earlier periods. Assume in one year, 6-month Treasury bill rates are 5% per year or 2.5% per six-month period. Then, the investor will receive in 18 months a coupon payment worth $2.50 and will have a bond worth $100. The present value as of one year is 102.5/1.025 = $100. Continuing to work back shows at the time the coupon is reset a riskless floating rate bond paying the Treasury bill rate will always sell at par.

Most floating rate bonds are not riskless. However, their coupon is set at the spread they normally sell above Treasuries. For example, the coupon might be set at the 6-month Treasury bill rate plus 2%. As long as the spread remains at a constant 2% per period, the principles discussed earlier hold; namely, at the time the coupon is reset, the bond sells at par.

What is the duration of a floating rate investment? After the reset date the next coupon payment is fixed. Since at the reset date the bond will sell at par, the bond will respond to interest rate changes like a bond that matures at the next reset date. Since between reset dates the bond has the cash flow pattern of a zero or pure discount bond with a maturity equal to the time to reset, and since the duration for zero coupon bonds is the maturity, the duration of a floating rate instrument ignoring any change in spread is the time to reset.

CONCLUSION

In this chapter, we have introduced bond terminology and the major features of bonds. The only principal feature we introduced but did not devote a section to was the effect of differing coupons. We did not devote a separate section to it because the effect of coupon payments has already been discussed in the tax and maturity sections. In the next chapter, we integrate bond management into portfolio theory.

APPENDIX A

SPECIAL CONSIDERATIONS IN BOND PRICING

The quoted price at which a bond is bought or sold is not the price the customer will pay or receive. The bond selling or purchase price is the quoted price plus accrued interest. Accrued interest is the proportion of interest that has accrued to the bondholder from the last interest payment until the sale or purchase date. For example, assume the quoted sale price is $96 on a bond paying interest at 10% semiannually. Further, assume there are 181 days between interest payments on the bond and that there are 70 days between the last interest payment and the date the payment will be made for a purchase or sale (settlement date). Then the bond sale price is

$$96 + \frac{70}{181} \times 0.05(100) = \$97.93$$

Rules for calculating accrued interest differ across bond types and countries. The reader calculating the price that will be paid needs to carefully check the rules for the particular bond being purchased.

Note that bond prices and stock prices are quoted on a different basis. Stock prices are quoted at prices at which they are bought or sold. Thus, when a stock pays a dividend, the stock decreases in value by an amount approximately equal to the dividend, and the price drops accordingly. Bonds, on the other hand, are sold at quoted price plus accrued interest. When a bond has an interest payment, the accrued interest becomes zero but the quoted price remains unchanged.

APPENDIX B

ESTIMATING SPOT RATES

As discussed in the text, spot rates are extremely important in bond valuation and investment decisions, and it is necessary to estimate them. Three techniques have been discussed in the literature. We discuss two of them in this appendix. These two differ in that one of them estimates discrete rates and the other continuous rates.

Consider the following equation relating the price of a bond to the cash flows accruing to the bondholder:

$$P = \frac{c}{(1+S_{01}/2)} + \frac{c}{(1+S_{02}/2)^2} + \frac{c}{(1+S_{03}/2)^3} + \cdots + \frac{1000+c}{(1+S_{0T}/2)^T} \tag{B.1}$$

where

P is the price of the bond

c is the coupon

S_{0t} is the t period spot rate

T is the number of periods where there are coupon payments

$\$1000$ is the principal payment

Alternatively,

$$P = cD_1 + cD_2 + cD_3 + \cdots + (c+1000)D_T \tag{B.2}$$

where

$$D_t = \frac{1}{(1+S_{0t})^t} \qquad t = 1,\ldots,T$$

The price and the cash flows are known.

As discussed in the text, if we fit Equation (B.2) to multiple bonds simultaneously and recognize that the equation can't hold exactly for each bond, then Equation (B.2) has the form of a multiple linear regression. D_1 through D_T are the regression coefficients to be estimated. In order to prevent estimates of forward rates being negative, it is normal to constrain the regression so that the D's are nonincreasing. Thus D_t is forced to be less than D_{t-1}. The spot rates estimated by this procedure are discrete. Since most bonds pay interest on a semiannual basis, these are spot rates for cash flows six months apart. Thus, $S_{01}/2$ is the spot rate for the first six months, $S_{02}/2$ is for the first 12 months, $S_{03}/2$ for the first 18 months, and so on. Furthermore, they are rates between specific dates. For example, the six-month intervals could be January to June and July to December. The difficulty with this procedure is that a large number of bonds pay interest on different dates, and the spot rates must be interpolated in some way for use on these dates. Furthermore, bonds with different payment dates cannot be used in the estimation and thus a fair amount of data are discarded. Carleton and Cooper [21] suggest the procedure just discussed.

The alternative is to estimate a continuous discount function. The procedure just described estimates $D(t) = 1/(1 + S_{0t}/2)^t$ where the t has integer values such as 1, 2, or 3. $D(t)$ is called a discount function. Consider the following diagram. Discount rates for different six-month intervals are plotted in the diagram. Using the technique just discussed, all we obtain are the points shown. As an alternative, the dashed line could be estimated. This would allow an estimation of discount functions for all maturities. Several forms of equations could be used to approximate the relationship between $D(t)$ and maturity. Since we have assumed some curvature to the relationship, let us approximate it by a quadratic equation. We can write it as

$$D(t) = a_0 + a_1 t + a_2 t^2 \tag{B.3}$$

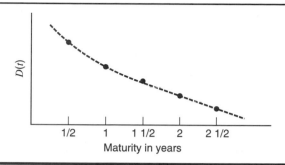

Once a_0, a_1, and a_2 are known, the spot rates for any time period are known. If the discount function for cash flow in $3\frac{1}{2}$ months is required, then t is set as 3.5/12. The task is thus to estimate a_0, a_1, and a_2. The price of a bond is the present value of its coupon and principal payment. This was written in Equation (B.2) and can be written in compact form as

$$P = \sum_{t=1}^{T} c(t)D(t) \tag{B.4}$$

where $c(t)$ is the coupon payment for all periods before the horizon and the coupon plus principal at the horizon.

Substituting Equation (B.3) into Equation (B.4) yields

$$P = \sum_{t=1}^{T} c(t)\left(a_0 + a_1 t + a_2 t^2\right)$$

Rearranging,

$$P = a_0\left[\sum_{t=1}^{T} c(t)\right] + a_1\left[\sum_{t=1}^{T} tc(t)\right] + a_2\left[\sum_{t=1}^{T} t^2 c(t)\right]$$

Once again this is in the form of a linear regression. The terms in the brackets and the price are known, and the a_t are regression coefficients. This is the procedure suggested by Schaefer [68] and McCulloch [54]. The equation used as a discount function by these authors is not exactly equal to that presented in Equation (B.3) but the general procedure is the same.[11]

APPENDIX C

CALCULATING BOND EQUIVALENT YIELD AND EFFECTIVE ANNUAL YIELD

		Normal Frequency of Interest	Quoted Yield	Bond Equivalent Yield	Effective Annual Yield
1.	Eurobond	Yearly	y	$2[(1 + y)^{1/2} - 1]$	y
2.	Government	Semiannual	y	y	$\left(1 + \dfrac{y}{2}\right)^2 - 1$

(continues on next page)

[11]Researchers have used a generalized polynomial curve fitting to estimate this relationship; we select a simple polynomial curve, the quadratic, to illustrate the procedure.

	Normal Frequency of Interest	Quoted Yield	Bond Equivalent Yield	Effective Annual Yield
3. Corporate	Semiannual	y	y	$\left(1+\frac{y}{2}\right)^2 - 1$
4. Ginnie Mae	Monthly	y	$2\left[\left(1+\frac{y}{12}\right)^6 - 1\right]$	$\left(1+\frac{y}{12}\right)^{12} - 1$
5. T-bills[a]	None	b	$2[(1+r)^{365/2N} - 1]$	$(1+r)^{365/N} - 1$

[a] b = banker's discount yield and $r = b\,\frac{N}{360}\,\frac{P_1}{P_0}$.

QUESTIONS AND PROBLEMS

1. Given the following, does the law of one price hold? If not, what action should an investor take?

	Cash Flows in Period		
Bond	1	2	Price
A	100	1100	970
B	80	1080	936
C	90	1090	980

2. Assume a bond with cash flows of $100 each year and a principal payment of $1000 in five years and a current price of $960. What is

   A. Its current yield?

   B. Its yield to maturity?

3. Given the following bonds and prices of bonds, what are the spot rates and forward rates?

Bond	Price	1	2	3	4
A	960	1000			
B	920		1000		
C	885			1000	
D	855				1000

4. Given the cash flows shown below, does the law of one price hold? If not, what is the price of bond C that will make it hold?

	Cash Flows in Period		
Bond	1	2	Price
A	80	1080	982
B	1100		880
C	120	1120	1010

5. Assume the data shown below. What tax rate would make the law of one price hold? Assume that the capital gains tax is one-half the ordinary income tax. Assume that the periods shown below are annual, and that any capital gain or loss is realized at the time the bond matures.

Bond	1	2	Price
A	80	1080	985
B	1100		900
C	120	1120	1040

BIBLIOGRAPHY

1. Ahu, Chang, Mo, and Thompson, Howard E. "Jump-Diffusion and the Term Structure of Interest Rates," *Journal of Finance*, **43**, No. 1 (Mar. 1988), pp. 155–174.

2. Alexander, Gordon J. "Applying the Market Model to Long-Term Corporate Bonds," *Journal of Financial and Quantitative Analysis*, **XV**, No. 5 (Dec. 1980), pp. 1063–1080.

3. Altman, Edward I. *Investing in Junk Bonds: Inside the High Yield Debt Market* (New York: John Wiley & Sons, 1987).

4. ——. *Default Risk, Mortality Rates and the Performance of Corporate Bonds: 1970–1988.* (Charlottesville, Va.: Foundation for Research of the Institute for Chartered Financial Analysts, 1989).

5. Altman, Edward, and Nammacher, Scott. "The Default Experience on High Yield Corporate Debt," *Financial Analysts Journal* (July–Aug. 1985), pp. 25–41.

6. Ananthanarayanan, A.L., and Schwartz, Eduardo S. "Retractable and Extendible Bonds: The Canadian Experience," *The Journal of Finance*, **35**, No. 1 (Mar. 1980), pp. 31–48.

7. Asquith, Paul, David Mullins, and Eric Wolff. "Original Issue High Yield Bonds: Aging Analysis of Defaults, Exchanges and Calls," *Journal of Finance* **44** (Sept. 1989), pp. 923–953.

8. Atkinson, T. R. *Trends in Corporate Bond Quality.* (New York: National Bureau of Economic Research, 1967).

9. Balduzzi, Pierluigi, Elton, Edwin J., and Green, T. Clifton. "Economic News and the Yield Curve: Evidence from the US Treasury Market," *The Journal of Financial and Quantitative Analysis,* **36** (Dec. 2001) pp. 523–543.

10. Black, Fischer, and Cox, John C. "Valuing Corporate Securities: Some Effects of Bond Indenture Provisions," *Journal of Finance*, **31** (May 1976), pp. 351–367.

11. Black, Fischer, and Scholes, Myron. "The Pricing of Options and Corporate Liabilities," *Journal of Political Economy*, **81** (May/June 1973), pp. 637–654.

12. Blume, Marshall E., and Donald B. Keim. "Risk and Return Characteristics of Lower Grade Bonds," *Financial Analysts Journal* (July/Aug. 1987), pp. 26–33.

13. Brennan, M.J., and Schwartz, E.S. "Convertible Bonds: Valuation and Optimal Strategies for Call and Conversion," *Journal of Finance*, **32** (Dec. 1977), pp. 1699–1715.

14. ——. "Conditional Predictions of Bond Prices and Returns," *The Journal of Finance*, **35**, No. 2 (May 1980), pp. 405–416.

15. ——. "An Equilibrium Model of Bond Pricing and a Test of Market Efficiency," *Journal of Financial and Quantitative Analysis*, **XVII**, No. 3 (Sept. 1982), pp. 301–330.

16. ——. "Bond Pricing and Market Efficiency," *Financial Analyst Journal*, **38**, No. 5 (Sept./Oct. 1982), pp. 49–56.

17. Brown, Stephen J., and Dybvig, Philip H. "The Empirical Implications of the Cox, Ingersoll, Ross Theory of the Term Structure of Interest Rates," *Journal of Finance*, **41**, No. 3 (July 1986), pp. 617–630.

18. Buse, A. "Interest Rates, the Meiselman Model and Random Numbers," *Journal of Political Economy*, **LXXV** (Feb. 1967), pp. 49–62.

19. Cagan, Philip. *Changes in the Cyclical Behavior of Interest Rates* (New York: National Bureau of Economic Research, 1966).
20. Campbell, John Y. "A Defense of Traditional Hypotheses about the Term Structure of Interest Rates," *Journal of Finance*, **41,** No. 1 (Mar. 1986), pp. 183–193.
21. Carleton, W. T., and Cooper, I. A. "Estimation and Uses of the Term Structure of Interest Rates," *Journal of Finance*, **31** (Sept. 1976), pp. 1067–1083.
22. Chambers, Donald R., Carleton, Willard T., and Waldman, Donald W. "A New Approach to Estimation of the Term Structure of Interest Rates," *Journal of Financial and Quantitative Analysis*, **19,** No. 3 (Sept. 1984), pp. 233–252.
23. Chance, Don M. "Default Risk And The Duration Of Zero Coupon Bonds," *The Journal of Finance*, **45,** No. 1 (Mar. 1990), pp. 265–274.
24. Conard, Joseph W. *Introduction to the Theory of Interest* (Berkeley, Calif.: University of California Press, 1959).
25. Constantinides, George M., and Ingersoll, Jonathan E., Jr. "Tax Effects and Bond Prices," *The Journal of Finance*, **37,** No. 2 (May 1982), pp. 349–351.
26. Cox, John C., Ingersoll, Jonathan E., and Ross, Stephen. "An Analysis of Variable Rate Loan Contracts," *The Journal of Finance*, **35,** No. 2 (May 1980), pp. 389–404.
27. Culbertson, John M. "The Term Structure of Interest Rates," *Quarterly Journal of Economics*, **LXXI** (Nov. 1957), pp. 485–517.
28. Dermoday, Jaime Cuevas, and Prisman, Eliezen Zeev. "Term Structure Multiplicity and Clientele in Markets with Transactions Costs and Taxes," *Journal of Finance*, **43,** No. 4 (Sept. 1989), pp. 893–911.
29. Duentz, Mark L., and Mahoney, James M. "Using Duration and Convexity in the Analysis of Callable Bonds," *Financial Analyst Journal*, **44,** No. 3 (May/June 1988), pp. 53–72.
30. Elton, Edwin J., and Green, T. Clifton. "Tax and Liquidity in Pricing of Government Bonds," *The Journal of Finance*, **53,** No. 5 (Oct. 1998), pp. 1533–1562.
31. Elton, Edwin J., Gruber, Martin J., Agrawal, Deepak, and Mann, Christopher. "Explaining the Rate Spread on Corporate Bonds?" *The Journal of Finance*, **LVI,** No. 1 (Feb. 2001), pp. 247–279.
32. Fama, E. "Forward Rates as Predictors of Future Spot Rates," *Journal of Financial Economics*, **3** (Oct. 1976), pp. 361–377.
33. ——. "The Information in the Term Structure," *Journal of Financial Economics*, **13,** No. 4 (Dec. 1984), pp. 509–528.
34. ——. "Term Premiums in Bond Returns," *Journal of Financial Economics*, **13,** No. 4 (Dec. 1984), pp. 529–546.
35. Fisher, Lawrence. "Determinants of Risk Premiums on Corporate Bonds," *The Journal of Political Economy*, **67** (June 1959), pp. 217–237.
36. Fitzpatrick, J.D., and J.T. Severiens. "Hickman Revisited: The Case for Junk Bonds," *Journal of Portfolio Management*, **4,** No. 4 (Summer 1978).
37. Fraine, H.G., and Mills, R.H. "The Effect of Defaults and Credit Deterioration on Yields of Corporate Bonds." *Journal of Finance*, **16** (Sept. 1961), pp. 423–433.
38. Galai, Dan. "Pricing of Optionable Bonds," *Journal of Business Finance*, **7,** No. 3, (Sept. 1983), pp. 323–337.
39. Hansen, L.P., and Hodrick, R.J. "Forward Exchange Rates as Optimal Predictors of Future Spot Rates: An Econometric Analysis," *Journal of Political Economy*, **88** (Oct. 1980), pp. 829–853.
40. Hickman, W. Braddock. *Corporate Bond Quality and Investor Experience.* (Princeton, N.J.: Princeton University Press and the National Bureau of Economic Research, 1958).
41. Hill, J.H., and L.A. Post. "The 1977–78 Lower-Rated Debt Market: Selectivity, High Yields, Opportunity," New York: Smith Barney Harris Upham & Co (Dec. 1978).
42. Ho, Thomas, and Singer, Ronald F. "The Value of Corporate Debt with a Sinking-Fund Provision," *Journal of Business*, **57,** No. 3 (Oct. 1984), pp. 315–336.
43. Johnson, Ramon, "Term Structure of Corporate Bond Yields as a Function of Risk of Default," *Journal of Finance*, **22** (May 1967), pp. 313–345.

44. Kane, Alex, and Marcus, Alan F. "Valuation and Optimal Exercise of the Wild Card Option in the Treasury Bond Futures Market," *Journal of Finance*, **41,** No. 1 (Mar. 1986), pp. 195–207.

45. Kessel, Reuben H. *The Cyclical Behavior of the Term Structure of Interest Rates* (New York: National Bureau of Economic Research, 1965).

46. Lang, Richard, and Rasche, Robert. "Debt-Management Policy and the Own Price Elasticity of Demand for U.S. Government Notes and Bonds," *Federal Reserve Bank of St. Louis Review*, **59** (Sept. 1977), pp. 8–22.

47. Lee, Wayne, Maness, Terry, and Tuttle, Donald. "Nonspeculative Behavior and the Term Structure," *Journal of Financial and Quantitative Analysis*, **15** (Mar. 1980), pp. 53–83.

48. Litzenberger, Robert H., and Rolfo, Jacques. "An International Study of Tax Effects on Government Bonds," *The Journal of Finance*, **39,** No. 1 (Mar. 1984), pp. 1–22.

49. ———. "Arbitrage Pricing, Transaction Costs and Taxation of Capital Gains: A Study of Government Bonds with the Same Maturity Date," *Journal of Financial Economics*, **13,** No. 3 (Sept. 1984), pp. 337–352.

50. Lutz, Friedrich A. "The Structure of Interest Rates," *Quarterly Journal of Economics*, **LV** (Nov. 1940), pp. 36–63.

51. Marsh, Terry. "Equilibrium Term Structure Models: Test Methodology," *The Journal of Finance*, **35,** No. 2 (May 1980), pp. 421–434.

52. McConnell, John J., and Schwartz, Eduardo S. "LYON Taming," *Journal of Finance*, **41,** No. 3 (July 1986), pp. 561–576.

53. McCulloch, J.H. "Measuring the Term Structure of Interest Rates," *Journal of Business*, **44** (Jan. 1971), pp. 19–31.

54. ———. "An Estimate of the Liquidity Premium." *Journal of Political Economy*, **83** (Feb. 1975), pp. 95–119.

55. ———. "The Tax-Adjusted Yield Curve," *Journal of Finance*, **30** (June 1975), pp. 811–830.

56. Malkiel, Burton G. "Expectations, Bond Prices, and the Term Structure of Interest Rates," *Quarterly Journal of Economics*, **LXXVI** (May 1962), pp. 197–218.

57. ———. *The Term Structure of Interest Rates* (Princeton, N.J.: Princeton University Press, 1966).

58. Meiselman, David. *The Term Structure of Interest Rates* (Englewood Cliffs, N.J.: Prentice Hall, 1962).

59. Merton, Robert, "On the Pricing of Corporate Debt: The Risk Structure of Interest Rates," *Journal of Finance*, **29** (May 1974), pp. 449–470.

60. Modigliani, Franco, and Sutch, Richard. "Innovations in Interest Rate Policy," *American Economic Review*, **LVI** (May 1966), pp. 178–197.

61. ———. "Debt Management and the Term Structure of Interest Rates: An Empirical Analysis of Recent Experience," *Journal of Political Economy*, **75** (Supplement: Aug. 1967), pp. 569–589.

62. Pinches, G.E., and Mingo, K.A. "A Multivariate Analysis of Industrial Bond Ratings," *Journal of Finance*, **28** (Mar. 1973), pp. 1–32.

63. Piros, Christopher D. "Taxable vs. Tax-Exempt Bonds: A Note on the Effect of Uncertain Taxable Income," *The Journal of Finance*, **42,** No. 2 (June 1987), pp. 447–451.

64. Rao, Ramesh K.S. "The Impact of Yield Changes on the Systematic Risk of Bonds," *Journal of Financial and Quantitative Analysis*, **XVII,** No. 1 (Mar. 1982), pp. 115–128.

65. Roll, Richard. *The Behavior of Interest Rates* (New York: Basic Books, 1970).

66. ———. "After-Tax Investment Results from Long-Term vs. Short-Term Discount Coupon Bonds," *Financial Analysts Journal*, **40,** No. 1 (Jan./Feb. 1984), pp. 43–54.

67. Sarig, Oded, and Warga, Arthur. "Some Empirical Estimates of the Risk Structure of Interest Rates," *The Journal of Finance*, **44,** No. 5 (Dec. 1989), pp. 1351–1360.

68. Schaefer, S.M. "Measuring a Tax Specific Term Structure of Interest Rates in the Market for British Government Securities," *Economic Journal*, **91** (June 1981), pp. 415–438.

69. ———. "Tax-Induced Clientele Effect in the Market for British Government Securities: Placing Bonds on Security Values in an Incomplete Market," *Journal of Financial Economics*, **X,** No. 2 (July 1982), pp. 121–160.

70. Shea, Gary S. "Pitfalls in Smoothing Interest Rate Term Structure Data: Equilibrium Models and Spline Approximations," *Journal of Financial and Quantitative Analysis*, **19,** No. 3 (Sept. 1984), pp. 253–270.

71. Smith, Clifford, and Warner, Jerold. "On Financial Contracting: An Analysis of Bond Covenants," *Journal of Financial Economics*, **7** (June 1979), pp. 115–161.

72. Sundaresan, M. "Constant Absolute Risk Aversion Preferences and Constant Equilibrium Interest Rates," *Journal of Finance*, **39,** No. 1 (Mar. 1983), pp. 205–212.

73. ———. "Consumption and Equilibrium Interest Rates in Stocastic Production Economies," *Journal of Finance*, **39,** No. 1 (Mar. 1984), pp. 77–92.

74. Telser, L.G. "A Critique of Some Recent Empirical Research on the Explanation of the Term Structure of Interest Rates," *Journal of Political Economy*, **75** (Supplement: Aug. 1967), pp. 546–561.

75. Torous, Walter N. "Differential Taxation and the Equilibrium Structure of Interest Rates," *Journal of Business Finance*, **9,** No. 3 (Sept. 1985), pp. 363–385.

76. Van Horne, James. "Interest-Rate Risk and the Term Structure of Interest Rates," *Journal of Political Economy*, **LXXIII** (Aug. 1965), pp. 344–351.

77. ———. "Interest-Rate Expectations, the Shape of the Yield Curve, and Monetary Policy," *Review of Economics and Statistics*, **XLVIII** (May 1966), pp. 211–215.

78. ———. "The Expectations Hypothesis, the Yield Curve, and Monetary Policy: Comment," *Quarterly Journal of Economics*, **LXXIX** (Nov. 1965), pp. 664–668.

79. Vanderhoof, Irwin T.F., Tenenbein, Albert A., and Verni, R. "The Risk of Asset Default." *Report of the Society of Actuaries*, C1 Task Force of the Committee on Valuation and Related Areas, 1989.

80. Van Horne, James C. "Implied Tax Rates and the Valuation of Discount Bonds," *Journal of Business Finance*, **6,** No. 2 (June 1982), pp. 145–159.

81. Van Horne, James C., and Bowers, David A. "The Liquidity Impact of Debt Management," *The Southern Economic Journal*, **XXIV** (April 1968), pp. 526–537.

82. Walsh, Carl E. "A Rational Expectations Model of Term Premium with some Implications for Empirical Asset Demand Equations," *Journal of Finance*, **40,** No. 1 (Mar. 1985), pp. 63–83.

83. Wood, John H. "Expectations, Error, and the Term Structure of Interest Rates," *Journal of Political Economy*, **LXXI** (Apr. 1963), pp. 160–171.

84. Zwick, Burton. "Yield on Privately Placed Corporate Bonds," *The Journal of Finance*, **35,** No. 1 (Mar. 1980), pp. 23–30.

21

The Management of
Bond Portfolios

In the previous chapter, we discussed the determination of interest rates and the characteristics of bonds that affect their return and value. In this chapter we discuss bond portfolio management. Modern portfolio theory has made less of an impact on bond management than it has on common equity management. Furthermore, some of the portfolio management techniques used in bond management are specific to the bond area and not outgrowths of modern portfolio theory. In this chapter we discuss the techniques specifically developed for the bond area as well as applications of general portfolio theory to the bond area.

The chapter is divided into four parts. First we discuss the major source of risk facing bond managers, changes in the yield curve, and measures used to examine a bond's sensitivity to this source of risk. Next we discuss ways of constructing a bond portfolio to insulate against this risk. These are normally referred to as passive portfolio strategies, although, as we will see, they generally involve actively adjusting the portfolio. Next we will discuss active bond management. We will discuss both techniques developed specifically for active bond management and bond management in a modern portfolio theory context, first discussing estimating expected return, then estimation of the variance-covariance structure. Finally we will discuss bond and interest rate swaps.

DURATION

The return on a bond has two components: interest income and capital gains or losses caused by a change in price. A price change can come about because of the passage of time or as a result of a shift in the yield curve. In what follows it will be convenient to assume interest is paid annually. Furthermore, we will assume a flat yield curve with all spot rates equal to i. In the appendix we will discuss the minor modification needed for bonds paying semiannual or monthly interest. We will also discuss the changes needed when there is an upward sloping yield curve.

Price Change Due to Passage of Time

Consider first a price change due to the passage of time. Assume a flat yield curve with an interest rate of 10%. Now consider a pure discount bond with three years to maturity. The price of a pure discount three-year bond that pays $1000 at maturity is

$$P_3 = \frac{1000}{(1.10)^3} = \$751.31$$

assuming that spot rates remain unchanged over the first year.[1] Then, at time 1 this bond must have the same yield as a two-year bond and thus have a price of

$$P_2 = \frac{1000}{(1.10)^2} = \$826.45$$

This price change would occur over the year. The price change over the year is $P_2 - P_3 = \$75.14$, which results in a rate of return of

$$\frac{P_2 - P_3}{P_3} = 10\%$$

The effect of the passage of time on the price of a bond should be easy to understand for pure discount bonds. Since pure discount bonds do not pay any interest, the full return is due to a change in price. Coupon paying bonds also can have an expected price change due to the passage of time. There are a large number of bonds that are comparable in every way except that they offer different coupons. These bonds must offer similar returns to investors. Thus, for these bonds, there are anticipated price changes. For example, a 4% coupon bond will sell at a discount and offer an expected price increase if current interest rates for a similar bond are 10%. Most bonds include an anticipated price change as part of their return.

Unanticipated Price Change

The other cause of a price change is a change in future expectations concerning interest rates (an unanticipated shift in the yield curve). Assume that the yield curve shifts and the new interest rate for all maturities is 14%. Further assume that the shift takes place immediately. In this case the three-year, pure discount bond would have a new price of

$$P_3' = \frac{\$1000}{(1.14)^3} = \$674.97$$

This results in a price change of

$$P_3' - P_3 = -\$76.34$$

If the yield curve remains constant over time or if expectations remain constant, the price change due to the passage of time is easy to calculate. The price change due to an unanticipated change in the yield curve is different.

If we knew how expectations concerning future interest rates would shift over time and others did not, then we would be able to calculate the price change of each bond and put all of

---

[1]This is the simplest example that can be constructed. It assumes a flat yield curve. The principle being demonstrated also holds under more complex shapes of the yield curve.

our money into the bond with the highest total return. However, this is not possible; the best that we can do is to calculate the sensitivity of each bond to a shift in the yield curve.

Sensitivity to Shifts in the Yield Curve

In earlier chapters we calculated a measure called Beta to measure a common equity security's sensitivity to changes in an index. An analogous measure is calculated for bonds: it is called "duration." Duration is a measure of the sensitivity of the price of a bond to a change in interest rates. More specifically, minus duration times the proportional change in 1 plus the interest rate is equal to the unanticipated return due to a change in price.[2]

In symbols

$$R_u = -D\,\Delta i \tag{21.1}$$

where

i is the interest rate

R_u is the unanticipated return due to a change in the interest rate

D is duration

Δi is the proportional change in 1 plus the interest rate $\left(\dfrac{d(1+i)}{1+i}\right)$

Note that we have dropped subscripts on the interest rate and have been referring to "the interest rate" as if there is a single rate that does not depend on maturity. Furthermore, to emphasize this change we use the symbol i. This is in contrast to earlier sections where we were clearly specifying the time horizon of the interest rate. For simplicity we are assuming a single rate for all maturities. A single rate is an assumption of a flat yield curve. In the appendix, we generalize the analysis.

To understand duration, consider a pure discount bond that matures in T years. Coupon paying bonds can be considered as combinations of pure discount bonds. Thus understanding duration for pure discount bonds will help us understand it for coupon bonds. Let P_0 be the current price of a pure discount bond that pays \$1000 in T years. If i is the yearly interest rate, then

$$P_0 = \frac{\$1000}{(1+i)^T} \tag{21.2}$$

---

[2]Security firms generally calculate a slight variation of this formula. Equation (21.1) is

$$R_u = -D\Delta i = -D\frac{d(1+i)}{(1+i)}$$

where $d(1+i)$ is the change in one plus the interest rate. Security firms divide duration by $(1+i)$ and call this adjusted or modified duration. Thus, modified duration (D_A) is

$$D_A = \frac{D}{1+i}$$

and Equation (21.1) becomes

$$R_u = -D_A d(1+i) - -D_A di$$

We derive the duration for this bond in the following section. The reader uninterested in the derivation can skip to the end of the dotted section.

Equation (21.2) can be written as

$$P_0 = (1000)(1+i)^{-T}$$

Recall that the derivative of X^N is $NX^{N-1}dX$. Thus

$$dP_0 = 1000(-T)(1+i)^{(-T-1)}d(1+i)$$

Rearranging yields

$$dP_0 = \frac{-1000T}{(1+i)^T}\frac{d(1+i)}{1+i}$$

Note that $1000/(1+i)^T$ is the price of the bond P_0; thus,

$$dP_0 = -TP_0\frac{d(1+i)}{(1+i)}$$

Dividing both sides by P_0 we have

$$\frac{dP_0}{P_0} = \frac{-TP_0}{P_0}\frac{d(1+i)}{(1+i)} = -T\frac{d(1+i)}{(1+i)}$$

The change in price divided by price dP_0/P_0 is the return due to an unanticipated change in the interest rate. $d(1+i)/(1+i)$ is the proportional change in 1 plus the interest rate.

Comparing this expression to Equation (21.1) and recognizing that $R_u = \frac{dP_0}{P_0}$ we see that $D = T$. Thus the duration on a pure discount bond is its maturity.

For a pure discount bond such as presented in Equation (21.2), duration is equal to its maturity. Thus, given the assumption of a flat yield curve, the sensitivity of a pure discount bond to a change in the yield curve should be directly proportional to its maturity. When the change in the interest rate divided by 1 plus the interest rate is equal to 1%, the change in the price of a pure discount bond with a maturity of one year should be 1%, and the change in price of a pure discount bond with a maturity of five years should be 5%, and so on.

Table 21.1 illustrates these ideas. The bonds in Table 21.1 are pure discount bonds with the maturity shown in the first column. All bonds are assumed to return a principal of $1000 at the horizon. The prices are shown in the next two columns under two alternative interest rate assumptions, 10% and 10.11%. The change in interest rate between the two columns is $0.1011 - 0.10$ or 0.0011. The percentage change in 1 plus the interest rate is $0.0011/(1.10)$ or 0.1%. The percentage change in price from the second to the third column should be minus duration times this 0.1 figure. Since for pure discount bonds, duration is maturity, the last column should be minus (0.1) times maturity, and it is. The analysis is

Table 21.1 The Effect of a Change in Interest Rates on the Price of a Pure Discount Bond

Maturity (year)	Price		Percentage Change in Price
	$i = 10\%$	$i = 10.11\%$	
1	$909.09	$908.18	−0.1
2	$826.45	$824.80	−0.2
3	$751.31	$749.07	−0.3
4	$683.01	$680.29	−0.4
5	$620.92	$617.83	−0.5

derived for very small changes in interest rates and it holds exactly for a very small change in rates. For large changes in rates, the duration measure provides only an approximation of the actual percentage change in prices. However, the approximation is a good one.

Coupon paying bonds can be viewed as combinations of pure discount bonds. Consider a bond with two payments, one in 5 years and one in 10 years. If we consider each payment separately, and designate the return on the payment in 5 years due to an unanticipated change in interest rates as R_u^5 and the return on the payment in 10 years due to an unanticipated change in interest rates as R_u^{10}, we have

$$R_u^5 = -5\,\Delta i$$

$$R_u^{10} = -10\,\Delta i$$

The bond with two payments can be viewed as a portfolio of the 5-year payment and the 10-year payment. Let P_5 be the present value of the 5-year payment and P_{10} be the present value of the 10-year payment, P_0 be the value of the bond, and R_u be the unanticipated return on the portfolio.

In earlier chapters, we showed that the return on a portfolio is a weighted average of the return on the assets comprising that portfolio and that the weights are the fraction of the money invested in the asset. The same principles apply here. Thus, the unanticipated return on the portfolio is simply the sum of the fraction of the portfolio invested in each payment times the unanticipated return on the appropriate payment. The fraction invested in each payment is the present value of that payment divided by the price of the portfolio. Thus[3]

$$R_u = \left(\frac{P_5}{P_0}\right)R_u^5 + \left(\frac{P_{10}}{P_0}\right)R_u^{10}$$

Substituting in for R_u^5 and R_u^{10} yields

$$R_u = \frac{P_5}{P_0}(-5\,\Delta i) + \frac{P_{10}}{P_0}(-10\,\Delta i)$$

$$= -\left[\frac{P_5}{P_0}(5) + \frac{P_{10}}{P_0}(10)\right]\Delta i$$

Thus the duration of a bond with two payments is a weighted average of the maturity of each payment where the weights are the proportion of the current value of the bond attributable to that payment. If the 5- and 10-year payment each contributed equally to the current value of the bond, then the duration would be $7\frac{1}{2}$ years. This can be generalized to T payments. The present value of a payment made in period t is $C(t)/(1 + i)^t$ where $C(t)$ is the payment in period t. If P_0 is the price of the bond, then the fraction of the present value of each payment is $[C(t)/(1 + i)^t]/P_0$. Each weight is multiplied by the duration of the payment that is its maturity. Thus the duration of a T-period bond with payments in each period is

$$D = \frac{\dfrac{C(1)}{(1+i)}}{P_0}1 + \frac{\dfrac{C(2)}{(1+i)^2}}{P_0}2 + \cdots + \frac{\dfrac{C(T)}{(1+i)^T}}{P_0}T$$

$$D = \frac{\displaystyle\sum_{t=1}^{T}\frac{tC(t)}{(1+i)^t}}{P_0} \tag{21.3}$$

---

[3]For the measure of duration under discussion, duration is additive only if there is a flat yield curve, which is what we have assumed.

Notice that the duration for coupon paying bonds is less than the maturity. Up to now we have assumed that the yield curve is flat and that a shift takes place in the flat yield curve. There are many other assumptions that could be made. Different assumptions change the definition of duration. We have set out several of these in Appendix A at the end of the chapter. Researchers have compared these measures to see which seems to be the most accurate representation of a bond's sensitivity to a change in interest rates. The surprising result is that the one we have presented in this chapter, which was the first one ever derived and is certainly the simplest, seems to do well in explaining unanticipated returns: Its performance and simplicity helps explain why this measure is the one most widely used in practice.

Table 21.2 shows the duration on a number of bonds with different maturities and different coupons. Notice how the duration of a bond is much shorter than its maturity, especially for bonds with long maturities.

Equation (21.3) shows that the duration of a bond is affected by the maturity of the bond, its coupon, and the interest rate. Holding changes in other variables constant:

1. An increase in the coupon lowers duration. This is illustrated in Table 21.2, and the logic behind it is easy to understand. As the coupon is increased, the value of the earlier cash flows increases relative to the present value of the terminal cash flow. This increases the weight of the early cash flows and lowers duration.

2. An increase in the interest rate lowers duration. The greater the interest rate, the less important are cash flows far in the future relative to near term flows. The greater the weight on near term flows, the lower the duration.

3. In general, the longer the maturity, the greater the duration. This is illustrated in Table 21.2.[4]

While this ends our presentation of the concept of duration, we return to duration and use it as a tool in bond portfolio management in the later section of the chapter.

Table 21.2 Duration of Bonds with Different Maturities and Coupons[a]

Years to Maturity			
Coupon	3	5	10
4	2.88	4.57	7.95
6	2.82	4.41	7.42
8	2.78	4.28	7.04
10	2.74	4.17	6.76
12	2.70	4.07	6.54
14	2.66	3.99	6.36

[a]The analysis assumes $i = 10\%$ and annual payment of coupons.

[4]A decrease would be rare. Only for deep discount bonds (low coupon) could duration shorten with an increase in maturity. If the coupon is sufficiently low, then receiving the principal later (longer maturity) may lower price by more than price is increased because of the extra coupons. If price is lowered, then the weight on the early payments (which is the present value of the payment divided by price) will be increased, and duration can be shortened.

Convexity

In recent years there has been an increased realization that although duration works well in explaining changes in price for small shifts in the yield curve, it does not work nearly as well for larger shifts. Duration assumes that the percentage price change is proportional to the percentage change in one plus the interest rate. This approximation becomes increasingly bad for large changes in interest rates.

A correction term has been developed that is generally known as convexity. The term "convexity" arises from the fact that percentage price change approximates a convex function rather than a linear function of changes in one plus the interest rate (see Figure 21.1). The derivation of convexity is described in the appendix, whereas the formula for unexpected return is given here.

$$R_u = -D\,\Delta i + C(\Delta i)^2$$

$$C = \left(\frac{1}{2}\right)\frac{\sum_{t=1}^{T}\dfrac{t(t+1)C(t)}{(1+i)^t}}{P_0} \tag{21.4}$$

and D is as described in Equation (21.3).

As an illustration of the use of convexity let us return to the example presented in Table 21.1. Consider the 5-year pure discount bond, which pays $1000 at maturity. Change the assumption in the table to a larger change in interest rates: in particular assume interest rates change from 10% to 12.2%. At a 10% interest rate the price of the 5-year pure discount bond is

$$\$620.92 = \left(\frac{1000}{(1.10)^5}\right)$$

whereas at a 12.2% interest rate the price is $562.39.

The rate of price change as interest rates rise from 10% to 12.2% is

$$\frac{P_{12.2} - P_{10}}{P_{10}} = \frac{562.39 - 620.92}{620.92} = -0.094 \text{ or } -9.4\%$$

The duration on the bond is 5 years, whereas $\Delta i = 0.022/1.10 = .02$. If we estimated the unexpected rate of return on the bond just using duration (Equation [21.1]), we would estimate it as

$$R_u = -5(0.02) = -0.10$$

This is a 6.4% error. To obtain a better estimate we wish to apply Equation (21.4), which corrects the duration measure for convexity.

The convexity on this bond is

$$C = \left(\frac{1}{2}\right)\frac{\dfrac{5(6)\,1000}{(1.10)^5}}{\$620.92} = 15$$

$$R_u = -5(0.02) + 15(0.02)^2 = -0.10 + 0.006 = -0.094 \text{ or } -9.4\%$$

The convexity measure has produced an exact estimate in this case. In general, even using duration and convexity, the estimate will only be an approximation, though often a very good one.

As a second example consider Figure 21.1, which plots the actual price of a bond when different flat yield curves are assumed. The bond prices being plotted are for an eight-year bond with a 10% coupon that pays interest semiannually. Also plotted on the curve is the estimated price of the bond using duration alone (the straight line) and using duration plus convexity (the dashed curve). For small changes in the yield curve, the actual price change is closely matched by both, the estimate using duration alone and the estimate using duration plus convexity.[5] For large price changes the introduction of convexity improves the estimation.

So far we have graphed only the relationship between price and yield for bonds without call features. For these bonds the relationship has the nice curved shape shown in Figure 21.1. The curved shape is known as the convexity, and for bonds without options such as those depicted in Figure 21.1, it is called positive convexity. When bonds have option features, the relationship between price and yield is not so simple. Figure 21.2 plots the relationship between price and yield for a callable bond. This relationship has negative convexity for yield below 10% but positive convexity for yields above. The reasons for the shape for yield below 10% is easy to understand. As the price of the bond exceeds the call price it pays the corporation to call. Investors knowing this will not pay much above the

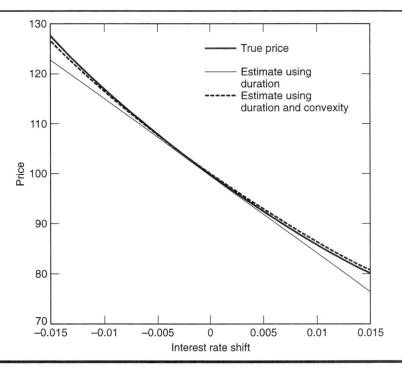

Figure 21.1   Actual price change and estimated price change.

[5]The plots of price using duration and using duration plus convexity were obtained as follows. When the yield changes, the bond price changes. The unanticipated return is the change in price divided by the preshift price or

$$R_u = \frac{\Delta P}{P} \text{ combining this equation with (21.4) we have}$$

$$\frac{\Delta P}{P} = -D\,\Delta_i + C\,\Delta_i^2 \quad \text{or} \quad \Delta P = -DP(\Delta_i) + CP(\Delta_i^2)$$

The plots were obtained with C equal to zero when calculating the approximation using duration alone, or its calculated value when calculating the approximation using duration plus convexity.

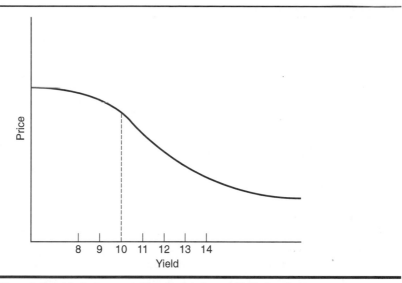

Figure 21.2   The relationship between yield and price for a callable bond.

call price for the bond in fear that the corporation will call. Thus below the yield of 10% the price curve flattens out.[6]

PROTECTING AGAINST TERM STRUCTURE SHIFTS

Shifts in the term structure are viewed by most managers as the major sources of risk to bond portfolios. Just as shifts in the market systematically affect all equity prices, shifts in the term structure affect all bond prices.

Two techniques have been devised to try to insulate a portfolio from shifts in the term structure. These techniques are known as exact matching and immunization.

Exact Matching or Dedication

Exact matching involves finding the lowest cost portfolio that produces cash flows exactly matching the outflows that are financed by the investment. Consider the example shown in Table 21.3. In this example we assume it is necessary to meet flows of $100, $1000, and $2000 over the next three years. These cash flows might be needed to meet pension payments. The bond portfolio is the investment used to meet these obligations. An exact matching program would determine a bond portfolio of one-, two-, and three-year bonds so that the coupons plus principal exactly match the three flows mentioned.

Portfolio A in Table 21.3 is a portfolio that is cash flow matched. Most investment organizations also consider portfolios with surplus cash flows in early periods that can be used to meet liabilities in latter periods as cash flow matched. This is illustrated by Portfolio B in Table 21.3. In this example $100 of the inflow of $195 in period 1 is used to meet the liability of $100 in period 1 and $95 is invested and carried forward to period 2 to finance the shortfall of $100 in period 2. As long as $5 in interest can be earned on the period 1 surplus the portfolio is cash flow matched.

---

[6]The corporation may not call exactly when the price exceeds the call price because of a belief that rates will fall even farther. Thus it is rational for the bonds to trade slightly above the call price, and they do.

534

Table 21.3   Cash Flow Matched Portfolios

	Period		
	1	2	3
Liability	$100	$1000	$2000
Portfolio A	$100	$1000	$2000
Portfolio B	$195	$900	$2000

In Appendix B, we discuss a procedure for determining a portfolio to accomplish this matching as well as variations on this procedure that can lead to lower-cost portfolios. Exact matching programs are a passive investment program. Once the portfolio is determined, no additional changes are required even if the yield curve changes in dramatic ways. The performance of the portfolio is insensitive to interest rate shifts in the sense that it meets a fixed set of obligations regardless of changes in the yield curve. In practice, when the yield curve shifts there may well be profitable bond swaps, and a firm using an exact matching program would use the procedures of Appendix C to evaluate these swaps.

There are two risks with exact matching programs. First, the cash flows may not materialize because of bonds defaulting or being called. Second, if the strategy involves cash carry forward (Portfolio B in Table 21.3), then there is risk that return on the funds carried forward will be inadequate. Nevertheless the manager is reasonably assured of meeting the liabilities even with shifts in the yield curve.

Immunization

The second category of techniques for protecting against interest rate shifts is immunization programs. Earlier we introduced duration as a measure of the sensitivity of a bond or a portfolio of bonds to interest rate shifts. Immunization theory attempts to eliminate sensitivity to shifts in the term structure by matching the duration of the assets to the duration of the liabilities. Thus, if duration is truly a measure of sensitivity to interest rate shifts, a shift in the term structure will have the same impact on the present value of both assets and liabilities and will leave unchanged the ability of the program to meet any obligations. If interest rates rise, the present value of assets and liabilities will fall by the same amount. Similarly, if interest rates fall, then the value of the assets and liabilities will rise by the same amount. Perhaps an analogy to Beta is helpful. If a liability had a Beta of 1.5, then purchasing an asset with a Beta of 1.5 would result in a zero Beta combination. This follows since the liability is an outflow and thus is a negative 1.5 Beta. The negative 1.5 Beta and the positive 1.5 Beta is a zero Beta combination insensitive to market movements.

To clarify further, consider a single liability of $100 at year 5. The goal of the investment program is to meet that liability. If a bond is purchased with a maturity of five years, the investor is certain about the value of the bond at the horizon but is uncertain about the rate at which coupon payments will be invested. If interest rates rise, the obligation will be more than met because the coupon payments will be invested at rates that were higher than anticipated. However, if interest rates fall, the obligation will not be met because the coupon payments will be invested at a rate below what was anticipated. If the investor purchases a bond with a maturity of longer than five years, the investor will also be uncertain about the value of the bond at year 5. Consider a rise in interest rates. With a rise in interest rates the aggregate value of the coupons at the horizon will be higher than anticipated because of the coupon payments being invested at more favorable rates. However, because interest rates rose, the value of the bond at the horizon will be less. These influences work in the opposite directions. If the bond is selected properly, these effects will exactly balance one another. Similarly, consider a decline in interest rates. With a decline, the coupon payments will be invested at rates less than anticipated. The aggregate value of the interest payments at the horizon will be less. However, if interest rates decline, the value of the bond will rise. Once again it might be possible to choose a maturity so that these influences exactly offset one another.

The principles discussed in this part of the chapter are exactly why immunization works. At a point in time equal to the duration of the assets the change in reinvestment income will exactly match the change in the value of the bonds. Table 21.4 illustrates these ideas. Assume that interest rates are currently at 11% for all maturities. Further assume that the bond pays annual interest of 13.52% and has a maturity of five years. These are the flows shown in the first column of Table 21.4. The duration of this bond is four years. The value of this bond as of period 4 if interest rates remain at 11% is 165.946.

If interest rates decline to 10%, the value as of period 4 is 165.946. The value is unchanged because the decrease in the value of the interest payments of 0.930 is exactly offset by an increase in the value as of period 4 of a payment of 113.52 in period 5. This increase is 0.930. If interest rates rise to 12%, the value of the coupon payments as of period 4 increases while the value as of period 4 of receiving 113.52 at period 5 decreases. Although these don't completely offset one another, they come close to doing so. This example illustrates the idea of immunization. If we had a liability at period 4, we could purchase a sufficient quantity of the bond to just meet the liability. For example, a $995 liability could be met with six bonds. Whether interest rates decrease or increase, the same liability could be met.

Why does the bond in Table 21.4 have these properties? The coupon for the bond in Table 21.4 was selected so that the bond has a duration of four years. Pure discount bonds have a duration equal to their maturity. Thus a pure discount bond with a maturity of four years also has a duration of four years. Earlier we argued that duration is a measure of sensitivity to interest rate changes. Two bonds with the same sensitivity have their value change by the same amount. If one bond could be swapped for a second before an interest change, it could also be swapped after the change. Since the pure discount bond has a constant value as of period 4, the bond that could be swapped for it would also have a constant value as of period 4.

In the last section we discussed how the addition of convexity improved the approximation of the estimated price change to the true price change. Many managers engaging in immunization match on convexity as well as duration. Their concern is that the convexity of the liabilities and assets might be quite different and the approximation utilizing duration alone might lead to large errors. The addition of convexity involves a tradeoff. The addition of convexity should provide better protection against term structure shifts.

Table 21.4   The Value of a Bond with Changing Interest Rates

Time	Cash Flow	Value as of Period 4		
		11%	10%	12%
1	13.52	$13.52(1.11)^3$	$13.52(1.1)^3$	$13.52(1.12)^3$
2	13.52	$13.52(1.11)^2$	$13.52(1.1)^2$	$13.52(1.12)^2$
3	13.52	$13.52(1.11)^1$	$13.52(1.1)^1$	$13.52(1.12)^1$
4	13.52	13.52	13.52	13.52
5	113.52	$113.52(1.11)^{-1}$	$113.52(1.1)^{-1}$	$113.52(1.12)^{-1}$
		165.946	165.946	165.974

However, fewer portfolios will be both duration and convexity matched. Thus, the match on both measures will likely result in higher cost portfolio.

Immunization strategies are widely used in order to mitigate the effect of interest rate changes. Extensive research has been done on designing immunized portfolios. We now discuss some implications of this research. The duration on a portfolio of bonds is a weighted average of the duration of the individual assets that make up the portfolio.[7] Let X_i be the proportion of bond i in the portfolio, D_i be the duration of asset i, and D_P be the duration on the portfolio with N bonds.

$$D_P = \sum_{i=1}^{N} X_i D_i$$

There are obviously an enormous number of ways to construct a portfolio of a particular duration. For example, assume that a bond portfolio with a duration of 10 years is required. Further assume that four bonds are being considered with a duration of 6, 8, 10, and 12 years. Simply holding the bond with a duration of 10 years would meet the constraint. Alternatively one-sixth of the money could be invested in the bond with 6 years' duration, one-fourth in the bond with 8 years' duration, and the remaining seven-twelfths in the 12-year bond. This results in a duration of 10 years since

$$\left(\frac{1}{6}\right)6 + \left(\frac{1}{4}\right)8 + \left(\frac{7}{12}\right)12 = 10$$

Two different strategies have been explored: a barbell strategy and a focused strategy. The focused strategy finds a portfolio of bonds with each bond having a duration close to the duration of the liability. For example, if the liability is 10 years, then the bonds might have a duration between 9 and 11 years. The bond portfolio is focused around the duration of the liability. The barbell strategy uses bonds with very different durations, for example, 5 and 15 years. The 10-year duration would be met by one-half in the 5-year duration bonds and one-half in the 15-year duration bonds. The advantage of a barbell strategy is that there is no necessity to construct individual bond portfolios to meet each liability. Instead, liabilities of different duration can be met by selecting different mixtures of the 5- and 15-year duration portfolios.

These two strategies have been explored to determine which one better meets the goal of having the asset and liability mix equally sensitive to changes in interest rates. The empirical evidence gives some support to the focused strategy. The reason seems to be as follows. All duration measures are approximations of the effect of the true shift in interest rate patterns. When individual assets and liabilities have similar durations, these errors are similar. When the individual assets in a portfolio have different durations from the liabilities even though the portfolio has the same duration, the error patterns can be very different. This latter pattern is what occurs with a barbell strategy. Thus inaccuracies in the duration estimate explain in part the evidence tending to support focusing.

Before closing this discussion, one more facet of immunization should be discussed. Immunization is often presented as a passive strategy, and therefore one by which a set of bonds is purchased and held to maturity. This impression is incorrect. Duration is calculated for a particular yield curve. As the yield curve shifts, duration changes and the assets and liabilities may no longer have the same duration. If the differences become large enough,

---

[7]This is a property of most duration measure. For the duration measure discussed here, it only holds if the yield curve is flat.

restructuring is required. Furthermore, even if the yield curve stays constant, the duration of the assets and the liabilities will move apart unless both assets and liabilities have the same cash flow pattern. This also requires restructuring. Thus immunization is an active strategy.

What are the risks of an immunized strategy? The principal one is the selection of the wrong duration measure. Each duration measure is derived assuming a different pattern of shifts in the yield curve. A portfolio is usually immunized using one measure but not another. For example using a measure that accurately measures price change for parallel shifts in a flat yield curve will not accurately measure price change if the yield curve steepens (long rates increase more than short).

Lest the reader become overly concerned, it is worth repeating that even the simplest measure discussed in this chapter works very well. The second risk of immunization concerns major yield shifts when the portfolio is not immunized. As discussed previously, either the passage of time or small changes in the yield curve will result in the portfolio not being immunized. Cash flows from the portfolio are used to purchase bonds to rebalance the portfolio so the duration of assets is closer to the duration of liabilities. Bond sales and purchases (rebalancing) could also be used to immunize the portfolio exactly. However, bond swaps are costly, so that a manager will let the duration of the assets drift away from the duration of the liabilities and not be immunized at all points in time.[8] The risk is that just before the manager engages in a bond swap to adjust the duration in order to immunize the portfolio, the interest rates may change dramatically.

A cash flow matched portfolio is, of course, immunized. Since its immunization comes from matched cash flows rather than the accuracy of a measure, it is generally less risky. Thus, the immunized portfolio has to be less costly than the cash flow matched portfolio for an organization to immunize. It is often optional to cash flow match part of the portfolio and immunize the remainder.

In this section, we have presented techniques for protecting against interest rate shifts. In the next section we discuss techniques for constructing portfolios when performance over a one-year period is being evaluated.

BOND PORTFOLIO MANAGEMENT OF YEARLY RETURNS

In the prior sections we have discussed designing portfolios of bonds that are reasonably insensitive to changes in the yield curve. The return on these portfolios can fluctuate dramatically from period to period because the concern is meeting some future liability rather than period-by-period returns. Many managers are interested not in meeting some future liability but in the year-by-year return on the portfolio. Managers of bond funds and many managers of pension funds are concerned with year-by-year variability.

This section is divided into three parts. In the first part we discuss indexation. Indexation is the passive strategy used by managers interested in period-by-period returns. The second section discusses active bond management techniques.

Indexation

Another passive strategy finding favor with bond managers is index replication. The major motivation behind index replication in the bond area is performance. Very few actively managed funds have outperformed the major bond indexes. Given this experience, many

---

[8]Futures can be used to adjust duration (see Chapter 23) as well as interest rate swaps. These are generally less expensive alternatives than bond swaps.

pension managers, in particular, have indexed a part of their assets. Indexation in the bond area is done differently than in the common stock area. There are thousands of corporate bonds, many of which are completely inactive. Thus, holding bonds in the same proportion as the index is infeasible. Rather, indexation is commonly done via cell matching. The major important characteristics of a bond are delineated. These generally include category (government, corporate, utility, etc.), duration, coupon, and bond rating. Then the proportion of the index with any set of characteristics is determined over all possible characteristics. For example, what percentage of the index is represented by corporate bonds rated Baa, with a duration between four and five years and a coupon between 8% and 9%? These percentages are calculated for all possible combinations of bond characteristics. A portfolio of bonds is then constructed that has roughly the same proportion in each cell as the indexes. This type of index replication is highly successful in matching the performance of the index.

Active Bond Management

There are essentially four categories of active investment strategies in the bond area. These are aggregate interest rate forecasting, sector selection or rotation, and individual bond selection.

Aggregate Interest Rate Forecasting   The major cause of variation in year-to-year return for a manager is unexpected shifts in the yield curve. Examining Table 20.1 shows that for most years the unanticipated return was considerably larger in absolute magnitude than the anticipated return. For example, in 1993 long-term bonds returned 16.38% while intermediate-term bonds returned 7.91%, even though the expected return on intermediate- and long-term bonds would have been very similar. Likewise, in the 1980s the long bond return varied from about -3% to $+42\%$ with much less variation in expected return. We know from our discussion of duration that if interest rates rise unexpectedly, that short duration bonds will be hurt less than long duration and if interest rates fall unexpectedly, short duration bonds will gain less than long duration bonds.

Thus, one investment strategy that managers follow is to shorten the duration when they expected rates to rise more is anticipated by the market (and reflected in the yield curve) and lengthen the duration when rates are expected to fall more than anticipated by the market. Bond managers pay a price for this timing. Most bonds are not as liquid as common equities. Those bonds that have a large market and can be readily traded in a short period of time are primarily government bonds of certain special maturities. Restricting purchases to these bonds can result in a lower expected return compared to purchasing corporate bonds with higher expected returns or bonds that are mispriced. In addition, folklore and possibly empirical evidence suggest that the bonds used in timing have a lower return than comparable risk bonds due to their marketability. Finally, concentrating on a few government issues to facilitate timing results in a relatively undiversified portfolio.[9]

No forecaster is accurate all of the time. For a forecast of future interest rates to be useful it has to be accurate and different from the consensus, since the consensus is already reflected in existing rates. A forecaster should be correct in estimating whether interest rates will rise or fall 50% of the time by chance. A forecaster who is accurate 60% of the time in calling direction would be doing extremely well in forecasting the market. Market timing involves one estimate each period: future interest rates. Since even a good

---

[9]An alternative technique for changing duration is the use of futures (see the discussion in Chapter 23). Using futures to change duration has two advantages: it's cheaper and it allows a separation of the selection decision and the duration decision. Thus, the manager selects the cheapest bonds and manages duration by using futures.

forecaster will often be wrong, it will take a number of periods before there is a high probability that a manager with timing ability has superior returns.

Some managers immunize and also engage in some market timing. For these managers the normal strategy is to have the duration of the assets and liabilities the same. If they anticipate rates to rise more than the market expects, then the duration of the assets is set less than the liabilities and if they expect rates to fall more than the market expects, the duration of the assets is set greater than the duration of the liabilities. Managers immunizing the portfolio are likely to be very cautious in utilizing market timing.

Sector Selection   Managers who engage in sector selection are doing so because they believe in the long run some sector will give superior performance. The most common type of sector selection is to lower the average credit rating on the portfolio. For example, a manager could believe that junk bonds offer a larger risk premium than is justified by any difference in risk and permanently invest in junk bonds in the belief that in the long run this premium will be earned and junk bonds will outperform other categories.

Sector Rotation   Sector rotation can be practiced using any of the characteristics of bonds discussed earlier. Sector rotation is related to sector selection. Sector rotation involves overweighting a sector in the belief that the relative performance of this sector will be better in the *next period*. For example, the yield to maturity on AAA corporates selling at par is higher than the yield to maturity on governments of the same maturity selling at par. This difference is partially a default premium and partially a risk premium. The spread would widen if investors believed that default risk increased. If a manager believed that the market was overreacting to a perceived risk increase, then the manager would switch to AAA debt. If the manager's assessment was correct, the manager would earn a larger than normal risk premium in the period and could earn an additional return if the default premium subsequently narrowed because of many investors realizing they have overreacted. For example, assume the normal default premium between government and corporates was $\frac{1}{8}\%$ and the default premium widened to $\frac{1}{4}\%$. If the spread goes back to an $\frac{1}{8}\%$, then the yield on AAA corporates is falling relative to Treasuries and AAA corporate prices will rise relative to governments.

As mentioned earlier, sector rotation can be practiced with respect to any of the factors affecting bond prices. As a second example, assume the investor feels the market is underestimating the volatility of interest rates. The more volatile the interest rates, the greater the change in interest rates that can occur. The greater the change in interest rates, the more likely very low interest rates will occur and it will pay a firm to call a bond. Thus, an investor believing that the market has underestimated volatility will believe that callable bonds are relatively unattractive and will rotate away from callable bonds.

Mispriced Bonds   There are generally two procedures for bond security selection. One is to accept bond classifications as accurate (e.g., AAA or AA) and to try to find the most attractive bonds in a given class. The second procedure is to look for misclassified bonds. For example, a firm might treat all AA noncallable bonds with 8 to 10 years' maturity as equivalent with respect to risk. The firm could then examine all bonds that met this criteria and select the most attractive. Brokerage firms generally utilize yield to maturity as a metric of desirability. Thus, they would suggest bonds with the highest yields as the most desirable.[10] Bonds services such as Barra or Gifford Fong utilize the difference between

---

[10]For some bonds such as Ginnie Maes, firms use spread over comparable Treasuries as a measure of desirability. We have discussed the difficulties with yield measures in the prior chapter.

actual price and theoretical price as a metric of desirability. Theoretical price is determined by discounting future cash flows at estimated spot rates and adjusting the price for any option value.

The other way firms practice bond selection is to look for misclassified bonds. This is especially prevalent with low-rated bonds. Implicit in the bonds' rating is a default probability and expected loss in event of default. The firm practicing this method of selection examines the issuing firms' characteristics and tries to find bonds that have default probabilities or expected loss that is different than what is implied by the bonds ratings. Those with more attractive characteristics are selected.

In the next section we discuss techniques for selecting bonds similar to those used for stocks.

Active Bond Selection Using Modern Portfolio Theory

Modern portfolio theory can be applied to bond management as well as stock management. In this section we will discuss how this can be done.

Estimating Expected Return   We start this section with a consideration of the simplest class of bonds: noncallable bonds issued by the federal government. Later we discuss expected return on nongovernment bonds and the impact of callability and tax considerations.

While any of the theories of the term structure of interest rates can be used to estimate the expected returns on a bond, let us start off illustrating the methodology with the simplest term structure theory: the expectations theory. Under the expectations theory, all bonds must give the same rate of return over any specific time horizon. Thus next period's expected return for any bond is simply the one-period spot rate.

This is modified if we recognize that bonds may be mispriced. Then the expected return will be a function of mispricing if it exists as well as the one-period spot rate. To see the impact of this on expected returns it is necessary to make an assumption about the period of time that elapses before the market corrects mispricing. We will follow common practice and assume that prices adjust to equilibrium within one period. This is the assumption implicit in most commercial services and seems consistent with empirical evidence. To calculate the expected rate of return on a bond we need to calculate its expected equilibrium value one period in the future. Then, from the interest payment expected during the period and the expected capital gain (change in price), we can calculate the expected rate of return.

To get a price for a bond one period in the future, we need expectations about what spot rates or forward rates will be at that time. In the previous chapter we showed how to derive forward rates from the spot rates. If the expectation theory holds, forward rates are not expected to change over time. A hypothetical set of rates is shown in Table 21.5. Assuming these rates, let us examine the expected return on a bond that will mature in five years and pays interest of $8 per period. The bond has $100 principal payment and its current price is $82.

If the bond were priced in equilibrium at the initial period, its price would be

$$P_0 = \frac{8}{1.10} + \frac{8}{(1.10)(1.11)} + \frac{8}{(1.10)(1.11)(1.12)} + \frac{8}{(1.10)(1.11)(1.12)(1.13)}$$
$$+ \frac{108}{(1.10)(1.11)(1.12)(1.13)(1.14)}$$
$$= \$86.16$$

Table 21.5 Hypothetical Set of Rates

Period	Current One Period Forward Rate (%)	Expected Forward Rate in One Period (%)
1	10	
2	11	11
3	12	12
4	13	13
5	14	14

The expected price one period in the future is

$$P_1 = \frac{8}{1.11} + \frac{8}{(1.11)(1.12)} + \frac{8}{(1.11)(1.12)(1.13)} + \frac{108}{(1.11)(1.12)(1.13)(1.14)}$$

$$P_i = \$86.77$$

Note that if the bond had been priced in equilibrium at time 0, the one-period cash flow would have been $8 in interest and 61¢ in capital gains for a total return of 8.61/86.16 or 10%. The 10% is, of course, the spot rate in the first period. If instead the bond could have been bought for $82, the return would be $8 in interest and $4.77 in capital gains or a return of 15.57%. This rate of return can be broken into its three components: 9.76% from interest income, 0.74% from the change in the equilibrium value of the bond, and 5.07% from the effect of mispricing.

If an alternative term structure theory is a better description of reality, there is a further element to expected return. However, the same techniques are applicable even if any of the other alternative term structure theories is a better description of reality. Consider the liquidity premium theory as an example. With the liquidity premium theory, the expected return is the one-period spot rate plus any adjustment so that the bond is priced in equilibrium plus the change in the liquidity premium. The same procedure can be used to value bonds as was discussed with the expectation theory, but the effect of the change in the liquidity premium has to be taken into account. Consider the example shown in Table 21.6.

Table 21.6 is divided into two parts: calculations associated with the current period and calculations associated with one period in the future. The table shows forward rates in the current period. These one-period rates can be determined from spot rates using the techniques discussed in the prior chapter. In the second column is a set of hypothesized

Table 21.6 Assumed Forward Rates (in Percent)

	Current Period			Next Period		
	Forward Rates	Liquidity Premium	Forward Rate (Liquidity Premium Removed)	Forward Rate (Liquidity Premium Removed)	Liquidity Premium	Forward Rates
1	10		10			
2	11	0.1	10.9	10.9		10.9
3	12	0.2	11.8	11.8	0.1	11.9
4	13	0.3	12.7	12.7	0.2	12.9
5	14	0.4	13.6	13.6	0.3	13.9

liquidity premiums. These are subtracted from the forward rates to arrive at the forward rates without the liquidity premium shown in the third column. These rates are assumed to remain unchanged. Thus the fourth column is the same as the third column. The column that is changed is the liquidity premium column. The liquidity premiums are the same; however, each premium is moved one period in the future. Thus the 0.1 liquidity premium that was the premium for two-year money as of the initial period appears in the third period rather than the second period since at time 1 two periods in the future is period 3.

Assume the same bond discussed previously: a bond with an 8% coupon and a $100 principal payment. Further assume that it sells for its equilibrium price. The forward rates shown in Table 21.6 as of the current period are identical to the rates in Table 21.5, and thus the equilibrium price is unchanged or

$$P_0 = \$86.16$$

The equilibrium price in one period using the rates shown in Table 21.6 is

$$P_1 = \frac{8}{1.109} + \frac{8}{(1.109)(1.119)} + \frac{8}{(1.109)(1.119)(1.129)}$$
$$+ \frac{108}{(1.109)(1.119)(1.129)(1.139)}$$
$$= \$87.05$$

Without an assumption of a liquidity premium, the equilibrium price in period 1 was $86.77. The difference between $87.05 and $86.77 is the effect of the additional capital gain due to bearing maturity risk. Total expected cash flow is interest income of $8, an expected capital appreciation without the liquidity premium of $86.77 − $86.16 or 61¢ and an effect of the liquidity premium applying to different cash flows of $87.05 − $86.77 or 28¢. Total expected return is (8 + 0.61 + 0.28) divided by $86.16 or 10.32%. The extra 0.32% is the liquidity premium effect. Any mispricing can be dealt with as discussed earlier for the expectations theory.

Up to now we have ignored the effect of default risk, callability, or tax effects in this discussion. Although there are many ways to deal with these influences, we will briefly discuss what has become the most widely used technique. To keep the discussion simple we will assume the expectations theory holds though the modifications for the liquidity premium theory are straightforward and follow from the discussion of how to deal with the liquidity premium presented before.

Let us look at callability. The future prices for noncallable government bonds are arrived at by the prior methods. Prices for callable bonds are arrived at by using the rates for noncallable bonds. The average difference between actual price for all callable bonds and the price arrived at for these bonds when they are priced as if they were noncallable bonds is then calculated. The theoretical price of any callable bond is arrived at by pricing as if it were a noncallable government bond and adding the average difference. Mispricing is the difference between the actual price and this theoretical price. This is obviously a crude procedure. A much more exact procedure would use the option pricing models of Chapter 22 to arrive at an estimate of the differential price due to callability. This differential price would be used to estimate possible mispricing. Taxes and default risk are evaluated in an analogous manner.[11]

---

[11]As an alternative to this procedure, some managers estimate spot rates and the effect of callability, default risk, and taxes simultaneously using a multiple regression and the techniques discussed in Appendix A at the end of the chapter. Once again an assumption is made that spot and forward rates remain unchanged and a new price is estimated one period in the future. This new price is used to calculate an expected return.

Index Models   In Chapters 7 and 8 we discussed methods of estimating the variance-covariance structure of common stock returns. The general principles discussed are equally as applicable to bonds as they are to stocks. However, there are special characteristics of bonds that suggest that some modification and respecification would be useful.

Single-index Models   In this section, we discuss the application of the single-index model to bond portfolio management. Consider first applying it to noncallable government bonds with no special tax effects. The return on government bonds can be divided into two parts: the anticipated return and the unanticipated return due to both changes in the yield structure and/or changes in the pricing of the bond in question relative to the yield structure. As discussed previously, if the expectations theory is correct and bonds are fairly priced, then all bonds should have the same expected return over the first period. If one of the other theories is correct or there is mispricing, then the bonds may have different returns and these returns will depend on the maturity of the bond. We will derive the single-index model under the assumption that the expectations theory holds.

The unanticipated return has two sources: a change in the yield curve or a change in the bond price relative to the yield curve. In the first section we showed that the return on a bond due to a shift in the yield curve was minus duration times a measure of interest rate change. We also emphasized that the duration measure is based on a simplified assumption about unanticipated shifts in the yield curve. Assume that the influence of shifts other than that assumed in deriving the duration measure is random. Further assume that shifts in the bond return relative to the yield curve are random. With these assumptions, the effect of these two influences on return are random and can be represented by e_i where the expected value of e_i is zero and the variance of e_i is represented by σ_{ei}^2.

Let us put these ideas together as follows:

$$\frac{\text{Total}}{\text{return}} = \frac{\text{Expected}}{\text{return}} + \begin{array}{c}\text{Return due to an}\\ \text{unanticipated shift}\\ \text{in the yield curve}\end{array} + \begin{array}{c}\text{Random}\\ \text{influence}\\ \text{on return}\end{array}$$

$$R_i = \bar{R}_i - D_i \Delta + e_i \tag{21.5}$$

where

R_i is the return on bond i

$\bar{R}_i$ is the expected return of bond i

D_i is the duration of bond i

Δ is the change in interest rate divided by 1 plus the interest rate

e_i is the random influence with a mean of zero and a variance of σ_{ei}^2

In Chapter 7 we expressed the single-index model in terms of an equity index. We can express the return on a bond in terms of a bond index. Let X_i^m be the proportion of bond i in the bond index. Then the return on the index called R_m is

$$R_m = \sum_i X_i^m R_i = \sum_i X_i \bar{R}_i - \sum_i X_i D_i (\Delta) + \sum_i X_i e_i$$

$$= \bar{R}_m - \sum_i X_i D_i \Delta + \sum_i X_i e_i$$

For a bond index with a large number of bonds $\Sigma_i X_i e_i$ should be approximately zero. This follows from assuming that the e_i are independent from one another. Define D_m as $\Sigma_i X_i D_i$ or the duration of the bond index. With these substitutions we have

$$R_m = \overline{R}_m - D_m(\Delta) \tag{21.5a}$$

Solving (21.5a) for Δ and substitutions into (21.4) yields[12]

$$R_i = \overline{R}_i + \frac{D_i}{D_m}\left(R_m - \overline{R}_m\right) + e_i \tag{21.6}$$

To complete the analogy with the model discussed in Chapter 7, define β_i as D_i/D_m. With the assumption of e_i being independent of the bond index, β_i has the same meaning as in Chapter 7, that is, β_i is the covariance of R_i with R_m divided by the variance of R_m. However, there is no reason to estimate β_i using historical or modified historical data. Instead, it can be measured directly as the ratio of durations.

Equation (21.6) is analogous to the single-index model presented for common stocks. If we make the assumptions of the single-index model that $E(e_i e_j) = 0$ for $i \neq j$ then we find

$$\text{cov}\left(R_i R_j\right) = \frac{D_i D_j}{D_m^2}\sigma_m^2$$

$$\text{var}\left(R_i\right) = \frac{D_i^2}{D_m^2}\sigma_m^2$$

This is not surprising since, as we have already stated, $\beta_i = D_i/D_m$. Single-index models have been used widely in stock selection. There is much less experience concerning their usefulness in the bond management area. Single-index models for bonds did not appear commercially until the 1980s. Similarly, there has been very little academic research of the applicability of single-index models to bond management. This is in contrast to the extensive research done in the common equity area.

Before leaving this discussion we want to mention some other influences affecting returns on bonds. These include liquidity premiums, tax effects, callability, and default risk. If the impact of all of these influences were constant over time, then the single-index model would be appropriate. However, if the premium for these influences changed over time, then bonds would have an added source of variance and covariance. These added influences might be an added source of covariance just as industry membership might be for common stocks. For example, two AAA-rated bonds might move more alike than two bonds picked at random. This leads us logically to the next section of this chapter on multi-index models.

Multi-index Models   There are a number of reasons why a multi-index model might be more relevant than a single-index model (several were discussed in the last section). The major reasons are

1. To more accurately measure the effect of interest rate changes.
2. To reflect the variability introduced by the change in the yield spread between bonds of a particular risk class and governments.
3. To reflect the variability introduced by the change in yield spread between bonds from various sectors: government, financial, and corporate.

---

[12]Using arbitrage pricing theory, this return generating process results in the following equilibrium model

$$\overline{R}_i = \overline{R}_z + \frac{D_i}{D_m}\left(\overline{R}_m - \overline{R}_z\right)$$

4. To reflect the variability introduced by the change in the value of a call.

5. To reflect the variability introduced by changes in the importance of taxes.

Any of these influences could be important enough so that a multi-index model would reflect the covariance structure better than a single-index model.

A number of studies have shown that two factors are necessary to capture changes in the term structure.[13] An example of the two factors researchers have used is changes in the long rate and changes in the spread between the long and short rate. Consider, for example, the following two-factor model

$$R_{it} = \bar{R}_i + \beta_{i1} F_{1t} + \beta_{i2} F_{2t} + e_{it}$$

where

R_{it} is the return on bond i in period t

$\bar{R}_i$ is expected return on bond i

β_{ij} is the sensitivity of bond i to factor j

F_{jt} is the value of factor j in period t

e_{it} is the random error term

Using two factors seems to substantially improve the explanatory power of these types of return-generating process. To be more concrete concerning the factors, consider an example. As a proxy for the long rate some investigators have used the rate on a 10-year government bond. Factor 1 in period t would be the change in the interest rate on a 10-year government bond from period t to period $t + 1$. The change in the interest rate measures the shift up or down in the term structure. One would expect β_{ij} to be negative so that if interest rates increased, the price on the bond would decline and the unexpected part of return due to an upward shift in the yield curve would be negative. Some investigators use a change in the short rate for factor 2, others use changes in the spread between long and short bonds as the second factor. For example, the spread could be the difference between 10-year and 1-year rates. The change in the spread between these rates from period t to $t + 1$ would be the value of the second factor. An increase in the spread between long and short rates while holding long rates constant implies a decrease in short rates. This should result in positive return for short bonds, thus b_{i2} should be positive.

Estimating the sensitivities in a return-generating process for bonds is more difficult than it is for common equities. In common equities, a time-series regression of return on factors is the usual starting point for most estimations. With bonds the maturity shortens as time passes. It is generally believed that sensitivity is related to maturity. For example, in the one-factor model, when sensitivity was related to duration as maturity shortened so did duration, and hence sensitivity changed. For time-series regression to be an appropriate method of estimating sensitivity, the sensitivity must remain constant over time. Thus time-series estimation of sensitivity for individual bonds is probably inappropriate.

What has been done is to estimate the sensitivities for a pure discount bond of constant maturity. Since coupon paying bonds can be viewed as portfolios of pure discount bonds and since the sensitivity on a portfolio is a weighted average of the sensitivity of the bonds comprising it, this procedure can be used to estimate a bond's sensitivity. For example, each month the return is calculated on the factors and on a 10-year pure discount bond. Of

---

[13]See, for example, Brennan and Schwartz [15], Nelson and Schaefer [39], Elton, Gruber, and Naber [27], and Elton, Gruber, and Michaely [26].

course, the bond that is a 10-year pure discount bond changes each month. The sensitivities are then estimated by regressing the return on the 10-year pure discount bond on the two factors. Any coupon paying bond can be viewed as a portfolio of pure discount bonds. The sensitivity on a portfolio is a weighted average of the sensitivities of the components where the weights are the proportion each component represents of the whole. For example, define

1. b_{t1}, b_{t2} as the sensitivities of a t-period pure discount bond to factor 1 and 2, respectively.
2. $PV(Cf_{ti})$ is the present value of the cash flow for bond i in period t.
3. P_i is the price of bond i.

The sensitivities for bond i are a weighted average of the sensitivities on the pure discount bonds or

$$\beta_{i1} = \sum_t \frac{PV(Cf_{ti})}{P_i} b_{t1}$$

$$\beta_{i2} = \sum_t \frac{PV(Cf_{ti})}{P_i} b_{t2}$$

There are other ways to estimate the sensitivities. For the one-factor model we could derive, using duration, a theoretical value for the sensitivities. There are two parameter duration models that allow a similar derivation of the sensitivities for two-factor models. Finally, other researchers have used duration for the first factor and convexity for the second. Both of these factors can be directly calculated.

Commercially available bond models generally estimate yield on bonds (and the corresponding price) rather than the period-by-period returns. Popular examples of these models are those sold by Barra and Fong. These models generally are multifactor models. They usually have two-term structure terms and additional terms to capture the spread between corporates and governments and option features of the bonds. These models can be used in two ways. One way is to try to select individual bonds that are mispriced in the sense that the model and theoretical price diverge. A second use of the models is to control the sensitivity to the factor. If one believes the spread between long and shorts is going to change, then one could adjust the sensitivity to spread accordingly. Finally, these models can be utilized to estimate risk for portfolio purposes. The discussion in Chapters 7 and 8 of how to use index models for portfolio risk estimation is equally applicable to models for returns on bonds.

SWAPS

In recent years, swaps have become an increasingly important part of bond management. Bond managers can swap bonds, or they can swap interest rate streams. We will discuss each in turn.

Bond Swaps

Bond swaps are divided into several categories based on the purpose of the swap. We will discuss the major categories.

Substitution Swap   The substitution swap is a swap of two bonds that are identical in characteristics, but have different prices. Assume two 10-year government bonds; both have coupons of 8% and one has a lower price than the second. A substitution swap is selling the higher priced bond and buying the lower priced. In Appendix C, we generalize a substitution swap to the case where a portfolio is being swapped for a second portfolio with the same cash flows and bond characteristics. For the existence of a substitution swap there must be a violation of the law of one price. Profitable substitution swaps are likely to be rare when one bond is being swapped for a second bond. They are more likely to exist when they involve complex combinations of large numbers of bonds.

Yield Pick-up Swaps   The yield pick-up swap is swapping a bond with a lower yield to maturity for a bond of like risk and maturity, but a higher yield to maturity. As we discussed in the last chapter, yield to maturity on a portfolio is not a weighted average of the yield to maturity of the bonds that comprise it. Thus, swapping one bond for a higher yield bond can actually reduce the yield on the portfolio. Furthermore, the bond with the higher yield to maturity could be overpriced when price is determined by discounting the cash flows at the spot rates, while the lower yield to maturity bond is fairly priced. Thus, although yield pick-up swaps are frequently discussed, the logic underlying them is tenuous.

Tax Swaps   Individuals in many countries including the United States are subject to tax on realized capital gains and losses. A tax swap involves generating a capital loss either to offset capital gains or to a limited extent ordinary income. Assume an investor has a bond that is selling for less than it was purchased but wishes to hold a security with the same characteristics as that bond. The investor can sell the bond whose value has declined, generating a capital loss, and purchase a bond with identical characteristics.[14] This action is a tax swap.

In the United States the Internal Revenue Service will not allow an individual to claim a capital loss if the purchase and sale involve the same security (wash sale). With bonds, however, it is usually easy to find a second bond that is almost identical to the first in coupon, maturity, and risk. Tax swaps are especially advantageous with municipal bonds. Assume an investor holds municipal bonds and interest rates rise. The investor's bonds fall in value. Since interest is not taxable on municipals (at least at the federal level), a sale of the municipals that declined in price and a purchase of a similar new municipal at par results in a capital loss with no corresponding tax obligation on the purchased bond.

Interest Rate Swaps

One of the major investment tools used in fixed income management is the interest rate swap. Interest rate swaps involve exchanging interest streams without exchanging the securities. The most basic type of swap is the fixed for variable swap. In this type of swap one party agrees to pay the other party a fixed coupon in return for a variable coupon. For example, party A might agree to pay a 6% coupon semiannually to party B over the next five years in return for a variable coupon equal to the six-month Treasury bill rate that exists at the beginning of each six-month period. The two parties have to agree not only on the rate, but also on the principal amount to which the interest rate is applied, called the notational principal. If the notational principal was 10 million, then the flows would be as depicted in Table 21.7.

---

[14]This swap may generate a capital gain in the future. For example, assume the investor bought the bond at $100 and it declined to $80. Selling the bond generates a $20 capital loss. Now assume the investor buys an identical bond at $80. When the bond matures at $100, the investor would need to pay a $20 capital gain. If this is in a subsequent tax year, the present value will be less than $20 and the investor will gain.

Table 21.7   Cash Flows of a Fixed for Floating Swap Assuming a 10 Million Notation Principal

Time Period (in half-years)	Six-Month T-bill Rate (annually)	Paid by B to A	Paid by A to B
1	6%	$300,000	$300,000
2	4%	$200,000	$300,000
3	7%	$350,000	$300,000
4	6%	$300,000	$300,000
5	5%	$250,000	$300,000
6	7%	$350,000	$300,000

Interest rate swaps are arranged by all the major brokerage firms. The parties engaged in the swap may or may not know who is on the other side. Swaps are an alternative to a direct sale. An investor interested in exchanging a long-term security for a sequence of six-month T-bills could potentially sell the long-term security and buy a series of six-month T-bills. Although it does not involve a physical sale, the swap serves the same purpose. Why the swap?

First, swaps are relatively inexpensive.[15] Thus, it may be cheaper to swap interest rate streams rather than sell a long-term bond and purchase a short-term bond. Second, one or more of the parties may not wish to sell the asset. For example, savings and loans hold mostly long-term mortgages on properties in their local community as their assets. One of their major liabilities is short-term savings accounts. To protect against term structure shifts, they would like to have the duration of the assets and liabilities matched. The savings and loan may feel that in order to maintain local goodwill, they need to hold the long-term mortgages. A fixed for floating swap can be used to duration match without physically selling off the assets. A third reason for a swap is comparative advantage. It has been argued that the risk premium that low-quality firms have to pay in issuing fixed debt is higher than they have to pay for variable rate debt. Further, since the interest rate swap doesn't involve the principal, only the interest stream, bankruptcy of one of the parties can only cost the other the opportunity cost of not having a favorable interest rate exchange.[16] Thus, it is argued that high-rated and low-rated corporations could gain by a swap. The swap involves a high-rated corporation, wanting to borrow at a variable interest rate, instead borrowing long at a fixed rate, and then swapping fixed for floating with a low-rated corporation that wants to borrow fixed.

APPENDIX A

DURATION MEASURES

There are at least a dozen different measures of duration. Duration measures the sensitivity of bond prices to a change in the yield curve. In the text we assumed that the yield curve was flat and there was a parallel shift in the yield curve. There are a large number of alternative assumptions that are possible. The yield curve could be upward or downward sloping, and the shift could be very different than parallel. Each of these alternative definitions

---

[15]Estimates the bid-ask spread are about 5 basis points.

[16]The fixed for variable swap is the most common swap. Other types of swaps involve interest rate swaps in different currency (used to manage currency risk) and floating rate swaps where the floating is tied to different instruments.

results in a different measure of duration. In the text we derive one measure of duration. This is the measure most often used. The second most common is derived as follows.

1. Macualay's Second Measure

Assume that the yield curve is not flat but that spot rates vary. Let S_{0t} be the spot rate for a t-year bond. Consider a pure discount bond that pays \$1000 at year t. Its price is

$$P_0 = \frac{1000}{\left(1+S_{0t}\right)^t} = 1000\left(1+iS_{0t}\right)^{-1}$$

Its sensitivity to a change in $1 + S_{0t}$ is

$$dP_0 = 1000(-t)\left(1+S_{0t}\right)^{-t-1}d\left(1+S_{0t}\right)$$

$$= \frac{1000}{\left(1+S_{0t}\right)^t}(-t)\frac{d\left(1+S_{0t}\right)}{1+S_{0t}}$$

Recalling that $P_0 = 1000/(1 + S_{0t})^t$ and dividing through by P_0 yields

$$\frac{dP_0}{P_0} = -t\frac{d\left(1+S_{0t}\right)}{\left(1+S_{0t}\right)}$$

The key assumption of the second measure of duration is that the proportional change in the t-period spot rate is the same as the proportional change in the one-period spot or

$$\frac{d\left(1+S_{0t}\right)}{\left(1+S_{0t}\right)} = \frac{d\left(1+S_{01}\right)}{\left(1+S_{01}\right)}$$

Making this substitution yields

$$\frac{dP_0}{P_0} = -t\frac{d\left(1+S_{01}\right)}{\left(1+S_{01}\right)} \qquad (A.1)$$

This equation holds for any t. A coupon paying bond can be considered a series of pure discount bonds. Let superscripts stand for the time of the flow, and let P_0^t be the current value of the tth-period flow. The price of a bond is the sum of the value of its components. Thus

$$P_0 = P_0^1 + P_0^2 + P_0^3 + \cdots + P_0^T$$

and

$$dP_0 = dP_0^1 + dP_0^2 + dP_0^3 + \cdots + dP_0^T$$

Dividing both sides by P_0 yields

$$\frac{dP_0}{P_0} = \frac{dP_0^1}{P_0} + \frac{dP_0^2}{P_0} + \frac{dP_0^3}{P_0} + \cdots + \frac{dP_0^T}{P_0}$$

or

$$\frac{dP_0}{P_0} = \frac{dP_0^1}{P_0^1}\frac{P_0^1}{P_0} + \frac{dP_0^2}{P_0^2}\frac{P_0^2}{P_0} + \cdots + \frac{dP_0^T}{P_0^T}\frac{P_0^T}{P_0} \qquad (A.2)$$

Substituting in the equations for dP_0^1/P_0^1 through dP_0^T/P_0^T and recognizing that P_0^T is the present value of the payment in t yields

$$\frac{dP_0}{P_0} = \frac{\dfrac{C(1)}{(1+S_{01})}}{P_0}(-1)\frac{d(1+S_{01})}{(1+S_{01})} + \frac{\dfrac{C(2)}{(1+S_{02})^2}}{P_0}(-2)\frac{d(1+S_{01})}{(1+S_{01})}$$

$$+\cdots+ \frac{\dfrac{C(T)}{(1+S_{0T})^T}}{P_0}(-T)\frac{d(1+S_{01})}{(1+S_{01})}$$

$$= -\frac{\displaystyle\sum_{t=1}^{T} t\,\frac{C(t)}{(1+S_{0t})^t}}{P_0}\frac{d(1+S_{01})}{(1+S_{01})}$$

$$= -D_2\,\frac{d(1+S_{01})}{(1+S_{01})}$$

D_2 measures the sensitivity of bond price to a change in the yield curve where the shift in the yield curve is such that the proportional change in all spot rates is the same.

2. Nonproportional Shift in Spot Rates

D_2 resulted from an assumption that the proportional change in all spot rates is identical. Empirical evidence suggests that long rates change less than short rates. Let $K(t)$ be the proportional change in the tth-period rate compared to the one-period rate. Then

$$\frac{d(1+S_{0t})}{1+S_{0t}} = K(t)\frac{d(1+S_{01})}{1+S_{01}}$$

One way of having long rates less volatile than short rates is if we define $K(t)$ as K^{t-1} and have K less than 1. With this definition the sensitivity of pure discount bonds to a change in interest rates is

$$\frac{dP_0}{P_0} = -tK^{t-1}\frac{d(1+S_{01})}{1+S_{01}} \tag{A.3}$$

For a coupon bond the proportional change in price is given by Equation (A.2). Substituting (A.3) into (A.2), recalling $P_0^t = C(t)/(1+S_{0t})^t$ yields

$$\frac{dP_0}{P_0} = \frac{\dfrac{C(1)}{(1+S_{01})^1}}{P_0}(-1)\frac{d(1+S_{01})}{(1+S_{01})} + \frac{\dfrac{C(2)}{(1+S_{02})^2}}{P_0}(-2)K^1\frac{d(1+S_{01})}{(1+S_{01})}$$

$$+\cdots+ \frac{\dfrac{C(T)}{(1+S_{0T})^T}}{P_0}(-T)K^{T-1}\frac{d(1+S_{01})}{(1+S_{01})}$$

or

$$\frac{dP_0}{P_0} = -\left[\sum_{t=1}^{T} \frac{tK^{t-1}\frac{C(t)}{(1+S_{0t})^t}}{P_0}\right]\frac{d(1+S_{01})}{(1+S_{01})}$$

Define the term in the brackets as D_3. This is the third measure of duration. It measures the sensitivity of bond price to a shift in the yield curve, if the change in the tth-period spot rate is K^t times the change in the one-period spot rate.

Measures of duration have been developed for quite a few other possible changes in the yield curve. For instance, Bierwag has developed a measure of duration for additive changes in the yield curve, multiplicative changes in the yield curve, and the combinations of additive and multiplicative changes. Basically, any reasonable way in which the yield curve can change can give rise to another definition of duration. The problem is that each measure assumes that the yield curve can shift in only one pattern (additive, multiplicative, proportional, etc.), and that once we know the change in one spot rate (e.g., S_{01}) we know the change in all spot rates. In reality, shifts in the yield curve may not follow any set pattern. The true test of the definition will be how effectively it measures the actual changes in the prices of bonds due to a change in the yield curve.

3. Numerical Estimation of Duration

An alternative to estimating duration using the analytical techniques discussed earlier is to estimate it numerically. Table 21.8 shows two hypothesized term structures. The unprimed is the current structure. The primed is a 1% increase in each spot rate in the term structure. From Equation (21.1) and footnote 2, we know that modified or adjusted duration is[17]

$$\frac{dP}{P} = -D_A\, di$$

Thus

$$D_A = \frac{\frac{-dP}{P}}{di}$$

We can calculate price assuming both term structures

$$P = \frac{10}{(1.10)} + \frac{10}{(1.11)^2} + \frac{10}{(1.12)^3} + \frac{10}{(1.13)^4} + \frac{110}{(1.14)^5}$$

$$P' = \frac{10}{(1.11)} + \frac{10}{(1.12)^2} + \frac{10}{(1.13)^3} + \frac{10}{(1.14)^4} + \frac{110}{(1.15)^5}$$

$$P = 87.589$$

$$P' = 84.522$$

---

[17]Modified duration is normally used since there often is ambiguity in defining $(1 + i)$ when complicated shifts in the term structure are assumed.

Table 21.8　Assumed Term Structures

t	S_{0t}	S_{0t}
1	10	11
2	11	12
3	12	13
4	13	14
5	14	15

thus

$$D = \frac{\dfrac{-(84.522 - 87.589)}{87.589}}{0.01}$$

$$D = 3.5$$

Multiple duration measures can be calculated. For example, it can be assumed that the short and long spot rates can move independent of one another. Movements of all intermediate rates are then linked to movements in these two key rates. A separate duration measure is calculated for movement in each rate. Immunization would be conducted by immunizing against movements in both rates. A possible advantage in numerical estimation is the ability to capture a greater variety of types of shifts in the yield curve. Another advantage is the ability to calculate duration for instruments with call features, since the price determination can reflect the impact of an option being exercised.

4. Duration Measures with Semiannual or Monthly Cash Flows

All of the duration measures were derived in a completely general manner with the length of the period left undefined. However, the reader must be careful in calculating duration for instruments with nonannual coupon payments. The proportional change in Equation (21.1) should be one plus the interest rate for the interval of the interest payments. Furthermore, since it is conventional to express duration in years the interval should be annualized. For example, consider a bond with 10 years to maturity paying semiannual payments. Then the t in Equation (21.3) would go from 1 to 20 (20 half years) and the resulting duration measure would be cut in half to annualize it. Alternatively, t could be expressed as part of a year or 1/2, 3/2, etc. In either case, the Δi in Equation (21.1) refers to the change in the six-month rate.

APPENDIX B

EXACT MATCHING PROGRAMS

One of the ways to reduce sensitivity to changes in interest rates is exact matching. Exact matching is an attempt to find the minimum cost portfolio such that the cash flows in each period are sufficient to cover all liabilities. Define the following elements:

1.　$L(t)$ as the liabilities in time t.
2.　$C(t, i)$ as the cash flows in period t from a bond of type i.
3.　$P(i)$ as the price of bond i.
4.　$N(i)$ as the number of bond of type i purchased.

The cost of the portfolio of bonds is the number of bonds of each type purchased times the price per bond summed over all bonds or $\sum_i N(i)P(i)$. This quantity is to be minimized. The aggregate cash flows from all bonds in time t is $\sum_i C(t,i)N(i)$. Note that some of these cash flows are coupon payments and some are principal payments. The restriction that cash flows be sufficient to meet liabilities is

$$\sum_i N(i)C(t,i) \geq L(t) \qquad \text{for all } t$$

The final constraint is that the investor cannot issue bonds. This requirement can be stated as $N(i) \geq 0$. Summarizing the exact matching problem is

$$\text{minimize} \sum_i N(i)P(i)$$

subject to

1. $\sum_i N(i)C(t,i) \geq L(t)$ for all t.

2. $N(i) \geq 0$ for all i.

Note that liabilities are being met by coupon payments or maturing bonds. Bonds are not sold to meet cash flows. Thus the only risk is default risk. Adverse interest rate changes do not affect the ability to meet liabilities. Thus matching programs do not necessitate changes in a portfolio as interest rates change. The foregoing problem is a linear programming problem and can be solved with standard algorithms.

The major variation in this problem is to allow cash carryforward. If cash can be carried forward, then there are two possible sources of funds that can be used to meet liabilities: cash flows from the bond investment and cash carryover from the prior period.

Let F_t represent the amount of short-term investment and r be the one-period interest rate. Then in time t the value of the short-term investment is the prior period's investment F_{t-1} plus the interest on the investment or $F_{t-1}(1 + r)$. In each period sources of funds (cash from the bond portfolio and short-term investments) must be equal to uses of funds (liabilities plus cash to be carried forward).

$$\text{Sources of funds} = \text{Uses of funds}$$

$$\begin{bmatrix} \text{From bond} \\ \text{portfolio} \end{bmatrix} + \begin{bmatrix} \text{From prior short-} \\ \text{term investment} \end{bmatrix} = [\text{Liabilities}] + \begin{bmatrix} \text{New one-period} \\ \text{investment} \end{bmatrix}$$

$$\sum_i N(i)C(t,i) + F_{t-1}(1+r) = L(t) + F_t$$

With the addition of cash carryforward the problem becomes

$$\text{minimize} \sum_i N(i)P(i)$$

subject to

1. $\sum_i N(i)C(t,i) + F_{t-1}(1 + r) \geq L(t) + F_t$ for all t.

2. $N(i) \geq 0$ for all i.

3. $F_t \geq 0$ for all t.

4. $F_{t-1} = 0$

Once again liabilities are being met out of interest payments and principal payments so that bonds are not being sold. Thus the cash flows from the bond portfolio do not depend on the future course of interest rates. However, r is a future interest rate. If r is set sufficiently low, there will be very little chance that future interest rates will be lower and very little risk that cash flows will be insufficient to meet liabilities. Allowing cash carryforward cannot result in more cost than not doing so. Thus the formulation allowing cash carryforward (perhaps at zero interest) provides the better solution. Firms that offer this type of product usually find that competitive pressures force r to approximate current expectations about future short-term rates. In this case the bond matching program becomes much riskier and once again its feasibility depends on the actual course of future interest rates.

APPENDIX C

BOND-SWAPPING TECHNIQUES

In the second part of this chapter, we discussed methods of actively managing a bond portfolio. Techniques discussed in these sections allow for bond switches resulting from changes in perceptions of which bonds are over- or underpriced or resulting from changes in risk perceptions. Using the techniques discussed in the second part of this chapter is clearly an appropriate technique for determining bond swaps.

An alternative procedure that makes many fewer assumptions is to attempt to find additional bonds that can be swapped for existing bonds that maintain the future cash flow pattern and yet earn immediate profit from the swap. This is the basic idea underlining a bond swap program. To be specific, define the following elements:

1. $P_B(i)$, the cost of buying bond i.
2. $P_S(i)$, the cash received from selling bond i.
3. $C(i,t)$, the cash flow of bond i in period t.
4. $N_B(i)$, the number of bonds of type i purchased.
5. $N_S(i)$, the number of bonds of type i sold.

With these definitions the cost of the bonds purchased is

$$\sum_i N_B(i)P_B(i)$$

The profit is the difference between the proceeds from the sale and the cost of the purchase or

$$\sum_i N_S(i)P_S(i) - \sum_i N_B(i)P_B(i)$$

The object of a bond swap program is to maximize this difference subject to not reducing cash flows. If the swap does not result in reduced cash flows, the bond portfolio will still meet any liabilities.

To express this constraint we write

$$\sum_i N_B(i)C(i,t) \geq \sum_i N_S(i)C(i,t) \qquad \text{for all } t$$

One swap model is

$$\text{maximize} \sum_i N_S(i)P_S(i) - \sum_i N_B(i)P_B(i)$$

subject to

1. $\sum_i N_B(i)C(i,t) \geq \sum_i N_S(i)C(i,t) \qquad \text{for all } t.$

2. $N_B(i), N_S(i) \geq 0$ for all i.

The ability to carry forward funds from an earlier to a later period can be added to the bond swap problem. This increases the risk since future interest rates are unknown. However, it increases the number of swap opportunities. Adding the ability to carry forward funds can be developed as follows. Let

1. F_t be the short-term investment in period t.

2. r be the one-period interest rate.

The value of the cash carried forward from period $t - 1$ is $F_{t-1}(1 + r)$. The investment in short-term cash in period t is F_t.

If short-term borrowing is not allowed, then F_t must be nonzero. The complete problem is

$$\text{maximize} \sum_i N_S(i)P_S(i) - \sum_i N_B(i)P_B(i)$$

subject to

1. $\sum_i N_B(i)C(i,t) + F_{t-1}(1+r) \geq \sum_i N_S(i)C(i,t) + F_t$ for all $t = 1, ..., T$.

2. $N_B(i), N_S(i) \geq 0$ for all i.

3. $F_t \geq 0$ for all t.

4. $F_{t-1} = 0$.

This is the standard bond swap problem.

APPENDIX D

CONVEXITY

In this appendix we derive Equation (21.4) and show how the mathematical definition of convexity is derived.

The formula for the first three terms in a Taylor series expansion of a function $f(i + h)$ in the region of i as h approaches zero is

$$f(i+h) = f(i) + \frac{f'(i)(h)}{1} + \frac{f''(i)(h)^2}{2 \times 1} + \cdots$$

where the prime denotes derivatives.

Define $P(i)$ as the price of a bond at an interest rate i. Then, writing the price of the bond at a new interest rate $(i + h)$ using the series expansion results in

$$P(i+h) - P(i) + P'(i)h + 1/2\, P''(i)h^2 \tag{D.1}$$

The price of the bond is

$$P(i) = \sum_{t=1}^{T} \frac{C(t)}{(1+i)^t}$$

Then the first derivative with respect to $(1 + i)$ is

$$P'(i) = \sum_{t=1}^{T} \frac{tC(t)}{(1+i)^t} \frac{1}{1+i} \tag{D.2}$$

and the second derivative is

$$P''(i) = \sum_{t=1}^{T} \frac{t(t+1)C(t)}{(1+i)^t} \frac{1}{(1+i)^2}$$

(D.3)

The return due to a change in interest rates is

$$R_i^u = \frac{P(i+h) - P(i)}{P(i)}$$

And using Equations (D.1), (D.2), and (D.3) together with the fact that Δ_i as defined in the text is $h/1 + i$

$$R_i^u = -D_i \Delta_i + C_i (\Delta_i)^2$$

where

$$D_i = \left[\sum_{t=1}^{T} \frac{tC(t)}{(1+i)^t} \right] / P(i)$$

$$C_i = 1/2 \left[\sum_{t=1}^{T} \frac{t(t+1)C(t)}{(1+i)^t} \right] / P(i)$$

alternative convexity measures could be derived by allowing the discount rate to vary over time.

QUESTIONS AND PROBLEMS

1. Consider a bond with semiannual coupon payments of $50, a principal payment of $1000 in 5 years, and a price of $1000. Assume that the yield curve is a flat 10%. What is the duration of the bond?

2. Consider a bond with annual coupon payments of $100, a principal payment of $1000 in 10 years, and a cost of $1000. Assume a flat yield curve with a 10% yield to maturity. What is the duration of the bond? If the yield curve remains unchanged, what is the bond's duration in three years? In five years? In eight years?

3. Given the following bonds

Bond	Duration (years)
A	5
B	10
C	12

construct three different portfolios of the three bonds, each with a duration of 9 years.

4. Assume liabilities of $250, $500, and $550 must be met in periods 1, 2, and 3, respectively. Find a portfolio of the bonds shown below that meets these cash outflows. What is the cost of the portfolio? (*Hint:* The question does not require a least cost portfolio. Thus the linear programming procedure of Appendix B isn't necessary.)

		Cash Flows in Period		
Number	Price	1	2	3
A	950	50	1050	
B	1000	100	100	1100
C	920	1000		

5. Assume that the yield curve for the data of Problem 3 is 10%. Further assume that the three bonds are of equal value and the only bonds existing. Set up a single-index representation of their covariance. What is the covariance between all pairs of bonds?

BIBLIOGRAPHY

1. Attari, Mukarram. "Discontinuous Interest Rate Processes: An Equilibrium Model for Bond Option Prices," *The Journal of Financial and Quantitative Analysis*, **34,** No. 3 (Sept. 1999), pp. 293–322.
2. Babble, D. "Duration and the Term Structure of Interest Rate Volatility," in G. Bierwag, G. Kaufman, and A. Toevs (eds.), *Innovations in Bond Portfolio Management: Duration Analysis and Immunization* (Greenwich, Conn.: JAI Press, 1983).
3. Bicrwag, G.O. "Immunization, Duration and the Term Structure of Interest Rates," *Journal of Financial and Quantitative Analysis*, **12,** No. 4 (Dec. 1977), pp. 725–742.
4. Bierwag, G.O., and Kaufman, George. "Coping with the Risk of Interest Rate Fluctuations: A Note," *Journal of Business*, **50,** No. 3 (July 1977), pp. 364–370.
5. ——. "Immunization Strategies for Funding Multiple Liabilities," *Journal of Financial and Quantitative Analysis*, **XVII,** No. 1 (Mar. 1983), pp. 113–124.
6. ——. "Durations of Non-Default-Free Securities," *Financial Analyst Journal*, **44,** No. 4 (July/Aug. 1988), pp. 39–46.
7. Bierwag, G.O., Kaufman, G.G., and Khang, C. "Duration and Bond Portfolio Analysis: An Overview," *Journal of Financial and Quantitative Analysis*, **13,** No. 4 (Nov. 1978), pp. 671–681.
8. Bierwag, G.O., Kaufman, George, G., and Toevs, Alden. "Single Factor Duration Models in a Discrete General Equilibrium Framework," *The Journal of Finance*, **37,** No. 2 (May 1982), pp. 325–338.
9. ——. *Innovations in Bond Portfolio Management: Duration Analysis and Immunization* (Greenwich, Conn.: JAI Press, 1983).
10. Boardman, Calvin M., and McEnally, Richard W. "Factors Affecting Seasoned Corporate Bond Prices," *Journal of Financial and Quantitative Analysis*, **XVI,** No. 2 (June 1981), pp. 193–206.
11. Boquist, J.A., Racette, G.A., and Schlarbaum, G. "Duration and Risk Assessment for Bonds and Common Stocks," *Journal of Finance*, **30,** No. 5 (1975), pp. 1360–1365.
12. Brennan, M.J., and Schwartz, E. "Savings Bonds, Retractable Bonds and Callable Bonds," *Journal of Financial Economics*, **5** (1977), pp. 67–88.
13. ——. "A Continuous Time Approach to the Pricing of Bonds," *Journal of Banking and Finance*, **3** (1979), pp. 133–155.
14. ——. "Conditional Predictions of Bond Prices and Returns," *Journal of Finance*, **35** (1980), pp. 405–417.
15. ——. "Duration, Bond Pricing, and Portfolio Management," in G. Bierwag, G. Kaufman, and A. Toevs (eds.), *Innovations in Bond Portfolio Management: Duration Analysis and Immunization* (Greenwich, Conn.: JAI Press, 1983).
16. Brown, Stephen, and Dybvig, Philip. "The Empirical Implications of the Cox, Ingersoll Ross Theory of the Term Structure of Interest Rates," *Journal of Finance,* **41,** No. 3 (1986), pp. 617–632.

17. Campbell, John Y. "Who should buy long-term bonds?" *The American Economic Review*, **91,** No. 1 (Mar. 2001), pp. 99–127.

18. Carr, J.L., Halpern, P.J., and McCallum, J.S. "Correcting the Yield Curve: A Re-interpretation of the Duration Problem," *Journal of Finance*, **29,** No. 4 (1974), pp. 1287–1294.

19. Chambers, Donald R., Carleton, Willard T., and McEnally, Richard W. "Immunizing Default-Free Bond Portfolios with a Duration Vector," *The Journal of Financial and Quantitative Analysis*, **23,** No. 1 (Mar. 1988), pp. 89–104.

20. Constantinides, George M., and Ingersoll, Jonathan E., Jr. "Optimal Bond Trading with Personal Taxes," *Journal of Financial Economics,* **13,** No. 3 (Sept. 1984), pp. 299–351.

21. Cornell, Bradford, and Green, Kevin. "The Investment Performance of Low-Grade Bond Funds," *The Journal of Finance*, **46,** No. 1 (Mar. 1991), pp. 29–48.

22. Cox, J.C., Ingersoll, Jr., J.E., and Ross, S.A. "Duration and the Measurement of Basic Risk," *Journal of Business*, **52,** No. 1 (Jan. 1979), pp. 51–61.

23. Dothan, U.L. "On the Term Structure of Interest Rates," *Journal of Financial Economics*, **6** (1978), pp. 59–69.

24. Ehrhardt, Michael C. "A New Linear Programming Approach to Bond Portfolio Management: A Comment," *The Journal of Financial and Quantitative Analysis*, **24,** No. 4 (Dec. 1989), pp. 533–537.

25. Elton, Edwin J., Gruber, Martin J., and Blake, Christopher R. "Fundamental Economic Variables, Expected Returns, and Bond Fund Performance," *The Journal of Finance*, **50,** No. 4 (Sept. 1995), pp. 1229–1256.

26. Elton, Edwin, J., Gruber, Martin, J., and Michaely, Roni. "The Structure of Spot Rates and Immunization," *Journal of Finance,* **XLV,** No. 2 (June 1990), pp. 621–641.

27. Elton, E., Gruber, M., and Naber, P. "Bond Returns, Immunization and the Return Generating Process," in M. Sarnat, and G. Szego, (eds.), *Studies in Banking and Finance, Essays in Memory of Irwin Friend* (New York: North-Holland, 1988).

28. Fisher, L., and Weil, R.L. "Coping with the Risk of Interest Rate Fluctuations: Returns to Bondholders from Naive and Optimal Strategies," *Journal of Business*, **44,** No. 3 (Oct. 1971), pp. 408–431.

29. Fong, Gifford H., and Vasicek, Oldrich A. "The Tradeoff between Return and Risk in Immunized Portfolios," *Financial Analyst Journal*, **34,** No. 5 (Sept./Oct. 1983), pp. 73–78.

30. ⸻. "A Risk Minimizing Strategy for Portfolio Immunization," *Journal of Finance*, **39,** No. 5 (Dec. 1986), pp. 1541–1546.

31. Hessel, Christopher A., and Huffman, Lucy. "The Effect of Taxation on Immunization Rules and Duration Estimation," *The Journal of Finance*, **36,** No. 5 (Dec. 1981), pp. 1127–1142.

32. Ingersoll, J. "Is Immunization Feasible?" in G. Bierwag, G. Kaufman, and A. Toevs (eds.), *Innovations in Bond Portfolio Management: Duration Analysis and Immunization* (Greenwich, Conn.: JAI Press, 1983).

33. Ingersoll, J.E., Jr., Skelton, J., and Weil, R.L. "Duration Forty Years Later," *Journal of Financial and Quantitative Analysis,* **13** (Nov. 1978), pp. 627–650.

34. Liebowitz, Martin L., and Weinberger, Alfred. "Contingent Immunization Part II: Problem Areas, *Financial Analysts Journal*, **39,** No. 1 (Jan./Feb. 1983), pp. 35–50.

35. Livingston, M., and Caks, J. "A 'Duration' Fallacy," *Journal of Finance*, **32** (March 1977), pp. 185–187.

36. Macaulay, F. R. *Some Theoretical Problems Suggested by the Movements of Interest Rates, Bond Yields, and Stock Prices in the United States since 1865* (New York: Columbia University Press, 1938).

37. Marshall, William J., and Yawtiz, Jess B. "Lower Bounds on Portfolio Performance: An Extension of the Immunization Strategy," *Journal of Financial and Quantitative Analysis*, **XVII,** No. 1 (March 1982), pp. 101–114.

38. Niederhoffer, V., and Regan, P. "Earnings Changes, Analysts' Forecasts, and Stock Prices," *Financial Analysts Journal*, **28,** No. 3 (May–June 1972), pp. 65–71.

39. Nelson, J., and Schaefer, S. "The Dynamics of the Term Structure and Alternative Portfolio Immunization Strategies," in G. Bierwag, G. Kaufman, and A. Toevs (eds.), *Innovations in*

Bond Portfolio Management: Duration Analysis and Immunization (Greenwich, Conn.: JAI Press, 1983).

40. Prisman, Eliezer Z. "Immunization as a Maximum Strategy," Journal of Business Finance, **20,** No. 4 (Dec. 1986), pp. 491–509.

41. Redington, F.M. "Review of the Principles of Life-Office Valuations," *Journal of the Institute of Actuaries*, **18** (1952), pp. 286–315.

42. Richard, S.F. "An Arbitrage Model of the Term Structure of Interest Rates," *Journal of Financial Economics*, **6** (1978), pp. 33–57.

43. Richards, Malcolm. "Analysts' Performance and the Accuracy of Corporate Earnings Forecasts," *Journal of Business*, **49,** No. 3 (July 1976), pp. 350–357.

44. Ronn, Ehud I. "A New Linear Programming Approach to Bond Portfolio Management," *The Journal of Financial and Quantitative Analysis*, **22,** No. 4 (Dec. 1987), pp. 439–466.

45. Schaefer, Stephen M., and Schwartz, Eduardo S. "A Two-Factor Model of the Term Structure: An Approximate Analytical Solution," *Journal of Financial and Quantitative Analysis*, **19,** No. 4 (Dec. 1984), pp. 413–421.

46. Vasicek, P. "An Equilibrium Characterization of the Term Structure," *Journal of Financial Economics* (Nov. 1977), pp. 177–188.

22

Option Pricing Theory

The markets for options are among the fastest growing markets for financial assets in the United States. While option trading is not new, it experienced a gigantic growth with the creation of the Chicago Board of Options Exchange in 1973. The listing of options meant more orderly and thicker markets for these securities.

The growth in option trading has been accompanied by a tremendous interest among academics and practitioners in the valuing of option contracts. In this chapter we discuss alternative types of options, examine the effect of certain characteristics on the value of options, and present explicit models for valuing options.

TYPES OF OPTIONS

An option is a contract entitling the holder to buy or sell a designated security at or within a certain period of time at a particular price. There are a large number of types of option contracts, but they all have one element in common: the value of an option is directly dependent on the value of some underlying security. Options represent a claim against the underlying security and thus are often called contingent claim contracts. The two least complex options are called puts and calls. These are the most widely traded options. In addition, most other options either can be valued as combinations of puts and calls or can be valued by the methodology developed to value puts and calls. Consequently, we will begin this section with a discussion of puts and calls and then we will discuss other types of options and combinations of basic options.

Calls

The most common type of an option is a call. A call gives the owner the right to buy a fixed number of shares of a stock at a fixed price, either before or at some fixed date. It is common to refer to calls which can only be exercised at a particular point in time as American calls and calls, which can be exercised at any time up to, and including the expiration date as European calls. Take as example a November 20 American call on Mobil at $70. This call gives the owner the right to buy a certain number of shares of Mobil at $70 a share anytime on or before November 20. Calls are normally traded in units of 100 shares. Thus, one call would be a right to buy 100 shares of Mobil. Each characteristic of the call has a name. For example, the $70 price is called the exercise price. The final date at which the call can be exercised is the expiration date.[1]

One of the distinguishing characteristics of a call is that if it is exercised, the exchange of stocks is between two investors. One investor issues the call (termed the call writer) and the other investor purchases the call. The call is a side bet between two investors on the future course of the security. Figure 22.1a shows the profit per share of stock for the holder of a call at the expiration date. The figure represents the pattern for a call originally purchased for $5 with an exercise price of $50. For a stock price below $50, it would not pay to exercise the call since shares could be purchased in the open market for less than the exercise price. For share prices above $50, it would pay to exercise the call and gain by the difference between the share price and exercise price. For example, if the share price is $54, then the holder of a call benefits from the ability to purchase the stock at $50 rather than $54. For share prices up to $55, the owner of the call loses money since the payoff from the stock purchase is less than the cost of the call. For a stock price above $55, there is a profit.

The position of the call writer is depicted in Figure 22.1b. The pattern of the profit is exactly opposite that of the call purchaser. For a stock price below $50 the call writer makes a profit equal to the $5 per share received from the issuance of the call; from $50 to $55 part of the $5 is lost by having to furnish the stock at a price below the market price; above $55, the call writer loses more than was received by selling the call.

Up to now we have referred to shares being traded between individuals as a result of exercise at the expiration of a call. We could have also discussed the exercise of a call before the expiration date. However, we have not done this so far since calls (even those that have an exercise price below the price of the stock) are rarely exercised before the

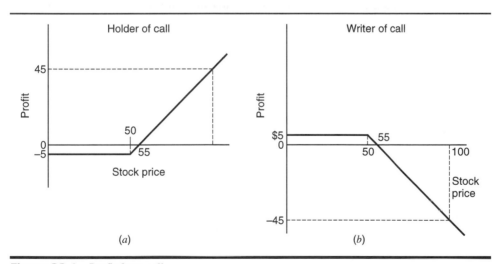

Figure 22.1   Profit from call.

---

[1]In the example we use an arbitrary date for expiration. For options not listed on the exchanges, any date is possible. However, options trading on the Chicago Board of Options have standardized expiration dates. Any single security will normally have options outstanding with three different expiration dates. These dates are three months apart (e.g., April, July, and October). These options expire at 10:59 A.M. Central Time on the Saturday after the third Friday of the month.

expiration date.[2] For example, assume the share price is $60 and the exercise price is $50. Clearly, a profit can be made by exercising the option. There is a third alternative. Instead of exercising the option, sell it.

The sale may be to someone who does not currently maintain a position in the option or it may be to an investor who wrote an option and also wishes to liquidate his or her position.[3] The listing of options on exchanges facilitates these sales. With options listed on the exchange, the mechanics of the purchase or writing of an option becomes identical to the mechanics of the purchase or sale of a stock except for differences in margin requirements.

There are actions that a firm might take that will affect the value of its shares. For example, a two-for-one stock split would be expected to cut the price of a share in half. Stock dividends and cash dividends are two other examples. The value of an option is affected by these actions of the firm. Clearly, if there were no adjustment in the exercise price when a stock splits, the value of an option would be substantially reduced. Most options are protected against stock dividends and stock splits by automatic adjustments in the exercise price and the number of shares that can be purchased with one option. Cash dividends are not as frequently protected against. For example, there are no adjustments for cash dividends for options traded on the exchanges. The price of a stock on average decreases by slightly less than the amount of the dividend when a stock goes ex-dividend. Thus, all other things being equal, the price of an option should be lower on a stock that will go ex-dividend before the expiration date.

The next most common type of option is a put, which we will discuss in the next section.

Puts

A put is an option to sell stock at a given price on or before a particular expiration date. Consider, for example, a $50 General Motors put of December 18. The person who owned such a put would have the right to sell the General Motors stock to the person who issued the put at $50 a share on or before December 18. Puts, like calls, are traded in units of 100 shares. Thus, one put involves the right to sell 100 shares. If the exercise can take place only at the expiration date, it is called a European put. If the exercise can take place at any time on or before the expiration date, it is called an American put. A put, like a call, involves a transaction between two investors. Thus, the writing of puts has no effect on the value of the firm.

Figure 22.2 shows the profit at the expiration date for a put with an exercise price of $50 that originally cost $5. Figure 22.2a shows the profit to the owner of the put. Figure 22.2b shows the profit to the writer of a put. Consider Figure 22.2a. For prices above $50, the owner of the put would prefer to sell shares in the regular market rather than to the writer of the put, since the price received is greater. Thus, for prices above $50, the exercise value is zero. For prices above $45 but below $50, the owner of the put would prefer to exercise her option instead of selling her stock on the open market. However, the owner of the put loses money, since she paid more for the put than she gains from the sale at a higher price.

---

[2]In a later section of this chapter we will discuss the well-established proof that (except for possible exceptions associated with dividend payments) it never pays to exercise an American call prior to the expiration date. It is always better to sell it rather than exercise it.

[3]When an individual sells an option, the person purchasing it need not be the original writer. Rather, the individual purchasing the option is whoever happens to wish to buy the option on the day of sale. This is identical to what happens with any other security. When you buy a share of stock and subsequently sell it, the individual from whom you buy or sell is unknown and normally different.

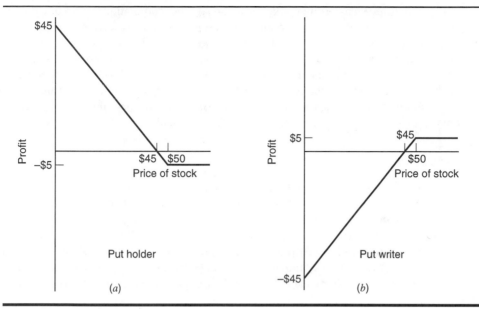

Figure 22.2   Profit from put.

Below $45, the owner of the put makes money, since the amount she gains from the sale at a more attractive price more than compensates for the cost of the put. The payoff pattern for the writer of the put is the exact opposite of the payoff pattern for the owner. For prices above $45, he makes money, and for prices below $45, he loses.

Puts, like calls, are rarely exercised before expiration. Assume the share price in our example declined to $40. At $40, it clearly pays to exercise rather than to let the option expire. Instead of exercising the option, the owner could sell the right. While an American put is more likely to be exercised before expiration than an American call, we will show that it generally pays to sell rather than exercise a put, for the sale price will almost always be higher than the exercise value. The exception can occur when the put is deep in the money.

Warrants

A warrant is almost identical to a call. Like a call, it involves the right to purchase stock at an exercise price at or before an expiration date. A warrant differs from a call in one way: A warrant is issued by the corporation rather than another investor. This seemingly small difference is very important. There are two instances when this difference has an effect on the value of the firm that issues the warrant. First, when the warrants are issued, the company receives the money for the warrant. Second, when the warrants are exercised, the following occurs:

1. The company receives the exercise price.
2. The number of shares of the firm that are outstanding goes up by the number of shares that are exercised.
3. The number of warrants still outstanding goes down.

Calls and puts are side bets by market investors and the corporation has no direct interest in transactions involving these options, either when they are created or exercised. Warrants, on the other hand, are used by the corporation to raise capital. The corporation and its shareholders have a definite interest in their issuance and exercise, since these transactions affect both the amount of cash the firm has raised and the ownership interest of its shareholders. Because the issuance and exercise of warrants affect the value of the security on which the warrant represents a contingent claim, the valuation of warrants becomes a more complex problem than the valuation of calls.

Combinations

Part of the fun of reading the options literature is the colorful terminology. One of the areas where it is especially colorful is the naming of combinations of options. An infinite number of combinations of puts and calls can be considered. A combination of a put and call with the same exercise price and expiration date is called a straddle. A similar combination of two puts and a call is a strip. If the combination is two calls and a put, it is called a strap. The payoff pattern at expiration is easy to determine using the techniques discussed earlier. Similarly, the valuation can be accomplished using the techniques discussed later in this chapter.

Consider a straddle. Figure 22.3a shows the profit at expiration from the point of view of the purchaser of the option. Figure 22.3b is the profit from the point of view of the writer. As we can see from examining these diagrams, a straddle should be purchased by someone who believes the price of the shares will move substantially either up or down, without being sure of the direction, and who also believes that other investors have underestimated the magnitude of future price changes. For example, a straddle could be purchased by someone who knew that major information was about to be announced that would seriously affect the company's fortune, was unsure whether the information would be good news or bad news, and believed that other investors were unaware of the existence of this information. In contrast, the writer of a straddle is an investor who believes that the share price will trade at close to the exercise price, while others believe differently.

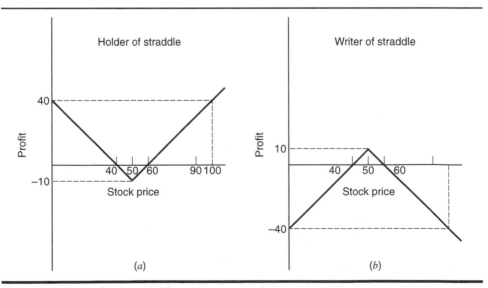

Figure 22.3   Profit from straddle.

One of the interesting ways to trade options is in combination with the stock on which they represent a claim. The investor who combines stocks with contingent claims on the stocks has two assets with very strong correlations. Consider the writer of a call who also owns the shares.[4] Figure 22.4 shows the payoff pattern at expiration. The exercise price is assumed to be $50, the cost of the stock to the holder is also assumed to be $50, and the call is assumed to cost $5. Three separate lines are shown: one for the stock, one for the call, and one for the combination. As Figure 22.4 shows, an investor who writes a call and owns the stock rather than simply owning the stock increases the return at low stock prices at the expense of returns at the higher share prices.

As a final example, consider the ownership of a put plus the ownership of stock. Once again, assume an exercise price of $50, a stock cost of $50, and a put cost of $5. Figure 22.5 shows the payoff pattern. This combination reduces the return at higher stock prices in exchange for guaranteeing that if the stock declines in price, the portfolio will not decline below a lower limit.

Another type of combination is an option that can be purchased only in combination with another security. A convertible bond is an example of this combination. A convertible bond has the same characteristics as a normal bond and in addition can be converted into the shares of a company. Thus, the convertible bond can be considered a bond plus a call. However, the call has a special feature. Conversion of the bond into shares of stock involves giving up the bond, plus sometimes cash for the stock. Since the value of the bond changes over time, the exercise price changes over time.

We have discussed a number of combinations of options and options plus security positions in this section. There are many others that are possible. We leave it to our readers to determine the payoff pattern for those they find interesting.

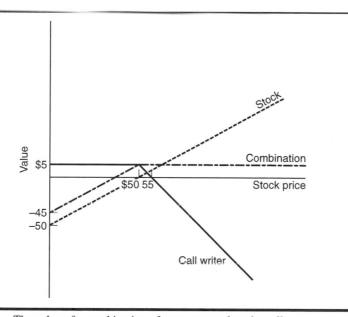

Figure 22.4   The value of a combination of common stock and a call.

---

[4]The writing of a call while owning the stock is called *writing a covered call*.

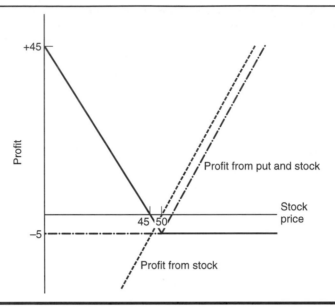

Figure 22.5   Profit from put and stock.

SOME BASIC CHARACTERISTICS OF OPTION VALUES[5]

In a short time we will examine formal option valuation models. However, before we do so we can infer the manner in which certain characteristics of options should affect their value in a rational market. Not only are these relationships interesting in themselves, they will also prove useful as a check on valuation models developed in the later sections. Any valuation model should be consistent with these basic relationships. It is interesting to note that some of the earlier option valuation models that were later proved incorrect were not consistent with these basic relationships.

Relative Prices of Calls with Alternative Characteristics

Recall that the European call gives the holder the right to purchase stock at the exercise price on a particular date (the expiration date). The American call differs from the European call in that it can be exercised at any time up to the expiration date. Since the American call is a European call with the added opportunity to exercise before the expiration date, it cannot be worth less than the European call. Thus, the first relationship established is that a European call with the same expiration date and exercise price as an American call cannot sell for more than the American call.

Consider two American calls with the same exercise prices and assume both calls are on the same stock. The one with the longer life offers the investor all the exercise opportunities of the one with the shorter life, plus some additional opportunities. Hence, it can't be worth less. It might bother the reader that we don't simply say that the longer lived call is more valuable. In general, this is true, but in some extreme cases (e.g., when both calls are worthless) this is not true. Hence the more cautious statement.

---

[5]The results in this section were developed by Merton [89].

The next relationship concerns the exercise price. Consider two calls with the same expiration date written on the same stock. The one with the higher exercise price cannot be more valuable than the one with the lower exercise price. This is obvious, since the holder of the latter can be in the same position as the holder of the former, upon exercise, except that she will have cash left over.

While these relationships seem quite simple, as discussed earlier, not all valuation models that have been developed were consistent with these principles, hence they are worth keeping in mind.

Minimum Value of a European Call

In this section we will show that the value of a European call on a non-dividend-paying stock is at least the greater of zero and the difference between the stock price and the present value of the exercise price. To see this, consider two different portfolios. Portfolio A involves the purchase of a call and a bond that matures at the expiration date of the call and which at that date will have a value equal to the exercise price. If R is the interest rate between the time the call is valued and the expiration date, and if E is the exercise price, then bonds in the amount of $E/(1 + R)$ should be purchased. An alternative to portfolio A is the purchase of stock directly. Call this portfolio B. The key characteristics to these investments are shown in Table 22.1. S_1 is the stock price at expiration, S_0 is the current stock price, E is the exercise price, and C is the current price of the call. The payoffs at the expiration date are shown in the last two columns of the table.

If $S_1 > E$, then the payoffs from both portfolios are the same. However, if $S_1 \le E$, the payoff from portfolio A is larger. Thus, portfolio A is at least as desirable as portfolio B, and if $S_1 \le E$ at expiration is possible, A is more desirable. Given that portfolio A is at least as desirable as B, it can't cost less than B; otherwise no one would purchase the stock (portfolio B). Therefore,

$$C + \frac{E}{1 + R} \ge S_0$$

or

$$C \ge S_0 - \frac{E}{1 + R}$$

The European call cannot sell for less than the stock price less the present value of the exercise price. Since the call cannot sell for a price below zero, we have completed the proof.

Table 22.1 Payoffs from Alternative Holdings

Action	Investment	Value at Expiration Date	
		If $S_1 > E$	If $S_1 \le E$
Portfolio A			
Buy call	$-C$	$S_1 - E$	0
Buy bonds	$\dfrac{-E}{1 + R}$	E	E
Total	$-C - \dfrac{E}{1 + R}$	S_1	E
Portfolio B			
Buy stock	$-S_0$	S_1	S_1

Early Exercise of an American Call

Probably the most surprising conclusion of modern option pricing theory is that it never pays to exercise an American call before the expiration date on a stock that doesn't pay dividends or whose exercise price is adjusted for dividend payments. Later we will present a simple proof. But before we do, it is worthwhile to discuss why this holds. The reason is simple but subtle. The American call is worth more alive than dead. It is worth more keeping the American call alive by not exercising it than killing it through exercise. Thus, an investor no longer wishing to hold the call is better off selling it than exercising it. Consider an example. Assume a stock is selling for $60 and an investor holds an American call with an exercise price of $50. Further, assume this investor believes that the stock price will decline between now and the expiration date. Clearly, the investor would prefer to exercise the call now rather than hold it and exercise it at a later date. There is another option: sell the call to another investor.

If the call has a market price higher than the $10 the investor makes on exercise ($60 stock price − $50 exercise price), selling the call is preferable. Why should the price of the call be more than $10? The American call has two sources of value: the value of an immediate call ($10) plus the value of the chance to call from now to the expiration date. As long as this latter opportunity has value, the American call should sell for more than $10. You might well ask why someone would wish to buy the call when the investor believes the stock price will decline. The answer is that this cannot be the general market belief or the stock price would have already declined. In other words, the aggregate market belief must be that the correct price is $60 and that at $60, the total return from the stock is competitive with securities of similar risk. Thus, the market must believe the return on the stock will be positive.

Now for the proof. Earlier, we argued that an American call cannot be worth less than a European call. We also showed that the European call was worth more than the maximum of zero and the difference between the stock price and the present value of the exercise price $[S_0 − E/(1 + R)]$. Thus, the value of the American call must be greater than the maximum of zero and $S_0 − E/(1 + R)$. However, if the call is exercised, its value is $S_0 − E$. Since $S_0 − E/(1 + R) > S_0 − E$, the call sells for more than its value if exercised.

The foregoing discussion assumed that the stock did not pay a dividend before the expiration date, or that the call was protected against dividends by having the exercise price adjusted by the amount of the dividend. If the stock is dividend paying or the call is not protected, early exercise is possible. Consider the example discussed earlier with a $60 stock price and a $50 exercise price. If the stock was about to pay a large dividend, then investors could rationally believe that the share price should be lower than $60 between the ex-dividend date and the expiration date and thus that the current difference is the best that can be obtained.[6]

Put Call Parity

A put and the underlying stock can be combined in such a way that the combination has the same payoff pattern as a call. Similarly, a call and the underlying equity can be combined so that they have the same payoff pattern as a put. This allows the put or call to be priced in terms of the other security.

---

[6]Stock prices are expected to drop by slightly less than the amount of the dividend when a stock goes ex-dividend.

This relationship is easiest to derive for European options. Furthermore, it is convenient to assume that the common equity will not pay a dividend in the period before the option expires. Define

S_0 as the current stock price

S_1 as the stock price at the expiration date

E as the exercise price

C as the call price

P as the put price

R_B as the borrowing rate

R_L as the lending rate

Now consider a combination of a share of stock, a put, and taking a loan for an amount $E/(1 + R_B)$. If $E/(1 + R_B)$ is borrowed and if the interest rate between the purchase of the combination and the expiration date is R_B, then $[E/(1 + R_B)] (1 + R_B) = E$ will have to be paid back. Thus, if $E/(1 + R_B)$ is borrowed, an amount equal to the exercise price will have to be paid back at the expiration date. The payoff of this combination at the expiration date is shown in Table 22.2. The payoff pattern is, of course, exactly the same pattern as for a call.

The investor has two possible investments: the call or the portfolio being discussed. Each investment has the same value at the expiration date. If they sell at different prices currently, then the investor can purchase the least expensive investment and issue the more expensive investment. Since they have the same payoff pattern at the expiration date, the investor can use the proceeds of the one investment to meet the obligations of the other. If they have different costs, a guaranteed profit can be made. Assuming the portfolio is less expensive than the call, then the investor would write the call and purchase the portfolio. If the call is more expensive than the portfolio, this combination then yields a guaranteed profit. The guaranteed profit is immediate and has zero risk. Such a possibility cannot last long in any efficiently functioning market. Thus, the call can't be more expensive than the portfolio, and writing the call plus purchasing the portfolio can't be profitable. Writing a call involves a cash inflow of C and purchasing portfolio A involves flows of $-S_0 - P + E/(1 + R_B)$. This implies

$$C - S_0 - P + \frac{E}{1 + R_B} \leq 0$$

or

$$S_0 + P - \frac{E}{1 + R_B} \geq C$$

Table 22.2   Payoffs of Portfolios Involving Puts

	Value at Expiration Date	
Security	If $S_1 > E$	If $S_1 \leq E$
Portfolio A		
Buy stock	S_1	S_1
Buy put	0	$E - S_1$
Borrow	$-E$	$-E$
Total	$S_1 - E$	0
Purchase of call		
Buy call	$S_1 - E$	0

Consider what happens if the call is less expensive than the portfolio. In this case, the investor would wish to issue the portfolio and buy the call. The flows would be $-C$ for the call and $S_0 + P - E/(1 + R_L)$ for portfolio A.

These flows closely resemble those discussed earlier, but R_L has replaced R_B. Since we assume the investor is short selling the portfolio rather than purchasing it, the investor is lending rather than borrowing and R_L is assumed to be the lending rate.

If the call is less expensive than the portfolio, then this combination yields a guaranteed profit. A guaranteed profit with no risk can't last long in the market, so buying the call and issuing the portfolio cannot be a profitable combination. This implies that

$$S_0 + P - \frac{E}{1 + R_L} - C \leq 0$$

or

$$C \geq S_0 + P - E/(1 + R_L)$$

Putting the equations together yields

$$S_0 + P - \frac{E}{1 + R_B} \geq C \geq S_0 + P - \frac{E}{1 + R_L}$$

If $R_L = R_B$, the preceding inequalities become equalities and we have the put call parity relationship.

Some comment on the two different arbitrage combinations is in order. The first combination was appropriate if the call was more expensive than the portfolio. This strategy involved buying stock and a put, borrowing, and writing a call. All of these are feasible, and the combination is a full description of the necessary actions.[7] The other combination was appropriate when the call was less expensive than the portfolio. This involved selling the stock short, writing a put, lending, and buying a call. The analysis assumed that the proceeds of the short sale were immediately available. This is unrealistic in general, as discussed earlier. However, it would represent a realistic situation for an investor who currently owned the shares and who engages in a transaction identical to a short sale by selling his or her existing shares. Since there are likely to be many of these investors, the put call parity theorem should hold reasonably well.

The previous analysis examined the payoff pattern at the expiration date of the option. This is, of course, the only relevant date to examine for European options. With American options, other dates are potentially relevant. One of the components of the portfolio is a put. It can be shown that it may pay to exercise a put before expiration, and the value of the American put may be higher than shown in the prior tables.[8] The issuance of an American put involves the risk of premature exercise and the arbitrage discussed earlier need no longer hold. Another problem with applying the prior analysis is the possibility of the payment of dividends. The payment of dividends would, of course, affect the payoffs depicted earlier. If the dividends are already announced, then the stock price can be adjusted by reducing it by the present value of the dividends. With this adjustment, dividends don't affect the prior analysis except insofar as they affect the probability of exercising a put. If dividends are not announced, then adjusting by the expected dividends is

---

[7]The only margin required is the margin on the call. The ownership of the stock is sufficient to meet this requirement.

[8]See Merton [89].

reasonably satisfactory. All these issues mean that the put call parity relationship may not hold perfectly for American options. Nevertheless, it should be a close approximation to market relationships. This is exactly what the empirical results (see Klemkosky and Resnick [73] and Gould and Galai [57]) have shown.[9]

VALUATION MODELS

In this section we will present and discuss two widely used option valuation models. The models we will present are for the European call. From the last section the reader will recall that it never pays to exercise an American call before its expiration date if it is either dividend protected or the stock will not pay dividends before the expiration date. An American call that meets these conditions will not be exercised before it expires and thus it can be valued as a European call. In the previous section we derived the relationship between the value of puts and calls. Thus, the valuation formula for a call can also be used to value puts.

The differences in modern valuation formulas stem from the alternative assumptions made about how share price changes over time. In this section we will present two models. One assumes that the percentage change in share price follows a binomial distribution; the other assumes it follows a log normal distribution.

Binomial Option Pricing Formula

The simplest of the option pricing formulas is the binomial option pricing formula.[10] Since the implications of the formula are similar to those of more complicated formulas and since the formula is easy to derive and understand, we will present a detailed derivation in this section.

Assume that a call is being valued one period before expiration. Further assume that the stock is currently selling at $50 and will either increase to $75 or decrease to $25. Further assume that the borrowing and lending rate is 25%. Under these conditions, what is the current value of a call with an exercise price of $50?

To answer this question, consider the portfolio shown in Table 22.3.

The way the portfolio is constructed, the investor receives nothing at period one whether the stock sells at $25 or $75. This suggests that the investment should cost nothing or that $2C - 50 + 20 = 0$ or that $C = \$15$. To confirm this, consider two other values of C: $C = \$10$ or $C = \$20$. If $C = \$10$, then the call is underpriced. This suggests buying the call,

Table 22.3   Cash Flows on a Zero Payoff Portfolio

		Flows at 1	
	Flows at 0	$S_1 = 25$	$S_1 = 75$
Write 2 calls	$+2C$	0	-50
Buy 1 share of stock	-50	$+25$	$+75$
Borrow $20	$+20$	$\underline{-25}$	$\underline{-25}$
		0	0

---

[9]The arbitrage involving the short sale of stock is sometimes profitable empirically. This part of the put call relationship has less empirical support.

[10]The earliest derivation of this formula is in Stone [123], Sharpe [114], Cox and Ross [36], and Rendleman and Bartter [101] have independently derived the formula.

Table 22.4   Cash Flows on a Zero Payoff Portfolio

	Flows at 0	Flows at 1	
		$S_1 = 25$	$S_1 = 75$
Purchase 2 calls	-20	0	$+50$
Short 1 share of stock	$+50$	-25	-75
Lend $20	-20	$+25$	$+25$
	$+10$	0	0

shorting the stock, and lending will lead to an instantaneous profit. Let us examine this combination in Table 22.4.

No matter which share price occurs at period 1, there are no net flows. The only flow occurs at zero and is a plus $10. This is a guaranteed return with no risk and as investors purchase the combination of securities shown before, prices will adjust until the profit disappears.

Now consider the case $C = \$20$. At this price, the call is overpriced and the investor issues the call, borrows, and buys stock. The flows are shown in Table 22.5.

Once again, there are no net flows at period 1, so that if this situation existed, the investor would have a guaranteed return with no risk. Such opportunities should disappear quickly if they exist, and the three securities should be so priced that riskless profits cannot occur. The call must sell at $15. Let's generalize this example.

The portfolio was constructed so that payoffs from the call plus the stock were the same, no matter what the value of the stock at time period 1. Then, by lending or borrowing, the payoff of the portfolio of calls, stock, and riskless bonds can be made to have zero return at time 1. In the example given a combination of two calls and one share of stock yielded 25—no matter what happened at period 1—and served the purpose. The number of shares of stock per call that makes the payoff from the combination independent of share price is called the hedge ratio. Let

S_0 = the stock price at period zero

E = the exercise price of the option

u = one plus the percentage change in stock price from time 0 to time 1, if the stock price increases

d = one plus the percentage change in stock price from time 0 to time 1 if the stock price decreases

C = the call price

α = the number of shares of stock purchased per share of the call

C_u = the value of the call if the stock increases in value (the maximum of $uS_0 - E$ or 0)

C_d = the value of the call if the stock decreases in value (the maximum of $dS_0 - E$ or 0)

Table 22.5   Cash Flows on a Zero Payoff Portfolio

	Flows at 0	Flows at 1	
		$S_1 = 25$	$S_1 = 75$
Write 2 calls	$+40$	0	-50
Buy 1 share of stock	-50	$+25$	75
Borrow $20	$+20$	-25	-25
	$+10$	0	0

Table 22.6   Cash Flows from a Portfolio of Calls and Stock

		Flows at 1	
Action	Flows at 0	$S_1 = uS_0$	$S_1 = dS_0$
Write call	C	$-C_u$	$-C_d$
Buy α shares of stock	$-\alpha S_0$	$\alpha u S_0$	$\alpha\, dS_0$

Consider Table 22.6. For this to be a hedged portfolio the flows at period 1 must be independent of the value of the stock. Thus

$$-C_u + \alpha u S_0 = -C_d + \alpha\, dS_0$$

or

$$\alpha = \frac{C_u - C_d}{S_0(u - d)}$$

In the previous example, $C_d = 0$, $C_u = 25$, $S_0 = 50$, $u = 1.5$, and $d = .5$. Thus,

$$\alpha = \frac{25 - 0}{50(1.5 - 0.5)} = \frac{25}{50} = \frac{1}{2}$$

Thus, to have the call plus the stock have the same payoffs, no matter what value the stock has at period 1, we must purchase one-half as many shares of stock as we write calls. Two calls and one share of stock, the hedged position used in the previous example, is consistent with this ratio. Utilizing a hedge ratio of α means that the flows at time 1 are the same or $-C_u + \alpha u S_0 = -C_d + \alpha\, dS_0$. To make the portfolio flows at one equal zero, we borrow an amount such that we owe $(C_d - \alpha\, dS_0)$ at time 1 (or, equivalently, $C_u - \alpha u S_0$). If r is one plus the interest rate, we borrow $(C_d - \alpha\, dS_0)/r$. This results in the flows shown in Table 22.7.

As discussed earlier, if the flows at period 1 on the portfolio are zero, the investment also must be zero. Thus,

$$C - \alpha S_0 - \frac{C_d - \alpha\, dS_0}{r} = 0 \qquad \text{or} \qquad C = \frac{\alpha r S_0 + C_d - \alpha\, dS_0}{r} \tag{22.1}$$

Substituting for α yields

$$C = \frac{\left(\dfrac{(C_u - C_d)}{S_0(u - d)}\right) r S_0 + C_d - \left(\dfrac{C_u - C_d}{S_0(u - d)}\right) dS_0}{r}$$

or

$$C = \frac{\dfrac{(C_u - C_d)r + C_d(u - d) - d(C_u - C_d)}{u - d}}{r}$$

or

$$C = \frac{C_u \dfrac{(r - d)}{(u - d)} + C_d \dfrac{(u - r)}{(u - d)}}{r}$$

Table 22.7   Cash Flows on a Zero Payoff Portfolio of Stock and Calls

| | | Flows at 1 | |
Action	Flows at 0	Price $= uS$	Price $= dS$
Write call	C	$-C_u$	$-C_d$
Buy α stock	$-\alpha S_0$	$\alpha u S_0$	$\alpha\, dS_0$
Borrow	$\dfrac{-C_d + \alpha\, dS_0}{r}$	$C_d - \alpha\, dS_0 = C_u - \alpha\, u S_0$	$C_d - \alpha\, dS_0$
Total	$C\,\alpha S_0 - \dfrac{C_d - \alpha\, dS_0}{r}$	0	0

This is the formula for the value of the call with one period remaining until it expires. It can be further simplified by defining $P = (r - d)/(u - d)$. With this definition

$$(1-P)=1-\frac{r-d}{u-d}=\frac{(u-d)-(r-d)}{u-d}=\frac{u-r}{u-d}$$

Making these substitutions into the previous formula, we have

$$C = \frac{C_u P + C_d (1 - P)}{r}$$

where

$$P = \frac{r - d}{u - d}$$

Before proceeding, one comment is in order. Notice that in this derivation we were never concerned with the probability of an up or down movement. We have never even discussed what it might be. P and $1 - P$ are not probabilities; rather, they are numbers that depend on the magnitude of the up and down movements and the riskless rate of interest. What does the value of the call depend on? Examining the formula shows that it depends on C_u, C_d, r, u, and d. However, C_u and C_d depend on the exercise price, the size of u and d, and the current stock price S_0. For example, if an up movement in the stock involves an exercise, then $C_u = uS_0 - E$. Thus, in a two-period example the call price ultimately depends on

u, the size of the up movement

d, the size of the down movement

E, the exercise price

r, one plus the riskless rate of interest

S_0, the current stock price

The type of factors that affect the call price carry over to the more complicated model discussed later.

There is a second way this formula can be derived that yields useful insight into the valuation of options. If we use the value of α derived earlier as the ratio of stocks to calls, then no matter whether the stock goes up or down, we get the same return. An investment that has the same outcome no matter what happens is riskless and should yield the riskless rate of interest. Thus, if we buy the stocks while writing sufficient calls to maintain the hedged position given by α, the return on the investment must be r.

$$(\text{investment}) \; r = \text{outcome}^{11}$$

$$(\alpha S_0 - C)r = \alpha \; dS_0 - C_d$$

A glance at Equation (22.1) shows that it is identical to the preceding expression. To move from Equation (22.1) to the option pricing formula involved substituting for α and rearranging. Thus, both procedures lead to the same result. The idea of valuing options by forming a riskless hedge carries over to models of more complicated stock movements that will be examined in a later section of this chapter.

The formula for pricing a call when there is more than one period to the expiration is a simple extension of the one-period formula just derived. Figure 22.6 shows what can happen to the share price when there are two periods to go to expiration.

The formula just derived allows us to determine the value of the call with one period to expiration (e.g., at period 1). However, knowing the value at time 1 allows the calculation of the value at time 0 by acting as if there is one period to go. In this iterative manner the binomial valuation can be derived. In Appendix A at the end of the chapter we go through a detailed derivation and show that the value of the call with n periods to go is

$$C = S_0 B[a, n, P'] - Er^{-n} B[a, n, P]$$

where

$$P = \frac{r-d}{u-d} \quad P' = \frac{u}{r} P$$

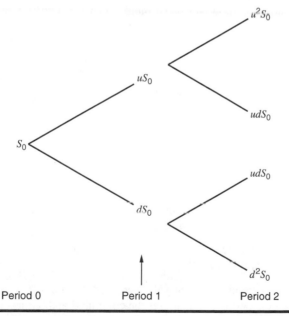

Figure 22.6   The movement of stock prices through time.

---

[11]The outcome could alternatively have been written as $\alpha u S_0 - C_u$.

and

S_0 is the current stock price

E is the exercise price

n is the number of periods to expiration

r is one plus the riskless rate of interest

a is the lowest number of upward moves in price at which the call takes on a positive value at expiration

$B[a,n,P']$ is the probability of a number of up moves in share price equal to or greater than a occurring out of n movements where the probability of an up move is P' (The probability is obtained from the binomial formula or can be looked up in a table of the binomial formula.)

u and d remain as defined earlier

Some additional comment on $B[a,n,P']$ or $B[a,n,P]$ is warranted. First, a is determined by examining the current price, the exercise price, and the expiration date. Assume, for example, that the current stock price was \$50, the exercise price was \$60, $u = 1.50$, $d = 0.80$, and $n = 10$. A little calculation will show that if there are four or more increases in share price, the stock price will exceed \$60 by the expiration date. Thus, $a = 4$ in this example.[12] The second comment necessary is that although in order to calculate $B[a,n,P']$ or $B[a,n,P]$ we act as if P' or P are probabilities, in actuality they have nothing to do with probabilities. P and P' depend on the size of the up and down movements and the risk-free rate. They are not connected with the probabilities of these up and down movements taking place. We refer to them as probabilities solely because we employ them as if they were probabilities in using the binomial formula.

The reader might well wonder how to determine the inputs in the binomial option pricing formula. In particular, how are the up and down price movements (u and d) determined? Values of u and d are set so that the return distribution resulting from their values is what the user considers reasonable. In practice the user specifies the standard deviation of the stock and the number of intervals until expiration over which a movement up or down takes place, and then calculates a value of u and d that would result in the return process having the standard deviation that was specified. The specific formulas are

$$u = e^{+\sigma\sqrt{t/n}}$$

$$d = e^{-\sigma\sqrt{t/n}}$$

where

   n is the number of intervals until expiration

   σ is the annual continuous time standard deviation of the return on the stock (the standard deviation of the log of returns)

   t is the time to expiration in years

   e is the exponential function

Specifying a larger number of intervals increases the number of possible returns the stock can have over the period but increases the computational burden. A fairly small number of intervals seems to produce accurate option valuation.

---

[12]$50(1.50)^4(0.80)^6 = 66.35$, whereas $50(1.50)^3(0.80)^7 = 35.39$. More formally, a can be defined as the number for which $u^{a-1}d^{n-(a-1)}S_0 < E \leq u^a - d^{n-a}S_0$.

Note that each of the factors that we demonstrated as affecting call price in the two-period model also affect call prices in the multiperiod model. The call is a function of the size of the up movement, the size of the down movement, the exercise price, the current share price, and the riskless rate of interest. In addition, the multiperiod model is a function of n, the number of periods remaining until expiration.

The binomial formula just derived can be utilized to derive two other valuation formulas that allow a continuous change in the share price. This is accomplished by letting the length of the period between up or down movements become very small, and hence the number of periods is very large. The most popular of these models is due to Black and Scholes, and is developed in the next section.

The Black–Scholes Option Valuation Formula

In the previous section of this chapter we derived an option pricing formula under the assumption that the rate of return on the underlying stock followed a binomial formula. As the number of time periods gets very large, the binomial distribution converges to the normal distribution.

If we assume that a stock's continuously compounded rate of return follows a normal distribution, then the option pricing model developed in the preceding section reduces to the Black–Scholes option pricing formula presented below.[13]

$$C = S_0 N(d_1) - \frac{E}{e^{rt}} N(d_2) \tag{22.1a}$$

$$d_1 = \frac{\ln(S_0/E) + \left(r + \frac{1}{2}\sigma^2\right)t}{\sigma\sqrt{t}} \tag{22.1b}$$

$$d_2 = \frac{\ln(S_0/E) + \left(r - \frac{1}{2}\sigma^2\right)t}{\sigma\sqrt{t}} \tag{22.1c}$$

where

r = the continuously compounded riskless rate of interest

C = the current value of the option

S_0 = the current price of the stock

E = the exercise price of the option

e = 2.7183

t = the time remaining before the expiration date expressed as a fraction of a year

σ = the standard deviation of the continuously compounded annual rate of return

$\ln(S_0/E)$ = natural logarithm of S_0/E

$N(d)$ = the value of the cumulative normal distribution evaluated at d

The Black–Scholes formula can be used to value any option. In the next section of this chapter we will discuss how to use it. Before we do, we will discuss the variables that affect the valuation of calls as well as the relationship of this formula to that discussed earlier.

---

[13]See Cox and Ross [36].

Perhaps the most interesting aspect of the Black–Scholes model is a variable that does *not* appear as a determinant of the value of a call. This variable is the expected rate of return on the stock. Any of the option models determines the price of the option in terms of the price of the underlying stock. The stock price, in fact, acts as the numeraire in which call prices are expressed. Expected return enters the model insofar as it determines current share price, but given current share price, it does not affect the value of the call.

The impact of the other variables on the value of the call can be seen by examining the properties of the Black–Scholes model as each changes. In general, the results are as follows: the higher the ratio of the current price of the stock to the exercise price of the call, the higher the value of the call. This is reasonable, for the higher this ratio, the less the price of the stock must increase for the call to have a value on its expiration date. The longer the time to maturity on the call, the higher the value of the call. This again is sensible, for the longer the time to maturity, the more the stock's price is likely to deviate from its present level at maturity. Since the payoff from deviations from price is asymmetrical, the longer time to maturity increases the value of the call.[14] Finally, the higher the riskless rate of interest, the greater the value of the call. This follows logically from the fact that the higher the riskless rate, the lower the present value of the amount that must be paid to exercise the call. The reader should note that these conclusions are consistent with the general statements we said must hold in a rational option pricing formula. They are also consistent with the conclusions we derived when we discussed the binomial formula.

Using the Black–Scholes Model   In examining the Black–Scholes formula we saw that the only data we needed to value an option were the current price of the stock, the exercise price of the option, the time remaining before expiration of the option, a cumulative normal probability table, the riskless rate of interest, and the standard deviation of the continuously compounded annual rate of return on the stock. All of these, except for the standard deviation, are easily observable.[15] One way to estimate the standard deviation of the continuously compounded annual rate of return on a stock is to use historic data on stock returns.[16] The Black–Scholes model was derived under the assumption of identically distributed rates of return over time. If this assumption in fact were strictly true over all periods, then estimates of the variance from historical data would be very good. As an example of this procedure, assume that we wish to estimate the appropriate variance for some stock using one year of historical weekly data. The price relative for each stock is simply the price at the end of the week plus any dividends divided by the price at the beginning of the week. The natural logarithm of the price relative is the continuously compounded rate of return per week. The standard deviation of the continuously compounded rate of return can easily be computed by applying the standard formula to the sequence of continuously compounded rates of return. For example, standard deviation is

$$= \left(\sum_{i=1}^{N} \left(\frac{\left(X_i - \overline{X}\right)^2}{N} \right) \right)^{1/2}$$

---

[14]For example, if the price of the stock is below the exercise price, then decreases in price up to the exercise time would result in the same value, zero, at the exercise time. In contrast, a rise in price could lead to a positive value for the call at the exercise time.

[15]The continuously compounded riskless rate of interest is usually found by taking the rate on a government security that has a maturity date equal to (or as close as possible to) the expiration date on the call.

[16]In the next section of this chapter we will discuss another method that uses the Black–Scholes model itself to prepare estimates of the standard deviation.

To convert the continuously compounded weekly standard deviation to a yearly standard deviation, simply multiply by the square root of 52.

The Black–Scholes model assumes that interest rates are continuously compounded. Because interest rates are generally stated using discrete compounding, some calculations are required to convert to the continuously compounded rate.

Assume the risk-free rate is calculated as ending value of the bond minus beginning value divided by beginning value (a discrete rate). As an example, assume the calculation results in a risk-free rate of 6%. Then the continuously compounded rate used in the Black–Scholes formula is r in the following formula

$$e^{-r} = 1.06 \quad \text{or} \quad r = 0.0582$$

Once inputs for the Black–Scholes valuation formula have been defined, one can easily solve for the value of a call option. Perhaps this can best be illustrated with an example.

$$S_0 = 90$$
$$E = 100$$
$$t = 0.5 \text{ (6 months)}$$
$$\sigma = 0.5$$
$$r = 0.10$$

Then d_1 and d_2 can be easily computed as follows:

$$d_1 = \frac{\ln(90/100) + (0.10 + \frac{1}{2}(0.25))(.5)}{0.5\sqrt{0.5}} \approx 0.02$$

$$d_2 = \frac{\ln(90/100) + (0.10 - \frac{1}{2}(0.25))(.5)}{0.5\sqrt{0.5}} \approx -0.33$$

From any table of the cumulative normal distribution, we can compute:

$$N(d_1) = N(0.02) = 0.5080$$
$$N(d_2) = N(-0.33) = 0.3707$$

The value of the call is

$$C = 90(0.5080) - \frac{100}{e^{.10(0.5)}}(0.3707) = \$10.46$$

Using the Black–Scholes formula we now have a theoretical value for the call of $10.46. Assume that the call was selling at $9.50. If the Black–Scholes formula is correct, the call is undervalued in the market. The investor can take advantage of this by buying the call directly. Alternatively, the investor could be protected against adverse stock price changes by buying the call and selling the stock short. Recall from the previous section that this combination is a riskless hedge.[17] It can be shown that if we accept the Black–Scholes option pricing formula as correct, the appropriate hedge ratio is given by $N(d_1)$ or, in our example, 0.5080. This means that for every call option purchased, 0.5080 or slightly more than half of the share of stock should be sold short.

The hedge ratio is sufficiently important to traders that it has been given a name of its own. It is called "Delta." The construction of portfolios to take advantage of any mispricing

---

[17]In the section discussing the binomial formula we derived a hedge ratio. A similar argument in the Black–Scholes model shows that the hedge ratio is $N(d_1)$. Examining d_1 shows that it should be expected to change over time and thus the hedge ratio also changes.

in either options or underlying securities is known as delta hedging. While at any moment in time the hedge ratio can easily be determined from the formulas for d and $N(d)$ presented above, examination of the formulas makes it clear that delta hedging is not a passive activity. This is because the size of the hedge changes with a change in the price of the underlying security, the passage of time, or a change in the volatility of the underlying security. The rate of change in the hedge ratio with respect to a change in the price of the underlying asset is known as "Gamma." The rate of change in the price of the option with respect to time is called "Theta." The rate of change of the option with respect to the volatility of the underlying asset is known as "Vega." Obviously, the smaller the size of Gamma, Theta, or Vega, the less often hedge ratios have to be adjusted and the easier and less costly it is to maintain a hedge portfolio. These parameters of hedging are sufficiently important so they are routinely computed by traders in the option market, and the exact formula for computing them can be found in any advanced text on options (e.g., Hull [65]).

Many traded calls are on securities that pay dividends over the life of the option. From previous discussion, early exercise, if it occurs, will occur immediately before the stock goes ex-dividend. Thus, a call will be optimally exercised either at maturity or just before the ex-dividend date. This pattern, that early exercise only occurs just before the ex-dividend date, can be used to value a call. The investor can view the problem of valuing a call on a dividend paying stock as owning two calls—one that expires just before the ex-dividend date, and one that expires at maturity. The value of the actual call is very close to the maximum value of each call considered separately. The call expiring just before the ex-dividend date is valued by the standard formula with the time to expiration, taken as the time between the current date, and the day before the ex-dividend date. The other call is valued similarly with two changes. First, the time to expiration is whatever it is for the call. Second, the price used in the option formula is the current price less the present value of the dividend. The logic is that when the stock goes ex-dividend, the value of the stock drops by the amount of the dividend. Unlike a stockholder, the option holder does not receive the dividend so the current value of the stock to the option holder is reduced by the dividend. Because the dividend is paid in the future, the current loss is the present value of the dividend.

Let's consider an example. Assume the following:

$S_0 = 50$

$E = 50$

$r = 3\%$ for 90 days

$r = 2\%$ for 60 days

$D = \$5$

$\sigma = 0.20$

Further assume the stock goes ex-dividend in 61 days and matures in 90 days. Then the value of the option, assuming exercise is 60 days just before it goes ex-dividend, is found by assuming $S_0 = 50$, $E = 50$, $r = 2\%$, and $\sigma = 0.20$. The option value using the Black–Scholes formula is $1.68.

Similarly, the value of the option, assuming exercise at maturity, is found by assuming $E = 50$, $r = 5\%$, $\sigma = 0.20$, and that S_0 is

$$S_0 = 50 - 5e^{-(0.02)(60/385)} = 45.02$$

The exponential e simply finds the present value of the dividend when continuous compounding is used.

The Black–Scholes option value, assuming no early exercise, is $0.41. The maximum of these two calculations is $1.68, and this would be considered the minimum option value. The call option value would be greater than these two numbers because of the opportunity to reconsider the decision immediately before the ex-dividend date.

Implicit Estimates of Stock's Own Variance from Option Formulas   In the previous section of this chapter we discussed the input needed to use option valuation models. All of the model input variables were easily observed except for one—the variance of the instantaneous rate of return on the stock. Up to now, we have assumed that the value of this variable is inferred from historical data. However, there is a second way in which option valuation formulas such as the Black–Scholes formula can be used. If we believe that option prices are such that the Black–Scholes model holds on average, then the market price of the option can be substituted for C in the model. The only remaining unknown in the formula is the instantaneous rate of variance of the stock.[18] Since we have one equation and one unknown, a formula like the Black–Scholes formula can be used to determine the variance of the stock. If the assumptions behind the Black–Scholes model are completely valid, and the model holds on average, then the variance implied by the Black–Scholes model should be a good estimate of the market's expectation about the variance of a stock's return. On any one stock there are likely to be many calls outstanding, and these calls will probably have different exercise prices and expiration dates. From each of these calls we can obtain an estimate of the standard deviation of the stock's continuously compounded rate of return. The efficiency of the estimate should be improved if we combine several independent estimates. Ways of doing this will now be discussed.

The simplest way to find an estimate of σ is to take an average of the estimates obtained from each call outstanding on the stock. If there are N calls outstanding, and if σ_j is the estimate of the standard deviation arrived at by employing data for the jth call, then

$$\sigma = \frac{1}{N} \sum_{j=1}^{N} \sigma_j$$

Not all authors weight the estimates equally. Many authors place less weight on estimates obtained from calls that have prices less sensitive to σ. This weighting scheme would place less weight on calls where the stock price is far from the exercise price, and more weight on calls where the stock price and exercise price are close. There are several variants of this weighting.[19] Some authors simply discard estimates from calls where the stock price is very different from the exercise price. Other authors have suggested weighting by the relative sensitivity of the call price of the option to changes in the standard deviation.[20]

---

[18]The Black–Scholes formula cannot be explicitly solved for variance. However, an iterative procedure can be used to find the implied variance for any stock that is consistent with this formula. See [75] for a discussion of search procedures.

[19]See [19] and [111] for additional suggestions as to plausible weighting schemes.

[20]This technique was used by [75]. Defining $\partial C_j / \partial \sigma_j$ as the change in the call price of call j to a change in standard deviation of call j, then the weight on the jth estimate of standard deviation (W_j) is

$$W_j = \frac{\partial C_j}{\partial \sigma_j} \Big/ \sum_k \frac{\partial C_k}{\partial \sigma_k}$$

and

$$\sigma = \sum_{j=1}^{N} w_j \sigma_j$$

Although calculating weights in the manner just discussed is only one of a large number of weighting techniques that have been advocated for arriving at estimates of the variance of a stock's return, it is one of the few subject to empirical tests. Latane and Rendleman [75] have used a weighting scheme similar to that described earlier to investigate the ability of estimates of variance from the Black–Scholes model to serve as forecasts of the future. To judge the usefulness of this technique, Latane and Rendleman perform two sets of tests. One set looks directly at whether better forecasts of actual future variance are achieved when (1) forecasts are prepared by computing variance over a historical period or (2) forecasts are prepared from the Black–Scholes model. They conclude that forecasts from the Black–Scholes model are more accurate. As a second test, they examine whether large profits are earned by arbitraging mispriced calls where the value of the call is computed by using the variances arrived at in (1) or (2). They again conclude that the use of variances inferred from the Black–Scholes model leads to a better valuation of assets (a higher excess return) than does the forecastings of variances from historical data. For an excellent analysis of forecasting variance see Figlewski [44].

While this technique for estimating variance has important implications for the pricing of options, it also can be important for portfolio selection. In earlier chapters, we have discussed how estimates of expected returns, variances, and correlation coefficients are necessary inputs to the portfolio selection process. We have devoted two chapters to estimating correlation coefficients. We have also mentioned that estimates of expected returns must come from security analysts and that analysts can be trained to produce estimates of variances. The latter is much more difficult than the former. The option literature seems to provide either a useful alternative measure of variances or, at the least, a useful benchmark to help the analysts in their estimation process.

ARTIFICIAL OR HOMEMADE OPTIONS

One of the existing insights in modern option theory is that an appropriate mixture of Treasury bills and a security creates a payoff pattern identical to the pattern of an option on the underlying security. This is exciting because options are written only on a limited number of securities and artificially created options can produce the payoff pattern of an option on securities or portfolios where actual options don't exist. Consider, for example, an arbitrary portfolio. Assume further that the portfolio does not resemble an index. In this case options would not exist on the portfolio. Assume further the portfolio has a value of $100. A homemade put at $105 can be created. This eliminates the risk of returns below 5% for the portfolio. Of course, homemade puts, like traded puts, have a cost. In the case of an artificial put, the cost comes in the form of a reduction in returns when returns on the portfolio are above 5%. Thus a homemade put changes the return distribution of the portfolio by eliminating returns below 5% and reducing the returns above 5% in the same manner as a traded put would. Whether this is desirable or not depends on the investor's taste for risk and return. The creation of an artificial put on a portfolio goes by the name of "portfolio insurance" since the portfolio is insured against returns below 5%.

Let's examine in more detail the construction of an artificial put. The first row of Table 22.8 shows the payoff pattern of a put if the stock price can end up at $50 or $40 in one period and if the exercise price is $45. Rows 2 and 3 show a combination of shorting the stock and buying T-bills that has the same payoff pattern as the put. If the put doesn't exist, then shorting the stock and owning T-bills create a homemade put that has the same payoff pattern as a publicly traded put.

Note that when a homemade put is written in conjunction with a portfolio or asset, the investor is not literally short. Consider a pension portfolio and an artificial put. The short

Table 22.8 Illustration of Homemade Put

	Value at Expiration Date	
	If Stock Price Is 40	If Stock Price Is 50
Buy put	5.00	0.00
Short $\frac{1}{2}$ share of stock	−20.00	−25.00
Buy T-bills	25.00	25.00
Sum	5.00	0.00

sale is accomplished by selling off part of the portfolio. Holding less of the portfolio is equivalent to owning the portfolio while simultaneously being short part of it.

Note also that the homemade put is created by selling off less than one share of stock. In the example it was one-half share. If there were more than one period, the fraction of shares sold short would change over time. Thus the creation of homemade options involves frequent readjustment of the combination of the underlying security and T-bills in order that the payoff pattern resemble that of an option. Early implementation of this idea involved literally selling and buying shares of an asset or portfolio. In order to replicate the payoff pattern of an option, frequent transactions were called for. Since frequent sales and purchases meant substantial transaction costs, shares were traded less frequently and the payoff pattern deviated substantially lower transaction costs. Furthermore, features can be used to construct an asset like stocks or bonds. Thus the growth of futures markets has been a spur to the creation of artificial options.

USES OF OPTIONS

In earlier sections of this chapter, we discussed the nature of options and their valuation. In this section, we will examine the major uses of options by individual investors and institutional investors.

Modifying the Return Pattern

In Chapter 5 we discussed the efficient frontier with riskless lending and borrowing. The efficient frontier was a straight line such as that shown in Figure 22.7. Note that as we increase the number of Treasury bills in the portfolio, we lower expected return and the standard deviation of return. However, we do not fundamentally change the distribution of return. If we plot two portfolios such as A, which is half Treasury bills and half risky assets and portfolio B, which is 100% in risky assets, to examine the distribution of returns we get the distributions shown in Figure 22.8. Note that the effect of reducing risk by adding Treasury bills is to squeeze the distribution and shift it to a lower mean return. Adding Treasury bills does not fundamentally change the shape of the return distribution. If we assumed that riskless lending and borrowing was not possible, then the same conclusion holds. Moving along the efficient frontier changes the mean return and variance but doesn't change the shape of the distribution.

One of the major uses of options is to modify the shape of the return distribution. Consider an index fund with the index currently valued at $300. Further, assume the investor believes the expected return is 10% with a standard deviation of 15%. Then, the investor holding the index fund expects to face a probability distribution such as that shown as a solid curve in Figure 22.9. Assume the investor buys a put on the S&P index with an exercise price of $310. Further, assume the put costs $12. Then the combination

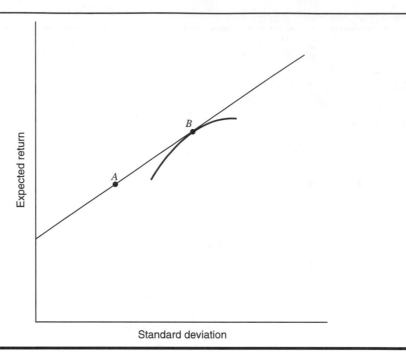

Figure 22.7   The efficient frontier.

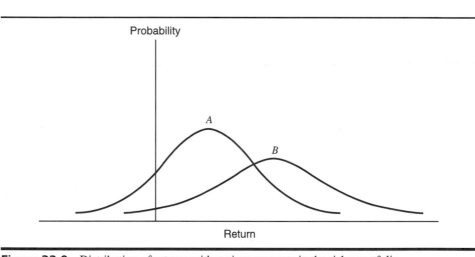

Figure 22.8   Distribution of returns with various amounts in the risky portfolio.

of the portfolio and put results in a return distribution such as the one shown by the dashed curve in Figure 22.9. The new distribution of returns is a result of two influences. If the Standard & Poor's (S&P) index ends up above 310, the put expires worthless and the return is lowered by the cost of the put (12/300 or 4%). If the S&P index ends up below 310, the put is exercised and the return is (310/300 − 1) minus the cost of the put or −0.67%. Thus, the effect on the return distribution of buying a put is to lower high returns and eliminate low returns. The worst outcome the investor could incur in our example is a return of −0.67%. This is true no matter how badly the stock market did. This modifica-

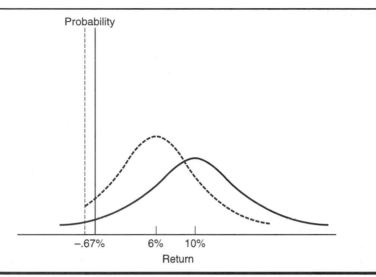

Figure 22.9   The effect of puts on the return distribution.

tion of the return distribution is not possible with a fixed combination of Treasury bills and a security portfolio.[21]

Another way that options are frequently used to modify the distribution of returns is to sell calls on stocks that are already owned in a portfolio. This gives some immediate income to the investor but has an opportunity cost in that the investor has sold off the right to receive a high potential payoff from the stock. Some investors (e.g., mutual funds), who have a target price above which they intend to close out a position in a stock, find that by selling calls at this price they can gain extra revenue while following their intended course of action. Some investors who follow this covered call writing strategy are less rational in that they have failed to consider the opportunity of high returns they give up for receiving the income from writing calls. The major use of options is to modify the return distribution in ways unattainable with fixed combinations of other assets.

Betting on Information

Investors receive a great deal of information about the prospective fortunes of company's shares. Information about the company's return can be utilized to buy or potentially short sell a company's stock. One type of information that is not easily utilized with nonoption strategies is information concerning the stock's variability. If an investor believes the company has undergone a large increase in risk, the investor might wish to sell stock if it's already owned, but there is no way with nonoption strategies to utilize this information to justify a purchase or short sale of the stock. Examining the option pricing formulas presented earlier, however, shows that the value of an option is directly related to the stock's underlying volatility. If the investor believes that the volatility of the company will increase dramatically and other investors have yet to discover this increase, then the purchase of options is a way to utilize this information. Thus, options are a convenient way to attempt to profit from information about a security's variance.

---

[21]As discussed earlier, dynamically changing the mix of T-bills and risky assets can create a portfolio with the payoff pattern of a put plus a risky portfolio.

Advanced Uses

There are other ways of employing options that depend on the ability to combine options with other securities to create a portfolio with identical characteristics to yet a third type of security. These are the security equivalencies discussed earlier. For example, combining options plus the underlying security with changing proportions of each can create a portfolio that has the same characteristics as a Treasury bill. If options are mispriced, this allows lending (or borrowing) at more attractive rates than the market. Further, if options are fairly priced, the portfolio of options and the underlying security allows the ability to borrow at the T-bill rate (ignoring transaction costs). Similarly, combinations of options and T-bills dynamically changed through time can create a security with the characteristic of a short position in the underlying security. Because there are limits to the size of the position an investor can short of the basic security, the use of options allows the investor to circumvent exchange restriction. Finally, it has been argued that because transaction costs are so low in options markets, and because options in conjunction with other securities can create new securities, options may be a less expensive way to buy the created security. All of the uses involve changing the mix of options and a second security over time to create a portfolio with a return pattern like a third security. This involves transaction costs. The value of options for these purposes when transaction costs are included, needs to be examined.

CONCLUSION

In this chapter we have examined the characteristics and valuation of contingent claim contracts. The development of a set of models for pricing contingent claims is a fairly recent and important contribution. We have explored the theory behind these models and their use in valuing options. In addition, we have shown how such models can be used to develop estimates of the variance of the return on the stocks against which they represent a claim. This may be an important input to portfolio management models.

APPENDIX A

DERIVATION OF THE BINOMIAL FORMULA

In the text we showed that with one period to go, the value of the call was

$$C = \frac{PC_u + (1-P)C_d}{r} \tag{A.1}$$

Now consider the possibilities with two periods to go. These are represented in the diagram shown here:

where

1. C_{u^2} as the value at expiration if there are two up movements in the stock $=$ maximum $[u^2S - E, 0]$

2. C_{ud} as the value at expiration if there is one up and one down movement in the share price $=$ maximum $[udS - E, 0]$

3. C_{d^2} as the value at expiration if there are two down movements in the share price $=$ maximum $[d^2S - E, 0]$

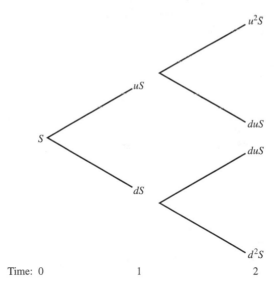

Time: 0   1   2

Applying Equation (A.1) we can determine the value of the calls at period 1 if the share price is uS at period 1 as

$$C_u = \frac{PC_{u^2} + (1-P)C_{ud}}{r}$$

Again, by applying Equation (A.1) we can determine the value at period 1 if the share price is dS at period 1 as

$$C_d = \frac{PC_{ud} + (1-P)C_{d^2}}{r}$$

Now consider period 0. Knowing the value at period 1, we can act as if there is only one period to go. This is shown as follows:

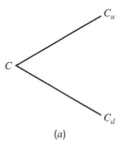

(a)

Applying Equation (A.1) again yields

$$C = \frac{P\dfrac{PC_{u^2} + (1-P)C_{ud}}{r} + (1-P)\dfrac{PC_{ud} + (1-P)C_{d^2}}{r}}{r}$$

Simplifying,

$$C = \frac{P^2 C_{u^2} + 2P(1-P)C_{ud} + (1-P)^2 C_{d^2}}{r^2} \qquad\qquad \text{(A.2)}$$

In exactly the same way we can derive the formula for the three-period case. The possible movements of the share price are shown in Figure 22.10.

Notice in this case that two periods before the expiration date the stock price is either uS or dS instead of S, as it was in the two-period example. If it is uS, then from Equation (A.2) the value at time 1 is simply

$$C_u = \frac{P^2 C_{u^3} + 2P(1-P)C_{u^2d} + (1-P)^2 C_{ud^2}}{r^2}$$

If the price of the stock were dS in period 1, then

$$C_d = \frac{P^2 C_{u^2d} + 2P(1-P)C_{ud^2} + (1-P)^2 C_{d^3}}{r^2}$$

where $C_{u^n d^R}$ = the value expiration if there are n up movements and R down movements. Apply Equation (A.1) yields the value of the call at time zero; we have

$$C = \frac{P\dfrac{P^2 C_{u^3} + 2P(1-P)C_{u^2d} + (1-P)^2 C_{ud^2}}{r^2} + (1-P)\dfrac{P^2 C_{u^2d} + 2P(1-P)C_{ud^2} + (1-P)^2 C_{d^3}}{r^2}}{r}$$

Simplifying,

$$C = \frac{P^3 C_{u^3} + 3P^2(1-P)C_{u^2d} + 3P(1-P)^2 C_{ud^2} + (1-P)^3 C_{d^3}}{r^3}$$

Recalling the determination of the value of the call at the horizon and examining the form of the preceding equations shows that for n periods before the horizon the value of the call is

$$C = \frac{\left[\displaystyle\sum_{j=0}^{n} \frac{n!}{j!(n-j)!} P^j (1-P)^{n-j} \max\left[0, u^j d^{n-j} S_0 - E\right]\right]}{r^n}$$

We can simplify the expression by defining a as the minimum number of up movements necessary for it to pay to exercise the option at the expiration date. For sequences with

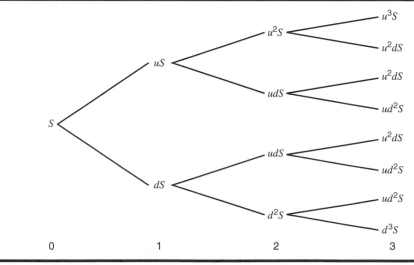

Figure 22.10   Stock price paths.

fewer than a up movements, the call will not be exercised and the value at expiration will be zero. Thus, the summation need start only at a. Furthermore, for more than a up movements we know that exercise pays. Thus, when the lower limit on the summation is a, the maximum can be rewritten as $u^j d^{n-j} S_0 - E$.

With these changes we have

$$C = \frac{\displaystyle\sum_{j=a}^{n} \frac{n!}{j!(n-j)!} P^j (1-P)^{n-j} \left(u^j d^{n-j} S_0 - E\right)}{r^n}$$

Rearranging,

$$C = S_0 \left[\sum_{j=a}^{n} \frac{n!}{j!(n-j)!} \frac{(Pu)^j \left[(1-P)d\right]^{n-j}}{r^n} \right] - E r^{-n} \left[\sum_{j=a}^{n} \frac{n!}{j!(n-j)!} P^j (1-P)^{n-j} \right]$$

The second expression in brackets is the binomial formula with R serving the role of a probability and can be represented as $B[a,n,P]$. The first expression in brackets also turns out to be a binomial formula. To see this, first write part of it as

$$\frac{(Pu)^j \left[(1-P)d\right]^{n-j}}{r^n} = \left(\frac{Pu}{r}\right)^j \left(\frac{(1-P)d}{r}\right)^{n-j}$$

Define P' as $(Pu)/r$. Then if $1 - P' = (1 - P)\, d/r$, we would have a binomial formula with P' serving the role of probability. A little algebra demonstrates that this is appropriate. Recall $P = (r - d)/(u - d)$. Thus,

$$1 - P' = 1 - \frac{Pu}{r} = 1 - \frac{u(r-d)}{r(u-d)} = 1 - \frac{ur - ud}{ur - dr} = \frac{ur - dr - ur + ud}{ur - dr}$$

$$= \frac{d}{r}\left[\frac{u-r}{u-d}\right] = \frac{d}{r}\left[\frac{u-d-r+d}{u-d}\right] = \frac{d}{r}\left[1 - \frac{r-d}{u-d}\right]$$

$$= \frac{d}{r}(1 - P)$$

This last expression is what we wanted to show. Thus, the first term in the brackets has the form

$$\sum_{j=a}^{n} \frac{n!}{j!(n-j)!} P'^{\,j} (1-P')^{n-j}$$

This can be represented as $B[a,n,P']$. Substituting the two expressions for binomials in the basic equation for a call yields

$$C = S_0 B[a, n, P'] - E r^{-n} B[a, n, P]$$

APPENDIX B

DERIVATION OF THE BLACK–SCHOLES FORMULA

The derivation of the Black–Scholes formula starts out in a similar manner to the derivation of the binomial formula. First, a portfolio is constructed that has the same return, no matter how well the stock performs. This portfolio, as in the case of the binomial formula, consists of writing a call and buying the stock. For simplicity, consider buying one share of stock. Then it can be shown that the amount of calls to write is one divided by the change in the value of the call with a unit change in the value of the stock.

The following example will clarify this. Assume that the call changes by one-half of the amount of the stock change. Thus, the rule just described says to write two calls. If the stock increased by $1, the ownership of the stock would cause an increase of $1 in the value of the hedge. However, if two calls are written, each call should increase in value by $0.50 or the two calls by $1. Since the hedge involves writing of two calls, this causes a loss of $1 in the value of the hedge.

Thus, the portfolio value is unchanged by a change in the share price. Such a riskless portfolio should yield the riskless rate of interest. Let

V_H be the initial value (cost) of the hedge

S be the market price of a share of stock

C be the value of a call

Q_s be the quantity of stock owned

Q_c be the quantity of calls owned

r be the riskless rate of interest

Then the value of the hedge is

$$V_H = Q_s S + Q_c C \tag{B.1}$$

and the change in the value of the hedge is

$$dV_H = Q_s dS + Q_c dC$$

This hedge is riskless and thus should yield the riskless rate of interest per each unit of time. Thus,

$$rV_H dt = Q_s dS + Q_c dC$$

Substituting for V_H from Equation (B.1), and recalling that if the hedge is formed in terms of writing calls,

$$Q_S = +1 \quad \text{and} \quad Q_C = \frac{-1}{\partial C/\partial S}$$

we have

$$r\left[S - \frac{C}{\partial C/\partial S} \right] dt = dS - \frac{1}{\partial C/\partial S} dC$$

Rearranging,

$$dC = \frac{\partial C}{\partial S} dS - r \frac{\partial C}{\partial S} \left[S - \frac{C}{\partial C/\partial S} \right] dt = \frac{\partial C}{\partial S} dS - rS \frac{\partial C}{\partial S} dt + rCdt \tag{B.2}$$

What is required next is a model of stock price and call price changes. The assumption that Black and Scholes make is that the instantaneous change in stock price follows a normal distribution.

$$\frac{dS}{S} = \mu dt + \sigma dZ$$

μ is the instantaneous expected return, σ is the instantaneous variance, and dZ is the zero mean unit standard deviation normally distributed variate. Given the stock price process described before, the change in the call price is well known from theorems in stochastic calculus.[22]

$$dC = \frac{\partial C}{\partial S} dS + \frac{\partial C}{\partial t} dt + \frac{1}{2} \frac{\partial^2 C}{\partial S^2} \sigma^2 S^2 dt$$

This expression should look somewhat familiar. The first two terms on the right-hand side are the terms that would be obtained in standard calculus if you take a total derivative of the value of a call. The last term arises because of the stochastic element in S. Substituting for dC in Equation (B.2) yields

$$\frac{\partial C}{\partial S} dS + \frac{\partial C}{\partial t} dt + \frac{1}{2} \frac{\partial^2 C}{\partial S^2} \sigma^2 S^2 dt = \frac{\partial C}{\partial S} dS - rS \frac{\partial C}{\partial S} dt + rCdt$$

Subtracting the term $(\partial C / \partial S) dS$ from each side, noting that there is a dt in each remaining term and thus that it can be eliminated by dividing by dt, and rearranging yields

$$\frac{\partial C}{\partial t} = rC - rS \frac{\partial C}{\partial S} - \frac{1}{2} \frac{\partial^2 C}{\partial S^2} \sigma^2 S^2 \tag{B.3}$$

This is a differential equation. At the horizon, the value of the call is

$$C = \begin{matrix} S - E & S - E \\ 0 & S \le E \end{matrix}$$

Solving the differential equation and using the value at the horizon as the boundary condition yields the expression shown in the text.

QUESTIONS AND PROBLEMS

1. A registered representative recently advised one of his clients to sell calls on all the stock he owned. He explained that the client wouldn't lose money, but would benefit by what he got paid for the call. Sounds foolproof. What's wrong?

2. Consider the purchase of a combination of two puts and a call. Assume that the call costs $5, the put $6, and the exercise price for the put or call is $50. Plot the profit versus the stock price at the expiration date.

3. Consider two calls, one with an exercise price of $40 and one with an exercise price of $45. Assume that the call with the $40 exercise price sells for $8 and the call with the $45 exercise price sells for $5. Assume that they have the same expiration date. Consider the strategy of issuing two $45 calls and purchasing one $40 call. Plot the profit versus the share price at the expiration date.

4. Assume the binomial pricing model. Assume that the share price is $50, the exercise price is $60, $u = 1.2$, $d = 0.9$, $r = 1.1$, and $N = 10$. What is the value of α? What is the call value?

5. Determine the value of the following call using the Black–Scholes model. The stock currently sells for $95 and the instantaneous standard deviation of the stock's return is 0.6. The call has an exercise price of $105, and has 8 months to go before expiration. The continuously compounded riskless rate of interest is 8%.

---

[22]The equation follows from Ito's Lemma. See [16].

BIBLIOGRAPHY

1. Arditti, Fred D., and John, Kose. "Spanning the State Space with Options," *Journal of Financial and Quantitative Analysis*, **XV,** No. 1 (Mar. 1980), pp. 1–10.
2. Baesel, Jerome B., Shows, George, and Thorp, Edward. "The Cost of Liquidity Services in Listed Options: A Note," *The Journal of Finance*, **38,** No. 3 (June 1983), pp. 989–996.
3. Bailey, Warren. "An Empirical Investigation of the Market for Comex Gold Futures Options," *Journal of Finance*, **42,** No. 5 (Dec. 1987), pp. 1187–1194.
4. Ball, Clifford A. "Estimation Bias Induced by Discrete Security Prices," *Journal of Finance*, **43,** No. 4 (Sept. 1988), pp. 841–865.
5. Ball, Clifford A., and Torous, Walter N. "A Simplified Jump Process for Common Stock Returns," *Journal of Financial and Quantitative Analysis*, **XVII,** No. 1 (Mar. 1983), pp. 53–66.
6. ——. "Bond Price Dynamics and Options," *Journal of Financial and Quantitative Analysis*, **XVIII,** No. 4 (Dec. 1983), pp. 517–532.
7. ——. "On Jumps in Common Stock Prices and Their Impact on Call Pricing," *The Journal of Finance*, **40,** No. 1 (Mar. 1985), pp. 155–174.
8. ——. "Futures Options and the Volatility of Futures Prices," *Journal of Finance*, **41,** No. 4 (Sept. 1986), pp. 857–870.
9. Ball, Clifford A., Torous, Walter N., and Tschoegel, Adrian E. "An Empirical Investigation of the EOE Gold Options Market," *Journal of Business Finance*, **9,** No. 1 (Mar. 1985), pp. 101–113.
10. Barone-Adesi, Giovanni, and Whaley, Robert E. "Efficient Analytic Approximation of American Option Values," *Journal of Finance*, **42,** No. 2 (June 1987), pp. 301–320.
11. Beckers, Stan. "On the Efficiency of the Gold Options Market," *Journal of Business Finance*, **8,** No. 3 (Sept. 1984), pp. 459–470.
12. Benninga, Simon, and Blume, Marshall. "On the Optimality of Portfolio Insurance," *Journal of Finance*, **40,** No. 5 (Dec. 1985), pp. 1341–1352.
13. Bhattacharya, Mihir. "Empirical Properties of the Black–Scholes Formula under Ideal Conditions," *Journal of Financial and Quantitative Analysis*, **XV,** No. 5 (Dec. 1980), pp. 1081–1106.
14. Bhattacharya, Sudipto. "Notes of Multiperiod Valuation and the Pricing of Options," *The Journal of Finance*, **36,** No. 1 (Mar. 1981), pp. 163–181.
15. Bick, Avi. "Producing Derivative Assets with Forward Contracts," *The Journal of Financial and Quantitative Analysis*, **23,** No. 2 (June 1988), pp. 153–160.
16. Black, Fischer, and Scholes, Myron. "The Pricing of Options and Corporate Liabilities," *Journal of Political Economy*, **81,** No. 3 (May/June 1973), pp. 637–654.
17. Blomeyer, Edward C., and Johnson, Herb. "An Empirical Examination of the Pricing of American Put Options," *Journal of Financial and Quantitative Analysis*, **23,** No. 1 (Mar. 1988), pp. 13–22.
18. Bookstaber, Richard, and Clarke, Roger. "Problems in Evaluating the Performance of Portfolios with Options," *Financial Analyst Journal*, **41,** No. 1 (Jan./Feb. 1985), pp. 48–62.
19. Boyle, Phelim. "Options: A Monte Carlo Approach," *Journal of Financial Economics*, **4,** No. 3 (May 1977), pp. 323–338.
20. Boyle, Phelim, and Ananthanarayanan, A. L. "The Impact of Variance Estimation in Option Valuation Models," *Journal of Financial Economics*, **5,** No. 3 (Dec. 1977), pp. 375–387.
21. Boyle, Phelim P., and Emanuel David. "Discretely Adjusted Option Hedges," *Journal of Financial Economics*, **8,** No. 3 (Sept. 1980), pp. 259–882.
22. Bracken, Jerome. "Models for Call Option Decisions," *Financial Analysts Journal*, **24,** No. 5 (Sept.–Oct. 1968), pp. 149–151.
23. Breeden, Douglas, and Litzenberger, Robert. "Prices of State-Contingent Claims Implicit in Option Price," *Journal of Business*, **51,** No. 4 (Oct. 1978), pp. 621–651.
24. Brennan, Michael J. "A Theory of Price Limits in Futures Markets," *Journal of Financial Economics*, **16** (1986), pp. 213–233.

25. Brennan, Michael, and Schwartz, Edwardo. "The Valuation of American Put Options," *Journal of Finance*, **XXXII,** No. 2 (May 1976), pp. 449–462.

26. Brennan, Michael J., and Solanki, R. "Optimal Portfolio Insurance," *Journal of Financial and Quantitative Analysis*, **XVI,** No. 3 (Sept. 1981), pp. 279–300.

27. Brennan, Michael J., Schwartz, Eduardo S., Grossman, Sanford J., and Vila, Jean-Luc. "Portfolio Insurance and Financial Market Equilibrium; Portfolio Insurance in Complete Markets: A Note," *The Journal of Business*, **62,** No. 4 (Oct. 1989), pp. 455–472.

28. Brenner, Menachem, and Galai, Dan. "On Measuring the Risk of Common Stocks Implied by Options Prices: A Note," *Journal of Financial and Quantitative Analysis*, **19,** No. 4 (Dec. 1984), pp. 403–412.

29. Brenner, Menachem, and Galai Dan. "Implied Interest Rates," *Journal of Business*, **59,** No. 3 (July 1986), pp. 493–507.

30. Brenner, Menachem, Courtadon, Georges, and Subrahmanyam, Marti. "Options on the Spot and Options on Futures," *Journal of Finance*, **40,** No. 5 (Dec. 1985), pp. 1303–1317.

31. Butler, J.S., and Schacter, Barry. "Unbiased Estimation of the Black/Scholes Formula," *Journal of Financial Economics*, **15** (1985), pp. 341–357.

32. Conover, James A., and Dubofsky, David A. "Efficient Selection of Insured Currency Positions: Protective Puts vs. Fiduciary Calls," *The Journal of Financial and Quantitative Analysis*, **30,** No. 2 (June 1995), pp. 295–312.

33. Courtadon, George. "The Pricing of Options on Default-Free Bonds," *Journal of Financial and Quantitative Analysis*, **XVII,** No. 1 (Mar. 1982), pp. 75–100.

34. ———. "A More Accurate Finite Difference Approximation for the Valuation of Options," *Journal of Financial and Quantitative Analysis*, **XVIII,** No. 5 (Dec. 1982), pp. 697–700.

35. Cho, D. Chinyung, and Frees, Edward W. "Estimating the Volatility of Discrete Stock Prices," *Journal of Finance*, **43,** No. 2 (June 1988), pp. 451–466.

36. Cox, Stephen, and Ross, Stephen. "A Survey of Some New Results in Financial Option Pricing Theory," *The Journal of Finance*, **XXXI,** No. 2 (May 1976), pp. 383–402.

37. ———. "The Valuation of Options for Alternative Stochastic Processes," *Journal of Financial Economics*, **3,** No. 112 (Jan.-Mar. 1976), pp. 145–166.

38. Dietrich-Campbell, Bruce, and Schwartz, Eduardo. "Valuing Debt Options: Empirical Evidence," *Journal of Financial Economics*, **16** (1986), pp. 321–343.

39. Dimson, Elroy. "Instant Option Valuation," *Financial Analysts Journal*, **33,** No. 3 (May-June 1977), pp. 62–69.

40. ———. "Option Valuation Nomograms," *Financial Analysts Journal*, **33,** No. 6 (Nov.-Dec. 1977), pp. 71–74.

41. Emanuel, David. "A Theoretical Model for Valuing Preferred Stock," *Journal of Finance*, **38,** No. 4 (Sept. 1983), pp. 1133–1155.

42. Eunine, Jeremy, and Rudd, Andrew. "Index Options: The Early Evidence," *Journal of Finance*, **40,** No. 3 (July 1985), pp. 743–756.

43. Eyton, T. Hanam, and Harpaz, Giora. "The Pricing of Futures and Options Contracts on the Value Line Index," *Journal of Finance*, **41,** No. 4 (Sept. 1986), pp. 843–855.

44. Figlewski, Stephen. "Forecasting Volatility," *Financial Markets and Instruments*, **6,** No.1 (1997).

45. Finucane, Thomas J. "Black–Scholes Approximations of Call Option Prices with Stochastic Volatilities: A Note," *The Journal of Financial and Quantitative Analysis*, **24,** No. 4 (Dec. 1989), pp. 527–532.

46. Fischer, Stanley. "Call Option Pricing When the Exercise Price Is Uncertain, and the Valuation of Index Bonds," *Journal of Finance*, **XXXIII,** No. 1 (Mar. 1978), pp. 169–176.

47. French, Dan W. "The Weekend Effect on the Distribution of Stock Prices: Implications for Option Pricing," *Journal of Financial Economics*, **13,** No. 4 (Dec. 1984), pp. 547–560.

48. Galai, Dan. "Tests of Market Efficiency of the Chicago Board Options Exchange," *Journal of Business*, **50,** No. 2 (Apr. 1977), pp. 167–197.

49. ———. "On the Boness and Black–Scholes Models for Valuation of Call Options," *Journal of Financial and Quantitative Analysis*, **XII,** No. 1 (Mar. 1978), pp. 15–27.

50. Galai, Dan, and Masulis, R. "The Option Pricing Model and the Risk Factor of Stock," *Journal of Financial Economics*, **13,** No. 1/2 (Jan.-Mar. 1976), pp. 53–81.

51. Garman, Mark B. "The Duration of Option Portfolios," *Journal of Financial Economics*, **14** (1985), pp. 309–315.

52. Geske, Robert. "The Pricing of Options with Stochastic Dividend Yield," *The Journal of Finance*, **XXXIII,** No. 2 (May 1978), pp. 617–625.

53. Geske, Robert, and Roll, Richard. "On Valuating American Call Options with the Black–Scholes European Formula," *The Journal of Finance*, **39,** No. 2 (June 1984), pp. 443–456.

54. Geske, Robert, and Johnson, H. E. "The American Put Option Valued Analytically," *The Journal of Finance*, **39,** No. 5 (Dec. 1984), pp. 1511–1524.

55. Geske, Robert, and Shastri, Kuldeep. "Valuation by Approximation: A Comparison of Alternative Option Valuation Techniques," *Journal of Financial and Quantitative Analysis*, **XX,** No. 1 (Mar. 1985), pp. 45–72.

56. Geske, Robert, and Shastri, Kuldeep. "The Early Exercise of American Puts," *Journal of Business Finance*, **9,** No. 2 (June 1985), pp. 207–219.

57. Gould, J. P., and Galai, Dan. "Transactions Costs and the Relationship Between Put and Call Prices," *Journal of Financial Economics*, **1,** No. 2 (July 1974), pp. 105–130.

58. Gultekin, N. Bulent, and Rogalski, Richard J. "Government Bond Returns, Measurement of Interest Rate Risk, and the Arbitrage Pricing Theory," *The Journal of Finance*, **40,** No. 1 (Mar. 1985), pp. 43–62.

59. Halpern, Paul J., and Turnbull, Stuart M. "Empirical Tests of Boundary Conditions for Toronto Stock Exchange Option," *The Journal of Finance*, **40,** No. 2 (June 1985), pp. 481–500.

60. Harrison, Michael J., Pitbladdo, Richard, and Schaefer, Stephen M. "Continuous Price Process in Frictionless Markets Have Infinite Variation," *Journal of Business*, **57,** No. 3 (Oct. 1984), pp. 353–365.

61. Hausman, W. H., and White, W. L. "Theory of Option Strategy Under Risk Aversion," *Journal of Financial and Quantitative Analysis*, **111,** No. 3 (Sept. 1968), pp. 343–358.

62. Heath, David C., and Jarrow, Robert A. "Arbitrage, Continuous Trading and Margin Requirements," *Journal of Finance*, **41,** No. 5 (Dec. 1987), pp. 1129–1142.

63. Hilliard, Jimmy, and Leitch, Robert. "Analysis of the Warrant Hedge in a Stable Paretion Market," *Journal of Financial and Quantitative Analysis*, **XII,** No. 1 (Mar. 1977), pp. 85–103.

64. Ho, Thomas S. Y., and Macris, Richard G. "Dealers Bid-Ask Quotes and Transaction Prices: An Empirical Study of Some AMEX Options," *The Journal of Finance*, **39,** No. 1 (Mar. 1984), pp. 23–46.

65. Hull, John. *Options Futures and Other Derivative Securities*. (Englewood Cliffs, N.J.: Prentice Hall, 2001.)

66. Hull, John, and White, Alan. "The Pricing of Options on Assets with Stochastic Volatilities," *Journal of Finance*, **42,** No. 2 (June 1987), pp. 281–300.

67. Jagannathan, Ravi. "Call Options and the Risk of Underlying Securities," *Journal of Financial Economics*, **13** (1984), pp. 425–434.

68. Jarrow, Robert, and Rudd, Andrew. "Approximate Option Valuation for Arbitrary Stochastic Processes," *Journal of Financial Economics*, **10,** No. 3 (Nov. 1982), pp. 347–370.

69. Johnson, H. E. "An Analytic Approximation for the American Put Price," *Journal of Financial and Quantitative Analysis*, **XVIII,** No. 1 (Mar. 1983), pp. 141–162.

70. Johnson, Herb, and Stulz, Rene. "The Pricing of Options with Default Risk," *Journal of Finance*, **42,** No. 2 (June 1987), pp. 267–280.

71. Jones, E. Philip. "Option Arbitrage and Strategy with Large Price Changes," *Journal of Financial Economics*, **10,** No. 4 (Mar. 1984), pp. 91–114.

72. Kassouf, Sheen. "Warrant Price Behavior—1945 to 1964," *Financial Analysts Journal*, **24,** No. 1 (Jan.–Feb. 1968), pp. 123–126.

73. Klemkosky, Robert C., and Resnick, Bruce G. "Put-Call Parity and Market Efficiency," *The Journal of Finance*, **34,** No. 5 (Dec. 1979), pp. 1141–1157.

74. ——. "An Ex Ante Analysis of Put-Call Parity," *Journal of Financial Economics*, **8,** No. 4 (Dec. 1980), pp. 363–378.

75. Latane, Henry, and Rendleman, Richard. "Standard Deviations of Stock Price Ratios Implied on Option Prices," *The Journal of Finance*, **XXXI,** No. 2 (May 1976), pp. 369–381.

76. Leabo, Dick, and Rogalski, Richard. "Warrant Price Movements and the Efficient Market Model," *The Journal of Finance*, **XXX,** No. 1 (Mar. 1975), pp. 163–177.

77. Leland, Hayne E. "Who Should Buy Portfolio Insurance?" *The Journal of Finance*, **35,** No. 2 (May 1980), pp. 581–594.

78. ——. "Option Pricing and Replication with Transactions Costs," *Journal of Finance*, **40,** No. 5 (Dec. 1985), pp. 1283–1301.

79. Levy, Haim. "Upper and Lower Bound of Put and Call Option Value: Stochastic Dominance Approach," *Journal of Finance*, **40,** No. 4 (Sept. 1985), pp. 1197–1217.

80. Litzenberger, Robert, and Sosin, Howard. "The Theory of Recapitalization and the Evidence of Dual Purpose Funds," *The Journal of Finance*, **XXXII,** No. 5 (Dec. 1977), pp. 1433–1455.

81. Lo, Andrew W. "Semi-Parametric Upper Bounds for Option Prices and Expected Payoffs," *Journal of Financial Economics*, **19** (1987), pp. 373–387.

82. MacBeth, James C., and Merville, Larry J. "Tests of the Black–Scholes and Cox Call Option Valuation Models," *The Journal of Finance*, **35,** No. 2 (May 1980), pp. 285–300.

83. Manaster, Steven, and Rendleman, Richard J., Jr. "Option Prices as Predictors of Equilibrium Stock Prices," *The Journal of Finance*, **37,** No. 4 (Sept. 1982), pp. 1043–1058.

84. Margrabe, William. "The Value of an Option to Exchange One Asset for Another," *The Journal of Finance*, **XXXIII,** No. 1 (Mar. 1978), pp. 177–198.

85. McDonald, Robert, and Siegel, Daniel. "Option Pricing When the Underlying Asset Earns a Below-Equilibrium Rate of Return: A Note," *The Journal of Finance*, **39,** No. 1 (Mar. 1984), pp. 261–266.

86. McGuigan, James, and King, William. "Security Option Strategy Under Risk Aversion: An Analysis," *Journal of Financial and Quantitative Analysis*, **VIII,** No. 1 (Jan. 1973), pp. 7–15.

87. ——. "Evaluating Alternative Stock Option Timing Strategies," *Journal of Financial and Quantitative Analysis*, **IX,** No. 4 (Sept. 1987), pp. 567–578.

88. Merton, Robert. "The Relationship Between Put and Call Option Prices: Comment," *The Journal of Finance*, **XXVIII,** No. 1 (Mar. 1973), pp. 183–184.

89. ——. "Theory of Rational Option Pricing." *Bell Journal of Economics and Management Science* (Spring 1973), pp. 141–183.

90. ——. "Option Pricing When Underlying Stock Returns Are Discontinuous," *Journal of Financial Economics*, **3,** No. 1/2 (Jan./March 1976), pp. 125–144.

91. ——. "The Impact on Option Pricing of Specification Error in the Underlying Stock Price Returns," *The Journal of Finance*, **XXXI,** No. 2 (May 1976), pp. 333–350.

92. Merton, Robert, Scholes, M., and Gladstein, M. "The Returns and Risk of Alternative Call Option Portfolio Investment Strategies." *Journal of Business*, **51,** No. 2 (Apr. 1978), pp. 183–242.

93. Parkinson, Michael. "Empirical Warrant-Stock Relationships," *Journal of Business*, **45,** No. 4 (Oct. 1972), pp. 563–569.

94. ——. "Option Pricing: The American Put," *Journal of Business*, **50,** No. 1 (Jan. 1977), pp. 21–36.

95. Perrakis, Stylianos, and Ryan, Peter J. "Option Pricing Bounds in Discrete Time," *The Journal of Finance*, **39,** No. 2 (June 1984), pp. 519–526.

96. Peterson, Richard. "Investor Preferences for Future Straddles," *Journal of Financial and Quantitative Analysis*, **XII,** No. 1 (Mar. 1977), pp. 105–120.

97. Phillips, Susan M., and Smith Clifford W., Jr. "Trading Costs for Listed Options: The Implications for Market Efficiency," *Journal of Financial Economics*, **8,** No. 3 (June 1980), pp. 179–189.

98. Protopapadakis, Aris, and Stoll, Hans R. "Spot and Futures Prices and the Law of One Price," *The Journal of Finance*, **38,** No. 5 (Dec. 1983), pp. 1431–1456.

99. Ramaswamy, Krishna, and Sundaresan, Suresh M. "The Valuation of Options on Futures Contracts," *Journal of Finance*, **40,** No. 5 (Dec. 1985), pp. 1319–1340.

100. Reback, Robert. "Risk and Return in CBOE and AMEX Option Trading," *Financial Analysts Journal*, **31,** No. 4 (July–Aug. 1975), pp. 42–52.

101. Rendleman, Richard, and Bartter, Brit. "Two-State Option Pricing," *The Journal of Finance*, **34,** No. 5 (Dec. 1979), pp. 1093–1110.

102. ———. "The Pricing of Options on Debt Securities," *Journal of Financial and Quantitative Analysis*, **XV,** No. 1 (Mar. 1980), pp. 11–24.

103. Ritchken, Peter H. "On Option Pricing Bounds," *Journal of Finance*, **40,** No. 4 (Sept. 1985), pp. 1219–1233.

104. Ritchken, Peter H., and Kuo, Shyanjaw. "Option Bounds with Finite Revision Opportunities," *Journal of Finance*, **43,** No. 2 (June 1988), pp. 301–308.

105. Rubinstein, Mark. "Displaced Diffusion Option Pricing," *The Journal of Finance*, **38,** No. 1 (Mar. 1983), pp. 213–217.

106. ———. "Displaced Diffusion Option Pricing," *Journal of Finance*, **38,** No. 1 (Mar. 1983), pp. 213–217.

107. ———. "A Simple Formula for the Expected Rate of Return of an Option over a Finite Holding Period," *The Journal of Finance*, **39,** No. 5 (Dec. 1984), pp. 1503–1510.

108. ———. "Nonparametric Tests of Alternative Option Pricing Models Using All Reported Trades and Quotes on the 30 Most Active CBOE Option Classes from August 23, 1976 through August 31, 1978," *The Journal of Finance*, **40,** No. 2 (June 1985), pp. 445–480.

109. Rubenstein, Mark, and Cox, John. *Option Markets* (Englewood Cliffs, N.J.: Prentice Hall, 1985).

110. Schaefer, Stephen M., and Schwartz, Eduardo S. "Time-Dependent Variance and the Pricing of Bond Options," *Journal of Finance*, **42,** No. 5 (Dec. 1987), pp. 1113–1128.

111. Schmalensee, Richard, and Trippi, Robert. "Common Stock Volatility Expectations Implied by Option Primia," *The Journal of Finance*, **XXXIII,** No. 1 (Mar. 1978), pp. 129–148.

112. Schwartz, Eduardo S. "The Pricing of Commodity-Linked Bonds," *The Journal of Finance*, **37,** No. 2 (May 1982), pp. 525–538.

113. Sears, R. Stephen, and Trennepohl, Gary L. "Measuring Portfolio Risk in Options," *Journal of Financial and Quantitative Analysis*, **XVII,** No. 3 (Sept. 1982), pp. 391–410.

114. Sharpe, William. *Investments* (Englewood Cliffs, N.J.: Prentice Hall, 1978.)

115. Shastri, Kuldeep, and Tandon, Kishore. "Valuation of Foreign Currency Options: Some Empirical Tests," *Journal of Financial Quantitative Analysis*, **21,** No. 2 (June 1986), pp. 145–160.

116. Smith, Clifford. "Option Pricing: A Review," *Journal of Financial Economics*, **3,** No. 1/2 (Jan.–Mar. 1976), pp. 3–51.

117. Smith, Keith. "Option Warrant and Portfolio Management," *Financial Analysts Journal*, **24,** No. 3 (May–June 1968), pp. 135–158.

118. Stapleton, R. C., and Subrahmanyam, M. G. "The Valuation of Multivariate Contingent Claims in Discrete Time Models," *Journal of Finance*, **39,** No. 1 (Mar. 1984), pp. 207–228.

119. ———. "The Valuation of Options When Asset Returns Are Generated by a Binomial Process," *The Journal of Finance*, **39,** No. 5 (Dec. 1984), pp. 1525–1540.

120. Sterk, William E. "Test of Two Models for Valuing Call Options on Stocks with Dividends," *The Journal of Finance*, **37,** No. 5 (Dec. 1982), pp. 1229–1238.

121. Stoll, H.R. "The Relationship between Put and Call Option Prices," *The Journal of Finance*, **XXIV,** No. 5 (Dec. 1969), pp. 801–824.

122. ———. "Reply," *The Journal of Finance*, **XXVIII,** No. 1 (Mar. 1973), pp. 185–187.

123. Stone, Albert. "Option Models." Ph.D. Dissertation, New York University, 1969.

124. Stulz, René M. "Options on the Minimum or the Maximum of Two Risky Assets: Analysis and Applications," *Journal of Financial Economics*, **X,** No. 2 (July 1982), pp. 161–186.

125. Vu, Joseph D. "An Empirical Investigation of Calls of Non-Convertible Bonds," *Journal of Financial Economics*, **16** (1986), pp. 235–265.

126. Weinstein, Mark I. "Bond Systematic Risk and the Option Pricing Model," *The Journal of Finance*, **38,** No. 5 (Dec. 1983), pp. 1415–1430.

127. Whaley, Robert E. "Valuation of American Call Options on Dividend-Paying Stocks: Empirical Tests," *Journal of Financial Economics*, **X,** No. 1 (Mar. 1982), pp. 29–58.

128. ———. "Valuation of American Futures Options: Theory and Empirical Tests," *Journal of Finance*, **41,** No. 1 (Mar. 1986), pp. 127–150.

129. Wiggins, James B. "Option Values Under Stochastic Volatility: Theory and Empirical Estimates." *Journal of Financial Economics*, **19** (1987), pp. 351–372.

23

The Valuation and Uses of Financial Futures

Forward contracts are commitments entered into by two parties to exchange a specific amount of money for a particular good or service at a specified future time. While the price is decided upon at the time of the agreement, no cash changes hands at that time. However, either or both parties to the transaction often have to post some funds to guarantee fulfillment of the contract. Forward contracts are a part of everyday life. When one orders a car not in stock from a dealer, one is buying a forward contract for the delivery of a car. The price and description of the car are specified. In this case the delivery date might not be exact. In addition, a deposit is often required to guarantee that the buyer will take delivery and pay the agreed-upon price.

In this chapter we will be primarily concerned with financial futures, though we will say a few words about other types of futures. Financial futures are similar to, but slightly different from, forward contracts. The name "financial future" is very descriptive. "Financial" means that the good to be delivered is a financial instrument (e.g., a stock or bond). The word "future" as opposed to "forward" reflects the fact that on these contracts, profits and losses are computed and settled on a day-to-day basis rather than at the end of the contract. This is called "marking to the market" and we will have more to say about it shortly. In addition, contracts for financial futures are traded on organized exchanges that set standard terms for the contracts.

This chapter is divided into four sections. In the first section we describe in more detail the characteristics of financial futures. In the second section we show how these contracts can be valued. In the third section we discuss how financial futures can be used in the investment process. Finally in the fourth section we briefly discuss commodity futures and commodity funds.

DESCRIPTION OF FINANCIAL FUTURES

A financial futures contract calls for the delivery of either a specific financial instrument or a member of a set of financial instruments at a specific date or during a specific period of time for an agreed-upon price. Financial futures are traded on organized exchanges and have standardized contract terms. The exact terms differ from financial future to financial future. Table 23.1 lists some of the financial instruments on which financial futures are

Table 23.1 The Underlying Instruments with Financial Futures

Debt Instruments	Stock Indexes	Currencies
Treasury Bills	S&P 500 Index	Australian Dollar
Treasury Bonds	S&P 400 MIDCAP	Brazilian Real
Treasury Note (2 Years, 5 Years, 10 Years)	Value-Line Index	British Pound
U.S. Bond Option	Russell Stock Indexes	Canadian Dollar
30-Day Interest Rate	NYSE Composite Index	Deutsche Mark
Canadian BAs—1 Month	Nasdaq-100 Stock Index	Eurodollar
Canadian BAs—3 Month	Mini Value-Line Index	Euroyen
Canadian Govt. Bond—10 Year	Major Markets Index	French Franc
LIBOR—1 Month	FT-SE 100 Index	Japanese Yen
Moody Corp. Bond	FT-SE Eurotrack 100 Index	Mexican Peso
Municipal Bond	CAC 40 Index	Swiss Franc
20-Year GILT	CAC 40 Index Options	U.S. Dollar Index
German Bund	Eurotop 100 Index	3-Month Eurodollar
German Bund Option	Maxi MMI	3-Month Eurodollar Option
Japanese Govt. Bond	Mexican IPC Stock Index	3-Month Sterling
ECU Bond	Nikkei 225 Index	3-Month Sterling Option
ECU Bond Option	Nikkei 225 Option	3-Month Euromark
Notional Bond	Bovespa Stock Index	3-Month Euromark Option
Notional Bond Option	Swiss Market Index Options	3-Month Euroswiss Franc
3-Month PIBOR	Swiss Market Index	3-Month Eurolira
Italian Bond	Australian All Ordinaries Index	3-month ECU
1-Day Interbank Rate		U.S. Dollar, Floating
Swiss Government Bond		U.S. Dollar, Commercial
3-Month Euroyen		5-Year Swiss Franc Rate

Abbreviations: BA; CAC; ECU; FT-SE; GILT; IPC; LIBOR, London Interbank Offered Rate; MIDCAP; MMI, ; Nasdaq, National Association of Security Traders; NYSE, New York Stock Exchange; PIBOR; S&P Standard & Poor's.

being or have been traded. We can categorize these instruments as debt instruments, stock indexes, and foreign currencies.

The terms of a futures contract are always specified in detail. These include

1. The amount and type of asset to be delivered—exactly what asset or set of assets must be delivered and in what quantities.

2. The delivery date or maturity date—the date or period of time at which the exchange is to be consummated.

3. The exact plane and process of delivery.

In addition, the exchanges often place certain restrictions on trading. For example, they set

1. Margin, the amount of funds that must be put up to ensure that each party will follow through with his or her side of the transaction.

2. Limits on the size of price changes that can occur within a trading day and the size of positions that can be taken.

These restrictions are imposed to ensure orderly markets.

Let's start by discussing the profits or losses from trading futures. Then we will return to an examination of some of the attributes of financial futures that affect their performance.

Profits and Losses from Futures Contracts

Futures contracts are traded on organized exchanges and have prices determined at any moment in time just as do stocks and bonds. In the next section of this chapter we will examine how these prices are determined in the marketplace. For now, let us consider the profit and loss that accrues to the parties to a futures contract. The purchaser of a futures contract is said to be long a contract. The purchaser agrees to take delivery of a certain financial instrument at a certain time. The seller is said to be short the contract; the seller agrees to deliver the instrument at a certain time. We will first examine the case of the purchaser of a specific contract.

Let us consider one contract of government bonds for delivery in 10 days. Government bond contracts are traded in amounts of $100,000 face value. Assume the settlement price series is as shown in Table 23.2. The price is per $1000. Thus 66 represents $66,000.

For a moment, let us assume that these prices were on a forward contract, rather than on a futures contract. For a forward contract gains and losses are settled at the maturity date. At the maturity, time 0, the forward price must be the same as the price for immediate delivery since the forward and spot contract each require immediate delivery of the same instrument. The original buyer of the forward contract has the right (obligation) to buy the bond at $66. At maturity, bonds cost $68. The profit to the buyer of the contract is $2 times the $1000, or $2000. Correspondingly, the seller of the contract is selling a bond at $66 when the market price is $68. This is a loss of $2 times $1000, or $2000.

Note that the profit to the purchaser is equal to the loss of the seller. Forwards and futures are zero-sum games; the profits (or loss) of the purchaser plus the loss (or profit) to the seller equals zero.

The cash flow pattern from the viewpoint of a buyer or seller of a futures contract is different from and more complex than the cash flow pattern from a forward contract. This is because, as mentioned earlier, futures contracts are marked to the market on a daily basis. At the close of each trading day, the gain or loss from the price change that occurred over that day is immediately credited or debited to the accounts of the individuals who are long or short. Furthermore, all contracts are rewritten so that the price at which parties are obliged to buy and sell the financial instrument is the price of the future at the close of the

Table 23.2   Cash Flows on a Forward and Futures Contract

Day	Settlement Price[a]	Cash Flow If Long 1 Forward	Cash Flow If Short 1 Forward	Cash Flow If Long 1 Future	Cash Flow If Short 1 Future
−9	66				
−8	67	0	0	+1000	−1000
−7	68	0	0	+1000	−1000
−6	65	0	0	−3000	+3000
−5	64	0	0	−1000	+1000
−4	66	0	0	+2000	−2000
−3	64	0	0	−2000	+2000
−2	68	0	0	+4000	−4000
−1	67	0	0	−1000	+1000
0	68	+2000	−2000	+1000	−1000
Total Cash Flow		+2000	−2000	+2000	−2000

[a]Prices are quoted in thousands of dollars to the nearest 1/32 of a thousandth.

day. This repricing is referred to as "marking to the market," and the price used to mark to the market is called the settlement price. The aggregate profit or loss from the contract over the life of the contract would be the same whether it is a forward or a futures contract, namely, $2000, but the timing of the cash flows is very different.

As just discussed, the person who shorted (wrote) a forward contract with the price behavior displayed in Table 23.2 would have one cash flow of −$2000 on day 0. The person who wrote a futures contract would have a much more complex pattern. On day −8, the futures price is $67. So the writer of the futures contract would then be debited by $1000 on day −8. The writer of the futures contract would then be considered to have a contract at $67. The contract is marked to the market. On day −7, futures go to $68. Since the contract is implicitly at $67, the loss is again $1000. The writer will have the account debited by $1000 and the price of the contract will be specified at $68. Thus the writer of the futures contract has the series of intermediate cash flows shown in Table 23.2. If the reinvestment rate were zero, an investor wouldn't care whether a future or forward contract was held. However, the potential of receiving cash or having to come up with cash on a daily basis makes futures contracts different from forward contracts.

Some Important Attributes of Futures Contracts

In this section we discuss three aspects of financial futures that can impact their performances. These are margin, limits, and delivery.

Margin   To purchase or sell a future is actually to enter into a promise to take a future course of action with associated cash flows over time. This is not a traditional investment because, at the time a futures position is bought or sold, no cash changes hands between the two parties. However, in order to ensure that the parties can fulfill their obligation, an initial margin or good faith deposit must be made with the broker. The size and terms of the good faith deposit vary from future to future. They are generally related to the size of the contract and the variability in the daily value of the contract. Relating to daily variability makes sense since the purpose of the good faith deposit is to see that contracts are fulfilled and that contracts are adjusted for profits or losses (marking to the market) on a daily basis. Margins for futures are small relative to other types of markets. For example, the initial margin needed to buy a future on 1 million dollars face value of Treasury bills (T-bills) is $1000. Furthermore, the margin can be put up in the form of earning assets such as T-bills or letters of credit. Nowadays, every futures market has a maintenance margin level, usually 75–80% of the initial margin level. If margin drops below the maintenance level due to marking of the market, then the investor must come up with additional funds to bring the account back to the original margin level. The cash flows needed to do so are called variation margin, and this added margin must be put up in the form of cash. If the investor doesn't deposit the added margin, the broker can liquidate the position at the going market price. The investor is liable for any shortfall that occurs when his portfolio is liquidated.

Limits   Another aspect of futures markets that should be discussed is the existence of limits. Most financial futures markets have limits on the size of the position any investor can take. Of more interest is that they have limits on the size of the price change that is allowed to take place during any day. For example, price moves on the one million dollar 90-day T-bill contract are limited to $1500 per day. When the price moves up or down by that amount during a day, trading essentially stops. What this can mean (and in fact has meant in the futures market for silver among others) is that a position can't be closed out during a period of time at any price. There have been periods of time where price has moved down by the limit for a number of days in a row and no one has traded at that price. Thus for a number of days it was literally impossible to trade on organized exchanges. While these limits were imposed to ensure orderly markets, they constitute an added risk to investing in futures markets.

Delivery   The delivery options of financial futures contracts are well specified. However, the person who has shorted the future often has several options as to which of several financial instruments to deliver and sometimes an option on exactly what day to deliver. For example, in dealing with the futures on Treasury bonds, the investor who has shorted such a future can deliver any government bond with more than a 15-year maturity and more than 15 years to first call. There are many bonds in the market at any time that fit the description and hence can be delivered. The amount of any bond that must be delivered to satisfy the contract is well specified. A set of "conversion factors" has been determined to ensure that a delivered bond would have the same yield to maturity or, if callable, yield to first call as an 8% coupon bond. The attempt was to make a large number of bonds equivalent for delivery. However, over most periods of time, these bonds are not equivalent. Generally, at any point in time there is a bond that is "cheapest" to deliver. This option to deliver any bond, along with the option to deliver at any point over a short period of time, adds value to the position of the future seller and correspondingly subtracts it from the value of the buyer. However, the seller always wants to deliver the cheapest bond. This bond has been stable over long periods of time. Thus the reader should not overemphasize the value of the option.

Not all financial futures are settled by delivery of an asset. Some (e.g., stock index futures) are always settled for cash. In this case, the final settlement price of the futures contract is set equal to the market price of the underlying assets on the last trading day of the contract.

Delivery of an asset rarely takes place, even for those contracts that are theoretically settled by delivery of an asset. Almost all futures positions are settled by an offsetting trade rather than by delivery. For example, a buyer of a June Treasury bond contract can close out that position at any time by selling a June Treasury bond contract. Less than 1% of all futures contracts traded are settled by delivery of the underlying asset.

VALUATION OF FINANCIAL FUTURES

The valuation of financial futures is greatly simplified by understanding the relationship between futures prices and the current (or spot) price of the underlying financial instrument. As we will show, a particular relationship must exist, for if it fails to hold, then an immediate riskless profit could be made. Since there are many individuals continuously looking for opportunities to profit from just such a failure, these basic relationships are reasonably descriptive of real markets. We will examine the relationship between spot and future prices for each of the major financial futures. All of the pricing relationships are derived from the ability to hold a financial instrument directly or to create a second instrument with almost identical cash flows by buying or selling futures contracts.

Treasury Bill Futures

Consider an investor who wants to hold a 151-day T-bill. The investor could do so in either of two ways. First, the investor could purchase it directly by simply buying the 151-day T-bill. Alternatively, the investor could purchase it indirectly. The investor could buy a forward contract on a 91-day T-bill for delivery in 60 days. Simultaneously, the investor could purchase a 60-day T-bill that matures for an amount exactly sufficient to take delivery of the forward contract. As we will show below, the resulting cash flows are identical. Both investments involve an immediate cash outlay and an inflow of the same size in 151 days. Since the future cash flows are the same, the price (initial cash flow) must be the same. Let's look at the two ways to purchase a 151-day T-bill in more detail.

1. *Directly.* Buy a 151-day Treasury bill at a cost of P.
2. *Indirectly.* Buy a forward contract that will lead to delivery in 60 days of a 91-day T-bill. Let's define F as the price the holder of a forward contract must pay to take delivery of bills in 60 days. Buy a 60-day T-bill that will have a value equal to F at the delivery date. This will cost $F/(1 + R)$, where R is the rate of interest on a 60-day T-bill.

The cash flows for these two strategies are shown in Table 23.3. Both of these strategies produce identical future cash flows (equivalent to that of holding a 151-day instrument). Since they have identical cash flows, they should have the same cost. Thus

$$F/(1+R) = P \qquad (23.1)$$

That two identical instruments should sell at the same price is known as the "law of one price."

If the prior relationship does not hold, then there are profit opportunities. The presence of such profit opportunities should lead reasonably alert investors to try to exploit them and in the process cause the relationship to hold. There are three types of profit opportunities that should force Equation (23.1) to be an equality.

Buy the Cheapest Instrument   The real 151-day T-bill and the homemade 151-day T-bill are identical instruments. Anyone who wished to hold a 151-day instrument should buy the least expensive of the two. This will bid up the price of the cheaper and cause the more expensive to decrease in price. To buy either of the two, the investor would incur transaction costs. If there are a sufficient number of investors with a desire to buy a 151-day instrument, the return of the two instruments could be affected only by the difference in transaction costs between the direct and the indirect purchase of a T-bill, and these should be exceedingly small. Thus Equation (23.1) should be extremely accurate.

Swap   Assume that the homemade 151-day T-bill is cheaper than the traded bill. In this case, anyone holding the 151-day T-bill would earn an immediate profit equal to the difference in their prices less transaction costs by selling the 151-day T-bill and purchasing the homemade 151-day T-bill. Such a trade will involve transaction costs on the purchase and on the sale. If the return differential is greater than two transaction costs, an alert

Table 23.3   Cash Flows on T-bill and Homemade T-bill Contract

Action	0	60	151
Direct			
Buy 151-day T-bill	P_0		1,000,000
Indirect			
Buy forward contract and take delivery		$-F$	1,000,000
Buy 60-day T-bill	$F/(1 + R)$	$+F$	
Sum	$F/(1 + R)$	0	1,000,000

investor will undertake the swap. This should force Equation (23.1) to be close to an equality. Since transaction costs in the T-bill and futures markets are very small, the equality should be very closely approximated.

Pure Arbitrage   The final force causing the law of one price to hold is pure arbitrage. Arbitrage involves selling short the more expensive instrument and using the proceeds of the sale to purchase the cheaper. Since subsequent cash flows are identical, this involves an immediate profit. The transaction costs are on the purchase and sale. In addition, the short seller usually incurs a $\frac{1}{2}$ of 1% cost on the short position. This last force causing the law of one price to hold is the most powerful in the sense that there are a large number of alert arbitrageurs prepared to take advantage of any discrepancies in the market. At the same time, since transaction costs are higher, the difference between a 151-day T-bill and a homemade 151-day T-bill can be larger without it paying to eliminate the differences.

Which of these three profit opportunities sets prices is still an open question. However, any of them should cause the returns of the 151-day T-bill and the homemade 151-day T-bill to be close and Equation (23.1) to be a reasonable equation for pricing forward Treasury bills.

There are several simplifications in our analysis. We used a forward contract in our discussion. However, futures contracts are the contracts that are available to most investors. The reason we used forward contracts was to avoid the intermediate cash flows associated with marking futures contracts to the market. Futures contracts, of course, involve marking to the market. Thus the homemade 151-day T-bill has intermediate cash flows. However, marking to the market does not have much of an impact for T-bill futures. Elton, Gruber, and Rentzler [17] found that marking to the market affected cash flows on a million dollar T-bill position by an average of only $4. A difference in cash flows due to marking to the market in the range of plus or minus ($31) occurred 75% of the time. To put these numbers in context, recall that T-bill futures are sold in million-dollar denominations, so that over 60 days at 9% interest the total cash flow is close to $15,000. Thus the effect of marking to the market is trivial and Treasury bill futures can be sensibly treated as if they were forwards. Elton, Gruber, and Rentzler [17] did an extensive analysis of the difference in returns of the actual bill and homemade bill. There were differences and any strategy that involves selling futures generally offered the higher return. While this is evidence that the law of one price does not hold exactly, and the market is not perfectly efficient, the differences were quite small.

Treasury Bond Futures

Treasury bills are government debt of one year or less to maturity. In addition, they are pure discount instruments with no intermediate cash flows. Treasury bills sell for less than their value at maturity. The increase in value from the time of the sale to the maturity provides the return to the investor. Treasury bonds, in contrast, have original maturities longer than one year and provide a periodic coupon payment as well as potential capital appreciation or loss. A futures market exists for Treasury bonds that have at least 15 years to maturity and are either noncallable or if callable are not callable for at least 15 years. There are a large number of different government bonds that meet these criteria, and any of them can be delivered to settle a Treasury bond futures contract. The standard bond to be delivered is an 8% coupon bond. Conversion factors have been computed for bonds with different coupon rates. Bonds with a different coupon are worth some fraction (for higher coupon bonds, a fraction greater than one) of the standard 8% bond. When the conversion factors were created, the hope was that there would be many different issues that would be equivalent and could be delivered. In practice there is generally a single bond that is cheapest to deliver and will be delivered if actual delivery takes place. This particular issue that is cheapest to deliver is fairly stable over time. Thus the bond that would be potentially delivered is fairly well known at the time the futures contract is written. There are two ways an investor who wished to purchase a government bond could do so:

1. *Purchase directly.* The investor purchases the bond at a current spot price, which can be represented as *P*.

2. *Purchase with delay.* The investor buys a Treasury bond future with a delivery price of *F* and simultaneously buys a T-bill with a face value of *F* that matures at the delivery date on the futures contract. The cost of the T-bill is $F/(1 + R)$, where *R* is the T-bill rate for the time until the future is delivered.

If the bond does not pay interest before the delivery of the future, these are equivalent positions, and if the law of one price holds, they should have the same cost. Thus,

$$F/(1+R) = P \tag{23.2}$$

If the Treasury bond has an interest payment before the delivery date, then the price of direct purchase should be reduced by the present value of this payment. If *I* is the payment and *PV(I)* is the present value of the payment, then the law of one price implies

$$F/(1+R) = P - PV(I) \tag{23.3}$$

Once again we are ignoring marking to the market. In addition, the foregoing analysis assumes we know which bond will be delivered. Historically, the bond that will be delivered, the so-called cheapest deliverable instrument, has remained stable over long periods of time, so that this assumption holds reasonably well in practice. In addition, all of the earlier discussion on what causes the law of one price to hold still follows. Thus Equation (23.2), while a very good estimate of the futures value, should not be expected to hold exactly.

There are other debt instruments with futures markets available. At the time this chapter was written, futures existed on Government National Mortgage Association (GNMAs) (mortgage pools with a government guarantee of interest), bank certificates of deposit (CDs) (short-term bank debt), and Treasury notes (intermediate-term government debt). Futures markets are developing rapidly, and we expect that futures will become available on additional instruments over time. The reader should be able to modify the preceding analysis to value these alternative instruments.

Stock Index Futures

Futures exist on a number of stock market indexes such as the Standard & Poor's (S&P) 500 Index, the S&P 100 Index, the Value Line Index, and the New York Stock Exchange (NYSE) Composite Index. The NYSE Composite is a value-weighted index of all the stocks on the New York Stock Exchange. Its return is equivalent to the capital appreciation on a portfolio of all stocks listed on the New York Stock Exchange where the weights in the portfolio are proportional to the market value of the stock (number of shares times price per share). The S&P 100 and 500, as the names imply, have 100 or 500 firms in the index, and these are generally the largest firms on the NYSE. They are also value-weighted indexes. The Value Line Index has a peculiar construction and, given its unimportance in the futures market, will not be discussed further here. The introduction of stock index futures was delayed by the lack of deliverable instruments. What facilitated their introduction was the acceptance of a cash settlement. For most stock index futures, the future is marked to the spot when the future expires. Cash is then transferred at that point in time; no instrument is ever delivered. While there are lots of ways to arrive at the value of stock futures, the easiest way is to assume that an investor looks at the following alternatives: buy an index fund leveraging the position so that the expected cash flow prior to a particular date is zero; or buy T-bills and futures so the same purchase of the index fund is accomplished at maturity.

1. *Direct purchase of an index fund, taking action to eliminate intermediate cash flows.* Assume the index fund can be bought for P dollars and the expected dividend on this amount of the fund is D. Let $PV(D)$ be the present value of the expected value of the future dividend stream. Borrow enough money so that the debt is repaid with the dividend. That is, borrow $PV(D)$ and use these borrowed funds to pay for part of the index fund. Thus the amount of cash that must be put up is $P - PV(D)$.

2. *Indirect purchase.* Buy futures that will represent the same amount of the index fund for an amount of money, F, and simultaneously buy a T-bill that will mature at a value F. The T-bill costs $F/(1 + R)$. Since the amount of the index fund purchased is the same, and since the dividend flows are used to repay the borrowing, the cost must be the same or:

$$F/(1 + R) = P - PV(D)$$

or

$$F = P\left[(1 + R) - \frac{PV(D)}{P}(1 + R)\right] \tag{23.4}$$

There are arbitrageurs who continually monitor this relationship and take action if it is out of line. Who are the arbitrageurs? One group is index fund managers. Brokerage firms continually monitor the relationship between stock index values and stock index futures prices. When the futures are cheap, they offer to buy a part of an index fund and to sell the fund T-bills and futures. Since the stock trading is not based on a belief that individual shares are mispriced, the brokerage firm believes that the shares can be rapidly resold and thus can offer very low transaction costs; $\frac{1}{8}$ of a dollar is not unusual. Likewise, if futures become overpriced, the reverse trade is made. In terms of our earlier discussion of how the law of one price comes about, this is considered a swap. In addition, there are arbitrageurs in the market who have constructed a small portfolio that is highly correlated with the index. This portfolio is bought or sold short depending on the value of Equation (23.4) with a corresponding action taken in the futures market.

Figure 23.1 was prepared for the book by traders at Kidder Peabody. It shows the difference in the theoretical value of the stock index future compared to the actual value of the index. The theoretical value depends on the traders' forecast of dividends. During this time period, futures on average were fairly valued. However, over time, futures have been systematically underpriced. At least one index fund has taken advantage of this relative cheapness and has consistently been invested in T-bills and futures. The performance of this fund has been superior to standard index funds, indicating that apparent inefficiencies are truly inefficiencies and can be used to earn an excess return.

Before leaving this section, it is appropriate to once again emphasize the factors that might cause the formula not to fit exactly. The formula depends on a forecast of dividends. However, these are dividends on an index, so they are relatively easy to forecast. Nevertheless, there is some small amount of risk in dividend forecasts and this could intro-

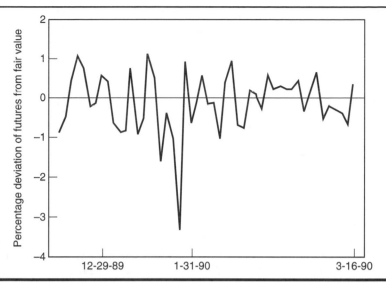

Figure 23.1   The premium of the S&P futures contract over time. *Source*: Goggin, Daniel B. Jr., and Kiou, Michael Co., "Daily Deviation of Basis from Co. Fair Value," Kidder Peabody and Company, Inc., May 2, 1990.

duce some added risks when attempting to duplicate the performance of an index fund with futures. The formula also ignores any effect of marking to the market. In the case of stock index futures, and insofar as a stock index is a proxy for a market portfolio in a capital asset pricing model (CAPM) sense, these flows may be correlated with the market and consequently may introduce systematic risk. We will now turn to a discussion of foreign currency futures.

Foreign Currency Futures

Futures exist on the major currencies. Table 23.1 shows the exact currencies for which futures contracts exist. Once again two equivalent instruments can be created that allow the valuation of the futures contract. The two equivalent instruments in this case are riskless domestic debt and riskless foreign debt. Foreign riskless debt is held as follows: convert dollars to a foreign currency, for example pounds. Invest the money in the foreign riskless debt. Guarantee the rate of conversion back to dollars with financial futures. This is accomplished by writing a futures contract converting pounds to dollars at the maturity of the foreign T-bill for an amount equal to the maturity value of the T-bill. Since the conversion to dollars is at a known rate, the foreign investment is riskless. Futures are quoted in number of dollars per pound. Let S be the initial number of dollars that can be bought with one pound. The initial conversion is to convert dollars to pounds. To convert dollars to pounds we use one over the rate or $1/S$. For example, if the rate is $2 per 1£, one dollar is worth half a pound (1/2). Finally let F be the futures price of one pound and R^B be the foreign (British) riskless rate. Consider an investment in British riskless debt. Then the number of pounds bought per dollar invested is $1/S$. The value of the debt at maturity is $(1 + R^B)/S$. Finally the value at the maturity in dollars is

$$\frac{\left(1 + R^B\right)}{S} F$$

and the return is

$$\left[\frac{\left(1+R^B\right)}{S} F \right] - 1$$

If the law of one price holds, all riskless debt should have the same return. If R^D is the rate of return on domestic debt then

$$R^D = \left[\left(1+R^B\right)F/S\right] - 1$$

or

$$F = \left[\left(1+R^D\right)/\left(1+R^B\right)\right]S \qquad (23.5)$$

Equation (23.5) is known as interest rate parity. Empirically, interest rate parity seems to hold fairly well. The risk element besides marking to the market is a fear of exchange controls. Governments can and do restrict conversion from one currency to another. In addition, governments can tax the returns to foreign investors. This affects the relative return and can be one element of risk insofar as a change in the tax law can occur during the time of the hedge.

In this section, we have discussed the valuation formula for commonly traded financial futures. The same principles should hold for the financial futures we have not discussed here.

THE USES OF FINANCIAL FUTURES

The growth in financial futures trading has been astronomic in recent years. For example, the dollar volume of shares commanded by futures contracts traded on the S&P index on an average day exceeds the dollar volume of direct trading in these shares. The major markets for financial futures are liquid and involve low transaction costs. Transaction costs are only a fraction of those involved in trading the underlying assets commanded by futures contracts. The combination of liquidity with low transaction costs has meant that there are a large variety of uses for financial futures contracts. We will attempt to review only a few of them here. We find it helpful to divide the uses to which financial futures can be put into three categories: hedging, investment management, and investment products. There is overlap between these categories, but they do serve as a useful characterization.

Hedging

The use of financial futures as a hedging mechanism has received the most attention in the financial literature. Hedging refers to the use of financial futures to reduce a type of risk to which the buyer or seller is subject. For example, the corporation about to sell a long-term issue of bonds (or the underwriter of such an issue) can eliminate most of the risk of interest rate movements by selling a future on a like amount of long-term government bonds. By doing so the corporation in essence locks in the current interest rate. If interest rates go up, the corporation will have to pay a higher interest rate to sell its bonds, but it will find that the value of its short position in futures has gone up by a similar amount. Unfortunately, this may not be an exact dollar-for-dollar movement because of basis risk. Basis risk is the risk that the spot price of the firm's corporate bonds and the futures price of government bonds do not move exactly alike. Corporate bonds and government bonds do move in similar but not identical ways over time. For example, when interest rates go up, the price of both long-term government bonds and long-term corporate bonds go down, but the amounts by which they go down need not be exactly the same because the spread in rates between the two instruments can change. However, the divergence of these rates over time is very small relative to the effect on the prices of either instrument as the level of rates changes.

As another example of hedging, consider a corporate treasurer who expects to receive a large sum of money in three months to invest in Treasury bills. By buying T-bill futures now, he or she can lock up a known rate on T-bills. In fact, if the treasurer takes delivery, the return will be certain.

Finally, consider an investor due to retire who is worried about the value of that portion of the pension fund that is invested in common stocks. By selling futures on a widely diversified portfolio like the S&P index, the investor can hedge away the risk that the stock market will go up or down between now and the time of retirement.

Changing Investment Policy

Financial futures have transaction costs that are dramatically less than those on stocks and bonds. This implies that they are likely to be the preferred way to change the risk exposure of individual assets or categories of assets. In addition, the use of financial futures allows a direct measure of the value added or subtracted by the policy change. Finally, using financial futures allows a wider choice of assets because of an ability to change risk exposure without having to buy and sell the individual assets in the portfolio. The ideas just presented need elaboration. The elaboration is best done with a few examples.

Changing the Market Exposure of a Stock Portfolio Consider a manager of a mutual fund with a particular exposure to changes in market level. Assume for a moment that the Beta on the portfolio is 1.5. Thus a 1% move in the market should be expected to lead to a 1.5% change in the rate of return on the portfolio. Assume further that the manager is pessimistic about the future course of the market and wishes to reduce the exposure. Without financial futures the manager would sell high Beta stocks and purchase lower Beta stocks or T-bills with the proceeds. With financial futures the Beta on the portfolio can be reduced in an alternative manner. If the manager sells stock index futures, the combination of the existing portfolio and the stock index futures will have a reduced Beta. By selling sufficient stock index futures, the manager can reduce the Beta to any level desired. Conversely, if the manager wished to increase the Beta on the portfolio, financial futures could be purchased.

There are a number of advantages in using futures to control the risk exposure of the portfolio to market fluctuations. First, transaction costs on futures are dramatically lower than transaction costs of selling stock and purchasing T-bills, or of using stock swaps to change the portfolio Beta. Second, if the firm feels that it has the ability to select individual stock issues, then changing the market exposure by selling stock and purchasing T-bills reduces the contribution of selection ability to the performance on the overall portfolio.

For example, if a manager who felt that the return on a particular stock portfolio would be 1% above equilibrium reduced its market exposure by being half in T-bills, the return on the full portfolio should be $\frac{1}{2}$ of 1% above equilibrium. By contrast, if futures were used to control risk exposure, the full 1% would generally be earned on the portfolio. Likewise, if the manager controls market risk exposure on the overall portfolio by constraining the Beta to be a particular level, then the performance should be reduced if there is forecasting ability, because less promising stocks must be selected in order to maintain a promised risk level. The final advantage of using futures is that they allow a direct evaluation of timing. Managers often try to vary their market risk exposure because of a belief in their ability to anticipate market moves. If the manager uses futures to time, then profits and losses on the futures position are a direct measure of the manager's timing ability. The use of futures separates performance due to timing from performance due to selection.

Changing Interest Rate Exposure on Bonds   In prior chapters we discussed the concept of bond duration. Bond duration is a measure of the sensitivity of a bond portfolio to changes in interest rates. Most bond managers are timers. They forecast the future course of interest rates. If they feel rates will rise more than they had previously anticipated, they shorten the maturity of their portfolio. If they feel rates will fall more than they had anticipated, then the maturity will be lengthened. Transaction costs across bonds can vary dramatically. The transaction costs of very liquid government bonds are substantially less than those of thinly traded government or corporate bonds. Because of this, timers generally hold very liquid governments as a large part of their portfolio. Thus, timers are giving up the greater expected return of corporates and less liquid governments in order to have lower transaction costs.

Futures can accomplish the same purpose without constraining the investor to holding lower return securities. The duration on a portfolio can be changed by buying or selling futures. If the manager wishes to shorten the duration, then futures are sold. For example, consider the issuance of a one-year future on a Treasury bond when Treasury bonds are held in the portfolio. The Treasury bond could be delivered against the future in a year. Thus the maturity of the bond has switched from long term to one year with a corresponding change in the duration. If the manager wishes to lengthen the maturity of the portfolio, then futures are bought.

There are a number of advantages in using futures to change interest rate exposure. These are the same reasons discussed earlier in using stock index futures. However, they bear repeating here. First, the transaction costs are substantially less. Second, using futures allows the manager to make the selection decision independent of the duration decision. Thus if the manager feels that certain sectors or bonds are especially attractive, these bonds can be selected even if they are illiquid and can be sold only with large transaction costs. Even if the manager does not profess to have selection ability, bonds that are illiquid but promise higher returns (such as corporates) can be selected. The reader should note that the manager can be exposed to basis risk by using futures on instruments that differ from those held in the portfolio to change duration. However, the impact on returns due to instrument types that are not perfectly matched should be small compared to the impact of interest rate changes on portfolios of different durations. Finally, profits and losses on the futures are a direct measure of the timing ability and the value added by the timing ability, if any exists. Many managers profess to have timing ability, but it is difficult to measure. Using futures gives a direct measure.

Before leaving this section one other issue will be briefly discussed. When interest rates were extremely high, the duration on even long-term bonds was fairly short. The problem was that the liabilities of many institutions (e.g., pension funds) had longer durations than even the longest maturity bond. Thus immunization, the matching of the duration on assets and liabilities, was infeasible using bonds alone. Futures can be used to change duration. A mixture of bonds and futures could be constructed with an arbitrarily long duration. Thus in periods of higher interest rates, employing futures was the only way that immunization was possible for many liabilities.

Changing the Bond–Stock Mix   Consider a manager of a balanced fund. One of the decisions that must be made is the relative exposure to the stock market and to the bond market. If the manager decides that the exposure to the stock market should be increased, it should be obvious from the prior sections that this change can be accomplished with futures. Purchasing stock index futures will increase the Beta on the stock portfolio and increase the stock market exposure. Selling bond futures decreases the duration and reduces the exposure to interest rate changes. All of the advantages of futures discussed in prior sections still hold for this use of futures. In particular, the use of futures lowers transaction costs, allows security selection to be independent of the market exposure decision, and gives an unambiguous measure of timing ability.

Creating New Products

Futures have been used to create products that could not exist or were inordinately expensive before futures existed. One such product is an Alpha fund. The idea behind such a fund is to capture the stock selection ability of a set of analysts without being subject to market risks. The implementation of the concept simply involves selling enough futures on the S&P index so that the sum of the Betas on the futures and the fund's stock portfolio equals zero. Thus the fund has a Beta of zero. Assume that the stock portion of the fund has a Beta of one. Then the amount of futures to be written equals the value of the fund. From an earlier section we know that the futures price is the spot price adjusted up by the risk-free rate and down by the dividend rate. If the stock portfolio has the same dividend rate as the S&P index, its dividend rate will match the minus dividend term in the equation valuing futures. Thus the return on the fund should be equal to the return on T-bills plus any Alpha or greater than equilibrium return earned on its stock portfolio. Such funds are called Alpha funds.

A second set of products involving futures stems from the fact that futures can be used to (almost) replicate puts and calls as well as to replicate stocks and bonds. In the section of this chapter on pricing, we have shown how futures are priced by their ability to replicate existing financial instruments. Holding T-bills and buying futures on the S&P index is almost the same as investing in the S&P index.[1] Similarly, selling T-bills and selling futures on the S&P index is almost the same as shorting the S&P index.

We showed in previous chapters that puts and calls can be replicated by dynamically changing the mix of instruments in a portfolio. For example, a put on a stock could be replicated by buying T-bills and shorting the stock. But now we know that shorting the stock can be replicated by borrowing and selling futures on the stock. Thus the put or call may be replicated by using futures in combination with lending and borrowing. This is particularly important in artificial puts (portfolio insurance) constructed through dynamic portfolio rebalancing. This rebalancing can take place at a much lower cost using futures than it can through changing the bond–stock mix. This has led to the creation of products using futures that attempt to replicate holding:

1.   T-bills plus calls on long-term bonds.

2.   T-bills plus calls on stocks.

3.   Long-term bonds or bond portfolios plus puts on these bonds.

4.   Stocks or stock portfolios plus puts on these stocks.

---

[1]The word *almost* is used because of the effect of marking to the market and the uncertainty of the dividend stream on stocks.

In closing we should mention that just as a position in futures plus a position in the underlying instrument plus T-bills can be used to replicate calls and/or puts, calls and/or puts can be used in combination with a position in the underlying instruments to replicate futures.

NONFINANCIAL FUTURES AND COMMODITY FUNDS

This chapter is primarily concerned with a discussion of financial futures. Before closing, though, we should mention that there are a tremendous number of nonfinancial commodity futures. Futures exist on a range of additional assets, from those that are thought of as being close to financial assets like silver and gold to those that are almost never thought of as financial futures like hog bellies. In the late 1960s and 1970s, with the tremendous increase in inflation in the American economy, interest grew in both commodity futures and financial futures as hedges against inflation. Actually, returns on commodity futures should reflect only unanticipated inflation as anticipated inflation should already be incorporated in the pricing of the commodity futures. One has to be cautious about interpreting the returns on commodity futures. Commodity futures are used heavily to hedge away the risk faced by producers and manufacturers of products; hence supply, demand, and prices, are heavily affected by end product demand and prices. Roll [40] found that orange juice futures prices were affected by and predictive of weather. In addition, since price is affected by unanticipated inflation rather than inflation itself, to decide on the timing of purchases of futures one has to predict unanticipated inflation. In other words one has to be a better predictor of inflation than the aggregate of investors (the market). Finally, there is the problem of computing a rate of return on a position in futures. Recall that no money changes hands when futures are bought or sold. Only a margin is posted and that can often be posted in the form of T-bills. Very little evidence exists on the rate of return on futures investing. That which does exist makes arbitrary assumptions about the way to compute rates of return and studies a period of time when inflation went from close to zero to over 10%. While it is worthwhile examining these results, one should be somewhat cautious about generalizing from them. Bodie [6] and Bodie and Rosansky [7] have studied the performance of an equally weighted portfolio of 23 commodity futures during the period of 1950 through the 1980s. Their data show that over the period the return and risk characteristics of financial futures were very close to that of the S&P 500, but because of a negative correlation between stocks and futures, a portfolio composed of long positions in commodity futures should be included in an investor's optimum portfolio.

There is another approach to the problem of the return on futures and that is to study the performance of publicly traded commodity funds. That is the subject to which we now turn.

In the 1980s, there has been an explosion of public commodity funds. These funds are similar to mutual funds in the sense that investors buy shares and the proceeds are pooled and managed by a professional manager. Commodity funds invest in financial futures as well as commodity futures. Managers can and will go short as well as long. Thus commodity fund managers are trying actively to guess the course of futures prices rather than taking a passive strategy. Table 23.4 shows the return characteristics of these funds relative to some standard market indexes. The S&P index and the Shearson index can be considered to be, respectively, the return on an index fund of stocks and the return on an index fund of bonds.

The striking feature of this table is the high variability of the return. The standard deviation of the commodity funds is $2\frac{1}{2}$ to 4 times that of either bond funds or stock funds. The correlation coefficient has been estimated as 0.12 between commodity funds and common equity and -0.03 with the Shearson bond index (see Elton, Gruber, and Rentzler [18]).

Table 23.4   Returns and Risk of Different Investments, 1980–1988

Instrument	Average Annual Returns	Standard Deviation of Monthly Returns
Common stocks	14.88%	4.91%
Shearson bond index	11.40%	2.38%
Commodity funds	2.26%	10.4%

Source: Elton, Gruber, and Rentzler [20].

Given the low realized returns and the high standard deviation of returns on these funds, evidence in this period indicates that an average commodity fund should not be added to a stock or bond portfolio despite the low correlation. Past return may not be predictive of future returns but the characteristics shown in Table 23.4 would suggest that commodity funds are not useful additions to a bond or stock portfolios.

QUESTIONS AND PROBLEMS

1. Given the following data, what is the arbitrage with no transaction costs? What is the size of the transaction costs necessary to negate the arbitrage?

A.	S&P 6-month futures contract	$200
B.	S&P current value	$190
C.	6-month interest rate	6%
D.	Present value of dividends on stocks in S&P index over 6 months	$4

2. Assume that General Mills, a user of wheat, and wheat farmers, have the same distributional assumptions about future wheat prices. Does a futures contract make economic sense from both points of view? If yes, why?

3. The spot rate (current rate) for Japanese yen is 120 yen to the dollar, whereas the one-year futures rate is 115. If one-year interest rates in Japan are 4%, what is the implied one-year interest rate in the United States assuming interest rate parity?

4. Assume you believe that the yield curve will flatten and therefore the spread between long and short rates will narrow. Furthermore assume others do not share this belief. What action in the futures market should you take to capitalize on your beliefs?

5. Assume you are a bond portfolio manager with 100 million of 20-year corporates. Further assume you wish to hold one-year corporates. Assuming for the moment the availability of any future you wish, design a strategy using futures to accomplish this switch. How would this be accomplished using futures that are traded? What is the additional risk?

6. As a treasurer of the company you wish to issue 40 million of 10-year bonds. You believe it will take three months before the issue can be floated and that interest rates will rise. You wish to lock in today's rates. Discuss how this can be done using futures contracts.

BIBLIOGRAPHY

1. Adler, Michael, and Detemple, Jerome B. "On the Optimal Hedge of a Non-traded Cash Position," *Journal of Finance*, **43**, No. 1 (Mar. 1988), pp. 143–153.

2. Aggarwal, Raj, and Sundaraghavan, P.S. "Efficiency of the Silver Futures Market," *Journal of Business Finance*, **11,** No. 1 (Mar. 1987), pp. 49–64.

3. Anderson, Ronald W., and Danthine, Jean-Pierre. "Hedging and Joint Production: Theory and Illustrations," *The Journal of Finance*, **35,** No. 2 (May 1980), pp. 487–497.

4. Bernard, Victor L., and Frecka, Thomas J. "Commodity Contracts and Common Stocks as Hedges Against Relative Consumer Price Risk," *The Journal of Financial and Quantitative Analysis*, **22,** No. 2 (June 1987), pp. 169–188.

5. Black, Fischer. "The Pricing of Commodity Contracts," *Journal of Financial Economics* (Jan.–Mar. 1976), pp. 167–179.

6. Bodie, Ziv. "Commodity Futures as a Hedge Against Inflation," *The Journal of Portfolio Management* (Spring 1983), pp. 12–17.

7. Bodie, Ziv, and Rosansky, Victor. "Risk and Return in Commodity Futures," *Financial Analysts Journal* (May 1980).

8. Breeden, Douglas T. "Consumption Risk in Futures Markets," *The Journal of Finance*, **35,** No. 2 (May 1980), pp. 503–520.

9. Capozza, Dennis, and Cornell, Bradford. "Treasury Bill Pricing in the Spot and Futures Markets," *Review of Economics and Statistics* (Nov. 1979).

10. Chang, Eric C. "Returns on Speculators and the Theory of Normal Backwardation," *The Journal of Finance*, **40,** No. 1 (Mar. 1985), pp. 193–208.

11. Cornell, Bradford. "Taxes and the Pricing of Treasury Bill Futures Contracts: A Note," *The Journal of Finance*, **36,** No. 5 (Dec. 1981), pp. 1169–1176.

12. Cornell, Bradford, and French, Kenneth R. "Taxes and the Pricing of Stock Index Futures," *The Journal of Finance*, **38,** No. 3 (June 1983), pp. 675–694.

13. Cornell, Bradford, and Reinganum, Marc R. "Forward and Future Prices: Evidence from the Foreign Exchange Markets," *The Journal of Finance*, **36,** No. 5 (Dec. 1981), pp. 1035–1046.

14. Cox, John C., Ingersoll, Jonathan E., and Ross, Stephen A. "The Relation between Forward Prices and Future Prices," *Journal of Financial Economics* (1981), pp. 321–346.

15. Dusak, Katherine. "Futures Trading and Investor Returns: An Investigation of Commodity Market Risk Premiums," *Journal of Political Economy* (Nov.–Dec. 1973), pp. 1306–1387.

16. Ederington, Louis. "The Hedging Performance of the New Futures Market," *The Journal of Finance* (Mar. 1979), pp. 157–170.

17. Elton, Edwin, Gruber, Martin, and Rentzler, Joel C. "Intra-day Tests of the Efficiency of the Treasury Bill Futures Market," *Review of Economics and Statistics* (Feb. 1984), pp. 129–137.

18. ———. "Professionally Managed, Publicly Traded Commodity Funds," *The Journal of Business*, **60,** No. 2 (Apr. 1987), pp. 175–199.

19. ———. "New Public Offerings Information, and Investor Rationality: The Case of Publicly Offered Commodity Funds," *Journal of Business* (Jan. 1989), pp. 1–15.

20. ———. "Publicly Offered Commodity Funds," *Financial Analyst Journal* (July–Aug. 1990).

21. Fama, Eugene. "Forward Rates as Predictors of Future Spot Rates," *Journal of Financial Economics* (Oct. 1976), pp. 361–377.

22. Figlewski, Stephen. "Futures Trading and Volatility in the GNMA Market," *The Journal of Finance* (May 1981).

23. ———. "Hedging Performance and Basis Risk in Stock Index Futures," *Journal of Finance*, **39,** No. 3 (July 1984), pp. 657–669.

24. Forsythe, Robert, Palfrey, Thomas R., and Plott, Charles R. "Futures Markets and Informational Efficiency: A Laboratory Examination," *The Journal of Finance*, **39,** No. 4 (Sept. 1984), pp. 955–982.

25. Gay, Gerard D., and Manaster, Stephen. "Hedging against Commodity Price Inflation: Stocks and Bills as Substitutes for Futures Contracts," *Journal of Business* (July 1982), pp. 317–344.

26. ———. "Hedging Against Commodity Price Inflation. Stocks and Bills as Substitutes for Futures Contracts," *Journal of Business*, **55,** No. 3 (July 1983), pp. 317–343.

27. ———. "The Quality Option Implicit in Futures Contracts," *Journal of Financial Economics*, **13,** No. 3 (Sept. 1984), pp. 353–370.

28. Hartzmark, Michael L. "Returns to Individual Traders of Futures: Aggregate Results," *Journal of Political Economy*, **95,** No. 6 (Dec. 1987), pp. 1292–1306.

29. Hilliard, Jimmy E. "Hedging Interest Rate Risk with Futures Portfolios Under Term Structure Effects," *The Journal of Finance*, **39,** No. 5 (Dec. 1984), pp. 1547–1570.

30. Ho, Thomas S. Y. "Intertemporal Commodity Futures Hedging and the Production Decision," *The Journal of Finance*, **39,** No. 2 (June 1984), pp. 351–376.

31. Hsieh, David A., and Kulatilaka, Nalin. "Rational Expectations and Risk Premia in Forward Markets: Primary Metals at the London Metals Exchange," *The Journal of Finance*, **37,** No. 5 (Dec. 1982), pp. 1199–1208.

32. Jacobs, Rodney L. "The Effect of Errors in Variables on Tests for a Risk Premium in Forward Exchange Rates," *The Journal of Finance*, **37,** No. 3 (June 1982), pp. 667–678.

33. Jagannathan, Ravi. "An Investigation of Commodity Futures Prices Using the Consumption-Based Intertemporal Capital Asset Pricing Model," *The Journal of Finance*, **40,** No. 1 (Mar. 1985), pp. 175–192.

34. Jarrow, Robert A., and Oldfield, George S. "Forward Contracts and Futures Contracts," *Journal of Financial Economics* (Dec. 1981), pp. 373–382.

35. Kamara, Avraham, and Siegel, Andrew F. "Optimal Hedging in Futures Markets with Multiple Delivery Specifications," *Journal of Finance*, **42,** No. 4 (Sept. 1987), pp. 1007–1021.

36. Kilcollin, Thomas Eric. "Difference Systems in Financial Futures Markets," *The Journal of Finance*, **37,** No. 5 (Dec. 1982), pp. 1183–1198.

37. Park, Soo-Bin. "Spot and Forward Rates in the Canadian Treasury Bill Market," *Journal of Financial Economics*, No. 1 (Mar. 1982), pp. 107–114.

38. Rendleman, Richard, and Carabini, Christopher. "The Efficiency of the Treasury Bill Futures," *The Journal of Finance* (Sept. 1979), pp. 895–914.

39. Richard, Scott F., and Sundaresan, M. "A Continuous Time Equilibrium Model of Forward Prices and Futures Prices in a Multigood Economy," *Journal of Financial Economics* (Dec. 1981), pp. 347–372.

40. Roll, Richard. "Orange Juice and Weather," *American Economic Review* (Dec. 1985), pp. 861–881.

41. Williams, Jeffrey. "Futures Markets: A Consequence of Risk-Aversion or Transactions Costs," *Journal of Political Economy*, **95,** No. 5 (Oct. 1987), pp. 1000–1023.

Part 5

EVALUATING THE INVESTMENT PROCESS

24

Evaluation of Portfolio Performance

An integral part of any decision-making process should be the evaluation of the decision. This is equally true whether investors make their own investment decisions or employ a manager to make them.

A large percentage of investments are made by professional managers. Professionally managed funds include mutual funds, pension funds, college endowments, and discretionary accounts, among others. It is important for an investor utilizing one of these managers not only to evaluate how well the fund has done relative to other funds, but also to understand the fund's general policies and to be able to tell how well the fund has followed them. How diversified is the fund? How actively does it try to pursue short-run aberrations in prices? What is the bond-stock mix and how much does it vary? In order for the individual investor to understand the risks he or she is undertaking, the fund's policies and how strictly the manager adheres to them must be known. For the institution that has engaged a professional manager, examining the manager's policies enables the institution to evaluate not only the risks they are undertaking, but also the costs of any restrictions they might have placed on the fund manager.

Evaluation is important, not only to the individual or institution who engages a professional money manager, but also to the individual who invests personal funds. Once again, evaluation involves more than rating how well the investor has performed compared to others. To the individual making investment decisions, it is important to understand what caused the performance. Were there extra benefits from market timing or only extra transaction costs? Was stock selection superior?

Portfolio evaluation has evolved dramatically over the last two decades. The acceptance of modern portfolio theory has changed the evaluation process from crude return calculations to rather detailed explorations of risk and return and the sources of each. Furthermore, two decades ago evaluation was not an integral part of many organizations. This has changed (in part from external pressure) so that at this time most investment organizations incorporate evaluation as an integral part of their decision-making process.

This chapter discusses the current state of portfolio evaluation principles. It is divided into four sections. In the first section we go through the measurement of the overall fund performance. In the second section we analyze how the overall evaluation can be decomposed into those factors that affect the overall performance. In the third section, we examine the implications of multi-index and the arbitrage pricing theory (APT) for performance evaluation. Finally, in the last section, we examine mutual bond performance and whether fund performance is predictable.

EVALUATION TECHNIQUES

The evaluation of portfolio performance is essentially concerned with comparing the return earned on some portfolio with the return earned on one or more other portfolios. It is important that the portfolios chosen for comparison are truly comparable. This means that they not only must have similar risk, but also must be bound by similar constraints. For example, an institution that restricts its managers to investing in bonds rated AA or better should not evaluate its managers by comparing their performance to the performance of portfolios that are unconstrained. Although such a comparison would be useful in evaluating the relevance of the constraint, it would not be relevant for evaluating the manager.

Often the return earned by a fund is compared to the return earned by a portfolio of similar risk. In other comparisons an explicit risk–return trade-off is developed so that comparisons can be made across funds with very different risk levels. In either case, it is necessary to be more precise about what is meant by risk and return.

Measures of Return

In earlier chapters when we computed return, we calculated the capital gains plus dividends from an initial investment. Thus, if a security paid dividends of $3.00 and had a capital gain of $7.00 on an investment of $100, the return was

$$\frac{7+3}{100} = 0.10 = 10\%$$

The 10% return was the return over the period in which the capital gain occurred.

When evaluating a portfolio, generalizing our simple idea of return requires care. A problem occurs because there are many inflows and outflows of funds to the portfolio and very different amounts of money are invested at different points in time. To illustrate this, consider the example shown in Table 24.1. The portfolio has increased in value by 10% in each period, yet the ending value is less than the beginning value because of net outflows. To determine the rate of return by comparing the ending value to the beginning value would not reflect these changes.

As a second example, consider Table 24.2. This table shows two different patterns of inflows and outflows. In both cases, over the entire period, the inflows equal the outflows. Furthermore, the rate of return earned by each fund is identical in each period. However, the ending value is very different because the fund manager of Fund *A* had the good luck to have the funds in the period that was highly profitable.

Table 24.1 Hypothetical Inflows and Outflows

	Period			
	0	1	2	3
1. Value before inflow or outflow	$100	$110	$231	$55
2. Inflow (outflow)	0	$100	($181)	
3. Amount invested	$100	$210	$ 50	
4. Ending value	$110	$231	$ 55	

Table 24.2　Cashflows and Returns for Two Funds

	Period			
	0	1	2	3
Rate of return earned by each manager	20%	−10%	10%	
Fund A				
1. Value before inflow or outflow	100	240	126	$138.60
2. Inflow (outflow)	100	(100)	0	0
3. Amount invested	200	140	126	
4. Ending value	240	126	138.60	
Fund B				
1. Value before inflow or outflow	100	120	198	$107.80
2. Inflow (outflow)	0	100	(100)	0
3. Amount invested	100	220	98	
4. Ending value	120	198	107.80	

If we just looked at the ending value, compared to the beginning value over the full period, Fund A's performance would look superior. However, the period-by-period return is identical and (ignoring risk for the moment) so is the manager's performance. *Unless* the inflows and outflows are under the control of the manager (and in most cases they are not), the manager should not be rewarded or penalized for the good or bad fortune of having extra funds available at a particular time.

We eliminate the effect of having different amounts of funds available if we calculate the rate of return in each time period and then compound the return to determine it in the overall period. When the rate of return is calculated this way, it is called the *time weighted rate of return.* For Fund A the return in the first period is $(240 - 200)/200 = 20\%$. In the second period the return is $(126 - 140)/140 = -10\%$. In the third period the return is $(138.60 - 126)/126 = 10\%$. The overall return is the product of 1 plus each of the three one-period returns minus 1, or $(1.20)(0.90)(1.10) - 1 = 0.188$, or 18.8%. This return is the same for A and B. Since the manager's performance was identical, this is appropriate. Also, in the first example, the time-weighted rate of return would show the actual 10% return that was earned for each period. It would not penalize the manager for the net out-flows encountered.

To calculate the time-weighted rate of return requires knowledge of the value of the fund anytime there is a cash inflow or an outflow. For a fund with frequent transactions, this involves substantial calculations. If the inflows and outflows are not related to the market performance, then less frequent calculations may yield a reasonable approximation. Often funds are sold in units. Inflows and outflows affect the number of units but any one unit reflects the same initial investment. In this case tracing the performance of one unit is equivalent to determining the time-weighted rate of return.

Having examined return, it is necessary to look at risk.

Measures of Risk

There are two possible measures of risk that can be used: total risk or nondiversifiable risk. Consider a college endowment fund. Clearly, the appropriate risk is the risk on the total assets. The college will find very little comfort in the fact that part of the risk could be diversified away if they held other assets when the portfolio under consideration contains their total assets. As an alternative, consider the pension fund of a large corporation. For example, at one time AT&T allocated its pension funds to 125 separate managers. The contribution to the risk of the pension fund as a whole from the portfolio under supervision of any of these managers is primarily the nondiversifiable risk. AT&T, in evaluating its managers, should look at return relative to nondiversifiable risk.

As discussed in earlier chapters, total risk is normally measured by standard deviation of return, whereas nondiversifiable risk is normally measured by the Beta coefficient. Having discussed risk and return, it is appropriate to look at techniques for examining portfolio performance.

Direct Comparisons

As discussed before, one way to compare portfolios is to examine the return earned by alternative portfolios of the same risk. This is the procedure used by Friend, Blume, and Crockett [30] in their examination of mutual funds. Mutual funds have been evaluated by academics more than any other group of investment vehicles. This attention, which may well be unwelcome, is due, primarily, to the fact that data on mutual funds' portfolios are publicly available. Throughout this chapter we illustrate the discussion of performance measurement with reference to mutual fund studies.

Table 24.3 from the Friend, Blume, and Crockett study shows the mean return earned by a group of mutual funds compared to randomly generated portfolios. In this table, variance was used as a measure of risk. The mutual funds were divided into three risk categories (high, medium, and low risk). Random portfolios with risks approximating the risk of the mutual funds were generated. The columns under mean variance show how closely they matched. The last two columns show the return on each group of random portfolios and mutual funds. In this period and for this measure, mutual funds did worse than randomly selected portfolios.

Friend, Blume, and Crockett repeated this analysis using Beta as a measure of risk. Table 24.4 illustrates this comparison. Once again, they divided mutual funds into low, medium, and high risk and matched these funds with randomly selected portfolios. The last four columns show the mean return on the mutual funds and three groups of random portfolios.

The three groups of random portfolios differ in how the stocks were selected and how they were weighted. Equally weighted random portfolios are constructed by randomly selecting securities from the New York Stock Exchange in a manner so that the odds of selecting any security are the same as the odds of selecting any other security. The stocks,

Table 24.3   Characteristics of Investment Performance of Mutual Funds and Random Portfolios with Variance as a Measure of Risk (Jan. 1960–June 1968)

	Number in Sample		Mean Variance		Mean Return	
Risk Class	Mutual Funds	Equally Weighted Random Portfolios[a]	Mutual Funds	Equally Weighted Random Portfolios[a]	Mutual Funds	Equally Weighted Random Portfolios[a]
Low Risk	43	62	0.00120	0.00118	0.102	0.128
Medium Risk	25	51	0.00182	0.00184	0.118	0.142
High Risk	18	50	0.00280	0.00279	0.138	0.162

[a]NYSE stocks only, assuming an equal investment as of beginning of period in each stock included.
Source: Friend, Blume, and Crockett [30].

Table 24.4 Comparison of Investment Performance of Mutual Funds and Random Portfolios (Jan. 1960–June 1968)

Risk Class	Number in Sample		Mean Beta Coefficient		Mean Return			
	Mutual Funds	Equally Weighted Random Portfolios[a]	Mutual Funds	Equally Weighted Random Portfolios	Mutual Funds	Equally Weighted Random Portfolios	Proportionally Weighted Random Portfolios, Variant 1	Proportionally Weighted Random Portfolios, Variant 2
Low risk (β = 0.5−0.7)	28	17	0.614	0.642	0.091	0.128	0.116	0.101
Medium risk (β = 0.7−0.9)	53	59	0.786	0.800	0.106	0.131	0.097	0.084
High risk (β = 0.9−1.1)	22	60	0.992	0.992	0.135	0.137	0.103	0.092

[a]Approximately the same number in a group for each of the variants.
Source: Friend, Blume, and Crockett [30].

once selected, are weighted equally. Proportionally weighted, variant 1 are random portfolios where the odds of selecting any one stock are proportional to the amount of the stock outstanding, but, once selected, an equal dollar amount is placed in each security. Finally, in variant 2, the odds of selecting any stock are equal, but, once selected, the amount invested in any stock is proportional to the dollar amount of that stock outstanding.

There is nothing special about the particular way each of these portfolios was constructed, but the variation illustrates an important point. Earlier we discussed that it is important to compare managers' performances with relevant alternatives. If a manager is restricted from undertaking certain types of investments, then the return on these investments should not be used to evaluate performance.

Mutual funds tend to invest in securities of large corporations and when they do purchase the securities of smaller companies, they tend to purchase them in small amounts. If this underrepresentation of small firms by mutual funds is by choice, then it is perfectly reasonable to use small firms in the evaluation, and the equally weighted random portfolios are a relevant alternative. However, the underrepresentation may not be by choice. Mutual funds are restricted by law from holding more than 5% of the shares of any one company. This may in fact mean that the mutual funds cannot invest as much in a small firm as they do in a large one. Thus, in evaluating whether mutual fund managers have outperformed random selection, variant 1 or 2 might well be the correct alternative.

There is an alternative viewpoint from which the relevancy of the three alternative randomly selected portfolios should be examined: the investor's viewpoint. If the investor is facing a choice as to whether or not to entrust funds to a mutual fund, then the equally weighted scheme may be relevant since the investor can make equally weighted investments even if the mutual fund cannot invest equally.

An examination of Table 24.4 shows that the method used to construct random portfolios affects the conclusions concerning mutual fund performance. During this period small firms had a higher return than large firms. Random portfolios with greater representation in these small firms performed best. During the period studied mutual funds were dominated by equally weighted random portfolios but not by the other two variants.

Most professional evaluation services chose as a benchmark not random portfolios but rather the performance of portfolios administered by other managers. Table 24.5 is a part of the report of one of the large services that evaluates fund managers (usually pension funds).[1] Table 24.5 shows the return earned by the manager over the last year compared with the return of other fund managers. The circle shown in the chart represents the return

Table 24.5 Balanced Funds: Total Fund Rates of Return (for Years Ending June 30)

	1980	1981	1982	1983	1984	1985	1986	1987	1988	1989
5th Percentile	20.6	23.4	7.1	64.5	3.4	35.7	38.0	20.2	6.0	18.8
25th Percentile	14.7	16.3	2.7	50.8	−0.7	30.1	30.9	15.3	3.0	16.0
Median	11.4	12.1	−1.0	44.1	−3.7	27.3	26.1	12.5	0.6	14.5
75th Percentile	9.0	7.6	−4.4	39.5	−8.0	24.5	22.5	10.3	−1.7	12.8
95th Percentile	5.0	1.1	−10.6	29.8	−13.3	20.1	16.6	5.9	−6.9	10.8
Fund H1874	9.2	11.2	0.3	47.2	1.5	29.5	32.2	11.5	0.9	14.1
Percent Rank	73	58	41	37	12	30	18	60	44	55

Source: Reprinted from S.E.I. Fund Evaluation Service with permission.

---

[1]The major fund evaluation services such as S.E.I., Wilshire, and Barra have similar reports. We selected one at random for illustrative purposes.

of the manager in each year relative to other managers. The solid line in the middle of each rectangle represents the return of the median (50th percentile) manager. The upper and lower solid lines forming the rectangle represent the return of the 5th percentile and 95th percentile, respectively. Thus 90% of the managers lie within the rectangle. Finally, the dashed lines represent the return for the 75th and 25th percentile, respectively. This same information is presented numerically at the bottom of the chart. This type of information shows how well all managers did (by the position of the rectangle) and how well the manager being evaluated performed relative to other managers (by the position of the circle).

Table 24.6 shows similar information about the fund's risk. Table 24.6 compares the fund's total risk as measured by the standard deviation of return. Once again the circle represents the fund's performance and the rectangle encompasses 90% of all funds' standard deviations. Generally, both standard deviation and systematic risk as measured by Beta are used as measures of risk. The same service will present comparisons using each measure separately.

Note that unlike the analysis of Friend, Blume, and Crockett, the return comparisons in Table 24.5 are not generally being made between funds of the same risk. Thus, although both return and risk measures are included as part of all evaluation services, it's often difficult to form an overall opinion about fund performance. Only in the two cases where risk and return are both adverse or good is it possible to form an overall opinion.

For example, if the performance evaluation indicated that the fund had a high risk relative to other funds and the return was consistently below average, the fund would be considered undesirable. Similarly, if the risk was consistently below average and the return consistently above average, the fund would be considered very desirable. Usually, however, there is no consistent pattern of return over time, and often the risk pattern varies as well. Thus the return pattern cannot be used to form an overall opinion about fund performance. The risk information may be useful in determining whether the manager has followed guidelines on risk. For example, if the manager was instructed to follow a strategy with a lower standard deviation than the average fund, was this policy in fact followed?

We have just shown that performance can be measured by comparing the return of any portfolio with the return on other portfolios with the same risk. Another possibility is to develop an explicit risk–return trade-off. In the next section we examine some techniques for measuring portfolio performance that allow a comparison of funds with differing risk.

Table 24.6   Balanced Funds: Total Fund Variability of Quarterly Returns for Moving Five-Year Periods Ending June 30

	1980–1984	1981–1985	1982–1986	1983–1987	1984–1988	1985–1989
5th Percentile	15.9	14.9	15.5	14.8	16.3	15.7
25th Percentile	13.5	11.6	12.9	13.1	13.7	12.6
Median	12.0	10.3	11.4	11.1	12.1	10.8
75th Percentile	10.4	9.1	9.6	9.6	10.1	9.2
95th Percentile	9.0	7.6	7.5	7.4	7.6	7.0
Fund H1874	11.7	10.4	11.3	10.0	10.1	9.7
Percent rank	53	49	52	70	75	67
Rates of return	12.7	16.6	20.7	23.3	14.3	17.0
Percent rank	23	14	6	15	19	38

Source: Reprinted from S.E.I. Fund Evaluation Service with permission.

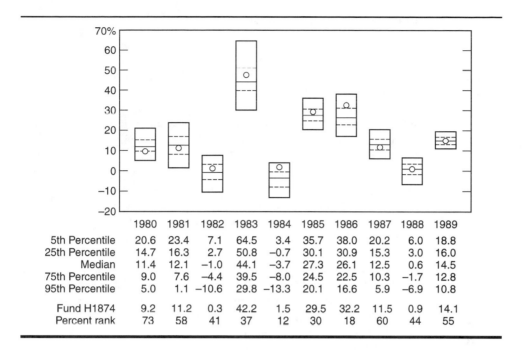

	1980	1981	1982	1983	1984	1985	1986	1987	1988	1989
5th Percentile	20.6	23.4	7.1	64.5	3.4	35.7	38.0	20.2	6.0	18.8
25th Percentile	14.7	16.3	2.7	50.8	−0.7	30.1	30.9	15.3	3.0	16.0
Median	11.4	12.1	−1.0	44.1	−3.7	27.3	26.1	12.5	0.6	14.5
75th Percentile	9.0	7.6	−4.4	39.5	−8.0	24.5	22.5	10.3	−1.7	12.8
95th Percentile	5.0	1.1	−10.6	29.8	−13.3	20.1	16.6	5.9	−6.9	10.8
Fund H1874	9.2	11.2	0.3	42.2	1.5	29.5	32.2	11.5	0.9	14.1
Percent rank	73	58	41	37	12	30	18	60	44	55

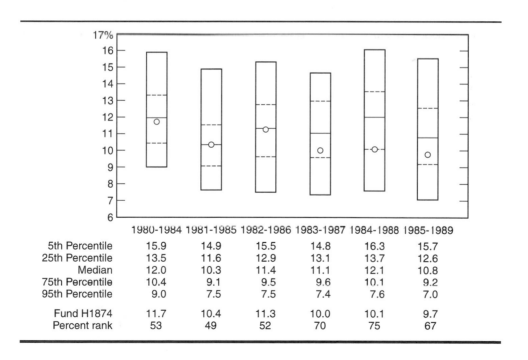

	1980-1984	1981-1985	1982-1986	1983-1987	1984-1988	1985-1989
5th Percentile	15.9	14.9	15.5	14.8	16.3	15.7
25th Percentile	13.5	11.6	12.9	13.1	13.7	12.6
Median	12.0	10.3	11.4	11.1	12.1	10.8
75th Percentile	10.4	9.1	9.5	9.6	10.1	9.2
95th Percentile	9.0	7.5	7.5	7.4	7.6	7.0
Fund H1874	11.7	10.4	11.3	10.0	10.1	9.7
Percent rank	53	49	52	70	75	67

One-parameter Performance Measures

There are four different one-parameter performance measures that have been proposed in the literature. We will discuss each measure in turn. These measures differ in their definition of risk and their treatment of the ability of the investor to adjust the risk level of any fund in which he or she might invest.

The Excess Return to Variability Measure   Consider the original portfolio problem. Figure 24.1 plots the return risk opportunities with riskless lending and borrowing.

As shown in Chapter 5, all combinations of a riskless asset and a risky portfolio lie along a straight line (in expected return standard deviation space) connecting the riskless asset and the risky portfolio. Thus, the line R_FA represents mixtures of the riskless asset and risky portfolio A, and R_FB represents mixtures of the riskless asset and risky portfolio B. As we argued earlier, all investors would prefer portfolio A to B because combinations along R_FA always give a higher return for the same risk. This idea can be and has been used for mutual fund evaluation.

Consider Figure 24.2. Portfolio A is being compared to portfolio B. If a riskless rate exists, then all investors would prefer A to B because combinations of A and the riskless asset give higher returns for the same level of risk than combinations of the riskless asset and B. All combinations of any portfolio and the riskless asset lie in a ray that intersects the vertical axis at R_F. The preferred portfolio is that which lies on the ray passing through R_F, which lies furthest in the counterclockwise direction. In Figure 24.2 the portfolios are ranked alphabetically. Stating that the preferred portfolio lies on the most counterclockwise ray is equivalent to stating that the slope of the ray is the highest. In Chapter 6 we showed that the slope of the line was $(\bar{R}_p - R_F)/\sigma_p$. This ratio is one of the measures first utilized in portfolio evaluation and is called the Sharpe measure. An examination of the ratio shows that funds are ranked by the fund's return above the risk-free rate (excess return) divided by the standard deviation of return. This ratio is often referred to as an excess return to variability measure.

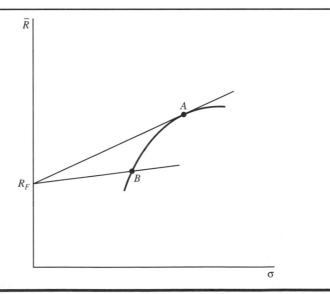

Figure 24.1   Combinations of a riskless asset and a risky portfolio.

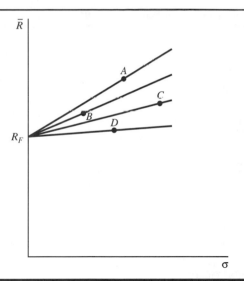

Figure 24.2   Combinations of a riskless asset and some mutual funds.

Table 24.7 applies this measure to mutual funds. The table is taken from Sharpe [75]. Column 1 is the return less a riskless rate of 3%. Sharpe chose 3% as his estimate of the riskless lending and borrowing rate. Column 2 is the standard deviation. Column 3 is column 1 divided by column 2, which is the Sharpe measure of mutual fund performance or excess return to variability. Figure 24.3 is a plot of these data and the Dow-Jones Index (designated by the symbol M). The ray connecting the risk-free asset and the Dow-Jones Index is shown on the diagram. Most of the mutual funds have a lower reward-to-variability index than the Dow-Jones Index. This implies that most mutual fund managers in this period did worse than they would have done if they had simply invested in the Dow-Jones Index and lent or borrowed to obtain their preferred risk.

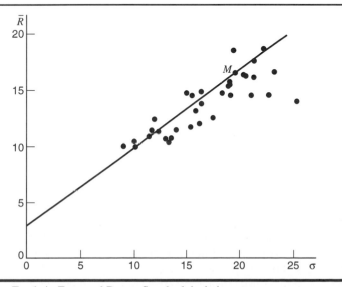

Figure 24.3   Funds in Expected Return Standard deviation space.

Table 24.7   Performance of 34 Mutual Funds, 1954–1963

Mutual Fund	Average Annual Excess Return (%)	Variability of Annual Return (%)	Reward-to-Variability Ratio (R/V)[a]
Affiliated Fund	11.6	15.3	0.75896
American Business Shares	7.0	9.2	0.75876
Axe-Houghton, Fund A	7.5	13.5	0.55551
Axe-Houghton, Fund B	9.0	16.3	0.55183
Axe-Houghton, Stock Fund	8.9	15.6	0.56991
Boston Fund	9.4	12.1	0.77842
Broad Street Investing	11.8	16.8	0.70329
Bullock Fund	12.7	19.3	0.65845
Commonwealth Investment Company	7.9	13.7	0.57841
Delaware Fund	11.4	21.4	0.58253
Dividend Shares	11.4	15.9	0.71807
Eaton and Howard, Balanced Fund	8.0	11.9	0.67399
Eaton and Howard, Stock Fund	12.2	19.2	0.63486
Equity Fund	11.6	18.7	0.61902
Fidelity Fund	13.4	23.5	0.57020
Financial Industrial Fund	11.5	23.0	0.49971
Fundamental Investors	13.0	21.7	0.59894
Group Securities, Common Stock Fund	12.1	19.1	0.63316
Group Securities, Fully Administered Fund	8.4	14.1	0.59490
Incorporated Investors	11.0	25.5	0.43116
Investment Company of America	14.4	21.8	0.66169
Investors Mutual	8.3	12.5	0.66451
Loomis-Sales Mutual Fund	7.0	10.4	0.67358
Massachusetts Investors Trust	13.2	20.8	0.63398
Massachusetts Investors—Growth Stock	15.6	22.7	0.63687
National Investors Corporation	15.3	19.9	0.76798
National Securities—Income Series	9.4	17.8	0.52950
New England Fund	7.4	10.2	0.72703
Putnam Fund of Boston	10.1	16.0	0.63222
Scudder, Stevens & Clark Balanced Fund	7.7	13.3	0.57893
Selected American Shares	11.4	19.4	0.58788
United Funds—Income Fund	13.1	20.9	0.62698
Wellington Fund	8.3	12.0	0.69057
Wisconsin Fund	10.8	16.9	0.64091

[a]R/V ratio = (Average return − 3.0%)/variability. The ratios shown were computed from original data and thus differ slightly from the ratios obtained from the rounded data shown in the table.
Source: Sharpe [75].

    The Sharpe measure looks at the decision from the point of view of an investor choosing a mutual fund to represent the majority of his or her investment. An investor choosing a mutual fund to represent a large part of his or her wealth would likely be concerned with the full risk of the fund, and standard deviation is a measure of that risk. Furthermore, if the investor desired a risk different from that offered by the fund, he or she would modify the risk by lending and/or borrowing. The relevant definition of performance may change if the problem is examined from the point of view of the fund manager. This leads directly to our second measure of performance.

Differential Return with Risk Measured by Standard Deviation   Let us assume for the moment that we are evaluating the manager of an all-equity portfolio who has the risk level determined by the client and that the manager is the only equity manager so that total risk is important. Such a situation is not atypical and may represent the situation for the manager of the equity portion of a pension fund. Pension funds often choose separate managers for the equity and bond portions of their portfolio and give target risk levels to each. What should be evaluated in this case is the ability of the manager to pick securities and combine them into a portfolio, given the risk level at which he or she is constrained to operate. The pension fund manager could obtain a portfolio of the desired risk through the naive strategy of placing part of the money in the market portfolio and part in the riskless asset (and, indeed, should have done so if the manager had no special selection skills). Thus, a measure of the manager's performance is how much better he or she did than this naive strategy. Consider Figure 24.4 and let A designate the fund being evaluated.

If the manager had followed the naive strategy of investing in the riskless asset and the market portfolio to obtain the same risk as A, a portfolio with the risk and return of A' would result. The differential return at the manager's chosen risk level (the distance AA') is a measure of how much better or worse the manager did than the naive strategy.[2]

The slope of the ray connecting R_F and M is, of course, $(\bar{R}_M - R_F)/\sigma_M$ and the intercept is R_F. Thus, the equation of the line is

$$\bar{R}_i = R_F + \left(\frac{\bar{R}_M - R_F}{\sigma_M}\right)\sigma_i$$

The return on portfolio A' is determined by substituting the standard deviation of A in the preceding formula and solving for the return of A'. The differential return is the difference, in return, between A and A'. For example, given

1. $R_F = 5\%$
2. $\bar{R}_M = 10\%$

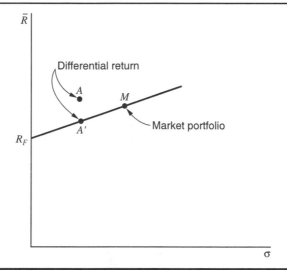

Figure 24.4   The determination of differential return.

[2]The measure just discussed is usually presented in return and Beta space and we will do so shortly. Depending on the relevant measure of risk, it may be more appropriate in standard deviation space.

3. $\sigma_M = 20\%$
4. $\sigma_i = 15\%$
5. $\overline{R}_A = 10\%$

then,

$$\overline{R}_{A'} = 5 + \left(\frac{10-5}{20}\right)15 = 8.75\%$$

and the differential return

$$\overline{R}_A - \overline{R}_{A'} = 10 - 8.75 = 1.25\%$$

With this measure, funds are ranked by their differential return with the best performing fund the one with the highest differential return.

   Figure 24.5 illustrates this measure with mutual fund data. It is taken from the Sharpe study and is exactly the same as Figure 24.3. The differential return for each fund is shown by the vertical lines. Table 24.8 lists the differential return. Both the Sharpe measure and the differential return measure will list the same mutual funds as performing better or worse than the market index. If a fund lies above line R_FM in Figure 24.5, it will have a positive differential return and lie on a ray with a higher slope than R_FM. The converse is true for funds that lie below the line R_FM. However, the relative ranking of the funds is affected by the choice of performance measure. This can be seen by comparing Table 24.8 with Table 24.7. Figure 24.6 illustrates why. The Sharpe measure would rank B as better than A since an investor through mixing the riskless asset and portfolio B would get a higher return for any level of risk than could be obtained by combining A with the riskless asset. The differential return index would rank A better than B. This is because the distance $A-A'$ is greater than the distance $B-A'$. This means that manager A was able to outperform a mixture of the market portfolio, and lending with the same risk as A by more than manager B could outperform a mixture of the market portfolio and lending at the same risk level as B.

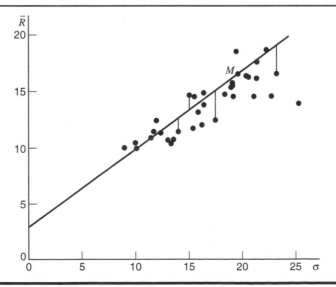

Figure 24.5   Measuring differential return.

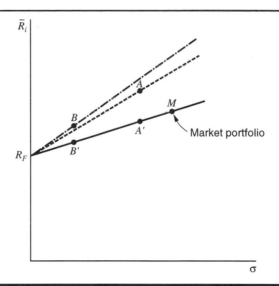

Figure 24.6 Effect of measure on ranking.

Each of the two measures just discussed has its counterpart when nondiversifiable risk (Beta) is chosen as the appropriate measure of risk.

Excess Return to Nondiversifiable Risk Consider portfolios in expected return Beta space. It is easy to show that all combinations of a riskless asset and a risky portfolio lie on a straight line connecting them. Furthermore, the slope of the line connecting the risky asset A and the risk-free rate is $(\bar{R}_A - R_F)/\beta_A$. Once again, an investor would prefer the portfolio on the most counterclockwise ray emanating from the riskless asset.[3] In Figure 24.7 the portfolio ranking is alphabetical.

This measure of portfolio performance was first suggested by Treynor [86] and is often called the *Treynor measure*. The final risk measure examines differential return when Beta is the risk measure.

Differential Return When Risk Is Measured by Beta Consider the line connecting the riskless rate and the market portfolio. A manager could obtain any point along this line by investing in the market portfolio and mixing this with the riskless asset to obtain the desired risk level. If the manager's choice is to actively manage the fund, then one

---

[3]Designate the Beta on a portfolio of the riskless asset and portfolio A as β_p. Designate the Beta on portfolio A as β_A and the Beta on the riskless asset as β_F. The Beta on a portfolio is a weighted average of the Beta on the individual securities. Thus $\beta_p = X\beta_A + (1 - X)\beta_F$. But the Beta on a riskless asset is zero or $\beta_F = 0$. Therefore, $X = \beta_p/\beta_A$. The expected return on a portfolio is a weighted average of the expected return on the individual assets. Thus, $\bar{R}_p = X\bar{R}_A + (1 - X)R_F$. Substituting β_p/β_A for X, we have

$$\bar{R}_p = \frac{\beta_p}{\beta_A}\bar{R}_A + \left(1 - \frac{\beta_p}{\beta_A}\right)R_F$$

Rearranging yields

$$\bar{R}_p = R_F + \left(\frac{\bar{R}_A - R_F}{\beta_A}\right)\beta_p$$

Table 24.8 Differential Returns with Standard Deviation as a Measure of Risk

	Average Annual Return	Return on a Portfolio of the Same Risk[a]	Differential Return
Affiliated Fund	14.6	13.20	1.40
American Business Shares	10.0	9.14	0.86
Axe-Houghton, Fund A	10.5	12.00	−1.50
Axe-Houghton, Fund B	12.0	13.87	−1.87
Axe-Houghton, Stock Fund	11.9	13.40	−1.50
Boston Fund	12.4	11.07	1.33
Broad Street Investing	14.8	14.21	0.59
Bullock Fund	15.7	15.87	−0.17
Commonwealth Investment Company	10.9	12.14	−1.24
Delaware Fund	14.4	17.27	−2.87
Dividend Shares	14.4	13.61	−0.79
Eaton and Howard, Balanced Fund	11.0	10.94	0.06
Eaton and Howard, Stock Fund	15.2	15.81	−0.61
Equity Fund	14.6	15.47	−0.87
Fidelity Fund	16.4	18.67	−2.27
Financial Industrial Fund	14.5	18.34	−3.80
Fundamental Investors	16.0	17.47	−1.47
Group Securities, Common Stock Fund	15.1	15.74	−3.64
Group Securities, Fully Administered Fund	11.4	12.40	−1.00
Incorporated Investors	14.0	20.01	−6.01
Investment Company of America	17.4	17.54	−0.14
Investors Mutual	11.3	11.34	−0.04
Loomis-Sales Mutual Fund	10.0	9.94	0.06
Massachusetts Investors Trust	16.2	16.87	−0.67
Massachusetts Investors—Growth Stock	18.6	18.14	0.46
National Investors Corporation	18.3	16.27	2.03
National Securities—Income Series	12.4	14.87	−2.47
New England Fund	10.4	9.80	−0.60
Putnam Fund of Boston	13.1	13.67	0.57
Scudder, Stevens & Clark Balanced Fund	10.7	11.87	−1.17
Selected American Shares	14.4	15.94	−1.54
United Funds—Income Fund	16.1	16.94	−0.84
Wellington Fund	11.3	11.00	0.30
Wisconsin Fund	13.8	14.27	−0.47

[a]Obtained by a mixture of market and risk-free rate.
Source: Sharpe [75].

measure of the manager's performance is the difference in return earned by actively managing the fund, compared to what would have been earned if the manager had passively invested in the market portfolio and riskless asset to achieve the same risk level. The slope of the line connecting the riskless asset and the market portfolio is $(\bar{R}_M - R_F)/\beta_M$, and the intercept must be the riskless rate. The Beta on the market portfolio is one. Thus, the equation of the line is

$$\bar{R}_p = R_F + \left(\bar{R}_M - R_F\right)\beta_p \qquad (24.1)$$

The differential return is the actual return less the return on the portfolio of identical Beta, but lying on the line connecting the riskless asset and the market portfolio. This return is

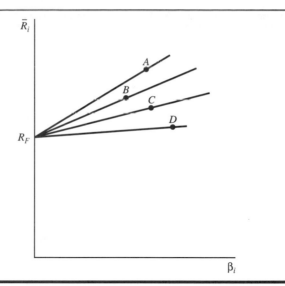

Figure 24.7   Treynor measure.

calculated, using the equation stated previously, along with the Beta of the portfolio being evaluated.

Assume the market return is 10% and the risk-free rate is 5% and the Beta on the portfolio being evaluated is 0.8. Then a mixture of the market portfolio and the riskless asset to obtain a Beta of 0.8 would have an expected return of

$$\overline{R}_p = 5 + (10 - 5)(0.8) = 9\%$$

The differential return is the difference between the return on the portfolio and the 9% just calculated.

This measure was first proposed by Jensen [44] and is often referred to as the Jensen differential performance index. As an illustration of its use, consider Table 24.9 taken from the Security and Exchange Commission study of mutual funds. As seen from this table, mutual funds over the period 1960–1969 seemed to outperform the passive strategy. By looking at the lower part of the table, which splits the period into two subperiods, it is easy to see that this is due to superior performance in the second subperiod.

The Jensen measure has a special appeal because of its relationship to the capital asset pricing models discussed in Chapters 13–15. We presented the Jensen model as a comparison between the return on the mutual fund and the return on a portfolio constructed by mixing the riskless asset and the market portfolio to obtain the same risk. There is an alternative way of viewing the Jensen measure. Equation (24.1) is, of course, the capital asset pricing line discussed in Chapter 13. The differential return can be viewed as the difference in return earned by the fund compared to the return that the capital asset pricing line implies should be earned. Viewed in this way, the Jensen measure becomes a special case of a large number of measures that could be used.

Chapters 13 and 14 discussed a number of different capital asset pricing models. Any of these could be used in calculating the differential return. The empirical evidence supporting the various capital asset pricing model (CAPM) models, discussed in Chapter 15, can help the reader decide which might be most relevant.

Table 24.9　Performance Summary—All Funds with Complete Data for 1960–1969 Period

Evaluation Period	Beta Range	No. Funds	Number of Observations (months)	Average Values (Unweighted)			
				Monthly Fund Return (%/month)	Average Beta	Monthly Market Return (%/month)	Differential Return
Jan. 1960	0–0.4	3	120	0.43	0.23	0.77	0.007
to	0.4–0.8	35	120	0.63	0.68	0.77	0.004
Dec. 1969	0.8–1.0	44	120	0.79	0.91	0.77	0.066
	1.0–1.2	30	120	0.86	1.07	0.77	0.056
	1.2+	13	120	1.05	1.33	0.77	0.130
	Total	125	120	0.78	0.91	0.77	0.051
Jan. 1960	0–0.4	4	60	0.60	0.16	1.05	0.245
to	0.4–0.8	47	60	0.83	0.65	1.05	0.064
Dec. 1964	0.8–1.0	43	60	0.82	0.91	1.05	−0.157
	1.0–1.2	22	60	0.73	1.11	1.05	−0.415
	1.2+	9	60	1.14	1.30	1.05	−0.162
	Total	125	60	0.82	0.85	1.05	−0.107
Jan. 1965	0–0.4	3	60	0.17	0.26	0.49	−0.250
to	0.4–0.8	22	60	0.46	0.69	0.49	0.001
Dec. 1969	0.8–1.0	46	60	0.68	0.91	0.49	0.194
	1.0–1.2	30	60	0.73	1.08	0.49	0.236
	1.2+	24	60	1.20	1.41	0.49	0.673
	Total	125	60	0.74	0.99	0.49	0.252

Source: SEC study [74].

For example, assume that the zero Beta version of the CAPM seems most reasonable. As discussed in Chapter 14, this implies that the expected return on portfolio i is given by

$$\bar{R}_i = \bar{R}_z + \left(\bar{R}_M - \bar{R}_z\right)\beta_i$$

This formula is used to calculate the expected return implied by the zero Beta CAPM for a portfolio with the same risk as the portfolio being evaluated. The differential return is the return on the portfolio being evaluated, less the return implied by the zero Beta CAPM.

Viewing the Jensen measure in this way also has implications for mutual fund evidence discussed earlier. Recall, when we were discussing the evidence on the CAPM, that empirical estimates of the CAPM have a higher intercept and a lower slope than the simple CAPM would suggest. In Figure 24.8 we have drawn these two lines. If the empirical line truly represents the risk–return opportunities available in the marketplace, then viewing the Jensen measure as a comparison to the CAPM line would imply that the differential returns should be calculated relative to the empirical line. Utilizing the empirical line rather than the theoretical line would result in portfolios with Betas less than one having smaller differential returns (if the differential returns are positive) and portfolios with Betas greater than one having large differential returns. Most mutual funds have Betas less than one. Therefore, calculating the differential returns from the empirical line would result in mutual funds being judged as having inferior performance. Utilizing the empirical CAPM might result in negative differential returns even though they were positive if the theoretical line is used.

We have presented the four single-index performance measures currently in use. The choice between them depends on the appropriate measure of risk and the appropriate

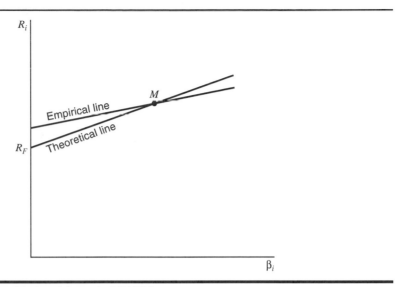

Figure 24.8 Empirical and theoretical CAPM.

viewpoint. In the next section we examine techniques for evaluating specific aspects of portfolio performance.

DECOMPOSITION OF OVERALL EVALUATION

In the previous section we examined a number of overall measures of performance. A number of attempts have been made to examine various aspects of performance that might affect overall performance. In this section we discuss these techniques.

One of the most widely referenced decompositions is one proposed by Fama [27]. Figure 24.9 shows Fama's decomposition. The line plotted in Figure 24.9 is the line representing all combinations of the riskless asset and portfolio M. As discussed earlier, one possible strategy for a manager with a desired risk level is to achieve this level by holding a portfolio composed of the riskless asset and the market. Line $R_F M$ plots the return on all such combinations. The Jensen measure of performance is, of course, the height above the line, or $A - A'$ in Figure 24.9. Fama calls this distance return from selectivity.

Portfolios A and A' have the same Beta and thus the same nondiversifiable risk. However, A and A' do not have the same total risk. All of the risk of the naive strategy comes about because of fluctuations in the market portfolio and thus the risk of portfolio A' is completely nondiversifiable. Portfolio A, however, is not strictly a market portfolio, or its return would lie on $R_F M$. In the process of earning extra return, diversifiable risk was incurred.

If this portfolio is a small part of the holdings of investors, this does not matter because diversifiable risk will wash out in looking at their total holdings. If the portfolio represents their entire portfolio, it does matter. The relevant question becomes, is the extra return worth the extra risk? These considerations are exactly the considerations discussed earlier when we discussed whether Beta or standard deviation was the appropriate measure of risk for evaluating portfolio management. If total risk is the appropriate measure of risk, then the easiest solution is to use one of the measures discussed earlier. However, many authors prefer working in the expected return Beta framework and the same analysis can be done

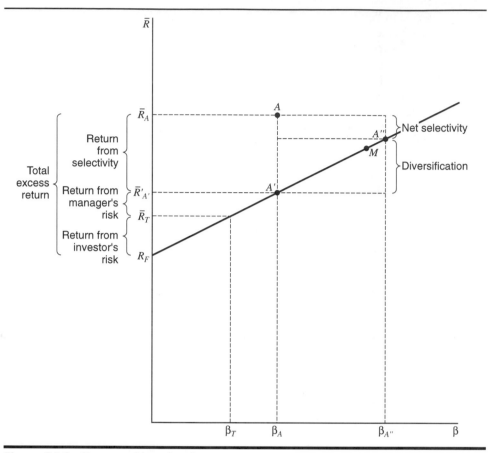

Figure 24.9   Decomposition of performance.

in that framework. Instead of comparing A with a naive portfolio with the same nondiversifiable risk, compare it with a naive portfolio with the same total risk. On Figure 24.9, portfolio A'' is such a portfolio.[4]

The quantity $\bar{R}_A - \bar{R}_{A''}$ is a measure of the extra return earned on portfolio A compared to a naive portfolio with the same total risk. It is the same size, of course, as would have been determined if we had used standard deviation directly as a measure of risk. Fama calls the distance $\bar{R}_A - \bar{R}_{A''}$ net selectivity. He calls the distance $\bar{R}_{A''} - \bar{R}_{A'}$ diversification, decomposing $\bar{R}_A - \bar{R}_{A'}$ into $\bar{R}_A - \bar{R}_{A''}$, and $\bar{R}_{A''} - \bar{R}_{A'}$ is his first decomposition.

The second part of the decomposition is to decompose the return $\bar{R}_{A'} - R_F$, which is the extra return earned on the naive portfolio for bearing risk. There are a large number of possible decompositions. One will be presented. Assume the manager was given a target risk level, say, β_T. Then the difference in return between the naive portfolio with risk β_T and the risk-free rate could be considered the extra return that the investor expected to earn, given the risk the investor was willing to bear. Fama calls this return, shown as $\bar{R}_T - R_F$,

---

[4]How can A'' be determined? As an example, assume total risk σ^2 is 20. Since the risk on the naive portfolio is totally nondiversifiable, its risk is $\beta^2 \sigma_M^2$, where σ_M^2 is the variance of portfolio M. If $\sigma_M^2 = 15$, then equating total risk $20 = 15\beta^2$, or the Beta on the naive portfolio with the same total risk as portfolio A is

$$\beta_{A''} = \sqrt{20/15}.$$

the return due to "investor's risk." The remaining return is $\bar{R}_{A'} - \bar{R}_T$. This is the return earned because the manager chose a different risk level than the target.

Decomposing $\bar{R}_{A'} - R_F$ into $\bar{R}_T - R_F$ and $\bar{R}_{A'} - \bar{R}_T$ is the second part of Fama's decomposition. The total decomposition is shown in Figure 24.9. We now examine in more detail specific aspects of portfolio performance that have been analyzed.

One aspect of portfolio performance generally measured is diversification. How much of the risk incurred by the portfolio is due to market movements and how much is due to unique movements of the individual securities in the portfolio? Diversification is usually measured by the percentage of total risk that can be accounted for by market movements. If, for the moment, we assume that an index like the Dow-Jones Index represents the market, then the first step is to correlate the returns on the Dow-Jones Index with the returns on the portfolio. The square of the correlation coefficient represents the percentage of total variation in portfolio returns explained by movements in the Dow-Jones Index. Almost all evaluation services provide this measure, and most academic studies also utilize this measure. Figure 24.10 presents this measure for 34 mutual funds. As can be seen by examining the figure, most mutual funds are well diversified and the majority of the risk they incur is risk of market movements. However, there are a number of mutual funds shown in Figure 24.10 that bear substantial nonmarket risk. If the mutual fund represents a substantial portion of the investor's portfolio, then the investor also bears the nondiversifiable risk. For the extra risk to be worthwhile, there needs to be substantial extra return. The mutual fund evidence reviewed in the earlier section would indicate that most mutual funds do not earn sufficient return to justify incurring this extra risk. In addition, there is no evidence to suggest that superior performance is related to a lack of diversification. Thus, the mutual funds

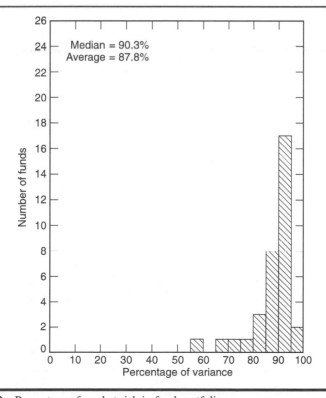

Figure 24.10   Percentage of market risk in fund portfolios.

that have substantial amounts of nonmarket risk are generally poor investments for individuals for whom the mutual fund represents their principal investment.

A second aspect of mutual fund performance that is often examined is timing. The question is, how successful have mutual funds been in timing market movements and how is timing measured? Managers use one of two techniques in an attempt to improve performance through timing. The first is to change the percentage committed to bonds and stocks in anticipation of market changes. If the market is expected to increase, then the manager increases the amount invested in common equities. If the market is expected to decline, then the manager switches from common equity to bonds. The alternative way managers attempt to market time is to adjust the average Beta on the portfolio in anticipation of changes in the market. Thus, when the market is expected to increase, the manager increases the Beta on the portfolio to obtain a portfolio with a greater responsiveness to market changes. When the manager feels the market might decline, high Beta securities are sold and low Beta securities purchased to reduce the Beta on the portfolio and make the portfolio less responsive to market movements.

Both the changes in the bond-stock mix and the changes in Beta on the common equity portion of the portfolio are attempts to change the average Beta on the total portfolio. Attempts to measure successful timing are best done utilizing Beta, since Beta captures both changes simultaneously. Nevertheless, both the bond–stock mix and the Beta on the common equity portion of the portfolio have been used as indications of timing ability.

The easiest way to examine the effectiveness of attempts to market time is to graphically examine market movements versus the bond–stock mix or average Beta. Figure 24.11 is an example using Betas. For this fund very little evidence of successful timing is present. If the fund has a well-specified policy regarding the average Beta or the bond–stock mix, then it is more illuminating to examine the relationship between deviations from the policy and changes in the market. Figure 24.12 is an example of this type of analysis.

Another measure of a manager's timing ability is to look at a plot of portfolio Beta or bond–stock mix compared to the market return. If there is significant timing ability, then there should be a relationship between these variables and this should be apparent from the plot.

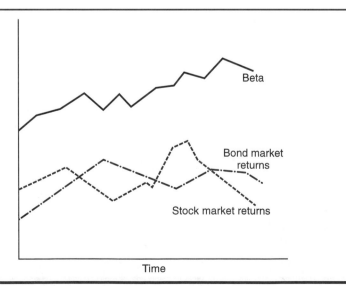

Figure 24.11   Beta and security returns.

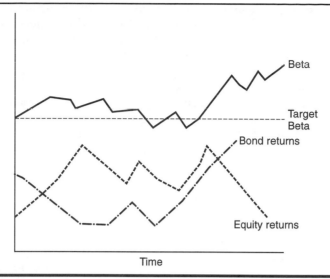

Figure 24.12 Measuring timing.

A third way to measure market timing is to look directly at the fund return compared to the market return. If the fund did not engage in market timing, then the average Beta on the overall portfolio should be fairly constant. If there was no diversifiable risk in the portfolio, then the portfolio return would be a constant fraction of the market return. A plot of market return compared to portfolio return would be a straight line. On an actual portfolio there is usually some diversifiable risk and some changes in both Beta and the bond–stock mix. If there was no successful timing, then these differences would simply cause the relationship between market return and portfolio return to be a scatter of points around a straight line, such as that shown in Figure 24.13. Assume a fund was able to engage in successful timing through changing Beta. In this case, when the market increased substantially, the fund would have a higher than normal Beta and would tend to do better than it would have otherwise done. This would cause the points to be above the normal line in

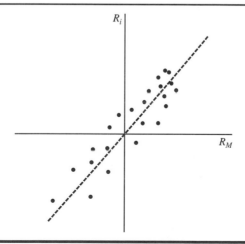

Figure 24.13 Returns for manager without timing.

Figure 24.13 for large market changes. Likewise, if the manager were able to anticipate a market decline, he or she would reduce the Beta and have a portfolio that declined less than it would otherwise. This would mean that for low market returns points would tend to scatter above the normal relationship. The points above the normal relationship for low and high market returns would give a curvature to the scatter of points if there were successful timing. An example is shown in Figure 24.14. Treynor and Mazuy [87] utilized this to analyze the timing ability of mutual funds. They found that only one fund out of the 37 they examined exhibited any significant timing ability. They did not examine the odds that one would observe one such fund when no timing ability existed.

The Treynor and Mazuy procedure to test for curvature is to fit a quadratic curve to the performance data. The following multiple regression is run

$$\left(R_{it} - R_{Ft}\right) = a_i + b_i\left(R_{mt} - R_{Ft}\right) + c_i\left(R_{mt} - R_{Ft}\right)^2 + e_i$$

where

R_{it}	is the return on fund i in period t
R_{mt}	is the return on the market index in period t
R_{Ft}	is the riskless asset
e_i	is the residual return
a_i, b_i, and c_i	are constants

If the relationship between the fund's returns and the market's returns are as shown in Figure 24.13, then a straight line will best fit the scatter of points. In this case the addition of a squared term will not improve the fit and c_i will be zero. If the relationship between the fund and the market is as shown in Figure 24.14, then the addition of a squared term (which results in a curved shape) will improve the fit and c_i will be positive. Thus c_i is a measure of the fund's timing ability.

An alternative way to analyze market timing is to fit two separate lines. One line is fit for the observations when the market outperforms the riskless asset (up markets) and the other line is fit when the market underperforms the riskless asset (down markets). A manager with market timing should have a high up market Beta and a low down market Beta.

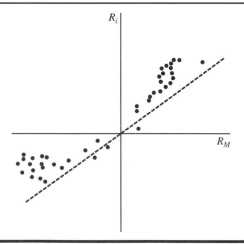

Figure 24.14   Returns for manager with timing.

This idea can be implemented by estimating the parameters in the following regression.

$$\left(R_{it} - R_{Ft}\right) = a_i + b_i\left(R_{mt} - R_{Ft}\right) - c_i D\left(R_{mt} - R_{Ft}\right) + e_i$$

where

$D = 0$ if $R_{mt} - R_{Ft} \geq 0$ an up market

     $= 1$ if $R_{mt} - R_{Ft} < 0$ a down market

To illustrate why this works consider what the equation looks like for different values of $R_{mt} - R_{Ft}$.

$R_{mt} - R_{Ft}$	EQUATION
+	$R_{it} - R_{Ft} = a_i + b_i(R_{mt} - R_{Ft}) + e_i$
0	$R_{it} - R_{Ft} = a_i$
−	$R_{it} - R_{Ft} = a_i + (b_i - c_i)(R_{mt} - R_{Ft}) + e_i$

Examining these equations shows that b_i is the up market Beta and $(b_i - c_i)$ is the down market Beta; c_i is the difference between the up market Beta and the down market Beta. A successful market timing will have a positive c_i. If c_i is statistically significant, it is some indication that the result is not due to luck but rather to skill.

Problems in Portfolio Measurement

For most individuals and institutions, riskless or near riskless investments are available. The purchase of the government bond of the appropriate maturity is riskless except for some potential risk on the rate to be earned on reinvested interest. Similarly, for individuals, savings accounts are essentially riskless. Note, however, that the single-parameter portfolio evaluation techniques, in general, assume lending and borrowing at the same riskless rate.

As an example, consider the Sharpe measure where portfolios are ranked by the slope of the ray connecting the risk-free asset and the portfolio being evaluated. Using this measure, we would say that portfolio A in Figure 24.15 dominated portfolio B, which dominated portfolio C, which dominated portfolio D.

To move out on the ray $R_F A$ beyond portfolio A required borrowing at the riskless rate and investing more than 100% in A. The argument of why A dominates C is that an investor desiring a portfolio with the risk of C would be better off holding A and borrowing to move to A'. If borrowing at the riskless rate is not possible, then it is no longer clear that A dominates C. If the borrowing rate is higher than the lending rate, say, R'_F, then the investor follows the line $R'_F A$ to move beyond A. The situation is depicted in Figure 24.16. In this case A dominates C for risk levels to A'', but beyond A'' portfolio C and lending (up to the risk level associated with C) or C and borrowing (for risk levels beyond C) dominate A and borrowing.

In many cases the choice is unambiguous. Clearly A dominates B in Figure 24.15, even if the borrowing rate is different from the lending rate. Combinations of lending or borrowing and A have higher return than lending and borrowing and B. This would be true for any portfolio that had lower risk than A. Portfolios with more risk than A may, or may not, be dominated by A. From the efficient set theorem A dominates D in Figure 24.15 since it has both higher return and less risk than D. Combining lending or borrowing with A or D will not change this relationship.

The portfolios that A would dominate can be seen from Figure 24.17. A dominates all portfolios that lie below $R_F AA''$.

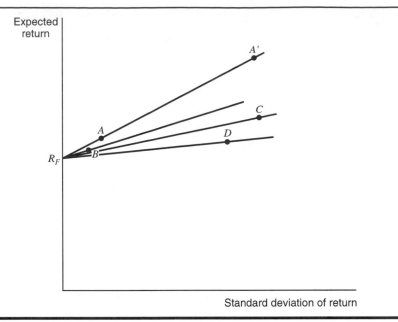

Figure 24.15   Combinations of risk and return.

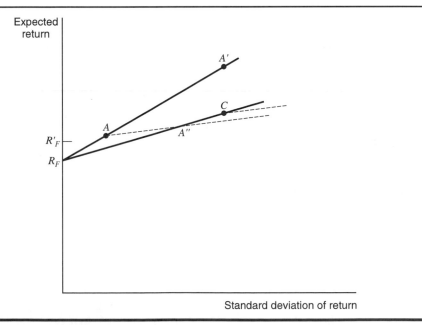

Figure 24.16   Combinations of risk and return with differential lending and borrowing.

Although the foregoing discussion utilized the Sharpe measure as an example, the same sorts of issues are present with the other measures. It is left to the reader to trace through the implications for the other models.

The second problem with implementing single-parameter risk measures is caused by changing risk levels. One style followed by managers is to try to earn an excess return by trying to anticipate market cycles and adjusting the portfolio accordingly. The standard

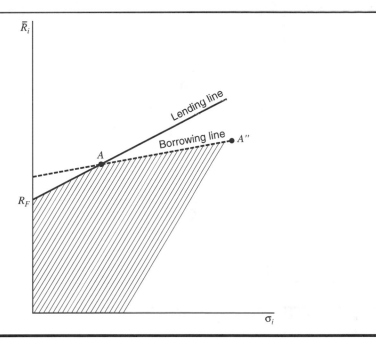

Figure 24.17   Regions of dominance.

method is to sell securities and purchase bonds in anticipation of a market decline and to sell bonds and purchase stocks in anticipation of a market increase. An alternative method utilized by some managers is to change the average Beta on the portfolio in anticipation of market movements by changing the type of stock held. If the market is expected to increase, the portfolio manager increases the average Beta on the portfolio in order to increase the sensitivity of the portfolio to the market. If the market is expected to decline, the manager decreases the Beta on the portfolio in order to make the portfolio less sensitive to market movements.

Many managers adopt one or more of these strategies in order to consciously adjust the risk on the portfolio. For many other portfolios, the risk changes as a by-product of adjustments in the portfolio's composition because of changes in expectations concerning individual security performance. In either case, the risk level of the portfolio is changing through time. Changing the risk level of the portfolio causes problems in the evaluation process. Most mutual fund evaluation studies and many portfolio evaluation services calculate the risk on the portfolio by examining the past sequence of returns for the portfolio. If the risk level of the portfolio has been changing through time, this procedure can lead to an estimate of risk very different from what it was at any point in time.

Perhaps this can best be illustrated by examining a possible set of circumstances when Beta is used as a measure of risk. Let us assume that the composition of a portfolio is unchanged for a six-month period. After the sixth month, the firm decides that the market is likely to go down and so it lowers the Beta on the portfolio for the next six months. Figure 24.18 shows the Beta that would be arrived at by using each of the six months of data separately and the overall Beta that would be found for the period.[5]

---

[5]The reader might note that the return in the market was higher in the second six months than in the first six months. This can be seen by noting that the points representing the second six months are farther to the right on the horizontal axis.

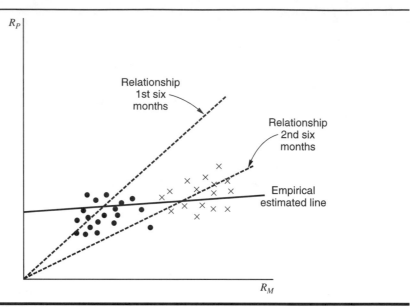

Figure 24.18 Returns with changing Beta.

Notice that the Beta for the year need bear no fixed relationship to the Beta for any six-month period. In this case, the Beta for the year is measured as being lower than the actual Beta on the portfolio at any point in time. The important point to keep in mind here is that estimating risk from a historical series of returns on a portfolio can produce a risk measure that bears no resemblance at all to the risk on the portfolio at any point in time.

We have raised an important problem. It would be convenient if we could produce a solution. Fortunately, we can. The risk on a portfolio at any point in time can be estimated by examining the risk of the individual securities and combining them using actual investment proportions to obtain the risk on the portfolio. For example, the Beta on a portfolio at a point in time can be found by estimating the Beta on each stock in the portfolio (using one of the techniques discussed in Chapter 7), and the risk on the portfolio found by taking a weighted average of the individual stock Betas. The weights are the fraction of the portfolio each stock represents. The differential return can then be found by measuring the returns between each portfolio change and compounding for the entire period.

A third possible problem has been emphasized by Roll, who points out that Beta is not an unambiguous risk measure. The Beta when using the S&P Index is not the same as the Beta calculated using the Dow-Jones Index as the market. Changing the definition of the market portfolio can change both the Beta and the ranking of portfolios. This is one more example of the principle we emphasized throughout this chapter. In evaluation one must be very careful to determine what is the purpose and what are the relevant alternatives. In this case it may pay the user to evaluate performance under several alternative definitions of the market portfolio. If the performance is robust (e.g., it appears good under a reasonable set of alternative market definitions), the user can feel confident in the result. If it is not robust, the user must either decide that performance is ambiguous or decide which market definition is the most relevant for judging performance in the particular problem under study.

Having examined some of the problems in single-parameter measures, it is worthwhile examining multiparameter measures.[6]

---

[6]The problem of Beta changing over time carries over to multiparameter measures.

MULTI-INDEX, APT, AND PERFORMANCE EVALUATION

The preponderance of literature on performance evaluation has, until quite recently, concentrated on single-index measures of performance or on measures that compare the manager with a single benchmark. The material we have reviewed so far in this chapter is based on this methodology. Development of arbitrage pricing theory (APT) models and the accompanying renewed interest in multi-index models has spurred the development of new performance measures. This development has also been accelerated by the fact that managers now place more diverse sets of assets in portfolios, necessitating the use of more complex benchmarks and models. We will divide this section into two parts. In the first, we discuss the use of multi-index and multi-benchmark measures to evaluate performance. In the second, we show how a full APT model can be used to evaluate and decompose performance.

The Use of Multiple Benchmark and Multiple Index Models for Performance Evaluation

Almost all of the early studies of portfolio performance compared performance of managed portfolios to a single-market index, usually the S&P index. In the last decade, this has changed. Researchers have recognized that managers hold a wide range of assets besides the large stocks that are contained in the S&P index. For example, certain funds hold only small stocks, whereas other funds (e.g., balanced funds) hold a mixture of bonds and stocks and still others, (e.g., international funds) hold assets from many different countries. The danger with comparing performance to a single index, such as the S&P index, is that types of assets held in the managed portfolios which are not contained in the benchmarks may perform differently than the benchmark. The researcher, finding differential performance cannot be sure if the performance is due to a manager's ability to select securities or simply due to the category from which securities are being selected that is not in the index having superior or inferior performance relative to the index.

The problem with using a single benchmark is illustrated in Elton, Gruber, Das, and Hlavka [25]. They examined a study by Ippolito [41]. Ippolito found an average Jensen's alpha of 0.4% when comparing mutual fund performance to the S&P index.[7] Over the period studied, however, the CRSP, a small stock index, had an Alpha of 10.06% when measured against the S&P index. Thus a manager of a small stock index fund would have shown enormous superior stock selection ability when measured against the S&P index. Ippolito had a number of small stock funds in his sample. Thus, the positive Alpha on average could be simply due to the superior performance of small stocks and small stock funds in this period. Using a multi-index model to correct for the differential performance of securities not in the index changed the Alpha to a negative −1.59% for the average fund.[8] Thus, Ippolito's results were due to an incorrect benchmark and not superior security selection on the part of fund managers.[9]

---

[7]See Elton, Gruber, Das, and Hlavka [25]. Ippolito had some data errors. This is the Alpha corrected for the data errors.

[8]This Alpha resulted from a three-index model using the S&P, a small stock and a bond index. Most of the difference in the results is due to including the small stock index. Some of it does arise from the inclusion of a bond index. A bond index was included because some of the funds in Ippolito's sample had more than 50% of their assets invested in debt instruments.

[9]Another problem with using an incorrect benchmark is that many of the characteristics of funds that are studied are likely to be correlated with the omitted index and incorrect inferences concerning the characteristic and performance will be made. For example, Ippolito found that high Beta funds outperformed low Beta funds. However, size and Beta are highly correlated. Once the performance of small size funds was accounted for, this relationship disappeared.

An alternative to using a single benchmark for all funds is to adopt a set of benchmarks, one of which is deemed appropriate for each fund. This approach has gained wide acceptance among individual investors and has become a standard feature of many commercial services. For example, Morningstar places every domestic stock fund into one of nine categories. These categories are defined by the intersection of two dimensions: (1) size (small, medium, or large) and (2) growth characteristics (growth, blend, or value). Any fund is characterized by the attributes of the securities it holds. While extremely useful for quick analysis, the problem with this approach is that it forces a fund into one of nine categories and doesn't allow consideration of how closely the fund fits that category. Funds hold securities that span multiple sets of characteristics rather than possessing only one set of characteristics. The way to adjust for this is to use a multi-index model.

The technique for controlling for multiple asset categories by using multiple indexes is a straightforward generalization of single-benchmark models. An example of a three-benchmark model to calculate Jensen's alpha would be

$$R_{it} - R_{Ft} = \alpha_i + b_{iL}\left(R_{Lt} - R_{Ft}\right) + b_{is}\left(R_{st} - R_{Ft}\right) + b_{iB}\left(R_{Bt} - R_{Ft}\right) + \epsilon_{it} \qquad (24.2)$$

where

R_{it} is the return on the portfolio being evaluated in period t

R_{Ft} is the return on the riskless asset in period t

b_{ij} is the sensitivity to the benchmark j

R_{jt} is the return on the benchmark in period t

ϵ_{it} is the random error

L is a large stock index

S is a small stock index

B is the bond index

The Alpha on the fund can be viewed as the difference between the actual return on the fund and the combination of the four passive portfolios that most closely matched the risk choice of the manager being evaluated.

One can think of this as a generalization of the Jensen model. Sharpe has proposed a generalized Sharpe measure, which is simply the Alpha from Equation (24.2) divided by the standard deviation of the residuals from that equation. This is a more general form of a reward-to-risk ratio originally proposed by Sharpe. In addition, it is a measure of the significance of Alpha.

Timing measures are a straightforward generalization of the ones discussed earlier. For example, to use the Treynor Black measure, squared terms would be added to the three measures of index returns.

Before leaving this section, one additional application of the multi-index model should be mentioned. By looking at a manager's average sensitivity to each factor (b's) one can get an idea of what type of investment strategy the manager is following (on average). Managers typically describe their style in brief terms (a growth stock manager or a value manager), but the description often lacks detail and in addition one should have an independent check on what the manager claims to be doing. For example, a typical growth stock manager has much more sensitivity to small stocks than the average manager. He or she also typically shows a much higher sensitivity to the S&P index and lower sensitivity to bonds than the nongrowth stock manager. These latter two facts are almost never contained in the description of the manager's policies or goals. Average profiles can be constructed for a growth stock manager, and the extent to which a particular manager conforms or differs from the average can be analyzed.

Because of these desirable characteristics, the examination and use of multi-index models for performance evaluation is increasing rapidly.[10] If one is willing to assume a multi-index equilibrium APT model, a more detailed decomposition of performance is possible.

However, before we do so, let's return to a reconsideration and reconciliation of the use of a single benchmark versus a multi-index model.

As noted before, an approach often used by practitioners is to evaluate performance relative to some pre-assigned style benchmark. If the portfolio manager is identified as belonging to a specific style of management, whether it be value, growth, yield, or some other style designation, then the manager's performance is typically evaluated relative to a benchmark comprising returns on funds managed by other managers within that specific style. In other words, if manager i belongs to style I, the relative performance measure α_i is defined in terms of the equation $R_{it} = \alpha_i + \bar{R}_{It} + \varepsilon_{it}$ and is computed by taking the time series mean of $R_{it} - \bar{R}_{It}$ where $\bar{R}_{It}$ is the average return as of time t for all funds managed according to style I. What is the relationship between this common industry practice and the generalized Jensen measure outlined above? The relationship between these approaches can be illustrated by taking the three-index benchmark model introduced in Section 4:

$$R_{it} - R_{Ft} = \alpha_i + b_{iL}\left(R_{Lt} - R_{Ft}\right) + b_{iS}\left(R_{St} - R_{Ft}\right) + b_{iB}\left(R_{Bt} - R_{Ft}\right) + \varepsilon_{it} \qquad (24.3)$$

In the practical context of active portfolio management, the benchmark loadings b may change through time as the underlying portfolios evolve as the manager buys and sells securities and changes sector allocations. One approach to this problem is to keep track of the investments of the fund and to change the benchmark loadings b accordingly.[11] However, this information is often available only on a quarterly basis. An alternative approach is to make the assumption that while the loadings may change, the definition of management styles imply that the loadings are the same for all managers who follow a specific style, in other words,

$$R_{it} - R_{Ft} = \alpha_i + \alpha_{It} + b_{ILt}(R_{Lt} - R_{Ft}) + b_{ISt}(R_{St} - R_{Ft}) + b_{IBt}(R_{Bt} - R_{Ft}) + \varepsilon_{it} \quad i\varepsilon I \quad (24.4)$$

which can be estimated using the cross section of fund returns at a point in time t.

We now have two approaches to evaluating performance based on a multi-index model. The use of Equation (24.3) assumed that the sensitivities of a fund to an appropriate set of indexes are stable, change slowly over time, or the changes are unrelated to the index return over the riskless rate. As an alternative, the sensitivity of each fund to each index can be measured at several points in time and those funds with major shifts in index sensitivities can be held out for separate consideration. Fortunately, research shows that the parameters of evaluation (24.3) change very slowly for the majority of mutual funds.

The alternative approach is to use Equation (24.4) which assumes that while the sensitivity of any fund to each index may changes rapidly over time, the sensitivity of all funds in a group to all the indexes is the same (for each fund) at a moment in time. If this is true, Equation (24.4) is an appropriate equation to evaluate performance.[12] Which assumption

[10]For some examples of multi-index models see Sharpe [77] and Elton, Gruber, Das, and Hlavka [25], which use market indexes in their multi-index models, and Lehmann and Modest [56], Connor and Korajczyk [13], and Grinblatt and Titman [37], which use empirically estimated indexes.

[11]See, for example, Hsiu-Lang Chen, Narashimhan Jegadeesh, and Russ Wermers [11].

[12]See Brown and Goetzmann (7) for the methodology and results of forming clusters of funds which behave homogeneously over time.

is better depends on the particular set of funds being analyzed and the characteristics of the funds in that set.

The Use of APT Models to Evaluate and Diagnose Performance

The use of an APT model in combination with a multi-index model allows for better diagnoses of what a portfolio manager is doing, a better development of appropriate benchmarks, and a better measurement and attribution of performance.[13]

The overall performance and reasons for the performance can be measured using an APT model such as the one discussed in Chapter 16. As an example, consider the model we described in the latter section of Chapter 16. Let's examine the return-generating process presented in Equation (16.11) with the APT model and the associated λ values presented in Chapter 16 inserted:

$$R_i - R_F = -4.32b_{iI} + 1.49b_{iS} + 0.00b_{iO} + 3.96b_{iM}$$
$$+ b_{iI}I_I + b_{iS}I_S + b_{iO}I_O + b_{iM}I_M \tag{24.5}$$

Recall that the subscript

I stands for inflation

S stands for aggregate sales

O stands for oil prices

M stands for the S&P index with other influences removed

Now assume a particular manager x who had the following values for the sensitivities (b's) on the portfolio:

$$b_{xI} = -0.5 \quad b_{xS} = 2.75 \quad b_{xO} = -1.00 \quad b_{xM} = 1.30$$

While the average b's for the S&P index were

$$b_{S\&P\ I} = -0.37 \quad b_{S\&P\ S} = 1.71 \quad b_{S\&P\ O} = 0 \quad b_{S\&P\ M} = 1.0$$

Let us further assume that the difference of each index from its expected value in the period where we are evaluating the manager is

$$I_I = 0.7 \quad I_S = 0.5 \quad I_O = 0.4 \quad I_M = 1.00$$

Assume that the manager is free to select the sensitivities to each index and we want to investigate why the manager does better or worse than the S&P index. Further assume that the manager was able to earn 14.52% excess return (above the riskless rate of interest). We can decompose the manager's return (compared to the S&P index) into the following categories: expected return from the S&P index, extra return on the S&P index that is earned from factors having returns which are different from their expected value, extra expected return earned from having sensitivities different from those on the S&P index, extra return earned from having sensitivities different from those of the S&P index that is earned because factors have returns that are different from their expected values, and extra return from security selection.

The expected return from the S&P index is simply from Equation (24.5) recognizing that all I's have an expected value of zero,

---

[13]There are many APT models. Whether using an APT model or the multi-index models of the prior section, results in better performance evaluation depends on how well the model that is used approximates the return-generating process or the true APT model.

$$\overline{R}_{S\&P} - R_F = -4.32\beta_{S\&P\,I} + 1.49\beta_{S\&P\,S} + 0.00\beta_{S\&P\,O} + 3.96\beta_{S\&P\,M}$$
$$\overline{R}_{S\&P} - R_F = -4.32(-0.37) + 1.49(1.71) + 0.00(0.0) + 3.96(1) = 8.103$$

Now, in any period the excess return on the S&P index will differ from this because the return on the factors over the period are not at their expected values (I_j's $\neq 0$). To see the influence of this, simply multiply the Betas for the S&P times the value that the I_j's take on over the evaluation period or

$$\left(R_{S\&P} - \overline{R}_{S\&P}\right) = \beta_{S\&P\,I}I_I + \beta_{S\&P\,S}I_s + \beta_{S\&P\,O}I_O + \beta_{S\&P\,M}I_M$$
$$\left(R_{S\&P} - \overline{R}_{S\&P}\right) = (-0.37)(0.7) + (1.71)(0.5) + (0.0)(0.4) + (1.0)(1.0) = 1.591$$

To this point we have seen that the excess return on the S&P was 9.694 with a return of 8.103 expected and 1.591 due to the fact that the factors driving security returns had returns different from expected returns over the period.

The choice of different sensitivities impacts performance in two ways. First, with different sensitivities, the return for risk bearing (expected return) will differ. Second, different sensitivities will affect the additional return that may be gained or lost because the return on an index was different from that required by the average investor (nonzero I's).

Let's think about this for a moment. The manager discussed earlier chose to have a higher sensitivity to the residual market influence than the S&P index had. Since the market price of this risk is positive, we would expect a manager with higher sensitivity to earn on average a higher return. However, this increase in expected return is simply what investors require for the extra risk. If we were to credit this extra return to the manager's performance, all managers who were not constrained, would on average hold portfolios with higher Betas with all factors that had positive λ's.

The extra return required (expected) by investors because this manager has chosen to take extra risk, is simply the difference in sensitivity between the portfolio and the S&P index times the associated λ. This is shown in Table 24.10 under the column entitled "Differential Expected Return."

We now come to the examination of any payoff that the investor receives due to the manager's ability to appropriately adjust factor sensitivities. This is the product of the difference between the factor sensitivities the manager chooses and the S&P index, and the return on any factor that was not required (expected) as compensation for risk. It is the sum of the differential b_{ij}'s times the I_j's and is shown in the column entitled "Differential Unexpected Return" in Table 24.10.

Adding together these four elements of return, we get 13.323%. Since the manager was able to earn an excess return of 14.52%, the difference of 1.197% is due to security selection. These ideas are summarized in Table 24.11.

Although this type of decomposition of performance is extremely useful, one must be careful in deciding what to attribute to management skill. How much of the return should be attributed to management skill? Clearly the 1.19 for security selection is attributed to management skill. However, the issue that needs to be addressed is whether the manager should be given credit for the return earned by having sensitivities different from the S&P index and having indexes having returns different from expected (0.329%). If the manager is free to choose the sensitivities, then one can argue that the extra return from a good choice of sensitivities should be attributed to management skill.

Note, however, that the factor sensitivities for this manager exactly match those of the average growth stock manager discussed in Chapter 16. If this manager was hired to act as a typical growth stock manager, then the extra return due to sensitivities differing from the

Table 24.10 Effect of Different Sensitivities on Performance

Common Influences	a Sensitivity of Manager's Portfolio b_{xj}	b Sensitivity of Market Portfolio $b_{S\&Pj}$	c Differential Sensitivity $c = a - b$	d Expected Return on Influence λ	e Unexpected Return on Influence l_j	f Differential Expected Return $f = c \times d$	g Differential Unexpected Return $g = c \times e$
Inflation	−0.5	−0.37	−0.13	−4.32	0.7	0.512	−0.091
Sales Growth	2.75	1.71	1.04	1.49	0.5	1.550	0.520
Oil Prices	−1.00	0.0	−1.00	0.00	0.4	0.000	−0.400
Market	1.30	1.0	0.30	3.96	1.0	1.188	0.300
						3.300	0.329

Table 24.11 Decomposition of Performance Using APT

Return on Benchmark		
a.	Expected	8.103
b.	From Factors Deviating from Mean	1.591
Return from Different Sensitivities (b)		
a.	Expected	3.300
b.	From Factors Deviating from Mean	0.329
	Return from Security Selection	1.197
	Total Return on Fund	14.52

S&P did not result from an active choice on the part of the manager. In this case the only extra return he or she can be credited for is the 1.197% due to selectivity.

In general, this raises the question of any appropriate benchmark to use in evaluating the manager. We have used the S&P index in our example and showed how the results would change had we used an average growth stock manager as the benchmark. In general, there are two types of benchmarks that seem appropriate. The first is a bogey that the investor selects as the target the manager is asked to outperform. This bogey can be an index, a portfolio, or another manager or group of managers. If this type of bogey is selected, then all of the analysis we have done previously holds, except that the b values for the bogey are used wherever we used b values for the S&P index.

The second type of bogey is the average b for the manager under question. If the manager is judged against the average Beta, then all excess returns that arise from differences from this average should be attributed to management performance.

MUTUAL FUND PERFORMANCE

In the earlier section we discussed mutual fund studies to illustrate some of the performance measurement techniques. In this section we intend to summarize the results.

When examining mutual fund performance figures, it is important to be careful to state the purpose of the evaluation. One purpose is to evaluate them as an alternative to individual direct investment, and this is the question we initially address. There are three types of transaction costs incurred directly or indirectly by investors in mutual funds. Mutual funds incur costs when they buy and sell securities. Second, mutual funds charge a yearly management fee. The typical size of this fee is $\frac{1}{2}$% of net asset value. Third, mutual funds have administrative costs that sometimes include sales expenses (so-called 12B1 fees). Finally, mutual funds often charge an initial fee to the purchaser of the fund's shares. This is typically 8% of the purchase made. Not all funds make this additional charge. Those that do not are referred to as no-load funds; those that do are referred to as load funds.

All of the tables in the earlier part of this chapter were prepared by deducting transaction costs of purchasing and selling the securities and the management fee from returns. However, the front load is not deducted. The argument for this choice is as follows. The alternative to mutual fund investment is direct investment. This involves a transaction cost for the initial purchase and final sale. Not deducting the front load is roughly equivalent to these transactions costs. This procedure is a rough approximation. It clearly distorts, some-what, the relative performance of load compared to no-load funds. Since no-load funds do not involve an initial purchase charge, the return or no-load funds is understated, relative to the return on an investor's direct purchase. Since the normal front load funds charge 8%, and 8% is larger than normal transaction costs, the return for load funds is overstated, rel-ative to individual direct purchase. Although this slightly affects the comparison between these types of funds, it probably has little effect on the overall conclusions concerning mutual fund performance.

The Evidence—Stock and Balanced Mutual Funds

A review of the evidence presented earlier in this chapter shows that, in general, mutual funds performed worse than a naive strategy of random selection or mixing passive port-folios with the riskless asset. This conclusion is broadly consistent with the other mutual fund studies that we did not examine of McDonald [61], Williamson [89], Crenshaw [15], Lehmann and Modest [56], and Elton, Gruber, Das, and Hlavka [25].

There are exceptions. The Securities and Exchange Commission (SEC) study showed one period of superior performance, the Friend, Blume, and Crockett [30] study showed good mutual fund performance compared to certain types of random selection; Connor and Korajczyk [13] found superior performance, as did Grinblatt and Titman [37].

With the exception of Elton, Gruber, Das, and Hlavka [25], all of the studies discussed earlier suffer from survivorship bias.[14] The sample of funds analyzed consists of the funds that exist at the end of the sample period studied by the researcher. Thus, if the researcher is studying data from 1980 to 1990, the sample consists of funds that exist as of 1990. An investor selecting in 1980 could select a fund that survives to 1990 or ceases to exist before 1990. The performance of funds that fail or are merged with other funds is generally poorer than those that succeed. Thus, a researcher examining the performance of funds that sur-vive will overstate performance. Furthermore, since failure is higher for the more volatile funds, a sample with survivorship bias will overstate performance of risky funds compared to safer funds.

As one might expect, the preponderance of evidence showing underperformance has not been happily received by the mutual fund industry. Is there any justification in light of these studies for an investor using mutual funds?[15] Mutual funds do provide substantial diversification.[16] Figure 24.10, taken from the Sharpe study, shows that about 88% of the total variance of return of mutual funds was due to market movements, leaving 12% diver-sifiable risk. Merrill Lynch, in their analysis of funds using their service, found that funds diversified away all but about 10% of the risk. Elton and Gruber [18] show that for an equally weighted randomly selected portfolio to be 90% diversified, 48 securities are required.[17]

---

[14]Grinblatt and Titman did estimate the impact of survivorship bias on their estimates.

[15]The advantages discussed shortly apply equally well to closed-end funds. Malkiel [60] suggests these funds may be more appropriate investment vehicles.

[16]Other reasons for owning mutual funds stem from conveniences provided to the investor. These include such items as check-writing privileges, the ability to switch types of investments costlessly (transfer money between different types of funds in the same family of funds), automatic reinvestment of income, and good investment reporting, among others.

[17]A careful selection of stocks can reduce this number significantly.

For an investor with limited capital, very large transaction costs are required to obtain the same degree of diversification. Thus, for small investors, mutual funds (even with some underperformance) still provide a reasonable alternative to direct purchase. If mutual funds are at times a good investment vehicle, a reasonable question to ask is: Are there any characteristics of mutual funds that are associated with superior performance?

The first variable to examine is sales charges. Table 24.12 shows such an examination. On average, the no-load outperformed the load funds. Funds in the category switch, involved in all cases, a change from load to no-load, performed the worst. Thus, an investor should only select a load fund if the investor has an ability to select a manager of a load fund with substantial selection ability and does not have the same ability to differentiate among no-load managers.

Table 24.12 Performance of Load and No-Load Funds

Fund	Number	α
Load	90	-1.55
No-load	19	-0.84
Switch	33	-2.17

Source: From Elton, Gruber, Das, and Hlavka [25].

The next three variables we examine are concerned with the techniques for managing mutual funds as well as characteristics that investors might use in selecting funds. First, do funds with high turnover have superior performance? Table 24.13 examines this question; this table indicates that managers with low turnover outperform managers with high turnover. Turnover causes transaction costs. The performance being examined is after transaction costs, thus the differential performance may simply reflect differences in the transaction costs that are incurred.

Table 24.13 Turnover and Alpha

Group	Average Turnover	α
High	$72\% < T < 162\%$	-2.21
2	$51\% < T < 72\%$	-1.87
3	$34\% < T < 51\%$	-2.17
4	$22\% < T < 34\%$	-1.11
Low	$T < 22\%$	-0.58

Source: From Elton, Gruber, Das, and Hlavka [25].

The second variable that has been examined is the ratio of expenses to assets. Expenses are the annual management fee and administrative costs. Table 24.14 shows that funds with greater expenses have poorer performance. Thus, high-expense funds do not seem to earn sufficient extra return to overcome the higher expenses.

Table 24.14 Effect of Average Expenses on α

Group	Average Expenses	α
High	$0.912 < E < 2.020$	-3.87
2	$0.753 < E < 0.912$	-1.68
3	$0.680 < E < 0.753$	-0.69
4	$0.590 < E < 0.680$	-1.19
Low	$E < 0.590$	-0.59

Source: From Elton, Gruber, Das, and Hlavka [25].

Another variable that has been examined is fund size. The argument can go either way. Large funds have an advantage in that they have more to spend for information and analysis. On the other hand, large funds may have more impact on the market when they engage in purchases and sales. When investigators examined this variable, they were unable to find any impact of size on performance. Table 24.15, taken from Friend, Blume, and Crockett, shows typical results.

There is another issue worth examining. Mutual funds have different stated objectives with respect to risk. If the actions of the funds differed from the stated objectives, then this would be an additional source of risk to the investors. Table 24.16 taken from the SEC study is typical. It shows that, in general, funds' stated objectives and performance are closely related.

Having examined performance for stock mutual funds, we will now turn to a similar analysis for bond mutual funds.

Table 24.15   Comparison of Investment Performance of Mutual Funds in Different Asset Size Groups (January 1960–June 1968)

	Number in Sample				Mean Return			
Risk Class (Beta Coefficient)	$10 to $50[a]	$50 to $100	$100 to $500	$500 and over	$10 to $50[a]	$50 to $100	$100 to $500	$500 and over
Low Risk ($\beta = 0.5-0.7$)	8	5	14	1	0.088	0.093	0.092	0.105
Medium Risk ($\beta = 0.7-0.9$)	11	12	18	12	0.101	0.111	0.105	0.110
High Risk ($\beta = 0.9-1.1$)	3	3	13	3	0.125	0.153	0.131	0.146

[a]Asset size in millions of dollars as of the end of 1967.
Source: From Friend, Blume, and Crockett [30].

Table 24.16   Relationship between Stated Investment Objectives and Mutual Fund Volatility, 125 Funds

	Investment Objective				
Volatility Range	Capital Gain	Growth	Growth Income	Income	Total
0–0.4	0	0	0	3	3
0.4–0.8	0	5	18	12	35
0.8–1.0	2	7	33	2	44
1.0–1.2	5	21	4	0	30
1.2+	8	5	0	0	13
Total	15	38	55	17	125

Source: SEC study [74].

The Evidence—Bond Funds

Bond mutual fund performance has not received nearly as much attention as equity fund performance. The principal study in this area is that of Blake, Elton, and Gruber [3]. Table 24.17 is reproduced from their article. They measure the performance of the bond funds for the five-year period ending in 1991 by comparing the return earned by the fund with

Table 24.17   Performance of Bond Funds

Fund Objective	Monthly Average Alpha	No. of Funds	No. of Negative Alphas	No. of Significant Alphas	
				Positive	Negative
Corporate	−0.051%	49	38	1	14
High Yield	−0.225%	42	38	0	11
Government Mortgage	−0.098%	30	30	0	15
Government Securities	−0.089%	96	81	2	42
All Funds	−0.107%	223	191	4	85

the return on a combination of passive portfolios of long-term government, long-term corporate, intermediate-term government, intermediate-term corporate, high-yield and mortgages with the same risk.

The first column in Table 24.17, which is labeled "Monthly Average Alpha," is the average difference in return between the fund and the combination of passive portfolios of equivalent risk. The data are monthly data. Thus, the negative monthly Alpha of −0.107% which is the average underperformance across all funds, corresponds to about 1.25% underperformance *per year* for the average bond mutual fund. Most bond mutual funds had negative Alphas. Over the full sample, 191 out of 223 had negative Alphas and 32 had positive Alphas. Furthermore, of the 89 funds whose Alphas were significantly different from zero, 85 were significantly negative. The average expenses for these funds were a little over 1%. Thus the amount of the underperformance was about equal to the expenses. Furthermore, when Alpha was regressed against expenses, the results were Alpha = −0.014 − 0.84 expenses. The slope of 0.84 means that every 1% increase in expenses results in a 0.84% reduction in Alpha. Put another way, for every 1% increase in expenses, the investor loses 84 basis points.

The slope was significantly different from zero, indicating that the relative performance across funds was significantly affected by their difference in expenses. The intercept of −0.01% translates into about −0.12% per annum. Thus, if funds did not charge any expenses, their average Alpha (α) would be about zero.

CONCLUSION

In this chapter we examined the state of the measurement and analysis of portfolio performance. We discussed alternatives for the overall evaluation of portfolios, as well as diagnostics to see what managers were doing and how well they accomplished their goals. Along the way we examined the actual performance of mutual funds and pointed out some deficiencies in the way that portfolio evaluation techniques are used.

QUESTIONS AND PROBLEMS

1.   Here are data on five mutual funds:

Fund	Return	Standard Deviation	Beta
A	14	6	1.5
B	12	4	0.5
C	16	8	1.0
D	10	6	0.5
E	20	10	2

What is the reward-to-variability ratio and the ranking if the risk-free rate is 3%?

2. For the data in Problem 1, what is the Treynor measure and ranking?

3. For the data in Problem 1, what is the differential return if the market return is 13%, the standard deviation of return is 5%, and standard deviation is the appropriate measure of risk?

4. For the data in Problem 1, what is the differential return if Beta is the appropriate measure of risk?

5. Assume that the zero Beta form of the capital asset pricing model (CAPM) is appropriate. What is the differential return for the funds shown in Problem 1 if $R_z = 4\%$?

6. For Funds A and B in Problem 1, how much would the return on B have to change to reverse the ranking using the reward-to-variability measure?

BIBLIOGRAPHY

1. Arditti, Fred. "Another Look at Mutual Fund Performance," *Journal of Financial and Quantitative Analysis*, **VI,** No. 3 (June 1971), pp. 909–912.
2. Ball, Ray, Kothari, S.P., and Shanken, Jay. "Problems in Measuring Portfolio Performance: An Application to Contrarian Investment Strategies," *The Journal of Financial Economics*, **38,** No. 1 (May 1995), pp. 79–107.
3. Blake, Christopher, Elton, Edwin, and Gruber, Martin. "The Performance of Bond Mutual Funds," *Journal of Business*, **66,** No. 3 (July 1993).
4. Blake, Christopher R., Elton, Edwin J., and Gruber, Martin J. "The Performance of Bond Mutual Funds," *The Journal of Business*, **66,** No. 3 (July 1993), pp. 371–403.
5. Blake, David. "Asset Allocation Dynamics and Pension Fund Performance," *The Journal of Business*, **72,** No. 4 (Oct. 1999), pp. 429–461.
6. Brown, Stephen J., and Goetzmann, William N. "Performance Persistence," *The Journal of Finance*, **50,** No. 2 (June 1995), pp. 679–698.
7. Brown, Stephen, Goetzmann, William, Ibbotson, Roger, and Ross, Stephen. "Survivorship Bias in Performance Studies," *Review of Financial Studies*, **5,** No. 4 (Dec. 1992), pp. 553–580.
8. Brown, Stephen J., and Goetzmann, William N. "Mutual Fund Styles," *Journal of Financial Economics*, **43,** No. 2 (1997), pp. 373–399.
9. Carlson, Robert. "Aggregate Performance of Mutual Funds: 1948–1967," *Journal of Financial Quantitative Analysis*, **V,** No. 1 (Mar. 1970), pp. 1–32.
10. Carpenter, Jennifer N., and Lynch, Anthony. "Survivorship Bias and Attrition Effects in Measures of Performance Persistence," *The Journal of Financial Economics*, **54,** No. 3 (Dec. 1999), p. 337.
11. Chen, Hsiu-Lang, Jegadeesh Narashimhan, and Wermers, Russ. "The Value of Active Mutual Fund Management: An Examination of the Stockholdings and Trades of Fund Managers," *Journal of Financial and Quantitative Analysis,* **35,** No. 3 (2000), pp. 343–368.
12. Cohen, Kalman, and Pogue, Jerry. "Some Comments Concerning Mutual Fund Versus Random Portfolio Performance," *Journal of Business*, **41,** No. 2 (April 1968), pp. 180–190.
13. Connor, George, and Korajczyk, Robert. "The Attributes Behavior and Performance of U.S. Mutual Funds," *Review of Quantitative Finance and Accounting*, **1,** (1991), pp. 4–25.
14. ———. "Performance Measurement with the Arbitrage Pricing Theory: A New Framework for Analysis," *The Journal of Financial Economics*, **15,** No. 3 (Mar. 1986), pp. 373–394.
15. Crenshaw, T.E. "The Evaluation of Investment Performance," *Journal of Business*, **50,** No. 4 (Oct. 1977), pp. 462–485.
16. Dahlquist, Magnus. "Evaluating Portfolio Performance with Stochastic Discount Factors," *The Journal of Business*, **72,** No. 3 (July 1999), pp. 347–383.
17. Dietz, Peter. "Components of a Measurement Model, Rate of Return, Risk and Timing," *Journal of Finance*, **XXIII,** No. 2 (May 1968), pp. 267–275.

18. Elton, Edwin J., and Gruber, Martin J. "Risk Reduction and Portfolio Size: An Analytical Solution," *Journal of Business*, **50,** No. 4 (Oct. 1977), pp. 415–437.

19. Elton, Edwin J., Gruber, Martin J., and Blake, Christopher R. "Fundamental Variables, APT, and Bond Fund Performance," *The Journal of Finance*, **50,** No. 4, (Sept. 1995).

20. ———. "The Persistence of Risk-Adjusted Mutual Fund Performance," *The Journal of Business*, **69,** No. 2 (Apr. 1996).

21. ———. "Survivorship Bias and Mutual Fund Performance," *Review of Financial Studies*, **8** (Winter 1996), pp. 1097–1120.

22. ———. "The Persistence of Risk-Adjusted Mutual Fund Performance," *The Journal of Business*, **69,** No. 2 (Apr. 1996), pp. 133–157.

23. ———. "A First Look At The Accuracy Of The CRSP Mutual Fund Database And A Comparison Of The CRSP And Morningstar Mutual Fund Databases," *The Journal of Finance*, **56,** No 6 (Dec. 2001).

24. Elton, Edwin J., Gruber, Martin J., Comer, George, and Li, Kai. "Spiders: Where Are the Bugs?" *The Journal of Business*, **75,** No. 3 (July 2002).

25. Elton, Edwin J., Gruber, Martin J., Das, Sanjiv, and Hlavka, Matthew. "Efficiency with Costly Information: A Reinterpretation of Evidence from Manager Portfolios," *Review of Financial Studies*, **6,** No. 1 (1993), pp. 1–23.

26. Fabozzi, Frank J., Francis, Jack C., and Lee, Cheng F. "Generalized Functional Form for Mutual Fund Returns," *Journal of Financial and Quantitative Analysis*, **XV,** No. 5 (Dec. 1980), pp. 1107–1120.

27. Fama, Eugene. "Components of Investment Performance," *Journal of Finance*, **XVII,** No. 3 (June 1972), pp. 551–567.

28. Fisher, Larry, and Weil, Roman. "Coping with the Risk of Interest Rate Fluctuations: Returns to Bondholders from Naive and Optimal Strategies," *Journal of Business*, **44,** No. 4 (Oct. 1971), pp. 408–431.

29. Friend, Irwin, and Blume, Marshall. "Measurement of Portfolio Performance Under Uncertainty," *American Economic Review*, **LX,** No. 4 (Sept. 1970), pp. 561–575.

30. Friend, Irwin, and Blume, Marshall, and Crockett, Jean. *Mutual Funds and Other Institutional Investors* (New York: McGraw-Hill, 1970).

31. Gaumnitz, Jack E. "Appraising Performance of Investment Portfolios," *Journal of Finance*, **XXV,** No. 3 (June 1970), pp. 555–560.

32. Gendron, Michel, and Genest, Christian. "Performance Measurement Under Asymmetric Information and Investment Constraints," *The Journal of Finance*, **45,** No. 5 (Dec. 1990), pp. 1655–1661.

33. Gepfert, Alan. "Does 'Good Portfolio Management' Exist?" *Management Science*, **15,** No. 6 (Feb. 1969), pp. B322–B324.

34. Gibb, J. William. "Critical Evaluation of Pension Funds," *Journal of Finance*, **XXIII,** No. 2 (May 1968), pp. 337–343.

35. Gordon, M., Paradis, G., and Rorke, C. "Experimental Evidence on Alternative Portfolio Decision Rules," *American Economic Review*, **LXII,** No. 1 (Mar. 1972), pp. 107–118.

36. Grant, Dwight. "Portfolio Performance and the 'Cost' of Timing Decisions," *Journal of Finance*, **XXXII,** No. 3 (June 1977), pp. 837–838.

37. Grinblatt, Mark, and Titman, Sheridan. "Mutual Fund Performance: An Analysis of Quarterly Portfolio Holdings," *Journal of Business*, **62** (1989), pp. 393–416.

38. ———. "Performance Measurement Without Benchmarks: An Examination of Mutual Fund Returns," *The Journal of Business*, **66,** No. 1 (Jan. 1993), pp. 47–68.

39. Gumperz, Julian, and Page, Evertee. "Misconceptions of Pension Fund Performance," *Financial Analysts Journal*, **26,** No. 3 (May–June 1970), pp. 30–37.

40. Guy, James. "The Performance of the British Investment Trust Industry," *Journal of Finance*, **XXXIII,** No. 2 (May 1978), pp. 443–455.

41. Ippolito, Richard. "Efficiency with Costly Information: A Study of Mutual Fund Performance," *Quarterly Journal of Economics*, **104,** No. 1 (1989), pp. 1–23.

42. Jagannathan, Ravi, and Korajczyk, Robert A. "Assessing the Market Timing Performance of Managed Portfolios," *The Journal of Business*, **59,** No. 2 (Apr. 1986), pp. 217–235.

43. Jensen, C. Michael. "The Performance of Mutual Funds in the Period 1945–1964," *Journal of Finance*, **XXIII,** No. 2 (May 1968), pp. 389–415.

44. Jensen, Michael. "Risk, the Pricing of Capital Assets, and the Evaluation of Investment Portfolios," *Journal of Business*, **42,** No. 2 (April 1969), pp. 167–247.

45. Jobson, J.D., and Korkie, Bob. "Potential Performance and Tests of Portfolio Efficiency," *Journal of Financial Economics*, **X,** No. 4 (Dec. 1982), pp. 443–466.

46. ———. "On the Jensen Measure and Marginal Improvements in Portfolio Performance: A Note," *The Journal of Finance*, **39,** No. 1 (Mar. 1984), pp. 245–252.

47. Joy, Maurice, and Porter, Burr. "Stochastic Dominance and Mutual Fund Performance," *Journal of Financial and Quantitative Analysis*, **IX,** No. 1 (Jan. 1974), pp. 25–31.

48. Kane, Alex, and Marks, Stephen Gary. "Performance Evaluation of Market Timers: Theory and Evidence," *The Journal of Financial and Quantitative Analysis*, **23,** No. 4 (Dec. 1988), pp. 425–435.

49. Kent, Daniel. "Measuring Mutual Fund Performance with Characteristic-Based Benchmarks," *The Journal of Finance*, **52,** No. 3 (July 1997), pp. 1035–1058.

50. Klemkosky, Robert. "The Bias in Composite Performance Measures," *Journal of Financial and Quantitative Analysis*, **VIII,** No. 3 (June 1973), pp. 505–514.

51. Kon, Stanley, and Jen, Frank. "Estimation of Time-Varying Systematic Risk and Performance for Mutual Fund Portfolios: An Application of Switching Regression," *Journal of Finance*, **XXXIII,** No. 2 (May 1978), pp. 457–475.

52. Kothari, S.P. "Evaluating Mutual Fund Performance," *The Journal of Finance*, **56,** No. 5 (Oct. 2001), pp. 1985–2012.

53. Kroll, Yoram, and Levy, Haim. "Sampling Errors and Portfolio Efficient Analysis," *Journal of Financial and Quantitative Analysis*, **XV,** No. 3 (sept. 1980), pp. 655–688.

54. Lee, Charles M.C., Shleifer, Andrei, and Thaler, Richard H. "Investor Sentiment and the Closed-End Fund Puzzle," *The Journal of Finance*, **46,** No. 1 (Mar. 1991), pp. 75–109.

55. Lee, Cheng, and Jen, Frank. "Effects of Measurement Errors on Systematic Risk and Performance Measure of a Portfolio," *Journal of Financial and Quantitative Analysis*, **XIII,** No. 2 (June 1978), pp. 299–312.

56. Lehmann, Bruce, and Modest, David. "Mutual Fund Performance Evaluation: A Comparison of Benchmarks and Benchmark Comparisons," *Journal of Finance*, **42** (1987), pp. 233–265.

57. Levitz, Gerald. "Market Risk and the Management of Institutional Equity Portfolios," *Financial Analysts Journal*, **30,** No. 3 (Jan./Feb. 1974), pp. 53–60.

58. Levy, Haim. "Portfolio Performance and Investment Horizon," *Management Science*, **18,** No. 12 (Aug. 1972), pp. B645–B653.

59. Mains, Norman. "Risk, the Pricing of Capital Assets, and the Evaluation of Investment Portfolios: Comment on [23]," *Journal of Business*, **50,** No. 3 (July 1977), pp. 371–384.

60. Malkiel, Burton. "The Valuation of Closed and Investment Company Shares," *Journal of Finance*, **XXXII,** No. 2 (June 1977), pp. 847–886.

61. McDonald, John. "Objectives and Performance of Mutual Funds: 1960–1964," *Journal of Financial and Quantitative Analysis*, **IX,** No. 3 (June 1974), pp. 311–333.

62. Meyer, Jack. "Further Applications of Stochastic Dominance to Mutual Fund Performance," *Journal of Financial and Quantitative Analysis*, **XII,** No. 3 (June 1977), pp. 235–242.

63. Miller, Tom W., and Gressis, Nicholas. "Nonstationarity and Evaluation of Mutual Fund Performance," *Journal of Financial and Quantitative Analysis*, **XV,** No. 3 (Sept. 1980), pp. 639–654.

64. Mills, D. Harlan. "On the Measurement of Fund Performance," *Journal of Finance*, **XXV,** No. 5 (Dec. 1970), pp. 1125–1131.

65. Monroe, Robert, and Treischmann, James. "Portfolio Performance of Property-Liability Insurance Companies," *Journal of Financial and Quantitative Analysis*, **VII,** No. 2 (Mar. 1972), pp. 1595–1611.

66. Peterson, David, and Rice, Michael L. "A Note on Ambiguity in Portfolio Performance Measures," *The Journal of Finance*, **35,** No. 5 (Dec. 1980), pp. 1251–1256.

67. Pohlman, R., Ang, J., and Hollinger, R. "Performance and Timing: A Test of Hedge Funds," *Journal of Portfolio Management*, **4,** No. 3 (Spring 1978), pp. 69–72.

68. Pontiff, Jeffrey. "Excess Volatility and Closed-End Funds," *The American Economic Review*, **87,** No. 1 (Mar. 1997), pp. 155–169.

69. Rothstein, Marvin. "On Geometric and Arithmetic Portfolio Performance Indexes," *Journal of Financial and Quantitative Analysis*, **VII,** No. 4 (Sept. 1972), pp. 1983–1992.

70. Sarnat, Marshall. "A Note on the Prediction of Portfolio Performance from Ex-Post Data," *Journal of Finance*, **XXVII,** No. 3 (June 1972), pp. 903–906.

71. Schlarbaum, Gary. "The Investment Performance of the Common Stock Portfolios of Property-Liability Insurance Companies," *Journal of Financial and Quantitative Analysis*, **IX,** No. 1 (Jan. 1974), pp. 89–106.

72. Schlarbaum, Gary, Lewellen, W., and Lease, R. "Realized Return on Common Stock Investments: The Experience of Individual Investors," *Journal of Business*, **51,** No. 2 (Apr. 1978), pp. 299–325.

73. ———. "The Common-Stock Portfolio Performance Record of Individual Investors: 1964–70." *Journal of Finance*, **XXIII,** No. 2 (May 1978), pp. 429–441.

74. Securities and Exchange Commission. *Institutional Investor Study* (Washington, D.C.: U.S. Government Printing Office, 1971) Part 2, pp. 325–347.

75. Sharpe, William. "Mutual Fund Performance," *Journal of Business*, **39,** No. 1, Part 2 (Jan. 1966), pp. 119–138.

76. ———. "Reply to [63]," *Journal of Business*, **41,** No. 2 (April 1968), pp. 235–236.

77. ———. "Determining a Funds Effective Asset Mix," *Investment Management Review* (June, 1988), pp. 5–15.

78. Shick, Richard, and Trieschmann, James. "Some Further Evidence on the Performance of Property-Liability Insurance Companies' Stock Portfolio," *Journal of Financial and Quantitative Analysis*, **XIII,** No. 1 (Mar. 1978), pp. 157–166.

79. Simon, Julian. "Does 'Good Portfolio Management' Exist?" *Management Science*, **15,** No. 6 (Feb. 1969), pp. B308–B319.

80. Simonson, Donald. "The Speculative Behavior of Mutual Funds," *Journal of Finance*, **XXVII,** No. 2 (May 1972), pp. 381–391.

81. Smith, Keith. "Is Fund Growth Related to Fund Performance?" *Journal of Portfolio Management*, **4,** No. 3 (Spring 1978), pp. 49–55.

82. Smith, Keith, and Tito, Dennis. "Risk-Return of Ex Post Portfolio Performance," *Journal of Financial and Quantitative Analysis*, **IV,** No. 4 (Dec. 1969), pp. 449–471.

83. Starks, Laura T. "Performance Incentive Fees: An Agency Theoretic Approach," *The Journal of Financial and Quantitative Analysis*, **22,** No. 1 (Mar. 1987), pp. 17–32.

84. Swadener, Paul. "Comment: Portfolio Performance of Property-Liability Insurance Companies," *Journal of Financial and Quantitative Analysis*, **VII,** No. 2 (Mar. 1973), pp. 1619–1623.

85. Tehranian, Hassan. "Empirical Studies in Portfolio Performance Using Higher Degrees of Stochastic Dominance," *The Journal of Finance*, **35,** No. 1 (Mar. 1980), pp. 159–220.

86. Treynor, Jack. "How to Rate Management of Investment Funds," *Harvard Business Review*, **43,** No. 1 (Jan./Feb. 1965), pp. 63–75.

87. Treynor, Jack, and Mazuy, M. "Can Mutual Funds Outguess the Market?" *Harvard Business Review*, **44,** No. 4 (July/Aug. 1966), pp. 131–136.

88. West, Richard. "Mutual Fund Performance and the Theory of Capital Asset Pricing: Some Comments," *Journal of Business*, **41,** No. 2 (Apr. 1968), pp. 230–234.

89. Williamson, Peter. "Measurement and Forecasting of Mutual Fund Performance: Choosing an Investment Strategy," *Financial Analysts Journal*, **28,** No. 5 (Nov./Dec. 1972), pp. 78–84.

25

Evaluation of Security Analysis

The selection of a portfolio of securities can be thought of as a multistage process. The first stage consists of studying the economic and social environment and the characteristics of individual companies in order to produce a set of forecasts of individual company variables. The second stage consists of turning these forecasts of fundamental data about the corporation and its environment into a set of forecasts of security prices and/or returns and risk measures. This stage is often called the valuation process. The third and last stage consists of forming portfolios of securities based on the forecast of security returns. Although, as we have seen in Chapter 24, a great deal of attention has been paid, both in the academic literature and in practice, to evaluating how well the entire process works, almost no attention has been paid to evaluating the component parts of the process. This is particularly surprising because the bulk of the evidence seems to indicate that the overall process does not work very well. The lack of extraordinary performance could be due to any of several causes, such as a lack of forecast ability, an inability to turn good forecasts of fundamental company data into good forecasts of returns, or a lack of ability to turn good forecasts of return into efficient portfolios. For example, it is perfectly possible that an organization has superior forecasting ability with respect to fundamental firm variables and market returns but does not capitalize on this information in forming portfolios.

In this chapter we are concerned with methods of analyzing how well an organization forecasts fundamental economic variables and how well it turns these forecasts into meaningful measures of security returns. To value a stock correctly, an organization must analyze and predict a large number of fundamental variables relating to each firm and the economy. In point of fact, the analysts at most institutions spend most of their time forecasting earnings (or growth in earnings). Because of this and because of the key role played by future earnings in any valuation scheme (see Chapter 18), we have selected forecasts of earnings per share as the fundamental firm variable examined in this chapter. The reader should keep in mind that the techniques we discuss for examining the accuracy of earnings estimates can be applied with a little imagination to forecasts of any fundamental variable. We start this chapter with a brief discussion of the sensitivity of price to earnings, and an overall look at the accuracy of earnings estimates. Then we present techniques that should be useful in evaluating and diagnosing the errors in earnings forecasts. Finally, we study some techniques for examining the valuation process itself.

WHY THE EMPHASIS ON EARNINGS?

In Chapter 18 we saw that a firm's value was generally considered to be a function of dividends, growth, and risk. Forecasts of future dividends are usually prepared by applying a forecasted payout ratio to forecasted earnings. At least in the short run payout ratios are easy to forecast and, to the extent they vary from historical levels, they usually do so as a function of earnings changes. We have already devoted a large amount of material to the analysis and forecasting of risk (Chapters 7 and 8). Thus the key remaining variable is the forecast of future earnings.

In Chapter 19 we showed that an ability to forecast future earnings can allow an excess return to be earned, even in the absence of a complex valuation model. For example, we saw that the 30% of firms that had the largest increase in earnings offered the investor a risk-adjusted excess return of 7.48% over a 13-month period, while those in the lower 30% offered a risk-adjusted excess return of −4.93%.[1]

The ability to earn an excess return by correctly forecasting earnings implies that the market's forecast of earnings (which determines price) is not perfectly accurate. Further evidence of this is supplied by the fact that the excess return we can earn from a perfect forecast of earnings becomes smaller and smaller as the end of the fiscal year approaches.[2] This is consistent with the market's estimate of future earnings becoming more and more accurate as information is released during the fiscal year.

A very good proxy for market expectation of future earnings is the consensus forecasts of security analysts. If the average forecast of security analysts is close to market expectations, then one should not be able to purchase stock on the basis of these expectations (e.g., forecasted growth) and make an excess return. Empirical evidence strongly suggests that this is, in fact, true.[3]

On the other hand, if the consensus forecasts are a good proxy for market expectations and one can forecast with more accuracy than the average analyst, then one should be able to make an excess return. In Chapter 19 we saw that this was, in fact, true. The next logical question to ask is how large has the error in consensus forecasts been. The answer is, quite large. If we examine forecasts made nine months before the end of the fiscal year, we find that for the 30% of the companies for which analysts most overestimated growth in earnings, their average error in forecasting growth was 63.6%. If we examine the 30% of the companies for which analysts most underestimated growth, we find their estimates were off, on average, by −38.9%. As the end of the fiscal year approaches, these errors shrink. But three months before the end of the fiscal year, they were still quite large: +26.4% and −27.0%, respectively.

It would be interesting to see how well individual analysts have performed compared to the consensus estimates. Unfortunately, no such studies exist. However, there are three studies of how accurately individual analysts' forecast compared to simple extrapolations of past earnings.

Cragg and Malkiel [3] analyzed predictions of long-term (five-year) growth rates prepared on each of a large sample of firms by analysts at five leading institutions. They concluded that there seems to be no clear-cut ability of the institutions examined to outperform simple extrapolations of historical growth rates.

---

[1] See Elton, Gruber, and Gultekin [7].

[2] See Elton, Gruber, and Gultekin [7] for evidence of this.

[3] See Elton, Gruber, and Gultekin [7].

Elton and Gruber [6] analyzed the ability of the analysts at three financial institutions to predict earnings nine months before the end of the fiscal year. They found that, of the three institutions examined, one performed slightly worse than historical extrapolation of past earnings, two performed slightly better, but none of the differences was statistically significant at even the 10% level. Brown and Rozeff [1] investigated the performance of Value Line estimates of earnings, once again comparing them with historical extrapolation methods. They found that Value Line outperformed the extrapolation techniques at a statistically significant level. A reasonable conclusion to draw from this evidence is that, while it is not easy to outperform historical extrapolation, there are individuals and perhaps institutions that might be able to do so. It may also be true that there are individuals and institutions that can outperform the consensus forecasts.

It is surprising, in light of the impact of the accuracy of earnings forecasts on stock selection and in light of the tremendous resources that financial institutions devote to the preparation of earnings forecasts, that more resources have not been devoted to the evaluation of earnings estimates. This is the subject with which the next section of this chapter deals.

THE EVALUATION OF EARNINGS FORECASTS

Although very little has been written about the evaluation of the estimates of security analysts, there is a broad literature in economics on the evaluation of forecasts. We draw heavily on this literature and, in particular, on the work of Henri Thiel in this section. We start by examining a meaningful overall measure of the accuracy of earnings forecasts. Then we look at both graphical and numerical techniques for diagnosing the sources of forecast error. We will end this section with an argument that any evaluation of earnings forecasts should be performed relative to the consensus (average) forecast of earnings. Anticipating this discussion and to provide a benchmark against which to measure analysts' performance, we provide data on the performance of the consensus forecast for several error measures discussed in this section.[4]

Overall Forecast Accuracy

In order to evaluate earnings forecasts in an exact manner, one should really have a loss function that measures the loss caused by any size error in the forecast. While this is indeed desirable, in many fields the evaluation of estimates must be performed in the absence of an explicit loss function. The most frequently assumed loss function is the quadratic, and the most frequently assumed measure of loss is the mean squared error.[5]

The mean squared forecast error for any set of forecasts can be easily computed as

$$\text{MSFE} = \frac{1}{N} \sum_{i=1}^{N} \left(F_i - A_i \right)^2$$

where

MSFE   is the mean squared forecast error

---

[4]The data used for the results reported in this chapter were extracted from the I/B/E/S data base. We include the consensus forecasts for all corporations with a December fiscal year, which were followed by three or more analysts for the years 1976, 1977, and 1978. Most tables are based on a total of 1242 consensus forecasts.

[5]See Thiel [11, 12].

F_i is a forecast of the earnings per share for firm i

A_i is the actual earnings per share that occurs for firm i

The mean squared forecast error is often developed in terms of the change in earnings. Define

P_i as the predicted change in earnings

R_i as the realized change in earnings

H_i as the level of earnings at the time the forecast was made.

Then,

$$P_i = F_i - H_i$$
$$R_i = A_i - H_i$$

The mean squared error in terms of the change in earnings can be written as

$$\text{MSFE} = \frac{1}{N} \sum_{i=1}^{N} (P_i - R_i)^2$$

The same MSFE results whether we perform the analysis in terms of the predicted change in earnings or the predicted level of earnings.[6]

It will prove convenient for error diagnosis to examine the forecast error as the error in forecasting the change in earnings. The mean squared forecast error can be used to rank forecasting techniques. However, it would be useful to scale the MSFE so that its value has a natural interpretation. One useful way to scale it has been suggested by Thiel [11, 12]. This measure, often referred to as Thiel's inequality coefficient (TIC), involves dividing the MSFE by the sum of the squared change in earnings, or

$$\text{TIC} = \left(\sum_{i=1}^{N} (P_i - R_i)^2 \right) \bigg/ \left(\sum_{i=1}^{N} R_i^2 \right)$$

Notice that two values of this measure have an easily interpreted economic meaning. If the predicted change in earnings always equaled the realized change in earnings (perfect forecasting), then the numerator would be 0 and TIC would be 0. Thus, a value of TIC equal to 0 implies perfect forecasting ability. If the predicted change in earnings always equaled 0, then P_i would equal 0 and TIC would equal 1. A value of TIC equal to 1 implies that the forecasts are exactly as accurate as a forecast of no change in next period's earnings. TIC allows us to obtain a sense of how well a forecaster performs, even before comparisons are made with other forecasters. A value below 1 indicates that the forecaster outperforms the naive no-change model. A value larger than 1 indicates that the forecasts could not outperform the most naive of all forecasting models.

Table 25.1 presents the values of TIC for the consensus estimates over the three years 1977, 1978, and 1979. Notice that 11 months before the last consensus forecast, the average

---

6

$$\text{MSFE} = \frac{1}{N} \sum_{i=1}^{N} (P_i - R_i)^2 = \frac{1}{N} \sum_{i=1}^{N} \left[F_i - H_i - (A_i - H_i) \right]^2 = \frac{1}{N} \sum_{i=1}^{N} (F_i - A_i)^2$$

Examination of the last term makes it clear that the MSFE of the change in earnings is identical to MSFE in terms of level of earnings.

Table 25.1   TIC over Time

Months before final forecast	11	10	9	8	7	6	5	4	3	2	1	0
TIC	0.75	0.70	0.62	0.54	0.49	0.44	0.41	0.35	0.28	0.26	0.20	0.15

analyst has a TIC value of 0.75, indicating that the performance of the consensus forecast is slightly better than the naive forecast. By the time analysts prepare their last forecast, the value of TIC has fallen to 0.15, indicating a great deal of accuracy. Table 25.1 also shows an extremely regular decrease of TIC for successive forecasts. The coefficient of determination between TIC and time is 0.99. As Elton, Gruber, and Gultekin [7] show, this same pattern occurs in each year, as well as on average over the entire period.

Before leaving this section we should mention an alternative to examining forecasts in terms of the error in forecasting earnings. Some researchers have suggested that forecasts be examined in terms of the *percentage* error in forecasting earnings. Ultimately, the test of which is correct depends on whether losses or gains are a function of the amount or the percentage by which earnings are misestimated. While this decision is up to the user, he or she should be aware that if percentage errors are used, results tend to be dominated by the huge percentage errors usually found in companies with very small earnings. Very small size earnings (a small denominator in the percentage calculation) make misestimation of any size appear quite serious. A problem also arises when the company has zero or negative earnings.[7] The analysis in this section can easily be recast in terms of percentage earnings error. The reader must decide which is the most relevant criterion.

Diagnosis of Forecasting Errors

There are infinitely many ways to examine forecast errors to learn more about them and perhaps correct future forecasts for their deficiencies. In this section we first present a diagrammatic scheme that can be used to learn a great deal about the pattern of forecast errors, and then we present some numerical techniques for computing diagnostics.

Graphical Analysis   One of the simplest, and yet most revealing, techniques for examining the pattern in forecast errors is the Prediction Realization Diagram (PRD) proposed by Thiel [11, 12]. This diagram is simply the plot of the predicted change in earnings against the realized change. The predicted change is plotted along the line that lies at a 45-degree angle to the horizontal axis, and actual change is plotted along a line that lies at a minus 45-degree angle to the horizontal axis. This is shown in Figure 25.1.

If we plot in this space the forecasted change in earnings versus the realized change, we can learn quite a lot about the type of forecast errors being made. Notice that if a point lies on the horizontal straight line, it indicates that the forecast change was exactly equal to the actual change. To the extent that points lie above the horizontal straight line, it indicates that estimates were too high. To the extent that points lie below the horizontal line, it indicates that estimates were too low. Now let us take a closer look at what each section of the graph represents. A point lying in section I of the PRD indicates that the forecaster successfully predicted that earnings would increase, but that the size of the increase was overestimated. A point lying in section II indicates that the analyst successfully predicted a

---

[7]When earnings are zero, the percentage change in earnings will be infinite. When earnings are negative, the meaning of percentage changes in earnings is ambiguous.

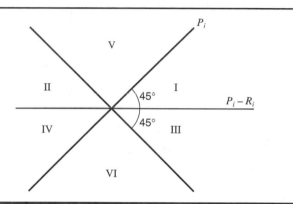

Figure 25.1   Prediction Realization Diagram.

decrease in earnings but that the size of the decrease was underestimated (earnings were overestimated). If a point lies in section V, it indicates that the analyst predicted the wrong direction for the change in earnings. That is, the analyst predicted they would increase when they, in fact, decreased. Sections III, IV, and VI are analogous to sections I, II, and V. Section III represents a successful prediction of an increase in earnings but an underestimate of the size of the increase. Section IV represents a successful prediction of a decrease but an overestimate of the size of the decrease. Finally, a point in section VI represents a forecast of a decrease in earnings when they actually increased. Sections V and VI indicate that the analyst misestimated the direction of the change in earnings movements whereas the other sections indicate the analyst got the direction right but the size wrong.

Examination of a group of forecasts on the PRD can reveal quite a lot of information about the source of error in analysts' forecasts. In Figures 25.2 and 25.3 we have constructed two hypothetical patterns that might be observed. Figure 25.2 presents the case where a forecaster is consistently optimistic. The forecaster consistently overestimates earnings changes when they are positive (section I) and consistently underestimates the size of a negative change (section II) or actually predicts a positive change when changes are negative (section V).

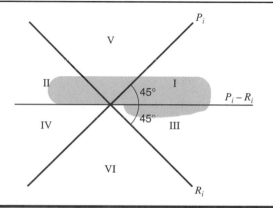

Figure 25.2   Prediction Realization Diagram: optimistic forecaster.

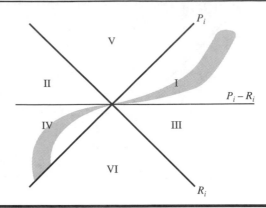

Figure 25.3   Prediction Realization Diagram: the overreactor.

A more interesting pattern is revealed in Figure 25.3. In this diagram we find the profile of an analyst who is excellent at predicting the direction of change. However, the analyst overreacts to change by becoming overoptimistic as large positive changes are expected and overpessimistic as large negative changes are expected. This can be seen by the fact that estimates lie further and further from the horizontal axis as the actual level of earnings change increases.

These are only two of the many potential patterns of forecaster behavior that can be seen through the PRD. The reader is encouraged to construct other series of points on this diagram and to interpret their meaning.

Numerical Analysis   While the graphical analysis of forecast errors is extremely useful, there are also several analytical decompositions of the mean squared forecast error that can provide useful insight into the sources of forecasting error. Let us take, as an example, a firm that has a collection of analysts making forecasts of a broad group of stocks in the economy. We discuss two meaningful decompositions of these errors. The first is based on the level of aggregation at which errors occur, while the second looks at the forecast error in terms of the characteristics of the forecasters.

Error Decomposed by Level of Aggregation   It would be extremely useful to determine at what level of aggregation errors in the forecasts occurred. One scheme for analyzing the level separates earnings errors into three components. This scheme is shown below.

$$
\text{MSFE} = \frac{1}{N} \sum_{i=1}^{N} \left(P_i - R_i \right)^2
$$

$$
= \left(\overline{P} - \overline{R} \right)^2 + \frac{1}{N} \sum_{i=1}^{N} \left[\left(\overline{P}_a - \overline{P} \right) - \left(\overline{R}_a - \overline{R} \right) \right]^2
$$

$$
+ \frac{1}{N} \sum_{i=1}^{N} \left[\left(P_i - \overline{P}_a \right) - \left(R_i - \overline{R}_a \right) \right]^2
$$

where

$\overline{P}$ = mean value of P_i across all stocks followed by all analysts

$\overline{R}$ = mean value of R_i across all stocks followed by all analysts

$\bar{P}_a$ = mean value of P_i for industry a to which i belongs. Each industry will have a different value of $\bar{P}_a$

$\bar{R}_a$ = mean value of R_i for each industry in turn

The first term measures how much of the forecast error is due to inability of the analysts, in total, to predict what average earning will be for the economy. This term is simply the squared difference between the average predicted change in earnings and the average realized change in earnings. The second term is a measure of how much of the total error is due to the individual analysts misestimating the differential performance of particular industries from the average for the economy.

Let us examine this term in more detail. For each firm (i) the difference between the mean predicted change in earnings for the industry to which it belongs ($\bar{P}_a$) and the mean predicted change in earnings for all firms ($\bar{P}$) is calculated. The same term is calculated for actual change in earnings ($\bar{R}_a - \bar{R}$). The difference between the two is squared and summed for all firms. Then the average value of this term is taken. The third term measures how much of the error is due to analysts not being able to predict the difference in performance of the individual stocks they follow from the appropriate industry average. The first part of this term is the difference between the predicted change in earnings for an individual stock P_i and the average predicted change for a stock in the industry to which i belongs. The second part has the same meaning, but deals with realizations. These differences are squared, summed, and then averaged.

By dividing through both sides of the equation by the MSFE, we express each source of error as a fraction of the total mean squared forecast error. Diagnosing the source of the error can be of great significance to the firm. For example, if the major source of error arises from misestimated aggregate earnings, then the company should concentrate more effort on preparing its forecasts of the general economy. If the analysts are provided with better information about the aggregate level of earnings and are explicitly encouraged to use this information, then improvement should occur in the firm's forecasting effort. Assuming that each analyst follows one industry or a group of closely related industries (economic sector), then a large value for the second term points to an error in understanding the economics of alternative industries. Large values of the third term indicate that errors are associated with being unable to differentiate between the performance of individual companies even when mistakes in forecasts of the level of the economy and industries are removed.

Obviously, this same type of decomposition can be repeated for all individual analysts with their error decomposed into their misestimate of how the stocks they follow will do, on average, and their inability to differentiate the performance of the companies they follow.

In Table 25.2 we present the decomposition of the mean square error by level of aggregation for the set of consensus forecasts discussed earlier. Perhaps the most striking aspect of this table is the small percentage of error that is due to misestimating the performance of the economy (the average company). This source of error never exceeds 3% of the total mean squared error. The percentage of error due to industry misestimates starts at 36.5% in January and declines continuously to 17.6% by the end of the fiscal year. Consequently, the error due to misestimating individual companies grows from 61.8% to 80.5% over the year. We have already seen that the size of analyst's errors shrinks over the year. Now we see that while analysts become more accurate in forecasting both industry and company errors, their ability to forecast industry influences grows relative to their ability to forecast company performance over the year.

Table 25.2　Percentage Error in Earnings Change by Level of Aggregation

	Economy	Industry	Company
January	1.7	36.5	61.8
February	1.8	36.4	61.8
March	1.9	35.6	62.4
April	1.9	33.7	64.4
May	2.4	33.4	64.2
June	2.7	31.8	65.6
July	2.8	31.7	65.5
August	2.8	30.9	66.2
September	3.0	28.2	68.9
October	2.7	27.2	70.1
November	2.2	23.6	74.3
December	1.9	17.6	80.5

Errors Decomposed by Forecast Characteristics　There is a second type of decomposition of forecast errors that is meaningful to management. This decomposition looks for the pattern of mistakes and is a numeric analogue to the graphical analysis presented earlier. We can write this decomposition as

$$\text{MSFE} = \frac{1}{N} \sum_{i=1}^{N} \left(P_i - R_i \right)^2$$

$$\text{MSFE} = \left(\overline{P} - \overline{R} \right)^2 + \left(1 - \beta \right)^2 \sigma_p^{\,2} + \left(1 - \rho \right)^2 \sigma_R^{\,2}$$

where

β　is the slope coefficient of the regression of R on P

ρ　is the correlation of P and R

σ_P^2　is the variance of P

σ_R^2　is the variance of R

The first term in this equation $(\overline{P} - \overline{R})$ represents bias. This is the tendency of the average forecast to either overestimate or underestimate the true average. The second term represents inefficiency or the tendency for forecasters to be systematically overoptimistic (or insufficiently optimistic) about good (or bad) events. If the Beta of actual earnings on forecasted earnings is greater than 1, then forecasts are overestimates of earnings at high values and underestimates at low values of actual earnings. If Beta is less than 1, then analysts underestimate earnings when they are high and overestimate earnings when they are low. The final component of this equation is the random disturbance term.

When we apply this decomposition to consensus estimates, we find some interesting results. The vast majority of analysts' errors are random rather than systematic in nature. In all months over 91%, and in one-half of the months over 94%, of the MSFE arise from random error. Inefficiency as well as bias contribute very little to MSFE. Furthermore, Betas are close to 1 and vary randomly around 1. There does not seem to be a systematic tendency of analysts to get overexcited or overly cautious about potentially good performance on the part of firms.

The Evaluation of Earnings Forecasts—Again

While it is important to examine the accuracy of earnings estimates and to diagnose where errors are being made, there is another step that should be taken. Forecast errors can more meaningfully be judged relative to some benchmark than they can on an absolute basis. The need for a benchmark is easy to see. It is less difficult to forecast earnings for some stocks and for some industries than it is for others. For example, the earnings of public utilities are more stable and easier to forecast than are the earnings for electronics manufacturers. If a benchmark is not used, the forecaster who follows utilities or the firm that specializes in utility stocks will be judged a better forecaster (if its ability is about the same) than the forecaster who follows electronics stocks.

Thus, one quality we would like a benchmark to have is to adjust for the difficulty of the forecasting process. A second quality we would like a benchmark to have is to represent an absolute base such that forecasting ability above the benchmark can be potentially transformed into superior security selection while performance below the benchmark is unlikely to lead to superior security selection. Fortunately, a benchmark exists that satisfies both these criteria. It is the consensus forecast introduced in Chapter 19. The accuracy of the consensus forecast reflects how easy or difficult it is to forecast the earnings for a particular company or group of companies. In addition, as we have already seen, the price of any stock reflects (incorporates) the consensus forecast. The ability to forecast with no more accuracy than the consensus should not lead to a superior return, while the ability to forecast with more accuracy should.

Thus, we propose that the benchmark against which all analysts and forecasts be judged should be the consensus forecast. As a first step in analyzing the performance of any analyst or group of analysts (institution), their mean squared forecast error can be computed and compared directly with the mean squared forecast error for the consensus forecast. The consensus mean squared forecast error should be computed over that same set of corporations for which the analyst or institution prepared forecasts. Then each of the diagnostics discussed earlier in this chapter can be computed for the consensus forecasts and compared directly with the diagnostics of the institution's forecasts. Alternatively, consensus forecasts can be used as the benchmark forecast and individual forecasts compared against it. This would involve defining realizations as the consensus forecast of change in earnings.

EVALUATING THE VALUATION PROCESS

The valuation process converts a set of forecasts about company fundamentals and economic data into a set of forecasts of market variables or a recommended course of action to take with respect to individual securities. The number of books and articles written about the valuation of securities far exceeds the number of publications on modern portfolio theory. It is surprising that, given the large number of publications on how to value securities, almost nothing has been written about how to value the valuation process itself.

Before turning to an evaluation of the valuation process, let us spend a little time thinking about what form the output from the valuation process should take. The problem becomes rather simple when we realize that the output from the valuation process is the input to portfolio analysis. We know what we need to perform portfolio analysis. We need estimates of the expected return for each stock, the variance of the return on each stock, and the correlation of returns between each pair of stocks. Chapters 7 and 8 dealt with alternative models for predicting correlations between securities as well as techniques for evaluating these alternative models. We mentioned at that time that we felt it unlikely that the analyst would ever produce direct estimates of correlation coefficients.

What analysts can produce are estimates of expected returns, perhaps variances, or estimates of the parameters of at least one of the models from Chapters 7 and 8 that can be used to estimate variance and covariances. For illustrative purposes, let us assume that analysts are preparing estimates of expected returns and Betas. Their estimates of Beta may well involve subjective modification of historical or fundamental Betas.

The question then remains, given that analysts produce estimates of the relevant risk and return parameters, how do we evaluate the quality of these estimates?[8]

Evaluating the Valuation Process with a Full Set of Outputs

There are really three steps that can and should be taken in evaluating the valuation process:

1. How well does each output from the valuation process predict the future?
2. If the output is examined in a simple way, does the output lead to undervalued and overvalued stocks being correctly identified?
3. If the output is used in an optimal manner, does it produce good results?

Let us now examine each in turn. The first step is to see if there is any predictive content in the output for the valuation process. For example, one type of output should be the expected return for each security. One question to analyze is how well does expected return forecast future returns, and what are the sources of error in the forecast? We have already designed the system for analyzing this question in the first part of this chapter. For all of the evaluation procedures outlined in this part of the chapter, we can simply substitute expected rate of return for change in earnings. For the naive model against which to judge expected rate of return, we can substitute the historical average rate of return on the stock for the consensus forecast of earnings.

Any other individual output from the valuation process can be analyzed in an analogous manner. For example, Beta estimates could be used in any of the diagnostic procedures outlined in the first part of this chapter.

Let us assume that there is some predictive content in one or more of the outputs from the valuation process. Where do we go from there? The next step is to begin to analyze the output in combination. The simplest way to do this is to examine the output in expected return Beta space and to see how stocks that appear to be underpriced (or overpriced) perform in subsequent periods. To be more specific, assume that analysts as of December 31, 1995, have forecasted the expected return and Beta for a group of stocks for the year 1996. Based on expectations about returns and Betas for the year 1996, an expected security market line could be constructed. The distance that a particular security lies above this line is a measure of its attractiveness as a candidate for purchase. The distance above or below the expected security market line is usually referred to as a stock expected Alpha. This is a measure of how much more or less than its equilibrium return a stock is expected to earn. At the end of 1996, the actual return and Beta for each stock can be measured as well as the security market line for 1996. This allows the computation of an actual Alpha for each stock for 1996. The expected Alpha for each stock can now be compared with the Alpha that occurred for each stock. In particular, the predictive power of expected Alpha can be compared with the naive prediction of all future Alphas equal to zero. If the expected Alphas predict better than this model, there is informational content in the valuation process.

---

[8]In this section we are presenting techniques for the evaluation of the valuation process given the quality of inputs to the valuation process. This should not be disturbing, since the previous section dealt with evaluating these inputs.

The final step in evaluating the output from the valuation process is to see if employing this output with the portfolio optimization rules of Chapters 6 and 9 leads to the selection of portfolios that perform well. Using the appropriate techniques from Chapters 7 and 9, we select that portfolio that would be optimum if the input from the valuation process were correct. We can then use any of the techniques outlined in the previous chapter to evaluate the portfolio we have selected. Hopefully, this portfolio will outperform naive strategies such as buying an index fund with the same risk.

Although we could end the discussion of evaluation of the valuation process at this point, there is one more step that should be taken. Using the techniques of the previous chapter, the portfolio discussed earlier should be compared with the portfolio actually held by the institution performing this analysis. If the institution's portfolio does not perform as well, it indicates that the portfolio manager is not making optimum use of the information supplied to him. If the manager's portfolio performs better, it indicates that he or she is introducing additional information not contained in the output of the valuation process.

Evaluating the Output of the Valuation Process: Incomplete Information

To perform portfolio analysis properly, one needs a full range of inputs on expected return, variances, and covariances. While more and more firms are recognizing this and encouraging their analysts to provide data in this form, the majority of firms have a much simpler form for output from the valuation process.

Many firms have their analysts provide data to portfolio managers (or provide data to the firm's clients) in terms of a recommendation to either buy, sell, or hold particular stocks.[9] This is less satisfactory than output provided, in terms of rate of return forecasts. It forces the analyst to compress a continuous rating of securities into a three-point scale. This prevents the analyst from passing along information to the portfolio manager or, perhaps worse, gives the analyst an excuse for not developing the information. The best evaluation that can be done in a case like this is to examine the performance of each of the three groups of stocks to see if the groupings contain information.

As an example of the type of analysis that might be done, let us assume that we have a group of stocks for which buy-sell-hold recommendations have been made as of December 31, 1995. The firm has a one-year time horizon and, it is now December 31, 1996. Then the returns on each stock for the year 1996 can be plotted in return Beta space. Furthermore, the best estimate of the security market line that existed in 1996 can be plotted on the same diagram. The alphas or distances above and below the line could be computed for each stock.[10] Figure 25.4 illustrates this analysis.

Hopefully the majority of the buy recommendations lie above the line and the majority of the sell recommendations lie below the line. The difference between the rate of return on the stock and the return expected on each stock given the security market line can be calculated for each buy recommendation, as well as for each hold and sell recommendation.[11] The average for each group can be computed. It should be positive for the buy

---

[9]Some firms use a five-point scale rather than a buy-sell-hold recommendation, but the evaluation will be similar to that described in this section.

[10]The estimate of the security market line should be made from all stocks, not just from those stocks followed by the firm.

[11]This distance is simply the vertical distance between the line and the point.

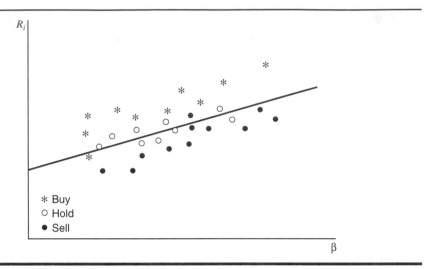

Figure 25.4   Examination of buy-hold-sell recommendations.

recommendations, close to zero for the hold, and negative for the sells. Notice that, even in computing the average distances for each group, we have implicitly made an assumption. The assumption is that in putting together a portfolio, the portfolio manager will place an equal dollar amount in each buy and an equal dollar amount in each sell. This is not an optimal course of action, even if the buy and sell ratings are perfectly accurate. There are bound to be differences in the relative rankings of stocks within each category, and this procedure fails to take account of these differences. However, the naive procedure of assuming equal investment can be used to get an indication of whether there is information in the estimates of buy, hold, and sell.[12]

CONCLUSION

Almost all the emphasis in the evaluation process has been placed on evaluating the performance of portfolios held by financial institutions. In light of the fact that the performance of these portfolios has been unsatisfactory, it is important to start examining the steps in the portfolio management process to see if there is information that is not being used. In this chapter we have suggested a series of steps for doing so. The first step is to examine the forecasts of fundamental data on corporations to see if they contain information. The second step is to evaluate the output from the valuation process to see if it has taken advantage of any information contained in the security analyst's basic forecast. The final step is to compare portfolios selected in an optimal fashion from the output of the valuation process with portfolios selected by portfolio managers to analyze what the portfolio manager adds to the process. It is only by breaking the portfolio selection and management process into stages that a firm can find what it does well and what it does poorly in the hope of improving portfolio performance.

---

[12]This naive procedure is necessary if one wishes to isolate the effect of information in the buy, hold, or sell recommendations. If one wished to simultaneously evaluate risk variables, a more complex procedure is possible.

QUESTIONS AND PROBLEMS

1. Assume that a brokerage firm concentrates on a few closely related industries. It has produced a set of estimates of earnings for 1985 and subsequently recorded the earnings that actually occurred. These data are given below:

Industry	Firm	Previous Earnings	Estimated Earnings	Actual Earnings
A	1	1.05	1.10	1.05
	2	1.32	1.37	1.35
	3	3.50	4.25	3.25
B	4	2.06	2.10	2.12
	5	2.08	2.13	2.12
	6	2.60	3.25	2.80
	7	1.07	1.06	1.06
C	8	2.00	2.70	2.40
	9	0.55	0.52	0.54
	10	1.18	1.16	1.20

A. Plot these points on a Predictive Realization Diagram. What can we learn about the forecast pattern of this firm from the PRD?

B. Calculate the mean square forecasted error for this firm.

C. Decompose the error by level of aggregation. That is, determine what percentage of the error was due to the inability to forecast earnings for this sector of the economy, what percent was due to an inability to forecast each industry, and what percent was due to inability to forecast differences for each firm.

D. Examine another level of decomposition. Assume that there are three analysts, each following one industry. What is the mean squared error of each analyst? How much of the error of each analyst is due to the analyst's inability to predict the future of the industry followed, and how much is due to an inability to differentiate between the firms in the industry?

E. Decompose the error by forecast characteristics. Find what percentage of the error is due to bias, what percentage is due to variance, and what percentage is due to covariance.

BIBLIOGRAPHY

1. Brown, Lawrence, and Rozeff, Michael. "The Superiority of Analysts' Forecast as Measures of Expectations: Evidence from Earnings," *Journal of Finance*, **XXXIII,** No. 1 (Mar. 1978), pp. 1–16.
2. Brown, Stephen J., and Warner, Jerold B. "Measuring Security Price Performance," *Journal of Financial Economics*, **8,** No. 3 (Sept. 1980), pp. 205–258.
3. Cragg, J. G., and Malkiel, B. G. "The Consensus and Accuracy of Some Predictions of Growth of Corporate Earnings," *Journal of Finance*, **23,** No. 1 (Mar. 1968), pp. 67–84.
4. Dybvig, Philip H., and Ross, Stephen A. "The Analytics of Performance Measurement Using a Security Market Line," *The Journal of Finance*, **40,** No. 2 (June 1985), pp. 401–416.
5. ——. "Performance Measurement Using Differential Information and a Security Market Line," *Journal of Finance*, **40,** No. 2 (June 1985), pp. 383–400.

6. Elton, Edwin J., and Gruber, Martin J. "Earnings Estimates and the Accuracy of Expectational Data," *Management Science*, **18,** No. 2 (Apr. 1972), pp. 409–424.

7. Elton, Edwin J., Gruber, Martin J., and Gultekin, Mustafa. "Expectations and Share Prices," *Management Science*, **27,** No. 9 (Sept. 1981).

8. ———. "Professional Expectations: Accuracy and Diagnosis of Errors," Working Paper, New York University, 1983.

9. Elton, Edwin J., Gruber, Martin J., and Grossman, Seth. "Discrete Expectational Data and Portfolio Performance/Comment," *The Journal of Finance*, **41,** No. 3 (July 1986), pp. 699–714.

10. Fama, Eugene F., and French, Kenneth R. "Size and Book-to-Market Factors in Earnings and Returns," *The Journal of Finance*, **50,** No. 1 (Mar. 1995), pp. 131–155.

11. Thiel, Henri. *Optimal Decision Rules for Government and Business* (Amsterdam: North-Holland, 1964).

12. ———. *Applied Economic Forecasting* (Amsterdam: North-Holland, 1966).

26

Portfolio Management Revisited

Throughout this book we have presented analysis and models that have major implications for the way money should be managed. Some of the analysis involved forecasts of economic or market characteristics for securities and optimal techniques for portfolio construction based on these forecasts. Other chapters imply that securities prices are in equilibrium or almost in equilibrium, and the investor should hold some sort of aggregate portfolio. We have not resolved this issue nor has the investment community resolved it.

It seems worthwhile to take a last look at how money management has evolved and how the financial community has dealt with these issues. In this chapter we will discuss the major investment strategies that modern portfolio managers follow. For each strategy we will discuss the assumptions under which the strategy should be successful. In addition to supplying a review of current approaches to investment analysis, this chapter should help the reader integrate earlier chapters of this book. Let's start by briefly reviewing the basic approaches to investment management. In general terms the approaches are labeled as passive management and active management. We present more of their overall characteristics in Figure 26.1. In earlier editions of this book we briefly described each approach. In recent years, however, because the investment process has evolved and resulted in the structuring of so many new investment management styles and products, we are going to devote more discussion to their analysis.

The chapter is divided into four sections. In the first section we discuss management styles for stock portfolios. In the second we discuss management styles for bond portfolios. The distinction is made for two reasons:

1. Types of investment products have developed in the bond area that have not yet been developed for stocks.

2. Because of both finite lives and liquidity considerations, bonds present some special challenges.

In the third section of this chapter we introduce some of the concepts of managing a portfolio when the manager is concerned with meeting a set of liabilities. In the final section we discuss the bond–stock mix.

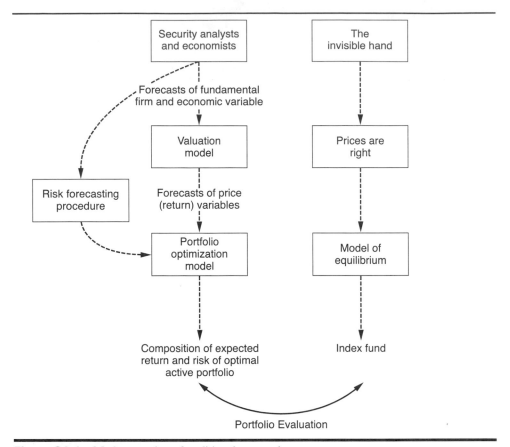

Figure 26.1   Modern version of traditional approach.

MANAGING STOCK PORTFOLIOS

In "olden days" (5 or 10 years ago), it was easy to discuss management styles for common stocks. One was a passive manager or an active manager. The passive manager held a market index [e.g., the Standard & Poor's (S&P) 500], and the active manager did something else. Although it would be easy to discuss management styles in this way, we would be overlooking recent developments in the area of passive management. Instead, we distinguish active versus passive management on the basis of whether action is predicated on forecast data. As we'll see, even with this definition, the line between passive and active management becomes increasingly fuzzy.

Passive Management

Funds under passive management have grown rapidly and reached significant size. For example, the *Institutional Investor* magazine estimated that $176 billion of institutional assets was invested domestically and $22 billion internationally in passive equity index matching portfolios as of 1990. The simplest case of passive management is the index fund that is designed to replicate *exactly* a well-defined index of common stock, such as the S&P 500. The fund buys each stock in the index in exactly the proportion it represents of the index. If IBM constitutes 4% of the index, the fund places 4% of its money in IBM stock.

The standard (Sharpe–Lintner–Mossin) capital asset pricing model could be considered the theoretical justification for such a fund, if one were willing to accept the S&P 500 as a suitable proxy for the market portfolio of risky assets. Perhaps a more practical justification is that index funds have outperformed more than 50% of active managers. One of the major companies evaluating manager performance estimated in 1989 that during the past 20 years the S&P index outperformed more than 80% of active managers. For the past five years the S&P outperformed more than 75% of active managers.

Although exact replication is the simplest technique for constructing an index fund, many index funds are not constructed this way. Managers of index funds must face a series of decisions in designing a fund. These decisions involve the trade-off between accuracy in duplicating the index (called tracking error) and transaction costs. Does the manager buy all 500 stocks in market proportions, or are some of the stocks with the smallest market weight excluded to save on transaction costs? How are periodic dividends reinvested to balance savings on transaction costs versus imperfections in tracking the index? How much cash should be kept on hand to accommodate withdrawals or as a result of cash inflows?[1] The more cash, the lower the transaction costs, but the less perfectly the index is tracked.

There are three commonly used approaches in constructing an index fund. Each makes a different tradeoff between accuracy in duplicating the index and transaction costs. These three approaches can be summarized as follows:

1. Hold each stock in the proportion it represents of the index.

2. Mathematically form a portfolio of not more than a specified number of stocks (e.g., 300), which best tracks the index historically. Standard mathematical programming algorithms can be used to do this.

3. Find a smaller set of stocks that matches the index in the percent invested in a pre-specified set of characteristics (e.g., same percent in industrial, utility, and financial stocks). Some of the frequently used characteristics are sector, industry, quality, and size of capitalization.

Although some index funds replicate market weights exactly, many use a combination of the first approach and either the second or third approach. Market weight matching is most likely to be used by funds that match an index of large capitalization stocks, such as the S&P 500 index. For funds that match a much broader index (e.g., the Wilshire 5000), large capitalization stocks are matched exactly in market weights and then one of the other techniques is applied to find a subset of low capitalization stocks to match the remaining part of the index. For most indexes, because a few stocks (e.g., 20%) make up more than one-half of the market value of the index, this approach has intuitive appeal.

Although an index fund designed to match the S&P index is a popular instrument, managers wanted to make it better almost immediately after it was created. The most obvious way to do this was to find a better proxy for the market portfolio. Index funds exist that track most major indexes such as the New York Stock Exchange (NYSE) Index and the Wilshire 5000 stock index. The higher transaction costs of duplicating a broader index mean that one or more of the techniques for matching an index with fewer stocks is almost always used in the construction of a broad-based index fund.

---

[1]Index funds available to the individual investor, such as the Vanguard funds, maintain cash to accommodate withdrawals. Index funds that invest funds for institutional clients such as pension funds often do not allow withdrawals without substantial notification. In addition, by using dividend reinvestment plans and futures many are essentially fully invested.

At first thought, one would expect most index funds to underperform the index on average. Index funds have management fees, and transaction costs are incurred in their management. However, two factors help performance. First, S&P occasionally missed small stock dividends in calculating the return on the index, thus understating the actual return. Second, index funds always deliver stock when a firm offers to buy it above market price (in a merger or stock repurchase), but some investors do not. Thus, the index fund obtains a higher price for some of its stock than is assumed when the return on the index is calculated. Because of these influences, some low-cost funds have outperformed the index they match over long periods of time.

No index fund has a performance that exactly matches the performance of the index it tracks on a month-by-month or year-by-year basis. Cash inflows from investors, the payment of dividends, and the response to changes in the composition of the index cause the cash position to change and transaction costs to be incurred. Index funds available to individual investors also maintain a cash position to smooth out cash flows. This results in Betas slightly below one with respect to the index they track. It also means they generally do slightly better in down markets and slightly worse in up markets. Despite these differences, many index funds earn returns within 0.05% per quarter of the index they track.

The index funds discussed thus far all have a theoretical justification based at least in part on the simple capital asset pricing model (CAPM). We should easily be able to design an index fund based on any of the other equilibrium models described in this book. One type of fund that met with some commercial success was the Wells Fargo yield-tilted index fund. From the post-tax equilibrium model developed in Chapter 14, we know that returns should be determined in part by dividends and that the attractiveness of any portfolio to an investor should be a function of the dividend yield on that portfolio and the relative tax rate of the investor.

Thus it makes sense to offer index funds tilted toward (or away from) high dividend-paying stocks to appeal to investors in different tax brackets. Although these dividend-tilted funds were a success when capital gains and dividends were taxed at different rates, the present tax codes, which tax dividends and realized capital gains at the same rate, have decreased their attractiveness.

The yield-tilted index fund just discussed is one example of a passive portfolio constructed on the basis of a nonstandard CAPM, which is discussed in detail in Chapter 14. It is possible to construct index funds based on any of the other nonstandard CAPM or arbitrage pricing theory (APT) models discussed in Chapters 14 and 16. For example, funds could be constructed with different sensitivities to inflation.

Other types of index funds are based on the kinds of anomalies discussed throughout this book. The investment community soon realized that the Wilshire 5000 tended, over long periods of time, to have a higher return than the S&P 500 (although recently this hasn't been true). The small stock anomaly was one justification for a more broadly based index. The small stock anomaly (Chapter 17) also has led to the creation of small stock (low capitalization) index funds (e.g., funds matching the Wilshire 4500, which excludes the S&P 500 or the Frank Russell 2000, which excludes the top 1000 stocks). Other new passive management strategies have followed. For example, there are passive portfolios that buy stocks with low price earnings (P/E) ratios. The design of these portfolios depends at least in part on unexplained deviations from theory rather than on theory itself.

Other innovations have also appeared. One popular one uses temporary mispricing across types of markets to increase the return on an index fund. An index fund can hold securities directly or can hold Treasury bills (T-bills) and a future on an index and be in the same risk return position. If futures are underpriced, T-bills plus futures will outperform the index fund that holds stock directly. Some index funds are based on the premise that futures on average will be underpriced and attempt to outperform holding securities directly by always holding T-bills and futures. Other index funds switch back and forth between the cash and futures markets to take advantage of any temporary mispricing that might arise between the two markets.

Are these passive or active management products? The line of demarcation has blurred. Although the first index funds bought a portfolio of stocks to match the index and did little but reinvest cash, some of the newer funds constantly monitor arbitrage conditions between the cash and futures market and switch between them. There is more of a continuum of products. Where one draws the line between active and passive management is somewhat arbitrary. We have chosen to draw it at the point where forecasts enter the picture. If the manager trades on a mechanical rule by using past data, we call it passive management. If the manager forecasts anything and acts on the forecast, we call it active management.[2]

ACTIVE MANAGEMENT

Active management involves taking a position different from that which would be held in a passive portfolio, based on a forecast about the future. A decision has to be made about which passive portfolio is best for an investor's goals. For ease of exposition, assume we have made that decision and have decided the appropriate benchmark is the S&P 500 portfolio. The neutral position is to hold each stock in the proportion it represents of the S&P 500. Any difference from these proportions represents a bet based on a forecast. Although there is no universal agreement about classification for active management styles, we find it useful to divide active managers into three groups: market timers, sector selectors, and security selectors. Market timers change the Beta on the portfolio according to forecasts of how the market will do. They change the Beta on the overall portfolio, either by changing the Beta on the equity portfolio (by using options or futures or by swapping securities) or by changing the amount invested in short-term bonds. Although we will have more to say about this in the fourth section of this chapter, market timing in stocks is used far less frequently than market timing decisions in managing bond portfolios.

At the other end of the spectrum from market timing is security selection. The search for undervalued securities and the methods of forming these securities into optimum portfolios have been the subject of much of this book. Investors practicing security selection are betting that the market weights on securities are not the optimum proportion to hold in each security. They increase the weight (make a positive bet) for undervalued securities and decrease it for overvalued securities. Most active stock managers practice security selection.

Another frequently used method of portfolio management is to practice sector or industry selection. This investment style often goes under the name of sector rotation. This is

---

[2]An alternative definition of passive management is to only call managers who try to replicate an established index as passive managers. This seems to us unduly arbitrary, because it would classify differently some managers who do essentially the same thing. As an example, consider the small stock manager. It would include the small stock manager who replicates the Wilshire 4500 stock index. However, it would exclude the small stock manager who buys the lowest decile of stocks in the NYSE. It would also exclude some portfolios such as the Wells Fargo yield-tilted index funds, which clearly were considered passive management by the investment community yet doesn't replicate an established market index.

Our definition would classify as passive managers those who construct portfolios on the basis of technical analysis. Under our definition, managers who bought on the basis of recent price increases (relative strength) as well as those who bought on low P/E ratios or low capitalization or any other mechanical rule would all be classified as passive managers. We find this more consistent than the convention of the financial community, which considers relative strength portfolios actively managed and low capitalization portfolios passively managed. We do not intend by our definition to imply that all styles of passive management are equally good.

like security selection, except that the unit of interest is an industry or a sector. On the basis of analysis, a positive or negative bet will be made on a sector. Although division of the population of stocks by industries is reasonably clear (there is some uncertainty as to how to divide stocks into industries), division by sectors is much more ambiguous.

Firms can divide stocks into sectors by

1. Broad industrial classification (e.g., industrial, financial, utilities).

2. Major product classification (e.g., consumer goods, industrial goods, services).

3. Perceived characteristics (e.g., growth, cyclical, stable). Other characteristics used to divide stocks into sectors are size, yield, or quality.

4. According to sensitivity to basic economic phenomena (e.g., interest-sensitive stocks, stocks sensitive to changes in exchange rates, etc.).

The type of analysis under discussion involves selecting one or more of these classifications in more than (less than) market weights according to the anticipated performance. Managers who practice this type of analysis will rotate their portfolios' overweighting (underweighting) sectors, or industries over time as they change forecasts of what sector is undervalued or overvalued.

Industry or sector selection should be contrasted to the security selection manager who just picks stocks within one sector. Many managers do not rotate among (select alternative) sectors over time, but choose always to select stocks from within one sector or group of industries. These are specialized managers; three examples are growth stock managers, utility stock managers, and technology managers. There are two reasons for specializing. The first is the belief that the sector is permanently undervalued. The second is the belief that one's staff is better able to select undervalued stocks in that sector or industry than in any other. Although the first is hard to justify, the second can be justified in a world of increasing complexity and specialization. The client can invest in sectors that are not covered by a particular manager by using either other active managers or a passive portfolio that covers these sectors (often called a "completion fund").

PASSIVE VERSUS ACTIVE

The case for passive versus active management certainly will not be settled during the life of the present edition of the book, if ever. Active management has some costs to overcome if it is to be effective. The predictive content of forecasts used in active management must be sufficiently large to overcome the following costs:

1. The cost of paying the forecasters either in the form of salaries or in the higher management fees charged by active managers relative to passive managers.[3]

2. The cost of diversifiable risk. Active portfolios, by their nature, have more diversifiable risk than an index fund (which has close to zero). The investor must be compensated for taking this risk.[4]

---

[3]In 1989, Vanguard's index fund had an expense ratio of 0.18%, whereas the active average fund had an expense ratio of 1.5%. In 1989, Vanguard's index fund had an 8% turnover of assets compared with the turnover for a typical stock mutual fund of 90%.

[4]As an approximation to this consider active managed stock mutual fund data. First mutual funds have coefficient of determination (R^2), with the market of between 0.90 and 0.95. To have the same total risk, an S&P index fund would need a Beta of 1.025–1.05. If the risk premium in the market is 6%, this implies that active funds would need to earn an added return of between 0.15% and 0.30% to compensate for their added risk.

3. The cost of higher transaction cost. Active decisions require turnover as opposed to the very low turnover of the buy and hold strategies of an index fund.

4. For the taxable investor, an early incidence of capital gains tax. Under current tax laws capital gains or losses are realized for tax purposes either because the fund sells stocks or the investor sells all or part of his or her share in the fund. An index fund has a very low level of turnover, so the taxable investor pays minimal capital gains taxes until he or she sells off part of the fund. An actively managed portfolio usually has a much higher turnover, and so capital gains taxes can be incurred by the investors even when the investors wish to leave their money fully invested.

Although index funds have outperformed most active managers, most investors who hire active managers believe they can spot the manager who will outperform the index. This belief persists despite the fact that there is very little evidence that superior performance is predictable. We are reminded of a recent survey of the entering class of one of the country's top-rated colleges. When students were asked if they expected to finish in the top 10% of their class, 87.5% responded that they did.

INTERNATIONAL DIVERSIFICATION

At several points in this book we have discussed the potential of international portfolio diversification. Although European portfolio managers have regularly diversified internationally, implementation of the concept is a much newer concept to American portfolio managers. Once again the portfolio manager has a choice involving passive and active management. At the most aggregate level the manager must decide whether to hold a passive portfolio of individual countries, weighting perhaps by the aggregate market value of each portfolio, or to try to select undervalued countries. Second, the manager must decide whether to bear the potential benefits and risk of currency movements or to hedge away changes in the relative value of currencies.

Once this decision is made the manager must decide whether to actively or passively manage the portfolio of stocks within each country. Any of the models discussed to this point can be applied within each country.

BOND MANAGEMENT

Many of the portfolio management strategies that are utilized for common stocks are also utilized for bonds. Although we will briefly review the justification for these strategies when applied to bond portfolio management, we will concentrate on those strategies that are unique to the bond area. Once again it is convenient to divide the strategies into passive and active strategies. In this section we will discuss strategies where the manager is concerned only with the return characteristics of the bond portfolio. In the next section we will discuss bond strategies that consider the existence of liabilities, such as immunization strategies.

Passive Strategies

As in common stock portfolio management, one passive strategy for bonds is to match an index. Institutional investor estimated that $67 billion of institutional assets was invested in domestic bond index funds and $1 billion in international index funds as of 1990. Index matching for common stocks is justified primarily by the equilibrium arguments of Chapters 13 and 14. Although some equilibrium models for bonds have been developed, empirical testing of the existing theories is virtually nonexistent. The justification for bond index funds rests primarily on the performance of active versus passive portfolios rather than on tests of a theory. Performance statistics reported in the industry press generally find that most active bond managers underperform the generally utilized bond indexes, such as the Shearson-Lehman index and the Salomon Brothers index.[5] If this past performance continues in the future, an investor could expect above average performance by investing in an index fund.

Some features of bond index funds differ from stock index funds and make bond index funds more difficult to manage. The first factor is the changing nature of the index. Stock indexes, such as Standard & Poor's 500, change occasionally as S&P decides that different firms are more appropriate or as firms in the index merge. The composition of all widely used bond indexes changes much more frequently as bonds mature and new bonds are issued. A second difference from stock indexes is that many bond indexes contain bonds that are illiquid and, in fact, might not be available to an investor. This means that the manager of a bond index fund will never attempt to duplicate an index exactly, but will employ one of the other techniques described in the section on stock index funds to match the index. Both of these influences mean that the passive manager will have to trade more frequently in running a bond index fund than he or she does in running a stock index fund.

Another type of passive product is unique to the bond area—the bond unit trust usually composed of municipal bonds. A unit trust buys a portfolio of bonds and does not buy or sell bonds over the life of the trust. A trust unwinds gradually over time and eventually dissolves as the bonds it initially buys are called or mature. An investor purchases a share of this fixed portfolio. Ignoring default and calls for the moment, the investor knows the cash flows associated with the portfolio and the bonds that comprise the portfolio. The important question is what benefits the unit trust provides that are not provided by other opportunities.

Investors could simply duplicate the holdings of the unit trust on their own, and by doing so, avoid management and sales fees. Investors of modest means would be faced with the problem that bonds can only be bought in large denominations (are not divisible) and that transaction costs of buying small amounts are high. Thus duplication is not feasible for most investors.

Two other opportunities suggest themselves—holding other bonds or index funds. A unit trust has the advantage of diversifying risk rather than holding a small number of bonds directly. In addition, since for most bonds the largest payment occurs when the principal is repaid, a portfolio of bonds with varying maturities can offer a more uniform cash flow. For retired people who want to consume capital as well as interest over time, the more uniform cash flow offered by a unit trust is often viewed as desirable.

The other comparison is with an index fund. A unit trust offers many of the benefits of diversifying default risks and, to a limited extent, call risks that an index fund offers.[6] However, it offers more predictable cash flows and larger cash flows in the early years, because a unit trust pays out principal as bonds mature or are called, whereas an index fund

---

[5]Standard indexes are market weighted and are therefore dominated by short-term bonds. The indexes have an average duration of three to five years. Bond managers generally hold portfolios of longer duration; thus performance of funds relative to the index is strongly affected by how interest rates changed during the period in which funds are being examined.

[6]The principal determinant of calls is the level of interest rates. The effect of the level of interest rates on calls is common to all bonds and is not diversifiable. However, bonds are called for other reasons such as firm restructuring. This part of the call risk can be diversified across bonds.

reinvests principal. Of course, this faster payment of principal can be an advantage or a disadvantage according to whether or not the investor wants money back earlier.[7] Unit trusts are the major passive strategy unique to bonds. Let us now examine active strategies.

Active Strategies

Active bond strategies are very similar to active stock strategies, although the popularity of each of the strategies differs. The most commonly employed active bond strategy is market timing. An estimate is made of what will happen to interest rates. If interest rates are expected to rise, prices are expected to fall and capital losses will be incurred on bonds. Thus, an investor expecting a rise in interest rates will shorten the duration of the portfolio, while an investor expecting a drop in interest rates will lengthen the duration of the portfolio. Although this is the standard argument underlying market timing, the argument is incomplete and additional comments are in order.

If a manager believes that interest rates will rise, and other investors share this belief, then market prices will reflect this expectation. In this situation, market timing will be ineffective, even with correct forecasting. Thus, successful market timing requires both accuracy in forecasting and beliefs different from those already reflected in market prices.

A second active bond strategy is to pursue the risk premium associated with lower-rated bonds. (This is one form of sector selection discussed in the section on common stocks.) Evidence discussed in Chapter 20 suggests that the extra promised return on riskier corporate bonds has historically more than compensated for the loss due to default. For example, Aaa corporates have minimal default risk and yet over the last several decades have offered a promised return well above similar government bonds. The same evidence indicates that historically the extra promised return of low-rated corporate debt relative to high-rated corporate debt more than compensated for the default losses.

A strategy followed by some portfolio managers is to try to earn an extra return by bearing credit risk. By holding a sufficiently large portfolio, the probability of a large portion of the portfolio defaulting is small, and with a positive risk premium, an extra return is earned. The manager of a high-risk portfolio will usually try to improve performance by using fundamental analysis to screen out the bonds that are most likely to default and to identify those most likely to show improvement in credit worthiness.

The risk of this strategy is twofold. First, the manager may have higher default experience than is expected. As shown in Chapter 20, default experience varies a great deal on a year-to-year basis and is related to current economic conditions. A manager using long-term experience as a guide to estimating the extra return from bearing credit risk might experience defaults in excess of historical experience and may have realized returns below those on higher-rated debt. The second risk involved in investing in lower rated debt is a change in the premium. For example, the difference between Aaa corporate debt and government debt with similar characteristics might be 0.3%. Historical experience would suggest that the default possibilities for Aaa corporate debt are exceedingly low. Thus, holding Aaa corporate debt rather than government debt would seem to almost guarantee an extra return. There have been a number of periods, however, when the realized return of government debt exceeded that of Aaa corporate debt. How can this occur? If the yield spread between Aaa corporate and governments widens from, for example, 0.3% to 0.5%, then

---

[7]The investor holding an index fund can, of course, obtain larger cash flows in early years by selling off part of the fund periodically. However, the size of cash flows is less predictable because of changes in the market value of the fund's portfolio.

Aaa corporates will experience a capital loss relative to governments. This is the second risk in pursuing a lower rated debt strategy.

The previous discussion suggests a third active strategy analogous to the strategy of sector rotation discussed for stocks. If a manager anticipates that the spread between Aaa corporates and governments would widen significantly, then a switch from Aaa corporates to governments should result in a better performing portfolio. Similarly, if the spread is expected to narrow or to remain unchanged, Aaa corporates should have the superior returns. This strategy can be classified as sector selection. A category such as Aaa corporates is selected based on the belief that this sector will have superior performance.

Although selecting a sector by comparing relative spreads between bonds of different rating category is the most obvious example of sector selection, the principle is perfectly general. Callable debt has a higher yield than noncallable debt because of the risk that the issuer will call debt at a disadvantageous time. Callable debt can be viewed by an investor as purchasing noncallable debt and issuing a call option (which reduces the value of the bond).

If the investor believes the market overprices the option (overestimates the probability of a call), then purchasing the callable debt should lead to superior returns. Both rating category and call features are examples of potential sector selection.

Security selection as a strategy in the bond area is the same as in the stock area; however, there is much less chance for excess returns. Security selection of bonds generally involves one of two approaches. One approach is to search for securities whose default risk is misestimated. For example, are there firms with A-rated bonds that have substantially less default risk than other A bonds (have been misclassified)? This strategy involves credit analysis. A second approach is to try to find bonds that are mispriced given their characteristics. A number of commercial services estimate the "fair" yield to maturity on a bond given its characteristics (bond rating, maturity, callability, etc.); Barra and Gifford Fong are two examples of such services. Buying bonds whose actual yield to maturity differs from model yield is a security selection strategy. The difference in model and actual yield is generally quite small. Thus, the extra return is also quite small even if actual yield moves to model yield. In the common equity area, finding a stock of a high-growth company before the market recognizes it can lead to spectacular returns. Thus security selection strategies in the common equity area have the potential for much higher returns.

We have discussed the major strategies in bond management when the investment manager is concerned only with returns. When the investor is also concerned with a liability stream, the strategies change considerably.

BOND AND STOCK INVESTMENT WITH A LIABILITY STREAM

Many portfolio managers are in charge of investing funds that are provided to meet future obligations. Managers of pension funds are the most obvious example; managers of insurance companies are another. There has been a greater awareness in recent years that the portfolio manager needs to consider the liability stream in making investment decisions. There are several reasons for this increased awareness. First, the accounting treatment of the return on pension assets has changed. This change means that changes in asset values relative to liabilities affect the earnings a company reports to its shareholders and affect the asset and liability values shown on the balance sheet. Second, regulatory bodies concerned with financial intermediaries such as insurance companies have forced the intermediaries to value more of their assets and liabilities at the price they would get if sold rather than at original cost. Third, in the 1980s many companies found that certain investment strategies, such as cash flow matching or dedication, resulted in surplus pension assets, and thus pension assets became a source of money.[8] All of these factors led to a greater awareness of the need to consider liabilities in selecting investment strategies.

When an investment manager considers the cash flow characteristics of liabilities as well as those of assets, investment strategies change. There are two ways to model the liability stream, which are useful for formulating investment strategies. One is to assume that the liability stream is known and fixed; the other is to assume that the liability stream is a function of one or more exogenous influences. Each of these will now be discussed in some detail.

Fixed Liability Stream

A manager is often called on to manage a portfolio of bonds so as to meet a fixed set of liability payments over time. Although liabilities often are not truly fixed, there are circumstances in which acting as if they were fixed is a close approximation to reality. Probably the clearest case was the sale of Guaranteed Insurance Contracts (GIC) by insurance companies, which were very popular in the early 1980s and still are. These contracts required that the insurance company pay a fixed sum at specified intervals to the purchaser. The contracted payments were fixed commitments (liabilities) of the insurance company, which had to put together portfolios of bonds so that it could meet these payments.

Another example is pension payments for retired employees. If the pension payments are fixed at the time of retirement, the amount per year that must be paid to any employee is fixed. Of course, the aggregate amount paid to all employees is not known because the mortality experience of the employees is not known. However, with a large number of retired employees the mortality experience can be predicted quite accurately. Hence, pension funds frequently require an investment manager to protect against a set of fixed forecasted pension liabilities. Low-risk strategies for managing bond portfolios to meet a fixed liability stream were discussed in Chapter 21. These include cash flow matching (often called dedication) and immunization.

An exact cash flow–matched portfolio employing only noncallable default-free (government) debt would have zero risk. Managers of cash flow-matched or dedicated portfolios are often selected on the basis of the initial value of the assets they require to meet the pension liabilities of a client. Managers in bidding on business wish to be competitive, and they can increase return (decrease initial assets) in two ways. The first, already discussed in Chapter 21, is to allow cash to be transferred between periods at a set rate. This is an assumed rate, and to the extent that it does not materialize, liabilities will not be matched.

The second is to introduce higher expected return debt into the portfolio. Managers frequently use corporate debt or callable debt to raise the expected return (lower the initial cash) necessary to match a set of liabilities. Although this might allow the manager to gain a customer, it increases the probability the liabilities will not be met. A corporate bankruptcy or an early call after a drop in interest rates will result in a shortfall in the return produced by assets.

The next most risky bond strategy is immunization. Because the liability stream is fixed in amount and timing, the only uncertainty involved in determining its value is the appropriate discount rates for valuing it. As the yield structure changes, the present value of the

---

[8]This was a major source of funds used in many leveraged buyouts. Surplus pension assets were recognized because actuaries were willing to value liabilities differently, depending on the investment strategy. If the firm's cash flow matched pension assets, the actuary used the return on the investment portfolio as the discount rate in valuing liabilities. This was a much higher rate than they normally used and resulted in a lower value of liability and excess pension assets.

liabilities also changes. If the investment manager is to have assets of at least equal value to the liabilities at all points in time, the manager will need to have the assets change in value in the same manner as the liabilities.

Because the value of the liabilities is dependent only on the term structure, the element in the investment policy that will affect risk is the sensitivity of assets to changes in interest rates. A policy of having the assets have the same sensitivity to interest rates as the liability stream (called an immunized policy) is a low-risk strategy. An immunized strategy is higher risk than cash flow matching because it depends on the accuracy of the measurement of the sensitivity of bonds to a change in interest rates.[9]

An immunized strategy can have a large component of active management. All of the active bond portfolio management techniques discussed in the previous section can be used in conjunction with immunization; these include sector selection and security selection. The manager maximizes the extra return subject to the constraint that the portfolio is immunized.[10]

Some managers attempt to do a modest amount of market timing while maintaining an immunized portfolio on average. A manager who wishes to market time would deviate from an immunized policy in some periods. Assume for a moment that duration is a reasonable measure of sensitivity to interest rate changes. If the manager believed that interest rates will rise, then a negative net duration would be set on the portfolio (duration on assets less than duration on liabilities). Similarly, if interest rates are expected to fall, a positive net duration would be set.

As a manager introduces more elements of active management into immunization strategies, he or she is attempting to increase expected returns but in doing so is increasing the probability that liability payments will not be met. In short, we are back to a risk-return choice, although a very restricted one. For example, because of their low correlation with interest rate movements, common stocks are not likely to be effective in immunization. Thus a manager investing in common stocks and concerned with a fixed liability stream has engaged in high-risk strategy in an attempt to earn a high return.

The choice of how immunized a manager should be depends in part on the ratio of assets to liabilities and in part on how the assets are funded. For example, a typical type of manager who practices immunization is the manager of a large financial intermediary, such as an insurance company. Many of these institutions have assets that are only slightly larger than their liabilities. An insurance company might have $20 billion in assets, $19.5 billion in liabilities, and $0.5 billion in net worth. For such an institution, a policy that results in a small fluctuation in asset value without a corresponding change in liabilities can be disastrous. In the example, more than a 5% decline in asset value without a decrease in the value of liabilities results in negative net worth. Thus for these types of highly levered institutions, a cash flow–matched or immunized bond investment policy is the only reasonable policy. In other circumstances a higher return investment strategy is more reasonable. For example, a company financing a pension plan for retired employees may be willing to risk a decline in assets to below liabilities because of the chance of a substantially higher return. Another possibility is an investment strategy called contingent immunization. The manager is active until the value of the assets just equals the value of the

---

[9]A cash flow–match strategy is, of course, also immunized. However, it is useful to distinguish those portfolios that are immunized, because they are cash flow matched, and those that are immunized by matching sensitivities to interest rates.

[10]There may be a cost to requiring the portfolio to be immunized when the manager believes that some bonds are mispriced. In this case there is a risk-return tradeoff. The manager may choose to incur the risk of a nonimmunized portfolio to make a heavier investment in bonds that are believed to yield an excess return.

liabilities (or) the value of the liabilities plus a fixed amount. At this point the active port-folio is liquidated and the portfolio is immunized. This strategy allows active management but has the guarantee of immunization.

When the liability stream is stochastic rather than fixed, management techniques become more complex. This is the situation that we now examine.

Stochastic Liability Stream

Stochastic liability streams arise in a number of realistic investment situations. Retired employees often have a cost-of-living adjustment (COLA) in their retirement plans. Their base pension is fixed, but is adjusted upward because of changes in some index such as the consumer price index. Casualty insurance (such as automobile insurance) companies are another example. A casualty insurance company receives premium income. The size of the liabilities (e.g., auto accident claims) takes a number of years to determine, because of the time needed to litigate claims. Although the number of claims can be estimated fairly accu-rately, the size of each claim is uncertain. The ultimate settlement is generally assumed to be a function of medical costs and general living costs. The assumption of a stochastic lia-bility stream with a fixed component and a variable component related to medical costs and inflation is reasonable for many casualty insurance companies.

To provide a concrete basis for subsequent discussion, let us consider the investment problem of a manager who is concerned with providing pension funds for retired employ-ees whose benefits include a COLA. Without the COLA the only uncertainty in determin-ing the present value of the liabilities is the appropriate discount rate to use. The rate of discount depends on the term structure of interest rates. Thus the rate of change in the value of liabilities is affected by shifts in the term structure. With a COLA the rate of change in liabilities is affected by two factors: changes in the term structure and the rate of inflation. We can then think of rates of change in the liabilities as being determined by a two-factor model.

If a manager is concerned only with variability of return on assets, then the sensitivity of the assets to a factor determines risk. When a manager is investing subject to a liability stream, the risk of movements in a factor is eliminated by making the net exposure (asset exposure less liability exposure) zero.

Previously, we discussed immunization as a strategy. This involves eliminating exposure to shifts in the term structure by setting the net exposure to shifts in the term structure to zero. With the two-factor model, the manager can choose to eliminate the exposure to any factor by making the net exposure to that factor zero.

Should a manager eliminate factor risk? To answer this question, consider two different scenarios. First, consider that the factor is unpriced so that exposure does not affect expected return in equilibrium. Second, consider that the factors are priced in the sense that exposure increases expected return.

If the factor is unpriced, then exposure to the factor in equilibrium produces extra risk without any additional expected return. If the manager does not have a special ability to forecast period-by-period values of the factor, zero net exposure (immunization) is the pre-ferred strategy. A belief by the manager of an ability to forecast the period-by-period value of the factor can mean a nonzero and changing exposure through time.

If the factor is priced, then the manager might choose to have exposure to the factor. Exposure to a factor increases the risk but also potentially increases the return. Thus, for priced factors, exposure to the factor involves a risk-return tradeoff.

Nothing in our prior discussion requires that the assets be only bonds. The inflation fac-tor for assets (and liabilities) is the effect of inflation holding changes in interest rates constant. For many bonds most of the effect of inflation will be impounded in a change in interest rate. Thus, investment managers concerned with a liability stream whose value is affected by inflation as well as interest rate changes might find both common equities and bonds to be useful hedging tools.

What is true of inflation is also true of other factors affecting the liability stream. Noninterest factors are generally better immunized by using common stocks. Return-generating models for common stocks tend to have many more components than bond return-generating models. Furthermore, many liability streams are likely to be sensitive to many of the additional influences that drive stock returns. Thus, the incorporation of stocks in the asset portfolio generally allows better hedging of noninterest rate factors in the liability stream.[11]

The concept of using a multi-index return-generating process to immunize a set of liabilities is new; so very little theoretical or empirical research exists in this area.[12] We expect it to be a fruitful area for future research.

Bond–Stock Mix

Management style with respect to bond–stock mix can be divided into two broad categories: managers who use fairly stable proportions through time and those managers who actively vary their proportions over time.

The managers who use fixed proportions generally make an assumption that the characteristics of various asset classes (e.g., mean return, variance) are fairly constant over time, or at least that changes in these parameters are not predictable. They generally examine the distribution of various combinations of asset classes and decide which combination is the most attractive. Often managers are concerned with the return characteristics over several multiperiod time horizons. In this case, simulation is frequently used to examine the characteristics of the return distributions for different mixes over several different time spans. Frequently, assumptions concerning asset characteristics are then varied to determine whether the chosen mix is reasonable with small changes in assumed values of the return distributions.[13]

Two management styles lead to varying mixes over time. The first is the market timer. Some managers believe that they can forecast the relative performance of the stock and bond market. The current term for this is tactical asset allocation. These managers have a variety of techniques for forecasting relative performance, which vary from a mechanical rule for utilizing past data to reliance upon forecasted changes in risk-return relationships.

One justification for this behavior is the empirical literature supporting changing risk premiums. In a series of papers, Fama and French [10] have shown that for holding periods beyond a year, expected returns on stocks and long-term bonds and, hence, relative returns are weakly predictable. They present results that variables such as dividend price ratios, default premiums, and term premiums can explain more than 30% of the variation

---

[11]An example of a more complex liability stream is the forecasted liability stream associated with a pension plan for active employees. The value of this stream is likely to depend on interest rates, cost-of-living changes, changes in the risk of the company and economy, changes in profitability, and so forth. Some of these influences affect the return on bonds, but more affect the return on stocks.

[12]See Elton and Gruber [7–9].

[13]Another condition necessary for fixed proportions is that the investor's utility function is not one that results in optimal asset proportions being a function of the current value of the portfolio (wealth). Managers who utilize fixed proportions either do not think in terms of utility functions or are explicitly making the assumption just discussed.

in returns. Among those who provide similar evidence are Keim and Stambaugh [16], Poteba and Summers [19], and Campbell and Shiller [2].

A theoretical justification for changing asset proportions is that the behavior of investors can be characterized by a utility function that implies optimal assets proportions are a function of the value of the portfolio. If the utility function depends on the value of the portfolio, the optimal asset mix at any point in time depends on the returns in all previous periods. Several firms use an explicit utility function to select the optimal bond–stock mix over time.

The second management style leading to changing asset proportions over time is one that uses changes in the asset mix to change the shape of the return distribution. As discussed in Chapter 22, a changing mix of stocks and T-bills can replicate the pattern of holding the stock portfolio along with a put on the stock portfolio. This trading strategy often goes under the name of portfolio insurance or dynamic asset allocation. Leland, O'Brian, and Rubinstein are leading proponents of this type of product.

Any manager who chooses to change the bond–stock mix over time can accomplish this goal through transactions in the futures market as opposed to the cash market. To increase the exposure to stocks relative to bonds the manager has to buy stock futures and sell bond futures. The use of futures has great appeal because of the low transaction costs and high liquidity in the futures market as compared with the cash market. Futures also allow the bond–stock mix to be easily modified without changing the exposure to specific issues that the manager may wish to maintain. This characteristic is especially useful for pension managers who employ multiple managers. Implementing the bond–stock choice by utilizing futures allows the bond–stock decision to be controlled at the level of the aggregate portfolio. This means that each of the multiple managers need not be concerned with the bond–stock mix and can manage assets in a segment or segments of the financial markets, which he or she believes is appropriate. Finally, if futures are used to implement timing decisions, it becomes easy to separate the return from timing decisions from the return due to selection ability.

BIBLIOGRAPHY

1. Admati, Anat R. "Does It All Add Up? Benchmarks and the Compensation of Active Portfolio Managers," *The Journal of Business*, **70,** No. 3 (July 1997), pp. 323–350.
2. Campbell, John Y., and Shiller, Robert. "The Dividend-Price Ratio and Expectations of Future Dividends and Discount Factors," Unpublished Manuscript, Princeton University, 1987.
3. Chevalier, Judith. "Risk Taking by Mutual Funds as a Response to Incentives," *The Journal of Political Economy*, **105,** No. 6 (Dec. 1997), pp. 1167–1200.
4. ———. "Career Concerns of Mutual Fund Managers," *The Quarterly Journal of Economics*, **114,** No. 2 (May 1999), pp. 389–443.
5. Cumby, Robert E., and Glen, Jack D. "Evaluating the Performance of International Mutual Funds," *The Journal of Finance*, **45,** No. 2 (June 1990), pp. 497–521.
6. Elton, Edwin J., and Gruber, Martin J. "A Multi-Index Risk Model of the Japanese Stock Market," *Japan and the World Economy*, **1,** No. 1 (1989), pp. 21–44.
7. ———. "Expectational Data and Japanese Stock Prices," *Japan and the World Economy*, **1,** No. 4 (1990), pp. 391–401.
8. ———. "Portfolio Analysis with a Non-Normal Multi-Index Return Generating Process," *Review of Quantitative Finance and Accounting*, **2,** No. 1 (Mar. 1992), pp. 100–120.
9. ———. "Optimal Investment Strategies with Investor Liabilities," *Journal of Banking and Finance*, **10,** No. 2 (Mar. 1991), pp. 210–230.
10. Fama, Eugene F., and French, Kenneth R. "Dividend Yields and Expected Stock Returns," Unpublished Manuscript, University of Chicago, 1987.

11. French, Kenneth R., Schwert, G. William, and Stambaugh, Robert. "Expected Stock Returns and Volatility," *Journal of Financial Economics* (1986), pp. 3–30.

12. Grinblatt, Mark, Titman, Sheridan, and Wermers, Russ. "Momentum Investment Strategies, Portfolio Performance, and Herding: A Study of Mutual Fund Behavior," *The American Economic Review*, **85,** No. 5 (Dec. 1995), pp. 1088–1105.

13. Gruber, Martin J. "Another Puzzle: The Growth in Actively Managed Mutual Funds," *The Journal of Finance*, **51,** No. 3 (July 1996), p. 783.

14. Hendricks, Darryll, Patel, Jayendu, and Zeckhauser, Richard. "Hot Hands in Mutual Funds: Short-Run Persistence of Relative Performance, 1974–1988," *The Journal of Finance*, **48,** No. 1 (Mar. 1993), pp. 93–130.

15. Ippolito, Richard A. "Efficiency With Costly Information: A Study Of Mutual Funds," *The Quarterly Journal of Economics*, **104,** No. 1 (Feb. 1989), p. 1.

16. Keim, Donald B., and Stambaugh, Robert F. "Predicting Returns in the Stock and Bond Markets," *Journal of Financial Economics*, **17,** (Dec. 1986), pp. 357–390.

17. Khorana, Ajay. "Top Management Turnover: An Empirical Investigation of Mutual Fund Managers," *The Journal of Financial Economics*, **40,** No. 3 (Mar. 1996), pp. 403–427.

18. Narayanan, M.P. "Form of Compensation and Managerial Decision Horizon," *The Journal of Financial and Quantitative Analysis*, **31,** No. 4 (Dec. 1996), pp. 467–491.

19. Poteba, James M., and Summers, Lawrence H. "Mean Reversion in Stock Prices," *Journal of Financial Economics*, **21,** (Oct. 1988), pp. 27–59.

20. Wahal, Sunil. "Pension Fund Activism and Firm Performance," *The Journal of Financial and Quantitative Analysis*, **31,** No. 1 (Mar. 1996), pp. 1–23.

Index
